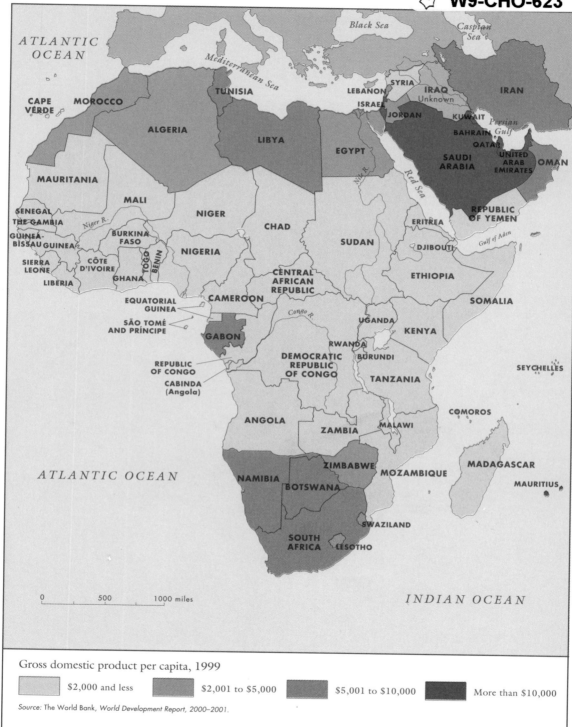

W9-CHO-623

ATLANTIC
OCEAN

Black Sea

Caspian
Sea

Mediterranean Sea

CAPE
VERDE

MOROCCO

TUNISIA

LEBANON

SYRIA

IRAQ
Unknown

IRAN

ALGERIA

LIBYA

ISRAEL

JORDAN

KUWAIT

Persian
Gulf

BAHRAIN

QATAR

MAURITANIA

EGYPT

SAUDI
ARABIA

UNITED
ARAB
EMIRATES

OMAN

NIGER R.

MALI

NIGER

CHAD

Red Sea

ERITREA

REPUBLIC
OF YEMEN

Gulf of Aden

SENEGAL
THE GAMBIA
GUINEA-
BISSAU GUINEA

Niger R.

BURKINA
FASO

SUDAN

DJIBOUTI

SIERRA
LEONE

CÔTE
D'IVOIRE

NIGERIA

TOGO

BENIN

CENTRAL
AFRICAN
REPUBLIC

ETHIOPIA

LIBERIA

GHANA

EQUATORIAL
GUINEA

CAMEROON

Congo R.

UGANDA

KENYA

SOMALIA

SÃO TOMÉ
AND PRÍNCIPE

GABON

RWANDA

BURUNDI

SEYCHELLES

REPUBLIC
OF CONGO

DEMOCRATIC
REPUBLIC
OF CONGO

TANZANIA

CABINDA
(Angola)

COMOROS

ANGOLA

ZAMBIA

MALAWI

MADAGASCAR

ATLANTIC OCEAN

NAMIBIA

ZIMBABWE

BOTSWANA

MOZAMBIQUE

MAURITIUS

SWAZILAND

SOUTH
AFRICA

LESOTHO

0   500   1000 miles

INDIAN OCEAN

Gross domestic product per capita, 1999

| $2,000 and less | $2,001 to $5,000 | $5,001 to $10,000 | More than $10,000 |

Source: The World Bank, *World Development Report, 2000–2001.*

AFRICA AND THE MIDDLE EAST

Economics of Development

Economics of Development

FIFTH EDITION

Dwight H. Perkins
HARVARD UNIVERSITY

Steven Radelet
HARVARD UNIVERSITY

Donald R. Snodgrass
HARVARD UNIVERSITY

Malcolm Gillis
RICE UNIVERSITY

Michael Roemer
LATE OF HARVARD UNIVERSITY

W. W. NORTON & COMPANY

Copyright © 2001, 1996, 1992, 1987, 1983 by W. W. Norton & Company, Inc.

The text of this book is composed in Adobe Garamond
with the display set in Meta Bold
Composition by UG / GGS Information Services, Inc.
Manufacturing by Maple–Vail
Book design by M Space

Library of Congress Cataloging-in-Publication Data
Economics of development / Dwight H. Perkins ... [et al.] — 5th ed.
      p. cm.
   Includes bibliographical references and index.
   ISBN 0-393-97517-7
   1. Developing countries—Economic policy. 2. Economic development. I. Perkins,
Dwight Heald.
HC59.7 .E314 2001
338.9—dc21   00-048078

W. W. Norton & Company, Inc., 500 Fifth Avenue, New York, N.Y. 10110
www.wwnorton.com

W. W. Norton & Company Ltd., Castle House, 75/76 Wells Street,
London W1T 3QT

4 5 6 7 8 9 0

To Michael Roemer. Friend, colleague, co-author: his contributions to the alleviation of world poverty will endure.

Contents

Part Two: Guiding Development

Part Three: Human Resources

Part Five: Production and Trade

Preface

Developing countries make the news when they are engulfed in crises. During the last few years since the publication of the fourth edition of this book, the financial crises in Asia, Russia, and Brazil were of such a magnitude that news about them made it to the front pages of newspapers around the world. The HIV/AIDS epidemic received special attention as well, as people began to realize the magnitude of its impact, particularly in Africa, where life expectancy actually has fallen and is falling further. Wars between Ethiopia and Eritrea, civil war within the Congo, and East Timor's struggle to gain independence from Indonesia also received attention. In the United States, one heard much about aid fatigue and how the general public, together with Congress, is tired of pouring huge sums into failed development efforts. The public in the industrialized countries is under the impression that vast sums of their tax dollars go to developing countries, when the reality is that far less than 1 percent of the GDP of these countries goes into such efforts. In the United States, less than a quarter of 1 percent goes for developing country assistance and much of that small amount has more to do with American security interests in the Middle East than with development.

For all the negative headlines, the reality is that much of the developing world has been transforming itself for the better. China, with 20 percent of the world's population, has enjoyed more than two decades of rapid sustained growth that has quadrupled the average income of its people. India, with almost as many people, struggled for decades with slow growth but, over the past decade, has experienced a marked acceleration in the pace at which per capita income is rising. The Asian financial crisis, severe as it was, has been followed by rapid recovery in all the crisis countries except Indonesia, where the financial crisis became entwined with an even more serious political crisis. In Latin America, the story continues to be the strengthening of democratic forces, most notably with the election in Mexico of the opposition party candidate. Latin America also has continued the process of moving away from economic policies based on extensive government intervention to ones that rely mainly on market forces. In sub-Saharan Africa, however, the story is mainly one of economic stagnation and a marked deterioration in public health, although there are a few notable exceptions in the region. And even in the countries elsewhere in the world that have achieved substantial growth large groups of people remain mired in extreme forms of poverty.

The main focus of the fifth edition of this textbook, as in the earlier editions, is not on the headlines but on the fundamentals of development. What underlying forces have made for rapid growth in the economies of some countries and the lack of growth in others? Why do some people get left behind in countries where the majority of their people enjoy steady improvement in their standard of living? Is the growth that is occurring sustainable, or is it based on policies that are exhausting natural resources and destroying the environment?

The issues of economic development have been around for a long time, going back to the late eighteenth century, and writing about development has an equally long history, beginning, as far as modern economics is concerned, with Adam Smith and David Ricardo. Over the past decade, however, interest in economic growth and development has renewed and produced a burgeoning theoretical and empirical literature on the subject. The biggest single change, in this fifth edition, from the earlier editions is the strengthening of our discussion of this new growth literature and breaking it out into a separate chapter of its own (Chapter 2).

Other changes in this edition include a full discussion of the causes and significance of the "Asian financial crisis." The dominant trend in the approach to development over the past two decades has been the stress on the importance of relying on market forces and the dismantling of many government controls that appeared to be impeding development. The other dominant trend has been the increasing emphasis on the importance of becoming integrated into international markets for goods, services, and capital. The Asian financial crisis, however, demonstrated that reliance on global markets works best when key institutions, such as the prudential oversight of banks, are in place. When they are absent, the rapid opening of financial markets to global pressures can lead to system failure as it did in 1997 and 1998. All the authors of this textbook share the view that developing countries should rely mainly on market forces but, from the first edition, recognize that there are many market failures in developing countries and not all of them are the product of earlier inappropriate government interventions that need to be dismantled. Some failures reflect the underlying problems inherent in countries that have not enjoyed decades of development of both income and institutions. Others are a result of the "public goods" nature of such services as health and education. This textbook, therefore, has tried to present the full range of arguments and approaches to these issues, not just a single point of view.

We also added a reference section at the beginning of the book describing several international development resources found on the Internet (see pp. xx–xxi). These resources provide students with easy access to a wealth of information on individual developing countries, databases, current development issues and debates, recent publications, and development projects around the world. The information found on these websites complements much of the material in the textbook and (since they are updated much more frequently than the textbook) provides a ready tool for research projects and other student initiatives.

While we have added new case studies and have brought the debates discussed in this text up to date in this fifth edition, our basic approach to the issues of development has not changed. The five distinguishing features of this text are these: (1) It makes extensive use of the theoretical tools of classical and neoclassical economics, in the belief that these tools contribute substantially to our understanding of development. (2) It draws heavily on decades of empirical studies by economists and economic historians, studies that have uncovered and explained the structure of development or at least narrowed our zones of ignorance. (3) It deals explicitly with the political and institutional framework in which economic development takes place. (4) It presents many real-country examples to illustrate major points, drawing on the authors' collective experience of more than a century of work on development issues. (5) It recognizes the diversity of development experience reflected in these country examples and acknowledges that the lessons of theory and history can be applied only within certain institutional and national contexts.

Finally, this edition differs from its predecessors with the addition of a new coauthor, Steven Radelet. Steve, like the other coauthors of this volume, has extensive experience in both research on development and the practice of development in the field. Two of the coauthors from the previous editions were unable to participate in this edition. Michael Roemer's death took from the development field one of its most thoughtful and productive writers and practitioners, with wide ranging experience in Africa, Asia, and Latin America. Mike, in many ways, was the single most important contributor to the earlier editions. His influence on this edition remains enormous, even though he passed away before we began its preparation. In recognition of that contribution and for so much else he gave to development and the developing world, we have dedicated this edition to Mike Roemer. The reduction in Malcolm Gillis's contribution arises from happier circumstances. Malcolm was the one who first got us started on writing this text, and his insights into development are still very much a part of the fifth edition. Malcolm left the Harvard Institute for International Development some years ago and has gone on to a distinguished career, first as a professor and dean at Duke University, and for much of the 1990s as president of Rice University. Unfortunately, the demands on the president of a major university leave little time for revising textbooks.

Organization

The basic structure of this book is similar to the earlier editions. Part 1 introduces the concept and measurement of development, theories that have arisen to explain development, and the body of data that has been amassed to recognize and define development when it takes place. Part 2 considers two broad issues, the role of markets versus planning and government control as the preferred means for guiding the economy and the question of how to make development sustainable.

The ultimate goal of development is the improved welfare of people. In turn, their improved welfare makes further development possible. Part 3 includes chapters on population, the role of labor, education, and health—all key elements in how development affects both human welfare and human productivity. Capital, the other major physical input into the growth process, is the subject of Part 4. The chapters in this part deal with capital and saving, fiscal policy, financial policy, and foreign capital, debt and financial crises. Part 5 deals with issues of production and trade in agriculture, other primary products, and industry; it concludes with a discussion of the principles involved in managing an open economy.

Supplements

To help meet the needs of students and instructors, two supplements accompany the text. A *Study Guide and Workbook*, originally created by Bruce Bolnick of Northeastern University and revised for this fifth edition by Berhanu Abegaz of the College of William and Mary, provides review material, self-tests, and problem sets that will help students grasp the major points more firmly. An *Instructor's Manual*, also originally created by Bolnick and revised by Abegaz, provides lecture notes and discussion topics along with answers to the problem sets in the workbook.

Acknowledgments

In the course of writing five editions, we have accumulated many debts to generous colleagues who have read chapters, reviewed the entire book, tested the manuscript in their classes, or otherwise encouraged us: Paul Albanese (Middlebury College), Ralph Beals (Amherst College), Richard Bird (University of Toronto), Bruce Bolnick (Northeastern University and now at Harvard), Paul Clark (Williams College), Ian Coxhead (University of Wisconsin at Madison), David Dapice (Tufts University), Shantayanan Devarajan (Harvard and now the World Bank), James Duesenberry (Harvard), Sebastian Edwards (University of Southern California), Alfred J. Field (University of North Carolina), Ira N. Gang (Rutgers University), Lester Gordon (Harvard University), Clive Gray (Harvard University), Arnold Harberger (University of Chicago), Sue Horton (University of Toronto), John Isbister (University of California, Santa Cruz), Alan Kelley (Duke University), Anne Krueger (Stanford University), Jong-Wha Lee

(Korea University), David Lindauer (Wellesley College), Charles McLure (Stanford University), Malcolm McPherson (Harvard University), Carrie A. Meyer (George Mason University), Vijayendra Rao (University of Michigan), Yana van der Muelen Rodgers and her students, who proofread some of the new material (College of William and Mary), Caroline Schwartz (Emory University), David Singer (University of Connecticut), Joseph Stern (Harvard University), Thomas Tushingham (Ryerson Polytechnic Institute), Jeffrey Vincent (Harvard University), and Louis Wells (Harvard University).

Work on the bibliography and data assembly was greatly assisted by the efforts of Ellen Gates, Mumtaz Hussain, Mark Gustafson, Carrie Workman, and Carol Zayotti.

At W. W. Norton and Company, Ed Parsons and Ann Marcy both encouraged and prodded us through the revision process and then transformed the manuscript into the book you are reading now.

We hope that we have produced a book that meets the expectations of all these people who played such an important role in making the process work.

D. H. P. Cambridge
S. R. Washington
D. R. S. Cambridge

International Development Resources on the Internet

The World Bank

http://www.worldbank.org/html/extdr/regions.htm
http://www.worldbank.org/html/extdr/thematic.htm
http://www.worldbank.org/poverty/

The World Bank website contains a wide range of information on specific countries and key development issues. The first of the three sites just listed contains brief economic overviews (including basic data) on every developing country. The second is a gateway to documents and information on a large assortment of development themes and issues. The third is a link to PovertyNet, a World Bank site aimed at providing resources for people and organizations working to understand and alleviate poverty.

The International Development Research Centre (IDRC)

http://www.idrc.ca/library/world/

Sponsored by the Canadian government, the IDRC gateway provides links to a large number of publications, databases, and development institutions.

Global Macroeconomic and Financial Policy Site

http://www.stern.nyu.edu/globalmacro/

Maintained by Professor Nouriel Roubini of New York University's Stern School of Business, this site provides links to newspaper and magazine articles on current issues, as well as academic and government analyses of exchange rate regimes, financial sector policies, financial crises, and the international financial system. It also provides links to information on specific countries and to selected macroeconomic and financial databases.

Netaid.org

http://www.netaid.org/

Netaid's mission is to use the power of the Internet to create opportunities to end the cycle of extreme poverty and to provide information on successful development projects and innovative organizations.

The World Factbook

http://www.odci.gov/cia/publications/factbook/index.html

Produced by the CIA, The World Factbook contains maps and information on government structures, key personnel, the economy, and other basic information on countries around the world.

IMF Directory of Economic, Commodity, and Development Organizations

http://www.imf.org/np/sec/decdo/contents.htm

The IMF directory provides background information on and links to over 100 regional economic organizations and intergovernmental commodity and development organizations.

ELDIS: The Electronic Development and Environment Information System

http://www.ids.ac.uk/eldis/eldis.html

The ELDIS gateway provides a wealth of information on development and the environment. Hosted by the Institute of Development Studies and the University of Sussex, ELDIS provides links to country-specific pages, full-text reports and research papers, recent news items, and other information.

Oneworld.net

http://www.oneworld.org/

Oneworld is an international network of cooperative centers with the objectives of promoting human rights and sustainable development. This site focuses on current news items and key development issues and includes information from a large number of development organizations.

PART ONE

Theory and Patterns

INTRODUCTION

In 1975, when she was 17 years old, Rachmina Abdullah did something no girl from her village had ever done before.[1] She left her home in a beautiful but poor part of the state of Kedah in Malaysia, where people grow rice in the valleys and tap rubber trees in the nearby hills, and went to work in an electronics plant in the busy city of Penang, 75 miles away. Rachmina's family was poor even by the modest standards of her village, and her parents welcomed the opportunity for their daughter to earn her own keep and possibly even send money back to help them feed and clothe the family, deal with recurrent emergencies, and raise their five younger children. With these benefits in mind, they set aside their reservations about their unmarried daughter's unheard-of plan to go off by herself to work in the city.

Rachmina got a job assembling integrated circuits (ICs) along with 500 other young women in a factory owned by a Japanese company. Every day, she patiently soldered hundreds of tiny wires onto tiny chips of silicon. It was tedious, repetitive work that had to be performed at high speed and, the management expected, with flawless accuracy. Each working day, Rachmina and her new colleagues rose very early and bicycled, walked, or bused to the factory. Being careful to arrive before the assigned hour of 7 A.M. to avoid being fined, the workers removed their shoes at the factory door, punched the time clock, and went to a room where they changed

---

1. This narrative is loosely based on Fatimah Daud, *"Minah Karan." The Truth about Malaysian Factory Girls* (Kuala Lumpur: Berita Publishing, 1985), and Kamal Salih and Mei Ling Young, "Changing Conditions of Labour in the Semiconductor Industry in Malaysia," *Labour and Society,* 14 (1989), 59–80.

into spotless white uniforms and slippers. Then they hurried to an assembly hall, where they heard a speech from the foreman about the day's production goals and sang the company song.

Except for one 5-minute break, which most of the young women used to fill in forms showing how much they had produced, they worked without stopping until noon, when it was time for a 45–minute lunch break. Rachmina spent this period eating and chatting with her friends in the lunch hall, where the Malay, Chinese, and Indian workers clustered in separate areas. After lunch, the women resumed the morning's routine, stopping only when the quitting bell rang at 4 P.M. Then they reversed the morning's procedure, returning to the assembly hall, singing the company anthem again, hearing another speech from the foreman, lining up to clock out, changing to street clothes, and leaving for home. By the end of her long day of steady activity, Rachmina had earned the equivalent of $2.50.

Since their hourly wages were low, the workers welcomed frequent opportunities to work overtime. Often they put in two or three extra hours in a day, for up to seven days a week. They particularly liked working Sundays and holidays, when double wages were paid. With overtime work and occasional bonuses, Rachmina was able to earn an average of $80 a month. She shared a small house in a squatter area with seven other factory workers. There was only one bedroom, so some of them slept in the lounge. By living simply and inexpensively, most of the young women managed to set aside $5 to $20 a month to send to their families in the villages. A few spent freely on clothes and cosmetics, and were criticized for it, but most led frugal lives. The young women enjoyed the unfamiliar freedom of living apart from their families.

In 1982, the electronics industry was hit by a recession. By this time, Rachmina had become a line leader, responsible for supervising the work of a team of newer workers. Her factory reduced its workforce, cut back on shift work, and virtually eliminated overtime. Rachmina, who was now 22 and had accumulated $400 in savings, decided it was time to return to her village, where she soon married a local man and settled down.

Rachmina's chance to work in an electronics factory came about because, in the 1970s, American and Japanese electronics manufacturers were moving into export processing zones (EPZs) established by the Malaysian government in several parts of the country. The government used the EPZs to tempt foreign investors to establish plants in Malaysia. The national unemployment rate was high, and the government was particularly anxious to find more urban, nonagricultural jobs for the indigenous Malay population, to which Rachmina and her family belonged. The Malays had long followed a rural lifestyle and generally were much poorer than the immigrants of Chinese and Indian stock. Now the government, which relied on Malay votes and had experienced terrifying race riots in 1969, was anxious to help Malays better their economic position.

Investors were drawn to Penang as a good place to set up semiconductor assembly plants. The electronics industry had originated in high-tech locations like Silicon Valley, California. By the mid-1970s, however, demand for ICs and other electronic devices was growing by leaps and bounds, and the firms were looking for overseas locations where they could carry out parts of their operations at lower cost. ICs are made in a four-step process. First, mask making, the process of designing the circuit and reducing the artwork to an overlay through high-resolution photography, is a high-skill operation. Second, wafer fabrication, the conversion of silicon into chips, is a capital-intensive process. Third, assembly, including mounting the chip on a frame, welding appropriate wires to it, and enclosing the completed chip in a resin, plastic, or ceramic covering, is very labor intensive. Finally, testing, although also done by hand, requires some skill.

It was becoming too costly for electronic firms to meet the booming demand while carrying out all four operations in California, Japan, and similar locations. The firms decided to move their assembly and testing operations to countries where labor was cheap, compliant, and capable of learning the relatively simple skills involved. The first beneficiaries of this migration in electronics and other industries were the newly industrializing nations of East Asia, South Korea, Taiwan, Hong Kong, and Singapore. In Malaysia, the city of Penang, with its good infrastructure and English-speaking workforce, also attracted foreign investors, even though the electronics industry was forced to recruit thousands of farmwomen like Rachmina and introduce them to the disciplines of factory labor.

Factories making 64K chips and other electronic components flourished in Penang and other Malaysian cities in the 1970s and early 1980s. Malaysia, a middle-income country previously known mainly for the export of rubber, tin, and palm oil, became the second largest exporter of electronic components, preceded only by Japan. The plants were almost all foreign owned. They bought and sold few goods and services in Malaysia itself, and only the simpler parts of the manufacturing process were carried out in Malaysia. Drawn by generous tax exemptions and wages that averaged as little as $30 a month in 1971, the companies experienced cost increases as wages rose to $120 a month by 1980, an increase only partly offset by rising productivity. Meanwhile, advances in technology in the 1980s made ICs both more complex and smaller, and so reduced the amount of work that could be done by hand. These changes contributed to the industry shakeout that Rachmina experienced in 1982. Employment of unskilled workers dropped sharply for a while in Malaysia and other developing countries involved in electronic component assembly.

In time, however, technological advances and continuing cost pressures
in the developed countries dictated that even some of the more complex
parts of the manufacturing process be shifted to lower-wage countries. As
wages rose in South Korea, Taiwan, Hong Kong, and Singapore, firms
moved their labor-intensive operations from these newly industrialized
countries (NICs) to the less-industrialized economies of Asia, such as
Malaysia and Thailand. In this second wave of foreign investment, some
of the migrating operations were owned by companies from Korea, Taiwan, Hong Kong, and Singapore. The Penang electronics industry revived. It now uses fewer unskilled and more skilled workers than before,
and it produces a wider range of products for both domestic and international markets. But it revived without Rachmina, happily engaged in raising a family in her Kedah village.

Rachmina Abdullah is a personification of the nearly 4 billion people
of the developing countries whose lives have been profoundly affected, in
many different ways, by economic changes in recent years. Her story raises
many issues of development that are addressed in this book. How does industrialization affect the lives of the majority of people in developing
countries who still are rural and poor? Who benefits from foreign investment and who loses, in both the developing and the industrial countries?
How do governments promote investment, industrialization, and exports?
How do countries educate their people to become productive workers in
more advanced industries? How do countries and their people cope with
the disparity between urban industrial workers and the vast majority of
still-poor farmers and marginal urbanites and between the advances of
some ethnic groups and the slow progress of others? This book explores
the economics of these and other issues in an attempt to understand why
some countries develop rapidly while others seem not to develop at all. We
are concerned with both the characteristics of development and the policies that can be employed to improve development performance.

Terminology: The Developing World

Before embarking on this complex task, we need to sort out some terms
commonly used to describe developed and less-developed countries and to
suggest some possible ways to measure where a country stands along the
continuum from industrial to developing.

RICH AND POOR COUNTRIES

The countries with which this book is concerned have been labeled with
many different terms. All these terms are intended to contrast their state or
rate of change with those of the more modern, advanced, developed coun-

tries, so that the terms tend to be found in pairs. The starkest distinction is between **backward** and **advanced** economies or between **traditional** and **modern** ones. The "backward" economy is traditional in its economic relationships. However precisely and neutrally the term can be defined, it retains pejorative connotations, a touch of condescension, and therefore is not much used today. In any case, the implication of stagnation is inappropriate, for in most countries economic and social relationships are changing in important ways.

The more popular classifications implicitly put all countries on a continuum based on their **degree of development.** Therefore, we speak of the distinctions between **developed** and **underdeveloped** countries, **more-** and **less-developed** ones, or to recognize continuing change, **developed** and **developing** countries. The degree of optimism implicit in *developing countries* and the handy acronym LDCs for *less-developed countries,* make these the two most widely used terms.[2] Developed countries frequently are called **industrial countries,** in recognition of the close association between development and industrialization. The highest income countries sometimes are referred to as **postindustrial countries,** in recognition that the modern service sector (finance, research and development, medical services, etc.), not manufacturing, accounts for the largest and most rapidly growing share of the economies of these countries.

A dichotomy based simply on income levels, the **poor** versus the **rich countries,** has been refined by the World Bank to yield a four-part classification that is useful for many analytical purposes.[3] The developing countries are divided by income into **low-income economies** (less than $785 per capita in 1996, converted into dollars at the current exchange rate) and **middle-income economies** (between $785 and $9,636 in 1996). The latter group is further divided into those with incomes below $3,115 per capita, the **lower-middle-income economies,** and from $3,115 to $9,636 per capita, the **upper-middle-income economies.** (A subset of upper-middle-income countries, mostly Asian and occasionally Latin American economies whose industrial output has been growing rapidly, sometimes is called the **newly industrializing countries** or **economies.**) The World

---

2. The initials also have been used, especially by the United Nations, to designate the "least-developed countries," those with the lowest incomes per capita (among other characteristics).

3. World Bank, *World Development Report 1994* (New York: Oxford University Press, 1994), pp. 178–79. The World Bank, formally the International Bank for Reconstruction and Development (IBRD), borrows funds on private capital markets in developed countries and lends to the developing countries and, through its affiliate, the International Development Association (IDA), receives contributions from the governments of developed countries and lends to the low-income countries at very low interest rates with long repayment periods. The bank perhaps is the world's most important and influential development agency.

Bank's classification is completed by the **high-income economies** (also called the *industrial countries*), mostly members of the Organization for Economic Cooperation and Development (OECD), with incomes over $9,636 per capita.

Three anomalous groups fit uneasily into this taxonomy. A number of Middle Eastern petroleum exporters such as Oman, Saudi Arabia, and the United Arab Emirates—whose incomes ranged from $8,000 to $17,000 per capita in 1996—have economies that are more traditional than the typical upper-middle income or industrialized country. Three other economies—Israel, Singapore, and Hong Kong—are considered by the United Nations (and many others) to be developing countries despite per capita incomes of over $18,000 in 1996. And the economies of Eastern Europe, including Russia, have incomes that qualify them as middle income, although some of them may be better described as industrial economies in decline or **transitional economies** moving from controlled to market-oriented development.

A term in vogue during the 1980s, especially in international forums, was the **third world.** Perhaps the best way to define it is by elimination. Take the industrialized (OECD) economies of Western Europe, North America, and the Pacific (the "first" world, although it was never called that) and the industrialized, formerly centrally planned economies of Eastern Europe (the "second" world); the rest of the countries constitute the third world. All third-world countries are developing countries, and these include all of Latin America and the Caribbean, Africa, the Middle East, and Asia except Japan. The geographic configuration of this group has led to a parallel distinction of **North** (first and second worlds) versus **South,** which still has some currency. But the South or third world encompasses a wide variety of countries, from wealthy oil exporters to very low-income, poorly endowed countries.

It is necessary to be aware of these various terms and classifications and recognize their exceptions and inconsistencies. But it is not wise to dwell too long on them. No system can capture all the important dimensions of development and provide a perfectly consistent, manageable framework. We generally refer to the less-developed, poorer countries as *developing countries,* although other terms are used where appropriate.

GROWTH AND DEVELOPMENT

While the labels used to distinguish one set of countries from another can vary, one must be more careful with the terms used to describe the development process itself. The terms **economic growth** and **economic development** sometimes are used interchangeably, but a fundamental distinction lies between them. *Economic growth* refers to a rise in national or per capita income and product.[4] If the production of goods and services in a country rises, by whatever means, one can speak of that rise as "economic growth." *Economic development* implies more. What has been happening in South Korea since 1960, for example, is fundamentally different from what has been happening in Libya as a result of the discovery of petroleum. Both countries experienced a large rise in per capita income, but in Libya this rise was achieved by foreign corporations staffed largely by foreign technicians who produced a single product consumed mainly in the United States and Western Europe. Although the government and people of Libya have received large amounts of income from their oil, they have had little to do with producing that income. The effect of petroleum development has been much as if a rich country decided to give Libya large amounts of grant aid.

Libya's experience is not usually described as economic development. Economic development, in addition to a rise in per capita income, implies fundamental changes in the structure of the economy, of the kind observed in South Korea since 1960. Two of the most important of these structural changes are the rising share of industry, along with the falling share of agriculture in national product, and the increasing percentage of people who live in cities rather than the countryside. In addition, countries that enter into economic development usually pass through periods of accelerating, then decelerating, population growth during which the country's age structure changes dramatically. Consumption patterns also change as people no longer have to spend all their income on necessities but instead move on to consumer durables and eventually to leisure-time products and services.

A key element in economic development is that the people of the country must be major participants in the process that brought about these changes in structure. Foreigners can be and inevitably are involved as well, but they cannot be the whole story. Participation in the process of development implies participation in the enjoyment of the benefits of development as well as the production of those benefits. If growth benefits only a tiny, wealthy minority, whether domestic or foreign, it is not development.

Modern economic growth, the term used by Nobel-laureate Simon Kuznets, refers to the current economic epoch as contrasted to, say, the epoch of merchant capitalism or the epoch of feudalism. The epoch of modern economic growth still is going on, so all its features are not yet clear, but the key element has been the application of science to problems of economic production, which in turn has led to industrialization, urbanization, and even explosive growth in population.

---

4. Income per capita is measured as the gross national product (GNP; the value of all goods and services produced by a country's economy in a year) divided by the population.

The widely used term **modernization** refers to much more than the economy. One can speak of the "modernization" of a society or political system, for example. But it is difficult to give the term a precise meaning. Too often there is a tendency to equate modernization with becoming more like the United States or Western Europe. Is it reasonable to say that the former Soviet Union was not modern because it was not democratic or that Japan is not modern because it still maintains certain ways of organizing business, based more on its own traditions than on practices in the West? Because of the vague and misleading nature of the term, we will not use it further here.

Finally, it always should be kept in mind that, while economic development and modern economic growth involve much more than a rise in per capita income or product, no development can occur without economic growth.

A Development Continuum

Much can be learned from a ten-minute perusal of Table 1–1 and Figures 1–1 to 1–4 about the nature of structural change during development and the many differences within the developing world. These data are from the World Bank's *World Development Report,* an annual publication that should become familiar to every student of development. The bank (and most sources) classifies countries by their income per capita, using the four-part division already discussed.

Although income per capita remains the most useful single indicator of development, it has many shortcomings, which we discuss in Chapter 2. One of these is that, to compare incomes among countries, all have to be converted into a common currency, typically into U.S. dollars. However, the fluctuation of exchange rates over time means that dollar incomes, and country rankings, change frequently even though the underlying situation—peoples' real welfare—has changed very little. One way to deal with this is to use a common set of prices, usually those of the United States, to measure the output of every country. Thus, a haircut in India is priced the same as one in the United States, as is a ton of wheat, a telephone, or a car.

This measure of average income is called the **purchasing power parity,** or PPP, method. It gives a more accurate comparison of incomes among countries and will be used throughout this book. In Table 1–1, countries are ranked in order of ascending PPP income per capita (column 1). The conventional measure of income, converted at the dollar exchange rate, is shown in the second column for comparison. The countries have been classified according to their PPP incomes: low-income countries have incomes below $2,000 per capita; lower-middle-income countries, $2,000

TABLE 1–1 DEVELOPMENT CHARACTERISTICS OF GROUPS AND SELECTED COUNTRIES, 1977

COUNTRY	GNP PER CAPITA (PPP DOLLARS)	GNP PER CAPITA (U.S. DOLLARS)	ENERGY CONSUMPTION PER CAPITA (KG OIL EQUIVALENT)	RURAL POPULATION SHARE (%)	LIFE EXPECTANCY AT BIRTH (YEARS)	ADULT ILLITERACY (%) MALES	FEMALES
LOW INCOME	1,400	350	198	72	59	35	59
LOWER MIDDLE INCOME	3,760	1,230	1,030	58	68.5	12	27
UPPER MIDDLE INCOME	7,700	4,520	1,579	26	69.5	12	17
HIGHER INCOME	22,770	25,700	5,118	22	77.5	N.A.	N.A.
ETHIOPIA	510	110	21	84	49.5	55	75
MALI	740	260	21	72	50	61	77
TANZANIA	N.A.	30	32	74	50.5	21	43
INDIA	1,650	390	260	73	62.5	35	62
BANGLADESH	1,050	270	67	81	58	51	74
KENYA	1,110	330	109	70	58.5	14	30
NIGERIA	880	260	165	59	53	33	53
SENEGAL	1,670	550	104	55	50.5	57	77
GHANA	1,790	370	92	63	59	24	47
CHINA	3,570	860	707	68	69.5	10	27
HONDURAS	2,200	700	236	55	67	27	27
PAKISTAN	1,590	490	243	65	63.5	50	76
BOLIVIA	N.A.	950	396	38	61	10	24
CAMEROON	1,980	650	117	54	56.5	25	48
PHILIPPINES	3,670	1,220	307	44	66	5	6
SRI LANKA	2,460	800	136	77	73	7	13
INDONESIA	3,450	1,110	442	63	65	10	22
PERU	4,390	2,460	421	28	68.5	6	17
EGYPT, ARAB REP. OF	2,940	1,180	596	55	65.5	36	61
BRAZIL	6,240	4,720	772	20	67	17	17
HUNGARY	7,000	4,430	2,454	34	70	N.A.	N.A.
COLOMBIA	6,720	2,280	655	26	70	9	9
ARGENTINA	9,950	8,570	1,525	11	73	4	4
MEXICO	3,130	1,250	1,456	26	72	8	13
MALAYSIA	10,920	4,680	1,655	45	72	11	22
KOREA, REP. OF	13,500	10,550	3,225	17	72.5	1	3
SAUDI ARABIA	N.A.	6,790	4,360	16	70	29	50
UNITED KINGDOM	20,520	20,710	3,786	11	77	N.A.	
JAPAN	23,400	37,850	3,964	22	80	N.A.	
GERMANY	21,300	28,260	4,156	13	77.5	N.A.	
UNITED STATES	28,740	28,740	7,905	23	77	N.A.	

Source: World Development Report 1998/99 (Washington, D.C.: The World Bank, 1999), pp. 190–91, 208–9. The energy use figures are for 1995.

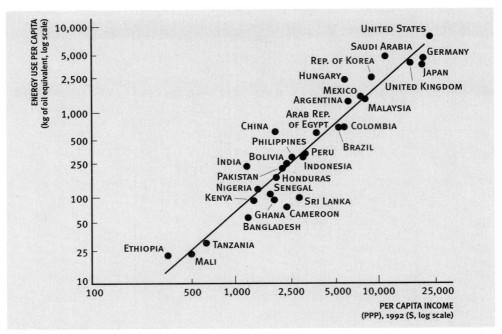

FIGURE 1–1 ENERGY CONSUMPTION PER CAPITA. There is a strong tendency for energy consumption to rise with average income, although some countries use much less energy than others at the same average income.

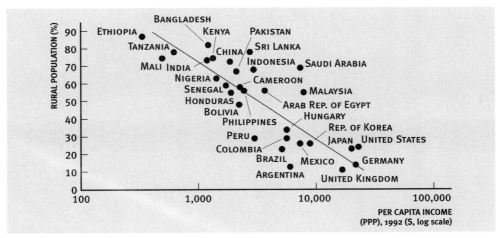

FIGURE 1–2 RURAL POPULATION. The share of the population living in rural areas declines as income grows.

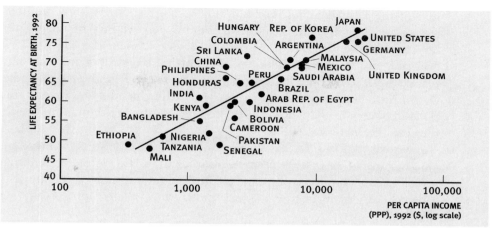

FIGURE 1–3 LIFE EXPECTANCY. Although life expectancy rises with average income, there are large differences among countries with similar incomes.

to $5,000; upper-middle-income countries, $5,000 to $10,000; and upper-income countries, above $10,000.

A major effect of using PPP incomes is to compress the differences between rich and poor countries. Table 1–1 shows that India, for example, has an income, converted at the dollar exchange rate, just over 1 percent that of the United States. But in PPP terms, India's income is 5 percent

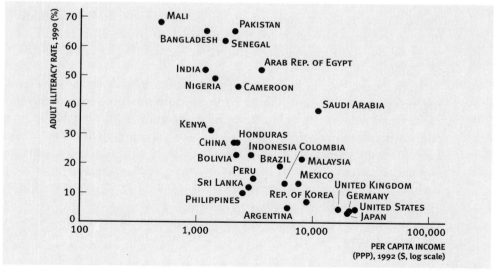

FIGURE 1–4 ADULT LITERACY. The rate of illiteracy among adults tends to fall as incomes rise, but some low-income countries have remarkably low rates of illiteracy.

that of the United States. For a middle-income country, say Colombia, the dollar exchange rate gives an income 6 percent that of the United States, while the PPP ratio is 25 percent, a very different picture. The PPP estimates also change the rankings of countries. Bangladesh and Pakistan, for example, move up in the rankings, while Mali and Senegal move down. At the upper end of the income scale, the United States remains the richest country in the world under the PPP standard, although not under the conventional measure.

One way to avoid the problems of comparing incomes is to use physical measures of economic modernization or industrialization. A common measure is a country's per capita consumption of energy. Figure 1–1 shows how closely energy use per capita is correlated with GNP per capita.[5]

A predominant structural characteristic of development is the growing share of both income produced and labor employed in industry. Table 1–1 and Figure 1–2 reflect this trend, inversely, in the share of the population living in rural areas. This share declines from an average of 73 percent for low-income countries to only 22 percent for high-income countries.

Rising income is not the only goal of development. People aspire to become healthier and better educated. Indicators for each of these aspects of well-being are included in Table 1–1, and they are correlated with per capita income in Figures 1–3 and 1–4. Life expectancy, averaging less than 60 years in low-income countries (excluding China), rises to 77 years on average for high-income countries. But the most dramatic contrast is in adult illiteracy. In the poorest group of countries, excluding China, more than 50 percent of the adult population is unable to read. Upper-middle-income countries have reduced their illiteracy to below 20 percent on average, while in the high-income countries, less than 5 percent of all adults are illiterate.

Each category includes considerable variance and hence some interesting exceptions. India and China consume substantially more energy per capita than other countries with similar incomes, while the Philippines consumes substantially less (Figure 1–1). The rural population share in Sri Lanka is more than twice that of Peru, a country with nearly the same income; the contrast between Malaysia, where 55 percent of the population is rural, and Argentina, where 13 percent is rural, is even sharper (Figure 1–2). Chinese and Sri Lankans live as long as Hungarians and Argentines, even though incomes in the latter countries are two to three times those in the former countries (Figure 1–3). The Philippines and Sri Lanka have

5. The regression lines shown in the graphs have been calculated for countries in our sample only. These countries have been chosen for their general interest rather than because they are a statistically representative sample.

adult illiteracy rates of 12 percent or less, little different from those of Colombia and Mexico, which have twice the income. In Pakistan and Egypt, with incomes similar to those in the Philippines and Sri Lanka, over half the adults are illiterate (Figure 1–4).

A Glance at History

This diversity in income and literacy is part of a much larger set of variations between developing countries that often have their origins in different historical experiences. A key characteristic of modern economic growth is that it did not begin everywhere in the world at the same time. Instead, it spread slowly across Europe and North America but, except for Japan, did not break out of areas dominated by European culture until the 1950s and 1960s. In parts of the world, it has yet to begin.

Even within Europe on the eve of industrialization, there were great differences among societies, and these differences had much to do with why development began first in Western Europe and spread only gradually to the East. In England, for example, laborers were free to change jobs and migrate to distant places, and commerce and banking had reached a high level of sophistication in the centuries preceding the Industrial Revolution. But Russia in the mid-nineteenth century was still feudal: Most peasants were tied to their lord's estate for life, and finance, industry, and transport was in a primitive state.

In Asia, Latin America, and Africa, the range of political and cultural experience is more diverse than that which existed within Europe. Great empires, such as those of China and Japan had over a thousand years of self-governing experience, and they thought of themselves as a single, unified people, rather than a collection of ethnically distinct tribes or regions. By premodern standards China and Japan also had high levels of urbanization and commerce, and they shared Confucian values, which emphasize the importance of education. Long years of comparative stability contributed to a population increase that resulted in the great shortage of arable land relative to population, which still exists in the region. Because of the comparative sophistication of premodern commerce in East Asia, European and American merchants never were able to play a significant role in the management of domestic commerce in the region. As Chinese and Japanese merchants gradually acquired an understanding of foreign markets, they were able to compete successfully with representatives of the industrialized world in that sphere as well.

At the other end of this historical spectrum of unified self-government and relative commercial sophistication are several Southeast Asian and most African nations. Indonesia and Nigeria, for example, really were the arbitrary creations of Dutch and British colonialism, which brought together diverse groups of people who spoke different languages and had no history of working together under a shared government. These diverse groups had little desire to maintain the externally imposed boundaries of the colonial powers. The result in the 1950s in Nigeria and the 1960s in Indonesia were wars fought to keep their new countries together. Similar civil wars threatened to break up the nation in the Republic of the Congo and the Sudan in the 1990s. Even Europe was not immune to this kind of antidevelopment chaos as the breakup of Yugoslavia into several independent nations in the late 1990s demonstrates.

Experience with commerce in many parts of Southeast Asia and Africa also was quite limited. Throughout the colonial era in Indonesia and many parts of sub-Saharan Africa, foreign trade and large-scale domestic commerce were almost entirely in the hands of Europeans. Local people sometimes controlled small-scale commerce, particularly in the countryside, but usually it was in the hands of minorities who had immigrated from other poor but commercially more advanced countries. Therefore, local commerce in much of Southeast Asia was in the hands of local Chinese, that in East Africa was managed mainly by immigrants from the Indian subcontinent, while in West Africa, Lebanese often played a central role. Because of inexperience, the local people could not effectively compete with either these immigrant groups or the Europeans; and because they could not compete, they gained little experience with trade or finance. This was one of the many vicious circles so common to the plight of poor countries.

Not all experiences with colonialism were the same. In India, a tiny number of British ruled a vastly populated subcontinent. By necessity, the British had to train large numbers of Indians to handle all but the very top jobs in the bureaucracy and army. At the time of independence in 1947, Indians already were running most of their own affairs because enough trained and experienced personnel were available to do so. But Indonesia had fewer than a thousand university or other post-secondary school graduates at the time of independence, and the Congo had hardly any. Prior to independence even the lower levels of the bureaucracy in Indonesia had been run by the Dutch and those in the Congo by Belgians. In comparison, India and China in the 1940s had hundreds of thousands of university graduates.

Latin America's historical heritage is different from that of either Asia or Africa. Independence in most of the region was achieved in the early nineteenth century, not after World War II as in Asia and Africa. Although there were local populations in the region when the Europeans first arrived, the indigenous populations were killed, suppressed, or enslaved. So, to meet growing labor requirements, the elites turned to voluntary and forced immigration of Europeans and Africans. Spanish and Portuguese immigrants ruled; the Africans were enslaved until late in the nineteenth century. Ignored or pushed aside, some of the original population continued to exist, but in varying numbers: Peru and Bolivia maintained large indigenous populations, whereas in Argentina, native peoples nearly disappeared.

North America above the Rio Grande also was peopled by immigrants who suppressed the local population. In both North and South America, slavery existed in some regions and not in others, but there were important differences between the types of colonial rule. In the North, the indigenous population was more thoroughly suppressed; hence, it was small and isolated and not a factor when economic development began. European immigrants were from the economically most advanced parts of Europe, where feudal values and structures already had been partially dismantled. But Spanish and Portuguese immigrants came from an area that, by the nineteenth century, was one of the more backward parts of Europe. The feudal values and structures that still dominated this region accompanied these colonists to the New World. Likewise, there were great differences within Latin America. Argentina, for example, is largely a nation of European immigrants; Mexico, Peru, and Bolivia have large indigenous populations; a large minority of Brazilians and virtually all Haitians are descended from former African slaves.

It is impossible to summarize all the important differences among countries in the developing world, but those with the greatest bearing on the potential for modern economic growth in the region would include differences between

- Countries with a long tradition of emphasis on education and an elite that was highly educated, as contrasted with countries where illiteracy was nearly universal.
- Countries with fairly highly developed systems of commerce, finance, and transport, mainly run by local people versus countries where these activities were monopolized at the time of independence by European or Asian immigrant minorities.
- Countries peopled by those who shared a common language, culture, and sense of national identity versus countries with a great diversity of language and culture and no common sense of national identity or shared common goals.
- Countries with long traditions of self-government versus those with no experience with even limited self-government until the 1950s or 1960s.

This list could be extended, but the point is made. Economic development requires both a government capable of directing or supporting a major growth effort and a people who can work effectively in and manage the enterprises and other organizations that arise in the course of development. Countries that have people with at least some relevant education and experience in economic affairs and governments able to support those people are better positioned for development than countries that have people with little relevant experience and diverse groups within the country that still argue over their share in what they believe, wrongly for the most part, to be a pie of fixed size.

The Concept of Substitutes

Given the great diversity in developing country experience, it would be a counsel of despair to suggest that the way to begin development is first to recreate the kinds of political, social, and economic conditions that existed in Western Europe or North America when those regions entered into modern economic growth. England prior to the Industrial Revolution had centuries of experience with merchant capitalism, but does it follow that Ghana or Indonesia also must acquire long experience with merchant capitalism before economic development is feasible? If the answer were yes, these countries would be doomed to another century or more of poverty.

Fortunately no standard list of barriers must be overcome nor must prerequisites be in place before development is possible. Instead, as economic historian Alexander Gerschenkron pointed out, for most presumed prerequisites there usually are substitutes. The main point of this concept is best illustrated with an example from Gerschenkron's own work.[6]

Capital, like labor, of course is necessary for development, and much more will be said about both in later chapters. But Karl Marx and others went a step further and argued that there must be an original or prior accumulation of capital before growth can take place. The basic idea came from looking at the experience of England where, Marx argued, trade, exploitation of colonies, piracy, and other related measures led to the accumulation of great wealth that, in the late eighteenth century, could be converted into investment in industry. Is such an accumulation a prerequisite for development everywhere or at least for a large number of countries? In the absence of a prior accumulation of capital, does economic development become impossible?

In Europe the answer clearly was no. One had to find funds that could be invested in industry, but they did not have to come out of the accumulated wealth of the past. Germany, for example, had little in the way of an original accumulation of capital when modern economic growth began there. But

6. Alexander Gerschenkron, *Economic Backwardness in Historical Perspective* (Cambridge, MA: Harvard University Press, 1962), Chap. 2.

Germany did have a banking system that could create funds, which then were lent to industrialists. How banks create funds is not our concern here; the point is that banks can create accounts that investors can draw on, and the creation of those accounts depends in no significant way on long years of prior savings and accumulation by merchants or other wealthy individuals.

Russia in the nineteenth century had neither an original accumulation of wealth nor a banking system capable of creating large enough levels of credit. Instead, Russia turned to the taxing power of the state. The government could and did tax funds from people and use this tax revenue for investment in industry. Russia also imported capital from abroad. Thus, in Russia, the government's use of taxation was a substitute for a well-developed banking system, and elsewhere a modern banking system was a substitute for an original accumulation of capital.

Similar examples of substitutes abound in today's world. Latin American countries, for example, rely heavily on financial institutions to mobilize and allocate savings. Sub-Saharan African countries, in contrast, rely more on fiscal institutions (the government budget). Factories in advanced countries with well-developed commercial networks rely on central distributors to supply them with spare parts. Rural industries in China, where commerce is less developed, make spare parts in their own foundries. A number of countries in the developing world today have substantial numbers of people with training and experience in areas relevant to economic development, while the number of such people in other countries, as already pointed out, is very small. The most common substitute for this lack of relevant experience is to import foreigners or to rely on nonindigenous residents who have the required experience. For reasons that will become apparent in later chapters, foreigners frequently are not very good substitutes for experienced local talent, but where the latter is missing, they can fill the gap until local talent is trained.

Therefore, in the chapters that follow, we do not look for three or four universal causes of poverty or a similar number of prerequisites that must be in place before growth is possible. Instead we attempt to identify some of the more common barriers to development and recognize that the presence of these barriers or the absence of some "prerequisites" does not condemn a country to stagnation and poverty. There usually are ways around, or substitutes for, any single barrier or "prerequisite," but the existence of many of these barriers or the absence of a wide variety of desirable preconditions will make economic development more difficult and in some cases impossible.

Despite the great diversity in historical experience and in policies and institutions used to promote growth, most less-developed countries have experienced growth in income since 1965 and many have enjoyed substantial growth, as Table 1–2 shows. All the most rapidly growing countries, with income per capita expanding by 4 percent a year or more, have been

TABLE 1–2   GROWTH OF POPULATION AND OUTPUT OF GROUPS AND SELECTED COUNTRIES, 1965–97 (PERCENT PER YEAR)

COUNTRY	POPULATION[a] 1965–80	1980–90	1990–97	GNP PER CAPITA, 1965–96	INDUSTRY VALUE ADDED, 1965–96
LOW-INCOME COUNTRIES	2.3	2.4	2.1	3.1	7.5
TANZANIA	2.9	3.2	3.0		N.A.
MALI	2.1	2.5	2.8	0.5	2.9
ETHIOPIA	2.7	3.1	2.3		N.A.
KENYA	3.6	3.4	2.6	1.5	5.8
BANGLADESH	2.6	2.4	1.6	1.0	4.1
INDIA	2.3	2.1	1.8	2.3	5.4
NIGERIA	2.5	3.0	2.9	0.1	4.3
SENEGAL	2.9	2.8	2.6	−0.5	3.9
GHANA	2.2	3.3	2.7	−0.9	0.4
CHINA	2.2	1.5	1.1	6.7	11.0
HONDURAS	3.2	3.3	3.0	0.5	4.5
LOWER-MIDDLE-INCOME COUNTRIES	2.4	1.6	1.2	0.8	N.A.
PAKISTAN	3.1	3.1	2.9	2.7	6.8
BOLIVIA	2.5	2.0	2.4	−0.5	0.0
CAMEROON	2.7	2.8	2.9	1.4	7.2
PHILIPPINES	2.8	2.6	2.3	0.9	3.6
SRI LANKA	1.8	1.4	1.2	3.1	4.8
INDONESIA	2.4	1.8	1.7	4.6	9.1
PERU	2.8	2.2	2.0	−0.4	N.A.
EGYPT, ARAB REP. OF	2.1	2.5	2.0	4.0	6.8
UPPER-MIDDLE-INCOME COUNTRIES	2.2	1.9	1.5	1.2	3.2
BRAZIL	2.4	2.0	1.4	2.4	4.6
HUNGARY	0.4	−0.3	−0.3	1.1	N.A.
COLOMBIA	2.4	1.9	1.8	2.1	4.5
ARGENTINA	1.6	1.5	1.3	−0.3	1.0
MEXICO	3.1	2.3	1.8	1.5	4.6
MALAYSIA	2.5	2.6	2.3	4.1	8.5
KOREA, REP. OF	2.0	1.2	1.0	7.3	13.8
HIGH-INCOME COUNTRIES	0.9	0.7	0.7	2.2	2.6
SAUDI ARABIA	4.6	5.2	3.4	−3.0	3.4
UNITED KINGDOM	0.2	0.2	0.3	1.9	N.A.
JAPAN	1.2	0.6	0.3	3.6	4.6
GERMANY	0.2	0.1	0.5	N.A.	N.A.
UNITED STATES	1.0	0.9	1.0	1.4	1.7

[a]Instantaneous rate of natural increase in 1992; that is, the rate of births less the rate of deaths per hundred.

Sources: World Development Report 1992 (Washington, DC: The World Bank, 1992) and *1998/99* (Washington, DC: The World Bank, 1999) for population growth rates and The World Bank, *World Development Indicators 1998* (Washington, DC: The World Bank, 1998) for GNP per capita and Industry growth rates.

in Asia: China, Indonesia, Malaysia, Korea, and Japan in the table plus Thailand, Taiwan, Hong Kong, and Singapore. There are many examples of countries with income growth over 2 percent a year. At 2 percent annual growth, the average income doubles in 35 years; at 4 percent, it doubles in less than a generation. Most of the countries with a declining average income since 1965 have been in Africa, although income also fell in Peru over the period. In most developing countries, manufacturing grew more rapidly than the gross national product and, thus, moved these economies through the inevitable structural change that reduces the share of income produced and labor employed in agriculture.

Perhaps the most remarkable changes in the third world since 1965 have been the virtually universal improvement in health conditions and the availability of education. From 1965 to 1992, the infant death rate reduced dramatically in every country listed in Table 1–3: Declines per 1,000 births from 177 to 78 in Nigeria and from 130 to 42 in Peru were typical. Primary school enrollment became universal in China, India, Kenya, and Sri Lanka and rose dramatically in most other low-income countries. With few exceptions, more than three quarters of the eligible children attend primary school in poor countries. That healthier populations also have meant higher population growth (Table 1–2) is an important consideration, as discussed in Chapter 8.

It sometimes is easy to become pessimistic about further progress in developing nations, especially when confronted by gloomy predictions about their future economic growth and the myriad problems afflicting LDCs, many of which will be cataloged in this book. As an antidote to discouragement, one needs to keep in mind the considerable economic development that already has taken place, the strong growth momentum of several countries in Asia, and the gratifying improvements in health and education that mark even the poorest countries. The question of how these benefits have been distributed among the populace will be taken up in Chapter 4 and in Part 3.

The study of economic development, however, is not mainly a review of what has and has not been accomplished in the past. It is a field concerned most of all about the future, particularly the future of the least-advantaged people in the world. To comprehend the future, one must first try to understand how we got to the point where we are now, but the future will not be just a replay or a projection forward of trends of the past. New forces are at work that will shape that future. Some of these forces can be seen clearly today. Others that will shape the economic progress of nations are only dimly perceived, if they are seen at all.

Any list of changes in the environment that will make the future of economic development different from the past should probably start with the information revolution. The role of greatly enhanced communication

TABLE 1–3   PROGRESS IN THE SOCIAL WELL-BEING OF GROUPS AND SELECTED COUNTRIES, 1965–96

COUNTRY	INFANT MORALITY RATE PER 1,000		PERCENTAGE OF AGE ENROLLED IN PRIMARY SCHOOL	
	1965	1996	1965	1995
LOW-INCOME COUNTRIES	122	80	76	95
TANZANIA	138	86	32	48
MALI	207	120	24	25
ETHIOPIA	149	109	49	24
KENYA	112	57	54	85*
BANGLADESH	144	77	49	92*
INDIA	150	65	74	100*
NIGERIA	177	78	32	89*
SENEGAL	126	60	40	54
GHANA	120	71	69	76*
CHINA	90	33	89	99
HONDURAS	128	44	80	90
LOWER-MIDDLE-INCOME COUNTRIES	123	35	74	92
PAKISTAN	149	88	40	74*
BOLIVIA	160	67	73	NA
CAMEROON	143	54	94	88*
PHILIPPINES	72	37	113	100
SRI LANKA	63	15	93	113*
INDONESIA	128	49	72	97
PERU	130	42	99	91
EGYPT, ARAB REP. OF	172	53	75	89
UPPER-MIDDLE-INCOME COUNTRIES	97	31	95	NA
BRAZIL	104	36	108	90
HUNGARY	39	11	101	93
COLOMBIA	86	25	84	85
ARGENTINA	58	22	101	108*
MEXICO	82	32	92	100
MALAYSIA	55	11	90	91
KOREA, REP. OF	62	9	101	99
HIGH-INCOME COUNTRIES	26	6	103	98
SAUDI-ARABIA	148	22	24	62
UNITED KINGDOM	20	6	92	100
JAPAN	18	4	100	100
GERMANY	25	5	—	100
UNITED STATES	25	7	104	96

*The star indicates that the figure is the gross enrollment ratio, whereas those figures without a star are the net enrollment ratio. The gross enrollment ratio is the ratio of total enrollment, regardless of age, to the population of the age group that officially corresponds to the primary level of education.

Source: World Development Report 1998/99, pp. 200–3, and The World Bank, Development Indicators, 1998, pp. 76–78.

around the world as represented by the Internet has sped up the flow of ideas across oceans and borders to an unprecedented degree and has made it possible for many kinds of services to be located far from the location where those services ultimately are used. An American business's accounting office might be in a building in Bangalore, India, rather than in a backroom of the business's operations in Chicago. Lower transport costs, together with better information contribute to global production networks and the expansion of global trade and investment. The rapid flow of information also is having an impact on politics, by making it harder for authoritarian regimes to control what their people are allowed to know. Partly for this reason, democratic regimes are becoming more the norm than the exception in developing countries, and there is reason to expect this trend to continue.

Not all the foreseeable trends of the future are positive. The scourge of HIV/AIDS is having a devastating impact on populations, particularly those hardest hit in Africa, where life expectancy actually is declining. Environmental degradation is much more serious today than it was a century ago, when Europe and North America were in the early stages of economic growth. Global warming, as a result, is a problem likely to play an important role in our future, whereas it played no role in the past. The one positive change in the environmental sphere is that people around the world are becoming aware of the danger at a much faster pace than in the past. Also a concern is that high technology and the information revolution benefit some groups in society, notably the better educated, while leaving behind other large groups.

Some changes likely to occur in the future are positive, but they still create problems for those that have to deal with them. Notable in this category is the rapid aging of populations in the industrialized countries, an aging process also underway in the many developing countries, which have experienced a sharp fall in both their birth and death rates. The result of this **demographic transition,** discussed at length in Chapter 7, is a longer life expectancy for the average person in these countries, clearly a positive change. But the size of the working-age population relative to the size of the retired older population is shrinking dramatically in more and more countries and that puts a large burden on those still in the workforce. The one group of countries that will not have to worry about this problem are those countries where the birth rate remains high and life expectancy low. Clearly, it is better to have to deal with the problem of an aging population than not to have the problem at all.

We probably are not even aware of many of the forces that will shape the future economic development of nations. No one at the end of the nineteenth century had heard of nuclear energy or DNA. No one in the

1970s had heard of HIV/AIDS. Given the pace of change in the current world of the new millennium, similar and possibly greater discoveries will influence profoundly how our economies develop. That said, we cannot rely on future discoveries to solve the problems of economic development and poverty among nations. We must try to understand how the nations of the world got to where they are today so that we can do a better job of raising living standards for all in the future.

Approaches to Development

This book is not for readers looking for a simple explanation of why some countries are still poor or how poverty can be overcome. Library shelves are full of studies explaining how development will occur if only a country will increase the amount it saves and invests or intensify its efforts to export. For two decades in the mid-twentieth century industrialization through import substitution—the replacement of imports with home-produced goods—was considered by many to be the shortest path to development. In the 1970s, labor-intensive techniques, income redistribution, and provision of basic human needs to the poor gained popularity as keys to development. Most economists now counsel governments to depend substantially on markets to set prices and allocate resources. Another school of thought suggests that development is possible only if preceded by a revolution that eliminates existing elites and replaces the market with central planning. A different theme is that development will be possible only with a massive shift of resources, in the form of foreign aid and investment, from the richest countries to the poorest.

No single factor is responsible for underdevelopment, and no single policy or strategy can set in motion the complex process of economic development. A wide variety of explanations and solutions to the development problem makes sense if placed in the proper context and makes no sense at all outside that set of circumstances. Mobilization of saving is essential for accelerated growth in most cases but sometimes may come second to a redistribution of income, if extreme poverty threatens political stability or forestalls the mobilization of human resources. Import substitution has carried some countries quite far toward economic development, but export promotion has helped others when import substitution bogged down. Prices badly distorted from their free-market values can stifle initiative and hence growth, but removing those distortions leads to development only when other conditions are met as well. Moreover, some, but certainly not all, centrally planned economies achieved sustained periods of development with prices that bore little relation to those determined by market forces. Finally, where leaders backed by interests hostile to development rule countries, those leaders and their constituents must be removed from power before growth can occur. But most developing countries have governments that genuinely want to promote development.

This book is not neutral toward all issues of development. Where controversy exists we shall point it out. Indeed, the authors of this book differ among themselves over some questions of development policy. But we share a common point of view on certain basic points.

First of all, this text extensively uses the theoretical tools of classical and neoclassical economics in the belief that these tools contribute substantially to our understanding of development problems and their solution. The text does not rely solely or even primarily on theory, however. For five decades and more, development economists and economic historians have been building up an empirical record against which these theories can be tested, and this book draws heavily on many of these empirical studies. We try to give real-country examples for virtually all the major points made in this book. In part, these examples come from the individual country and cross-country comparative studies of others, but they also are drawn extensively from our own personal experiences working on development issues around the world. The five authors who have contributed to this textbook have been fortunate enough to study and work over long periods of time in Bolivia, Chile, China, Colombia, Fiji, The Gambia, Ghana, Indonesia, Kenya, Korea, Malaysia, Peru, Sri Lanka, Tanzania, and Vietnam. At one time or another, at least one from this group of nations has exemplified virtually all the approaches to development now extant.

While this book draws on classical and neoclassical economic theory, development involves major issues for which these economic theories provide no answers or at best provide only partial answers. Economic theory tends to take the **institutional context** (the existence of markets, of a banking system, of international trade, etc.) as a given. But development is concerned with how one creates institutions that facilitate development in the first place. How, for example, does a country acquire a government interested in and capable of promoting economic growth? Can efficiently functioning markets be created in countries that currently lack them, or should the state take over the functions normally left to the market elsewhere? Is a fully developed financial system a precondition for growth, or can a country do without at least some parts of such a system? Is land reform necessary for development, and if so, what kind of land reform? These institutional issues and many others like them are at the heart of the development process and will reappear in different guises in the following chapters.

Organization

This book is divided into five parts. Part 1 examines the main factors that contribute to differing rates of economic growth and the kinds of structural change—including changes in income distribution—that occur once growth is underway. Structural change often is the result of deliberate choices by governments, and Part 2 provides an introduction to issues of market-based versus command systems of development and to economic planning models. It also raises issues of sustainability: How far or fast can development proceed without exhausting natural resources or irreversibly degrading the environment?

Economic development first and foremost is a process involving people, who are both the prime movers of development and its beneficiaries. Part 3 deals with how human resources are transformed in the process of economic development and how that transformation contributes to the development process itself. There are chapters on population, labor, education, and health.

The other major physical input in the growth process is capital, and Part 4 is concerned with how capital is mobilized and allocated for development purposes. From where, for example, do the savings come, and how are they transformed into investment? How does government mobilize the resources to finance development? What kind of financial system is consistent with rapid capital accumulation? Will inflation enhance or hinder the process, and what role will foreign aid and investment play?

Especially in the early stages of development, countries depend heavily on agriculture and on the export of food, fuel, and raw materials. Part 5 discusses strategies to enhance the productivity of such primary industries as a first, and often a continuing, task in stimulating economic development. Ultimately, however, development depends on industrialization. Part 5 also extends the discussion of industrial development, explores trade policies to promote manufactured exports, and analyzes the macroeconomic management of a developing economy open to world markets.

ECONOMIC GROWTH: THEORY AND EMPIRICAL PATTERNS

Why are some countries rich and others poor? Why do some economies grow quickly, while others grow slowly or not at all? How is it that some East Asian countries that were relatively poor in the early 1960s grew extremely rapidly to join the ranks of the middle- and upper-middle-income countries in the space of just 30 years? Why do some African countries remain mired in deep poverty, with few signs of sustained growth and development? These are some of the most important questions in the study of economics and indeed touch on some of the deepest problems facing human society.

Rapid economic growth and wide divergences of economic performance across countries actually are a fairly recent phenomena in world history. Up until about 500 years ago—a relatively short period of time in human history—most people lived in conditions that we now would consider abject poverty. Housing was poor, food supplies were highly variable and dependent on the weather, nutrition was inadequate, disease was common, health care was rudimentary, and life spans rarely exceeded 40 years. Even as recently as 120 years ago, the vast majority of people living in the world's most modern cities, including New York, London, and Paris, lived in extremely difficult conditions on very meager incomes. At the end of the twentieth century, however, income levels around the world generally are much higher and far more diverse. A significant minority of the world's population recorded relatively rapid and sustained income growth and now enjoys much longer and healthier lives, high levels of education, and generally much improved standards of living. Other countries have achieved important but more modest gains and now are considered to be middle-income countries. The majority of the world's population, however, continues to live in poverty, surely better off than their ancestors but living at levels of income and welfare far below those of the world's richest countries.

The next two chapters explore in some detail the puzzles of economic growth and divergent levels of income. Our objectives are to better understand the processes by which economies grow and develop and the characteristics that distinguish rapidly growing economies from those with slower growth. We examine both theories of economic growth and empirical patterns of growth across countries. Of course, economic growth is not synonymous with economic development and widespread improvements in the welfare of the population, which are taken up at greater length in Chapter 4. However, economic growth and increases in average income are central to the development process, and sustained development cannot occur in the absence of economic growth. This chapter begins by exploring the concept of gross national product and the related measure of per capita income and then examines the basic empirical data on rich and poor countries. It introduces some basic theories of economic growth and examines recent empirical studies on the factors most closely associated with economic growth. The next chapter examines the specific roles of different productive sectors in the growth process (focusing on the interrelationship between agriculture and industry) and explores empirical data on the broad patterns of changes in consumption and production generally associated with growth.

Estimating Gross National Product

At the outset of our exploration of economic growth and the patterns of development, it is important to understand both the strengths and weaknesses of the basic data. At the core of studies of economic growth are changes in average income, or gross national product per capita. **Gross national product** (GNP) is the sum of the value of finished good and services produced by a society during a given year and excludes **intermediate goods** (goods used up in the production of other goods, such as the steel used in an automobile or the chips that go into a computer). GNP counts output produced by citizens of the country, including the value of goods and services produced by citizens that live outside the country. **Gross domestic product** (GDP) is similar to GNP, except that it counts all output produced within the borders of a country, including output produced by resident foreigners but excluding the value of production by citizens living abroad. For example, during the last two decades a large numbers of Filipinos have found work in Malaysia, where there are abundant opportunities for low-skilled and semi-skilled workers. The value of the output produced by these workers counts as part of the Philippines' GNP (since these workers are Philippine nationals) but not as part of the Philippines' GDP (since the work is performed outside of the country). By contrast, the value of this work counts as part of Malaysia's GDP but not its GNP.

The share of a sector or component of GNP such as manufacturing or agriculture is measured by the value added by that sector. **Value added** refers to the addition to the value of the product at a particular stage of production. Thus, the value added of the cotton textile industry is the value of the textiles when they leave the factory minus the value of raw cotton and other materials used in their production. At the same time, value added is equal to the payments made to the factors of production in the textile industry: wages paid to labor plus profits, interest, depreciation of capital, and rent for buildings and land. Since the total value added at all stages of production equals total output, GNP is a measure of both total national *income* and total national *output*. GNP divided by the total population gives the standard measure of **per-capita income.**

The great strength of the GNP concept is that it encompasses all of a country's economic activity in a few mutually consistent summary statistics. The alternative of describing growth in terms of tons of steel and kilowatt-hours of electricity either leaves out much economic activity or, in an effort to be inclusive, involves the hopelessly complex discussion of thousands of individual products. The analysis of individual products in physical terms can be misleading, particularly in the measurement of broad economic change over time. Cotton textile output, for example, may fall over time, but the output of textiles made from artificial fibers may be increasing by more than enough to offset that fall. Gross national product provides a consistent technique for adding these two different trends together.

If the concept of gross national product has certain advantages, it also has certain important limitations, particularly when comparing patterns of development in a wide variety of developing countries. One difficulty is that low-income countries usually have poor-quality statistics; data from certain sectors of low-income countries, such as agriculture and handicrafts, are the worst of all. Estimates of the gross national product of many developing nations are based on fairly reliable statistics of modern industrial and mining enterprises combined with estimates of rural-sector performance based on small samples or outright guesses.

In addition to data limitations are basic methodological issues that reduce the accuracy of GNP estimates, which we discuss in the ensuing paragraphs.

WHAT IS INCLUDED IN GNP?

To begin with, a problem arises in the definition of *gross national product.* The proper way to calculate GNP is to add up the value of all the goods and services produced by the citizens of a country and then sold on the market.[1] However, many valuable contributions to society are excluded from gross national product. When housework and childcare are performed by paid servants or day-care employees, for example, they are included in GNP, since these services are "sold in the market." However, when unpaid members of the household perform these same services, they do not enter GNP. In developing countries, a very large number of activities do not enter the market. Much of what is produced by the agricultural sector, for example, is consumed by the farm household and never reaches the market. Strictly speaking, because of the way that GNP is defined, one cannot meaningfully discuss the changing share of agricultural production in GNP but only the changing share of the *marketed* agricultural production in GNP. Because this strict definition of GNP would severely limit the usefulness of comparing structural change among countries in which agriculture is the dominant sector, the usual practice is to include farm output consumed by the producer, valued at the prices of marketed farm produce. While making GNP a more meaningful indicator of the productive capacity of a developing economy, this procedure turns GNP into a somewhat arbitrary concept. If nonmarketed agricultural produce is included, for example, why not include household-provided childcare services? Since GNP excludes the value of nonmarketed services performed in the home, tasks that generally are performed by women are systematically underrepresented in GNP estimates. This problem is particularly severe in developing countries, since the share of women working in nonmarketed activities tends to be larger in low-income countries than in high-income countries. A related issue that works in an opposite way from subsistence agriculture and household services is the treatment of nonrenewable resources such as petroleum or silver. The value added of mining products includes the original value of the ore as well as the value added by the labor and capital needed to mine that ore. But the original value of the ore was not produced by the economy and hence does not really belong in GNP.

EXCHANGE-RATE CONVERSION PROBLEMS

A second methodological problem arises when attempting to convert the GNP of several different countries into a single currency. To compare the changing economic structure of several countries as per capita income

---

1. In calculating GNP, goods and services can be valued by using either the prices at which they are sold in the market (**GNP at market prices**) or the cost of all factor inputs (labor, capital, land) used in their production (**GNP at factor cost**).

rises, one must measure the per capita income figures in a common currency. The shortcut to accomplishing this goal is to use the official exchange rate between U.S. dollars and each national currency. For example, to convert India's GNP from rupees into U.S. dollars, the official exchange rate between Indian rupees and U.S. dollars (about 43 rupees per U.S. dollar in mid-1999) is used.

One problem with this procedure is that exchange rates, particularly those of developing countries, frequently are highly distorted. Trade restrictions make it possible for an official exchange rate to be substantially different from a rate determined by free trade. But even an accurate estimate of the free-market exchange rate would not eliminate the problem. A significant part of GNP is made up of what are called **nontraded goods and services;** that is, goods that do not and often cannot enter into international trade. Electric power, for example, can be imported only in rare cases from an immediate neighbor with a surplus to sell (the United States imports some electricity from Canada, for example). For the most part electric power must be generated within a country, and it makes little sense to talk about the international market or the international market price for electric power. By definition, internal transportation cannot be traded, although many transport inputs, such as trucks, can be imported. Wholesale and retail trade or elementary school teachers are nontraded services. The wages of workers in these nontraded services are not strongly influenced by any international market. Generally speaking, whereas the prices of traded goods tend to be similar across countries (since trade could quickly exploit any price differences), the prices of nontraded goods can differ widely from one country to the next (we explore the concepts of traded and nontraded goods and services in more detail in Chapter 19).

Exchange rates are determined largely by the flow of traded goods and international capital flows and generally do not reflect the relative prices of nontraded goods. As a result, gross national product converted to U.S. dollars by market exchange rates will give misleading comparisons if the ratio of prices of nontraded goods to prices of traded goods is different in the countries being compared. The way around this problem is to pick a set of prices prevailing in one of the countries and use that set of prices to value the goods and services of all countries being compared. In effect, one is calculating a **purchasing power parity** exchange rate. Thus, a cement block or a haircut is assigned the same value no matter if is produced in New Delhi or New York.

The essence of the procedure can be illustrated with the simple numerical exercise, presented in Table 2–1. The two economies in the table are called the United States and India, and each economy produces one traded commodity (steel) and one nontraded service (retail

TABLE 2–1   EXCHANGE RATE VERSUS PURCHASING POWER PARITY METHODS OF CONVERTING GNP INTO A SINGLE CURRENCY

| | UNITED STATES | | | INDIA | | |
	QUANTITY	PRICE (U.S. DOLLARS)	VALUE OF OUTPUT (BILLION U.S. DOLLARS)	QUANTITY	PRICE (RUPEES)	VALUE OF OUTPUT (BILLION RUPEES)
STEEL (MILLION TONS)	100	200 PER TON	20	8	9,000 PER TON	72
RETAIL SALES PERSONNEL (MILLIONS)	2	5,000 PER PERSON PER YEAR	10	4	60,000 PER PERSON PER YEAR	240
TOTAL GNP (LOCAL CURRENCY)			30			312

Official exchange rate, based on steel prices = 9,000/200, or Rs 45 = U.S. $1.

1. Indian GNP in U.S. dollars calculated by using the official exchange rate:

    312/45 = U.S. $6.9 billion.

2. Indian GNP in U.S. dollars calculated by using U.S. prices for each individual product or service and applying that price to Indian quantities (i.e., using purchasing power parity, PPP):

    | Steel | 8 million × $200 = $1.6 billion |
    | Retail sales personnel | 4 million × $5,000 = $20 billion |
    | GNP | = $21.6 billion. |

3. Ratio of PPP calculation to official exchange rate calculation: 21.6/6.9 = 3.1

sales). The price of steel is given in U.S. dollars in the United States and rupees in India, and the exchange rate is based on the ratio of the prices of the traded good (in this case, steel). The value of the services of retail sales personnel is estimated in the most commonly used way, which is to assume the value of the service is equal to the wages of the worker providing the service. These wages are likely to differ widely across countries and be determined almost exclusively by domestic labor supply and labor demand conditions, because workers cannot easily migrate from one country to another to take advantage of any differences in wages (partly because of immigration rules and partly because the cost of moving to a new country can be high). The two methods of converting Indian GNP into U.S. dollars are presented in the table. Clearly, one gets very different results depending on which method is used.

Systematic estimates from the World Bank using the two different methods on a select group of countries are presented in Table 2–2. While many of the differences in results between the two methods are not as

TABLE 2–2	GROSS NATIONAL PRODUCT PER CAPITA IN 1998 (U.S. DOLLARS)		
	MEASURED USING OFFICIAL EXCHANGE RATES (1)	MEASURED AT PURCHASING POWER PARITY (PPP) (2)	RATIO OF PPP CALCULATION TO OFFICIAL EXCHANGE RATE CALCULATION (3)
UNITED STATES	29,340	29,340	1.00
JAPAN	32,380	23,180	0.72
GERMANY	25,850	20,810	0.81
UNITED KINGDOM	21,400	20,640	0.96
SOUTH KOREA	7,970	12,270	1.54
MEXICO	3,970	8,190	2.06
COLOMBIA	2,600	7,500	2.88
CHINA	750	3,220	4.29
BOLIVIA	1,000	2,820	2.82
INDONESIA	680	2,790	4.10
INDIA	430	1,700	3.95
GHANA	390	1,610	4.13
KENYA	330	1,130	3.42

Source: World Bank, *World Development Report 1999/2000: Entering the 21st Century* (Washington, DC: World Bank, 2000), pp. 230–31.

great as in our numerical illustration, they still are substantial. Furthermore, there is a reasonable systematic relationship between the degree to which the exchange-rate conversion method understates GNP and the average income of the country. For Germany and the United States, whose per capita GNPs were not far apart in 1997, the exchange-rate conversion is a reasonable approximation of what is obtained when converting German GNP into U.S. dollars using the better method. For India, however, the ratio between the two measures is 3.95 to 1, even larger than in our illustration. With differences of that magnitude, exchange-rate conversions can be very misleading.

OTHER INDEX-NUMBER PROBLEMS

The issue being discussed here is part of a larger group of issues, generally referred to as **index-number problems.** Index-number problems arise not only in the comparison of two countries using two different currencies but also in the study of the growth of a single country over a long period of time. As growth occurs, relative prices usually change; that is, the prices of some commodities fall while the prices of others rise. If the country is experiencing **inflation,** which is a sustained increase in the general price level, usually all prices rise, but some rise faster than others so that relative prices still change. To eliminate the

TABLE 2-3	BASE-YEAR VERSUS CURRENT-YEAR PRICE CALCULATION OF GNP			
	BASE YEAR (1972)		CURRENT YEAR (2000)	
PRODUCT PER YEAR	QUANTITY	PRICE (U.S. DOLLARS)	QUANTITY	PRICE (U.S. DOLLARS)
TELEVISION SETS (MILLIONS)	1	300	50	100
WHEAT (MILLION TONS)	100	100	200	150

1. GNP index in 2000 using base-year prices:

$$100 \times \frac{(50 \times 300) + (200 \times 100)}{(1 \times 300) + (100 \times 100)} = 340$$

2. GNP index in 2000 using current-year prices:

$$100 \times \frac{(50 \times 100) + (200 \times 150)}{(1 \times 100) + (100 \times 150)} = 232$$

impact of inflation on the statistics, economists measure *real* increases (growth in the actual quantity of goods produced) rather than nominal increases (where the prices also grow) in GNP. The proper procedure is to recalculate GNP in each year using the prices of only one year. But this poses a problem: Which year should we pick? Estimates of the growth rate will differ as one uses the prices of different years, just as the ratio of Indian to U.S. GNP will vary if one uses the Indian prices to value both countries' GNPs in one case and the U.S. prices in another.

A hypothetical illustration of the impact of base-year versus current-year prices is presented in Table 2–3. In this example, a higher growth rate is achieved using base-year rather than current-year prices. This happens because the relative price of the industrial product (television sets) is higher in the base year (when TV sets were scarce) than in the current year (when they are more abundant). As a result, the faster-growing industrial product accounts for a larger share of total product when base-year prices are used. In most countries, the industrial sector grows faster than the agricultural sector, and hence a set of prices that gives the industrial sector more weight in the national product will result in a higher GNP growth rate.

Data problems, therefore, are pervasive whenever one studies the aggregate performance of an economy as it evolves over time or compares the aggregate performance of two different economies When comparing the steel ingot output of two countries, it is possible to say precisely how many more tons of steel one of the countries produces when compared with the other. There is no comparable precision when one compares large aggregate measures such as GNP. A certain ambiguity always is present when these figures are used to compare income levels, rates of growth, or development patterns across countries or over time.

Income Levels and Economic Growth around the World: A Brief Overview

Economic historian Angus Maddison has estimated economic growth and income levels for the world economy as far back as the year 500 A.D. According to his calculations, average world income in 1500 was exactly the same as it had been 1,000 years earlier.[2] In other words, growth in per capita income between 500 and 1500 was zero. The next 320 years (from 1500 to 1820) was only slightly better, with world income per capita growing just 0.04 percent per year, for a cumulative increase of 15 percent. The little bit of economic growth that did take place was centered in Western Europe and in what Maddison calls the Western "Offshoots" (Australia, Canada, New Zealand, and the United States). By 1820, these regions already had a decided advantage of the rest of the world. For example, whereas China and India probably were the richest countries in the world in 1500, average income in these two countries had fallen well behind the European average by 1820.

Maddison's research suggests that rapid economic growth as we know it really began around 1820. He estimates that over the subsequent 170 years, average world income increased by 1.2 percent per year. Note that the difference between annual growth of 0.04 percent and 1.2 percent is huge. With the world economy growing at 0.04 percent per year, it would take more than 1,700 years for average income to double. With annual growth of 1.2 percent, average income doubles in just 58 years.[3] Therefore, the world has changed from no growth at all for 1,000 years

---

2. The data in this section for the years 500–1500 come from Angus Maddison, *Phases of Capitalist Development* (Oxford: Oxford University Press, 1982), Table 1.2. For the period after 1500, the data are from Maddison's *Monitoring the World Economy 1820–1992* (Paris: Organization for Economic Cooperation and Development, 1995).

3. The "rule of 70" is useful in thinking about the time necessary for incomes (or anything else) to double for a given growth rate. As a close approximation, 70 divided by the annual growth rate gives the doubling time. Thus, at a growth rate of 2 percent per year, income will double in about 35 years. More precisely, the equation is $(1 + g)^x = 2$, where g is the annual growth rate and x is years. By taking logs of both sides and using a bit of algebra, we find that $x = \ln(2)/\ln(1 + g) = 0.693/\ln(1 + g)$. By multiplying the numerator and denominator of this ratio by 100, we get $x = 69.3/(100 \times \ln(1 + g))$, which is approximately equal to $x = 70/g$. With Madisson's estimated annual growth rate of 1.2 percent, we set $g = 0.012$ and solve to find $x = 58.1$ years.

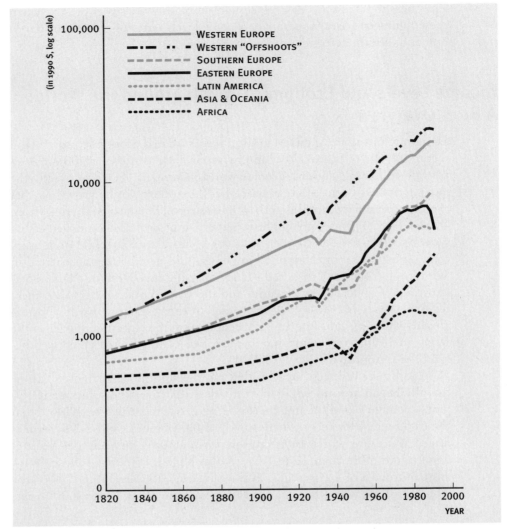

FIGURE 2–1   LEVELS OF GDP PER CAPITA BY REGION: 1820–1992. Note: Western "Offshoots" include Australia, Canada, New Zealand, and the United States. Source: Maddison, *Monitoring the World Economy,* Figure 1–1.

to a situation where the average real income doubles in less than three generations.

Maddison's estimates of average income levels for the world's major regions between 1820 and 1992 are shown in Figure 2–1. Several features of this data are notable. First, economic growth rates clearly accelerated around the world during this period, especially after 1880. Second, and perhaps most striking, the richest countries recorded the fastest growth rates and the poorest countries, the slowest growth rates until 1950, just after the end of World War II. Per capita income in the Western "Offshoots" grew by about 1.6 percent per year between 1820 and 1950, while in Africa it grew by just 0.5 percent. As a result, the ratio between the average incomes in the richest regions to those in the poorest regions grew from about 3:1 in 1820 to about 12:1 in 1950.

Between 1950 and 1992 the patterns of economic growth changed, at least in several regions. The poorest region in 1950—Asia—recorded the fastest growth rate (3.5 percent), thereby substantially closing the income gap with other regions of the world. Southern Europe also grew very quickly, with its average income jumping past that of Eastern Europe and Latin America. The gap between the Western "Offshoots" and Western Europe, which had been widening through 1950, narrowed significantly. By contrast, Latin America's growth stagnated after 1980, and Eastern Europe's collapsed after the fall of the Berlin Wall in 1989. Africa's average growth rate first accelerated then faded after 1980, averaging about 1 percent over the period. As a result, the income gap between the Western "Offshoots" and Africa grew to 16:1.

These regional averages disguise a wide range in individual country performance. Some countries that initially were relatively wealthy grew slowly, falling well behind their counterparts, while some poorer countries recorded rapid economic growth. For example, the average income in Argentina in 1870 was about the same as that in Spain and Norway and higher than that of Portugal and Finland. Many people expected Argentina to be among the most rapidly growing economies in the world. But, by 1992, Argentina's average income was little more than half the average of those four countries. By contrast, Japan's average income was only about one third that of Western Europe and the "Offshoots" in 1870, but by 1992, it had the third highest average income in the world.

The growth performance of individual countries between 1960 and 1996 is shown in Table 2–4. The table shows an extraordinary range of economic performance. Four economies—Hong Kong, Korea, Singapore, and Japan—recorded average per capita growth rates of 5.5 percent or better. As a result, average real income increased *by a factor of 7* in each of these economies in the space of just two generations. Several other Asian countries recorded per capita growth rates of 4 percent or better, leading to a fourfold increase in average income during the period. The fastest growing country outside of Asia was Botswana, which is a major diamond exporter and benefited from very good economic management. At the other end of the spectrum, in several countries per capita income fell during the period, some disastrously so. In Chad and Madagascar, for example, average income in 1996 was only about half of what it had been in 1960.

TABLE 2–4   REAL GDP PER CAPITA (PPP) FOR SELECTED COUNTRIES, 1960–96 (1985 CONSTANT PRICES)

COUNTRY	1960	1996	AVERAGE ANNUAL GROWTH, 1960–96 (% PER ANNUM)
HONG KONG	2,231	18,339	6.02
KOREA	898	7,135	5.92
SINGAPORE	1,626	11,392	5.56
JAPAN	2,943	20,415	5.53
THAILAND	940	5,194	4.88
MALAYSIA	1,409	7,180	4.65
BOTSWANA	525	2,328	4.25
INDONESIA	641	2,754	4.16
CHINA	564	2,374	4.11
ISRAEL	3,447	11,669	3.48
SPAIN	3,128	10,338	3.42
EGYPT	804	2,088	2.73
MAURITIUS	2,840	7,313	2.70
TURKEY	1,615	4,137	2.69
FRANCE	5,820	14,466	2.60
PAKISTAN	644	1,563	2.53
THE NETHERLANDS	6,087	14,304	2.44
BRAZIL	1,780	4,135	2.41
COLOMBIA	1,686	3,781	2.31
DOMINICAN REPUBLIC	1,188	2,543	2.17
SOUTH AFRICA	2,185	4,626	2.14
MEXICO	2,825	5,906	2.11
INDIA	769	1,546	2.00
SRI LANKA	1,253	2,516	1.99
UNITED STATES	9,908	19,243	1.90
NIGERIA	560	1,015	1.70
SAUDI ARABIA	3,869	6,644	1.54
PHILIPPINES	1,133	1,813	1.34
PERU	2,031	3,157	1.26
EL SALVADOR	1,433	2,147	1.16
JAMAICA	1,761	2,452	0.95
MALAWI	380	526	0.93
KENYA	646	874	0.86
ARGENTINA	4,481	5,739	0.71
HONDURAS	1,034	1,315	0.69
THE GAMBIA	614	757	0.60
GHANA	886	1,002	0.35
SENEGAL	1,062	1,116	0.14
VENEZUELA	6,313	6,085	−0.10
RWANDA	535	440	−0.56
HAITI	921	545	−1.50
ZAMBIA	946	556	−1.52
CHAD	743	383	−1.89
MADAGASCAR	1,187	584	−2.03

Sources: Summers and Heston, *Penn World Tables;* World Bank, *World Development Indicators CD, 1998.*

The Progression of Growth Theory

What determines the rate of growth of an economy and its aggregate level of output? A broad range of factors plausibly could be important. Countries with a higher level of output tend to have a larger capital stock—more roads, bridges, power generators, factories, ports, and the like. Output clearly is influenced by how many people work and how productive they are. Labor productivity, in turn, depends on levels of education and the general health of the population. Natural resource endowments, such as petroleum deposits, gold, rubber, land, rich agricultural soil, forests, lakes, and oceans, also are important. Countries that can develop and adapt new technologies more quickly than others are likely to grow rapidly. In addition, most people would agree that government policies influence economic output by affecting the allocation of economic resources and creating the incentives to use the factors of production in different ways. A country's history, culture, political system, and geography may play important roles, too.

PRODUCTION FUNCTIONS: AN OVERVIEW

Most models of economic growth focus primarily the basic factors of production: the capital stock and the labor force. Natural resource endowments, including land, sometimes are incorporated as a third factor of production but most often are subsumed as part of the capital stock. Standard growth models have at their core one or a series of **production functions.** At the individual firm or microeconomic level, these production functions tell how much the output of a firm or factory, such as a textile mill, will increase if the number of workers or the number of spindles and looms (i.e., the capital stock) rises by a given amount. Production functions often are derived from engineering specifications that relate given amounts of physical input to the amount of physical output that can be produced with that input. Often, for convenience, microeconomic production functions are expressed in money values rather than physical quantities.

At the national or economywide level, production functions describe the relationship of the size of a country's labor force and its stock of capital with the level of that country's gross national product. These economywide relationships are called **aggregate production functions.** They measure the value of output or national product, given the value of the aggregate capital stock and labor force. Because both input and output are measured in aggregate terms (national capital stock, GNP), index-number and other measurement problems of the kind described earlier in the chapter introduce some ambiguity into the interpretation of the economy-wide production functions. Still, this is the best tool we have for relating input and output at the national level within a consistent framework. For that reason, it is useful to see what this aggregate production function can tell us about how capital and labor contribute to growth, before turning in later chapters to how those inputs can be mobilized.

THE BASIC GROWTH MODEL

We now examine some of the basic frameworks used to explain the process of economic growth. We begin with the simplest growth models that examine aggregate economic growth and do not distinguish between the types of goods and services that an economy produces. That is, for the moment we ignore the key differences between agricultural and industrial products, goods traded in international markets and those produced and consumed at home, and simple products and more sophisticated high-technology products.

The most fundamental models of economic output and economic growth are based on a small number of equations that relate savings, investment, and population growth to the size of the workforce and capital stock and, in turn, to aggregate production. The version we examine here has five equations: (1) an aggregate production function, (2) an equation determining the level of saving, (3) the saving-investment identity, (4) a statement relating new investment to changes in the capital stock, and (5) an expression for the growth rate of the labor force.[4] We examine each of these in turn.

First, the production function relates total output to the size of the capital stock and the labor force. If Y represents total output (and therefore total income), K is the capital stock, and L is the labor supply, at the most general level, the aggregate production function can be expressed as follows:

$$Y = F(K, L) \qquad [2\text{--}1]$$

This expression simply means that output is a function (denoted by F) of the capital stock and the labor supply. As the capital stock and labor supply grow, output expands. The exact form of the function F—stating precisely *how much* output expands in response to changes in K and L—is what distinguishes many different models of growth, as we will see later in this and the next chapter. In this framework, economic growth occurs by increasing either the capital stock (through new investment in factories,

---

4. This five-equation presentation is based on teaching notes compiled by World Bank economist Shantayanan Devarajan, to whom we are indebted.

machinery, equipment, roads, and other infrastructure), the size of the labor force, or both. The other four equations of the model describe how these increases in K and L come about.

Equations 2–2 through 2–4 are closely linked and together describe how the capital stock (K) changes over time. These three equations first calculate total saving, then relate saving to new investment, and finally describe how new investment changes the size of the capital stock. To calculate total saving, we take the most straightforward approach and assume that saving is a fixed share of income:

$$S = s \times Y \qquad [2\text{--}2]$$

In this equation, S (upper case S) represents the total value of saving, and s (lower case s) represents the average saving rate. For example, if the average saving rate is 20 percent and total income is \$10 billion, then the value of saving in any year is exactly 20 percent of total income, or \$2 billion.

The next equation relates saving (S) to investment (I). The most basic form of the investment-saving relationship is for a closed economy (i.e., one without trade or foreign borrowing), in which saving must be equal to investment. This is because, without trade, all output of goods and services produced by the economy is used for either current consumption or investment, while all income earned by households must be either consumed or saved. This relationship is expressed as follows:

$$S = I \qquad [2\text{--}3]$$

We are now in a position to show how the capital stock K changes over time. Two main forces determine changes in the capital stock: new investment (which adds to the capital stock) and depreciation (which slowly erodes the value of the existing capital stock over time). Using the Greek letter delta (Δ) to represent the *change* in the value of a variable, we express the change in the capital stock as ΔK, which is determined as follows:

$$\Delta K = I - (d \times K) \qquad [2\text{--}4]$$

In this expression d is the rate of depreciation. The first term (I) indicates that the capital stock *increases* each year by the amount of new investment. The second term $-(d \times K)$ shows that the capital stock *decreases* every year because of the depreciation of existing capital. We assume here that the depreciation rate is a constant, usually in the range of 2–10 percent (i.e., d is between 0.02 and 0.10).

To see how this works, let us continue our earlier example, in which total income is \$10 billion and saving (and therefore investment) is \$2 billion. Say that the value of the existing capital stock is \$30 billion and the annual rate of depreciation is 3 percent, so $d = 0.03$. In this example, the capital stock will increase by \$2 billion because of new investment but also will decrease by \$0.9 billion (3 percent $\times$ \$30 billion) because of depreciation. Equation 2–4 puts together these two effects, calculating the change in the capital stock as $\Delta K = I - (d \times K) = \$2$ billion $- (0.03 \times \$30$ billion$) = \$1.1$ billion. Thus, the capital stock increases from its original value of \$30 billion to its new value of \$31.1 billion. This new value of the capital stock then is inserted into the production function in equation 2–1, allowing for the calculation of a new level of output, Y.

The fifth and final equation of the model focuses on the supply of labor. To keep things simple, we assume here that the labor force grows exactly as fast as the total population. Over long periods of time, this assumption is fairly accurate. However, as we discuss in Chapter 8, the labor force can grow faster or slower than the total population for several generations, as birth rates and death rates change over time. If n is equal to the growth rate of both the population and the labor force, then the change in the labor force (ΔL) is represented by

$$\Delta L = n \times L \qquad [2-5]$$

Thus, if the labor force consists of 1 million people and if the population (and labor force) is growing by 2 percent (that is, $n = 0.02$), then the labor force increases by 20,000 (1 million $\times$ 0.02). The new labor force is 1.02 million people, a figure that can be inserted into the production function for L to calculate the new level of output.

These five equations represent the complete model.[5] Collectively they can be used to examine how changes in population, savings, and investment affect the capital stock and labor supply and ultimately economic output. New saving generates additional investment, which adds to the capital stock and allows for increased output. New workers add further to the economy's capacity to increase production.

One way these five equations can be simplified slightly is to combine equations 2–2, 2–3, and 2–4. The aggregate level of saving (in equation 2–2) directly determines the level of investment in equation 2–3, which (together with depreciation) determines changes in the capital stock in equation 2–4. Combining these three equations in this way gives

$$\Delta K = sY - dK \qquad [2-6]$$

---

5. Note that since the model has five equations and five variables (Y, K, L, I, and S) it always can be solved. In addition, there are three fixed parameters (d, s, and n), the values of which are assumed to be fixed exogenously, or outside the system.

This equation simply states that the change in the capital stock (ΔK) is equal to saving (sY) minus depreciation (dK). This expression allows us to calculate the change in the capital stock and enter the new value directly into the aggregate production function in equation 2–1.

The Harrod-Domar Growth Model

As we have stressed, the aggregate production function (shown earlier as equation 2–1) is at the heart of every model of economic growth. This function can take many different forms, depending on what we believe is the true relationship between the factors of production (K and L) and aggregate output. This relationship depends (among other things) on the relative abundance of each factor, how efficiently each is used, and the mix of economic activities, including agriculture, heavy industry, light labor-intensive manufacturing, high-technology processes, services, and others. Indeed, much of the debate in the academic literature on economic growth is about how to best represent the aggregate production process.

THE FIXED-COEFFICIENT PRODUCTION FUNCTION

The simplest production function used in basic models of economic growth assumes that capital and labor are used in a constant ratio to each other to determine the level of total output. This **fixed-coefficients production function** is shown in Figure 2–2. Output in this figure is represented by **isoquants,** which are combinations of inputs (labor and capital in this case) that produce equal amounts of output. For example, on the first (innermost) isoquant, it takes capital (plant and equipment) of $10 million and 100 workers to produce 100,000 tons of cement. Only two isoquants are shown in this diagram, but a nearly infinite range of isoquants are possible for different levels of capital and labor inputs.

The L-shape of the isoquants are characteristic of fixed-coefficient production functions. The term *fixed coefficients* reflects the assumption that capital and labor always are used in a fixed proportion to produce different levels of output. In Figure 2–2, for the first isoquant, the **capital-labor ratio** is 10 million:100, or 100,000:1. In other words, one worker must be matched with $100,000 in capital to produce the given output. For the second isoquant, the ratio is the same: $20 million:200, or 100,000:1. Note, however, that with this kind of production function, if more workers are added *without* investing in more capital, output will *not* rise. Look again at the first isoquant in Figure 2–2, starting at the elbow (with 100 workers and $10 million in capital). If the firm adds more workers (say, increasing to 200 workers) without adding new capital, it moves horizon-

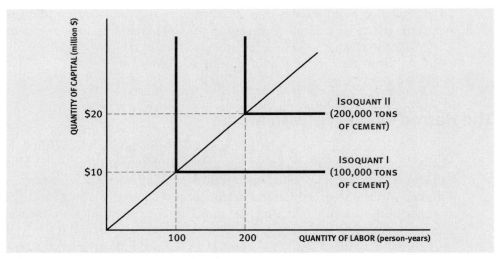

FIGURE 2–2   PRODUCTION FUNCTION WITH FIXED COEFFICIENTS. With constant returns to scale, the isoquants will be L-shaped and the production function will be the straight line through their minimum-combination points.

tally along the first isoquant to the right. But, at any point on this iso-quant, the firm still is producing just 100,000 tons of cement. In this very simplified kind of production function, new workers need more machines to increase output. Adding new workers without machines will result in only idle workers, with no increase in output. Similarly, more machinery without additional workers will result in only underused machines. For each isoquant, the most efficient production point is at the elbow, where the minimum amounts of capital and labor are used. The production function is the ray that connects these points.

The production function depicted in Figure 2–2 also is drawn with **constant returns to scale,** so if capital in the cement industry is doubled to $20 million and labor is doubled to 200 workers, output also exactly doubles to 200,000 tons per year.[6] With this further assumption, two more ratios remain constant at any level of output: capital to output and labor to output. If cement is valued at $50/ton, then 100,000 tons is worth $5 million. In this case, in the first isoquant, the **capital-output ratio** is $10 million : $5 million, or 2 : 1. In the second isoquant the ratio is the same ($20 million : $10 million, or 2 : 1). Similarly, for each isoquant the **labor-output ratio** is a constant 1 : 50,000, meaning that each worker produces $50,000 worth (or 1,000 tons) of cement.

6. More generally, in a constant returns to scale production function, if we multiply both capital and labor by any number, w, output will multiply by the same number. In other words, the production function has the following property: $wY = F(wK, wL)$.

THE CAPITAL-OUTPUT RATIO AND THE HARROD-DOMAR FRAMEWORK

The fixed-coefficient, constant returns to scale production function is the centerpiece of a well-known early model of economic growth that was developed independently during the 1940s by economists Roy Harrod of England and Evsey Domar of MIT, primarily to explain the relationship between growth and unemployment in advanced capitalist societies.[7] It ultimately focuses attention on the role of capital accumulation in the growth process. The **Harrod-Domar model** has been used extensively in developing countries to examine the relationship between growth and capital requirements. In the model, the production function has a very precise form, in which output is assumed to be a *linear* function of capital, as follows:

$$Y = 1/v \times K \qquad \text{or} \qquad Y = K/v \qquad\qquad [2\text{--}7]$$

where v is a constant. In this equation, the capital stock is simply multiplied by the fixed number $1/v$ to calculate aggregate production. It is difficult to imagine a simpler production function than this one. The constant v turns out to be the capital-output ratio, since by rearranging the terms in Equation 2–7 we find

$$v = K/Y \qquad\qquad [2\text{--}8]$$

The capital-output ratio is a very important parameter in this model, so it is worth dwelling for a moment on its meaning. This ratio essentially is a measure of the productivity of capital or investment. In the earlier example in Figure 2–2, it took $10 million in investment in new plant and new equipment to produce $5 million worth of cement, implying a capital-output ratio of 2 : 1 (or just 2). A larger v implies that more capital is needed to produce the same amount of output. So, instead, if $20 million in investment is needed to produce $5 million worth of cement, v would be 4.

The capital-output ratio captures two characteristics of the production process: capital intensity and efficiency. More capital-intensive production activities, like steel, will display a larger v than more labor-intensive processes, such as computer assembly. Therefore, countries with a large share of production in capital intensive activities (such as automobiles, petrochemicals, and machinery) will show a larger aggregate capital-output ratio than a country that concentrates on labor-intensive activities (such as textiles, basic agriculture, and footwear). A larger v also can imply less efficient production. A factory with lots of idle machinery and poorly

7. Roy F. Harrod, "An Essay in Dynamic Theory," *Economic Journal* (1939), 14–33; Evsey Domar, "Capital Expansion, Rate of Growth, and Employment," *Econometrica* (1946), 137–47; and "Expansion and Employment," *American Economic Review,* 37 (1947), 34–55.

organized production processes will have a higher capital-output ratio than a more efficiently managed factory.

Economists often calculate the **incremental capital-output ratio** (ICOR) because, in studying growth, one is interested mainly in the impact on output of additional (or incremental) capital. The incremental capital-output ratio measures the productivity of additional capital, while the (average) capital-output ratio refers to the relationship between a country's total stock of capital and its total national product. In the Harrod-Domar model, since the capital-output ratio is assumed to remain constant, the average capital-output ratio is equal to the incremental capital-output ratio, so the ICOR = v.

So far we have been discussing total economic output, not growth. The production function in equation 2–7 easily can be converted to relate *changes* in output to *changes* in the capital stock:

$$\Delta Y = \Delta K / v \qquad [2\text{–}9]$$

The growth rate of output, g, is simply the increment in output divided by the total amount of output, $\Delta Y/Y$. If we divide both sides of equation 2–9 by Y, then

$$g = \Delta Y/Y = \Delta K/Yv \qquad [2\text{–}10]$$

Finally, from equation 2–6, we know that the change in the capital stock ΔK is equal to saving minus the depreciation of capital ($\Delta K = sY - dK$). Substituting equation 2–6 into equation 2–10 and simplifying[8] leads to the basic Harrod-Domar relationship for an economy:

$$g = (s/v) - d \qquad [2\text{–}11]$$

Underlying this equation is the view that capital created by investment in plant and equipment is the main determinant of growth and that saving by people and corporations make investment possible.[9] It rivets attention on two keys to the growth process: saving (s) and the efficiency with which capital is used in production (v). The message from this model is clear: Save more and make productive investments, and your economy will grow.

For economic policy makers, given this simple equation the task is straightforward. The first step is to try to come up with an estimate of the incremental capital-output ratio (v) and depreciation rate (d) for the

8. Substituting 2–6 into 2–10 leads to $g = (sY - dK)/Y \times 1/v$, which can be simplified to $g = (s - dK/Y) \times 1/v$. Since $K/Y = v$, we have $g = (s - dv) \times 1/v$, which leads to $g = s/v - d$.

9. For an important early contribution to the discussion of the importance of capital accumulation to the growth process, see Joan Robinson, *The Accumulation of Capital* (London: Macmillan, 1956).

country. Policy makers then can set a target for the rate of economic growth (g) they wish to achieve; in which case, the equation will tell them the level of saving and investment necessary to achieve that growth. Alternatively, policy makers can decide on the rate of saving and investment that is feasible or desirable; in which case, the equation will tell them the rate of growth in national product that can be expected. For example, if the saving (or investment) rate is 20 percent, the capital-output ratio is 4, and the depreciation rate is 2 percent, then the economy can be expected to grow by 3 percent (since 0.20/4 − 0.02 = 0.03).

This procedure can be applied to the economy as a whole, or it can be applied to each sector or each industry. Incremental capital-output ratios, for example, can be calculated separately for agriculture and industry. Once planners decide how much investment will be allocated to each sector, the Harrod-Domar equations determine the growth rates that can be expected in each of the two sectors.

How does this model work in practice? Consider Korea, which between 1991 and 1995 had one of the highest investment rates in the world, at 37 percent, and (not coincidentally) recorded very rapid average GDP growth of 7.5 percent per year. Assuming a depreciation rate of 3 percent, then the implied capital-output ratio was approximately $v = 3.5$.[10] Would these figures have helped the Korean government predict the 1996 growth rate? In 1996, the investment rate was 35.4 percent, so the Harrod-Domar would have predicted growth of 7.1 percent ($g = 0.354/3.5 − 0.03$). The actual growth rate for 1996 was 7.0 percent, not too far off the model's predictions.

STRENGTHS AND WEAKNESSES OF THE HARROD-DOMAR FRAMEWORK

The basic strength of the Harrod-Domar model is its simplicity. The data requirements are small, and the equation is easy to use and to estimate. And, as we saw with the example of Korea, the model can be accurate from one year to the next. Generally speaking, over short periods of time (a few years) and in the absence of severe economic shocks (such as a drought or large changes in export or import prices), the model does a surprisingly good job of estimating expected growth rates in most countries. For this reason, the model has been used widely in many developing countries for economic planning.

The model, however, has some major limitations. The most important is that, with this model, the economy remains in equilibrium (with full employment of both the labor force and the capital stock) only in very special circumstances. Since the fixed-coefficient production function re-

---

10. Since $g = s/v - d$, then $v = s/(g + d)$. For Korea between 1991 and 1995, $v = .37(0.075 + 0.03) = 3.52$.

quires the capital-labor ratio to be constant, the capital stock and the labor force must always grow at the same rate to maintain equilibrium. But this is unlikely to happen. Consider first the growth rate of capital. To keep the capital-output ratio constant, the capital stock must grow at exactly the same rate as output, which in the model is the rate g. If the capital stock grew any faster or slower than g, the capital-output ratio would change. Now consider the labor force. In our original five-equation model, we stipulated (in equation 2–5) that the labor force would grow at exactly the same pace as the population at rate n. Therefore, the only way that the capital stock and the labor force can grow at the same rate is if n happens to be equal to g. This happens only when $n = g = s/v - d$, and there is no particular reason to believe the population will grow at that rate.

On the one hand, if n is larger than g, the labor force is growing faster than the capital stock. In essence, the saving rate is not high enough to support investment in new machinery sufficient to employ all new workers. A growing number of workers will not have jobs and unemployment will rise indefinitely. On the other hand, if g (or $s/v - d$) is larger than n, the capital stock is growing faster than the workforce. There will not be enough workers for all the available machines, and capital will become idle. The actual growth rate of the economy no longer will be g, as the model stipulates, but will slow to n, with output constrained by the number of available workers. In other words, unless $s/v - d$ (or g) is exactly equal to n, either labor or capital will not be fully employed and the economy will not be in a stable equilibrium. This characteristic of the Harrod-Domar model has come to be known as the *knife-edge* problem. As long as $g = n$, the economy remains in equilibrium, but as soon as either the capital stock or the labor force grows faster than the other, the economy falls off the edge with growing unemployment of either capital or labor.

The essence of this problem is the twin assumptions of fixed capital-output and capital-labor ratios, which allow for no flexibility in the model and no internal adjustment when g and n are not equal. The rigid assumption that the incremental capital-output ratio always is a fixed number may be reasonably accurate for short periods of time or in very special circumstances but usually is inaccurate over time, as an economy evolves and develops. The incremental capital-output ratio tends to vary among countries and, for a single country, over time. The efficiency with which capital is used can change in response to policy changes, affecting v. Moreover, the capital intensity of the production process can and usually does change over time. A poor country with a low saving rate and surplus labor (unemployed and underemployed workers) can achieve higher growth rates by utilizing as much labor as possible and thus less capital. Such an economy typically will record a low v. As economies grow and per capita income rises, the labor surplus diminishes and economies shift gradually toward

TABLE 2-5	SELECTED INCREMENTAL CAPITAL-OUTPUT RATIOS		
COUNTRY	1970–79	1980–89	1990–97
UNITED STATES	3.4	3.6	2.8
JAPAN	4.9	4.6	6.5
SOUTH KOREA	2.7	2.8	3.7
INDIA	3.7	2.8	2.9
INDONESIA	2.2	3.2	3.0
ARGENTINA	4.8	9.8	2.0
BRAZIL	2.2	4.2	3.4
IVORY COAST	2.6	4.3	1.8
VENEZUELA	5.6	6.7	2.8
KENYA	2.3	3.7	4.0

Note: These ratios were derived by dividing the average share of gross domestic investment in gross domestic product by the average growth rate in gross domestic product, and subtracting an assumed annual depreciation rate of 3 percent. All numbers are expressed as a ratio to 1. For example, the full incremental capital-output ratio for the United States in the first period is 3.4:1.
Source: World Bank, *World Development Indicators*, 1999 CD-ROM.

more capital-intensive production. As a result, the ICOR shifts upward. This suggests that a higher v does not necessarily imply inefficiency or slower growth.

Consider again the example of Korea. The ICOR changed from approximately 2.7 between 1970 and 1980, to 2.8 between 1981 and 1990, and (as stated previously) to 3.5 between 1990 and 1995 as Korea gradually moved into more capital-intensive production processes. To continue to use the 1970–80 ICOR during the 1990s would have been very misleading and would have led to increasingly imprecise growth forecasts. The structure of the economy had changed significantly during that time period and, with it, the ICOR.

Therefore, generally speaking, the Harrod-Domar framework tends to become increasingly inaccurate over longer periods of time as the actual ICOR changes and with it the capital-labor ratio. These shifts in the ICOR can come about through market mechanisms, as prices of labor and capital change in response to changes in supplies. As growth takes place, saving tends to become relatively more abundant and hence the price of capital falls while employment and wages rise. Therefore, all producers increasingly economize on labor and use more capital and the ICOR tends to rise. Data on incremental capital-output ratios for a few selected countries are presented in Table 2–5. These ratios vary from 1.8 (that is, a capital-output ratio of 1.8:1) to 9.8 and even higher. Some of these differences can be explained by the point made earlier, that richer countries such as the United States, Norway, and Japan tend to have higher ratios because capital is less expensive relative to labor than in poorer

ECONOMIC GROWTH IN THAILAND

In the 1960s, Thailand's agrarian economy depended heavily on the production of rice, maize, rubber, and other agricultural products. About three quarters of the Thai population derived their income from agricultural activities. GNP per capita (measured in 1997 purchasing power parity terms) was around $1,500, about one tenth the average income in the United States. Life expectancy was 55 years and the infant mortality rate was 95 per 1,000 births. Few observers expected the Thai economy to develop rapidly.

However, between the mid-1960s and the mid-1990s the Thai economy grew steadily, benefiting from sound economic management and a relatively favorable external environment. The government regularly achieved surpluses on the current account of its budget, and used these funds (plus inflows of foreign assistance) to finance investments in rural roads, irrigation, power, telecommunications, and other basic infrastructure. The government's fiscal, monetary, and exchange rate policies kept the macroeconomy relatively stable with fairly low inflation, even through the turbulent period of world oil price shocks in the 1970s and 1980s. Beginning in the 1970s, the government began to remove trade restrictions and promote the production of labor-intensive manufactured exports. These products found a ready market in the booming Japanese economy of the 1980s and provided a growing number of jobs for Thai workers.

countries in the early stages of development. Other differences, however, such as those between Korea and Argentina in the 1970s, have little to do with differences in the relative scarcity of capital and are more likely to be the result of the differences in the efficiency with which capital and other inputs are managed.

The rigidity in the model extends to the capital-labor ratio. In a world with fixed-coefficient production functions, little room is left for a factory manager to increase output by hiring one more worker without buying a machine to go with the worker or to purchase more machines for the current workforce to use. In economics parlance, we say that the fixed-proportion production function does not allow for any substitution between capital and labor in the production process. In the real world, of

Thailand's ability to make investments and deepen its capital stock depended on its capacity to save. The country's saving rate averaged about 20 percent in the 1960s, already high for developing countries, and increased steadily over time to an average of 35 percent in the early 1990s. These high saving rates, combined with sound economic management and Japan's economic boom all supported very rapid economic growth in Thailand. GNP growth averaged 6–7 percent per year between 1965 and 1995, with GNP per capita rising by about 4.8 percent per year. As a result of this growth, average income in real terms more than quadrupled in just 30 years.

During this period, the structure of the economy changed significantly. By the mid-1990s, manufacturing accounted for over 30 percent of GNP, up from just 14 percent in 1965, while the share of agricultural production dropped commensurately. The composition of exports shifted away from rice, maize, and other agricultural commodities toward labor-intensive manufactured products, which by the mid-1990s accounted for 80 percent of all exports. As the Harrod-Domar model predicts, Thailand's high saving rate and resulting capital accumulation was accompanied by a dramatic increase in output (and income) per capita. Contrary to the model, however, the ICOR did not remain constant over time. As the stock of capital grew and the economy shifted toward more capital-intensive production techniques, the ICOR increased from 2.6 in the 1970s to 4.1 in the early 1990s. The rising ICOR indicated that, as the Thai economy expanded and the level of capital per worker increased, an ever-larger increment of new capital was required to bring about a given increase in total output, a characteristic captured by the neoclassical model of economic growth.

course, at least some substitution between labor and capital is possible in most production processes. As we see in the next section, adding this feature to the model allows for a much richer exploration of the growth process.

A final weakness of the Harrod-Domar model is the absence of any role for technological change. Advances in technology generally are thought to play a critical role in long-term growth and development by contributing to increased productivity of all factors of production. In Figure 2–2, increased factor productivity and technical change can be represented by an inward shift of each isoquant toward the origin. The simplest way to capture this in the Harrod-Domar framework is to introduce a smaller ICOR, but of course this would contradict the idea of a constant ICOR.

The Solow (Neoclassical) Growth Model

THE NEOCLASSICAL PRODUCTION FUNCTION

In the mid-1950s, MIT economist Robert Solow introduced a new model of economic growth that represented an important step forward from the Harrod-Domar framework.[11] Solow recognized the problems that arose from the rigid production function in the Harrod-Domar model, which did not allow for substitution between the factors of production. Solow's answer was to drop the fixed-coefficients production function and replace it with a **neoclassical production function** that allows for more flexibility and substitution. In effect, in the Solow model, the capital-output and capital-labor ratios no longer are fixed but vary depending on the relative endowments of capital and labor in the economy and the production process.

The neoclassical production function is shown in Figure 2–3. In this figure, if one starts with output of 100,000 tons at point *a*, using $10 million of capital and 100 workers (not shown in the figure), output could be expanded in any of three ways. If the firm's managers decided to expand at constant factor proportions and move to point *b* on isoquant II, the situation would be identical to the fixed proportions case of Figure 2–2. The capital-output ratio at both point *a* and point *b* would be 2 : 1, as it was before. But production of 200,000 tons could be achieved by using more labor and less capital, a more labor-intensive method, at a point like *c* on isoquant II. In that case, the capital-output ratio falls to 1.4 : 1. Alternatively, a more capital-intensive method could be used, such as the production technique given by *d* on isoquant II. In this case, the capital-output ratio would rise to 2.8 : 1.

If the production function facing a country is neoclassical, then the capital-output ratio becomes a variable that to some extent is under the control of policy makers in the government. Considering production functions like those in Figure 2–3 from the industry level, policy makers in developing countries in which capital is scarce can try to induce manufacturers and farmers to employ more labor-intensive technologies. Then, for a given amount of saving and investment, both output and employment can be higher. At the level of the whole economy, policy changes

11. The two classic references of Solow's work are "A Contribution to the Theory of Economic Growth," *Quarterly Journal of Economics,* 70 (February 1956), 65–94; and "Technical Change and the Aggregate Production Function," *Review of Economics and Statistics* 39 (August 1957), 312–20. For an excellent and very thorough undergraduate exposition of the Solow and other models of economic growth, see Charles I. Jones. *Introduction to Economic Growth* (New York: W. W. Norton and Co. 1998). In 1987, Solow was awarded the Nobel Prize in Economics, primarily for his work on growth theory.

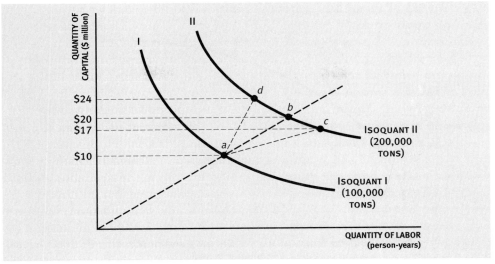

FIGURE 2–3   NEOCLASSICAL (VARIABLE PROPORTIONS) PRODUCTION FUNCTION. Instead of requiring fixed factor proportions, as in Figure 2–1, output can be achieved with varying combinations of labor and capital. This is called a *neoclassical* production function. The isoquants are curved, rather than L-shaped.

could encourage labor-intensive technologies as well as investment in the more labor-intensive industries, and so reduce the demand for investment and saving on both counts. The kinds of tools that policy makers may use to accomplish this reduction in the capital-output ratio are discussed in depth in several chapters later in this text.

THE BASIC EQUATIONS OF THE SOLOW MODEL

The Solow model is understood most easily by expressing all the key variables in per-worker terms. To do so, we divide both sides of the production function in equation 2–1 by L, so that it takes the form

$$Y/L = F(K/L, 1) \tag{2–12}$$

The equation shows that output per worker is a function of capital per worker.[12] If we use notation in which small case letters represent quantities in per-worker terms, then y is output per worker (that is, $y = Y/L$) and k is

12. We can divide both sides by L because the Solow model (like the Harrod-Domar model) assumes the production function exhibits constant returns to scale, so that the production function has the property that $wY = F(wK, wL)$. To express the Solow model in per-capita terms, we let $w = 1/L$.

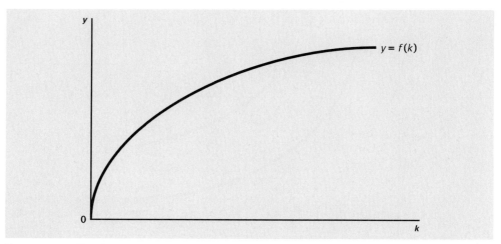

FIGURE 2–4   THE PRODUCTION FUNCTION IN THE SOLOW GROWTH MODEL. The neoclassical production function in the Solow model displays diminishing returns to capital, so that each additional increment in capital per worker (k) is associated with smaller increases in output per worker (y).

capital per worker ($k = K/L$). This gives us the first equation of the Solow model, in which the production function can be written simply as

$$y = f(k) \qquad\qquad [2\text{–}13]$$

Solow's model assumes a production function with the familiar property of **diminishing returns to capital.** With a fixed labor supply, giving workers an initial amount of machinery to work with will result in large gains in output. But as these same workers are given more and more machinery, the addition to output from each new machine gets smaller and smaller. For example, a bread company that purchases its first oven can rapidly increase its output. A second oven will further expand production but probably not by quite as much as the first oven. By the time the company buys its hundredth oven (without adding any new workers), the increment to bread production will be much smaller than it was with the first oven.

A production function with this property is shown graphically in Figure 2–4. The horizontal axis represents capital per worker (k), and the vertical axis shows output per worker (y). The slope of the curve declines as the capital stock increases, reflecting the assumption of diminishing returns to capital (or more precisely, a diminishing marginal product of capital). Each movement to the right on the horizontal axis yields a smaller and smaller increase in output per worker.

The first equation of the Solow model tells us that capital per worker is fundamental to the growth process. In turn, the second key equation of the model focuses on the determinants of change in capital per worker.

This second equation can be derived from equation 2–6[13] and shows that capital accumulation depends on saving, the growth rate of the labor force, and depreciation:

$$\Delta k = sy - (n + d)k \qquad\qquad [2\text{--}14]$$

This is a very important equation, so we should understand exactly what it means. It states that the change in capital per worker (Δk) is determined by three things:

1. Δk is positively related to saving (or investment) per worker. Since s is the saving rate and y is income (or output) per worker, the term sy is equal to saving per worker. As saving per worker increases, so does investment per worker, and the capital stock per worker (k) grows.
2. Δk is negatively related to population growth, shown by the term $-nk$. Each year, because of growth in the population and labor force, there are nL new workers. If there were no new investment, the increase in the labor force would mean that capital *per worker* (k) would fall. Equation 2–14 states that capital per worker would fall by exactly nk.
3. Depreciation erodes the capital stock. Each year, the amount of capital per worker will fall by the amount $-dk$ simply because of depreciation.

Therefore, saving (and investment) add to capital per worker, while labor force growth and depreciation reduce capital per worker. When saving per capita, sy, is larger than the amount of new capital needed to compensate for labor force growth and depreciation ($(n + d)k$), then Δk is a positive number. This implies that capital per worker, k, is increasing.

---

13. To derive equation 2–14, we begin by dividing both sides of equation 2–6 by K so that
$$\Delta K/K = sY/K - d.$$
We then focus on the capital per worker ratio, $k = K/L$. It can be shown that the growth rate of k is equal to the growth rate of K minus the growth rate of L:
$$\Delta k/k = \Delta K/K - \Delta L/L$$
With a little rearranging of terms, this equation can be written as $\Delta K/K = \Delta k/k + \Delta L/L$. We earlier assumed that both the population and the labor force were growing at the rate n, so $\Delta L/L = n$. By substitution we obtain
$$\Delta K/K = \Delta k/k + n$$
Note that, in both the first equation of the footnote and this most recent equation, the left-hand side is equal to $\Delta K/K$. This implies that the right-hand sides of these two equations are equal to each other, as follows:
$$\Delta k/k + n = sY/K - d$$
By subtracting n from both sides and multiplying through by k, we find that
$$\Delta k = sy - nk - dk \qquad \text{or} \qquad \Delta k = sy - (n + d)k.$$

The process through which the economy increases the amount of capital per worker, k, is called **capital deepening.** Economies in which workers have access to more machines, computers, trucks, and other equipment have a deeper capital base than economies with less machinery, and these economies are able to produce more output. In some economies, however, the amount of saving is just enough to simply provide the same amount of capital to new workers and make up for depreciation. An increase in the capital stock that just keeps pace with the expanding labor force and depreciation is called **capital widening** (referring to a "widening" of both the total amount of capital and the size of the workforce). Capital widening occurs when sy is exactly equal to $(n + d)k$, implying no change in k. Using this terminology, equation 2–14 can be restated as saying that capital deepening (Δk) is equal to saving per worker (sy) minus the amount needed for capital widening ($(n + d)k$).

A country with a high saving rate easily can deepen its capital base and rapidly expand the amount of capital per worker, thus providing the basis for growth in output. In Singapore, for example, where the savings rate has averaged more than 40 percent for many years, it is not difficult to provide capital to the growing labor force and make up for depreciation and still have plenty left over to supply existing workers with additional capital. By contrast, Kenya, with a saving rate of about 15 percent, has much less saving to spare for capital deepening after providing machines to new workers and making up for depreciation. As a result, capital per worker will not grow as quickly, and neither will output (or income) per worker. Partly because of this large difference in saving rates, output per person in Singapore grew by an average of 5.6 percent per year between 1960 and 1996, while Kenya's growth averaged less than 1 percent.

We can summarize the two basic equations of the Solow model as follows. The first ($y = f(k)$) simply states that output per worker (or income per capita) depends on the amount of capital per worker. The second equation ($\Delta k = sy - (n + d)k$) says that changes in capital per worker will depend on saving, the population growth rate, and depreciation. Thus, as in the Harrod-Domar model, saving plays a central role in the Solow model. However, the relationship between saving and growth is not linear because of diminishing returns to capital in the production function. In addition, the Solow model introduces a role for the population growth rate and allows for substitution between capital and labor in the growth process.

Now that we are equipped with the basic model, we can proceed to analyze the effects of changes in the saving rate, population growth, and depreciation on economic output and economic growth. This is accomplished most easily by examining the model in graphical form.

THE SOLOW DIAGRAM

The diagram of the Solow model consists of three curves, shown in Figure 2–5. The first is simply the production function $y = f(k)$, given by equation 2–13. The second is a saving function, which is derived directly from the production function. The new curve shows saving per capita, sy, found by multiplying both sides of equation 2–13 by the saving rate, so that $sy = s \times f(k)$. Since saving is assumed to be a fixed fraction of income (with s between 0 and 1), the saving function has the same shape as the production function but shifts it downward by the factor s. The third curve is the line $(n + d)k$, which is a straight line through the origin with the slope $(n + d)$. This line represents the amount of new capital needed as a result of growth in the labor force and depreciation just to keep capital per worker (k) constant. Note that the second and third curves are diagrammatic representations of the two right-hand terms of equation 2–14.

The second and third curves intersect at point A, where $k = k_0$ (and, on the production function, $y = y_0$ on the vertical axis). At other points along the horizontal axis, the *vertical difference* between these curves shows the *change* in capital per worker. To the left of point A (say, where $k = k_1$ and $y = y_1$), the amount of saving in the economy per person (sy) is larger than the amount of saving needed to compensate for new workers and depreciation ($(n + d)k$). As a result, the amount of capital per person (k) grows (capital deepening) and the economy shifts to the right along the horizontal axis. The economy will continue to do this as long as the sy

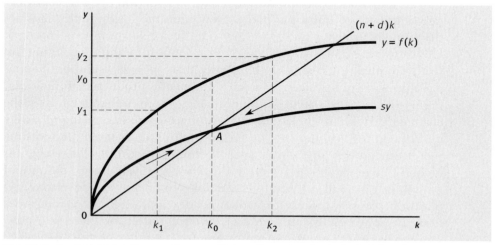

FIGURE 2–5 **THE BASIC SOLOW GROWTH MODEL DIAGRAM.** In the basic Solow diagram, point A is the only place where the amount of new saving, sy, is exactly equal to the amount of new capital needed for growth in the workforce and depreciation ($n + d$). Point A is the *steady state* level of capital per worker and output per worker.

curve is *above* the $(n + d)k$ curve, until eventually the economy reaches point A. In terms of the production function, the shift to the right implies an increase in output per worker, y (or income per capita), from y_1 to y_0. To the right of point A (say, where $k = k_2$ and $y = y_2$), saving per capita is smaller than the amount needed for new workers and depreciation, so capital per worker is falling and the economy shifts to the left along the horizontal axis. Once again, this shift will continue until the economy reaches point A. The shift to the left corresponds to a decline in output per worker from y_2 to y_0.

Point A is the only place where the amount of new saving, sy, is exactly equal to the amount of new capital needed for growth in the workforce and depreciation. Therefore, at this point, the amount of capital per worker, k, remains constant. Saving per worker (on the vertical axis) also remains constant, as does output per worker (or income per capita), with $y = y_0$. As a result, point A is called the **steady state** of the Solow model. Output per capita at the steady state (y_0) is alternatively referred to as either the **steady state, long run,** or **potential level of output per worker.**

It is very important to note, however, that all the values that remain constant are expressed as *per worker*. Although output per worker is constant, *total* output continues to grow at rate n, the same rate the population and workforce are growing. In other words, *at the steady state GNP (Y) is growing at the rate n (that is, the economy is growing), but GNP per capita (y) is constant (average income remains unchanged)*. Similarly, although capital per worker and saving per worker are constant at point A, total capital and total saving are growing.

The graphical representation also tells us something crucial about the rate of growth of k and y at points away from the steady state. Consider the situation when k and y are low (i.e., in a relatively poor country). Under these circumstances, the requirements for capital widening are relatively small, so sy tends to be greater than $(n + d)k$, and both k and y are growing. The relatively steep slope of the production function at points where k and y are low implies that, for a given increment in k, the change in y is relatively large, so per-capita income is growing relatively quickly. As the economy grows and moves toward point A (and income increases), growth in y slows until it stops at point A. Therefore, for higher-income countries (where y and k are relatively large), the rate of growth in y is smaller. Therefore, the Solow model has a very strong implication for the process of economic development: When countries have the same steady state level of y, *poorer countries are expected to grow faster than richer countries and to eventually "catch up" to the same level of income per capita at point A*. Later in the chapter, we investigate the empirical evidence to see the extent to which this actually occurs in the world economy.

CHANGES IN THE SAVING RATE AND POPULATION GROWTH IN THE SOLOW MODEL

Both the Solow model and the Harrod-Domar model place saving (and investment) at the center of the growth process. In the Harrod-Domar model, an increase in the saving rate translates directly (and linearly) into an increase in aggregate output. What is the impact of a higher saving rate in the Solow model?

An increase in the saving fate from s to s' shifts the saving function sy up to $s'y$, without shifting either the production function or the capital widening line $(n + d)k$, as shown in Figure 2–6. The increase in the saving rate means that saving per worker (and new investment per worker) now is greater than $(n + d)k$, so k gradually increases. The economy shifts to a new long-run equilibrium at point B. In the process, capital per worker increases from k_0 to k_3 and output per worker increases from y_0 to y_3. The aggregate economy initially grows at a rate faster than its steady state growth rate of n until it reaches point B, where the long-run growth rate reverts to n. Thus, the higher saving rate leads to more investment, a permanently higher stock of capital per worker, and a permanently higher level of income (or output) per worker. (The increase in per-capita income, however, is smaller than for a similar increase in s in the Harrod-Domar model, since the Solow model has a diminishing returns production.) It also leads to a *temporary* increase in the economic growth rate as the steady state shifts from A to B. However, the increase in the saving rate does *not* result in a permanent increase in the long-run rate of growth, which remains at n.

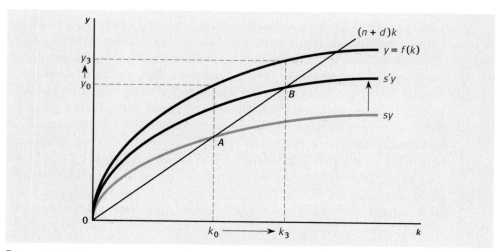

FIGURE 2–6 AN INCREASE IN THE SAVING RATE IN THE SOLOW MODEL. An increase in the savings rate from s to s' results in an upward shift in the capital deepening curve, so that capital per worker increases from k_0 to k_1.

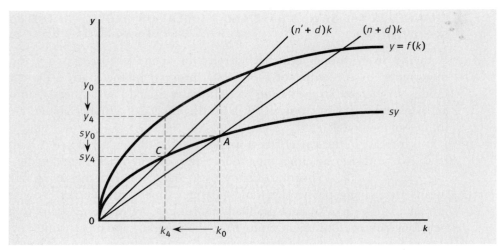

FIGURE 2-7   CHANGES IN THE POPULATION GROWTH RATE IN THE SOLOW MODEL. An increase in the rate of population growth from n to n' causes the capital widening curve to rotate to the left. Equilibrium capital per worker drops from k_0 to k_4.

The Solow diagram also can be used to evaluate the impact of a change in the population (or labor force) growth rate. An increase in the population growth rate from n to n' rotates the capital widening line to the left from $(n + d)k$ to $(n' + d)k$, as shown in Figure 2–7. The production and saving functions do not change. Since now there are more workers, savings per worker (sy) becomes smaller and no longer is large enough to keep capital per worker constant. Therefore, k begins to decline and the economy moves to a new steady state, C. Since there are more workers, capital per worker declines from k_0 to k_4 and saving per worker falls from sy_0 to sy_4. Output per worker (or income per capita) also declines, from y_0 to y_4. Thus, an increase in the population growth rate leads to lower average income in the Solow model. Note, however, that the new steady-state growth rate of the entire economy has increased from n to n' at point C. In other words, with a higher population growth rate, Y needs to grow faster to keep y constant.[14] By contrast, a *reduction* in the population growth rate leads to a process of capital deepening, with an increase in both k and in the steady-state level of income per worker, y.

The Solow growth model (to this point) suggests that growth rates differ across countries for two main reasons. First, two countries with the same current level of income may experience different growth rates if one

14. A similar exercise can be used to determine the impact of an increase in the depreciation rate, d. Such an increase will result in a reduction in k and y to a lower steady-state income per capita. The subtle difference between an increase in n and an increase in d is that the latter case does not lead to a change in the long-run growth rate of Y, which remains equal to n.

has a higher steady-state level of income than the other. To the extent that two countries with the same current level of income have different savings rates, population growth rates, rates of change in technology, and other factors that affect the production function, their steady-state income levels will differ, and so will their growth rates during the transition to their respective steady states. Second, two countries with the same long-run steady-state level of income may have different growth rates if they are in different points in the transition to the steady state. For example, consider two countries that are identical in every way except that one has a higher saving rate than the other and, so, initially has a higher steady-state level of income. At the steady states, the country with the higher saving rate will have a higher level of output per worker, but both will be growing at the rate *n*. If the country with the lower saving rate suddenly can increase saving to match the other country, its growth rate will be higher than the other country until it catches up at the new steady state. Thus, even though everything is identical in the two countries, their growth rates may differ during the transition to the steady state, which may take many years.

TECHNOLOGICAL CHANGE IN THE SOLOW MODEL

The Solow model as described to this point is a powerful tool for analyzing the interrelationships between savings, investment, population growth, output, and economic growth. However, the unsettling conclusion of the basic model is that, once the economy reaches its long-run potential level of income, economic growth simply matches population growth, with no chance for sustained increases in average income. How can the model explain the empirical fact that many of the world's countries have seen steady growth in average incomes since 1820?

Solow's answer was **technological change.**[15] According to this idea, a key reason why the United Kingdom, France, Germany, the United States, and other high-income countries have been able to sustain growth in per-capita income over very long periods of time is that technological progress has allowed output per worker to continue to grow. To incorporate an economy's ability to produce more output with the same amount of capital and labor, we slightly modify our original production function and introduce a variable, *T*, to represent technological progress, as follows:

$$Y = F(K, T \times L) \qquad\qquad [2\text{--}15]$$

15. See Robert Solow, "Technical Change and the Aggregate Production Function." For an early discussion about the relationship between capital accumulation and technological progress, see Joan Robinson, *Essays in the Theory of Economic Growth* (London: Macmillan, 1962).

In this specification, technology is introduced in such a way that it directly enhances the input of labor. This type of technological change is referred to as *labor augmenting*.[16] As technology improves (and T rises), the efficiency and productivity of labor increases, since the same amount of labor can now produce more output. Increases in T can result from improvements in technology in the mechanical sense (e.g., new computers or machines) or in terms of **human capital,** such as improvements in the health, education, or skills of the workforce.[17]

The combined term $T \times L$ is sometimes referred to as the amount of **effective units of labor.** $T \times L$ measures both the amount of labor and its efficiency in the production process. An increase in either T or L increases the amount of effective labor and therefore increases aggregate production. For example, an insurance sales office can increase its effective workforce by either adding new workers or giving each worker a new, faster computer. An increase in T differs from an increase in L, however, since the rise in aggregate income from new technology does not need to be shared with additional workers, so output (and income) per actual worker will increase.

Solow specified technological change as exogenous to the model, that is, determined independent of all the variables and parameters specified in the model. He did not spell out exactly how technological change takes place or how it might be affected by the growth process itself. Wherever it came from, however, new technology clearly added to the ability of the factors of production to increase output. In this sense, technological change has been likened to "manna from heaven" in the Solow model. The usual assumption is that technology improves at a constant rate, which we denote by the Greek letter theta, so that $\Delta T/T = \theta$. If technology is growing at 1 percent per year, for example, then each worker is becoming 1 percent more efficient each year. With the workforce growing at n, growth in the effective supply of labor is equal to $n + \theta$. In other words, if the workforce (and population) is growing at 2 percent per year and technology is growing at 1 percent per year, the effective supply of labor is increasing by 3 percent per year.

To show technological change in the Solow diagram, we need to slightly change our notation. Whereas we earlier expressed y and k in

16. Two other possibilities are "capital-augmenting" technological change ($Y = F(T \times K, L)$), which enhances capital inputs, and "Hicks-neutral" technological change ($Y = F(T \times K, T \times L)$), which enhances both capital and labor input. For our purposes, the specific way in which technology is introduced does not affect the basic conclusions of the model.

17. Keep in mind, however, that while these two broad categories of improvements in technology have similar general effects in this aggregate model, their true effects are somewhat different in the real world. Technological change in the mechanical sense or from the spread of a new idea can be shared widely across the workforce and can be considered a kind of public good. Improvements in human capital, by contrast, are specific to individual workers and are not necessarily widely shared. However, both have the effect of augmenting the supply of labor and increasing total output.

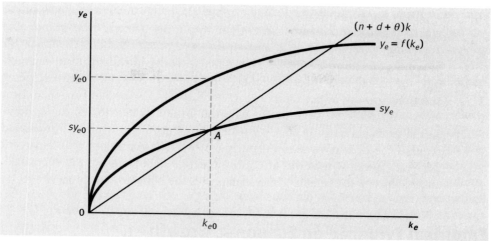

FIGURE 2–8   THE SOLOW MODEL WITH TECHNICAL CHANGE. Here, the equilibrium level of effective capital per worker (k_{e0}) is determined by point A, the intersection of the effective capital widening curve ($n + d + \theta$) and the effective saving curve (sy_e).

terms of output and capital *per worker*, we now need to express these variables in terms of output and capital *per effective worker*. The change is straightforward. Instead of dividing Y and K by L as previously (to obtain y and k), we now divide each by ($T \times L$). Thus, **output per effective worker** (y_e) is defined as $y_e = Y/(T \times L)$. Similarly, **capital per effective worker** (k_e) is defined as $k_e = K/(T \times L)$.[18]

With these changes, the production function can be written as $y_e = f(k_e)$, and saving per effective worker expressed as sy_e. With effective labor now growing at the rate $n + \theta$, the capital accumulation equation (2–14) changes to

$$\Delta k_e = sy_e (n + d + \theta)k_e \qquad [2\text{–}16]$$

The new term $(n + d + \theta)k_e$ is larger than the original $(n + d)k$, indicating that, with θ a positive number, more capital is needed to keep capital *per effective worker* constant.

These changes are shown in Figure 2–8, which looks very similar to the basic Solow diagram, with only a slight change in notation. There still is one steady-state point at which savings per effective worker is just equal to the amount of new capital to compensate for changes in the size of the workforce, depreciation, and technological change in order to keep capital per effective worker constant.

18. Note that this is consistent with the earlier notation. If there is no technological change (our earlier assumption), so that $T = 1$ (and remains unchanged), then $y_e = y$ and $k_e = k$.

One change, however, is very important. At the steady state, output per *effective* worker is constant, rather than output per worker. *Total output now is growing at the rate n + θ, so that output per actual worker (or income per person) is increasing at rate θ.* Therefore, with the introduction of technology, the model now incorporates the possibility of an economy experiencing sustained growth in per capita income at rate $θ$. This mechanism, then, provides a plausible explanation for why the United States, for example, never seems to reach a steady state with constant output per worker but instead regularly records growth in output per worker of between 1 and 2 percent per year. We now turn our attention to actual data from around the world, and see how well the Solow model captures the basic growth process.

Empirical Evidence on Economic Growth

CONVERGENCE

A key implication of the Solow growth model is that, if all countries have the same potential (or steady-state) level of income, poor countries will grow faster than rich countries and eventually will catch up at the steady state. In other words, in a strict interpretation of the model, we should observe the levels of income of countries around the world "converging" toward one another over time. Has this actually happened?

The short answer is no. Figure 2–9 shows the initial level of per capita income in 1965 and subsequent rates of growth for 124 countries from

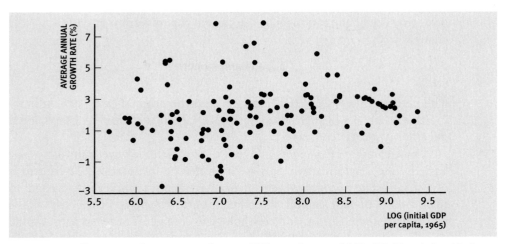

FIGURE 2–9   ECONOMIC GROWTH AND INITIAL GDP PER CAPITA, 1965–97. No relationship is apparent between initial levels of income and subsequent rates of economic growth when other factors affecting growth are not controlled for. The sample includes 124 countries from all areas of the world with a wide range of incomes. Sources: GDP data are from *Penn World Table,* vol. 5.6, 1994, and *World Development Indicators 1999* CD-ROM.

around the world. If it were true that poor countries were growing faster than rich countries, the graph would show a clear downward slope from left to right. Poor countries would record a high rate of growth (and appear in the upper left part of the figure) and rich countries would display a slower growth rate (and be in the bottom right). But there is no clear pattern evident in the figure. Some poor countries have grown quickly, but others have recorded very low (even negative) rates of growth. The same is true for middle-income countries. The only part that seems accurate is that almost all the rich countries display relatively slow growth rates, as expected. These results have been documented in many studies using more sophisticated techniques. The empirical fact is clear: There has been no *general* tendency for poor countries to catch up to the world leaders. If anything, the opposite has been true. As we saw earlier in Figure 2–1, for the last two centuries the gap between the richest and poorest regions of the world has grown, implying a divergence of incomes.

However, this simple graph does not really do justice to the Solow model. The model predicts that poorer countries will grow faster than richer countries *if the two countries have the same long-run, or steady-state, level of income.* That is, we should expect to find convergence of incomes for countries with the same underlying production function and the same rates of saving, population growth, depreciation, and technology growth. Some of the poor countries in Figure 2–9, for example, have low saving rates or very little growth in technology compared with other countries and, therefore, have lower steady-state levels of income. To see if the Solow model holds under these stricter conditions, we have to dig a little deeper.

The trick is to find a group of countries that plausibly have the same (or at least similar) potential levels of income. William Baumol initially tackled this issue by examining the evidence for convergence among a group of industrialized countries.[19] The plausible assumption is that production processes, technology accumulation, and other factors are roughly similar across this group of economies. Figure 2–10 shows the evidence for convergence between 1965 and 1990 among the 24 countries that were members of the OECD in 1975. The pattern is strikingly different from in Figure 2–9. The six OECD countries with the lowest average incomes in 1965 (Turkey, Portugal, Greece, Ireland, Japan, and Spain) recorded economic growth rates of 3.0 percent or better between 1965 and 1997, whereas the four highest income countries (the United States, Switzerland, Sweden, New Zealand) all grew at less than 2.1 percent per year. The downward slope of the figures shows a clear tendency toward convergence of average incomes across these countries.

---

19. William J. Baumol, "Productivity Growth, Convergence, and Welfare: What the Long-Run Data Show," *American Economic Review,* 76 (December 1986), 1072–85.

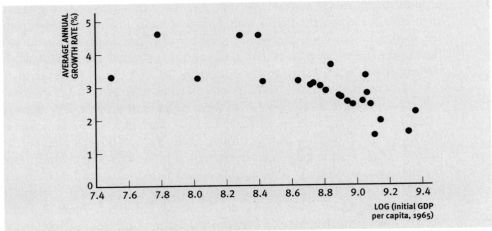

FIGURE 2–10   CONDITIONAL CONVERGENCE WITHIN THE OECD. The 24 countries that were members of OECD in 1975 are likely to have similar long-run (steady-state) levels of income. Within this group of countries, lower-income countries recorded faster rates of economic growth, as predicted by the Solow model, giving a downward slope to the graph. Sources: GDP data are from *Penn World Table,* vol. 5.6, 1994, and *World Development Indicators 1999* CD-ROM.

Another approach is to pick a group of countries from all income levels that are similar in their policy choices, geographic characteristics, or some other variable that might be a determinant of the steady state level of income. Economists Jeffrey Sachs and Andrew Warner, for example, examined the evidence for convergence among all countries that had been consistently open to world trade since 1965.[20] A group of "open" economies might have similar long-run levels of income, since they can acquire new technology relatively quickly from other open economies through imports of new machinery and their connections to global production networks (we discuss these issues more in Chapter 19). Figure 2–11 shows a strong tendency for convergence of incomes among the group of 30 countries identified as "open" by Sachs and Warner. Among poorer countries that have been open to world trade, there has been a propensity for rapid economic growth and catching up with richer countries. Prominent examples of this tendency include Singapore, Korea, Taiwan, Malaysia, Mauritius, Indonesia, and Thailand.

A growing body of more sophisticated econometric studies that control for a wide range of other variables has reached the same conclu-

20. A country was considered to be "open" if it met five criteria: (1) its average tariff rates were less than 40 percent, (2) its nontariff barriers (e.g., quotas) covered less than 40 percent of imports, (3) the premium on the unofficial parallel market exchange rate did not exceeding 20 percent, (4) there were no state monopolies on major exports, and (5) it was not a socialist economy. We discuss these issues more in Chapter 19. Source: Jeffrey Sachs and Andrew Warner, "Economic Reform and the Process of Global Integration," *Brookings Papers on Economic Activity,* 1 (1995), 1–118.

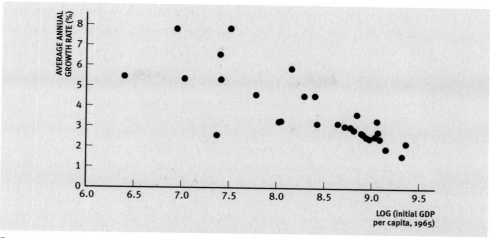

FIGURE 2–11 CONDITIONAL CONVERGENCE AMONG OPEN ECONOMIES. The 30 countries among those most open to trade (as defined by the Sachs-Warner openness index) between 1965 and 1997 show convergence in income, as predicted by the Solow model. Lower-income countries grew more quickly than higher-income countries, giving a downward slope to the figure. Sources: GDP data are from *Penn World Table* vol. 5.6, 1994, and *World Development Indicators 1999* CD-ROM. Openness data are from Sachs and Warner, "Economic Reform and the Process of Global Integration."

sion.[21] Once we take into account differences in important government policies, saving (or investment) rates, natural resource abundance, and geographic characteristics (such as being landlocked) that affect the production process, there is a clear tendency for poorer countries to grow faster than rich countries. Therefore, while there is no evidence for "absolute convergence" of income levels among all countries, there is a large body of evidence for "conditional convergence" of incomes once we control (or condition) for differences in steady-state income levels.

CHARACTERISTICS OF RAPIDLY GROWING ECONOMIES

The same body of research that examined convergence across countries has searched for broad characteristics common to rapidly growing economies. Until relatively recently, it was difficult for researchers to systematically examine these issues due to severe data limitations. A few pioneering efforts,

21. Some of the most important studies in this body of research include Robert Barro. "Economic Growth in a Cross Section of Countries," *Quarterly Journal of Economics,* 106, no. 2 (May 1991), 407–43; Bradford DeLong and Lawrence Summers, "Equipment Investment and Economic Growth," *Quarterly Journal of Economics,* 106, no. 2 (May 1991), 445–502; Gregory Mankiw, David Romer, and David Weil, "A Contribution to the Empirics of Economic Growth," *Quarterly Journal of Economics,* 107, no. 2 (May 1992), 407–38; and Sachs and Warner, "Economic Growth and the Process of Global Integration." For a review of this literature, see Jonathan Temple, "The New Growth Evidence," *The Journal of Economic Literature,* 37, no. 1 (March 1999), 112–56.

such as Irma Adelman and Cynthyia Taft Morris's *Society, Politics, and Economic Development—A Quantitative Approach*,[22] paved the way for today's cross-country empirical growth research. In recent years, this type of research has grown very rapidly, in line with the emergence of many new and large datasets on income in PPP terms, education levels, health characteristics, quality of governance, and a host of related items. Most of the recent studies are modeled on research completed by economist Robert Barro in the early 1990s. In essence, these studies control for the initial (current) level of income and incorporate several variables that might affect the long-run level of income. These include levels of education and health, policy choices, resource endowments, geographic characteristics (latitude, whether the country is landlocked, etc.), political systems, and so on. The growth rate depends on the difference between the long-run level of income and the current level of income.[23]

This type of research has been controversial, and there is far from a consensus on the exact group of variables that affect the steady state (and therefore growth rates). For one thing, while this research starts with the Solow model, for many of the variables tested there is no well-developed theoretical link between the variable and either long-run income levels or economic growth. The existing theories on economic growth simply are not explicit enough about exactly what variables determine the shape of the production function and the steady state. As a result, some characteristics may appear as statistically important in one research study that includes a certain group of variables but unimportant in another study with a different group of variables.[24] A second issue has to do with statistical interpretation of the results. For example, most economists would agree that high saving rates are associated with rapid economic growth. But which causes which? Higher savings can lead to more rapid growth, as suggested by the Solow model, while faster economic growth might provide more disposable income and a higher saving rate. In practice, it is a

---

22. Irma Adelman and Cynthyia Taft Morris, *Society, Politics, and Economic Development— A Quantitative Approach* (Baltimore: Johns Hopkins University Press, 1967).

23. These studies usually estimate the parameters of an equation of the form

$$g = \alpha y_0 + \beta_1 x_1 + \beta_2 x_2 + \cdots \beta_n x_n + v$$

In this equation, g is the growth rate of output per worker and y_0 is the level of output per worker in the initial year of the study. The variables x_1 through x_n represent a group of characteristics that are thought to influence the long-run (or steady state) level of income, and therefore the current growth rate during the transition to that steady state. The variables α_0 and β_1 through β_n are the parameters estimated in the study that tell us the magnitude and the statistical importance of y_0 and x_1 through x_n on economic growth, and v is an error term.

24. A seminal study on the robustness of explanatory variables across different specifications is Ross Levine and David Renelt, "A Sensitivity Analysis of Cross-Country Growth Regressions," *American Economic Review*, 82, no. 4 (September 1992), 942–63.

major statistical challenge to precisely estimate the magnitude of these two effects.[25]

Despite these issues, this empirical growth research has helped analysts better understand the broad characteristics associated with rapid economic growth (even if not the exact channel through which each variable affects growth). While the debate is far from over about which variables influence long-run growth, how they do so, and the magnitude of the effect, this research has helped provide broad clues about why some economies grow faster than others. Economist Xavier Sala-i-Martin has neatly summarized this research by formulating a list of variables that most consistently are found to be closely associated with economic growth.[26] These variables include the following:

- *Level of income.* Almost all studies find a strong negative relationship between the level of income in the initial year of the study and the subsequent growth rate *after controlling for other variables.* This, of course, is the conditional convergence effect discussed in the previous section.
- *Life expectancy.* Many studies have shown a strong relationship between longer life expectancy and more rapid economic growth. A longer life expectancy is indicative of general improvements in the health of a population, which in turn probably indicates a healthier and more productive labor force. In addition, a higher life expectancy might boost saving and capital accumulation, since people are more likely to invest in skill and education if they expect to live longer to reap greater benefits.
- *Level of education.* In the extended Solow model with technological change, increased levels of education are expected to translate into a more highly skilled workforce and an increase in the amount of effective units of labor and, therefore, a higher steady-state level of income. (The same is true for a healthier workforce.) Although most studies verify the expected positive relationship between education and economic growth, the statistical strength of the relationship often is relatively modest. This may be due to difficulties in accurately and consistently measuring the quantity and quality of education across a large number of countries.

25. Researchers can get around this problem partially by choosing their observation of the x variable (say, the saving rate) at the beginning of the research period. Thus, if the saving rate in 1960 is included, it is hard to argue that the growth rate from 1960 to 1990 influenced the 1960 saving rate, so researchers are more confident that the measured effect shows how the saving rate influences the subsequent growth rate. This approach has its problems, too, however. The 1960 saving rate may change shortly thereafter and so may not be indicative of the saving rate actually influencing growth over the entire period.

26. Xavier X. Sala-i-Martin, "I Just Ran Two Million Regressions," *American Economic Review,* 87, no. 2 (May 1997), 178–83.

- *Geography.* A striking fact is that there are no rich economies in the tropics other than Singapore, the Hong Kong territory of China, and a few small, oil-rich countries. Tropical countries have to deal with greater numbers of virulent diseases, erratic rainfall, and generally poor quality soil for agriculture. Similarly, landlocked countries face higher transport costs, greater isolation, and fewer economic opportunities than coastal economies.[27] In the Solow framework, these geographic factors influence the production function (and possibly the saving rate) and tend to lead to a lower potential level of income.[28]

- *Saving and investment.* Investment in equipment has a large and strong positive relationship to economic growth in many studies. Nonequipment investment also shows a positive relationship but not nearly as large as for equipment investment. Many studies also show a strong relationship between saving and growth, as expected in the model. A few studies have found a particularly strong relationship between government saving (that is, the government's budget surplus on current revenue and expenditure) and growth.

- *Trade and exchange rate policies.* Sala-i-Martin's analysis found a strong negative relationship between measures of distortion in the exchange rate (for example, a large difference between the official exchange rates and the "street" rate) and economic growth. Furthermore, the Sachs-Warner study and others have found that countries that have been consistently "open" to the world trading system have recorded more rapid rates of economic growth.

- *Natural resource endowments.* Historically, many countries with rich natural resource endowments have had very strong economic performance, including the United States, Australia, New Zealand, Denmark, and the Netherlands. But, in recent years, the relationship between natural resource endowments and economic growth generally has been negative. A large number of resource-rich developing countries have fared poorly and recorded very slow growth rates, including Nigeria, Angola, Bolivia, Colombia, Congo, Venezuela, Mozambique, Nicaragua, Myanmar, and others.

27. Switzerland and Austria are the exceptions that prove the rule. Although landlocked, these countries are far from being economically isolated and have been very successful. Most landlocked countries are in fact very isolated from major markets, which raises production costs for their firms and reduces their potential level of income.

28. Recent studies that explore the impact of geographical factors on levels of income and growth rates include Robert Hall and Charles Jones, "Why Do Some Countries Produce So Much More Output per Worker Than Others?" *Quarterly Journal of Economics* 114 (February 1999), 83–116; Steven Radelet and Jeffrey Sachs, "Shipping Costs, Manufactured Exports, and Economic Growth," Harvard Institute for International Development, January 1998; and John Gallup and Jeffrey Sachs, "Geography and Economic Development," in Boris Pleskovic and Joseph Stiglitz, eds., *World Bank Annual Conference on Development Economics 1998* (Washington, DC: World Bank, 1998), pp. 127–78.

- *Political variables.* Many studies have found a positive relationship between economic growth and the strength of the rule of law, political rights, civil liberties, and other measures of governance and institutional quality. Conversely, but not surprisingly, a strong negative relationship exists between economic growth and incidence of revolutions, coups, and war. Political stability, like macroeconomic stability, is good for growth and development.

SOURCES OF GROWTH ANALYSIS

A different, but in many ways complementary, approach to studying the empirical evidence on economic growth is to focus directly on the contribution of each term in the production function to economic growth. This approach, also pioneered by Robert Solow, is more of an accounting framework based on actual data than an economic model. It seeks to answer the following question: What proportions of recorded economic growth can we attribute to growth in the capital stock, growth of the labor force, and changes in overall efficiency?[29] Solow's procedure usually is referred to as **growth accounting** or **sources of growth analysis.** It starts with the basic production function, as in equation 2–1, and extends it by adding a term, A, to capture the general efficiency with which inputs are used:

$$Y = F(K, L, A) \qquad [2\text{--}17]$$

The parameter A is meant to capture the effects of things other than the capital stock and labor supply that might influence growth, such as policies, institutions, and the level of technology.[30] Efficiency could be improved, for example, by changing policies (such as removing price subsidies that distort the allocation of resources), strengthening institutions (such as the court system), or introducing new technologies (including improvements in productive techniques and the introduction of products with improved quality). The parameter A generally is referred to as **total factor productivity** (TFP).

Before we examine the actual data, we must convert this production function into a form that makes it possible to measure the contribution of each factor (K, L, and A) to overall growth. The derivation of this new form of the equation involves calculus and so is presented in the appendix to this chapter. The resulting equation is

$$g_Y = a + (W_K \times g_K) + (W_L \times g_L) \qquad [2\text{--}18]$$

29. Solow, "Technical Change and the Aggregate Production Function."

30. Some specifications denote this parameter as T for technology, but we wish to stress that the efficiency parameter encompasses more than technology.

EXPLAINING DIFFERENCES IN GROWTH RATES

Many recent studies have shown that initial levels of incomes, openness to trade, healthy populations, high levels of education, favorable geography, and high savings rates all contribute to rapid economic growth. But which are most important? One study sought to explain differences in growth during the period 1965–90 between three groups of countries: 10 East and Southeast Asian countries (in which per capita growth averaged 4.6 percent), 17 sub-Saharan African countries (in which growth averaged 0.6 percent), and 21 Latin American countries (in which growth averaged 0.7 percent).[31]

Policy variables explained much of the difference in growth rates. For example, the East and Southeast Asian countries recorded higher government saving rates, were more open to trade, and had higher quality government institutions. Together, the differences in these policies accounted for 1.7 percentage points of the 4.0 percentage point difference between the East and Southeast Asian and sub-Saharan African growth rates, and 1.8 percentage points of the difference between East and Southeast Asia and Latin America. Openness to trade stood out as the single most important policy choice affecting these growth rates.

Initial levels of income also were important, as the Solow model predicts. Since the Latin American countries had higher average income (and therefore greater output per worker) than the East Asian countries in 1965, the Solow model would predict somewhat slower growth for the Latin American countries. Sure enough, this study estimates that Latin America's higher initial income slowed its growth rate by 1.2 percentage points relative to East and Southeast Asia. By contrast, the sub-Saharan African countries had lower average initial income, indicating that (all

31. Steven Radelet, Jeffrey Sachs, and Jong-Wha Lee, "Economic Growth in Asia," Harvard Institute for International Development, July 1997. These results are also summarized in the Asian Development Bank's study *Emerging Asia: Changes and Challenges* (Manila: Asian Development Bank 1997), pp. 79–82.

in which g_Y, g_K, and g_L are the growth rates of Y, K, and L, respectively. W_L and W_K are the shares in total income of wages and returns on capital, respectively. For example, if 60 percent of all income comes from wages and the remaining 40 percent comes from returns on capital (e.g., interest and rent), then $W_L = 0.60$ and $W_K = 0.40$. The parameter a is the rate of

else being equal) these countries could have grown 1.0 percentage point faster than the East and Southeast Asian countries, rather than the actual outcome of 4.0 percentage points slower. This suggests that the other factors had to account for a full 5.0 percentage point difference in growth rates between East and Southeast Asia and sub-Saharan Africa.

Initial levels of health, as indicated by life expectancy at birth, were a major factor contributing to sub-Saharan Africa's slow growth. Life expectancy at birth averaged 41 years in sub-Saharan Africa in 1965, compared to 55 years in East and Southeast Asia. The study estimates that this reduced sub-Saharan Africa's growth rate by 1.3 percentage points relative to East and Southeast Asia. By contrast, since average life expectancy in Latin America in 1965 was almost the same as in East and Southeast Asia, health explains little of the difference in growth between these regions.

Favorable geography helped East and Southeast Asia grow faster. The combination of fewer landlocked countries, longer average coastline, fewer countries located in the deep tropics, and less dependence on natural resource exports all favored Asia. (Chapter 16 explores why a dearth of natural resources might have actually helped Asia.) Taken together, these factors accounted for 1.0 percentage points of East and Southeast Asia's rapid growth compared to sub-Saharan Africa, and 0.6 percentage points relative to Latin America. Differences in initial levels of education and the changing demographic structure of the population accounted for the remaining differences in growth rates across these regions.

Of course, this simple accounting framework does not fully explain the complex relationships that underlie economic growth. Each of the variables in the study captures a range of other factors that affect growth rates. For example, differences in government saving rates probably reflect differences in fiscal policy, inflation rates, political stability, and many other factors. Because of lack of sufficient data, the analysis omits several factors (such as environmental degradation) that may be important. And it certainly does not begin to explain why different policy choices were made in different countries. As a result, studies like these should be seen as a first step to understanding growth, rather than as a precise explanation for the many complex differences across countries.

change in A, measuring the shift in the production function resulting from greater efficiency in the use of inputs.

The basic procedure is to substitute actual data for all the variables in equation 2–18 except a, which cannot be measured directly. Values for all the other variables usually can be found in the statistical handbooks of most countries. Once all the other values are inserted into the equation, *a* can be calculated as the residual to balance the equation. In this way, the contribution of each of these variables to growth can be measured and identified.

A simple numerical example illustrates the way in which this equation is used. From the statistical records of a developing country, we find the following values for the variables in the equation:

g_Y = 0.05 (GNP growth rate of 5 percent a year)
g_K = 0.07 (capital stock growth of 7 percent a year)
g_L = 0.02 (labor force growth of 2 percent a year)
W_L = 0.6 (the share of labor in national income is 60 percent)
W_K = 0.4 (the share of capital is 40 percent).

By substituting these figures into equation 2–19, we get

$$0.05 = a + 0.4(0.07) + 0.6(0.02)$$

Solving for *a*, we find that *a* = 0.01. These figures tell us that TFP growth is 1 percent a year and thus accounts for one fifth (0.01/0.05) the total growth of the GNP. The growth in the capital stock accounts for slightly more than half (56 percent) the total growth (.4 × .07/.05). The remaining 24 percent of growth is accounted for by growth in the labor force (0.02 × 0.6/0.05).

This type of accounting analysis has been used widely in many countries to examine the sources of growth, with particular attention paid to calculating TFP growth. Before briefly examining some of these results, however, it is important to recognize the limits of this kind of study. There are two kinds of problems. First, *a* represents a combination of influences that this analysis cannot entirely disentangle. Should improvements in *a* be attributed, for example, to better trade policies, reduced corruption, or the introduction of faster computers or other technologies? Is a change in *a* the result of more efficient use of existing inputs or the introduction of a new technology? The limited growth accounting framework cannot definitively answer these questions without adding many more variables for which data do not exist (although that has not stopped analysts from assigning their own favorite explanation to the results). Second, *a* invariably is measured inaccurately, since it is the residual in the equation. All economic data are measured with some inevitable errors, including all the data used in equation 2–19. As a result, *a* captures the net effect of errors and omissions in all the other data. Thus, what is labeled *TFP* actually, in practice, is a combination of errors in the data, omission of other factors that should be included in the growth equation, as well as efficiency gains and changes in technology. As a result, there is a danger in trying to read too much into these data when analysts interpret them as strictly efficiency gains or the effects of new technology. In reality, rather than truly being TFP growth, *a* simply is the part of measured growth than cannot be explained by data on the traditional factors of production. For this reason, the residual *a* sometimes has been referred to as a *measure of our ignorance* about the growth process.

Sources of growth analyses have been carried out for many countries. Solow's initial study on the United States attributed a surprisingly large share of growth to the residual and a correspondingly small share to changes in the capital stock. In fact, he attributed 88 percent of the increase in output per worker to TFP growth and only 12 percent to increases in capital per worker. Subsequent work by economists Edward Denison, Dale Jorgenson, and others attempted to measure in a more precise way the contribution of various inputs to the growth process. For example, they divided labor into different skill categories based on the amounts of formal education that workers had received. A worker having a high school education and earning $20,000 a year is treated as the equivalent of two people having only primary school education and earning $10,000 a year each. Similar procedures are used to measure the increase in productivity that occurs when workers shift from low-productivity occupations in rural areas to higher-productivity occupations in urban areas. Other methods are used to measure improvements in the quality of capital and increasing use of economies of scale. Many of these more detailed analyses of the U.S. economy found results very similar to Solow's initial work: The bulk of the growth process could be attributed to the residual, with relatively small amounts apportioned to various categories of labor, capital, and other inputs. Over the years, many more studies have been completed for the industrialized countries. Increases in the capital stock frequently account for less than half the increase in output, particularly in rapidly growing countries. These results came as a bit of a surprise for most economists, since most basic models put capital formation at the heart of the growth process.

Similar studies have now been carried out for a wide range of developing countries. Data problems and price distortions tend to be more severe for developing countries than for the industrialized countries. Few developing countries, for example, have reliable measures for differences in the quality of alternative capital input and labor skill categories. Generally speaking, TFP studies in developing countries attribute a larger role to capital formation than in the industrialized country studies. This is consistent with the idea that developing countries have lower levels of capital per worker than the industrialized countries and can catch up (or converge) through the investment process. Furthermore, much of the capital equipment imported by developing countries (which shows up as investment)

TABLE 2-6   SOURCES OF GROWTH IN THE FOUR TIGERS, 1966-90 (AVERAGE ANNUAL GROWTH RATES, PERCENT)

REGION/PERIOD	OUTPUT	WEIGHTED CAPITAL	WEIGHTED LABOR	TOTAL FACTOR PRODUCTIVITY
HONG KONG (1960–91)	7.3	3.0	2.0	2.3
SINGAPORE (1960–90)	8.5	6.1	2.7	−0.3
SOUTH KOREA (1960–90)	10.4	4.4	4.4	1.7
TAIWAN (1960–90)	9.6	3.6	3.6	2.4

Source: Young, "The Tyranny of the Numbers."

embodies advances in technology. Therefore, the mobilization of capital remains a major concern of policy makers in developing countries.

In recent years, much of the debate on TFP growth in developing countries has centered on the experiences of the East Asian economies, which, even after taking into account the financial crises of 1997–98, have recorded remarkably rapid growth rates since the late 1960s. Some analysts have argued that, at the core of East Asia's growth, were rapid increases in efficiency and technological gains. If true, East Asia's growth might not be susceptible to a slowdown in growth from diminishing returns to capital, and growth could continue at a rapid rate long into the future. However, in one widely cited study, economist Alywn Young found that the main engine for growth in the "four tigers"—Singapore, Hong Kong, Taiwan, and South Korea—was capital accumulation rather than TFP growth.[32] His basic results are shown in Table 2–6. The most surprising finding was the negative TFP growth in Singapore between 1966 and 1990. In the three other economies, average TFP growth varied between 1.7 percent (South Korea) to 2.4 percent (Taiwan). In each case, capital accumulation was the largest contributor to growth and, in all except Hong Kong, labor was the second largest contributor. In other words, substantial investment in physical and human capital provided the main foundation for growth in these economies.

Although TFP growth in the four tigers contributed less to growth than capital accumulation, how did TFP growth in these countries compare to other regions of the world at the same time? A study by Susan Collins and Barry Bosworth addressed this issue by measuring TFP growth for a large

32. Alwyn Young, "The Tyranny of the Numbers: Confronting the Statistical Realities of the East Asian Growth Experience," *Quarterly Journal of Economics,* 110, no. 3 (August 1995), 641–80.

TABLE 2–7   SOURCES OF GROWTH IN EAST ASIA AND OTHER REGIONS, 1973–94 (AVERAGE ANNUAL GROWTH RATES, PERCENT)

| | | | CONTRIBUTION BY COMPONENT | | |
REGION/PERIOD		GROWTH OF OUTPUT PER WORKER	PHYSICAL CAPITAL PER WORKER	EDUCATION PER WORKER	TOTAL FACTOR PRODUCTIVITY
INDONESIA	1973–84	4.3	3.3	0.5	0.5
	1984–94	3.7	2.3	0.5	0.9
KOREA	1973–84	5.3	3.4	0.8	1.1
	1984–94	6.2	3.3	0.6	2.1
MALAYSIA	1973–84	3.6	2.7	0.5	.4
	1984–94	3.8	1.8	0.5	1.4
PHILIPPINES	1973–84	1.2	2.0	0.6	−1.3
	1984–94	−0.3	0.2	0.4	−0.9
SINGAPORE	1973–84	4.3	3.1	0.2	1.0
	1984–94	6.0	2.3	0.6	3.1
THAILAND	1973–84	3.6	2.0	0.5	1.1
	1984–94	6.9	2.6	0.8	3.3
TAIWAN	1973–84	4.9	3.0	0.9	0.9
	1984–94	5.6	2.3	0.5	2.8
CHINA	1973–84	4.3	1.7	0.4	2.2
	1984–94	8.0	2.9	0.3	4.6
EAST ASIA	1973–84	4.0	2.8	0.6	0.5
	1984–94	4.4	2.2	0.6	1.6
SOUTH ASIA	1973–84	2.5	0.9	0.4	1.2
	1984–94	2.7	1.0	0.3	1.5
AFRICA	1973–84	−0.6	1.2	0.2	−2.0
	1984–94	−0.6	−0.4	0.3	−0.4
MIDDLE EAST	1973–84	0.5	2.2	0.6	−2.2
	1984–94	−1.1	0.0	0.5	−1.5
LATIN AMERICA	1973–84	0.4	1.1	0.4	−1.1
	1984–94	0.1	0.1	0.4	−0.4
UNITED STATES	1973–84	0.2	0.3	0.5	−0.5
	1984–94	0.9	0.3	0.0	0.7
OTHER INDUSTRIALIZED COUNTRIES	1973–84	1.8	1.1	0.6	0.2
	1984–94	1.7	0.8	0.2	0.7

Source: Collins and Bosworth, "Economic Growth in East Asia."

number of countries between 1960 and 1994.[33] Their results are summarized in Table 2–7. As with other studies, they found a fairly consistent pattern that capital accumulation was the main contributor to growth for developing countries. For industrialized countries, the main contributions were more evenly split between capital accumulation and TFP growth. In comparing TFP growth across countries, they found that the rapidly grow-

33. Susan Collins and Barry Bosworth, "Economic Growth in East Asia: Accumulation versus Assimilation," *Brookings Papers on Economic Activity*, 2 (1996), 135–203.

ing East Asian economies (including China) recorded much faster TFP growth than developing countries from other regions of the world. In fact, the average TFP growth for countries in Africa, Latin America, and the Middle East actually was *negative* between 1973 and 1994. The East Asian countries also recorded faster TFP growth than the average for industrialized countries over the same period. Therefore, TFP growth was higher in the East Asian countries than in other countries. TFP growth seems to have risen around the world between 1984 and 1994 compared to the earlier 1973–84 period, probably reflecting the end of the major commodity price and exchange rate swings of the 1970s. The increase in TFP growth was particularly large in Singapore, Thailand, Taiwan, and China.[34] Thus, while TFP growth was not the prime mover of Asian growth, in most countries it made an important contribution to growth.

In summary, sources of growth analyses suggest that capital accumulation is the main source of growth for developing countries, consistent with the Solow growth model. TFP can play an important part in growth process in the appropriate policy and structural context. In rapidly growing economies, both factor accumulation and TFP growth appear to play an important role. TFP growth appears to become more important as incomes rise, and is a major contributor to growth in the higher income industrialized countries.

Beyond Solow: New Approaches to Growth

Although the Solow model provides a relatively powerful framework for analyzing economic growth, it makes many simplifying assumptions about the real world. For example, the model simply assumes the saving rate, the rate of growth of the labor supply, the skills of the workforce, and the pace of technological change. In reality, the values of these parameters are not just given but partially determined by government policies, economic structure, and the pace of growth itself. Economists have begun to develop more sophisticated models in which one or more of these variables is determined within the model (that is, these variables become endogenous to the model).[35]

---

34. In the interesting case of Singapore, Collins and Bosworth calculated 1 percent TFP growth between 1973 and 1984 (slightly larger than the numbers found by Alwyn Young), but the figure jumped to 3.1 percent between 1984 and 1994.

35. The seminal contributions to the new growth theory are Paul Romer, "Increasing Returns and Long-Run Growth," *Journal of Political Economy,* 94 (October 1986), 1002–37; Robert Lucas, "On the Mechanics of Economic Development," *Journal of Monetary Economics,* 22 (January 1988), 3–42; and Paul Romer, "Endogenous Technological Change," *Journal of Political Economy,* 98 (October 1990), S71–S102.

These models depart from the Solow framework by assuming that the national economy is subject to **increasing returns to scale,** rather than the constant returns to scale of the Solow model. That is, a doubling of capital, labor, and other factors of production leads to more than a doubling of output. One implication is that the impact of both physical capital and human capital would be larger than suggested by the Solow model. For example, investments in research or education not only will have a positive effect on the firm or the individual making the investment but also may have a positive "spillover" effect on others in the economy. This beneficial effect on others, called a **positive externality,** results in a larger impact from the investment on the entire economy. The benefits from Henry Ford's development of the production line system, for example, were certainly large for the Ford Motor Company, but they were even larger for the economy as a whole because knowledge of this new technique soon spilled over to other firms that could benefit from Ford's new approach. Similarly, investments in research and development (R&D) lead to new knowledge that accrues not only to those that make the investment but to others that eventually gain access to the knowledge. The gain from education is determined not just by how much a scientist's or manager's productivity is raised by that individual's investment in his or her own education. If many scientists and managers invest in their own education, there then will be many educated people who will learn from each other, increasing the benefits from education. An isolated scientist working alone will not be as productive as one who can interact with dozens of well-educated colleagues. This interaction constitutes the externality. Such externalities suggest that the measured contribution of physical and human capital to growth may be larger than that captured by the Solow framework. This could account for a significant portion of the residual in the Solow accounting framework, meaning that actual TFP growth is smaller than many studies have suggested.

Another important implication is that economies with increasing returns to scale do not necessarily reach a steady-state level of income as in the Solow framework. When the externalities from new investment are large, diminishing returns to capital do not necessarily set in, so growth rates do not slow, and the economy does not necessarily reach a steady state. As a result, an increase in the saving rate can lead to a *permanent* increase in the rate of economic growth. These models, therefore, can explain the observed fact of continued per capita growth in many countries without relying on the exogenous technological change (θ) of the Solow model. Moreover, they do not necessarily lead to the conclusion that poor countries will grow faster than rich countries, so there is no expectation of convergence of incomes. Initial disparities in income can remain, or even enlarge, if richer countries make investments that encompass larger externalities. Since growth can perpetuate in these models without relying on an assumption of exogenous technological change, they often are referred to as **endogenous growth models.** For developing countries, the new models emphasize the importance of investments in human capital and the potential gains from the transfer of technology from countries with more-advanced research capacity. The new models remain a subject of debate, however, since many empirical studies have shown that the Solow model (allowing for different steady states across countries) can capture the vast majority of the variation in economic growth rates across countries.[36]

Appendix: Deriving the Sources of Growth Equation

There are six steps to deriving the sources of growth equation from the standard aggregate production function. To simplify the presentation, we assume only two factors of production, capital and labor.

1. Assume an aggregate production function:

$$Y = F(K, L, t) \qquad [2\text{–}19]$$

which is continuous and homogeneous to degree 1, where
$$Y = \text{national income or product,}$$
$$K = \text{capital stock,}$$
$$t = \text{time (shift in basic production function),}$$
$$L = \text{labor force.}$$

2. Differentiate this production function with respect to time.

$$\frac{dY}{dt} = \left(\frac{\partial F}{\partial K} \cdot \frac{dK}{dt}\right) + \left(\frac{\partial F}{\partial L} \cdot \frac{dL}{dt}\right) + \left(\frac{\partial F}{\partial t} \cdot \frac{dt}{dt}\right) \qquad [2\text{–}20]$$

where the symbol ∂ is used to represent the partial derivative.

3. Divide through by Y, and insert L and K in the equation.

$$\frac{1}{Y} \cdot \frac{dY}{dt} = \frac{1}{Y}\left[\left(\frac{\partial F}{\partial K} \cdot \frac{dK}{dt} \cdot K \cdot \frac{1}{K}\right) + \left(\frac{\partial F}{\partial L} \cdot \frac{dL}{dt} \cdot L \cdot \frac{1}{L}\right) + \frac{\partial F}{\partial t}\right] \qquad [2\text{–}21]$$

---

36. See the references cited in footnote 21, but especially Gregory Mankiw, David Romer, and David Weil, "A Contribution to the Empirics of Economic Growth," *Quarterly Journal of Economics,* 107, no. 2 (May 1992), 407–38.

4. Rearrange the terms.

$$\frac{dY/dt}{Y} = \frac{(\partial F/\partial K)K}{Y} \cdot \frac{dK/dt}{K} + \frac{(\partial F/\partial L)L}{Y} \cdot \frac{dL/dt}{L} + \frac{\partial F/\partial t}{Y} \quad [2\text{-}22]$$

where

$$G_Y = \frac{dY/dt}{Y} = \text{growth rate of income,}$$

$$G_K = \frac{dK/dt}{K} = \text{growth rate of capital,}$$

$$G_L = \frac{dL/dt}{L} = \text{growth rate of the labor force,}$$

$$W_K = \frac{(\partial F/\partial K)K}{Y} = \text{share of product of capital}$$
$$\text{in the national income.}$$

5. Assume perfect competition, so that wages and the interest rate equal the marginal product of the labor and capital respectively. If

$$\frac{\partial F}{\partial L} = \text{wage rate}$$

then

$$W_L = \frac{(\partial F/\partial L)L}{Y} = \text{share of wages in national income;}$$

and if

$$\frac{\partial F}{\partial K} = i \text{ (rate of interest),}$$

then

$$W_K = \frac{i \cdot K}{Y} = \text{share of income of capital in the national income,}$$

$$a = \frac{\partial F/\partial t}{Y} = \text{increase in output as a share of income}$$
$$\text{not explained by the increase in factors.}$$

6. Substitute G_Y, G_L, G_K, W_L, W_K, and a into equation 2–10, which then gives one the sources of growth equation:

$$G_Y = (W_K \cdot G_K) + (W_L \cdot G_L) + a \quad [2\text{-}23]$$

This equation can be rewritten in the form

$$a = \text{(the residual)} = G_Y - (W_K \cdot G_K) - (W_L \cdot G_L) \quad [2\text{--}24]$$

Countries with reasonably good statistical systems regularly publish data on the growth rate of national product (G_Y) and the labor force (G_L). Data on the growth rate of the capital stock (G_K) are more difficult to find, because estimates of the capital stock are readily available only for industrialized nations. Economists who work with developing-country data, therefore, sometimes rewrite the $W_K \cdot G_K$ component of equation 2–11. By not inserting K into equation 2–10, that part of equation 2–10 becomes

$$\frac{\partial F}{\partial K} \cdot \frac{dK/dt}{y}$$

where

$$\frac{\partial F}{\partial K} = \text{the interest rate as previously assumed,}$$

$$\frac{dK/dt}{Y} = I = \text{the share of gross domestic investment}$$
$$\text{in the gross domestic product.}$$

The share of gross domestic investment (I), or capital formation, in the gross domestic product regularly is calculated for most countries.

Data on the share of labor income in national income (W_L) are the total wages and salaries paid to workers plus the inputted wages of farmers. The share of capital income in national income (W_K) is made up of interest income and profits. In a two-factor model, W_K would encompass all property income, including the rent on land.

When economists such as Edward Denison calculate the sources of growth, they generally use more than two factors of production. Labor, for example, usually is divided into unskilled and skilled labor of various types. Foreign exchange earnings sometimes are treated as a separate factor of production from capital, and so on. There often is an attempt to break down the residual measure of productivity increases (a) into its various components. Some of these refinements can be used in estimating the sources of growth in developing countries, but others cannot because of the limited availability of relevant developing-country data.

3

STRUCTURAL CHANGE

Modern economic growth involves more than increases in per capita output and rises in total factor productivity. As per capita income rises, the structure of the economy also changes. The best-known structural shift is the decline in the number of people working on farms and rise in their number working in industry and the service sector. Within the industrial sector, there is also structural change. Countries starting down the path of industrialization usually begin with simple labor-intensive processes such as making shoes and garments and then move to more complex, capital-intensive industries such as petrochemicals and automobiles. Industrialization usually is accompanied by urbanization, and many goods and services that used to be produced by households for their own use are produced instead by enterprises that then sell these goods and services to the individual households. These shifts in the structure of output or national product are the subject of this chapter. In this chapter, we are concerned mainly with the relationship between these sectors as growth takes place. In later chapters (notably Chapters 15 and 17), we look at development within each of these sectors individually.

One clear pattern of changing economic structure in the course of economic development is that, as per capita income rises, the share of industry in gross national product rises also. Although it is possible to conceive of a situation in which a country moves from a condition of poverty to one of wealth while concentrating on agriculture, this kind of growth has yet to occur. Every country that has achieved a high per capita income also has experienced a population shift, in which the majority moves from rural areas and farming to cities and industrial jobs. All also have experienced an increase in industrial value added in gross national product.

There are two principal reasons for this. The first is **Engel's law.** In the nineteenth century, Ernst Engel discovered that, as incomes of families rose, the proportion of their budget spent on food declined. Since the main function of the agricultural sector is to produce food, it follows that demand for agricultural output would not grow as rapidly as demand for industrial products and services; hence, the share of agriculture in national product would decline. This relationship holds for all countries that experienced sustained development.

A second reason has reinforced the impact of the first: Productivity in the agricultural sector has risen as growth has progressed. People require food to survive, and if a household had to devote all its energy to producing enough of its own food, it would have no surplus time to make industrial products or to grow surplus food, which could be traded for industrial products. In the course of development, however, increased use of machinery and other new methods of raising crops have made it possible for an individual farmer in the United States, for example, to produce enough food to feed, and feed very well, another 70 to 80 people. As a result only 3 percent of the workforce of the United States is in farming, while the others have been freed to produce elsewhere.

The rising share of industry also helps explain why, as incomes rise, an increasing percentage of every country's population lives in cities rather than in the countryside. There are **economies of scale** in the manufacture of many industrial products, which implies that output per unit of input rises as the firm size increases. That is, a large industrial enterprise in an industry such as steel will produce more steel per dollar cost (made up from the cost of coal, iron ore, limestone, labor, plant machinery, and electricity) than a smaller enterprise. Furthermore, it makes sense for many different kinds of industrial enterprises to locate in the same place, so that common support facilities, such as electric power stations, transport, and wholesalers, also can operate at an efficient level. The result is that industry leads to the growth of cities, and the growth of cities itself tends to increase the share of manufacturing and some services in the gross national product. In the rural economies of most poor countries, for example, food processing is done in the home and usually not included in gross national product calculations at all. In urbanized countries, in contrast, food processing often is done in large factories, and the value added produced by these factories is included in the share of the manufacturing sector.

Even though the rising share of manufacturing in gross national product and the declining share of agriculture is a pattern common to all countries, it does not follow that the rates of change are the same in each country. In fact, planners around the world have been plagued by the question of how much to emphasize agriculture versus industry during the course of development. The Chinese in the 1950s, for instance, tried to follow the Soviet example of putting most of their investment into industry, hoping that agriculture would somehow take care of itself. Disastrous harvests in 1959 through 1961 forced the government to put more resources, notably chemical fertilizer, into agriculture, but machinery, steel, and related industries continued to receive the lion's share of investment. Food production grew but only fast enough to hold per capita consumption constant, since population grew at 2 percent a year. When wages and farm incomes began to rise in the late 1970s, however, constant per capita output was perceived as insufficient, and the government once again greatly increased the share of investment going to agriculture. In the 1980s, it took the even more radical step of abandoning collectivized agriculture in what proved to be a successful move to raise agricultural production at an accelerated rate.

For a decade and more after independence, some African countries also felt that agriculture required little help. Increased food requirements could be met by the simple expedient of expanding the amount of land under cultivation. But the population continued to grow, at rates over 3 percent a year in many countries, and the supply of readily available arable land was exhausted. On the edge of the Sahel desert, the overuse of fragile land has contributed to severe ecological damage that, together with a change in weather patterns, has brought about widespread famine in the region.

In fact, virtually every government in the developing world has struggled with the question of the proper relationship between agricultural and industrial development. Would a greater awareness of the historical relationship between agriculture and industry in countries undergoing development improve performance in these countries? If planners knew that the share of agriculture in national product always remained above 40 percent until per capita income rose above $500, those planners would have a target to aim at. Investment in agriculture could be kept at a level to ensure that the share did not fall below 40 percent. But what if no consistent patterns were found among countries at comparable levels of development?

Hollis Chenery and his coauthors, for example, found no single pattern for the changes in shares and that, to talk meaningfully about consistent patterns at all, the countries of the world had to be divided into three subgroups: large countries, meaning countries with a population over 15 million in 1960; small countries that emphasize primary (agriculture plus mining) exports; and small countries that emphasize industrial exports.[1]

Subsequent work in this same tradition has divided nations into very large (with populations over 50 million in 1980), large (populations of 15–50 million in 1980), and small (under 15 million people). The patterns for these three categories of countries are presented in Figure 3–1. The figure also includes the individual country patterns for the years 1960–1982 or 1983 for 11 of the largest nations. As is apparent from this figure, the average performance of the very large, large, and small nations is similar, although the share of industry begins rising at a lower per capita GNP in large countries than in small ones. An individual country's performance, however, can deviate substantially from these average trends at least for a period of two decades. None of the 11 very large countries in Figure 3–1 is right on the average trend line for industry's share in GNP.

Chenery and his coauthors once spoke of the trends they estimated as being the **normal pattern** of development for large (or small) countries. The term has contributed to a good deal of misunderstanding and misuse of the results. Planners compared these estimated trends with the actual performance of their country, and if their own industrial share grew more rapidly than the trend, they congratulated themselves for a good performance. Or, if their share grew at a rate below the general trend line, they concluded that something had to be done to correct a poor performance. In either case, a deviation from the trend was seen as cause for concern. But these patterns are nothing more than the average results obtained from comparing many diverse patterns. They are not a guide to what a country ought to do. Perhaps, someday, we shall be in a position to say that one trend makes more efficient use of a nation's resources than another or leads to a faster overall growth rate. Today, all we have are data and estimates that give us a general idea of the trends to expect as economic development occurs. Under the circumstances, it is better to drop the term *normal pattern* and speak of an **average pattern.** On the average, the primary share (agriculture plus mining) of GNP in large countries falls from 32 percent at $600 per capita (in 1983 prices) to 19 percent at $1,600 per capita, but the variation around that trend is so great that these patterns provide only the crudest of guides for planners.

For all their limitations, these studies of the quantitative patterns of structural change in the course of economic development have provided us a guide to what kind of patterns are typical and need to be explained. Patterns analysis alone, however, cannot provide us the required explanations. For that, we need the help of economic theory.

1. Hollis B. Chenery and Moises Syrquin, *Patterns of Development, 1950–1970* (London: Oxford University Press, 1975); and Hollis B. Chenery and Lance J. Taylor, "Development Patterns: Among Countries and over Time," *Review of Economics and Statistics* (November 1968), 391–416.

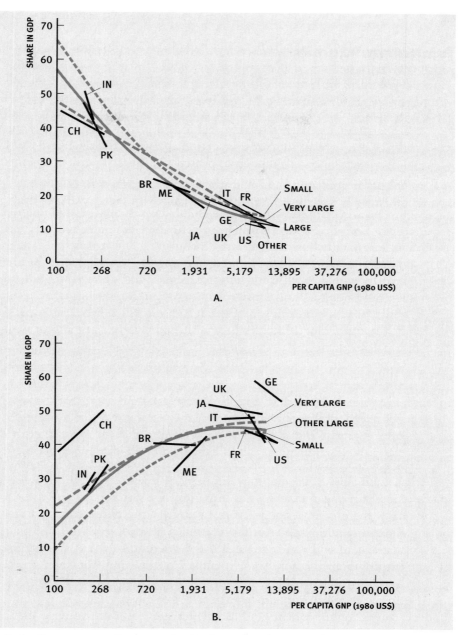

FIGURE 3–1 DEVELOPMENT PATTERNS. In this figure the Chenery methodology for making cross-country comparisons is used to compare the patterns of the share of industry and agriculture in GNP for very large (over 50 million people), large (15–50 million people), and small (under 15 million people) countries. Part A depicts the share of agriculture and part B the share of industry. The very large countries for which individual country trends are given are China (CH), India (IN), Pakistan (PK), Brazil (BR), Mexico (ME), Japan (JA), West Germany (GE), Italy (IT), United Kingdom (UK), France (FR), and the United States (US).

Source: Dwight H. Perkins and Moshe Syrquin, "Large Countries: The Influence of Size," in Hollis B. Chenery and T. N. Srinivasan, eds., *Handbook of Development Economics,* Vol. 2 (Amsterdam: Elsevier, 1989), pp. 1725–26.

Two-Sector Models

Long before the concept of GNP was invented or economists had many statistics of any kind to work with, they recognized the fundamental importance of the relationship between industry and agriculture. To better understand the nature of that relationship, they began to design simple models to explain the key connections between the two sectors. The best known of the earlier models appeared in David Ricardo's *The Principles of Political Economy and Taxation,* published in 1817. In his model, Ricardo included two basic assumptions that have played an important role in two-sector models ever since. First, he assumed that the agricultural sector was subject to **diminishing returns:** Given increases in inputs lead to continually smaller increases in output. The reason is that crops require land and land is limited. To increase production, Ricardo felt, farmers would have to move onto poorer and poorer land, and therefore it would be more and more costly to produce a ton of grain. Second, Ricardo put forward the concept that today is called **labor surplus.** Britain, in the early nineteenth century, still had a large agricultural workforce, and Ricardo felt that the industrial sector could draw away the surplus labor in the rural sector without causing a rise in wages in either the urban or rural area.

The concept of labor surplus is closely related to concepts such as **rural unemployment** and underemployment or disguised unemployment. Rural unemployment formally is much the same as urban unemployment. When there are people who desire to work, are actively looking for work, and cannot find work, they are said to be **unemployed.** Very few people in rural areas of developing countries are unemployed in this sense. While most rural people have jobs, those jobs are not very productive. In many cases there is not enough work to employ the entire rural workforce full time. Instead members of farm families all work part time and share what work there is. Economists call this **underemployment** or **disguised unemployment,** because some members of the rural workforce could be removed entirely with no fall in production. Some remaining workers would simply change from part-time to full-time effort.

Underemployment and other features of developing-country labor markets will be discussed at greater length in Chapter 8. Here we are interested mainly in how an agricultural sector with diminishing returns and surplus or underemployed labor affects the development of the industrial sector. Put differently, if the industrial sector grows at a certain rate, how fast must the agricultural sector grow to avoid a drag on industry and overall economic development? And will accelerated population growth help or make matters worse? To answer these and related questions, we develop a **simple two-sector model.**

The modern version of the two-sector labor-surplus model was first developed by W. Arthur Lewis.[2] Lewis, like Ricardo before him, pays particular attention to the implications of surplus labor for the distribution of income; hence the Lewis version of that labor surplus model is most relevant to the discussion in Chapter 5. The concern in this chapter, however, is with the relationship between industry and agriculture. The model we use to explore that relationship was developed by John Fei and Gustav Ranis.[3]

THE PRODUCTION FUNCTION

Our starting point is the agricultural sector and the **agricultural production function.** A production function, as indicated earlier, tells us how much output we can get for a given amount of input. In our simple agricultural production function, we assume two inputs, labor and land, produce an output, such as grain. The production function of Figure 3–2 differs from that of Figure 2–2 in the previous chapter, because instead of showing two inputs, labor and capital, on the axes, it shows output and one input, labor. Because increases in labor must be combined with either a fixed amount of land or land of decreasing quality, the production function indicates diminishing returns. Put differently, the **marginal product of labor** is falling; this means that each additional unit of labor produces less and less output.

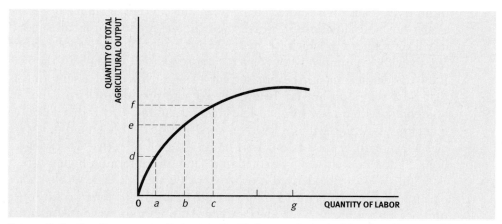

FIGURE 3–2   THE PRODUCTION FUNCTION. In this figure, a rise in the labor force from *a* to *b* leads to an increase in output of *de*; an equal increase in labor from *b* to *c* leads to a smaller rise in output. At point *g*, further increases in the amount of labor used lead to no rise in output at all. Beyond point *g*, the marginal product of labor is zero or negative, so additional labor causes no increase or reduction in output.

2. W. Arthur Lewis, *The Theory of Economic Growth* (Homewood, IL: Irwin, 1955).

3. John C. H. Fei and Gustav Ranis, *Development of the Labor Surplus Economy* (Homewood, IL: Irwin, 1964).

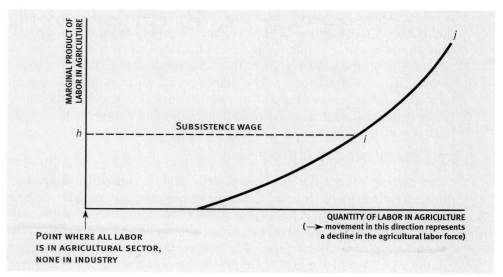

FIGURE 3–3   MARGINAL PRODUCT OF LABOR IN AGRICULTURE. As the quantity of agricultural labor decreases, the marginal product increases.

The next step in constructing our model is to show how rural wages are determined. The standard assumption in all labor surplus models from Ricardo to the present time is that rural wages will not fall below a minimum level. Thus, in its more general form, the concept of labor surplus includes not only situations in which the marginal product of labor is zero, but also situations in which the marginal product of labor is above zero but less than the minimum below which rural wages will not fall. In the Fei-Ranis model and in other labor surplus theories, the usual assumption is that rural wages do not fall below the **average product** of farm labor in households with a labor surplus. The logic behind this view is that a laborer in a farm household will not look for work outside the household unless he or she can earn at least as much as he or she would receive by staying at home. These concepts are presented in diagrammatic form in Figure 3–3.

Figure 3–3 can be derived directly from Figure 3–2. The *total product* per unit of labor in Figure 3–2 is converted into the *marginal product* per unit of labor of Figure 3–3. The concept of a minimum wage (represented by the dotted line *hi*) then is added to the diagram. This minimum wage sometimes is called an **institutionally fixed wage** to contrast it with wages determined by market forces. In a perfectly competitive market, wages will equal the marginal product of labor for reasons that will be discussed at greater length in Chapter 8. So, once labor is withdrawn from agriculture to a point where the marginal product rises above the minimum wage (point *h* in Figure 3–3), wages in agriculture will follow the marginal product curve. To hire away from the farm, factories in the city will have to pay at least as much as the workers are earning on the farm. Therefore, the line *hij* in Figure 3–3 can be thought of as the **supply curve of labor** facing the industrial sector. Actually the usual assumption is that the supply curve of labor in industry is a bit above the line *hij* because factories must pay farmers a bit more than they receive in agriculture to get them to move.

The key feature of this supply curve of labor is that, unlike more common supply curves, it does not rise steadily as one moves from left to right but has a substantial horizontal portion. Formally, this means that the supply curve of labor up to point *i* is **perfectly elastic. Elasticity** is a measure of responsiveness. Technically, it is the percentage change occurring in one variable (in this case, the supply of labor) arising from a given percentage change in another variable (in this case, wages).[4] Perfect elasticity occurs when the ratio of these two percentages equals infinity. From the point of view of the industrial sector, this means that this sector can hire as many workers as it wants without having to raise wages until the amount of labor is increased beyond point *i*.

The final steps are to add a demand curve for labor in the industrial sector (Figure 3–4) and combine the three figures into a single model. As we see in Figure 3–4, this demand curve can be derived from the industrial production function. To simplify our model, we ignore this step and draw in the demand curve *m*. The supply curve in Figure 3–4 is derived from Figure 3–3. The amount $0k$ in Figure 3–4 is assumed to be slightly higher than the subsistence wage in Figure 3–3. The supply curve of labor to industry turns up when the withdrawal of labor from agriculture no longer can be accomplished without a decline in the agricultural output (when the marginal product of labor rises above 0), because at that point, the relative price of agricultural produce will rise and this will necessitate a commensurate rise in urban wages. The demand curve for labor in industry is determined by the marginal product of labor in industry; hence, the demand curve can be derived from the industrial production function.[5]

To combine Figures 3–2, 3–3, and 3–4, one additional piece of information is needed, the size of the country's labor force. Many models use

4. The term **elasticity** refers to the percentage change in one variable that results from a percentage change in another variable and is presented as a ratio. In the case discussed here, the elasticity is the ratio of the percentage change in the supply of labor ($\Delta L/L$) to the percentage change in the wage rate ($\Delta W/W$):

$$\text{Elasticity} = \Delta L/L \div \Delta W/W$$

In the case of perfect elasticity, this ratio approaches infinity.

5. A factory owner under competitive conditions is willing to pay up to but no more than what a laborer contributes to increase the volume of output of the factory. The increase in output value contributed by the last laborer hired, by definition, is the marginal revenue product of that laborer.

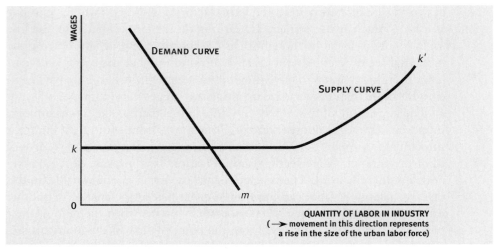

FIGURE 3–4   THE SUPPLY AND DEMAND FOR INDUSTRIAL LABOR. The supply curve kk' is drawn directly from Figure 3–3. Demand m is derived from the industrial production function.

total population rather than the labor force, and this switch has little effect if the labor force is closely correlated with total population. The size of the labor force in Figure 3–5 is represented by the line 0 to p, as labeled in part A. To combine the three figures, Figure 3–2's relation to the others is made clearer if it is flipped so that an increase in labor in agriculture is represented by moving from right to left rather than the reverse. Handled this way, a movement from left to right represents both a decline in the agricultural labor force and a rise in the industrial labor force; that is, a transfer of labor from agriculture to industry.

If a labor-surplus economy starts with its entire population in agriculture, it can remove a large part of that population (pg) to industry or other employment with no reduction in farm output. Industry will have to pay that labor a wage a bit above subsistence (the difference between $p''k$ and $p'h$) to get it to move, but as long as there is some way of moving the food consumed by this labor from the rural to the urban area, industrialization can proceed without putting any demands on agriculture. Even if agriculture is completely stagnant, industry can grow. As industry continues to grow, however, it eventually will exhaust the supply of surplus labor. Further removal of labor from agriculture will lead to a reduction in farm output. A shift in industrial demand to m will force industry to pay more for the food of its workers; that is, the *terms of trade* between industry and agriculture will turn against industry and in favor of agriculture. This shift in the terms of trade accounts for the rise in the supply curve of labor between g'' and i''. Industry must pay more to get the same amount of food to feed its workers.

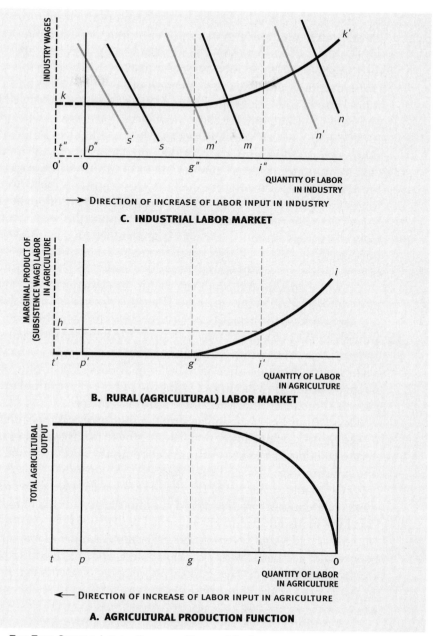

FIGURE 3–5 THE TWO-SECTOR LABOR-SURPLUS MODEL. The limit imposed by the country's population (0 to *p* in Part A), coupled with the agricultural production function, allows us to analyze the effects of industry wages on the mix between agricultural and industrial labor.

The Fei-Ranis model can be used to explore the implications of population growth and a rise in agricultural productivity, among other things. To simplify, if one assumes a close relationship between population and the labor force, then an increase in population from, say, p to t will not increase output at all. The elastic portion of both the urban and rural labor supply curves will be extended by $p't'$ and $p''t''$ respectively, and thus postpone the day when industrialization will cause wages to rise.[6]

The point where wages begin to rise sometimes is referred to as the *turning point*. Most important, if the population rises with no increase in food output, the average amount of food available per capita will fall. From the standpoint of everyone but a few employers who want to keep wages low and profits high, population growth is an unqualified disaster. Wages actually may fall in the urban areas, and the welfare of the great mass of farmers certainly will fall. It is a model such as this, even if only imperfectly understood, that people often have in mind when they speak of population growth in wholly negative terms.

How fast agricultural production must grow depends on what happens to a number of different variables. If industry's demand for labor is growing very rapidly, for example, agricultural productivity must grow rapidly enough to keep the terms of trade from turning sharply against industry and thereby cutting into industrial profits and slowing or halting industrial growth.[7] On the other hand, as long as there is a surplus of labor and no population growth, it is possible to ignore agricultural productivity growth and concentrate one's resources on industry.

David Ricardo, using similar although not identical reasoning, was concerned with keeping down population growth to avoid using poorer and poorer land in order to get a sufficient food supply. He also feared the impact of increasing wages, which he saw as leading to a twofold disaster. Following Thomas Malthus, he argued higher wages would lead to workers having more children. Further, they would cut into the profits that initially had provided the funds for investment in capital and allowed the rural surplus labor to move to cities and be employed in industry. Modern labor-surplus theorists would not agree with Ricardo's harsh policy prescriptions, but they would see the problems facing today's developing countries in a similar light.

6. In the industrial labor supply and demand part of Figure 3–5, part C, it also is necessary to move the labor demand curves to the left since the 0 point on the horizontal axis has been moved to the left. These new demand curves, s', m', and n', therefore, really are the same as s, m, and n. That is, the quantity of labor demanded at any given price is the same for s', as s, and so on.

7. *Agricultural productivity,* in the model presented here, refers to a shift in the agricultural production function causing a given amount of labor input in agriculture to produce a larger amount of agricultural output.

LABOR SURPLUS IN CHINA

In China, by the 1950s, most arable land already was under cultivation and further increases in population and the labor force contributed little to increases in agricultural output. Urban wages rose in the early 1950s but then leveled off and remained unchanged for 20 years, between 1957 and 1977. If allowed to do so, tens of millions of farm laborers would happily have migrated to the cities despite urban wage stagnation. Only legal restrictions on rural-urban migration, backed by more than a little force, held this migration to levels well below what would have been required to absorb the surplus. Population growth that averaged 2 percent a year up until the mid-1970s continued to swell the ranks of those interested in leaving the countryside. In short, China over the past three decades was a labor-surplus country.

As pointed out earlier, China did invest in agriculture but only enough to maintain, not to raise, per capita food production. The rural-urban migration that occurred was not fast enough to eliminate the agricultural labor surplus, but it was enough to require farmers to sell more of their production to the cities. Thus, the prices paid to farmers for their produce were gradually raised, while the prices paid by farmers for urban products remained constant or fell; that is, the rural-urban terms of trade shifted slowly but markedly in favor of agriculture.

To get out of this labor-surplus situation, Chinese planners after 1978 had to both accelerate the transfer of workers from agricultural to urban employment and take steps to keep the agricultural pool of surplus labor from constantly replenishing itself. Accelerating the growth of urban employment was accomplished by encouraging labor-intensive consumer goods (textiles, electronics, etc.) and service industries (restaurants, taxis, etc.). To feed this increase in urban population, the government increased food imports, shifted more investment funds to agriculture, and allowed a further improvement in rural-urban terms of trade.

To keep the rural pool of surplus labor from replenishing itself, planners attacked the surplus at its source by a massive effort to bring down the birth rate. By 1980, the population growth rate in China had slowed from 2 to 1.2 percent a year, and the rate stayed below 1.5 percent throughout the 1980s and 1990s. From the early

1980s through the end of the century, rapid industrial and services growth in and around the cities and in the countryside itself was absorbing roughly 10 million new workers a year. In 1991, the workforce in agriculture reached its peak and began to decline steadily through to the end of the century. In percentage terms, the agricultural labor force that accounted for 70.5 percent of total employment in 1978 fell to 59.7 percent in 1991 and 49.9 percent in 1997. For the first time in Chinese history, less than half the people employed in the country were farmers.

THE NEOCLASSICAL TWO-SECTOR MODEL

By changing many of the assumptions in the labor-surplus model, many of its implications can be explored. Here, we take up the implications of one assumption, the labor-surplus assumption. Many economists simply do not agree that a surplus of labor exists in today's developing countries, even in India or China. These economists have developed an alternative two-sector model, sometimes referred to as a **neoclassical model.**

The framework developed in Figure 3–5 also can be used to explore the implications of the neoclassical assumptions. A simple neoclassical model is presented in Figure 3–6.

The implications of population or labor force growth in the neoclassical model are quite different from what they were in the labor-surplus model. An increase in population and labor in agriculture will raise farm output (see dashed line *t* in Figure 3–6A), and any removal of labor from agriculture will cause farm output to fall. That is, the neoclassical model is different from the labor-surplus model: The marginal product of labor is never 0; and wages, instead of being set above the marginal product of labor, are equal to it. Thus, in a neoclassical model, population growth is not such a wholly negative phenomenon. The increase in labor is much less of a drain on the food supply, since that labor is able to produce much or all of its own requirements, and there is no surplus of labor that can be transferred without a consequent reduction in agricultural output.

If industry is to develop successfully, simultaneous efforts must be made to ensure that agriculture grows fast enough to feed workers in both the rural and urban sectors at ever-higher levels of consumption and prevent the terms of trade from turning against industry. A stagnant agricultural sector, that is, one with little new investment or technological progress, will cause wages of urban workers to rise rapidly and thereby cut into profits and the funds available for industrial development. Where in the labor-surplus model planners can ignore agriculture until the surplus

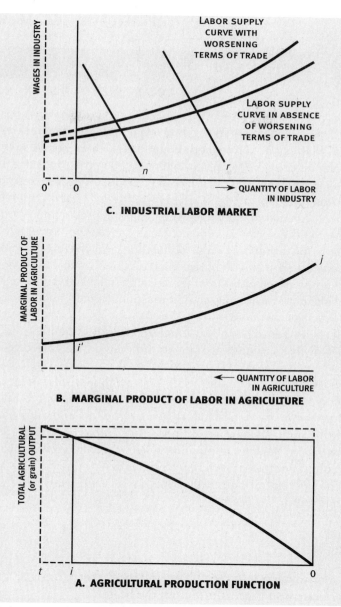

FIGURE 3–6 NEOCLASSICAL TWO-SECTOR MODEL. The key difference between Figures 3–5 and 3–6 is the agricultural production function (Figure 3–6A). Limited land resources do lead to slightly diminishing returns in the agricultural sector, but the curve never flattens out; that is, the marginal product of labor never falls to a minimum subsistence level, so there is no minimum subsistence or **institutionally fixed** wage in Figure 3–6B. Instead wages always are determined by the marginal product of labor in agriculture. Finally, the supply curve of labor to industry no longer has a horizontal section. Since the removal of labor from agriculture increases the marginal product of labor remaining in agriculture, industry must pay an amount equal to that marginal product plus a premium to get labor to migrate to the cities. The supply curve of labor to industry rises for another reason as well. As labor is removed from agriculture, farm output falls; and to extract enough food from the agricultural sector to pay its workers, industry must pay higher and higher prices for food. Only if industry is in a position to import food from abroad will it be able to avoid these worsening terms of trade. If imports are not available, rising agricultural prices will lead to a higher value of output and hence higher wages for workers in agriculture. As in the labor-surplus case, industry will have to pay correspondingly higher wages to attract a labor force.

LABOR SURPLUS IN AFRICA

Africa, as already pointed out, had low population densities relative to the availability of arable land. In nations such as Kenya, increases in population could be readily accommodated in the 1950s and 1960s by opening new land or converting land to more intensive uses (for example, from pasture to crops). Therefore, the increased population was more or less matched by rises in agricultural production. Food output, at least in the richer countries such as Kenya, kept up with the needs of both the expanding rural population and the even more rapidly growing urban sector. Planners felt little pressure to either improve the rural-urban terms of trade or increase state investment in agriculture. In short, until recently, Kenya fit reasonably well the assumptions of the neoclassical model.

Because Kenya's land resources were not unlimited and population growth continued at the extraordinarily high rate of close to 4 percent per annum, by the late 1970s, Kenya was beginning to acquire some of the characteristics of a labor-surplus economy and planners had to adjust to the policy implications (more investment and better prices for agriculture, a greater effort to reduce population growth) of these new conditions. But, throughout the 1980s and early 1990s, Kenya's population grew at 3.6 percent per year while agricultural output growth lagged behind at 2.3 percent per year. Per capita agricultural output by 1997, as a result, was 11 percent less than in 1980.

of labor is exhausted, in the neoclassical model there must be a balance between industry and agriculture from the beginning.

Two-sector models of both the labor-surplus and neoclassical types can become very elaborate, with dozens or even hundreds of equations used to describe different features of the economy. These additional equations and assumptions also have an influence on the kinds of policy recommendations an economist will derive from the model. But at the core of these more elaborate models are the labor-surplus and neoclassical assumptions about the nature of the agricultural production function.

These same points can be made in a less abstract way by turning to Chinese and African examples of the relationship between industry and agriculture during economic development.

This discussion of the relations between the agricultural and industrial sectors during the process of economic development has gone as far as we productively can go at this stage. Analysis of the patterns of development using data on shares of the two sectors of the GNP provides insight into the patterns that have occurred in the past and might be expected to recur in the future. Two-sector models have made it possible to go a step further and acquire an understanding of some of the reasons why different patterns of industrial and agricultural development might occur. In later chapters, the validity of the labor-surplus versus neoclassical assumptions for today's developing world are explored at greater length. There also are extended discussions of the nature and problems of industrial and agricultural development that include further consideration of the nature of relations between the two sectors.

Industrial Patterns of Growth

To know precisely which industries would develop at each stage in a country's growth would be a very valuable piece of information for economists. Plans could be drawn up that could concentrate a country's energies on particular industries at particular stages. If all industrial development began with textiles, for example, then planners could focus their attention on getting a textile industry started and worry about other sectors later. Similarly, if only countries with high per capita incomes could support the efficient production of automobiles, planners in countries beginning development would know that they should avoid investing resources in the automobile industry until a later stage.

EMPIRICAL APPROACHES

Chenery and Taylor use the terms *early industries, middle industries,* and *late industries.*[8] **Early industries** are those that supply goods essential to the populations of poor countries and are produced with simple technologies, so that their manufacture can take place within the poor country. In statistical terms, the share of these industries in GNP rises at low levels of per capita income but stops rising when income still is fairly low and stagnates or falls thereafter. Typically included in this group are food processing and textiles. **Late industries** are those whose share in GNP continues to rise even at high levels of per capita income. This group includes many consumer durables (refrigerators, cars) as well as other metal products. **Middle industries** are those that fall in between the other two categories.

8. Chenery and Taylor, "Development Patterns."

Unfortunately, it frequently is difficult to decide in which category a particular industry belongs. For many industries, the nineteenth century experience of European nations or the United States is a poor guide because many industries that are important today did not even exist then. The nuclear power industry, for example, did not exist prior to World War II, and even the chemical-fertilizer sector as we think of it today really did not begin until well into the twentieth century.

A way around the problem of changing technologies over time is to use data for countries at different levels of development at a given point in time. Data of this sort, called **cross-section data,** while they solve the one problem, introduce others. In several Arab states, petroleum accounts for a large share of GNP because these nations have unusually rich underground resources. In Malaysia, soil and climate have been favorable to producing rubber, palm oil, and timber. Singapore and Hong Kong, which have no natural resources to speak of, have taken advantage of their vast experience in foreign trade to develop textiles, electronic equipment, and other manufactures and services for export. In short, the share of particular industries in the GNP of individual countries is determined by endowments of natural resources, historical heritage of experience with commerce and trade, and many other factors. There is no single pattern of industrial development, or even two or three patterns, that all nations must follow as they progress out of poverty. Some industries where the techniques used are easier to master, such as textiles, are more likely to get started in the early stages of development than others, such as the manufacture of commercial aircraft. And there is some regularity in the patterns of what people consume as they move from lower to higher incomes. Engel's law already has been mentioned as part of the explanation for the declining share of agriculture in GNP. The same law has much to do with why the share of food processing within industry falls as per capita income rises. But, before planners can decide which industries to push in one country, they must know the particular conditions facing that country as well as these more general patterns.

THEORETICAL APPROACHES

Economists' debates on balanced and unbalanced growth predate much of the quantitative work on patterns of development. **Balanced-growth** advocates such as Ragnar Nurkse or Paul Rosenstein-Rodan argue that countries have to develop a wide range of industries simultaneously if they are ever to succeed in achieving sustained growth.[9] What would happen in the absence

9. Ragnar Nurske, *Problems of Capital Formation in Underdeveloped Countries* (New York: Oxford University Press, 1953); and Paul N. Rothstein-Rodan, "Problems of Industrialization of Eastern and Southeastern Europe," *Economic Journal* (June–September 1943), reprinted in A. N. Agarwala and S. P. Singh, eds., *The Economics of Underdevelopment* (New York: Oxford University Press, 1963).

of balanced growth often has been illustrated with a story of a hypothetical country that attempted to begin development by building a shoe factory. The factory is built, workers are hired and trained, and the factory begins to turn out shoes. Everything goes well until the factory tries to sell the shoes it is producing. The factory workers themselves use their increased income to buy new factory-made shoes; but of course, they are able to produce far more shoes than they need for themselves or their families. The rest of the population is mainly poor farmers whose income has not risen, and hence they cannot afford to buy factory-made shoes. They continue to wear cheap homemade sandals. The factory in turn, unable to sell its product, goes bankrupt, and the effort to start development comes to an end.

The proposed solution to this problem is to build a number of factories simultaneously. If a textile mill, a flour mill, a bicycle plant, and many other enterprises could be started at the same time, the shoe factory could sell its shoes to the workers in these factories as well. In turn, shoe factory workers would use their new income to buy bicycles, clothing, and flour and thus keep the other new plants solvent. This kind of development sometimes is referred to as **balanced growth on the demand side,** because the industries developed are determined by the demand or expenditure patterns of consumers (and investors). Balanced growth on the supply side refers to the need to build a number of industries simultaneously to prevent supply bottlenecks. Therefore, in building a steel mill, planners need to make sure that iron, coal mines, and coking facilities also are developed, unless import of these inputs is readily available. At a more aggregated level, it also is necessary to maintain a balance between the development of industry and agriculture. Otherwise, as pointed out earlier, the terms of trade might turn sharply against industry and thereby bring growth to a stop.

One problem with the balanced-growth argument is that, in its pure form, it is a counsel of despair. A poor country with little or no industry is told that it must either start up a wide range of industries simultaneously or resign itself to continued stagnation. This across-the-board program sometimes is referred to as a **big push** or a **critical minimum effort.** By whatever name, it is discouraging advice for a poor country that is taxing its managerial and financial resources to the limit just to get a few factories started.

In the discussion of patterns of industrial development, however, we pointed out that little evidence suggests all countries have to follow a set pattern. Some countries have emphasized one set of industries while other countries concentrated on different ones. Proponents of unbalanced growth, especially Albert Hirschman, recognize these differences and use them to suggest a very different pattern of industrial development.[10] Na-

10. Albert O. Hirschman, *The Strategy of Economic Development* (New Haven, CT: Yale University Press, 1958).

tions, they say, could and did concentrate their energies on a few sectors during the early stages of development. In most cases, there was little danger of producing more shoes than could be sold.

Certain industrial products have ready markets, even among the rural poor and even in the absence of a big push toward development. A worker in a nineteenth century factory, for example, could produce 40 times as much cotton yarn per day as a peasant with a spinning wheel in a dark rural cottage. From the peasant's point of view, therefore, it made sense to buy factory yarn and concentrate effort on a more-productive activity, such as weaving that yarn into cloth. Initially much of this yarn was imported by places like India and China from factories in Britain, but it was not long before entrepreneurs in China and India discovered that cotton yarn could be produced more cheaply at home than purchased as an import. Therefore, they substituted domestic production for imports. **Import substitution,** as this process is called, is one way a nation can find a ready market for one of its own industries. The market is already there, and all a country's planners have to do is ensure that the domestic industry can compete effectively with the imported product. How this can be done is a subject to which we shall return in Chapter 16. Here the main point is that import substitution is one way to begin industrialization on a limited and selective basis rather than with a balanced big push. Another way is to rely on exports, as England did during the Industrial Revolution. If it is impossible to sell all a factory's product at home, it often is possible to sell the product abroad, assuming that product could be produced at a competitive cost. Some of the most rapidly developing nations from the 1960s through the 1990s have begun exporting manufactures at a very early stage in their development process.

BACKWARD AND FORWARD LINKAGES

Unbalanced growth advocates such as Hirschman, however, did not content themselves with simply pointing out an escape from the dilemma posed by balanced-growth proponents. Hirschman developed the unbalanced-growth idea into a general interpretation of how development ought to proceed. The central concept in Hirschman's theory is that of **linkages.** Industries are linked to other industries in ways that can be taken into account in deciding on a development strategy. Industries with **backward linkages** use inputs from other industries. Automobile manufacturing, for example, uses the products of machinery and metal processing plants, which in turn use large amounts of steel. Building an automobile manufacturing plant, therefore, will create a demand for machinery and steel. Initially, this demand may be supplied by imports, but eventually local entrepreneurs will see that they have a ready market for domestically made machinery and steel, and this demand stimulates them to set up such plants. Planners interested in accelerating growth, therefore, will emphasize industries with strong backward linkages because these industries will stimulate production in the greatest number of additional sectors.

Forward linkages occur in industries producing goods that then become inputs into other industries. Rather than start with automobiles, planners might prefer to start at the other end by setting up a steel mill. Seeing that they had a ready domestic supply of steel, entrepreneurs might be stimulated to set up factories to use this steel. In a similar way successful drilling for oil will encourage a country to set up its own refineries and petrochemical complexes rather than ship its crude oil to other countries for processing.

Both forward and backward linkages set up pressures that lead to the creation of new industries, which in turn create additional pressures, and so on. These pressures can take the form of new profit opportunities for private entrepreneurs, or pressures can build through the political process and force governments to act. Private investors, for example, might decide to build factories in a given location without, at the same time, providing adequate housing facilities for the inflow of new workers or roads with which to supply the factories and transport their output. In such cases, government planners might be forced to construct public housing and roads.

While, on the surface, the balanced- and unbalanced-growth arguments appear to be fundamentally inconsistent with each other, when stated in less extreme forms they can be seen as opposite sides of the same coin. Almost everyone would agree that there is no single pattern of industrialization that all countries must follow. On the other hand, quantitative analysis suggests that some patterns are broadly similar among large groups of countries. While countries with large amounts of foreign trade can follow an unbalanced strategy for some time, a country cannot pick any industry or group of industries it desires and then concentrate exclusively on those industries throughout the country's development; it cannot in effect follow an extreme form of an unbalanced-growth strategy. The very concept of linkages suggests that extreme imbalances of this sort will set up pressures that force a country back toward a more balanced path. Thus, the ultimate objective is a degree of balance in the development program. But planners have a choice between attempting to maintain balance throughout the development process or first creating imbalances with the knowledge that linkage pressures eventually will force them back toward the balance. In terms of Figure 3–7, the issue is whether to follow the steady balanced-growth path, represented by a "straight" line, or the unbalanced-growth path, represented by a curved line. The straight line is shorter, but under certain conditions, a country might get to any given point faster by following the curved line.

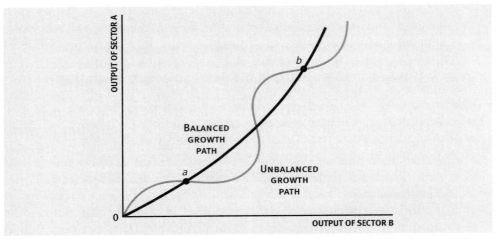

FIGURE 3–7   BALANCED- AND UNBALANCED-GROWTH PATHS. The "straight" line between points *a* and *b* is shorter than the curved line, but because of the impact of linkages, a country traveling along the curved line may get from point *a* to *b* in less time than a country traveling along the straight line or balanced-growth path.

Quantitative Interindustry Models

The quantitative tool most widely used to explore these interindustry linkages is the **input-output** table. The tool was first developed by the Russian-born economist Wassily Leontief in the 1930s, while at Harvard, and the Russian economist Leonid Kantorovich at about the same time. Both later were to win the Nobel Prize for their efforts.

The essence of an input-output table is to display the flow of output from one industry to another and industries to final users (consumers, investors, and exporters). A highly simplified example is shown in Table 3–1, which contains only four sectors: primary products, manufactured consumer goods, manufactured producer goods, and services. The sectors shown in rows are producing industries, whereas those shown in columns are users. For example, row 1, Primary industry, indicates that agriculture, forestry, and mining produced $20 (million, billion, or whatever unit is convenient) worth of products used within the sector (for example, feed for livestock); it produced $65 worth sold to consumer goods manufacturers (such as wheat for bakeries or cotton for textiles), $50 worth sold to producer goods industries (for instance, wood pulp or iron ore for steel), and $10 worth sold to services (perhaps, meat for restaurants). These intermediate uses totaled $145 (column 5). Final products, such as corn for consumption or cocoa for export, were valued at $245, so total output was $390. Similarly, producer goods manufacturers sold $60 worth of output, such as chemicals, to consumer goods manufacturers (row 3, column 2), and so on.

TABLE 3–1	SIMPLIFIED INPUT-OUTPUT TABLE (FLOW MATRIX), VALUE IN DOLLARS						
			AS USERS				
AS PRODUCERS	1. PRIMARY INDUSTRY	2. MANU- FACTURED CONSUMER GOODS	3. MANU- FACTURED PRODUCER GOODS	4. SERVICES	5 TOTAL INTER- MEDIATE USES	6. FINAL USE	7. TOTAL USE
1. PRIMARY INDUSTRY	20	65	50	10	145	245	390
2. MANUFACTURED CONSUMER GOODS	0	30	0	0	30	260	290
3. MANUFACTURED PRODUCER GOODS	50	60	70	15	195	50	245
4. SERVICES	40	15	50	70	175	200	375
5. TOTAL PURCHASES	110	170	170	95	545		
6. VALUE ADDED	280	120	75	280		755	
7. TOTAL OUTPUT	390	290	245	375			1,300

Each producer also is a user of intermediate goods, and its purchases are shown in the columns of the input-output table. For example, consumer goods manufacturers (column 2) bought $65 worth of primary products, which we know from inspecting row 1, and $30 from within the sector (for example, textiles used in clothing), $60 from producer goods industries (such as chemicals or paper used in printing), and $15 from services (for instance, banking services or transportation of goods). Total purchases for this sector, given in row 5, were $170. These industries added value of $120, including wages, rents, depreciation, interest, and profits, so total output was valued at $290. This must be equal to the total output shown in row 2 for manufactured consumer goods. Each row shows output allocated according to uses (including final demand), whereas each column shows the costs and profit of producing the output. Rules of accounting tell us that these must give the same total. This applies to the total columns (5, 6, and 7) and rows as well. Column 6, Final use, gives the sum of consumption plus investment plus exports less imports by sector. Add these and the result must be the gross national product, $755. Row 6 gives value added by sector, and the sum of its entries also must yield the GNP.

National input-output tables are much larger than the example shown here. Small ones may have 15 to 20 sectors, while those developed for the United States economy have close to 500 sectors. Moreover, the columns giving final uses and the rows giving value added may be broken down into their components and considerably refined. Quantities of capital, labor, and essential imports (goods not produced in the country) can be added as rows to the bottom of the table and show the investment, labor,

TABLE 3-2	COEFFICIENTS MATRIX			
	1. x_1	2. x_2	3. x_3	4. x_4
1. PRIMARY GOODS (X_1)	0.05	0.23	0.20	0.03
2. CONSUMER GOODS (X_2)	0.00	0.10	0.00	0.00
3. PRODUCER GOODS (X_3)	0.13	0.21	0.29	0.04
4. SERVICES (X_4)	0.10	0.05	0.20	0.18
5. TOTAL PURCHASES	0.28	0.59	0.69	0.25
6. VALUE ADDED	0.72	0.41	0.31	0.75
7. TOTAL OUTPUT	1.00	1.00	1.00	1.00

and foreign exchange requirements of expanded output. In this form, the input-output table also is called a **flow matrix.**

To turn the input-output flow matrix into a usable tool for planning or analysis, a crucial assumption is required. Inter-industry tables are based on observations of a single year's activity for each sector, merely a snapshot of the economy. If the ratio of purchases and value added to total production is assumed to be fixed for every industry and will prevail in the future, then this accountant's snapshot of costs becomes an economist's production function with fixed coefficients. It says that, for any industry, inputs and costs must expand proportionately with output. Table 3–1 can be converted into a matrix of ratios, called **input-output coefficients;** this is done in Table 3–2. Each column in Table 3–1 has been divided through by its total, so that the second column, for example, now gives the ratios of inputs to output for consumer goods industries: Each unit requires 0.23 of primary goods, 0.10 of consumer goods, 0.21 of producer goods, 0.05 of services, and 0.41 of value added.

The resulting table of coefficients, known as the **A-matrix,** can be seen as a set of production functions for each sector shown in the columns. These fixed-coefficient production functions often are called **Leontief production functions.** The **elements** (coefficients) of input-output tables usually are designated a_{ij}; the subscripts referring to the row (i, for input) and column (j) in that order. Thus, a_{12} is the output of primary products needed per unit of consumer goods, a value of 0.23, while a_{43} is the 0.20 unit of services needed to produce 1 unit of manufactured producer goods.

The input-output matrix is particularly suited to analyzing the following kind of problem: Starting with a target growth rate for an economy over five years, planners can estimate a bill of final goods—those commodities and services purchased by private consumers, investors, government, and foreign importers—that will be demanded at the higher income level. Approximately how much output will be required from each branch of industry to produce that set of final goods? If we can estimate the required output, then it should be possible to determine roughly the amount and kinds of investment needed to produce it.

The answer to the central question (how much of each good?) is not immediately obvious. Let us say that 100 units of manufactured consumer goods will be needed. We know from Table 3–2 that this will require, for example, 21 units of producer goods (coefficient $a_{32} \times 100$). But the story does not end there, because to manufacture those inputs, producer goods industries will in turn purchase, for example, 4.2 units of primary goods (21 units needed for consumer goods times a_{13}, or 21×0.20). To produce this 4.2 units, primary industries require 0.55 units (4.2×0.13) of producer goods, and so on, through an endless chain of outputs and inputs. How can we solve the problem?

Start by asking a simple question: For any level of output of the four products, which we now label X_1 through X_4, how much of one product, primary goods X_1, will be required? The answer is

$$X_1 = a_{11}X_1 + a_{12}X_2 + a_{13}X_3 + a_{14}X_4 + F_1 \qquad [3\text{--}1]$$

This says that enough X_1 must be produced to cover the input needs of each of the producing sectors, given by the input-output coefficient times the level of output, or $a_{ij}X_j$, plus the amount of X_1 needed for final demand F_1. The same is true for each of the other products, so the complete model is

$$X_1 = a_{11}X_1 + a_{12}X_2 + a_{13}X_3 + a_{14}X_4 + F_1 \qquad [3\text{--}2]$$

$$X_2 = a_{21}X_1 + a_{22}X_2 + a_{23}X_3 + a_{24}X_4 + F_2 \qquad [3\text{--}3]$$

$$X_3 = a_{31}X_1 + a_{32}X_2 + a_{33}X_3 + a_{34}X_4 + F_3 \qquad [3\text{--}4]$$

$$X_4 = a_{41}X_1 + a_{42}X_2 + a_{43}X_3 + a_{44}X_4 + F_4 \qquad [3\text{--}5]$$

We already know the values for F_1 through F_4, because these are the final goods required by our growth targets. Since we have four equations (equations 3–2 through 3–5) and four unknowns (the values of total output, X_1 through X_4), we can solve this set of linear simultaneous equations for each of the outputs and get our answer that way. This is a mechanical process that any student of intermediate algebra (or a computer) easily can complete.[11]

11. For those who know matrix algebra, this set of equations can be solved by inverting $I -$ A, where I is the identity matrix and A is the input-output matrix of Table 3–2. The result is a matrix of **direct plus indirect** input coefficients, usually labeled r. The matrix is called the **Leontief inverse.**

This basic calculation, yielding the total production needed for any bill of final goods, was at the heart of planning in the former Soviet Union, where it was called the method of **material balances,** and in other command economies. While material balances planning no longer exists outside a few isolated cases such as North Korea, the input-output technique continues to be used by industrial planners elsewhere when they have to decide whether to build a new steel plant or when to begin the development of a petrochemical complex. When the requirements of total production in one sector or another are checked against the capacity in each sector, the input-output technique becomes a test of consistency: Is present capacity adequate for projected final uses, industry by industry? If not, as is likely in any growing economy, plans must provide enough investment in additional capacity so that each sector can produce the required output. The resulting requirement for investment then can be checked against available savings and foreign investment, one of the constraints of the macroeconomic model. Similarly, requirements for labor of varying skills, for imports (foreign exchange), and for other scarce factors of production can be measured against anticipated supplies. One of these constraints, **labor requirements,** has received considerable attention from education planners who utilize input-output techniques to project the demand for education implied by growth targets.

Thus, the input-output table can provide a comprehensive but detailed model of the economy, one capable of tracing through the implications for all resources of any output or growth target. This is the most complete form of consistency planning that has been done, although only a minority of developing countries, including South Korea, Malaysia, India, and Mexico, have used it in this way. Despite its power, the input-output model has some serious drawbacks. First, the assumption of fixed coefficients rules out the real possibility that targets may be met not by proportional growth of all factors of production but through the substitution of abundant factors, like unskilled labor, for scarce ones, like capital This possibility was suggested in Chapter 2, when the Harrod-Domar model was contrasted with a neoclassical production function. The concept of substitution is central not only to neoclassical economic theory but also to much real-world economics. The fuel crisis of the 1970s, for example, was solved partly by substitution of more abundant fuels, like coal, for oil. Solutions to the greenhouse effect and other environmental problems will require substitution of cleaner-burning fuels or solar energy for coal and oil.

The fuel crisis and environmental concerns also suggests the need for **technological innovations,** or improvements, another possibility not handled easily by interindustry methods. Any time new technologies appear, new coefficients are required in the Leontief table. If planners anticipate such changes, they can make approximate allowances by adjusting the initial coefficients; for example, by reducing petroleum inputs relative to output as oil prices rise. Nor can tables of fixed coefficients handle economies of scale and learning by doing, both of which increase factor productivity with growth.[12]

SOCIAL ACCOUNTING MATRIX

As complex as an input-output matrix can become, it describes only a portion of an economy and leaves many essential policy concerns untouched. An innovation of the 1970s, the **social accounting matrix,** or SAM, amplifies the Leontief model to accommodate far more economic data. Table 3–3 shows a simplified schematic diagram of a typical social accounting matrix. The SAM is laid out as an input-output table. Rows represent amounts received by suppliers of goods, services, and factors of production; these are the producers of the interindustry matrix, Table 3–1. Columns represent expenditures, amounts paid by users of goods and services, the users in Table 3–1. Each row and column taken together can be seen as an account for each entity, covering receipts and expenditures, so that each row and column must balance.

To see how the matrix works, follow column 1, Activities, which are productive units such as the steel industry or the restaurant industry. In row 2, we find that the activities account purchased intermediate inputs for the commodities account, such as coke and iron ore for the steel industry or food for the restaurant industry; this is the interindustry core of the input-output matrix of Table 3–1, subsumed into one cell of our simplified SAM. Row 3 shows the payments by activities to factors of production—land, labor, and capital. Add indirect taxes (sales and excise taxes) paid to government (row 6), and the total represents payments to all suppliers or total cost of production. Follow across row 1, representing receipts (sales) by these same activities, and we find that they receive payments from domestic sales (under column 2, Commodities); from exports (column 8, Rest of world); and from Government (column 6) if export subsidies are paid. The sums of column 1 and row 1 must be equal, because total payments must equal total receipts; profits are implicitly included under factor payments.

The information contained in rows and columns 1 to 3 can be found in most input-output tables. The major innovation of the social accounting matrix is the addition of a row and a column representing each of the institutions that make up the economy: enterprises, households, and government. In addition, the matrix adds an account for capital and one for the rest of the world. Now we find that commodities (row 2) are sold to

12. For an introductory text on input-output analysis, see Hollis B. Chenery and Paul Clark, *Interindustry Economics* (New York: Wiley, 1959).

TABLE 3–3 SIMPLIFIED SOCIAL ACCOUNTING MATRIX

RECEIPTS	1. ACTIVITIES	2. COMMODITIES	3. FACTORS	4. ENTERPRISES	EXPENDITURES 5. HOUSEHOLDS	6. GOVERNMENT	7. CAPITAL	8. REST OF WORLD	9. TOTAL
1. ACTIVITIES		DOMESTIC SALES				EXPORT SUBSIDIES		EXPORTS	TOTAL SALES
2. COMMODITIES	INTERMEDIATE DEMAND				HOUSEHOLD CONSUMPTION	GOVERNMENT CONSUMPTION	INVESTMENT		TOTAL DEMAND
3. FACTORS	FACTOR PAYMENTS								VALUE ADDED
4. ENTERPRISES			GROSS PROFITS			TRANSFERS			ENTERPRISE INCOME
5. HOUSEHOLDS			WAGES	DISTRIBUTED PROFITS		TRANSFERS		FOREIGN REMITTANCES	HOUSEHOLD INCOME
6. GOVERNMENT	INDIRECT TAXES	TARIFFS	FACTOR TAXES	ENTERPRISE TAXES	DIRECT TAXES				GOVERNMENT RECEIPTS
7. CAPITAL				RETAINED EARNINGS	HOUSEHOLD SAVINGS	GOVERNMENT SAVINGS		NET CAPITAL INFLOW	TOTAL SAVING
8. REST OF WORLD		IMPORTS							IMPORTS
9. TOTAL	TOTAL PAYMENTS	TOTAL ABSORPTION	VALUE ADDED	ENTERPRISE EXPENDITURE	HOUSEHOLD EXPENDITURE	GOVERNMENT EXPENDITURE	TOTAL INVESTMENT	FROEIGN EXCHANGE	

Source: Sherman Robinson, "Multisectoral Models," in Chenery and Srinivasan, Handbook of Development Economics, Vol. 2, p. 897. Reprinted with permission.

activities (intermediate demand, column 1), for household consumption (column 5), for government consumption (column 6), and for investment (column 7); the total represents domestic demand. Reading down column 5, we learn that households pay for (consume) commodities (row 2), pay direct or income taxes (row 6), and save (row 7).

The SAM is a comprehensive account for the entire economy. Each of the national accounting aggregates can be found in the table. Gross domestic product at factor cost can be found as the sum of either row 3 or column 3. Gross domestic expenditure (consumption plus investment plus exports minus imports) can be read from elements of the commodities and rest-of-world accounts. Account 6 presents the government budget; the row gives revenues and the column shows expenditures. Row 7 shows the source of savings, which must be matched by column 7, its uses as investment. Account 8 provides the balance of payments and shows the sources of foreign exchange (column 8) used to purchase imports (row 8).

Table 3–3 is a highly simplified SAM. These accounts can be subdivided in many ways. You already know that accounts 1 and 2 can be broken into many industrial sectors, covering all producers of goods and services in an economy. By dividing households into different income categories and firms into different types and sizes (publicly owned versus private firms, large versus small firms, corporations versus partnerships or family-owned businesses), we could obtain a detailed picture of who owns and supplies the different factors of production, who receives various kinds of income and how much, in what kinds of industries and organizations workers of various skills are employed, and so forth. This detail gives a comprehensive picture of how production in an economy results in the observed income distribution among households (or, in the jargon of mathematically minded economists, how production relationships **map** onto income distribution).

Social accounting matrices serve four purposes in economic analysis. At the most basic level, a SAM provides comprehensive and consistent frameworks to organize masses of economic data, including the national accounts, balance of payments, household budget surveys, government accounts, income tax information, financial market accounts, and other sources. Once organized into a SAM and added up in the relevant rows and columns, these data can be checked to ensure internal consistency. Second, when this has been done, the SAM provides a detailed and comprehensive picture of the economy. Third, the SAM highlights areas where data are missing and thus defines an agenda for research. Fourth, when this economic picture has been completed, the SAM can be converted into a dynamic model of the economy and used to determine how various interventions might affect the economy in detail.[13]

13. Social accounting matrices were introduced by Graham Pyatt and Eric Thorbecke in *Planning Techniques for a Better Future* (Geneva: International Labour Office, 1976).

COMPUTABLE GENERAL EQUILIBRIUM MODELS

The input-output matrix and the SAM are useful tools for checking for the consistency between objectives and available resources, but they are accounting devices that do not include how consumers and producers are likely to behave in response to changes in industrial strategies. To represent the complex market-based behavior of consumers and producers and the kinds of policy interventions that are feasible, economists have developed the **computable general equilibrium model** or CGE. CGEs come in many forms, from relatively simple models of a few equations to models as comprehensive as the social accounting matrix, on which they can be based.

The key technical innovation of CGEs is that they escape the constraints of linearity present in the earlier **linear programming models** used to explore consumer and producer behavior in a general equilibrium context. The Leontief and linear programming models would represent production of a commodity X_j as

$$X_j \leq a_{ij}X_i, \qquad X_j \leq b_jK_j, \qquad X_j \leq c_jL_j \qquad [3\text{–}6]$$

where X_i is one or more commodity inputs in the production of X_j; K_j is the capital used in the X_j industry and L_j is its labor force; and the coefficients a, b, and c are the required inputs of the commodity, capital, and labor, respectively, used in producing X_j. The is the **fixed-proportions production function** pictured as an L-shaped production isoquant in Figure 2–2; it comes directly from the a coefficients matrix of an input-output table, such as that shown in Table 3–2. We already have discussed the shortcomings of a model employing these linear relationships.

A CGE model, in contrast, uses the **neoclassical** (or **variable-proportions**) **production function,** depicted in Figure 2–3, to represent some input-output relationships. With this innovation, not only can the interindustry format be represented, but factor substitution, productivity increases, and economies of scale also could be included. A fairly simple neoclassical function would be

$$X_j \leq a_{ij}X_i, \qquad X_j \leq L_j^{\alpha_j}K_j^{\beta_j} \qquad [3\text{–}7]$$

The input-output relation is unchanged from the linear production function, but the contributions of labor and capital to value added can be variable. Moreover, economies of scale can be accommodated by having the sum of the coefficients, a_j and b_j, exceed 1. Productivity increases could be represented by inserting a time trend into equation 3–7. Similarly, a CGE would contain consumption functions that permit substitutability among consumers goods, such as

$$p_jX_j = h_jY_d \qquad [3\text{–}8]$$

which says that consumers spend a constant proportion, h_j, of their disposable income, Y_d, on good X_j; if p_j, the price of the good, rises, consumers will buy a proportionately smaller quantity of X_j. This very simple demand equation yields a map of indifference curves like that of Figure 3–2.

CGEs can become quite complex and represent each cell of a disaggregated SAM model as a nonlinear expression like equation 3–7 or 3–8. These are **behavioral relationships,** the supply and demand functions that describe in mathematical terms the ways in which producers utilize factors and consumers respond to market prices. In addition, the model must contain equations representing constraints on the availability of each of the factors used in production and **balance equations** representing each of the accounting relationships of the rows and columns in the SAM. Because a CGE can incorporate substitution, productivity increases, and economies of scale, it can be a much better representation of real economies than its linear predecessors, without resorting to the artificial constraints needed to make a linear programming model behave.

This major improvement in economic modeling has a cost: A sophisticated computer program is required to solve these complex models. However, such programs exist and can be handled routinely by an experienced operator with a modern desktop computer. Once a CGE model has been built, it can be tested and run repeatedly at low cost: as a consistency model; as a simulation model, tracing out many different solutions with varying specifications of the model; or as an optimizing model. With the development of the CGE, it has become feasible to test hypotheses about economic development and to try out policy recommendations within a general equilibrium framework, accommodating the many interactions that mark a real economy.[14]

This chapter began with an analysis of the changing structure of the economy in the course of economic growth based on quantitative analysis without much reliance on formal models or theory. It proceeded to develop a simple two-sector model to explore the relationship between agriculture and industry as income rises. Many of the theories about structural change in the course of development, however, notably theories about the advantages and disadvantages of balanced and unbalanced growth, require models that disaggregate the economy into many sectors, not just two. To deal with issues of this sort, economists first developed the input-output model then expanded it to the SAM. Finally, to place

14. Advanced students should consult Kemal Dervis, Jaime de Melo, and Sherman Robinson, *General Equilibrium Models for Developing Countries* (London: Cambridge University Press, 1982); and Sherman Robinson, "Multisectoral Models," in Chenery and Srinivasan, *Handbook of Development Economics,* Vol. 2.

these interindustry relationships in a complete general equilibrium model that included the behavior relationships of consumers and producers, economists developed the CGE. Because the CGE is such a complex model and the skills needed to develop and use the model are more appropriate to a graduate level course in development, only the basic idea behind the CGE is presented here.

DEVELOPMENT AND HUMAN WELFARE

Between 1965 and 1998, most developing countries (although far from all) experienced rising per capita income. Does this mean that their people became better off? Did the poor benefit as well as the nonpoor? Did women gain as well as men, children as well as adults? For that matter, what does it mean to be better off? Our discussion of these issues is organized around two important concepts: **inequality** (the relative welfare of different groups) and **poverty** (the number of poor and their state of well-being).

Economic growth is a necessary but not sufficient condition for improving the living standards of large numbers of people in countries with low levels of GNP per capita. It is necessary because if there is no growth, people can become better off only through transfers of income and assets from others. In a poor country, even if a small segment of the population is very rich, the potential for this kind of redistribution is severely limited. When GNP per capita is $1,000 (PPP), the most a country can do through static income redistribution is to create shared poverty in which each citizen receives $1,000 a year.[1] Economic growth, by contrast, enables some or even all people to become much better off without anyone necessarily becoming worse off.

Economic growth is not a sufficient condition for improving mass living standards, however, because the distribution of the income created

---

1. There is a view, however, that argues that, if assets are redistributed first, faster growth will result. This is taken up in the last section of this chapter.

also is important. For at least three reasons, it would be wrong to assume that higher per capita GNP necessarily means higher income for all, or even most, families.

First, governments promote economic growth not just to improve the welfare of their citizens but also, and sometimes primarily, to augment the power and glory of the state and its rulers. Much of the wealth of ancient Egypt was invested in the pyramids. Modern LDCs may buy ballistic missile systems, develop nuclear weapons, or construct elaborate capital city complexes in deserts and jungles. When the gains from growth are channeled to such expensive projects, they provide little immediate benefit to the country's citizens.

Second, resources may be heavily invested in further growth, with significant consumption gains deferred to a later date. In extreme cases, such as the Soviet collectivization drive of the 1930s, consumption can decline dramatically over long periods. When the Soviet Union fell in 1991, its consumers were still waiting, with growing impatience, for the era of mass consumption to arrive. Normally, the power to suppress consumption to this extent in the name of economic growth is available only to totalitarian governments.

Third, income and consumption may increase, but those who already are relatively well-off may get all or most of the benefits. The rich get richer, the old saw says, and the poor get poorer. (In another version, the poor get children.) This is what poor people often think is happening. Sometimes they are right.

The question of who benefits from economic growth is not new. In Victorian England, rising inequality in income and wealth and persistent poverty among the lower classes were widely perceived and frequently discussed. Social philosophers like Karl Marx and novelists like Charles Dickens made these issues their major themes. Defenders of the status quo either denied that things were as bad as the critics charged or argued that the conditions they deplored were a necessary part of a process of change that would ultimately benefit all strata of society.

Despite the efforts of a few nineteenth century statistical pioneers and those of later economic historians, the dimensions of nineteenth century inequality and poverty cannot be measured precisely. What is clear is that improvement occurred during the late nineteenth and early twentieth centuries in England and other countries that we now consider developed. These gains came as real wages rose and governments enacted reforms (antitrust legislation, progressive taxation, unemployment insurance, social security, and after 1930, stabilizing monetary and fiscal policies) that helped to mitigate against the worst inequalities and assure some minimal living standard for all members of society. Contrary to Marx's prediction of ever-worsening inequality and social instability leading to the collapse of the "bourgeois system," workers in the rich capitalist countries ultimately did reach an era of mass consumption that allowed them to share in the gains from economic development.

What concerns us now is the prospects of more than 1 billion Asians, Africans, and Latin Americans who remain desperately poor by the standards of the ordinary citizen of a rich Western country or even by those of "transition" (post-Communist) economies in Central and Eastern Europe. As industrialization proceeds and their nations' GNPs rise, what will happen to their individual economic welfare? When can they hope to reach an era of mass consumption?

Back in the 1950s and early 1960s, most development specialists ignored the problems of poverty and inequality, tacitly assuming that when per capita GNP rises everyone becomes better off. Evidence that certain sections of the population were not benefiting from growth sometimes was shrugged off with assurances that, in due course, the benefits of economic development would "trickle down" to them. The lack of statistics on income distribution in developing countries at this time made it easier to ignore distributive issues.

The question of whether economic development really was helping the poor arose first in India around 1960. By the late 1960s, enough data had been compiled to rock the complacent. These numbers confirmed that, as some already suspected, income inequality generally is higher in poor countries than in rich ones. Further, they suggested that inequality was rising in many developing countries and the mass of people in some countries were receiving no benefits at all from development. Finally, and more controversially, some writers claimed that the poor were actually becoming worse off, at least in large and very poor countries such as India and Bangladesh.

Interest in the problems of poverty and inequality waned in the 1970s and nearly vanished in the 1980s. Sadly, this occurred not because these problems had been solved but rather because they were eclipsed by seemingly larger and more immediate difficulties. With economic growth slowing or even being replaced by decline for several years, the pressing need in many African and Latin American countries seemed to be to deal with the factors that had brought growth to a halt: the foreign debt crisis in the case of Latin America and a host of troubles, much debated, in sub-Saharan Africa.

Recently, interest in poverty—but not inequality—has revived. East Asia, an area of rapid growth up to 1997, saw a dramatic decline in the extent and severity of poverty. In sub-Saharan Africa, where economic decline has become more common than growth, critics charged that economic stabilization programs cause poverty to deepen as social services and subsidies to the poor are cut back. Particular concern was expressed about the impact of these policies on children and women. The critics were challenged, however, by others who asked whether poverty was really getting worse and, if so, whether economic stagnation or decline (the "disease") should not be blamed rather than stabilization programs (the prescribed "cure"). The economic crisis of 1997–99 reversed the earlier trend in several East Asian economies, pushing millions of people who earlier had escaped poverty back below the poverty line. Now poverty reduction has been accepted by major development institutions as the main touchstone of efforts to develop the low- and middle-income countries.

While the level and nature of interest thus has changed over the years, the relationship between economic growth and human welfare remains a vital topic. The following pages review our knowledge of inequality and poverty in the developing countries. They deal first with concepts of economic welfare, then with the recent historical record, next with theories about the causes and effects of inequality and poverty, and finally with policies to help ameliorate inequality.

Concepts and Measures

INCOME DISTRIBUTION

The **size distribution of income** shows the amounts of income received by rich, poor, and middle-class individuals or families and often is interpreted as a direct measure of welfare.[2] The shape of the size distribution depends on ownership patterns of the productive factors (including the value of the labor services that one "owns") and the role each factor plays in the production process. For example, ownership of land and capital often is highly concentrated, so anything that enhances the returns to these factors will make the size distribution of income more unequal. Conversely, higher wages for unskilled labor, the most widely distributed factor of production, will lead to a more equal size distribution of income.

Many practical problems are involved in measuring the size distribution of income. Ideally, average income over several years should be used, since earners in developing countries often experience wide income fluctu-

---

2. One could argue that the distribution of consumption or wealth should be measured instead. Consumption measures the volume of goods and services actually consumed, so it could be equated with material welfare. But income represents potential consumption, including a part of the potential that is not realized in the current period because it is saved to yield higher consumption later on. Wealth, finally, defines the potential to earn and to consume, especially when human capital is included in the definition of wealth (see Chapters 9 and 10). But the distribution of wealth is notoriously hard to measure, and statistics on wealth distribution are rare.

ations as a result of the vagaries of nature, markets, and their own governments. Cumulated lifetime income would be an even better measure, because earnings vary systematically with age. But such refinements seldom are practical, and most studies are based on estimated income in one recent year. Other practical issues are precisely how to define income and collect data.

Usually a sample survey of households is undertaken. Even when great care and ingenuity are exercised, the resulting statistics are likely to be of questionable accuracy. Respondents may not know what their true income is, or they may be afraid to disclose it, perhaps thinking that their taxes will go up. Generally, reported incomes are understated. If a household income survey is projected over all households, the total ought to equal the aggregate household share of national income implied in the national income estimates.[3] In practice a shortfall of "only" 15 or 20 percent of national income is regarded as a good result for a household income survey. These statistics thus require careful interpretation.

Once the data have been collected, they must be analyzed. Most procedures begin by ranking respondents (either individuals or households) by income size. The best ranking criterion is household income per capita, since family members in LDCs usually pool their incomes; welfare is thus enhanced by an increase in total household income received and reduced when a larger number of family members must be supported from a given level of income.

The data can be arranged in various ways. The most common method is the **Lorenz curve,** shown in Figure 4–1. To draw a Lorenz curve, income recipients are arrayed from lowest to highest income along the horizontal axis. The curve itself shows the share of total income received by any cumulative percentage of recipients. Its shape indicates the degree of inequality in the income distribution. By definition the curve must touch the 45° line at both the lower-left corner (0 percent of recipients must receive 0 percent of income) and the upper-right corner (100 percent of recipients must receive 100 percent of income). If everyone had the same income, the Lorenz curve would lie along the 45° line (perfect equality). If only one individual or household received income, the curve would trace the lower and right-hand borders of the diagram (perfect inequality). In all actual cases, of course, it lies somewhere in between. Inequality is greater the farther the Lorenz curve bends away from the 45° line of perfect equality (the larger the shaded area, *A*).

3. **National income** equals gross national product less depreciation and indirect taxes; the household share of national income also would exclude profits retained (not distributed as dividends) by corporations.

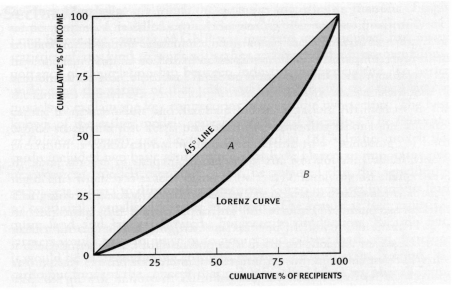

FIGURE 4-1   LORENZ CURVE. The farther the Lorenz curve bends away from the 45° line, the greater is the inequality of income distribution. Dividing the shaded area (*A*) by the total area under the 45° line (*A* + *B*) gives one measure of inequality, the Gini concentration ratio.

INEQUALITY MEASURES

Statisticians have long sought to define a single number that would express the degree of overall inequality present in an income distribution. Such simple measures as the range and standard deviation have serious flaws. The most frequently used statistic, the **Gini concentration ratio,** is derived from the Lorenz curve. This ratio is understood most easily as the value of area *A* divided by area *A* + *B* in Figure 4–1. That is, the larger the share of the area between the 45° line and the Lorenz curve, the higher is the value of the Gini concentration ratio. One can see from Figure 4–1 that the theoretical range of the Gini ratio is from 0 (perfect equality) to 1 (perfect inequality). In practice, values measured in national income distributions have a much narrower range, normally from about 0.28 to 0.60. Some examples are shown in Table 4–1.

Like other indicators that have been proposed to measure inequality, the Gini concentration ratio has its problems. For one thing Lorenz curves can intersect. It is even possible for curves with different shapes to generate the same Gini ratio. This happens when one distribution is very unequal in one part of its range—say, from the bottom to around the middle—while another is unequal in a different part—say, in terms

TABLE 4–1   INCOME DISTRIBUTION IN SELECTED COUNTRIES

| COUNTRY | PERCENT OF INCOME RECEIVED BY | | GINI CONCENTRATION RATIO[a] |
	LOWEST 40%	HIGHEST 20%	
LOW-INCOME COUNTRIES			
TANZANIA	17.8	45.4	0.318
ETHIOPIA	N.A.	N.A.	0.324
ZAMBIA	15.2	49.7	0.435
BANGLADESH	22.9	37.9	0.283
KENYA	10.1	61.8	0.544
PAKISTAN	21.3	39.7	0.312
GHANA	19.9	42.2	0.339
INDIA	21.3	41.1	0.320
COTE D'IVOIRE	18.0	44.1	0.369
SRI LANKA	22.1	39.3	0.301
INDONESIA	21.0	40.7	0.317
BOLIVIA	15.3	48.2	0.420
MIDDLE-INCOME COUNTRIES			
CHINA	16.7	41.7	0.378
PHILIPPINES	14.3	52.5	0.457
BULGARIA	19.3	41.7	0.344
PERU	14.1	50.4	0.449
TUNISIA	16.3	46.3	0.402
THAILAND	11.3	58.5	0.515
BRAZIL	7.4	65.2	0.596
POLAND	19.2	39.5	0.331
MALAYSIA	12.9	53.7	0.484
COLOMBIA	12.4	54.4	0.513
HUNGARY	23.6	38.1	0.279
MEXICO	11.9	55.3	0.503
VENEZUELA	10.7	58.4	0.538
HIGH-INCOME COUNTRIES			
SOUTH KOREA	19.7	42.2	0.336
SWEDEN	18.9	39.0	0.324
AUSTRALIA	14.3	46.4	0.417
UNITED KINGDOM	20.3	40.8	0.324
GERMANY[b]	19.4	38.9	0.322
HONG KONG	15.1	49.4	0.450
FRANCE	19.0	42.0	0.349
JAPAN	17.7	41.8	0.348
CANADA	20.3	34.8	0.277
SWITZERLAND	21.0	41.1	0.329
SINGAPORE	17.3	46.6	0.410
UNITED STATES	15.2	44.1	0.379

Note: Dates of the surveys underlying these estimates vary by country: they range from 1981 to 1994. Countries are categorized and ranked by their GNP per capita in 1998. Low-income countries have GNP per capita (PPP) of less than $3,000; middle-income countries fall in the $3,000–10,000 range; high-income countries are those over $10,000 in 1996. Estimates are regarded as of acceptable quality, except for Ethiopia and Switzerland.

[a]Approximate Gini concentration ratios calculated from grouped data (that is, from data that have been aggregated by income size groups).

[b]Data refer to West Germany in 1989 (before reunification).

Source: Database compiled for the World Bank by Klaus Deininger and Lyn Squire.

TABLE 4-2	COMPARISON OF TWO HYPOTHETICAL INCOME DISTRIBUTIONS	
INCOME GROUP	DISTRIBUTION NO. 1	DISTRIBUTION NO. 2
LOWEST 25%	7.5	13.3
NEXT 25%	7.5	13.3
NEXT 25%	42.5	13.3
HIGHEST 25%	42.5	60.0
GINI COEFFICIENT	.35	.35

of the income shares of the very richest families. Another problem is that the Gini ratio's extreme reference standard, perfect equality, makes the measure generally insensitive to changes in distribution. This insensitivity is greatest for changes in the income of low-income groups, which may be small in relation to total income but large in relation to the income of the poor households themselves and often an important policy issue.[4]

Any measure that tries to encompass the entire Lorenz curve in a single statistic must be arbitrary to some degree. One way around this is to look only at a particular part of the curve. Thus, if we are most interested in how the poor are faring, we might examine the absolute and relative incomes of the poorest 30 or 40 percent of the distribution. Conversely, if our main concern is the concentration of wealth near the top of the distribution, then the top 5, 10, or 20 percent could be studied. This tells what we want to know for particular purposes but at the cost of generality; it ignores what is going on in the rest of the distribution.

Some of these points are illustrated in Table 4–2, which compares two hypothetical income distributions. In one country, income is equally distributed both within the lower half of the income distribution and within the upper half, but mean income differs greatly between the two halves. In the other country, people in the lower three quarters of the distribution receive the same income while people in the upper one quarter receive a larger sum. These two distributions turn out to have the same Gini coefficients (0.35), but their Lorenz curves are of different shapes and cross, as shown in Figure 4–2.

4. In Mexico in 1995, the lowest 20 percent of the income distribution received only 3.6 percent of total income while the top 10 percent of households got 42.8 percent of total income. Taking 1 percent of total income from the richest group and giving it to the lowest group would raise the incomes of the poor by 28 percent, a meaningful increase. Yet it would lower the Gini concentration ratio only from 0.537 to 0.502 (assuming that the redistributive gain is shared equally by the lowest two deciles), a fall of less than 7 percent.

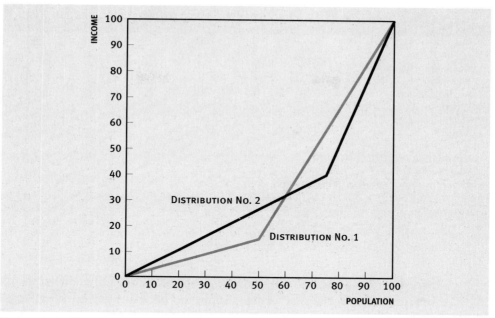

FIGURE 4-2 TWO HYPOTHETICAL LORENZ CURVES. Although these two income distributions differ substantially, the fact that their Lorenz curves cross permits them to yield the same measures of relative inequality (Gini coefficient = 0.35).

POVERTY MEASURES

While inequality clearly is a matter of relative income, **poverty** refers to the low absolute income received by certain households. An objective definition of *poverty* is surprisingly hard to formulate. Calculations of the minimum income level necessary for physical survival indicate that one can get by on very little if one chooses.[5] Efforts to link poverty to its specific manifestations—starvation, severe malnutrition, illiteracy, substandard clothing and housing—also are inconclusive. In fact, poverty is not just a matter of absolute income; it also implies something about relative income. In social terms, the poor are those who must live below what most people in a particular time and place regard as the minimum acceptable standard. Thus, while almost everyone in the United States receives a higher income than almost everyone in, say, Chad, there still are (relatively) poor people in the

5. George Stigler calculated that Americans could purchase a physiologically adequate diet for $8 per month per person (in 1950 prices) by limiting themselves to wheat flour, evaporated milk, cabbage, spinach, and dried navy beans. See George Stigler, *The Theory of Price,* rev. ed. (New York: Macmillan, 1952), p. 2. That very few chose to do so indicates the importance of the psychological and social aspects of poverty.

TABLE 4-3	CHANGES IN INCOME DISTRIBUTION AND POVERTY IN SRI LANKA, 1953–73		
MEASURE	1953	1963	1973
INCOME SHARES OF QUINTILES			
BOTTOM 20%	5.2	4.5	7.2
SECOND QUINTILE	9.3	9.2	12.1
THIRD QUINTILE	13.3	13.8	16.3
FOURTH QUINTILE	18.4	20.2	21.6
TOP 20%	53.8	52.3	42.9
GINI CONCENTRATION RATIO	.46	.45	.35
MEAN MONTHLY INCOME PER CAPITA (RUPEES)*	117	134	150
MEAN MONTHLY INCOME OF BOTTOM 40% (RUPEES)*	42	46	72
PERCENT OF HOUSEHOLDS BELOW 100 RUPEES/MONTH*	63	59	41

*In 1963 prices.

Source: Gary S. Fields, *Poverty, Inequality and Development* (London: Cambridge University Press, 1980), p. 197.

United States and (relatively) nonpoor people in Chad. Different standards apply in the two places. Psychologically, the poor are those who feel deprived of whatever is enjoyed by other members of the society of which they consider themselves to be a part (their reference group). Reference groups probably are expanding as education and communication improve. Formerly, peasants may have compared their own status with that of the village elites at most. Now they are becoming more aware of how urban elites in their own countries live and even of the standards that prevail in rich countries. The sense of deprivation well may be growing.

Those interested in measuring the amount of poverty in a country usually begin by drawing a poverty line. Ideally, this line is defined in terms of household income per capita. Households with per capita incomes below the poverty line are defined as *poor,* while those with incomes above the line are not poor. The simplest and most common measure of poverty (the "poverty head count") is the percentage of all households that are poor. More complex measures also take account of the extent to which the income of the poor falls below the poverty line. A reduction in poverty then can mean either that the percentage of poor households falls or that the absolute income of the poor rises.

Table 4–3 illustrates these points, using as an example one of the most successful cases of poverty and inequality alleviation. Sri Lanka in 1953 had a low per capita income, relatively great inequality (as measured by the Gini ratio), and a large population of poor people (defined here as receiving a monthly per capita income below 100 rupees in 1963 prices). Over the succeeding two decades, inequality declined and outstanding progress was made in reducing poverty, as can be seen from the rise in the mean income of the bottom 40 percent of the income distribution and from the sharp decline in the percentage of households below the poverty line. Note that this was achieved with only modest growth in average income; according to the statistics, monthly income per capita rose only 28 percent in 20 years, while the average income of households in the lowest four deciles of the distribution rose by 71 percent. Few developing countries have been able to duplicate this achievement.

The poverty analyst can apply similar or different standards across varying times and places. World Bank publications sometimes refer to the quantity and distribution of "absolute poverty" in the world; these calculations are made using a simple global poverty line of about $1 per capita per day.[6]

EQUALITY AND EQUITY

Equality means simply that everyone gets the same income (or owns the same wealth). Although this never occurs in practice, equality is an objective standard against which actual distributions can be judged. Equity, on the other hand, is a normative (ethical) concept: What is equitable depends on one's sense of right and wrong. Many Americans, for example, believe in equality of opportunity but think that considerable inequality of results can be justified by interpersonal differences in ability, effort, training, willingness to take risks, and stage in the life cycle. Even societies that favor substantial equality of income and wealth find they must offer extra rewards for hard work, education, saving, and ability to achieve economic growth. Most concepts of equity therefore allow for some degree of inequality in the distribution of income.

BASIC HUMAN NEEDS AND SOCIAL INDICATORS

Some students of development, including many from disciplines other than economics, reject all definitions of *poverty* based on income. Of course, they say, higher incomes *help make it possible* for people to live better and longer, but why not ask directly whether these changes actually occur? Efforts to measure a wide variety of **social indicators** go back many years. More recently, interest has centered on seeing whether **basic human needs** are satisfied. Lists of basic human needs vary but most include minimal levels of nutrition, health, clothing, shelter, and opportunities for individual freedom and advancement. Some of these, at least, can be measured.

The World Bank periodically releases data on social indicators obtained from various sources. Table 4–4 summarizes part of this information. Some

6. For a probing discussion of these measurement problems, see Amartya K. Sen, *On Economic Inequality* (New York: W.W. Norton, 1973). A good overview of inequality measures is provided in Stephen P. Jenkins, "The Measurement of Income Inequalty," in Lars Osbert Webb, ed., *Economic Inequality and Poverty: International Perspectives* (Armonk, NY: Sharpe, 1991), pp. 3–38.

TABLE 4–4   ILLUSTRATIVE SOCIAL INDICATORS FOR THE EARLY 1990S (GDP PER CAPITA, PPP)

	LESS THAN $1,000	$1,000–2,000	$2,000–5,000	$5,000–10,000	MORE THAN $10,000
INFANT DEATHS/1000	107	73	33	30	6
LIVE BIRTHS	(31)	(32)	(19)	(19)	(3)
LIFE EXPECTANCY	49	57	68	69	76
AT BIRTH (YEARS)	(8)	(8)	(4)	(6)	(2)
PHYSICIANS/1000	33	88	161	181	231
INHABITANTS	(63)	(139)	(140)	(93)	(64)
ACCESS TO SAFE WATER	35	54	72	81	95
(% OF POPULATION)	(9)	(20)	(21)	(12)	(4)
ENERGY CONSUMPTION PER	46	189	977	2029	4857
CAPITA (KG OF OIL EQUIVALENT)	(33)	(159)	(955)	(1469)	(2472)
MALNOURISHED CHILDREN	35	30	16	12	N.A.
UNDER 5 (% OF TOTAL)	(7)	(15)	(11)	(7)	
ADULT LITERACY (%)	52	60	85	83	96
	(20)	(22)	(15)	(14)	(5)
RADIOS/1000	144	148	284	396	795
INHABITANTS	(82)	(147)	(189)	(201)	(381)
TELEVISIONS/1000	61	77	194	215	463
INHABITANTS	(91)	(82)	(109)	(109)	(127)
PERSONAL COMPUTERS/	N.A.	N.A.	7	21	148
1000 INHABITANTS			(6)	(10)	(84)

Note: Data points vary. Most are in the 1987–92 range, but some are from 1980 to 1985. Figures in parentheses are standard deviations.
Sources: World Bank, *World Development Indicators 1999* CD-ROM.

of the indicators listed—infant death, life expectancy, child malnutrition, and adult literacy—reflect the degree to which basic human needs are satisfied in countries at different levels of GNP per capita. Other indicators are related less directly to welfare. Some, such as energy consumption and the prevalence of personal computers, measure the sophistication of the economy and society. Still others, represented in Table 4–4 by the provision of physicians and access to safe water, indicate levels of services that may contribute to basic needs satisfaction, which itself is measured more directly by other indicators.[7]

Two interesting points emerge from an examination of Table 4–4. One is that improvement in social indicators generally goes hand in hand with a rise in per capita GNP. Nearly every time we move to a higher-income group in Table 4–4, the average value of each social indicator for the countries covered by the World Bank's data changes in the expected direc-

7. In addition to being an approach to measuring welfare, the satisfaction of basic human needs is also a strategy for welfare-oriented development. This aspect is discussed in the last section of this chapter.

tion.[8] But the second point is that, within each income class, variations among countries are large. This is demonstrated by the high values for standard deviations shown in the table.[9] A third important point, not seen in the table, is that most social indicators have improved over time in most countries, whether they have raised per capita income or not. For example, health status has tended to rise and become less dependent on per capita income (see Chapter 10).

OVERALL INDICATORS OF DEVELOPMENT

Social indicators are hard to combine into an overall measure of a country's social development. The best-known effort to do so is the **human development index** (HDI), which was introduced in 1990 by the United Nations Development Program (UNDP) in its *Human Development Report*.[10] The HDI combines measures of life expectancy, educational attainment (encompassing mean years of schooling and adult literacy), and GNP per capita. Like other such indexes, the HDI is somewhat arbitrary and may reflect the political opinions of its compilers. Prior to the 1999 edition of the HDI, increments of GDP per capita above the global average were heavily discounted. This implied that raising per capita income from the level of Turkey or Poland to that of Switzerland or the United States contributes little to human development. The current (1999) HDI continues to discount the contribution or rising income to human development but does so less severely, especially for middle-income countries.

Rankings of countries according to their HDI values correlate fairly well with their per capita GNP or GDP rankings, especially when the purchasing power parity measure is used. The largest deviations are for obvious cases such as the oil-exporting countries, which have high per capita income (at least in years when oil prices are high) but low values on the social development indexes. Table 4–5 gives recent values of all three measures for a number of countries.

8. In other words, "good things" like life expectancy and access to safe water rise, while "bad things" like infant deaths and malnutrition fall. The sole exception is that adult literacy declines slightly from the $2,000–5,000 income class to the $5,000–10,000 income class.

9. The standard deviation is a measure of the average variation among observations. It can be defined as

$$(d^2/n)^{1/2}$$

where d is the deviation of each observation from the mean and n is the number of observations. A large standard deviation indicates a wide spread among the observations, while a small one suggests that most observations have values close to the mean. In a normal, or bell-shaped, distribution, over 60 percent of all observations lie within one standard deviation of the mean.

10. United Nations Development Program, *Human Development Report 1990* (New York: Oxford University Press, 1990). The *Human Development Report* has appeared annually since then, and several minor adjustments have been made to the HDI.

TABLE 4–5   COMPARISON OF PER CAPITA INCOME AND HUMAN DEVELOPMENT INDEX FOR SELECTED COUNTRIES, 1998

	GDP PER CAPITA (PPP)	GNP PER CAPITA (EXCHANGE RATE)	HUMAN DEVELOPMENT INDEX[a]
LOW-INCOME COUNTRIES			
TANZANIA	490	210	0.421
ETHIOPIA	500	100	0.298
ZAMBIA	860	330	0.431
BANGLADESH	1,100	350	0.440
KENYA	1,130	330	0.519
PAKISTAN	1,560	480	0.508
GHANA	1,610	390	0.544
SRI LANKA	1,610	810	0.721
INDIA	1,700	430	0.545
IVORY COAST	1,730	700	0.422
INDONESIA	2,290	690	0.681
BOLIVIA	2,820	1,000	0.652
LOWER-MIDDLE-INCOME COUNTRIES			
CHINA	3,220	750	0.701
PHILIPPINES	3,540	1,050	0.740
BULGARIA	4,280[b]	1,230	0.758
PERU	4,410[b]	2,460	0.739
TUNISIA	5,160	2,050	0.695
THAILAND	5,840	2,200	0.753
BRAZIL	6,160	4,570	0.739
UPPER-MIDDLE-INCOME COUNTRIES			
POLAND	6,740	3,900	0.802
MALAYSIA	6,990	3,600	0.768
COLOMBIA	6,720	2,140	0.850
HUNGARY	6,730	4,340	0.857
MEXICO	7,660	3,670	0.855
VENEZUELA	8,130	3,020	0.860
HIGH-INCOME COUNTRIES			
SOUTH KOREA	12,270	7,970	0.852
SWEDEN	19,480	25,620	0.923
AUSTRALIA	20,130	20,300	0.922
UNITED KINGDOM	20,640	21,400	0.918
GERMANY	20,810	25,850	0.906
HONG KONG	22,000	23,670	0.880
FRANCE	22,320	24,940	0.918
JAPAN	23,180	32,380	0.924
CANADA	24,050	20,020	0.932
SWITZERLAND	26,620	40,080	0.914
SINGAPORE	28,620	30,060	0.888
UNITED STATES	29,340	29,340	0.927

Notes:

[a]1997.

[b]1996.

Source: World Development Indicators 1999 and United Nations Development Program, *Human Development Report 1999.*

Although further efforts improve the measurement and comparison of welfare across countries can be expected in the future, one can safely predict that universally acceptable measures never will be found. Development brings about many changes, and an evaluation of its effect on welfare inevitably depends on the importance one attaches to each type of change. Varying degrees of emphasis on growth, inequality, and poverty lead to differing assessments. A particular measurement scheme can express one evaluator's values, but the values of other observers well may diverge. There is general agreement, however, that successful development (in welfare terms) requires rising per capita output, reduced poverty, and improved health and longevity, with at least no dramatic worsening of inequality.

Patterns of Inequality and Poverty

INEQUALITY AND ECONOMIC DEVELOPMENT

Economists and statisticians long have been intrigued by the idea that a systematic relationship might be found between inequality and the level or pace of economic development. Much research was inspired by Simon Kuznets's 1955 presidential address to the American Economic Association, which suggested that the relationship between per capita GNP and inequality in the distribution of income may take the form of an inverted *U.* That is, as per capita income rises, inequality may initially rise, reach a maximum at an intermediate level of income, and then decline as income levels characteristic of an industrial country are reached.

Kuznets based this proposition on the mere fragments of data available at the time for estimating income distribution in a few rich and poor countries and on trends in distribution over time in a few European countries. His insight later was both supported and challenged by studies based on much larger bodies of data. Most of these studies looked at **cross-section data** (that is, estimates made for a number of different countries at about the same time) while a few worked with **time-series data** (comparable estimates at different times for particular countries). Often there were serious problems with the quality of the data used. Recently, the World Bank sponsored a project that systematically screened all available estimates of the distribution of either income or consumption and rated them by degree of reliability.[11] Table 4–6, based on the latest estimates for the 100 countries for which acceptable data are available, shows that the relationship postulated by Kuznets generally is present in the cross-section data: middle-income countries average higher levels of inequality than ei-

11. See Klaus Deininger and Lyn Squire, "A New Data Set Measuring Income Inequality," *World Bank Economic Review* 10, no. 3 (September 1996), 565–91.

TABLE 4–6   ESTIMATES OF INEQUALITY AND POVERTY IN RELATION TO GNP PER CAPITA (PPP)

COUNTRY GROUPS	NUMBER OF COUNTRIES INCLUDED	PERCENTAGE OF INCOME RECEIVED BY LOWEST 40%	PERCENTAGE OF INCOME RECEIVED BY HIGHEST 20%	GINI CONCEN-TRATION RATIO	MEAN INCOME OF LOWEST 40% (DOLLARS PPP)	GNP PER CAPITA (DOLLARS PPP)
LOW-INCOME COUNTRIES	28	15.7	48.8	0.423	420	1,110
LOWER-MIDDLE-INCOME COUNTRIES	22	14.9	50.1	0.438	1,110	5,340
UPPER-MIDDLE-INCOME COUNTRIES	10	11.7	55.7	0.511	1,750	6,030
HIGH-INCOME COUNTRIES	24	18.7	40.4	0.338	7,000	15,620
TRANSITION ECONOMIES	16	21.0	39.0	0.307	2,930	5,400

Note: Unweighted averages are taken within groups. For this table, low-income countries are those with GNP per capita of less than $2,000 (PPP) in 1990; lower-middle-income countries are in the $2,000–5,000 range; upper-middle-income countries are in the $5,000–10,000 range; and high-income countries in the over-$10,000 range.
Source: Same as Table 4–1. Only income distribution data rated acceptable by Deininger and Squire have been used.

ther low-income countries or high-income countries.[12] There are many exceptions, however, and the relationship does not hold up when time-series data are examined. Several studies found that inequality can either rise, fall, or remain the same as incomes rise. As a result, we no longer can argue with confidence that rising inequality can be tolerated because it is temporary and can be counted on to reverse itself in a later stage of development. Countries that adopt favorable social politics (in particular, commit themselves to mass education) *and* achieve economic growth however may be able to bring about the decline in inequality at higher levels of income predicted by Kuznets.[13]

OTHER INFLUENCES ON INEQUALITY

Many individual countries have substantially more or less inequality than might be expected at their per capita income level. Sri Lanka often is cited as an example of relatively equal income distribution in a low-income country (discussed later), while South Korea and Taiwan are

12. Transition economies, which generally have low levels of inequality, are treated separately.

13. See Albert Fishlow, "Inequality, Poverty and Growth: Where Do We Stand?" in Michael Bruno and Boris Plekovic, eds., *Annual World Bank Conference on Development Economics 1995* (Washington, DC: World Bank, 1996), pp. 25–39.

famed for their ability to combine rapid growth with relatively equal income distribution. Latin American countries are known for high inequality, but inequality in Argentina and Uruguay has been measured in the past as far below the normally high levels for the region. Developing countries with unusually high inequality include Ethiopia, Kenya, Zambia, the Philippines, Colombia, Peru, Thailand, Brazil, Malaysia, Venezuela, and Mexico. Transition economies (such as Bulgaria, Poland, and Hungary in Table 4–1) had very low inequality in the past but experienced some increases recently. Among developed countries, Hong Kong, Australia, Singapore, and the United States (where inequality has risen in recent years) have considerably more inequality than the average for their income level.

Efforts to identify factors other than per capita income that might explain the amount of inequality present in a given country have had mixed results. An early World Bank study found that higher enrollment rates in primary and secondary schools and a higher GNP growth rate are associated with less inequality, given the level of GNP per capita, while a higher growth rate of population goes with more inequality.[14] Later research yielded similar findings, but no one has been able to explain much more than half the intercountry variation in inequality and some of the results obtained have been contradictory.

HOW GROWTH REDUCES POVERTY

Logically, if the income share of the poor rises with growth, their absolute income also must rise, since they then receive an increasing share of an increasing total. But what if their share declines, as it may in the early stages of development? Even in this case, poverty alleviation is closely associated with per capita GNP or GDP. A recent analysis found that, on average across many countries, the incomes of the poor rise at virtually the same rate as GDP.[15] Other factors were found to influence income growth for the poor as well, notably political and economic stability. In summary, therefore, while people may be poor for many different reasons, the most important one is that they live in poor countries. Raising per capita income almost certainly will increase the absolute income of the poor and probably also will reduce the propor-

---

14. See Montek S. Ahluwalia, "Income Inequality: Some Dimensions of the Problem," in *Redistribution with Growth;* Hollis Chenery et al., eds., *Redistribution with Growth* (London: Oxford University Press, 1974), pp. 3–37, and Montek S. Ahluwalia, "Inequality, Poverty and Development," *Journal of Development Economics,* 3 (1976), 307–42.

15. John Luke Gallup, Steven Radelet, and Andrew Warner, "Economic Growth and the Poor." Harvard Institute for International Development, 1998.

tion of the population living in poverty, as measured by a global poverty line.

Another indication that poverty and low national income per capita go together is the geography of world poverty. In 1993, 84 percent of the world's 1.3 billion poor (defined as those living on less than $1 per day) lived in either China or the low-income countries of South Asia and sub-Saharan Africa (Table 4–7). There were absolutely poor people in other regions, of course, but their numbers were much smaller.

Sharp differences in rates of economic growth in 1970–97 reduced the incidence of poverty in Asia while raising it in sub-Saharan Africa. Asia's share in world poverty still is large, but it is declining (East Asia's especially rapidly up to 1997), while sub-Saharan Africa's share is rising. The World Bank estimates that between 1987 and 1993 the number of poor people in East Asia and the Pacific fell from 464 million to 446 million, or from 28.2 percent of the population to 26.0 percent. In South Asia over the same period, the absolute number of poor people increased (from 480 million to 515 million), but allowing for population growth, the incidence of poverty fell from 45.4 percent to 43.1 percent. Over the same period, poverty in sub-Saharan Africa rose from 180 million to 219 million, or from 38.5 percent of the population to 39.1 percent. Although South Asia still has the largest number of poor people and the highest incidence of poverty, faster economic growth eventually could cut the incidence of poverty in South Asia below that of virtually stagnant Africa. Faster population growth in Africa is contributing to this outcome (see Chapter 7).

In all third world regions and countries, poverty is more prevalent in rural than urban areas. World Bank estimates suggest that, in most Asian

TABLE 4–7	GEOGRAPHICAL DISTRIBUTION OF WORLD POVERTY, 1993		
REGION	NUMBER OF POOR (MILLIONS)	PERCENT OF REGION'S POPULATION	PERCENT OF WORLD POOR
EAST ASIA AND THE PACIFIC	446	27	34
(EXCLUDING CHINA)	74	15	6
EASTERN EUROPE AND CENTRAL ASIA	15	7	1
LATIN AMERICA AND THE CARIBBEAN	110	24	8
MIDDLE EAST AND NORTH AFRICA	11	4	1
SOUTH ASIA	515	43	39
SUB-SAHARAN AFRICA	219	40	17
ALL DEVELOPING COUNTRIES[a]	1299	28	100

[a]Excludes Europe and Central Asia.
Source: World Bank, *World Development Indicators, 1999.*

and African countries, 80 percent or more of the poor lived in rural areas in the 1980s. In Latin America, which is more urbanized than Africa or Asia, the urban poor are a larger share of the total, but the prevalence of poverty (the percentage of the population that is poor) still is greater in the countryside. Although many countries have urban slums, urbanization clearly is an important part of the poverty reduction process.

We emphasize that the strong association of poverty with low national per capita income and of poverty reduction with economic growth applies to absolute poverty measured using a global poverty line. Relative poverty is far more persistent. Few people live on $1 per day in the United States, but many receive incomes far below a reasonable U.S. standard.

GENDER, INEQUALITY, AND POVERTY

Whether economic development improves or worsens the status of women is an old and complex debate. In addition to the distribution on income *among* households, we can conceptualize a distribution *within* households. This, however, is difficult to measure. Households can be modeled as patriarchal, more democratic, or subject to bargaining between husband and wife. To the extent that the bargaining model is realistic, economic change might be expected to improve the status of women when it increases their income-earning opportunities; for example, by offering a better chance to work for pay outside the home. Alternatively, the status of women might suffer if, say, there is a shift from food crops that they traditionally control to cash crops that are regarded as the province of men. There is no doubt that many forms of injustice toward women persist in the developing world. While some of these appear to be associated with poverty, many others have origins that are more culture specific. South Asia is one world region in which gender inequality, for example, between the educational and health status of boys and girls, is severe. Yet there are large differences among the countries of the region (men and women are relatively equal in Sri Lanka, for instance) and even within India and Pakistan. For example, the ratio of female to male child mortality in one Indian state (Haryana) is higher than in any country in the world, while in another (Tamil Nadu) it is lower than in all but three countries.[16] Worldwide, while the absolute educational and health status of both girls and boys is strongly related to per capita income, disparities between boys and girls are not. The *absolute* welfare of women and girls therefore is likely to

---

16. Deon Filmer, Elizabeth M. King, and Lant Pritchett, "Gender Disparity in South Asia: Comparisons between and within Countries," World Bank Policy Research working paper no. 1867, 1999.

SOUTH KOREA

South Korea continued to enjoy an extraordinarily high rate of economic growth up to the crisis of 1997–99. GNP per capita more than tripled between 1980 and 1996. This helped greatly to alleviate poverty and satisfy basic needs. The Korean development pattern has been highly equitable, compared with virtually all other developing countries, for two reasons. First, assets, especially land, were distributed relatively equally before rapid growth began; second, Korea pursued a pattern of development that did not greatly concentrate income or wealth. When Korea emerged from Japanese colonial rule at the end of World War II, the many large production units that had been Japanese owned were either nationalized or broken up and redistributed. Two land reforms subdivided the larger agricultural holdings and virtually eliminated tenancy (in which land is owned by one person but farmed by another, who pays rent for its use).

The rapid economic growth that began in the early 1960s emphasized the modernization of small- and medium-sized firms (although by the 1970s, large-scale firms were formed). Foreign ownership was held to a minimum. Manufacturing for export boomed and absorbed a larger share of labor-force growth than in almost any other country. The Korean educational system, which accommodated all children at its lower levels and then rigorously selected the few best performers for continuation to its higher levels, supported both equity and growth. All these factors contributed to a rapid decline in poverty. Inequality has risen slightly as the country transformed itself economically and began to emphasize growth in larger firms, but it has remained lower than in other developing countries and comparable to inequality in the most-developed Western countries. Korea, then, is a clear-cut case of rapid growth with equity. Its economy now is recovering rapidly from the 1997–99 recession.

benefit from economic development, particularly when it is accompanied by efforts to provide jobs and small-scale credit to lower-income women and educational and health services to women and girls. Improving the status of women *relative to men,* however, is likely to depend more on vigorous social, political, and legal efforts than on economic development.

BRAZIL

Brazil has one of the most unequal income distributions in the world. Its economy has grown faster during some periods than most other Latin American countries, but the consequences for human welfare have been equivocal. A large, naturally rich country, Brazil has made impressive strides toward the creation of a modern, diversified economy. Some of its industries and modern cities bear comparison with those in the rich countries. Brazilian agriculture also has progressed in important areas, such as the development of soybeans as a major export crop alongside coffee and other traditional items. But economic growth has been uneven in both time (there have been several stop-and-go phases) and space.

Whole sections of the country, such as the poor northeast, have been largely excluded from development. Even the big, modern cities in the south (Rio de Janeiro, São Paulo, Belo-Horizonte) have appalling urban slums, sometimes located right next to luxurious, architecturally impressive, new construction. Many of the factors that led to equitable growth in Korea are reversed in Brazil: Asset ownership is highly concentrated; there has been no land reform; access to education is uneven and heavily influenced by wealth; production, both manufacturing and agricultural, is concentrated in large production units; and technologies adopted have tended to be capital intensive. Public expenditures on education, health, and social insurance have been distributed inequitably and, thus, have worsened inequality instead of alleviating it. The overall result is very high inequality and little progress toward poverty alleviation, despite some increases in the real income of the poor.

In 1990, the average income of the lowest 40 percent of the income distribution in Brazil was only modestly higher than that of a comparable group in Bolivia, a country with less than half the per capita income of Brazil but a more equitable income distribution.

Four case studies help round out the picture of world poverty created by the global statistics and research that we have been discussing. If they achieve nothing else, these case studies show that one should be cautious in generalizing about development, inequality, and poverty. Much depends on the circumstances of the individual country and the pattern of development pursued.

SRI LANKA

Sri Lanka has grown at low or average rates through most of its history. As a result of the country's open democratic system of government and the articulateness of its well-educated electorate, all Sri Lankan governments since independence in 1948 have had to be populist to survive. A system of social benefits that included cheap staple foods and free schooling and medical services helped to produce a healthy, literate populace. Inequality was kept relatively low, and despite low income levels, the worst manifestations of poverty (premature death, malnutrition, illiteracy) were avoided to a remarkable degree. The trouble was that economic growth was too slow to provide either adequate financing for the welfare system or employment for the growing labor force, especially the educated youths seeking white-collar jobs. Chronic popular dissatisfaction led to repeated changes in government at the polls and an unsuccessful youth revolt in 1971. In 1977, a new government inaugurated an effort to accelerate growth by emphasizing labor-intensive manufacturing, irrigation, and tourism. This led to faster economic growth but also rising income inequality. Tragically, although pro-growth policies have been maintained, bitter conflict between the island's majority Sinhalese community and the minority Tamils has severely limited the benefits realized.

Theories of Inequality and Poverty

During the classical period of economic thought, poverty and inequality and their relationship to economic growth were a principal concern of theorists. This is particularly evident in the work of David Ricardo, who wrote in the early 1800s, when England was a developing country.

RICARDO'S TWO-SECTOR MODEL

We saw in Chapter 3 that Ricardo pioneered the two-sector model of development. His analysis suggested that, if England did not abolish the corn laws, which protected grain farmers from foreign competition, and allow imports of food to fuel its industrial revolution, income would be redistributed from capitalists to landlords. (Wages, he assumed, would remain at the subsistence level.) Since Ricardo regarded landlords as spendthrifts and believed that economic growth was financed by the sav-

INDIA

India, like Brazil, is a big country with areas of both dynamism and stagnation. Also like Brazil, it has emphasized inward-looking development to build a self-sufficient, subcontinental economy. Like Sri Lanka, India is a poor country, which generally has not grown very rapidly. Substantial development has taken place in some regions, such as Bombay and the Punjab, through either industrialization or successful adoption of the Green Revolution in food-grain production. Other areas, like Bihar state, remain desperately poor. One southern state, Kerala, has a Sri Lanka-like pattern of high basic-needs satisfaction together with low income and growth. Overall inequality measures for India usually come out rather low because there are so many poor people and relatively small classes of the comfortable or rich. More than 50 percent of the population lived below the officially defined poverty line in 1970; this proportion declined modestly to 40 percent by 1993–94. Most of the villages in which the majority of Indians live experienced declining poverty in the 1970s and 1980s, but progress was slow and irregular and did not occur in all areas. Market-oriented policy reforms initiated in 1991 were blamed by some for a rise in rural poverty in 1991–93 but poor agricultural performance was an important additional cause. Economic growth slowed once more in the mid-1990s, as implementation of the policy reforms was retarded by complex political problems. In poverty reduction, as in economic growth, India continues to lag behind Asia's other massively populous nation, China.

ings of the thrifty capitalist class, he concluded that this redistribution would harm economic growth.

Although his theory was innovative and internally consistent, all Ricardo's predictions about income distribution and economic growth turned out to be wrong. Rent (income to landlords) has not taken a growing share of national income in industrializing countries but instead remained a rather small share. The profit share (income to capitalists) has not been squeezed out. And wages have not been held to the subsistence level but have risen, at least in the later stages of industrial development; the share of wages in the national income, if anything, has tended to increase. Several reasons explain why actual trends have not matched those predicted in Ricardo's model. One is that England did adopt free trade, as

Ricardo wanted. But, even if it had not, diminishing returns probably would have been largely offset by technological change, which would have made it possible to grow increasing amounts of food on land of given quantity and quality. Ricardo also overestimated the strength of the Malthusian population mechanism (see Chapter 7), which he thought would hold wages at the subsistence level.

MARX'S VIEW

Karl Marx also believed that capitalist development would create an increasingly unequal distribution of income. Capitalists, he thought, had an incentive to create a "reserve army of the unemployed," whose brooding presence would ensure that the wages of employed laborers stayed at the subsistence level. (Marx hotly rebutted the Malthusian theory that demographic forces created the labor surplus, calling this line of thinking an insult to the working class.) In Marxian thought, the owners of capital dominate both the economy and the "bourgeois state." But, as capitalism develops, the rate of profit falls and crises occur, causing firms to fail and industrial concentration to rise. Eventually, in an apocalyptic crisis, capitalism itself collapses, to be replaced by socialism. Only then, according to Karl Marx, can the lot of the workers improve.

Although Marx was enormously influential as a critic of capitalism and revolutionary prophet, his prediction of how income distribution would evolve over time was no more accurate than Ricardo's.

NEOCLASSICAL THEORY

The dominant theory used today to explain income distribution in developed countries was worked out in the late nineteenth and early twentieth centuries. The **neoclassical (marginal productivity) theory** postulates that all factors of production (now more numerous than land, labor, and capital, to take account of quality differences) are in scarce supply and their rates of return are set equal to their marginal products in competitive factor markets. This theory also is relevant to developing countries, but its applicability there is more debatable because the theory's assumption that product and factor markets are perfectly competitive is less valid in such a setting.

LABOR-SURPLUS MODEL

An alternative to the neoclassical theory for analyzing income distribution in developing countries is provided by the labor-surplus model of W. Arthur Lewis. It was Lewis who first observed that conditions in less-developed countries are in some ways more similar to those that prevailed in the industrialized countries before the Industrial Revolution than they are to conditions in those countries today. A useful theory to analyze the workings of a low-income economy, therefore, might be built on classical rather than neoclassical assumptions. This insight led Lewis to his celebrated model of "economic development with unlimited supplies of labor," which utilized the Ricardo-Marx assumption that labor is available in unlimited quantity at a fixed real wage, rather than being a scarce factor of production that must be bid away from other uses, as in the neoclassical theory. The implications of the labor-surplus model for the importance of agricultural development and the role played by population growth were discussed in Chapter 3. Here we bring out the model's implications for the distribution of income.

The labor-surplus model suggests that inequality first will increase and later diminish as development takes place. It therefore is consistent with Kuznets's generalization about what actually occurred. Lewis gives two reasons why an initial rise in inequality might be expected. One is that the income share of the capitalists (i.e., those who control capital, including state-owned enterprises) rises as the size of the modern, or capitalist, sector increases. The second reason is that inequality in the distribution of labor income also rises during the early period, when increasing but still relatively small numbers of laborers begin to move from the subsistence wage level to the capitalist-sector wage level, which Lewis says tends to run about 30 percent higher in real terms.

If this seems counterintuitive, imagine that there are no wage differentials within either sector of the dual economy but a 30 percent differential between the two sectors, as Lewis assumes. In this case, inequality in the distribution of labor income would be zero at the beginning of the development process, when all the workers were employed in the low-wage sector, and zero again at the end of the process, when all the workers are employed in the high-wage sector. At all points between these two extremes, there would be some inequality in the distribution of labor income. In our simple model, inequality in the distribution of labor income would rise up to the point at which half the labor force is employed in the high-wage sector and then decline.

The tendency for inequality to rise during the early stages of development is strongly reversed (as explicitly depicted in the Fei-Ranis extension of the Lewis model; see Chapter 3) when all the surplus labor finally is absorbed into modern-sector employment. At that point, labor becomes a scarce factor of production, and further increases in demand require increases in real wages to bid labor away from marginal uses. The model suggests that the resulting rise in the general wage level brings about not only an eventual downturn in inequality but also the long-awaited abolition of poverty, at least by former standards.

In the Lewis version of the labor-surplus model, inequality is not just a necessary effect of economic growth; it is a cause of growth. A distribution of income that favors high-income groups contributes to growth because profit earners save to obtain funds for expanding their enterprises. The more income they receive, the more they invest. Their saving and investment increase the productive capacity and thus bring about output growth. In a famous quotation, Lewis says that "the central problem in the theory of economic development is to understand the process by which a community which was previously saving and investing 4 or 5 percent of its national income converts itself into an economy where voluntary saving is running about 12 to 15 percent of the national income or more."[17] The answer, he argues, lies with the 10 percent of the population that receives 40 percent or more of national income in labor-surplus countries. Growth occurs when the well-off save more, not because their marginal propensity to save increases but because their aggregate income and share in total income go up. This happens because the profit share of income increases with the growth of the modern sector while the wage share remains constant.

Not only does inequality contribute to growth according to Lewis, but attempts to redistribute income "prematurely" run the risk that economic growth will be stifled. As in Ricardo's theory, anything that raises urban wages cuts into profits and, hence, into savings, investment, and economic growth. Factors that could have this effect include a rise in the price of food relative to the price of manufactured goods and actions by trade unions or government to bargain for or legislate increased modern-sector wages. Such efforts would gain little anyway because, as noted earlier, in poor countries, there is little to redistribute; all will benefit in time, Lewis suggests, if they wait for the development process to run its course. A temporary increase in inequality is the price that must be paid for these gains.

The implications of the labor-surplus model have been presented at some length because this long has been the dominant paradigm. It is far from universally accepted, however, and often has been challenged. Several questions have been raised about the model. Will the capitalists save or will they indulge in luxury consumption? If they do save, will they necessarily invest at home or will they seek higher rates of return abroad? How fast will the capitalist (modern) sector absorb labor, particularly since it may be using capital-intensive technology imported from the developed countries and inappropriate to the factor endowment of a poor labor-surplus economy? (See Chapter 8 for discussion of this issue.) Finally, can governments in today's developing countries afford to wait for the accumulation process to work and the benefits of growth eventually to be dis-

17. W. Arthur Lewis, "Economic Development with Unlimited Supplies of Labor," *Manchester School*, 22 (May 1954), 155.

tributed throughout the society? Or do poverty, population growth, and political instability require intervention to redistribute income sooner?

No firm, categorical answers to these important questions can be found. Some capitalists will save and invest their savings locally, while others will consume their high income or invest abroad. What they do probably depends on a complex set of factors relating to the characteristics of the upper-income group in a particular country and the local investment climate. Nor does making the government the capitalist necessarily solve the problem. Few governments have been able to follow the Soviet model of rapid accumulation under a system of state capitalism; most of those that tried were unable to evolve the combination of discipline and incentives needed for publicly owned enterprises to generate surpluses.

Strategies for Growth with Equity

Countries in Asia, Africa, and Latin America have demonstrated the difficulty of trying to redistribute wealth before growing. "Socialism" has been a popular slogan in many countries, connoting immediate redistribution through direct controls on economic activity, elaborate social service networks, consumer subsidies, reliance on cooperatives, and other populist devices. Especially when undertaken by "soft states," which find it hard to enforce their own mandates on the populace, these measures often have slowed economic growth without achieving their redistributive objectives. Burma under Ne Win, Ghana under Kwami Nkrumah, and Jamaica under Michael Manley are three examples among many in recent history. Even when carried out relatively successfully, directly redistributive policies often succeed in redistributing income only in a rather narrow sense. For example, the Peruvian "national revolution" of the 1970s redistributed income to the urban working class but left the poorest elements of society (Andean peasants, mainly of indigenous origin) almost untouched.

Is there then no alternative to the stern trade-off between growth and equality postulated by Lewis? Contemporary development thinking and experience in fact have suggested three alternative models. If Lewis's classical model may be characterized as "grow first, then redistribute," the alternatives could be described as a radical "redistribute first, then grow" model and two reformist models: "redistribution with growth" and "basic human needs."

REDISTRIBUTE FIRST, THEN GROW

The radical model is epitomized by the experience of the Asian socialist economies, especially the People's Republic of China, prior to their recent conversion to more market-based policies. Socialist development in these countries began with the expropriation of capitalists and landlords. Their property then was either subdivided among small-scale producers or, more often, placed under a system of collective ownership. Confiscation has two kinds of effects on income distribution. The immediate impact is to eliminate the property income of the previous owner and assign it to either the state or the new owners of the subdivided property. This can substantially alter income distribution if the profit or rent share is large. In the longer run, however, the second effect of confiscation is likely to be more important. This works through the productivity of the confiscated asset (factory, farm, etc.) under its new management. If the asset is managed at least as efficiently as under the prior ownership, then the initial redistributive effect holds up in the long run. If, however, the asset is less productive under the new arrangement, then some or all of the redistributive effect is dissipated. The old owner has lost the property income, but the new owners have not gained as much as the old owner lost. The management of a confiscated asset thus is an important determinant of its redistributive effect.

Countries that pursue a radical pattern of development are not exempted from the need to amass a surplus and reinvest it productively if they wish to grow. Development in the Soviet Union, which followed a basic-industry strategy, involved a concerted effort to hold down consumption and squeeze a surplus out of the general population, particularly the peasants. Inequality was limited because most property income accrued to the state, but the system came under fire and ultimately broke down because it could not substantially improve the consumption standards of the Soviet people.

The People's Republic of China followed a more balanced development pattern. While it, too, aimed at building up heavy industry, it simultaneously paid attention to smaller-scale, decentralized, and more labor-intensive production units. By "walking on two legs" and not stinting on basic human services, China was able to achieve a more equitable pattern of development than the Soviet Union, and in a much poorer country.

By the late 1980s, however, dissatisfaction with the radical approach to economic development had become nearly universal. Mikhail Gorbachev failed to introduce market principles into the Soviet economy and the Soviet Union itself broke up in 1991. Its successor republics have tried, with varying degrees of seriousness and success, to undo much of the old economic structure and establish market-oriented systems. China's government also freed up markets and avoided political collapse. It shifted responsibility for farm production decisions from collectives to families and permitted foreign investors to establish factories in some regions. These reforms accelerated production growth so dramatically that China became the world's fastest-growing economy, but they created large income gaps among individuals and regions, which led to political strains.

Although many of the radical redistribution policies followed by the Chinese Communists in their earlier phase probably are available only to a strong regime that gained power through a revolution, a modified version of the redistribute-then-develop approach has been used in Taiwan and South Korea, where large rural landholdings were broken up shortly after World War II and development has proceeded rapidly and comparatively equitably.

REDISTRIBUTION WITH GROWTH

The desire to avoid both the extremes of concentrated industrial development as depicted by the Lewis model and radical restructuring of asset ownership has led naturally to a search for a middle way—"redistribution with growth," as a study sponsored by the World Bank called it. In other words, is there a way in which the gains from economic growth can be redistributed, so that, over time, the income distribution gradually improves—or at least does not worsen—as growth proceeds?

The basic idea of redistribution with growth (RWG) is that government policies should try to shape the pattern of development so that low-income producers (in most countries, located primarily in agriculture and small-scale urban enterprises) see improved earning opportunities and simultaneously receive the resources necessary to take advantage of them. According to the World Bank study group, seven types of policy instruments can be employed to this end:

1. Measures to make labor cheaper relative to capital and thus encourage the employment of more unskilled labor.
2. Dynamic redistribution of assets by encouraging the creation of assets that the poor can own, such as improved agricultural land or small shops.
3. Greater education to improve literacy, skills, and access to the modern economy.
4. More progressive taxation.
5. Public provision of consumption goods, such as basic foods, to the poor.
6. Intervention in commodity markets to aid poor producers and consumers.
7. Development of new technologies that help make low-income workers more productive.

How these elements can be best combined into an effective national policy package naturally will depend on a country's circumstances. A rural-based, equity-oriented development strategy often is proposed for large, predominantly rural countries such as India.[18] For these countries, it is argued, the time required for the modern sector to soak up all the surplus labor in the traditional sector would be far too long for any reasonable standard of equity to be achieved or political stability maintained. A strategy that emphasizes rural development, it is hoped, will bring about a much more equitable pattern of development than ever could be attained through emphasis on urban and industrial growth. (Rural development is discussed in Chapter 18.)

On the other hand, countries in which the modern sector is larger relative to the traditional sector face a less severe trade-off. These nations can hope to create an integrated, modern economy in a much shorter period and, in the meantime, have a much larger surplus available to redistribute to the traditional sector through social services and rural development projects.

The RWG approach attracted a lot of interest among those who wanted to see the welfare of the third world poor improve without violent social revolution. Indeed the reader may note that many of the ideas included in the RWG package are treated sympathetically in this book. In practice, RWG is the approach used by most developing-country governments that regard poverty reduction as a serious policy objective. Yet, one must accept that the changes brought about by such a strategy will occur slowly in most countries. Development almost always is a gradual business, and even the changes in equality and poverty projected by the World Bank's study group, which was intellectually and emotionally committed to the approach, struck many readers as disappointingly small and gradual.

BASIC HUMAN NEEDS

Pessimism about how fast economic development, even when it is poverty focused, can improve the well-being of the poor in most developing countries feeds interest in the **basic human needs** (BHN) approach. Although advocates of RWG and BHN share the same objectives, they differ on the best means of achieving them. While RWG stresses increases in the productivity and purchasing power of the poor, BHN emphasizes the provision of public services, along with entitlements to the poor to make sure they get access to the services provided.

The BHN strategy aims at providing the poor with several basic commodities and services: staple foods, water and sanitation, health care, primary and nonformal education, and housing. The strategy requires two important elements for success. First, financing must be adequate to en-

18. For example, see John Mellor, *The New Economics of Growth. A Strategy for India and the Developing World* (Ithaca, NY: Cornell University Press, 1976).

sure that the commodities and services needs can be provided at costs affordable to the poor. Second, service networks are needed to distribute these services in forms appropriate for consumption by the poor, especially in areas where the poor live.

The possibility of using fiscal policy to ameliorate poverty is discussed in Chapter 12. Redistribution of income through a combination of progressive taxation and public expenditures on social service programs has been an important part of twentieth century reform movements in Western industrial countries. The potential of this form of redistribution for less-developed countries used to be downplayed because the public sector is smaller in these countries and therefore has less revenue-raising power, because the government pursues multiple objectives in its tax and expenditure policies and so cannot devote itself wholeheartedly to redistribution, and because of the many difficulties in identifying, designing, and implementing public consumption and investment projects that can affect the income of the poor.

However, there is a more positive side to the picture. Many LDCs now collect 20 percent or more of their GNPs in government revenue. While the room for progressive taxation often is limited in developing countries, their tax systems at least can be made less regressive, even when direct (income) taxes are paid by only a small fraction of the population. Indirect taxes, such as customs duties, excises, turnover taxes, and sales taxes with exemptions, can lend a modest element of progressivity. Finally, much can be done on the expenditure side of the budget to improve the distribution of benefits from public services. Some of these possibilities will be discussed in Chapters 9 and 10, which deal with education and health.

For BHN programs to redistribute income, basic services must be subsidized. Otherwise, redistribution will not work because the poor will either spend too much of their meager incomes on the services offered or be deterred by high user charges and not take advantage of them at all. If the poor fail to use the services offered, the income transfer provided by subsidies can be perverse. In many countries, for example, government-run universities selectively admit only the well-qualified secondary school graduates, yet charge low fees, and thus subsidize the well-to-do. For the poor to be reached, appropriate forms of service must be emphasized: primary schools over universities, village clinics over intensive-care units in urban hospitals. Second, the system must be extended to the poor in their villages and urban slums. There must be schools and clinics with teachers and primary healthcare workers where the poor live. So far, most LDC social service networks have not met this challenge, despite some honorable exceptions.

Much of the appeal of BHN derives from its link to the notion of investment in human capital. Many kinds of education, health, and other social expenditures can improve the quality of human resources. When such expenditures are directed particularly toward the poor, as for instance in primary education or rural community health programs, they become ways to reduce poverty by increasing the productivity of the poor.

The World Bank's review of the problem of third world poverty in its *World Development Report 1990* spotlights two basic actions for poverty reduction: policies to increase the productivity of the main resource owned by poor—their labor—and the provision of basic social services to the poor. This supports the importance of satisfying basic needs as a complement to a RWG-influenced strategy but not as an alternative. Countries that are not achieving economic growth usually find it extremely difficult to satisfy basic human needs.

STRUCTURAL ADJUSTMENT AND THE POOR

Many of the countries in sub-Saharan Africa, Latin America, and elsewhere that experienced slow economic growth or none at all in the 1980s undertook programs of "structural adjustment" in cooperation with the International Monetary Fund (IMF) and World Bank. As explained in Chapter 5, these countries agreed to make major policy changes—correcting macroeconomic imbalances and reforming macro and sectoral policies—in exchange for external assistance. The transitional costs of these programs, for example, the termination of consumer and producer subsidies, can be substantial, and critics charge that they fall disproportionately on the poor. The impact of structural adjustment on the children of the poor was documented by a group of analysts assembled by UNICEF, the United Nations Children's Fund. Their report called for "adjustment with a human face," a set of policies that would permit growth to resume, raise the productivity of the poor, improve the equity and efficiency of social services, compensate the poor for deficits in nutrition and health services during adjustment periods of limited duration, and improve monitoring of the conditions of affected low-income groups, particularly children.[19] "Adjustment with a human face" can be regarded as an adaptation of the BHN and RWG ideas to fit the circumstances of the 1980s, especially in sub-Saharan Africa.

While macroeconomic adjustment programs undoubtedly can be carried out in ways that give more attention to the plight of the poor, the analysis of this chapter suggests that a more fundamental solution to the problem of poverty in third world countries that have not been growing is

19. See Giovanni Andrea Cornia, Richard Jolly, and Frances Stewart, eds., *Adjustment with a Human Face*, 2 vols. (New York: Oxford University Press, 1987).

a resumption of economic growth itself, combined with the provision of basic social services to the poor and policies that seek to increase their participation in the development process.

GROWTH AND EQUITY: KEY POLICY ISSUES

The single most promising way of improving equity during growth under the reformist approach is to put more emphasis on employment creation. By appropriate price incentives and other measures to absorb more labor in relatively productive forms of employment, the inequality generated by the Lewis-type employment shift can be mitigated and the labor surplus can be eliminated in a shorter time, as discussed in detail in Chapter 8.

Another touchstone of equitable growth is the relationship between the prices of rural and urban output. If farm prices are held down to depress urban wages and increase the investible surplus, then the majority of the poor who live in the rural areas and depend mainly on agriculture for a living will suffer. (There also are likely to be food supply problems; see Chapter 18.) Of course, if farm prices rise too high, growth will be choked off. But a concern for equity rules out the squeeze-the-farmer approach often attempted in the past and still is in effect in some LDCs (for example, many in Africa) today.

Finally, one can ask whether governments of less-developed countries in fact will take advantage of these opportunities to reduce inequality arising during the course of economic growth. This is an important question of political economy. Marxists argue that governments are controlled by particular social classes and act in the best interests of those classes. Certainly, many third world governments are heavily influenced by civilian or military elites and, for this reason, are much less likely to undertake egalitarian reforms than to talk about them. But political motivations perhaps are more mixed than Marxists believe. Some governments may be inclined to make limited reforms for essentially conservative reasons: to forestall upheavals or demands for more radical changes. Others may be motivated toward reform by a different kind of political incentive: In countries where ethnic, tribal, or religious distinctions form an important basis for political activity, it may not be the rich but rather a large, less-wealthy social group whose interests are primarily reflected in government policy. In such cases—for example, the Malays of Malaysia—ambitious redistributive programs may be launched even by relatively conservative governments.

Poverty reduction increasingly has become the focal point of world development efforts. The United Nations and Organization for Economic Cooperation and Development recently set a target of reducing the incidence of world poverty to half its 1996 level by 2015. Accelerated economic growth in low-income countries is a necessary condition for attaining this goal. Related goals are improved child nutrition, universal primary education, improved gender equality in schooling, reduced infant and child mortality, and expanded access to reproductive health services. All these topics are discussed in Chapters 8, 9, and 10.

PART TWO

Guiding Development

GUIDING DEVELOPMENT: MARKETS VERSUS CONTROLS

Market forces can propel the processes of development described in the last three chapters. But skillful policies can accelerate these changes, and virtually all governments have attempted to push development faster than market forces might have allowed. Two sets of policy tools are available. The first depends on a **capitalist** or **market economy** and its competitive energies but tries to make the market work more efficiently and comprehensively. The second rejects the autonomous, self-regulating nature of a market economy and substitutes government controls, resulting in a **socialist** or **command economy.** In this chapter, we compare these two very different systems for guiding development and show why and how governments have moved away from controls toward market-based policy tools in the last decade or so.

Managing Development

From World War II until the 1980s, capitalism and socialism competed for adherents throughout the world and nowhere more intensely than in the developing countries. Neither system was ever pure. All market economies were managed by their governments and for that reason were sometimes labeled **mixed economies.** And all command economies were tempered by unregulated and often illegal markets. In the 1980s, and especially after the fall of the Berlin Wall in 1989, even the socialist countries began adopting market systems. By the end of the decade, the command economy in its pure form was rapidly disappearing. Debates about economic management still range over a continuum of market mechanisms versus controls, but largely within the context of a mixed economy. Still, it is useful to keep in mind the capitalist-socialist dichotomy that marked the postwar world.

MARKET ECONOMIES

Most countries depend on market mechanisms, rather than government controls, to allocate most goods, services, and factors of production. Three arguments favor market allocation. First, the market can allocate thousands of different products among consumers, reflecting their preferences, and thousands of productive inputs among producers, getting the maximum output from available inputs.[1]

These complex allocative tasks, if handled by the state, require enormous government responsibility with attendant high costs for decision making and control. Second, markets frequently are more flexible than governments and better able to adapt to changing conditions, automatically providing incentives for growth, innovation, and structural change that governments either cannot manage or are slow to achieve. Third, reliance on markets encourages private economic activity, providing greater scope for the dispersion of economic power. Economic pluralism, in turn, is one element tending to encourage democratic government and individual liberties.

Despite these substantial advantages, in some circumstances markets do not perform well on their own. Economists have identified a number of such **market failures:**

1. Modern economies are marked by growing concentration and **monopoly** or **oligopoly power,** where one or a few sellers gain control of a market. In developing countries, **economies of scale** (the decline of unit costs as output rises) may be so large relative to market size that monopoly is inevitable in some industries, while oligopoly is the rule in many others. Truly competitive markets, where no one seller or buyer has any influence over market prices, typically exist in agriculture, fishing, handicraft industries, construction, transportation, retail trade, personal services, and sometimes in banking. In much of mining, manufacturing, utilities, airlines, communications, and wholesale trade, monopoly or oligopoly are common. One or a few firms can raise their prices, and consequently their

---

1. The principles of market economies underlying these allocations are familiar to those who have taken an introductory course in microeconomics.

profits, by restricting output, so that consumers pay more and obtain less than they would in a competitive market. In large economies, governments can try to limit the exercise of monopoly pricing in some sectors by regulating the size of firms and breaking up the largest ones. In all economies, competing imports—actual or potential—curtail monopoly power in manufacturing industries and in some services by forcing domestic firms to meet competition from abroad. However, this antimonopoly weapon seldom is used in developing countries. Price controls often are employed instead. If the government cannot prevent monopoly pricing, it can capture some of the benefits from monopolists by taxing the resulting profits at high rates.

2. **External economies** are the benefits of a project, such as a hydroelectric dam, enjoyed by people not connected with the project, such as the downstream farmer whose production rises because the dam prevents floods. External economies are important benefits in many **overhead** investments, such as dams, roads, railroads, and irrigation schemes. Although in principle the beneficiaries could be charged for all external benefits, in practice they cannot be. It may be difficult and costly to control access to the facilities and difficult even to identify the beneficiaries or the extent to which they benefit. Hence, a private investor would not be able to realize revenue from this aspect of the project's output. Because private investors cannot easily charge for externalities and such projects take large investments with long repayment periods, private investors are unlikely to undertake them. Governments do so instead. Another kind of external economy is central to the balanced growth strategy discussed in Chapter 3. If several industries are started at the same time, the resulting labor force may be large enough to create an internal market for the output of all industries and backward linkages may create adequate markets for producer goods industries. But a single private investor who depended on these newly created markets would not invest without strong assurances that the other investments would take place simultaneously. Government must intervene to ensure that these external benefits can be realized.

3. **External diseconomies** are costs not borne by the firm. The pollution of air and water is a widely recognized problem in the industrial world and increasingly so in developing countries. Polluters could bear all the costs of reduced emissions and effluents, but they benefit only as average members of the population of the affected area, so have little incentive to control pollution on their own. The same situation arises with **common resources,** such as forests, fisheries, or open grazing land, which can be used by many people who do not own them. For example, the first cattle to graze on open range land find abundant grass, so costs to the herders are low. But, as more cattle graze, there is less grass for each and herders

must go farther afield to find it. The *tragedy of the commons* is that over-grazing so degrades the rangeland that fewer and fewer cattle can be fed there, yet each private herder continues to have an incentive to graze cattle on the open range. Both pollution and common resources require some kind of intervention by government as discussed in Chapter 6.

4. Markets may not accommodate the changes in economic structure required for development. The most frequently cited example is the **infant industry,** one brand new to a society, whose productivity increases and costs fall over time because managers and workers are "learning by doing." Although the industry can become profitable over several years, investors may be too shortsighted to finance the new firms. This can justify a **protective tariff** (a tax on competing imports) or **initial subsidy** (where the government bears some start-up costs) to make an infant industry more profitable in the short run. But the long-run gains in productivity may be realized only if the tariff or subsidy is gradually reduced and the new industry eventually is forced to compete with imports (or other domestic firms). The infant industry argument has even greater force for the economy as a whole, because experience in all industries creates a more skilled and productive labor force and this makes all activities more attractive for investors. This "infant economy" phenomenon is closely akin to the balanced growth strategy because it also depends on external economies: As trained, experienced workers leave one employer to work for another, the second firm benefits from the training provided by the first. Sectorwide (or even economywide) protective tariffs could be justified by this effect, although a depreciated exchange rate combined with offsetting taxes on traditional exports would be a superior intervention, for reasons that will be explored in Chapters 18 and 19.

5. **Underdeveloped institutions** exclude large numbers from the market. In developed economies, consumers "vote" with their dollars for the goods the economy should produce. But, in developing economies, remoteness, poverty, and illiteracy prevent many subsistence farmers, rural laborers, and their families from "voting" in goods, services, and financial markets, so these groups have little influence on the types of goods and services supplied. Special efforts are required to bring them into the monetary economy. Even for those in the monetary economy there is **inadequate information** about markets and products, so many consumers remain ignorant about the goods and services being offered, workers know little about job opportunities, and producers cannot easily learn about changing market conditions. Perhaps the best example is in banking, which generally remains urban based and employs standards of services, modeled on Western banking methods, that exclude most of the rural and much of the poor urban population. Similarly, investors, producers, and traders find it difficult to hedge against the **risks** of doing business in

changing circumstances, because financial, commodity, and insurance markets are underdeveloped or missing altogether. The government may have to encourage or establish some of these missing institutions to help markets function better.

6. Economywide markets for labor, credit, and foreign exchange do not always adjust rapidly enough to balance supply and demand as conditions change, and **macroeconomic imbalances** characterize every modern economy. Wages that adjust slowly, low short-run elasticities of supply or demand, and misinformed expectations cause shortages and surpluses that can require government interventions, such as monetary management, fiscal policy, exchange rate adjustments, and incomes policies. We will hear more about such **macroeconomic management** tools through this book, particularly in Chapter 19.

7. To a considerable extent market economies require intervention not only because of inherent market failures but also because societies impose on them **national goals** that even well-functioning markets cannot satisfy. Establishing policies that favor poorer majorities over entrepreneurially accomplished minorities is one example. If the ethnic Chinese in Malaysia and Indonesia or the ethnic Indians and Pakistanis ("Asians") in Kenya and Tanzania already dominate the production and distribution system of those countries, then unguided economic growth may further improve their relative position over time. To expand the role of the indigenous majority and allow it to "catch up" requires government intervention. Markets can be very effective in stimulating rapid growth that automatically generates demands for the output of small farmers and the self-employed, creates jobs to absorb poor workers, and generally helps to relieve poverty. Nevertheless, these market forces are often led by—and hence favor—people and firms that already are successful. Thus, market-oriented growth may concentrate incomes initially, as we saw in the discussion of Kuznets's proposition in Chapter 4, even while relieving poverty. Only after growth has been rapid for some time does the income distribution begin to equalize. But the reduction of inequality often is considered too urgent to await the operation of market forces, and intervention is considered necessary. This may be true for other goals as well, such as creation of greater employment or reduced dependence on foreign goods, capital, technology, and skills. Even accelerated growth, typically served well by market economies, may require intervention if savings levels initially are low.

These market failures provide some of the reasons that governments intervene in market economies. The particular interventions chosen are not always ideal. Worse, they often work against the goals they are supposed to achieve. The most egregious examples will be explored in later chapters: legislation on wages, pensions, and job security that concentrates incomes and reduces employment; interest rate ceilings that reduce and bias investment; tariffs and import controls that intensify dependence on imports; and food price controls that discourage farm production. Nevertheless, because markets are imperfect and governments have political goals that markets must serve, intervention is the rule. Usually interventions work best and avoid undesired side effects if they are aimed to improve the functioning of markets and to work indirectly through prices to alter supply and demand, rather than operate directly through controls. A central aim of development policy in a mixed economy is to structure these interventions to achieve their aims with minimal incidental costs.

SOCIALIST ECONOMIES

Socialism can be defined as government ownership and control of the means of production. Whether a country is socialist or not is a matter of degree. The clear examples have been the Communist countries—the Soviet Union, the Eastern European countries until 1989, China, North Korea, Vietnam, and Cuba—in which government ownership and control dominated industry and services and strongly influenced agriculture. Some Western European countries, such as Sweden and Great Britain, were for a time governed by socialist political parties that nationalized key industries. Many other countries have large state-owned enterprise sectors, but these economies retain the market character of mixed economies.

What distinguished the Soviet and other command economies was government control over production. Whereas *in mixed economies the market sets prices* as signals for production and consumption, *in Soviet-style economies central planners controlled the quantities* produced and consumed. Official prices became irrelevant to production and investment decisions. But prices, along with quantity rationing, still regulated demand, because no government is able to give directives to each household about its complete consumption basket. Prices also served an accounting function; they determined how much income was transferred from households to government-owned producers (and vice versa, through wage payments), among producers, and from producers to the government.

To manage a Soviet-style economy, it was necessary to begin with a plan. Typically, governments operated with one-year plans for controlling current output and five-year plans to guide major investment projects. The planning methods used in the Soviet Union and until the 1980s in China were based on approaches similar to the interindustry or input-output models described in Chapter 3. What separated a centrally planned economy from the kind of industrial planning and analysis described in Chapter 3 was the way in which plans were carried out. Once broad goals and quantitative targets for individual industries had been decided, planners gave direct orders to firms on how much to produce and the quantity of inputs that could be used in production. Firms could not buy the necessary inputs in a market but had to apply to government organizations for the delivery of needed items. The firm paid for these items, but willingness to pay did not determine whether it got them. Only if the plan said it should receive a certain amount of steel, for instance, was that amount delivered.

In reality, the Soviet-type system did not follow the plan quite so rigidly. A variety of both legal and illegal devices, including markets, provided some flexibility. Nevertheless many allocations that were handled by impersonal market forces in mixed economies were decided by the command of bureaucrats in centrally planned economies. The command system therefore needed large numbers of people trained to manage the complex tasks of deciding which firms ought to get particular inputs. Hundreds and even thousands of different kinds of inputs had to be parceled out to tens of thousands of individual enterprises. If the inputs got to the wrong enterprises, those enterprises would have surpluses piling up in their warehouses while other enterprises operated below capacity. Large inventories were characteristic of this kind of system.

The advantage of the command system was that it gave central planners a high degree of control over the economy and, with that control, the power to restructure key sectors. The system, however, did not put a high premium on the productive use of resources. The problems of inefficiency increased if people with the skills adequate to manage such a system were in short supply, as often was the case in developing countries. Even though China had sufficient numbers of such people or was able to train them with Soviet help in the 1950s, after 1978, China began to experiment with greater use of market forces to reduce inefficiency.

The leaders who designed the Soviet economic system began from the premise that prices determined by the market could not be relied on to guide production. This basic view of the market was reinforced by the pronounced emphasis in the Soviet Union, and later in China, on machinery and steel as leading sectors in their industrialization programs. Since neither economy had much of a steel or machinery industry to begin with, planners were faced with an extreme form of the infant industry problem and very large external economies, because the main demand for steel was from a machinery sector that did not yet exist. In general, the price system is less effective when the change in economic structure being contemplated is rapid and massive. What the Soviet Union desired in the 1930s when it introduced this system and what China wanted in the 1950s was precisely such a rapid and massive restructuring of economies that were fundamentally agricultural into ones that were based on machinery and steel.

Recent history has demonstrated the limitations of the centrally planned economy. It was effective in mobilizing resources in the early days of communism: Few countries have ever industrialized as rapidly as the Soviet Union. The heavy industrial base so created contributed to the Soviet Union's ability to make the weapons that helped throw back the German invasion in World War II. But the Soviet system was not efficient in allocating the myriad of goods, services, and factors of production among thousands of competing uses. It was particularly ineffective in producing consumer goods. And, once the economy became more industrialized, the command system was unable to adjust easily to changes in the economic environment. Pressure built up in the 1980s in both Eastern and Central Europe and the Soviet Union as stagnant economies had to be propped up with increasing amounts of international debt. Wages and consumption grew hardly at all, which fed worker and consumer discontent. When President Gorbachev made it known that the Soviet army would no longer prop up the Communist Party-dominated governments then in power throughout Eastern and Central Europe, most of these governments collapsed and were replaced by democratically elected leaders. Soon thereafter the Soviet empire collapsed and was replaced by a number of republics of which Russia was by far the largest. It was not only the political system that collapsed. The Council for Mutual Economic Assistance (Comecon), the organization that governed trade among the Soviet Union, Eastern Europe, and Vietnam, also collapsed, and so all these nations were forced to develop new foreign trade relationships.

Many of the democratic governments that came to power in Central and Eastern Europe after 1989 were determined to dismantle the Soviet command economies as rapidly as possible and replace them with market systems much like the ones they observed in Western Europe. Poland was the boldest in attempting to create a market economy almost overnight by what came to be called **shock therapy.** Hungary, having begun to move toward a market system long before 1989, moved more cautiously to introduce further market reforms. Under President Boris Yeltsin, Russia also attempted to move rapidly toward a market system by freeing prices and introducing across-the-board privatization of much of the state-owned economy. For reasons that we shall go into later in this chapter, however, the move to a market system proved to be more difficult than many of the reformers anticipated. Recessions in the economies of the countries of Eastern Europe and the republics of the former Soviet Union were long and deep. The resulting hardships for many individuals, although by no means for everyone, created political resistance to reforms that led to votes for many antimarket parliamentarians in the elections of 1993 and 1994.

Among developing countries with per capita incomes less than $2,000, only China, Vietnam, North Korea, and Cuba ever succeeded in introducing the full Soviet-style command system, although a few other countries not ruled by Communist parties, notably Tanzania, tried. China, Vietnam, and North Korea arguably had the administrative and decision-making capacity to control production through central planning without the use of market forces, and they did achieve sustained increases in gross national product for a time under this system. But discontent with the inefficiency and slow growth of the command system led China to begin moving toward a market system after 1978 and Vietnam to do so after 1986. North Korea and Cuba, both of which resisted moves toward the market into the late-1990s, experienced economic stagnation and declining standards of living.

Tanzania was one of the few countries in Africa to attempt to introduce parts of a command system, one patterned in large part after the model of China. In the 1970s, Tanzania, avowedly socialist, placed the majority of modern industries under public ownership, nationalized much wholesale and retail trade, and attempted to socialize its agriculture. Nevertheless, the government did not try to set output targets and most units, public or private, continued to respond to market-determined prices. Interventions in setting these prices, although substantial, were not markedly greater in socialist Tanzania than in many nonsocialist developing countries, such as Bolivia, Kenya, and Indonesia. India based its first development plans on Soviet models that emphasized investment in capital goods and other heavy industries and espoused public ownership of these sectors. Yet, even when India's economy was ostensibly socialist, less output was produced in public enterprises than in avowedly capitalist South Korea.

The March toward Markets

It is clear from the perspective of the beginning of the twenty-first century that all kinds of governments—capitalist and socialist, industrial and developing—have been reducing the scope of controls and adopting market mechanisms instead to guide their economies. What explains the popularity of controls before reforms became common? And what explains this historic march away from controls toward market mechanisms?

THE APPEAL OF CONTROLS

We already have given two reasons why governments might want to resort to controls to hasten development. Controls may be essential if policy makers desire large structural changes, like the leaders of the Soviet Union before World War II and China after 1949. And within a mixed economy, controls can be used to correct for market failures that otherwise might retard development, make it unsustainable, or yield politically and socially undesirable outcomes. After World War II, a confluence of historical factors pushed many governments of developing countries to employ controls rather than market mechanisms as a means to accelerate economic development.

The Great Depression of the 1930s had destroyed confidence in market capitalism. The antidote to depression offered by John Maynard Keynes—and accepted for decades by most economists and governments—was active intervention to stimulate the economy through fiscal policy. Price controls and quantity rationing helped guide the U.S. economy through World War II. In the 1930s and 1940s, when trade wars and real wars made export-oriented development strategies almost impossible, building one's own industrial capacity behind high tariff walls seemed to make sense. After the war, European recovery was substantially aided by the U.S. Marshall Plan. The U.S. government not only provided vast amounts of capital (equivalent to 1.5 percent of its GNP over four years) but also encouraged governments of war-torn economies to plan for public investment in postwar recovery.

In Asia and Africa, economies had been highly regulated by the colonial powers before and after the war. After independence in 1947, India's new leaders followed the interventionist tendencies of Fabian socialism and the British Raj to a planned and regulated economy. As other countries in Asia and Africa emerged from colonialism over the next two decades, many of them emulated India. The Soviet Union's rapid industrialization under communism also impressed the leaders of these newly emerging countries. The older countries of Latin America, especially Argentina, Brazil, and Mexico, had taken advantage of the war to build their own industries to supply goods once imported from the United States. After the war, Argentine dictator Juan Peron and others built on this base a highly protected manufacturing system that spurred industrial growth for a time. Even in the capitalist United States, as in Western Europe, government intervention in markets was the norm, from the New Deal of President Franklin Roosevelt during the depressed 1930s to the Great Society of President Lyndon Johnson in the 1960s.

Economic thought encouraged these tendencies. Underlying the views of many thinkers, ancient and modern, is the view that markets lead to outcomes that are arbitrary, capricious, or worse. Karl Marx's belief in the chaotic nature of markets had a major influence on those who designed the economic systems of the Soviet Union and China. More recent times, as described in Chapter 3, saw Paul Rosenstein-Rodan's 1943 theory of the big push and Albert Hirschman's 1958 retort, the strategy of unbalanced growth. Both strategies assumed that markets would not work adequately for rapid development and both invited some form of government intervention. Latin American economist Raul Prebisch and European economist Hans Singer were influential in arguing that world demand could not grow fast enough to accommodate the rapid growth of food and raw material exports on which most developing countries depended.[2] This **export pessimism** was taken as strong support for a strategy of **import substitution,** which required government intervention to protect local manufacturers. Perhaps the most influential article of all was W. Arthur Lewis's 1954 theory of the labor-surplus economy, also explained in Chapter 3. Although Lewis did not advocate intervention, one implication of his theory was the need to transform a developing economy rapidly away from traditional, stagnant agriculture toward dynamic industry. This, as the Soviet Union and China appeared to show, could be accomplished by a command economy. These treatises and others like them set the tone for development economics at least until the mid-1960s. Even if national leaders did not know about these works, their economic advisers were strongly influenced by them.

These historic and intellectual tendencies influenced many governments to try a range of interventions in search of economic development. By the early 1970s, the vast majority of third world countries could be characterized as mixed economies with a strong dose of controls. A development adviser, flying into almost any developing country picked at random, could expect to find high protective tariffs and quantitative restrictions over imports, strict controls over foreign exchange dealings, ceilings on interest rates and floors under wages, government-set prices of vital commodities from food grains to fuel, restrictions on private investment, many government-owned firms displacing private companies, harassment of people operating in the informal sector, and many other interventions.

RESURGENCE OF THE MARKET

Most of these interventions still are visible in the developing world, but they no longer are so ubiquitous and many countries have begun to shed many of the controls. The pronounced trend of the 1980s and 1990s was toward economic reform that substituted market mechanisms for controls in many aspects of economic policy. No corner of the world has been im-

2. United Nations (by Paul Prebish), *The Economic Development of Latin America and Its Principal Problems* (Lake Success, NY: United Nations, 1950); and Hans W. Singer, "The Distribution of Trade between Investing and Borrowing Countries," *American Economic Review*, 40 (1950), 470–85. See also Ragnar Nurske, *Equilibrium Growth and the World Economy* (Cambridge, MA: Harvard University Press, 1961).

mune. Deregulation was a byword of economic policy in the United States under President Jimmy Carter in the 1970s, although the approach was later associated with President Ronald Reagan. Western Europe moved toward open, integrated markets throughout the 1980s, completed many key elements of a full economic integration by 1992, and adopted a common currency, the euro, in 1998. The Uruguay round of negotiations further freeing up worldwide international trade was completed successfully in 1994. The roll call of developing countries undertaking market reforms, including Chile, Bolivia, Ghana, Kenya, Tanzania, India, South Korea, and Indonesia, grew throughout the 1980s and 1990s. In the communist world, China led the way after the death of Mao Zedong in 1976. The changes in Central and Eastern Europe after 1989 already have been described.

Many factors combined to stimulate market reforms in the developing world. First was a series of negative causes: Controls and other market interventions just did not work very well. Protection and import substitution spurred industrial growth at first, but then industrial development sputtered in country after country. Price interventions generally had unintended consequences: High protective barriers bred inefficient manufacturing; interest rate ceilings suppressed the evolution of financial systems, depressed monetary savings, and encouraged unproductive investment; minimum wages, if they had any impact at all, stifled employment growth and exacerbated inequalities; and ceilings on food prices and taxes on agricultural exports discouraged farmers and retarded productivity growth in agriculture.

Controls by government engendered just political and bureaucratic reactions by private entrepreneurs and managers, instead of the innovative and competitive behavior needed for sustained development. Regulations created higher-than-necessary profits, which economists call **rents,** for those able to gain favorable treatment from bureaucrats or to evade the rules. Widespread corruption and other forms of **rent seeking** diverted the energy of entrepreneurs, investors, managers, and traders from productive activities; wasted scarce resources; and reduced economic growth.[3] The almost universal proliferation of public enterprises extended ineffectual bureaucratic behavior into activities that private enterprises could have handled more effectively and more efficiently.

The consequences of these interventions were apparent as early as the end of the 1960s. In 1970, influential studies by economists at Williams College and Oxford University chronicled the failures of import substitu-

---

3. Ann O. Krueger, "The Political Economy of Rent-Seeking," *American Economic Review,* 64, no. 3 (1974).

tion and all the interventions that generally accompanied it.[4] The explosive rise of oil prices in the 1970s, then their precipitate fall in the 1980s, and the accompanying accumulations of unserviceable debt exposed the failures of some interventionist development strategies. These swings in economic fortune required flexible, creative responses from all economies. But regimes mired in controls were too rigid to cope with the unstable economic environment.

The near stagnation of many developing economies in the 1970s and 1980s stood in stark contrast to the rapid and sustained growth of four East Asian "newly industrialized countries" during the same period. South Korea, Taiwan, Hong Kong, and Singapore, all of which grew by 8 to 10 percent a year for 20 years or more, provided the positive reasons for the conversion to economic reforms. Hong Kong and Singapore had economies governed largely by market forces. In South Korea and to a lesser degree Taiwan, however, the government intervened forcefully. What these four had in common was a strategy of depending heavily on export growth to lead development. This "outward-looking" strategy is explored in Chapter 18. In essence, by inducing private firms to seek markets overseas, these countries took advantage of the large world market and simultaneously exposed their manufacturing firms to the discipline of competition in international markets. This competitive industrial base permitted the four East Asian countries to sail through the economic crisis of the 1970s and 1980s with relative ease.

Development economists of the **neoclassical school** began to promote the virtues of market-oriented, outward-looking development even before the oil and debt crises. Chicago economist Theodore Schultz won his Nobel Prize partly for his work in the early 1960s showing that so-called traditional farmers were rational decision makers whose techniques were well adapted to the conditions and constraints they faced. One implication was that market incentives, accompanied by new technologies, would induce farmers to change their methods and raise productivity.[5] The promise of a dynamic agriculture was realized with the coming of the Green Revolution in Asia. The 1970 studies of import substitution, mentioned previously, suggested the obvious alternative strategy of more open, market-oriented economies. By the late 1970s, a series of country studies by trade economists Bela Balassa, Jagdish Bhagwati, and Anne Krueger had established a strong empirical

---

4. Henry J. Bruton, "The Import Substitution Strategy of Economic Development," *Pakistan Development Review,* 10 (1970), 123–46; and Ian Little, Tibor Scitovsky, and Maurice Scott, *Industry and Trade in Some Developing Countries* (London: Oxford University Press, 1970).

5. Theodore W. Schultz, *Transforming Traditional Agriculture* (New Haven, CT: Yale University Press, 1964).

THE DECLINING EFFECTIVENESS OF INDUSTRIAL POLICY: KOREA FROM THE 1960S TO THE 1990S

South Korea in the 1960s and 1970s pursued an industrial policy that involved heavy intervention by the government to promote exports, in general, and specific industries, in particular. The government provided bank loans to favored industries at below market rates, gave these industries special access to government controlled foreign exchange, and helped build the infrastructure required by them. The president of the country even met monthly with the heads of the major industries to review and help solve their problems. The government saw itself as correcting for market failures even though many of these market failures were the creation of earlier and continuing government import-substituting policies.

These industrial policies in the 1960s and 1970s appear to have worked reasonably well, although the heavy industry and chemical industry drive of the 1970s remains controversial to this day. President Park Chung Hee, who led this effort, kept politics and corruption out of most of these industrial policy decisions. Because he ran an authoritarian regime supported mainly by a modern army, he felt no need to use industrial policies to pay off his political supporters. By the early 1980s, however, many Korean economists and others felt that this activist government industrial policy was causing too many economic distortions and that the country should move toward a more market-oriented system. Moving toward a market system proved to be difficult because of promises made to private compa-

case that outward-looking strategies work better than import substitution.[6] We further explore the reasons for this in Chapter 18.

At the core of the argument for market-guided development is the proposition of neoclassical economics that markets create competition and competition stimulates the growth of productivity. The discussion of growth accounting in Chapter 2 showed how the growth of income per

6. Bela Balassa, "Exports and Economic Growth: Further Evidence," *Journal of Development Economics,* 5, no. 2 (1978), 181–89; Jagdish Bhagwati, *Foreign Exchange Regimes and Economic Development: Anatomy and Consequences of Exchange Control Regimes* (Cambridge, MA: Ballinger Press, 1978); and Anne O. Krueger, *Foreign Exchange Regimes and Economic Development: Liberalization Attempts and Consequences* (Cambridge, MA: Ballinger Press, 1978).

nies that had carried out the government's wishes in the past. They felt that they had an implicit guarantee that they would be helped out if, by doing the government's bidding, they got into trouble. In the 1980s, they did get into trouble and the government spent much of its time in that decade providing subsidies and other means of support to these firms.

By the 1990s, Korea had a democratic government led, after 1992, by President Kim Young Sam, who had little interest in an activist industrial policy. Like his predecessors, however, he saw how these policies could be used to raise large sums of money to support his political campaigns. Increasingly the criteria for getting government support for a particular firm or industry depended on whether that firm contributed to the political campaigns. Such contributions existed in the 1960s and 1970s as well but they were not allowed to influence major industrial policy decisions. By contrast, in the 1990s, industrial policy interventions were driven more by politics than by a concern for building efficient competitive industries. Industrial policy in the earlier period had produced such firms as POSCO, one of the largest and most efficient steel companies in the world, a firm that remained profitable right through the Asian financial crisis of 1997–1999. Industrial policy in the 1990s produced such firms as the Hanbo steel company, whose bankruptcy contributed in a significant way to Korea's involvement in the Asian financial crisis.

Finally, in the 1998–2000 period, the Korean government under a new president, Kim Dae Jung, began to make a major effort to get the government out of the business of supporting particular industries and firms. The objective was to create a level playing field for all but to do so without triggering another financial crisis caused by the collapse of the older firms that had relied so much on government support.

capita can be attributed to two sources: growing supplies of the productive factors, especially capital available to each worker, and increases in the productivity of all factors used in production. Rapid capital accumulation—high investment rates—has been achieved for sustained periods by both well-functioning market economies (Japan and the four newly industrialized countries of Asia) and command economies (the Soviet Union and China). But when it comes to raising **factor productivity**—the productivity of capital, labor, land, and other resources—some market economies do quite well while command economies have a notoriously poor record. In mixed economies, greater market orientation—less government intervention and more openness to world markets—appears to promote gains in factor productivity.

There are several reasons why this should be so. In market economies, competition and the profit motive force producers—farmers, industrial firms, service industries, and individual workers—to operate as efficiently as possible and to reduce costs (raise productivity) whenever they can. Those who cannot use their resources efficiently or cannot find profitable markets for their output earn less than others who can, and their businesses may fail. These individual attempts to operate more efficiently, compelled by market forces, translate into a more productive economy so long as the market failures are compensated. When market forces do not guide production decisions, the incentive for productivity gains is weaker. Price distortions draw labor, capital, and other factors into less productive employment; for example, from efficient export industries into protected import-substituting ones. Government regulations establish incentives for rent seeking and bribery; entrepreneurs and managers then spend more time dealing with and influencing government officials and less time making their plants run more efficiently. Protection behind high tariffs, other import barriers, and investment restrictions insulates firms from competition, both foreign and domestic, and so permits them to earn profits even when they use resources inefficiently. When governments themselves enter into production through state-owned enterprises, the profit motive of their managers is diluted by political and bureaucratic concerns: noneconomic goals are imposed by the government; bureaucratic rules and procedures govern key decisions on investment, finance, and wages; and managers' careers often depend more on their ties to government leaders than their firms' performances.

Some empirical support can be found for the proposition that markets, particularly foreign markets, within which firms are exposed to competition contribute to factor productivity growth. A cross-country comparison by economists Moshe Syrquin and Holllis Chenery suggests that outward orientation has some impact on the growth of both gross domestic product and total factor productivity.[7] The results for 106 countries are summarized in Table 5–1. For Syrquin and Chenery, outward orientation means that a country has a higher-than-average ratio of exports to GDP, given its per capita income and population. They also distinguish between **primary-oriented** countries, which have higher-than-average shares of primary good (agricultural and raw material) exports to total exports, and **manufacturing-oriented** countries. Regardless of this classification, outward-oriented countries had significantly higher GDP growth rates than inward-oriented ones from 1950 to 1983 (column 1).

7. Moshe Syrquin and Hollis B. Chenery, "Three Decades of Industrialization," *World Bank Economic Review,* 3, no. 2 (1989), 145–81. See also World Bank, *The East Asian Miracle* (Oxford: Oxford University Press, 1993), Chap. 6.

TABLE 5–1	IMPACT OF OUTWARD ORIENTATION ON GROWTH			
		GDP GROWTH	TOTAL FACTOR PRODUCTIVITY GROWTH	
	COUNTRIES	1950–83	1960–70	1970–82
PRIMARY ORIENTED	55			
INWARD ORIENTED	37	3.9	1.1	0.4
OUTWARD ORIENTED	28	5.0	2.0	−0.2
MANUFACTURING ORIENTED	41			
INWARD ORIENTED	23	4.7	2.2	0.2
OUTWARD ORIENTED	18	5.5	2.4	0.9

Note: Growth rates in percent per year.
Source: Moshe Syrquin and Hollis B. Chenery, "Three Decades of Industrialization."

The impact on factor productivity is not so clear-cut, however. For the primary-oriented countries, openness led to substantially higher productivity growth during the relatively stable decade of the 1960s. During the 1970s, however, when oil prices forced major readjustments and other commodity prices first rose and then fell, all countries' productivity growths were much lower. The outward-oriented primary exporters then had lower productivity growth than their inward-oriented counterparts, perhaps because they had more severe adjustments to make. In contrast, very little difference in productivity growth occurred among manufacturing-oriented countries during the 1960s, but the outward-oriented economies did better when major adjustments were required in the 1970s. However, in manufacturing-oriented countries, where resource endowments matter less and trade strategies matter more, a clear if moderate margin seems to favor outward orientation.

A more recent study by Harvard economists Jeffrey Sachs and Andrew Warner confirms the importance of market orientation in economic growth.[8] They establish two sets of criteria for market-based economic policies: the security of property rights, defined as the absence of socialist economic structures, civil or external war, and extreme deprivation of civil or political rights; and economic openness, defined as a low proportion of imports covered by quantitative restrictions and a free market exchange rate that is within 20 percent of the official rate. Sachs and Warner identify only 13, out of 75, countries meeting all these criteria over the period from 1970 to 1989. Of those 13, 11 had growth

8. Jeffrey Sachs and Andrew Warner, "Economic Convergence and Economic Policies," Harvard Institute for International Development, development discussion paper no. 502, March 1995.

rates of income per capita over 3 percent a year and the other 2 had rates over 2 percent. Of the 75 countries that did not meet all these criteria, only 6 grew by more than 3 percent a year and 51 grew by less than 2 percent a year.

These studies suggest that market orientation is important for rapid growth of income and productivity. But market-based policies are not sufficient to ensure growth, nor do these studies rule out the possibility that growth can be achieved through other policy regimes. Market orientation is not the only factor contributing to growth; entrepreneurial talent, educated workers, and well-run governments also are important. Several countries that are open in the sense of having high ratios of exports to gross national income may lack other requirements for growth, while some inward-looking countries may have them in abundance. Under the circumstances, the apparently narrow differences in productivity growth in the Syrquin-Chenery data and the stronger results on income growth in the Sachs-Warner study support the proposition that openness contributes to economic growth. Economists believe that openness works because it introduces competition (as well as wider markets and the ability to attain economies from larger-scale production). Then, by extension, we conclude that markets, which create competition, also work to raise productivity.

By the mid-1990s, the conclusions reached in the previous paragraphs had become widely accepted and were the intellectual underpinning for the movement toward "globalization" of most economic activity in a large majority of countries around the world. The economic crisis that began in Asia in 1997 and then spread beyond Asia to Russia and Brazil, however, led some analysts to question whether the rush to open up the world's economies was really such a good thing. The Asian economic crisis is discussed at length in Chapters 13 and 14. Here we note only that the economic crisis that began in 1997 and continued to the end of the century had little to do with the opening up of the crisis-hit countries to the import of manufactures and agricultural products or to the export orientation of these economies. Rather, the removal of restrictions on the flow of capital in and out of these countries, together with the weakness of their financial institutions, contributed to the crisis. The opening up or globalization of the financial system, therefore, was a problem and has led many economists to question whether full liberalization of a country's financial system is a good idea, at least before that financial system is greatly strengthened. The crisis has not affected most economists' views of the importance for economic growth of opening up the economy to the unhindered flow in and out of most manufactures, agricultural products, and even many financial services.

Implementing Market Reforms

Over the past several decades, therefore, a strong case has been built favoring a greater role for market forces in the management of the economy. How does a country used to widespread government intervention wean itself from overuse of bureaucratic commands in favor of more market influence? Is it simply a matter of dismantling the government's role in the economy and allowing market forces to take over? Or do market-oriented reforms require a different role for government, not necessarily a lesser role?

To make the transition from a regulated economy to a well-functioning market economy, five conditions need to be met, each of which will be explored in greater depth in subsequent sections:

1. *Prices must become reasonably stable* and the macroeconomy should be close to equilibrium. Macroeconomic instability—large budget deficits, rampant inflation, and a severe drain on the balance of foreign payments—discourages productive activity and invites widespread government interference with market forces.

2. *Most goods and services must be bought and sold through market mechanisms* and not allocated through administered arrangements, such as import licensing, output quotas, ration shops, government agencies, and public enterprises. Before the 1990s, most developing countries and all socialist countries allocated a significant share of goods and services through nonmarket mechanisms.

3. *There must be competition,* either within the domestic market or from abroad, if productivity gains are to be achieved. In some cases the economy is too small to sustain more than one firm in an industry and government restrictions on imports eliminate competition from foreign firms. In other instances there are several firms in the industry but their own collusion or government allocation of quotas for critical inputs effectively removes competitive pressure. Centrally planned economies favor monopolies in part because it makes planning easier.

4. *Relative prices should reflect relative scarcities* in the economy. It is possible to have a market system with highly distorted prices, but it is not possible to have an efficient market system under such circumstances. Price distortions have been pervasive in many developing economies and "getting prices right" is a major objective of most market-oriented reforms.

5. *Firm managers, farmers, and other decision makers must be able and willing to respond to market signals.* Firms must maximize profits by increasing their sales or cutting their costs, or they must follow some rule that is a close approximation of profit maximization. Economists tend to assume that firms will maximize profits because it is in their own interest to do so.

But, when economies are riddled with government intervention, profits are obtained by extracting greater subsidies, price supports, and the like from the government, not by increasing the economic efficiency of the firm.

These five transitional requirements incorporate two market failures discussed earlier: macroeconomic stability is in both lists and competition is the antidote to monopoly power. Other market failures also are relevant to reform. Prices that reflect relative scarcities suggest taxation or other corrections for external costs and benefits as discussed in Chapter 12. And economies in transition from controls to market mechanisms are deficient in the market institutions, especially those for diversifying risk and conveying information, necessary to make markets work efficiently. Although essential to long-term development, corrections for these market failures usually are not addressed in transitional reforms and are mentioned only incidentally in the next sections.

1. STABILIZATION OF THE MACROECONOMY

In theory, a market can work while prices are rising rapidly. In practice, price increases above a certain level will trigger government intervention in the form of general price freezes or specific price controls. If price controls are put in place without first curing the underlying causes of inflation, the result will be excess demand for the goods whose prices were frozen. To deal with this excess demand, the government must either introduce rationing or stand by while long lines form at shops selling the goods in short supply, an informal kind of rationing. Either way the goods end up being distributed by some nonmarket mechanism, through ration coupons or to those who are first into line and most willing to wait. In the Soviet Union, it was normal for citizens to carry shopping bags with them at all times on the chance that some shop had just gotten a new supply of some scarce item. Under rationing, those who first obtain scarce goods frequently turn around and sell them in the **parallel** or **black market,** where prices are higher than in the official market and can exceed the prices that would prevail in an uncontrolled market.

What level of inflation triggers this kind of intervention? The answer is in part political. Some societies, such as those in South America, are accustomed to very rapid inflation and rates of 20 or 30 percent a year are considered relatively stable. Other societies, China, for example, consider any rate above 20 percent intolerable, while Germans feel uncomfortable with inflation of 5 percent a year.

Inflation leads to distortions in relative prices and the decisions based on them. Groups organized to wield political power, such as unionized labor, large firms, the military, and civil servants, compete

CHINA JOINS THE WTO TO SPEED THE TRANSITION TO THE MARKET, 1999–2000

In the early 1990s, China had largely completed the process of putting in place a market system in agriculture, domestic commerce, and for its small- and medium-scale township and village industrial enterprises. But the large state-owned enterprises that dominated such sectors as steel, machinery, and automobiles resisted the changes required by a market system. They continued to fight for easy credit from the banking system, and when that was not available, they simply stopped paying their suppliers. The government, they assumed, always would bail them out because the government was afraid of the political consequences of the rising unemployment that would occur if these enterprises stopped production and laid off workers. As long as the state-owned industrial enterprises remain unreformed, it also was difficult to make the banks behave the way they should in a market system.

In 1997 and 1998, however, the government began to push hard to reform the state-owned enterprises and the banks. Redundant workers began to be laid off and the unemployed in the cities rose to over 20 million workers. To further emphasize how serious they were, Premier Zhu Rongji, on a trip to the United States in 1999, announced that he was willing to open up the Chinese economy to foreign competition to an unprecedented degree. His immediate purpose was to conclude a trade agreement with the United States that would allow China to become a member of the World Trade Organization (WTO). The magnitude of the concessions that China said it would agree to, however, made it clear that China's goals had as much to do with its own domestic reforms as it did with its desire for membership in the WTO. Foreign competition for the banks as well as such industries as automobiles was to be the vehicle for forcing these sectors to reform. All manner of protection for these industries and financial institutions was to be abolished or sharply reduced, and foreign ownership was to be allowed in many financial sectors where previously it had not been allowed. The European Union agreed to a similar list of concessions in May 2000, and the way was paved for Chinese WTO membership and a wave of competitive pressures that would assist China to complete its transition to a market economy.

intensely to protect their shares of the national income. The result is a distortion of relative prices away from scarcity values to reflect instead the outcome of these political struggles. Relative prices themselves become volatile and so reduce the information they convey to participants in the economy. For example, **real interest rates** (interest rates corrected for inflation) often become negative; this reduces the supply of long-term funds for investment. Exchange rates usually become **overvalued:** The central bank, for instance, offers too few pesos (the local currency) to people with dollars to sell, and this discourages exports and encourages imports.

These distortions and the uncertainty about future rates of inflation cause people to acquire land, gold, and other assets whose prices will rise with inflation rather than productive assets or to transfer their financial wealth overseas. With rapid inflation, entrepreneurs and managers spend more time trying to profit from inflation and devote correspondingly less energy to producing more efficiently. After all, large and sustained productivity gains might reduce costs by 3 to 5 percent a year, not much compared to rates of inflation from 10s to 100s of percent a year.

Impressive evidence demonstrates that macroeconomic stability is necessary—although far from sufficient—to promote economic growth. Figures 5–1 and 5–2 assemble data on rates of inflation, exchange rate overvaluation, and economic growth for 29 countries from 1980 to 1992. They show that none of the countries with rapid inflation, such as Ghana, Zambia, and several in Latin America, was able to generate growth in per capita income. Conversely, all the countries with very rapid growth, especially those in East and Southeast Asia, had low rates of inflation. Similarly, all countries with per capita income growth greater than 2 percent a year kept their official exchange rates within 20 percent of the free market rate. But low inflation and low exchange rate overvaluation were not always sufficient to generate growth, as evidenced by Kenya and Cameroon.

More comprehensively, MIT economist Stanley Fischer, later to become first deputy managing director of the International Monetary Fund, compiled data for 80 countries over 25 years, covering the early 1960s to the middle 1980s. His regressions demonstrate that higher inflation, higher budget deficits, and more overvalued exchange rates are closely correlated with reduced economic growth. And there is some indication that the macroeconomic imbalances cause slower growth, not the other way around.[9]

9. Stanley Fischer, "The Role of Macroeconomic Factors in Growth," *Journal of Monetary Economics,* 32 (1993), 485–512. Exchange rate distortions are measured by the percentage deviation of the parallel market exchange rate from the official rate.

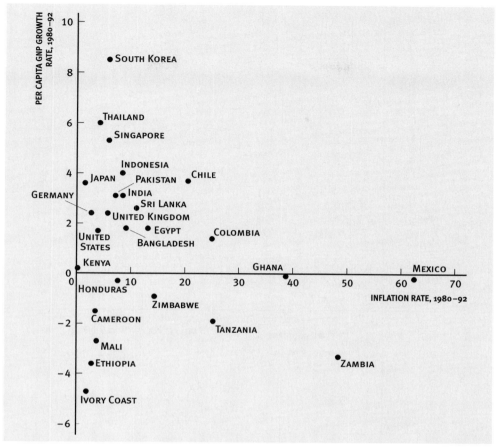

FIGURE 5–1   INFLATION AND ECONOMIC GROWTH, 1980–92. All countries with per capita income growth greater than 2 percent a year kept inflation below 20 percent a year and the most rapidly growing countries all kept annual inflation below 10 percent.

Stabilization programs are designed to stem inflation and correct the other imbalances associated with it, notably deficits in the government budget and the balance of foreign payments. Often, the International Monetary Fund (IMF) works with the country to introduce a package of stabilization policies. At the core of the package is the notion that inflation is caused when the supply of money increases faster than the demand for it. To correct this and other imbalances, a typical program will contain some or all of the following remedies. (1) A reduction in the government's budget deficit, through higher taxes and reduced expenditure, is needed because deficits are financed either by money creation or borrowing from private savers, which "crowds out" private investment. (2) To control growth of the money supply, restrictive tar-

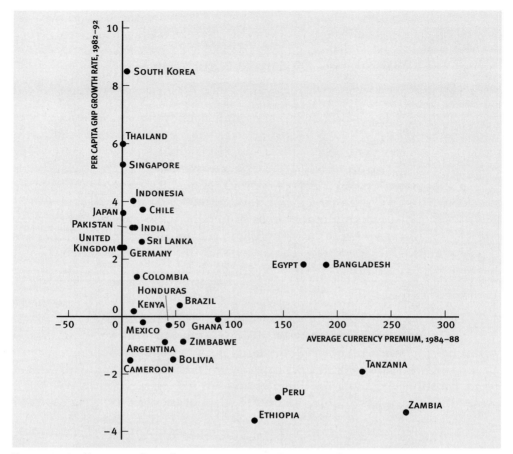

FIGURE 5–2   EXCHANGE RATE OVERVALUATION AND ECONOMIC GROWTH, 1980–92. All countries with per capita income growth exceeding 2 percent a year had exchange rate premia (excess of free market over official market rates) of less than 20 percent, while most countries with high premia suffered declines in average income.

gets are set for central bank credit to the government and commercial banks. (3) The exchange rate may be devalued, which raises the price of foreign exchange in domestic currency and helps correct a balance-of-payments deficit by stimulating exports and restraining the demand for imports. (4) Price controls may be removed so that markets can reduce the distortions in relative prices; administered prices may be adjusted for the same reason. Interest rates, food prices, utility rates, and transport fares often are affected. (5) Targets are set for restraining wage increases. Wages that increase faster than productivity push up the cost of production and thus contribute to inflation. We discuss macroeconomic stabilization further in Chapter 19.

When deficits in the budget or balance of payments occur, they must be either reduced through economic adjustment or financed from overseas. To assist in financing deficits, the IMF may help the government reschedule its foreign debt payments, especially those due commercial banks. The IMF itself offers loans, called **standby credits,** for three to five years at moderate interest rates to help close the balance-of-payments gap. This is intended to ease the pain of stabilization by permitting the corrective measures to be less drastic than they otherwise would have to be. However, disbursement of the loan (as well as debt relief) is contingent on successful implementation of the measures designed to stabilize the economy. This quid pro quo—loans and debt relief in return for policy reform—is known as **conditionality.**

The IMF stabilization package is controversial, at no time more so than at the beginning of the Asian financial crisis in 1997. Most economists accept that imbalances, particularly budget deficits, have to be corrected and inflation curbed if growth and development are to be sustained. One issue, however, is the speed of adjustment. Stabilization is likely to require some rise in unemployment and a decline in income for some groups, although the imbalances themselves might have caused similar problems. The more abruptly these measures are enforced, the greater will be the dislocations. Yet a gradual implementation may undermine the government's credibility and make it more difficult to complete the stabilization.

When control of inflation has to be combined with a major restructuring of the economy, the dislocations can be particularly severe. This situation, in essence, was the case in much of Central and Eastern Europe, Russia, and Vietnam during the first half of the 1990s. The structural changes there led to both a loss in revenue, as existing sources of tax revenue disappeared, and an increase in government expenditures to bail out the many loss-making state enterprises—losses due in large part to the difficulties these enterprises were having in adjusting to a market system. Formally these enterprises received loans from the central bank, but since no one expected the loans to be repaid, in reality they were subsidies from the government budget. Closing down the loss-making enterprises would have reduced expenditures and hence inflation pressure, but it also would have thrown large numbers of people out of work. Russia was unable or unwilling to face the political consequences of what the leaders believed would be large-scale unemployment, so inflation continued at 10 to 20 percent per month (300 to 900 percent per year). Vietnam, with a much smaller state enterprise sector, cut back sharply on subsidies to state enterprises and thereby reduced inflation from around 70 percent a year in 1990 and 1991 to well under 20 percent a year in 1992 and 1993.

Even where the restructuring of the economy is less drastic than what has been attempted in Russia or Eastern Europe, inflation may be more difficult to bring down than many orthodox economists believe. A school of heterodox economists, led by Lance Taylor of the New School for Social Research, believes that many wages and other prices are set by predetermined, nonmarket rules. For example, in inflation-prone countries in Latin America, labor agreements sometimes adjust wage rates to compensate for inflation, a practice called **indexing.** And many firms set their prices by calculating a fixed percentage, or margin, over the costs of production, a practice called **markup pricing.** To the extent that these practices prevail, a reduction in the growth of the money supply will not reduce inflation for some time, as unions and firms continue their habit of raising wages and prices to make up for past losses to inflation and to protect against future inflation. Instead, with prices rising faster than the money supply, the result is layoffs and bankruptcies. Eventually, perhaps, the unions and firms will adjust their expectations and inflation will abate, but it can take years and may require more than the economic measures contained in stabilization packages. Fundamental agreements among employers, workers, and government may be needed to change the entrenched habits of indexing and markup pricing; sometimes these "agreements" are forced by coercive measures, often by military governments.[10]

Ultimately this is an empirical matter: Are prices **flexible,** moving up and down with demand, or **fixed** and insensitive to reductions in demand? Most economies have a mixture of both kinds. Prices for most agriculture, many services, and some manufactured goods are flexible. But, in some industries, especially those with a few large-scale firms, fixed pricing may prevail. In countries with entrenched and politicized labor unions and concentrated industries, prices are more likely to be inflexible. When, in addition, the income distribution is very unequal, a government often is unable to win a broad consensus on stabilization measures. These conditions seem characteristic of some Latin American countries, where the experience with stabilization programs has been mixed, with many notable failures, such as Brazil and Argentina in the 1980s, and some successes, notably Bolivia in 1985 (see the case study on page 178). In Asia, governments have been better able to use stabilization packages to correct budget and payments imbalances and control inflation.

10. For a review of these controversies, see Tony Killick, ed., *The Quest for Stabilization: The IMF and the Third World* (London: Heinemann, 1984); Lance Taylor, *Varieties of Stabilization Experience: Toward Sensible Macroeconomics in the Third World* (London: Oxford University Press, [Clarendon], 1988); and John Williamson, ed., *IMF Conditionality* (Washington, DC: Institute for International Economics, 1983). The Taylor book is for advanced readers.

The role of the IMF in the Asian financial crisis beginning in 1997 was controversial for reasons quite different from the kinds of typical IMF interventions designed to control inflation or a balance of payments deficit. The hard-hit Asian economies had neither high inflation nor, except for Thailand, major and unsustainable balance of payments deficits in the months immediately preceding the crisis. The cause of the Asian crisis, as already mentioned, was due to financial panic by both domestic and foreign investors, combined with financial institutions that had been dangerously weakened by decades of state-directed lending. Critics of the IMF argued that the IMF applied its usual orthodox solutions to a problem that was very different from that usually tackled by the IMF and that those orthodox solutions were inappropriate to the new circumstances. We return to the IMF's handling of the Asian financial crisis in Chapters 13 and 14. For the discussion here of the transition from a controlled to a market economy, the main point remains that, one way or another, a country must avoid serious inflation or balance of payments difficulties if it wants a well-functioning market economy.

2. DISMANTLING CONTROLS

Once stabilization has been achieved, or even while it is being achieved, the other four elements of a well-functioning market system must be put in place. Many of the measures designed to accomplish this task come in the category the World Bank calls **structural adjustment.**

A critical step at the outset is to make as many goods as possible available for purchase on the market rather than through some allocation mechanism of the government bureaucracy. Therefore, an important element in trade reform is to remove government quotas on imports. Import licensing is a way of transferring allocations from the market to the government. In many developing countries firms starting up a new factory must get licenses to purchase land, to get foreign exchange for imports of capital equipment and intermediate inputs, and even to buy electricity. Negotiations to acquire these licenses can drag on for years. In the agricultural sector, fertilizer and pesticides sometimes are distributed through a state commercial network in amounts determined by the government, rather than by farmers' willingness to purchase and use these inputs. Most of these interventions in mixed economies were justified at their origin by the market failure and distributional arguments outlined at the beginning of this chapter. Others, restrictions on foreign investment for example, are justified on political or security grounds. When restriction is piled on restriction, however, the cumulative effect is to remove large parts of the economy from participation in the market.

STABILIZATION THAT WORKED: BOLIVIA, 1985–86[11]

From August 1984 to August 1985, prices in Bolivia rose by 20,000 percent, the most rapid inflation in Latin American history. During September 1985, inflation was stopped cold and prices actually began to fall. How did this happen?

The hyperinflation of 1984–85 was the culmination of events under the regime of President Siles Zuazo, which in 1982 became Bolivia's first elected government in 18 years. Declining foreign aid and commercial bank lending, combined with rising international interest rates and debt payments, led to a growing payments deficit: Net resource flows into Bolivia declined by 10 percent of the GDP over three years to a net outflow of $190 million in 1983. To compensate for this loss of revenue, the government resorted to central bank credit and thus increased the money supply. This, combined with wage increases granted to organized labor, caused accelerating inflation. Rising prices caused a precipitate decline in tax revenues, from 9 percent of the GDP in 1981 to only 1.3 percent in 1985, and led to a rapid depreciation of the exchange rate, both of which fed back into higher inflation. By 1985, the public had lost all confidence in the boliviano and most transactions were denominated in dollars.

11. This account is drawn from Juan Antonio Morales and Jeffrey D. Sachs, "Bolivia's Economic Crisis," in Jeffrey D. Sachs, ed., *Developing Country Debt and the World Economy* (Chicago: University of Chicago Press, 1989), pp. 57–79; and Jeffrey D. Sachs, "The Bolivian Hyperinflation and Stabilization," *American Economic Review,* 77, no. 2 (May 1987), 279–83.

In command economies, such as those of China, the Soviet Union, and Vietnam, allocation of goods through the market, except for retail sales to consumers, was rejected altogether. Industrial and agricultural inputs were allocated by government bureaus to enterprises in accordance with a central plan. An enterprise that needed more of one kind of input had to go back to the central planners or the government bureau to get an increased allocation. Buying the item on the market was not possible because no such market existed.

Dismantling such controls over production, marketing, and consumption, in both mixed and command economies, is a central feature of structural adjustment packages. Reforms that end controls are called **liberalization** or **deregulation**.

In August 1985, the newly elected government of President Victor Paz Estenssoro took power and instituted a radical stabilization program along orthodox lines. The boliviano was devalued and made fully convertible into dollars; a sharp rise in the prices of goods and services sold by government corporations, together with a freeze on public sector wages, immediately cut the budget deficit; a tax reform was proposed and later enacted to increase revenues and avoid future deficits; the treasury went on a cash-flow basis, spending no more than its incoming cash revenues. The elimination of the deficit reduced the need to obtain central bank credit and so restricted the money supply; this in turn curbed price increases and stabilized the new exchange rate. In contrast to other Latin American stabilizations, no price controls were employed and some existing controls were eliminated. The stabilization was aided by a standby agreement with the IMF and the subsequent resumption of lending by the aid donors, including the World Bank. But the moratorium on debt payments to commercial banks, begun under the Siles government, was maintained.

The abrupt elimination of the government's deficit and its ability to stabilize the exchange rate made its program credible to the public. The Paz government's task was easier because the previous government's policies had been completely discredited and the economy was in a shambles. The government was even able to carry out the kind of unpopular measures that might have toppled other regimes, notably the layoff of 21,000 workers employed by the inefficient government tin mining company, COMIBOL, and the sharp curtailment of government expenditures. After the first few months of dramatic reform, inflation did resume, but at levels of 10 to 15 percent, some of the lowest rates in Latin America.

3. ENSURING COMPETITION

In many developing countries competition has been avoided. Foreign competition in particular is considered "unfair," because foreign firms have years more experience than the country's new domestic firms. The solution often is to prohibit entry into the domestic market by foreign firms. Competition between domestic firms also is seen to waste resources. Why have three firms when one or two can produce all that is required? Fewer firms can achieve economies of scale and produce at lower average cost. Competition is disorderly, so the argument goes, and some firms will fail and put people out of work.

Waste caused by the bankruptcy of a company is visible to all, but waste is not so apparent if caused by lack of pressure to produce more efficiently. Hardly anyone noticed that the U.S. automobile companies largely had ignored the demand for smaller cars until the Japanese came along with their compacts and subcompacts. Competition is the force that pressures everyone to do better. The desire to produce goods that were competitive in international markets was one reason for the rapid growth of the four East Asian tigers. State-owned enterprises often are inefficient in part because the state frequently awards monopoly control of their market to these enterprises. With monopoly control they can set prices high enough to cover their high costs and sell goods of inferior quality. Under the circumstances, why bother working hard to lower costs? Industries built behind a wall of protection from foreign imports may never be able to compete in foreign markets. Managers in these industries, as already pointed out, will put most of their energy into lobbying to maintain that protection, rather than learning how to meet the competition.

Centrally managed economies, such as those of the Soviet Union and China before the recent reforms, allowed little real competition among enterprises. In China in the 1970s even small-scale county-owned enterprises were given a monopoly over the local county market. When demand in the local market for the output of the small enterprise was saturated, production was stopped and the enterprise retooled to produce something else. In this kind of system, the government allocates inputs and tells firms how much to produce. Pressure to surpass the targets set by the state provides some impetus to produce more efficiently, but this kind of pressure is a poor substitute for competition between firms where the loser will have a smaller market share, lower profits, and fewer employees—and may go out of business. Command economies are notorious for their profligate waste of resources.

Reform programs attempt to introduce competition into markets where it has been limited or absent. In larger countries, or in industries with few economies of scale, there can be several firms in any industry. Competition among these domestic firms can be fostered simply by dismantling import or investment licensing, quotas over output, controls over prices, or other government interventions that give some firms advantages over others. In China, one of the first reform steps was to abolish all regional or local monopolies and thus force enterprises in different regions to compete with each other.

If the domestic market is small and one or a few firms dominate the industry or if domestic firms fail to compete vigorously, the only viable competition comes from abroad, in the form of competing imports. Therefore, the deregulation of import controls and reduction of tariffs provide the competitive stimulus for improved productivity and higher quality. Another way to infuse domestic industry with competitive urges is to bias the entire structure of incentives toward exports, away from domestic sales. Import liberalization should be part of this strategy, but it also encompasses exchange rate devaluation, direct and indirect subsidies, preferential credit, investment in ports and other types of infrastructure, and many other measures to support exporters. To take advantage of more profitable sales in foreign markets, domestic firms must improve both their quality and their productivity and learn to market aggressively. This is the outward-looking approach used by the four East Asian "tigers."[12]

4. MOVING TOWARD SCARCITY PRICES

While competition creates the stimulus for firms to maximize profits and improve productivity, **relative prices** are the signals that tell firms how to manage their resources to earn the highest rewards. If the relative prices reflect the real scarcities in the economy, firms that maximize profits and consumers who maximize their utility automatically will act to make the most out of all resources on behalf of the economy as a whole. This is called **static efficiency.** Scarce resources, such as capital or energy, should have relatively high prices to conserve their use; abundant resources, such as unskilled labor in poor economies and educated workers in rich ones, should receive relatively low wages so they will be used more intensively in production. When market prices dictate these allocations of scarce and abundant resources, a greater value of output can be achieved for any given expenditure on inputs.

Despite these advantages of market-determined prices, governments regularly have intervened to set prices and shield them from market influences. In principle, these price controls were designed to correct for market failures and thus to bring prices in line with real scarcities. In reality, price setting generally is a process based on political and not economic objectives. More often than not, government interventions lead prices further away from real economic scarcities.

A major objective of structural adjustment reforms, therefore, is to reduce or remove these distortions generated by government intervention. In the majority of developing countries, the list of distorted prices is a long one. (1) Tariffs raise the price of imports and competing domestic goods. If tariffs were at a uniform rate on all imports, the distortions would not be so great. But tariffs typically vary from 0 to 50 percent, and rates of 200 percent are not uncommon. (2) Interest rates on loans frequently are held well below market rates in a misguided attempt to promote investment by reducing the cost of finance. Low rates discourage saving, however; and this reduces the availability of finance. Also, cheap loans meant for the

12. Not all measures listed always are advocated for outward-looking strategies. Subsidies and preferential credit, although they promote exports, also distort the economy away from scarcity prices.

poor usually are siphoned off by the well-connected rich, while the poor pay very high rates on the loans available to them through informal credit markets. (3) Small numbers of well-organized urban workers sometimes can pressure governments to support demands for high wages and non-wage benefits or to restrict layoffs. Poorer, unorganized workers in both the urban and rural areas continue to receive lower, market-set wages. The larger factories, faced with higher labor costs, cut back on employment and substitute machines where they can. (4) Gasoline and other fuels often are sold at prices below those of the world market; this encourages the wasteful use of energy and generally favors well-off consumers. (5) Food prices frequently are kept low for urban workers, even though this can mean that the poorer rural people get paid less for their crops.

The political nature of price setting is readily apparent. For every government-determined price, there are winners, who receive more for their output or pay less for their inputs, and losers. Price distortions most often occur when the beneficiaries of a price change are few and concentrated, while the losers are large in number and dispersed. A tariff on bicycles, for example, will raise the profits to the owners of a country's handful of bicycle factories. A small increase in prices may mean very large increases in profits. Those paying the higher price will number in the millions in a large country, but they will be scattered unevenly across the country and are unlikely to organize to protest the increase. Since the tariff is built into the price of the bicycle, these consumers may not even be aware that government intervention caused the higher prices. The producers will know, however, and be in positions with their increased profits to help those who helped them. Where the beneficiaries of price distortions are large in number, as in the case of food price subsidies, other kinds of political pressures can arise. Removal of a food subsidy frequently triggers rioting that can topple governments.

Structural adjustment reforms designed to correct price distortions, therefore, frequently run into stiff resistance. Nowhere is this more true than in the former command economies of Central and Eastern Europe, Russia, and China. In these countries most state enterprises saw themselves as beneficiaries of state price controls because it meant that they received key inputs at artificially low prices. To get around the resistance of large state enterprises, China created a dual price system where steel going to a large enterprise in accordance with the annual plan was charged a low state-set price, while all other steel was sold on the market at much higher market-determined prices. This dual system overcame much of the political resistance to price reform, but it also created opportunities for corruption by those who could use their influence to buy at the low state price and quickly resell at the high market price—corruption that contributed to the discontent that fueled the demonstrations on Tiananmen Square in

1989. Many of the other socialist and former socialist countries, from Russia to Vietnam, therefore, opted for eliminating state-set prices altogether and using one market-determined price for most goods and services. By the latter half of the 1990s, China as well had largely eliminated the two-price system in favor of a unified market-price system. The gradual elimination of the dual price system resulted in part from deliberate decisions by the Chinese government to reduce the quantity of goods sold at low state-set prices. For the most part, however, the state-set prices disappeared because producers increasingly were unwilling to sell their goods at below market prices, and they found numerous ways to circumvent government instructions requiring them to do so.

There is no question that removing the distortions in prices caused by state intervention normally will raise the welfare of the nation as a whole, even as it hurts select groups and individuals. But how large are these welfare improvements? This question has no easy answer. Potentially, in the former socialist economies, the gain should be very large given the size of the previous distortions, but only China and Vietnam have experienced unequivocal benefits in the form of high growth rates, while in Russia and much of Eastern and Central Europe price reforms were followed by deep recessions. Some economists argue that the gains from price reforms in most developing countries are quite modest. Others suggest that, where distortions are large, as was true in much of the developing world in earlier decades, the gains will be large and are the very essence of reform. Because structural adjustment reforms such as those in Russia and China or in Latin America involve much more than the freeing up of prices, however, it usually is not possible to separate out the impact of efforts to correct price distortions from the effects of the four other elements that make markets work. Most successful reform packages, therefore, involve a combination of reforms of which removing price distortions is only one.

5. RESPONDING TO MARKET SIGNALS

Perhaps the least understood of the reforms needed to make markets work are those that induce producers to act in accordance with market signals. The rule is simple enough: Producers should maximize profits by cutting their costs or increasing their sales. Economists typically assume that producers automatically maximize profits.[13] A firm's owners try to earn high incomes for themselves. But what happens when the firm is run by managers who are hired by the owners? What happens if the firm is owned by the state and managers are appointed to their posts by the government?

13. Recall the structuralists, led by Lance Taylor, who assume firms mark up their prices to cover costs plus a percentage of profit; this is not the same as maximizing profits.

Some of the early socialist theorists, the Polish economist Oscar Lange, for example, thought this problem could be solved by simply ordering managers of state-owned enterprises to maximize profits. These orders would be necessary because, with the state receiving the profits, higher profits no longer necessarily mean higher income for the managers. It is to the credit of these early theorists that they recognized that the issue had to be solved. If firms did not maximize profits, getting prices right would not necessarily lead to a better allocation of resources. Prices work by raising profits to producers of goods in short supply. The prospect of earning higher profits stimulates producers to increase production of scarce items. If the producers are not rewarded by higher profits, they may not respond to higher prices. The early theorists had correctly diagnosed the problem, but their solution—ordering managers to maximize profits—was insufficient.

Increasing the role of the market often works most easily in agriculture. As Theodore Schultz emphasized, farmers, like owners of small businesses, are profit maximizers.[14] If prices are raised on a particular crop, say, coffee in Kenya, farmers will plant more land in coffee but less in grain, because by doing so they will raise their income. Reform therefore can be effective simply by freeing up prices of agricultural products so that prices reflect society's demand for those products and by making inputs such as fertilizer available through the market rather than through state trading companies. Family farmers respond to deregulated prices and supplies because it is profitable for them to do so.

A key reason for the success of the Chinese and Vietnamese reform efforts was that both countries began with reforms in agriculture and small-scale trading. The collective farms and communes were broken up, and the land was turned over to be farmed by individual profit- or income-maximizing households. The crops raised on this land then could be sold on the freed-up rural markets. In both China and Vietnam, farm output increased dramatically after these reforms were introduced, and so added credibility to the overall reform effort.

Small-scale industrial and commercial enterprises behave much like family farmers. Managers and owners are the same people and increased profits go directly to the managers. In developing countries, this direct link between ownership and management holds even for moderately large firms, which often are owned by one or a few families. But as firms increase in size and complexity, the direct link is broken. Owners hire professional managers whose ownership stake in the firm is limited. Incentive bonuses based on profits can help motivate managers but are no perfect substitute for direct ownership. Single or family owners give way to many stockholders whose control over managers is diffuse and often ineffective. In the United States, boards of directors often do not restrain managers

14. Schultz, *Transforming Traditional Agriculture.*

and many large shareholders, especially pension funds and other institutions, are not even represented on the boards.

In the case of **state-owned enterprises,** even the owner has goals other than profit maximization. Government-appointed managers often are directed to keep their prices low to help consumers, to employ more people than needed, to invest and locate in less-developed (and less-profitable) regions, to contribute to the political campaigns of the ruling party, and much else. Profits and efficiency may not even be a specified goal.

A more fundamental problem is that state-owned enterprises are owned by all the people in the country; this usually means that no individual or group of individuals feels any real sense of ownership. It is left up to the state to make sure that the enterprise does not waste its assets or sell its output to a favored few at below market prices. But the state often is a rather remote entity with little real knowledge of what is going on within the enterprise. State rules with special auditors to enforce them can prevent theft but they also can tie up an enterprise in so much red tape that it cannot respond to market signals and hence loses money. To help get around this problem, many state enterprises are required to sign performance contracts in which the state specifies the goals that managers are expected to achieve and managers' rewards if they do achieve them. But performance contracts do not always elicit the kinds of changes in managerial behavior that are required. The limitations of the ownership problem have led many countries to implement more radical changes, including outright privatization.

One critical issue is how to create property rights or a full sense of ownership for those who have decision-making authority over the enterprise. **Property rights,** to be meaningful, must be **well defined** and **exclusive.** If they are neither, then others will lay claim to the property and no one will know who really has decision-making authority. Property rights must also be **secure** for long and indefinite periods. Otherwise, those who have these rights will take a very short-term view, knowing that they will not be around to reap either the rewards or the punishments for long-run success or failure. Normally, property rights also must be **transferable** through sale or lease for much the same reason. An enterprise decision maker who can sell the enterprise will want to maintain its value and not lower its price by running the enterprise into the ground. And property rights must be **enforceable** usually through a well-established legal system, although there are other enforcement mechanisms.[15]

Most state enterprises fail to meet these property rights requirements. Neither the managers nor the supervising ministry officials have well-defined, secure, and transferable rights to the enterprise in most cases. They can be removed from control by the stroke of a pen of some higher

---

15. Theodore Panayotou, *Green Markets: The Economics of Sustainable Development* (San Francisco: ICS Press, 1993), pp. 35–37.

government official. Only the voting public or a small oligarchy, if it is an authoritarian system, have any real property rights; and they usually are too remote to exercise effective control.

Increasingly, in the 1980s and 1990s, privatization of all or most state-owned firms is seen as the solution to the property rights problem. Efforts have been made to privatize state-owned firms in both mixed economies and in the former Soviet-style command economies. In some cases, usually in mixed economies, enterprises are sold off one by one over a long period. In other cases, the effort has been rapid and across the board.

The Russian privatization program of the first half of the 1990s is one of the more interesting cases of the latter approach. Vouchers were given to four groups: the general public, local governments, managers of privatizing state enterprises, and workers of those enterprises. These vouchers through an auction system could then be used to purchase a share of ownership in enterprises undergoing privatization, which by 1994 represented more than two thirds of all state-owned firms.[16]

Russia represented a particularly severe case of an absence of property rights prior to privatization. The central government was too weak to protect the state assets. Workers, managers, and local governments had little incentive to help the center because there was nothing in it for them. So workers and managers who had temporary control of state assets took the opportunity to sell them for personal profit. Privatization therefore was designed to end the theft of assets by giving those with control over them a stake in their preservation and efficient use. Unfortunately for Russia, there is more to obtaining secure property rights and good enterprise management than just privatization of state assets, so the performance of Russian industry did not improve as much as many of the advocates of privatization had hoped. Support for privatization and secure property rights was further undermined when, at a later stage, the government transferred some of the states most valuable assets to political friends in private deals rather than through an open voucher process.

Privatization may not always be necessary to create the required property rights. China's county, township, and village enterprises, for example, often are owned by the county, township, or village. In many cases, the local government officials at this level behave as profit-maximizing entrepreneurs and the township population as a whole clearly sees the relationship between the effectiveness of the local enterprise and its own personal rewards. Public pension funds and other forms of public mutual funds also may serve as effective owners of state firms, if those funds are clearly profit oriented and have the right to hire and fire enterprise managers by electing their represen-

16. Maxim Boycko, Andrei Shleifer, and Robert Vishny, *Privatizing Russia* (Cambridge, MA: MIT Press, 1995).

tatives to the enterprise board of directors. Experiments of this sort are underway in places as diverse as Central Europe, China, and Malaysia.

Whether or not privatization is necessary, it almost never is sufficient. Privatization that creates secure and transferable property rights but does nothing to force the enterprise to compete will not create efficient enterprises capable of sustaining high productivity growth. A firm sold to a cousin of the country's president, who then gets monopoly rights over the sale of its product and state subsidies of various kinds, will be no more efficient than a state-owned enterprise with similar forms of protection.

Whether public or private, the umbilical chord tying the enterprise to the government must be cut. Management energy, as already pointed out, must go into raising sales and cutting costs, not into generating more government support. Government reform, therefore, often is an integral part of making both state and private enterprises work better. If a tax system removes all or most discretion from the tax collector, then the enterprise does not have to spend time negotiating with or bribing the collector for favorable treatment. The government also must disengage from setting the firm's prices or from providing other kinds of subsidies, such as import quotas when the firm gets in trouble. Only then will the enterprise, whatever its ownership, be a truly independent, competitive firm capable of playing a leading role in the development effort.

The Transition to a Market System

The implementation of stabilization and structural adjustment measures raises another set of issues for a reforming government: the credibility of the whole reform package, the timing of measures, and the magnitude of change.

Success in reforming an economy depends crucially on the **credibility** of the entire package.[17] If budget deficits remain high or, for any other reason, money creation is not slowed, the public will anticipate continued or higher inflation. If the real exchange rate is allowed to appreciate because inflation outruns nominal devaluation, as happened in Chile and elsewhere, export industries become unattractive to investors. If import liberalization is undertaken tentatively or if past attempts are reversed, investors will put their money into the old protected industries. To establish credibility, governments need to manage their reform programs decisively, despite their complexity. They also may need to "lock in" reforms by making commitments that are difficult to reverse. Many reforms, espe-

17. Political scientist Joan Nelson explored issues of credibility, timing, and magnitude as director of a multicountry study of stabilization programs. See "The Political Economy of Stabilization: Commitment, Capacity and Public Response," *World Development,* 12, no. 10 (1984), 983–1006.

cially in Africa, now start by freeing the exchange rate and foreign exchange flows from all controls; this forces the government to reduce its deficit and contain money supply growth to avoid massive depreciation and capital outflow. One of the more decisive government efforts to establish the credibility of trade liberalization was the decision of Mexico to negotiate and sign the North American Free Trade Agreement (NAFTA). Opponents desiring to reverse these reductions in trade barriers must first contend with an international treaty.

Credibility also depends on the public's perceptions about stabilization and liberalization. In judging the effects of policies, the public is most likely to compare situations before and after, when the proper comparison is with and without. A stabilized economy may look worse than the observed precrisis economy but could well be an improvement over the situation that might have developed without stabilization, which of course cannot be observed. Leaders and officials in many countries have a deep-seated statist bias toward controls and often maintain an illusion that government controls are effective when they are not. These perceptions by government and the public make it more difficult to plan and implement reforms. Disappointing results with past stabilization and reform efforts make it more difficult to convince the public to support new initiatives.

The influence of foreign aid institutions on credibility is two edged. The International Monetary Fund and the World Bank provide additional resources that can ease the transition to an open economy and help protect income during the transition. Foreign aid can enhance the position of reforming elements within a government and be used by government to sell stabilization programs to the public. However, additional resources also make the crisis seem less intense and reforms less necessary. Moreover, an IMF presence has increasingly become a focal point for opposition to economic change. Although governments of countries such as Egypt, Russia, and Zambia have deflected public ire by ceasing to negotiate with the IMF, the result has been only to delay stabilization, not eliminate its necessity.

Public debt plays a similarly dual role. To a point, the need to pay off foreign creditors can be used to steel the public to a degree of austerity. But, at some point, debt becomes a liability, as the public begins to wonder why its standard of living should decline so that foreign bankers' profits can be maintained. In the long run, debt probably requires convincing arguments about the population's own well-being to sustain either stabilization or reform efforts.

Implicit in the discussion of credibility are the questions of **timing** and **magnitude.** Should reforms be pushed through quickly or phased in gradually? There are times in a country's history when economic and political forces provide a brief opportunity for dramatic reforms. Probably the single most convincing observation on timing, by political scientist Joan Nelson, is that the beginning of a new regime is the time to act.[18] Recently elected regimes have the momentum of popular support, used to good effect by President Jayawardana in Sri Lanka in the late 1970s and dramatically by President Victor Paz Estenssoro in Bolivia in 1985 (see the example on pages 178–179). New regimes of any kind have a brief initial period when they can blame problems on the previous government. Early success obviously has political benefits for the regime. But, as time goes on, growing ties between the government and its supporters in the private sector (*clients*) make policy change increasingly dangerous for any regime. In these circumstances, credibility probably is served by rapid, decisive, comprehensive action.

The more complex and multifaceted the reform process becomes, however, the more difficult it is to act in a way that achieves across-the-board changes. The main task in Bolivia in 1985 was to stop rampant inflation in what already was a market economy. The task in Russia, Vietnam, and much of Central and Eastern Europe was to control inflation, but it also was to create a complete market economy where little or none had existed before. Enterprises, private or public, had to learn how to act in a completely different environment. Property rights had to be established where none had existed before, and a supporting legal system had to be designed and made to work.

Poland, in what came to be called **shock treatment** or the big-bang approach to reform, tried to do everything at once. The early reform efforts in Russia associated with Yegor Gaidar attempted to do something similar. The approach called for an immediate halt to inflation by stopping the growth in the money supply, freeing up all prices, and privatizing the state-owned sectors of the economy. In terms of economic theory, abstracted from politics, doing everything at once made sense. If all of the elements of a market system are in place, the market will work better than if only some elements are in place.

In practice, shock treatment, at least in its initial form, proved impossible to implement. State enterprises could not adjust to the new situation quickly, so many of them ran deeply into the red. Rather than letting these enterprises go bankrupt, thus throwing large numbers of people out of work, the central bank, as pointed out earlier in this chapter, kept the enterprises alive by giving them large loans, which no one expected them to pay back to the bank. Increased loans raised the money supply and so kept inflation at high levels. Freeing up prices put goods back on the shelves of stores, but left those with incomes that did not adjust to inflation in a difficult situation. This, in essence, is what happened in Russia in the first half of the 1990s. Some former socialist countries did better, others worse.

Virtually all of Central and Eastern Europe and the republics of the former Soviet Union experienced deep declines in the gross national product that lasted for years. The problems of introducing a market system

---

18. Nelson, "The Political Economy of Stabilization."

were compounded by the need to downsize the overblown military establishment and establish new trading relationships after the breakup of the
communist trading bloc Comecon. Recession brought parties to power
promising to slow the reform or even to reverse it. By the late 1990s, however, the countries that had gone the furthest in transforming their economic system to one based mainly on market forces with secure property
rights also were the economies where full recovery and renewed growth
were first achieved. Poland, in particular, stood out in this respect.

China and Vietnam in the 1980s and 1990s demonstrated, for some
countries at least, that there was a more gradual approach to replacing a
command system with a market system. Both began by freeing up prices
and reestablishing household-based farming in the agricultural sector. They
then freed up inputs and prices to the industrial sector and so created the
conditions, in China at least, for a boom in small- and medium-scale industries. These industries in turn put competitive pressure on the large enterprises to become more effective at marketing their products and
lowering their costs. While these changes were going on, Chinese GNP
grew at an average of 9 percent a year, and Vietnamese GNP rose to over 7
percent a year by 1992 through 1997, although both economies began to
slow down as the Asian financial crisis affected their exports. China's and
Vietnam's experience, however, does not prove that gradualism is the right
answer for all countries. The large-scale state enterprise sector, the most difficult to reform, was a much smaller share of the economy in China and
Vietnam than in Russia or Poland. China and Vietnam could afford to
delay the full marketization of the large-scale state sector while they transformed the other three-quarters of the economy. In Russia and much of
Eastern Europe, the large-scale state sector constituted most of the economy. Delaying reform of that sector meant delaying the entire effort to introduce a market economy.

Most developing economies, however, have at least some elements of a
market system in place, and few have economies completely dominated by
large-scale state enterprises. In these economies, piecemeal reform of one sector rather than the whole economy often is possible. Import liberalization can
occur across the board, or it can begin with a few commodities and then
spread to others. Customs procedures can be streamlined even if many tariffs
remain high, and quotas can be abolished and replaced with tariffs. There is a
danger that political resistance to gradual change will build because the costs
may be more apparent than the benefits, but this could happen with across-
the-board liberalization as well. What is feasible in individual countries will
depend on the nature of the government and the base of its political support.

Even in market-dominated economies, however, structural adjustment
reforms may not always be able to be carried out gradually over time and
in a piecemeal fashion. In many Latin American countries, for example,
trade liberalization is difficult if one cannot control inflation. And control-

ling inflation is difficult because the government is committed to support-ing large vested interests at a level that cannot be paid for from existing sources of revenue; hence, there is a rise in the money supply and more in-flation. Many of these vested interests are the very workers and capitalists who own and work in the import-substituting industries that will be hurt by trade liberalization. Structural impediments to reform of this type are deeply rooted in the social and political systems of the country and may not be changeable without some radical across-the-board restructuring.

Some argue that the structural barriers to rapid reform are more eco-nomic than political. For a devaluation to improve the balance of pay-ments, for example, people must cut back their consumption of imports and producers of exports must be able to move quickly to expand pro-duction and sales. In technical terms, the **demand elasticities** for im-ports and the **supply elasticities** for exports must be large. If they are low, even if they are low only in the short run, the response to devalua-tion will be slow and the economy is more likely to be disrupted. Rapid change, to avoid disruption, requires elastic responses. Much of the re-sistance to reform comes from "elasticity pessimists," who feel that re-form will cut back on key inputs without eliciting a dynamic production response that will overcome the impact of the reduction in inputs on in-come and employment. Sometimes elasticity pessimists create self-fulfill-ing prophesies by not carrying through with reforms that would allow producers to respond with alacrity.

For all the complexity involved in meeting these conditions for effi-cient markets, an increasing number of countries are making the effort to do so. Some of the most successful efforts have been in Asia. Hong Kong and Singapore were relatively free market economies from the beginning. South Korea used government controls extensively in the 1970s but sys-tematically dismantled many of the controls in the 1980s and 1990s. Even when the Asian financial crisis hit Korea hard after 1997, the government, rather than backing away from market-oriented reforms, redoubled its ef-forts to dismantle most of the restrictions on the free movement of goods, services, and capital that remained. Taiwan has based its remarkable growth on small firms guided by market forces. China was one of the first avowedly socialist developing economies to introduce market reforms, first into agriculture and, after 1984 with less complete success, into industry. Indonesia moved from a government-regulated industrial and financial system in the 1970s to a more market-oriented economy in the 1980s and 1990s, although the financial crisis of the late 1990s forced some back-tracking as the government attempted to deal with the collapse of the In-donesian financial system (see the case study on page 192).[19]

19. David Lindauer and Michael Roemer, *Asia and Africa: Legacies and Opportunities in De-velopment* (San Francisco: ICS Press, 1994).

STABILIZATION AND DEREGULATION, INDONESIA 1986–90

Indonesia is an oil-producing country that suffered major losses when, from 1984 to 1986, world oil prices fell by half. Indonesia's annual export earnings were cut by $6 billion, about a quarter of total export revenues. At the same time, with export revenues denominated in dollars and much of its debt denominated in Japanese yen, the falling dollar added nearly 40 percent to Indonesia's annual debt service payments. These two external shocks forced the Indonesian government first to stabilize its economy then to make it less dependent on oil exports for both foreign exchange earnings and government revenue.

The government of President Suharto had been in office for two decades when the crisis struck and already had laid the groundwork for stabilization and reform. Indonesia's currency, the rupiah, had been fully convertible into foreign currencies since 1970. Devaluations in 1978 and 1983 had kept the rupiah in reasonable alignment with the dollar. The government was prevented by law from financing budget deficits from domestic sources, although it could, and did, borrow overseas. A tax reform enacted in 1983, which introduced a 10 percent value-added tax, already had begun to shift the burden of government revenue from oil exports to domestic taxes. When the oil market collapsed in 1985–86, the government acted quickly to correct imbalances: Civil service salaries were frozen for four years, overall government spending net of debt service fell by 6 percent of GDP, and a 33 percent devaluation of the rupiah in September 1986 enhanced the competitiveness of nonoil exports, on which export growth now depended. Because budget deficits were kept small and not financed by bank credit, money creation and hence inflation could be kept under control. Despite the devaluation, prices rose by only 9 percent a year in 1986 and 1987, then by around 6 percent in the next two years.

With the economy stabilized, policy makers instituted a strong but gradual five-year reform, called a *deregulation,* of Indonesia's international trade regime and its financial markets. In 1985 the president responded to corruption and costly delays in the customs service by bringing in a foreign private firm to manage the customs, a bold and unprecedented reform. In 1986 exporters were exempted from paying duties on imported inputs and allowed to buy them without regard to existing import restrictions. From 1986 to 1988, a series of deregulation "packages" eased the nontariff barriers to many imports. Financial reform packages in 1988 and 1990 allowed banks to determine their own deposit and lending rates, phased out subsidized credit, and otherwise deregulated financial markets. In some respects, the banks were slow to respond to market signals, but they competed vigorously for savers' deposits and vied to open new branches to serve customers all over the country, in urban and rural areas. Restrictions on domestic and foreign investment were reduced substantially in 1989; and the Jakarta stock exchange, now encouraged by government, experienced a boom in 1989 and 1990.

These reforms showed results almost immediately. The dollar value of nonoil exports rose by 22 percent a year from 1985 to 1989 and from 32 to 61 percent of total export earnings. As money flowed into the bank deposits, domestic credit expanded from 15 percent of GDP in 1985 to 32 percent in 1989. Government revenues rebounded. And GDP growth resumed, averaging nearly 7 percent a year between 1989 and 1993. A long-serving government, with shrewd policy leadership and a history of cautious reform, had acted quickly to adjust to a major external shock, then took deliberate steps to transform its economy into one of the more dynamic export-led developers in Asia.

Seven years later, in 1997, Indonesia was hit by another external shock from which it did not emerge unscathed as in the late 1980s. There were two fundamental differences from the earlier period. The external shock that came in the form of an Asia and then worldwide financial panic was much more severe than in 1985–86. Second, the reform effort itself had slowed down particularly with respect to the banking sector and the government's interference in that sector, interference that frequently took the form of government-directed loans to increasingly questionable projects supported by individuals close to President Suharto. The result was a collapse of the Indonesian financial system and then of the Suharto government. (See Chapters 13 and 14 for a more complete discussion of the financial crisis that began in 1997.)

In Latin America, many market reforms have stumbled over failed stabilization programs, including those in Argentina and Brazil during the 1980s. Among the exceptions, Bolivia's successful stabilization and reform already has been described. In its almost two decades of stabilization and structural adjustment, Chile took many wrong turns but seems to have found a workable formula during the 1980s and 1990s. Mexico deregulated its trade and industry in the 1990s while meeting large debt payments—a process reinforced by signing the North American Free Trade Agreement. In Africa, the most notable reforms have been attempted in countries such as Ghana, Uganda, and Tanzania, which had fallen into stagnation or even economic anarchy before righting themselves. The Ivory Coast and Kenya, never in such dire straights, have flirted with mild reforms that produced marginal results.

SUSTAINABLE DEVELOPMENT

An abundance of natural resources should be an advantage in economic development. Well-endowed countries such as Brazil, Nigeria, and Indonesia should be able to exploit their natural capital—climate, soil, natural forests, fisheries, and mineral deposits—to generate income in the early stages of development. If a large share of that income is saved, natural wealth can be converted into human-made capital such as an educated workforce, roads, power and telecommunications systems, productive agriculture, modern industry, growing cities, and the other assets of developed countries.

Many resource-rich countries, in fact, have achieved sustained economic growth and development. The United States, Canada, Australia, Denmark, New Zealand, and other high-income countries all relied heavily on their resource bases to fuel economic development. More recently, many countries with large petroleum deposits suddenly achieved great wealth during the oil price hikes of the 1970s, including Saudi Arabia, Kuwait, Brunei Darussalam, and others. In addition, a small number of resource-rich developing countries, notably Botswana, Indonesia, and Malaysia, have converted natural wealth into sustained rapid economic growth.[1] Yet, in recent decades, many if not most resource-rich developing countries, especially those in the tropics, actually have grown more *slowly*

---

1. Even after the effects of the Asian financial crisis, average per capita income in Malaysia and Indonesia still was more than three times larger in 1999 than it had been in 1965, with each country averaging annual per capita growth of well over 3 percent over the 35-year period.

than countries with scarce natural resources.[2] And, if we allow for the depletion of the resource base with development, as national income accounting systems do not, the performance of resource-rich developing countries would be even worse. This mixed record is a reflection of the difficulties inherent in managing natural resources in the development process. How should developing countries manage their resources to use them most productively in the short term and convert natural wealth into sustainable economic growth and development in the long term?

A country's environment—its air, water, diversity of biological species, and natural surroundings—are also valuable natural resources. However, to some extent all economic activity uses the environment as a dump for waste products, and environmental damage can have substantial effects on health and welfare. For example, contaminated water and the resulting diarrheal disease kills about 2 million children and causes about 900 million episodes of illness every year. Dust and soot in city air cause between 300,000 to 700,000 premature deaths every year.[3] In addition, soil erosion, water and air pollution, and deforestation can cause substantial economic losses to a wide variety of economic activities. Further, natural resources and wildlife have certain intrinsic value above their relationship to economic activity and human welfare.

Economic development and environmental management often are assumed to be at odds with each other, with many people supposing that an improved environment can come only at the cost of reduced growth and development. In some situations, in fact, real costs accrue to environmental management and preservation, and hard choices need to be made. Rapid but polluting growth today reduces welfare and incurs clean-up costs in the future. Is it rational for developing countries to pollute now and pay later? Can growth be sustained if it depletes the natural environment? However, in a great many situations development and environmental goals are complementary, and reducing environmental degradation can help lower production costs and directly improve economic output and welfare. Reduced air and water pollution, for example, should help support tourism, fisheries development, and agricultural production.

---

2. Harvard economists Jeffrey Sachs and Andrew Warner systematically examined a group of 95 countries from around the world between 1971 and 1989 and found that countries with larger primary product exports grew more slowly than resource-poor countries. In their study, an increase of 10 percentage points in the ratio of primary exports to GDP was associated on average with a decline of 0.7 percentage points in the rate of growth of per capita income. These findings are discussed in more detail in Chapter 16. See Jeffrey Sachs and Andrew Warner, "Natural Resource Abundance and Economic Growth," Harvard Institute for International Development discussion paper 517a, October 1995.

3. *World Development Report 1992: Development and the Environment*, (Washington, DC: World Bank, 1992).

These issues take on greater meaning when the whole planet is considered. Are we depleting the world's fisheries and cutting down its rainforests so fast that neither can regenerate and large numbers of species are becoming extinct? Will the world run out of minerals, especially fuels, before our ingenuity can develop technologies to harness renewable sources of energy and develop alternative materials? Is humankind polluting the air and contaminating water supplies faster than these resources can absorb our waste and cleanse themselves by natural processes? Are we heating earth's atmosphere so much with emissions of carbon dioxide from burning fossil fuels that economic development will change the world's climate, with dramatic and unpredictable effects on human welfare? And will these uses of our natural resource base have cumulative effects that are irreversible if we do not act soon enough?

In this chapter, we try to provide some frameworks that can be used to answer these questions. At the national level, it is not difficult to design policies that promote sustainable development, although governments often find it difficult to implement them. For the earth as a whole, the answers are more speculative and there are few mechanisms to enforce solutions to environmental problems.

Market Failures

The central theme of this chapter, and the main thrust of economists' approach to sustainability, is that, within a single country, properly working (efficient) markets can be the most effective mechanism available to promote efficient resource use, reduce environmental degradation, and generate sustainable development. At first blush, that proposition may be hard to accept. In Chapter 5, we developed the idea that competition among private producers, disciplined by markets, is more likely to promote rapid economic development than an economy dominated by government intervention. But Chapter 5 also discussed the conditions that cause markets to fail, when market prices deviate from scarcity values and lead private agents to make decisions that would maximize their earnings but cause uncompensated losses for others and society as a whole.

Prominent among these conditions are *externalities—costs* borne by the population at large but not by individual producers and *benefits* that accrue to society but cannot be captured by producers. The most important externalities are those caused by the depletion or degradation of natural resources, including the environment. If resources are depleted at rates faster than they can be replenished or substituted by human-made capital, development will be **unsustainable,** either nationally or globally. If markets fail in this fundamental way, how can they promote sustainable development? To resolve this apparent conflict, we first need to analyze in greater depth the reason that markets fail to allocate natural resources efficiently.

THE COMMONS

During the eighteenth century, as the Industrial Revolution began in England, cows still grazed on the commons of many villages in England and its American colonies. The essence of a village commons was **open access,** free of charge, to any member of the village. The first villages to take advantage of open access would have ample grazing for their livestock; their only cost was the time it would take to herd their animals to the commons, allow them to graze, and herd them home. But the amount of land was fixed and soil fertility and climate limited the quantity of grass. As more villagers used the commons, the grass became sparse, so the animals took longer to feed or, in the case of open rangeland, the herder was forced to travel farther to find forage, so that everyone's costs rose. The rising average cost to each herder eventually discouraged grazing on the commons. But none of the new entrants had to pay the rising costs to each of the previous entrants and more grazing took place than was in the interests of the village as a whole. Eventually, overgrazing destroyed the commons as a useful source of feed.

The disappearance of the grazing commons from eighteenth century villages probably was inevitable and certainly no global tragedy. But the dilemma of the commons is a widespread phenomenon, applicable to any limited resource to which access is unlimited by fee or regulation. Grazing on open range, whether in the U.S. West or the African savannah, has the same outcome. Open access to timberlands or access at fees well below the social cost results in overlogging and the destruction of native forests in Brazil, Ghana, Thailand, and many other tropical countries. Open access to fishing grounds in the North Atlantic, in Peru's Pacific waters, and in some inland lakes in Africa already has depleted fish stocks beyond their ability to regenerate. Free use of water from a stream benefits upland farmers, who have first access to the water, at the expense of downstream farmers, who get less water. Even traffic congestion in a city like Bangkok, Mexico City, or New York fits the description of a common property: City streets, to which access is free, are the common resource; each new vehicle causes worse traffic jams, forcing all previous entrants to drive more slowly.

The earth's environment, on which life depends, itself is composed of several common resources: air and the atmosphere, fresh water and the oceans, the earth's soils and minerals, and the diverse plant and animal species that live in this biosphere. Access to the environment typically is free. When manufacturers and farmers vent their waste into the air or water or create toxic dumps in the ground, they create health problems for the affected population, reduce the value of land in the affected area, destroy recreational potential, and generally reduce the welfare of people who value a clean environment. When lumber companies cut down a rainforest, they destroy the habitat of plant and animal species that are of value to others, including local populations that may harvest them or ecotourists who simply like to see them. They also may alter local climates, change patterns of water availability to surrounding farmers, and cause soil erosion. When we include the environment as a common resource, then much private activity generates external costs and market failure becomes a very general phenomenon.

EXTERNALITIES: A CLOSER LOOK

External costs and benefits are at the core of the common resource problem. A new producer creates higher costs for all previous entrants or all producers impose external costs on the general population. In either case, in the absence of regulation, taxes, or property rights for environmental quality, external cost are not borne by the producers who cause them and the prices of their products do not reflect the social costs of production. Thus, more of these resource-depleting or -polluting goods and services are produced and consumed than would be the case if prices reflected external costs. Hence, societies pollute more than their people would choose if markets reflected all social costs.

Figure 6–1 shows this. In a market with competitive producers, the supply curve S represents private marginal costs. Market equilibrium occurs at price P_1 with output Q_1. But, if this is a polluting industry, the external costs would make the social marginal cost, SMC, higher. If these costs were reflected in the market, the price would jump to P_2 and demand, and therefore output, would be reduced to Q_2. As less of the offending product would be grown or manufactured, there would be less environmental degradation.

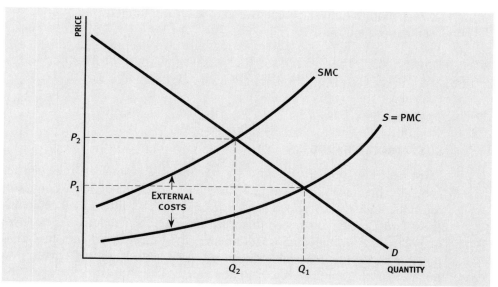

FIGURE 6–1 EXTERNAL DISECONOMIES. Polluters impose costs on others. If these external costs were reflected in the firms' costs, the social marginal cost curve, SMC, would prevail, the market price would be P_2, and output would be Q_2. But, because the firms do not bear these costs, their private marginal cost curve, PMC, is lower, so more, Q_1, of the polluting product is produced and consumed.

SOIL EROSION IN JAVA, INDONESIA[4]

Soil erosion in the uplands of Java is thought to be the main determinant of downstream siltation, water flow irregularities, and agrochemical runoff. Because the costs to low-lying areas from upland conservation are external to the upland farmers, taking on additional costs to conserve soil would not be economically sound for upland farmers. Costs for soil conservation include the time spent during the dry season constructing terraces and the cost of paid labor to complete the work, which takes far more time than a single farmer can spend. Assuming a four-month dry season and a holding of an acre, a single farmer could provide a maximum of 100 person days each dry season for soil conservation. The time required for terracing a plot of this size ranges from 375 person-days for gradual slopes and up to 900 person-days for steep slopes. If the farmer intends to add an intensive livestock system with the terracing, there are costs for adding a grass cover to the terraces and for the livestock itself. For slopes steeper than 45 to 50 percent, where the preferred method of soil conservation is to take land out of annual food-crop production to produce tree crops for cash income, there are both planting costs of around US$100/hectares in 1982 and opportunity costs while the trees mature. Unless compensated, the upland farmer will not undertake these measures.

4. From Edward B. Barbier, *Economics, Natural Resource Scarcity and Development* (London: Earthscan, 1989), pp. 160–80.

SUSTAINABLE HARVESTS

Most common property resources are **renewable resources:** they can regenerate themselves, given time. The village common or open rangeland reproduces grass each year. Fish breed new stocks, wild animals replenish their herds, and forests reseed themselves. Air and water cleanse themselves of pollutants through biological, chemical, or mechanical transfers. It is possible to exploit renewable resources sustainably if annual harvests do not exceed the annual growth of the stock. The difference between the rate of harvest and the rate of growth is called the **rate of depletion.** The faster these resources can be replenished, the greater the rate of economic growth that can be sustained indefinitely.

For renewable resources, three questions arise: What is the maximum sustainable harvest? What is the economically optimal harvest? And what is the danger of overexploiting the resource to the point of irretrievable loss or extinction? To answer these questions, it is convenient to explore a simple model of a fishery. Fish stocks are typically renewable within a relatively short period. Anything we can conclude about fisheries must apply with greater force to forests or the environment, which take longer to regenerate.

Before fishing begins, the stock of fish (in a lake or an ocean fishery) is large and cannot grow rapidly because its supply of food is limited. When fishing begins, food becomes relatively more abundant, the fish can replenish their numbers more rapidly, and the sustainable catch rises. But as the fishing effort increases, this process reaches a peak, after which the annual growth of the stock declines and so does the sustainable catch. If the fishing effort continues to grow, the fish stock may be so small or so scattered that reproduction cannot replace the catch at any level; this leads to extinction. The fishery model is an alternative way to describe the common resource problem. With the village common, we assumed that more entrants raise the cost for all. With the fishery, even if the costs of operating a boat are constant, the catch per boat, and hence fishermen's revenues, decline.

Fishing's total costs and revenue are shown in Figure 6–2, which gives total revenue for the fishery on the y axis and the total effort by all those fishing on the x axis. Assuming a constant price for fish, the total revenue curve, TR, first rises with effort, then peaks and begins to fall. At some point, overfishing depletes the stock so much that the fish cannot reproduce at the rate of extraction and become extinct. The total cost of fishing, TC, is assumed to rise linearly: Each boat puts to sea at the same cost, so total cost is simply the unit cost times the number of boats. Note that costs include the minimal profit necessary to keep those fishing in business.[5]

If fishing is done by small, independent operators who have open access, the level of effort will increase as long as new entrants earn some net revenue over costs and necessary profit. Fishers earn net revenues up to E_1, the point where TC intersects TR. The last boat to enter the fishery just balances costs and revenues. Note that, because these are total revenue and cost curves, once the marginal boat is in the fishery, no net revenues are left for any of the fishing units. The external costs of exploiting the common fishery have caused this result.

5. For a complete discussion of the fisheries model, see any of a number of texts on natural resources listed in the readings at the end of the book. This abbreviated version is based on Tom Tietenberg, *Environmental and Natural Resource Economics*, 5th ed. (New York: Addison-Wesley, 2000).

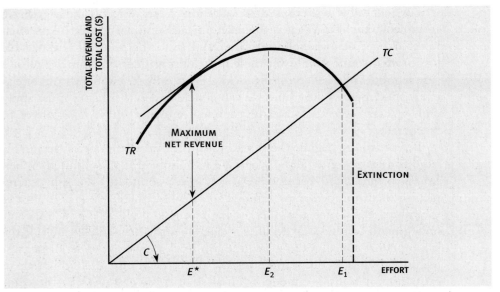

FIGURE 6-2 FISHERY ECONOMICS. As the level of fishing effort increases, sustainable total revenue (*TR*) at first rises, then peaks at E_2, and begins to fall, until the fish cannot reproduce fast enough to replace the catch and extinction occurs. The total cost of effort is *TC*, assuming each boat puts to sea at the same unit cost. With open access, effort reaches E_1. The optimal outcome would maximize the net revenue from the fisheries—the difference between *TR* and *TC*—at E^*, where marginal revenue (the slope of *TR*) equals marginal cost (the slope of *TC*).

In Chapter 12, we will see that a society wishing to maximize its economic welfare will utilize resources to the point where net present value is maximized for any activity. In the fishery case, that rule is equivalent to maximizing the net revenue to all fishers, the difference between total revenue and total cost.[6] We know from microeconomic principles that maximum net revenue is achieved by equating marginal cost and marginal revenue. In Figure 6-2, the marginal cost is the slope of the total cost line. Marginal revenue is the increase in the catch for a unit increase in effort, valued at a constant price, which is the slope of the *TR* curve at any point. The slope of *TR* is the same as the slope of *TC* at level of effort E^*. This level of effort, maximizing net revenue, would be achieved by a fishing company that had exclusive rights to the fishery or by a government that regulated access by individual fishermen.

Another term for *net revenue* in this case is **resource rent.** A *rent* is a return to producers in excess of that necessary to keep them in production. Because the total cost curve in Figure 6-2 includes necessary profit, any revenue in excess of *TC* is a rent. Therefore the rule to optimize the ex-

6. It is assumed implicity that the discount rate is 0, so that net benefits tomorrow have the same weight as those today. We relax that assumption in the next section.

ploitation of a natural resource—maximize net revenue—is equivalent to prescribing the maximization of resource rents. This is the rule a private owner of the fishery would follow, just as the private owner of agricultural land would seek to maximize the rental payments from tenant farmers.

Note that the optimal level of effort E^* is much lower than E_1, the effort expended by fishers with open access. The economically optimal effort also is less than that needed to achieve the biologically determined maximum catch E_2. So long as there is some cost to fishing effort, the economically optimal effort occurs where the TR curve has positive slope, to the left of E_2. It is not in society's interest to extract the maximum sustainable yield from the fishery or from any renewable resource; a society gains maximum welfare by extracting less than the maximum yield.

Can profit-maximizing fishers cause extinction? This could happen in an open-access fishery if the unit cost were so low that the TC line intersected the TR curve along the dashed line, where the stock had become too small to replace the annual catch. It also could happen at a lower level of effort, such as E_1, if environmental conditions caused a reduction in fishes' reproduction rates for a time, so that what had been a sustainable catch became unsustainable. Once overfishing has become apparent, fishers might adjust by reducing their effort. However, consider a lake fisher in Africa: once he has a boat and net, his cost of fishing is only the opportunity cost of his time, which is probably quite low, while the benefits of withdrawal accrue not to him but to other fishermen. Hence, there is little incentive to withdraw from the industry. The exhaustion of fisheries in the North Atlantic, in the Humboldt Current off the coast of Peru, and in some lakes in Africa shows that overfishing is not just a theoretical possibility.

Similar models can be used to describe the exploitation of other renewable resources. The application to game hunting is clear. Where hunting is effectively controlled, as is deer hunting in the United States or the hunting of large cats in many African countries, stocks can be maintained. Where hunting is less effectively controlled, extinction becomes a real possibility, because the cost of hunting is so low. For poachers of elephant and rhinoceros in Africa, costs are low, the value of tusks or horns is very high, and poachers place little value on sustaining stocks into the future. The African tourist industry benefits from big game and tries to conserve it, but the poachers do not share in the benefits from this lucrative industry. The reduction in earnings from tourism slows economic growth.

Natural forests regenerate over much longer periods than fish or mammals, and second-growth forest is likely to be different from native stands. Tropical rain-forest species can take 70 years or so to grow to harvestable maturity, and economic rotation of northern species such as Douglas fir are about the same length.[7] Moreover, if harvesting greatly alters the habitat, regeneration can take longer or become impossible. In parts of Indonesia, inappropriate logging techniques allow the generation of a grass, called *alang-alang*, that has no economic value and prevents both reforestation and farming; forest land literally is laid to waste.

Environmental amenities, such as clean air and water, have similar properties. Waste can be dumped in them and water can be consumed without permanent impairment, so long as these uses do not exceed the capacity of air and water to cleanse themselves or rainfall to replace ground water. But, at least until environmental regulation became common over the past two decades, air and water were common properties with virtually free access. The extreme air pollution of cities such as Los Angeles, Mexico City, Bangkok, and Jakarta testify to the overuse of this common resource. Industrial pollution of many waterways in North America, the "killing" of the Aral Sea in Uzbekistan by excessive irrigation that reduced its supply of river water, and the dumping of household waste in Asian rivers are examples of burdening water resources beyond their medium-term abilities to cleanse themselves. Private and public wells have seriously depleted aquifers in many places, sometimes to the point of permitting the incursion of seawater, which renders them permanently useless.

THE VALUE OF TIME

So far, we have skirted the issue of time by discussing sustainable harvests as if all years were of equal value. That is unrealistic and especially difficult to sustain in talking about exhaustible resources. We know from the discussion of discounting in Chapter 12 that benefits and costs realized in the future have less present value than those that are realized immediately. If the discount rate (the real interest rate) is r percent per year, then in any future year n, the present value placed on resource flows is $1/(1 + r)^n$.[8]

The more productive is capital and the scarcer are savings that finance investment, the higher is the discount rate and the lower is the value placed on future benefits and costs. In developing countries, we expect real discount rates of 10 percent a year or so; at that rate, a benefit of $100 accruing 15 years from now would be worth only $24 today ($100 \times 1/1.10^{15} = \$24$). This indicates that people are not so willing to wait long for benefits from their investments. The more developed a country becomes, the lower is the likely return on new investments (because the capital stock has become larger), the more can be saved (because incomes are

---

7. Tom Tietenberg, *Environmental and Natural Resource Economics,* 4th ed. (Glenview, IL: Scott, Foresman, 1988), p. 245.

8. See page 433.

higher), and the more willing is the population to be to wait for future benefits; hence the appropriate discount rate is lower. If a country's discount rate were 5 percent a year, the value of $100 of benefits received in 15 years would be $48.

To see how discounting affects the allocation of scarce resources over time, consider an oversimplified but instructive hypothetical example. Zambia has a copper deposit that is expected to last two decades and the government is trying to decide how much copper to extract and export in each of the first and second decades. Zambia's output is large enough to affect the world price. For each decade, the higher the rate of extraction and the more Zambia exports, the lower it will drive the price of copper on world markets. If extraction costs are constant, then in each decade the net revenue from copper exports (world price less mining cost) will decline as more ore is extracted. How much should be mined in each decade?

The answer depends on the **marginal net benefit** (MNB), or the additional revenue net of additional costs from producing one more unit (mining one more ton of copper ore) in each period. The rule for maximizing net benefits over time is to equate the present value of the marginal net benefit for each period; that is, $MNB_1 = MNB_2/(1 + r)$. (In this example, r is the discount rate between decades, not years.) The discount factor $(1 + r)$ on the right-hand side of the equation indicates that Zambia places a lower value on benefits received in the second decade than in the first, since it generally can expect to earn higher income in the future if it can save and invest more today. If the marginal net benefit is higher in period 1 than the discounted benefit in period 2, it pays the country to mine more copper in period 1 and less in period 2, until the present value of the net benefits are equal at the margin. Note that the maximizing condition can be satisfied only if MNB_1 is less than the undiscounted value of MNB_2. Because the price and thus MNB decline as output rises, net benefits are maximized over both decades if Zambia mines and exports more copper in the first decade than in the second.[9]

This highly simplified example has important implications for resource management. First, even though the current generation, mining in the first decade, is concerned about the welfare of the next generation, it will consume some of the nonrenewable resource. Second, the current generation should consume more of the resource than the next generation so long as time has value and the discount rate is positive. This will be the case whenever profitable investments are to be made and savings are there to finance them, so that the next generation will have higher income than

9. If Zambia's exports of copper were too small to affect world market prices, this result still would hold if the marginal cost of mining increased with the quantity mined in each period, as well it might.

the current one. Third, the higher the discount rate and the higher the expected level of future income, the more should be exploited by the current generation.

This two-period example easily can be extended to the more realistic case of annual discounting over many years or generations, for both renewable and nonrenewable resources. Discounting applies with particular force to the harvesting and regeneration of natural forests. Assume that a private firm owns a large area of forest with secure rights along into the future, and for simplicity ignore the nontimber products of the forest. The timber company has three choices. It can fell all the marketable timber now for immediate profit and then invest the proceeds in another business. It can wait for some future time to do the same thing. Or it can harvest the timber continuously over time. These three options are depicted in Figure 6–3.

Felling all trees now brings in the revenue, net of costs, shown in rectangle *A*. Because this is done in the present, no discounting is necessary. Waiting until some future time to harvest the entire forest yields the revenue in rectangle *B*. Because world timber prices have been rising at about 2 percent a year in real terms and because the trees may produce more volume in the future, the company can expect to earn higher current revenues by waiting, as indicated by the dashed rectangle. But, to compare future revenues *B* with current revenues *A*, future revenues must be discounted; this yields the clear rectangle at *B*. The decision to harvest continuously is shown by option *C*, the solid line rising continuously over time as prices rise and trees grow; its discounted value is the area under the solid line.

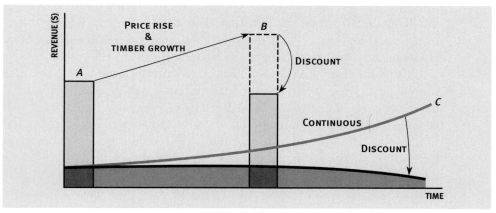

FIGURE 6–3 DISCOUNTED VALUE OF FOREST HARVEST OPTIONS. Option *A* is to cut all trees now. Option *B* is to wait for benefits from tree growth and rising real prices, but discounting reduces the present value of future net revenues. Option *C* is a continuous harvest, made more attractive by rapid tree growth and price rises but less so by a high discount rate.

If the discount rate exceeds the rate of price increase plus the rate of timber growth, the value of option *A* will exceed the discounted value of either *B* or *C*. Immediate harvest is likely to be the optimal choice for mature forests, with little or no potential timber growth. But if the forest is not mature, so that potential growth is substantial, and if the discount rate is not very high, discounted net revenues from a future harvest at *B* or a continuous harvest, option *C*, may exceed those at *A*.

Any of these options can result in a sustainable harvest. Whether trees are logged all at once or continuously, the natural forest can regenerate itself if nearby forests can provide seeds and if the logged land is protected from encroachment by loggers, fuelwood gatherers, herders, and farmers. For some forests, clear-cutting large tracts, as under options *A* and *B*, are compatible with sustainable harvesting. For others, selective and continuous logging may be more sustainable. The period for complete regeneration can be long, however. In the Indonesian rainforest, it takes up to 70 years for trees to mature, although it may not be economically efficient to wait for full maturity.

Environmental protection has the same time dimension. Cleaning up a degraded environment or forgoing pollution altogether entails current costs, or the loss of current output, in favor of greater environmental benefits in the future. The most serious deterrents to such investments are that the benefits of clean air and water and more attractive scenery are external to the firm and most environmental benefits cannot be valued or marketed easily. But, leaving this aside, high discount rates—implying a low regard for the future compared to the present—also work against environmental protection or cleanup.

This is one reason why poorer countries, with high discount rates, may place less emphasis on environmental amenities than richer countries. High discount rates can help to explain why Brazil and Malaysia cut down their tropical rainforests at unsustainable rates and why authorities in Mexico City and Bangkok appear less concerned about air pollution then authorities in Los Angeles.

Policy Solutions

The market failures that lead to overexploitation of natural resources stem from external costs that are not borne by producers. Even in a well-functioning market economy, externalities require government intervention to reach efficient market outcomes. The government can bestow property rights on private users, regulate access to common resources, impose taxes that reflect external costs, and issue tradable access rights. We discuss each in turn.

PROPERTY RIGHTS

Common properties generate external costs because no one owns or controls the right to exploit them. For some resources, a simple solution would be to confer ownership, which economists call **property rights,** on a single individual or company. As long as the owner is a profit maximizer and sells output in a competitive market, the socially optimal outcome will be achieved without further government intervention.[10] Nor does the owner have to be the producer to achieve optimal resource use. The owner who rents the resource to some of the same producers who previously had common property access will maximize profit by charging rents that limit access and production to the optimal level.

Property rights, to be effective, must be exclusive and well defined, leaving no doubt to the owners and possible competing claimants about what has been conferred and to whom. Rights need to be secure, so that the risk of loss through legal challenge or expropriation is reduced and enforceable through the judicial system. Ownership must be valid over a long enough horizon that the owners have a stake in the long-term, sustainable exploitation of the resource. Longevity converts the resource into an asset for the producer, who can reap the benefits from investments in improving and sustaining its productivity. And the rights must be transferable, so the owner can realize the benefits of the resource asset by selling the property at any time.[11]

For some resources, such as forests, rangeland, or mineral deposits, the application of property rights is straightforward. The resource is a tangible property and exclusive ownership is enforceable. The government can privatize the asset by granting or selling rights to private producers. If the right is granted, then the producer gains all the resource rents. If it is sold for a fixed fee, government shares part of the rent. But, if the property right is auctioned, potential owners will bid up the price to the point where they still can earn a reasonable profit on their investment of capital and labor[12] but have forgone most or all the resource rents, which then are captured by the government. Such auction systems now commonly are employed in a few developing and transi-

10. If the owner is a monopolist in the product market, output would be below, and the price above, the social optimum. with the possible exception of a few minerals such as diamonds, markets for the products of common resources are fairly competitive (i.e., firms face elastic demand), especially when close substitutes are considered.

11. Theodore Panayotou, *Green Markets: The Economics of Sustainable Development* (San Francisco: ICS Press, 1993), pp. 35–37.

12. Remember that rents are defined as revenue net of costs and that costs include the profits necessary to keep capital engaged in the industry.

COMMUNAL FOREST MANAGEMENT IN INDIA[13]

In the village of Arabari in West Bengal, officials began in 1970 to experiment with a form of communal management of the forest that had some of the desirable characteristics of property rights. Villagers had been cutting the forest and earning much of their income from the sale of fuelwood. The Arabari experiment employed villagers in planting trees and grass and provided fuelwood and construction materials to the village from outside sources at cost. Villagers also received 25 percent of the sales of mature trees. In return, villagers were asked to prevent encroachment of the forest. After 15 years, the forests had been restored and village incomes were higher than before the experiment. The Forest Department expanded the arrangements to cover 700 village groups and so rehabilitated some 170,000 acres of forest.

13. Reported in Panayotou, *Green Markets,* pp. 118–19.

tional economies, including Malaysia and Romania. Short-run revenue maximization does not necessarily translate into long-run maximization of resource rents, however, if the structure of concession agreements does not promote use of logging methods that ensure regeneration. Concessions to exploit the tropical rainforest are common in Indonesia and Malaysia, although the terms are badly flawed and do not result in optimal regeneration. Most timberland in the United States is privately owned and harvested and replanted on a sustainable basis, although the result often is plantations of uniform species rather than regenerated natural forest.

Property rights can be held by communities. If local populations have traditional access to the forest, for example, and can enforce this right, it is in their interest to achieve optimal output because they benefit from the resulting rents. The struggle over property rights in Brazil's Amazon is in part a conflict between local communities that traditionally have exploited the rainforest sustainably (though perhaps not optimally) and modern companies whose incentives are to overexploit this resource. In Kenya, county councils have been given property rights to some of the game parks that attract international tourists in large numbers; the entry fees charged give local governments an incentive to preserve these assets against poaching and grazing by cattle.

For some common property resources, however, it is difficult (and in some cases impossible) to convey property rights as these usually are understood. Both law and ease of access make it impractical to own an ocean and difficult (although not impossible) to own a lake fishery. Nor can a company own the air and water that accommodate its waste, because the polluter cannot easily exclude other users and therefore cannot charge for access to clean air and water. Nevertheless, governments can create property rights even in these common resources by legislating, granting, and enforcing quotas, access permits, licenses to operate, and other legal instruments that give some agents the right to fish, harvest, pollute, or otherwise use a common resource. Because these instruments convey only limited access, they have value to the holder and can be treated as any other asset.

GOVERNMENT REGULATION

As an alternative to conveying private property rights, governments themselves can act as the owners of common resources and directly regulate their use. Governments can limit the quantity of a hunter's kill, a fisher's catch, a logger's haul, a rancher's herd, or a polluter's emissions. And they can regulate the kinds of equipment that can or must be used: Some kinds of fishing nets, boats, or navigation equipment have been banned; hunters may be restricted in their choice of weapons; polluters are required to install equipment that scrubs gas emissions and treats wastewater.

Quantity regulations raise two issues. First, how do the regulators know the optimal levels of access and output? If property rights can be conveyed, efficient outcomes will be approached through market forces and no government judgments are needed. But if regulation replaces the market, regulators need to estimate the characteristics of both producers' costs and users' demand for the products of a common resource. To get a sense of these information requirements, consider the regulation of air pollution.[14]

The external costs of pollution are manifest in the reduced welfare of others: poor health, unsightly environment, lower property values, fewer and more expensive recreational possibilities, and possibly reduced productivity and income. If these costs could be measured, they would be depicted by a curve such as MEC in Figure 6–4, which shows the marginal external cost of pollution (measured along the horizontal axis). Any reduction in pollution means a reduction in this cost or, equivalently, an increase in the marginal external benefit of abatement.

---

14. This approach to the economies of pollution abatement is based on the treatment by David W. Pearce and R. Kerry Turner, *Economics of Natural Resources and the Environment* (Baltimore: Johns Hopkins Press, 1990), Chaps. 4–7.

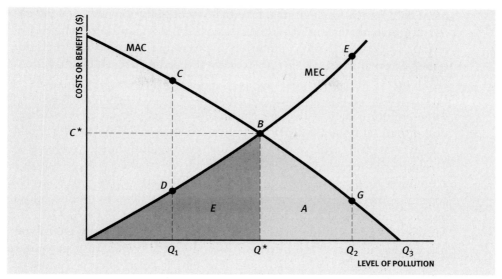

FIGURE 6–4   OPTIMAL LEVEL OF POLLUTION. The marginal external cost of pollutants, borne by the population, is given by MEC; the marginal cost of abatement, borne by the firm, is MAC. The total cost to society (the area under E plus A) is minimized and pollution is optimal at Q^*, where MEC = MAC.

However, there is a cost to abating pollution. The polluting firm, say, a petrochemical plant, can reduce its effluents either by changing its production process, by installing abatement equipment such as gas scrubbers and water treatment plants, or by reducing output. Schedule MAC traces these marginal abatement costs. At any point along MAC, the cost shown is that of the lowest-cost method of abatement. Moving from right (high pollution) to left (lower pollution), MAC rises because it becomes increasingly costly to clean up air or water the stricter are the standards or the lower the level of contamination. It is important to recognize that these costs of abatement, although borne by the petrochemical firm, also are costs to society because they involve either less consumption of steel or savings spent on abatement that otherwise might have been spent on investment in other goods or services people want. These abatement costs thus have equal weight to the benefits gained by reducing pollution.

Society's (and government's) aim should be to minimize the combined costs of pollution and its abatement. This is achieved at Q^* in Figure 6–4, where MEC = MAC; $Q_3 - Q^*$ of pollution has been abated (assuming for convenience that Q_3 is the maximum amount of pollution), and Q^* of pollution remains. Because these are marginal cost curves, the total external cost of pollution is the area E under MEC from 0 to Q^*. And the total cost or abatement is given by the shaded area A under the MAC curve between Q^* and Q_3. With less pollution, such as Q_1, the marginal abatement cost exceeds the marginal external cost of pollution and the total cost of additional abatement, $Q_1 Q^* BC$, exceeds the net gain from reduced pollution, $Q_1 Q^* BD$. If more pollution is permitted, such as Q_2, the additional external cost, $Q^* Q_2 EB$, exceeds the reduced cost of abatement, $Q^* Q_2 GB$.

Therefore society is better off, in that it suffers minimal costs, with some pollution than with none, just as society gains from some exploitation of natural resources, even nonrenewable ones. But how do the regulators, who wish to achieve this optimal level of pollution, know what it is? To find Q^*, they would have to know all the external costs of pollution as a function of the levels of contaminants in the air, water, and soil. The costs in some cases are substantial. Soil erosion reduces economic output by an estimated 0.5–1.5 percent per year in Costa Rica, Malawi, Mali, and Mexico.[15] Various studies have estimated the economic costs of environmental degradation in countries in Asia to range from 1 to 9 percent of GNP (Table 6–1). Particulates and lead emissions in Jakarta, Indonesia, cause damage estimated to be up to 2 percent of GNP. In Pakistan, damage from air and water pollution combined with productivity losses from deforestation and soil erosion amount to more than 3 percent of GNP. And the costs of environmental, degradation and pollution in China may be the equivalent of a staggering 8.5 percent of GNP.[16]

In addition to these estimates of direct economic costs, finding Q^* requires having some method of estimating the values people place on environmental amenities such as clean air, water, and soil. Survey and other methods are being developed to measure such valuations, but these still are experimental and beyond the scope of governments in many developing countries.[17] Finally, the regulators need to know the costs of abatement. Yet firms subject to regulation have an incentive to overstate these costs in the hope of being allowed to emit more pollutants and avoid abatement costs.

In the absence of such knowledge, regulators must, and do, set arbitrary standards based on studies estimating the impact of pollutants on human health, animal survival, forest dieback (from acid rain) and regeneration, and presumed climate changes. Because of the large uncertainty in such estimates and the conflicting objectives of environmental policy, these standards become political issues, subject to contention by interest groups speaking for the environment, the public, industry, and developers. These policy struggles, the establishment of compliance staffs in both the govern-

15. *World Development Report 1992: Development and the Environment,* p. 56.

16. These findings are summarized in the Asian Development Bank study *Emerging Asia: Changes and Challenges* (Manila: ADB, 1997), p. 223.

17. Paul R. Portney, "The Contingent Valuation Debate: Why Economists Should Care." *Journal of Economic Perspectives,* 8, no. 4 (Fall 1994), 3–17.

TABLE 6–1	COSTS OF ENVIRONMENTAL DEGRADATION IN ASIA			
			ANNUAL COST	
COUNTRY	FORM OF DAMAGE	YEAR	$ MILLION	% GNP
CHINA	SOIL EROSION, DEFORESTATION, WATER SHORTAGE, WETLAND DESTRUCTION	1990	13,900–26,000	3.8–7.3
	HEALTH AND PRODUCTIVITY LOSSES FROM CITIES' URBAN POLLUTION	1990	6,300–9,300	7.1–2.5
	GENERAL ENVIRONMENTAL DEGRADATION AND POLLUTION	1989	31,000	8.5
INDONESIA	HEALTH EFFECTS OF PARTICULATES AND LEAD IN JAKARTA	1989	2,164	2
PAKISTAN	HEALTH IMPACTS OF AIR AND WATER POLLUTION AND PRODUCTIVITY LOSSES FROM DEFORESTATION AND EROSION	EARLY 1990S	1,700	3.3
PHILIPPINES	HEALTH AND PRODUCTIVITY LOSSES FROM WATER AND AIR POLLUTION IN MANILA VICINITY	EARLY 1990S	335–410	0.8–1.0
THAILAND	HEALTH EFFECTS OF PARTICULATES AND LEAD	1989	1,602	2

Source: Asian Development Bank, *Emerging Asia: Changes and Challenges.*

ment and polluting firms, and the ensuing lawsuits all add significant costs to the imposition of environmental standards and so reduce the gains to society. In developing countries where rent seeking is an important feature of political and legal systems, polluting industrialists are likely to use their financial and political muscle to thwart environmental regulation.

The second question raised by regulation is its efficiency compared to other methods. Governments have imposed many different methods for restricting access to common resources. They have specified hours or days of access to fisheries; completely barred access to some forests or fisheries; set quotas for individual hunters, loggers, and fishers; limited the specific levels of pollution for each plant in a region; prohibited particularly efficient equipment such as gill nets or even, in Alaska for a time, motorized boats;[18] mandated the use of abatement equipment; and shut off electricity to conserve water in hydroelectric sites. These methods may get the economy closer to the optimal rate of use but are unlikely to achieve it. Even if they did, the outcome would not be optimal for society because the controls themselves impose costs on producers and consumers.

18. Tietenberg, *Environmental and Natural Resource Economics,* 4th ed., p. 271.

In Figure 6–4, regulators might achieve output Q^* by requiring certain equipment for each plant or setting output quotas for each producer. But, while the MAC curve assumes that each polluter makes the most efficient choice of technique for abating pollution, regulators are unlikely to know the costs of each option and have little incentive to find the most efficient way to reduce emissions. So their required method of achieving Q^* is likely to raise the MAC schedule above its minimum and unnecessarily raise the costs borne by society. In controlling the fisheries depicted in Figure 6–2, regulators might achieve optimal catch E^* by enforcing certain practices or prohibiting certain equipment, and so raise the cost of fishing to each entrant. But the higher costs would dissipate the rents available from the optimum level of effort, and these rents no longer would be available to society for other uses.[19]

TAXATION

In principle, the government also could achieve optimal rates of resource use by imposing taxes that reduce the incentive for producers to enter common properties or manufacture polluting products.[20] A tax might be imposed on output that represents the external costs of production, so that the private marginal cost schedule shifts up to equal the social marginal cost schedule.[21] This might take the form of a tax on each ton of steel or petrochemicals at a rate representing the external cost of pollution or a tax on gasoline to cover the costs of both pollution and traffic congestion. A tax, equal to the maximum resource rent, could be levied on the level of effort or on the quantity harvested by fishers or foresters, so that their private costs would induce them collectively to take the optimal harvest.[22]

If the tax is on output or level of effort, the incentive is to reduce production of the good with external costs. If the tax can be levied on the externality itself, there is an additional incentive to invest in reducing external costs. For example, a tax on the quantity of pollutants would give petrochemical plants an incentive to abate pollution, because the tax then would be reduced. Malaysia has had success with emissions fees on its palm oil industry (see the case study example). China has introduced emissions fees on industrial and urban wastewater, air pollution, and solid waste. Several of the transitional economies in Central and Eastern Europe

---

19. Ibid., p. 270.

20. See Gunnar Eskeland and Shantayanan Devarajan, *Taxing Bads by Taxing Goods: Pollution Control with Presumptive Charges* (Washington, DC: World Bank, 1996).

21. In Figure 6–1, the tax would shift the PMC schedule up to coincide with the SMC schedule.

22. In Figure 6–2, a tax equal to the maximum resource rent would move the cost schedule up to TC' and induce fishers to expend the optimum effort E^*.

(including Poland, Estonia, Latvia, Russia, Romania, and Bulgaria) have experimented with a range of pollution charges, based largely on modifying systems that were in place before the breakup of the Soviet Union in 1989.[23] In general, however, attempts to tax pollutants have had limited success (and even less success in high-income countries than in developing and transitional economies). Monitoring is difficult (and expensive), charge rates are generally set too low, and tax avoidance can be relatively easy. An alternative might be to tax the polluting product but to reduce or eliminate the tax if pollution abatement equipment is in operation.

Taxes that internalize external costs have two important advantages over regulation. First, they allow the producer to choose the method of reducing access to a common resource, so that rents are not dissipated in wasteful expenditures forced by regulators. The cost savings with this flexibility can be substantial. Studies in the United States comparing the costs of water pollution abatement indicate that "command and control" approaches with strict regulation can cost up to three times more than the alternative least cost method of achieving the same goal. For air pollution, command and control approaches have been found to cost from 2–22 times more than the least cost alternative.[24] An optimal tax, however, requires the same information as optimal regulation: In the case of pollution, knowledge of the relation between pollution and output, of the cost of abatement, and of the external costs to the population. However, given a consensus that pollution is too great or a common resource is being overexploited, the government can move in the right direction by imposing some tax, observing outcomes, and adjusting the tax rate if necessary.

Second, taxes can generate substantial revenues for the government. Carbon taxes (mainly on gasoline) can contribute an estimated 2–8 percent to government revenues in many countries, as shown in Table 6–2. In Indonesia, increasing stumpage fees on logging concessions could add an estimated 6–8 percent to government revenues, pollution charges for the greater Jakarta area could generate 1–2 percent, and congestion charges on urban roads could add another 2–3 percent to government revenues.[25] These revenues can be used to fund environmental programs or in other ways to compensate citizens for the harm caused by pollution and other environmental degradation.

23. See Robert Bohm, Chazhong Ge, Milton Rusell, Jinnan Wang, and Jintian Yang, "Environmental Taxes: China's Bold New Initiative," *Environment,* 40, no. 7 (September 1998); and Randall Bluffstone and Bruce A. Larson, eds., *Controlling Pollution in Transition Economies* (Cheltenham, UK: Edward Elgar, 1997).

24. These estimates are summarized in Tietenberg, *Environmental and Natural Resource Economics,* 5th ed. pp. 372 and 453.

25. The figures are from Theodore Panayotou, *Instruments of Change: Motivating and Financing Sustainable Development* (London: Earthscan, 1998).

REDUCING WATER POLLUTION FROM PALM OIL MILLS IN MALAYSIA[26]

Between 1970 and 1989, Malaysia's output of palm oil, a major export, grew 12-fold. Unfortunately, the processing of palm oil in rural mills generates 2.5 tons of wastewater for every ton of crude palm oil produced. By the late 1970s, effluents from the mills had severely polluted over 40 rivers in Malaysia, mainly by depleting their oxygen. Pollution killed freshwater fish, endangered mangroves on the coast that are essential for traditional marine fisheries, contaminated the major source of drinking water for many rural Malays, and emitted a stench that made several villages uninhabitable.

Water pollution became so serious that, in 1974, the government passed the Environmental Quality Act and in 1975 established the Department of the Environment (DOE). In 1977, the DOE announced standards for the quality of effluents from palm oil mills that were to become increasingly stringent over time. To provide the reluctant mills with incentives to comply, the DOE established a two-part licensing fee with a constant charge per unit of effluent plus an excess fee that varied with the oxygen-depleting potential of the discharge. Therefore the mills could choose their least-cost option: Either pay the costs of reducing and treating their effluent or pay the higher fees for discharging waste that exceeded the environmental quality standard.

The industry responded by developing and installing improved treatment technologies; by developing commercial products, such as fertilizer and animal feed, from their waste products; and by recovering methane that could be used to generate electricity. Over time, the economic incentives became less important as inflation eroded their value, and direct controls became less important. Nevertheless, the market-oriented regime set in motion a sharp reversal of polluting practices. By 1989, even though palm oil production had reached an all-time high, three out of four mills complied with the stringent sixth-generation standards and the oxygen-depleting potential of emitted waste was only 1 percent of its mid-1970s level.

---

26. From Jeffrey R. Vincent, "Reducing Effluent While Raising Affluence: Water Pollution Abatement in Malaysia," Harvard Institute for International Development, March 1993.

TABLE 6–2	POTENTIAL REVENUE OF A CARBON TAX IN SELECTED COUNTRIES, 1991		
COUNTRY	US$ MILLIONS	% GOVERNMENT REVENUE	% GDP
GERMANY	1,773	0.54	0.16
JAPAN	2,371	0.73	0.10
UNITED SATES	12,461	1.37	0.28
BRAZIL	503	0.50	0.17
CHINA	5,699	8.81	1.87
INDIA	1,454	3.85	0.57
INDONESIA	263	1.62	0.35
MEXICO	772	3.16	0.55
NIGERIA	90	2.33	0.37
POLAND	1,257	5.07	1.97
FORMER SOVIET UNION	10,129	N.A.	N.A.
WORLD	54,810	N.A.	N.A.

Source: A. Shah and B. Larsen, "Carbon Taxes, the Greenhouse Effect, and Developing Countries," policy research paper no. 095, Washington, DC: World Bank.

MARKETABLE PERMITS

A fourth intervention is to create a property right where none exists by issuing **marketable permits,** granting the holders the right to harvest a common resource up to a given limit or giving producers a license to pollute the environment up to specified amounts. Although environmentalists sometimes scoff at the notion of a "right" to pollute or exploit resources, in fact these permits may be the most efficient way to reduce pollution and resource overuse.

Figure 6–5 shows how a pollution permit works.[27] The MAC and MEC curves are copied from Figure 6–4. Say that the government knows the optimal level of pollution and auctions off emissions permits totaling Q^*. Any firm polluting without a permit would, if detected, be fined or shut down. (Thus, permits have the same enforcement requirements as regulations or taxes.) If MAX represents the cost of pollution abatement for all firms in the market, they would bid up the price of permits to P^*. The MAC schedule shows that firms can reduce pollution from Q_3 to Q^* at costs less than P^*. Without permits, however, they would have to reduce pollution below Q^* at costs higher than P^*. Therefore the MAC schedule is the demand curve for permits. Either the government can issue a given number and observe the auction price paid for them or it can set a price and issue whatever number of permits is demanded by polluters.

27. This figure is adapted from Pearce and Turner, *Economics of Natural Resources,* pp. 110–13; and Tietenberg, *Environmental and Natural Resource Economics,* 4th ed., pp. 319–20.

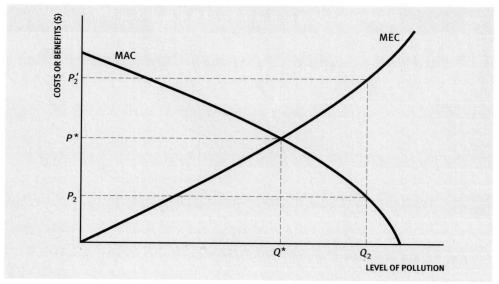

FIGURE 6–5   MARKETABLE PERMITS TO POLLUTE. The MAC schedule shows the demand for pollution rights. If rights are issued to pollute up to Q_2, these are worth P_2 to polluters, but the public places a value of P_2' on reducing pollution. This could be the basis for a bargain to reduce pollution to the optimal level Q^*.

What if the government overshoots and either issues Q_2 permits or offers permits at a price P_2? There would be more pollution than the public would like, as indicated by the MEC schedule; with Q_2 permits, the public's marginal cost due to pollution is P_2'. If there is an effective market for permits, sufferers from pollution could offer to buy permits from producers. At first, they should be willing to offer a price of P_2', the marginal benefit to them of less pollution. This would be more than enough to induce a polluter to sell a permit and reduce emissions at a cost of only P_2. Such bargains would continue, until the public's benefits, given by MEC, just equaled the polluters costs, MAC, which would occur at the optimum level of pollution Q^*, where permits would sell for P^*.

Economist Robert Coase theorized that this is precisely what could happen, even in the absence of government-issued permits.[28] But the requirements of the Coase theorem are stringent and probably not often met in practice. Some countries, such as Indonesia, have had some success with informal regulation to reduce pollution, based largely on making polluters more aware of the pollution they are generating and by providing positive

28. Ronald Coase, "The Problem of Social Cost," *Journal of Law and Economics*, 3 (October 1960), 1–44.

publicity to those that reduce their emissions.[29] But to actually move to the optimum level of pollution Q^*, the suffering public would have to incur the costs of organizing to make their bargaining power effective and would have to mobilize funds to match the benefits they would gain from reduced pollution. But as many of those benefits, such as improved health, better recreational facilities, or more attractive scenery, have no market price, it would be difficult to convert them into cash that could compensate polluters. And, in poor societies or among the poor in any country, it seems highly unlikely that the demand for an improved environment could be made effective in a permits market.

Some environmental groups, which are organized to solicit contributions for environmental causes, could overcome these obstacles and behave as Coase predicted. They could purchase and then withdraw tradable emission permits from the market, for example. Conservation groups have purchased fishing rights in New Zealand and other countries to reduce the catch. And the programs of the Nature Conservancy and other groups to purchase rainforest land in tropical countries, while using a different mechanism, has the same effect of expressing consumer interests in an improved environment through the market.[30]

Even if the market between polluters and suffers is not fully effective, the market among polluters can be highly effective in minimizing the costs of meeting any government-imposed standard for emissions or other limitations to resource use. Assume that the government issues an arbitrary quantity, Q_p, of permits to pollute that would reduce emissions below their current level and divides these among existing firms by any method, for example, in proportion to their output. Firm 1, with old technology, would find it very costly to reduce its emissions to the new standard represented by the permits. Firm 2, built recently, is capable of reducing its emissions below the level of its permits at lost cost. Here is the basis for a bargain between the two firms that would benefit society. Firm 1 sells some of its permits to Firm 2 at a price above its marginal abatement cost but below the MAC of Firm 2. Both firms are better off: Firm 1 has earned revenue in ex-

29. Sheoli Pargal and David Wheeler, "Informal Regulation of Industrial Pollution in Developing Countries: Evidence from Indonesia," *Journal of Political Economy,* 104, no. 6 (December 1996), 1314–27; Shakeb Afsah and Jeffrey Vincent, "Putting Pressure on Polluters: Indonesia's PROPER Program, available at www.worldbank,org/nipr/work-paper/vincent/index.htm (February 1997).

30. In one version of this transaction, an environmental group will buy some of the host country's debt from disappointed bondholders on the international market, usually at a heavy discount, and then agree not to seek repayment of the loans from the host government. In return, the host country sets aside a negotiated area of rainforest to be preserved as a national park. These are called *debt-for-nature swaps.*

cess of its costs of abatement while Firm 2 has paid less than it would have to reduce its pollution. The public also is better off because the reduced emission standard has been met, but at a lower cost than would have been incurred had the initial allocation of permits been enforced.

This powerful result is quite general. It suggests that, whenever a limitation is to be imposed on private activity, the creation of a marketable property right can achieve an efficient outcome with minimal government intervention. For that reason, economists recommend that traditional property rights to natural resources, such as forest concessions or licenses to fish and hunt, should be marketable. The use of marketable permits is in its infancy. Considerable experience has been gained in the United States with pollution permits issued to public utilities. The sulfur allowance program in the United States allows utility companies to buy and sell from each other the rights to emit sulfur oxides and penalizes companies that emit more than authorized by their holdings of allowances.[31] In developing and transitional economies, where policy dependence on market forces is a more-recent phenomenon, marketable permits hardly have been tried (although some pilot programs have been introduced in Kazakhstan and Poland[32]) but hold promise for the future if the problems of enforcement can be overcome.

Policy Failures

Although some government intervention is necessary to correct for the market failures associated with natural resources, it is equally true that, all over the world, government policies frequently contribute to wasteful use of resources and the degradation of the environment. We have seen that, when production has external costs, one approach is to internalize those costs by taxing output or granting marketable property rights. But governments commonly suppress the prices or subsidize the production of commodities that degrade natural resources and often compromise property rights in ways that encourage rapacious exploitation. Examples are not hard to find.

Forestry policy has been especially destructive in many tropical countries. Until recently, Brazil subsidized ranching and other activities that encroach on the Amazon rainforest (see the following case study). Indonesia grants logging concessions for only 20 years with no clearly defined conditions for renewal, which encourages wasteful logging practices because regeneration times are 70 years. It also charges no fees for the concessions,

31. For a brief description of this program, see Tietenberg, *Environmental and Natural Resource Economics,* 5th ed., pp. 396–98.

32. Jeffrey Vincent and Scott Farrow, "A Survey of Pollution Charge Systems and Key Issues in Policy Design," in Randall Bluffstone and Bruce A. Larson, eds., *Controlling Pollution in Transition Economies* (Cheltenham, UK: Edward Elgar, 1997).

SUBSIDIZED DEFORESTATION OF THE AMAZON[33]

The government of Brazil, wishing to promote development in the Amazon, has been subsidizing ranchers to cut down the vast rainforest. Each year throughout the 1970s, 3,000 to 4,000 square miles of the Amazon was deforested, and almost a quarter of the Amazonian state of Rondonia was converted from rain forest to pasture from 1970 to 1985. Not only does pastureland replace the rainforest, but rainforest occupations provided more jobs than the ranching that replaced them. Despite this, the government provided new ranchers with 15-year tax holidays, investment tax credits, exemptions from export taxes and import duties, and loans with interest substantially below market rates. Although a typical subsidized investment was estimated to yield a loss to the economy equivalent to 55 percent of the initial investment, a private rancher was able to earn a return, due to subsidies, equivalent to 250 percent on the amount invested.

33. From Panayotou, *Green Markets,* pp. 14–15.

discourages transfers of the concessions, imposes inadequate taxes and fees that do not encourage conservation, and is ineffective in policing the regulations aimed at conservation. Thailand's policies were so wanton that its rainforest has all but disappeared, and the Philippines is on the same path.

Trade policy has been equally destructive. Ghana, Indonesia, and Malaysia, for example, placed bans on log exports as a means of promoting wood-processing industries. Export bans drive down the domestic price of tropical hardwood, and so make it profitable for sawmills and plywood mills to purchase logs and export semifinished products. But these industries have been inefficient and consumed resource rents in higher production costs. Because timber companies cannot export tropical hardwoods, such as ebony and mahogany, as logs, these valuable species are used along with low-value timber to make inexpensive products, such as plywood sent to Japan to make forms for pouring cement. The role of self-imposed log export bans in destroying rainforests should be a warning to northern countries that want to preserve tropical forests by imposing their own import bans on these logs.[34]

34. On forest policies, see Robert Repetto and Malcolm Gillis, eds., *Public Policies and the Misuse of Forest Resources* (Cambridge: Cambridge University Press, 1988); and Jeffrey Vincent, "The Tropical Timber Trade and Sustainable Development," *Science,* 256 (1992), 1651–55.

Energy pricing is another common policy failure. In oil-rich countries, like Nigeria and Venezuela, energy has been kept cheap as a stimulus to industrialization and diversification. This has multiple adverse effects. It encourages wasteful domestic consumption and reduces the country's petroleum and gas reserves and its export-earning potential. It encourages the use of cars and minibuses, and so adds to congestion. Cheap energy promotes industry ill-suited to the country's endowments. Firms and consumers have little incentive to adopt energy-saving technology. Because burning oil is an important source of air pollution, all these overuses contribute to environmental degradation. Not all oil exporters underprice energy. Indonesia now values its fuel at world prices and has begun to recognize environmental externalities as a factor in domestic oil pricing. But some oil importers, such as Egypt, Argentina, China, and India, have subsidized petroleum products by as much as 50 percent of the world price, and so encouraged imports they cannot afford, industries that cannot compete in world markets, and environmental degradation that market pricing would have discouraged.[35]

Figure 6–6 shows commercial energy use per unit of GDP (using the purchasing power parity estimates for 1990) for almost 90 countries. The

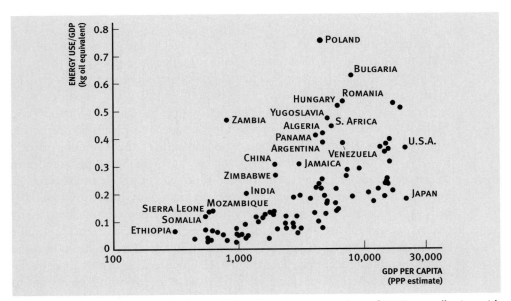

FIGURE 6–6   ENERGY USE AND INCOME. Although energy use as a share of GDP generally rises with income per capita, some countries have especially high energy use, in many cases because of distorted prices and subsidized energy.

35. Bjorn Larsen and Anwar Shah, "World Fossil Fuel Subsidies and Global Carbon Emissions," World Bank working paper WPS 1002 (October 1992), especially Chart 1.

KEROSENE SUBSIDY IN INDONESIA[36]

From 1972 to 1984, the government of Indonesia heavily subsidized the consumption of kerosene and other fuels. The kerosene subsidy was justified as an aid to poor rural dwellers, who were thought to use it for cooking, and as a disincentive to harvest fuelwood. The cutting of fuelwood was denuding mountain slopes and causing soil erosion on Java, Indonesia's most densely populated island. But research subsequently discovered that rural families used kerosene predominantly for lighting, not for cooking, so that only about 50,000 acres of forest land was protected each year by the subsidy at a cost of almost U.S.$200,000 a year per acre. Replanting programs, in contrast, cost only $1,000 per acre. Moreover, most kerosene turned out to be consumed by the wealthy, not the poor. And the low price of kerosene made it necessary to subsidize diesel fuel as well, because the two fuels could be partially substituted in truck engines, and this caused greater environmental damage. Recognizing the costs of this policy, the government sharply reduced its subsidy on kerosene and other fuels in the mid-1990s. However, large subsidies reemerged following the 1997 Asian financial crisis.

36. Malcolm Gillis, "Indonesia: Public Policies, Resource Management and the Tropical Forest," in Repetto and Gillis, *Public Policy and the Misuse of Forest Resources.*

variance, even among poor countries, is notable. Countries with especially high energy use are labeled in the diagram; the United States and Japan are labeled for comparison. Among the high energy users, mistaken energy policies are not entirely to blame but must be suspected in countries like Zambia, India, Argentina, South Africa, and Venezuela, where market prices generally have been distorted until the economic reforms of the 1980s and 1990s; even today, Venezuela prices gasoline at about 25 U.S. cents a gallon. The consequences of price distortions are particularly notable in the former communist countries (China, Poland, Bulgaria, Hungary, and Romania), where markets played very little role in resource allocation until recently. Among industrial countries, Norway and Canada stand out as particularly high users of energy. The United States, often castigated as a wanton consumer of fuel, does not show an especially high rate of use for its income, partly because energy is priced at or above world market levels.

Investment in infrastructure is a third area of widespread policy failure. In forestry and energy pricing, governments typically underprice the resource and fail to force private operators to account for external costs. In infrastructure investment, governments often create new external costs and fail to account for them in project planning. Environmental groups have focused much of their fire on investments in power dams, irrigation and flood control systems, roads, and power plants that damage their environments. Dams that flood their upstream areas displace local populations, who seldom fare as well in new locations, and destroy natural habitat. Egypt's huge Aswan Dam controlled the floodwaters of the Nile. But those floodwaters had beneficial effects, replenishing soil and leaching out unwanted salts, so the dam may have reduced agricultural productivity over the long run. Irrigation schemes in Africa encourage diseases such as schistosomiasis and river blindness. Roads into the rainforest in Brazil and elsewhere not only destroy habitat along the right of way but encourage overexploitation of the forest and surroundings.

Project analysis, discussed in Chapter 12, to some extent can accommodate the external costs of large projects. The commercial value of land, forests, and inland fisheries can be calculated and added to the costs of projects. More controversially, the cost of illness from some kinds of environmental change can be estimated. Recreational benefit and costs also might be quantified (see the following case study). To the extent possible, the inclusion of these costs and the use of cost-benefit analysis in public investment decisions would help avoid environmentally damaging projects or change designs and reduce external costs. However, many environmental costs cannot be quantified so readily, although applications of nonmarket valuation techniques have expanded readily in the past decade, including in developing countries.[37] Probably more critically, too many governments do not take project appraisal at all seriously. The World Bank, under considerable pressure from environmental groups, now undertakes impact analyses of the investments it finances. This practice is likely to spread.

In one important respect, then, the economic reform agenda discussed in Chapter 5 also is an agenda for more sustainable development. The core of structural adjustment is to depend as much as possible on markets to determine prices and allocate resources.[38] As part of this, subsidies and protective tariffs are to be reduced or eliminated. Where this agenda is implemented, all resources, including marketable natural resources and sources of pollution, will bear prices closer to their true scarcity costs. That

37. For a summary of valuation studies in developing countries, see Stavios Georgiou, Dale Whittington, David Pearce, and Dominic Moran, *Economic Values and the Environment in the Developing World* (Cheltenham, UK: Edward Elgar, 1997).

38. On the relationship between structural adjustment and the environment, see David Reed, *Structural Adjustment, the Environment, and Sustainable Development* (London: Earthscan, 1996).

VALUING A RECREATIONAL FACILITY IN BANGKOK, THAILAND[39]

For environmental amenities, valuation techniques are either market oriented or survey oriented. Market-oriented techniques use information on observed behavior, especially market prices. Survey techniques ask affected populations about their willingness to pay for amenities or to accept compensation for losses. Lumpinee Public Park, in downtown Bangkok, provides many benefits to its users. Because no admission fee is charged, no direct expression of its value can be observed, so two survey techniques have been employed. The first, called the *travel cost approach,* uses the money and time costs of getting to the park as an estimate of the demand schedule for environmental amenities associated with the park. The value of the park is calculated as consumer surplus, the area under the estimated demand curve. The second approach, called *hypothetical valuation,* asks users how much they would contribute annually to the upkeep of the park if the government no longer could maintain it. The two approaches gave similar results: the park's services were valued at about 13 million baht in 1980, or U.S.$650,000 using the 1980 exchange rate. Capitalizing these annual benefits at a discount rate of 10 percent per annum in perpetuity gives an asset (or present) value of U.S.$6.5 million.

39. From John A. Dixon and Maynard M. Hufschmidt, eds., *Valuation Techniques for the Environment* (Baltimore: Johns Hopkins Press, 1986), 121–40.

is the first step toward an incentive regime to promote sustainable resource use. Because external costs and benefits are not reflected in market prices, it is not the only step. Marketable property rights and permits, taxes, or even regulation also will be necessary to internalize the externalities and complete the incentive regime. But it is important to recognize that there is no necessary conflict between economic reform and sustainable development.

Measuring Sustainability

Most societies and their governments aim to increase income as rapidly as possible over long periods. How do they ensure that economic growth does not depend unsustainably on the consumption of natural resources? This chapter so far has answered this question in terms of the markets for individual resources, such as fisheries, forests, mineral deposits, and the environment. If a government wished to track the country's success in sustaining its growth, what concepts could it use and how would these be measured?

NATURAL CAPITAL

The economic growth models presented in Chapter 3 show that rising income depends on increases in the capital stock and the productivity with which labor and capital produce goods and services. In those models, and in most economic analysis, capital stock has meant **human-made capital:** machines, buildings, and infrastructure **(made capital),** as well as the education and experience of the labor force **(human capital).**[40] What if production also consumes natural resources, however? The productivity of made capital and labor will decline as natural resources are depleted, unless more resources are discovered, greater amounts are invested in made capital, or technological change increases productivity. This suggests that natural resources also ought to be included in economic growth models and measures of national output.

To incorporate natural resources in our thinking about economic growth, economists have developed the concept of **natural capital,** analogous to that of made capital. Natural capital is the value of a country's existing stock of natural resources, including fisheries, forests, mineral deposits, water, and the environment. Natural capital produces goods and services, just like labor and made capital. It can be, and usually is, depleted in the process of production, just as made capital is depreciated. It also, through natural growth of renewable resources and investment in discovery of new reserves, can be augmented, just as investment augments the stock of made capital.

The concept is clear, but how can natural capital be measured? Made capital is measured as the cost of investment: If a factory cost $30 million to build and equip, that is the value of the capital stock recorded in the national accounts. In any year, such as 1995, the *gross capital stock* of a country is the sum of such investments over the previous many years, with each year's investment adjusted for inflation. Because the capital stock wears out in the course of production, the stock is reduced each year by a percentage called *depreciation.*[41] Thus, each year the beginning capital stock is increased by the value of investment and decreased to calculate the *net capital stock.* If the economy is to grow sustainably, net capital stock must grow at the same rate.

Obviously there is no analogous way of valuing natural capital. But an alternative and economically preferable way of valuing made capital can be applied to natural capital. Capital of any kind produces goods and services

---

40. Economists have defined *human capital* as the value of learning and experience embodied in workers, which, like made capital, increases productivity and income. Chapter 9 deals with this important concept.

41. The rate of depreciation varies with the kind of asset. It usually is low, say, 2 percent, on buildings and infrastructure, around 10 percent on equipment, and perhaps 20 percent on vehicles.

into the future. A measure of the net benefits from producing these goods and services is the difference between their market price and the cost of the other inputs—materials and labor—used to produce them. The capital then can be valued as the sum of these future benefits, discounted by the appropriate interest rate. That is, the capital is valued as the *net present value* of the future stream of value added by the capital.

This approach can be used to value natural capital. If a forest is harvested, the logs have a market value determined by their price less the costs of harvesting; that is, their resource rent.[42] The cost of harvesting includes materials, wages, and the minimum necessary return to made capital; that is, the opportunity cost of made capital engaged in logging. The market price of timber will vary depending on the quality and volume of the timber, something that can be roughly estimated from the characteristics of the forest and logging practices. Then, the value of the forest can be calculated as the discounted present value of the future resource rents, using the prevailing interest rate (see equation 12–1). The annual depletion of the forest simply is the change in this present value.

The application of this approach to fisheries, water supplies, mineral deposits, and soil fertility is straightforward. The estimation of the recreational value of an urban park is discussed in the case study on page 225. But the valuation of clean air and water and other environmental amenities is not so simple. The physiological impact of particular pollutants on human well-being is complex, indirect, and not completely understood. Many forms of the impact have no market values. And environmentalists suspect that pollution has cumulative, nonlinear effects that are not easily estimated, such as climate change due to the venting of carbon dioxide into the atmosphere (the *greenhouse effect*). Until scientists and economists understand more about the costs of environmental degradation, the valuation of natural capital is likely to be confined to marketable resources like fish, timber, minerals, and water supplies.

A CONCEPT OF SUSTAINABILITY

If an economy consumes natural capital in producing current income, then the economy's capacity to generate income will decline in the future unless the natural capital is replaced. For the moment, consider a constant population. A test for a sustainable economy is its capacity to maintain consumption at a constant level indefinitely. To achieve this, the depletion of natural capital must be replaced by made capital, technological change must be generated to increase the productivity of all capital and labor, or both must be done. This suggests an alternative, if partial, criterion for sustainability: the maintenance of the total stock of capital, both natural

42. Strictly speaking, the resource rent should be measured using the *marginal* cost of extraction.

and made.[43] The depletion of natural capital must be compensated for by net investment in made capital.

Therefore sustainability can involve the depletion of natural resources and the eventual decline of farming, fishing, forestry, mining, petroleum, and other sectors dependent on natural resources. As these industries decline, others grow, including manufacturing, utilities, construction, finance, transportation, telecommunications, trade, health, education, and other services. Indeed, this transformation is what most people have in mind when they speak of development. When an economy develops from a natural resource base, the net benefits or rents from the primary sectors provide much of the finance for secondary and tertiary industries. And some of the finance may go into research and development of new technologies that will increase productivity.

One other kind of transformation should be noted. In countries almost entirely dependent on natural resources for income, such as oil exporters Kuwait and Brunei, there is little scope for transforming resource rents into other productive capital within the economy. Instead, these countries invest their resource rents in bonds and stocks in the international capital markets or even in the industries of other countries. Brunei, for example, has invested in cattle ranching in Australia and hotels in the United States. As the oil runs out, these countries begin increasingly to live off their investments. They become *rentier* economies, another path to sustainability.

The transformation to made capital does not justify the wanton use of resources. Resources should be exploited efficiently, in ways described earlier in this chapter. The substitution of made capital for natural capital may not be productive or even possible forever. Natural resources also are used in manufacturing and services, as raw materials, fuel, and waste sinks. Unless technology continues to reduce this dependence on raw materials, it is possible that a country, or even the planet, may run out of needed resources. Further, if the population is growing and a society wants its income per capita to grow as well, then it becomes necessary to invest more than resource rents to continuously increase the total capital stock. Within these limits, however, some societies may choose to accelerate resource depletion in favor of investment in other industries and can do it sustainably if resource rents are invested productively.

RESOURCES AND NATIONAL INCOME

The concept of sustainability as the transformation of natural into made capital can be reflected in the national accounts. Chapter 3 defined **gross national** (or **domestic**) **product** (GNP or GDP) as the sum of value added in the production of finished goods and services in an economy.

---

43. Human capital could be included in this criterion.

GNP is *gross* because it makes no allowance for the depreciation or consumption of capital. Another income measure, **net national product** (NNP), is equal to GNP less the depreciation of made capital (D_m):

$$NNP = GNP - D_m \qquad [6\text{--}1]$$

Net national product is an appropriate measure of the resources available for consumption once allowance has been made for the consumption of capital. Because GNP consists of consumption (C) and national saving (S),

$$NNP = C + S - D_m \qquad [6\text{--}2]$$

As long as saving equals or exceeds depreciation, consumption is less than net product and can be sustained indefinitely. In effect, the stock of capital together with labor produces NNP each year; if enough is saved to replace the worn-out capital, production is sustainable.

Once there is a measure of the stock of natural capital, its annual depletion (D_n) can be estimated and included in net product. The result has been called **adjusted net national product** (ANNP):

$$ANNP = GNP - D_m - D_n = C + S - D_m - D_n \qquad [6\text{--}3]$$

This corrected definition of net product has the same implication as NNP. If enough is saved each year to cover the depreciation of both made and natural capital, the economy can sustain its level of consumption. In other words, the basic sustainability criterion is that net saving (NS) must be greater than 0, where NS is measured as

$$NS = S - D_m - D_n \qquad [6\text{--}4]$$

Estimates of ANNP and net saving for several resource-rich countries are given in Table 6–3. Note the high estimated rates of resource

TABLE 6–3	ADJUSTED NET NATIONAL INCOME					
COUNTRY	**GNP**	**D_M**	**D_N**	**ANNP =** $GNP - D_M - D_N$	**SAVING (S)**	**NET SAVING =** $S - D_M - D_N$
COSTA RICA	100	3	8	89	21	+10
INDONESIA	100	5	17	78	30	+8
BRAZIL	100	7	10	83	21	+4
THE PHILIPPINES	100	11	4	85	18	+3
NIGERIA	100	3	17	80	23	+3
MEXICO	100	12	12	76	17	−7
MALAWI	100	7	4	89	2	−9

Sources: Saving rates, *World Development Report 1994*, Table 9 (for 1992); depreciation of made and natural capital (D_m and D_n), David Pearce and Giles Atkinson, "Capital Theory and the Measurement of Sustainable Development: An Indicator of 'Weak' Sustainability," *Ecological Economics*, 8 (1993), 103–8.

SUSTAINABLE DEVELOPMENT IN MALAYSIA[44]

Malaysia has used its rich natural resource base—oil, tin, timber, and fertile tropical land—to transform its economy and generate rapid growth in per capita income, averaging 3 percent a year from 1965 to 1990. Has it done so sustainably? To find out, Harvard economist Jeffrey Vincent estimated natural resource depletion for three parts of the country: the Malay Peninsula, on mainland Asia, and Sabah and Sarawak, two timber-rich Malaysian states on the nearby island of Borneo. In Peninsular Malaysia, with a diverse resource base and rapidly growing industry, adjusted net domestic product (ANDP) has equaled or exceeded consumption in every year from 1970 to 1990. That had also been the pattern in the outlying state of Sarawak until the late 1980s, when the situation reversed. Sabah, however, has been consuming unsustainably for the entire 20-year period; from 1970 to 1980, ANDP was only about half of consumption, which declined over those 10 years. Peninsular Malaysia was making a highly successful transformation while Sabah, in effect, was consuming its rainforest.

44. From Jeffrey Vincent and Rozali bin Mohamed Ali, "Natural Resources, Environment, and Development in Malaysia: An Economic Perspective," unpublished manuscript, 1994. Chap. 2, and Jeffrey Vincent and Yusuf Hadi, "Deforestation and Agricultural Expansion in Peninsular Malaysia," Harvard Institute for International Development, development discussion paper no. 396, September 1991.

depletion (D_n) for Indonesia and Nigeria; however, these were more than balanced by high saving rates so net saving remained positive. In Mexico and Malawi, however, the sum of the estimated values of D_m and D_n is larger than total saving, suggesting that consumption is not sustainable. Measurement of natural capital depletion still is experimental, and these estimates should be considered highly approximate and illustrative. Even the standard depreciation of made capital (D_m) is estimated only approximately, if at all, for most developing countries. Partly for that reason, neither NNP nor ANNP has been used much in official estimates, and they have hardly affected policy discussions. Yet even rough allowances for natural depletion would be an improvement on current estimates of national product and should lead to better pol-

> The development of Peninsular Malaysia shows how resource use and industrialization can interact to generate sustainable growth. The expansion of plantations in rubber (during the first 60 years of the century) and oil palm (in the 1960s and 1980s) caused rapid rates of deforestation, felling most of Malaysia's original, species-rich lowland forest, but leaving about half the country's forest, mostly on hillsides. Rubber and palm oil exports were profitable to the private growers, earned positive returns to the economy, and contributed importantly to its growth. Government policies and structural change in the economy combined eventually to end deforestation. Property rights to plantation land were secure; the government invested in infrastructure and promoted crop research, which was financed by charges to the growers; and it avoided subsidies that would have encouraged overexpansion of plantations. Consequently, after 1980, growers had incentives to invest in the intensification of production on existing land, rather than to further expand the area under cultivation.
>
> Growing plantation exports supported investment in economic diversification. Rapid, export-oriented industrialization was encouraged by open market policies akin to those described in Chapter 5, expanding employment opportunities at rising wages. Industrialization led to the migration of workers from rural to urban areas, raising rural wages and further encouraging intensification of agriculture. In textbook fashion, natural capital had been converted into made capital that fueled Malaysia's continuing development, while setting in motion forces that eventually limited the further depletion of natural resources.

icy.[45] The United Nations and the World Bank, however, are encouraging countries to begin keeping resource and environmental accounts as satellites to their standard national income accounts.[46] As more experience is gained, resource and environmental accounting may become an integral part of the standard national income accounts of many countries.

45. The omission of natural capital depletion is not the only important fault with standard national accounts. Among others, failure to include the services provided by unpaid housewives and children causes underestimates of gross income similar in size to the overestimates of net income from the omission of natural depletion.

46. See the collection by Ernst Lutz, ed., *Toward Improved Accounting for the Environment* (Washington, DC: World Bank, 1993).

Global Sustainability

Is economic development sustainable? For any one country, given appropriate economic and resource policies, the answer is "yes," because any single, well-managed country can draw on resources, saving, and technology from other countries. The answer becomes less certain when the whole planet is considered. Scientists are developing complex models to predict whether our economies will exhaust the earth's minerals, soils, forests, and fisheries or cause irreversible damage to the environment, including changes in climate. But the existing models give uncertain, sometimes unstable and often conflicting, results. In this state of uncertain scientific knowledge, what are the biases for gloom and for hope?

MALTHUSIAN VIEWS

In the early nineteenth century, the famous English demographer Thomas Malthus predicted that growing populations would exhaust the earth's capacity to produce food, until rising death rates and falling birth rates harshly would keep populations in check.[47] Malthusian ideas remain influential in the late twentieth century, although the focus has shifted from land and agriculture to all natural resources and the global environment.

The heart of the Malthusian view is the notion that the demand for natural resources is based on the exponential growth of both population and income, while the supply of resources either is absolutely limited or can increase only linearly. No matter how slow the growth rate, any exponentially expanding demand eventually must overwhelm any fixed or linearly increasing supply, as shown in Figure 6–7. Historically, human societies have been able to avoid the Malthusian trap in three ways. First, science and technology have moved fast enough to increase the productivity of land and other natural resources. Second, when resources became scarce, such as wood in England in the seventeenth century or coal in the nineteenth, substitutes (coal, then petroleum) were found. Third, people have chosen to reduce family size and thus population growth.

The question is whether these processes can continue indefinitely to avoid Malthusian scarcity. Although the world population growth is slowing, it remains high enough to expect a doubling of the world's population by the middle of the next century.[48] As development proceeds, especially in populous Asia and in Latin America, a rising share of this expanding population will aspire to the consumption standards of the northern middle class, which suggests more intensive consumption of resources and pollu-

---

47. Malthus is discussed in Chapter 7.
48. *World Development Report 1992*, p. 26.

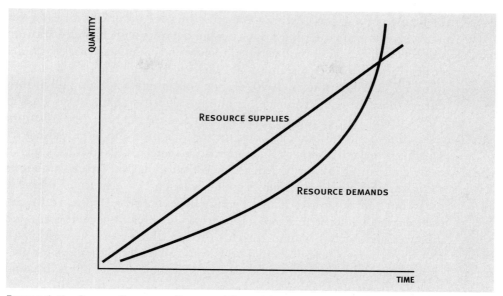

FIGURE 6–7   GLOBAL RESOURCE BALANCE. The Malthusian view is that resource supplies rise at a linear rate, at best, while demand rises exponentially. If so, demand eventually must exceed supply.

tion of the environment. As nonrenewable fuels run out and the environment becomes saturated with waste, alternative sources of materials or new technologies may be substantially more costly than current ones, and so growth may be slowed. And, if the impact of resource depletion and pollution accelerate and become irreversible, it may be beyond the capability of humans to develop new technologies fast enough to compensate.[49]

NEOCLASSICAL VIEWS

The basis for optimism lies in both history and economics. Human societies in fact have been able to evade the Malthusian trap. The hopeful interpretation of this experience comes from neoclassical economists, who argue that the growing resource scarcity itself has been the main inducement to changes in behavior and technology. As one country or the entire earth runs out of resources such as wood and then petroleum for fuel or supplies of fresh water or clean air, either the market price of these resources rises or, in the case of unpriced amenities, the cost of using them increases. Higher costs, which often are anticipated, become a signal for several changes that ameliorate the growing resource scarcity.

49. These views are discussed by Edward B. Barbier. *Economics, Natural-Resource Scarcity and Development.*

Rising costs of fuels and raw materials make it profitable to search for new deposits and to exploit less-accessible deposits with higher extraction costs. The fuel crisis of the 1970s led to new finds of oil and natural gas deposits: Proven reserves rose from 50 billion tons of oil equivalent in 1950 to over 250 billion tons in 1990, despite consumption of 100 billion tons during those 40 years. Estimates of ultimately recoverable reserves are 600 times current rates of usage.[50] Higher costs also mean greater rewards from research into new technologies that increase the productivity of waning resources or make it cheaper to use alternative materials. Even if the costs of using alternatives cannot be reduced, substitutes may become economic as the prices of exhaustible resources go up. Solar energy technically is feasible today but too expensive. If fuel deposits become more expensive to tap, solar energy would be relatively more attractive, even at current costs, and more research would be undertaken to reduce these costs. It is estimated that solar energy already is competitive with the use of natural gas for generating electricity during peak loads and that, on current trends, it could become competitive with fuel oil for base load generation by 2020.[51]

Increased scarcity also forces users to conserve. World energy consumption fell substantially as a result of the oil crises of 1973–1980. In 1971, a dollar of world GNP required more than a kilogram of energy (in oil equivalents); by 1992, the same output could be produced by a third of a kilogram.[52] Much of the decline was due to improved technology, such as improvements in automobile engines, that reduced fuel consumption with no reduction in output or change in consumers' behavior. In the United States, the stock of cars in 1973 averaged 13 miles per gallon of gasoline; by the mid-1980s average mileage had almost doubled.

As with resource use, so with environmental pollution. Even though many environmental amenities are not marketed, pollution entails costs felt by producers and consumers. Some of these work through the market, for example, as land values fall in polluted areas. Others may have to be artificially imposed by government policies, of the kinds discussed in this chapter, that impose external costs on producers or consumers. As these costs are felt, the demand rises for new technology or behavioral changes that reduce pollution. Gas scrubbers seemed to be a costly imposition on industry at first, but they have become economic and less costly as societies become willing to pay for cleaner air. The relationship between income levels and environmental indicators tends to follow three broad patterns, as discussed in the next case study and shown in Figure 6–8. Some environmental problems tend to diminish as incomes grow, such as lack of access to safe water and adequate sanitation. Other problems tend

50. *World Development Report 1992*, p. 115.
51. Ibid., p. 123.
52. *World Development Report 1994*, p. 171.

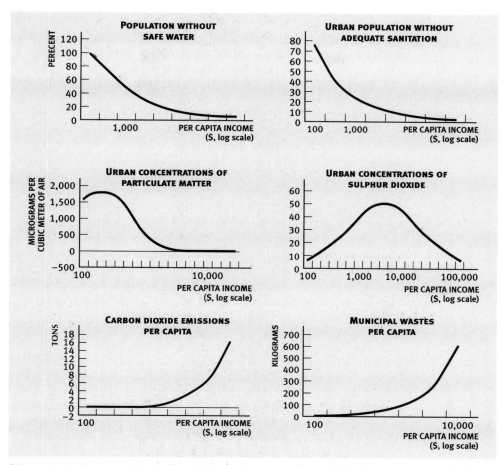

FIGURE 6–8 INCOME LEVELS AND VARIOUS ENVIRONMENTAL INDICATORS. Source: Shafik and Bandyopadhyay, background paper, World Bank, *World Development Report, 1992,* Figure 4.

to worsen continually as economic output and incomes rise, including municipal wastes and carbon dioxide emissions. In still other cases, environmental problems tend to worsen as incomes grow at low levels of income, then reach a turning point, after which the problem tends to diminish with economic growth. Both air and water pollution tend to follow this pattern.[53]

53. This last pattern is sometimes referred to as an environmental *Kuznets's curve,* since its inverted U shape is reminiscent of the pattern between income levels and income distribution hypothesized by Simon Kuznets (Chapter 4). For further discussion of the relationship between environmental indicators and income, see *World Development Report 1992: Development and the Environment;* Gene Grossman and Alan B. Krueger, "Economic Growth and the Environment," *The Quarterly Journal of Economics* (May, 1995), 353–77; and Kenneth Arrow et al., "Economic Growth, Carrying Capacity, and the Environment," *Science* (April 28, 1995), 520–21.

ENVIRONMENTAL DEGRADATION AND INCOME LEVELS: THREE PATTERNS[54]

Figure 6–8 illustrates how rising economic activity can cause environmental problems but can also, with the right policies and institutions, help address them. Three patterns emerge:

- Some problems decline as income increases. This is because increasing income provides the resources for public services such as sanitation and rural electricity. When individuals no longer have to worry about day-to-day survival, they can devote resources to profitable investments in conservation. These positive synergies between economic growth and environmental quality must not be underestimated.
- Some problems initially worsen but then improve as incomes rise. Most forms of air and water pollution fit into this category, as do some types of deforestation and encroachment on natural habitats. There is nothing automatic about this improvement; it occurs only when countries deliberately introduce policies to ensure that additional resources are devoted to dealing with environmental problems.
- Some indicators of environmental stress worsen as incomes increase. Emissions of carbon and of nitrogen oxides and municipal wastes are current examples. In these cases abatement is relatively expensive and the costs associated with the emissions and wastes are not yet perceived as high—often because they are borne by someone else. The key is, once again, policy. In most countries individuals and firms have few incentives to cut back on wastes and emissions, and until such incentives are put into place—through regulation, charges, or other means—damage will continue to increase. The experience with the turnaround achieved in other forms of pollution, however, shows what may be possible once a policy commitment is made.

Figure 6–8 does not imply an inevitable relationship between income levels and particular environmental problems; countries can choose policies that result in much better (or worse) environmental conditions that those in other countries at similar income levels. Nor does it imply a static picture; as a result of technological progress, some of these curves have shifted downward over recent decades, providing an opportunity for countries to develop in a less damaging manner than was possible earlier.

54. Extracted from World Bank, *World Development Report 1992: Development and the Environment*, p. 10.

None of this guarantees that the resource barriers, cumulative effects, and irreversibilities emphasized by Malthusian views can be overcome. Perhaps, the economic behavioral and technological mechanisms of the past will be swamped by global resource exhaustion. Much depends on both government policy designs and individual choices. But predictions of exhaustion that ignore proven adaptive mechanisms are just as likely to be wrong as predictions of sustainable growth that ignore possible irreversibilities. And the cost of acting on wrong predictions, in either direction, can be large.

From an economics perspective, the soundest strategy for global sustainability would be to move quickly toward more effective markets, including property rights, marketable permits, and taxes, so that real resource scarcities will be reflected in the prices people pay for all commodities and services. An end to subsidies on fuels, fertilizers, pesticides, water, timber, land clearing, and other destructive uses of resources would be a major step toward sustainability. Most countries are far from this ideal market environment and can reduce resource wastage without jeopardizing economic growth.[55] While this is happening, we need to invest in better scientific observations and models to see how close humankind really is to exhausting the earth.

ENVIRONMENTAL STANDARDS, INTERNATIONAL COMPETITIVENESS, AND TRADE

The relationship between international trade and environmental quality has been a topic of growing concern in recent years. At the heart of the issue is the convergence of increased globalization of production processes and differences in environmental standards across countries. Some business leaders and policy makers fear that environmental regulations may substantially raise production costs and adversely affect the ability of firms to compete in international markets. Environmental advocates are concerned that the globalization of production will induce firms to move to locations with lax environmental standards to avoid tougher standards at home (the "pollution haven" hypothesis).

These concerns have manifested themselves in several ways. The World Trade Organization (WTO) increasingly is called on to arbitrate disputes that arise from differences in environmental standards across countries. For example, the WTO has been involved in disputes between the United States and India, Pakistan, and Malaysia over exports of shrimp caught by fishing gear that may be environmentally harmful. It also has arbitrated cases affecting pollution, such as high-sulfur oil exported from Venezuela

---

55. These ideas are developed in Panayotou, *Green Markets*.

to the United States. Concerns about the environmental impact of trade led to the negotiation of elaborate side agreements as part of the North American Free Trade Agreement between Canada, Mexico, and the United States. Countries with stricter environmental standards have threatened (and sometimes imposed) special duties on imports from countries with weaker standards. Policy makers in many developing countries fear that wealthier countries will use such duties and other regulations as a disguised way to protect industries in high-income countries from competition from abroad. While some people advocate global environmental standards, difficult issues arise about who would set those standards and how they would be enforced.[56]

Many of these concerns are based on the notion of a trade-off between environmental standards, on the one hand, and firm productivity and international competitiveness, on the other hand. In this view, strict environmental standards raise production costs by more than the benefits received by the firm, and these additional costs are large enough to harm a firm's competitiveness, perhaps enough to push firms to relocate in other countries.[57] However, as we have seen, this trade-off does not always apply. Stricter environmental standards will reduce the costs of some industries. For example, fisheries will gain from reduced water pollution, agriculture from improved soil quality, and tourism from lower pollution and improved overall environmental management. And improved worker health should be reflected in higher labor productivity across all industries. In addition to these kinds of benefits, Harvard Business School professor Michael Porter has suggested that environmental regulations may improve a firm's productivity by encouraging efficient use of inputs, improved overall management, and technological innovation.[58]

56. For a succinct and accessible review of the relationships between competitiveness and environmental regulation, see Theodore Panayotou and Jeffrey Vincent, "Environmental Regulation and Competitiveness," in the *World Competitiveness Report 1997* (Geneva: World Economic Forum, 1997), pp. 64–73. For a more thorough review, see Adam Jafee et al., "Environmental Regulation and the Competitiveness of US Manufacturing: What Does the Evidence Tell Us?" *Journal of Economic Literature*, 33, no. 1 (March 1995), 132–63.

57. See Rudiger Pethig, "Pollution, Welfare, and Environmental Policy in the Theory of Comparative Advantage," *Journal of Environmental Economic Management*, 1975, no. 2, pp. 160–69; Horst Seibert, "Environmental Quality and the Gains from Trade," *Kyklos*, 3, no. 4 (1975), 657–73; and Martin McGuire, "Regulation, Factor Rewards, and International Trade," *Journal of Public Economics*, 17, no. 3 (April 1982), 335–54.

58. Michael Porter, "America's Green Strategy," *Scientific American* (April 1991), 168; and Michael Porter and Claas van der Linde, "Toward a New Conception of the Environment-Competitiveness Relationship," *Journal of Economic Perspectives*, 9, no. 4 (Fall 1995).

Research into these topics is made difficult by the statistical need to create meaningful measures of environmental regulations and environmental quality that are consistent over time and across countries.[59] Studies in the United States have found relatively modest productivity losses from environmental regulations, with small losses in some industries and larger losses in others (such as paper and pulp). Economists Dale Jorgenson and Peter Wilcoxen estimated that pollution controls in the United States reduced GNP by 0.2 percent per year between 1974 and 1985. In a follow-up study, they estimated that, following the enactment of amendments to the Clean Air Act in 1990 that allowed for more flexible, market-based instruments, the loss in annual GNP would fall to 0.004 percent per year. These studies, however, did not try to estimate the economic benefit from these controls.[60] There also is some suggestive, but not conclusive, evidence supporting Porter's hypothesis that environmental standards will induce technological innovation and reduce production costs.

The "pollution haven" hypothesis, while a seemingly logical concept, does not gain much support from the available evidence. Environmental standards do not appear to have a strong impact on a firm's decision on where to invest, and are dwarfed by concerns about macroeconomic and political stability, geographical location, labor costs, and other issues. This is consistent with the finding that the costs of environmental regulation are relatively modest in most industries. These costs would have to be much larger to induce firms to close factories in one country and open new operations in a different country.[61]

Similarly, environmental standards appear to have relatively little impact on trade patterns, again consistent with the idea that, in most industries, these standards have a modest impact on production costs. For example, economists Gene Grossman and Alan Krueger found that higher pollution abatement costs in the United States had no effect on U.S. imports from Mexico, contrary to the fears that some had expressed that

---

59. This research is summarized in Panayotou and Vincent, "Environmental Regulation and Competitiveness."

60. Dale Jorgenson and Peter Wilcoxen, "Environmental Regulation and US Economic Growth," *Rand Journal of Economics,* 21, no. 2 (Summer 1990), 314–40; and Dale Jorgenson and Peter Wilcoxen, "Impact of Environmental Legislation on US Economic Growth, Investment, and Capital Costs," in Donna Brodsky, ed., *US Environmental Policy and Economic Growth: How Do We Fare?* (Washington, DC: American Council for Capital Formation, 1992).

61. See David Wheeler and Ashoka Mody, "International Investment Location: The Case of US Firms," *Journal of International Economics,* 33, nos. 1–2 (August 1992), 57–72; Robert Repetto, "Jobs, Competitiveness, and Environmental Regulation: What Are the Real Issues?" World Resources Institute, March 1995; and Panayotou and Vincent, "Environmental Regulation and Competitiveness."

these costs would lead to a surge of imports from less-regulated Mexican firms.[62] Moreover, more open trade actually may help reduce pollution in many developing countries. A country completely closed off from trade would have to produce everything for itself, including capital- and pollution-intensive products, such as steel. There is a long history in many developing countries of partially closing off the economy from world trade to protect nascent domestic industries, as discussed in Chapter 19. This strategy can lead to growth of inefficient, high-cost firms that face little competition and have no incentive to reduce costs or use the most appropriate technologies that might reduce pollution. Some of the most heavily polluting industries in developing and transitional economies are "smokestack industries" insulated from trade and competition. One study found that the toxic intensity of manufacturing increased more rapidly in inward-oriented developing countries with policies designed to inhibit trade, while more outward-oriented developing countries recorded either slowly increasing or decreasing levels of toxic intensity in manufacturing.[63]

In sum, the available evidence suggests that the fear that environmental regulations will substantially increase production costs and inhibit the international competitiveness of firms *in developing countries* appears to be overstated. At the same time, increased trade does not seem to be creating a "race to the bottom," with firms locating where they can pollute more, but rather may create incentives for developing countries to focus production on less pollution-intensive goods and services.

POVERTY AND THE ENVIRONMENT

The two major threats to the earth's capacity to sustain living standards are seen to be growing population, especially of poor people in developing countries, and rising consumption standards, especially of the expanding middle class. The middle class, wherever it prospers, not only consumes more resources but eventually wants, and exerts political pressure to get, a cleaner, more sustainable environment. Whether these opposing tendencies are balanced enough to promote sustainability remains to be seen.

What about the poor? Asian, African, and Latin American farmers and migrants use slash-and-burn techniques to clear land for farming; African herders graze their livestock on deteriorating common land; poor, rural

---

62. Gene Grossman and Alan Krueger, "Environmental Impacts of a North American Free Trade Agreement," in Peter Garber, ed., *The US-Mexico Free Trade Agreement* (Cambridge, MA: MIT Press, 1993), pp. 13–56.

63. Hemamala Hettige, Robert Lucas, and David Wheeler, "The Toxic Intensity of Industrial Production: Global Patterns, Trends, and Trade Policy," *American Economic Review*, 82, no. 2 (May 1992).

households throughout the developing world encroach on the forest to obtain wood for charcoal, their most common fuel; local fishermen in Africa deplete inland fisheries; and the rivers of densely populated Asia are used simultaneously as common sewers and sources of water. The poor have little margin for subsistence. Struggling to survive today, they heavily discount the future and choose consumption over conservation. In countries where the majority of people are poor enough to exert such pressure on the environment, it is both infeasible and unfair to regulate and tax the access of the poor to common resources. Development itself is then seen as a solution to resource degradation: As incomes rise, the poor will move away from the margin of subsistence and open opportunities for more sustainable resource use.[64]

Although there is considerable truth to this view of poverty and resource use, it is not the whole story. The poor also are victims of resource degradation and have a stake in efficient resource use. Land in central Kenya is exquisitely planted to derive the maximum output from small plots, farmers of arid land in Sudan have developed techniques to make the most of the occasional rainfall, and complex irrigation systems are effectively managed by small farmers in Indonesia. Photographs from the semiarid Machakos District of Kenya show evidence of better soil conservation and more trees today than in the 1920s.[65] Small, poor farmers in the Philippines have organized to prevent the destructive logging of the nearby rainforest. The murder of Chico Menendez, who organized local rubber tappers to protect the Amazon from commercial exploitation, made headlines everywhere. Greenbelt and other grassroots organizations have sprung up in Africa and Asia to protect the environment.[66]

Although extreme poverty undoubtedly makes resource conservation more difficult, the principles of resource policy seem as applicable to poor producers and consumers as to rich ones. Where poor farmers, foresters, or fishers are invested with secure property rights, they will act in their own interest to use resources sustainably. Where poor nomads, migrants, and the landless have no properties to protect, they are more likely to degrade the environment.

64. See, for example, World Commission on Environment and Development (the Brundtland Commission), *Our Common Future* (New York: Oxford University Press, 1987), pp. 3, 28; and *World Development Report 1992,* pp. 23, 30.

65. Mary Tiffen and Michael Mortimore, "Malthus Controverted: The Role of Capital and Technology in Growth and Environment Recovery in Kenya," *World Development,* 22, no. 7 (July 1994), 997–1010.

66. Robin Broad, "The Poor and the Environment: Friends or Foes?" *World Development,* 22, no. 6 (June 1994), 811–22.

RICH NATIONS AND POOR NATIONS

Today the industrial countries are pressing for global action for sustainable resource use. The developing countries, with more untapped resources, higher discount rates, and greater pressure for rapid economic growth, resist. Industrial countries would like to preserve tropical rainforests for their many environmental amenities and productive uses. The tropical countries see timber as an important export of growing value and forest land as an opportunity for agricultural expansion. Northern countries are concerned about global warming, produced mainly by burning fossil fuels. Southern countries wonder why they, at lower incomes, have to slow development to help compensate for a problem caused, until now, mainly by industrial growth in the North. China wants to use its abundant coal to fuel rapid income growth for a fifth of the world's population, a vanguard of which is already moving into middle-class consumption patterns. Environmentalists in Europe and North America shudder at the idea of so much production and consumption growth fueled by the most-polluting source of energy in the world.

Therefore the North places a high value on resource and environmental sustainability, while the South is more concerned about rapid economic growth. These are the conditions for a bargain. Industrial countries should be willing to help finance programs to preserve resources and the environment and permit developing countries to invest in growth. Debt-for-nature swaps, in which environmental groups from rich countries have paid off poor countries' debts in return for the protection of natural habitats, have been one popular example of such bargains. National and multilateral aid agencies condition their assistance on the kinds of market reforms that promote more efficient resource use, but they could do this in a more focused way. They also are taking more explicit care about the environmental impact of large projects. Industrial countries might finance the use of new technology that uses resources more efficiently and reduces industrial effluents.[67]

The sustainability of global development therefore may require a transfer of financial and made capital from the industrial to the developing countries in return for the preservation of natural capital in the South, which also will benefit the North. The measure of the North's sincerity in promoting efficient global resource use will be its willingness to make these transfers. But increased efficiency and greater sustainability in resource and environmental management will be beneficial to the developing countries themselves and should be undertaken whether or not a bargain can be struck.

67. Theodore Panayotou, "Financing Mechanisms for Agenda 21," Harvard Institute for International Development, 1994.

PART THREE

Human Resources

POPULATION

The chapters in Part 2 deal with the human factor in economic development. People play a dual role in the development process: On the one hand, they are its ultimate beneficiaries; on the other, they provide the most important input into the process of production growth and transformation, that is called *economic development.*

In view of this dual role, what attitude should one take toward the growth of population at the family, national, and global levels? Should population growth be limited on the ground that it creates more mouths to feed and bodies to clothe, frequently in households and societies having trouble feeding the mouths and clothing the bodies they already have? World population projections and estimates of natural resource availability can make frightening reading. Yet each new individual also can bring additional labor power and, even more important, additional human spark and creativity to help solve the many problems that society faces. The argument for some form of population limitation is strong, but agreement is not universal, and important social, political, and moral issues must be weighed.

The decision of how many children to have is an intimately personal one. Traditionally, it has been left to the choice of the couple involved, but all societies condition these individual decisions in many ways. Arguments for conscious policy intervention to limit population growth depend either on the rationale that couples do not know how to achieve their desired family size or find it too expensive to do so and thus must be helped to achieve it or, alternatively, on the belief that individual reproductive choices impose excessive social costs at the national or international level. A few governments have intervened to *promote* reproduction; they have argued that the national interest requires that more children be born than people would have if left on their own. Arguments *against* intervention in reproductive decision making may appeal either to the value of freedom for the individual or the supposed advantages of a larger population for a nation or social group.

The view of humans as an economic resource has quantitative and qualitative dimensions. In the past, economic theory often emphasized the quantitative aspect while downplaying or ignoring the qualitative aspect. Many economic models assume that labor is homogeneous (undifferentiated) and therefore can be measured satisfactorily by counting bodies or hours or days of work. Other models make only a broad distinction between skilled and unskilled labor. Few take account of the importance of gender. Such models, although useful for revealing particular truths, are extreme simplifications, since the study of economic development clearly demonstrates that the qualitative aspects of the human contribution to production is at least as important as the quantitative aspects.

In the past 30 years, however, interest in the quality of human resources as a contributor to economic growth has increased. Specialists now talk about "developing human resources" or "investing in human capital." The analogy to natural resources and physical capital is appropriate in many ways. But it should not be taken to imply that the nature of "human resources" and their contribution to production are understood as fully as the contributions of a lathe, a road, or a ton of bauxite. The role of human resources is far more complex and mysterious than any of these. To what extent, and in what ways, human resources can be created through an investmentlike process are questions to be addressed in Chapter 8 to 10. This chapter lays a foundation for the later discussion by reviewing some of what is known about population and development.

Demographic Measures

Demography, the study of population, has its own specialized vocabulary. The **birthrate,** also called the **crude birthrate,** is births per thousand of population. Similarly, the **(crude) death rate** is deaths per thousand of population. The **rate of natural increase** is the difference between the birth rate and the death rate, but it is conventionally measured in percentage terms (per hundred rather than per thousand). Say a developing country has a population of 10 million at the start of a given year. During that year it experiences 400,000 births and 150,000 deaths. If net international migration is 0 (that is, if the number of immigrants equals the number of emigrants), its population at the end of the year will be 10,250,000. The midyear or average population is used to calculate the birth rate, death rate, and rate of natural increase, which in this case turn out to be 39.5, 14.8, and 2.47, respectively.

The growth potential of a population can be expressed through its **doubling time.** For a population rising at a constant rate, doubling time is approximately 70 divided by the growth rate. Hence, growth at 1 percent a year doubles the population in about 70 years, while a steady 2 percent annual growth doubles it in just 35 years, and a 3 percent growth in 23 years and a few months.[1]

Crude birth and death rates reflect the interaction between the *age structure* of a population and its *age-specific fertility and death rates.* Comparisons of crude birth and death rates across populations with different **age structures** (different shares of various age groups in the total population) can be misleading. For example, some LDCs have crude death rates as low as those in the developed countries, yet more people die each year in all age groups in these LDCs. The reason is that LDC populations are much younger on average and emphasize age groups (older children and youth) in which death rates are low.

Therefore, for some purposes, it is important to use age-specific demographic rates. One such rate, the **infant death rate,** differs sharply between rich and poor countries. It is defined as deaths in the first year of life per thousand live births. Thus, if 40,000 of the 400,000 babies born in our hypothetical country die before reaching their first birthday, the infant death rate is 100. Similar age-specific death rates can be calculated for other age groups, using mean population in the age group as a base.

Life expectancy is the number of additional years the average person of a given age will live if age-specific death rates remain constant. It is a purer measure of mortality than the crude death rate because it is unaffected by the age distribution of the population. **Life expectancy at birth** is the most frequently used version of this measure.

---

1. The formula for exponential growth is

$$P_t = P_0 e^{rt}$$

where P_0 = population in the base year, P_t = population t years later, e = the base of the natural logarithm (2.7183), and r = the annual growth rate. If $P_t = 2P_0$, then

$$2P_0 = P_0 e^{rt}$$

$$2 = e^{rt}$$

It turns out that $2 = e^{.7}$ (approximately). This means that rt, the product of the growth rate (expressed as a decimal) and the number of years, must equal 0.7. At 2 percent annual growth, for example, $0.02 \times 35 = 0.7$.

The **fertility** of a population refers to its propensity to have children. An **age-specific fertility rate** is the average number of children born each year to women in a particular age group. The **total fertility rate** is the sum of the age-specific fertility rates applying to a particular group (cohort) of women as they move through their reproductive years. In other words, it is the number of children the average woman will have in her lifetime if age-specific fertility rates remain constant.

A Brief History of Human Population

Concern is frequently expressed over high rates of population growth and rising population densities in places such as Egypt, Mexico, and Bangladesh. But rising population densities are a very old story. For years people have been saying, "This cannot continue"; yet it does. How do current demographic trends fit into the history of human experience?

World population has been growing more or less continuously since the appearance of life on earth, but the rate of growth was accelerating from 200 years ago until very recently. Four eras of demographic history can be distinguished.[2]

THE PREAGRICULTURAL ERA

For perhaps half a million years, humans lived a precarious existence as hunters, gatherers, and sometimes cannibals. Population density (the number of people per square kilometer) necessarily was very low, since a given population required a vast extent of land to sustain itself. The birthrate probably was high, but the death rate was nearly as high and the rate of natural increase was very low. When this unimaginably long era ended with the introduction of settled agriculture about 12,000 years ago, the world's population was perhaps no more than 100 million.

FROM SETTLED AGRICULTURE TO THE INDUSTRIAL REVOLUTION

The introduction of settled agriculture revolutionized the earth's capacity to sustain human life. During the years leading up to the Industrial Revolution of the late eighteenth and early nineteenth centuries, the food supply grew and became more reliable. The death rate fell, life expectancy increased, and population growth gradually accelerated to around 0.5 per-

2. Based on Lester R. Brown, *In the Human Interest* (New York: W.W. Norton, 1974), pp. 20–21; for informative and enjoyable longer presentations, see Carlo Cipolla, *The Economic History of World Population,* 7th ed. (New York: Barnes and Noble, 1978); and Massimo Livi-Bacci, *A Concise History of World Population,* 2nd ed. (Malden, MA: Blackwell Publishers, 1997).

cent a year. This growth, however, was set back at intervals by plagues, famines, and wars, any of which could wipe out as much as half of the population in a given area. As late as the fourteenth century, the Black Death (bubonic plague) killed one third of the population of Europe. Nevertheless, by 1800 the world's population was about 1.7 billion.

FROM THE INDUSTRIAL REVOLUTION TO WORLD WAR II

The Industrial Revolution, which marked the start of modern economic growth, further expanded the earth's population-carrying capacity. Innovations in agriculture matched innovations in industry, permitting labor to be transferred to industry while the productivity of the remaining agricultural laborers rose fast enough to feed the growing urban population. Transcontinental railroads and fast, reliable ocean shipping further boosted world food output in the late nineteenth century, making it possible to grow more basic foodstuffs in the areas best suited for this activity and get supplies to food-deficit areas quickly in emergencies. Famines decreased in frequency and severity. Food prices fell. Meanwhile, modern medicine, sanitation, and pharmaceutical production began to develop. All these factors helped to reduce the death rate. Population growth accelerated, reaching about 1 percent per annum by World War II. When this third demographic era ended in 1945, the population of the world was slightly less than 2.5 billion.

The third demographic era saw major shifts in the location of world population. Between 1846 and 1930, more than 50 million people left Europe to settle in other parts of the world. The United States received the bulk of them, while smaller numbers went to Canada, Brazil, Argentina, Chile, South Africa, Australia, and New Zealand. The proportion of world population that was of European stock grew from an estimated 22 percent in 1846 to 35 percent in 1930, when the Great Depression ended mass international migration.[3] During the same period, millions of laborers and merchants from densely populated India and China moved to more sparsely settled areas in Southeast Asia, Africa, the South Pacific, and elsewhere. The existence of colonial empires facilitated this movement.

THE POST-WORLD WAR II PERIOD

After the war, there were further dramatic improvements in food supply and disease control. Techniques introduced in the developed countries during the preceding era spread throughout the globe. People became

---

3. For discussion, see Cipolla, *The Economic History of World Population.*

more aware of famines and epidemics in "remote" parts of the world and less willing to tolerate them. The result was a veritable revolution in death rates and life expectancy. Plummeting death rates in many areas raised rates of natural increase to 2 or even 3 percent. As its doubling time shortened drastically, world population passed 5 billion in 1987 and 6 billion in 1999.

It appears that this fourth demographic era, with its dramatic acceleration of population growth, will be short-lived. Population growth is slowing down in most parts of the world, as many developing countries follow the industrial countries in a **demographic transition.** Initially, countries experiencing this transition have high birth and death rates. Then they experience a fall in the death rate, which raises the rate of natural increase. Some years later, this is followed by a drop in the birthrate, which cuts natural increase to around 1 percent. The demographic transition, as it occurred in England and Wales, is depicted in Figure 7–1.

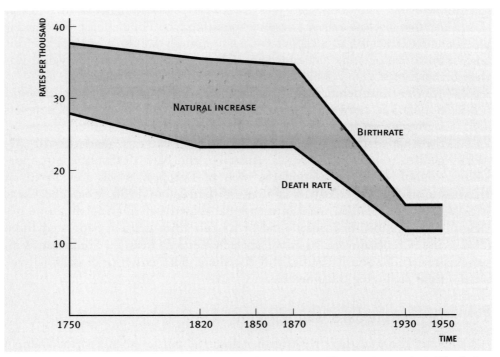

FIGURE 7–1 THE DEMOGRAPHIC TRANSITION IN ENGLAND AND WALES, 1750–1950. The decline in the death rate preceded the decline in the birthrate; this created a period of fairly rapid (about 1 percent per annum) natural increase in the late eighteenth and early nineteenth centuries. After 1870, the birthrate fell more rapidly; this sharply reduced the rate of natural increase. *Source:* Cipolla, *The Economic History of World Population.*

Some of the developing countries that experienced their own demographic transitions have seen far more rapid change than occurred in England and Wales. Shortly after World War II, for reasons discussed in Chapter 10, death rates started to fall almost everywhere. In the developing countries, the mortality decline began at much lower levels of per capita income and fell much faster than it had earlier in the developed countries. An example is given in Figure 7–2 (drawn to the same vertical scale as Figure 7–1), which depicts the demographic experience of Ceylon (now Sri Lanka) during the twentieth century. These early and sharp death rate declines, which by now have been achieved for practically the entire population of the world, were not always followed by such rapid decline in the birthrate as occurred in Sri Lanka after 1955. But, as time goes by, it is becoming increasingly evident that the phenomenon of falling birthrates is widespread. A "new demographic transition" has become visible in most of the developing world, although it probably will continue to differ in important ways from the classic demographic transition experienced earlier by the developed countries.

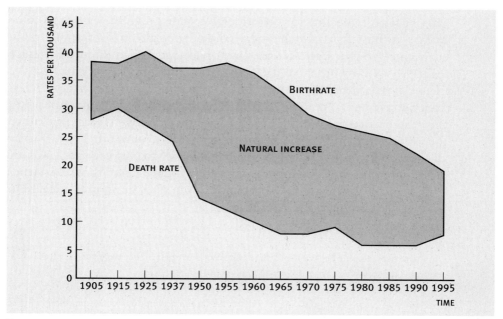

FIGURE 7–2   THE DEMOGRAPHIC TRANSITION OF CEYLON (SRI LANKA). The death rate fell very sharply after 1920 but the birthrate remained high until about 1960. Very high rates of natural increase were experienced in the 1950s and 1960s. Later, however, the crude death rate bottomed out as the population aged and permitted the continuing birthrate decline to bring down the rate of natural increase.

The Present Demographic Situation

Although recent data provide strong evidence that fertility now is falling almost everywhere (see Table 7–1), rates of decline differ greatly among countries and regions. Europe and North America have completed the demographic transition and now have crude birthrates below 20 and rates of natural increase well under 1 percent. Their aging populations and low total fertility rates (TFRs) suggest that natural increase will contribute little if anything to their future population growth.[4] In many developed countries and even some developing countries, current fertility already is too low to replace the existing population.[5] Zero population growth (ZPG), promoted by some as a desirable target in view of limitations on natural resources, soon may be a reality in the industrialized countries.

The developing countries show unmistakable signs of fertility decline.[6] All developing countries with GDP per capita of $1,000 or more (PPP) had lower fertility in 1997 than in 1980.[7] The great majority of countries below this income level also have joined in the move toward lower fertility. Fertility did not rise anywhere in 1980–97 and remained unchanged only in Guinea-Bissau, Niger, and Somalia.

Although nearly everyone is joining the movement to lower fertility, rates of fertility decline vary considerably across regions. The drop came earliest in East Asia, which by no coincidence also had the most rapid economic growth. East Asian women had just 2.1 children on average in 1997, while women in Latin America and the Caribbean had 2.7 (Table 7–1). Although women in sub-Saharan Africa still had 5.5 children on average and those in the Middle East and North Africa 3.7, they too participated in the birthrate decline. Change is least evident in the 18 countries that still had birthrates of 40 or more in 1997. Nearly all these nations are located in sub-Saharan Africa and very poor. Crude death rates in these countries, although higher than those in richer countries, have fallen in recent years, causing rates of natural increase to

---

4. But demographic behavior sometimes surprises the experts. They were confounded, for example, by the post-World War II "baby boom" in the United States.

5. Clearly, women must have at least two children each during their childbearing years for the population to replace itself. Allowing for infant and child mortality, the replacement level of total fertility is around 2.1. In 1996, three important developing countries (China, South Korea and Thailand) had TFRs below 2.1, as did most ex-Communist countries.

6. The data are summarized in Table 7–1 and presented country by country in the *World Development Indicators*.

7. A minor exception is the small African country of Gabon.

TABLE 7–1   CHANGES IN TOTAL FERTILITY RATE BY REGION AND LEVEL OF GNP PER CAPITA (PPP), 1970–97

	1970	1980	1990	1997
REGION				
SUB-SAHARAN AFRICA	6.7	6.7	6.0	5.5
EAST ASIA & PACIFIC	5.4	2.9	2.3	2.1
SOUTH ASIA	6.0	5.3	4.1	3.5
EASTERN EUROPE & CENTRAL ASIA	2.7	2.5	2.4	1.6
WESTERN EUROPE	2.7	2.1	1.8	1.5
MIDDLE EAST & NORTH AFRICA	6.9	6.3	4.9	3.7
UNITED STATES & CANADA	2.5	1.8	2.1	2.0
LATIN AMERICA & CARIBBEAN	5.4	4.2	3.2	2.7
INCOME GROUP				
BELOW $1,000	6.7	6.9	6.5	6.0
$1,000–4,000	5.9	4.2	3.3	2.9
$4,000–7,000	4.8	3.7	2.8	2.1
$7,000–12,000	5.5	4.5	3.5	3.0
ABOVE $12,000	2.5	1.9	1.8	1.7
WORLD	5.2	4.0	3.2	3.2

Source: World Bank, *World Development Indicators, 1999* CD-ROM.

rise.[8] Even a slightly higher income level produces a better situation, however, as Tables 7–1 and 7–2 show. In countries with $1,000–4,000 per capita (PPP), women now have fewer than three babies in their lifetimes and the rate of population growth is down to 1.5 percent.

These widespread fertility declines are causing world population growth to slow down. As Table 7–2 shows, the world's population grew at a rate of 1.4 percent in 1997, an average that masks large differences in regional population growth rates. These regional differences are altering the global population distribution (Table 7–3): 84 percent of humanity lives in developing countries, 35 percent lives in low-income countries, 56 percent lives in Asia. Only 11 percent are sub-Saharan Africans, but this share will rise sharply in the future. As these population-share figures indicate, further reductions in world population growth depend heavily on demographic behavior in the developing countries.

Table 7–2 reveals some demographic characteristics of countries at different levels of GNP per capita. With only a few aberrations, birthrates de-

8. The AIDS epidemic, which is severe in some parts of Africa, has slowed the mortality decline in several countries and contributed significantly to increase in the crude death rate between 1990 and 1997 in Botswana, Kenya, Tanzania, Uganda, and Zambia. This situation will worsen in the future because many Africans are HIV-positive and means of treatment (as well as financing for them) generally are unavailable. Violence is primarily to blame for rising death rates in Rwanda, Sierra Leone, and Somalia in the early 1990s.

TABLE 7–2 DEMOGRAPHIC CHARACTERISTICS OF COUNTRIES BY REGION AND LEVEL OF GNP PER CAPITA (PPP), 1997

	CRUDE BIRTHRATE (PER 1,000)	CRUDE DEATH RATE (PER 1,000)	RATE OF NATURAL INCREASE (%)	INFANT DEATH RATE (PER 1,000 LIVE BIRTHS)
REGION				
SUB-SAHARAN AFRICA	41	15	2.6	89
EAST ASIA & PACIFIC	18	8	1.0	32
SOUTH ASIA	28	9	1.9	75
EASTERN EUROPE & CENTRAL ASIA	12	12	0	17
WESTERN EUROPE	13	9	0.4	10
MIDDLE EAST & NORTH AFRICA	27	7	2.0	46
UNITED STATES & CANADA	15	8	0.7	7
LATIN AMERICA & CARIBBEAN	23	6	1.7	31
INCOME GROUP				
BELOW $1,000	44	16	2.8	80
$1,000–4,000	24	9	1.5	59
$4,000–7,000	18	9	0.9	59
$7,000–12,000	24	7	1.7	25
ABOVE $12,000	12	8	0.4	6
WORLD	23	9	1.4	42

Source: World Bank, *World Development Indicators, 1999* CD-ROM.

TABLE 7–3 WORLD POPULATION BY REGION AND DEVELOPMENT CATEGORY, 1997

	TOTAL POPULATION NUMBER (MILLIONS)	PERCENT OF TOTAL	POPULATION DENSITY (PER SQUARE KM)	ANNUAL GROWTH RATE, 1990–97 (%)
REGION				
SUB-SAHARAN AFRICA	613	11	62	2.8
EAST ASIA & PACIFIC	1,978	34	182	1.2
SOUTH ASIA	1,281	22	357	1.9
EASTERN EUROPE & CENTRAL ASIA	413	7	68	−0.1
WESTERN EUROPE	451	8	137	0.7
MIDDLE EAST & NORTH AFRICA	290	5	53	2.4
UNITED STATES & CANADA	298	5	26	1.0
LATIN AMERICA & CARIBBEAN	495	9	42	1.8
WORLD BANK DEVELOPMENT CATEGORY				
DEVELOPING COUNTRIES	4,898	84	162	1.6
LOW-INCOME COUNTRIES	2,037	35	254	2.1
MIDDLE-INCOME COUNTRIES	2,861	49	96	1.3
HIGH-INCOME COUNTRIES	922	16	206	0.7
WORLD TOTAL	5,820	100	169	1.5

TABLE 7–4 DEMOGRAPHIC CHARACTERISTICS OF SELECTED DEVELOPING COUNTRIES, 1997

	CRUDE BIRTHRATE (PER 1,000)	CRUDE DEATH RATE (PER 1,000)	RATE OF NATURAL INCREASE (%)	TOTAL FERTILITY RATE	INFANT DEATH RATE (PER 1,000 LIVE BIRTHS)
LATIN AMERICA					
BOLIVIA	33	9	2.4	4.4	66
BRAZIL	21	7	1.4	2.3	34
CHILE	20	6	1.4	2.4	11
COLOMBIA	25	6	1.9	2.8	24
PERU	27	6	2.1	3.2	40
AFRICA					
GHANA	36	9	2.7	4.9	66
KENYA	37	13	2.4	4.7	49
TANZANIA	41	16	2.5	5.1	85
ASIA					
CHINA	17	8	0.9	1.9	32
INDIA	27	9	1.8	3.3	71
INDONESIA	24	8	1.6	2.8	47
SOUTH KOREA	15	6	0.9	1.7	9
MALAYSIA	26	5	2.1	3.2	11
PAKISTAN	36	8	2.8	5.0	95
SRI LANKA	19	6	1.3	2.2	14

cline steadily as one moves up the income scale from the poorest countries, with per capita incomes below $1,000 (PPP), to the richest, with annual incomes of $10,000 or more. Death rates, however, are sensitive to per capita income only below $4,000 per capita; almost all countries above that level now have relatively low death rates. The highest rates of natural increase now are in the low-income countries. (Formerly, the middle-income countries had the highest rates, but their birthrates have fallen enough to cut down their rates of natural increase.) The infant death rate is a particularly sensitive measure of death rate decline; it falls by 93 percent from the poorest group of countries in Table 7–2 to the richest group. Table 7–4 gives similar information for selected countries and thus provides some idea of the range of intercountry variation.

The high birthrates still found in most low-income countries give them populations in which children make up large shares of the total—46 percent on average in the poorest countries versus only 19 percent in high-income countries (see Table 7–5). Elderly people are a more significant (and growing) component of the population in developed countries, but China and a few other developing countries that rapidly depressed fertility already are experiencing a rapid aging of their populations (Tables 7–5

TABLE 7-5   POPULATION CHARACTERISTICS OF COUNTRIES BY REGION AND LEVEL OF GNP PER CAPITA (PPP), 1997

	POPULATION BELOW 15 YEARS (% OF TOTAL)	POPULATION 65 OR OLDER (% OF TOTAL)	GROWTH RATE OF URBAN POPULATION 1990–97 (%)	URBAN POPULATION (% OF TOTAL)
REGION				
SUB-SAHARAN AFRICA	44	3	5.0	34
EAST ASIA & PACIFIC	27	7	2.2	37
SOUTH ASIA	36	4	3.3	27
EASTERN EUROPE & CENTRAL ASIA	23	11	1.2	67
WESTERN EUROPE	19	14	1.2	75
MIDDLE EAST & NORTH AFRICA	38	4	4.0	61
UNITED STATES & CANADA	22	12	1.3	77
LATIN AMERICA & CARIBBEAN	33	5	2.3	74
INCOME GROUP				
BELOW $1,000	46	3	5.0	30
$1,000–$4,000	32	5	2.7	31
$4,000–$7,000	28	8	2.9	70
$7,000–$12,000	33	6	2.4	71
ABOVE $12,000	19	14	1.1	79
WORLD	31	7	2.6	46

Source: World Bank, *World Development Indicators 1999* CD-ROM.

and 7–6). A country with a large share of either young or elderly population is said to have a high **dependency ratio,** or ratio of non-working-age population (conventionally defined as 0 to 14 and 65 and over) to working-age population. A high dependency ratio depresses per capita income by requiring the output of a given number of producers to be shared among a larger number of consumers.

The spatial distribution of population is another concern in many low-income countries. **Urbanization** is a well-known concomitant of development. In low-income countries, the majority of people live in rural areas; in middle- and high-income countries, most live in towns and cities (Table 7–5). Fear that migration from the countryside is causing urban areas to grow too fast and creating serious social problems frequently is expressed. Yet when third world governments have tried to stanch the flow, they enjoyed little success. The reason is that people have found they can better themselves in several ways by moving to the cities. They earn higher income than in the rural areas and gain access to better schooling for their children and social services of other kinds. This is what people seek in rural-urban migration, and studies have shown that, by and large, they find it.

TABLE 7–6	POPULATION CHARACTERISTICS OF SELECTED DEVELOPING COUNTRIES, 1997			
	POPULATION BELOW 15 YEARS (% OF TOTAL)	POPULATION 65 OR OLDER (% OF TOTAL)	GROWTH RATE OF URBAN POPULATION 1990–97 (%)	URBAN POPULATION (% OF TOTAL)
LATIN AMERICA				
BOLIVIA	40.2	3.9	4.1	62
BRAZIL	30.7	4.8	2.4	80
CHILE	29.0	6.8	1.8	84
COLOMBIA	33.7	4.5	1.1	72
PERU	35.3	4.4	2.3	72
AFRICA				
GHANA	44.1	3.1	4.0	37
KENYA	44.9	2.9	6.3	30
TANZANIA	45.7	2.5	6.1	26
ASIA				
CHINA	25.7	6.8	1.7	29
INDIA	34.8	4.7	2.9	27
INDONESIA	32.2	4.4	4.6	37
SOUTH KOREA	22.5	6.0	2.8	83
MALAYSIA	33.0	3.9	4.0	54
PAKISTAN	42.5	3.1	4.0	35
SRI LANKA	28.1	6.2	2.2	23

This raises an important question: If rural-urban migration is good for the people who move, can it really be bad for society? It is true that external social costs are associated with the migration process: Congestion may make it harder to provide adequate urban infrastructure (housing, roads, sewers, etc.) and social services. This can be seen as a problem of **common property.** We all benefit from having fresh air to breathe, and we all lose when the air becomes polluted, but as individuals we have little incentive to avoid polluting because doing so has little effect on the air we ourselves breathe. Is not some form of social intervention therefore needed to limit pollution so that we all may have fresher air to breathe?

Probably, but many of the social costs of urbanization arise because governments feel obliged to provide facilities for urban populations that they do not provide for rural populations. If they choose to provide better facilities in the cities than in the villages, they can hardly complain when people avail themselves of the opportunity to get improved educational, health, and recreational services. The common perception of urbanization as a problem contains an element of class bias. Ruling elites sometimes feel threatened by rapid growth in the number of poor people who live, so to speak, within marching distance of the palace.

Some third world governments have tried to accelerate the development of secondary towns or backward regions of the country. To the extent that these policies attempt to counteract the existing pattern of incentives affecting the location of population and economic activity, they frequently fail. To make them succeed, governments have to commit large amounts of their own resources to the backward areas in the form of infrastructure and public facilities. It would take nothing less than a radical shift in development strategy to a genuine emphasis on the intensification and diversification of the rural economy to do the job.

The Demographic Future

When extrapolated into the future, even modest-seeming population growth rates generate projected total populations that may seem unthinkable. Continued growth at the 1.4 percent rate that prevailed in 1997 would bring the world's population to 12.2 billion by 2050 and 24.4 billion by 2100.

This type of projection, beloved by popular writers, is frightening to many. It is hard to imagine life in a world with two to four times as many people as there are today. How will this expanded population live? How will the globe's finite supplies of space and natural resources be affected? Should population growth be slowed down? Can it be slowed down? These obviously are vital questions that concern everyone.

In the first place, linear extrapolations of current trends are invalid because, as we have seen, after accelerating for more than two centuries, world population growth now is slowing down. While the demographic transition clearly has spread to the developing countries, the speed of future birthrate decline remains uncertain. The World Bank has projected that further declines in fertility will slow the world population sufficiently that the 2050 figure will be 9.6 billion and that of 2100 will be 11.0 billion, less than half the figure produced by linear extrapolation.[9] No one knows for sure, however; fertility could rise again, as it has in the past. Long-term projections are useful illustrations of the dramatic power of population growth over time, but they cannot be taken literally. On a sobering note, Joel Cohen of Rockefeller University pointed out that we are approaching global population levels at which various thinkers have calculated that natural limits to the earth's carrying capacity might be encountered.[10]

9. World Bank, *Population and Development: Implications for the World Bank* (Washington, DC: World Bank, 1994), p. 29.

10. Joel E. Cohen, *How Many People Can the Earth Support?* (New York: W.W. Norton, 1996).

We do know for certain that world population growth will continue to grow for some time yet because of **demographic momentum.** Populations that have been growing rapidly have large numbers of people in, or about to enter, the most fertile age brackets. Even if all the world's couples today were to start having just enough children to replace themselves in the population—what is called the *replacement level of fertility*—growth would continue well into the twenty-first century. If the replacement level of fertility were reached around 2025, world population would stabilize at about 10 billion near 2100.[11]

The Causes of Population Growth

So, world population growth will continue for at least another 100 years. The bulk of this growth will occur in the developing countries, with an increasing share in Africa. Viewpoints on this prospect vary widely, and discussions of world population often turn acrimonious. Questions of whose population is to be limited and by what means clearly are sensitive. Before we can confront such issues intelligently, we must consider what is known about both the causes and the effects of rapid population growth. In particular, a course on economic development must concern itself with the two-way relationship between the growth of population and the combination of rising average income levels and structural change that we term *economic development.* We deal first with economic development as a cause of population growth.

MALTHUS AND HIS WORLD

The most famous and influential demographic theorist of all time was Thomas R. Malthus (1766–1834). His pessimistic view of the principles underlying human reproduction and the prospects of economic development is well-known. Malthus believed that "the passion between the sexes" would cause population to expand as long and far as food supplies permitted. People generally would not limit procreation below the biological maximum. Should wages somehow rise above the subsistence level, workers would marry younger and have more children. But this situation could be only temporary. In time, the rise in population growth would create an increase in labor supply, which would press against fixed land resources and eventually, through diminishing returns, cause wages to fall

---

11. See Thomas W. Merrick, "World Population in Transition," *Population Bulletin,* 41, no. 2 (January 1988), 8–16.

back to the subsistence level. If this process went too far, famines and rising deaths would result. Malthus did not think that the growth of the food supply could stay ahead of population growth in the long run. In a famous example, he argued that food supplies grow according to an arithmetic (additive) progression while population follows an explosive geometric (multiplicative) progression.

We can see that, in the grim Malthusian world, population growth is limited primarily by factors working through the death rate, what he called *positive checks*. In this deceptively mild phrase, Malthus included all the disasters that exterminate people in large numbers: famines, wars, and epidemics. These phenomena, he believed, generally constitute the operative limitation on population. Only in the late editions of his famous *Essay on the Principle of Population* did he concede the possibility of a second, less drastic, category of limiting factors: "preventive checks" that work through the birthrate. Here, Malthus had in mind here primarily measures of "restraint," such as a later age of marriage. Unlike latter-day "Malthusians" he did not advocate birth control, which as a minister he considered immoral. Although he grudgingly admitted that humanity might voluntarily control its own numerical growth, Malthus invested little hope in the possibility.

The gloominess of the Malthusian theory is understandable when one considers that its author lived during the early years of the Industrial Revolution. In all prior history (that is, through the first two demographic eras outlined previously), the population had tended to expand in response to economic gains. With unprecedented economic growth underway in the world he knew, what could Malthus expect except an acceleration of natural increase as death rates fell? That indeed was happening during his lifetime.

Malthus did not live to witness the rest of the European demographic transition. As Figure 7–1 showed, the early decline in deaths rates was followed, with a lag, by a fall in fertility; beginning in the middle of the nineteenth century, wages began to increase dramatically. Why did all this happen? Wages rose, despite accelerating population growth, because capital accumulation and technical change offset any tendency for the marginal product of labor to decline. It appears that the death rate fell through a combination of the indirect effects of higher incomes (better nutrition and living conditions) and the direct effects of better preventive and curative health measures. The fall in the birthrate is harder to understand. There are both biological and economic reasons to expect, as Malthus did, that fertility would rise, not fall, as income went up. Healthier, better-fed women have a greater biological capacity to conceive, carry a child full term, and give birth to a healthy infant. Also, people marry earlier when times are good, and better-off families have the financial capacity to support more children. Why, then, do increases in income seem to lead to declines in fertility? An answer to this question must be sought in post-Malthusian demographic theory.

MECHANISMS FOR REDUCING BIRTHRATES

The first stage of the demographic transition is marked by a decline in the death rate, particularly a reduction in deaths among infants and young children. This in itself is a very good thing and no humane person or government would wish to reverse the trend. The question of how to reduce the rate of population growth therefore narrows down to ways of lowering the birthrate.

Three kinds of demographic change affect the crude birthrate. The first is change in the population shares of different age groups and sexes. A rise in the share of people of reproductive age (roughly 15 to 45) increases the birthrate, as we saw earlier in the discussion of demographic momentum. Conversely, if the proportion of older people in the population goes up, as is happening in many industrial countries today, the birthrate drops. Similarly, unbalancing the sex ratio (for example, through migration of men) reduces the birthrate, whereas correcting a previously unbalanced ratio increases it. However, these structural effects are quantitatively important only in rather special circumstances.

The second demographic mechanism that influences the birthrate is change in the share of people of reproductive age who are married. This in turn is affected by the proportion who marry at some time in their lives, by the average age of first marriage and by the divorce rate.

The third factor is marital fertility, the rate at which married couples reproduce. Historical birthrate declines have come about mainly because of declines in marital fertility. A later age of marriage also has been important in some cases, for example, in the drop of the Irish birthrate after the potato famine of the 1840s.

It has been suggested that three basic preconditions are needed for a significant decline in marital fertility. (1) Fertility must be subject to conscious choice; it must be socially acceptable for a couple to decide how many children they want to have. (2) Reduced fertility must be seen as advantageous; social and economic benefits to having fewer children must be perceived. (3) Effective techniques of fertility reduction must be available; couples must know about them and agree to employ them.[12] Some theorists regard the first and third preconditions as merely facilitating influ-

---

12. Michael S. Teitelbaum, "Relevance of Demographic Transition Theory for Developing Countries," *Science*, 188 (May 2, 1977), 420–25.

ences. The active force working for lower birthrates, they argue, is perceived incentives for individuals to have fewer children.

MODERN THEORIES OF FERTILITY

Modern theories of fertility try to explain how people use the available mechanisms for determining the number of births. Many of these theories employ a supply and demand framework. Looked at this way, family planning programs work mainly on the supply side. They can reduce the birthrate by making it easier and cheaper for people to regulate the number of births and come closer to their desired family size. They also may affect the demand side of this equation (the number of children people want to have) through propaganda but probably not much. The social motivations that lead governments to undertake family planning programs—perceived crowding and strain on national resources, perhaps some pressure from foreign aid organizations—are unlikely to carry much weight with individuals. Couples are unmoved by general, remote-sounding arguments.

Why, then, do people have children? Is it because they are moved by Malthus's "passion between the sexes" and do not know how to prevent the resulting births? Or do they have many children because they are tradition bound, custom ridden? Or is it perhaps rational in some social settings? All three positions have some merit. The case for the first one was stated by a Latin American doctor at an international conference a few years ago. "People don't really want children," he said. "They want sex and don't know how to avoid the births that result." This viewpoint captures the element of spontaneity inevitably present in the reproductive process. Yet the evidence suggests that all societies consciously control human fertility. In no known case does the number of children that the average woman has over her childbearing years even approach her biological capacity to bear children. All societies practice methods of inhibiting conception, aborting pregnancies, and disposing of unwanted infants, even societies that have had no contact with modern birth control methods.

It has been said that many children are the social norm in traditional societies, that society looks askance at couples who have no or few children, that a man who lacks wealth at least can have children, and that a woman's principal socially recognized function in a traditional society is to bear and rear children. Such norms and attitudes are important, but they probably are not the decisive factors in human fertility. Fertility evidently is determined by a complex combination of forces, but social scientists in recent years have given increasing credence to the elements of individual rationality in the process. Simply stated, they believe that most families in traditional societies have many children because it is rational for them to do so. By the same token people in modern societies have fewer children because that is rational behavior in the settings in which they live. It follows that, to reduce fertility in developing countries, it is necessary to alter the incentives.

Although some would regard it as a cold, inhumane way of looking at the matter, it is nevertheless true that children impose certain costs on their parents and confer certain benefits. To the extent that couples are influenced by these benefits and costs, are able to calculate them, and are able to carry out their reproductive plans, it follows that, to reduce the birthrate, it will be necessary to raise the ratio of costs to benefits.

The benefits of having children can be classified as economic and psychic. Within a few years of their birth, children may supplement family earnings by working. On family farms and in other household enterprises there usually is something that even a very young child can do to increase production. In many poor societies, large numbers of children work for wages outside the home. In the longer run, children also provide a form of social security in societies that lack institutional programs to assist the elderly. In some cultures it is considered especially important to have a son who survives to adulthood; if infant and child mortality is high, this can motivate couples to keep having children until two or three sons have been born, just to be safe. In addition to these economic benefits, which are probably more important in a low-income society than a more affluent one, children also can yield psychic benefits, as all parents know.

The costs of children also can be categorized as economic and psychic. Economic costs can be further divided into explicit (monetary) and implicit (opportunity) costs. Children entail cash outlays for food, clothing, shelter, and sometimes for hired child-care services and education. Implicit costs arise when child care by a member of the family, usually the mother, involves a loss of earning time. Psychic costs include anxiety and loss of leisure-time activities. Some of the costs felt by parents parallel the costs of population growth experienced at the national level. For example, more children in a family may mean smaller inheritances of agricultural land, an example of a natural resource constraint operating at the family level. Similarly, it may be harder to send all the children in a larger family to school; this reflects the pressures on social investment felt when population growth is rapid.

Viewing childbearing as an economic decision has several important implications. (1) Fertility should be higher when young children can earn income or contribute to household enterprises than when they cannot. (2) Reducing infant deaths should lower fertility because fewer births will be needed to produce a given desired number of surviving children. (3) The introduction of an institutionalized social security system should lower fertility by reducing the need for parents to depend on their children for support in their old age. (4) Fertility should fall when there is an increase in opportunities for women to work in jobs that are relatively incompatible with childbearing, essentially work outside the home. (5) Fertility should be higher when income is higher because the explicit costs are more easily borne.

The first four theoretical predictions have received substantial support from empirical studies. The fifth, however, conflicts sharply with observed reality. In the real world, fertility usually is negatively related to income, not positively related as simple theory predicts. The negative relationship shows up both in time-series data (that is, fertility usually declines through time as income rises) and in cross-section data (fertility generally is higher in poor countries than in rich ones; also, in most societies, middle- and upper-income families have fewer children than poor families).

Several theorists have wrestled with this anomaly. Gary Becker of the University of Chicago, a pioneer of "the new household economics," views children as a kind of consumer durable that yields benefits over time. Couples maximize a joint (expected) utility function in which the "goods" they can "buy" are (1) number of living children, (2) "child quality" (a vector of characteristics including education and health), and (3) conventional goods and services. The constraints faced by parents in Becker's model are (1) their time and (2) the cost of purchased goods and services. Becker explains the fall in fertility as income rises over time by saying that the cost of children tends to rise, especially because the opportunity cost of the parents' time goes up. He believes that the spread of contraceptive knowledge also plays a part. Given the rising cost of child *quantity,* Becker argues, many parents opt to invest in child *quality* and spend more money on a decreasing number of children.[13]

Whereas Malthus erred in basing his theory of population on the assumption that people always would be driven by their passions, Becker has been charged with going too far in the opposite direction and exaggerating the extent to which couples consciously select their family sizes using a cost-benefit calculus. Others argue that socially conditioned changes in tastes and values are an important part of the demographic transition, but Becker regards tastes as given.

Rivaling Becker's purely economic model of fertility is the more eclectic framework of University of Pennsylvania demographer Richard Easterlin, who directly addresses people's motivation to use the available means of fertility control. He says this is determined by two factors. One is the demand for children, defined as the number of surviving children a couple would have if fertility regulation were costless; this essentially is a matter of taste, which Easterlin, unlike Becker, believes does change over time. The

13. See Gary Becker, *A Treatise on the Family* (Cambridge, MA: Harvard University Press, 1981).

second factor influencing people's interest in fertility control is natural fertility, which Easterlin defines as their potential number of children if fertility were not deliberately limited; this is determined partly by biology and partly by culture. Besides motivation to limit fertility, Easterlin believes the cost of controlling fertility is another important influence on the use of means to limit births. To Easterlin, the cost includes not only market costs, such as the cost of contraceptives, but also psychic costs deriving, for example, from social disapproval of particular fertility limitation practices. Easterlin thus explains declining fertility in the real world as the combined effect of changing tastes and the declining cost of fertility control.

For the population policy maker, Becker's theory emphasizes the importance of changing incentives to have children if one wishes to reduce fertility, while Easterlin's approach points to the need to change tastes and reduce the market and psychic costs of practicing birth control.[14]

The demographer John Caldwell explains the demographic transition in somewhat different terms that still are consistent with the general idea of rational choice. He argues that the main reason why large families are rational in traditional societies is that extended family relationships cause net intergenerational wealth transfers to flow from younger to older generations. According to Caldwell, as nuclear families become more common and the emotional and economic ties between generations weaken in the course of modernization, the direction of the intergenerational flow of wealth reverses. Since parents must now transfer net wealth to their children, rather than receive net wealth from them, they opt to have fewer children.[15]

Analyzing the Effects of Rapid Population Growth

Two questions are important for population policy. What are the effects of population growth on development and human welfare? And, if population growth is thought to have harmful effects, how can these harmful effects best be reduced or eliminated?

OPTIMUM POPULATION

The theory just reviewed implies that, at the family level, population tends toward an optimum, in the sense that people have the number of children they consider beneficial to their overall welfare. Yet, when asked, many

14. See Richard Easterlin, "Modernization and Fertility: A Critical Essay," in R. Bulatao and R. Lee, eds., *Determinants of Fertility in Developing Countries,* Vol. 2 (New York: Academic Press, 1983), pp. 562–86.

15. See John C. Caldwell, "Toward a Restatement of Demographic Transition Theory," *Population and Development Review,* 2, nos. 3–4 (September–December 1976), 321–66.

parents in developing countries say that they would rather have fewer children than they have. Also, several studies show that rates of sickness and death are higher among children in large families, especially those born later. So perhaps spouses' judgments about optimal family size change after they become parents and form a more realistic appraisal of the costs and benefits of children.

When we consider the relationship between population and welfare at the national level, the main question is whether individual preferences should be allowed to determine how large a population a country has. What are the effects of population growth on development and human welfare? Is there a case for the state to intervene to curb, or in some instances perhaps to encourage, human reproduction?

We can begin to attack this issue by considering the relationship between per capita income and the size of a country's population. Would per capita income be higher or lower if the population were larger than it is? In dynamic terms, which are more relevant for policy, the question is whether the future growth of per capita income would be faster or slower if the rate of population growth were increased or reduced.

An answer to this equation can be reached through successive approximations. The oldest and simplest answer is that with every mouth comes a pair of hands. This implies that economic activity is scale neutral, that per capita income is unaffected by the size or growth rate of the population. But this ancient piece of folk wisdom is all too obviously oversimplified. It ignores the role of nonlabor resources and particularly the possibility (which so concerned Ricardo and Malthus) that diminishing returns will be encountered as population expands.

A somewhat more sophisticated approach that meets this objection is the optimum population theory: For any given country with a fixed supply of nonlabor resources at any particular time, there is a unique population size at which per capita income is maximized. At suboptimal levels of population, per capita income is lower than it could be because there is not enough labor to utilize efficiently the available nonlabor resources. At levels above the optimum, per capita income also is lower than it could be because there is too much labor and diminishing returns set in. This relationship is graphed in Figure 7–3.

Optimum population theory is consistent with the intuition that countries can be either underpopulated or overpopulated. It is not hard to believe that immigration into the United States, Canada, and Australia during the nineteenth century raised per capita income in those countries. (It is harder to think of underpopulated countries in today's world.) Nor is it implausible to think that Bangladesh's per capita income would rise if some millions of its population could somehow be made to disappear. The trouble is that this is a static approach that takes only limited account of

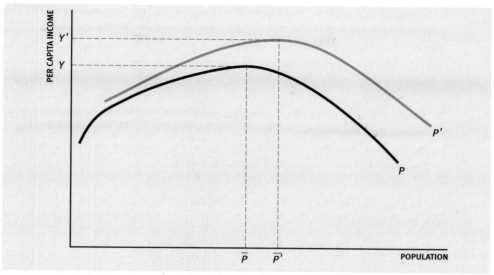

FIGURE 7–3 THE THEORY OF OPTIMUM POPULATION. Curve *P* shows that, at levels of population below *P*, an increase in population leads to an increase in income per capita, but beyond *P*, more population reduces average income. *P* is the optimum level of population. Discoveries of new resources, capital accumulation, or technological change can shift the curve upward to *P′*, with a new, higher optimum population *P′*.

dynamic factors. Capital accumulation, technical change, and natural-resource discoveries make it possible simultaneously to raise per capita income and increase the optimum population over time.

DYNAMIC MODELS OF POPULATION GROWTH

Figure 7–3 depicts what economists call comparative statics. Optimum population theory shows how income per capita is determined at a point in time, given population, stocks of other resources, and technology. It also indicates how income per capita is affected by, say, a one-time improvement in technology; but it does not show what would happen through time as population and capital stocks grow, as resource supplies stabilize or decline, and as technology changes. A dynamic model would try to do that.

The pioneering dynamic model of population's effect on material welfare was written in 1958 by Princeton University demographer Ansley Coale and Duke University economist Edgar Hoover.[16] According to their

16. Ansley J. Coale and Edgar M. Hoover, *Population Growth and Economic Development in Low-Income Countries: A Case Study of India's Prospects* (Princeton, NJ: Princeton University Press, 1958).

analysis of population and economic growth in India, a reduction in the birthrate would help raise per capita income in two important ways. First, slower population growth would lower the dependency ratio, reducing consumption and increasing saving at any given level of income. Second, as labor force growth slowed about 15 years later, the amount of investment needed to provide a constant amount of capital per worker for a growing number of workers (called *capital widening*) would go down and permit more investment to be used to increase capital per worker *(capital deepening)*. These two benefits from slower population growth would be felt both at the household and national levels.

CONCERN ABOUT THE EFFECTS OF POPULATION GROWTH ON DEVELOPMENT

Later model builders generally supported the findings of Coale and Hoover and endorsed the long-standing view that rapid population growth impedes development. During the 1970s, the U.S. Agency for International Development, the World Bank, and other international aid agencies gave heavy emphasis to population policy as a criterion for judging the seriousness of the development effort of a potential aid recipient. A comprehensive review of population change and development conducted by the World Bank in 1984 found that rapid population growth depresses private savings, necessitates more capital widening, and discourages capital deepening that would raise productivity and per capita income.[17] In addition, many writers called attention to the deleterious effects of population growth on the environment. They noted that rising population densities have contributed to deforestation in many parts of the third world, as rural people move up the hillsides in search of more agricultural land and firewood. Indeed, depletion of all nonrenewable resources is accelerated by rapid population growth. Maintaining a stable or rising per capita food supply has been less of a problem than Malthus anticipated, but it has proven difficult in wide areas of sub-Saharan Africa. The World Bank, among many others, also has pointed to the impact of a growing total population on urbanization, which brings with it extra costs that society must bear.

The proposition that population growth retards increases in per capita income has obvious appeal in developing countries (including many in Asia, Egypt, and most Caribbean islands) where population density already is so high in relation to land and other natural resources that diminishing returns probably have set in. Even in areas where population density is lower, however—relatively land-rich areas in sub-Saharan Africa and South America— rapid population growth can press on scarce capital resources and inhibit

---

17. See *World Development Report 1984*, pp. 51–206.

capital deepening and efforts to improve public services. It thus can be argued that it reduces the growth of per capita income in both types of LDCs.

Recall from the earlier discussion of fertility determinants that, although some of the pressures created by high population growth and density are felt by individuals, others are not. For example, excessive growth in the number of school-age children makes it difficult for society to provide schooling of adequate quality for everyone. Although a reduction in the average number of children per family would contribute to a solution of this problem, particular couples would not find publicly financed educational facilities any better if they had fewer children (although they would be better able to meet the private costs of schooling). One argument for policy intervention to bring about a more moderate rate of population growth is that such social diseconomies can be avoided.

Also contended is that rapid population control in particular countries produces external diseconomies at the international level. There are nationalistic reasons, related to prestige and sometimes also to military power, why particular states may want larger populations. But this can disrupt international relations and injure other countries. Policies to expand national populations may raise the likelihood of war by making larger armies possible and heightening competition for land and other resources. These may create pressures for migration from densely populated countries to countries whose population growth is under control. For all these reasons, a case can be made for an international effort to limit world population. The problem is to decide whose population is to be limited. Possibilities for doing much about population at the global level are limited by the linkage of the population problem to other issues of international politics and by the locus of population policy, which is at the national level.

DOUBTERS AND DISSENTERS

Despite the arguments for limiting population growth in developing countries, the results of population modelers, and the views of powerful aid organizations, there always have been dissenters from the majority opinion that rapid population growth is harmful to economic development in the third word. These contrary views have received some support recently from empirical researchers who found it difficult to identify or measure population growth's deleterious effects.

Some analysts have doubted that faster population growth retards growth in per capita income or even claimed that it is beneficial.

1. Australian economist Colin Clark was one of the first to note the lack of empirical support for the proposition that population growth impedes economic growth. He claimed that the empirical relationship

between the growth rate of population and that of per capita income in fact was positive.[18]

2. Danish economist Ester Boserup concluded from her historical studies of agricultural development that population growth serves as a stimulus to agricultural intensification and technological impirovement.[19]

3. Julian Simon of the University of Illinois mustered a variety of arguments in favor of population growth, notably that a larger population is likely to contain more entrepreneurs and other creators, who can make major contributions to solving the problems of humanity. He called human ingenuity the "ultimate resource" that can overcome any depletion of other resoures.[20]

4. Rati Ram of the University of Illinois and Theodore W. Schultz of the University of Chicago have pointed out that the longer life spans that accompany falling death rates and faster population growth in the LDCs increase the incentives for investment in human capital and make labor more productive.[21]

5. A 1986 review of population and development sponsored by the National Academy of Sciences addressed a series of assertions about the negative effects of population growth and generally found that empirical evidence to support them is weak.[22]

CONCLUSION

Despite these doubts, dissents, and inconclusive evidence, most analysts continue to believe that, in the circumstances of nearly all LDCs, slower population growth would permit per capita income to rise more rapidly. The experience of East Asian countries over the past three decades shows how rapid economic growth and falling fertility can interact to create a "virtuous circle" that is the antithesis of the better-known "vicious circle" of poverty and high fertility accompanied by high rates of sickness and death. It also indicates that the growth rate of a population may be less important for economic development than the effect of the demographic

---

18. See Colin Clark, "The 'Population Explosion' Myth," *Bulletin of the Institute of Development Studies* [Sussex, England] (May 1969); and Colin Clark, "The Economics of Population Growth and Control: A Comment," *Review of Social Economy,* 28, no. 1 (March 1970), 449–66.

19. See Ester Boserup, *The Conditions of Agricultural Growth* (Chicago: Aldine, 1965).

20. See Julian L. Simon, *The Ultimate Resource* (Princeton, NJ: Princeton University Press, 1981); and Julian L. Simon, *Theory of Population and Economic Growth* (Oxford: Basil Blackwell, 1986).

21. Rati Ram and Theodore W. Schultz, "Life Span, Savings, and Productivity," *Economic Development and Cultural Change,* 27, no. 3 (April 1979), 394–421.

22. See National Academy of Sciences, *Population Growth and Economic Development: Policy Questions* (Washington, DC: National Academy Press, 1986).

transition on the age structure of the population.[23] Getting from a vicious circle to a virtuous one, however, is no simple matter. Population growth is affected by many different policies and development programs. Which ones should a developing country select?

Population Policy

Most LDC governments today are on record as favoring slower population growth and have formulated policies for attempting to achieve it. The strongest commitments generally have come from Asian governments. In Latin America, governments may provide family planning services officially or permit private organizations to do so, but their actions usually are rationalized as efforts to promote the welfare of mothers and children. Some African governments are committed to population growth limitation, while others have been indifferent or even hostile (see the case study on Kenya). The population policies of Communist regimes have varied among countries and from time to time. China achieved what is probably the most effective control over population ever attained by any government through its "planned births" campaign (see the case study).

Population policy has raised political, moral, and religious issues in a number of countries. Some countries are pronatalist for nationalistic reasons, perhaps because they want enough people to hold areas of low population density against external challenges. Others (Guyana, Lebanon, Nigeria, Malaysia, and Singapore, to name a few) have internal racial, tribal, religious, or ethnic divisions that make population policy a sensitive matter, since it involves the balance of power among the various groups. Still other countries have provoked adverse political reactions by adopting methods of population control regarded as excessively zealous, offensive to local belief, or callous in their disregard of individual rights. Indira Gandhi's surprising defeat in India's 1977 general election was attributed in part to the population policy of her emergency government. Despairing

---

23. A rise in the proportion of working-age adults in the population benefited economic development in East Asia substantially between 1965 and 1990. Matthew Higgins of the Federal Reserve Bank of New York, and Jeffrey Williamson and David Bloom of Harvard University show that this change in population boosted savings, reduced dependence on foreign capital, and accelerated the growth of the labor force. They estimate that this demographic shift contributed as much as one third of observed economic growth over the period. See Matthew Higgins and Jeffrey G. Williamson, "Age Structure Dynamics in Asia and Dependence on Foreign Capital," *Population and Development Review,* 21, no. 2 (June 1997), 261–93; David E. Bloom and Jeffrey G. Williamson, "Demographic Transitions and Economic Miracles in Emerging Asia," *World Bank Economic Review,* 12, no. 3 (September 1998), 419–55.

POPULATION AND FAMILY PLANNING IN KENYA

Kenya is an African country with relatively low population density but a high population growth rate and explosive demographic potential. Until the early 1980s, Kenya's total fertility rate was 8 and its population growth rate well above 3 percent, both among the highest in the world. A survey taken in the late 1970s found that the average Kenyan regarded eight children as an ideal family size, up from six in the 1960s. Nevertheless, fertility began to fall in the 1980s. The total fertility rate dropped to 5.6 by 1990 and 4.7 in 1997. Although the population still is growing at 2.4 percent, fast enough to double in 29 years, a demographic transition clearly is underway.

Why were Kenyans so very fertile, and why are they now becoming less so? The decline in the 1980s and 1990s seems to have resulted from a combination of economic and social change and the increased availability of family planning services. Although Nairobi, the capital, is a prosperous, modern city, the country still is 70 percent rural. The per capita GNP of $1,160 (PPP, 1997) is distributed very unequally. Water shortages severely restrict the cultivability of much of Kenya's land, and in some of the fertile areas, there are large farms. Many Kenyans, therefore, must make a living from holdings that are either too small or too poorly watered to ensure an adequate income.

Although the Kenyan government adopted a policy of population limitation as early as 1966, the national family planning program received only tepid political backing before the 1980s. The late president Jomo Kenyatta, who issued the 1966 policy statement, later refused to lend public support to family planning. Kenya's keen tribal rivalries made the issue a sensitive one, since each group feared that if it adopted birth limitation it would become weaker relative to its competitors. In recent years, however, as the dangers of continued rapid population growth have become both evident and imminent, President Daniel Arap Moi's government has actively supported a revived family planning effort, which is widely regarded as having contributed to the fertility declines observed since 1980.

of controlling population growth by conventional means, the government added male sterilization to its list of promoted family planning methods. Incentives were offered to those who agreed to be sterilized, and quotas were assigned to officials charged with carrying out the program in different parts of the country. Problems arose when force allegedly was used against low-status individuals by officials anxious to fill their quotas. The result was a setback not only for Indira Gandhi's government but also for Indian family planning.

The thinking about population and development reviewed here casts light on both the rationale for population policy in the LDCs and the proper design of programs to reduce fertility. Population policy must be grounded in a consideration of the effects of rapid population growth in a low-income country. Its design should pay attention to the modern theories of fertility determination.

Two main rationales are used for the promotion of family planning in an LDC. One is that, through information dissemination and access to contraceptives, couples can be helped to realize their reproductive plans. The second rationale is that high fertility has social costs not taken into account by individuals but that should be offset by the government on behalf of society by subsidizing family planning, penalizing couples who have many children, or both. The first argument enjoys wide support; the second is more controversial.

POLICY ALTERNATIVES

A policy maker who wishes to reduce population growth can consider family planning, integrated programs of reproductive health, population redistribution, more drastic measures like abortion or sterilization, and policies that alter reproductive incentives.

In essence, **family planning programs** do two things: make one or more forms of contraception more widely or cheaply available or both and undertake information and propaganda activities to urge people to use them. These programs have achieved good results in some cases but had little or no discernible effect in others. They appear to work best where at least some people in the population already want smaller families. Most of the family planning programs that have been relatively successful in reaching a large number of acceptors and retaining a large stock of current users over time are to be found in countries rapidly attaining higher literacy, reduced infant death rates, and more widespread employment of women outside the home.[24] In countries where these factors are absent, family

---

24. This list of factors is based on empirical research. Some of the reasons why these factors should be influential were suggested earlier.

POPULATION AND FAMILY PLANNING IN CHINA

Since 1971, China has made spectacular and unique progress toward controlling the growth of its massive population. By doing so, it not only has made a large numerical impact on world population growth but also provided important lessons to other low-income countries interested in fertility reduction. Yet some of the techniques used to reduce the number of births in China may not be transferable to other political and cultural settings, and others would not be widely acceptable because of the loss of personal freedom they involve.

Population policy in China has been anything but constant. After the Communist takeover in 1949, Chairman Mao Zedong repeatedly asserted that "revolution plus production" would solve all problems, with no need to limit population growth. China's first census, conducted in 1953, revealed such a large population (nearly 600 million) that it shook this complacency. But birth control campaigns from 1956 to 1958 and from 1962 to 1966 had only limited results and were interrupted by Mao's famous policy reversals, the Great Leap Forward of 1960 and the Cultural Revolution of the late 1960s. Only in 1971 was a serious and sustained effort launched. At that time, the crude birthrate, already reduced by the disruptions of the Cultural Revolution, stood at 30. By 1983 it had been cut to 19.

The "planned births" campaign of 1971 reportedly was launched at the personal initiative of Premier Zhou Enlai. It established three reproductive norms *(wan xi shao):* later marriage, longer spacing between births, and fewer children. To implement these norms, the highly committed post-Mao leadership set birth targets for administrative units at all levels throughout China. The responsibility for achieving these targets was placed in the hands of officials heading units ranging from provinces of 2 to 90 million people down to production teams of 250 to 800. The national government held information and motivation campaigns to persuade people to have fewer children, but

planning tends to catch on among the relatively well-off, the urbanized, and the educated, but it spreads very slowly among the rest of the population. The record, however, is not clear-cut. In some parts of rural Indonesia, family planning has had a measurable effect on the birthrate, despite comparatively low levels of income, education, and health services (see the case study on page 276).

it was left to local officials to fill out many details of the program and finance much of its cost. A wide range of contraceptives was offered, and family planning was closely linked to efforts to improved child and maternal health care.

While national spokespeople maintained that participation in the program was voluntary, local officials with targets to fulfill often applied pressure. At the production-team level, birth planning became intensely personal, as couples were required to seek approval to have a child in a particular year. (The application might be accepted or they might be asked to wait a year or two.) Such extreme methods seem to have worked and been reasonably well accepted in China, presumably because of its cohesive social structure and strong government authority from the national down to the neighborhood level.

The most popular form of birth limitation in China has been the intrauterine device (IUD). Two other major forms have been abortion and sterilization of both women and men.

The *wan xi shao* campaign lowered fertility, but population projections continued to cause concern and, in 1979, the "one child" campaign was promulgated. Couples were not told that "only children are better children" and urged to take a pledge to stop at one. Those who do so often receive special incentives, such as an income supplement, extra maternity leave, and preferential treatment when applying for public housing. The "one-child" campaign flew in the face of traditional son preference by asking half of China's couples to stop reproducing before they had a male child and appears to have been associated with some resurgence of female infanticide or neglect of girl babies, but it did succeed in reducing fertility to the replacement level by the mid-1980s. China's population now is expected to stabilize early in the twenty-first century.

Although some aspects of China's population program will doubtless remain unique, countries interested in strengthening their own programs could learn from China's strong information activities, its use of a wide range of contraceptive methods, and its decentralization of many aspects of planning and implementation to local authorities.

Integrating contraceptive services with other services, especially maternal and child health services, seems to help. Even if population growth is not reduced, enabling women to improve the spacing of births has health and welfare benefits that women recognize and that contribute to acceptance of the program. The 1994 Cairo International Conference on Population and Development endorsed the idea that family planning be

POPULATION AND FAMILY PLANNING
IN INDONESIA

Indonesia is the world's fourth most populous country. Its 200 million people (1997) inhabit a chain of islands stretching some 3,000 miles along the equator. Yet two thirds of all Indonesians cluster on Java and Bali, small islands that make up only 7 percent of the land area. In rural sections of Java and Bali, population densities are among the highest in the world, land holdings are small and shrinking, and decent jobs remained hard to find, even before the economic crisis that struck in 1997.

For many years transmigration to the less fertile but relatively uncrowded outer islands of Sumatra, Kalimantan, and Sulawesi was promoted as a way of easing population pressure in Java and Bali. But the program was unable to make a significant impact on population growth in these core islands, let alone reduce existing densities. Indeed, about as fast as migrants were moved to available agricultural land in the outer islands, others flocked to Java's cities, where the best income-earning opportunities were concentrated.

Indonesia's population policy reversed gears in the late 1960s. Sukarno, the ardent nationalist who was president from 1945 to 1966, often avowed that Indonesia had too few people, not too many. "We have rich natural resources," he said. "We need more people to exploit them." Yet Sukarno's government failed to develop the country's re-

replaced by a broader program known as **reproductive health.** This "implies that people are able to have a responsible, satisfying, and safe sex life and that they have the capability to reproduce and the freedom to decide if, when, and how often they do so. Implicit in this last condition are the right of men and women to have access to safe, affordable, and acceptable methods of fertility regulation of their choice, and the right of access to appropriate health care services that will enable women to go safely through pregnancy and childbirth and provide couples with the best chance of having a healthy infant."[25] The Cairo conference also addressed the issues of completing the demographic transition in the poorest countries and of linking population programs more effectively to other efforts to improve the welfare and status of women and children.

25. See World Bank, *Population and Development,* p. 81.

sources, and by the mid-1960s, Indonesia's masses were desperately short of food, clothing, and medical care.

Suharto, the second president, tried to rebuild the economy. He also declared approval of population limitation, and in 1970, an official family planning program was launched. Although most people in Indonesia remain poor and ill educated, this program has succeeded beyond anyone's expectation. Greatest attention was paid to, and greatest success achieved in, the rural parts of Java and Bali. The program was imaginatively conceived, well managed, and implemented largely through existing village institutions. Pills were used as the main method of contraception. By 1980, fertility in key areas had fallen by 15–20 percent. In other areas, fertility remained high; in still others, it was low but only because of low female fecundity resulting from ill health and malnutrition.

During the 1980s fertility reduction in Indonesia was further spurred by rapid expansion of educational opportunities. Parents came to see greater possibilities for sending their children to high school and college and began to limit the number of children they had as a way to save more and thus realize these dreams. Between 1970 and 1997, the total fertility rate fell from 5.5 to 2.8. This reduction met a goal adopted in the early years of the family planning program—to cut fertility in half by the year 2000—which then was regarded as highly ambitious. Indonesia's experience thus shows what an effective family planning program launched by a determined government can achieve, even in circumstances that experts considered quite unfavorable for family planning.

A third approach to population policy would try to move people from one part of the country to another to improve the fit between population and the availability of land and other resources. **Population redistribution** may help to accommodate a growing total population in limited circumstances, but the magnitude of the effect is unlikely to be great. First, there must be empty but habitable space into which people can be moved. Then, particularly if the government is going to organize the movement, considerable investment and formidable organizing capacity is required. It is hard to move enough people to make a real difference, as experience in Brazil, Indonesia (see the preceding case study), and elsewhere shows. We already have noted that the kind of mass international population redistribution common in the nineteenth century is unlikely to occur in today's world, although smaller movements of people (motivated by political as well as economic considerations) still take place.

Methods of population control more drastic than contraception, such as abortion and sterilization, have played an important part in the slow-down of population growth in several European, South American, and East Asian countries. These methods often are regarded as objectionable on moral grounds. When forced on resisting populations, as in India during the emergency of the mid-1970s, they can backfire. Yet, when acceptable to local mores, they may help to bring about a rapid decline in fertility.

In addition to planning, many other government policies indirectly influence fertility levels by altering the incentives to have children. Some governments have used these policies to complement the effects of their family planning efforts. The policies include increased education for girls, especially the attainment of basic literacy for all women in countries that have not yet reached this target; increased job opportunities for women outside the home; formal social security systems—a realistic option only for middle-income countries; a ban on child labor; compulsory schooling up to a certain age; and improvement in the status of women, which will give them greater control over their own lives. The use of monetary incentives and disincentives geared to the number of children per family also has been advocated. The trouble with these measures is that, although they may discourage parents from having an additional child, they frequently penalize those children already born. For example, levying higher charges for the medical care and schooling of third and subsequent children indeed may cause parents to have fewer children, but it also may result in lower-quality care for children who, through no fault of their own, are born late into large families.

Reduction of infant mortality can be considered an indirect population policy. According to the child replacement thesis, the number of children that a couple has is geared to the number it expects to survive; accordingly, if survival prospects improve, then the birthrate—if not necessarily the rate of natural increase—will fall.

A country that once emphasized policies to provide disincentives for large families, albeit in rather special circumstances, is Singapore. There 60 percent of the population lives in public housing, and nearly everyone is heavily dependent on the government for a variety of social services. In its campaign to limit population growth, the government of Singapore discriminated among users of public services on the basis of how many children they have. People with large families paid higher maternity fees, got lower priority in school selection, and received no extra income tax deductions or housing space. Abortion and sterilization (both male and female) were made available on demand at nominal fees. All this was backed up by a determined information campaign. Singapore's tough policy contributed to a dramatic fall in population growth, although rapid economic and social change in the Southwest Asian city-state probably had an even greater impact. In fact, the campaign was so successful in reducing fertility that the prime minister later reversed himself and urged educated women to have more children so that the quality of the population could be maintained.

A final idea for indirectly influencing fertility is that improvement in the distribution of income will cut the birthrate. (The complementary proposition, that unequal income distribution leads to higher fertility, also has been advanced.) This makes sense, since poor households have perhaps three quarters of the babies born in a developing society, and their income must rise if an increase in income is to bring about a decline in fertility. A related notion is that a generally equitable pattern of development, including improving social services for the poor, will convince people that their lives are improving and they are gaining increasing control over their own destinies; and this leads to an especially rapid decline in fertility. These are attractive hypotheses and some evidence supports them, but it is not conclusive.

FAMILY PLANNING VERSUS DEVELOPMENT?

Some people, with diverse perspectives, argue that governments should worry less about population policy, concentrate more on economic development, and leave it to the demographic transition to bring about a decline in fertility. At the first United Nations World Population Conference, held in Bucharest in 1974, a popular slogan was, "Take care of the people and the population will take care of itself." There and elsewhere, verbal wars have been waged between "family planners" and "developmentalists." Ideology often becomes entwined in the debate. Marxist spokespeople routinely contend that population pressure in capitalist countries is merely one more manifestation of class conflict. In a socialist society, the problem will disappear because it will be possible to organize society "scientifically" and thus provide full employment and satisfaction of everyone's basic needs. In the meantime, capitalist efforts to promote family planning are seen as just one more futile attempt to stave off the coming revolution. Interestingly, the United States delegation to the second World Population Conference, held in Mexico City in 1984, provided a mirror image of this argument by contending that population would be less of a problem if LDC governments gave freer rein to private enterprise.

The earlier review of facts and theories suggests that family planning *versus* development is a false dichotomy. The fertility decline that completes the demographic transition can be hastened *both* by family planning *and* by economic development and both are supported by improvements in health (see Chapter 10). Family planning alone is unlikely to reduce the birthrate; we have seen that it seldom works well in settings where there has been little development. Moreover, its effects on marital fertility need support from a trend toward a higher age of marriage, and this also is more likely to come about in a more rapidly developing society.

Yet family planning has made its own independent contribution to LDC fertility decline in recent years, as studies have shown.[26] In many countries of Latin America and Asia, more than 50 percent of married couples now practice family planning.[27] In reality, family planning and development are more complements than substitutes.

26. W. Parker Mauldin and Berhard Berelson, "Conditions of Fertility Decline in Developing Countries, 1965–75," *Studies in Family Planning,* 9, no. 5 (1978). See also "Fertility and Family Planning Surveys: An Update," *Population Reports,* series M, no. 8 [Baltimore: Johns Hopkins University] (September–October 1985).

27. Based on *World Development Indicators 1999.* There are many countries for which data are unavailable.

LABOR'S ROLE

The dual role of people as both the beneficiaries of economic development and a major productive resource is particularly evident in discussing labor and employment. Labor employment in economic activity is likely to be costly (that is, it has an alternative use, as discussed later) in the same way that the use of other scarce resources is costly. But employing the available labor supply offers two important benefits. First, because of market imperfections, it may be possible to increase production through policies that encourage better use of available labor and the adoption of technologies more appropriate to the factor endowments of less-developed countries. Second, even if total output does not rise, increased employment of poor people can be an effective and relatively low-cost way to increase their share of total income and thus diminish poverty and distributive inequality.

A perplexing program is how best to measure the quality of labor used in production. Given the supplies of capital and natural resources available, as well as a range of applicable technologies, the level of GNP attainable depends on the amount of labor available. But what is the "amount of labor available"? We could simply count the number of people potentially available for work—the number of people who are not underage, overage, or infirm—but this could be misleading. Labor productivity, or quality, varies widely in the real world, depending on several factors.

One of these is people's attitudes and values. How highly do they value the goods and services that can be earned by working? Are people willing to abandon traditional social settings and take up jobs in unfamiliar environments, such as factories, mines, and plantations? Do they come to work on time? Do they exert themselves on the job? Can they tolerate routine operations? Is saving for the future important to them or do they live for the moment? Although economic theories usually abstract from the effects of values and attitudes on productivity, in the real world they are significant. Values and attitudes are acquired, not inborn. The work of sociologists and psychologists indicates that they are shaped by experiences in the home, in school, and on the job. In a sense they are a consequence of economic development, but they also are one of its causes. The subject is not yet understood well enough for values and attitudes to be readily manipulated as a means of promoting development, although many governments try to do so.

A second set of influences on labor productivity is made up of the skills possessed by the population. If values and attitudes refer to the way people look at the world, skills are what they know how to do. Some skills are widely usable; others are specific to particular environments. One needs to know different things to work effectively in an Asian rice field, a Detroit auto factory, or an Arctic fishing community; skills that are vital in one of these settings may be useless in another. Compared to attitudes and values, skills are acquired in a more straightforward and easily understood manner. The process can be called education, although the term is used here in a broader sense than is usual.

Finally, labor productivity is affected by the health and nutrition of the working population. People must possess the physical and mental stamina necessary, first to learn economically useful skills and then to apply them in the workplace. Education and health merit extended treatment and are taken up in Chapters 9 and 10. Here we concentrate on quantitative aspects of the human factor in development.

Analyzing Employment Issues

Quantitative aspects of labor's role include growth in the number of laborers, patterns of employment, structure of labor markets, and methods of measuring labor supply and its utilization. We take up these issues in turn.

GROWTH OF THE LABOR SUPPLY

A major difference between the development challenge faced by developing countries today and the one overcome by the industrial countries in the early phase of their own development is that the supply of labor is growing much faster in the developing countries. In most low-income countries, the number of people who want to work currently is increasing at 2.5 percent a year or more. Since nearly all men and many women seek work outside the home, the rise in the number of potential workers is closely related to the increase in total population. Labor force growth lags population growth by 15 years (more or less, depending mainly on how long children stay in school). When health improves and more children survive from infancy to adulthood, population growth accelerates; this leads to faster labor force growth after 15 years. Similarly, a fall in the birthrate leads to reduced labor force growth, with a lag of 15 years or so. During the 1980s and 1990s, the labor force growth began to slow down in all regions except South Asia (Table 8–1). But it will remain rapid, higher than current population growth, at least into the early part of the twenty-first century.

PATTERNS OF EMPLOYMENT

One of the best-known characteristics of labor in developing countries is that most people work in agriculture. Agriculture's share of the labor force is highest in the poorest countries and declines systematically as the GNP per capita rises. The shares of both industrial and service workers rise to offset this decline (Table 8–2). Individual countries generally follow this pattern with case-to-case variations, as depicted in Table 8–3.

Another well-known fact about LDC labor is that wages generally are low by the standards of industrial countries. In developing countries, labor is plentiful relative to the supply of complementary resources that could raise its productivity and permit higher wages to be paid. Nearly all complementary resources tend to be scarce: capital equipment, arable land, and foreign exchange, as well as those less tangible but important resources, entrepreneurship and managerial capacity. Therefore, low wages easily are understood from the perspective of an elementary supply-demand analysis.

TABLE 8–1 GROWTH OF LABOR FORCE BY REGION, 1970–97	1970–80	1980–90	1990–97
SUB-SAHARAN AFRICA	2.5	2.8	2.7
EAST ASIA & PACIFIC	2.3	2.2	1.6
SOUTH ASIA	2.3	2.2	2.6
EASTERN EUROPE & CENTRAL ASIA	1.3	0.3	0.3
WESTERN EUROPE	0.8	1.0	0.9
MIDDLE EAST & NORTH AFRICA	2.9	3.2	3.1
UNITED STATES & CANADA	2.2	1.4	1.3
LATIN AMERICA & CARIBBEAN	3.2	3.0	2.5
ALL DEVELOPING COUNTRIES	2.2	2.0	1.8

Source: World Bank, World Development Indicators 1999 CD-ROM.

TABLE 8–2	EMPLOYMENT SHARES AT DIFFERENT LEVELS OF DEVELOPMENT, 1990–94		
	PERCENT OF LABOR FORCE EMPLOYED IN		
LEVEL OF GNP PER CAPITA (PPP), 1994	AGRICULTURE	INDUSTRY	SERVICES
LESS THAN $1,000	70	6	23
$1,000–4,000	64	16	20
$4,000–7,000	26	30	43
$7,000–12,000	19	27	54
MORE THAN $12,000	5	28	67

Note: Data are for different years in the 1990 to 1994 range, depending on the latest available source (usually a national population census).
Source: World Bank, *World Development Indicators 1999* CD-ROM.

It is not demeaning to LDC workers, however, to note that another cause of low productivity and pay is the characteristics of the workers themselves. Through no fault of their own, few have the education and work experience required for high productivity. Indonesia's 1980 population census revealed that only 32 percent of adults had completed primary school, a mere 10 percent had gone on to secondary education, and a microscopic 0.5 percent had been to a university. Few indeed had ever worked in a factory or had other good opportunities for on-the-job training. In many developing countries, these proportions are even lower. All too many LDC workers lack even the capacity to do sustained physical labor because their health and nutritional status is low. Yet developing countries also have in their workforce persons of consummate learning and outstanding abilities.

Another characteristic of LDC labor is that differentials among the wages received by different skills and education levels are wider than in developed countries. Skilled manual workers in developed countries may earn 20 to 40 percent more than their unskilled counterparts. In Asia, they are likely to earn 40 to 80 percent more, in Latin America 70 to 100 percent, and in Africa the skill differential can be 100 percent or more. Earnings differentials attributable to higher levels of education also are much larger in developing countries. In part, these large earnings differentials exist because the rarity of skills and schooling attracts a larger market premium. Other factors may be segmented labor markets and "efficiency wage" considerations, discussed in the following section.

A final characteristic of labor in the poorest economies is widespread underutilization of the available labor supply. For reasons discussed later, much of this underutilization takes the form of **disguised unemployment,** rather than the visible unemployment familiar in industrial countries. That is, people do have some kind of a job, and may even work long

TABLE 8-3   EMPLOYMENT SHARES IN SELECTED COUNTRIES, 1990–94

COUNTRY	PERCENT OF LABOR FORCE EMPLOYED IN		
	AGRICULTURE	INDUSTRY	SERVICES
LOW-INCOME COUNTRIES			
ETHIOPIA	86	2	12
TANZANIA	85	5	10
MALI	87	2	11
NIGERIA	43	7	50
BANGLADESH	65	16	18
KENYA	79	8	13
INDIA	64	16	20
GHANA	59	13	28
PAKISTAN	50	16	34
SENEGAL	78	5	16
CAMEROON	71	10	20
HONDURAS	37	16	47
SRI LANKA	36	19	45
CHINA	72	15	13
EGYPT	31	18	52
MIDDLE-INCOME COUNTRIES			
BOLIVA	48	17	34
INDONESIA	41	17	42
THE PHILIPPINES	41	15	44
PERU	35	17	48
RUSSIA	14	42	44
COLOMBIA	1	32	48
HUNGARY	15	38	48
MALAYSIA	26	24	50
MEXICO	27	21	52
ARGENTINA	12	32	56
SOUTH KOREA	13	32	54
HIGH-INCOME COUNTRIES			
UNITED KINGDOM	2	24	74
GERMANY	4	38	58
JAPAN	6	33	61
UNITED STATES	3	23	74

Note: Data are for different years in the 1990 to 1994 range. They are classified by World Bank groupings and, within groups, by ascending order of GNP per capita (PPP) in 1994.
Source: World Bank, *World Development Indicators 1999* CD-ROM.

hours, but their contribution to output is small. With some reallocation of resources and improvement of institutions, their labor could be made more productive. This is a major challenge for development policy.

To recapitulate, low wages and productivity, large wage differentials, rapid growth of the labor supply, and underutilization of the existing supply of labor all characterize developing countries. There are many inter-

PRIMARY EDUCATION AND CHILD LABOR IN INDIA

In india around 1990, fewer than half of children ages 6–14 were in school. Some 44 million in fact were working, either for wages or as unpaid contributors to family enterprises.

> They stay at home to care for cattle, tend younger children, collect firewood, and work in the fields. They find employment in cottage industries, tea stalls, restaurants, or as household workers in middle-class homes. They become prostitutes or live as street children, begging or picking rags and bottles from trash for trade. Many are bonded laborers, tending cattle or working as agricultural laborers for local landowners. (Myron Weiner, *The Child and the State in India: Child Labor and Education Policy in Comparative Perspective*. Princeton, NJ: Princeton University Press, 1991, p. 3)

Education is not compulsory in India and child labor is legal, except in factories. Most children who start school drop out before completing the primary segment. Although official statistics now show high enrollment ratios at the primary level, many unofficial inquiries have found irregular attendance by teachers as well as pupils, along with low-quality instruction when schools do meet.

country variations, however. The degree of labor underutilization also varies greatly, depending mainly on the supply of arable land and other complementary resources in relation to the working-age population.

THE STRUCTURE OF LABOR MARKETS

It is useful to think of labor services as bought and sold in markets like other goods and services. In the economist's "perfect market," given certain assumptions, prices are set to cause goods to be allocated efficiently. But labor markets are notoriously imperfect, none more so than those of the LDCs. Wages (the "price" of labor) are not determined entirely by competitive forces. This section describes a pattern of segmented labor markets, which may help explain wage and employment determination in the LDCs.

A "typical" developing country could be represented by a three-tiered employment structure, consisting of an urban formal sector, an urban in-

Why is India such a glaring exception to the global trends of de-creasing child labor and universal basic education? Poverty is part of the reason, but other countries have done much better at similar in-come levels. Moreover, the South Indian state of Kerala, which is no richer than India as a whole, has nearly universal literacy in the younger age cohorts and very little child labor. According to the late Massachusetts Institute of Technology political scientist Myron Weiner, India's main problem is not poverty but the belief system of the bureaucracy and other middle-class Indians. This assumes a strati-fied social order, in which education differentiates the upper from the lower class and "excessive" or "inappropriate" education for the poor would disrupt existing social arrangements.

How can the twin problems of child labor and nonenrollment in basic education be solved? Child labor could be banned and schooling made compulsory by legal action, but poverty and the attitudes cited by Weiner might undermine such efforts. Jean Dreze and Amartya Sen deplore the existing situation but argue that compulsory education alone would be an inadequate response. "Making it legally compul-sory for children to attend schools that cannot receive them would not be a great gift" (Jean Dreze and Amartya Sen, *India: Economic Develop-ment and Social Opportunity.* Delhi: Oxford University Press, 1995, p. 132). Dreze and Sen advocate gradual introduction of compulsory schooling, beginning with the more prosperous states. Yet, the Indian states have long had the authority to institute compulsory schooling, have frequently promised to do so, and have not followed through.

formal sector, and rural employment. Figure 8–1 is a schematic represen-tation of these three markets.

The **urban formal sector** is where almost everyone would like to work if he or she could. It consists of the government and large-scale enterprises such as banks, insurance companies, factories, and trading houses. People welcome the opportunity to work in a modern facility and be associated with a prestigious name, but the main attractions of formal-sector employ-ers are that they pay the highest wages and offer the steadiest employment. One reason they pay more is that they hire virtually all the university- and secondary-school-educated labor in the country. But they also tend to pay more for given types of labor than the smaller firms—more, indeed, than they would have to pay just to attract the number of workers they need.

Why do formal-sector firms pay as much as they do, when there are many unemployed people who would work for less? Sometimes formal-

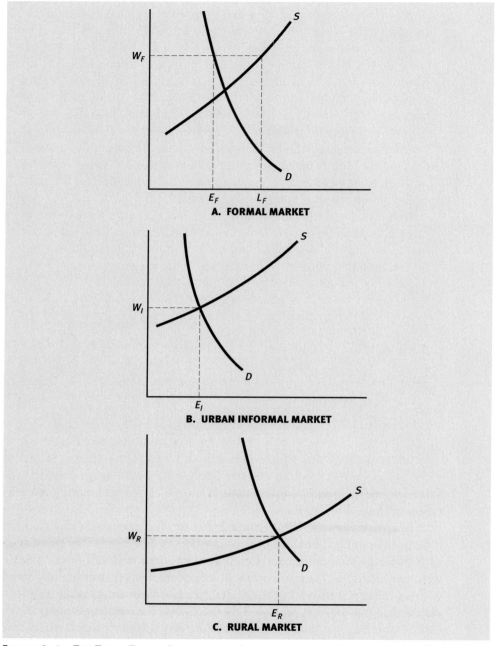

FIGURE 8–1   THE THREE-TIERED EMPLOYMENT STRUCTURE. In the formal market (A) the wage (W_F) is too high for the market to clear; not everyone can find work and there is a queue ($L_F - E_F$) of job applicants. In the urban informal sector (B), the wage (W_I) clears the market but is lower than the formal-sector wage (W_F). Finally, the rural labor market (C) the wage (W_R) also clears the market but is lower yet; the supply of labor to this sector is highly elastic.

sector firms pay more because the government presses them to do so (for example, through minimum wage laws or pressures to be model Employers), but often they do so quite voluntarily. The efficiency wage theory postulates that worker productivity is a positive function of the wage paid.[1] For several reasons, better-paid workers may be more productive. First, they may be better nourished and therefore physically better able to work. Second, they may be inherently better workers, since firms that pay higher wages can be more selective about whom they hire. Next, they may stay where they are longer, learn by doing, and reduce the firm's labor turnover. Finally, higher wages may make them work harder because they fear to lose such a good job. With wages held above market-clearing levels by some or all of these factors, there always is a queue of workers ($E_F - L_F$ in Figure 8–1A) waiting for jobs with urban formal-sector employers. A routine job-opening announcement may attract hundreds, or even thousands, of applicants.

Alongside the large urban formal-sector establishments—or, more likely, in the alleys behind them—are the smaller enterprises of the **urban informal sector.** These shops and curbside establishments produce and trade a wide range of goods and services. Sometimes, they compete with the larger enterprises; more often, they meet market demands that formal-sector firms do not find profitable. Often, the urban informal sector provides jobs for migrants who have come to town from the rural areas to seek work in the urban formal sector but have been unable to find it. However, studies in several third world cities indicate that many of the people who earn their income in this way are long-time urban residents and veterans at their particular lines of work. The majority of urban informal sector participants in most developing countries are women.

The urban informal sector can be easy to enter; often one can become a street hawker or enter dozens of other lines of work with only a tiny amount of capital. Those who lack even the $10 to $100 of capital needed to be self-employed may be able to work for others, although frequently at low wages and under harsh working conditions. Domestic servants form one such group, a large and important one in every low-income country (servants then disappear gradually as wages rise in middle-income countries). The urban informal sector can provide incredible amounts of low-wage employment and a useful array of goods and services (see the case study on page 290).

1. On efficiency wage theory, see Joseph E. Stiglitz, "Economic Organization, Information, and Development," in H. Chenery and T. N. Srinivasan, eds., *Handbook of Development Economics,* Vol. 1 (Amsterdam: North-Holland, 1989), pp. 93–160; George A. Akerlof and Janet L. Yellen, eds., *Efficiency Models of the Labor Market* (Cambridge: Cambridge University Press, 1986); and Lawrence F. Katz, "Efficiency Wage Theories: A Partial Evaluation," *NBER Macroeconomics Annual 1986* (Cambridge, MA: National Bureau of Economic Research, 1986), pp. 235–76.

THE URBAN INFORMAL SECTOR IN INDONESIA

Although the informal sector is hard to define and often ignored by local policy makers and elites, it is an important source of jobs, income, and a wide array of goods and services in many developing countries.

In-depth studies carried out in Jakarta by the Center for Policy and Implementation Studies under the direction of Harvard anthropologist Marguerite S. Robinson focused on three specific activities that are important in the Indonesian capital: *becak* driving (a *becak* is a three-wheeled pedal rickshaw); scavenging of waste materials such as metal, rags, and glass; and curbside retailing (hawking). The studies showed that these activities provide jobs for hundreds of thousands of workers at earnings levels that compare favorably, on average, with what the same workers could earn in the formal sector. Informal-sector workers often are migrants from rural areas who regularly remit substantial sums to relatives left behind in the villages. They produce low-priced goods and services (e.g., short-distance transportation, input for small-scale industries, and small-lot retailing) that help hold down the cost of living for working-class households and, ironically, permit formal-sector employers to pay lower wages. Jakarta's scavengers recycle a variety of waste materials with an efficiency that should be envied by modern industrial societies, which lack an equally efficient technology (at their high wage rates) for separating different types of materials so that they can be reprocessed.

Although informal-sector entrepreneurs provide many benefits to their families, their numerous employees (often family members), and their customers, municipal authorities often fail to understand or sympathize with them. Their activities frequently are suppressed, while efforts to help them often are misguided. For example, new markets may be developed at sites less favorably located than those habitually used by traders; the authorities then wonder why many of the new sites remain empty whereas traders who move to them may fail to repay their government loans. More enlightened policy must be based, not only on empathy for people who are struggling to survive, but also on an understanding of how their enterprises really contribute to development.

Because it is easily entered, the urban informal-sector labor market tends to be in equilibrium (Figure 8–1B). New entrants generally can find something to do, even if their presence tends to drive down wages slightly for all participants.

Although in visualizing the urban informal sector one tends to think first of massive urban agglomerations such as Mexico City, Lagos, and Calcutta, smaller cities and towns also provide significant amounts of urban informal-sector employment. Market towns often draw rural workers to participate in activities linked to the farm economy: marketing and processing local agricultural produce, distributing basic consumer goods and farm inputs, transportation, and repair services.

Even the urban informal sector is likely to pay higher wages than the **rural labor market.** In part, this wage differential is illusory, because urbanities have to pay higher prices for food and housing than rural residents and they often are forced to buy things (water, fuel, building materials) obtainable at no monetary cost in rural areas (although large expenditures of time and effort often are required). But, even after allowance has been made for differences in living costs, surveys indicate that more urban residents, even recent rural-urban migrants, are better off than all but the wealthiest rural residents.

As assumed by dual-economy models of development (presented in Chapter 3), rural employment in low-income countries commonly means work by family members, not for wages but a share in the output of a family enterprise. Yet almost always there is a market for hired labor, particularly in seasons of peak labor demand. Depending on the degree of population pressure and the prevailing pattern of land tenure, a large or small number of people will be forced to depend on wage employment because they have no land to farm or not enough to support their families. These agricultural laborers typically make up the very lowest income stratum in a poor country. Even when there are few agricultural laborers as such, rural households commonly trade labor back and forth at different times of the year, sometimes on a cooperative or barter basis but more often for wages in cash or kind. While rural people work primarily in agriculture, they often rely on small-scale nonagricultural activities such as trade, services, and handicrafts to provide important supplements to agricultural income.

MEASURING THE LABOR SUPPLY AND ITS UTILIZATION

The structural complexity of labor markets in developing countries makes it hard to apply concepts that are relatively straightforward in developed countries. In both types of countries, policy makers want to measure the supply of labor available to the economy and determine how fully the available labor supply is being utilized.

In developed countries, the labor supply is measured through the **labor force** concept. The labor force includes everyone who has a job or is actively looking for work. Its size is determined by three factors: (1) the size of the population, (2) its composition in terms of age groups and sexes, and (3) the labor force participation rates of these groups, which reflect social factors such as educational patterns and the willingness of women to work outside the home. The short-term responsiveness (elasticity) of the labor supply can be large under unusual circumstances, as when women in many countries went to work in factories for the first time during World War II, but normally it is low. Developed countries experiencing full employment easily can have their economic growth constrained by the available supply of labor.

In low-income countries, the size of the labor force generally is not a constraint on development, although skilled labor and management can be very scarce. Typically, more people would like to work than are working, and many who are working are underutilized. Moreover, the meaning of *having a job* or *actively looking for work* is harder to pin down in this context, where multiple job holding, part-time work, and work for one's own family all tend to be common, than in a developed country. The number of "discouraged workers" (those who have stopped looking for work because they believe none is available) also is likely to be greater in less-developed than in developed countries. Using the conventional definitions, women participate increasingly in the labor force as development proceeds and the number of jobs outside the home rises. This suggests that, at low levels of development, a large reserve of female labor is not apparent in the statistics but is ready to come forth when reasonably attractive work opportunities open up. In fact, of course, these women already are working hard in the home, where by convention they are not counted as part of the labor force.

In developed countries, labor underutilization is measured primarily through the concept of **unemployment.** The *unemployed* are defined as those who do not have a job but are actively looking for one. The familiar **rate of unemployment** is total unemployment as a percentage of the labor force. In industrial countries this rate is a closely watched indicator of economic performance.

In developing countries the rate of unemployment understates labor underutilization, often by a large factor. Surveys have indicated that India has a lower rate of unemployment than the United States. Yet most observers would agree that underutilization of labor supply is much greater in India than in the United States. Surveys in middle-income countries such as Malaysia, the Philippines, and several Latin American countries also have indicated far higher rates of unemployment than in very poor countries. One reason for these anomalies is suggested by analyzing the types of people who are reported as unemployed when labor force surveys are carried out in developing countries. Many of them are young and live in urban areas; they are far better educated than the population in general, and many have never worked before. The inference is clear. The unemployed, as measured in these surveys, tend to be those who can afford to remain unemployed while they search for the type of job, undoubtedly in the urban formal sector, that they want and for which they believe their educational attainments qualify them. They in fact may come from the better-off families in society and are supported by their parents through an extended period of search for the "right" job.

The very poor may appear less often in the unemployment statistics of developing countries, and when they are caught by the labor force surveys, they do not remain unemployed for long. Because they lack resources, they cannot be without work for more than a brief period or they and their families may starve. Therefore, the poor must accept almost any job that becomes available. It has been observed ironically that, in a poor country, unemployment is a luxury. Unemployment usually is part of a job search that can be long and costly. Those best situated to make this search are the relatively privileged. Because LDCs lack unemployment insurance and other forms of social support common in the developed countries, job seekers must be supported either by their families (which sometimes make large sacrifices for the purpose) or by such casual work as they can find.

If the standard concept of unemployment is an inadequate measure of labor underutilization in developing countries, what better measure might be devised? This is a complex matter because, in fact, several different kinds of underutilization are common in developing countries (Table 8–4) and it is hard to encompass them all in any single measure.

It has been argued that disguised unemployment (the lower right-hand quadrant of Table 8–4) is the major form of labor underutilization in poor countries. Workers in this category are fully but unproductively employed in the rural sector or urban informal sector. Standard examples include the street vendor who sits for hours just to make one or two small sales, the shoeshine hawker, and the goatherd. These people, it is argued, contribute little or nothing to production. Like those classified as unemployed, they could be put to work somewhere else in the economy at little or no opportunity cost. We discuss the merits of this argument as a guide to development policy later. The important point here is that, although this category

TABLE 8–4	TYPES OF LABOR UNDERUTILIZATION IN DEVELOPING COUNTRIES	
TYPE	UNEMPLOYMENT	UNDEREMPLOYMENT
VISIBLE	MOSTLY URBAN NEW ENTRANTS	RURAL LABOR; SEASONAL
INVISIBLE	MOSTLY WOMEN ("DISCOURAGED WORKERS")	RURAL + URBAN INFORMAL SECTOR ("DISGUISED UNEMPLOYMENT")

of labor underutilization may be large and important, it is exceedingly difficult to define and measure precisely.

One country profile of labor underutilization, based on a framework similar to that of Table 8–4, was provided by the 1970 International Labor Office (ILO) employment mission to Colombia.[2] Visible unemployment in urban areas was running at 14 percent of the labor force, but the mission estimated that, when discouraged workers and the underemployed (those involuntarily working short hours) were taken into account, urban labor underutilization rose to at least 25 percent. Adding disguised unemployment, as indicated by extremely low income, raised it to one third of the labor force. In rural areas everyone apparently was employed at the peak season, but at least one sixth of the labor force earned incomes low enough to be characterized as disguised unemployment.

The many difficulties of defining and measuring labor utilization make it uncertain just how the overall degree of labor utilization varies with the level of economic development. The highest rates of visible unemployment, often reaching 10 to 20 percent of the labor force, have been measured in the urban areas of low- and middle-income countries. According to broader definitions of underutilization, still larger shares of the labor force are underutilized and overall underutilization probably is greatest in the poorest countries. Disguised forms of underutilization are relatively more important in the poorest countries than in the somewhat richer ones. In the semideveloped countries covered by labor utilization surveys, disguised unemployment was significant but quantitatively somewhat less than open unemployment.

Nor is it easy for trends to be established with certainty. In the 1960s it was widely feared that accelerated population growth would lead to massive unemployment in the developing countries. During the decade of the 1970s, many observers thought that the degree of labor underutilization in most LDCs was increasing. However, a careful review of the data showed that this probably was not the case.[3] The point is that nearly everyone in developing countries must work to live. The main issue, therefore, is not how many job seekers find employment but rather what kind of work they find to do—how productive they are and how good an income they earn.

Labor Reallocation

We cannot talk about employment policy in developing countries without broaching an issue that has been debated extensively by development theorists: How can underutilized labor be used in a development strategy?

2. International Labor Office, *Towards Full Employment* (Geneva: ILO, 1970), pp. 12–28.

3. Peter Gregory, "An Assessment of Changes in Employment Conditions in Less-Developed Countries," *Economic Development and Cultural Change*, 28, no. 4 (July 1980), 673–700.

Early theoretical writings frequently asserted that large numbers of people engage in work that adds nothing to national output. Two well-known writers who emphasized this idea and made it a cornerstone of their analyses of how development proceeds were Finnish economist Ragnar Nurkse and Nobel laureate W. Arthur Lewis.[4] Nurkse saw the reallocation of surplus labor to more productive uses, especially labor-intensive construction projects, as a major source of capital formation and economic growth. Lewis envisaged a similar reallocation process, but he pictured the "capitalist sector," essentially industry, as the principal employer of the surplus labor. (Chapters 3 and 4 discuss Lewis' theory in detail.) Both theorists regarded the labor reallocation process as nearly costless, but they worried about how to capture, from the agricultural sector, the food necessary to feed the reallocated laborers.

This approach to development theory started a debate on two issues: what extra laborers actually contribute to LDC agricultural production and how readily any excess labor can be mobilized in industry or construction projects. Three conclusions emerged from this debate. First, extra laborers do increase agricultural production, contrary to Nurkse's and Lewis' assumption. The marginal product of labor almost always is positive, not 0, but it may be very low in densely populated countries. At least this is true on a year-round basis. If there really is such a thing as zero marginal product labor, the condition is likely to be seasonal. Second, even if forgone output were 0 or negligible, other costs would be associated with the physical movement of labor from agricultural pursuits to industry or construction. These will be discussed shortly. Third, although long-term growth consists of reallocating labor to more productive uses, no free, or even very easy, gains are to be had in the short run.

A more positive restatement of this conclusion is that, in almost all countries and times, there are opportunities to work at some positive wage and marginal product, although these may be very low. If workers remain unemployed despite such opportunities, the most likely reason is that they reject the wage offered as too low to compensate for their loss of leisure or chance to search for a better-paid job.

COSTS AND BENEFITS OF REALLOCATING LABOR

Given these findings, how should an LDC government look at an employment-creating development project? Any development project can be evaluated using social cost-benefit analysis. An important part of the so-

4. Ragnar Nurkse, *Problems of Capital Formation in Underdeveloped Countries* (Oxford: Blackwell, 1957; first published in 1953); and W. Arthur Lewis, "Economic Development with Unlimited Supplies of Labour," *Manchester School*, 22 (May 1954), 139–91.

cial cost of any input is its **opportunity cost,** its value in its next best alternative use. Labor hired for an urban formal-sector project might well be drawn from the urban informal sector. The worker who moves out of the urban informal sector in turn may be replaced by someone from the rural sector. In this example, the output lost is that of the worker who formerly was in the rural sector, the worker at the end of the employment chain. For this reason, some analysts believe that the wage paid to casual agricultural laborers provides a good measure of the social cost of unskilled labor.

However, this measure, although a good indicator of output forgone through labor reallocation, probably understates the true social cost of employing labor, which has other components that are likely to be significant.

One such component is **induced migration.** An influential model of rural-urban migration, developed by John R. Harris and Michael P. Todaro and described more fully in the following section, implies that migrating workers essentially are participants in a lottery of relatively high-paid jobs in the towns.[5] When new urban jobs are created, the lottery becomes more attractive to potential migrants. Depending on their responsiveness to this improved opportunity, it is possible that more than one worker will migrate for each job created. If so, the output forgone may be that of two or more agricultural workers, not just one. Family ties may multiply this effect. If a male worker migrates and brings his family with him, additional output may be lost because the wife and children find fewer employment opportunities in the town than in the rural areas; for example, they do not have land on which to grow food.

In addition to forgone output, certain **costs of urbanization** should be included in computing the social cost of urban job creation. Some of these costs are internalized by the worker and presumably taken into account in the migration decision: the higher cost of food, housing, and other items in the town. Other costs are external and must be borne by society as a whole: social services provided only to the urban population or more expensive in the town, pollution, congestion, and additional security requirements. These costs make many third world governments frown on urbanization, however much they may desire industrialization.

Finally, there is the possibility of a reduction in national savings, which has worried development theorists and Soviet-style economic planners alike. If labor that has been adding little to agricultural output but has been consuming a larger share of that product is withdrawn from the sector, who controls the food so freed up? Government planners may want to transfer the food that the rural worker was consuming to feed the same

5. John R. Harris and Michael P. Todaro, "Migration, Unemployment and Development: A Two-Sector Analysis," *American Economic Review,* 60 (March 1970), 125–42.

worker in the city. Their fear is that the remaining rural population simply will increase its per capita consumption. Since the urban labor force must be fed—from imports, if not from domestic production—the planners' concern is that aggregate national consumption will rise and national savings will fall and reduce the growth of GNP. The problem is exacerbated when the new urban workers get higher wages and want to consume more food than they were consuming in the rural areas.

During the 1930s, this concern moved Soviet planners to drastic measures to extract a surplus from a resistant rural population. Governments of developing countries generally have neither the means nor the desire to suppress food consumption, so they may indeed experience some decline in savings. This is far from a pure loss, however, because the added consumption is a gain to some members of society. In any case, there are better ways to increase saving than through coercive controls on food consumption.

The primary benefit of urban employment is added output. A highly productive project easily can repay all the costs just discussed, but low-productivity make-work projects in urban areas may incur costs with few offsetting benefits. Labor-intensive projects in rural areas, especially those employing seasonally underutilized labor, also may waste resources but are likely to be more beneficial on a net basis because they do not require workers to migrate. These projects are discussed near the end of this chapter.

A secondary benefit of urban job creation is the training it may provide. In developing countries, opportunities to learn skills useful in the modern economy are concentrated in urban areas. For example, the ability to operate and repair machinery of all kinds typically is rare. A worker who comes to town can acquire these skills. In doing so, the worker may benefit and obtain higher wages if employment as a skilled worker can be found. But the worker also confers an "external benefit" on society, because everyone gains when bus drivers, auto mechanics, appliance repair people, and others who work with machinery learn to do their jobs better. The gainers include both employers, who can hire labor from a more-skilled pool, and consumers, who get better service at lower prices.

Thus, developing through the reallocation of low-productivity labor is a more complex business than Nurkse and Lewis imagined in the 1950s. Nevertheless, employment expansion remains vital for both increasing output and redistributing income. Economies that can create jobs with a marginal product of labor above its social cost, taking into account all the elements discussed here, can achieve both objectives simultaneously. Output rises and more income goes to unskilled workers from low-income families. Less-productive forms of employment creation, in which the social cost of labor exceeds its marginal product, can be acceptable as redistributive measures if income redistribution is desired and other ways of achieving it are unavailable. But they achieve more equity only by sacrificing growth.

INTERNAL MIGRATION

Most of the internal labor migration that occurs in the course of economic development is from rural to urban areas. Theorists have long argued that economic factors dominate the decision to migrate. Some early writers distinguished between "pull" and "push" factors, saying that rural-urban migration can result from either favorable economic developments in the town or adverse developments in the countryside. The Harris-Todaro model of rural-urban migration, introduced previously, integrates these two sets of factors by posting the urban-rural wage differential as the motivating force behind migration. Yet there is something to the older notion. Just as eighteenth century English cottagers were pushed into the town by the Enclosure Movement, so peasants in eastern India move to Calcutta primarily because of wretched conditions in the surrounding countryside, rather than outstanding income or employment opportunities in Calcutta. By contrast, the growth of dynamic third world cities such as Saō Paulo and Nairobi could be attributed at least partly to pull factors.

The Harris-Todaro model is an important formulation of the role of economic incentives in the migration decision. The model assumes that migration depends primarily on a comparison of wages in the rural and urban labor markets. That is,

$$M_t = f(W_u - W_r) \qquad [8-1]$$

where M_t = the number of rural to urban migrants in time period t, f = a response function, W_u = the urban wage, and W_r = the rural wage. Since there is unemployment in the town (assume that there is none in the countryside) and every migrant cannot expect to find a job there, the model postulates that the expected urban wage is compared with the rural wage. The expected urban wage is the actual wage times the probability of finding a job, or

$$W_u^* = pW_u \qquad [8-2]$$

where W_u^* = expected urban wage and p = probability of finding a job.

A simple way of defining p is

$$p = \frac{E_u}{E_u + U_u} \qquad [8-3]$$

where E_u = urban employment and U_u = urban unemployment. In this formulation, all members of the urban labor force are assumed to have equal chances of obtaining the jobs available, so W_u^* becomes imply the urban wage times the urban employment rate. Migration in any given time period then depends on three factors: the rural-urban wage gap, the urban employment rate, and the responsiveness of potential migrants to the resulting opportunities:

$$M_t = h(pW_u - W_r) \qquad\qquad [8\text{--}4]$$

where M_t = the migration in period t and h = the response rate of potential migrants.

As long as W_u^* exceeds W_r, the model predicts that rural-urban migration will continue. It will stop only when migration has forced down the urban wage or forced up urban unemployment sufficiently that $W_u^* = W_r$. It also is possible that W_r is greater than W_u^*, in which case there will be a flow of disappointed urban job seekers back to the countryside.

An interesting feature of this model is that an increase in the urban wage (W_u) requires an increase in unemployment to restore equilibrium. In other words, an increase in the demand for labor or anything else that raises wages in the cities is likely to induce more migration and thereby worsen urban unemployment.

Critics of the Harris-Todaro model point out that the equilibrium condition specified by the model seldom is attained. It is common for urban wages to be, say, 50 to 100 percent higher than rural wages and for urban unemployment to run at 10 to 20 percent of the labor force. If the figures stay in this range, the expected urban wage (W_u^*) remains above the rural wage (W_r). Migration in practice does not seem to close the gap between W_u^* and W_r as the model predicts. The model can be rescued, however, by assuming (realistically) that not all urban jobs turn over, that is, are available in the "lottery." In this case, the probability of a migrant not finding a job is lower than the employment rate. For example, if the unemployment rate is 20 percent, the probability of a migrant's finding a job might actually be 50 percent or less, not 80 percent as implied by the simplest version of the model.

Reverse migration from town to country is significant in many countries. Although Harris and Todaro interpret such movement as disappointed urban job seekers returning home in despair, much of this two-way or *circular* migration is clearly intentional. Young, unattached men are particularly likely to migrate temporarily to towns, mines, or plantations, to work there for a while and amass savings, which they take back to the rural areas to invest in land, farm improvements, or marriage. This pattern of cyclical migration has been especially common in parts of Africa, perhaps because in many African cultures women customarily tend the crops after the men have planted them. The opportunity cost of absent men outside the planting season is thus low.

Economic factors are not the only important influences on migration decisions. Studies show that distance and social ties also are significant. Migrants to expanding urban areas tend to come from nearby rural regions, and peasants pushed out of their native districts by a calamity are likely to go to the nearest large town. People often move to areas where members of their family, village, or ethnic group have settled.

Although most internal migration in developing countries is from rural to urban areas, interregional differences in economic opportunity can bring about substantial rural-to-rural movement as well. Countries fortunate enough to possess lightly settled yet cultivable regions may try to bring about such movement as a matter of public policy, as we saw in Chapter 7. Unless massive physical or legal barriers prevent the settlement of relatively empty areas, however, such interregional movements tend to occur spontaneously. This happened in Nepal, for instance, where farmers moved from the densely packed Kathmandu Valley into the southern *terai* region, and in many parts of Africa and South America. Unforced movement of a population from one region of a country to another is likely to be socially beneficial. People make these moves to improve their own living standards and those of their families. Even in the most congested slums of such major LDC cities as São Paulo, Lagos, and Jakarta, migrants report that they are better off than they were in the rural areas and generally do not want to go back.

Society is likely to benefit as well from an improved spatial allocation of labor relative to other resources. But two factors could make the social costs greater than the benefits. First, distorted incentives, such as artificially high wages and subsidized urban services, can inflate private benefits. Second, external costs such as congestion, pollution, and crime are borne equally by migrants, who benefit from migration, and by their predecessors, who do not. If these distortions and externalities are large, social costs may exceed benefits.

INTERNATIONAL MIGRATION

International migration, which has continued at high levels in recent years,[6] frequently is regarded as a different matter altogether. To bring a degree of cool rationality to this often heated subject, it is helpful to dis-

---

6. From 1985 to 1990, eight developing countries each supplied 200,000 or more net emigrants: Mexico, the Philippines, China, Lebanon, Pakistan, India, El Salvador, and Colombia. The United States was by far the largest receiving country, with nearly 3 million net immigrants, including an estimate of illegal immigrants. Australia, Canada, and Saudi Arabia each admitted more than 300,000 in this period. See Fred Arnold, "International Migration: Who Goes Where?" *Finance and Development*, 27, no. 2 (June 1990), 46–47.

tinguish between unskilled labor and skilled or educated labor. This distinction may not matter when we look at the problem from the global point of view: It has been argued that world GNP is maximized when everyone works where the salary, and therefore presumably the productivity, is greatest. But it is important from the viewpoint of the developing countries, because skilled and unskilled labor have different opportunity costs.

The migration of educated, highly skilled labor is abhorrent to most developing countries and has been stigmatized as the "brain drain" for two reasons. One is that such people represent one of the LDCs' scarcest resources. The other is that, in most cases, their education has been time consuming, expensive, and heavily subsidized by the state. If they depart for foreign lands, not only are their services lost but a high cost must be incurred to train replacements. Yet if they are so productive, why are they not paid enough to keep them at home? The answer may be nonmarket influences on the salary structure. For example, if most doctors and engineers work for the government and their salaries are held down to avoid politically embarrassing salary differentials, it is not surprising that many of them seek an opportunity to emigrate. International agencies, which recruit in a worldwide labor market, typically pay far more for the same skills than national governments. This is why one finds Pakistani experts working in Egypt, for example, even as Egyptian experts are employed in Pakistan, although both groups probably could work more effectively in their own countries.

Although it surely does raise the world GNP, international migration of the educated worsens the distribution of income between rich and poor countries. To offset this effect, Jagdish Bhagwati of Columbia University has proposed a tax on the brain drain, to be collected by the governments of developed countries to which professional and technical personnel from underdeveloped countries have migrated.[7] The proceeds of the tax would be transferred to the poor countries of origin as compensation for their loss of talent.

In contrast, the international migration of unskilled labor can be beneficial to the country of emigration. Unskilled workers are more plentiful, so their loss is likely to be felt less keenly by the sending economy. There even are significant offsetting benefits. One is remittances: Unskilled migrants are less likely to take their families along and therefore are more likely to send back money. This makes labor a kind of national export. Countries such as Turkey, Algeria, and Egypt have long relied on worker remittances as a significant source of foreign exchange earnings. A second

7. Jagdish Bhagwati and Martin Partington, *Taxing the Brain Drain: A Proposal* (Amsterdam: North-Holland, 1976).

potential benefit is training. Unskilled workers who go abroad generally return to their native lands after a few years and bring back usable skills acquired abroad.

Some LDC governments have begun to look more favorably on worker emigration. Despairing of generating enough employment at home, they have begun to encourage their people to go abroad, at least for a while. South Asian countries, for example, took advantage of lucrative employment opportunities in the Middle East in the 1970s and 1980s. When education is particularly cheap, even the emigration of trained personnel may be encouraged. The Philippines has been exporting doctors and nurses in quantity for years.

Employment Policy

The main cause of the employment problem in the developing countries has been the rapid growth of the population and labor force relative to the natural resource base and sometimes also the stock of physical capital. But problems also have occurred on the demand side of the labor market. Even when capital stock has risen faster than the labor force, it often has been deployed in ways that kept labor absorption well below its potential. Import-substituting industrialization (ISI) was once expected to readily solve the employment problem in most LDCs. This was the premise, for example, of India's first two five-year plans. But experience has shown that although industrial-sector employment has grown rapidly in many cases of ISI, it has been unable to absorb the expanding labor force. A simple example will help to explain why this is so.

LABOR ABSORPTION THROUGH INDUSTRIALIZATION

Industrial sectors in developing countries typically grow rapidly from a low base. In low-income countries between 1965 and 1983, the value added in industry (defined to include manufacturing, utilities, and construction) grew at an average rate of 7.1 percent a year. Yet employment growth in the sector was only 60 percent as fast, or 4.3 percent a year. The amount of industrial employment growth expected from a given rate of output growth can be expressed by

$$\Delta E_i = \eta g(V_i) S_i \qquad [8\text{--}5]$$

where ΔE_i = annual employment growth in industry, expressed in percentage points of labor force growth; η = an elasticity relating the growth of employment to the growth of value added; $g(V_i)$ = growth in industrial value added, expressed in percentage points; S_i = industrial employment as a fraction of total employment. Industry absorbed 9 percent of the labor force in low-income countries in 1965, so

$$\Delta E_i = 0.6 \times 7.1 \times 0.09 = 0.4 \qquad [8\text{--}6]$$

This means that only 0.4 of 1 percent of the labor force was absorbed by industrial expansion each year. Yet the labor force grew at 2.1 percent a year from 1965 to 1983. Therefore, fewer than one fifth of the workers entering the labor force found jobs in industry. The rest had to do the best they could in primary production or the service sector.

Is this too pessimistic a depiction of the problem? On the brighter side, it can be noted that only direct employment creation in industry has been taken into account. Some **indirect job creation** can be expected in sectors with either forward or backward links to the industrial sector, such as service activities that distribute its products and agricultural and mining activities that supply its inputs (links within the industrial sector already are accounted for in the calculation). Indirect job creation can be significant in some circumstances, as when the capacity to process domestically produced primary commodities is expanded, but it frequently is limited for industrialization of the import-substituting type, which has few forward or backward links. Chapter 15 will discuss this in detail. **Secondary job creation** also occurs as workers employed in high-paying industrial jobs spend their income. Businesses supplying them with consumer goods of various kinds prosper, and this creates additional employment.

Since industrial jobs often are among the most productive and best paid in the economy, it is important to ask what can be done to improve industrial-employment creation. In the formula just given, raising ΔE_i requires increasing η, $g(V_i)$, S_i, or some combination of them. Industry's share in employment (S_i) will rise only gradually through time. In the medium term, industrial labor absorption can be increased by raising either the growth rate of sectoral value added, $g(V_i)$, or the employment elasticity, η.

When economic growth slowed in the 1980s, particularly in many Latin American and African countries, the labor market situation tended to deteriorate. Governments and private formal-sector employers shed workers in some cases and trimmed the wage premiums that they traditionally paid in others. One result was accelerated growth of the urban informal sector.

A few countries were able to expand industrial employment much faster than average. These nations achieved most success in exporting labor-intensive manufactured products. This path to industrial job creation was pioneered by South Korea, Taiwan, Hong Kong, and Singapore, known collectively as the *four tigers.* More recently, Malaysia, Thailand,

and even Indonesia and the coastal areas of China have followed in their footsteps, along with a few other countries including tiny Mauritius. Many other developing countries in all regions are eager to join the trend. It therefore is important to understand what, exactly, is involved. The four tigers' achievement has two separate aspects. First, by breaking into the export market, they were able to reach higher growth rates of industrial output, $g(V_i)$, because they freed themselves from dependence on growth of the domestic market for manufactured goods. Second, they achieved high values of η because the goods they chose to export, at least at the start of their export drives, were those that used large amounts of their most plentiful resource, labor. These countries have experienced values of η of around 0.8 instead of the more typical 0.4 to 0.6. Thus, South Korea, when its development accelerated after 1963, was able to absorb as much as half its total labor force growth in manufactured exports alone, at a time when most LDCs were absorbing less than 5 percent of their labor force growth in this activity.[8] How many other LDCs will be able to take lessons in employment policy from South Korea and the other tigers? We take up this question in the next section.

Critics have noted that, in countries that have been able to expand employment in export-oriented manufacturing rapidly, wages in the export industries often have been lower, at least in the early years, than in older import-substitution industries. This disadvantage to the working poor has been more than offset by the far larger number of jobs created by the export industries. Later on, wages in export industries are likely to rise, but they still may appear very low from the viewpoint of a developed country. Dismay has been expressed in the United States recently about low wages and poor working conditions in factories that produce garments, footwear, and other consumer products for the U.S. market. For example, workers who make expensive athletic shoes in Indonesia are said to earn only $2 per day. What the U.S. protesters may not know is that, just a few years ago, the daily wage of an unskilled urban worker in Indonesia was $1 per day or less. The growth of export industries has significantly raised wages, as well as dramatically expanded employment opportunities.

Low wages (by developed country standards) often are accompanied by long hours and unsafe or unsanitary working conditions. Of course, workers in developing countries would like to see higher wages and better working conditions in these industries. Often they join labor unions dedicated to these goals. Several LDC governments have impeded labor organization and labor union activities, fearing that labor costs will rise,

---

8. Susumu Watanabe, "Exports and Employment: The Case of the Republic of Korea," *International Labour Review,* 106, no. 6 (December 1972), 495–526.

making their industries less competitive in global markets and perhaps even causing investment to shift to other countries. Yet comparative international studies have shown that labor unions often share their members' interest in preserving their jobs and therefore act as a constructive force in the industrial relations of developing countries.

The vexing problem of how to define and enforce international labor standards appropriate to the widely varying conditions that prevail around the world frequently is discussed in bodies such as the International Labor Organization and the World Trade Organization. Although there is much to lament in the wages, working conditions, and industrial relations of export industries in developing countries, critics from wealthy countries should remember that these problems reflect national poverty and are not specific to the industries concerned. Those interested in the development of poor countries should guard against the use of these negative conditions as justifications for protectionism, which will harm not only developing countries but also consumers in developed countries.

The weak employment performance of industry in most developing countries is particularly distressing when one recalls that this sector not only should be soaking up a good share of labor force growth, but also should gradually draw labor away from less productive forms of employment in peasant agriculture, petty services, and cottage industries. When industry fails to do this, employment in these less productive sectors must rise rather than fall. This can lead to stagnant, or even declining, levels of worker productivity and income. These conditions are far more injurious than the problems in the export industries of those few developing countries that have succeeded in developing some kind of export base.

Although most of the discussion so far has been couched in terms of manufacturing, it has growing relevance to the formal service sector. In this era of plummeting communication costs, many services once thought of as untradable can be exported successfully from developing to developed countries. Data entry for airlines, medical establishments, and many other types of business now often can be performed more cheaply in developing countries and the results transmitted rapidly by electronic means. Countries with relatively large computer-literate populations are in a strong position to benefit from these opportunities. India and the Philippines, countries that have not done particularly well in manufactured goods exports, can reap large benefits. As with manufactured goods exports, however, appropriate policies must be adopted and necessary infrastructure provided to facilitate the export of information-intensive services. Telephone and Internet services must be provided or upgraded, and they must be priced appropriately to facilitate business use. Meanwhile, more advanced countries like Hong Kong and Singapore are making a broad-based move into modern service activities and away from manufacturing as part of the structural transformation that normally accompanies economic growth.

ELEMENTS OF EMPLOYMENT PROMOTION POLICY

In principle the problem of labor underutilization could be attacked on either the supply or demand side. In practice, however, little can be done to bring about a supply-side adjustment. Labor supply grows steadily from year to year. It is hard to discourage people from seeking work. Nor would most policy makers wish to do so, given the advantages of employment creation as a means of income redistribution and the psychological and political advantages of enabling everyone to participate in the economy. The only realistic supply-side potential is to reduce the growth of labor supply in the long run by limiting population growth.

At one time it was widely believed that increasing the supply of certain types of skilled labor would produce a strong expansionary effect on employment generally through the increased absorption of complementary unskilled labor. Therefore, India in its early post-independence years tried to eliminate a perceived labor bottleneck by expanding the supply of engineers, on the supposition that employment in construction and other activities could be increased in this way. The number of Indian engineers increased rapidly. The effect on general employment is hard to determine, but the effect on the engineers was clear-cut: Soon there were far too many of them, and many were unemployed. The moral is that, although skill shortages can constrain employment and output growth, they sometimes can be eliminated relatively quickly and easily through the expansion of education and training programs or through migration. In other countries, where education is less developed, skill formation may be much more difficult and time-consuming.

Given the limited potential for correcting the labor market disequilibrium by working on the supply side, policy must concentrate on the demand side of the equation. Many different kinds of policy affect the economy's ability to create jobs for a growing labor force. Wage, industrial promotion, fiscal, foreign trade, and education policies all have important implications for employment.

Earlier we identified two different approaches to employment creation. One is to stimulate output, especially in the relatively high-productivity and high-wage sectors of the economy. The other is to try to increase the amount of labor used to produce a given amount of output. The first approach will be discussed in Chapters 15, 16, and 17, which deal with the growth of exports, agriculture, and industry. The second is examined here.

In general, production can be made more labor intensive in two ways. One is to alter relative prices and thus create incentives for businesses to substitute labor for capital. The other is to develop technologies more appropriate to the factor proportions prevailing in developing countries.

FACTOR PRICE DISTORTIONS

The prices of labor and capital faced by modern-sector firms in less-developed countries frequently are distorted in ways that make capital artificially cheap relative to labor. This distortion can inhibit labor absorption at several levels. At the sectoral level, it can promote the growth of sectors that are technologically better suited to capital-intensive production (for example, basic metals) and hinder the growth of sectors that tend to be more labor intensive (for example, textiles). At the level of interfirm competition, it can promote the appearance and growth of plants using relatively capital-intensive technologies (these may be large scale, foreign owned, or both) and accelerate the decline and disappearance of more labor-intensive units. At the plant level, it can promote the use of machines in place of people.

These factor price distortions usually result from some form of government action. Artificially high wages may be imposed on modern-sector firms by minimum-wage laws intended to protect workers' incomes, by government support of trade union demands, or by pressure (especially on foreign- and state-owned enterprises) to be model employers. Some governments levy payroll or social security taxes on modern-sector payrolls and thus raise the cost of labor to the employer. In Latin America, restrictions on firing workers frequently are so severe that employers think twice before hiring them in the first place. When jobs once done by foreigners are taken over by citizens, nationalist pressure can cause salaries to be kept at their previously high, internationally competitive levels.

All these policies promote the welfare of relatively small groups at the expense of much larger ones. Minimum-wage laws and similar measures, if effectively enforced (and often they are not), can improve wages and working conditions for those workers fortunate enough to get jobs in modern-sector firms. But by raising the cost of labor, these measures limit the ability of existing firms to absorb more workers and inhibit the creation of more enterprises like them. In this way, they harm the much larger group of workers who either are unemployed or work in the informal and rural sectors.

Why do governments of countries with serious employment problems enact such measures as minimum-wage laws? The answer is that relatively small but well-organized, vocal, and visible groups of modern-sector workers, nearly always located in urban areas, have enough political power to lobby effectively for enactment of these laws or for increases in the statutory minimum wage once a system of minimum wages is established. In some Latin

American countries, minimum wages are indexed to inflation; this ensures that they remain high in real terms. Under a minimum-wage system, the government accepts direct responsibility for the earnings of workers in the protected sectors. If it resists a strongly backed demand for a rise in the minimum wage, it is inviting political trouble. Of course, the government also is responsible for the welfare of those who lose from the wage increase because their chances of ever getting a job in the protected high-wage sector are reduced. But their loss is less easily perceived than the wage gain of the protected workers, and the government is less likely to be held accountable for it.

Artificially cheap capital reinforces the effect of artificially expensive labor. In many developing countries, interest rate ceilings make capital equipment cheaper for those preferred customers who can obtain the credit necessary to buy it. (For the rest, of course, capital may become more expensive, or even unobtainable, as banks and other financial institutions direct the available funds to their preferred customers.) Overvaluation of the domestic currency in terms of foreign exchange can have a similar effect. It forces the imposition of a licensing system for foreign exchange, imports, or both; this in turn makes artificially cheapened capital goods available to those who can obtain the necessary licenses.

Like minimum wages, interest ceilings, foreign exchange control, and import licensing all serve the interests of influential minorities. New York University economist Lawrence White shows how preferred access to imports and credit in Pakistan led to the increasing concentration of industry and commerce in the hands of an elite group known as the *twenty families*.[9] Licensing systems also receive strong support from officials of the license-granting authorities, who can earn substantial illicit income from the bestowal of their favors.

Another way governments make capital artificially cheap is by gearing investment incentives to the amount of capital invested. Often a firm that invests $50 million is given a longer tax holiday or a shorter write-off period than one that invests only $5 million. This creates incentives for capital-intensive industries to be established in the country and for firms facing a range of possible technologies to select more capital-intensive modes of production.

CORRECTING FACTOR PRICE DISTORTION

What can be done to correct these factor price distortions? The most straightforward approach is for governments to avoid the kinds of price-distorting policies just mentioned or, if they have already instituted them,

9. Lawrence White, *Industrial Concentration and Economic Power in Pakistan* (Princeton, NJ: Princeton University Press, 1974).

to deregulate as soon as possible. While there has been a trend toward liberalization in recent years, many governments remain reluctant to deregulate, out of either concern for the welfare of workers already holding modern-sector jobs or fear of the political power of those who benefit from artificially high wages or artificially cheap capital and foreign exchange.

Price distortions that cannot be removed can be offset, in theory, by taxes or subsidies. Economists have argued that the artificially high labor costs faced by modern-sector employers should be countered by a wage subsidy. While this advice rarely has been followed, a few countries have adopted investment incentives that depend in part on the number of jobs an investor creates.

An important question about all proposals for correcting factor price distortions is exactly how much employment they are likely to create. Technically speaking, this depends on the **elasticity of substitution,** which can be defined as

$$\sigma = \frac{\Delta(K/L)(w/r)}{\Delta(w/r)(K/L)}$$

where $K =$ the amount of capital, $L =$ the amount of labor, $w =$ the wage rate, $r =$ the cost of capital, and Δ signifies a change. The elasticity of substitution thus is the percentage change in the capital-labor ratio, $\Delta(K/L)/(K/L)$, that results from a given percentage change in the ratio of the price of labor to that of capital, $\Delta(w/r)/(w/r)$. (The expression w/r also is called the **wage-rental ratio.**) Therefore, if a 10 percent decline in the wage-rental ratio leads to a 5 percent fall in the capital-labor ratio, then the elasticity of substitution is 0.5. Under these circumstances, a 10 percent decline in the wage-rental ratio would mean that, in the future, it would take 5 percent less investment (capital) to employ a given amount of labor; alternatively, a given amount of investment would employ 5 percent more workers.

Debates over the efficiency of employment creation through the correction of factor price distortions pit elasticity optimists against elasticity pessimists. The optimists argue that the employment effects are likely to be large because investors tend to be rational profit maximizers who have a range of possible outputs and technologies open to them. When faced with cheaper labor relative to capital, they therefore will adjust by (1) concentrating on goods that can be produced relatively efficiently using a lot of labor relative to capital and (2) using more labor-intensive technologies in some or all their operations. (The optimists assume that investors have a "shelf" of appropriate technologies available to them, an issue to be explored in the following section.)

The pessimists, on the other hand, contend that the response to a change in the wage-rental ratio may be small or nonexistent. They note that, in some modern industries, technology permits little substitution of labor for capital. Examples include **process industries** such as petrochemicals and wood pulp. In such industries, highly capital-intensive technologies may be absolutely more efficient than any less-capital-intensive alternatives. That is, they may use less capital per unit of output as well as less labor. In many cases, these technical characteristics are linked to economies of scale: To be efficient, a plant must be very large, as well as highly capital intensive. An LDC government should think twice before establishing such an industry, but it would be ill advised to try to make it either small scale or labor intensive.

Elasticity pessimists also point out that many firms sell in protected markets and therefore do not necessarily have to maximize profits, that they may prefer the most modern (capital-intensive) technologies for their own sake, and that they may produce goods mainly for middle-class consumption, to which capital-intensive technologies are better suited than labor-intensive technologies. For all these reasons, the pessimists argue against the policies advocated by the optimists. They would expect, for example, that a wage subsidy would do more to increase business profits than to expand employment.

Figures 8–2 and 8–3 show the differences between what the pessimists and the optimists have in mind. Which is the better depiction of the real world? It might seem simple to calculate the elasticity of substitution in developing countries and settle the argument once and for all. Indeed, many econometric estimates have been made. Quite a number of these studies have found the value of s to range from 0.5, not a dramatically high value but high enough to encourage the elasticity optimists, up toward 1.0. Other writers have criticized these estimates on various grounds: They assume labor and capital to be **homogeneous,** that is, of uniform quality, when in fact they are not; they ignore the roles of other factors of production, such as management; they often deal with industries that are defined so broadly as to encompass a variety of outputs; and so on. Modest changes in assumptions, the critics note, can lead to large differences in conclusions.

Therefore, the debate between the optimists and the pessimists is not so easily resolved. However, there remain good reasons for believing that the relative prices of labor and capital can make a significant difference for employment creation. First, whatever the range of technologies available for producing a particular item, factor prices can have an important influence on employment by affecting the choice of goods to be produced. Recall the example of the successful exporters of labor-intensive manufacturers mentioned earlier. Second, even if the technology of a core produc-

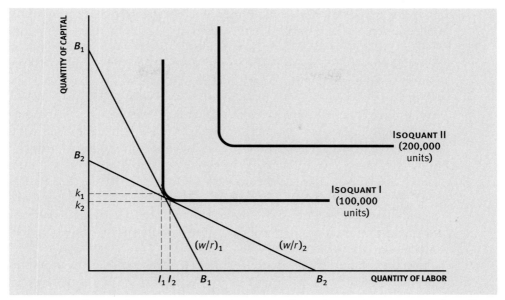

FIGURE 8–2   FACTOR SUBSTITUTION WITH RELATIVELY FIXED FACTOR PROPORTIONS (LOW ELAS-TICITY OF SUBSTITUTION). Possibilities for producing given levels of output with different factor combinations are severely limited. When the wage-rental ratio falls from $(w/r)_1$ to $(w/r)_2$, there is little effect on the amounts of labor and capital used to produce 100,000 units of output.

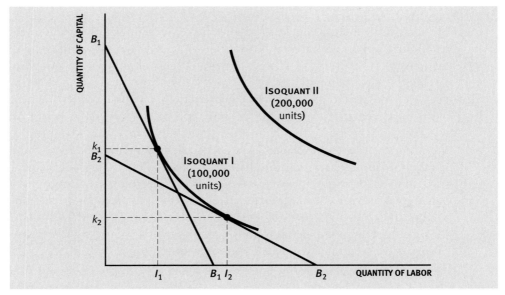

FIGURE 8–3   FACTOR SUBSTITUTION WITH RELATIVELY VARIABLE FACTOR PROPORTIONS (HIGH ELASTICITY OF SUBSTITUTION). Possibilities for producing given levels of output with different factor combinations are much greater than in Figure 8–2. When the wage-rental ratio falls, the amount of capital used is sharply reduced while employment expands significantly.

tion process is fixed and capital-intensive, opportunities exist for using large amounts of labor in subsidiary operations such as materials handling. Similarly, in construction, some operations are best done by machines at almost any wage-rental ratio while other tasks lend themselves to labor-intensive methods if labor costs are low enough.

Third, employers are far more responsive to relative factor prices when they are forced to sell their products in competitive markets than if they can sell in protected markets. An important study conducted in Indonesia by Harvard Business School professor Louis Wells showed that, while the nonmaximizing behaviors cited by the elasticity pessimists are real enough, business executives indulge them much more freely in protected markets.[10] When competition forces them to seek the most-profitable technology and factor proportions, both domestic and foreign business executives find ways to economize on capital and substitute more labor in labor-rich, capital-scarce countries.

Together these three points suggest that open competition promotes appropriate factor choices. Increasing competition, both within a given economy and among economies (as we will see in Chapters 15 and 16), can do much to validate the assumptions of the elasticity optimists and make it possible to promote employment by reducing factor price distortions.

THE ROLE OF TECHNOLOGY

For the employment problem to be solved, or even significantly ameliorated, technology appropriate to the factor endowments of the low- and middle-income countries clearly is needed. How can such technology be acquired?

The LDCs face a paradox: They must depend on the developed countries to provide the great bulk of their modern technology, yet most of what these countries have to offer is inappropriate for use in countries with plentiful labor and scarce capital and skills. Since the beginning of their industrialization processes, the United States and Europe have had a scarcity of labor relative to other factors of production. Nearly all their innovations accordingly aimed at saving labor. The result in almost every productive sector has been a sequence of increasingly mechanized and automatically controlled technologies, each more appropriate than the last for a country with scarce labor and plentiful capital, but less and less appropriate for a country with the opposite factor endowments.

10. Louis T. Wells, "Economic Man and Engineering Man: Choice of a Technology in a Low-Wage Country," in Peter Timmer et al., eds., *The Choice of Technology in Developing Countries: Some Cautionary Tales* (Cambridge, MA: Harvard University Center for International Affairs, 1975), pp. 69–93.

Excessive capital intensity is only one dimension of the inappropriateness of developed-country technology for the developing countries. Since the economies of even the smaller industrial countries generally are much larger than those of even the most populous developing countries, technology frequently is designed to be efficient at a much larger scale of operation than the developing countries can hope to attain in the foreseeable future. In addition, borrowed technology may necessitate the use of skills unavailable in poor countries and thus require the importation of foreign technicians. Finally, it may be designed to produce the wrong type or grade of product: for example, no-iron synthetic fabrics in countries where cotton is cheaper and there is plenty of labor to wash and press cotton garments.

Despite all these dimensions of inappropriateness, rich countries remain the main source of technology for poor countries. Well over 90 percent of the world's expenditure on technology research and development is made in rich countries. Third world countries invite multinational corporations to invest in their leading sectors. They obtain equipment through official aid programs. The investors and aid givers can provide only what they know and have available. In the absence of appropriate policies in the developing country, the result often is the transfer of inappropriate technology.

TECHNOLOGY POLICIES

Four possible ways of adapting technology available from developed countries to LDC needs have been suggested.[11] First, LDC can use developed-country technologies but make peripheral modifications; for example, in materials handling. Second, they can borrow old technologies from the industrial countries. The U.S. technology of 20, 30, or even 50 years ago may be more appropriate to the setting of, say, India, than the methods and machines used in the United States today. A third possible source of appropriate technology is selective borrowing from the industrial countries. Former British, French, U.S., and Dutch colonies in Southeast Asia learned after independence that Japanese equipment often was better suited to their needs than the machines they had been importing from the metropolitan country. Later, machines from Korea, Taiwan, and mainland China often replaced Japanese equipment. Fourth, LDCs can do their own research and development to evolve technology specifically designed to fit local conditions. Sometimes indigenous technology developed

11. See Frances Stewart, "Technology and Employment in LDCs," in Edgar O. Edwards, ed., *Employment in Developing Nations* (New York: Columbia University Press, 1974), pp. 88–132; and Henry Bruton, "Technology Choice and Factor Proportions Problems in LDCs," in Norman Gemmell, ed., *Surveys in Development Economics* (Oxford: Blackwell, 1987), pp. 236–65.

over the years by local farmers, craftspeople, and fishers provide a promising basis for this work.

Making appropriate selections and adaptations is neither simple nor straightforward. U.S. economist Larry E. Westphal and his colleagues have suggested that what is needed is a broad-based "acquisition of technological capacity," which can be developed only through "learning by doing."[12] South Korea purposely set out to acquire technological capability in several industries in which it thought it could develop a comparative advantage. Making the ability to export increasing amounts, initially with the aid of government subsidies, its criterion for continued support, Korea succeeded in developing industries that could hold their own in international competition without further subsidization. Some economists have argued that this result also can be achieved through judicious import substitution.[13] Either way, the key point is that productivity must be raised through learning by doing; this will permit the industry in question to stand on its own after a few years.

Despite this potential, few countries have succeeded in making the development of appropriate technology a dynamic force in their economic development. One important reason already has been suggested: When competitive pressures are absent, incentives to adapt technology to local conditions are weak. Barriers to communication also are significant. It is hard for someone sitting in Surabaya or São Paulo to know just what technology—new and modern or older vintage—is available in New York or Nagasaki. Finally, it must be said that most third world governments have not yet fully awakened to the need to promote local research and development. Their universities usually are preoccupied with teaching, and official research institutes established in various fields often are slow to develop, in part because of severe staffing difficulties. Sometimes, under these circumstances, the most useful research and development work is done by foreign firms with long histories of operations in the country.

British economist Frances Stewart has identified three broad schools of thought on technology policies for third world countries. The first group, which she called the **price incentive school,** stresses "getting the prices

12. See Larry E. Westphal, Linsu Kim, and Carl J. Dahlman, "Reflections on the Republic of Korea's Acquisition of Technological Capacity," in Nathan Rosenberg and Claudio Frischtak, eds., *International Technology Transfer: Concepts, Measures, and Comparisons* (New York: Praeger, 1985), pp. 167–221; and Howard Pack and Larry E. Westphal, "Industrial Strategy and Technological Change: Theory versus Reality," in Simon Teitel, ed., *Trade, Stability, Technology and Equity in Latin America* (New York: Academic Press, 1982), pp. 225–79; and Bruton, "Technology Choice and Factor Proportions Problems in LDCs."

13. See Larry E. Westphal, "Fostering Technological Mastery by Means of Selective Infant-Industry Protection," in Teitel, *Trade, Stability, Technology and Equity in Latin America,* pp. 255–79; and Bruton, "Technology Choice and Factor Proportions Problems in LDCs."

right," because it believes factor prices that reflect social costs n(
lead to the selection of the most efficient techniques out of th(
available range but also create incentives for more appropriate te
to be developed. The opposing **technologist school** believe(
mechanism of induced innovation cannot be relied on to do the job and
urges a conscious decision to invest more in technological development. Finally, a **radical reform school** takes a broader view of the matter. It argues
that both the array of goods produced and the methods used to produce
them are inherent features of social systems. How can one expect anything
but capital-intensive methods and products targeted for middle-class consumption from the multinational corporations? The creation of appropriate
technology and the use of appropriate factor proportions, this last group argues, require that production be reoriented toward a multitude of cheap
items for mass consumption. This in turn requires massive redistribution of
income, which cannot be achieved without a social revolution. Hence, the
problem of inappropriate technology and inadequate job creation can be
solved only in the context of a radical reform of society.

As Stewart sensibly concludes, there is a degree of truth in each school
of thought. Evidence for the efficacy of radical reform comes from the experience of China, which was able to find social and technological solutions
that permitted that nation's vast labor force to be employed more fully and
productively than ever before. Chinese industry "walks on two legs," combining large-scale, relatively capital-intensive production units with smaller,
more labor-intensive, and decentralized plants. Large-scale public works
projects, such as dams and irrigation channels, have been another important form of labor absorption. Finally, intensified agricultural technologies
using much larger amounts of fertilizer and other modern inputs have
made it possible to increase agricultural employment productively. Appropriate technology is combined with strong production organization at the
local level. The rural commune contrives to provide full employment for all
its members in a combination of agricultural and nonagricultural activities.

Other socialist developing countries have had trouble deciding just
which way they want to go. Different conceptions of African socialism
prevalent in Tanzania in the early 1970s stressed decentralized small-scale
industry, increased processing of domestic raw materials, and creation of a
modern, self-sufficient, state-run economy but did not show how these
ideas could be reconciled.

OTHER EMPLOYMENT POLICIES

Some theorists have argued that *improving income distribution* would accelerate job creation. According to this argument, goods consumed by
poor people tend to be more labor-intensive than items consumed by

those who are better off, so redistribution of income in favor of the poor would make the pattern of demand more favorable to employment creation. Unfortunately, most of the studies undertaken to evaluate this proposal have concluded that the amount of employment generated by such a shift in demand would not be very great. A major stumbling block seems to be that, although the goods consumed by the middle- and upper-income groups indeed are more capital-intensive than those consumed by the lower-income group, the better-off groups also consume more services, many of which are almost pure labor, such as household services. Moreover, goods consumed by the rich and poor often use the same intermediate inputs, for example, steel. Thus a shift in the pattern of final demand may have only a limited impact on the structure of production.

One useful approach to employment creation is to seek out *investments that complement labor* rather than substitute for it. Such investment opportunities probably exist in every sector of the economy. In agriculture, for example, mechanization of the planting and harvest functions may displace massive quantities of labor, but investments in irrigation actually create employment by making it possible to cultivate the same land more intensively and through a greater proportion of the year. A different kind of complementary investment, discussed earlier, is training to fill skill bottlenecks.

Even though capital is scarce in low-income countries, paradoxically their stocks of capital equipment often are underutilized. In many countries, factories produce at only 30–60 percent of capacity, shift work is rare, tractors sit idle in fields, and bulldozers rest by roadsides. If a way could be found to *increase capacity utilization* and put this idle capital to work, there would be a sharp upswing in the demand for labor, achievable in the short run, without having to wait for new investments to be made and mature. Unfortunately, this appealing prospect is hard to realize. Unused capacity may result from many causes, including fluctuations in demand and inadequate supplies of materials. Despite the scarcity of capital, distorted prices in some developing countries may make it cheaper for firms to let equipment stand idle part of the time than use it more intensively.

Generally speaking, *small informal-sector establishments* use less capital and more labor to produce a given type of output than larger formal-sector firms. One reason may be that small firms face prices for labor and capital closer to their social opportunity costs. Minimum-wage laws, unions, and payroll taxes all have little or no application to informal-sector firms. And not being preferred customers of the banks—indeed, often not dealing with banks at all—they have no access to rationed credit at artificially low interest rates. This situation has led many governments and international agencies to pay special attention to small-scale industry, as further discussed in Chapter 19.

TABLE 8–5	SHARE OF SMALL ESTABLISHMENTS IN TOTAL MANUFACTURING EMPLOYMENT, 1980s			
GNP PER CAPITA ($)	DISTRIBUTION OF EMPLOYMENT BY SIZE CLASS (%)			
	1–4 WORKERS	5–19	20–99	100+
$100–500	64	8	4	25
$500–1,000	41	12	10	37
$1,000–2,000	11	13	14	61
$2,000–5,000	8	11	17	64
OVER $5,000	4	6	20	70

Source: Donald R. Snodgrass and Tyler S. Briggs, *Industrialization and the Small Firm: Patterns and Policies* (San Francisco: International Center for Economic Growth and the Harvard Institute for International Development, 1996).

Small firms often provide much-needed jobs to workers who cannot find work in larger firms. This valuable social function sometimes is impeded by government policies that discriminate against small firms. Such policies range from overvalued exchange rates and investment incentives available only to large firms to regulatory harassment and disruptively selective enforcement of tax and licensing requirements. Although discrimination against small-scale industry obviously is inappropriate, the long-term potential of small-scale industry is more debatable. Normally, the relative importance of small firms declines in the course of economic development (see Table 8–5). Small firms that survive the transition to industrialization are progressive enterprises that have adapted to changing economic conditions and found ways to use resources just as productively as large firms. In some countries, such as Japan historically and Taiwan in recent decades, small-scale industry has continued to play a major role in industrial employment and value added up to high levels of per capita income. These small firms have been able to flourish in a competitive environment, unlike the subsidized and protected small-scale industry of India, which has stagnated and remained a drain on the exchequer.

When all else fails, governments may institute **food-for-work programs** to provide at least part-time or temporary employment to groups particularly distressed or well placed to give the government trouble if their needs are not looked after. Many of these programs have been financed by foreign food aid, either by paying the participants with food or by selling the food and using the counterpart funds thus earned to help pay the cost of the program.

Food-for-work programs promise to combine construction of a socially useful facility with income redistribution to some of the poorest elements in society. It has been discovered, however, that the promise has been fulfilled only occasionally in the dozens of such programs that have been undertaken.[14] Many food-for-work programs have been plagued by bad management. In some countries, local elites have found ways to capture most of the benefits; sometimes, they have even forced peasants to labor at low wages to provide a road or irrigation ditch that increases the value of only the landlord's property. Implementing an effective food-for-work program is a challenging task, best undertaken by governments (such as China's) that possess both a strong commitment to economic and social equity and the capacity to enforce that commitment.

Employment Creation Strategies

The desirability of accelerating the creation of productive employment, especially in countries hoping to combine a reasonable measure of equity with economic growth, is evident. Its feasibility is much less straightforward. Many different types of public policy impinge on employment creation. It is not really possible to draw up an employment plan for a developing country, only a general development plan stressing employment as one in a set of interrelated objectives.[15] The importance of employment as an objective of development policy and planning has received full recognition only since 1970. Policy makers and scholars alike still are learning what is involved in increasing productive employment in developing countries.

What is clear is that the context of the particular developing country— its size and economic structure—makes a difference for the kind of employment creation strategy to be pursued. South Korea and Singapore were able to solve their employment problems by emulating the Japanese pattern of whirlwind industrialization based largely on the export market. Medium-sized, semi-industrialized countries like Malaysia and the Philippines appear to be following a similar path, with modifications permitted by their richer natural-resource endowments. Larger, more agricultural countries must take a more-balanced approach. At best, they may be able to develop rapidly following a continental model, as Brazil seems to be doing. At worst, as in Bangladesh and the other very poor countries, a long period of primary reliance on job creation in agriculture and other rural activities will be required.

14. J. W. Thomas et al., "Public Works in Developing Countries: A Comparative Analysis," World Bank staff working paper no. 224, February 1976.

15. This did not prevent the ILO, under its World Employment Programme, from preparing a series of such plans through the use of visiting missions for Colombia, Sri Lanka, Iran, Kenya, the Philippines, and the Sudan. While useful as a means of publicizing the goal of employment creation and as illustrations of how employment-oriented development planning can be carried out, these plans have not in any literal sense been implemented by the governments concerned.

9

EDUCATION

The previous chapter discussed labor as a homogenous resource in economic development, a quantity of human power available to produce goods and services. But numbers of workers cannot tell the whole story. Attempts to attribute economic growth to growth in the factors of production always leave an unexplained residual, as we saw in Chapter 3. One important explanation for that residual is the improvement in the quality of human resources that leads workers to be more productive. Labor quality may be enhanced by education of either children or adults, as well as by improved health and nutrition for children and working adults, by migration of workers to placed with better job opportunities, and by fertility reduction.

Some of these activities are discussed in other chapters. At this point we want to stress their common characteristics. In each case some people—either the community as a whole, employers, the individuals concerned, or their parents—make a decision to use scarce resources to improve the productivity, present or future, of human beings. In an influential presidential speech to the American Economic Association in 1960, Nobel laureate Theodore Schultz suggested that such activities should be considered a process of accumulating capital, which could later be drawn on to increase a worker's productivity and income. He called this *investment in human capital.* This form of investment, said Schultz, is every bit as important as investment in physical capital, but until his speech it largely had been neglected by academics and policy makers alike.[1] Subse-

---

1. See Theodore W. Schultz, "Investment in Human Capital," *American Economic Review,* 51 (January 1961), 17.

quent work by Schultz and others elaborated the idea of investment in human capital, applying it to all the human resource development activities mentioned previously. A fuller idea of what the concept implies should emerge from discussion of it in the context of education later in this chapter.

Many studies support the idea that human resource development has an important bearing on economic growth. There is reason to believe that the relationship is two way and mutually supporting. On the one hand, growing economies can and do devote increasing resources to improvement of educational, health, and nutritional standards. But also apparent is that investment in human resources helps accelerate economic growth. It does this by increasing labor productivity, encouraging greater physical investment, and reducing the dependency burden of the population. These contributions to growth are especially evident in the case of education.

Trends and Patterns

Education can be defined broadly as all forms of human learning or more narrowly as the process that occurs in specialized institutions called *schools*. Unquestionably, this is the most important form of human resource development, in several senses.

First, there is tremendous popular demand for education, particularly for schooling, in virtually all countries, developing and developed alike. Often, in developing countries, the number of people seeking admittance to schools far exceeds the number of places available. In Indonesia (see the case study) the popular response was tremendous when the government made primary schooling widely available. Obviously, people everywhere believe that education is beneficial for themselves and their children.

A second reason for believing that education is important is that education and income are highly correlated at both the individual and societal levels. Figure 9–1 shows typical patterns relating age, educational attainment, and earnings in two developing countries. Although not all high school graduates, for example, earn more than all who completed only primary school, the majority do, and on average their earnings are much higher. People the world over intuitively recognize this correlation and consequently try to obtain the largest possible amount of schooling for themselves and their children.

The correlation between national income levels and educational attainment also is strong. As we saw in Chapter 1, illiteracy is rife in the very poorest countries and diminishes steadily as one goes up the in-

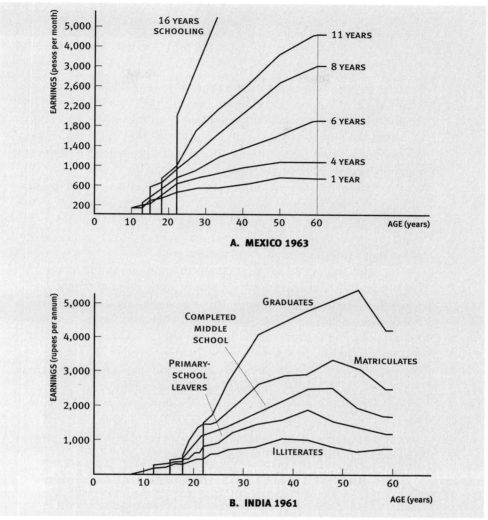

FIGURE 9–1   AGE EARNINGS PROFILES IN MEXICO AND INDIA. The lines of the graph represent mean earnings at different ages of people with varying amounts of formal education. On average, people who stay in school longer earn higher incomes.
Sources: Martin Carnoy, "Rates of Return to Schooling in Latin America," *Journal of Human Resources* (Summer 1967), 359–74; and M. Balug, R. Layard, and M. Woodhall, *Causes of Graduate Unemployment in India* (Harmondsworth, UK: Allen Lane, Penguin Press, 1969), p. 21.

come scale (see also Table 9–1). Mass education still is a relatively recent phenomenon in the poorer countries. When most adults now living were children, schooling was far less prevalent than it is today. Yet all but the very poorest countries currently educate rather large fractions of their school-age populations (middle columns of Table

EDUCATION IN INDONESIA

In 1973, as he was working on the country's second five-year plan, the chairperson of Indonesia's National Development Planning Board registered displeasure at statistics received from the Ministry of Education. The data showed that only 54 percent of 7- to 12-year-olds were enrolled in primary school. Worse, the ministry projected no rise in the percentages of children enrolled over the next five years. The major reasons were too few of Indonesia's 60,000 villages had primary schools, trained teachers were in short supply, textbooks were scarce and expensive, and many poor rural households were unable to pay even the modest fees charged to attend school. The chairperson decided that something drastic had to be done.

The solution was a special program to improve rural children's access to schools by cutting red tape and building primary schools in villages that did not yet have them. These new schools were staffed with newly trained teachers and provided with millions of just-printed library books and textbooks. Meanwhile, school fees were abolished at the primary level. The program was funded through loans from the World Bank and the high oil revenues that Indonesia was fortunate to receive during the 1970s. Would rural parents respond to the improved opportunity by sending their sons and daughters to school? They did. By 1983, after more than 60,000 new schools had been built and over 100,000 existing schools rehabilitated, 95 percent of 7- to 12-year-olds had signed up for school. The program was a great success.

But every development success brings new problems in its wake. In the 1980s, the Indonesian government struggled to cope with the rising tide of primary school graduates who wanted to go on to secondary school and eventually university. By then, oil prices had fallen, and the government could not afford to build enough public high schools to accommodate all who wanted to attend them. Many parents could not afford to send their children to private schools. Nevertheless, Indonesia is something of an education success story. By 1996, illiteracy had fallen to 15 percent of the adult population. Nearly all primary school age children were in school, along with half those of secondary school age. Higher education reached three times as large a share of young adults as it had in 1980. For a country where educational attainments were extremely low 50 years ago, these are considerable achievements.

9–1), so the educational attainment of the adult population is rising fast.[2]

The relationships shown in Figure 9–1 and the top of Table 9–1 are averages. There are many contrary cases: of rich individuals and societies that have received little schooling and of well-educated individuals and highly schooled societies whose incomes are relatively low. Some of the intercountry variations are shown in the bottom part of Table 9–1. On average, however, the correlation between education and income is strong. Does this necessarily mean that education *causes* a person's or a country's income to rise? Could causation not flow in the opposite direction, indicating merely that richer countries and families spend more on education, as they do on goods and services? Or, finally, are higher income and education perhaps the common results of some unidentified third factor? These questions are explored later in the chapter.

A third reason why education is important is that large sums are spent to acquire it. Education is a big item in both household and national budgets. Because their people want it and to some extent also because they think it will stimulate national development, governments of developing countries devote a substantial fraction of their resources to the creation and operation of school systems. Table 9–1 indicates that the expenditure of 4 to 6 percent of GNP in public funds is typical in middle-income countries while many low-income countries spend lower proportions of GNP. Private expenditure on education, which is harder to measure, is omitted from most published statistics but is significant in many countries. Some 15 to 20 percent of the government budget commonly goes for education. If one considers education an industry, it is one of the largest in all economies, ranking high in both value added and employment.

TYPES OF LEARNING

We have been treating the terms *education* and *schooling* as if they were synonymous, as one does in everyday parlance. Modern usage by specialists, however, applies the term *education* to a broader concept, akin to the notion of learning. This calls attention to the fact that several different forms of learning are important and may substitute for each other in some

2. It is rising rapidly from a very low starting point. Barro and Lee calculate that the average years of schooling of adults 25 years and over rose from 2.1 years in 1960 to 4.4 years in 1990. For women, the rise was from 1.5 years of schooling on average to 3.6 years. Children in developing countries currently are receiving considerably more schooling than this. See Robert J. Barro and Jong-Wha Lee, "International Data on Education," paper presented to National Bureau of Economic Research Conference on Human Capital in Aggregate Models, August 1996.

TABLE 9–1   EDUCATION STATISTICS IN RELATION TO GDP PER CAPITA AND FOR SELECTED COUNTRIES (AROUND 1995)

GDP PER CAPITA (PPP)	PERCENT OF ILLITERATE ADULTS	ENROLLMENT RATIOS[a] PRIMARY SCHOOL GROSS	PRIMARY SCHOOL NET	SECONDARY SCHOOL, GROSS	HIGHER EDUCATION, GROSS	PUBLIC EXPENDITURE PERCENT OF GNP	PER PUPIL ($) PRIMARY	SECONDARY	HIGHER
BY INCOME GROUP									
Below $1,000	49	68	42	20	1	2.4	25	100	1950
$1,000–4,000	31	105	93	55	8	2.9	120	400	950
$4,000–7,000	12	105	91	67	25	4.5	400	400	1300
$7,000–12,000	12	108	92	72	23	5.7	870	900	2700
Above $12,000	5[b]	103	97	106	59	5.0	4500	5800	8500
FOR SELECTED COUNTRIES									
Tanzania	28	66	48	5	1	3.4	N.A.	N.A.	N.A.
Kenya	21	85	N.A.	24	2	6.5	230	N.A.	N.A.
Ghana	34	75	N.A.	36	1	4.2	N.A.	N.A.	N.A.
Pakistan	59	74	N.A.	23	3	2.7	N.A.	637	N.A.
India	47	100	N.A.	49	7	3.2	43	N.A.	277
Sri Lanka	9	109	100	75	5	3.4	N.A.	119	678
Bolivia	16	95	91	37	24	4.9	N.A.	N.A.	N.A.
China	17	120	100	75	5	2.3	56	129	2110
Indonesia	15	115	97	48	11	3.4	N.A.	73	143
Peru	9	104	91	68	32	5.1	N.A.	N.A.	1266
Brazil	16	120	90	45	12	5.1	N.A.	N.A.	N.A.
Colombia	9	113	85	67	19	4.4	227	249	815
Hungary	1	103	97	98	25	4.6	929	916	2120
Chile	5	101	88	75	30	3.6	487	521	906
South Korea	3	94	92	102	60	3.7	1983	1361	633
United Kingdom	2	115	100	133	50	5.3	2924	4299	8536
Japan	2	102	100	103	43	3.6	7365	7250	5304
United States	2	102	95	97	81	5.4	5380	6921	7183

Note: Year of most recent estimate varies by country.

[a]Enrollment ratios express enrollment as a percentage of the school-age population. Gross enrollment ratios relate total enrollment of students of all ages to the size of the age group that normally attends that level of schooling; they can exceed 100 percent. Net enrollment ratios show the percentage of the pertinent age group that is enrolled.

[b]Rough estimate, many high-income countries with very high literacy rates no longer publish statistics on literacy.

Sources: UNESCO Statistical Yearbook 1999 (Paris: UNESCO, 1999) and World Bank, World Development Indicators 1999 CD-ROM.

circumstances. Usually three principal types of learning—education in the broad sense—are identified.

Formal education takes place in institutions called *schools*. It usually involves young people who have not yet begun their working lives.

Nonformal education can be thought of as organized programs of learning that take place outside schools. Often the participants are adults. Programs of nonformal education usually are shorter, more narrowly focused, and more concerned with applied knowledge than programs of formal education. They may teach occupational skills or other subjects such as literacy, family life, or citizenship.

Informal education is learning that takes place outside any institutional framework or organized program. People learn many important things at home, on the job, and in the community.

Although other definitions of the three terms easily can be found, these formulations indicate the basic differences among them. In the rest of this chapter we will use them in these senses.

CHARACTERISTICS OF DEVELOPING-COUNTRY EDUCATION

School systems in developing countries have expanded tremendously in the past 50 years. Countries that emerged from colonialism after World War II usually inherited narrow-based systems designed to educate only the local elite and a small cadre of literate clerks. Most colonial regimes distrusted the educated "native" and feared the consequences of mass education. Even in Latin America, where most countries became independent early in the nineteenth century, a rigid class structure confined schooling essentially to the rural elite and better-off urbanites.

After independence, the political imperatives changed radically. Pledged to change so much in so short a time, newly independent governments found that one of the most popular things that could be done relatively quickly was to build schools. While a modern economy might be decades away, a modern-looking school system could be built in just a few years. Now the incentive was to expand schooling rapidly.

As Table 9–2 shows, school enrollments at all levels in developing countries grew from about 400 million in 1970 to 906 million by 1997. Enrollment growth was rapid in the 1970s (especially at the secondary and higher levels) but tapered off in the 1980s, a troubled decade for many developing countries. By this time, primary school enrollments were approaching 100 percent in most countries and financial problems constrained expansion at higher levels, where unit costs were much higher (Table 9–1). As economic growth improved in the 1990s, enrollment growth at the secondary and higher levels picked up again while remaining well below the growth rates of the 1970s.

Enrollment growth came in waves. It hit the primary schools first. Then, as more children finished primary schooling, high school enrollment soared. Some time later, universities, technical colleges, and other institutions of higher education were affected. The spread of the system differed from country to country. A relatively westernized Asian country like Sri Lanka, which adopted a free-schooling policy at independence in 1948, was able to achieve practically universal primary schooling by the 1950s, then press on

TABLE 9–2	SCHOOL ENROLLMENT IN DEVELOPING COUNTRIES, 1970–97 (MILLIONS)			
	1970	1980	1990	1997
PRIMARY				
SUB-SAHARAN AFRICA	25	51	64	81
ARAB STATES	13	21	30	37
LATIN AMERICA & CARIBBEAN	44	65	76	85
EAST ASIA & OCEANIA	153	211	195	215
SOUTH ASIA	72	96	136	158
TOTAL	313	449	507	579
SECONDARY				
SUB-SAHARAN AFRICA	3	9	15	21
ARAB STATES	4	9	15	19
LATIN AMERICA & CARIBBEAN	11	17	22	29
EAST ASIA & OCEANIA	38	79	82	113
SOUTH ASIA	26	42	71	95
TOTAL	85	159	209	283
HIGHER				
SUB-SAHARAN AFRICA	*	1	1	2
ARAB SATES	*	1	2	4
LATIN AMERICA & CARIBBEAN	2	5	7	9
EAST ASIA & OCEANIA	1	5	11	17
SOUTH ASIA	3	4	6	9
TOTAL	7	17	29	43
GRAND TOTAL[a]	404	625	746	906

[a]Includes enrollments in a small number of developing countries in Europe.

Sources: UNESCO Statistical Yearbook 1999 and previous years.

rapidly with expansion of the higher levels until financial difficulties forced a slowdown of enrollment expansion in the 1960s. Other countries—in Latin America, India, and elsewhere—began rapid enrollment expansion at the higher levels of schooling long before universal primary schooling was attained. Often this pattern resulted from a concentration of political power that gave more weight to elite interests than to those of the general population. Elsewhere, as in the more conservative Muslim countries, it was a consequence of reluctance to provide education for girls. Worldwide, the educational participation and attainment of girls have continued to lag behind those of boys, especially at the secondary and higher levels. If girls are not expected to work outside the home, parents may see little sense in investing in their education. Significant social benefits are lost through such decisions, however, since more education for girls has been shown to improve the health and education of the children whom they eventually will rear. To prevent such losses, programs have been launched in several countries to encourage girls to stay in school.

TABLE 9–3 CHANGES IN ENROLLMENT RATIOS AND CENTRAL GOVERNMENT EXPENDITURES ON EDUCATION, 1980 AND 1996

	PRIMARY		SECONDARY		TERTIARY		PUBLIC EXPENDITURE AS A PERCENT OF GNP	
	1980	1996	1980	1996	1980	1996	1980	1996
LOW-INCOME COUNTRIES	78	93	25	42	4	5	3	N.A.
LOWER-MIDDLE-INCOME COUNTRIES	108	114	52	69	10	14	4	5
UPPER-MIDDLE-INCOME COUNTRIES	101	111	47	61	13	19	4	5
DEVELOPING COUNTRIES IN								
SUB-SAHARAN AFRICA	78	77	15	27	1	3	4	4
EAST ASIA & THE PACIFIC	111	118	49	69	3	8	3	3
SOUTH ASIA	76	100	27	48	5	6	2	3
EUROPE & CENTRAL ASIA	99	100	87	83	30	32	N.A.	5
MIDDLE-EAST & NORTH AFRICA	87	96	42	64	11	16	5	5
LATIN AMERICA & CARIBBEAN	105	113	42	52	14	19	4	4
ALL DEVELOPING COUNTRIES	96	108	41	58	8	11	4	4

Sources: Based on data given in World Bank, *World Development Indicators 1999* CD-ROM.

Rapid school expansion often created teacher shortages that led to increasing class sizes and the use of less highly trained teachers. Sometimes, it proved possible to expand teacher training and overcome the worst of the shortages after a few years. In many countries, however, teacher shortages persist to this day, particularly in poor and remote regions where teachers, like other public servants, are reluctant to go.

Fiscal strains caused by the expansion of schooling began to appear in the 1960s. Few developing countries have been able to satisfy all the social demand for education from public funds. In low-income countries, the problem is threefold. First, only a small percentage of GNP typically is allocated to public expenditure on education (Table 9–3). Second, because GNP per capita is low, this allocation yields a tiny absolute amount; most parents also have little private money to spend on education. Third, because the relatively few educated people in the society command large salary premiums, relatively high teachers' salaries (the largest cost element in education) mean that money spent on education does not go very far. All three of these unfavorable influences moderate as countries develop. African and Latin American nations that experienced slow economic growth, stagnation, or even declines in GNP per capita during the 1980s found it difficult even to maintain past educational standards. Nevertheless, as Table 9–3 indicates, enrollment ratios generally continued to rise in 1980–96. Government expenditures on education grew little during the 1980s, however, so the quality of schooling probably declined in some of the more hard-pressed countries. Private funding probably paid a larger share of the bill as private schools and colleges sprang up to offer places to disappointed applicants to the public institutions.

Developing country school systems have been plagued by large number of **dropouts** (those who withdraw from schooling before completing an academically meaningful course of study) and **repeaters** (those who require more than the prescribed number of years to complete an educational program). Most educators believe that a child who does not complete at least five or six years of school gains little from attendance; yet millions fail to do so. In large measure, these problems result from poverty. The various costs of keeping a child in school simply become too heavy an imposition on the poor household after a while.

In view of such problems, it is not surprising that learning achievements in developing country schools often are low. The World Bank reports that scores on standardized arithmetic and science achievement tests administered to fourth to eighth graders during the 1970s and early 1980s averaged 35 to 40 percent in low- and lower-middle-income countries, compared to 50 top 60 percent in high-income countries. In reading tests, the difference was 49 percent versus 70 percent.[3] There even is evidence that those who master specific skills in school sometimes lose them in later life through lack of use. Functional literacy is likely to be retained only when one has access to written materials and some incentive to read and write daily. Many people in low-income countries have neither.

Increasingly, computer literacy is becoming a basic in global educational systems. India, the Philippines, and a few more developing countries have been able to establish new information industries on a base of good computer skills and low salaries. For most people in the developing countries, including the great majority in those two countries, computer literacy is a distant dream. Only the wealthy few can buy personal computers, and the introduction of computers into the public schools still is in its infancy.

Severe inequalities among regions and social classes characterize most developing-country school systems. In many countries a child who lives in a major city or comes from a favored socioeconomic background is much more likely to receive schooling—and vastly more likely to get high-quality schooling—than a student from a rural area or a more ordinary socioeconomic setting. Since education frequently leads to a better job and a higher income, this pattern of educational provision worsens the distribu-

---

3. *Primary Education. A World Bank Policy Paper* (Washington, DC: World Bank, 1990), p. 13.

tion of opportunity and income. Some economists believe that an improved distribution of schooling would be a major force for achieving a
more-equal distribution of income. Governments in developing countries
have only begun to address these problems and potentials.

Education's Role in Development

Education is many things to many people. In addition to the economic
benefits already mentioned, education up to a certain level often is seen as
an inherent right. Education also has been promoted because it can socialize people. Through a common schooling experience, it often has been
thought, people from different national, social, ethnic, religious, and lin-
guistic backgrounds can be encouraged to adopt a common outlook on
the world. Since many developing countries have diverse populations and
must place a high premium on the attainment of greater national unity,
this is an important objective for them. Education is thought to confer
civic benefits, too. Some political scientists believe that at least a minimal
level of schooling is a prerequisite for political democracy.[4]

Thinking about how education can be used to promote economic development has changed considerably over the years. During the 1950s much of
the discussion centered on the need for trained personnel. "Manpower planning," outlined later, became a popular way to analyze a developing country's human resource needs. Its emphasis on middle- and high-level trained
personnel implies that secondary and higher education are most in need of
expansion. Yet, as we have seen, the 1950s also was a period of rapid growth
in primary school enrollment. In 1959, a number of Asian governments
subscribed to the **Karachi Plan,** which pledged them to provide at least
seven years of compulsory, universal, and free schooling by 1980.

Disillusionment with this approach followed in the 1960s. Many governments found their budgets strained by the attempt to expand all levels of
schooling simultaneously. The demand began to seem unquenchable; expansion of capacity at one level of schooling only increased the numbers applying
for places at the next-higher level. Paradoxically, the continuing boom demand for schooling was accompanied by an apparent decline in its benefits to
the individual. The rise of unemployment among the educated caused officials to wonder whether more and more resources should be devoted to expanding the school system, just so people could be unemployed. Thus, the
excess demand for schooling resulted from a market failure: because individu-

4. Yet education does not guarantee the existence of democracy, as many examples of countries with educated populations but undemocratic governments attest. (The role of education in
the recent upsurge of democracy in Latin America and Eastern Europe could be debated.) And
there are many examples of democratic systems in countries with relatively little education: India,
Jamaica, Guyana, and Colombia. So the relationship of education to democracy is not clear-cut.

als lacked information about educational trends, they expected higher returns to investments in schooling than they were able to realize.

Growing cost consciousness fit well with a new method of analyzing educational investments, introduced during the 1960s. Cost-benefit analysis, based on human capital theory, compares the costs and benefits of education, as we shall see later; manpower analysis, in contrast, considers only the benefits. By the 1970s, however, the disillusionment had spread to the human capital approach. A search for alternative concepts of education's role began and still is underway.

Education remains tremendously important in developing countries. Indeed, larger numbers of people and sums of money are involved than ever before. Current concerns include how to finance the amounts of education that people want, how to improve the quality of schooling, and how to provide basic education to those who are still excluded, especially (in some countries) girls. In March 1990, four United Nations agencies sponsored the **World Conference on Education for All** at Jomtien, Thailand, which focused on problems in basic education: More than 100 million children, including at least 60 million girls, have no access to primary schooling; more than 960 million adults, two thirds women, are functionally illiterate; more than one third of all adults have no access to printed knowledge; more than 100 million children fail to complete basic education programs; and millions satisfy the attendance requirements but do not acquire essential knowledge and skills. The conference tried to raise consciousness and mobilize resources to solve these problems.

When stock was taken of these efforts in 1996, progress on key priorities was found to be slower than had been hoped for at Jomtien. The enrollment rate of girls had virtually stagnated. While some 50 million more 6- to 11-year-olds were enrolled in primary school than in 1990, this barely kept up with population growth. Meanwhile, the poor quality of schooling in most developing countries had contributed to high rates of repetition and dropout.[5]

MANPOWER PLANNING[6]

In any economy, there is a tendency for people with given levels of education to hold certain types of jobs. In developing countries, for example, nearly all employed university graduates work at professional, technical, or

---

5. See UNICEF, *State of the World's Children 1999* (New York: Oxford University Press for UNICEF, 1999).

6. The term *manpower planning* refers to a specific analytical approach, which is described here. Since it covers female as well as male labor, the term is gender-insensitive by contemporary standards. Unfortunately, there is no good gender-neutral synonym. *Human resource planning* is a more general phrase and does not refer to this particular approach.

managerial jobs, usually either in government or as independent professionals. People whose schooling ended at the secondary level tend to hold middle-level jobs in the clerical, sales, and service occupations. Half or more of the labor force in the typical developing country is made up of farmers and agricultural laborers who received little or no formal education.

It is tempting to jump from these observable facts to the assumption that a certain level of education is *required* if a person is to fill a particular occupational role. If this were the case, it would follow that a growing economy, which is expected to undergo a shift in occupational structure toward more professional, technical, and industrial workers, must follow a defined pattern of educational development to obtain the kinds of trained people it will need.

Manpower planning is based on this assumption. It presumes that the economy's need for educational labor can be predicted and the growth of the educational system planned to avoid both manpower shortages, which may retard economic growth, and manpower surpluses, which waste educational resources and may lead to educated unemployment or "brain drain."

Manpower planning starts with a prediction of manpower needs. This can be based on employer projections or an extrapolation of past trends, although both are highly unreliable. A more-sophisticated method, developed by Dutch Nobel laureate Jan Tinbergen and U.S. economist Herbert Parnes, tries to deduce the future employment pattern from a projection of GNP growth. It starts from a target growth rate of GNP during the planning period, which must be at least several years long, since the training of middle- and high-level manpower takes time. Next, it estimates the structural changes in output by sector of origin needed to achieve that overall growth rate. Third, employment by sector is estimated, using assumptions about labor productivity growth or the elasticity of employment growth relative to output growth, which is its inverse. Fourth, employment by industry is divided into occupational categories using assumptions about the "required" structure in each industry; these are then summed across industries to get the economy's required occupation mix. Finally, occupational requirements are translated into educational terms via assumptions about what sorts of education are appropriate for each occupational group.

These five steps lead to an estimate of manpower requirements in some future year. To project manpower supply in that year, one first adjusts the current stock of manpower for expected losses through retirement, death, emigration, and withdrawal from the labor force. Next, one projects increases to manpower supply resulting from output of the school system, immigration, and labor force entry by nonworking adults. The projected manpower supply then is compared with projected requirements. If a gap results, it usually is assumed that it must get closed through accelerated school enrollment. Occasionally, other ways of increasing manpower supply, such as upgrading less-skilled workers or bringing in foreign workers, are considered.

A major weakness of the manpower-planning approach is that the relationships it assumes fixed often are unstable and unpredictable in the real world. Labor productivity is affected by many factors and often changes unexpectedly. The occupational mix also changes, for both exogenous (external) and endogenous (internal) reasons. For example, new technology may be introduced and bring into being a new set of occupational requirements. Or a change in relative wages may induce employers to hire a different mix of workers; such price adjustments are assumed away in the model. In the long run, changes in the occupational mix occur as a direct result of changes in the supply of educated labor. People with more schooling increasingly do jobs that previously were done by less-educated persons. This can be called **educational deepening.**

Further undercutting the logic of manpower planning is the absence of a unique education-occupation linkage. The knowledge required to do virtually any job can be acquired through formal, nonformal, or informal education. Similarly, only a small fraction of what is learned in most educational programs is unique to a specific occupation; much more of it is applicable to a range of jobs.

Manpower planning also fails to account for the cost of education. Manpower "requirements" are assumed to be absolute, and the conclusion always seems to be that a projected gap should be filled through educational expansion, generally of secondary and higher formal education. Yet these types of schooling are relatively expensive in many developing countries (the right-hand columns of Table 9–1). Alternative, possibly cheaper, ways of dealing with the problem, such as nonformal education or on-the-job training, seldom receive adequate consideration.

These objections, plus the emergence of the competing cost-benefit approach, long ago doomed manpower planning to limbo as far as most academic specialists are concerned. However, the approach still is used by practical planners to gain at least a rough idea of what a developing country's possible manpower problems are. It often appeals to politicians, who like its apparent precision. They enjoy being told, say, that 125 architects need to be trained by the year 2015. As a matter of political economy, manpower planning is more likely to be heeded when it projects deficits than when it projects surpluses. Deficits offer an apparently strong rationale for expanding a particular type of education. In many developing countries, however, schooling has expanded so much that few manpower deficits can be projected legitimately. In these circumstances, society's demand for education and the political pressures that go with it generally ensure that the school system continues to expand at a faster rate than would be indicated by manpower planning, which tends to be ignored.

COST-BENEFIT ANALYSIS

The assumption underlying human capital theory is that the main reason why individuals, or their governments on their behalf, spend money on education, health, and other human services is to raise their income and productivity. The added income and output that result in future years then can be seen as a return on the investment made. Application of this idea to formal education begins with a set of **lifetime earnings curves,** such as those in Figure 9–1. These curves, which show average earnings at various ages for people with particular amounts of schooling, have been calculated for many populations. Nearly all of them have three characteristics. First, given the amount of schooling, defined in terms of either years of school or the highest level attained, earnings increase up to a maximum level that is reached around age 40 or later, and then level off or decline. Second, for those with larger amounts of schooling, the curve is higher, and steeper in its rising phase; although people with more schooling start work a bit later in life, they usually begin at a higher earnings level than those with less schooling who already are working. Third, more schooling leads to later attainment of maximum earnings and to higher earnings in retirement. All three features can be seen in the curves for Mexico and India shown in Figure 9–1.

Cost-benefit analysis frequently is employed to calculate both the private and social values of education. To understand the *private rate of return,* begin by imagining a set of parents faced with a decision on how much schooling to provide a child. They have a rough idea of what the lifetime earnings curves look like and regard them as a prediction of what their child could earn if he or she had different levels of educational attainment. Although it may strain one's credulity, it is necessary to think of these parents as calculating the discounted present value of the future earnings stream attached to each level of schooling and comparing it with the cost of attaining that level of school.

The present value of prospective earnings in any future year can be defined as

$$V_0^t = \frac{E_t}{(1 + i)^{t'}} \qquad\qquad [9\text{--}1]$$

V_0^t = the present value of earnings in year t, E_t = the earnings in year t, and i = the rate of interest (opportunity cost of the parents' capital). The earnings are discounted to the present, using the rate of interest i.

The discounted present value of the entire stream of earnings until year n therefore is

$$V = \sum_{t=1}^{n} \frac{E_t}{(1+i)^{t'}} \qquad [9\text{--}2]$$

This is the benefit side of the cost-benefit calculation. The private costs of schooling—those borne by private households—are of two types, explicit and implicit. **Explicit costs** involve actual outlays of cash. The most obvious example is tuition fees, but it is important to recognize that even "free"—that is, tuition free—schooling entails costs, explicit as well as implicit. Some cash outlays almost always are required for books, uniforms, transportation, and other purposes. Even such modest explicit costs can present a significant barrier to school attendance for children from poor families. Moreover, education has important **implicit costs.** These take the form of the forgone earnings of students who would be working, either as wage earners or as unpaid but productive workers on family farms and in family enterprises, if they were not in school. In general these opportunity costs are highest for older students and higher levels of schooling (since their earning potentials are greatest), but in settings where young children can work productively, opportunity costs may be a factor even at the primary level, particularly for the poorer households which need the modest income that young children can earn.

All the costs of schooling typically are incurred before any of its benefits can be reaped. Since benefits and costs occur at different times, cost-benefit analysis requires that **discounting** be used to make their values comparable. Whether a particular educational investment is worthwhile can be determined by comparing the discounted present values of the benefit and cost streams. If discounted benefits exceed discounted costs, using a relevant rate of interest to discount both streams, then the investment should be made. If discounted costs exceed discounted benefits, the investment is not worth making. More commonly in educational analysis, however, the **internal rate of return** on the investment is calculated. This is the discount rate that equates the discounted present values of the benefit and the cost streams. We can solve for the internal rate of return using

$$\sum_{t=1}^{n} \frac{E_t}{(1+r)^{t}} = \sum_{t=1}^{n} \frac{C_t}{(1+r)^{t'}} \qquad [9\text{--}3]$$

or

$$\sum_{t=1}^{n} \frac{E_t - C_t}{(1+r)^{t}} = 0 \qquad [9\text{--}4]$$

where $C_t =$ the private costs (explicit and implicit) incurred in year t and $r =$ the internal rate of return. Using this approach, the family's rate of return on an investment in education would be compared with the returns on other investments they might make. The family would invest in education if it offered a higher rate of return than, say, putting the money in the bank or expanding its herd of livestock.

There also is a **social** or **economic rate of return,** which is calculated using a more comprehensive measure of cost: All costs of education, public as well as private, are included on the cost side of the calculation. In other words, public-sector outlays not reimbursed by tuition are added in here. Because income taxes are a cost to the individual but not to society as a whole, income should be measured after payment of income taxes when the private rate of return is estimated and before payment of income taxes when the social (economic) rate of return is estimated. This would make both benefits and costs higher in the social rate-of-return calculation than in the private rate-of-return calculation. Depending on the relative magnitude of the cost borne directly by the government and the income tax collected, the social (economic) rate of return to education could be either higher or lower than the private rate of return.

In practice, however, calculations done for developing countries generally measure income before taxes in estimating both the private and the social rates of return. This is done partly because personal income taxes are less important in developing countries than in developed countries and partly because tax data are difficult to obtain. If the same measure of benefits (income before taxes) is used in the social rate-of-return calculation, it follows that the private rate of return must be higher than the social rate of return when this less satisfactory method of calculation is used (as in Table 9–4).

The usual form of social cost-benefit analysis of education therefore is more comprehensive than private cost-benefit analysis only on the cost side. The many and varied social benefits of education that are not reflected in higher earnings are excluded from the calculation, even in social cost-benefit analysis. It would be better to include them, but benefits such as greater social cohesion and enhanced ability to participate in politics are hard to quantify.[7]

Many private and social rates of return to investment in education have been estimated for both developed and developing countries. Average results for countries at different per capita income levels and in different re-

---

7. One bold attempt to list and value some nonmarket benefits of education suggested that their total value may be roughly equal to that of the benefits reflected in higher earnings in the labor market. See Robert H. Haveman and Barbara L. Wolfe, "Schooling and Economic Well-Being: The Role of Nonmarket Effects," *Journal of Human Resources,* 19, no. 3 (Summer 1984), 377–407.

TABLE 9–4   AVERAGE ESTIMATED RATES OF RETURN TO EDUCATION FOR INCOME GROUPS AND REGIONS

	SOCIAL			PRIVATE		
	PRIMARY	SECONDARY	HIGHER	PRIMARY	SECONDARY	HIGHER
BY INCOME GROUP[a]						
LOW-INCOME COUNTRIES	23.4	15.2	10.6	35.2	19.3	23.5
LOWER-MIDDLE-INCOME COUNTRIES	18.2	13.4	11.4	29.9	18.7	18.9
UPPER-MIDDLE-INCOME COUNTRIES	14.3	10.6	9.5	21.3	12.7	14.8
HIGH-INCOME-COUNTRIES	N.A.	10.3	8.2	N.A.	12.8	7.7
WORLD	20.0	13.5	10.7	30.7	17.7	19.0
BY REGION						
SUB-SAHARAN AFRICA	24.3	18.2	11.2	41.3	26.6	27.8
ASIA[b]	19.9	13.3	11.7	39.0	18.9	19.9
EUROPE/MIDDLE EAST/NORTH AFRICA[b]	15.5	11.2	10.6	17.4	15.9	21.7
LATIN AMERICA/CARIBBEAN	17.9	12.8	12.3	26.2	16.8	19.7
OECD COUNTRIES	14.4	10.2	8.7	21.7	12.4	12.3
WORLD	18.4	13.1	10.9	29.1	18.1	20.3

Note: Averages of latest estimates for countries in which rates of return have been calculated. Most estimates were made in the 1980s.

[a]Low income = $610 or less; lower-middle income = $611–$2,449; upper-middle income = $2,450–$7,619; and high income = $7,620 or more (exchange rate conversion method).

[b]Excluding OECD countries.

Source: George Psacharopoulos, "Returns to Investment in Education: A Global Update," *World Development,* 22, no. 9 (September 1994), 1328.

gions are displayed in Table 9–4. All the rates shown in the table are marginal rates. That is, they indicate the return on the additional investment needed to move from one level of educational attainment to the next-higher level.

Four principal conclusions emerge from Table 9–4 and similar calculations. First, rates of return to education in developing countries generally are high; often they are higher than the rates of return earned on investments in physical capital. Education looks like a good investment in most low- and middle-income countries. Second, the highest social rates of return usually are earned on primary schooling, particularly in countries where primary schooling is still far from universal. In countries where almost everyone has completed primary schooling, the rate of return at the primary level becomes indeterminate because there is no lower level with which to compare it. Third, the spread between private rates of return (where income is measured before taxes) and social rates of return can be large because the government sometimes bears most of the costs. When more of the costs of schooling are financed privately, as with higher education in OECD countries, the spread between the two rates of return is smaller. Fourth, returns to education tend to diminish as countries become more developed. The basic reason is that workers with a given amount of schooling become less scarce and thus command a smaller premium in the labor market.

Cost-benefit analysis can be used to value the human capital created by the educational process. The value of human (or any) capital is derived from the stream of income it will earn in the future. This income stream is capitalized by discounting it to the present. The formula for discounting the earnings created by a person's schooling—from primary school through the highest level attained—is given in equation 9–5. E_t in the formula represents the additional sum earned each year, compared with someone who received no schooling. Conceptually, the value of human capital created by forms of investment other than education also could be measured by discounting additional future earnings, but actually measuring the amount of human capital created would be more difficult in these cases because the added earnings are harder to measure:

$$\text{NPV} = \sum_{t=1}^{n} \frac{E_t}{(1+r)^{t'}} \qquad [9\text{--}5]$$

COST-BENEFIT ANALYSIS IN EDUCATIONAL PLANNING

Of what practical value are cost-benefit calculations of education? The idea is that private rates of return can serve as guides to individual educational choices whereas social rates can inform public investment and policy decisions. But doubts surround the validity of both claims.

From the private point of view, the main problem is predicting what the structure of earnings will be in the future. The procedure just outlined implicitly assumes that the current earnings structure provides an accurate guide to the future, but in fact relative earnings can change considerably for reasons originating on either the demand or supply side of the labor market. In many developing countries in recent years, the number of people possessing all kinds of academic credentials has increased much faster than the number of jobs traditionally held by people with these credentials. The result, discussed in Chapter 8, is that school leavers tend to be unemployed for a long period of time, following which they may have to accept lower salaries than their predecessors obtained. When such educational deepening is taking place, the incomes earned by previous school leavers become a poor guide to the future, since the rate of return to a particular level of schooling is likely to decline.

Despite this tendency, applicants continue to besiege the secondary schools and universities of most developing countries. How is this to be explained? Some observers interpret it as evidence that applicants for schooling are not motivated exclusively, or even primarily, by a desire for economic gains, but want more schooling mainly for social or psychological reasons (an economist would say that they value education as a consumption good). An alternative explanation is that, when schooling is heavily subsidized by the government, the private rate of return can remain reasonably high, even when the social rate dips in response to educated unemployment and the ongoing devaluation of academic credentials. This latter thesis has been used to explain the continuing strong demand for secondary and higher education in countries such as India and Sri Lanka. It suggests that education can be simultaneously a good investment for the individual and a bad investment for society.

When the cost-benefit approach is used in educational planning, the starting point again is data on lifetime earnings by level and type of education, along with information on the total costs—explicit and implicit, private and public—of providing each level and type of education. The social rates of return on the various levels of education (primary, secondary, higher) and types of education (academic, vocational, nonformal, on the job) then can be calculated and compared. A rational government would expand those forms of education showing high social rates of return and cut back on those showing low rates of return.[8]

However, a number of questions can be raised about this procedure. As with manpower planning or any other planning methodology, its results are only as good as its assumptions, and some of these are questionable. Like the hypothetical parents discussed earlier, cost-benefit analysts must worry about how the structure of earnings may change in the future. In addition, they must weigh factors that are of no concern to the private decision maker.

If education is to be treated as an investment that must compete for scarce resources with roads and steel mills, it must be justified in terms of its contribution to national output. From the social point of view, higher earnings are not sufficient justification unless they are caused by higher productivity. The usual way of linking earnings to productivity is to assume that wages are equated to the marginal product of labor through the workings of a perfectly competitive labor market. This enables us to interpret wages as measures of marginal product. But, if other factors—for example, the salaries paid to expatriates in colonial days; see Chapter 8—have a significant effect on the wages actually paid, then wages or earnings are not necessarily equal to the marginal product and so become unreliable indicators of social benefits. In theory, this problem could be dealt

8. More precisely, activities showing a rate of return higher than the opportunity cost of capital (the return thought to be obtainable if the funds were invested outside the education sector) would be expanded and those with lower rates would be contracted.

with by using shadow wages or opportunity costs (estimates of what wages would be under competitive conditions) instead of actual wages, but this is difficult in practice.

A second and closely related issue is whether the relationship between education and earnings truly is causal. Up to now, we in effect have assumed that differences in average earnings are both associated with differences in education and caused by these differences. This is not strictly the case, since both education and earnings also partly are the result of other factors, such as individual ability and socioeconomic origin. People who are more able or who come from favored backgrounds may do better both in school and the workplace. According to the screening hypothesis, the main role of education is not so much to train people as to select those individuals who will do best in the job market.

Even if we agree that education raises earnings, there is a question of how this works. Do schools teach skills that turn out to have economic value or do they only socialize people to work better—to be punctual in their attendance and conscientious in completing their assignments? These issues have been much debated, but recent research lends strong support to the view that underlies cost-benefit analysis of education: Skills learned in school, especially literacy and numeracy, account for most of the differential in earnings associated with higher levels of schooling.[9]

The cost-benefit approach implicitly assumes that educational categories adequately specify the types of labor relevant to the labor market. In other words, it assumes perfect substitutability within each educational category. This assumption is obviously crude, particularly when categories are specified only by level (primary, secondary, higher). Surely there are significant differences between graduates of academic and vocational high schools or between graduates of medical and legal faculties. Separate calculations should be made for these major different types of education, but even this fails to capture the quality dimension. In the real world, graduates of the "best" schools, which may be best solely or mainly in terms of popular perception, earn far more than graduates of the "inferior" institutions. Finally, alternatives to schooling—nonformal education and on-the-job training—tend to be left out of the comparison altogether. If the Ministry of Education is responsible for educational planning while training programs are provided by other ministries, there is a strong tendency to downplay them.

9. See M. Boissiere, J. B. Knight, and R. H. Sabot, "Earnings, Schooling, Ability, and Cognitive Skills," *American Economic Review*, 75, no. 5 (December 1985), 1016–30; and John B. Knight and Richard H. Sabot, *Education, Productivity and Inequality: The East African Natural Experiment* (New York: Oxford University Press for the World Bank, 1990).

EDUCATIONAL POLICY IN KENYA AND TANZANIA AND ITS RESULTS

Kenya and Tanzania are neighboring East African countries that are similar in size, colonial heritage, resource endowment, economic structure, and level of development. After gaining independence in the early 1960s, each country tried to provide all its children with seven years of primary schooling. When growth in the numbers of primary school graduates pushed the demand for secondary schooling beyond the governments' limited financial capacity to provide places in government secondary schools, however, the two countries' policies diverged. Influenced by manpower forecasts that projected limited need for secondary school graduates, Tanzania severely restricted its provision of secondary school places and rationed admissions on the basis of performance on a national examination. As in Kenya, government secondary schools were highly subsidized. Kenya also limited the creation of government schools (although less severely than Tanzania), but it permitted the establishment of private *harambee* (self-help) schools that met much of the excess demand that could not be satisfied by the government schools. As a result, by the 1980s, Kenya had far more secondary school graduates than Tanzania.

The results of this policy divergence in otherwise similar circumstances have been intensively analyzed by researchers funded by the World Bank.[10] Their studies indicate that Kenya's educational

10. Knight and Sabot, *Education, Productivity and Inequality;* see also Arthur Hazelwood et al., *Education, Work and Pay in East Africa* (Oxford: Oxford University Press [Clarendon], 1990).

Like any planning tool, cost-benefit analysis can provide useful information, but it cannot be used mechanically to dictate solutions. It does furnish a useful measure of the productivity of the existing pattern of investment in education. If, for example, the social rate of return to primary schooling is high, this suggests that investment at this level is likely to be socially remunerative. Similarly, large differences between private and social returns may help explain patterns of educated unemployment, as we have seen. But the value of these calculations always is limited by the assumptions on which

policy performed much better than Tanzania's, in both raising labor productivity and spreading education more equitably among the population. Although earnings differentials related to education narrowed as the supply of educated people increased and some of Kenya's secondary school graduates had to accept jobs beneath their expectations, Kenya's heavier investment in human capital paid off handsomely in productivity gains. Kenya's more permissive policy also was more equitable, particularly in permitting greater intergenerational mobility as students from farm or working-class families had better opportunities to obtain secondary-level education. This was true even though access to Kenya's private secondary schools depended on ability to pay. By limiting access as it did, Tanzania created larger rents for those who were able to obtain secondary schooling. Those from favored backgrounds were able to perform better, on average, on the qualifying exam, and they received large subsidies once admitted.

Methodologically, the Kenya-Tanzania comparison supports the cost-benefit approach to analyzing educational decisions and casts doubt on the manpower planning approach. Although the Tanzanian planners were correct that their economy would not "need" the additional high school graduates that faster expansion of secondary schooling would have provided, the productivity benefits of an additional investment in secondary schooling would have more than repaid its cost. Given the Tanzanian government's well-known commitment to socialism, it is particularly ironic that the equity consequences of its educational policy also were less favorable than those of the policy followed by the capitalist-minded government of Kenya.

they are based. It is particularly hard to determine how fast the social rate of return will decline as a particular variety of education is expanded. To know this, we would have to calculate the elasticities relating earnings differentials to the relative supplies of different kinds of labor.

In spite of the attractiveness of its base in human capital theory—at least for those who admire neoclassical economic theory—the cost-benefit approach is of only limited use in practical educational planning. This brings us to the question of what alternatives might exist.

ALTERNATIVE VIEWPOINTS

Most educational policy decisions are made pragmatically, in response to whatever political pressures bear most strongly on the decision makers at any particular moment. Manpower projections and cost-benefit analyses are undertaken from time to time, but they seldom have more than a small impact on what actually happens. Because of the intellectual limitations of these two analytical approaches, more elaborate *formal modeling* sometimes has been attempted, but it has had even less influence. This was the case with several linear programming models of education and its relationship to the economy constructed in the 1960s and 1970s, as well as with efforts to synthesize the manpower and cost-benefit approaches.

Some economists and sociologists—*radical critics*—altogether reject the idea that education raises productivity. An element in their critique, mentioned earlier, is that education acts as a screen or sieve to select the fortunate few who are then "credentialed" to hold elite positions in society. To this, the more radical critics add that those who pass through the sieve and receive the prized credentials tend strongly to be individuals who started from privileged positions in life. The school system, they say, essentially reproduces the class structure from generation to generation. Those not destined for elite positions receive a form of education intended to make them more amenable to playing a subservient role in society They are taught diligence, punctuality, and respect for authority. The solution to all this lies not in any conceivable reform of the school system within the framework of capitalist society but in the radical reform of the social structure and economic system. Less-conventional radical critics argue that efforts should be made to revamp schooling as we know it to permit true learning to take place or to use mass education as a means of raising the consciousness of the poor regarding their oppressed condition.[11]

In view of these criticisms and proposals, it is interesting to see how Communist regimes managed their school systems. They strongly emphasized universal attainment of basic literacy and numeracy, and then restricted secondary and higher education rather severely (or just higher education in the richer Communist states), while heavily emphasizing the attainment of specific vocational skills. In the Soviet Union and other East European countries, as in the West, opportunities to obtain the more restricted types of schooling went disproportionately to those from favored

11. Iconoclastic analyses of education in developing countries include Ivan Illich, *Deschooling Society* (New York: Harper and Row, 1970); Paolo Freire, *Pedagogy of the Oppressed,* translated from the Portuguese by Myra Bergman Ramos (New York: Seabury Press, 1970); and Ronald Dore, *The Diploma Disease. Education, Qualification, and Development* (Berkeley: University of California Press, 1976).

social positions. The Communist regime most noted for radical reform efforts was that of China, especially during the Cultural Revolution of the 1960s, but Chinese educational policy subsequently returned to something much closer to the Soviet or Western model.

A very different critique and reform proposal argues for market-based reforms. Educational planning has failed, say these critics: All proposed methodologies are flawed and choices about what kinds of schooling to provide and whom to educate therefore should be left to market forces. An obvious objection to this proposal is that, if the market gives the wrong price signal, it will encourage people to respond in only the wrong ways. As long as education is subsidized, people will tend to purchase too much of it relative to other goods and services. This bias could be corrected by reducing the degree of subsidization and charging people something much closer to the actual cost of providing schooling. But that would only strengthen another objection to the market solution: that it takes no account of equity considerations. Proposed means of making a market system more equitable include liberal use of scholarships for the poor but deserving and—more far-reaching—creation of educational vouchers, a special currency that could be distributed according to any criteria deemed equitable and used to purchase any kind of schooling that the consumer thinks most beneficial.

Like the radical reform proposals, those coming from the right have been more discussed than implemented. Most governments prefer to retain a much tighter grip on educational activities than this type of reform would permit. The main role of the market in developing-country education, as noted earlier, is to provide places for those who are unable to gain admittance to public institutions, and even this is permitted only in certain countries.

An older reform proposal is that school curricula should be made more practical; for example, by replacing schools that offer traditional, academically oriented curricula with agricultural, technical, and **vocational schools,** emphasizing the teaching of practical skills. Some vocational schools have succeeded and made valuable contributions to development, but many others have failed. In a well-known article, University of Chicago educationist Philip Foster traced a series of unsuccessful experiments in Ghana, going all the way back to the middle of the nineteenth century. He attributed the persistent failure to "the vocational school fallacy," the idea that certain manual skills regarded as necessary for economic development should be stressed, when in fact the structure of incentives favors "impractical" academic training that opens the door to employment in the urban formal sector.[12] A major problem with govern-

12. Philip J. Foster, "The Vocational School Fallacy in Development Planning," in C. A. Anderson and M. J. Bowman, eds., *Education and Economic Development* (Chicago: Aldine, 1966), pp. 142–63.

ment-run vocational schools is that they often fail to provide the skills actually required by private employers. Yet, when adequately funded and run in close coordination with potential employers, vocational schools can make a real contribution to development.

A final reform proposal is to give much greater emphasis to **nonformal education.**[13] Proponents of nonformal education argue that it is more practical, cheaper, more flexible, and better able to reach lower-income groups than formal education. Although there indeed have been successful nonformal education projects—in basic education (literacy and numeracy), family education (health, nutrition, child care, family planning), community education (cooperatives, community projects), and occupational training—it seems more realistic to regard nonformal education as a complement to formal education than as its rival. Nonformal training courses generally teach different skills and reach a different audience (mainly adults) from the schools. One criticism of nonformal education is that, like vocational schools, it perpetuates a two-tiered social system. Members of the favored class get into the schools, while the less-favored have to make do with the programs of nonformal education.

13. Philip H. Coombs with Manzoor Ahmed, *Attacking Rural Poverty: How Nonformal Education Can Help* (Baltimore: Johns Hopkins University Press, 1974).

HEALTH AND NUTRITION

The goal of improving health conditions in developing countries often has been accorded a low priority, both by the developing-country governments and by development specialists. In nearly every country, the Ministry of Health has little bureaucratic clout and receives one of the smallest budget allocations. Development specialists have participated in this downgrading of health; as far as we know, ours was the first development economics textbook to include a chapter on health and nutrition.

Neglect of the subject, however, has been partially reversed in the past 30 years. Interest in health and development was boosted in the 1970s by the attention given to equity-oriented development strategies and later by concern about the effect that slower economic growth in the 1980s was having on the health of children, especially in Africa. Since the 1960s, expenditures on health, like those on education, have been regarded increasingly as investments in human capital.

The health-development relationship is a reciprocal one. Economic development tends to improve health status, while better health contributes to economic development. But proponents of health-sector programs frequently warn that development alone cannot be relied on to cut morbidity and mortality, that special programs in nutrition, health care, and environmental sanitation also are needed. Occasionally, they cite examples of how development can worsen health or argue that the provision of appropriate health programs can do the job by itself, even in the absence of significant overall development. Critics of this view stress the relationship of health status to income level and observe that the benefits of specific health measures are sharply reduced when the surrounding socioeconomic and physical environments remain unfavorable to health. We will return to this debate later in the chapter, as well as to the related issue of how health contributes to economic development.

Health in the Developing Countries

What exactly is health? What determines whether an individual, or a society, is healthy or sick? Health is a surprisingly elusive concept. The World Health Organization (WHO), the United Nations agency responsible for programs to improve health standards, defines it as a "state of complete physical, mental and social well-being," but this goes far beyond what normally is meant by *health*. For most people, health simply is the absence of disease and infirmity. But even this commonsense definition can be hard to pin down in practice. Conditions such as infection with intestinal parasites or first-degree (mild) malnutrition, which are perceived as disease in countries with high health standards, may be so common in countries with lower standards that they are not even recognized as abnormal.

The health status of an individual can be determined through clinical examination by a qualified health professional. But this would be an expensive way to measure the health status of an entire population, so for that we usually rely on statistics. Health statistics attempt to measure **morbidity** (sickness) and **mortality** (deaths). Statistics on morbidity seldom are adequate. Not only is a clear-cut definition of sickness lacking, but many sick people in poor countries never consult a doctor or enter a hospital, so they fail to come into contact with the statistical system. Mortality data are considerably better: Death seldom goes unnoticed, and most countries now have reasonably complete official systems of death registration, although significant gaps remain in some cases. Death statistics are most useful for assessing the health status of a population when they include detailed information on the person who has died (age, sex, place of residence, and so on) and on the cause of death. However, data on the cause of death usually are weak in low-income countries.

PATTERNS AND TRENDS

Despite justifiable concern and even alarm over famine, AIDS (acquired immune deficiency syndrome), and many other serious challenges to health in developing countries, the fact is that health conditions in most developing countries have been improving gradually for many years. Life expectancy has risen almost everywhere. Life expectancy is the average number of years members of a given population are expected to live. We cannot know, of course, how long any particular individual actually will live. But it is possible to predict the average longevity of a class of people (for example, boys age 3), using the recent mortality experience of the rele-

TABLE 10–1   LIFE EXPECTANCY AT BIRTH BY INCOME GROUP AND FOR SELECTED COUNTRIES, 1970 AND 1997

	LIFE EXPECTANCY	
GNP PER CAPITA (PPP)	1970	1997
BY INCOME GROUP (PPP)		
BELOW $1,000	42	49
$1,000–4,000	54	65
$4,000–7,000	57	68
$7,000–12,000	61	71
ABOVE $12,000	71	74
IN SELECTED COUNTRIES		
LATIN AMERICA		
BOLIVIA	46	61
BRAZIL	59	67
CHILE	62	75
COLOMBIA	51	70
AFRICA		
GHANA	49	60
KENYA	50	52
TANZANIA	46	48
ASIA		
CHINA	62	70
INDIA	49	63
INDONESIA	48	65
SOUTH KOREA	60	72
MALAYSIA	62	72
PAKISTAN	49	62
SRI LANKA	65	73

Source: World Bank, *World Development Indicator 1999* CD-ROM.

vant group (in this case, all males) as a guide. Life expectancy at birth is the form of the statistic most often cited, as in Table 10–1, but the concept really refers to expected years of *remaining* life and therefore can be applied to people of various ages, as in Table 10–2.

The average crude death rate (CDR) for low-income countries is now 10 deaths per 1,000 population, far less than in earlier decades. However, this average is strongly influenced by the successful experience of China, where the CDR was 8 in 1997. In low-income countries other than China and India, where the CDR was 10, the crude death rate averaged 12 per 1,000 in 1997. In middle-income countries, the rate was 8, even lower than in high-income countries, where the CDR was 9.

Recall from Chapter 7, however, that the crude death rate is strongly affected by the age structure of the population. Young populations in developing countries pull down their CDRs. There are still big differences between the richest and poorest countries in life expectancy (see Table 10–1) and infant death rates (look back at Table 7–2, where we saw that

TABLE 10–2 COMPARISON OF MALE LIFE EXPECTANCIES IN BANGLADESH AND SWEDEN, MID-1970S					
	ADDITIONAL YEARS A MALE IS EXPECTED TO LIVE IF HE IS NOW				
	NEWBORN	AGE 1	AGE 5	AGE 15	AGE 65
SWEDEN (1976)	72.1	71.8	67.9	58.1	13.9
BANGLADESH (1974)	45.8	53.5	54.5	46.3	11.6
DIFFERENCE	26.3	18.3	13.5	11.8	2.3

Source: United Nations, Demographic Yearbook, Historical Supplement (New York: United Nations, 1979), pp. 553, 558.

the infant death rate falls from 97 per 1,000 in countries with a GDP per capita of $1,000 or less measured in purchasing power parity to 6 per 1,000 in countries with $10,000 or more). The average male in a high-income economy lives 13 years longer than his counterpart in a low-income economy—19 years longer if we compare the industrialized economies with low-income economies other than China and India. Women live six years longer than men on average in developed countries, but in developing countries their longevity advantage is smaller (just two years on average in low-income countries). In parts of the developing world—China, South Asia, the Middle East, and North Africa—female life expectancy is less than would be expected.[1]

The correlation between income level and mortality, although strong, is far from perfect. In the recent past, a few countries had a life expectancy far longer than the average for their income group. China and Sri Lanka were particularly notable in this regard. By 1997, however, many countries had achieved life expectancy of 70 years or more. This included 13 countries with a GNP per capita of $1,000–4,000 (PPP), only 4 of which had a life expectancy that high in 1970, and 15 in the $4,000–7,000 group (versus 5 in 1970). Except for Botswana and South Africa, all countries with a GNP per capita of $7,000 or more (PPP) in 1997 had a life expectancy above 70 years.

Although the strong global trend was toward longer life, life expectancy declined in 1970–97 in three groups of countries. In Russia and other post-Soviet countries, a mortality crisis among men reduced life expectancy. In Rwanda and Burundi, ethnic violence raised the death rate. And in Botswana, Uganda, and Zambia, the AIDS epidemic was so destructive that life expectancy declined. In several other African countries, life expectancy in-

1. A comparison of sex ratios in various national populations has led Cambridge University economist, philosopher, and Nobel Laureate Amartya Sen to conclude that "More than 100 Million Women Are Missing." See his article of that title in the New York Review of Books (December 20, 1990), 61–66; also Development as Freedom (New York: Alfred A. Knopf, 1999). Females in these countries receive inferior nutrition and health care for a combination of cultural and economic reasons, and this adversely affects their longevity.

creased less than it otherwise would have because of AIDS. By 1999, more than 33 million people had been infected by HIV, the virus that causes AIDS, according to a United Nations estimate. Of these, 95 percent were in developing countries, including 23 million in sub-Saharan Africa. Further declines in life expectancy are in prospect for the most severely affected African countries and major epidemics are possible in India and other Asian nations.

The great gains in life expectancy experienced by most developing countries came about mainly through reduction in mortality among the very young. This is illustrated dramatically in Table 10–2, which compares male life expectancies at various ages in Sweden and Bangladesh in the mid-1970s. These two countries differed enormously in life expectancy at birth. Yet for males who survived the early years of life, differences in remaining life expectancy fell sharply. Whereas in Sweden and other countries with high health standards, expected years of further life decline steady as a person ages, in Bangladesh a surviving 5-year-old actually could expect to live eight more additional years than a newborn. As Table 10–2 shows, in 1974 the average newborn boy in Bangladesh would not live to age 46 whereas a 5-year-old could expect to survive to age 59. This is testimony to the terrible extent of infant and child mortality in the poorest countries.

The cross-section data in the upper part of Table 10–1 are consistent with the history of mortality in the industrial countries. Figure 10–1

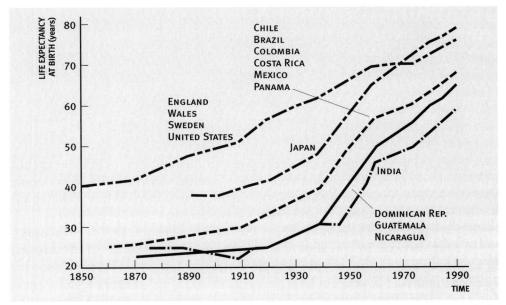

FIGURE 10–1 TRENDS IN LIFE EXPECTANCY IN SELECTED COUNTRIES. Life expectancy rose gradually in Europe and the United States and more rapidly in Japan. It is rising rapidly in the LDCs, too, but they still are far behind the developed countries.
Sources: World Bank, *Health Sector Policy Paper,* 2d ed. (Washington, DC: World Bank, 1980), p. 10; updated using data from World Bank, *World Tables,* 1989–90 ed. (Washington, DC: World Bank, 1990).

HIV/AIDS IN AFRICA

The HIV/AIDS epidemic (human immunodeficiency virus/acquired im-munodeficiency syndrome) struck Africa in the early 1980s. By 1999, according to United Nations estimates, 22.3 million adults and children were living with HIV or AIDS in sub-Saharan Africa. This was more than two thirds of the global total and implied an adult prevalence rate of 8 percent, far above any other world region. In some countries, one fifth or more of adults were infected. HIV/AIDS in Africa is spread primarily through heterosexual contact. Of HIV-positive adults, 55 percent are women, who tend to contract the disease at younger ages than men. This reflects their lack of power in negotiating sexual contact and the poverty that induces young girls to enter into "sugar daddy" relationships. The epidemic has severely affected all levels of society. The educated middle class is at least proportionately affected and may have been hit even harder than the poor. Deaths through 1999 total 13.7 million; a similar number can be expected to die in the first decade of the twenty-first century. Life expectancy at birth in southern Africa rose from 44 years in the early 1950s to 59 in the early 1990s but will probably fall back to 45 by 2010 because of AIDS. The epidemic's concentration on young adults has created millions of AIDS orphans and is reducing the growth rate of the labor force.

HIV/AIDS has begun to affect production and will have a significant impact on per capita income in the near future. Even before the epi-

shows how life expectancy has risen over the long run in different groups of countries. The early-developing countries experienced a slow, steady rise in life expectancy after 1850. Japan, a later developer, was able to extend life more rapidly and reach a level close to that of the early developers by about 1960. Despite the rapid increases in life expectancy experienced in developing countries over the past 50 years, life expectancy in the poorest countries remains far below those in the rich countries (Table 10–1).

The general improvement in life expectancy and other health statistics does not belie the fact that serious and sometimes worsening child health problems remain in sub-Saharan Africa and other low-income regions. Malaria is resurgent in some regions, while AIDS affects children both didemic struck, labor productivity in the region was low. In many countries, it had stagnated or declined since 1980, or even since 1965. About 80 percent of workers in sub-Saharan Africa are in agriculture and the informal sector. Another 10 percent work for government bodies, while the remaining 10 percent are private-sector employees. In agriculture, the main problem is to maintain productivity as experienced farmers become ill and have to be replaced by old people whose skills are outdated or by inexperienced young people. Although they represent only 20 percent of employment, employees who work for wages or salaries produce half or more of GNP. In wage employment, education and training are important means of raising productivity. Shorter life expectancy lowers the return to investments in education, particularly higher education, whose benefits are felt over a long period of time. The decline in life expectancy brought about by AIDS is making the investment in education less attractive, both for individuals and for governments and other sponsoring bodies. Yet skills are still needed to operate public and private enterprises and institutions. One form of adjustment is to invest smaller amounts per person in skill formation for larger numbers of people. Another is to substitute capital for labor, but this is bad for income distribution and at least a few professionals and skilled workers still are needed to keep the machines working. Ways must be found to keep productive enterprises working after key employees become incapacitated or die. The private sector also faces a challenge to competitiveness. Firms that provided relatively generous health, retirement, and death benefits are finding that they must cut back on such benefits to avoid ruinous increases in the cost of production.

rectly (through infection with HIV) and indirectly (through decreased attention from because adult caregivers are sick or have died). Diarrheal diseases and pneumonia remain serious health problems in many areas. Nevertheless, infant mortality declined in 118 of 121 developing countries for which data are available between 1980 and 1997, including 36 of 38 countries in sub-Saharan Africa. Under-age-5-mortality showed a similar trend, with declines in 88 of the 93 countries for which comparable data are available.

Although large gaps remain between the health status of populations in rich and poor countries, in general these gaps have narrowed in recent decades and continue to do so. This contrasts with gaps in GNP per capita, which have continued to widen. Next we need to consider why.

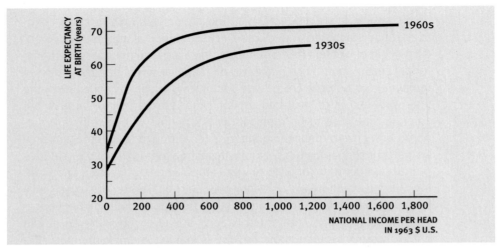

FIGURE 10–2   RELATIONSHIP BETWEEN LIFE EXPECTANCY AT BIRTH AND NATIONAL INCOME PER HEAD. In both decades, people in richer countries could expect to live longer. Between the 1930s and the 1960s, the curve shifted up; citizens of countries with given real income levels lived longer on average. Note also that the curve for the 1960s is flatter than the curve for the 1930s; except for very poor countries (below $500), per capita income no longer was so important a determinant of mortality as it had been in the 1930s.
Source: Preston, "The Changing Relationship Between Mortality and Level of Economic Development," adapted from p. 235.

CAUSES OF SICKNESS AND DEATH

Interesting research by University of Pennsylvania demographer Samuel Preston shows that the cross-section relationship between income and life expectancy is parabolic in form and has been shifting upward during the twentieth century (Figure 10–2).[2] That is, at any given level of real income per capita, people tend to live longer as time goes by. However, the relationship between income and life expectancy has become looser in recent decades. Preston found that rising income accounted for only 10–25 percent of the rise in life expectancy between the 1930s and 1960s. Other factors accounted for 75–90 percent of the increase.

What could explain this loosening of the relationship between income and life expectancy? Increasing literacy may have contributed. Preston

2. Samuel H. Preston, "The Changing Relationship between Mortality and Level of Development," *Population Studies,* 29, no. 2 (July 1975), 231–48. Continuing subsequent rises have been charted by the World Bank. See *World Development Report 1993,* p. 34, for the latest version.

stresses the international spread of health technology and a growing similarity of values regarding its application.

Although the international spread of health technology has been a major factor in the worldwide decline in death rates and rise in life expectancy that occurred since World War II, its impact sometimes has been exaggerated. An early debate concerned a 43 percent fall in the crude death rate between 1945 and 1949 in Sri Lanka (then still called Ceylon). This improvement in mortality initially was attributed almost entirely to the control of malaria through the use of DDT. Later, it became evident that DDT was only part of the story and that longer-run and more general factors such as rising income, widespread literacy, and availability of low-priced foodstuffs also were influential.

National statistics on causes of death, although weak, are good enough to permit comparison between rich and poor countries and illuminate the historical pattern of death rate decline by cause. Important causes of death in poor countries, affecting mainly the young and accounting for more than half of all deaths, have included infectious, parasitic, and respiratory diseases such as diarrhea, pneumonia, malaria, whooping cough, polio, tetanus, and diphtheria. All these diseases—many of which came to be known as tropical diseases in the twentieth century, although they were major killers in temperate countries in earlier centuries—now are well controlled in rich countries, where diseases of the circulatory system and cancer have replaced them as major causes of death. Now, infectious, parasitic, and respiratory diseases are being brought under control in developing countries as well. As people in these countries live longer, they, too, are succumbing in increasing numbers to heart disease and cancer, since they have been spared an earlier death from another cause.[3]

Despite these improvements, a number of endemic and epidemic diseases continue to affect large populations in the developing countries. Some of these diseases—tuberculosis, malaria, cholera—are prominent causes of death. Others do not kill large numbers but limit people's lives and may contribute to a premature death, which officially is ascribed to some other cause. One such kind of disease is parasitic conditions, which are almost universal in some areas. It has been estimated that perhaps one fourth of the world's population has roundworms. Another is malnutrition, which is rare in its easily recognized clinical form but common at a subclinical level, where its effects, although destructive, are more subtle and difficult to detect.

3. The exception is affected areas of sub-Saharan Africa, where increasing numbers of adults (including many members of the educated elite) are succumbing to AIDS.

HEALTH IN SRI LANKA

The small Asian country of Sri Lanka enjoys unusually good health and life expectancy compared with other low-income countries. This favorable experience is attributable to a combination of good fortune and the policies followed in the period since independence in 1948.

A small island located on the trade routes between Europe and East Asia, Sri Lanka had early contact with Western colonialism. The British, who controlled the island after earlier periods of Portuguese and Dutch domination, began to introduce modern medicine in the early nineteenth century. Campaigns to eradicate smallpox and yaws began in 1802. A civil medical department was started in 1858, a Contagious Diseases Ordinance enacted in 1866, and a medical school opened in Colombo, the capital, in 1870. In the early twentieth century, Ceylon's tea, rubber, and coconut plantations were required to provide medical care for their workers and their families, and a school health program was started. In the 1940s a network of rural hospitals was built. The compact, self-contained nature of the island supported these efforts, and when it gained its independence in 1948, Ceylon already had unusually high health standards compared with other Asian countries.

Credit for continued improvement since 1948 belongs primarily to the government of Sri Lanka, which consistently has accorded a high priority to improving the health of its people. From the start, medical care was free to all. More important, efforts were made to extend the service network to all parts of the island. These efforts were continuously hampered by shortages of funds. Sri Lankan hospitals always have been crowded,

Effects of Health on Development

Having considered the effect of development on health, it is now time to ask what better health can contribute to development. Can health expenditures legitimately be regarded as a form of investment in human capital? Before addressing this question, it is important to recognize that the validity of health services as a development activity does not rest entirely on our ability to prove that health expenditures increase national output. Better health is an important goal in its own right. Health increases human potentialities of all kinds and rightly is regarded as a basic human need. Everyone can benefit from better health in the present, and improved health for the young will lead to a healthier population in the future.

and the provision of additional beds ran only marginally ahead of population growth between 1950 and 1980. Efforts to train more doctors were partially offset by the emigration of physicians to countries where much higher incomes could be earned. The only dramatic change was in the supply of nurses and paramedics, which nearly tripled in relation to population between 1950 and 1980. This increase provided essential support for the extension of primary care to the rural areas.

Measures of mortality and morbidity show striking improvement in the past 50 years. Epidemics have been eliminated and diseases such as typhoid, tuberculosis, and malaria have declined sharply as causes of death. Crude and infant death rates have fallen, and life expectancy has climbed to 72 years. Sri Lanka has become, with China (where life expectancy at birth is 69 years), one of the rare examples of a country whose generally poor population is nearly as healthy as people in the high-income countries.

Not all the improvement in Sri Lankans' health is attributable to medical services. The island country also is unusually advanced in education. Near-universal literacy appears to have promoted better health conditions. Another positive factor is the comparative rarity of malnutrition, which results from a relatively equal distribution of income and a policy of subsidizing basic foods. Although the average calorie intake in Sri Lanka is not very different from other countries at similar income levels (see Table 10–4), total available calories probably are better distributed among the population than in most other countries.

Medical services in Sri Lanka form a colorful mosaic. The indigenous ayurvedic system coexists with Western medicine and receives some official support. Psychological disorders are treated by trance dancers or exorcists in some cases and by Western-trained psychiatrists in others.

Like education, health services improve the quality of human resources, both now and in the future.[4] Better health for workers can provide direct and immediate benefits by increasing the workers' strength, stamina, and ability to concentrate while on the job. Better child health and nutrition promote future productivity growth directly by helping children develop into stronger, healthier adults. In addition they contribute indirectly by improving children's ability to acquire productive skills and attitudes through schooling. It has been shown that healthy, well-fed children have

4. For a comprehensive statement of the case for regarding health expenditures as investments in human capital, along with some U.S. examples, see Selma Mushkin, "Health as an Investment," *Journal of Political Economy,* 70, no. 5, part 2 (Supplement, October 1962), 127–57.

higher attendance rates and are able to concentrate better while they are in school. Moreover, children who enjoyed better health and nutrition in their preschool years achieve more after they enter school.

Unlike education expenditures, which increase only the quality of human resources, moreover, health expenditures also increase their quantity in the future by lengthening expected working life. This, too, complements educational investments, since other things being equal, returns to education will be higher if people can work and earn for longer periods.

Although expenditures on health promises several different kinds of private and social benefits, returns to the investment in health unfortunately are even harder to quantify and verify empirically then returns to investment in education. For one thing, there is no simple measure, analogous to years of schooling, for the amount invested in the health of any particular individual. The economic effects of better health also are hard to measure. The quantitative effects (extended working life) can be gauged in additional years worked, but what value should be put on them? In a private cost-benefit analysis expected additional earnings can be used, but in a social cost-benefit analysis the social marginal product of labor should be estimated to determine the value to society of an extended working life. This recalls the complex question, already addressed in Chapter 8, of what the productivity of the marginal worker really is. In an economy in which marginal productivity is very low, the production benefits of an extended working life are necessarily small. The qualitative effects of health expenditure (increased worker productivity and earnings) also are hard to measure because increases in productivity or earnings attributable to improvement in health may be difficult to identify.

Research to measure the effects of better health on labor productivity has yielded varying results. Several attempts have been made to measure the effects of improved health and nutrition on workers whose productivity easily can be measured (for example, plantation and road construction workers). While some of these studies have revealed the expected positive effects on productivity, others indicated smaller impact than expected or none at all.[5] In some cases, people seem to find ways to adapt to wide ranges of ill health and malnutrition without greatly reducing their productivity. They may not feel well, but they still work. In such cases, im-

---

5. Two types of study have been undertaken: (1) socioeconomic studies, in which the productivity effects of different health statuses are measured, controlling for interpersonal differences, and (2) experimental studies, in which health improvement measures (e.g., iron supplementation) have been undertaken for one set of workers, whose productivity then is compared with that of a control group. The results of these studies are analyzed in Jere R. Behrman and Anil B. Deolalikar, "Health and Nutrition," in Chenery and Srinivasan, *Handbook of Development Economics*, Vol. 1, pp. 631–711 (especially pp. 683–92); and Jere R. Behrman, "Health and Economic Growth: Theory, Evidence, and Policy," in *Macroeconomic Environment and Health* (Geneva: WHO, 1993), pp. 21–61.

proving health will not necessarily increase productivity, but it remains desirable from a humanitarian point of view.

In addition to increasing the quantity and improving the quality of human resources, health expenditures can increase the availability or productivity of nonhuman resources. The clearest example is the large tracts of land rendered uninhabitable or unusable by endemic disease. Malaria and yellow fever blocked access to many parts of Latin America, Africa, and Asia before these diseases were brought under relatively effective control in the twentieth century. Even today, schistosomiasis makes it unsafe for people to enter lakes and streams in sections of Africa, and trypanosomiasis (African sleeping sickness) restricts the range of the livestock industry. So far no chemical means of control has been discovered for either of these diseases. China, however, has made progress against schistosomiasis through mass campaigns aimed at ridding lakes and streams of the snails that transmit the parasite. Improved control of ankylostomiasis (hookworm) and other parasitic conditions would increase resource availability in a different way. The effective productivity of resources devoted to food production would be increased.

Finally, better health can save money spent on curative health care. This frees up resources for other uses.

We have seen that the productive benefits of health expenditures, although easy to hypothesize, have proven difficult to verify empirically. But even the effects on health status sometimes are hard to measure. The main reason is the multiplicity of factors that go together to determine health status. For example, a study of the health effects of projects to provide safe water supplies to a number of villages in Lesotho found, surprisingly, that provision of a clean water source failed in many cases to lead to a significant reduction in the prevalence of waterborne and water-related diseases. One explanation was that waterborne diseases also are transmitted by other means, such as contaminated food, and the provision of a safe water source alone does not protect villagers from infection through other sources.[6]

Health improvement has one effect that could be considered a social cost: by reducing the death rate, it increases population growth. Admittedly, the decline in the death rate may in turn encourage a drop in fertility, which would reduce the overall positive impact on population growth; but studies indicate that the magnitude of this replacement effect, if it exists at all, is likely to be small. Another consideration at this point is a question of ethical values. Even if population growth is acknowledged to be injuriously high, universally espoused values make it unacceptable to reduce that growth by allowing persons already born to die when the

---

6. Richard Feuchem et al., *Water, Health, and Development: An Interdisciplinary Evaluation* (London: Tri-Med Books, 1974), Chap. 9.

TABLE 10–3   ACCESS TO SAFE DRINKING WATER AND SANITATION IN DEVELOPING COUNTRIES, 1990S (PERCENT OF POPULATION)

REGION	SAFE DRINKING WATER[a]	SANITATION[b]
URBAN POPULATION		
AFRICA	79	N.A.
ASIA	N.A.	N.A.
LATIN AMERICA	84	62
RURAL POPULATION		
AFRICA	41	81
ASIA	74	23
LATIN AMERICA	41	40

[a]Defined as reasonable access to an adequate amount of water (including untreated but uncontaminated water). An adequate amount is generally defined as 20 liters per day per person.
[b]Defined as at least adequate excreta disposal facilities.
Source: World Bank, *World Development Indicators 1999* CD-ROM.

means to save them are at hand. It follows that this "cost" should not be used as an argument against health improvements and that other means should be found to limit population growth if this is considered to be an important social objective.

Environmental Health

The health planner, like the physician, should carefully diagnose before he or she prescribes. Health planning must address the real health problems found in the developing countries. Some of the causes of sickness and premature death in the developing countries that deserve more careful examination are environmental health problems, malnutrition, and lack of medical care of adequate quantity, quality, and type.

The principal problem of **environmental sanitation** in low-income countries is the contamination of the water supply, and sometimes also food and soil, with human waste. This occurs in villages and cities alike. Although most urban residents have access to piped drinking water, the public water supply often is rendered unsafe by contamination in the distribution process as a result of a faulty or nonexistent sewage system. A majority of rural residents still enjoyed neither safe drinking water nor decent sanitation in the 1990s, as Table 10–3 indicates.[7]

Many of the infectious, parasitic, and respiratory diseases that afflict poor countries are waterborne. Typhoid, dysentery, and cholera are leading examples. Their prevalence results in much sickness among adults and

7. The exception is that most in rural Asia now enjoy safe drinking water.

frequent deaths among infants and malnourished children. A second type of environmental sanitation problem arises from housing with insufficient space, ventilation, and access to sunlight. This situation, which is more likely to occur in urban than in rural areas, promotes the spread of airborne diseases such as tuberculosis.

Sanitary improvement programs involve primarily the problems of waste disposal and water supply, particularly the need to keep one system from contaminating the other. In villages, this means safe wells and properly constructed privies or latrines. Simple but effective technologies are available for such improvements. In urban areas, matters become more expensive and complex. It will be a long time before all cities in the developing countries have decent sewage disposal and water supply systems, let alone adequate housing for their growing populations.

In the historical experience of the developed countries, improvements in sanitation were closely associated with reduction in diseases and became effective long before successful treatments were discovered. So far, in the developing countries, the experience has been mixed. Some projects to improve water supply and waste disposal methods have led to dramatic reductions in disease. Others, as noted earlier, have had no discernible effect.

Malnutrition

Malnutrition is a major source of ill health and premature death in the developing countries. Average daily caloric intake has risen since the 1960s in all major regions, in most (but not all) individual countries, and at all levels of GDP per capita (PPP), including the lowest. By 1989, estimated caloric intake exceeded the minimum daily requirement of approximately 2,300 calories in nearly all countries with GDP per capita (PPP) of $2,000 or more and in most regions of the world. Countries with a per-capita GDP of less than $1,000, sub-Saharan Africa, and South Asia fell below the prescribed minimum. While this may appear to be a generally favorable situation and the shortfalls in the deficit income groups and regions, at 4–12 percent, may seem relatively small, one should be aware of two major pitfalls in interpreting these figures.

First, it must be recognized that the minimum daily requirement is not so simple a concept as it may appear. People can survive at lower levels of caloric intake, but to do so they must maintain a lower body weight and become less active. Such people generally do not appear ill, and it has even been suggested that some Asian groups, for example, should be regarded as "small but healthy." Arguing against this view, however, is considerable evidence that Asian workers who receive higher caloric intake and can maintain greater weight for their height outperform their smaller counterparts at physical tasks such as farm work. It should be added that Asian smallness is not entirely genetic, but is at least partially attributable to inadequate nutrition in the past. When Asians regularly get enough to eat, as the Japanese have since World War II and the Chinese and Koreans more recently, their average weight and height, and thus their caloric requirements, increase rapidly from one generation to the next.

The second problem is that these averages can make the situation look better than it actually is because available food may be distributed very unequally. Even in a country where the average daily intake is less than 2,000 calories, at least a few people eat as well as people in the developed countries (3,500 calories or more). Meanwhile, as discussed later, large parts of the population are likely to experience significant caloric deprivation. The problem is that although the ample—even excessive—intake of the well-fed few raises the national average, it in no way diminishes the deficit suffered by those who cannot obtain the recommended minimum. Averages computed for large and diverse populations are particularly likely to understate the nutritional problem by offsetting surpluses against deficits in this misleading way.

Because of these problems, it is more revealing to count malnourished people than count calories. Table 10–4 shows percentages of children under the age of 5 who were either "stunted" (far too short for their age) or "underweight" (far too light for their age). The table indicates that these signs of malnutrition are widely prevalent in countries where GNP per capita (PPP) was less than $4,000 in 1997. Above that income level, the number of stunted and underweight children falls off rapidly. In regional terms, the highest prevalence of child malnutrition is in South Asia, where more than half of all children under 5 are affected. Things are somewhat better in sub-Saharan Africa, despite the low income level in that region. Nutritional standards have improved substantially in East Asia and the extent of child malnutrition is comparatively low in Latin America and the Caribbean.

Most of the malnutrition in the world today is of the type known as *protein-calorie malnutrition* (PCM). Conditions caused by deficiencies of specific nutrients, such as rickets, scurvy, and beriberi, generally have declined in importance. Among the remaining deficiency diseases the most important are vitamin A deficiency, which can cause blindness, and iron-deficiency anemia. At one time it was thought that shortage of protein was the principal nutritional problem of the developing countries, since protein is necessary for physical and mental development. Later, however, it was discovered that most of the children whose diets are protein deficient also suffer from a deficiency of calories, and if protein is added to the diet while calories remain insufficient, development is little affected because the added protein is used up as energy. Accordingly, calories are now re-

TABLE 10–4	PERCENTAGE OF MALNOURISHED CHILDREN BY INCOME CLASS, REGION, AND SELECTED COUNTRIES, 1990S	
INCOME GROUPS (PPP)	HEIGHT FOR AGE[a]	WEIGHT FOR AGE[a]
BELOW $1,000	45	87
$1,000–4,000	40	33
$4,000–7,000	16	8
$7,000–12,000	13	9
ABOVE $12,000	N.A.[b]	N.A.[b]
DEVELOPING REGIONS AND SELECTED COUNTRIES		
SUB-SAHARAN AFRICA	32	33
GHANA	N.A.	24
KENYA	34	23
TANZANIA	43	31
SOUTH ASIA	52	51
INDIA	52	53
PAKISTAN	50	38
SRI LANKA	24	38
EAST ASIA AND THE PACIFIC	33	20
CHINA	31	16
INDONESIA	42	34
SOUTH KOREA	25	11
MALAYSIA	N.A.	20
LATIN AMERICA AND THE CARIBBEAN	14	9
BOLIVIA	29	8
BRAZIL	11	6
CHILE	2	1
COLOMBIA	15	8
PERU	26	8

[a]Percentage of children below the age of 5 who are more than two standard deviations below the median for a U.S. population.
[b]Statistics are not reported for most high-income countries but presumed to be low.
Source: World Bank, *World Development Indicators 1999* CD-ROM.

garded as the limiting factor in nutrition, and most programs attempt to supplement calories first and protein, vitamins, and minerals only secondarily.

FOOD CONSUMPTION

What causes malnutrition, and how could nutritional improvement contribute to economic development? The determinants of human nutritional levels can be analyzed using microeconomic consumption theory. The consumption of food, like that of other goods and services, can be thought of as determined by three elements: income, relative prices, and tastes. Engel's law, introduced in Chapter 3, says that households spend an increasing amount, but a decreasing proportion, of income on food as their income rises. Very poor households devote more than half their income to food and have relatively high income elasticities of demand for food; that is, a significant proportion of any additional income will be used to buy food. At higher income levels, the share of income devoted to food purchases falls to one-quarter or less, and the income elasticity of demand for food becomes quite low. Thus, income is an important determinant of food consumption levels, particularly at lower levels of household income. However, research has indicated that increases in income are less likely to raise calorie intake in the population as a whole than previously thought, because people evidently spend a large share of increased income on better quality or a greater variety of food, rather than on more calories.[8]

Prices also have considerable influence, through income effects and substitution effects. A change in the price of the basic foodstuff—rice, wheat, or corn, depending on the country—can have a significant effect on the purchasing power of a poor household. If the household spends, say, 30 percent of its income on rice and the retail price of rice increases by 20 percent, this amount to a 6 percent cut ($0.3 \times 0.2 = 0.06 = 6$ percent) in the household's already low purchasing power. For this reason, staple food grain prices are a basic indicator of welfare levels among the poor and also political stability—in many low-income countries.

Substitution effects can be significant as well. Even if people strongly prefer particular foods, large price differences can cause them to shift to cheaper substitutes for the more-expensive foods that they prefer. This is especially true for the very poor. Hence, it was possible to induce large numbers of people in East Pakistan (now Bangladesh) to consume U.S. surplus wheat instead of rice, the favored food grain, when there was a rice shortage during the 1960s. Similarly, desperately poor families sometimes are forced to "trade down" from the preferred food grain to a cheaper source of calories, usually either a hard grain like sorghum or a starchy root crop such as manioc (cassava).

A powerful argument for the influence of income on food consumption and nutritional status has appeared in discussions of famine. Most people associate famine with a precipitous drop in the overall food supply, usually as a result of crop failure, but Cambridge University economist Amartya Sen has shown that, in several historical famines, the total availability of food did not decline. The real problem, Sen argues, is likely to be people's food **entitlements:** Their ability to obtain food, whether through purchase, rationing, or other forms of distribution.[9] Contempo-

---

8. Behrman and Deolalikar, "Health and Nutrition."

9. Amartya Sen, "Ingredients of Famine Analysis: Availability and Entitlements," *Quarterly Journal of Economics,* 96, no. 3 (August 1981), 433–64.

rary food policy analysts define their goal as **food security,** a situation in which all people, at all times, have access to enough food to permit them to lead active, healthy lives.

Both income and price influence the consumption of *food,* not necessarily or directly the consumption of nutrients derived from food. When people spend more on food, they may or may not obtain better nutrition. Some of their additional expenditure goes for a larger *quantity* of food, but much of it, especially above minimal income levels, goes for higher *quality.* *Quality* is defined subjectively by the consumer, following his or her tastes. Foods regarded as higher in quality need not be more nutritious than less-favored competitors, and they may even be nutritionally inferior. Every nutritionist can tell horror stories about the deterioration in nutritional standards as development proceeds: Carbonated beverages replace natural drinks, commercial infant foods replace mother's breast milk, and various junk foods increasingly are consumed by children and adults. Statistics make it clear, however, that these cases run against the general pattern of improved nutrition in relation to increasing income. In general, people with higher incomes have at least a somewhat higher caloric intake and a more varied diet, which is superior in terms of nutrients other than calories.

Food beliefs and tastes can impede nutritional improvement. Every culture has beliefs about the health effects of various foods that are not supported by modern nutritional science. Traditional feeding taboos for infants and new mothers are particularly injurious in many developing countries. In most human environments one can point to nutritional potentials that remain underexploited for reasons of taste and habit. For example, soybean products provide a much cheaper source of protein than animal products, yet they are eaten in quantity only in East Asian countries, where they are standard protein sources. Nutritionists can counter the economists' assertion that income is the main influence on nutritional status by demonstrating that even very poor households could eat more nutritiously if they had the necessary information and chose to do so.

Therefore, all three of the factors we have examined—income, prices, and tastes—are significant contributors to the determination of nutritional status. Emphasis on the role of each factor leads to a different approach to nutritional policy, as will be seen.

The distribution of food within a family is another important aspect of individual nutritional status. When there is not enough food to go around, children and older adults tend to find their rations disproportionately reduced.[10] It is understandable that, in dire circumstances, families

10. Children with *high parity*—those born into families where there are several older siblings—are particularly likely to suffer. Studies have shown that such children have higher mortality rates, presumably because large families strain supplies of income, food, and parental attention.

channel scarce food to the working adults on whose continued health and strength the survival of all family members ultimately depends. This makes it hard to devise programs to improve the nutritional status of the more vulnerable family members, such as infants and new mothers, since if they get more food at a clinic, the family may compensate by giving them less at home. In the end, the net increase in the family's food supply may go to the breadwinner, rather than the intended recipients.

NUTRITIONAL INTERVENTIONS

The first problem to be solved when designing a nutrition improvement program is to select a target group.

Infants and children face the greatest nutritional problem in the developing countries. Infants usually are adequately fed through the breast-feeding stage, but they may suffer a nutritional decline after weaning. If not corrected, this decline will reduce their energy levels and physical growth. This, in turn, may decrease their resistance to disease and impair their ability to learn in school. It also has been argued that malnutrition causes severe, even irreversible, retardation of mental development, but this assertion is regarded as controversial at best. Even so, nutritional deficiencies among children in developing countries must be viewed as important because they are widespread and have such serious consequences.

Pregnant and lactating women also merit special attention because of their relationship to the child nutrition problem. While carrying or nursing a child, a woman has especially high nutritional requirements, because she is "eating for two," as the saying goes.

Whether working adults should be specially targeted for nutrition intervention is more debatable. Conceivably, improved nutrition for this group could have the most direct and immediate effect on economic growth if its productivity were thereby increased. But we have seen mixed evidence on whether their productivity is reduced by the degrees of malnutrition prevailing in most developing countries and whether it would be improved by nutrition intervention. In any case, since working adults tend to get favored access to whatever food is available, it is not clear to what extent their food supply is cut when the family as a whole is short of food.

Several different types of nutrition intervention are possible. In the 1950s, attention focused on the severely malnourished, who required hospital treatment. Later emphasis shifted to treatment of milder cases outside hospitals. Supplementary feeding programs were instituted in a number of countries. Their greatest difficulty turned out to be reaching the intended beneficiary group at reasonable cost. School lunch programs can be helpful, but the worst nutritional deficiencies are likely to be among preschool children. Even when the intended beneficiaries are reached and fed, evaluators of feeding programs suspect that substitution frequently takes place in the home: Children are fed less to compensate for the school lunch, and the net increase in the family's food supply thus goes to the adults rather than the children.

The best way to get supplementary food to infants and small children is to integrate food distribution with **maternal and child health** (MCH) programs. These programs aim to provide health services to mothers and infants through local clinics while also providing nutritional surveillance. The food offered can serve as an inducement for mothers to bring their children into an MCH center regularly for weighing, examination, and treatment, if necessary. Persuasion and links with other services that may be desired, such as family planning, also promote these programs. Without such efforts, very few mothers in developing countries bring their babies in for examination by a health professional unless they are obviously sick.

Other conventional nutrition improvement programs include the promotion of **backyard gardens** to supplement the local diet and **nutritional education,** conducted in schools, adult education courses, and the like. Since these programs are inherently limited in scope, attempts have been made to develop broader, more general programs. **Food supplementation** (fortification) sometimes has had dramatic success in overcoming specific nutritional deficiencies, such as through the addition of iodine to the salt supply in goiter-prone areas. Fortification of bread and other basic foodstuffs to increase their protein content has been attempted in several areas, with mixed results. Still less successful have been efforts, some of them widely heralded for a time, to develop commercially compounded **new foods,** whose exceptional nutritional values would overcome the problem of malnutrition. The high cost of new foods usually puts them beyond the reach of those low-income consumers likely to be malnourished.

Growing interest in malnutrition and the limited success of conventional approaches have led to increasing attention to still broader programs, such as **campaigns to increase national food production** and **food price subsidization** for low-income urban consumers. There is no doubt that food-growing peasants, such as small-scale rice or corn producers, eat better when their farms become more productive. Similarly, a price cut for staple food items—made possible by higher farm production and greater supplies—can provide a substantial boost in both purchasing power and nutritional status for the urban poor, as we have seen.

Staple-food subsidization programs pose two major problems: how to limit them to the intended beneficiaries and how to finance them. Recipients of subsidized foodstuffs (or food stamps, as in the U.S. program) may sell them to buy other goods they prefer. While this practice is consistent with the idea of consumer sovereignty, it may defeat the purpose of nutritional improvement. Subsidy programs can be expensive, especially when their scope is broad. Egypt and Sri Lanka have had food subsidy programs that extended to nearly the entire population. In both cases subsidization of basic foodstuffs (wheat, beans, lentils, vegetable oil, meat, fish, and tea in Egypt; rice, wheat, and sugar in Sri Lanka) probably increased the real income of the poor and improved their nutritional and health status. But the cost of the program grew to around 15 percent of government expenditure in both countries and became a threat to fiscal stability. In both cases efforts to cut back on the subsidy bill led to political instability: riots in both countries, and in Sri Lanka the defeat at the polls of more than one government.

The cost-effectiveness of different approaches to nutritional improvement has been debated.[11] Targeted programs that deliver nutritional services to specific groups of beneficiaries—for instance, school lunch programs or baby-weighing programs—can involve high logistical and supervision costs per beneficiary served. More general programs, such as food fortification or food subsidies, may achieve a lower cost per recipient but entail a different kind of cost problem: Leakage of program benefits to people other than the intended beneficiaries. Providing nutritional services, especially food subsidies, to large segments of the population can be costly, as the experiences of Egypt and Sri Lanka illustrate. Experience with World Bank-sponsored projects in Brazil, Colombia, Indonesia, and the Indian state of Tamil Nadu suggests that well-designed targeted programs can be more cost-effective than general programs.[12]

Medical Services

Most developing countries have too few health services, and those are too poorly distributed. Public expenditures on health services are much smaller in developing than in developed countries, even as a percentage of GNP (Table 10–5). In terms of dollars per capita, these outlays are woefully inadequate. Governments in the poorest countries typically spend only a few dollars per capita, even when measured in purchasing

11. Cost-effectiveness is a concept akin to the benefit-cost ratio. But, whereas in the benefit-cost ratio both benefits and costs are measured in money terms, cost-effectiveness uses a nonmonetary measure of benefits. In the case of a nutritional intervention, for example, greater cost-effectiveness would consist of achieving a larger amount of nutritional benefit for a given program expenditure. Alternatively, it could be defined as achievement of a given amount of nutritional benefit for less program expenditure.

12. Alan Berg, *Malnutrition. What Can Be Done? Lessons from World Bank Experience* (Baltimore: Johns Hopkins University Press for the World Bank, 1987).

TABLE 10–5	HEALTH PERSONNEL, FACILITIES AND EXPENDITURES (1990S)					
COUNTRY'S GDP PER CAPITA (PPP)	PER 1,000 POPULATION		EXPENDITURES[a]			
			PERCENT OF GNP			
	HOSPITAL BEDS	PHYSICIANS	PUBLIC	PRIVATE	TOTAL	DOLLARS PER CAPITA
BELOW $1,000	0.1	1.1	1.2	1.1	2.5	14
$1,000–4,000	0.9	2.6	1.5	2.6	4.1	73
$4,000–7,000	1.9	5.4	3.0	2.4	5.5	290
$7,000–12,000	1.5	3.2	3.5	1.7	6.9	544
ABOVE $12,000	2.4	7.4	6.0	3.5	9.8	2,293

[a]Public and private spending on health do not necessarily add to total spending on health because of inconsistencies in the original data and differences in country coverage.

Source: World Bank, *World Development Indicators 1999* CD-ROM.

power parity.[13] The inadequacy becomes clearer when we consider that in developing countries, in contrast to the United States, the public sector finances the bulk of the modern, Western-style medical and health services.[14] Private doctor and hospitals typically are few and patronized mainly by well-to-do urban residents. As a percentage of GNP, private expenditure on health services also is very small (see Table 10–5). Most countries also have indigenous practitioners of various kinds: herbalists, exorcists, and acupuncturists. Typically, the masses of people consult both modern and indigenous healers, depending on the nature of the ailment and on their access to the various systems of medicine.

Low medical expenditures in the past have led to an inadequate stock of health facilities and personnel in most developing countries and particularly in the poorest ones, as Table 10–5 indicates. Medical training in many of the poorest countries may not benefit society because doctors are highly mobile, and once trained, many emigrate to seek higher income elsewhere (see the case study on Cuba). In many cases, increasing the supply of nurses and other health auxiliaries may be a better way to improve services.

13. Conventional figures, which show government health expenditures of only $1–2 per capita per year, are distorted by the extreme disparity in the pay of medical personnel, especially doctors, between rich and poor countries. The purchasing power parity used in Table 10–5 roughly triples the per capita expenditure figures for the poorest countries and doubles those for the somewhat less poor. By any measure, however, the figures remain abysmally low. See Frederick Golladay, "Health Problems and Policies in Developing Countries," World Bank staff working paper no. 412, August 1980.

14. In the United States, total (public plus private) health expenditures in 1992 amounted to about 12 percent of the GNP. Yet central government expenditure, as reported in the *World Development Report 1994,* was less than 4 percent.

In addition to being inadequately supplied, health services in poor countries are very unevenly distributed among the population. Capital cities and other major urban areas usually have several times as many doctors in relation to the population as rural areas. Similar if slightly smaller disparities exist for hospital beds and primary health workers.

The usual public health service is organized on a referral basis, so in theory, patients from rural areas with acute medical problems are sent to better facilities in the towns and, if necessary, the major cities for care. Generally, however, this referral system works poorly. The lower reaches of the system seldom provide easily accessible services to the whole country. For large parts of the population in most low-income countries, even the most rudimentary public health facility is so far away that, given the prevailing poor transportation systems, in practice it is inaccessible. When patients do go to a government clinic or hospital, they often find that they have to wait many hours and possibly pay unauthorized fees before receiving any attention. Even then, the care they obtain may be slipshod and halfhearted. As a result, rather than using the systems for routine services and referrals, as intended, people tend to ignore it except in acute emergencies and then go directly to a hospital.

Managerial and logistical problems overwhelm some developing country health systems. Many of the vaccines administered, for example, have been rendered ineffective by age and exposure to heat, and sterile conditions for medical procedures are all but impossible to maintain. Reuse of needles without proper sterilization and other unsanitary procedures, always a means of spreading diseases such as hepatitis, now threaten to accelerate the spread of AIDS.

Medical resources often are distributed ineffectually among different types of ailments and forms of treatment. In many countries, large fractions of tight health budgets have been devoted to acquiring state-of-the-art medical technologies for hospitals in the capital city or at the local medical school. Does it make sense for a country that is not providing even rudimentary medical care to sick infants to acquire the capacity to do open-heart surgery? For the cost of a single complicated medical procedure, basic attention could be provided to hundreds of rural patients. Why then do so many countries opt for what appears to be a severe maldistribution of their scant health resources? One reason appears to be urban bias, the general tendency in developing countries for urban populations to benefit disproportionately from government expenditure and policies.[15] Urban bias in the provision of medical services has many causes: One is that the powerful national elites centered in urban areas, especially the

15. *Urban bias* was defined and analyzed by Michael Lipton in *Why Poor People Stay Poor: Urban Bias in World Development* (Cambridge, MA: Harvard University Press, 1977).

capital city, want good medical care for themselves and their families. A second reason is nationalism: "Our doctors are just as good as doctors in the advanced countries; they can do open-heart surgery, too." Yet a third reason is the technology-mindedness that many doctors share with engineers and other professionals. Medicine often is regarded as an outstanding example of the transfer of inappropriate technology from developed to developing countries. These three factors can interact, as when the self-interest of the elites prompts them to indulge the technology-mindedness of the doctors.

Still another shortcoming of public health services in most developing countries relates to the balance between preventive and curative services. Since, as we have seen, curing all the sick is beyond the means of many poor countries, the possibility that sickness and death can be reduced more cheaply through preventive measures deserves careful examination. Measures such as inoculation campaigns, mosquito spraying, and rat killing have produced dramatic improvements in health conditions in some low-income countries, most notably in China. Many developing countries still spend too much on curative services relative to preventive activities.

It is thus evident that inadequate, maldistributed, and inappropriate medical services in poor countries are themselves contributors to sickness and premature death. What can be done about it?

Improved medical services depend on the extension of coverage to the entire population and on the development of service patterns more appropriate to the health needs and resource availability of a developing country. Many experts believe that a reformed health system would include (1) active and continuous promotion of community health, instead of intermittent treatment of specific conditions in individuals; (2) management of the system by nonphysicians; (3) training health care auxiliaries recruited from the community to diagnose and treat simple ailments; and (4) limited referral of difficult cases.

The health care systems evolved by socialist developing countries such as China and Cuba sometimes are taken as models by those interested in similar reforms. In 1976, China reported spending over 60 percent of its health care budget in rural areas and sending half its medical school graduates to assignments in the countryside. Like other developing countries, it has experienced difficulty in getting health professionals to live in rural areas. China has countered this tendency, however, and through its well-known system of health auxiliaries, for the first time it is providing decent health care to its enormous peasant population. As of 1976, official sources reported 1.5 million "barefoot doctors" were working in the country, doing preventive work, treating patients at home and in the fields, assisting with mass health and sanitation cam-

SUPPLYING MEDICINES TO POOR COUNTRIES

Pharmaceutical companies justify high prices for prescription drugs as a way of recapturing the huge development costs of some new drugs. But this policy often prices low-income countries out of the market. In some cases, companies have agreed to sell medicines to poor countries at reduced rates, but they worry about the possible leakage of drugs into markets where prices are higher.

In early 2000, under pressure from developing country governments, several manufacturers of extremely high-priced drugs to treat HIV/AIDS agreed to supply African countries with these drugs at 20 percent of the price charged in developed countries. Since a year's dosage costs $15,000 in developed countries, however, even the reduced price is far beyond the reach of most Africans. Moreover, effective treatment of disease involves far more than the availability of drugs, so the ability to deal with HIV/AIDS and other diseases afflicting Africa remains a daunting challenge.

Malaria, tuberculosis, and AIDS kill almost 5 million Africans annually. Yet research on vaccines for these diseases remains minimal, largely because vaccine developers believe that the low income of those who suffer from these diseases would make it impossible to recoup their research costs. To overcome this problem, Harvard University economists Michael Kremer and Jeffrey Sachs proposed a vaccine precommitment mechanism in the form of a promise to purchase newly developed vaccines and distribute them to poor countries in exchange for modest copayments. This would provide incentive for vaccine development and ensure that poor countries could acquire the vaccines once they were developed. The funds would be pledged by developed country governments, international organizations, and foundations, and would not be spent until effective vaccines were developed. A major question about this creative proposal is whether such promises and pledges would be credible enough to bring about the desired vaccine development effort by the pharmaceutical companies.

paigns, and disseminating information on family planning and maternal and child health care. In addition, some 3 million part-time health auxiliaries were said to be assisting in these activities. Such efforts have contributed to levels of health and life expectancy unusual for a country with China's still-low income level.

In the 1990s, however, after three decades of striking improvement, China's health gains began to erode in some respects. Mortality rates rose in some provinces, especially among infants and children under 5. A World Bank study attributes these setbacks to three factors. First, changes in health finance reduced the efficiency and equity of medical treatment. Second, changes in the disease pattern required a shift of emphasis from conditions that the public health system was accustomed to treating (problems associated with maternity and infectious diseases) to others with which it had less experience (noninfectious diseases and injuries). Finally, the shift to a more market-oriented economy changed environmental and behavioral risk factors, diversifying the types of diseases across regions.

The development and dissemination of simple cures for widespread health problems must accompany the spread of medical services into the rural areas. For example, at present, about 10 percent of all children born in the developing countries die of diarrhea before reaching the age of 10. Yet, a simple inexpensive technology can prevent most of these deaths: oral rehydration therapy (ORT), which is nothing more than a solution of sugar and mineral salts in water. ORT counteracts dehydration, which is the direct cause of diarrhea deaths. A scientifically designed and tested ORT formula is being disseminated by organizations such as the United Nations Children's Fund, but even folk versions of the remedy, such as rice water and simple mixtures of sugar and table salt, may be effective. Sickness and early death among children in poor countries could be sharply curtailed by spreading knowledge and availability of this remedy throughout the world and developing others like it.

Health Services and the Market

We saw in this chapter that public health services in developing countries are severely underfinanced. Prices traditionally have played only a minor role, either in generating resources to finance health services or in determining who should have access to them.[16] According to the World Bank, only 7 percent of the cost of publicly provided services in developing countries was recovered through user fees in the 1980s. These observations led to proposals to increase fees charged for health services and institute charges for services currently provided free. The revenue thus generated would be used to expand health services. Since this is a textbook on the *economics* of development, it behooves us to conclude this chapter on

16. Emmanuel Jimenez, *Pricing Policy in the Social Sectors. Cost Recovery for Education and Health in Developing Countries* (Baltimore: Johns Hopkins University Press for the World Bank, 1987).

health and development by considering the merits of this proposal to increase the role of prices in the provision of health care in developing countries.

In this analysis of the possibility of charging higher prices for educational and health services, World Bank economist Emmanuel Jimenez proposes that we distinguish between services that yield personal benefits enjoyed by only the individual recipient and those that have substantial external benefits for the broader society. When external benefits are large, the price charged for the service must be set below its cost, or else society will be deprived of valuable benefits. Broadly speaking, one probably would not want to charge for most preventive health services, but one might be more willing to place a reasonably high fee on many curative services. If there is excess demand for these services, fees probably could be raised without reducing the quantity of services provided. Additional revenue would be generated; if this were reinvested in service provision, services could then be expanded, perhaps by enough to meet the previously unfulfilled demand. If there is no excess demand for services, the effect of a fee increase on revenue and the level of service would depend on the elasticity of demand for health services. Available evidence suggests that this demand is highly inelastic, since people regard at least some kinds of health services—particularly, one suspects, curative services in health emergencies—as necessities. Jimenez notes, however, that user fees for the highest-cost services can be brought close to the cost of providing them only if medical insurance is widely available, since few of the people unfortunate enough to require such services are likely to be able to afford them.

One should approach the possibility of financing expanded health services in developing countries through higher user fees with a critical frame of mind. There is little doubt that increasing expenditure on health services would benefit both economic growth and human welfare in the short run in most developing countries. Yet this kind of earmarked tax is neither necessarily the best way to raise the funding for such an expansion nor a sure way of garnering additional resources for this purpose (in a society that places a low priority on health, the funds might be diverted to other programs in any case). Serious objections also can be raised to fee charging, not only because of the external benefits mentioned by Jimenez but also on equity grounds.

As discussed earlier, the kinds of services on which the developing country governments *should* be spending the bulk of their health budgets are those that yield major benefits to society in general and particularly to poor people in rural and urban areas. One wishes to expand these services substantially in most countries, not to discourage their use through the imposition of substantial fees. Government expenditures on health and other social services cannot fulfill its potential for improving income distribution and lessening the grinding effects of poverty if it is accompanied by fees that discourage the use of these services by the very people the government wants to reach.

Health services therefore may be one area where potentials for using the price system, so frequently advocated in this textbook, are limited. It should be noted, however, that this skepticism about the desirability of charging for health services is warranted only *if* the emphasis in health services is on primary and preventive services aimed at the masses of people, as advocated in this chapter. If, on the contrary, the services offered are primarily those that benefit the rich, then of course high fees should be charged. But this, as we hope to have made clear by now, is no way to run a public health service in a developing country.

PART FOUR

Capital Resources

CAPITAL AND SAVING

Of all the approaches to economic growth discussed in Chapters 2 and 3, the emphasis on capital formation perhaps was the most influential and durable. The view that capital formation is the single most important determinant of growth and development, called **capital fundamentalism,** was at the heart of development strategies in many countries for several decades. Until relatively recently, the development problem was widely seen as one of simply securing investment resources sufficient to generate some chosen target rate of national income growth.

There are several reasons for the longevity and prominence of capital fundamentalism as a core idea in development. First, it had respectable theoretical underpinnings—the simple but elegant Harrod-Domar and Solow models, discussed in Chapter 2. Properly viewed, the Harrod-Domar model provides insight into vital aspects of the development process, because it focuses on the difficulties involved in meeting the investment requirements for assuring substantial and steady growth without high rates of inflation or unemployment. However, more mechanistic interpretations of the Harrod-Domar model postulated a lockstep relationship between growth in investment and national income. The Solow model introduced diminishing returns into the story, but still put a major emphasis on capital formation.

Second, capital fundamentalism resonated with the aims and approaches of foreign aid donors of the 1950s and 1960s, by furnishing a readily explicable, apparently clear-cut basis for the justifying aid "needs." Capital shortage then was widely judged to be the single most important barrier to accelerated economic development. Most governments put a heavy premium on framing **development plans**—blueprints for multiyear public sector investment—that reflected this point of view. The best-crafted of such plans, such as Pakistan's third five-year plan in the early 1960s, were able to show heavy initial capital requirements and a need for large early injections of foreign capital, especially foreign aid. Large initial contributions of aid, it was thought, would generate new flows of domestic savings and reduce aid requirements in the long run.

Third, capital fundamentalism was durable because its framework was flexible enough to incorporate new economic ideas of the 1960s, especially the concept of human capital discussed in Part 3 of this book. The selective embedding of human capital considerations into the framework further strengthened the argument that capital formation was the linchpin of development. The incorporation of human capital was no minor embellishment, for the size of the human capital stock relative to the physical capital stock can be quite large. In the United States, for example, estimates place the value of the human capital stock as roughly equal to that of the stock of physical capital.

Of course, both theory and practical evidence tell us that the quality of investment can matter almost as much as the quantity. The key parameter in the Harrod-Domar model is the capital-output ratio, which essentially is a measure of the efficiency of investment. In the Solow model, a country with less productive investment will have a lower steady-state level of income per worker. High levels of capital formation made possible by initial abundance of savings matter little for income growth—much less for employment creation and improving income distribution—when capital is deployed in projects of low productivity. These include the much-ridiculed, large-scale showcase steel mills and thousands of inefficiently small hydroelectric plants common in many developing countries, expensive and misdirected higher education systems, and ultramodern cardiac care centers serving small elites in capital cities. Further, massive investment projects financed by foreign savings, however productive, may have little impact on income growth when host country policies are poorly suited for capturing an equitable share of the returns from such projects. Particularly before the mid-1960s, sometimes host countries, especially those with sizable natural resource endowments, ultimately had little to show from major foreign investment projects other than the scrap content of equipment left behind at the end.

Accumulation of physical capital no longer is viewed as a simple panacea for poor countries, since we now more widely recognize the important roles played by international trade, macroeconomic stability, investments in health and education, institutional development, and a range of other issues. Nevertheless, clearly, even mildly robust growth rates can be sustained over long periods only when societies are able to maintain saving and investment at a sizable proportion of GDP. This proportion rarely can be much less than 15 percent and in some cases it must be as high as 25 or even 35 percent, depending on investment efficiency and the desired rate of growth, as we see in the next section.

Saving and Investment: The Basic Data

Table 11–1 shows basic investment and saving ratios for a group of 26 developing countries in Asia, Africa, and Latin America, representing a wide range in per capita income, natural resource endowments, and ideological orientation. It also shows the averages for groups of countries classified by the World Bank as low income, lower-middle income, upper-middle income, and upper income. Average investment ratios increased substantially between 1965 and 1998 for the low-income countries (excluding China and India) from 14 to 24 percent. China had the highest investment rate of any country in this group, at 39 percent. The average investment ratio also increased for the group of lower-middle-income countries, from 16 to 23 percent. However, investment rates declined for several countries in this group, including Pakistan and Bolivia. For the group of upper-middle-income countries, the average investment ratio rose only slightly, from 21 to 23 percent. Korea showed one of the largest changes, increasing its investment ratio from 15 percent to a very high 35 percent. By contrast, Brazil's investment ratio fell from 25 to 21 percent. Interestingly, investment ratios on average fell for the upper-income countries from 24 to 19 percent. The United Kingdom, the United States, and Germany all saw their investment ratios decline during the period. Japan's investment ratio also declined slightly but remained at a high 30 percent. Notice that, by 1998, the upper-income countries had a lower average investment ratio than any of the other three groups.

Saving ratios followed the same basic patterns, albeit with more variation. In general, domestic saving ratios have been slightly less than investment ratios, creating the **resource gap** (defined as investment minus domestic saving) shown in the fifth and sixth columns. This gap has to be filled by **foreign saving** (capital inflows from abroad) in the form of foreign aid, foreign borrowing, or foreign investment, as we discuss later in this chapter. Developing countries as a group significantly increased rates of domestic saving between 1965 and 1998. For example, the average domestic saving rate for the low-income group of countries (excluding China and India) rose from 13 percent to 20 percent. These averages (as usual) mask some major differences in the saving performances of different countries, but the general picture is one of some success in mobilizing additional domestic saving since 1965. Among countries in this table,

TABLE 11-1   GROSS DOMESTIC INVESTMENT AND SAVING, 1965 AND 1998

COUNTRY OR CATEGORY	GROSS DOMESTIC INVESTMENT[a] (AS % OF GDP)		GROSS DOMESTIC SAVING[b] (AS % OF GDP)		RESOURCES GAP[c]		GNP GROWTH PER CAPITA
	1965	1998	1965	1998	1965	1998	1965-97
ETHIOPIA	13	20	12	9	1	11	0.3
MALI	12	21	4	10	8	11	0.8
TANZANIA	15	16	17	6	−2	10	0.9
INDIA	18	23	14	18	4	5	2.5
BANGLADESH	11	21	8	15	3	6	1.3
KENYA	14	18	15	13	−1	5	1.7
NIGERIA	19	20	17	12	2	8	0.5
SENEGAL	12	20	8	15	4	5	−0.4
GHANA	18	23	8	13	10	10	−0.4
CHINA	25	39	25	43	0	−4	7.1
HONDURAS	15	30	15	25	0	5	0.9
LOW-INCOME COUNTRIES	20	30	19	32	1	−2	
(W/O CHINA AND INDIA)	14	24	13	20	1	4	
PAKISTAN	21	17	13	23	8	6	2.7
BOLIVIA	22	19	13	9	9	10	4.5
CAMEROON	13	18	13	20	0	−2	0.7
PHILIPPINES	21	25	15	15	6	11	1.3
SRI LANKA	12	24	13	17	−1	7	3.0
INDONESIA	8	31	8	31	0	0	4.6
PERU	34	25	27	20	7	5	0.6
EGYPT, ARAB REP.	18	19	14	10	4	9	3.3
LOWER-MIDDLE-INCOME COUNTRIES	16	23	12	22	4	1	
BRAZIL	25	21	27	19	−2	3	3.1
HUNGARY	26	27	25	27	1	0	2.7
COLOMBIA	16	18	17	14	−1	4	2.2
ARGENTINA	19	22	23	19	−4	3	1.4
MEXICO	22	26	21	24	1	2	1.9
MALAYSIA	20	32	24	47	−4	−15	4.3
KOREA, REP. OF	15	35	7	34	8	1	6.7
UPPER-MIDDLE-INCOME COUNTRIES	21	23	21	21	0	2	
UNITED KINGDOM	20	16	19	15	1	1	2.0
JAPAN	32	30[d]	33	30[d]	−1	−1	4.1
GERMANY	28	21	29	22	−1	−2	0.7
UNITED STATES	20	18	21	16	−1	2	1.8
UPPER-INCOME COUNTRIES	24	19	25	19	−1	0	

[a]Gross domestic investment is defined as all public- and private-sector expenditures for additions to the stock of fixed assets plus the net value of inventory changes.

[b]Gross domestic saving is calculated by deducting total consumption from gross domestic product.

[c]Gross domestic investment minus gross domestic saving.

[d]1996 data.

Sources: World Bank, *World Development Report 1987* (Washington, DC: The World Bank, 1987), Table 5; *World Development Report 1994: Infrastructure for Development* (Washington, DC: The World Bank, 1994), Table 9; *World Development Report 1999/2000: Entering the 21st Century* (Washington, DC: The World Bank, 1999), Table 13; *World Development Indicators* 1999 CD-ROM.

domestic saving rates in 1998 ranged from 6 percent in Tanzania to an astonishing 43 percent in China. The relationship between income levels and saving rates has become less clear over time. We ordinarily would expect a lower ratio of savings in poor countries relative to middle-income countries simply because in poor countries less for savings is available after subsistence needs are met. This appeared to be the case in 1965, when the upper-middle-income and upper-income groups had the highest average saving rates. By 1998, however, these differences had largely disappeared, and only small differences are found between the average saving ratios of the four country groups shown in the table. Several of the low-income countries had saving rates higher than those in the United Kingdom and the United States, including India, China, Honduras, Pakistan, Cameroon, and others. This partly is due to the large numbers of retirees living in the United Kingdom and the United States, which tends to dampen saving rates, but clearly there is no simple relationship between saving and income. We discuss the determinants of private saving rates later in the chapter.

The data in Table 11–1 suggest that the more prosperous developing countries tend to cover a larger share of their investment needs with local savings and rely less on foreign saving. Most of the upper-middle income and upper-income countries have small or negative resource gaps (the latter implying that the country is a net lender to the rest of the world). The table also shows that, although domestic saving rates increased appreciably from 1965 to 1998 in many low-income countries, the share of domestic saving in total investment finance rose only slightly in developing countries in general and actually declined in a considerable number. In particular, excluding China and India, the average resource gap increased from 1 to 4 percent of GDP for the low-income countries. In most countries, since domestic saving nearly equaled investment, the resource gap was relatively small. However, in several countries the resource gap was substantial, reaching 10 percent or more in 1998 in Ethiopia, Mali, Tanzania, Ghana, Bolivia, the Philippines, and several other countries not shown in the table.

Table 11–1, however, does not begin to portray adequately the diversity of saving performances across more than 100 developing countries. In 1998, at least 11 developing and transition countries had negative rates of domestic saving; in Albania, Armenia, Eritrea, Lebanon, and Lesotho, negative savings amounted to more than 10 percent of GDP. But, in that year, 16 developing countries, including the 6 depicted in Table 11–1 had positive saving rates of 25 percent or more per year.

Government policies have had a major impact on the ability of developing countries to mobilize domestic saving. We see in the next three chapters that some countries have actively sought to deploy policies to encourage savings growth and have utilized instruments well suited for that purpose. In still more countries, governments have been no less concerned with the promotion of domestic saving but relied on policy tools ill suited for saving mobilization. Finally, in a small group of countries, government policies appear to have been designed with little or no regard for their implications for domestic saving. As might be expected, saving generally has responded positively to policy initiatives in the first groups of countries, less so in the second group, and has tended to stagnate or decline in the third.

The data in Table 11–1 also indicate that countries with higher saving and investment rates generally have recorded faster growth rates, as theory would suggest. From an empirical standpoint, the critical role of saving and capital formulation in creating income growth has been well established through sources of growth analysis and studies of total factor productivity growth, as described in Chapter 2. In industrial societies, the expansion of physical capital inputs typically is responsible for about half the growth in aggregate income. Similarly, the rapid growth of East Asia's "miracle economies" owes much to high levels of saving and investment in both physical and human capital. Studies on other developing countries attribute a very high share of growth to capital accumulation. These studies take us only so far, however. While pointing to the importance of capital accumulation, they tell us very little about why some societies have been more successful in generating high rates of saving and investment, and why some economies have invested their resources more productively than others.

Investment Requirements for Growth

TYPES OF INVESTMENT

Investment spending comes in many forms. The first important distinction is between public and private investment. In many countries, **public investment** by the government is one of the most important components of both annual budgets and longer-range development strategies. The basic rationale for public investment is that individual private firms and households will not make certain critical investments, even though these would be beneficial to society as a whole. For example, while all firms and households benefit from roads that connect cities, villages, farms, factories, markets, and ports, it typically will not be financially profitable for any single firm to build roads for its own benefit. The cost of building the road simply is too high. Moreover, once the road is built, others can use it without having borne the cost of the initial investment, so every firm has the incentive to wait for someone else to do it. This benefit to those that do not bear the cost is called an **externality** of the investment. One possible solution to this dilemma is toll roads that charge a fee to users, but these generally are unworkable except for certain highways and bridges. The more common solution is that each firm and household indirectly pays a relatively small share of the cost of the road through tax payments, and the government builds the road for public use.

Governments in developing countries play the central role in building roads, ports, power, water, and telecommunications facilities. Roads are important not only to connect urban commercial facilities but to connect remote villages to markets so they can buy goods more cheaply and sell their products at better prices to a larger market. In this way, rural roads can be an important ingredient in the alleviation of rural poverty. Deep-sea ports help facilitate fast and inexpensive international shipments of both imports and exports. Reliable power supplies help avoid costly production shutdowns and reduce production costs. Appropriate telecommunication facilities have become ever more important for telephone, fax, and Internet connections, and they open new opportunities for developing country firms to provide services (such as "backroom accounting") to global markets. In addition to these kinds of investments, the public sector plays the major role in building schools, hospitals, clinics, and other related facilities in essentially all developing countries. Of course, this does not mean that all public sector infrastructure investments are a good idea—governments have been known to build fancy superhighways connecting the capital city to the president's village or large showcase dam projects that never pay for themselves. As discussed in the next chapter, the acid test for public investment decisions is whether the net present value (NPV) of the investment (using shadow prices) is greater than 0 and is greater than the NPV of other possible public investments. In other words, each investment project should generate more economic resources that it costs to undertake and should generate a greater return than all of the other available investment options. Unfortunately, many investment projects in developing countries fail to meet this simple test.

While public investment lays much of the foundation to create an environment conducive to growth, **private investment** provides the dynamism for growth by creating jobs, introducing new technologies, and accounting for the vast majority of economic output. According to data from the World Bank, in 1997, private investment accounted for two thirds of gross domestic investment (GDI) in East and South Asia and sub-Saharan Africa, three quarters of GDI in Europe and Central Asia, and fully 84 percent of GDI in Latin America.[1] In some countries, of course, the share is much lower, such as in China, Haiti, and Mozam-

---

1. World Bank, *World Development Report 1999/2000.* (Washington, DC: World Bank, 1999), Appendix Table 16.

bique, where the private sector accounts for about half of GDI. But, in most developing countries, the private sector is the main channel for investment. Private investment usually is grouped into three categories. First, fixed business investment includes spending on "plant" (factories, offices, warehouses, etc.) and "equipment" (machines, vehicles, and the like). Second, inventory investment measures changes in unfinished goods, stocks of input and raw materials, and finished products that are not yet sold. Increases in the stocks of each of these items from one year to the next are considered a form of investment, since they will affect production and sales in the future. Third, at the household level, the major form of investment is in residential structures, including both construction and maintenance of housing stock.

EFFECTIVE USE OF CAPITAL

Governments in developing countries generally face the dual challenges of creating an environment that will encourage both *high levels* of private investment and *more productive* investment. In fact, the two are closely related. The more productive is investment in terms of rates of return to investors, the easier it will be to encourage a greater volume of investment. At the same time, however, the Solow model points out that, as the volume of investment increases, its marginal productivity tends to fall, unless policy changes or new technologies are introduced that further enhance productivity. In developing countries where basic macroeconomic prices (exchange rates, interest rates, wage rates) are approximately equal to scarcity values for factors of production, scarce capital is likely to be deployed where it can be applied most effectively. Since developing countries tend to be relatively capital scarce, a given addition to the capital stock can generate increments to output that exceed those in industrial countries where capital is more abundant. This is the insight from the Solow model, that poorer countries can grow faster than richer countries, on the condition that they have similar steady-state levels of income (see Chapter 2). In many developing countries, however, distortions in prices (e.g., through subsidies on certain types of fuel or high tariffs on imported capital goods) negatively affect both the volume and allocation of investment, lowering the productivity of investment and ultimately the rates of economic growth.

Perhaps the simplest way to think about the productivity of investment is the incremental capital-output ratio of the Harrod-Domar model. Depending on the geographic and resource endowments of a particular country and its major policy stances, the ICOR can vary from under 3:1 to 7:1 and even higher, as discussed in Chapter 2. Consider the investment implications of an ICOR of 3.0 compared with an ICOR half again as high, or 4.5. For countries with an ICOR of 3.0, a necessary, but not sufficient, condition for achieving sustained aggregate growth in output of 5.0 percent per year (or around 3 percent per capita) is securing capital resources equivalent to 15 percent of GNP (ignoring depreciation). However, countries with an ICOR of 4.5 will need to invest 22.5 percent of GNP to attain the same rate of output growth. Thus, more efficient deployment of capital can substantially reduce the savings effort required for sustained growth.

CAPITAL-INTENSIVE OR LABOR-INTENSIVE INVESTMENT: A HYPOTHETICAL CASE

When the factors of production cannot move easily from one sector to another or across international boundaries, a pervasive pattern of capital-intensive production in capital-scarce countries tends to lead to either lower rates of economic growth, strong suppression of consumption, or both. To illustrate, consider two small low-income countries that initially are identical in all important respects: per capita income of $400 in 2000, population of 2.5 million, an investment ratio in 2000 of 15 percent, and similar patterns of exports, imports, agriculture, and industry. From 1990 to 2000, both followed essentially the same development strategy, which produced in an incremental capital-output ratio (ignoring depreciation) of 3.5 in each country. And each experienced a real GDP growth rate of about 4.3 percent over the ten-year period.

In 2000, new governments in both countries decided to change their development policies. For the next decade country A's government chose a strategy involving heavy outlays on large-scale, capital-intensive investments, such as oil refining, paper mills, and steel mills. As a result of this change, and supported by other government policies, the ICOR was expected to rise from 3.5 to 4. Country B, on the other hand, decided in 2000 to shift to a strategy emphasizing more labor-intensive investments in agriculture and industry, including textiles, commercial firewood forests, coastal fisheries, and shoe manufacture. Decision makers in country B expect the ICOR to decline from 3.5 to 3 as a result. These two capital-output ratios are within the high range for developing countries discussed in Chapter 2 (see Table 2–5). In this example, we overlook contributions of other factors to growth.

We assume both countries have access to similar amounts of investment finance during the period 2000–2005. Specifically, investment is likely to expand by between 5 percent per year (the "low" case) and 10 percent per year (the "high" case). The implications of these alternative investment ratios for GDP growth are presented in Table 11–2.

A striking implication can be drawn from Table 11–2. The table shows that the efficiency with which capital is used can be much more important

TABLE 11–2   GDP AND INVESTMENT UNDER TWO DIFFERENT STRATEGIES ($U.S. MILLION)

	2000	INVESTMENT GROWTH RATE (%)	2001	2002	2003	2004	2005	AVERAGE ANNUAL GROWTH (%)	2005 INVESTMENT/ GDP (%)
AVAILABLE INVESTMENT FUNDS									
I. Low	150.0	5.0	157.5	165.4	173.6	182.3	191.4	5.0	—
II. High	150.0	10.0	165.0	181.5	199.6	219.6	241.6	10.0	—
GDP IN COUNTRY A (CAPITAL-INTENSIVE STRATEGY, ICOR = 4)[a]									
I. Low	1000.0	5.0	1037.5	1076.9	1118.3	1161.7	1207.3	3.8	15.9
II. High	1000.0	10.0	1037.5	1078.8	1124.2	1174.1	1229.0	4.2	19.7
GDP IN COUNTRY B (LABOR-INTENSIVE STRATEGY, ICOR = 3)[a]									
I. Low	1000.0	5.0	1050.0	1102.5	1157.6	1215.5	1276.3	5.0	15.0
II. High	1000.0	10.0	1050.0	1105.0	1165.5	1232.0	1305.2	5.5	18.5

[a]To simplify presentation, the example assumes that all investment resources in any given year are available by the beginning of that year and there is only a one-year lag between the time investment resources are available and the time they begin to yield output. Therefore, the calculation for GDP in country A in 2001 is as follows: Investable funds in year 2000 ($150 million) divided by country A's ICOR (4) leads to the increment in output ($37.5 million). Thus GDP in 2001 is the initial $1,000 million plus $37.5 million, or $1037.5 million.

for GDP growth than raising the volume of investment. Note that, in country B (with the lower ICOR), GDP is higher than in country A after just five years, *even when the growth rate of investment in country A is twice as large as in country B.* With investment in country B growing by 5 percent each year, average annual GDP growth also is 5 percent, whereas in country A even 10 percent growth in investment leads to only 4.2 percent average annual GDP growth. In this scenario, after five years, investment in country A reaches 19.7 percent of GDP, whereas it remains at 15 percent of GDP in country B. Even with this large difference in investment ratios, country B grows faster because of its more efficient investment and lower ICOR.

On the other hand, if investment resources available to both countries were to grow at 10 percent per annum, aggregate income in country B would be 6 percent higher than in country A by 2005, even though they began at the same level. Although a 6 percent difference in total income after five years may not seem large, when placed in proper perspective it can be quite significant. For one thing, at this rate, after just 58 years, total income in country B would be *double* that of country A. Moreover, even if the growth rates in the two countries were the same after 2005 and the difference in GDP remained at 6 percent, only a few developing countries spend this much on education, and only a handful spend as much as 3 percent on public health. Merely because it uses capital more efficiently than country A, country B would, in the extreme, possess the capacity to more than double real outlays for education or triple expenditures on public health programs. Alternatively, with a higher domestic saving rate, country B has much less need to resort to foreign capital to finance a substantial share of its development effort. An investment ratio of 15 percent clearly is much easier to support from domestic resources than the 20 percent required for country A to attain the same level of GDP growth.

We began this example by stating that country A was pursuing a capital-intensive investment strategy, while country B focused on more labor-intensive industries. The heavy emphasis on capital-intensive investment often found in developing countries to some extent is the unintended result of government policies. But it also may be attributed to a pervasive belief that only capital-intensive technology is efficient, that to become rich a country must first master capital-intensive technologies, and that the appropriate choice of the most efficient technology does not depend on the relative prices of labor and capital. The discussion in Chapter 8, however, shows that this is not the case. Policies that result in underpricing capital and overpricing labor cause firms and government agencies to adopt techniques involving more capital and less labor than would be the case in the absence of such policies. However, Chapter 8 also reminds us that a bias toward capital intensity in investment cannot always, or even usually, be fully explained in terms of distorted price signals. Nor is it legitimate to assume that capital intensity always represents vice and that labor-using investment always denotes virtue. For example, those who would advocate a conscious, reverse bias in favor of labor-intensive methods of underground coal or tin mining have either never visited the hazardous labor-intensive facilities for these activities (for example, in Bolivia and Indonesia) or are unaware of the large financial surpluses available from capital-intensive mining that can be deployed for investment in labor-intensive activities in other fields. Even in agriculture there are sound arguments, advanced in Chapter 15, for mechanization to increase both productivity and employment. In the end, at the most general level, the best strategy is for investment decisions to be based on the relative scarcity values of capital and labor, which should be reflected as much as possible in the prices of these factors of production.

Sources of Savings

All investment ultimately must be financed by saving by either domestic entities (e.g., firms, the government, households) or foreigners. A private firm, for example, finances much of its investment through contributions by equity holders, which ultimately are these individuals' personal savings. Many corporations in developing countries finance investment by borrowing from foreign banks, which in turn raise their funds primarily through saving deposits. Governments finance public investments through tax contributions, which can be thought of as a form of forced saving. Before exploring various theories and empirical evidence on the determinants of saving, we begin by distinguishing different types of saving.

A TAXONOMY OF SAVINGS

When households and firms choose to save, they decide to reduce present consumption in order to increase the resources available to them to finance consumption in the future. The allocation of resources between present consumption and future consumption (saving) is one of the most fundamental economic choices facing the individuals and firms in any economy. This choice affects not only the rate of economic growth but also the standards of living for future generations.

For a country, the total supply of available savings, S, is simply the sum of domestic saving (S_d) and foreign saving (S_f). Domestic saving[2] may be broken down into two components: government, or public-sector, saving (S_g) and private domestic saving (S_p). Government saving consists primarily of budgetary saving (S_{gb}) that arises from any excess of government revenues over government consumption, where public consumption is defined as all *current* government expenditure plus all capital outlays for military hardware. Examples of public sector consumption include expenditures for food subsidies; meeting recurring costs, such as salaries for civil servants and police; purchasing stationery, fuel, and arms; and maintaining roads and bridges; plus interest on the national debt. It does not include expenditures for building roads, bridges, schools, and other physical infrastructure, which are classified as capital or investment spending. Of course, most or all of a government's saving (from the surplus of revenue over consumption spending) is used to fi-

---

2. A further distinction can be made between domestic saving and national saving, which is roughly equivalent to the difference between gross domestic product (GDP) and gross national product (GNP). Domestic saving measures all saving that takes place within the borders of a country, whether by citizens or foreigners resident in the country (including foreign corporations). It does not include saving by citizens living abroad or the foreign operations of domestic firms operating abroad. National saving includes savings of all citizens of a country regardless of where they live. It does not include the saving of foreign residents or firms inside a country's borders. The distinction is important in some countries, such as the Philippines, where the remittances of citizens working overseas constitutes an important part of national saving. In this chapter, we use the two terms interchangeably.

nance public investment. Therefore, it is important to recognize that a country could have positive public saving even when the overall government budget is in deficit, when consumption plus investment spending is larger than total revenue. In a very few countries, saving by government-owned enterprises (S_{ge}) also contribute to public-sector savings (see Chapter 12).

Private domestic saving arises from two sources: corporate saving (S_{pc}) and household saving (S_{ph}). **Corporate saving** is defined as the retained earnings of corporate enterprises (corporate income after taxes minus dividends paid to shareholders). **Household saving** (S_{ph}) simply is the part of household income not consumed. Household saving includes saving from unincorporated enterprises (single proprietorships, partnerships, and other noncorporate forms of business enterprise). In most developing countries, unincorporated business enterprise is by far the dominant form of business organization.

Foreign saving also comes in two basic forms. **Official foreign saving** (S_{fo}), usually referred to as *foreign aid* or *official development assistance,* consists of grants and loans from other governments or international government organizations such as the World Bank or the United Nations. **Private foreign saving** (S_{fp}) is made up of **external commercial borrowing,** or *debt* finance (symbolized S_{fpd}), and **equity finance** (symbolized S_{fpe}). Whereas principal and interest on commercial debt payments must be paid for both good and bad projects alike, returns to equity (dividends) are paid only when profits are made. Foreign equity finance usually is classified as either **direct foreign investment** (when foreigners take a direct equity share in a domestic firm) or **portfolio investment** (when foreigners purchase equities through the domestic stock market).

To recapitulate, total available saving may be viewed in the first instance as

$$S = S_d + S_f = (S_g + S_p) + (S_{fo} + S_{fp}) \qquad [11\text{–}1]$$

For understanding saving patterns and policies, saving may be disaggregated further to

$$S = [(S_{gb} + S_{ge}) + (S_{pc} + S_{ph})] + (S_{fo} + S_{fpd} + S_{fpe}) \qquad [11\text{–}2]$$

Reliance on different sources of saving differs greatly among developing countries, depending not only on country characteristics such as the level of per capita income, natural resource endowments, and sectoral composition of GDP but also on the nature of saving mobilization policies adopted by particular governments. The balance of this chapter identifies the determinants of domestic saving and its various components and discusses one component of foreign saving, foreign aid. Chapter 14 examines private foreign saving, its patterns, and the controversies surrounding it.

GOVERNMENT SAVING

Where present, government saving has arisen almost wholly from an excess of total tax revenues over public consumption expenditures (S_{gb}). Chapter 12 shows that in very few cases does saving by government enterprises (S_{ge}) ever materially contribute to aggregate government saving. Given the very minor role of S_{ge}, the discussion of government saving in this chapter is confined to budgetary saving.

During the 1950s and 1960s, a basic tenet of typical development strategies was that the investment expansion required for sustained income growth could not proceed in the absence of major efforts to increase the share of government saving in GDP. It commonly was held that growth in private saving was inherently constrained by such factors as low per capita incomes and high private consumption propensities among wealthy families with the greatest capacity for saving. Limited availability of foreign saving also led policy makers, as well as aid donors, to stress the necessity for mobilizing government saving. In almost all cases, the preferred means for achieving this goal was to raise the ratio of tax collections to GNP (the tax ratio) through significant reform of the tax structure, if possible, or through increases in existing tax rates, if necessary.

Underlying this view was an important assumption: The propensity to consume out of an additional dollar of income was substantially less in the public sector than in the private sector. Raising government revenue through increasing the tax ratio increases total national saving only if the government saves more out of each tax dollar than the private sector would have had it kept that dollar. In the 1950s and 1960s, the widely held view was that diversion of income to the government in developing countries, in fact, would increase national saving rates. This belief, in turn, engendered a prevailing view among many development planners that rising tax ratios were associated with successful development strategies, a view reinforced by the policies of foreign aid donors. During this period many donors, including the United States, utilized tax ratios and tax effort indices as prime indicators of national commitment to belt-tightening in recipient countries. Countries willing to "suffer" higher domestic taxes were seen as committed to development and more deserving of aid, other things being equal.

This raises two important questions. First, to what extent can governments actually increase the tax ratio, if they want to do so? Second, will an increase in the tax ratio lead to an increase in total national saving?

On the first question, it is not easy to increase tax collections in developing countries. Except for those countries blessed with valuable natural-resource endowments, developing countries cannot be expected to have tax ratios nearly as high as is common in the industrial countries, if for no other reason than their much lower per capita income allows a much smaller margin for taxation after subsistence needs are met. Whereas typical tax ratios for developing countries range between 12 and 18 percent, the ratio of central government taxes to GNP in the industrialized countries averages between 25 and 30 percent. Despite the difficulties involved, many developing countries have been able to raise the shares of their taxes in GNPs since the 1960s. One early study showed small advances in the average tax ratio for a group of 47 developing countries from 1950. For these countries as a group, the typical share of tax in GNP hovered at about 11 percent in the 1950s. By 1972–76, the average tax ratio had risen to 16 percent.[3]

The average tax ratio has fluctuated about that level ever since; it increased to nearly 18 percent in the early 1980s, when sharply higher world oil prices resulted in pronounced increases in tax collections in several oil-exporting developing countries, such as Mexico, Indonesia, and Venezuela; it then slipped to about 15 percent during the subsequent period of depressed world oil prices (1982–87). Table 12–6 suggests that the tax ratio tends to rise with per capita income, from about 10 percent of GNP in the poorest countries to 28 percent in the richest.

Turning to the second question, a higher tax ratio does not necessarily lead to a higher national saving rate. The question turns on the extent to which two things happen: (1) Higher tax ratios result in higher government saving, and (2) higher government saving leads to higher national saving. Unfortunately, for some developing countries, evidence suggests that the government's marginal propensity to consume out of taxes has been sufficiently high that increased taxation easily may have resulted in less, not more, total domestic saving. This phenomenon has become known as the *Please effect,* after Stanley Please of the World Bank, who brought it to widespread attention in the 1960s.[4] Experience over most of the past three decades shows rather strong consumption propensities by governments, so that an increase in the tax ratio may have only a small effect on raising government saving.

While tax ratios in developing countries typically rose marginally over the 1960s and 1970s, before leveling off in the mid-1980s, the share of public-sector consumption expenditures showed a mixed pattern. In low-income countries (exclusive of India and China), the share of public-sector consumption expenditures in GNP rose from 8 percent in 1960 to 12 percent in 1983, then declined to 9 percent in 1998. In middle-income countries, the share of public-sector consumption in GDP rose even more

3. Alfred Tait, Wilfred Gratz, and Barry Eichengreen, "International Comparisons of Taxation for Selected Developing Countries." *International Monetary Fund Staff Papers,* 26, no. 1 (March 1979), 123–56.

4. Stanley Please, "Saving through Taxation: Reality or Mirage?" *Finance and Development,* 4, no. 1 (March 1967), 24–32.

sharply over the past three decades: from 11 percent in 1960, to 13 percent in 1983, to around 15 percent in 1992, and down slightly to 14 percent in 1998.[5] Between 1980 and 1998, central government consumption rose from 14 to 17 percent of GDP in sub-Saharan Africa but fell from 13 to 11 percent in East Asia.[6]

It is worth emphasizing that, in many countries, much of the growth in public-sector consumption has been intended to promote development. Some government salary adjustments have been meant to keep and attract qualified civil servants, and many governments have strengthened their efforts to maintain roads, schools, health facilities, communication networks, and the like. But, when higher government consumption has been traceable to a rapid buildup of military purchases (which we look at in the next chapter), excessive procurement of materials, or upkeep of a large government vehicle fleet dominated by Mercedes Benzes, the effect have been unhelpful to national development.

If the government is successful in raising public saving, will national saving increase? Debates on this issue date back at least as far as the early part of the nineteenth century, to the writings of the great British economist David Ricardo. Ricardo postulated—and largely rejected—the idea that, under certain circumstances, a change in taxes will have absolutely no effect on total domestic saving. Ricardo's theory has come to be known as **Ricardian equivalence:** Any increase in public saving will be offset by an equivalent decline in private saving, with total domestic saving remaining unchanged. The basic idea is that, when private actors receive a tax cut and see that government spending does not change, they anticipate a commensurate tax increase in the future and prepare for it by increasing their current saving. Thus, if the government reduces taxes, government saving may fall, but households and firms will increase private saving in anticipation of a future tax increase. The fall in government saving will be offset exactly by a rise in private saving, and the tax cut will have no impact on total saving. Similarly, a tax increase may lead to higher government saving, but private saving would be expected to decline by the same amount with no change in total saving. Ricardo's original idea was rejuvenated and formalized by Harvard economist Robert Barro in 1979.[7]

Ultimately, of course, this is an empirical issue that comes down to measuring the extent to which private agents alter their saving behavior in response to changes in government tax and expenditure policies. The abundance of evi-

5. World Bank, *World Development Report 1985.* (Washington, DC: World Bank, 1985); *World Development Report 1990: Poverty* (Washington, DC: World Bank, 1990); *World Development Report 1994: Infrastructure* (Washington, DC: World Bank, 1994).

6. World Bank, *World Development Report 1999/2000,* Appendix Table 13.

7. Robert Barro, "Are Government Bonds Net Wealth?" *Journal of Political Economy* (November–December 1979).

dence suggests partial, but only partial, truth to Richardo's hypothesis. Many studies have shown that an increase in government saving tends to be associated with a decline in private saving, but by less than the strict one-to-one relationship postulated by Ricardo. Most studies have found an offset of between 0.40 and 0.65, meaning that a 1 percentage point increase in the government saving rate is associated with a 0.40–0.65 percentage point decline in the private saving rate. This would imply a net increase in the total national saving rate of between 0.35 and 0.60 percentage points.[8]

The salutatory impact of higher government saving may go beyond the effect on national saving. Since higher government saving is derived largely from smaller budget deficits, it reduces the government's borrowing requirements. Government deficits typically are financed through domestic money creation (i.e., borrowing from the central bank, which prints money to fund the deficit) or by borrowing in either local or overseas markets. As a result, larger budget deficits can lead to higher rates of inflation (from money creation), larger government debts, or both. Lower budget deficits (or higher public saving) tend to have the opposite outcomes: lower inflation and indebtedness. Thus, higher public saving is likely to enhance general macroeconomic stability.

Some recent studies have gone beyond looking at the relationship between public and national saving and found a strong relationship between government saving and economic growth. Recent empirical studies on economic growth (discussed in Chapter 2) have found that countries with higher government saving rates generally record faster rates of growth in per capita income.[9] For example, government saving rates in the rapidly growing "four tigers" (Hong Kong, Korea, Singapore, and Taiwan) averaged 5.6 percent of GDP between 1970 and 1992, and in Southeast Asia government saving averaged 3.5 percent of GDP. By contrast, over the same period, government saving in sub-Saharan Africa, Latin America, and South Asia averaged 3 percent, 1.2 percent, and 1.0 percent of GDP, respectively. To some extent, of course, this relationship works both ways, since saving helps growth and rapid growth makes it easier for the government to save more. There probably is a positive mutually reinforcing relationship between public saving and growth, in which increases in public saving help increase investment and growth, which in turn help to further increase the saving rate.

8. See, for example, Sebastian Edwards, "Why Are Saving Rates So Different across Countries? An International Comparative Analysis," National Bureau of Economic Research working paper no. 507 (April 1995); Luis Servon Schmidt-Hebbel and Andros Solimano, "Saving and Investment: Paradigms, Puzzles, and Policies," *World Bank Research Observer* 11, no. 1 (February 1996), 87–117; and Steven Radelet, Jeffrey Sachs, and Jong-Wha Lee, "Economic Growth in Asia," Harvard Institute for International Development, May 1997.

9. See, for example, Radelet et al., "Economic Growth in Asia."

PRIVATE DOMESTIC SAVING

Public saving and foreign saving, while important, account for relatively small shares of total saving in most developing countries, as shown in Table 11–3. Private saving typically accounts for three quarters or more of total saving in most developing countries, and between 10 and 20 percent

TABLE 11–3 NATIONAL SAVING, PRIVATE SAVING, AND PUBLIC SAVING, 1975 AND 1994 (PERCENT OF GNDI)

COUNTRY	GROSS NATIONAL SAVING		PRIVATE SAVING		GOVERNMENT SAVING	
	1975	1994	1975	1994	1975	1994
BANGLADESH	3.2	15.6	1.2	11.0	2.0	4.6
CHINA	37.9	41.2	37.6	39.4	0.3	1.7
ETHIOPIA	4.3	13.7	4.2	12.3	0.1	1.3
GHANA	13.8	10.5	16.4	5.7	−2.6	4.8
HONDURAS	9.1	12.8	5.8	7.5	3.3	5.3
INDIA	21.1	21.3	19.4	23.1	1.7	−1.8
KENYA	11.4	20.0	12.2	17.8	−0.8	2.2
MALI	7.4	19.5	7.7	13.7	−0.4	5.8
NIGERIA	18.6	16.5	14.3	18.5	4.2	−2.0
SENEGAL	13.9	12.9	11.8	10.0	2.0	2.9
TANZANIA	20.6	16.4	21.6	14.5	−1.0	1.9
BOLIVIA	30.0	8.3	28.6	8.1	1.4	0.2
CAMEROON	10.4	12.4	7.7	12.2	2.7	0.2
EGYPT	18.9	16.0	22.1	9.9	−3.2	6.1
INDONESIA	24.0	33.3	18.4	23.6	5.6	9.7
PAKISTAN	8.4	20.8	9.5	22.4	−1.1	−1.6
PERU	12.7	16.9	11.4	16.0	1.2	0.9
PHILIPPINES	26.2	20.9	24.2	19.8	2.0	1.1
SRI LANKA	9.3	19.5	8.5	21.0	0.8	−1.4
ARGENTINA	30.2	16.6	31.8	15.6	−1.6	1.0
BRAZIL	21.8	20.6	3.3	34.3	18.5	−13.7
COLOMBIA	17.1	14.4	13.9	14.0	3.2	0.4
MALAYSIA	23.3	34.4	22.7	25.5	0.6	8.9
MEXICO	19.7	15.1	18.9	12.9	0.8	2.2
S. KOREA	18.1	35.0	16.6	30.5	1.5	4.6
GERMANY	21.3	21.6	22.3	22.0	−1.0	−0.4
JAPAN	32.7	31.2	30.7	28.7	2.0	2.5
UNITED KINGDOM	17.7	13.6	127.9	18.1	−0.2	−4.5
UNITED STATES	18.6	15.8	22.6	17.8	−4.0	−2.0

Notes: (1) Saving data for China, Ethiopia, and Tanzania were not available in 1975. We used data from 1978 for China and 1981 for Ethiopia and Tanzania. Data on Cameroon and Brazil are for 1993 instead of 1994. (2) (According to definitions used by the World Bank, gross national saving is calculated by deducting aggregate consumption from gross national disposable income (GNDI). Government saving is the saving of the consolidated central government. Private saving is calculated by subtracting government saving from national saving.
Source: World Bank Saving database (on-line)

of disposable income. In a few countries, the ratio is higher. For example, private saving accounted for more than 25 percent of disposable income in 1994 in Malaysia, Korea, Brazil, and China, with China leading the way with an extraordinary rate of 39 percent. In a handful of countries, the private saving ratio is less than 10 percent of disposable income, including Ghana, Honduras, Bolivia, and Egypt. Moreover, in most of the countries shown in Table 11–3, private saving rose steadily between 1975 and 1994.

Until fairly recently, economists, aid donors, and many decision makers in developing countries tended to view private domestic saving from both households and businesses as decidedly secondary to government saving and foreign aid as a source of investment finance. Partly, this was due to the belief that government saving and foreign saving could be more easily influenced by policy than private saving. However, in recent years, much more attention has been given to issues of mobilizing private saving and channeling it into productive investments. To better understand how this might be done and to gain further insight into this fundamental relationships in the development process, it is useful to consider the economic theory of private-sector saving behavior.

Determinants of Private Saving

Theories of household saving behavior initially were developed as part of the postwar Keynesian revolution in economic thought to explain saving patterns in industrial countries. The applicability of these theories to the study of saving behavior in developing countries frequently has been called into question in recent years.[10] Nevertheless, current controversies over the determinants of saving behavior in developing countries are almost impossible to understand without reference to earlier studies developed for the analysis of private saving in industrial nations.

HOUSEHOLD SAVING BEHAVIOR

All theories of household saving behavior seek to explain the following three observed patterns: (1) within a particular country at a given time, higher-income households tend to save larger fractions of their income than lower-income households; (2) within a particular country over time, household saving ratios tend to be roughly constant, more so in industrial than in developing countries; and (3) across countries, household saving

10. See especially Angus Deaton, "Saving in Developing Countries: Theory and Review," *Proceedings of the World Bank Annual Conference on Development Economics* (Washington, DC: World Bank, 1989).

ratios vary with no clear relation to income. To help reconcile these "stylized facts," we consider five alternative explanations of household saving behavior: the Keynesian absolute-income model, the relative-income hypothesis, the Friedman permanent-income model, the life-cycle hypothesis, and the Kaldor class-savings hypothesis.

Economists once widely believed in the general applicability of a simple income-saving relationship. Household saving was viewed as directly dependent on current disposable income (household income after direct taxes). The propensity to save out of current disposable income was thought to rise with income. This was known as the **Keynesian absolute-income hypothesis,** after the famed British economist John Maynard Keynes, who propounded the idea in the 1930s. In this view the saving-income relationship would be expressed as

$$S = a + sY^d \qquad\qquad [11–3]$$

where S = the value of domestic saving, Y^d = current disposable income, a = a constant (with $a < 0$), and s = the marginal propensity to save ($0 < s < 1$). The constant a generally is taken to be negative to signify that, at low levels of income, saving will be negative. Under this formulation saving ratios (saving as a fraction of GDP) should be expected to rise over time in all countries where income is growing. But the historical record in both developed and developing countries provides very weak support for the Keynesian hypothesis.

At best, the Keynesian formulation may depict saving behavior over the very short term, but it breaks down as a long-run proposition. The Keynesian formulation explains only the first household saving pattern but not the second or third. An alternative view of the income-consumption relationship, the **relative-income hypothesis,** focuses on the longer term. In its simplest form this hypothesis holds that consumption (and therefore saving) depends not only on current income but also on previous levels of income and past consumption habits. One form of the relative-income hypothesis, called the **Duesenberry hypothesis** after Harvard economist James Duesenberry, who originated the concept in the late 1940s, may be expressed as

$$C_1 = a + (1 - s)Y_1^d + bC_h \qquad\qquad [11–4]$$

where C_1 = consumption in period 1, Y_1^d = income in period 1, C_h = previous high level of consumption, b is the share of the previous year's consumption that will be maintained regardless of the current level of saving, $0 < s < 1$ as before, and $0 < b < 1$. Note the relationship between the middle term of equation 11–4 and the second term of equation 11–3. In equation 11–3 sY^d represents the fraction of disposable income saved, whereas in equation 11–4, the term $(1 - s)Y_1^d$ represents the share of disposable income consumed. The two are equivalent. The key difference between 11–3 and 11–4 is the third term of equation 11–4, which states that consumption is partly dependent on the previous high level of consumption. Therefore, under the relative-income hypothesis, the short-run consumption (saving) function in an economy tends to ratchet upward over time. As income grows over the long term, consumers adjust their spending habits to higher levels of consumption. But, in the short run, they are reluctant to reduce consumption levels and slow to raise them in response to temporary changes in disposable income. In essence, consumers are expected to adjust their saving more quickly than their consumption when income changes. The relationship between the Keynesian absolute-income hypothesis and the Duesenberry relative-income hypothesis is depicted in Figure 11–1.

The Duesenberry hypothesis was formulated as an explanation for consumption and saving behavior for the United States. Later researchers argued that it also may be applicable to developing countries. Some have suggested that a *demonstration effect* operates to cause consumption in developing countries to ratchet upward as incomes grow. Internationally mobile and worldly wise upper-income groups in the developing countries

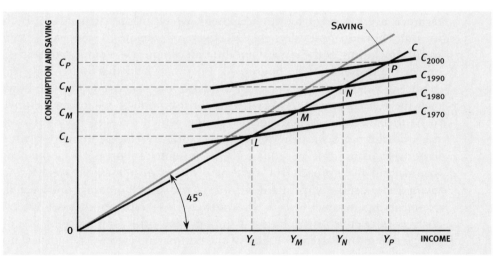

FIGURE 11–1 CONSUMPTION AND SAVING IN THE SHORT AND LONG TERM WITH RISING INCOME OVER TIME. The 45° line shows all points at which consumption is equal to income. Four short-run consumption functions are shown for each of the years 1970, 1980, 1990, and 2000, representing what people would have spent at various levels of income in those years. Consumption lines for each year plot equation 11–3, with

$$C = Y_d - S = -a(1 - S)Y_d$$

because $a < 0$, $-a > 0$. The flatness of these curves reflects consumers' reluctance to change consumption habits in the short run. In each of these years, actual (current) income was Y_L, Y_M, Y_N, and Y_P, respectively. Therefore, actual consumption in each of those years was C_L, C_M, C_N, and C_P. The points L through P trace out a long-term consumption. Consumption, and therefore savings, tend to be a constant proportion of income over time.

are thought to emulate high-consumption patterns of the wealthiest income groups in developed countries; successively lower-income groups tend to emulate the patterns of higher-income groups, so that consumption in the society as a whole tends to be a high and stable function of income. Indeed, British economist Nicholas Kaldor once estimated that if the richest families in Chile had the same consumption propensities as families at the same *relative* income position in developed nations (but at higher absolute levels of income), the Chilean savings rate in the 1950s could have been doubled.[11] The relative-income hypothesis explains all three of the observed saving patterns cited earlier.[12]

Other approaches developed to explain consumption and saving behavior in developed countries have been applied to developing countries. The most influential of these has been the **permanent-income hypothesis,** first formulated by Nobel-Prize laureate Milton Friedman at the University of Chicago in the 1950s. In the Friedman view, income consists of two components: permanent income and transitory income. The basic idea is simply that individuals expect to live for many years and they make consumption decisions over a horizon that includes their entire life span. The permanent-income component is not to be regarded as expected lifetime earnings. Rather it should be viewed as the mean income at any age regarded as permanent by the household, which in turn depends on both its time horizon and foresight. **Permanent income** is the yield from wealth, including both physical and human capital assets (education and so on) at the disposal of the household. Friedman held that individuals can predict with a reasonable degree of assurance the magnitude of these flows over their lifetimes and they gear their consumption to what they perceive to be their normal, or permanent, income, which tends to be stable over time. Furthermore, in the most-restrictive variant of the permanent-income hypothesis, consumption tends to be a constant proportion of permanent income and to approach 100 percent of permanent income. Hence, any saving that occurs will primarily be out of **transitory income:** unexpected, nonrecurring income such as that arising from changes in asset values, changes in relative prices, lottery winnings, and other unpredictable windfalls. In the most extreme version of the permanent-income hypothesis, individuals are held to save 100 percent of any transitory income. But

11. Nicholas Kaldor, "Problemas Económicos de Chile," *El Trimestre Economico,* 26, no. 102 (April–June 1959), 193, 211–12.

12. Other studies of factors affecting saving behavior among high-income elites in developing countries include Robert H. Frank, "The Demand for Unobservable and Other Non-Positional Goods," *American Economic Review,* 75 (March 1985), 101–16; and Philip Musgrove, "Income Distribution and Aggregate Consumption Function," *Journal of Political Economy,* 2, no. 88 (June 1980), 504–25.

econometric research has called into question this assumption; some studies show a fairly high propensity to consume out of transitory income.

The permanent-income hypothesis may be expressed

$$S = a + b_1 Y_p + b_2 Y_t \qquad\qquad [11\text{--}5]$$

where S = saving, a = constant, Y_p = permanent income, and Y_t = transitory income. As noted, in the most extreme version, $b_1 = 0$ and $b_2 = 1$, so all saving arises from the transitory component of income and all this component is saved. Modified versions of the permanent-income hypothesis hold only that saving out of permanent income is constant over a person's lifetime but can be positive and that, although the propensity to save out of transitory income is high, all transitory income may not be saved. Equation 11–5 can represent this version with $0 < b_1 < b_2 < 1$.

Several studies have sought to test the applicability of the permanent-income hypothesis to a variety of developing countries in Asia and Latin America. The results are far from conclusive, but in toto they lend some support to the modified versions of the hypothesis: People tend to save a higher proportion of transitory, as opposed to permanent, income.

A particularly interesting study by Angus Deaton in 1989, based on the framework of permanent-income models, stresses the importance of precautionary motives in household saving behavior, particularly among poor rural families in developing countries. Deaton argues that, for these groups, saving is not so much a matter of accumulation as it is a method of smoothing consumption in the face of volatile income. Essentially, Deaton says that poor rural households dissave as often as they save and behave as if their primary motive for saving is to protect their living standards against disasters.[13] In general, the permanent-income hypothesis has proven helpful in understanding all three observed saving patterns.

The **life-cycle model** of saving is similar to the permanent income model in that it postulates that saving and consumption depend on expectations about future income in addition to actual current income. The life-cycle model, associated most closely with Nobel Prize-winning economist Franco Modigliano, is more specific about how saving and consumption would be expected to vary systematically during a person's lifetime.[14]

13. Deaton, "Saving in Developing Countries," pp. 61–81.

14. See Franco Modigliano and Richard Brumberg, "Utility Analysis and the Consumption Function: An Interpretation of Cross-Section Data," in K. Kurihara, ed., *Post Keynesian Economics* (New Brunswick, NJ: Rutgers University Press, 1954); and Alberto Aldo and Franco Modigliano, "The Life-Cycle Hypothesis of Saving: Aggregate Implications and Tests," *American Economic Review* (March 1963). For a classic early work on the subject, see Ansley J. Coale and Edgar M. Hoover, *Population Growth and Economic Development in Low-Income Countries* (Princeton, NJ: Princeton University Press, 1958).

In this model, young adults tend to have lower saving rates because they have lower incomes (and expect higher incomes in the future) and are raising children. Indeed, many people would be expected actually to dissave (go into debt) during this stage of life. Savings rates tend to rise and peak toward the middle and end of a person's working years, when incomes are higher and there are fewer consumption-related expenses for children. During this stage of life, people accumulate the bulk of their saving to be used during retirement. Once workers retire, their income falls and they again dissave by drawing down on their previous saving. Thus, saving rates tend to be low or even negative during the younger years, high during middle age, and negative again after retirement.

The life-cycle hypothesis suggests that the demographic structure of a society may have a strong effect on saving rates. As discussed in Chapter 7, all societies tend to pass through a demographic transition with three basic stages: (1) high birth and death rates, with low population growth; (2) falling death rates, with continued high birth rates and consequently high population growth rates; and (3) falling birth rates with continued low death rates and lower population growth. As countries pass through these stages, the share of the population too young to work, of working age, or retired tends to change dramatically, and saving rates may change with them. A society in stage 2 of the demographic transition is likely to have a relatively large number of surviving children because of falling death rates and continued high birth rates. Children, of course, earn very little or no income and do not contribute directly to saving. However, each worker in the society will have more young dependents to care for, so saving rates would be expected to be relatively low. Later on, as a country enters stage 3 of the transition, the number of children tends to fall and the large number of children from the previous generation enter the workforce. As a result, society as a whole tends to have a far larger share of workers and fewer dependents. Since each worker has fewer children to care for, saving rates would be expected to rise. Later still, these workers will retire and saving rates will tend to decline. In Japan, for example, saving rates rose very quickly after World War II as the country rapidly passed through the demographic transition. As the population has continued to age in recent decades, with more Japanese workers entering retirement, however, saving rates have fallen.

Although some empirical studies have found very little connection between the composition of the population and saving rates, many others have detected a strong relationship. The relationship seems to be most robust with respect to the share of the young (i.e, under age 16 years) in the population: The larger is the share of young children, the lower the saving rate. The evidence is weaker with respect to the old, suggesting that this cohort may not reduce its saving as much as the life-cycle theory suggests.[15]

One further model of household saving behavior merits attention: the **class theory** of the British economist Nicholas Kaldor. This approach views consumption (saving) habits to be sharply differentiated by economic class. Workers, who receive mainly labor income, are thought to have far weaker saving propensities than capitalists, who receive primarily property income (profits, interests, rents). The class-savings hypothesis is represented as

$$S = s_w L + s_c P \qquad\qquad [11\text{--}6]$$

where s_w = workers' saving propensities out of labor income, s_c = capitalists' saving propensities out of property income, L = labor income, P = property income, and $0 < s_w < s_c < 1$.

The class-savings hypothesis explains the first pattern and also explains the third pattern, if factor shares (relative shares of labor and capital income) differ across countries. But the difference between the class-savings hypothesis and the permanent-income hypothesis may be more apparent than real. It is difficult to see why households, in their spending-saving decisions, treat labor income any differently than property income: A peso is a peso, a rupee of property income is no different from a rupee of labor income. However, the property income of households, particularly that from unincorporated enterprises, tends to fluctuate more than labor income. The permanent-income hypothesis suggests that propensities to save out of variable income streams are higher than out of more-stable streams. In addition, property income is more concentrated in higher-income groups. Therefore, studies of saving behavior based on the class model that show markedly higher saving out of property income really may be recording the effects of higher propensities to save out of more-fluctuating income.

All these hypotheses view income, whether current, relative, or permanent, as the principal determinant of saving behavior. But income by no means is the only determinant of aggregate private-sector saving behavior, particularly in developing countries. Analysts have suggested a range of

---

15. Studies that find no relationship between demographic structure and saving include Angus Deaton, *Understanding Consumption* (Oxford: Clarendon Press, 1992); and M. Gersovitz, "Savings and Development," in Hollis Chenery and T. N. Srinivasan, eds., *Handbook of Development Economics,* Vol. 1 (Amsterdam: North-Holland, 1988). Studies that reach the opposite conclusion include Sebastian Edwards, "Why Are Saving Rates So Different across Countries?"; P. Masson, T. Bayoumi, and H. Samiei, "International Evidence on the Determinants of Private Saving," IMF working paper no. 51, 1995; and Radelet et al., "Economic Growth in Asia."

other possible influences on private saving. As mentioned earlier, the life-cycle hypothesis suggests the age structure is critical. Others have stressed the location (rural versus urban) of a country's population. There appears to be some tendency around the world for rural households to save higher fractions of their income than urban households with comparable income levels—a phenomenon observed in a number of countries, including both Korea and Yugoslavia in the early 1970s. This behavior is consistent with the permanent-income hypothesis, because farmer's incomes are more variable than those of urban wage earners.

Financial markets may be an important ingredient in mobilizing saving, as discussed in Chapter 13. While many analysts have suggested that low interest rates discourage saving and high interest rates have the opposite affect, there is little empirical support to this proposition. More recent studies have focused attention on the institutional basis (or lack thereof) for saving in developing countries. Formal saving and credit markets often are segmented and closed to much of the population in developing countries. The absence of mortgage markets means that people must accumulate a large share of saving in advance of the purchase. Similarly, "missing" markets for pensions, insurance, and consumer credit may be associated with higher rates of saving. Indeed, precautionary motives may play a large role in mobilizing saving, as households save out of current income to protect themselves from adverse shocks in the future. Thus, more sophisticated financial markets may be associated with lower rates of saving.[16]

In the end, despite many plausible theories about the determinants of private saving, the empirical evidence is fairly weak. Private saving data from developing countries are notoriously poor, since they often are measured as the residual from the national accounts and therefore include large errors and omissions. Even with good data, saving studies are bedeviled by identification, causality, and bias problems. Therefore, further work on private saving in developing countries is a high priority for future research.

CORPORATE SAVING BEHAVIOR

We have seen that there is no shortage of hypotheses purporting to explain the determinants of household saving. However, there is little consensus among economists about the determinants of corporate saving, even in the industrialized countries. For example, in the United States, a major question in research on business finance has been to explain why U.S. corporations pay such a high proportion of their after-tax income in dividends,

---

16. For more discussion of these issues, see T. N. Srinivasan, "Saving in the Development Process," in James H. Gapinski, ed., *The Economics of Saving* (Norwell, MA: Kluwer Academic Publishers, 1993).

despite strong tax and other incentives to retain earnings (save) within the firm. There is even less understanding of the determinants of corporate saving in developing countries.

In the industrialized countries, the share of corporate savings in total income typically is less than 5 percent, and the share of corporate saving in total net private saving typically is less than 25 percent. For example, in the early 1990s, corporate saving was about 2 percent of disposable income in Japan and the United States, 3 percent in Belgium and France, and about 1 percent in Canada. Only in Denmark, the Netherlands, and Spain did the figure exceed 5 percent. Such data are available for only a few developing countries and not always very reliable. World Bank data suggests that, in 1991, corporate saving accounted for 7 percent of disposable income in Colombia, 2 percent in Korea, and around 0 percent in the Philippines.[17]

Corporate saving is relatively small in most developing countries primarily because the corporate sector is relatively small. For a variety of reasons, there are fewer pressures and incentives in developing countries for doing business in the corporate form. The principal reasons for organizing as a corporation in the private sector are to limit the liability of enterprise owners to amounts invested in a business and to facilitate enterprise finance through the issue of equity shares (stocks). Although these advantages are substantial in higher-income countries with well-developed commercial codes, civil court systems, and capital markets, they are smaller in most developing countries, where the collection of commercial claims (for example, company debts) through the courts is relatively difficult and where, as shown in Chapter 13, capital markets are poorly developed when they exist at all.

As usual, however, there are important exceptions to these generalizations. In some developing countries, corporations are both numerous and quite large. Each year since 1980, *Fortune* magazine's annual list of the 500 largest corporations outside the United States includes several dozen from developing countries.[18] Examples include conglomerates such as Bavaria (beverages and food processing) in Colombia and Hyundai (automobiles) in Korea and enterprises such as Alpargatus (textiles and shoes) in Argentina, the diversified firm Tata in India, and Villares (steel products) in Brazil. But, except in Korea and Brazil, even in middle-income countries, such corporations are not numerous, ordinarily do not account for a large share of private-sector business activity, and clearly do not provide a high proportion of domestic saving.

In all but a few of the highest-income developing countries, the great bulk of private sector farming and commercial and manufacturing activity

17. World Bank Saving database (on-line).

18. *Fortune* magazine, "World Business Directory," annual.

is conducted by unincorporated, typically family-owned enterprises, which will be discussed in Chapter 17. Some of these fall into the category of medium-scale establishments (from 20 to 99 workers). Very few are large-scale enterprises. The great majority are small-scale operations (fewer than 20 employees), which, in spite of their abundance, do not account for a sizable share of either value added or saving.[19] Nevertheless, the noncorporate sector manages to generate more than half of all domestic saving in most developing countries, and this sector is the only consistent source of surplus in the sense that its saving exceeds its investment. For those closely held, largely family-owned and -managed firms, enterprise profits become an important part not of corporate saving but of gross household income. The available evidence indicates, and economic theory suggests, that household saving accounts for the overwhelming share of private saving in developing countries and the chief source of household saving probably is household income from unincorporated enterprises.

Foreign Saving

Countries unable to generate sufficient domestic saving to finance economic growth historically have sought resources from other countries. The United States relied heavily on foreign saving, particularly during the antebellum period from 1835 to 1860. Likewise, Russia needed foreign saving to propel its development in the three decades before World War I and the Communist revolution. Yet Japan became a modern nation even though it actively discouraged inflows of foreign saving and investment throughout its history. Foreign saving can help development but is not essential for it. When capital is permitted to flow freely across borders, it tends to move from higher-income countries (where capital is more abundant and rates of return are relatively low) to developing countries (where capital is scarce and potential rates of return are relatively high), although this is not always the case. Most developing countries consider foreign saving to be an important ingredient in their development efforts. But controversy surrounds foreign aid, foreign investment, and the debt that has accrued from foreign borrowing. The remainder of this chapter examines the basic concept of foreign saving and explores in detail one major component—foreign aid. Chapter 14 examines issues related to private capital flows, foreign debt, and recent financial crises related to short-term foreign capital flows.

The concept of foreign saving can be approached from two different directions. Foreign saving (F) can finance the amount by which invest-

---

19. See Donald Snodgrass and Tyler Biggs, *Industrialization and the Small Firm: Patterns and Policies* (San Francisco: ICS Press, 1996).

TABLE 11–4 FOREIGN SAVING AND BALANCE OF PAYMENTS FOR DEVELOPING COUNTRIES (AVERAGE 1995–97, $U.S. BILLION)		
	RECEIPTS (+)	EXPENDITURES (−)
1. TRADE		
TRADE IN GOODS	EXPORTS = 1,793	IMPORTS = 1,789
TRADE IN NONFACTOR SERVICES[a]	EXPORTS = 371	IMPORTS = 413
2. NET RESOURCE TRANSFER (IMPORTS − EXPORTS)	INFLOW = 38	
3. INCOME PAYMENTS[b]	EARNED = 107	PAID = 205
4. TRADE IN GOODS AND ALL SERVICES	EXPORTS = 2,271	IMPORTS = 2,407
5. NET RESOURCE FLOW (NET FOREIGN SAVING)	INFLOW = 136	
6. REPAYMENT OF PRINCIPAL ON DEBT		REPAID = 170
7. TOTAL PAYMENTS	RECEIVED = 2,271	PAID = 2,577
8. GROSS RESOURCE FLOW (GROSS FOREIGN SAVING)	INFLOW = 306	

[a]Services include freight, transportation, insurance, and tourism.
[b]Income payments include dividends, interest payments, and wages. Total includes interest payments on foreign debt of 106 billion.
Source: IMF, *Balance of Payments Statistics Yearbook 1998,* and World Bank, *Global Development Finance 1999.*

ment (I) exceeds domestic saving (S), so that $F = I - S$. Alternatively, foreigners can finance the trade deficit, which is the amount by which imports exceed exports, $F = M - E$. Because of the way gross domestic or gross national product is measured, $I - S$ always is equal to $M - E$, so foreign saving must be the same whichever definition we use.[20]

Table 11–4 places foreign saving in the context of the balance of payments, consistent with the second preceding definition, using actual data from the period 1995–97. Receipts represent payments of foreign exchange to people or institutions inside the home country; expenditures are payments by the country to the outside world. By far the largest source of receipts for most countries is exports, while the largest expenditure is imports. If we consider only trade in goods and services, excluding income payments (interest, dividends, and wages) to and from foreign sources,

20. Recall from the national accounts that $Y = C + I + G + E - M$. In addition, all income must be consumed (C), given to the government as tax payments (T), or retained as private saving (S_p), so $Y = C + T + S_p$. Combining these two identities and rearranging terms yields ($T - G$) + $S_p = I + E - M$. Since $T - G$ is equal to government saving, the left-hand side of the last equation simply is equal to total domestic saving, S. Substituting this into the equation and rearranging terms yields the identity $I - S = M - E$.

then the trade balance represents the **net resource transfer** (line 2 of the table). This is the contribution that foreign saving makes to development in goods and services that cannot be financed by exports. In Table 11–4, this is a net inflow that averaged $38 billion to the developing countries between 1995 and 1997.

If instead we include income receipts and payments as part of exports and imports, the trade balance is that **net resource flow** (line 5), an inflow averaging $136 billion between 1995 and 1997. This concept of net foreign saving suggests that foreign resources finance goods and services for development (net transfers) as well as the payments of interest and dividends on earlier flows of foreign capital. Net resource flow also can be measured as the inflow of capital net of repayments of principal on loan obligations incurred by the home country. Adding debt principal repayments to the net flows would yield the *gross resource transfer* (or gross foreign saving, line 8), which averaged $306 billion between 1995 and 1997.

Foreign saving includes both official saving and private saving. Most **official saving** is on **concessional terms,** made available either as *grants* (outright gifts) or as *"soft" loans,* bearing lower interest rates and longer repayment periods than would be available in private international capital markets. Governments and international agencies also make some loans on commercial terms *("hard" loans).* Most governments and multilateral organizations (such as the World Bank and regional development banks[21]) make both soft and hard loans to developing countries. Concessional flows technically are called **official development assistance** (ODA) but popularly are called **foreign aid.** Aid can be further divided into *bilateral aid,* given directly by one government to another, and *multilateral aid,* in which the funds flow from governments to international agencies like the United Nations, the World Bank, and the regional development banks, which in turn grant or lend the funds to recipient developing countries. Finally, aid can be in the form of *technical assistance,* the provision of skilled individuals to augment national expertise, or *capital assistance,* the provision of finance or commodities.

Foreign private saving consists of four elements. *Foreign direct investment* is made by nonresidents, typically but not always by multinational corporations, in enterprises located in host countries; direct investment implies full or partial control of the enterprise and physical presence by foreign firms or individuals. *Portfolio investment* is the purchase of host country bonds or stocks by foreigners, without managerial control. This was a very important form of foreign investment in the nineteenth and

---

21. The regional development banks include the African, Asian, and Inter-American Development Banks and several smaller subregional banks. Most of these are patterned on the World Bank.

TABLE 11–5   NET RESOURCE FLOWS TO DEVELOPING COUNTRIES, 1970–97 ($U.S. BILLION)

	1970[a]	1983	1990	1997
OFFICIAL DEVELOPMENT FINANCE	12	31.5	58.0	39.0
OFFICIAL GRANTS	8[b]	9.9	29.4	25.7
OFFICIAL LOANS	4[c]	21.6	28.5	13.3
BILATERAL	3	10.6	13.5	−7.7
MULTILATERAL	1	11.0	15.0	21.1
PRIVATE FINANCE	7	36.7	63.5	320.0
COMMERCIAL BANK LOANS	3	19.8	3.2	60.1
BONDS	0	1.0	1.2	42.6
OTHER PRIVATE LOANS	N.A.	7.3	11.4	2.6
SHORT-TERM DEBT FLOWS	N.A.	N.A.	19.5	21.1
PORTFOLIO INVESTMENT	0.3	0.2	3.7	30.2
FOREIGN DIRECT INVESTMENT	3.7	8.5	24.5	163.4
TOTAL NET RESOURCE FLOW	19	68.2	121.5	359.0
VALUE OF TECHNICAL ASSISTANCE	N.A.	N.A.	14.4	17.0
TOTAL WITH TECHNICAL ASSISTANCE	19	68.2	135.9	376.0
(TOTAL IN CONSTANT 1997 DOLLARS)[d]	76.9	77.2	147.9	376.0

[a]Figures for 1970 are from a different source than the other years and may not be exactly comparable.
[b]Includes technical assistance and concessional loans.
[c]Nonconcessional loans only.
[d]Deflated using the import unit value index for developing countries from IMF, *International Financial Statistics 1999*.
Sources: World Bank, *Global Development Finance 1999* and OECD Development Assistance Committee, *Development Cooperation in the 1990s* (Paris, 1989) p. 150 (1970 data).

early twentieth centuries, but fell into disuse after World War II. Portfolio investment revived in the 1990s, however, as rich-country investors showed interest in emerging stock and bond markets, especially in Asia and increasingly in Latin America. *Commercial bank lending* to developing country governments and enterprises supplanted portfolio investment in importance for a time but waned with the debt crisis of the 1980s. Finally, exporting firms, their commercial banks, and official banks offer *export credits* to importing countries as a way of promoting sales by permitting delayed payment for imports, often at commercial interest rates. We discuss these various forms of foreign private saving, the 1980s debt crisis, and the related financial crises of the mid-1990s in more detail in Chapter 14.

From 1970 to 1997, total net resource flows more than quadrupled in constant prices, a growth rate of 5.7 percent a year (Table 11–5). Net resource flows grew most rapidly between 1990 and 1997 at an astonishing real rate of 13.3 percent per year. The net resource flow of $376 billion in 1997 was equivalent to 5.7 percent of gross domestic product for the developing countries, an increase from almost 4 percent in 1970, and to roughly $76 per person. The value of official development finance actually fell in the 1990s, so the growth is due wholly to extraordinary increases in private flows, including commercial bank loans, bond placements, portfolio equity investment, and foreign direct investment. Although official flows made up two thirds of the total in 1970, their share had fallen to one ninth by 1997. Direct investment accounted for half of all private flows in 1997. However, during the intervening years, commercial bank lending played a more important role: In 1983, it accounted for 54 percent of private resource flows but then dried up as the debt crisis eroded international banks' confidence and profits. Chapter 14 discusses private international capital flows in more detail, where we see that these private flows are highly concentrated into a small number of developing countries.

Foreign Aid

HISTORICAL ROLE

Foreign aid as now conceived is a product of the post-World War II era. Its roots are in the Marshall Plan, under which the United States transferred $17 billion over four years, equivalent to about 1.5 percent of the U.S. GNP, to help rebuild Europe after the war. Two elements of the Marshall Plan were believed at the time to have been crucial for its success: an influx of financial capital from the United States and coordinated plans to employ it productively to rebuild Europe's devastated physical capital stock.

The two decades after World War II saw the emergence of independent nations from Europe's colonies, especially in Asia and Africa. Encouraged by the success of Marshall Plan aid in rebuilding Europe, the United States took the lead in trying to help the newly emerging nations by providing that same element, capital, in the form of foreign aid, especially to countries that had development plans for investing the aid they received. Early aid programs also recognized that developing countries lacked certain kinds of skills and expertise, so donors also offered technical assistance programs, which supplied foreign experts in fields from economic planning to engineering to construction.

The motives behind the U.S. aid programs of the postwar years were complex and ranged from the selfish to the generous. The security of the United States was the center of Congress's concerns in approving both the Marshall Plan and the Point IV program, under which President Truman began to shift U.S. attention and resources toward the developing countries. This meant "containing Communism" around the perimeter of the Soviet bloc as well as trying to ensure access to raw materials needed by U.S. industry. The prosperity of both the United States and its allies required expanding trade and investment, also promoted by aid. It was believed that development would serve both security and economic interests

| TABLE 11–6 | NET OFFICIAL DEVELOPMENT ASSISTANCE (DISBURSEMENTS) FROM THE OECD COUNTRIES TO DEVELOPING COUNTRIES AND MULTILATERAL AGENCIES, 1965–97 | | | |

| | PERCENT OF GNP | | | $U.S. BILLION, |
SOURCE	1965	1991	1997	1997
CANADA	0.19	0.45	0.34	2.0
FRANCE	0.76	0.62	0.45	6.3
GERMANY[a]	0.40	0.41	0.28	5.9
ITALY	0.10	0.30	0.11	1.2
JAPAN	0.2	0.32	0.22	9.3
THE NETHERLANDS	0.36	0.88	0.81	2.9
SWEDEN	0.19	0.92	0.79	1.7
UNITED KINGDOM	0.47	0.32	0.26	3.4
UNITED STATES	0.58	0.20	0.09	6.8
OECD TOTAL	0.48	0.33	0.22	48.3[b]

[a]West Germany only in 1965; unified Germany in 1991, 1997.

[b]Table 11–6 counts disbursements as they are made by the donor countries to the developing countries and to multilateral agencies; Table 11–5 counts disbursements as they are received by the developing countries from both the bilateral and multilateral agencies. This difference in treatment helps to explain the slight differences in total ODA.

Source: World Bank, *World Development Report 1994*, Table 18; and OECD Development Assistance Committee, 1999, Table V-1.

by reducing instability and giving the emerging nations a stake in the capitalist world order. The U.S. aid policy also was intended to encourage the new countries to maintain or adopt democratic political institutions and private-enterprise-based economies in the U.S. image. There was a core of humanitarian concern for the welfare of the world's poor as well. Indeed, the strength of the early aid programs depended on this mixture of nationalistic and altruistic motives, which drew political support from a wide spectrum of opinion.

In the early postwar years of aid, the United States, the United Kingdom, and France were the most important contributors; The latter two contributed mainly to their former colonies. As the other industrial countries began to recover and prosper, however, some of them became important donors. Table 11–6 shows net official development assistance from the countries of the Organization for Economic Cooperation and Development, including bilateral aid and contributions to multilateral organizations, from 1965 to 1997. Although some OECD donors, including several not shown in the table, increased their aid efforts by significant amounts, on the whole, the aid effort of the OECD countries declined substantially. Aid flows as a share of GNP have declined in France, Germany, Japan, the United Kingdom, and especially the United States, whose aid effort shrank from 0.6 to 0.1 percent of GNP over these years. Only four countries—Denmark, the Netherlands, Norway, and Sweden—exceeded the United Nations target of 0.7 percent of GNP. The decline in bilateral assistance has been offset to some extent by an increase in the share of aid given as grants (up from 47 percent in 1970 to 77 percent in 1997), but not by enough to make up for the decline in the total. In terms of dollar amounts, Japan is by far the largest donor, with France and Germany providing nearly as much aid as the United States. Over this period, also, the multilateral agencies, especially the World Bank, became important dispensers of capital. By 1997, net lending by the multilateral agencies accounted for about 54 percent of all official development finance.

As the flow of aid expanded and more countries and multilateral agencies became important players, the economic development rationale for aid changed as well. During the 1950s and 1960s, the main economic goal was rapid growth of output and incomes, to be achieved by increasing the amount of domestic and foreign saving available for investment. Human capital received emphasis beyond the recognized role of technical assistance, and aid programs spread into education, health, and other human services. During the late 1960s and the 1970s, aid programs began to incorporate goals other than the promotion of economic growth: Income redistribution, poverty alleviation, satisfaction of basic needs, and rural development became motivators for the aid programs of most donors. In the 1980s and early 1990s, the shift toward market-oriented economic policies (described in Chapter 5) led donors, particularly the World Bank, to focus more on macroeconomic stabilization and structural adjustment as goals of aid. More recently, environmental sustainability and democratization have become important aims of donors.

Total official development assistance increased from $12 billion in 1979 to $63 billion in 1991 but dropped sharply thereafter to $39 billion in 1997. These flows amounted to 0.6 percent of GNP (about $8 per capita) for the recipient low- and middle-income countries in 1997, down from around 1 percent of GNP (about $12 per capita) in 1991. In real terms, of course, the decline is even larger. However, there are major and moderately systematic variations around this rather low average, as Table 11–7 reveals. First, there is a strong tendency for donors to use scarce concessional aid in favor of the poorest countries: Aid tends to represent a higher fraction of GNP for the poorer countries in Table 11–7. Some of the exceptions to this rule point to a second strong tendency. Among the 15 countries with the lowest incomes, 5 of the most populous have very low aid-GNP ratios: India, China, Pakistan, Nigeria, and Indonesia. Donors, faced with a choice of spreading their aid proportionally (to GNP or population) and thus having scant impact anywhere or concentrating it where they can make a lager impact, choose the latter. Small countries thus get greater relative amounts of aid than large countries.

TABLE 11–7	NET RECEIPTS OF OFFICIAL DEVELOPMENT ASSISTANCE BY SELECTED DEVELOPING COUNTRIES, 1997			
COUNTRY	GNP PER CAPITA ($)	$U.S. MILLION	PERCENT OF GNP[a]	DOLLARS PER CAPITA
ETHIOPIA	500	637	10	11
TANZANIA	620	964	15	31
MALI	720	455	17	44
NIGERIA	860	202	1	2
BANGLADESH	1,090	1,010	2	8
KENYA	1,160	459	5	16
PAKISTAN	1,580	597	1	5
GHANA	1,610	498	7	28
INDIA	1,660	1,678	0	2
SENEGAL	1,690	427	9	0
SRI LANKA	2,460	347	2	19
BOLIVIA	2,810	717	9	92
CHINA	3,070	2,054	0	2
EGYPT	3,080	1,949	3	32
INDONESIA	3,390	850	0	4
THE PHILIPPINES	3,670	694	1	9
GUATEMALA	4,060	303	2	29
BRAZIL	6,350	487	0	3
COLOMBIA	6,570	274	0	7
MALAYSIA	7,730	−241	0	−11
MEXICO	8.110	108	0	1
SOUTH KOREA	13,430	−158	0	−3
ISRAEL	17,680	1,192	0	204

[a]In this column, 0 means less than 0.5 percent.
Note that, in the second column, GNP per capita is expressed in terms of purchasing power parity to rank countries by average income. In the fourth column, the calculation of ODA as a percentage of GNP uses GNP expressed in nominal US dollars, since ODA is expressed in these terms.
Source: World Bank, World Development Indicators 1999 CD-ROM.

Finally, Table 11–7 includes some examples of countries favored for political and strategic reasons. Mali and Senegal benefit disproportionately, as do all francophone African states, from France's generous aid program. Egypt, along with Israel, has been favored by the United States' involvement in the Middle East. Bolivia, both small and poor by Latin American standards, receives considerable U.S. aid to help suppress the cocaine trade. During the 1950s and 1960s, South Korea, Taiwan, Pakistan, Turkey, and other allied governments were favored recipients of U.S. aid. Although the manifestations of politically inspired aid are strongest in these cases, they are present to some extent in many other countries.

AID INSTITUTIONS AND INSTRUMENTS

Bilateral aid donors usually plan and dispense loans and grants through an aid agency, such as the United States Agency for International Development (USAID), Britain's Department for International Development (DFID), the International Development Agencies of Canada (CIDA) and Sweden (SIDA), and others. The main **multilateral aid** agencies are the World Bank, the International Monetary Fund, the regional development banks, and the United Nations.

The largest and most influential of the multinationals is the **World Bank,** which consists of five affiliated institutions: the International Bank for Reconstruction and Development (IBRD), the International Development Association (IDA), the International Finance Corporation (IFC), the Multilateral Investment Guarantee Agency (MIGA), and the International Centre for Settlement of Investment Disputes (ICSID). The World Bank operates in over 100 developing and transitional economies. Its main activities are financing specific projects (e.g., roads, power plants), providing general financing to support policy reform programs, and offering technical assistance in a range of areas. Despite its leading role in the aid community, most of the capital supplied by the World Bank is not aid. The IBRD obtains its funds by borrowing on world capital markets at prevailing prime interest rates and relends to developing countries at slightly higher rates. Since the IBRD has an excellent credit rating, it is able to make more capital available and at lower interest rates than could be obtained by the developing countries on their own. Its affiliate, the IFC, lends on commercial terms and takes minority equity positions in support of private foreign investments. Only the IDA, which channels contributions from the richer member countries to the poorer countries on very soft terms, dispenses aid in the strict sense.[22] During the 1970s the World Bank became the world's leading center for research, information, and policy advice on economic development. In 1998 the World Bank group disbursed about $25 billion in loans and concessional aid; when loan repayments to the bank are included, however, the net resource flow was about $14 billion, or 49 percent of total official development finance.[23]

The word *reconstruction* in the bank's title stems from its origin, at the Bretton Woods (New Hampshire) conference in 1944, when its first task was to help finance the reconstruction of war-torn European countries.

---

22. MIGA and ICSID do not dispense loans. MIGA provides guarantees to foreign investors against loss caused by noncommercial risks, and ICSID provide facilities for the settlement of investment disputes between foreign investor and the host countries. See the World Bank website, available at www.worldbank.org.

23. World Bank, *World Debt Tables 1994–1995* (Washington, DC: World Bank, 1994), p. 171.

One of the other institutions founded at the conference was the **International Monetary Fund,** whose main charge was to reestablish an international system of national currencies in stable relation to each other, in support of a rejuvenated world trade system. The IMF played a significant role in the unprecedented expansion of world trade during the 1950s and 1960s. Although not primarily concerned with promoting development, the IMF practices and resources have had a major effect on developing countries. Since the 1980s debt crisis, the fund increasingly has turned its attention toward working with developing countries by offering balance-of-payments support in a variety of ways. It typically provides financing for a one- to three-year period for countries facing macroeconomic instability and an acute shortage of foreign exchange. To receive these loans, the government must agree to undertake a series of policy reforms, typically aimed at reducing the government budget deficit, tightening monetary policy, and quickly reducing the current account deficit. As of early 1999, the IMF had programs in 58 developing and transitional economies, making it one of the most important institutions working in developing countries. Although these programs are designed to be short term, in many instances they are renewed for many years. For example, for the period 1980–96, the IMF had continuous or nearly continuous programs in Jamaica, the Philippines, Malawi, Togo, Uganda, and several other countries.

Each of the developing world's continents—Africa, Asia, and Latin America—has its own **regional development bank,** including the African Development Bank, the Asian Development Bank, and the Inter-American Development Bank. These each have separate "windows" that dispense hard and soft loans to member countries. Regional members and the major aid donors contribute to the capital of these banks, which also borrow on private capital markets to finance hard loans and receive contributions from aid donors for their soft loan windows. Other multilateral donors include the European Union (EU) and the Arab countries of the Organization of Petroleum Exporting Countries (OPEC). The EU originally concentrated its aid on the former French colonies in Africa but now spreads its assistance more widely, especially in Africa. Arab OPEC, which was especially active during the late 1970s and early 1980s when oil prices were high, concentrates its assistance on Islamic states.

The United Nations concessional programs have amounted to about $1.5 billion of technical assistance each year in the 1990s. This effort is coordinated by the United Nations Development Programme (UNDP), which grants to member countries. However, the specialized agencies of the United Nations, such as the UN Industrial Development Organization (UNIDO), International Labor Organization (ILO), and World Health Organization (WHO), among others, execute the technical assistance projects financed by UNDP.

Development assistance agencies deal with a wide range of aid instruments, both technical and capital assistance. Most capital aid is disbursed against specific projects, such as hydroelectric dams, roads, or rural development projects, and is called **project aid.** However, some bilateral agencies have made **program loans,** which finance general categories of imports and are conceived as broad support for the balance of payments. *Structural adjustment loans,* made especially by the World Bank to support economic reforms as described in Chapter 5, are program loans. *Food aid* is a kind of bilateral program loan, since it provides commodities, mostly grains, that otherwise would have to be purchased with a country's own foreign exchange earnings.

AID AND DEVELOPMENT

The simplest way to think of the contribution of aid (and other foreign saving) to development is that it adds to available saving and investment. In the simple Harrod-Domar model, for example, the role of foreign saving of all kinds is to augment domestic saving to increase investment and thus accelerate growth. If aid and other foreign saving added, say, 6 percent of GNP, if the capital-output ratio were 3.0, then the growth rate would increase by 2 percentage points. In a neoclassical model in which the share of GNP earned by capital was 50 percent, the growth rate would increase by 1 percentage point.[24]

A glance at Table 11–7 shows that for some countries—Ethiopia, Mali, Tanzania, Sensegal, and Bolivia—ODA is a large fraction of GNP and could contribute 2.5 percent or more to the growth rate in this simple neoclassical world. For countries like India, China, Indonesia, Mexico, and Brazil, ODA is a small fraction of GDP and could not have much impact on growth. In fact, no strong correlation is found across countries between aid receipts (as a share of GNP) and economic growth. This suggests either the limitations of the neoclassical model or that aid is not always used very effectively. Developing countries of course may lack some important complementary inputs to development, such as human skills, administrative capacity, infrastructure, economic institutions, and political stability, without which even high saving rates may not stimulate growth.

---

24. From equation 2–18, $g_Y = a + (W_K \times g_K) + (W_L \times g_L)$. An increase in the growth rate of capital stock, dg_K, would cause an increase in the growth of the GNP, $dg_Y = W_K dg_K$. How much does foreign aid contribute to the growth of the capital stock? If all of it were invested, then $dg_K = S/K = (S_f/Y)(Y/K)$. We know that the aid share in GNP, S_f/Y, is 0.06 and the capital output ratio, K/Y, is 3, so $dg_K = .02$. If W_K, the share of capital income in GNP, is 50 percent, then this 2 percent increase in the annual growth rate of the capital stock adds $dg_Y = W_K dg_K = 0.5(.02) = .01$, or 1 percent, to the annual growth of income.

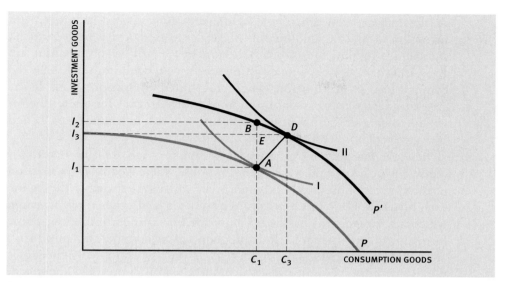

FIGURE 11–2 IMPACT OF AID ON INVESTMENT AND CONSUMPTION. Foreign aid totaling AB turns into actual new investment of only AE, because the country maximizes welfare on the new frontier, P', at point D, not B. P' is not really a "production" frontier but a "supply" frontier; see footnote 25.
Source: Adapted from Paul Mosley, "Aid, Savings and Growth Revisited," *Oxford Bulletin of Economics and Statistics* 42, (May 1980), 79–91.

In addition, some economists have argued that foreign aid may not contribute much to additional saving or imports, but instead at least some of it could be used to finance higher consumption or to reduce exports.

Figure 11–2 shows why these doubters are at least partly correct. A developing country, before it obtains aid, can produce consumption goods and capital goods along the production possibilities frontier P. To simplify, the diagram ignores international trade. Community tastes are defined by a set of indifference curves, of which two, labeled I and II, are shown. Without aid, the country's welfare is maximized if it produces and consumes at point A, where the indifference curve I is tangent to the frontier P, with consumption at C_1 and investment at I_1. Now donor countries contribute an amount AB of aid. They intend that the full amount should be invested and raise total investment to I_2. However, the offer of aid AB in effect moves the production frontier outward from P to P'.[25] With these added resources the country maximizes its welfare by producing at point

25. The purist will worry about this shift in the production frontier. It is not production that has been increased but the supply of goods through additional imports, financed by aid. Graphically, this is equivalent to an outward shift in the frontier, in the same sense that additional income shifts the budget line outward for an individual consumer. Strictly speaking, however, the production frontier in Figure 11–2 remains P.

D, the tangency between P' and indifference curve I_2. It consumes C_3 and invests I_3. Of the aid amount AB, AE (equal to $I_3 - I_1$) has been invested, as intended by the donors, but BE (equal to $I_2 - I_3$) has been consumed. Even if all the new aid money is invested as intended, some of what the country had invested before would be shifted to consumption. If the country's tastes favored consumption over investment even more, then it would reach equilibrium at a point along P' to the southeast of D and convert even more of its aid into consumption.

The diagram demonstrates that the amount of aid actually used to increase investment rather than consumption will depend on production possibilities, community tastes, and other variables left out of the figure, such as trade. How can a country convert aid and other foreign saving, which are intended to be used for investment, into consumption? Some forms of foreign saving, such as program aid or commercial bank loans, are designed to provide finance for general purposes and deliberately give the recipient the kinds of choices demonstrated in Figure 11–2. Food aid, of course, is intended to increase or maintain consumption rather than investment. But, even if all foreign saving were dispensed as project aid and targeted to specific investment projects, substitution would be possible. Project aid might be used, for example, for investment projects that the government or private investors would have made even without aid. In that case, resources are freed up for other purposes, including consumption. When aid finances projects that otherwise might not be implemented, a government may simply cut back on preferred projects because it wants to raise the share of consumption, for economic or political reasons. Whey substitutions of these kinds are possible, aid is called *fungible*.

Perhaps more important, a host of subtle influences of foreign saving on relative prices also may contribute to substitution. More capital in general conceivably could mean lower returns on investments and hence a greater tendency to consume in the recipient countries. More foreign exchange tends to lower its price (that is, to appreciate the exchange rate) and cause greater demand for imports, as intended by donors, but also creates a reduced incentive to produce for export, which is not intended.[26] And food aid has a similar effect; it lowers food prices because it satisfies part of domestic demand and hence reduces the incentive for domestic farmers to produce grains and other foods. These influences could be overcome by countervailing government policies, but governments may not undertake such measures for a variety of reasons. In sum, the contribution of aid and other foreign savings to development is not that they provide specific amounts of additional investment, imports, or food. Rather, foreign aid provides additional purchasing power and thus gives recipient

26. This effect is a form of the Dutch disease, described in Chapter 16.

governments and citizens more room to choose between consumption and investment, more imports and less exports, more food consumption or less food production, and so forth.

Additional macroeconomic resource flows are not the only mechanism by which donors try to enhance development, however. Aid can have four other kinds of influences on a country's development. First, most capital assistance goes to specific projects. Donors frequently use project aid to give special attention to particular sectors or kinds of activities, hoping to improve practices in those areas and to initiate developments that eventually become self-sustaining. Investment in wheat and rice production was a high priority for project aid during the late 1960s, for example, especially in Asia, while rural development projects were emphasized during the 1970s. It had become evident that neglect of rural investment, in many countries, had slowed economic growth and made it difficult to reduce poverty. Foreign assistance played a major role in spreading the Green Revolution, which delivered new seed varieties for wheat and rice, together with a "package" of inputs, including fertilizers, pesticides, and water, and made countries such as India and Indonesia much less vulnerable to famine and better able to promote widespread economic development. Although horror stories about failed aid projects are common enough, these and other examples suggest that project assistance can have a beneficial impact.

A second avenue to influence development is **technical assistance.** In 1997, technical cooperation grants were the equivalent of about 44 percent of official development finance (Table 11–5). Although the United Nations perhaps is the largest provider of technical assistance, all donors supply it to some extent. They provide experts in fields as diverse as agronomy, computer programming, economics, education, engineering, forestry, geology, law, management, medicine, and public health. Foreign experts are sent to perform jobs for which local professionals are not qualified or are in short supply. Technical assistance is not always effective. In the best cases, however, expatriate professionals become agents of change when they put new systems in place, influence local professionals to try new or improved ways of performing tasks, train local professionals, and help build new development institutions.

The third route for aid to influence development is through **conditionality,** the attempt by aid donors to use their assistance as a lever to influence policy in recipient countries. Some conditions tied to assistance do not advance development. Donors offer aid to reward political friends and military allies and withhold it from those perceived as enemies. This was a common practice, especially during the cold war, as both East and West tried to win support (and votes at the United Nations) through their aid programs. In addition, donors tie aid funds to the purchase of goods and services in their own countries as a way of increasing their own markets for exports and dampening the impact of aid on their own balance of payments. They channel it toward countries and institutions that adhere most closely to the donor's own views of economics and politics in ways that may be of more benefit to the donor than the recipient. These perhaps are the crassest uses of aid, and they generally are confined to bilateral donors.

But donors, both bilateral and multilateral, also use aid to induce recipient governments to change their development policies in what donors believe to be the recipients' own best interests. Chapter 5 discussed donors' conditioning of aid on economic reforms such as currency devaluation, market liberalization, changes in tax systems, adoption of new wage and income policies, adjustments in food and other agricultural prices, and many other policy actions. To the extent these reforms are appropriately designed to support long-term growth and development, policy leverage may be as important a contribution of aid programs to development as the resource flows they finance. It is an open question, however, whether donors can do more than push governments in directions they already wish to go. If host governments wish to resist conditions attached to aid, they have ways of appearing to accept conditions but not implementing them fully, and donors have reasons to continue offering their aid even if conditions are not met.

Fourth, aid can influence development by supporting the generation of new ideas and best practices. The international aid establishment directly and indirectly supports a large group of their own expert staff, university scholars, professional consultants, aid administrators, and others, from both the industrial and developing countries, who conceive and eventually popularize new ways of thinking about development issues. This diverse group, over time, has influenced the way developing country scholars and policy makers think about many issues including economic reform, trade strategy, fiscal policy, rural development, and so on. Once this general and diffuse influence changes the minds of policy makers, foreign aid can become far more effective in serving national development strategies because recipients and donors share its basic premises.[27]

Nevertheless, despite the many ways that aid could support development, skepticism has grown about the actual effectiveness of aid. These doubts are one reason why donor countries cut back sharply on aid in the 1990s. Many donors felt that there was little to show for the large increases in aid that took place in the 1980s. And, indeed, several studies have shown weak or nonexistent links between aid and investment and be-

---

27. For a comprehensive review of the impact of foreign aid on development, see Robert Cassen et al., *Does Aid Work?* (London: Oxford University Press, 1986).

tween aid and growth.[28] One reason, as discussed earlier, is that aid is fungible, so at least some aid ends up financing consumption rather than investment. But even taking this into account, aid projects do not always work very well. Sometimes, this is due to restrictions placed on aid by the donors that require the funds be spent on materials purchased in the donor country. This kind of aid, known as tied aid, can result in much higher costs of needed equipment, as well as purchases of machinery that are inappropriate for the recipient country. But often aid loses its effectiveness because of poor economic policies in the recipient country. In highly distorted, overregulated, slow-growing economies, most investments have low payoffs, including aid-financed investments. Recent studies by the World Bank indicate that aid is effective in supporting investment, growth, and poverty reduction in countries with good economic policies and relatively strong institutions but has little effect in countries with a poor environment.[29]

28. See, for example, Richard Reichel, "Development Aid, Saving and Growth in the 1980s: A Cross-Section Analysis," *Saving and Development,* 19, no. 3 (1995); and Mark McGillivray and Akhter Ahmed, "Aid, Saving and Investment Reexplored: The Cases of Bangladesh, India, Nepal, Pakistan, and Sri Lanka," *Asian Economic Review,* 36, no. 3 (December 1994).

29. Craig Burnside and David Dollar, "Aid, Policies, and Growth," policy research working paper No. 1777, World Bank, June 1997; David Dollar and William Easterly, "The Search for the Key: Aid, Investment, and Policies in Africa," World Bank, 1998; and Paul Collier and David Dollar, "Aid Allocation and Poverty Reduction," World Bank, 1998.

FISCAL POLICY

The next two chapters focus on two sets of government policy instruments that operate across all sectors of an economy: fiscal policy and financial policy. Both sets of instruments can play critical roles, for good and ill, in the mobilization of domestic saving. Moreover, both types of policies have far-reaching effects on income distribution, employment, efficiency, and economic stability. In this chapter, we focus on **fiscal policy,** which encompasses all measures pertaining to the level and structure of government expenditures and revenues. **Financial policy,** the subject of Chapter 13, includes monetary policy and a wide variety of policy measures affecting the growth and allocation of financial assets in an economy.

As the terms are used in this book, **government revenues** consist of all tax and nontax revenues flowing to the government treasury, including surpluses of public enterprises owned by governments and domestic borrowing by the treasury. **Government expenditures** are all outlays from the government budget, including those for current expenditures, such as civil service salaries, maintenance, military costs, interest payments, and subsidies to cover losses by public enterprise. The other major category on the expenditure side is capital expenditures, sometimes also referred to as *development expenditures,* such as outlays for construction of irrigation canals, roads, and schools and for the purchase of nonmilitary equipment owned by government.

Fiscal policy operates through both the tax and expenditure sides of the government budget. The locus of decision making on fiscal policy in developing countries typically is split between two agencies: the Ministry of Finance (the Treasury Department) and the Ministry (or Board) of Planning. In most countries the Ministry of Finance is assigned primary responsibility for the design and implementation of tax policy and decisions concerning current government consumption expenditures. The Ministry of Planning sometimes holds sway on decisions concerning government capital expenditures. Some economists and policy makers reserve the term *fiscal policy* for that which is done by the Ministry of Finance and the term *development policy* for that which is under the ultimate control of the Ministry of Planning. But the distinction between public capital and consumption spending essentially is an arbitrary one, in both theory and practice.

The Government Budget: General Considerations

Much of economic policy operates through the expenditure and tax sides of the government budget. To be sure, many government activities have an importance out of proportion to their relative significance in the overall government budget. This is particularly true for the conduct of financial policy; government regulation of competition, trade, and investment; and operations of public enterprises (except in countries where public enterprises receive heavy subsidies from the government budget). In any case, in this chapter, the term *public sector* refers only to that part of government operations reflected in the expenditure side of the budget.

All societies, from those organized under laissez-faire principles to those organized under socialism, require a public sector, simply because, even under the best conditions, the market mechanism cannot perform all economic functions desired by households. Because of *public goods* and other types of *market failures* discussed at the beginning of Chapter 5, the market alone cannot satisfy all consumer wants, even when societies have a strong preference for decentralized decision making. For private goods, such as rice, saris, or TV sets, the signals provided by unfettered competitive market mechanisms guide producers to satisfy consumer demand efficiently. For pure public goods, the market fails entirely. There are few examples of pure public goods; national defense and lighthouses generally are cited as illustrations. The term *public good* refers to a good or service that exhibits two traits: nonrival consumption and nonexcludability.

In *nonrival consumption,* one person's use of a good does not reduce the benefits available to others. That being the case, no one has any incentive to offer to pay for the good: If it is available to one, it is available to all. *Nonexcludability* means that it is either impossible or prohibitively expensive to exclude anyone from the benefits once the good is available. In either case, the private market cannot provide the good: Market failure is total. For most public goods the characteristics of nonrival consumption and nonexcludability are present but less pronounced and the market can function only in an inefficient way. Examples include vaccination against contagious diseases, primary education, police protection, and mosquito abatement. Therefore, it is evident that the appropriate role of the public sector, to a significant degree, is a technical issue. Extension of the public sector beyond that required to provide public goods and to correct for other market failures is an ideological issue, to be settled through a political process. Most countries, industrial and developing, have extended the size of the public sector well beyond that required for technical reasons, to include income redistribution, provision of pension schemes, and ownership and operation of airlines, shipping, utilities, manufacturing enterprises, and banks. Government investment, particularly in developing countries, also tends to account for a large share, often as much as half, of all capital formation.

Government Expenditures

In the late 1800s, German political theorist Adolph Wagner propounded his famous *law of expanding state activity*. The thrust of Wagner's law was that the relative size of the public sector in the economy has an inherent tendency to grow as per capita income increases. Although few fiscal economists accept Wagner's law without several qualifications, poor countries do have smaller public sectors than rich ones, when size of the public sector is measured as the ratio of government expenditure to GDP. As may be noted from Table 12–1, the overall proportion rises with per capita income, from about 17 percent in the lowest-income countries (including India) to 23 percent in the middle-income countries and 32 percent in the high-income economies.

TABLE 12–1	CENTRAL GOVERNMENT EXPENDITURES AS SHARE OF GNP, 1992				
SPENDING CATEGORY	LOW-INCOME COUNTRIES	EXCLUDING INDIA	LOWER-MIDDLE-INCOME COUNTRIES	UPPER-MIDDLE-INCOME COUNTRIES	HIGH-INCOME COUNTRIES
MILITARY SPENDING	3	2	3	2	5
EDUCATION	1	4	2	3	2
HEALTH	0	1	1	1	4
HOUSING, SOCIAL SECURITY, WELFARE	1	1	1	5	11
ECONOMIC SERVICES	3	8	5	4	2
OTHER	10	29	10	28	28
TOTAL SPENDING	17	24	22	23	32

Source: World Bank, *World Development Report 1994* (Washington, DC: World Bank, 1994), Table 10, pp. 180–81.

Three classes of expenditure account for most of the difference between high-income and developing countries' outlays as a share of GNP. Military expenditures in the industrial countries, at 5 percent, are about double the share of national product in the developing countries. Expenditures on health are 1 percent or less in developing countries but 4 percent of GNP in the high-income countries. But social welfare programs account for most of the difference: These are 11 percent of GNP in the high-income countries, about half that in upper-middle-income countries, and only 1 percent in other developing countries as a group. However, the costs of economic services, which include direct government investments and subsidies to state-owned enterprises, are higher in the poorer market economies than in the richer ones.

Hundreds of books and articles have been written on the reasons for differences in government expenditure across countries and through time. The results of the studies often conflict. Although associated with income growth, these differences do not seem to be related in any systematic way to population growth, but may be strongly influenced by other demographic factors, such as urbanization.

CURRENT AND RECURRENT EXPENDITURES

The current expenditure side of the budget includes expenditures that must be made annually as long as the government is involved in any particular activity. These expenditures also often are referred to as *recurrent expenditures,* because they recur year after year, in contrast with capital expenditures, which come to an end when a bridge or highway is completed and turned over to the operating authorities. Table 12–2 breaks down recurrent expenditure into five categories: (1) outlays for wages and salaries of civil servants, teachers, and the military; (2) outlays on nondurable goods and services, including equipment and materials for use by public sector employees, maintenance, and all spending on military equipment; (3) interest payments on the government debt; (4) subsidies and other transfers to individuals; and (5) transfers to subnational governments. The table shows a wide variance in the proportions of total expenditure devoted to each category. Some of this is related to the stage of development: Richer countries have larger social welfare programs that cause subsidies and other transfers to be a much higher share of expenditures than in most lower-income countries. Some variations have to do with government structures: In India, Indonesia, Peru, Brazil, and Korea, the central government transfers 13 percent or more of its expenditures to subnational governments. Huge differences in interest payments on public debt reflect differing policy choices and alternative ways to manage—or mismanage—economies. And, in some cases, ac-

TABLE 12−2   COMPOSITION OF GOVERNMENT RECURRENT EXPENDITURE BY TYPE (SHARE OF TOTAL EXPENDITURE, %)

COUNTRY	YEAR	RECURRENT SHARE OF TOTAL EXPENDITURE[a]	WAGES AND SALARIES	OTHER PURCHASES OF GOODS AND SERVICES	INTEREST PAYMENTS ON PUBLIC DEBT	SUBSIDIES AND OTHER TRANSFERS[b]	TRANSFERS TO SUBNATIONAL GOVERNMENTS
LOW-INCOME COUNTRIES							
ETHIOPIA	1995	76	28	25	10	13	N.A.
INDIA	1997	76	11	10	23	32	19
KENYA	1996	88	28	17	26	17	N.A.
GHANA	1993	85	28	17	16	23	0
LOWER-MIDDLE-INCOME COUNTRIES							
BOLIVIA	1997	67	64	2	1	0	1
CAMEROON	1995	89	37	16	23	13	N.A.
THE PHILIPPINES	1996	87	30	21	19	17	N.A.
SRI LANKA	1997	87	21	18	26	22	1
INDONESIA	1993	52	18	8	12	1	0
PERU	1997	85	18	20	10	36	19
EGYPT, ARAB REPUBLIC	1995	75	17	14	20	24	N.A.
UPPER-MIDDLE-INCOME COUNTRIES							
BRAZIL	1994	92	7	5	40	40	11
HUNGARY	1997	96	8	10	24	58	16
COLOMBIA	1989	81	16	9	10	46	0
ARGENTINA	1996	92	16	5	11	60	6
MEXICO	1996	86	17	9	19	43	N.A.
MALAYSIA	1997	51	15	17	N.A.	3	6
KOREA, REPUBLIC	1997	63	10	11	2	39	43
HIGH-INCOME COUNTRIES							
UNITED KINGDOM	1995	95	9	21	9	56	19
GERMANY	1997	32	32	20	3	26	4
UNITED STATES	1997	97	8	14	15	60	11

[a]Subsequent columns are components of this column. Total expenditure is net of repayments of loans to government, so it is possible for recurrent expenditure to exceed 100 percent of the total.
[b]Excluding transfers to subnational governments.
Source: IMF, *Government Finance Statistics Yearbook 1999* (Washington, DC: International Monetary Fund, 1999), country tables.

counting practices may be responsible for differences in the way expenditures are reported.

A pervasive belief is that recurrent expenditures in some sense are less important and should have a lower priority than public investment or capital expenditures. Recurrent costs of public investment programs by convention are labeled *government consumption,* implying that increases for such purposes do not increase productive capacity. But governments often focus so much on capital expenditures that they make inadequate provision for the recurrent operational and maintenance costs of previous investments. In many parts of the developing world, public sector capital is underutilized and allowed to decay because of inadequate provision for the recurrent expenditure requirements of the project.

As indicated already, the division between recurrent and capital expenditures also can be somewhat arbitrary. Recurrent outlays on education and health, for example, are investments in human capital that can have major long-term benefits to economic development as discussed in Chapters 9 and 10.

WAGES AND SALARIES

Wages and salaries constitute a large fraction of recurrent outlays of governments, especially in the low- and lower-middle-income countries: In Table 12–2, 6 of the 11 countries in this category devote more than a quarter of their current expenditures to wages and salaries.

The stereotypical image of public sector bureaucracies in developing countries is one of bloated payrolls and inefficient, corrupt, even indolent behavior. The evidence for this view essentially is anecdotal. Reliable international comparisons of civil service performance are almost nonexistent. It is easy to accumulate anecdotes involving bureaucratic snafus, stupidities, corruption, and shortsightedness in both developing and developed societies. No firm judgment can be made on the extent of overstaffing of public agencies or overremuneration of officials or bureaucratic extravagance in developing countries relative to industrial countries: Civil service payrolls in Massachusetts and New Jersey may be as bloated as in many developing countries. And, despite examples of gross venality and blatant use of political patronage in public sector hiring in segments of the civil service systems of some developing countries (and many U.S. cities), there also are examples of first-rate professionalism and codes of conduct that may rival those found in industrial countries, as in the Indian and Malaysian civil service systems.

In some countries, the salary bill for civil servants could be compressed sufficiently to augment government savings. But, in others, like Bolivia, Peru, and Kenya, civil service salaries remain so low relative to those available in the private sector that it has been difficult to attract and hold the type of qualified public-sector managers, secretaries, and technicians essential for efficient government operation.

About the only safe generalization that can be made about civil service systems in developing countries is that they appear no more, or less, responsive to the socioeconomic changes that accompany development than any other group in society. In the 1950s, it was almost impossible to discuss Latin American development without hearing repeated mention of the "antidevelopmental" effects of the famous *mordida* (bite) then commonly demanded by civil servants for doing what they should—or should not— be doing. It was commonly believed then that such behavior was the result of both low civil service salaries and unalterable cultural habits. Low civil service salaries contribute to the problem, but culture probably has relatively little explanatory power. When low salaries are combined with high customs duties, government licensing of all kinds of economic activity, and other such discretionary authority in the hands of government officials, the temptation on the part of many of those officials to ask for side payments can become irresistible. One powerful motive behind the decision of many countries to move toward greater reliance on unfettered market forces is that this eliminated many of the opportunities for inappropriate side payments. That made it easier for the government to focus on the more limited number of cases of inappropriate official behavior that remained. Singapore and Hong Kong are good examples of how government actions of this sort have reduced rent seeking to levels well below those found in much of the rest of the world, including in the richest nations.

PURCHASES OF GOODS AND SERVICES

Governments need supplies, such as paper, computers, and fuel, to perform their functions; and they also purchase services, such as construction, transportation, and janitorial work, from private firms. If a road maintenance crew consists of employees of the Ministry of Works, their salaries come under the heading *wages and salaries* and their supplies are categorized as *other purchases* in Table 12–2. But, if the ministry hires a private contractor instead, all the expenditure falls under *other purchases*. Two important items in this category are *maintenance and repair* and nonwage *military spending*.

If there is waste in government procurement in some areas, there are other areas where, for lack of funds, governments have been too miserly in appropriating funds. As already suggested, this is particularly true with regard to **maintenance costs** for the upkeep of the public-sector capital stock and many vital operating expenses. The phenomenon is aptly characterized by Peter Heller:

> In Colombia, new tarmac roads have suffered rapid and premature deterioration for lack of maintenance. Throughout West Africa, many new schools have opened without qualified teachers, educational materials, or equipment. Agricultural projects are often starved for extension workers, fertilizer, or seeds. In the Sahel, pastoral wells constructed for livestock projects have fallen into disrepair. In Bolivia, doctors are often stranded at rural health centers for lack of gasoline for their vehicles.[1]

1. Peter Heller, "Underfinancing of Recurrent Development Costs," *Finance and Development,* 16, no. 1 (March 1979), 38–41.

Underfinancing of recurrent costs is pervasive across countries, including the United States, where items such as bridge maintenance have been long postponed in many states. In developing countries, however, this pattern is exacerbated by the policies of aid donors, who strongly support capital projects but as a matter of policy have been reluctant to support the recurrent costs of these projects. As a result, painfully accumulated public-sector capital stock tends to deteriorate rapidly until eventually it is beyond maintenance and requires new construction. Few countries are in a position to expand public savings by further compressing this category of recurrent expenditures.

The share of **military spending** in recurrent expenditures shows no trend as incomes rise (Table 12–3), but on average the low- and middle-income countries spend less of their national incomes (3 percent or less) on the military than upper-income countries (4 percent). Israel and Jordan spend substantially more of their national income on defense than any other countries in Table 12–3, a consequence of their position in the war-

TABLE 12–3 MILITARY EXPENDITURE AS SHARE OF RECURRENT EXPENDITURE AND GNP (PERCENT)

COUNTRY	SHARE OF CENTRAL GOVERNMENT EXPENDITURE	SHARE OF GNP	COUNTRY	SHARE OF RECURRENT EXPENDITURE	SHARE OF GNP
MADAGASCAR	5.0	0.9	TURKEY	17.6	4.0
MALAWI	3.5	1.6	BRAZIL	3.9	1.7
NEPAL	5.8	0.9	IRAN, ISLAMIC REPUBLIC	13.6	2.6
INDIA	12.7	2.4	PANAMA	5.3	1.4
KENYA	6.2	2.3	HUNGARY	4.6	1.5
			THAILAND	19.7	2.5
			URUGUAY	7.3	2.4
			MEXICO	5.1	1.0
			MALAYSIA	12.4	3.0
PAKISTAN	25.3	6.1	CHILE	11.4	3.8
BOLIVIA	9.5	2.3	KOREA, REPUBLIC	13.6	3.4
THE PHILIPPINES	8.5	1.5			
SRI LANKA	15.7	4.6			
INDONESIA	8.9	1.8			
MOROCCO	13.8	4.3	ISRAEL	21.1	9.6
JORDAN	21.7	7.7	SINGAPORE	24.0	4.7
ECUADOR	18.3	3.7	UNITED KINGDOM	7.2	3.0
			AUSTRALIA	8.8	2.5
			THE NETHERLANDS	4.4	2.1
			DENMARK	4.1	1.8
			FRANCE	6.6	3.1
			UNITED STATES	17.4	3.8

Source: World Bank, *World Development Indicators 1998* (Washington, DC: The World Bank, 1998), pp. 278–80. The data are for the year 1995.

torn Middle East. Otherwise, the high spenders are Pakistan, Singapore, and the United States, all at 5–6 percent of GNP.

Military spending is directed toward noneconomic goals, such as defense against external threats and internal instability. What is known about the impact of military spending on economic growth? Clearly, all countries could expand public savings significantly by reducing military spending. Beyond that, the topic is controversial. Nevertheless, research suggests that high military spending has many more negative effects on growth than positive ones, including the large contributions made by military spending to debt in some countries, the diversion of scarce resources from more productive civilian uses, and the effects of highly import-intensive military outlays on balance-of-payments deficits.[2]

INTEREST PAYMENTS

Interest on government debt is a major cost for many developing countries, ranging as high as a quarter of expenditures for India, Kenya, the Philippines, and Sri Lanka and about half of all outlays for the debt-ridden governments of Brazil and Mexico (Table 12–2). Chapter 14 discusses the debt crisis caused by overborrowing by developing countries, especially in Latin America and Africa. The Asian financial crisis that began in 1997 also involved excessive borrowing, but unlike the earlier Latin American and African cases, most of the Asian borrowing was by the private sector and the banking system. In the Asian case, therefore, the borrowing did not show up on the expenditure ledgers of the government. In situations where the government is or has been a major borrower, interest on government debt reflects past decisions about deficit finance and external borrowing. Interest outlays are difficult to reduce in the short term, even if budgets are balanced and borrowing ceases. Debt payments can be radically reduced only if a government defaults on its debt obligations, like Bolivia and Peru in the 1980s. Indonesia in the late 1990s did not formally default on its government debt, but it did restructure that debt in agreement with the Paris Club, thus reducing its interest payments.

SUBSIDIES

A variety of subsidies and other transfers account for substantial shares of expenditures in developing and industrial countries. In Table 12–2, the shares range from less than 10 percent in Ethiopia, Kenya, and Indonesia to 40 percent and more in Hungary, Colombia, Argentina, Germany, and

---

2. Anita Bhatia, *Military Expenditure and Economic Growth* (Washington, DC: World Bank, 1987).

the United States. This category includes subsidies to consumers, social welfare payments, and subsidies to loss-making state-owned enterprises.

Consumer subsidies are particularly common for basic foods. Countries such as Colombia, Egypt, India, Indonesia, and Sri Lanka have provided large subsidies on purchases of staple foods such as rice or wheat flour. A typical mechanism is to distribute price-controlled foods through state-owned entities then absorb losses in food distribution through budgetary transfers to these enterprises (see Chapter 15). When the world price of oil rose during the 1970s, most oil-producing countries (and a few oil importers) generously subsidized the domestic use of refined products; a few, such as Venezuela, still do. Budgetary subsidies also have been common for rural electrification (Malaysia and the Philippines), contraceptive devices (Indonesia), fertilizer (Indonesia and Sri Lanka), bank interest payments on savings deposits (Indonesia), and urban bus services (Colombia, Indonesia, and others).

As incomes rise, countries typically undertake social welfare programs that transfer funds to citizens for medical care and retirement. The high share of subsidies and other transfers for the industrial countries in Table 12–2 reflects programs such as Medicare, Medicaid, and Social Security in the United States. The transition economies took on heavy obligations of this sort under their communist regimes (note Hungary's 55 percent share in Table 12–2) and now find these obligations especially burdensome. Developing countries, especially middle-income economies, also are moving toward medical and pension plans that may swell their outlays on transfers in the future. Some of these will fund themselves through contributions from those who will benefit, as is true for some of the programs in the rich countries. But experience suggests that contributions will fall short of benefits and governments will bear part of the burden.

In virtually all developing countries employing budgetary subsidies, the stated purpose has been income redistribution. For foods, especially grains, the argument appears plausible, even if the ultimate effect is not always what was intended. Heavy subsidies on fertilizer use in Indonesia had a high payoff in greater rice production and rural income. The role of many other subsidies in securing goals of income redistribution is less clear, however, as we shall see. Whatever the ultimate impact of budget subsidies on income distribution, clearly, in many countries, substantial sums are involved and efforts to remove or reduce them meet with strong resistance virtually everywhere. Riots have occurred following the reduction of food subsidies in Sri Lanka, Egypt, Turkey, Zambia, and other countries; and social disturbances followed the reduction of gasoline subsidies in Indonesia, Colombia, and Thailand, when these were coupled with increases in urban bus fares. It is clear why governments often view proposals to reduce subsidies with even more reservation than proposals for tax increases. Yet, by the late 1980s and 1990s, the need to stabilize economies by reducing budget deficits had become so acute that many countries were forced to shrink their subsidies.

STATE-OWNED ENTERPRISES

A significant portion of governmental outlays for subsidies and other transfers (Table 12–2) has been devoted to covering large deficits in state-owned enterprises (SOEs). Four decades ago, SOEs were not numerous in developing countries and, with notable exceptions such as Turkey and Mexico, typically were confined to a few sectors of their economies. Commonly, SOEs were limited to the so-called natural monopolies (decreasing-cost public utilities); monopoly production of sumptuary products such as liquor, beer, and tobacco; and so-called basic necessities such as salt and matches.[3]

With independence after World War II, there was a rapid expansion in the number and relative importance of state enterprises in developing economies. This was particularly so in Africa, where more than half the SOEs were established between 1967 and 1980; in Tanzania alone, the number of state enterprises increased tenfold from 1965 through 1985.[4] By 1980, SOEs were common, and often dominant, in manufacturing, construction, banking services, natural resource industries, and agriculture. Although SOEs typically were small-scale undertakings in most developing countries prior to 1950, many now are among the largest firms in their countries, and some are among the largest enterprises in their fields anywhere the world.

Deficits in the state enterprises averaged 4 percent of the GDP across all developing countries in the mid-1970s. The problem worsened in the early 1980s, particularly in such countries as Brazil, Costa Rica, the Dominican Republic, Ecuador, Egypt, the Philippines, Turkey, and Venezuela, where SOE deficits reached between 3 and 12 percent of the GDP. In all these countries, the rest of the public sector would have generated a fiscal surplus, excluding the net transfers to the state enterprises.[5] By the late 1980s and throughout the 1990s, the drain of SOE subsidies on government budgets has led to efforts by many developing countries to eliminate these subsidies by privatizing their SOEs. International aid agencies

---

3. For a good discussion of some of the reasons for the development of large public enterprise sectors in developing nations, see R. P. Short, "The Rule of Public Enterprises: An International Statistical Comparison," IMF dept. memo 83/34, 1983.

4. *World Development Report 1988.* New York: Oxford University Press for the World Bank, 1988.

5. *World Development Report 1988,* p. 171.

frequently have made SOE privatization a condition for further assistance. Privatization, however, has been a slow process, because it has been actively resisted by SOE managers and workers, not to mention politicians that use SOE employment as a patronage machine for their supporters. In countries where a large part of the private sector is controlled by minorities, as is the case with the Chinese minority in Southeast Asia or the South Asian minority in East Africa, the majority population often fears that privatization is simply a way of turning even more of modern business over to the minority.

INTERGOVERNMENTAL TRANSFERS

Transfers from central to subnational governments conventionally are treated as recurrent expenditures, even though subnational governments (provinces, departments, counties, municipalities) may use the proceeds for capital formation, such as construction of schools and hospitals. However, some countries, such as Indonesia, classify some transfers as capital spending and others as consumption, so international comparisons are difficult. Table 12–2 shows that transfers to subnational governments (including revenue sharing) constitute a sizable proportion of recurrent spending in a few countries (India, Indonesia, Brazil, Korea) and a very small share in most others. In a few cases, subnational governments with small transfers have access to rich sources of revenue. This is true for Bolivia, where oil-producing provinces receive large oil royalties, and for Malaysia, where the state governments of Sabah and Sarawak earned substantial tax revenues from the export of tropical timber. In most unitary states, such as Chile, government affairs at virtually all levels are run from the capital, and subnational units of governments have few responsibilities to go with their limited sources of local revenue.

Elsewhere, including many federal countries, transfer of funds from the central government to subnational units is essential because the center has monopolized the most productive sources of tax revenue. In most cases, national governments impose income taxes because subnational governments lack the resources and skill required to administer such a complex tax and could not do so effectively anyway because the income tax base easily can migrate within a country. Similarly, the major source of tax revenue for some developing countries—import duties—must remain a central government resource, since most countries have only a few serviceable ports.

We have just seen that there are few easy ways to reduce government recurrent expenditure to achieve higher public savings. The scope for doing so often is greatest in the areas of military spending and subsidies to cover deficits of state-owned enterprises. Together, these two categories of recurrent spending can account for 7–10 percent of GDP.

Project Appraisal and the Capital Account

As indicated previously, the government's capital or development expenditures account for as much as half of all investment in many developing countries. No attempt will be made here to list all of the different kinds of capital expenditures that can be undertaken through the government budget. Suffice it to say that many of the investment expenditures described in many of the chapters in this book can be undertaken by the private sector, government, or both. Particularly in the early stages of development, government often takes responsibility for large-scale capital projects because it believes that the private sector, particularly the domestic private sector, lacks access to sufficient financing to carry out these projects.

A central issue for fiscal stability and the overall rate of economic growth is how to ensure that these government, and private, investments are carried out in the most efficient manner possible. One of the most commonly used tools for this purpose is **cost-benefit analysis,** or **project appraisal.** This technique has its genesis in the kind of analysis done by private firms on their alternative investment prospects, but as we shall see, the technique is equally or more useful in analyzing government development projects.

When a private firm lays out its investment plans (called *capital budgets*), it tries to select investments that will yield the highest profit for a given amount of finance. The firm's calculation involves three steps, as explained in the next section.

PRESENT VALUE

The first step in the firm's investment decision is to forecast the **net cash flow** of an investment. Net cash flow measures the difference between the cash revenues from the sale of the product and the cash outlays on investment, material inputs, salaries and wages, purchased services, and so forth. Costs that do not deplete the cash resources of the firm, of which depreciation is the most prominent example, are not counted.

The second element involves the observation that cash received in the future is less valuable than cash received immediately, because in the interim the firm could earn interest (or profits) on these funds by investing them in bonds or savings accounts (or in additional, revenue-earning production facilities). For example, a firm or individual, asked to choose between $1,000 today or $1,000 next year, would take the money now and place it in a savings account earning, say, 8 percent a year. Then, after one year, the interest payment would boost the savings account balance to $1,080. So the prospect of $1,000 a year from now should be evaluated as equivalent to only $1,000/1.08 = $926. This process, reducing the value of future flows because funds earn interest over time, is called **discounting.** Because interest also is earned on previous interest, discounting must allow for **compound interest.** In the second year another 8 percent would be earned on the balance of $1,080, and increase it to $1,166. The payment of $1,000 two years from now would then be discounted to yield a **present value** of only $1,000/1.166 = $858. A general expression for the present value, P, is

$$P = F/(1 + i)^n \qquad [12\text{--}1]$$

where F = the value to be realized in the future ($1,000, in our example), i = the interest rate (8 percent), and n = the number of years. As the interest rate or the delay in payment increases, the present value decreases.

An investment project will result in a series of net cash flows over time: They flow out in the early years as investments are made; then they become positive, perhaps gradually, as the new facilities begin to generate revenue in excess of recurrent costs. Such a **time profile** of net cash flow is depicted in Figure 12–1; it is the most common of several possible profiles. To summarize the value of this net cash flow in a single number, each year's net cash flow is multiplied by the respective dis-

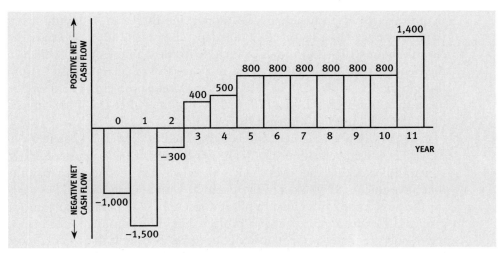

FIGURE 12–1 TIME PROFILE FOR INVESTMENT: NET CASH FLOW. The cash flow of a project can be represented by a bar diagram. Cash outflows are shown by bars below the horizontal axis, inflows by bars above the axis. Years 0 and 1 show investment in construction and equipment, and hence negative cash flows; year 2 is the start-up period; years 3 and 4 show gradually increasing output and cash inflows; years 5 through 10 show steady output and cash inflows; and the project is assumed to end in year 11, when the salvage value of equipment swells the cash inflow.

count factor and the resulting present values are added to give the **net present value** (NPV):

$$\text{NPV} = \sum_{t=0}^{n} (B_t - C_t)/(1 + i)^t \qquad\qquad [12\text{--}2]$$

where B_t and C_t = the benefits (revenue) and costs, including investment, in each year t; i = the discount rate; and n = the life of the project. For a firm, the correct discount rate is the average cost at which additional funds may be obtained from all sources, the firm's cost of capital.

If the net present value of a project, discounted at the firm's average cost of capital, happens to equal 0, this implies that the project will yield a net cash flow just large enough to repay the principal of all funds invested in the project and pay the interest and dividends required by lenders and shareholders. In that case, when NPV = 0, the discount rate has a special name, the **internal rate of return** (IRR). If the net present value is positive, then the project can cover all its financial costs with some profit left over for the firm. If negative, the project cannot cover its financial costs and should not be undertaken. Clearly the higher is the net present value, the better the project.

Another measure of project desirability is the **benefit-cost ratio** (BCR):

$$\text{BCR} = \sum_{t=0}^{n} B_t(1 + i)^{2t} / \sum_{t=0}^{n} C_t(1 + i)^{2t} \qquad\qquad [12\text{--}3]$$

When NPV = 0, BCR = 1, so desirable projects have an NPV greater than 0 or a BCR greater than 1. Although the BCR can be useful, it has the disadvantage that its precise value depends sometimes on arbitrary decisions about which cash flows to include in the numerator and which in the denominator. Neither the NPV nor the IRR calculation suffers from this ambiguity. However, the IRR has a different problem: There will be more than one IRR for a cash flow if at any time after the initial investment the cash flow again turns negative.

The cash flow of Figure 12–1 is discounted at a rate of 12 percent in Table 12–4, using equation 12–2. The net present value is a positive $518, which indicates that the investment project will earn enough to repay the total investment ($2,500 over years 0 and 1) with a surplus of $518.

We now come to the final step in project appraisal, comparison among projects. We already know that a project should be considered for investment only if its net present value is positive. But how does one choose among many projects, all with positive NPVs? The answer is to select the set of projects that will yield the highest total net present value for the entire investment budget. This assumes that the firm has a set of alternative projects to consider at any one time and an investment budget that can accommodate several but not all of these.

TABLE 12–4	NET PRESENT VALUE		
YEAR	CASH FLOW[a] FROM FIGURE 12–1 (DOLLARS)	DISCOUNT FACTOR[b] AT 12%	PRESENT VALUE[c] (DOLLARS)
0	−1,000	1.000	−1,000
1	−1,500	0.893	−1,340
2	−300	0.797	−239
3	400	0.712	285
4	500	0.636	318
5	800	0.567	454
6	800	0.507	406
7	800	0.452	362
8	800	0.404	323
9	800	0.361	289
10	800	0.322	258
11	1,400	0.287	402
NET PRESENT VALUE[d]			+518

[a]Cash flow = $(B_t - C_t)$ from equation 12–3.
[b]Discount factor = $1/(1 + i)^t$ from equation 12–2. In this example, $i = 12$ percent; t takes the value of each year, 0 to 11. Discount factors for a range of discount rates are readily available in discount tables. See, for example, the appendix table in Michael Roemer and Joseph J. Stern, *The Appraisal of Development Projects* (New York: Praeger, 1975).
[c]Present value = cash flow × discount factor.
[d]Net present value = algebraic sum of the present values.

OPPORTUNITY COSTS

A country or government wishing to derive the greatest possible future income (or consumption) from its development budget faces the same problem as the investing firm. The only difference is that the country or government is interested in resource flows and their **opportunity costs,** rather than cash flows. When any project in the public or private sector uses goods and services, it denies these to other possible projects. For example, investment in a dam requires utilization of savings that otherwise could be invested in a rural road or a textile factory. Cotton used in that factory otherwise could have been exported to earn foreign exchange, or the labor used to build the road might have otherwise been used to build the dam or to grow cotton. For society, the cost of undertaking a project is the value of the resources—goods and services—used to invest in and operate the new facilities. The value of these resources is measured in terms of the net benefits they would have provided if used in some alternative project, the opportunity cost.

A simple illustration should capture this point. A textile factory is built and hires labor away from the rural areas. For the textile firm, the cost of labor is the wages paid. For society, however, the cost is the reduction in the value of production, net of costs, in the rural areas. If ten laborers migrate to take jobs in the new factory, their opportunity cost would be the reduction in agricultural output due to their leaving the farm, net of the nonlabor recurrent costs of producing that output. This reduction in net output is the value of the marginal product of price theory and the opportunity cost of labor in this situation.[6] Similarly, if the investment in the textile mill means that savings will be drawn away from other projects that on average would have earned a return of 12 percent, then the opportunity cost of capital is 12 percent, and this should be used as the discount rate in evaluating the textile mill. Because project appraisals are most conveniently done at **constant prices,** netting out inflation, the discount rate is a **real rate of interest,** net of inflation. If, in this example, inflation were 10 percent a year, the corresponding nominal interest rate, the rate observed in the market, would be 23 percent.[7]

Foreign exchange plays a special role in cost-benefit analysis. Most developing countries face a shortage of foreign exchange, in the sense that export revenues and foreign investment are inadequate to finance the imports needed to achieve growth and other development targets. When a project requires imports, such as capital equipment or raw materials, it reduces the foreign exchange available to other projects. If it yields additional foreign exchange, by exporting its output or by substituting domestic production for imports, it benefits other projects by providing more foreign purchasing power. Therefore, the opportunity cost or benefit of any good that could be imported or exported should be measured as the net amount of foreign exchange the good represents. For example, the cotton used in the textile mill otherwise might have been exported; if so, its opportunity cost would be the foreign currency it would have earned as an export. If the cloth produced by the mill would have been imported in the absence of the project, its opportunity cost (a benefit in this case) would be the foreign exchange that otherwise would have been spent on cloth imports.

---

6. The value of the marginal product of a factor of production can be calculated as the price of a commodity multiplied by the additional physical output that results when one unit of the factor is added to the production process with all other factors held constant.

7. The formula relating these is $1 + i = (1 + r)(1 + p)$, where i = the nominal rate of interest, r = the real rate, and p = the rate of inflation. Normally, we know the nominal rate and need to calculate the real rate:

$$r = \frac{1 + i}{1 + p} - 1 = \frac{i - p}{1 + p}$$

For small values of p, r can be approximated by $r = i - p$.

SHADOW PRICES

The opportunity costs of goods and services are estimated for the economy as a whole and called **shadow prices** or **social opportunity costs.** The first approximation of a shadow price—for land, labor, capital, and foreign exchange—is the price paid by private participants in the market. Interference in the market distorts market prices from their social opportunity cost: taxes and subsidies of all kinds, monopoly power, minimum wages, interest rate controls, tariffs and import quotas, price controls, and so forth. Prices observed in the market need to be adjusted for these effects before a good approximation of shadow prices can be found. A simple example is the wage of textile workers. If the government imposes minimum-wage regulations, the factory probably will have to pay a wage above the opportunity costs of rural migrants and urban workers who are outside the formal, protected urban wage sector.

Estimation of shadow prices is a research task that requires intimate knowledge of the workings of an economy, both its macroeconomic relationships and the microeconomic behavior of its factor markets. It is a task to be undertaken by a government planning agency, which then instructs other planning units—ministries, public enterprises, regional and local governments—in the application of these economywide shadow prices to the appraisal of development projects. Not only does shadow price estimation help improve the selection of development projects, the estimation of these opportunity costs teaches the researchers a great deal about the working of the economy, an important by-product for a government agency.

Despite much controversy among economists on the precise estimation of shadow prices, some general results have emerged for a wide range of developing countries. First, and most significant, the shadow foreign exchange rate tends to be higher than the official rate in terms of local currency per dollar, perhaps 10–50 percent higher. This reflects the widespread use of import duties and quotas, as well as the reluctance of many countries to devalue their exchange rate despite the inflation of domestic prices.[8] As a consequence, any export project that earns more foreign exchange than it uses or any import-substituting project that saves more than it uses gets a boost from the shadow exchange rate. In terms of the net cash flow profile of Figure 12–1, application of the shadow rate to such projects will raise the positive net cash flows of years 3–11 proportionately more than it raises the negative flows of years 0–2, giving the project a higher net present value at the same discount rate.

8. When countries undertake market reforms, as described in Chapter 5, these distortions are reduced and the official exchange rate becomes a closer approximation of the shadow rate.

Although the salaries and wages of skilled employees probably require no adjustment from market to shadow prices, frequently the opportunity cost of unskilled workers is lower than the wage in formal, urban labor markets. Therefore, any project using unskilled labor, especially if it is located in a rural area, gets a boost because the shadow wage reduces costs without changing benefits.

The social discount rate can represent either the opportunity cost of investment and saving in the private sector or the rate at which policy makers wish to discount future benefits. The first method yields discount rates of 10–15 percent for developing countries. The second approach usually employs a lower discount rate but entails a shadow price of investment that raises the effective cost of capital. In either case, discounting at social rates treats capital as a very scarce factor and so discourages any project with high initial investment costs, long gestation periods, and low net cash flows in the productive years. This system favors projects that generate their net benefits early, because these can be reinvested in other productive projects for continued growth, and projects that use abundant resources, especially labor, instead of scarce ones, like capital.

PROJECT APPRAISAL AND NATIONAL GOALS

Project appraisal using social opportunity costs is a simple and powerful device to further certain national goals. Its underlying tenet is that saving should be allocated to investments yielding the greatest future income or consumption. This automatically accommodates the goal of efficient resource use to promote maximum growth. It further implies that scarce resources, like foreign exchange, are more highly valued than the market would indicate. The subsidiary goals of improving foreign exchange earnings or reducing dependence on imports also are built in, because any project that efficiently increases exports or reduces imports is given a correspondingly higher net present value by the shadow exchange rate. Once the government planners establish a system of appraisal with shadow prices, every agency that designs, evaluates, and proposes investment projects automatically incorporates these national goals in its work and hence in the government's capital budget.

An illustration of the power of shadow pricing is contained in Table 12–5, which depicts two projects with identical cash flows. However, one project (the textile mill) earns more foreign exchange than the other (a telecommunications system), net of foreign exchange expenditure and uses more labor. Because the shadow wage rate is below the market rate, the economic net present value of both projects is raised, but the more labor-intensive textile project benefits more (part 2). When the shadow exchange rate is applied, the net present value of the exchange-earning textile mill is

TABLE 12–5	EFFECTS OF SHADOW PRICING ON COST-BENEFIT ANALYSIS		
PROJECT	INVESTMENT (FIRST YEAR)	NET ANNUAL CASH FLOW (NEXT 5 YEARS)	NET PRESENT VALUE (10%)
1. TAKE TWO PROJECTS WITH IDENTICAL CASH FLOWS. PROJECT A EARNS MORE NET FOREIGN EXCHANGE AND USES MORE LABOR THAN PROJECT B:			
A. TEXTILE MILL, OF WHICH	−1,000	+300	+137
NET FOREIGN EXCHANGED EARNED	−500	+400	
WAGES PAID	−350	−100	
B. TELECOMMUNICATIONS SYSTEM, OF WHICH	−1,000	+300	
NET FOREIGN EXCHANGE EARNED	−800	0	
WAGES PAID	−100	−50	+137
2. THE SHADOW WAGE IS 75% OF MARKET WAGE, SO ALL WAGE COSTS ARE REDUCED BY 25%. THIS RESULTS IN THE FOLLOWING NET CASH FLOWS:			
A. TEXTILE MILL	−913	+325	+319
B. TELECOMMUNICATIONS SYSTEM	−975	+313	+212
3. THE SHADOW EXCHANGE RATE IS 20% ABOVE OFFICIAL RATE, SO THE NET FOREIGN EXCHANGE FLOW IS RAISED BY 20%. THIS RESULTS IN THE FOLLOWING NET CASH FLOWS:			
A. TEXTILE MILL	−1,100	+380	+340
B. TELECOMMUNICATION SYSTEM	−1,160	+300	−23

raised considerably, but that of the telecommunications system, which is a net user of foreign exchange, falls and becomes negative (part 3).

Not all national goals can be incorporated conveniently into government project appraisals, however. Two are of particular concern. The use of low shadow wages for unskilled workers will encourage employment creation but only insofar as this is efficient, in the sense that the workers' opportunity cost is below the net benefit they would produce in the project. The government, however, may want to encourage employment beyond this point, because a job is the most significant way that people can participate in development and employed workers may be deemed politically more stable than the unemployed. If projects such as rural public works employ people inefficiently for the sake of employment, then the role of cost-benefit analysis is to estimate the cost of the employment in terms of the greater net benefits that might be earned if investment and labor were allocated to other projects that employ fewer people.

A second class of goals, income redistribution or poverty alleviation, also can be served by project appraisal, because low shadow wages encourage the employment of low-income labor. The impact may be weak, however, because distributional goals still are subordinate to efficient growth in the cost-benefit framework. Situations requiring structural change and large investments to alleviate poverty may not measure up to the high efficiency standard of project analysis in the short run. For this reason some economists have suggested, and some governments have considered, using welfare weights in a project analysis. These would place a higher value on net additional income to certain target groups, such as families in the lower 40 percent of the income distribution. Then projects generating such incomes would have higher NPVs than otherwise and tend to be selected more frequently.

The method potentially is powerful but has its dangers as well. The welfare premiums are arbitrary weights, subject to planners' or politicians' judgment. This, in itself, is not bad, but these weights can so overwhelm economically based shadow prices that project selection comes down to a choice based almost entirely on arbitrary weights. This gives a false sense of precision.

Shadow prices based on existing economic conditions are not value free, either. They imply a welfare weighting scheme that accepts the existing income distribution and the resulting pattern of demand. A compromise is to keep the two goals separate, make measurements of net present values using only the economic variables, then identify separately the redistributional benefits of projects. The two can be compared; this gives government decision makers a trade-off to consider and the opportunity to make clear choices of goal priorities.

We skirt an issue of terminology. When a firm undertakes investment analysis, it can be called **commercial project appraisal,** which uses *market prices.* Traditionally, once *shadow prices* are introduced to reflect the goal of efficient growth and the real scarcities of productive factors, it has been called **social project appraisal.** The implication may be too broad, however, because only economic and not other social goals are incorporated. The World Bank, which undertakes a large fraction of the project analysis done in the world, has shifted to a more accurate terminology. It calls the second form **economic project appraisal.** The term *social appraisal* is reserved for a third stage, in which welfare weights are applied to reflect distributional goals. But readers should be wary, because this distinction has not been accepted universally.

TRANSFORMING MARKET PRICES INTO SHADOW PRICES

If governments undertake projects on the basis of economic appraisals, using shadow prices, an implementation problem arises. A firm, whether public or private, can be financially sound only if it covers its costs and earns a profit at market prices. The shadow prices of planners exist only on paper; no one pays them or receives them in the marketplace. For example, consider a public enterprise producing paper; its investment is encouraged by the government because it employs many workers whose opportunity cost is low. However, the enterprise must pay its workers not the low shadow wage but the higher minimum wage set by the government. If this causes the firm to lose money, it could go bankrupt, in which case the economic benefits to the country would be lost. (A private firm, of course, would never undertake such an investment.) Hence, a government that wants the project implemented would have to do it itself or compensate the enterprise. The most effective compensation would be a direct subsidy to wages, up to the difference between the shadow and minimum wages. Not only would this improve the firm's cash flow, it would also give the firm an incentive to use more labor because its wage costs would be lower. This is precisely what government wants: to employ more workers, an abundant resource with low opportunity costs, and less of other, relatively scarce, factors of production, like capital and foreign exchange.

The same holds for any production factor that is shadow priced: labor, capital, foreign exchange, and specific commodities. Whenever shadow prices push projects that are commercially unprofitable into the realm of the economically profitable, a subsidy may have to be paid to induce a firm to undertake the project or the government must include the project in its own capital budget. And, conversely, if economically undesirable projects nevertheless are profitable at market prices, the government should consider imposing taxes to discourage firms from undertaking such projects.

This leads to a more general point about shadow prices. They represent the opportunity costs that, ideally, functioning markets should be generating to give the right price signals to private producers and consumers. Market prices deviate from shadow prices for two reasons. First, government interventions—controls and taxes—cause artificial price distortions. These *policy failures* can be reduced substantially (although not entirely) through market deregulation and tax reform, as discussed in Chapter 5. Second, inherent *market failures,* such as externalities, natural monopolies, infant industries, and institutional deficiencies, cause price distortions that require counteracting policies by the government. If the government can correct its own policy failures and intervene to counteract market failures, then resources would be used efficiently; that is, according to their relative scarcities; this would promote economic growth.

As this discussion makes clear, governments should follow the dictates of project appraisal in determining which projects belong in the government's development budget and deciding when and when not to subsidize wages or impose additional taxes on capital. Governments, of course, often do not use project appraisal techniques in making these decisions. Projects can be selected because they bring prestige to a government or because they are a reward to supporters of the government. Or projects can be chosen on the basis of their engineering feasibility, whatever their economic rate of return. If the results of these alternative approaches deviate significantly from the dictates of project appraisal, however, the government capital budget (and government-subsidized projects in general) contribute less to economic growth than otherwise would be the case. In extreme cases, as occurred in several oil-rich countries during the 1970s oil price boom, poorly selected projects can turn the government development budget into a net drag on the entire economy. Public saving in this latter situation is largely wasted.

Tax Policy and Public Saving

For much of the postwar period, extending well into the 1970s, the most widely prescribed measures to boost public saving were policies to raise tax collections, especially increased tax rates and new taxes. This tendency was reinforced by policies of aid donors and the advice of foreign experts, who encouraged countries to generate high tax ratios, by making full use of their taxable capacity. **Taxable capacity** was determined in terms of an index composed of per capita income, mineral and oil exports, and the share of foreign trade in the GDP. High values for these variables suggested higher taxable capacity, either because of a higher margin of income over subsistence (high per capita income) or because of the accessibility of the tax base in oil- and mineral-exporting economies and highly open economies. Exports and imports easily are taxed, because they pass through bottlenecks (ports), where they are tracked more easily than items in domestic trade.

By the mid-1980s and throughout the 1990s, however, a wide consensus shared by development specialists and government officials was that high tax ratios were not necessarily a virtue, nor low tax ratios a vice, in mobilizing domestic savings. Tax ratios reflect both opportunity and ideology. Sub-Saharan African countries in particular tend to tax themselves more heavily relative to their taxable capacities than countries in Asia.[9] Ideology may be a factor, but a high tax ratio may reflect that opportunities for mobilizing other types of savings, especially private savings, are limited because of poorly developed and organized financial systems. Latin American countries tend to dominate any list of countries with low tax effort. This may merely reflect the relatively greater ease with which private savings can be mobilized through the financial system in Latin America. Since 1945, extended periods of robust growth of organized financial markets have occurred in many Latin American countries, particularly in Mexico, Brazil, Argentina, and Chile and more recently in Colombia and Venezuela.

Tax measures can be used to expand public saving or to shrink a destabilizing government deficit except where taxes are so high that they result in lower domestic savings overall. Even when the government's marginal

9. For the late 1970s, the average tax ratio for sub-Saharan African countries was 18 percent; that for Asia was but 15 percent. By 1985, tax revenues as a percent of GDP were about 23 percent in Africa, 16 percent in East Asia, and only 12 percent in South Asia. See Vito Tanzi, "Quantitative Aspects of Tax Systems in Developing Countries," in David Newberry and Nicholas Stern, eds., *The Theory of Taxation for Developing Countries* (London: Oxford University Press, 1987); and World Bank, *World Development Report 1988,* p. 82.

TABLE 12–6	COMPOSITION OF TAX SYSTEMS BY MAJOR TYPE OF TAX, 1995						
	TOTAL TAXES SHARE OF GDP (%)	COMPOSITION OF TAXES (%)					
		TAXES ON INTERNATIONAL TRADE	DOMESTIC GOODS & SERVICES TAXES	DOMESTIC INCOME TAXES	SOCIAL SECURITY TAXES	OTHER TAXES[a]	NONTAX REVENUES
LOW-INCOME COUNTRIES	9.9	25.2	32.9	18.8	0.1	23.0	—
LOWER-MIDDLE-INCOME COUNTRIES	20.0	13	36	17	6	3	15
UPPER-MIDDLE-INCOME COUNTRIES	23.3	5	32	19	10	3	12
HIGH-INCOME COUNTRIES	28.0	0	28	28	22	3	10

[a]For low income countries, this figure includes all other revenue sources.
Sources: All data except for the composition of tax data for low-income countries are taken from the World Bank, *Development Indicators 1998*, pp. 220 and 228. The composition of taxes for low-income countries are for the year 1992.

propensity to consume is significantly less than 1, there is no guarantee that the higher public saving made possible by higher tax revenues will result in an appreciable expansion of *overall* national saving. As shown later in this chapter, some part of any higher taxes will come out of private saving.

Where the Please effect is no concern, a number of tax measures are available for increasing public saving or reducing destabilizing deficits. These include (1) periodic increases in rates imposed under existing taxes; (2) enactment of new taxes to tap previously unutilized sources of revenue; (3) improvements in tax administration that allow greater collection under existing taxes at present tax rates, by reducing tax avoidance and evasion; and (4) major reform of the entire tax structure, involving elements of options 1, 2, and 3. For many countries, options 1 and 2 offer only slight hope for increased collections. Options 3 and 4 perhaps are the more difficult to implement but, if feasible, are much more likely to achieve the desired results.

Recall from Chapter 11 that, as incomes rise, so does the share of GNP collected in tax revenues, from 16 percent on average for low-income countries to 27 percent for high-income countries. Table 12–6 shows that the composition of tax revenue also differs markedly between developing and developed countries. Taxes on commodities—including imports, a few primary exports, and domestically produced goods—account for over half of revenues in low-income countries but less than a fifth in high-income countries. Import and export duties in particular decline as incomes rise. In contrast, income, social security, and property taxes levied on households and corporations make up less than a fifth of total revenue in low-income countries but account for about two thirds of revenues in the high-income economies. Some of the reasons for these variations are explored in the next sections.

TAXES ON INTERNATIONAL TRADE

Although reliance on the taxes of foreign trade has diminished in recent years, particularly in middle-income countries, tax revenue structures in developing countries historically have depended heavily on import duties. Many low-income countries remain markedly dependent on import duties. This is particularly so for countries like the Gambia, Uganda, Rwanda, Sudan, Togo, and Yemen, where at least half of total government revenue comes from taxes on imports. Dependence on import duties is much less marked in middle-income countries, which have developed alternative sources of tax revenue.

For most countries, attempts to raise further revenues through higher duties is infeasible and undesirable on economic grounds. Higher import duties intensify the incentive for smuggling or evading tariffs. Various studies have shown that, for countries with already high duty rates, the incentive to smuggle increases disproportionately with further increases. Therefore, a 10 percent rise in duty rates can result in an increase in smuggling activity by more than 10 percent, as illustrated by the case study of Colombia. And in mountainous countries, such as Afghanistan and Bolivia, or archipelago countries, such as Indonesia and the Philippines, borders are especially porous to smuggled imports.

Reliance on import duties for additional revenues may be infeasible for another reason. Except in open economies such as Hong Kong, Singapore, and Malaysia, the typical structure of import duties in developing countries, as explained in greater detail in Chapter 18, is heavily cascaded: The highest rates of duty in virtually all countries are imposed on consumer durable goods, particularly luxury goods (appliances, cameras, and so on); lower rates are applied on such intermediate goods as cement and leather; and the lowest duty rates are put on capital goods and imported items viewed as basic necessities (food, grains, fish, kerosene). When countries have sought additional revenues from tariffs, consumer goods already subject to high tariffs have been taxed even higher. Higher rates on necessities were considered inadvisable for equity reasons, and higher rates on capital goods and intermediate goods were deemed unacceptable for fear this would retard industrialization programs. But the enactment of higher duties on consumer goods, particularly luxury consumer goods, generally did not produce higher revenue. The reason is simple: The price elasticity of demand is not 0 for any consumer good, and for many already subject to very high duties, price elasticity is relatively high, in some cases -2.0 or more. For an import already subject to a 150 percent duty, such as stereos,

TAX RATES AND SMUGGLING: COLOMBIA

In Colombia, before 1969, when the import duty rate on cigarettes was over 100 percent, it was virtually impossible to purchase duty-paid cigarettes. At such high rates, import duty collections on cigarettes were nil and the market was flooded with smuggled foreign brands. In 1969, the duty rate was reduced to 30 percent. Cigarette smuggling on the poorly policed Caribbean coast of that country continued, but duty-paid packages began to appear in the mountainous interior, and duty collections on this product soared. Smuggling profits possible under a 30 percent duty were no longer high enough to compensate smugglers for the risks of arrest. Similar phenomena have been observed in Indonesia, Bolivia, and elsewhere.

and with a demand price elasticity of -2.0, a 10 percent increase in duty rates actually would decrease tax revenue on this item by about 2 percent.[10]

Export taxes are constitutionally prohibited in the United States and extremely rare in other industrial countries. But export taxes are not uncommon in developing countries, particularly in tropical Africa and Southeast Asia. Taxes ordinarily are imposed on exports of raw materials such as timber (Ivory Coast and Liberia), tin (Malaysia), jute (Pakistan), and diamonds (Botswana) and on foodstuffs such as coffee (Colombia), peanuts (the Gambia and Senegal), cocoa (Ghana), and tea (Sri Lanka).

Twenty developing countries relied on export taxes for more than 10 percent of total tax revenue in the 1980s, but in only seven countries, primarily low-income African countries, do export taxes account for more than 20 percent of revenue. Export taxes often are imposed in the belief that they are paid by foreign consumers. That is, the taxes themselves are thought to be exported to consumers abroad, along with the materials. But the conditions necessary for exporting taxes on exports to foreign consumers rarely are present.

Export taxes also are employed to promote nonrevenue goals, including increased processing of raw materials within natural-resource-exporting developing countries. This is done by imposing high rates of export tax on unprocessed exports (cocoa beans or logs) and lower or no rates of tax on

10. This result comes from applying the formula

$$\frac{\mathrm{d}R/R}{\mathrm{d}t/t} = 1 + E\left(\frac{t}{1+t}\right)$$

where R = total duty collections on stereos, t = rate of duty, and E = price elasticity of demand.

processed items fabricated from raw materials (chocolate and plywood). In principle, this use of export taxes should increase local value added on natural resource exports and thereby generate greater employment and capital income for the local economy. Unfortunately, in many cases, the result has been that a government gives up more in export tax revenues than its country gains in additional local value added, particularly when processed raw materials are exported tax free. One study documents several instances in Southeast Asia and Africa where the additional value-added gained in heavily protected local processing of logs into plywood typically was less than half the amount of export tax revenue that would have been collected had timber been exported in the form of logs.[11]

PERSONAL AND CORPORATE INCOME TAXES

Harried ministers of finance, perceiving slack in personal and corporate income taxes, often resort to rate increases in these taxes, with no change in the tax base. The results usually are disappointing, particularly for the personal income tax. Even in middle-income countries, only a very small proportion of the population is covered by the personal income tax: only 2 percent in the 1970s in Ghana, Peru, and almost all other developing countries, although higher in Burma, Kenya, and Turkey. In contrast, well over half the adult population in the United States filed income tax returns in the 1990s. Therefore, few developing countries can rely heavily on the personal income tax for revenues. Whereas the personal income tax accounts for just over two thirds of all federal tax in the United States (not including Social Security and Medicare payments), rarely does the personal income tax account for as much as 10 percent of total central government revenues in developing countries.

In Colombia, for instance, the personal income tax is as well developed as in any developing country. Yet, even though this tax typically is responsible for as much as 15–18 percent of national government revenues, a large share of it is paid by a small number of people: In the early 1970s, the top 4 percent of households paid two thirds of the total tax.[12] In general, personal income taxes are paid largely by urban elites. Not only are these groups usually the most vocal politically, but over the years, they have developed such a variety of devices for tax evasion and avoidance that rate increases stand little chance of raising additional revenues.

Rate increases for corporate taxes usually are not productive, either. In only 16 of 82 developing countries did the corporation income tax ac-

11. Robert Repetto and Malcolm Gillis, eds., *Public Policies and the Misuse of Forest Resources* (New York: Cambridge University Press, 1988), "Conclusions," Chap. 10.

12. Malcolm Gillis and Charles E. McLure, Jr., "Taxation and Income Distribution: The Colombian Tax Reform of 1974," *Journal of Development Economics,* 5, no. 3 (September 1978), 237.

count for more than 20 percent of total taxes in the 1980s. In 1996, corporate taxes and personal income taxes taken together accounted for more than 30 percent of all revenue in only a third of a sample of 60 developing countries. And, in most of these countries, corporate tax collections usually originated with foreign natural-resource firms. Except for several middle-income countries, such as Argentina, Korea, Taiwan, and Mexico, the corporate form of doing business covers but a small portion of the private sector. To be sure, most state-owned firms are corporations, but few such firms outside the natural-resources sector earn sizable taxable profits. Even fewer pay substantial income taxes.

SALES AND EXCISE TAXES

A much more promising source of additional government revenue is indirect taxes on domestic transactions, such as sales and excise taxes. **Sales taxes,** including **value-added taxes,** are broad-based consumption taxes imposed on all products except those specifically exempted, such as food, farm inputs, and medicine. **Excise taxes** also are taxes on consumption, but these levies are imposed only on specifically enumerated items—typically tobacco, alcoholic beverages, gambling, and motor fuel. On average, developing countries depend on domestic commodity taxes for nearly a third of total revenues (Table 12–6).

Virtually every developing country imposes some form of sales tax. In most, the tax is not applied to retail sales because of the burdensome administrative requirements of collecting taxes from thousands of small retailers. In the past, as in Chile before 1970 and in some Indian states, the tax was imposed as a gross turnover tax collected at all levels of production and distribution, with harmful implications for efficiency, income distribution, and virtually every objective of tax policy. In developing countries, administrative problems are more tractable when the sales tax is confined to the manufacturing level: A much smaller number of firms is involved and the output of manufacturers is far more homogeneous than sales of retailers or wholesalers. For these reasons many low-income countries have utilized either the single-stage or the value-added form of manufacturers' tax, usually exempting very small producers. This kind of sales tax, however, involves more economic distortions than either a wholesale or a retail tax, and for that reason, as well as for revenue motives, more and more middle-income countries have turned to taxes at the retail level.[13]

Increasingly, these taxes have taken the form of one or another variant of the value-added tax (VAT), widely seen as the most effective method of

---

13. For a full discussion of the distortions involved in different forms of sales tax, see John Due and Raymond Mikesell, *Sales Taxation: State and Local Structure and Administration* (Baltimore: Johns Hopkins Press, 1983).

taxing consumption yet developed. Nearly 60 countries, including all members of the European Community, have adapted the VAT since it was first adopted in its comprehensive retail form in Brazil in 1967.[14] Nearly 40 developing countries had adopted the tax by 1989, either to replace older, outdated forms of sales taxes or to allow them to reduce reliance on harder-to-collect income and property taxes. Table 12–7 provides a chronology of adoption for the VAT in over 40 selected developing countries, as well as the share of the VAT in GDP and in overall tax revenues.

Virtually all developing and industrial countries using the VAT have chosen to extend the tax through the retail level. A VAT extended through the retail level has a tax base virtually identical to a single stage of retail sales tax and, when imposed at the same rate as the latter tax, will generate almost identical revenues. Both are indirect taxes on consumption.[15]

Excise taxes might appear to represent an ideal source of additional tax revenue. These typically are imposed on sumptuary items having relatively inelastic demand. When the price elasticity of demand for such products is very low (as for tobacco products) or relatively low (as for alcoholic beverages), an increase in excise tax rates will induce little reduction in consumption of the taxed good. If price elasticity is as low as -0.2—not uncommon for cigarettes—then an additional 10 percent excise tax on this product would yield an 8 percent increase in tax revenues. Moreover, it is a hallowed theorem in optimal tax theory that taxes levied on items with inelastic demand and supply involve the smallest losses in economic efficiency, or what is the same thing, the least excess burden. **Excess burden** is defined as a loss in private welfare above the amount of government revenue collected from a tax.[16] Further, many agree, with much justification, that consumption of both tobacco and alcohol should be discouraged on health grounds.

All three considerations would seem to argue for heavy reliance on excise taxes in developing countries. However, unfortunately, in addition to low price elasticity, items such as tobacco and alcoholic beverages have low income elasticity and so tend to be more important in the budgets of low-income than high-income households. It follows that excise taxes on sumptuary items are decidedly regressive: Poor people pay a higher proportion of their income in excise taxes than rich people—a serious matter

14. Carl Shoup, "Choosing among Types of VAT," in Malcolm Gillis, Carl Shoup, and Gerry Sicat, eds., *Value-Added Taxation in Developing Countries* (Washington, DC: World Bank, 1990).

15. As used in virtually all developing and in all industrial countries, the VAT properly is seen as an indirect tax on consumption: The base of the tax includes only consumption goods and services. A VAT can be structured so that the tax base is all income, but this tax is more difficult to administer and has been used in few countries (Argentina, Turkey). See Shoup, "Choosing among Types of VAT."

16. For a further discussion of optimal taxation and excess burden, see Figure 12–2, later in this chapter, and also Joseph Stiglitz, *Economics of the Public Sector* (New York: W.W. Norton, 1988).

TABLE 12-7 VALUE-ADDED TAXATION

COUNTRY	YEAR VAT INTRODUCED	VAT REVENUES AS % OF GDP	VAT REVENUES AS % OF TOTAL TAX REVENUE	BASIC VAT RATE (%)	OTHER VAT RATES (%)
LOW-INCOME COUNTRIES					
MALAWI	1989	6	31	20	
KENYA	1990	8	31	18	
LOWER-MIDDLE-INCOME COUNTRIES					
PAKISTAN	1990	2	10	15	
NICARAGUA	1975	2	13	10	
EL SALVADOR	1992	4	37	10	
BOLIVIA	1973	5	32	14.92	
THE PHILIPPINES	1988	2	10	10	
ROMANIA	1993	7	19	18	
SRI LANKA	1995	6	30	25	
INDONESIA	1985	4	22	10	
PERU	1976	3	32	18	
MOROCCO	1986	6	21	19	
PARAGUAY	1993	3	24	10	
ECUADOR	1970	3	17	10	
UPPER-MIDDLE-INCOME COUNTRIES					
BULGARIA	1994	3	7	18	
TUNISIA	1988	3	10	17	6, 29
TURKEY	1985	5	24	15	1, 8, 23
BRAZIL	1967	1	4	11	9
PANAMA	1977	2	6	5	10
HUNGARY	1988	8	14	25	10
THAILAND	1992	3	19	7	
URUGUAY	1968	7	22	22	12
MEXICO	1980	3	19	10	
GREECE	1987	14	39	18	4, 8
CHILE	1975	9	37	18	
VENEZUELA	1993	1	3	10	
KOREA, REPUBLIC	1977	4	23	10	2, 3, 5
HIGH-INCOME COUNTRIES					
PORTUGAL	1986	7	17	16	5, 30
IRELAND	1972	8	19	21	12.5
SPAIN	1986	4	14	15	3, 6
NEW ZEALAND	1986	6	18	12.5	
ISRAEL	1976	12	31	17	6.5
FINLAND	1994	9	27	22	9, 12
UNITED KINGDOM	1973	7	19	17.5	
THE NETHERLANDS	1969	7	14	17.5	6
SWEDEN	1969	9	21	25	12, 21
ITALY	1973	5	13	19	4, 9, 12
NORWAY	1970	9	18	22	
BELGIUM	1971	7	16	20.5	1, 6, 12
AUSTRIA	1973	6	16	20	10, 32
DENMARK	1967	10	25	25	
FRANCE	1968	8	19	18.6	2.1, 5.5
JAPAN	1989	1	8	3	4.5
GERMANY	1968	4	14	15	7

Source: World Bank, *World Development Report 1994* (Washington, DC: The World Bank, 1994), Table 11; IMF, *Government Finance Statistics Yearbook 1994*, pp. 42–43; and Glenn P. Jenkins, "Economic Reform and Institutional Innovation," unpublished paper, April 11, 1995.

when the sumptuary items constitute a substantial portion of spending by poor people, as in most developing countries. In Indonesia, for example, the poorest 20 percent of Javanese households spent about 5 percent of total income on heavily taxed cigarettes in 1976, as opposed to 3.5 percent of income for persons with income more than five times as high.

NEW SOURCES OF TAX REVENUES

If higher rates on existing taxes are unlikely to raise revenues much, a second option for increasing public savings is to tap entirely new sources of tax revenues. In many developing countries, whether by accident, design, or simply inertia, many sources of tax revenue may have been overlooked entirely. Many countries have not collected taxes on motor vehicle registrations; some have not utilized urban property taxes as a significant source of revenue; many have not applied corporation income taxes to the income of state-owned enterprises. Kenya, for example, does not seriously tax farm land, and a few countries, such as Indonesia until 1984, do not collect personal income taxes on the salaries of civil servants.

The service sector furnishes other examples. Telephone service exists in all but the very poorest countries and is widespread in many but often untaxed. Some service establishments, such as restaurants and cabarets, are commonly taxed, but services of beauty shops, parking lots, tire-recap businesses, photo-finishing firms, modern laundries, and foreign-travel agencies are among the more common items excluded from the tax base. Not only is taxation of this category of spending attractive from a revenue standpoint, in developing countries, such services typically face relatively income-elastic demand. Because families with higher incomes purchase proportionately more of these items, they would tend to bear the greater burden of taxation, consistent with the equity objectives of fiscal policy. However, these services constitute a small fraction of consumption, even for upper-income groups, so their revenue potential is limited.

CHANGES IN TAX ADMINISTRATION

A far more significant option for increasing tax revenues is to implement changes in tax administration that permit more taxes to be collected from existing tax sources, even at unchanged tax rates. The potential for increased revenues from such action is very large, and seldom realized, in virtually all developing countries. Shortages of well-trained tax administrators, excessively complex tax laws, light penalties for tax evasion, corruption, and outdated techniques of tax administration combine to make tax evasion one of the most intractable problems of economic policy in developing countries.

TAX ADMINISTRATION IN INDIA
AND BOLIVIA IN THE 1980S

India during the 1980s provides one of the more egregious examples of poor tax administration. During the fiscal year 1981, for example, it was found that taxes were avoided on at least 40 and possibly 60 percent of potentially taxable income. Almost 70 percent of the taxpayers covered by a survey openly admitted bribing tax officials and three quarters of the tax auditors admitted accepting bribes to reduce tax payments. The cost of a bribe was commonly known to be about 20 percent of the taxes avoided.[17]

In Bolivia during the same period, the tax system was chaotic. More than 400 separate taxes were levied by the national, regional, and city governments. Taxpayer records were out of date, and tax collections were recorded more than a year after they had been paid. Of 120,000 registered taxpayers, one third paid no taxes at all, while 20,000 taxpayers who did pay were not on the register. The administration had all but ceased its data processing. Administration had gotten so bad that the government was helpless to collect taxes during the hyperinflation of the mid-1980s (see the case study in Chapter 5). Tax collections fell to only 1 percent of the GDP. Faced with this chaos, the Bolivian government reformed its tax administration, simplifying it drastically. This, together with price stabilization (see Chapter 5), enabled the government to collect revenues equivalent to over 7 percent of the GDP by 1990, a low ratio by world standards but a vast improvement for Bolivia.[18]

17. Omkar Goswami, Amal Sanyal, and Ira N. Gang, "Taxes, Corruption and Bribes: A Model of Indian Public Finance," in Michael Roemer and Christine Jones, eds., *Markets in Developing Countries: Parallel, Fragmented and Black* (San Francisco: ICS Press, 1991), pp. 201–13.

18. Carlos A. Silvani and Alberto H. J. Radano, "Tax Administration Reform in Bolivia and Uruguay," in Richard M. Bird and Milka Casanegra de Jantscher, eds., *Improving Tax Administration in Developing Countries* (Washington, DC: International Monetary Fund, 1992), pp. 19–59.

The case studies, which suggest the magnitude of the problem in India and Bolivia, are typical of many, perhaps most, other developing countries. These examples suggest that efforts to collect a greater share of the taxes due under current law can increase revenues substantially. But the kinds of administrative reforms required are difficult to implement and especially difficult to sustain. Even Bolivia's successful reform raised its tax ratio to only 7 percent of GDP. Korea, a country noted for efficient and determined administration, failed in the 1960s to reach its goal of increasing collections by 40 percent through more effective enforcement, although it was able to reduce underreporting of nonagricultural personal income from 75 percent to slightly under 50 percent. Although administrative reform can help and can be important at any stage of development, better tax administration tends to improve with economic development. In a lower-middle-income country like Jamaica, more than a third of the potential tax base escapes taxation, compared to less than 15 percent in the United States or Canada.[19]

FUNDAMENTAL TAX REFORM

The final policy option available for increasing tax revenues is the most difficult to implement but the most effective when it can be done. Fundamental tax reform requires junking old tax systems and replacing them with completely new tax laws and regulations. Implementing tax reform engenders enormous technical and informational, not to mention political, difficulties in all countries. In general, governments resist genuine efforts to reform the tax structure until fiscal crisis—in the form of massive budgetary deficits—threatens. Even during a fiscal crisis, it is difficult to mobilize a political consensus to allow unpopular tax measures to pass. Tax policies that protect favored groups and distort the allocation of resources did not just happen; more likely, they were enacted at the behest of someone, ordinarily the privileged and the powerful.

Probably, more has been said, to less effect, about tax reform than almost any topic in economic policy. This is no less true for the United States than for the 50-odd developing countries where major tax reform efforts have been mounted since 1950. That the process is painful and slow is evident from the experience of several countries: In the United States, the time lag between the birth of tax innovations (tax credit for child-care expenses, inflation proofing of the tax system) and their implementation usually is at least 15 years. If anything, the lag may be slightly shorter in developing countries.

In spite of the difficulties involved, some countries were able to carry through fundamental reforms in tax structure and administration before 1980. The classic example is Japan in the 1880s, when that society began its transformation to a modern industrial power. Korea implemented a major tax reform program in the early 1960s, as did Colombia (see the following case study) and Chile in the 1970s. But, also during the 1970s,

19. James Alm, Roy Bahl, and Matthew Murray, "Tax Base Erosion in Developing Countries," *Economic Development and Cultural Change,* 39, no. 4 (July 1991), 849–72.

LESSONS FROM COMPREHENSIVE
TAX REFORM: COLOMBIA

In 1974, Colombia implemented one of the most ambitious tax reform programs undertaken. The Colombia experience illustrates both the potential payoffs and the difficulties involved in any serious tax reform effort.

In the last quarter of 1974, the new government of Alfonso Lopez Michelsen, in the midst of a national crisis, enacted a tax reform of very large magnitude. The reform, nearly a decade in the making, was engineered by an extraordinary group of officials as well versed in fiscal economics as any treasury department in the world. The reform package was comprehensive: It involved nearly all tax sources. It was geared to all four fiscal policy objectives: growth, equity, stability, and efficiency. The instruments employed were well suited to the objectives sought. The reform contained measures to increase progressivity that still are absent in tax systems of the United States and Canada. Numerous anomalies in the tax system that encouraged waste and inefficiency in the private sectors were introduced and allowed to stand for a short time before they were struck down by the Colombian Supreme Court.

The reform's most striking initial achievements were its effects on tax-revenue growth and income distribution. In the first year following the reform, tax revenues grew by 45 percent, more than twice the growth rate in revenues in the years prior to the reform. The early impact on income distribution was just as striking: In its first year, the reform shifted as much as 1.5 percent of GDP away from the top 20 percent of the income earners—a rare feat.

Many of the achievements of the reform effort proved short-lived, however. The reform initially caught most powerful economic interests with their defenses down. But by 1976, groups injured by the reform were able to have many key measures watered down or repealed, and taxpayers began to develop defense mechanisms against the new law and exploit loopholes uncovered by the best legal minds in the country. Also, the reform effort paid far too little attention to the practical problems of implementation and to the strengthening of tax collection procedures. Nevertheless, many of the innovations introduced in 1974 survived relatively intact through 1980, and many revenue-hungry and equity-oriented tax officials in other Latin American countries viewed much of the 1974 reform package as a model worth detailed study.

major tax reform efforts went for naught in many more countries: Bolivia, Ghana, Liberia, and Peru, among others.

Since 1980, however, the pace of tax reform has quickened notably, in both developing and industrial countries, with many similarities in the various reform programs. Throughout much of the postwar period, tax systems commonly were fine-tuned to achieve a wide variety of nonrevenue objectives. In particular, governments in developed and developing nations alike commonly sought substantial income redistribution through the use of steeply progressive tax rates. Also, complex and largely impossible to administrate systems of tax incentives were widely used in attempts to redirect resources to high-priority economic sectors, to promote foreign investment, regional development, and even stock exchanges.

While fine-tuning tax systems someday may yield the desired results, this requires, at a minimum, strong machinery for tax administration and traditions of taxpayer compliance. Within developing countries, at least, there has been growing recognition that these conditions seldom prevail. Consequently, governments increasingly have turned away from reliance on steeply progressive tax rates and complicated, costly tax incentive programs.

The 1980s and 1990s saw a worldwide movement toward an entirely different type of tax system, with a shift toward vastly simplified taxes imposed at much flatter rates and with much broader bases[20] and with increasingly greater reliance on consumption rather than income taxation. Tax reform programs in Bolivia, Chile, Colombia, India, Indonesia, Jamaica, and Malawi exemplify most of these trends.[21]

Two aspects of this worldwide movement in tax reform are especially salient. First, the top marginal income tax rates of 60–70 percent were not uncommon from 1945 to 1979. But, since 1984, country after country has slashed the top marginal rate, often substantially. Table 12–8 shows that 31 developing countries have reduced the top marginal rate of income tax, many of them quite dramatically. During the same period, 20 industrial nations ranging from Australia and Austria through the United Kingdom and the United States also cut the top rate sharply.

In many of these cases, sharp cutbacks in the highest tax rates were accompanied by reforms involving a very substantial broadening of the income tax base, through the reduction of special tax incentives, abolition of tax shelters, and the like. This pattern was especially notable in Bolivia, Colombia, Indonesia, Jamaica, and Sri Lanka, so that even with a rate reduction, higher-income groups often ended up paying a higher proportion of total taxes than before.

20. Joseph A. Pechman, ed., *World Tax Reform: A Progress Report* (Washington, DC: Brookings Institute, 1988), "Introduction," p. 13.

21. A number of these cases are discussed in Malcolm Gillis, ed., *Tax Reform in Developing Countries* (Durham, NC: Duke University Press, 1989).

TABLE 12–8	COUNTRIES REDUCING HIGHEST RATES OF INCOME TAX, 1984–97	
COUNTRY	1984	1997
LOW-INCOME COUNTRIES		
TANZANIA	75	35
MALAWI	50	38
UGANDA (1985)	70	30
INDIA	62	40
BANGLADESH	60	25[a]
KENYA	65	35
NIGERIA	70	25
SENEGAL (1985)	65	50
GHANA	65	35
ZIMBABWE (1985)	61	40
LOWER-MIDDLE-INCOME COUNTRIES		
PAPUA NEW GUINEA	50	35
PAKISTAN (1985)	60	35
BOLIVIA	40	13
THE PHILIPPINES (1985)	60	35
SRI LANKA	55	35
INDONESIA	45	30
PERU (1985)	50	30
GUATEMALA	42	30
JAMAICA	58	25
UPPER-MIDDLE-INCOME COUNTRIES		
TURKEY (1985)	55	55
BOTSWANA	75	40[a]
BRAZIL (1985)	60	25
COSTA RICA (1985)	50	25
COLOMBIA	49	35
THAILAND (1985)	65	37
ARGENTINA (1985)	45	33
MEXICO (1985)	55	35
MALAYSIA	55	30
CHILE (1985)	56	45
TRINIDAD AND TOBAGO	70	35
HIGH-INCOME COUNTRY		
SINGAPORE	45	28

[a]Refers to the year 1994.

Sources: George J. Yost, III, ed., *1994 International Tax Summaries, Coopers & Lybrand International Tax Network* (New York: Wiley, 1994); Glenn P. Jenkins, "Tax Reform: Lessons Learned," in Dwight H. Perkins and Michael Roemer, eds., *Reforming Economic Systems in Developing Countries* (Cambridge, MA: Harvard Institute for International Development, 1991); and *World Development Report 1998/99* (Washington, DC: The World Bank, 1999), pp. 222–23.

Reasons for the worldwide shift toward lower tax rates on broader income tax bases are not difficult to find. First, income taxes imposed at high marginal rates have proven difficult or impossible to administrate, even in wealthy countries such as the United States. With high marginal tax rates, the incentives to evade taxes (through concealment of income) or avoid taxes (by hiring expensive legal talent to devise tax shelters) is very high. Second, the growing mobility of capital across international boundaries has meant that the risk of capital flight from a particular country increases when that country's top rates of income tax exceed those prevailing in industrial nations, where tax rates have been falling.[22] Third, the operation of the income tax systems of such developed nations at the United States and Japan has placed downward pressure on the tax rates everywhere. This is because of the *foreign income tax credit,* wherein a country like the United States allows foreign income taxes to be credited (subtracted) from U.S. taxes due on income repatriated from abroad. This credit could be used, however, only up to the amount of tax payable at U.S. rates, which was reduced from 50 to 28 percent in 1986. Finally, high marginal rates of income tax did not prove to be particularly efficacious in correcting severe inequalities in income distribution in either rich or poor countries.

The second striking feature of recent tax reforms worldwide has been the steadily growing number of countries adopting the value-added tax. Several reasons account for the popularity of the VAT: The two most important are its reputation as a "money machine" and its administrative advantages, relative to other forms of sales taxes and to income taxes.[23]

The record of the VAT in generating large amounts of revenue quickly, and in a comparatively painless fashion, has given it a reputation as a money machine. Although this reputation stems largely from the experience in European countries, the record in developing countries does lend some support to the alleged revenue advantages of the VAT. In Indonesia, the 4 percent share of the value-added tax in GDP in 1987 was nearly three times the share garnered in 1983 by the taxes it replaced. And, for 14 of the 27 developing countries in Table 12–7, the share of the VAT in GDP was higher than 3 percent; in all but 10 of these cases, the VAT constituted at least 20 percent of total tax revenue. Still, in five of the countries listed in Table 12–7, the VAT revenues were less than 2 percent of GDP. Notwithstanding the marked revenue success of the VAT in nations such as Brazil, Chile, and Indonesia, its reputation as a money machine appears to have been at least slightly overstated.

Twenty years ago, it was common to hear the claim that the VAT was largely self-administering. This is not so, but the tax-credit type of VAT

---

22. For a cogent discussion of the implications for taxation of growing international mobility of financial and physical capital, see Dwight R. Lee and Richard B. McKenzie, "The International Political Economy of Declining Tax Rates," *National Tax Journal,* 42, no. 2 (March 1989), 79–87.

23. For a full statement of these reasons, see Alan A. Tait, *Value-Added Tax* (Washington, DC: International Monetary Fund, 1988), Chap. 1.

has three principal advantages over single-stage retail and nonretail sales taxes in limiting the scope for evasion. First, the VAT is self-policing to some extent because underpayment of the tax by a seller (except, of course, a retail firm) reduces the tax credit available to the buying firm. Even so, firms that also are subject to income taxes have incentives to suppress information on purchases and sales to avoid both the value-added and income taxes. Also, this possible advantage of the VAT is diminished when evasion at the final (retail) stage of distribution is endemic. Second, cross-checking of invoices enables the tax administration to match invoices received by purchasers against those retained by sellers. The cross-check feature is a valuable aid in audit activities but no substitute for a true, systematic audit. Third, that a large share of the VAT is collected prior to the retail level is an advantage particularly because, in most developing countries, an abundance of small-scale retail firms do not keep adequate records. In sum, the administrative advantages of the VAT are very real, if sometimes exaggerated by enthusiastic proponents.[24]

Taxes and Private Investment

Fiscal policy influences capital formation in the private sector by affecting both the capacity and the incentive to save and by affecting incentives to invest in private projects. Taxes impinge more directly, but not necessarily more importantly, on both sets of incentives than government expenditures and will be our prime focus here.

TAXES AND PRIVATE SAVING

An increase in taxes on households will come partly out of consumption and partly out of saving, but the effects of taxes in reducing consumption and saving, respectively, is a matter of some dispute. Some cross-country studies of saving behavior suggest that increases in taxes in developing countries merely reduce private-sector consumption with little or no effect on saving. Other studies cited in Chapter 11 conclude that there is a high degree of substitutability between private savings and taxes. The truth probably lies slightly closer to the latter observation.

Different taxes will have different types of impact on the **capacity to save.** Although heavy sales taxes on highly price-elastic items of luxury consumption will curtail rates of growth in the consumption of such items, heavy taxes on corporate income may come in large part at the ex-

24. For a succinct summary of some of these issues, see John F. Due, "Some Unresolved Issues in Design and Implementation of Value-Added Taxes," *National Tax Journal,* 42, no. 4 (December 1990), 383–98.

pense of business savings that might have been plowed back into company investment. Where upper-income groups have a high propensity to consume, as often has been argued to hold for the elite in many Latin American countries, increased taxes on them may have little impact on private savings. But where the same groups display strong saving propensities, as many argue is true for some ethnic minorities in Africa and Southeast Asia, higher taxes will have a relatively greater impact on saving. Further, heavier taxes on foreign natural-resource firms ordinarily will have minimal negative impact on the availability of private domestic savings unless such firms have local joint-venture partners and cut their dividends to them in response to reduced profitability.

There is less uncertainty concerning the effect of different forms of taxes on **incentives to save,** but even here, offsetting considerations are present. Taxes on consumption probably impinge less severely on private savings than taxes on income in most developing societies. Perhaps the only exception to this statement arises when households save primarily for the later purchase of items subject to heavy consumption taxes. Some observers have argued that this motivation for saving is common in many low-income countries, where the nature of extended-family relationships makes household saving difficult. In some societies, households with incomes above subsistence share resources with poorer households within the family group to help them meet subsistence needs. This pattern is characteristic of many African countries and of many parts of rural Asia. Under such circumstances household saving is devoted largely to the purchase of prized durable goods, such as transistor radios, bicycles, and sewing machines. In high- and middle-income countries these typically are viewed as consumer goods that are strong candidates for taxation. But, in some poorer countries, heavy taxation of such items may well reduce incentives to save. It is even questionable whether products such as bicycles, sewing machines, and even small outboard motors should be viewed as consumer goods in many low-income societies. Purchasing a bicycle or a small outboard may allow a rural family to market garden produce and fish more easily, whereas sewing machines ordinarily are bought to generate extra income for the household.

On balance, consumption-based taxes probably are more favorable for growth in private saving than income-based taxes. Virtually all developing countries tax consumption through such indirect means as sales and excise taxes. These levies, although not inherently regressive, often are perceived to be. This perception has led many tax reformers to argue for direct taxes on consumption. Under a direct consumption tax, taxpayers annually would report total consumption as well as income. Consumption below the level thought minimally necessary for an adequate living standard would be exempt, and any consumption above that level would be taxed at rates that rise progressively with total consumption. If such a levy could be administered, it would stimulate savings, since a household could reduce its tax liability by not spending. Direct consumption taxes have been seriously proposed for the United States (1977), Great Britain (1978), Sweden (1976), and Australia (1976). Among developing countries, they have been proposed for India, Guyana, and Sri Lanka and actually enacted in India in the 1950s. The Indian experiment was short-lived, however, as the tax involved required information beyond the capacities of the tax administration at the time; it proved impossible to administer. But, in the 1990s, the administrative problems, both real and imaginary, of direct consumption taxes are not so great as to preclude their consideration in many developing and industrial countries.

Taxes can affect incentives to save in other ways. To the extent that national savings rates are responsive to the after-tax rate of return on savings (a question examined in the next chapter), heavy taxes on income from capital (dividends and interest) reduce the volume of private savings available for investment. Likewise, to the extent that people save mainly to finance retirement, social security taxes also can reduce private and aggregate national saving if the social security system is financed on a pay-as-you-go basis (that is, from current revenues), as in the United States, Colombia, the Philippines, and India. Under a social security system financed in this manner, it is argued that individuals covered by the system will reduce their saving in anticipation of receiving future social security benefits. But there will be no corresponding increase in public saving because the social security taxes paid by those covered now are not set aside and invested, but rather are used to pay benefits to those already retired.

This is an important point, because many proposals have been made—and some enacted—for social security systems in Asia and Latin America intended to help increase the national saving rate. The argument that social security systems can foster domestic saving is correct only under two circumstances, both relatively uncommon in developing countries. First, social security systems that operate as true retirement funds clearly can help mobilize capital resources provided the funds are invested in projects with an adequate social marginal rate of return. Under such *provident funds,* the taxes collected from those covered are invested by the government in assets that earn returns; payments are made to retirees out of these returns rather than from taxes collected by those still working, as under the pay-as-you-go system. Under this approach, used in Chile and Singapore and for some workers in Malaysia and a few other countries, any decline in the private savings of those paying social security taxes largely is offset by a concomitant rise in public savings. But the use of provident funds is not widespread.

Even the pay-as-you-go system can increase national saving rates in its early years of operation if benefits are denied to those who retired before the system was implemented and if social security tax rates are set high enough to cover benefit payments for the first decade or so. In the early years, the number of workers covered is large relative to the number of retirees, so that the disbursement of benefits is small compared to the inflow of revenues. Therefore, a government seeking new temporary sources of public saving could enact a pay-as-you-go system for social security that would serve this purpose for a few years. Sooner or later, however, such a system would tend to reduce overall domestic saving, although not necessarily by as much as the social security taxes paid by covered workers.

TAXES AND CAPITAL MOBILITY

If a country's tax system operates to reduce private savings, it will tend to curtail private domestic investment. Beyond that effect, taxes can affect both the amount and allocation of private domestic investment undertaken out of any given volume of private capital available for investment.

We saw in Chapter 11 that, in spite of exchange controls and similar restrictions, capital tends to be fairly mobile across international boundaries. If opportunities for earning returns abroad promise higher after-tax returns than those available in a particular developing country, domestic capital will tend to flow to these opportunities. Of course, a critical factor determining after-tax returns in a given country is the nature of taxes on capital there. Suppose, for example, that capital owners in the Philippines can secure, on the average, before-tax returns equal to 15 percent of their investments and that capital income in that country is subject to a 50 percent tax. After-tax returns are then 7.5 percent. The same funds invested in well-developed capital markets in Hong Kong, where capital is less scarce, might obtain only a 12 percent return before taxes, but are taxed at only, say, 15 percent. The after-tax return in Hong Kong is therefore 10.2 percent. The difference of 2.7 percent in after-tax returns may be large enough to induce movement of Philippines savings to Hong Kong. In general, countries that attempt to impose substantially heavier taxes on capital income often experience outflows of domestic savings to countries employing lower tax rates on capital. This movement is quite distinct from the type of *capital flight* from developing to developed countries often observed in countries experiencing severe domestic political turmoil or exchange-rate uncertainties.

No shortage of low-tax foreign opportunities faces domestic savers in developing countries. *Tax havens* such as Panama and the Bahamas have been attractive to Latin American investors since the 1960s. Likewise, the Hong Kong and Singapore financial markets draw substantial inflows of savings from other Asian countries. Increasingly, enterprises from countries such as India, with relatively high taxes on capital income, have become major investors in other developing countries where after-tax returns are higher than at home.

Most countries have recognized that capital is fairly mobile across national boundaries and sought to keep taxes on capital income from reaching levels much above those prevailing worldwide. This is evident from an inspection of corporate income tax rates prevailing in most developing countries. In Latin America corporate tax rates typically are found in a band of from 25 to 40 percent, compared to 34 percent in the United States in 1990. In Southeast Asia, corporate tax rates—other than those of Hong Kong—cluster in a narrow range of 30–40 percent; the rate in Hong Kong is less than 20 percent.

Countries have sought to impede the outward mobility of capital through such devices as controls on movement of foreign exchange, imposition of domestic taxes on worldwide income of residents, and other devices. Flourishing business in tax-haven countries, coupled with very large investment holdings by citizens of developing countries in the United States, Switzerland, Hong Kong, and Singapore, are ample testament to the limited effectiveness of such controls.

Partly to stem capital outflow and to direct private investment into high-priority areas, such as basic industry, exports, or backward regions, many developing country governments selectively offer substantial tax incentives to domestic investors. The two main types of incentives are income tax holidays, in which approved investments are exempted from income tax obligations for specified periods ranging from three to ten years, and tax credits for investment, in which a government allows an investor to subtract some portion of initial investment (usually 20–25 percent) from his or her income tax liabilities. On rare occasions, these types of incentives for domestic investment have produced the desired results, but these devices suffer from a number of administrative and efficiency limitations. Because of these limitations, Indonesia in 1984 abolished all tax incentives and replaced them with the most effective tax incentive ever offered: lower tax rates for all firms.

Income Distribution

As indicated in Chapter 4, a basic thrust of economic policy in many developing countries has been the mitigation of extreme income inequality. For decades, developed and developing countries alike have sought to use the fiscal system, particularly taxation, to redress income inequalities generated by the operation of the private market. Social philosophers from John Stuart Mill and eminent nineteenth-century Chilean historian Francisco Encina to John Rawls in the 1970s have sought to establish a philosophical basis for income redistribution, primarily through progressive taxes. Karl Marx also favored steeply progressive taxes in bourgeois societies, but for reasons other than income redistribution. Rather, in Marx's view, heavy taxes on capitalists were essential for speeding the decline of the capitalist state and its replacement by a socialist order.

No scientific basis is used to determine the optimal degree of income redistribution in any society. And across developing countries different views prevail as to the ideal distribution of income. But, in virtually all countries, the notion of *fiscal equity* permeates discussions of budgetary operations. In the overwhelming majority of countries, fiscal equity typically is defined in terms of the impact of tax and expenditure policy on the distribution of economic well-being. Progressive taxes, those that bear more heavily on better-off citizens than on poor ones, and expenditures whose benefits are concentrated on the least advantaged are viewed as more equitable than regressive taxes and expenditures.

TAXATION AND EQUITY

On the tax side of the budget, the materialistic conception of equity requires that most taxes be based on the **ability to pay.** The ability to pay can be measured by income, consumption, wealth, or some combination of all three. Clearly, individuals with higher incomes over their life spans have a greater ability to pay taxes, quite apart from the moral question of whether they should do so. Indeed, the redistribution impact of taxation almost always is expressed in terms of its effects on income. However, philosophers since the time of Hobbes have argued that consumption furnishes a better index of ability to pay than income; in this view, tax obligations are best geared to what people take out of society (consume) rather than what they put into society (as measured by income).

In practice, developing countries have relied heavily on these two measures of ability in fashioning tax systems. Personal and corporate income taxes employ income as the indicator; sales taxes and customs duties are indirect assessments of taxes on consumption. But the ability to pay is not the exclusive guide to the assessment of taxes in all countries. Religious and cultural values often provide other bases for establishing tax liability. Nevertheless most societies largely define equity in taxation as requiring taxation on the basis of ability to pay, and this is commonly interpreted to mean progressivity. At a minimum, equity usually is assumed to require the avoidance of regressive taxes whenever possible. A number of tax instruments have been employed to secure greater progressivity in principle, if not in practice; all suffer from limitations to one degree or another.

PERSONAL INCOME TAXES

The most widely used device for securing greater progressivity has been steeply progressive rates under the personal income tax. In some countries in some periods, nominal or legal marginal income tax rates have reached very high levels, even for relatively low incomes. Thus, for example, tax rates applicable to any income in excess of $1,000 in Indonesia in 1967 reached 75 percent, largely because tax rates were not indexed to rapid inflation; in Algeria in the 1960s, all income in excess of $10,000 was subject to marginal tax rates of nearly 100 percent; Tanzania imposed top marginal rates of 95 percent as late as 1981.

Although, in most developing countries, marginal income tax rates are considerably lower than the preceding examples and, as is apparent from Table 12–8, have been falling, some countries still attempt to impose rates in excess of 50 percent.[25] Countries such as Brazil, Colombia, Costa Rica, Mexico, Singapore, and Sri Lanka generally hold maximum marginal rates to 40 percent or slightly less, and the maximum income tax rate in Indonesia has been 35 percent since that country implemented tax reform in 1984.

If the tax administration machinery functioned well and if capital were immobile among countries, the pattern of actual tax payments of high-income taxpayers would resemble the legal, or theoretical, patterns just described. In fact, in most countries, **effective taxes**—taxes actually collected as a percent of income—fall well short of theoretical liabilities. Faced with high income tax rates, taxpayers everywhere tend to react in three ways: (1) They evade taxes by concealing income, particularly capital income not subject to withholding arrangements; (2) they avoid taxes by altering economic behavior to reduce tax liability, whether by supplying fewer labor services, shipping capital to tax havens abroad, or hiring lawyers to find loopholes in the tax law; and (3) they bribe tax assessors to accept false returns.

For all these reasons, the achievement of substantial income redistribution through progressive income taxes has proven difficult in all countries, including the United States and the three Scandinavian nations where tax rates were long among the world's most progressive. Tax avoidance is the favored avenue for reducing tax liability in the United States, where use of the other methods can result in imprisonment. But where tax enforcement is relatively weak, particularly where criminal penalties for evasion are absent and tax officials deeply underpaid, tax evasion and bribery are utilized more commonly. The scope for substantial redistribution through the income tax therefore is even more limited in developing countries than in the United States or Sweden.

25. Ten of the 16 countries imposing income tax rates in excess of 50 percent in 1989 were in Africa, two were in Latin America, and the remainder were in Asia. Bruce Bartlett, "The Worldwide Tax Revolution."

Notwithstanding these problems, a significant share of the income of the wealthiest members of society is caught in the income tax net in many developing countries. Revenues from personal income tax collections in countries such as Colombia, South Korea, and Chile have been as high as 15 percent of total taxes and in a few others have run between 5 and 10 percent of the total. In virtually all developing countries, the entirety of such taxes is collected from the top 20 percent of the income distribution. This means, of course, that the very presence of an income tax, even one imposed at proportional rather than progressive rates, tends to reduce income inequality. Income taxes, together with taxes on luxury consumption, constitute about the only feasible means of approaching income redistribution goals through the tax side of the budget.

TAXES ON LUXURY CONSUMPTION

In view of the difficulties of securing a significant redistribution through income taxes, many countries have sought to employ heavy indirect taxes on luxury consumption as a means of enhancing the progressivity of the tax system. Efforts to achieve this goal usually center on internal indirect taxes, such as sales taxes, and on customs duties on imports, but not excises on tobacco and alcohol.

Several developing countries have found that, provided tax rates are kept to enforceable levels, high rates of internal indirect taxes on luxury goods and services, coupled with lower taxes on less income-elastic items, can contribute to greater progressivity in the tax system. For revenue purposes, countries typically impose basic rates of sales taxes on nonluxuries at between 4 and 8 percent of manufacturers' values. This is equivalent to retail taxes of between 2 and 4 percent because taxes imposed at this level exclude wholesale and retail margins. Food, except that consumed in restaurants, almost always is exempted from any sales tax intended to promote redistributive goals. In developing countries, the exemption of food by itself renders most sales taxes at least faintly progressive, given the high proportion (up to 40 percent in many middle-income countries) of income of poor households spend on food. Sales taxes involving a limited number of luxury rates of between 20 and 30 percent at the manufacturers' level have been found to be workable in countries such as Colombia, Chile, Taiwan, and Korea.

The redistributive potential of sales tax rates differentiated in this way, however, is limited by the same administrative and compliance constraints standing in the way of the heavier use of income taxation in developing countries. While sales taxes are not as difficult to administer as income taxes, they do not collect themselves. A manufacturer's sales tax system employing three or even four rates may be administratively feasible in most countries, even when the highest rate approaches 40 percent. Rates much higher than that or reliance on a profusion of rates in an attempt to fine-tune the tax lead to substantial incentives and opportunities for tax evasion. Jamaica had over 15 rates prior to 1986, and Chile had over 20 from 1960 to 1970. In recognition of these problems, Indonesia adopted a flat-rate manufacturers' tax in 1985: The tax applies at a rate of 10 percent on *all* manufactured items and all imports. The tax nevertheless is slightly progressive, since it does not apply to items that do not go through a manufacturing process, including most foodstuffs consumed by low-income families.

Although the use of internal indirect taxes, such as sales taxes, can contribute to income redistribution goals without causing serious misallocation of resources, the same cannot be said for the use of customs duties. Sales taxes are imposed on all taxable goods without regard to national origin, including goods produced domestically as well as abroad. Tariffs apply only to imported goods. Virtually all countries, developed and developing, utilize customs duties to protect existing domestic industry. Developing countries in particular employ customs duties as the principal means of encouraging domestic industry to produce goods that formerly were imported. This strategy, called **import substitution,** is examined at length in Chapter 18.

Deliberate policies to encourage import substitution through the use of high protective tariffs, under certain conditions, might lead to results sought by policy makers. But accidental import substitution arises when tariffs are used for purposes other than protection, and this is unlikely to have positive results. Many countries, as already pointed out, use high tariffs to achieve heavier taxation of luxury consumption. Often heavy tariffs are imposed on imported luxury items for which there is no intention of encouraging domestic production. Therefore, many Latin American and some Asian countries have levied customs tariffs of 100–150 percent of value on such appliances as electric knives, hair dryers, sporting goods, videocassette recorders, and mechanical toys. For most countries, these items are clearly highly income elastic and apt candidates for luxury taxation.

But efforts to tax luxuries through high customs duties lead to unintended—and almost irresistible—incentives for domestic production or assembly of such products. In virtually all countries save the very poorest, alert domestic and foreign entrepreneurs have been quick to seize upon such opportunities. By the time local assembly operations are established, they usually can make a politically convincing case that the duties should be retained to enable local production to continue, even when the value added domestically is as low as 10 percent of the value of the product. Such operations, if subject to any local sales taxes, usually succeed in being taxed at the basic tax rate, usually 5 to 10 percent. By relying on tariffs for luxury taxation, the government ultimately forgoes the revenues it previously collected from duties on luxury goods, as well as severely undermining the very aims of luxury taxation.

If, instead, higher luxury rates on imports are imposed under a sales tax collected on both imports and any domestic production that may develop, unintended import substitution can be avoided. The use of import tariffs for luxury taxation—indeed, for any purpose other than providing protection to domestic industry—is one illustration of the general problem of using one economic policy instrument (tariffs) to achieve more than one purpose (protection, luxury taxation, and revenue). Reliance on import duties for revenue is subject to the same pitfalls just discussed. If it is desired to increase government revenue from imports, a 10 percent sales tax applied both to imports and any future domestic production will yield at least as much revenue as a 10 percent import duty, without leading to accidental protection.

CORPORATE INCOME AND PROPERTY TAXES: THE INCIDENCE PROBLEM

Income taxes on domestic corporations and property taxes often are mentioned as possible methods for securing income redistribution through the budget. Corporate income ultimately is received, through dividends and capital gains, almost exclusively by the upper 5–10 percent of the income distribution. Also, ownership of wealth, which in many lower-income countries largely takes the form of land, tends to be even more concentrated than income. But, to a greater extent in developing than in developed countries, efforts to secure significant fiscal redistribution through heavier taxes on domestic corporations and property are limited both by administrative and economic realities.

Administrative problems bedevil efforts to collect income taxes from domestic firms to at least as great an extent as for income taxes on individuals. Hence, in many countries, such as China and Pakistan, where corporate taxes on local firms have been important, as much as two thirds to three fourths of nonoil corporate taxes flow from state-owned firms not from private firms owned by high-income individuals. Taxes on land should be subject to less-severe administrative problems, since it is an asset that cannot be hidden easily. However, land valuation for tax purposes has proven difficult even in Canada and the United States. It is more difficult in developing countries. Other than Colombia, few developing countries have been able to assess property at anything approaching its true value.

Economic realities hinder efforts to achieve greater progressivity in the tax system through heavier use of corporate and land taxes, because of the tendency for taxation to unintentionally burden groups other than those directly taxed. This is the **incidence** problem. The incidence of a tax is its ultimate impact: not who actually pays the tax to the government, but whose income finally is affected by the tax when all economic agents have adjusted in response to the tax. The point of incidence is not always the point of initial impact. Taxes on domestic corporations may reduce the income of capitalists, who in turn might shift their investment patterns to reduce taxation. The income of the workers they employ and the prices charged to consumers may be affected as well. In the end, taxes on land and improvement may not much reduce the incomes of landholders but may be reflected in higher prices charged to consumers. Ultimately, all taxes are paid by people, not by things such as corporations and property parcels.

The implications of incidence issues may be illuminated by a simple application of incidence analysis to the corporation income tax. Consider a profit-maximizing company that has no significant monopoly power in the domestic market. If taxes on the company's income are increased in 1999, then after-tax returns to its shareholders in 1999 will be reduced by the full amount of the tax. In the short term, the incidence of the tax clearly is on shareholders. Since shareholders everywhere are concentrated in higher-income groups, the tax will be progressive in the short run. If capital were immobile, unable to leave the corporate sector, the long-term incidence of the tax also would rest on shareholders, and the tax would be progressive in the long run as well.

But, in the long run, capital can move out of the corporate sector. To the extent that capital is mobile domestically but not internationally, the corporate tax also will be progressive in the long run. Returns on capital remaining in the corporate sector will be reduced by the tax. Untaxed capital owners employed outside the corporate sector also will suffer a reduction in returns, because movement of capital from the taxed corporate sector will drive down the rate of return in the nontaxed sector. Because the corporate tax reduces returns to capital throughout the economy, all capital owners suffer, including owners of housing assets, and in a closed economy, the long-run incidence again is progressive.

However, few if any developing economies are completely closed; indeed, we saw in Chapter 11 that capital in recent years has become much more mobile internationally. To the extent that capital can move across national borders and higher returns are available in other countries, domestic capital will migrate to escape higher corporate taxes. But, as capital leaves an economy, both new and replacement investment and, ultimately, output will be curtailed and the marginal productivity of workers will fall. Prices of items produced with domestic capital therefore will rise. In this way, an increase in corporate taxes may be borne by domestic consumers, who pay higher prices for the reduced supply of corporate-sector goods. Similarly, domestic workers, whose income is reduced when production is curtailed, may bear a part of the burden of the corporate tax.

Hence, the corporate tax may be regressive (worsen the income distribution) in the long run. The degree of regressivity will depend on whether consumption by low-income groups is more or less capital intensive and on the relative position in the income distribution of workers losing their jobs or suffering declining real wages. In the end, capital owners may suffer no significant decline in income. Although, under other plausible conditions, an increase in the corporation income tax may not result in greater relative burdens on capitalists, this scenario is sufficient to illustrate that often the intentions of a redistributive tax policy may be thwarted by all the workings of the economy. Therefore, policy makers cannot be sure that all taxes imposed on wealthy capital owners ultimately will be paid by them.

LIMITED EFFECTS OF REDISTRIBUTION POLICY

The foregoing discussion suggests that, whereas some tax instruments may achieve income redistribution in developing countries, the opportunities for doing so are limited in most countries—a conclusion supported by a large number of empirical studies. With few exceptions, these studies show that the failure to administer personal income taxes effectively—the failure to utilize the limited opportunities for heavier taxes on luxury consumption, overreliance on revenue-productive but regressive excise taxes, and inclusion of food in sales taxes, all these combined—reduces significantly the redistribution impact of tax systems. By and large, tax systems in developing countries tend to produce a burden roughly proportional across income groups, with some tendency for progressivity at the very top of the income scale. As a result, the very wealthy pay a somewhat greater proportion of their income in taxes than the poor, but the poor still pay substantial taxes: at least 10 percent of their income in many cases studied (Argentina, urban Brazil, Colombia, Jamaica, and six others).[26] This is the predominant pattern even in countries, such as Colombia, Jamaica, Tanzania, and Chile before 1970, that placed strong policy emphasis on the use of tax tools to reduce income inequality. Of course, in the absence of such efforts, the after-tax distribution of income may have been even more unequal. This suggests that, although difficult to implement and often disappointing in results, tax reforms intended to reduce income inequality are not futile exercises and they may prevent taxes from making the poor worse off.

26. These Latin American studies have been summarized in Richard M. Bird and Luc Henry DeWulf, "Taxation and Income Distribution in Latin America: A Critical View of Empirical Studies," *International Monetary Fund Staff Papers,* 20 (November 1975), 639–62. Results of studies on Indonesia and Jamaica may be found in Gillis, *Tax Reform,* Chaps. 4 and 5.

EXPENDITURES AND EQUITY

The limits of tax policy suggest that, if the budget is to serve redistribution purposes, the primary emphasis must be on expenditure policy. Indeed, where redistribution through expenditures has been a high priority of governments, the results generally have been encouraging. The effects of government expenditure on income distribution are even more difficult to measure than those of taxes. But both the qualitative and quantitative evidence available strongly indicate that, in developing countries, budget expenditures may transfer very substantial resources to lower-income households, in some cases as much as 50 percent of their income. And the pattern of benefits tends to be progressive: A much higher fraction of income goes to the poor households than to those in the upper reaches of the income distribution.

One study found that, in Malaysia in the late 1960s, the combined effect of taxes and recurrent government consumption expenditures was to transfer 5 percent of GNP from the two highest income classes to the two lowest income groups, with more than three-quarters of the transfer going to the poor. This figure understates the actual extent of the redistribution impact of expenditures since it does not include the effects of public investment, which was perhaps the most important tool of fiscal redistribution in Malaysia from 1968 well into the 1990s.[27] Another study found that, in Indonesia in 1980, the tax system was only slightly progressive. But the expenditure side of the budget, with its emphasis on food subsidies and primary education, markedly helped the poor: Benefits from government expenditure were slightly more than 50 percent of the income of the poorest income group.[28] Similarly, an exhaustive study of the net incidence of the Chilean budget for 1969 shows that, although the tax system had virtually no effect on income distribution, government expenditures favored the poor. The lowest-income groups received only about 7.5 percent of national income but about 15–18 percent of the benefits from government expenditures.[29]

Obviously, not all government expenditures are effective in reducing income inequality. Some, like interest payments on government debt, have the opposite effect because interest income is concentrated in upper-income groups. But it is not difficult to identify those categories of budget

27. Donald R. Snodgrass, "The Fiscal System of Malaysia as an Income Redistributor in West Malaysia," *Public Finance,* 29, no. 1 (January 1972), 56–76.

28. Malcolm Gillis, "Micro and Macroeconomics of Tax Reform: Indonesia," *Journal of Development Economics,* 19, no. 2 (1986), 42–46.

29. Alejandro Foxley, Eduardo Aninat, and J. P. Arellano, *Redistributive Efforts of Government Programs* (Elmsford, NY: Pergamon Press, 1980), Chap. 6.

outlays that tend to have the most marked effects on the income of the poor. Public expenditures on primary, but not university, education tend strongly to reduce income inequality (Chapter 9). Government spending for public health programs, particularly water supplies, sanitation, nutritional programs, and rural health clinics, also can have a clearly progressive impact (Chapter 10). Although many poor people live in huge cities such as Jakarta, São Paulo, Mexico City, Lagos, and Calcutta, in most developing countries most of the poorest people tend to live in rural areas and wealthy people tend to live in urban areas. Hence, programs that reallocate government spending to rural areas (irrigation programs, secondary roads, erosion control) may tend to reduce income inequality overall, particularly in the case of irrigation.

Subsidies for consumption of basic foodstuffs also can result in substantial redistribution, provided food subsidy programs are not accompanied by oppressive price controls on the production of food by poor farmers. Subsidies to subnational governments often are used to finance the provision of basic human needs, such as water, sewerage, education, and health services, all of which have benefits concentrated in lower-income classes. Housing subsidies favor the poor less frequently, since many programs for housing subsidies (Indonesia, Ghana, Pakistan) in reality are confined largely to government employees, a group that in most countries is relatively well off.

Not all subsidy programs contribute to income redistribution, even when redistribution is the announced goal. The most striking example has been that of subsidies for the consumption of petroleum products, particularly kerosene, in Bolivia, Colombia, Indonesia, Pakistan, and several other oil-producing countries. In all four cases mentioned, a principal justification offered for such subsidies was to assist low-income groups. In Bolivia through 1980 and in Colombia through 1974, this argument was extended to cover gasoline consumption, even though in both countries automobile ownership was confined largely to the upper 5 percent of the income distribution and, in both, urban bus transport already was heavily subsidized. In Indonesia, gasoline was subsidized only lightly, but budget subsidies held the prices of kerosene and diesel fuel at less than half the costs of production and distribution. Although it seems plausible that kerosene subsidies strongly favor the poor, this is not the case. The poorest 40 percent of families consume only 20 percent of the kerosene sold. Therefore, for every $1 of subsidy to the poor, relatively high-income families received $4 of benefit. And, since kerosene can be substituted for diesel fuel, the subsidy program included it as well to prevent diesel users from switching. The result was that subsidies to kerosene and diesel fuel averaged about 5 percent of total tax revenues in Indonesia from 1979 to 1981, a figure exceeding total capital expenditures for education during that period.

IRRIGATION AND EQUITY

Many economists have long believed that government investment in irrigation in developing countries was bound to result in significant benefits for poor rural households, primarily by the effects of increased irrigation on agricultural productivity. However, this view was widely questioned by many analysts in the 1970s. They claimed that irrigation tends to be adopted faster and more completely by large farmers at the expense of small farmers and landless laborers, because the large farmers then are better able to buy out the small ones and because the technology associated with irrigation is laborsaving.

Studies sponsored by the International Food Policy Research Institute (IFPRI) tend to confirm the older view: Government investment in irrigation has not benefited the larger farmers more than small farmers and landless laborers. Rather, these studies find that the latter groups have made major increases in their incomes as a result of irrigation. This research focused on ten project sites in Indonesia, Thailand, and the Philippines. It found no tendency to merge farms after the introduction of irrigation and, particularly in Indonesia, the gains to landowners accrued primarily to small farmers. Further, gains to landless labor were substantial, however these are measured, because irrigated areas use more workers per acre than nonirrigated farms.[30]

30. *IFPRI Report,* 8, no. 1 (January 1986).

Fiscal policy to redistribute income must be viewed in perspective. It is not the only, and not always the most effective, instrument for redistribution. Other chapters, especially Chapter 4, draw attention to the pivotal importance for income distribution of land tenure, the terms of trade between rural and urban areas, the growth of employment, the relative prices of labor and capital, the openness and market orientation of the economy, and other factors. Taxation and government expenditures can affect most of those factors to some extent, but other, more direct policy instruments may have greater impact on income distribution. Each of these instruments, some of which force radical changes in the economy, has its economic and political dangers. But a government determined on a more equitable income distribution probably needs to employ all these measures—including progressive taxation and expenditure policies—to some degree.

Economic Efficiency and the Budget

SOURCES OF INEFFICIENCY

On the expenditure side of the budget, the tool we call *social cost-benefit analysis* earlier in this chapter can be deployed to enhance efficiency (reduce waste) in government spending. On the tax side, promotion of economic efficiency is more problematic.

All taxes, save lump-sum levies (poll taxes), lead to inefficiencies to one degree or another. Lump-sum taxes are not realistic options for raising government revenues given their high degree of regressivity. The objective therefore is to minimize tax-induced inefficiencies consistent with other goals of tax policy. In most developing societies, this objective largely reduces to the necessity to identify examples of waste engendered by taxes and purge them from the system. If a particular feature of a tax system involves large efficiency losses, called *excess burden* in fiscal economics, and at the same time contributes little or nothing to such other policy goals as income redistribution, then that feature is an obvious candidate for abolition. A full discussion of those elements of tax systems that qualify for such treatment is properly the subject of an extended public finance monograph. We can do little more here than indicate some of the principal examples.

A major source of inefficiency in taxation is excessive costs of tax administration. In some countries and for some taxes these costs have been so high that they call into question the desirability of using certain taxes for any purposes. This is true for certain kinds of narrow-based stamp taxes widely used in Latin America to collect government revenue on the documentation of transfer of assets, rental agreements, checks, and ordinary business transactions. Many stamp taxes cost more to administer than they collect in revenue.

In some countries even broad-based taxes have had inordinately high costs of collection. For example, sales taxes in Chile and Ecuador in the 1960s cost $1 in administration for every $4 collected, as opposed to about $1 per $100 for most state sales taxes in the United States. And because taxes on capital gains are so difficult to administer everywhere, including North America, the cost of collecting this component of income taxes often exceeds the revenue in developing countries.

Many developing countries, from Ghana to Colombia to Indonesia, have offered substantial tax incentives to encourage investment in particular activities and regions. Many of these, particularly income tax holidays for approved firms, have proven very difficult to administer and few have led to the desired result.[31] Given persistently pressing revenue require-

---

31. See, for example, Arnold C. Harberger, "Principles of Taxation Applied to Developing Countries: What Have We Learned?" in Michael Boskin and Charles E. McLure, Jr., eds., *World Tax Reform: Case Studies of Developed and Developing Countries* (San Francisco: ICS Press, 1990).

ments in most countries, granting liberal tax incentives may have no effect other than requiring higher rates of tax on taxpayers who do not qualify for incentives. It is a dictum of fiscal theory that economic waste (inefficiency) arising from taxation increases by the square of the tax rate employed, not proportionately. Therefore, it is not difficult to see that unsuccessful tax incentive programs involve inefficiencies for the economy as a whole that are not compensated for by any significant benefits. Largely for this reason, Indonesia abolished all forms of tax incentives in a sweeping tax reform in 1984.

Finally, some features of major tax sources involve needless waste. From the earlier discussion of the use of import duties for luxury tax purposes, it is clear that this often is a major source of inefficiency. The use of progressive tax rates in a corporation income tax (as in Colombia until 1974, Venezuela, Mexico, Brazil, Ghana, and a score of other countries) is another example. Progressive rates of corporate tax, where they cannot be enforced, do little to contribute to income redistribution, and where they can be enforced, they lead to several kinds of waste. Two of the most important are fragmentation of business firms and inefficiency in business operations. The incentive for fragmentation is evident: Rather than be subject to high marginal rates of taxes, firms tend to split into smaller units and lose any cost advantages of size. Where high progressive rates are employed for company income, the tax will take a high proportion (say, 70 percent) of each additional dollar of earnings, so the incentive to control costs within the firm will be reduced. For example, for a firm facing a marginal tax rate of 70 percent, an additional outlay of $1,000 for materials will involve a net cost to the firm of only $300, because at the same time taxes are reduced by $700.

NEUTRALITY AND EFFICIENCY: LESSONS FROM EXPERIENCE

Experience around the world, both in developed and developing countries, seems to indicate that, in societies where efficiency in taxation matters, this objective is best pursued by reliance on taxes that are as neutral as possible. A **neutral tax** is defined as one that does not lead to material change in the structure of private incentives that would prevail in the absence of the tax. A neutral tax system, then, is one that relies, to the extent possible, on uniform rates: a tax on all income at a flat rate or a sales tax with the same rate applied to all food and services. A neutral tax system cannot be an efficient tax system.

An **efficient tax system** involves a minimum amount of excess burden for raising a required amount of revenue, where the *excess burden* of a tax is defined as the loss in total welfare, over and above the amount of tax revenues collected by the government. Figure 12–2 demonstrates how the ex-

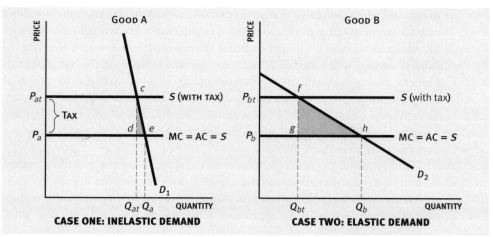

FIGURE 12–2   TAXATION AND EFFICIENCY: EXCESS BURDEN OF COMMODITY TAXES WITH CONSTANT MARGINAL (MC) AND AVERAGE COSTS (AC), UNDER COMPETITION. The shaded area in each case represents the excess burden of equal tax rates imposed on different goods. The greater is the elasticity, the greater the excess burden.

cess burden of, say, a commodity tax is the greater the more elastic is the demand or the supply of the taxed item. The left-hand diagram depicts the inelastic case, good A, while the right-hand diagram shows the elastic case, good B. Constant marginal costs (MC) are assumed in both cases, and at the same level for both goods, to portray more starkly the contrasting results achieved in those cases. Before the tax is imposed on either good, the equilibrium price and quantity are P_a and Q_a for good A and P_b and Q_b for good B. Now, we impose a tax rate (t)on both goods. The new equilibrium (posttax) magnitudes are P_{at} and Q_{at} for good A and P_{bt} and Q_{bt} for good B. For good A, the total amount of government revenue is the rectangle $P_a P_{at} cd$. The total loss in consumer surplus arising from the tax is the trapezoid $P_a P_{at} ce$. The excess of the loss in consumer surplus over the amount of government revenue is the conventional measure of efficiency loss from a tax, or excess burden. For good A, the excess burden is the small triangle *cde*. By similar reasoning, the excess burden in the case of good B is the larger triangle *fgh*. We may see that taxes of equivalent rates involve more excess burden when imposed on goods with elastic demand.

We can see that efficient taxation requires neither uniformity nor neutrality but many different tax rates on different goods, with tax rates lower for goods with elastic demand and higher for goods with inelastic demand. This is known as the **Ramsey rule,** or the **inverse elasticity rule.** The problem is that a tax system under this rule would be decidedly regressive: The highest taxes would be required on foodstuffs, drinking water, and sumptuary items. Taxes would be lower on items such as clothing, services, and foreign travel, which tend to be both price and income elastic.

The principle of neutrality in taxation is not nearly as intellectually satisfying a guide to tax policy as efficient taxation. Nevertheless, neutral taxation is to be preferred as one of the underlying principles of taxation, along with equity, until such time as analysts are able to identify optimal departures from neutrality—and uniformity in tax rates—in real-world settings. More intellectually satisfying tax policies also must wait until such time as administrative capacities are equal to the task of operating necessarily complicated structures of efficient or optimal taxes.

There is a paradox here. Neutral, uniform-rate taxes are less suited for efficiency goals than perfectly administered efficient taxes. Yet neutral tax systems are more likely to enhance efficiency in the economy than efficient or optimal systems, since neutral systems with uniform rates can be administered most easily and are much less vulnerable to evasion. This is not to say that neutrality has ever been or should be the overriding goal of tax policy. Governments often undertake very deliberate departures from neutral tax treatment of certain sectors or groups of society to achieve other policy goals. But, in real-world settings, these departures involve costs, not only in terms of tax administration but often in both equity and efficiency terms as well. It is important that these costs be made as transparent as possible, so that policy makers may weigh them against expected gains from nonneutrality, including efficiency gains. Under the present technology, major departures from neutrality in taxation are not likely to yield benefits commensurate with the costs. Neutrality in taxation may be the most advisable guide to efficiency in taxation for some time to come.

13

FINANCIAL POLICY

A country's **financial system** consists of a variety of interconnected financial institutions, both formal and informal. Except in a handful of countries (including Liberia, Panama, and several Francophone African countries), a central bank lies at the core of the organized financial system and is responsible for the control of the money supply and the general supervision of organized financial activity. Virtually everywhere, and particularly in developing countries, the commercial banking system is the most visible and vital component of the formal financial system, as acceptor of deposits and grantor of shorter-term credit. Other elements of the formal financial system include savings banks, insurance companies, and in a growing number of middle-income countries, pension funds and investment banks specializing in long-term credit, as well as emerging stock exchanges. Coexisting with these modern financial institutions are the informal and largely unregulated systems of finance, including pawnshops, local moneylenders, trade credit, and other informal arrangements involving the borrowing and lending of money, such as intrafamily transfers and cooperative credit. In very low-income countries, or even in some middle-income countries, the informal financial sector may rival the formal system in size.

Financial policy embraces all measures intended to affect the growth, utilization, efficiency, and diversification of the financial system. In North America and Western Europe, the term *financial policy* ordinarily is used as a synonym for *monetary policy:* the use of monetary instruments to reduce instability caused by fluctuations in either internal or external markets. In the United States, these instruments include open-market operations, changes in legal reserve requirements of commercial banks, and shifts in central bank (Federal Reserve) lending (rediscount) rates to commercial banks; these terms are explained later in the chapter. In developing countries, the term *financial policy* typically has a much broader meaning. Monetary policy is part of financial policy but so are measures intended to encourage the growth of savings in the form of financial assets, to develop money and capital markets, and to allocate credit between different economic sectors. Also of central importance, as the Asian financial crisis of 1997–98 reminds us, are regulatory and supervisory systems that oversee capital markets.

The Functions of a Financial System

The financial system provides four basic services essential for the smooth functioning of an economy: First, it provides a medium of exchange and a store of value, called *money,* which also serves as a unit of account to measure the value of the transactions. Second, it provides channels for mobilizing savings from numerous sources and channeling them to investors, a process called *financial intermediation.* Third, it provides a means of transferring and distributing risk across the economy. Fourth, it provides a set of policy instruments for the stabilization of economic activity.

MONEY AND THE MONEY SUPPLY

An economy without money as a **medium of exchange** is primitive. Trade between individuals must take the form of high-cost, inefficient barter transactions. In a barter economy, goods have prices, but they are expressed in the relative prices of physical commodities: so many kilos of rice for so many liters of kerosene, so many meters of rope for so many pairs of sandals, and so on. Trading under such circumstances involves onerous information costs.

Few societies have ever relied heavily on barter because of the high costs implicit in this means of exchange. At some point, prices of goods and services begin to be expressed in terms of one or more universally accepted and durable commodities, like gold and silver, or even beads and cowrie shells. The rise of commodity money diminishes the transaction and storage costs of trade but still involves problems of making exchanges across space and time. Gold and silver prices fluctuate, and the commodities therefore are not fully reliable as **units of account.** As specialization within an economy increases, financial instruments backed by commodities appear. In the last century, with the rise of central banking all over the world, currency has evolved into *fiat* money: debt issued by central banks that is legal tender. It is backed not by commodities of equivalent value but only by the full faith and credit of the central bank.

As markets widen and specialization proceeds apace, a need arises for still another financial instrument, **transferable deposits.** In the normal course of development, *checking* or *demand deposits*—deposits that may be transferred to any economic agent at the demand of the depositor—appear first and ordinarily bear little or no interest. Rising levels of economic activity, however, create increasing needs for transaction balances; individuals always will maintain some balances in demand deposits to meet these needs but tend to economize on the levels of such deposits if no interest is paid on them. With further monetization still another financial instrument begins to grow in importance: *time deposits,* which also are legally transferable on demand but sometimes only after stated periods. Time deposits involve contractual interest payments; higher interest rates induce people to hold greater amounts of deposits in this form.

While checking (demand) and time deposits are **liabilities** (or debts) of commercial banks, they are **financial assets** for the persons who hold them. Both demand and time deposits are known as *liquid financial assets.* Unlike *nonfinancial assets* that also can be held by households and businesses (inventories, gold, and land), demand and time deposits can be quickly and conveniently converted into their currency equivalents. *Currency,* by definition, is the most liquid of all assets. The concept of liquid financial assets is an important one in any discussion of financial policy in developing countries. For most developing countries, the movement of savers in and out of liquid financial assets may be the prime factor behind the success or failure of a financial policy. We will see that long-term shifts from tangible, or nonfinancial, physical assets to financial assets, particularly liquid assets, bodes well not only for economic growth but also for economic stability.

A country's **money supply** may be defined as the sum of all liquid assets in the financial system. While not all economists agree about what constitutes a liquid financial asset, most vastly prefer this money supply concept to those commonly employed in early postwar monetary analysis. Formerly, the money supply was conventionally defined as the sum of only two liquid financial assets: currency in circulation outside banks (C) plus demand deposits (D), which together are known as M1 *(narrow money).* However, it later became clear that, because depositors tend to view time and savings deposits (T) as almost as liquid as demand deposits, the former also should be included in any workable concept of money supply, called M2 *(broad money).* Finally, for high-income countries, specialized deposit-taking financial institutions have arisen and offer an array of options to savers other than those available in commercial and savings banks. The liabilities of these specialized institutions (O) are included in M3, *total liquid liabilities,* the broadest measure of money. Thus,

$$M1 = C + D \qquad [13\text{--}1]$$

$$M2 = M1 + T \qquad [13\text{--}2]$$

$$M3 = M2 + O \qquad [13\text{--}3]$$

For most low-income countries and many middle-income countries, liquid financial assets constitute by far the greatest share of outstanding financial assets. But, as income growth continues and the financial system matures, less-liquid financial assets assume progressively greater importance. These include primary securities such as stocks, bonds (issued both by government and firms), and other financial claims on tangible (physical) assets that are convertible into currency equivalents with only some risk of loss to the asset holder and are hence less liquid than demand or time deposits.

The evolution of financial activity follows no set pattern across countries. Differing economic conditions and policies may result in widely divergent patterns of financial growth. Nevertheless, as per capita income rises, money increases as a ratio to GDP. Table 13–1 shows these patterns for broad money, M2. For all income classes shown in the table, the ratio of M2 to the GDP rose substantially from 1970 to 1997. This reflects both economic growth and changing policies. Looking across countries, however, the pattern is not so clear-cut. On average, the advanced, high-income economies had much higher monetization ratios than the middle- and low-income countries. But no clear differences are found in the averages for lower-, lower-middle-, and upper-middle-income country groups. The variance among countries, even with similar income, is notable, as is the range among developing countries. The ratio of M2 varies from lows of 14–15 percent for low-income Nigeria and middle-income Peru and Argentina to highs of over 70 percent for Ethiopia, one of the poorest countries in the world, and middle-income Egypt and Malaysia. Even among industrial countries, Japan's ratio is two-thirds higher than those of Germany and the United States.

Liquid assets are not the only source of financial growth, however. As financial markets widen with the spread of the money economy, they also tend to deepen as a greater variety of financial assets begin to appear. With rising incomes, a growing proportion of financial growth tends to come in the form of nonliquid financial assets, such as primary securities, suitable as a basis for the type of longer-term finance that commercial banking systems cannot easily provide. The **financial ratio** (the ratio of net financial assets to GNP) tends to rise steadily from less than 20 percent of GNP in very poor countries, such as Haiti or Chad, to between 60 and 80 percent in higher-income countries, such as Brazil, South Korea, and Venezuela.

TABLE 13–1	BROAD MONEY (M2) AS A PERCENTAGE OF GDP, 1970 AND 1997						
	PERCENT OF GDP					**PERCENT OF GDP**	
	1970	1997				1970	1997
LOW-INCOME COUNTRIES	23	24[a]	*UPPER-MIDDLE-INCOME COUNTRIES*			27	44[a]
EXCLUDING INDIA	23	24[a]	COLOMBIA			19	20[a]
ETHIOPIA	14	44	ARGENTINA			31	24
TANZANIA	25	19	MEXICO			16	27
INDIA	23	47	MALAYSIA			34	100
BANGLADESH	31	38	KOREA, REPUBLIC			33	48
KENYA	30	46					
NIGERIA	17	17[a]	*HIGH-INCOME COUNTRIES*			59	74[a]
GHANA	19	17	SAUDI ARABIA			18	50
HONDURAS	20	36	UNITED KINGDOM			35	106
			JAPAN			74	111
LOWER-MIDDLE-INCOME COUNTRIES	25	44[a]	GERMANY			51	35
PAKISTAN	43	48	UNITED STATES			63	62
BOLIVIA	15	47					
CAMEROON	15	61					
THE PHILIPPINES	29	14					
SRI LANKA	23	32					
INDONESIA	10	56					
PERU	24	25					
EGYPT	35	78					

[a]1996 data.

Source: IMF, *International Financial Statistics 1999*; IMF, *International Financial Statistics Yearbook, 1994*, country tables; World Bank, *World Development Indicators* (Washington, DC: The World Bank, various years).

Malaysia by 1985 had reached the extraordinarily high level for a developing country of 200 percent. In very high-income countries, including Canada and the United States, total financial assets are also nearly twice as large as GNP, and three times GNP in Japan.[1] Here again, there is no evidence of immutable laws of financial development. Many very high-income industrial countries, including France and Holland, have financial ratios a third that of Japan. And many higher-income developing countries, particularly those with long inflationary histories (Uruguay, Brazil, Argentina), display a lower ratio of financial assets to GNP than poorer countries such as India and Thailand (89 and 65 percent, respectively).

FINANCIAL INTERMEDIATION

As financial structures become increasingly rich and diversified in terms of financial assets, institutions, and markets, the function of money as a medium of exchange, store of value, and unit of account tends to be taken

1. World Bank, *World Development Report 1989*, p. 39.

for granted except in the context of situations of runaway inflation. As financial development proceeds, the ability of the financial system to perform its second major function—financial intermediation—grows as well. The process of financial intermediation involves gathering savings from multitudinous savers and channeling them to a much smaller but still sizable number of investors. With a few exceptions, households are the only net savers in developing countries. At early stages of economic development, a preponderant share of intermediation activities tends to be concentrated in commercial banks. As development proceeds, new forms of financial intermediaries begin to appear and gradually assume a growing share of the intermediation function. These include investment banks, insurance companies, pension funds, and securities markets.

Financial intermediation activities are best measured through use of **flow-of-funds accounts,** which display the uses of finance by different economic sectors together with the sources of savings by sectors. These are akin to the flow matrix of input-output tables and social accounting matrices (see Chapter 3). Unfortunately, reliable flow-of-funds tables are available for only a few countries at present and cross-country generalization about intermediation based on such tables is not yet possible. In the absence of flow-of-funds accounts, we employ the liquid asset-GDP ratio as an approximate measure of financial intermediation.

Financial intermediation is best seen as one of several alternative technologies for mobilizing and allocating savings. The fiscal system discussed in Chapter 12 furnishes another alternative, and we see in the next chapter that reliance on foreign savings constitutes still another. Further, we will observe in this chapter that inflation also has been employed as a means of mobilizing resources for the public sector. Indeed a decision to rely more heavily on financial intermediation as a means of investment finance is tantamount to a decision to rely less heavily on the government budget, foreign aid and foreign investment, and inflation to achieve the same purpose.

TRANSFORMATION AND DISTRIBUTION OF RISK

Another major service provided by a well-functioning financial system is the transformation and distribution of risk. All economic activities involve risk taking, but some undertakings involve more risk than others. Individual savers and investors tend to be risk averse; the marginal loss of a dollar appears more important to them than the marginal gain of a dollar. But the degree of risk aversion differs among individuals. When risk cannot be diversified, or pooled, across a large number of individuals, savers and investors will demand greater returns, or premiums, for bearing risk; and activities involving high risk will tend not to be undertaken. But high-risk activities may well offer the greatest returns to the economy as a whole. A well-functioning financial system furnishes a means for diversifying, or pooling, risks among a large number of savers and investors. The system may offer assets with differing degrees of risk. Financial institutions that specialize in assessing and managing risks can assign them to individuals having different attitudes toward, and perceptions of, risk. Indeed, a perfectly functioning financial system can reduce all risk premiums to zero, except for those *systematic risks* that never can be diversified away from the domestic economy, such as those arising from national disasters and recessions in the world economy.

STABILIZATION

Finally, the financial system provides instruments for the stabilization of economic activity in addition to those available under fiscal policy and direct controls. All economies experience cyclical changes in production, employment, and prices. Governments often attempt to compensate for these fluctuations through policies affecting the money supply. Because unemployment in developing countries rarely is of the type that can be cured by monetary expansion, the use of financial policy for stabilization purposes generally focuses on efforts to control inflation. As the economic crisis that began in Asia in 1997 demonstrated, however, the financial system itself can become a major source of instability in the country. From 1998–99 on, as a result, financial policy also has focused on more than simply whether the supply of money is growing too rapidly or too slowly. Policy makers have had to devote much attention to ensuring the integrity and stability of banks and other, nonbank financial institutions to avoid a severe recession brought on by financial panic. In the discussion that follows, we focus first on the use of the financial system to control inflation and then return to the issue of how the financial system should be designed and managed to avoid panic and recession.

Inflation and Savings Mobilization

By the 1980s and 1990s, **price inflation,** defined as a sustained increase in the overall price level, generally was regarded as a malady, which in its milder forms was annoying but tolerable and in its moderate form corrosive but not fatal. Runaway inflation, also known as *hyperinflation,* however, always has been recognized as severely destructive of economic processes, with few offsetting benefits. Whereas a number of influential thinkers in the 1950s and 1960s advocated some degree of moderate inflation (for example, inflation rates between 8 and 12 percent) as a tool for promoting growth, few adherents of this view remain, for reasons discussed later. Many others did not actively advocate inflation but tended to have a higher threshold of tolerance for a steadily rising general price level than now is common. They believed that development inevitably involved trade-offs between inflation and unemployment and that the wise course was to resolve the trade-off in favor of less unemployment and more inflation. Today, few economists still believe in a fixed, long-term relation between inflation and unemployment, and a growing body of evidence, some of it presented in Chapter 5, demonstrates that restraining inflation may enhance, rather than retard, prospects for long-run growth.

INFLATION EPISODES

Inflationary experiences vary widely among developing countries and generalizations are difficult to make. Nevertheless, postwar economic history offers some interesting national and regional contrasts in both susceptibility to and tolerance for different levels of inflation. The period prior to the early 1970s was one of relative price stability in developing countries. In the southern cone of Latin America, however, particularly in Argentina, Brazil, and Chile, **chronic inflation**—prices rising 25–50 percent per year for three years or more—was an enduring fact of economic life for much of the past four decades. The experience of these countries indicates that a long period of double-digit inflation does not necessarily lead to national economic calamity in all societies. In all, 35 countries experienced chronic inflation from 1950 to 1997, as shown in Table 13–2.

However, a tolerable rate of inflation in one country may constitute economic trauma in another. This may be seen more readily by considering the often progressive inflationary disease called **acute inflation.** Acute inflation, defined here as inflation in excess of 50 percent for three or more consecutive years, was experienced by 33 countries over the postwar period, in some cases more than once per country. For Brazil, the progression from chronic to acute inflation did not result in any noticeable slowing of that country's relatively robust economic growth, whatever it may have meant for income distribution. In Ghana, on the other hand, a decade of acute inflation coincided with a decade of decline in GDP per capita. Although it may be tempting to attribute economic retrogression in Ghana to acute inflation, it is more likely that the same policies that led to sustained inflation, not the inflation itself, were responsible for declines in living standards there.[2]

2. For a diagnosis of the causes of the Ghanian economic decline after 1962, see Michael Roemer, "Ghana, 1950 to 1980: Missed Opportunities," and Yaw Ansu, "Comments," both in Arnold C. Haberger, ed., *World Economic Growth* (San Francisco: ICS Press, 1984), pp. 201–30.

TABLE 13-2 INFLATION OUTLIERS: EPISODES OF CHRONIC, ACUTE, AND RUNAWAY INFLATION AMONG DEVELOPING COUNTRIES, 1948–97 (AVERAGE ANNUAL RATES)

	CHRONIC INFLATION (25–50%, 3 YEARS)		ACUTE INFLATION (50–100%, 3 YEARS)		RUNAWAY INFLATION (+200%, 1 YEAR)	
	YEARS	RATE	YEARS	RATE	YEARS	RATE
ANGOLA					1995–97	1,053
ARGENTINA	1950–74	27	1977–82	147	1976	443
			1986–87	111	1983–85	529
					1988–90	1,400
ARMENIA					1990–96[a]	897
AZERBAIJIAN					1990–96[a]	590
BELARUS					1990–96[a]	715
BOLIVIA	1979–81	33	1952–59	117	1983–86	1,132
BRAZIL	1957–78	36	1979–84	108	1985	227
			1986	145	1987–92	831
CHILE	1952–71	29			1973–76	308
	1978–80	36				
	1983–85	26				
COLOMBIA	1979–82	26				
	1988–92	28				
DOMINICAN REPUBLIC			1988–92	51		
GEORGIA					1990–96[a]	2,279
GHANA	1986–90	32	1976–83	73		
INDONESIA					1965–68	306
KAZAKHSTAN					1990–96[a]	605
KYRGYZ REPUBLIC					1990–96[a]	256
LATVIA					1990–96[a]	111
LITHUANIA					1990–96[a]	179
MEXICO			1982–88	70		
NICARAGUA	1979–84	33			1985–91	2,130
PARAGUAY			1951–53	81		
PERU	1975–77	32	1950–55	102	1988–91	1,694
			1978–87	85		
ROMANIA					1991–93	132
RUSSIA					1993–95	376
SIERRA LEONE			1983–92	81		
SOUTH KOREA			1950–55	95		
TAJIKISTAN					1990–96[a]	394
TURKMENISTAN					1990–96[a]	1,074
TANZANIA	1980–89	27				
TURKEY	1981–87	38	1978–80	69		
			1988–92	67		
UGANDA	1990–92	37	1981–89	101		
THE UKRAINE					1993–95	1,167
URUGUAY	1948–65	26	1965–68	83		
	1981–83	34	1972–80	68		
			1984–92	76		
VENEZUELA	1987–92	40				
ZAIRE/CONGO	1981–82	36	1976–80	68	1991–92	2,987
			1983–90	68	1992–95	3,206
ZAMBIA	1985–87	44	1988–92	113		

[a]For a number of the former Soviet republics, the GDP price deflator data are given for the entire period, 1990–96, not broken down by year. See The World Bank, *World Development Indicators 1998,* pp. 230–32.

Source: IMF, *International Financial Statistics Yearbook 1994.*

Although acute inflation has proven toxic to economic development in some settings and only bothersome in others, **runaway (hyper-) inflation** almost always has had a devastating effect. Inflation rates in excess of 200 percent per year represent an inflationary process that is clearly out of control; 22 countries have undergone this traumatic experience since 1950. One recent major bout of runaway inflationary experience occurred in three Latin American countries: Bolivia and Argentina in 1985, Argentina again in 1988–90, and Peru in 1988–91. In Bolivia the annual rate of inflation over a period of several months in 1985 accelerated to a rate of nearly 4000 percent. In Argentina, the monthly rate of price increases was 30.5 percent in June 1985 alone; on an annual basis that would have been an inflation rate of 2340 percent. In both Bolivia and Argentina for much of 1985, workers had little choice but to spend their paychecks within minutes of receipt, for fear that prices would double or triple over the next week. In Peru, hyperinflation in 1989 gave birth to publications devoted only to the tracking of inflation (see the case study). In the 1990s, hyperinflation was experienced by virtually all the new republics formed after the breakup of the Soviet Union. In the first part of the 1990s, inflation reached a rate of nearly 400 percent a year in Russia over a period of several years and over 1000 percent a year in Georgia and Turkmenistan. In the latter two countries, civil war put heavy demands on government expenditures while reducing the ability of those governments to collect taxes, leading them to finance their activities by printing money. In Africa in the 1990s, civil war in Angola and the Congo also led to inflation rates of over 1000 percent per year.

The 35 countries in Table 13–2 brought on inflation in three different ways. In one group—including Argentina, Chile, Ghana, Indonesia, Peru, Russia, and the Ukraine—large budget deficits relative to GDP were financed by borrowing from the central bank. In a second group—Paraguay in the early 1950s and Brazil and Uruguay before 1974—inflation was caused by a massive expansion of credit to the private sector. And in Nicaragua, Sierra Leone, Uganda, Angola, the Congo, and several of the nations created out of the former Soviet Union, political strife or civil war exacerbated the fiscal and monetary causes of inflation. Whatever the initial impetus to inflation, as we shall see, once it begins to accelerate, the public begins to expect inflation to continue, and this leads to even higher more-sustained price increases.

For developing countries as a group, Table 13–3 shows that, on average, inflation was only 13 percent a year until the oil crisis began in 1973 but jumped to 21 percent a year during the period of rising oil prices until 1981. Inflation then accelerated to more than 30 percent a year even as oil prices began falling and exceeded 50 percent a year after oil prices collapsed in 1986. In the 1990s, these high rates of inflation continued

HYPERINFLATION IN PERU: 1988–90

The economic and social havoc wrought by hyperinflation is difficult to comprehend for those who have not lived through the experience. The Peruvian hyperinflation, which began in 1988 and continued until 1991, provides some rueful examples.

The inflationary process was triggered by large budgetary deficits and sustained by subsequent ongoing deficits, virtual economic collapse, and steadily rising inflationary expectations. Peru already had experienced two serious bouts with acute inflation since 1950 (see Table 13–2), but the pace of inflation in 1989 was the highest in the nation's history: 28 percent per month, or about 2000 percent per year. Moreover, inflation accelerated in the first six weeks of 1990, as prices rose by 6 percent per week, or about 1 percent per day. From January 1989 to December 1990, the value of the Peruvian currency (the intis) on the free market fell from 1,200 intis per dollar to 436,000 intis per dollar.

This hyperinflation may turn out to be one of the best documented in history: In 1988, Richard Webb, an internationally respected Peruvian economist, began to publish a magazine devoted essentially to helping producers and consumers cope with the chaos associated with runaway inflation. The magazine, called *Cuanto?* (*How Much?*) appeared monthly. It not only provided details on price developments for a large number of commodities and services but managed to extract what little humor there is in a situation where the price of a

TABLE 13–3	INFLATION BY REGIONAL GROUPINGS, 1964–98 (PERCENT PER ANNUM)					
	1963–73	1973–81	1981–86	1986–92	1992–95	1995–98
WORLD	26.3	13.8	14.1	21.1	19.2	6.8
INDUSTRIAL COUNTRIES	24.6	10.3	24.9	4.0	2.5	1.9
DEVELOPING COUNTRIES	12.9	20.7	32.0	55.0	47.9	12.6
AFRICA	24.9	17.3	29.0	25.4	40.2	12.1
ASIA	13.5	28.8	26.8	9.0	11.6	6.9
MIDDLE EAST	24.2	16.6	18.8	14.0	15.0	9.5
LATIN AMERICA & CARIBBEAN	18.4	43.7	98.0	232.8	216.5	15.5

Source: IMF, *International Financial Statistics Yearbook 1994, 1998*, pp. 108–9.

movie ticket rises while people are waiting in line to buy it or where a taxi driver must carry his fare money in a burlap bag because the domestic currency collected in fares each evening is too bulky to fit in his trousers.

But precious little is funny about hyperinflation. In Peru, it was a story of government employees going without pay for weeks at a time, of indices of poverty nearly doubling from 1987 to 1989, further impoverishing the poorest 40 percent of the population. It was a story of precipitous decline in gross domestic product and the rise of pervasive black markets in everything from dollars to gasoline to cement. It was a time when, on each payday, laborers rushed to the market to buy their weekly food supplies before they were marked up overnight. It was a tale of wide variations in price rises, where prices for such items as pencils and chicken increased by more than 25 times from February 1989 to February 1990, but prices of light bulbs and telephone services increased "only" tenfold.

Imagine life in Lima, the capital city, in the first few weeks of 1990, for a middle-income family trying to survive. For the first 40 days of the year, increases in the price of dying outpaced the price of living: the cost of funerals rose 79 percent, while house rent rose by 56 percent and the price of restaurant meals and haircuts increased by 44 percent.

By mid-1990, the economic paralysis of Peru was virtually complete. Peru's hyperinflation ended in 1992 (although inflation remained acute at 75 percent) as government reduced its budget deficit to 1 percent of GDP.

through the first half of the decade and then slowed markedly after 1995. The industrial countries, in contrast, had much lower inflation throughout and the highest price increases coincided with the rise in oil prices.

These averages conceal more than they reveal, however. Asian countries, with moderate inflation before the oil crisis, were adept at stabilizing their economies and reducing inflation to single digits during and after the rise in energy prices. African countries went in the opposite direction; they accepted the "imported" inflation from higher oil prices (and their own commodity price boom) during the 1970s and then, in the 1980s, chose to finance their deficits, using foreign aid and domestic borrowing, rather than to reduce them. Latin America stands out as the region of highest inflation prior to the 1990s and prior to the breakup of the Soviet Union into independent republics. Not only did many Latin American countries borrow extensively during the 1970s to cover external deficits, they also refused to reduce their fiscal deficits when those loans had to be repaid, at higher interest rates, during the early 1980s. Inflationary deficit financing intensified throughout the 1980s in many countries. By the 1990s, however, particularly after 1995, there was a strong trend in both Africa and Latin America toward reduced deficits and lower inflation, as it became clear that economic growth was unlikely until inflation had been quenched. In Latin America in the 1990s, only Brazil continued to experience triple digit inflation while major economies such as Argentine, Mexico, Chile, and Bolivia saw the rate of price increase fall below 20 percent a year.

FORCED MOBILIZATION OF SAVINGS

Chapter 12 identified a number of problems involved in the use of conventional taxes, such as income and sales taxes, for mobilizing public-sector savings. Another form of taxation is inflation. Governments from the time of the Roman Empire have recognized inflation as an alternative means of securing resources for the state. All that is required is that the stock of money be expanded at a sufficiently rapid rate to result in increases in the general price level and that people be willing to hold some money balances even as the values of these holdings decline. Inflation then acts as a tax on money holdings. At 15 percent inflation, the annual tax on currency is 13 percent, and at 40 percent inflation the tax is 29 percent.[3] These are higher annual tax rates than any country has ever managed to impose successfully on any physical asset, such as housing, automobiles, or equipment. Under extremely high rates of inflation, as in the German hyperinflation of 1922–23 or the Peruvian inflation of 1988–90, households attempt to reduce holdings of money balances to virtually nothing. However, except during runaway inflation, because money is so convenient as a means of exchange and unit of account, people always will hold some money balances even if they must pay fairly heavy inflation taxes for the convenience.

---

3. Say the nominal value of money balances at the beginning of a year is M_n, equal to the real value, M_r. Now, if price inflation proceeds at a rate p per year, then after one year the real value of money balances M_r' would be

$$M_r' = M_r/(1 + p)$$

The tax on these balances is $T = M_r - M_r'$, and the tax rate is

$$t = \frac{M_r - M_r'}{M_r} = 1 - \frac{1}{1 + p} = \frac{p}{1 + p}$$

If $p = 40$ percent, $t = p/(1 + p) = 29$ percent.

Difficulties in collecting conventional taxes, the apparent ease of collecting inflation taxes, the convenience properties of money balances, and the view that inflation taxes are progressive (richer people hold higher money balances) have led some policy makers and economists to view inflation as a desirable means of development finance. During the 1950s and 1960s, the influential United Nations Economic Commission for Latin America saw moderate inflation as a means of "greasing the wheels" of development, forcing savings from holders of money balances and transferring such savings to governments that were strapped for investment resources. Accordingly, much effort was expended in the search for what was viewed as an "optimal" rate of inflation for developing societies: The rate that maximizes tax collections, including both conventional taxes and inflation rates.

Implementation of such a forced-saving strategy will tend to curtail private investment, since some of the inflation tax will come out of money balances that would have been used for investment in the private sector. However, proponents of tax maximization through inflation assumed that the government's marginal propensity to invest out of inflation taxes exceeded that of the private sector and that the government would invest in real assets as productive as the private investment it displaced. Therefore, it was thought, forced-savings strategies would never reduce total investment.

Two implicit assumptions lay behind the argument that the forced-savings strategy would improve economic welfare in developing countries. Collections of conventional taxes were believed to be highly responsive to inflationary growth; that is, the revenue elasticity of the conventional tax system with respect to nominal income growth is greater than 1.[4] And efficiency losses from inflation taxes were thought to be less than efficiency losses from the use of conventional taxes to increase government revenues. Indeed, it can be shown that under circumstances where (1) a government's marginal propensity to invest out of inflation taxes is unity or greater, (2) the revenue elasticity of the tax system also is unity or greater, and (3) the marginal efficiency costs of inflation taxes are less than those for explicit taxes, the growth-maximizing rate of inflation may be as high

---

4. The revenue elasticity (E_R) measures the responsiveness of the tax system to growth in GDP. It is defined as the percent of change in tax collections divided by the percent of change in GDP, where $Y = $ GDP, or

$$E_R = \frac{\Delta T/T}{\Delta Y/Y}$$

If $E_R > 1$, then the tax system is revenue elastic and taxes rise proportionally more than national income. For example, if $E_R = 1.2$, then, for every 10 percent increase in GDP, tax collections rise by 12 percent. If $E_R < 1$, the tax system is revenue inelastic; if $E_R = 0.8$, then, with a 10 percent increase in GDP, tax collections rise by 8 percent.

as 30 percent. However, these assumptions are so far divorced from economic realities in developing countries as to undermine severely, if not demolish, the case for forced savings through inflation.

First, little evidence has found that governments anywhere have a marginal propensity to invest out of inflation taxes that is near unity. For tax maximization through inflation to simulate growth, a government's marginal propensity to invest would have to rise with inflation. Research by George von Furstenberg of the IMF and others find no support at all for even the weakest form of this hypothesis. Second, the net result of even moderate inflation on a government's total revenues (conventional taxes plus inflation taxes) actually may be to decrease the government's ability to expand total investment. This may occur easily if the revenue elasticity of the tax structure is less than unity, as is the case in many, but not all, developing countries. In such cases, the growth in collections from conventional taxes lags well behind nominal GNP growth. Particularly in the early stages of an inflationary process, part of the higher inflation tax collections will be offset by a decline in the real value of conventional tax collections. Third, available evidence suggests that, once inflation exceeds 2 percent per annum, the incremental efficiency losses from inflation taxes tend strongly to outweigh those from conventional taxes.[5] And it is well to note that, since 1973, typical inflation rates in developing countries have been far above 2 percent (Table 13–3).

At best, then, government mobilization of resources through inflation is a knife-edge strategy. Inflation rates must be kept high enough to yield substantial inflation taxes but not so high as to cause holders of liquid assets to undertake wholesale shifts into real assets to escape the tax. Inflation rates must be kept low enough that collections from conventional taxes do not lag far behind growth in nominal income and that efficiency losses from inflation do not greatly exceed efficiency losses from higher conventional tax revenues. Paradoxically, then, the inflation tax device can work best where it is needed the least: in those countries having tax systems most responsive to growth in the overall GDP and involving low efficiency costs. Countries with revenue-elastic tax systems do not need to resort to inflation in an attempt to finance expanded government investment. In this sense, tax reform can be seen as a substitute for inflationary finance but not the other way around.

INFLATION AS A STIMULUS TO INVESTMENT

The forced-savings doctrine was not the only argument employed in favor of purposeful inflation. For more than 50 years, some economists argued that, even in industrial countries, rising prices can act as a stimulus to pri-

---

5. George M. von Furstenberg, "Inflation, Taxes and Welfare in LDCs," *Public Finance,* 35, no. 2 (1980), 700–1.

vate business enterprise, as inflation was thought to be helpful in drawing labor and capital out of declining sectors of the economy and into dynamic ones. If true for industrial societies, then, it was reasoned, the argument might apply with special force in developing countries, where rigidities, bottlenecks, and barriers to mobility were such that resources were particularly likely to be trapped in low-productivity uses. Inflation, it was argued, would help to speed the reallocation of labor and capital out of traditional or subsistence sectors into the modern sectors with the greatest development potential. Therefore, moderate inflation was seen not only as inevitable but desirable: A progressive government would actively seek some target rate of inflation, perhaps as high as 10 percent, to spur development.

Experience with development since 1950 strongly suggests that some inflation indeed is inevitable in developing societies seeking rapid growth in per capita income: Factors of production are relatively immobile in the short run, and imbalances and bottlenecks in supply develop in spite of the most careful planning. However, the deliberate use of sustained inflation to spur development is likely to achieve the desired results only under a limited set of circumstances.

First, if inflation is the result of deliberate policy or can otherwise be anticipated, then in a sustained inflationary process, the approaching rise in prices will cause individuals and firms to adjust their expectations of inflation. To the extent that the inflation is anticipated, the supposed beneficial effects will never occur; people already will have taken them into account in their decision making.[6] For industrial societies, it would be difficult, at least for an economist, to accept the idea that behavior does not ultimately adjust to expectations of inflation. In developing countries, where all markets, including the market for information, tend to be more imperfect than in developed countries, it might be argued that firms and individuals are less efficient in collecting and using information, including that pertinent to the formation of price expectations. Thus, inflation may not be fully foreseen throughout the economy, and consequently rising prices may result in some stimulus to development in the short term. But it should be recognized that, over the longer run, a successful policy of deliberate inflation depends on people not understanding the policy.

Second, the argument that deliberate inflation enhances private-sector performance overlooks the effects of inflation on risk taking. Inflation increases the risk of all investment decisions. Suppose that businesses can anticipate inflation with a margin of error of plus or

6. This observation dates at least as far back as the early 1930s, to Swedish economist Knut Wicksell. It contains the germ of the idea behind the rational-expectations school of thought of the 1970s and 1980s.

minus 20 percent of the actual rate. (If the margin of error is wider, the effects about to be described will be more pronounced.) If inflation has been running at 5 percent per year, there may be a general expectation that it will settle within the range of 4–6 percent in the near future. But, if inflation has been running at substantially higher rates, say, 30 percent, then expectations of future inflation rationally may be in the much broader range of 24–36 percent. The entrepreneur therefore faces far higher levels of uncertainty in planning investments and production. The more uncertain the future and future returns are, the more likely is the entrepreneur to reduce his or her risks. Investments with long lives (long gestation periods) tend to be more risky than those with short lives. Thus, inflation tends to reduce private-sector investment in projects with a long-term horizon; the inhibiting effects rise with the rate of inflation. Unfortunately, these often are precisely the types of investments most likely to involve high payoffs in terms of income growth for society as a whole.

Finally, inflation may severely curtail private-sector investment by constricting the flow of funds to the organized financial system if nominal interest rates are not allowed to rise as rapidly as the expected rate of inflation. As we see in the next sections, such situations are typical under strategies of shallow financial development.

In any case, many of the arguments developed in favor of deliberate inflation may have been little more than efforts to rationalize the failure of many governments (particularly in Latin America) to bring inflation under control. In most cases inflation in developed and developing countries has been more a consequence of policy miscalculation or economic dislocation (oil-price shocks, civil wars, agricultural disasters, and so on) than a consciously chosen instrument of economic growth. Some reflective observers of inflationary dynamics, such as Albert Hirschman, have maintained that inflation usually is not the outcome of a systematic set of choices designed to promote growth and other policy objectives. Rather, inflation usually represents the consequences of government temporizing, postponing difficult decisions that might shatter a fragile consensus in governments with sharply divided constituencies.[7] Measures to increase collections from conventional taxes or reduce government spending on programs enacted at the behest of powerful vested interests are examples of such difficult decisions. Avoiding such stabilizing changes is tantamount to choosing inflation, in the hope that, at some point in the future, a more enduring coalition of constituencies can be assembled to

7. Albert O. Hirschman, *Journeys toward Progress: Studies of Economic Policy-Making in Latin America* (New York: Twentieth Century Fund, 1963), pp. 208–9.

directly confront difficult issues. Seen this way, inflation results not by design but by default.

INFLATION AND INTEREST RATES

The concept of real interest rates is central to the understanding of the implications of financial policy for growth and development. Interest rates may be viewed as the price of financial assets. The **nominal interest rate** on loans is the stated rate agreed between lender and borrower at the time of contracting a loan. The nominal rate of interest on deposits is the rate offered savers at the time the deposit is made. The nominal rate is an obligation to pay (on loans) or a right to receive (on deposits) interest at a fixed rate regardless of the rate of inflation. Currency, which is debt of the central bank but a financial asset for currency holders, bears a *nominal* interest rate of 0. In some countries, such as Indonesia, Turkey, and South Korea, interest is paid on demand deposits, but typically this asset also receives a nominal return of 0. Time deposits (including savings accounts) always bear positive nominal interest rates, ranging from as high as 30 percent in Indonesia in 1974 (for deposits committed for a two-year term) to as low as 4 percent in Ghana in the early 1970s. When an enterprise borrows from a commercial bank, the interest rate it agrees to pay usually is quoted in nominal terms; that is, independent of any changes in the general level of prices. Because costs are incurred in intermediating between savers and investors, the nominal lending rates must exceed nominal deposit rates or financial intermediaries will operate at a loss. However, in some countries, governments, as a part of broader antiinflationary programs, deliberately have set lending rates below deposit rates and subsidized banks to cover their losses, as in Korea (1960s) and Indonesia (1968–80).

Nominal interest rates—those quoted by banks on loans and deposits—often are subject to maximum ceilings imposed by governments. For example, usury laws and conventions throughout much of the history of the United States limit nominal interest rates that can be charged on loans both to private citizens and the government. Similar laws have operated in developing countries. Also, several organized religions support limitations on nominal rates to limit usury; this adds moral force to conventions limiting interest rates.

Nominal interest rates are significant for financial development because the nominal rate governs the *real* interest rate. The **real interest rate** is the nominal interest rate adjusted for inflation, or more precisely, the inflation rate expected by the public. Consider two depositors in different countries in otherwise identical circumstances, except that in one country the inflation rate is expected to be 5 percent and in the other at 10 percent. If both receive nominal interest rates of 6 percent, then the real rate of interest in the first case is a positive 1 percent and in the second case is a negative 4 percent. The prospective value of the deposit will rise in the first and fall in the second.

Borrowers as well as depositors respond ultimately to real, not nominal, rates of interest. At sustained high rates of inflation, say, 30 percent per year, borrowers will be quite willing, indeed eager, to pay nominal interest rates of 30 percent per year, for loans then are costless: They can be repaid in money with purchasing power well below that at the time of borrowing. Where legal ceilings do not apply on nominal interest rates, they will tend to adjust as expected inflation rises and falls. However, in many countries, at least until recent financial market reforms, governments placed ceilings on nominal interest rates. Inflation often exceeded these ceilings, and this resulted in negative real rates.

The relationship between real and nominal interest rates can be illustrated with a one-year deposit of $1 that pays a nominal rate of interest, i. At the end of the year, the deposit is nominally worth $1 + i$. If inflation is p per year, then the *real* value of the deposit at the end of the year is only $(1 + i)/(1 + p)$. Then, the real rate of interest, r, is this value minus the original deposit of $1, or

$$r = (1 + i)/(1 + p) - 1 \qquad [13-4]$$

Note that in this formula we must express rates in fractions, not percentages: 6 percent becomes 0.06.

For example, in Ecuador in 1992, the deposit rate was 34 percent and inflation was 45 percent. The real rate of interest on deposits was

$$r = (1 + 0.34)/(1 + 0.45) - 1 = -0.076 = -7.6 \text{ percent}$$

This means that a depositor, at the end of a year, would have lost 7.6 percent of the value of his or her funds, equivalent to a tax of 7.6 percent on those assets.

When inflation and interest rates are low, say, below 10 percent, the real rate of interest can be approximated by a simple formula:

$$r = i - p \qquad [13-5]$$

In Malaysia, where the deposit rate was 7 percent in 1992 and inflation was nearly 5 percent, the real rate of interest was $7 - 5 = 2$ percent a year.

In cases where conventional income taxes are collected on interest income, the tax (at rate t) also must be deducted from the nominal rate to arrive at the real deposit rate net of taxes r_n.

$$r_n = \frac{1 + i(1 - t)}{1 + p} - 1 = \frac{i(1 - t) - p}{1 + p} \qquad [13-6]$$

Therefore, with only a 20 percent income tax on interest, equation 13–6 shows that the real rate of deposit interest in Ecuador would have been -12 percent. Most countries impose taxes on interest income.

This discussion of inflation and real interest rates brings us to the point where we may evaluate the role of financial policy in a systematic fashion. We shall see that the real interest rate is critical in determining the extent to which the financial system will be able to *mobilize and allocate* savings for development finance. It is important to note that this is not the same thing as saying that higher real interest rates will induce households to save higher proportions of their income than would be the case at lower real interest rates. This would imply that the interest elasticity of savings is greater than 0. But, if savings and consumption decisions are responsive to the real rate of interest, the effects of financial policy on income growth are magnified.

Interest Rates and Saving Decisions

In evaluating the impact of financial policy on economic growth, it is important to distinguish between the implications of real interest rates for consumption-saving decisions, on the one hand, and for decisions about the uses of savings, including the channels through which savings flow, on the other. Debate over the first question revolves around estimates of the interest elasticity of savings (ϵ_{sr}); debate over the second is couched in terms of the elasticity of demand for liquid assets with respect to the real interest rate (ϵ_{lr}).

Where both elasticities are 0, financial policy can play only a minimal role in the development process. Where both elasticities are high and positive, the scope for growth-oriented financial policy can be substantial. Where ϵ_{sr} is small or 0 but ϵ_{lr} is positive and large, financial policy still may have a significant impact on savings mobilization through the financial system. Virtually all economists can agree that the real interest rate has a significant impact on the demand for liquid assets; that is, with higher real rates, a higher proportion of savings will be channeled through the financial system.

But the evidence is mixed on the extent to which higher real interest rates may stimulate savings and, thus, increase the ratio of national savings to gross national product.

Econometric tests on national savings rates by financial economist Maxwell Fry note that, in Asia, where real interest rates generally have been positive over the past two decades, the ratio of gross national saving to GNP rises about 0.1 percentage point for each 1 percentage point rise in the real deposit rate. This response, although statistically significant, is too small to justify a rise in interest rates as the main approach to raising national savings. But Fry cites other studies that find higher elasticities of savings to real interest rates in much of the developing world except Latin America, where the elasticity is close to 0. There does appear to be a consensus that saving rates are determined more by income and by economic and demographic structure than by interest rates. In Asia, it appears that savings rates are strongly affected by the availability of banking services, as measured by the number of bank branches per 1,000 people.[8]

INTEREST RATES AND LIQUID ASSETS

Whereas the role of the real interest rate in consumption-saving decisions is a matter of some dispute, the role of real interest rates in influencing the demand for liquid assets rarely is questioned, whether in developed or developing countries. Indeed, there is evidence that the real interest rate paid on deposits plays an even greater role in liquid asset demand in developing than industrial countries. Furthermore, experience with marked adjustments in real interest rates in Korea (1965), Indonesia (1968–69, 1974, and 1983), Taiwan (1962), and a host of Latin American countries strongly indicates the significance of real interest rates for growth in money holdings and demand and time deposits (M2).

Liquid assets, or financial assets in general, represent one form in which savings out of past or current income can be held. The demand for liquid assets in economies where nominal interest rates are not allowed to adjust fully to expected rates of inflation, as has been true for many developing countries, typically is represented as a function of income, the real interest rate, and the real rate of return available on nonfinancial assets:

$$L/P = d + d_1 Y + d_2 g + d_3 r \qquad [13\text{--}7]$$

where L = liquid asset holdings; P = price level; Y = real income (that is, money income deflated by the price level); g = real return on nonfinancial assets; r = the real interest rate on deposits; and d = a constant; d_1 and d_3 are expected to be positive, and d_2 negative.

The values for the parameters in equation 13–7 are readily understandable. As real income (Y) grows, the public will want to hold more purchasing power in the form of cash and demand and time deposits, the principal forms of financial assets available in developing countries. In particular, d_1 is positive because, at higher levels of real income, higher real levels of liquid balances will be needed to carry out transactions and meet contingen-

---

8. Maxwell J. Fry, *Money, Interest and Banking in Economic Development,* 2d ed. (Baltimore: Johns Hopkins Press, 1995), pp. 162–69.

cies. Clearly, liquid asset balances furnish a convenience service to asset holders. In industrial societies with highly developed financial systems and securities markets, it might be reasonable to expect something like a proportional relationship between the growth in income and the growth in demand for liquid assets. However, in developing countries, the demand for liquid assets, given relative price stability, may rise at a faster rate than income because of the paucity of other financial assets in which to hold savings. That is, in developing countries, the income elasticity of demand for liquid assets may be expected to exceed unity. Indeed, even for middle-income countries such as Malaysia, the demand for liquid assets grew twice as fast as real income from 1970 to the eve of the financial crisis in 1997–98. For many Latin American countries the long-run income elasticity of money demand also often is above unity. In such circumstances the rate of increase in the supply of liquid assets (M2) can exceed the rate of income growth by a substantial margin and price stability still can be maintained.

The sign for d_2, the coefficient of the return on nonfinancial assets, is negative since liquid assets are not the only repository for domestic savings. A range of assets, including nonfinancial assets and, in higher-income countries, nonliquid financial assets such as securities, are available to savers. Higher returns on these nonliquid assets relative to liquid assets will induce a shift of savings out of the latter.

The coefficient d_3 of the real deposit rate has a positive sign, for at higher levels of real interest rates, the public will be willing to hold larger liquid balances. Where r is negative, holders of all liquid assets pay hidden inflation taxes on their balances. Because higher rates of the inflation tax are imposed on non-interest-bearing assets (cash and demand deposits) than on interest-bearing time deposits, savers will be less willing to hold liquid assets.

Numerous studies have been made of the demand for liquid assets in a variety of developing countries over the past several decades. In these studies, estimates of the elasticity of demand for liquid assets with respect to real interest rates vary according to differing economic conditions across countries. However, in country after country, real interest rates have been a powerful factor affecting liquid asset demand. In Asia, where controls over interest rates have been most widely liberalized for the longest time, sharp increases in the real interest rate on time deposits (from negative to positive levels) have resulted in dramatic growth in the share of liquid assets in GNP. On the other hand, many Latin American and African countries have allowed real interest rates to remain negative over long periods. Consequently, growth in the demand for liquid assets was minimal in these countries. In most, the share of liquid assets in the GDP either declined or remained constant until after financial reforms were implemented in the 1980s or 1990s.

Table 13–4 presents the real interest rates on deposits and bank loans for a number of developing countries. In 1980, there was a preponderance

TABLE 13-4   REAL INTEREST RATES, 1980 AND 1992

	REAL DEPOSIT RATE		REAL LENDING RATE	
	1980	1992	1980	1992
LOW-INCOME COUNTRIES				
ETHIOPIA	—	26.2	—	22.3
MALI	—	8.1	14.5	17.2
TANZANIA	220.2	—	214.4	0.0
INDIA	—	—	4.6	6.4
BANGLADESH	24.5	5.9	21.9	10.3
KENYA	27.1	212.2	22.9	28.3
NIGERIA	24.3	218.4	21.5	213.7
SENEGAL	22.3	7.9	5.3	16.9
GHANA	225.7	5.6	220.7	—
HONDURAS	29.4	3.2	0.3	11.9
LOWER-MIDDLE-INCOME COUNTRIES				
BOLIVIA	219.8	9.9	213.0	29.8
CAMEROON	21.9	6.2	3.1	14.4
THE PHILIPPINES	25.0	5.0	23.6	9.7
SRI LANKA	29.2	6.2	25.6	1.4
INDONESIA	210.2	12.0	—	15.3
PERU	—	28.0	—	57.8
EGYPT	210.3	20.1	26.1	6.2
UPPER-MIDDLE-INCOME COUNTRIES				
BRAZIL	17.6	49.7	—	—
HUNGARY	25.8	0.1	20.3	5.8
COLOMBIA	—	20.2	—	8.1
ARGENTINA	210.6	26.5	26.9	27.8
MEXICO	24.6	0.2	1.3	—
MALAYSIA	20.5	2.3	1.0	3.1
KOREA	27.1	3.6	28.3	3.6
HIGH-INCOME COUNTRIES				
UNITED KINGDOM	23.3	3.5	21.5	5.5
JAPAN	22.1	1.0	0.6	4.4
GERMANY	2.5	3.8	6.3	9.2
UNITED STATES	—	—	1.6	3.2

Source: World Bank, *World Development Report 1994,* Table 12; and IMF, *International Financial Statistics Yearbook 1994,* pp. 106–9.

of negative real rates on both deposits and loans. But, by 1992, after financial market reforms and stabilization programs in many countries, most countries had positive real rates. Comparison with Table 13–1 shows many cases in which a marked rise in real interest rates or the maintenance of positive real rates over the period was accompanied by a jump in the ratio of broad money to GDP: India, Honduras, Bolivia, the Philippines, Sri Lanka, Indonesia, Egypt, Mexico, and Korea.

Financial Development

SHALLOW FINANCE AND DEEP FINANCE

Policies for **financial deepening** seek to promote growth in the real size of the financial system: the growth of financial assets at a pace faster than income growth. In all but the highest-income developing countries, private-sector financial savings predominantly take the form of currency and deposits in commercial banks, savings and loan associations, postal savings accounts, and in some countries, mortgage banks. For most developing countries, growth in the real size of the financial system is reflected primarily in growth in the share of liquid assets in GDP. In contrast, under **shallow finance,** the ratio of liquid assets to GDP grows slowly or not at all over time and typically will fall: The real size of the financial system shrinks. Countries able to mobilize large volumes of government or foreign savings can sustain high growth rates even under shallow finance policies, although even these countries may find financial deepening attractive for reasons of employment and income distribution. But, for countries where mobilization of government savings is difficult and foreign savings scarce or unwanted, deep finance may be essential for sustained income growth. This is because growth in the share of liquid assets in GDP provides an approximate indication of the banking system's ability to increase its lending for investment purposes. We will see that the hallmark of deep financial strategy is avoidance of negative real interest rates; shallow finance, on the other hand, typically involves sharply negative real interest rates.

Growth in the real size of the financial system enhances its capacity for intermediation: gathering savings from diverse private sources and channeling these savings into productive investment. The need for financial intermediation arises because savings endowments do not necessarily correspond to investment opportunity. Those individuals with the greatest capacity to save usually are not those with the entrepreneurial talents required for mounting new investment projects. Except in very simple, rudimentary economies, mechanisms are required to channel savings efficiently from savers to entrepreneurs. In rudimentary economies, production in farming, industry, and other activities is small scale and involves traditional technologies. Producers ordinarily can finance most of their modest investment requirements from their own current savings or those of their families (self-finance). Small-scale enterprises employing traditional technologies have an important role to play in development (see Chapter 17). Yet, at some stage, improvement in productivity (and therefore living standards) in any economy requires adoption of newer technologies. These typically involve lumpy investments that ordinarily are well beyond the financial capacity of all but the wealthiest families. Where enterprise finance is restricted to current family savings, only very wealthy groups can adopt such innovations. Thus, a heavy reliance on self-finance tends to be associated with both low productivity and, usually, persistent income inequality.

Restriction to self-finance also guarantees that many productive opportunities involving high private and social payoffs will never be seized, because the resources of even the small number of very wealthy are not unlimited. Innovative, smaller-scale investors are not the only groups that fare poorly where financial intermediation is poorly developed; savers are penalized as well. Let us first examine the case where even the most basic financial intermediaries—commercial banks—are absent. Under these circumstances the domestic options open to savers are limited to forms of savings such as acquisition of gold and jewelry, purchase of land and consumer durable goods, or other relatively sterile forms of investment in physical assets. Alternatively, wealthier savers may ship their savings abroad. The common feature of all such investments is that the resources devoted to them are inaccessible to those domestic entrepreneurs who would adopt new technology, begin new firms, or expand production in existing enterprises. Savings in the form of physical assets like gold may be plentiful, as in France or India, but this type of savings effectively is locked away from investors. At a minimum, such investments may be trapped in declining sectors of the economy, unable to flow to sectors with the brightest investment prospects.

However, even where financial intermediation is poorly developed, individuals have the option of holding some of their savings in the form of currency. Additions to cash hoards are superior to investment in unproductive physical assets from an economywide point of view, since at least this serves to curtail the demand for physical assets, reduce upward pressures on their prices, and thus moderate domestic inflation. Nevertheless, savings held in this form still are relatively inaccessible to investors.

There now are virtually no societies where financial systems are as rudimentary as those just sketched. All developing countries have financial institutions, however embryonic, to serve as intermediaries between savers and investors, even where these intermediaries are limited to commercial banks that accept checking (demand) and time (savings) deposits from savers, to relend to prospective investors for a short term. Intermediation flourishes under deep finance, but under strategies of shallow finance intermediation is constricted and the financial system can contribute little to further the goals of economic growth. Later, we see that shallow finance may have unintended effects on employment and income distribution as well.

SHALLOW FINANCIAL STRATEGY

Shallow financial policies have a number of earmarks: high legal reserve requirements on commercial banks, pervasive nonprice rationing of credit, and most of all, sharply negative real interest rates. Countries rarely, if ever, have consciously and deliberately adopted strategies of shallow finance. Rather, the repression of the financial system flows logically from certain policies intended to encourage, not hinder, investment.

In developed and developing countries alike, policy makers often have viewed low nominal rates of interest as essential for expansion of investment and controlled interest rate levels tightly. Indeed, so long as the supply of investment funds is unlimited, low interest rates will foster all types of investment activities, as even projects with low returns will appear more attractive to investors. In accordance with that observation and in the belief that low interest rates are particularly essential to assist small enterprises and small farmers, governments often have placed low ceilings on nominal interest rates charged on all types of loans. These low ceilings are quite apart from special credit programs involving subsidized credit for special classes of borrowers. Because financial institutions ultimately must cover costs (or else be subsidized by governments), low legal ceilings on nominal loan rates mean low nominal interest rates on deposits as well.

As long as inflation is held in check, low ceilings on nominal loan and deposit interest rates may not retard growth, even when these ceilings are set below the opportunity cost of capital. Indeed, the United States over the period 1800–1979 managed rather respectable rates of income growth even in the presence of a set of archaic usury laws and other interest rate controls that (particularly before 1970) often involved artificially low, administered ceilings on interest rates. Even so, throughout most of the period before 1979, real interest rates in the United States remained positive; periods in which real interest rates were sharply negative were intermittent and confined to wartime (1812, 1861, 1917–18, and 1940–46).[9]

Usury laws and other forms of interest rate ceilings have been common in developing countries as well. For all the reasons just given plus one more, financial officials in many developing countries, observing gross imperfections in financial markets, have concluded that the market should not be permitted to determine interest rates. Monopoly (or oligopoly) power in financial markets—particularly in commercial banking—in fact provides ample scope for the banks and other lenders to exercise market power in setting interest rates on loans at levels higher than the opportunity cost of capital.

There are ample observations of gross imperfections in financial systems in developing countries. Barriers to entry into banking and finance often allow a few large banks and other financial institutions to possess an inordinate degree of control over financial markets and thus to exercise monopoly power in setting interest rates. Often these barriers are a direct

---

9. Steven C. Leuthold, "Interest Rates, Inflation and Deflation," *Financial Analysis Journal* (January–February 1981), 28–51.

result of government policies. Governments have prohibited new entrants into the field, adopted such stringent financial requirements for entry that only the very wealthy could amass the needed capital, or reserved permission for entry to political favorites who were attracted to banking and finance largely by the monopoly returns available when entry was restricted.

In this way, one set of government policies—entry restrictions—helps give rise to the need for extensive controls on price charged by financial institutions. Typically, these controls take the form of interest rate ceilings imposed to limit the scope of monopoly power in the financial system. Controls by themselves do not necessarily lead to shallow finance. Rather, combination of rigid ceilings on nominal interest rates and inflation impedes financial development and ultimately retards income growth.

Few economists believe that steeply positive real interest rates are essential for healthy growth in the real size of the financial system. In fact, the Chilean experience with very high real interest rates from 1981 to 1983 strongly suggests the opposite. Indeed, there is no widely accepted answer to the question, What level of real interest rates is required for steady development of the financial system? Clearly the required real rate will differ across countries in different circumstances. In some, financial growth may continue even at 0 or mildly negative real interest rates; for others, moderately high positive real rates of between 3 and 5 percent may be essential.

Apart from a few Latin American countries and Indonesia, most developing countries were able to keep rates of inflation at or below 5–6 percent prior to 1973. Inasmuch as nominal deposit rates typically were between 3 and 5 percent, real interest rates tended to be slightly positive or only mildly negative. When inflation accelerated in many developing countries after 1973, because few countries made more than marginal adjustments in nominal deposit rates, real interest rates turned significantly negative in many nations, as Table 13–4 shows for 1980. Negative interest rates endured in a few African and Latin American countries in the period 1983–89.

When real interest rates turn significantly negative, the maintenance of low nominal rates for promoting investment and income growth becomes counterproductive. Inflation taxes on liquid financial assets bring real growth in the financial system to a halt. Sharply negative real rates lead to a shrinkage in the system, as the demand for liquid assets contracts. This tendency is evident from a comparison of Tables 13–1 and 13–4, which shows the tendency for negative real interest rates to be associated with decreases in the degree of monetization in countries such as Argentina, Ghana, Nigeria, and Peru.

Contraction in the financial system results in a reduction in the real supply of credit and thus constricts investment in productive assets. Under such circumstances, nonprice rationing of investible resources must occur and can take many forms. In most developing countries, only those borrowers with either the highest-quality collateral or the "soundest" social and political connections or those willing to make the largest side payments (bribes) to bank officers will be successful in securing finance from the organized financial system. These criteria do not yield allocations of credit to the most productive investment opportunities.

Negative real interest rates make marginal, low-yielding, traditional types of investment appear attractive to investors. Banks and financial institutions find such projects attractive as well, since they may be the safest and the simplest to finance and involve the most creditworthy borrowers. Satisfying the financial requirements of such investors constricts the pool of resources available to firms with riskier projects offering greater possibilities for high yields. Additionally, in the presence of substantial inflation, interest rate ceilings discourage risk taking by the financial institutions themselves, since under such circumstances they cannot charge higher interest rates (risk premia) on promising but risky projects. Also, negative real interest rates are inimical to employment growth, as they make projects with relatively high capital-output ratios appear more attractive than if real interest rates were positive. This implicit subsidy to capital-intensive methods of production reduces the jobs created for each dollar of investment, even as the ability of the financial system to finance investment is shrinking.

Negative real rates of interest tend to lower the marginal efficiency of investment in all the ways described. In terms of the Harrod-Domar model described in Chapter 2, shallow financial strategies cause higher capital-output ratios. Consequently, growth in national income and, therefore, growth in savings tend to be lower than when real rates are positive. Therefore, shallow finance retards income and employment growth even if the interest elasticity of savings is 0. And, if savings decisions are responsive to real interest rates, then shallow finance will have even more serious implications for income growth, as the ratio of private savings to the GDP also will contract.

DEEP FINANCIAL STRATEGIES

Deep finance as a strategy has several objectives: (1) mobilizing a larger volume of savings from the domestic economy, that is, increasing the ratio of national savings to the GDP (where the interest elasticity of savings is thought to be positive and significant); (2) enhancing the accessibility of savings for all types of domestic investors; (3) securing a more efficient allocation of investment throughout the economy; and (4) permitting the financial process to mobilize and allocate savings to reduce reliance on the fiscal process, foreign aid, and inflation.

A permanent move toward policies involving positive real interest rates or, at a minimum, avoidance of sharply negative real rates is the essence of deep finance. In turn, this requires either financial liberalization that allows higher nominal rates on deposits and loans, curbing the rate of inflation, or some combination of both.

Given the difficulties involved in securing quick results in reducing inflation to levels consistent with positive real rates of interest, the first step involved in a shift from shallow to deep financial strategies ordinarily is to raise the ceilings on nominal rates for both deposits and loans. In some cases this has required nominal interest rates as high as 30 percent on time deposits (Korea in 1966, Indonesia in 1968 and 1974).[10] In extreme cases of acute inflation, the initial step has involved raising ceilings on nominal deposit rates to as much as 50 percent in Argentina and Uruguay in 1976 and to nearly 200 percent in Chile in 1974 (where real interest rates nevertheless remained negative until 1976). As the real rate moves toward positive levels, savers strongly tend to increase their holdings of liquid assets; this allows a real expansion in the supply of credit to investors. Marked increases in flow of savings to financial institutions have been observed when nominal rates were increased substantially, as in Uruguay in 1976, Indonesia in 1968–69 and 1983, and Taiwan and South Korea in 1965. Notable responses also have occurred in countries where mildly negative real rates were moved closer to positive levels through increases in nominal rates: These include India and Sri Lanka after 1977 and Turkey after 1980.

Available evidence suggests that countries that attempt to maintain modestly positive real interest rates over long periods tend to be among those with the highest rates of financial growth, as we have already noted in comparing Tables 13–1 and 13–4. Nevertheless, one can have too much of a good thing. One factor contributing to sharply negative real GDP growth rates in Chile in 1982 and 1983 was the emergence of very high real interest rates in 1981 and 1982. The nominal interest rate on loans increased sharply, while at the same time there was a very large and unexpected drop in inflation: The real interest rate soared above 30 percent.[11]

---

10. Ceilings rarely need be increased to the point where they match the *current* rate of inflation. For example, in Indonesia in 1974, the nominal ceiling on two-year time deposits was raised to only 30 percent, even though inflation over the previous 12 months was 42 percent. The increase in nominal rates, coupled with a battery of other measures, convinced depositors that real rates soon would be positive. All that is required is that the inflation expected by savers be reduced to levels closer to the nominal deposit rate.

11. The Chilean real GDP declined by 13.2 percent in 1982 and by 2.3 percent in 1983. For a comprehensive discussion of the Chilean economic debacle of 1982–83, see Sebastian Edwards "Stabilization with Liberalization: An Evaluation of Chile's Experiment with Free-Market Policies 1973–83," *Economic Development and Cultural Change,* 27 (September 1985), pp. 224–53.

Where finance is deep, inflation tends to be moderate; therefore savers are not subject to persistently high inflation taxes on liquid asset holdings. That being the case, they are less inclined to shift their savings into much more lightly taxed domestic assets such as gold, land, or durable goods and foreign assets such as currencies or land and securities. Rather, financial resources that otherwise may have been utilized for these purposes flow to the financial system, where they are more accessible to prospective investors. Nonprice rationing of credit, inevitable under shallow finance, diminishes as well. As a result, the capacity of the financial system to identify and support socially profitable investment opportunities expands: Higher-risk, higher-yielding investment projects stand a far better chance of securing finance under deep than shallow finance. Growth prospects are enhanced accordingly.

The preceding discussion represents but a sketch of policies designed to promote financial deepening. The focus has been on the real interest rate on deposits and loans when in fact a variety of other policies may be involved. These include central bank payment of interest on commercial bank reserves and avoidance of high legal reserve requirements to commercial banks. That positive real interest rates tend to lead to growth in the real size of banking systems now rarely is questioned. Such a development substantially enlarges the real flow of short-term credit, the stock-in-trade of commercial banks. However, investment finance problems do not end with provision of a growing real flow of short-term credit. As economies move to higher levels of per capita income, the pattern of investment shifts toward longer horizons. Longer-term investment requires longer-term finance. Commercial banks everywhere are ill suited for providing substantial amounts of long-term finance, given that their deposits primarily are of a short-term nature.

Therefore, as financial and economic development proceeds, the need for institutions specializing in longer-term finance rises accordingly: Insurance companies, investment banks, and ultimately equity markets (stock exchanges) become important elements in financial intermediation. Nevertheless, the type of well-functioning commercial bank system that tends to develop under deep finance almost always is a necessary condition for the successful emergence and long-term vitality of institutions specializing in longer-term investment finance. Where entry into financial activities is only lightly restricted, longer-term financial institutions may appear spontaneously.

Earlier we observed that entry into the financial field is rarely easy, and other factors also often lead to gross imperfections in financial markets. Under such circumstances, many developing country governments have found intervention essential to develop financial institutions specializing in longer-term finance. Intervention may take the form of establishment of government-owned development banks and other specialized institutions to act as distributors of government funds intended as a source of longer-term finance, as in Indonesia and Pakistan. In Mexico, Colombia, and Venezuela, governments have provided strong incentives for private-sector establishment of long-term financial institutions. Other governments have sought to create conditions favorable for the emergence of primary securities (stocks and bonds) markets, the source par excellence for long-term finance. In cases where these measures have been undertaken in the context of financial markets with strong commercial banking systems (Hong Kong, Singapore, Brazil, and Mexico), efforts to encourage long-term finance have met with some success. In cases where commercial banking has been poorly developed as a consequence of shallow finance (Ghana, Uruguay before 1976) or where government has sought to "force feed" embryonic securities markets through tax incentives and other subsidies (Indonesia before 1988, Kenya, Turkey), the promotional policies have been less effective.

PANIC, MORAL HAZARD, AND FINANCIAL COLLAPSE

Prior to the late 1990s, policy makers and students of financial systems development were concerned largely with how to gradually achieve financial deepening over the long term through the kinds of measures discussed in the previous sections of this chapter. In 1994, however, Mexico was hit by very rapid withdrawals of foreign capital and a cessation of international lines of credit, leading to what became known as the *peso crisis*. The Mexican economy contracted sharply, and the crisis spread to Argentina, Venezuela, and several other economies. In the middle of 1997, financial panic struck again, hitting first in Thailand and then in three other Asian countries and eventually spreading as far as Russia and Brazil. These events reminded policy makers and analysts alike of the risk of outright collapse of the financial system. Nations that had appeared to have developed deeper and stronger financial systems suddenly found themselves with large numbers of bankrupt commercial banks and nonbank financial institutions that were in even worse condition. On these countries' stock markets, share values of listed companies fell to a small fraction of what they had been only a few months earlier.

Financial panics have occurred throughout the history of banking. Economists have long recognized that financial markets tend to be prone to instability and panic. Events similar to the Asian financial crisis have been recurring in slightly different forms since the development of banks and the emergence of international capital flows several centuries ago. Prominent examples include the Dutch tulip mania of 1636, the bank panics in the United States in the late nineteenth century, and the global financial collapse and Depression that began in 1929. Economist Charles Kindleberger chronicled the long history of these phenomena in his classic work *Manias, Panics, and Crashes: A History of Financial Crises.*[12]

Banks, as pointed out previously, must be prepared to pay their depositors immediately on demand, but banks lend for longer periods. This situation does not create a problem as long as only a few depositors ask for their money at any given time. But, sometimes, rumors spread that the bank may be in trouble and in danger of defaulting on its obligations to its depositors. It may not matter whether the rumor is true or not as long as a large number of depositors believe it might be true. Depositors will rush to the bank to get their money, and the bank will not have enough cash on hand or readily available from nearby sources to satisfy so many customers. As a result, the bank will have to sell off its assets (long-term loans, for example) to other banks and financial institutions, often at a large discount. Even a previously healthy bank under such circumstances can go bankrupt. Panics of this sort were common through the nineteenth century and the early part of the twentieth century.

Financial crises occur less frequently in industrialized economies today because these countries have put into place mechanisms and institutions specifically designed to reduce the frequency and severity of financial crises. The United States' experiences with severe banking crises in 1873, 1893, and 1907 helped bring about the establishment of the Federal Reserve System beginning in 1913. The Federal Reserve, like other central banks around the world, stands ready to act as a "lender of last resort" and provide financing to commercial banks that face a sudden creditor run. With this mechanism in place, there is no need for a bank to hurriedly sell off its assets at discounted prices.[13] Industrialized countries also provide deposit insurance, ultimately backed by the government, to assure bank depositors that they will get their money back even in the event that their bank runs out of funds. The Federal Deposit Insurance Corporation insures deposits in U.S. banks up to $100,000. Depositors therefore no longer had to rush to the bank and remove their money every time they feared the bank might be in trouble. In addition, most industrialized countries have well-defined and transparent systems for managing bankruptcies and other debt workouts. These mechanisms provide a way to both stop a creditor panic (the court has the authority to declare a standstill on debt payments) and to sort out creditor claims on a bankrupt corporation. These institutions have re-

---

12. New York: John Wiley and Sons, third edition, 1996.

13. The United States used this mechanism effectively in October 1987 to mitigate the impact of a severe stock market crash.

duced (but not completely eliminated) financial crises in the industrialized countries.[14]

As Southeast Asia in 1997 demonstrated, however, some situations still could lead to financial panic and a run on the banks and other financial institutions. A critical feature of the Southeast and East Asian situation was that the banks of Thailand, Indonesia, Malaysia, and South Korea had borrowed heavily outside their countries and thus had acquired debts that had to be repaid in foreign exchange such as U.S. dollars or yen. The next chapter will deal with the circumstances that led the banks to borrow abroad. Here, we simply note that these Asian banks acquired large liabilities that were not protected by deposit insurance. The ability of the banks to repay also depended on their ability to buy foreign exchange from the central bank, preferably at the same exchange rate at which they had borrowed the money. But, in the case of the Southeast and East Asian countries, the central banks ran out of foreign exchange and had to allow the exchange rate to devalue. Where, in early 1997, 25 Thai baht could buy 1 U.S. dollar, by the end of the year it took 50 baht to buy a dollar. A bank that had borrowed $100 million, expecting to use 2.5 billion baht to repay the loan (plus interest) now had to find 5 billion baht to do so. In effect, the size of the bank's debt, in terms of baht, had doubled almost overnight.

As foreign lenders began to realize what was happening, they panicked much like depositors in the days before deposit insurance would have panicked. Even lenders who previously felt there was nothing to worry about rushed to get their money out because the first people in line were the ones most likely to get their money. As with a fire in a crowded theater, those first out the door are the most likely to survive. The panic that began in Thailand soon spread to Malaysia and Indonesia and then even to the considerably more advanced economy of South Korea. When the panic finally subsided, many of the banks and nonbank financial institutions in these countries were insolvent. In the case of Indonesia in 1998, despite nearly a decade of banking reform, virtually all the banks were insolvent.

If foreign borrowing by the banks created conditions that could lead to panic, why did so many banks and nonbank financial institutions take the risk of borrowing so much in foreign exchange? Why, in turn, did the foreign lenders lend? Some of the behavior of both the borrowers and lenders can be attributed to ignorance. Neither fully realized the dangers entailed in their actions. Among foreign lenders, for example, there was a widespread belief that Asia was the place to make high rates of return on

---

14. The most prominent recent example of a financial crisis in the United Sates is the savings and loan crisis of the early 1990s.

their investments, a belief often based on little more than that everyone else in their business thought this was the case. It is not uncommon for investors to behave more like a herd of animals than careful calculators of risks and rewards. This kind of behavior, therefore, often is referred to as **herd** behavior.

But there was another important reason why borrowers and investors alike were willing to take these risks. They believed the risks were not that great because they counted on being helped out if they got into trouble. The investors counted on their own governments (in Japan, Europe, and the United States) together with the International Monetary Fund to protect them from default by the Asian banks. The Asian banks and nonbank financial institutions, in turn, counted on their own governments to bail them out if they got into trouble. The political and personal ties between the bankers and the government were very close in all four of the hard-hit Asian countries, and in the past, the government frequently had stepped in to help out when one bank or another got into trouble. The willingness of governments to step in when these borrowers and lenders got into trouble created a situation that economists refer to as **moral hazard.** *Moral hazard* refers to the situation where an effort to protect people or institutions from risky behavior actually tends to encourage people and institutions to increase their willingness to practice risky behavior. Governments, by protecting lenders and borrowers in the past, thus contributed to the risky behavior that led to the Asian financial crisis of 1997–98.

The development of a sound financial system, therefore, requires more than a government that ensures that real interest rates are positive, important as that is. Financial institutions, if they are to survive a crisis like the one that occurred in 1997–98, must learn that they have to be able to stand on their own feet in such a crisis. They must carefully calculate the risks of their actions and avoid practices that would require them to turn to the government in a crisis. The Asian banking systems that came closest to meeting this standard, those of Singapore and Hong Kong, weathered the 1997–98 crisis without getting into serious trouble. We return to the lessons of the Asian financial crisis and the role of the International Monetary Fund, in particular, in the next chapter.

INFORMAL CREDIT MARKETS

The discussion of financial development has dealt with modern credit institutions, the formal market. But, in many developing countries, **informal credit markets** coexist with modern financial institutions. These markets arise in many forms. In rural India, village moneylenders make loans to local farmers who have no access to commercial banks. In Ghana and other West African countries, market women give credit to farmers by paying for crops in advance of harvest, and they assist their customers by selling finished goods on credit. In South Korea, established lenders actually make loans on the street outside modern banks; this justifies their designation as the *curb market*. In much of rural Africa, wealthy family members make loans to less fortunate kin; and all over the developing world, there are cooperative arrangements to raise funds and share credit among members. Even in modern economies, pawnbrokers and others give credit outside the formal credit system.

Informal credit generally is financed by the savings of relatively wealthy individuals, such as local landowners, traders, family members who have moved into lucrative jobs or businesses, and the pooled efforts of cooperative societies. But informal lenders also may have access to the formal banking system and borrow there, to relend to customers with no access to banks. How can they do this if the banks cannot? First, because they know their borrowers so well and may have familial, social, or other ties to them, informal lenders face lower risks than distant, large banks that might loan to the same borrowers. Loan recovery rates are higher (usually much higher than found in large banks in developing countries) because those who borrow in informal markets know that the availability of loans in the future is dependent on repaying current loans. Second, they also face lower administrative costs in making loans. Of course, moneylenders charge very high interest rates; and this is a third reason they coexist with banks, which are often prevented by law from charging rates high enough to cover the risks and costs of loans in small amounts to very small firms and low-income borrowers.

As modern credit institutions evolve, especially under deep financial policies, they draw customers and resources from the informal market. First, some of the largest and most creditworthy borrowers from informal lenders eventually qualify as borrowers in the formal market. Second, some moneylenders themselves may establish credit institutions within the informal system. Third, banks begin to attract savings from a wider group of households, some of which previously had directed their savings into informal channels. On all counts, the informal market is likely to shrink in size and coverage, although it is likely to exist in tandem for some time. The process may leave behind several kinds of borrowers, such as small farmers, traders, artisans, and manufacturers, who will still depend on the shrinking informal market for their credit. Competitive, efficient, and varied financial institutions—the kind encouraged by deep financial policies—have incentives to integrate borrowers into the modern market and thus reduce the adverse impacts of financial development on those who once depended upon informal credit markets.

SMALL-SCALE SAVINGS AND CREDIT INSTITUTIONS: BANGLADESH AND INDONESIA

In a number of countries, most notably in Bangladesh and Indonesia, formal credit institutions have attempted to bridge the gap between small-scale borrowers in the informal sector and the formal financial system.

In Bangladesh, the Grameen Bank, founded by Muhammad Yunus roughly three decades ago, provides credit to people in about a third of the country's 68,000 villages. The average loan is under $100 and the maximum is $200. Of the borrowers, 65 percent are landless women and all loan recipients are poor. Loans are made to individual women, but only through local groups that provide social pressure for repayment. The loans are not heavily subsidized and the recovery rate exceeds 97 percent. Grameen Bank is more than a financial institution, however. Its loans require recipients to accept certain "social disciplines" such a cleanliness and family planning, and the bank provides such services as advice on home construction and access to education for some borrowers.[15]

In Indonesia, a government bank, the Bank Rakyat Indonesia, or BRI, provides full banking services, both loans and savings deposit facilities, to farmers, traders, and other small-scale borrowers, through their branches in over 3,000 villages. BRI charged market rates of interest, around 30 percent a year, on its loans and paid attractive rates, about 12 percent, on deposits. These rates changed during the financial crisis of 1997–98, largely because of the high inflation in that period, but the basic rate-setting principles remained the same. In the absence of inflation, rates of 30 percent on loans may seem high, but they were considerably below the rates charged by informal money lenders. At these rates the BRI was able to attract sufficient savings deposits to more than finance its loan program. Roughly 97 percent of the loans are repaid on time. In addition, the program is a major generator of profits for the BRI, something that cannot be said about many of its credit programs for large-scale producers and borrowers.[16]

15. World Bank, *World Development Report 1989,* p. 117; and A. Wahid, *The Grameen Bank: Poverty Relief* (Boulder, CO: Westview Press, 1993).

16. Richard H. Patten and Jay Rosengard, *Progress with Profits: The Development of Rural Baking in Indonesia* (San Francisco: ICS Press, 1991); and Marguerite Robinson, "Rural Financial Intermediation: Lessons from Indonesia," development discussion paper No. 434, Harvard Institute for International Development, October 1992.

Monetary Policy and Price Stability

We have seen from Table 13–3 that inflation largely was conquered in Asia during the 1970s, but accelerated in Latin America and Africa during and especially after the oil-price boom of the 1970s. By the 1990s, however, attempts to control inflation have been more serious and widespread with the notable exception of the republics formed out of the collapse of the Soviet Union. Monetary policy is the principal instrument used to achieve price stability.

MONETARY POLICY AND EXCHANGE-RATE REGIMES

Appropriate use of monetary policy in controlling inflation depends critically on the type of exchange-rate regimes used by a country. Exchange-rate regimes form a continuum with fixed (pegged) exchange rates at one end and floating (flexible) exchange rates at the other. Under a **fixed-exchange-rate** system, a country attempts to maintain the value of its currency in a fixed relation to another currency, say, the U.S. dollar: The value of the local currency is **pegged** to the dollar. This is done through intervention by the country's monetary authorities in the market for foreign exchange and requires the maintenance of substantial **international reserves** (reserves of foreign currencies), usually equivalent to the value of four or more months' worth of imports.

For example, consider the case of Thailand, where from 1987 to early 1997 the Thai currency, the baht, was fixed at an exchange rate close to 25 baht to $1 U.S. Because the exchange rate, if left to its own devices, would change from day to day to reflect changes in both the demand for and supply of exports and imports and in capital flows, to defend the peg, the government must be prepared to use the country's international reserves to buy or sell dollars at an exchange rate of 25 to 1 to keep the exchange rate from moving. If, for example, a poor domestic harvest caused the nation to increase its food imports, the baht-dollar exchange rate would tend to rise (the baht would depreciate, as its dollar value falls) in the absence of any net sales of dollars from Thailand's international reserves. To sustain a fixed exchange rate, of course, the country must have sufficient foreign exchange reserves to keep on buying baht at that fixed rate. In 1997, as already pointed out, because of large capital outflows, Thailand actually ran out of foreign exchange and had to abandon its support of the pegged rate.

Under freely **floating rates,** the authorities simply allow the value of local currency vis-à-vis foreign ones to be determined by market forces. Between the two ends of this continuum (see Figure 13–1) lie a number of

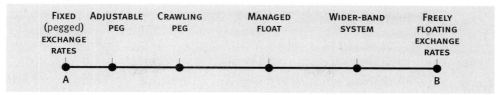

FIGURE 13–1 CONTINUUM OF PROTOTYPES OF EXCHANGE-RATE REGIMES. As one moves from point *A* on the left to point *B* on the right, both the frequency of intervention by domestic monetary authorities and the required level of international reserves tend to be lower. Under a pure fixed-exchange-rate regime (point *A*) authorities intervene so that the value of the currency vis-à-vis another, say the U.S. dollar, is maintained at a constant rate. Under a freely floating-exchange-rate regime, authorities do not intervene in the market for foreign exchange, and there is minimal need for international reserves; indeed, there can be no balance-of-payments deficit.

intermediate options.[17] Closest to the floating-exchange-rate option is the *wider band* system, where the exchange rate of a country is allowed to float or fluctuate within a predefined band of values, say, between 23 and 27 baht to $1 U.S. But, when conditions threaten to push the value of the currency beyond the band, the authorities intervene by buying or selling local currency as appropriate to stay within the band. Further along the continuum away from floating rates is the *managed float,* where the authorities are committed to defend no particular exchange rate, but they nevertheless intervene continuously at their discretion. A country with steadily shrinking international reserves, for example, might allow the value of its currency to depreciate against the value of other currencies; that is, allow the exchange rate to rise against other currencies.

Two other systems are closely related hybrids of fixed and floating rules. The *crawling peg,* used over a long period by Brazil, Colombia, and Indonesia, involves pegging the local currency against some other currency but changing this in gradual, periodic steps to adjust for any differential between the country's inflation rate and the world inflation rate. Closest to a fixed-exchange-rate system is the *adjustable peg,* involving a commitment by the monetary authorities to defend the local exchange rate at a fixed parity (peg), while reserving the right to change that rate when circumstances require.

Two very rigid forms of pegged exchange rates that a small number of countries have adopted are currency boards and "dollarization." With a *currency board,* the government issues domestic currency only when it is

17. For a full discussion of these and other types of exchange-rate regimes, see John Williamson, *The Open Economy and the World Economy* (New York: Basic Books, 1983), pp. 238–41; or Anne O. Krueger, *Exchange Rate Determination* (New York: Cambridge University Press, 1983), pp. 123–36.

fully backed by available foreign exchange reserves at the given exchange rate. Currency in circulation increases when additional foreign exchange becomes available (say, through increased export receipts) and decreases when foreign exchange becomes scarcer (e.g., through an increase in imports or capital outflows). This system assures that the country will not run out of foreign exchange. However, the main instrument of adjustment becomes domestic interest rates, which increase when foreign exchange (and domestic currency) becomes scarcer, and declines when foreign exchange becomes more available. Hong Kong, Bulgaria, Argentina, Brunei, Djibouti, Estonia, and Lithuania all have currency boards. With *dollarization,* one country adopts another country's currency, as Panama did many years ago when it adopted the U.S. dollar as its currency. Most economists believe that currency boards and dollarization are appropriate in only a very limited number of developing countries that are small, very open to trade, and not vulnerable to large commodity price swings.

The currencies of all the major industrial countries have floated vis-á-vis one another since the early 1970s, with occasional intervention by national monetary authorities to prevent very sharp swings in rates. Most developing countries have adhered to either the adjustable-peg or the crawling-peg system, although an increasing number, particularly in Africa, have been adopting floating-rate systems as part of stabilization programs. Since, in practice, both pegged systems are like fixed-rate regimes, for our analysis we focus most of our attention on monetary policy issues arising under fixed exchange rates in small open economies.

SOURCES OF INFLATION

In open developing economies with fixed exchange rates, the rate of monetary expansion no longer is under the complete control of domestic monetary authorities. Rather, countries with fixed exchange rates may be viewed as sharing essentially the same money supply, because the money of each can be converted into that of the others at a fixed parity.[18] Under such circumstances, the stock of money (M) by definition is the sum of two components: the amount of domestic credit of the banking system that is outstanding (DC) and the stock of international reserves of that country (IR), measured in terms of domestic currency. There therefore is a domestic component and an international component to the money supply. Thus, we have

$$M = DC + IR \qquad\qquad [13\text{--}8]$$

18. This section draws substantially on syntheses of monetary and international economics by Arnold C. Harberger. See his "A Primer on Inflation," and "The Inflation Syndrome," papers presented in the Political Economy Lecture Series, Harvard University, March 19, 1981.

Changes in the domestic money stock can occur either through expansion of domestic credit or by monetary movements that lead to changes in international reserves. That is,

$$\Delta M = \Delta DC + \Delta IR \qquad\qquad [13\text{--}9]$$

Under fixed exchange rates, a central bank of any small country can control DC, the domestic component, but has only very limited control over IR, the international component. Under such circumstances, developing countries that attempt to keep the rate of domestic inflation below the world inflation rate (through restrictive policies on domestic credit) will be unable to realize this goal. If, fueled by monetary expansion abroad (growth in the world money supply), world inflation initially is running in excess of domestic inflation, the prices of internationally traded goods will rise relative to those of domestic, nontraded goods.[19] Imports will fall, exports will rise, and the balance of payments will move toward surplus and cause a rise in international reserves. Therefore, the foreign components of the money stock will rise. This is tantamount to an "importation of money" and eventually will undo the effort to prevent importation of world inflation. Again, a small country on fixed exchange rates can do little to maintain its inflation rate below that of the rest of the world. For very open countries with few restrictions on the movement of goods and capital into and out of the country, the adjustment to world inflation can be very rapid (less than a year). For less-open countries with substantial restrictions on international trade and payments, the process takes longer, but the outcome is inevitable under fixed exchange rates.

The fact that financial policy for stabilization in countries with fixed exchange rates is heavily constrained by international developments sometimes is taken to mean that changes in the domestic component of the money stock have no impact on prices in economies adhering to fixed exchange rates. On the contrary, excessive expansion in money and credit surely will result in domestically generated inflation that, depending on the rate of expansion, for a time can be well in excess of world inflation rates. However, such a situation cannot continue for long, as excess money creation will spill over into the balance of payments via increased imports and lead to a drain on international reserves and, ultimately, an inability to maintain the fixed exchange rate. As reserves dwindle, the country no longer can defend its exchange rate and devaluation becomes inevitable.[20]

19. This is but one of several mechanisms that led to changes in international reserves sufficient to thwart efforts by developing countries to insulate themselves from world inflation.

20. Import controls frequently are used to stem the drain of reserves and avoid devaluation for a time. But import controls engender another set of distortions and inefficiencies—explored in Chapter 18—that eventually require more drastic measures, including devaluation.

Inflation therefore can be transmitted to small, open economies through the working of the world economy or generated by domestic developments.

A growing number of developing countries have begun to employ floating exchange rates (point B on the continuum in Figure 13–1). A floating exchange-rate regime allows countries to insulate themselves from world inflation. Under such a system, the rise in world prices attendant on world inflation would initially favor exports from the country and discourage imports. As a consequence, the current account of the country's balance of payments would improve, international reserves would rise, and the exchange rate soon would appreciate (fewer baht would be required to buy dollars, for instance). The appreciation in the country's exchange rate would cancel out external price increases and prevent the importation of world inflation.

Under any exchange-rate regime, domestically generated inflation may result from excessive increases in domestic credit from the banking system to either the public or the private sector. Budget deficits of the central government, for example, must be financed by borrowing, but the embryonic nature of money and capital markets in most developing countries generally means that governments facing deficits ordinarily must resort to borrowing from the central bank. Borrowing from the central bank is equivalent to direct money creation via the printing press. The result is a direct addition to the reserve base of the monetary system, an increase in so-called high-powered money. It is important, however, to recognize that not all budgetary deficits are inflationary. We have seen that a growing economy will be characterized by a growing demand for liquid assets, including money. Moderate budgetary deficits year after year, financed by the central bank, can help satisfy this requirement without leading to inflation. In general, the money stock may expand at least as fast as the growth in real income, with little or no inflationary consequences.

Earlier we saw that liquid assets normally are between 40 and 50 percent of GDP in developing countries (with wide variations), equivalent to roughly four to six months of income. Therefore, the public generally is willing to hold this much in money balances. A deficit of 2 percent of GDP financed by money creation would add only marginally to the money supply and easily may be accepted by the public. But a deficit of 8 percent GDP would increase the stock of money by an amount equal to one more month of income, an amount the public may be unwilling to hold (unless nominal interest rates on deposits are greatly increased). The excess would spill over into higher prices.

Use of bank credit to finance government deficits has not been the only source of inflationary monetary expansion in developing countries. Sometimes excessive growth of credit to the private sector has played a more-significant role in domestically generated inflationary processes. Nevertheless, as a general rule, inflation rates that are much in excess of world inflation usually have been traceable to budgetary deficits.

It is evident, then, that for countries attempting to maintain fixed exchange rates, efforts to avoid price increases in excess of world inflation must be a matter primarily of fiscal policy, not monetary policy. If budget deficits are not held to levels consistent with world inflation, even very deft deployment of monetary policy instruments will be unable to prevent rapid inflation, devaluation, or both. There still is a role for monetary policy in developing countries, but that role must be largely passive. Resourceful use of monetary policy can help by not making things worse and by moderating strong inflationary pressures until the budget can be brought under control, provided the latter is done fairly quickly.

We have seen that monetary factors are causes of inflation in both fixed- and floating-exchange-rate countries. In the case of fixed exchange rates, both world monetary expansion and domestic monetary expansion generate inflation; in flexible-exchange-rate countries, inflation arises from domestic monetary sources. But, thus far, no mention has been made of so-called nonmonetary causes of inflation. It seems plausible that internal and external shocks, such as those arising from widespread crop failure in the domestic economy or a drastic increase in prices of imported energy, could have important effects on inflation in countries suffering such shocks. This is true, but the mechanism whereby nonmonetary factors may initiate or worsen inflation needs to be clearly portrayed.

Nonmonetary disturbances indeed may precipitate policy reactions that lead to domestic monetary expansion large enough to accommodate higher relative prices of food or oil and large enough to cause inflation. In the absence of accommodating monetary expansion in the face of such shocks, inflation can be contained, but at some cost. In practice failure to allow the money supply to expand to accommodate higher relative prices of important goods leads to increases in unemployment that most governments find unacceptable. Therefore, as a matter of course, governments in such cases usually attempt to allow monetary expansion sufficient to avoid unwanted consequences for employment. But it is important to remember that, however advisable monetary accommodation may be on social and employment grounds, expansion in the money stock is required to fuel inflation, whatever external or internal factors may precipitate the expansion. This truth, known for centuries, often is incorrectly interpreted to mean that nonmonetary factors cannot "cause" inflation. They can, but only through an expansion of the national or international stock of money or both.

CONTROLLING INFLATION THROUGH MONETARY POLICY

The array of available instruments for antiinflationary monetary policy in developed countries include (1) open-market operations, in which the central bank can directly contract bank reserves by sales of government securities;[21] (2) increases in legal reserve requirements of banks, so that a given volume of reserves will support a lower stock of money (and reduce the credit expansion multiplier as well); (3) increases in rediscount rates, so that commercial bank borrowing from the central bank becomes less attractive; and (4) moral suasion, where the exhortations of monetary authorities are expected to lead to restraint in bank lending policies.

For virtually all developing countries, the first instrument—open market operations—is not available for inflation control. Securities markets typically are absent or not sufficiently well developed to allow the exercise of this powerful and flexible instrument, although some countries, including the Philippines and Brazil, have utilized the tool to a limited degree. The other three monetary policy instruments are employed, with varying degrees of success, in developing countries. In addition, developing countries often resort to two other tools employed only infrequently in developed countries: (5) credit ceilings imposed by the central bank on the banking system and (6) adjustments in allowable nominal rates of interest on deposits and loans. Governments attempting to control inflation usually resort to all these instruments, often together but sometimes separately, occasionally experiencing temporary success, as in Argentina in 1985, and occasionally enjoying transitory success, as in Indonesia in 1967 and 1968 and in Bolivia in 1985–86.

RESERVE REQUIREMENTS

All central banks require commercial banks to immobilize a portion of their deposits in the form of legal services that may not be lent to prospective customers. For example, legal reserve requirements for Indonesian and Malaysian banks in the late 1970s were expressed as 30 percent of deposits in domestic currency in the former and 20 percent of all deposits in the latter. Thus, in Malaysia, for example, banks were required to add 20 units of currency to reserves for every 100 units of deposits. These figures are not too far out of line with legal reserve requirements in many industrial nations, where reserve ratios of 15 percent for demand deposits and 5 percent for time deposits are common.

---

21. Open-market operations are used as an instrument of monetary policy in countries with well-developed financial markets. When the Federal Reserve System in the United States or a central bank in Europe wants to curtail the growth of the money supply, it sells government securities (bonds, bills) on the open market. When a buyer pays for the securities, the effect is to reduce directly the reserves of the banking system, since the funds are transferred from commercial bank deposits or household cash holdings to the account of the Federal Reserve. When the Federal Reserve wants to expand the money supply, it buys securities on the open market and thus directly adds to bank reserves.

Increases in reserve requirements can be used to help moderate inflation. An upward adjustment in reserve requirements works in two ways: It reduces the stock of money that can be supported by a given amount of reserves, and it reduces the money multiplier. The first effect induces banks to contract credit outstanding; the second reduces the growth in the money stock possible from any future increment to reserves.[22] Changes in legal reserve requirements usually are employed only as a last-ditch measure. Even small changes in the required ratio of reserves to deposits can have a very disruptive impact on commercial bank operations unless banks are given sufficient time to adjust.

CREDIT CEILINGS

In some countries, such as Indonesia from 1947 to 1983 or China in 1994 and 1995 and at various other times in Malaysia, Sri Lanka, and Chile, credit ceilings have been used as supplementary instruments of inflation control. Indeed, the International Monetary Fund often requires countries seeking balance-of-payments support to adopt credit ceilings as a prerequisite for IMF assistance. General ceilings of domestic credit expansion represent a useful method of controlling growth in domestic components of the money supply. Credit ceilings, however, do not allow full control of money supply growth in developing countries operating under fixed-exchange-rate regimes, since the monetary authorities have no control over foreign components of the money supply. Nevertheless, general credit ceilings sometimes can be usefully deployed in combating inflation in countries not experiencing major imbalances in external payments. Unfortunately, ceilings work the least well where they are needed the most, since countries attempting to deal with chronic inflation usually are those experiencing the most destabilizing changes in their international reserve positions. Finally, general credit ceilings are unlikely to have much effect on inflation unless the government simultaneously takes steps to reduce the budgetary deficits that—except in major oil exporting countries—typically are the root causes of chronic, acute, and especially runaway inflation.

Countries often supplement general credit ceilings with specific ceilings on lending to particular sectors of the economy. Indonesia attempted to fine tune credit controls in this way from 1974 to 1983, with poor results. The

22. In its simplest form the money multiplier (m) can be expressed as

$$m = (c + 1)/(c + k)$$

where c = the ratio of currency outside banks to deposits and k = the ratio of reserves to deposits. If k is raised, then m falls.

system of ceilings was so detailed and cumbersome that domestic banks were unable to come close to exhausting the ceilings. Excess reserves arose. The banks had little choice but to place their excess reserves in deposits overseas, primarily in banks in Singapore. As a result, many domestic firms in Jakarta were forced to seek credit from Singapore banks, which held well over a billion dollars of deposits from Jakarta banks that might have been lent to domestic firms at a lower rate in the absence of credit ceilings.

INTEREST RATE REGULATION AND MORAL SUASION

In most industrial countries, the central bank can influence interest rates by varying the *rediscount rate* charged on central bank loans to commercial banks that require additional liquidity. Because the rediscount rate is central to commercial banks' operations, it is important in determining the market rate of interest on both deposits and loans. As more developing countries adopt financial reforms that free interest rates from central bank control, they are better able to use the rediscount rate as a tool for influencing market interest rates.

In developing countries that have controlled rates on loans and deposits, the controlled rates have been instruments of antiinflationary packages. Since 1973, the use of such interest rate adjustments have been common in Latin America, and increases in deposit rates and loan rates were major elements in the stabilization programs of South Korea and Taiwan in the mid-1960s and of Indonesia in both 1968 and 1974. The objective in each case was twofold: to stimulate the demand for liquid assets and to discourage the loan demand for marginal investment projects by private-sector borrowers. The extent to which such measures can be successful depends on the interest elasticity of the demand for liquid assets and the interest elasticity of the demand for loans. In most of the cases just cited, particularly in the three Asian countries, both sets of elasticities evidently were sufficiently high, as the stabilization packages succeeded to a large degree.

Moral suasion by the monetary authorities, sometimes called *open-mouth operations* or *jawbone control,* is practiced no less extensively in developing than in developed countries. Warnings and exhortations to commercial banks to restrict lending or to encourage them to focus lending on particular activities have been quite common in Ghana. They also were used at various times in Malaysia, Singapore, Brazil, and elsewhere, sometimes prior to the imposition of credit ceilings and often to reinforce pressure on banks to adhere to ceilings. In both developed and developing countries, however, moral suasion has proven credible only when accompanied by forceful use of more tangible instruments of monetary control.

PRIVATE FOREIGN CAPITAL FLOWS, DEBT, AND FINANCIAL CRISES

Private foreign capital has taken on an increasingly important role in developing countries in recent decades. At the most basic level, private foreign capital flows are an important part of foreign saving (described in Chapter 11) that add to total investable funds and can help accelerate economic growth. But private capital flows play a more complex role. Depending on its form, private capital can help open new foreign markets for export sales, bring knowledge of new products and production techniques, and encourage the transfer of new technologies. However, it also can come in forms that bring relatively few benefits and may leave developing countries vulnerable to sudden capital withdrawals and financial crises. Private capital flows raise complex policy issues about repatriation of profits, incentives to either encourage or discourage certain types of flows, and macroeconomic management in a globalized financial system. This chapter discusses various forms of private foreign capital, focusing especially on foreign direct investment and foreign debt, and explores in some detail both the developing country debt crises of the 1980s and the emerging market financial crises of the 1990s.

Private foreign capital flows to developing and transitional economies grew very rapidly during the 1990s, from $64 billion in 1990 to $320 billion in 1997, before dropping off in 1998 following the Asian financial crisis (Table 14–1). Private flows to developing countries were comparable in

TABLE 14–1　　PRIVATE CAPITAL FLOWS TO DEVELOPING COUNTRIES, 1990–98 (BILLION U.S. DOLLARS)

TYPE OF CAPITAL FLOWS	1990	1991	1992	1993	1994	1995	1996	1997	1998[a]
PRIVATE DEBT FLOWS	35.3	40.7	75.7	87.9	95.7	121.1	131.4	126.4	62.9
COMMERCIAL BANKS	3.2	4.8	16.3	3.3	13.9	32.4	43.7	60.1	25.1
BONDS	1.2	10.8	11.1	37.0	36.7	26.6	53.5	42.6	30.2
OTHERS	11.4	3.0	10.7	8.6	3.7	1.0	3.0	2.6	2.7
SHORT-TERM DEBT	19.5	22.1	37.6	39.0	41.4	61.1	31.2	21.1	4.9
PORTFOLIO EQUITY FLOWS	3.7	7.6	14.1	51.0	35.2	36.1	49.2	30.2	14.1
FOREIGN DIRECT INVESTMENT	24.5	34.4	46.1	67.0	88.5	105.4	126.4	163.4	155.0
TOTAL PRIVATE CAPITAL FLOWS	63.5	82.7	135.9	205.9	219.4	262.6	272.9	320.0	232.0

[a]Preliminary data.

Source: World Bank, *Global Development Finance 1999.*

size to official flows in 1990 but were fully eight times larger in 1997. Although this growth is impressive, it is worth recalling from Chapter 11 that these flows still constitute a relatively small share of total saving and investable funds. Private foreign capital flows typically are the equivalent of no more than 4–5 percent of the GDP in developing countries and therefore account for perhaps one fourth or less of available investable funds. From the perspective of the most basic economic growth models (such as the Harrod-Domar and Solow models), which emphasize the role of capital formation in the growth process, private foreign capital flows are only modestly important. Only when one takes a more expansive and dynamic view, incorporating the positive and negative effects of private foreign capital flows on macroeconomic stability (through the effects of inflows and outflows on the exchange rate and interest rates), debt, and technology transfer and learning by doing (which often accompany direct investment by foreign firms in developing countries), do they take on more importance.

Broadly speaking, foreign private capital flows come in two forms: equity and debt. The largest type of equity flow, in fact the largest of all capital flows to developing countries, is **foreign direct investment** (FDI). FDI generally is a long-term investment that involves significant management control. The World Bank defines FDI as investment made to acquire a lasting management interest (usually at least 10 percent of voting stock) in an enterprise operating in a country other than that of the investor. With FDI, equity holders are concerned with their returns over a period of years rather than weeks or months. This characteristic makes FDI more difficult for developing countries to attract compared to other capital flows but also more important for long-term growth and development. A second type of equity flow is **portfolio equity,** in which an investor takes a smaller stake in an enterprise, either directly or through a stock exchange. Portfolio equity includes direct purchases of shares by foreign investors as well as share purchases through country funds and depository receipts. Portfolio equity flows to developing countries grew very rapidly in the 1990s, from $4 billion in 1990 to $30 billion in 1997, but were still less than one fifth the size of FDI and about one half the size of long-term commercial bank loans. For developing countries, one important distinction between equity (both FDI and portfolio) and debt flows is that, with equity, capital is repatriated only when an investment is profitable. If an investment project loses money, no one is obliged to make payments to the equity holder. This is very different from foreign debt, in which the debtor promises to make a series of payments to the creditor, regardless of the profitability of the investment.

Foreign debt flows come in several forms. Chapter 11 discusses lending to developing countries by international agencies such as the World Bank and the International Monetary Fund, as well as by other governments. For many developing countries, this continues to be the dominant form of foreign borrowing. For a growing group of middle-income developing and transitional economies, however, borrowing from private creditors exceeds financing from official sources and is the second largest type of capital flows, behind FDI. Private credit can be in the form of commercial bank loans, trade credits, or bonds. Short-term commercial bank loans were at the heart of the Asian financial crises of the late 1990s and have become much more controversial as a result, as discussed later in the chapter.

Foreign Investment and the Multinationals

In the 1960s and 1970s, many developing countries were suspicious of FDI and often took steps to actively discourage it. At the time, because of the recent colonial history in many countries, the sometimes outrageous behavior of certain foreign investors in taking advantage of weak political and legal systems to make huge profits, and the tendency for many foreign investors to gain monopoly rights in some countries, this suspicion often was well founded. Since the mid-1980s, however, developing countries increasingly have sought to attract FDI. Between 1986 and 1997, FDI to developing countries increased by a factor of *16* from $10 billion to $163 billion before dropping off slightly in 1998. As a result of this astonishing growth, FDI accounted for about 45 percent of total net foreign resource flows to developing countries in 1997, compared with just 16 percent in 1986. The sharp increase in FDI is due partly to worldwide advances in technology (and accompanying reduction in costs) in communications and transportation, and it goes hand in hand with the rapid expansion in world trade during the period. However, it also is the result of a substantial relaxation of rules that had restricted FDI in many developing countries. Direct investment still generates much controversy, however. Its influence is magnified because foreign investment usually comes in a package that may include not only equity finance, but often much larger amounts of loan finance, management expertise, modern technologies, technical skills, and access to world markets. Indeed, often the nonfinancial element of the investment package are more desired by developing countries. Moreover, this package is controlled by multinational corporations, whose size and control over resources often match and sometimes outstrip that of the recipient country governments. Investment by a multinational corporation raises the specter of interference by, and dependence on, foreign economic powers beyond the control of the host country. This section examines the basis for these fears and the potential benefits and costs of foreign investment.

MULTINATIONALS' INVESTMENT PATTERNS

The overwhelming proportion of direct foreign investment in third world countries is done by **multinational corporations** (MNCs); *transnational corporations* (TNCs) is an alternative term. A multinational is an enterprise that produces in more than one country and considers overseas operations to be central to its profitability. Multinational enterprises come in all sizes and from all regions of the world, including the developing countries, but most multinationals are based in the industrial countries. Not surprisingly, the vast majority of FDI comes from rich country investors. However, the share of FDI coming from developing countries grew rapidly during the 1990s, with most of the growth coming from Asia. Whereas about 95 percent of all FDI came from the industrialized countries in the late 1980s, by 1997 the share had fallen to 85 percent. Asian developing countries were the source of 12 percent of total global FDI flows.[1] Most multinational investment also is directed toward other wealthy countries, but the share aimed at developing countries has been rising sharply. According to the World Bank, in 1991, developing countries received less than one fourth of global FDI flows; by 1998, the share had reached 42 percent. Although this growth is impressive, it is important to recognize that FDI is highly concentrated in a few developing countries. In 1997, 70 percent of all FDI in developing countries was directed at just ten countries. One

---

1. United Nations Conference on Trade and Development (UNCTAD), *Transnational Corporations,* 7, no. 3 (December 1998), 131.

country—China—received an incredible 27 percent of the total. By contrast, the 61 countries that the World Bank classifies as low-income received less than 7 percent and sub-Saharan Africa received just 3 percent of the total.

CHARACTERISTICS OF MULTINATIONALS

Not very long ago, the word *multinational* implied a giant, private, U.S. manufacturing company with lots of overseas operations. Today, multinationals are a much more diverse group. Only 184 of the world's largest 500 companies were American in 1998, according to *Fortune* magazine; 102 of them were Japanese. Multinationals are not even necessarily from the industrial countries. Eight developing countries had companies in the top 500, including Korea (nine entries), China (six), and Brazil (four).[2] Nor are multinationals always private firms; the top 500 includes a number of giant, state-owned companies producing petroleum and steel, especially from the developing countries.

Nor are multinationals always large; small companies, especially in East and Southeast Asia, have been investing overseas for many years. The largest of the multinationals, however, are very large indeed, as Table 14–2 shows. Many multinationals have worldwide sales and assets that exceed the GDPs of some large developing countries. General Motors, the largest MNC, had sales in 1998 equivalent to more than the total GDP of Poland, the tenth largest developing country economy. The sales of Hitachi, the 25th largest multinational, exceeded the GDP of Algeria, the 25th largest economy.[3]

FDI is aimed at a very wide range of economic activities, making generalizations difficult, but at least three broad groups can be identified. First, from a historical perspective, the largest share of FDI has been in activities related to a country's natural resource endowments, such as mining, agricultural production, and tourism. Prominent examples include Firestone Tire Company's investments in West Africa (attracted by rubber), Freeport McMoran's copper and gold mining operations on the island of Irian Jaya in Indonesia, Shell Oil Company's investments in petroleum in Nigeria, and United Fruit Company's investments in agricultural production in Latin America. Second, some FDI in manufacturing is aimed at producing for the domestic market in the host developing country, often with protec-

2. "The Fortune Global 500 Ranked by Performance," *Fortune,* August 2, 1999.

3. Of course, sales and GDP are not directly comparable. Sales measures gross output, whereas GDP measures value added or net output and is equal to the sum of payments to labor, capital, and other factors of production. Nevertheless, the comparisons in the table are indicative.

TABLE 14–2   THE SIZES OF MULTINATIONALS AND DEVELOPING COUNTRY ECONOMIES, 1998 (BILLION U.S. DOLLARS)

RANK IN 1998[a]	COMPANY (COUNTRY)	SALES	ASSETS	EMPLOYEES (000s)
1	GENERAL MOTORS (U.S.)	161.3	257.4	594.0
10	TOYOTA (JAPAN)	99.7	124.7	183.9
25	HITACHI (JAPAN)	62.4	81.7	328.4
50	SEARS ROEBUCK (U.S.)	41.3	37.7	324.0
100	MOTOROLA (U.S.)	29.4	28.7	133.0
500	NOTHROP GRUMMAN (U.S.)	8.9	9.7	49.6
LARGEST DEVELOPING COUNTRY MNCs				
73	SINOPEC (CHINA)	34.0	51.6	1,190.0
102	SAMSUNG (KOREA)	28.8	11.2	7.4
103	SK (KOREA)	28.8	28.0	24.0
126	PDVSA (VENEZUELA)	25.7	48.8	50.8
133	BANCO DO BRASIL (BRAZIL)	25.1	107.2	72.4
140	HYUNDAI (KOREA)	24.4	1.0	0.7
DEVELOPING COUNTRIES' GDP IN 1998[b]		GDP		
1	CHINA	960.9		
5	ARGENTINA	344.4		
10	POLAND	148.9		
25	ALGERIA	49.6		
50	KENYA	11.1		
100	REPUBLIC OF THE CONGO	2.0		

[a]Ranked according to sales.
[b]Ranked according to GDP.
Source: "The Fortune Global 500 Ranked by Performance," *Fortune*, August 2, 1999; and World Bank, *World Development Report 1999/2000*, Table 12.

tion against competing imports. These investments can be either capital or labor intensive, but their main goal is to capture part of the domestic market. Third, an increasingly larger share of FDI in recent decades has focused on firms engaged in labor-intensive manufacturing aimed for export on world markets. These firms tend to be very efficient and competitive and can create many jobs for low- and semi-skilled workers. However, they also can move quickly from one country to another in response to changes in production costs or macroeconomic or political instability (these issues are discussed in more detail in Chapter 18).

BENEFITS OF FOREIGN DIRECT INVESTMENT

As mentioned earlier, viewed as a **transfer of capital** from rich to poor countries, foreign direct investment is relatively small but of growing importance. Table 14–3 shows the flow of direct investment to the largest re-

TABLE 14–3   FOREIGN DIRECT INVESTMENT IN LARGEST RECIPIENT DEVELOPING
COUNTRIES, 1980–97

| | MILLION U.S. DOLLARS | | | SHARE OF GDP (%) |
	1980	1990	1997	1997
CHINA	0	3,487	44,236	5.4
BRAZIL	1,911	989	18,765	2.4
MEXICO	2,156	2,634	12,000	3.6
ARGENTINA	678	1,836	6,326	2.0
RUSSIAN FEDERATION	—	0	6,241	1.4
CHILE	213	590	5,417	7.0
COLOMBIA	157	500	5,330	5.6
VENEZUELA	55	451	4,893	5.6
INDONESIA	180	1,093	4,677	2.2
POLAND	—	89	4,500	3.3
MALAYSIA	934	2,333	4,100	4.2
INDIA	79	162	3,100	0.9
THAILAND	190	2,444	3,029	1.9
KOREA, REPUBLIC	6	788	2,844	0.6
PERU	27	41	2,030	3.2
HUNGARY	0	0	2,000	4.4
THE PHILIPPINES	−106	530	1,253	1.5
PANAMA	−47	132	1,030	12.5
NIGERIA	−740	588	1,000	2.5
EGYPT, ARAB REPUBLIC	548	734	850	1.1
TURKEY	18	684	805	0.4

Source: World Bank, *Global Development Finance, 1999;* and World Bank, *World Development Report, 1998/99.*

cipients among the developing countries. FDI rose in all of these countries between 1980 and 1990 with the single exception of Brazil, and each country experienced especially large increases during the 1990s. FDI was the equivalent of more than 2 percent of GDP in 14 of these countries in 1997 and more than 5 percent of the GDP in 5 countries. Growing evidence shows a positive association between FDI and other forms of investment and between FDI and economic growth. Recent studies have found that a 1 percentage point increases in the share of FDI in GDP is associated with an increase in per capita GDP of between 0.3 and 0.8 percent.[4]

An advantage of FDI flows is that they tend to be much less volatile than other types of foreign private capital flows. FDI tends to be attracted by resource endowments and long-term fundamental economic strengths, factors that generally do not change as quickly as interest rates

4. See Romain Wacziarg, "Measuring the Dynamic Gains from Trade," World Bank policy research working paper No. 2001, November 1998; and Eduardo Borensztein, Jose de Gregorio, and Jong-Wha Lee, "How Does Foreign Direct Investment Affect Economic Growth?" *Journal of International Economics,* 45 (June 1998), 115–35.

and exchange rates, which are stronger determinants of short-term flows. Moreover, since FDI is characterized by significant management control in large, fixed production facilities such as factories and mines, investors are less likely (and less able) to flee at the first hint of economic trouble. During the 1997–98 Asian financial crises, for example, FDI flows fell somewhat but were the most stable capital flows to the crisis economies. Although many foreign investors sold their assets during the crisis, almost as many new investors were prepared to purchase the assets at depressed prices.

The contribution of multinationals to **employment creation** in developing countries differs by country and economic activity but is modest at best. In most developing countries, multinationals account for less than 1 percent up to 6 percent of the *total* employment in all sectors. This small number is not surprising, considering that multinationals account for a relatively small share of total investment and overall economic activity. The contribution of MNCs to employment is more significant in manufacturing alone, ranging from 10 to 23 percent in Argentina, Vietnam, Brazil, and Mexico and reaching over 40 percent in Malaysia, Singapore, and Sri Lanka.[5]

The issue is not gross employment, however, but net new employment. How many jobs have been created by multinationals that otherwise would not have been created? The answer turns on a subsidiary question: Do multinational firms use more or less labor-intensive techniques than domestic firms? The spotty empirical evidence on this issue is hardly convincing one way or the other. To the extent that multinationals invest in sectors such as petrochemicals and metals that are inherently capital intensive, they will employ relatively fewer workers per unit of investment than domestic firms that work in more labor-intensive industries. But the relevant comparison is between foreign and domestic firms in the same industries. Some studies find that foreign firms, wedded to capital-intensive techniques developed in their home markets where labor is expensive, tend to use these less appropriate techniques in developing countries as well. Yet there also are examples of multinationals using more labor-intensive techniques than comparable domestic firms. Much appears to depend on the extent of competition: When multinationals invest to produce for domestic markets protected from competition, they can afford to import capital-intensive production techniques. When they produce for export, however, or when they enter competitive domestic markets, competitive pressures force both multinationals and domestic firms to employ the lowest-cost techniques, and this frequently means more labor-intensive

5. UNCTAD, *World Investment Report 1999* (New York: United Nations, 1999), Annex Table A.I.7.

methods.[6] So job creation may depend as much on the host country's policies as on the multinationals' practices.

A third major benefit expected from foreign investment, and perhaps the most important, is the **transfer of technology,** skills, and know-how. Because much of the world's research and development activity takes place within large firms in North America, Europe, and Japan, firms from these areas are a potentially rich source of valuable information about innovative products, manufacturing processes, marketing methods, and managerial approaches. Smaller multinationals, particularly those from other developing countries, offer other kinds of technological benefits: successful adaptation to local conditions of older technology from developed countries and new, cost-saving innovations in small-scale manufacture. If this information is transplanted to host countries, innovation and adaptation eventually can become consistent with less future dependence on multinational investors.

For some kinds of operations, such as logging, many manufacturing activities, and open-pit mining, acquisitions of new information and methods by host-country workers and supervisors requires only a basic educational background and a willingness to work in a modern, structured enterprise with clear standards for work schedules and work pace. But, in other activities, particularly in natural-resource-based industries such as steelmaking, copper smelting, and chemical manufacturing, absorptive capacity depends on a locally available stock of more highly trained technical personnel, such as chemical engineers, metallurgists, geologists, biologists, industrial economists, and experienced managers.

A few developing countries, such as India and Mexico, have trained relatively large numbers of technical industrial personnel and are able to absorb new technologies across a broad spectrum. Other countries have made strong efforts to train technical personnel specifically to take over important foreign-owned industries. Venezuela trained petroleum engineers and managers who now successfully run that sector; South Korea used its first chemical fertilizer plant, built and operated by a foreign firm, to train Koreans who soon were operating several other nationally owned fertilizer plants; and Malaysia became capable not only of operating its own rubber industry but of conducting its own research on new species and methods of cultivation. Yet most developing countries do not have sufficient cadres of technically educated people to manage complex industries, and only a few have the educational establishments needed to begin rectifying this shortage.

6. Joseph M. Grieco, "Foreign Investment and Development: Theory and Evidence," in Theodore H. Moran et al., *Investing in Development: New Roles for Foreign Capital?* (Washington, DC: Overseas Development Council, 1986), pp. 47–48.

Perspectives on technology transfer differ markedly between multinationals and developing countries. The firms view their investments in production of technology as a continuing process that should earn financial returns just like any investment. Host countries, however, are concerned primarily with access to existing knowledge and, with some justification, regard past multinational investments in technology as sunk costs requiring no reimbursement. Public goods theory, as well as casual observation, tells us that multinationals will withhold information on technology when they would not otherwise be able to appropriate the returns.

A fourth benefit sought from multinational investment is **managerial capacity,** without which access to technology is largely ornamental. To be sure, many developing countries have gifted entrepreneurs and innovators, including the market women in West African countries such as Ghana and Nigeria, clusters of industrialists in such Latin American cities as Monterey and São Paulo, the Gujaratis of India, and communities of Chinese and Indians who have long resided in developing countries from East Africa to Southeast Asia. Nevertheless, only a few developing countries possess sufficient numbers of managers capable of organizing and operating large industrial projects such as those undertaken by multinational firms, and virtually all are short of people with advanced training and experience in management. The number of MBAs and experienced managers in a single company such as IBM can rival the entire population of MBAs and other managers in even some well-endowed developing countries. Still, managers are created all the time in the most dynamic of the developing countries, and the multinationals in particular employ and train them. The growth of MNCs from the development countries themselves attests to their growing competence in management.

A fifth benefit is **access to world markets.** Developing countries capable of producing at competitive costs often find it difficult to penetrate foreign markets. Many multinationals, particularly in natural resources, chemicals, and other heavy industries, are vertically integrated, oligopolistic firms, for which many transactions take place within the firm. In the early 1980s, over 60 percent of all imports by multinational manufacturers in the United States were from affiliates overseas, while almost 40 percent of exports also were within firms.[7] Multinationals developed preferential access to customers by fashioning and adhering to long-term contracts in standardized products, such as petroleum, or by acquiring a reputation for delivering a specialized product of satisfactory quality on a reliable schedule, as in construction and engineering. Developing country firms often re-

---

7. UN Centre on Transnational Corporations (UNCTNC), *Transnational Corporations in World Development* (New York: United Nations, 1988), p. 93. The ratios for Great Britain and Japan are lower, 27 percent, covering all industries.

quire years to overcome such marketing advantages of the multinationals, although it increasingly is being done by firms in East Asia and elsewhere.

A sixth benefit, especially relevant for FDI in manufacturing for export, is **specialization.** When firms in developing countries are part of a global production process, they can focus on the particular activity where they have a comparative advantage (see Chapter 16) and can produce most efficiently. Firms in the automobile business need not make the entire car (and if they do, they might not be able to compete on world markets). Instead, they can specialize in assembly, production of basic components (such as door parts or wiring), manufacturing of more sophisticated parts (e.g., engines or transmissions), design, or other aspects of the production process. In today's production environment, it is difficult to classify an automobile as American, German, Japanese, or Korean, since various parts are made all over the world. Moreover, the particular activity that makes sense in an economy can change over time as resource endowments, skills, and economic policies change. When Intel made its first investments in the electronics industry in Malaysia in the early 1970s, for example, it focused on low-skill activities such as simple assembly. Over the years, as the Malaysian workforce gained new skills and more Malaysians became experienced managers, activity shifted toward production of basic parts (e.g., keyboards), then to more advanced components (such as microprocessors), and later to testing and research. More recently, electronics production in the Philippines has followed a similar progression.

Historically, these benefits of multinational investment for decades were made available to host countries only as an **investment "package,"** incorporating equity capital (that is, ownership and control), management, technology, and marketing. The Firestone Tire Company, for example, owned both a rubber plantation and a tire factory in Ghana. It supplied the equipment (and thus the technology) for both facilities, along with financing and top management. Rubber was sold to its own tire plants, either in Ghana or the United States. Such investment packages traditionally have been offered "all or nothing," in the probably correct belief that the whole is more valuable than the sum of its parts and as a means of protecting the most crucial element, patented technology.

In recent years, developing countries have made some progress in "unbundling" the package to capture more benefits for themselves. At the same time, some multinationals have seen benefits in avoiding the risks of equity participation and maximizing the profits on sales of unbundled technology, management, or marketing access. Different contractual forms have been developed to transfer elements of the old package to host countries, including joint ventures in which the foreign firm takes less than a majority partnership; agreements in the petroleum industry to share production rather than ownership; licensing technology, as in the Korean automobile industry; management contracts in which a foreign firm runs the enterprise but may have little or no equity share; franchising products and brands, as done by McDonalds in the United States and worldwide; and turnkey projects that are handed over to the host country firm after being started up by a multinational, a form used in building electric power plants, for example.

Another much-used route has been gradually to take over the management and ownership of existing foreign investments as the host country's capacities increase. Harvard economist Raymond Vernon has called this the "obsolescing bargain," in recognition of the shift in negotiating strength that occurs once the foreign investment is in place and the host country increases its ability to operate the facility.[8] Through these and other means, industrializing countries such as Brazil, Mexico, India, Korea, and Taiwan not only have developed their own petrochemical industries, for example, but have become suppliers of technology and management to less-advanced countries.[9]

Unbundling is not suitable in every case, however. Some countries have begun to reconsider arrangements in which multinationals make their profits on the provision of technology, management, or market access but have little or no profit incentive to manage the firm productively and leave all the risks to host-country firms. This reconsideration is one factor, together with the growing burdens of foreign debt, that has led developing countries to view multinational investment more tolerantly in recent years.[10]

FDI is most beneficial when the host country can capture some or all of these advantages, such as providing new jobs, increasing managerial capacity, enhancing competition and specialization, and inducing the transfer of new technologies. But FDI is not always beneficial. One recent study found that 25 percent or more of all FDI projects had a negative impact on the economic welfare of the host country.[11] The major reason was lack of competition in input and output markets in which the foreign firm operated. When foreign firms are given monopoly rights to operate in protected domestic markets, they tend to misallocate resources, generate less

8. Raymond Vernon, *Storm over the Multinationals: The Real Issues* (Cambridge, MA: Harvard University Press, 1977), p. 151.

9. Charles P. Oman, "New Forms of Investment in Developing Countries," in Moran et al., *Investing in Development: New Roles for Private Capital?* pp. 131–55.

10. UNCTNC, *Transnational Corporations in World Development,* p. 71.

11. Theodore H. Moran, "Foreign Direct Investment and Development: The New Policy Agenda for Developing Countries and Economies in Transition," Washington, DC, Institute for International Economics, November 1998.

employment, induce smaller productivity gains, and transfer less technology, perhaps making the host country worse off than it would have been without the investment.

POLICIES TOWARD FOREIGN DIRECT INVESTMENT

Host governments use a range of restrictions and incentives to capture as much as possible of the expected benefits from foreign direct investment, including performance requirements, local ownership requirements, restrictions on profit repatriation, monopoly privileges, and tax holidays. When well designed, these policies can increase the benefits to the host country; however, when poorly designed, they easily can discourage and even repel FDI. **Performance requirements** generally are tailored to fit each industry. Multinationals that assemble cars and other vehicles often are forced to increase annually the share of local content in each vehicle, for example, while those entering mining may commit themselves to future investments in domestic minerals processing. Policies that make foreign firms utilize local personnel are aimed not only at job creation but also at increasing absorptive capacity for the transfer of technology from multinationals. Developing countries have tried to promote technology transfer by imposing standards requiring multinationals to import only the most-advanced capital equipment rather than used machinery. But such measures work against other development goals because older equipment is likely to be more labor intensive and less costly to operate. Ecuador has imposed special taxes on multinationals to finance government research and development, while India has required firms to invest in local research and development activities.[12]

Many host countries, particularly in Latin America and Southeast Asia, have made it mandatory for foreign investors to sell a specified share of equity, usually 51 percent, to local partners to form **joint ventures.** Through local ownership requirements, host governments hope to appropriate technology, limit the repatriation of profits, and maintain local control. Host countries assume that local joint-venture partners will become capable of matching technological and managerial capacities with foreign firms. However, many local joint-venture partnerships are pro forma arrangements involving local elites close to the centers of political power with little interest in business matters. And parent multinationals often are more reluctant to allow diffusion of technology to joint ventures than to wholly owned subsidiaries. Even when joint ventures succeed in asserting greater national control over foreign investments, Raymond Vernon stresses that

---

12. Jack N. Behrman and William A. Fischer, *Overseas R&D Activities of Transnational Corporations* (Cambridge, MA: Oelgeschlager, Gunn and Hain, 1980), pp. 107–9.

if local owners, in buying out their foreign partners, pay a price fully commensurate with the earnings they expect to receive, then the net effect is an export of scarce capital to the foreign multinational.[13]

Other common restrictions include ceilings on repatriation of profits to the parent corporation and stiff taxes on profit remittances. In Colombia, profits remitted by a firm to a parent abroad at one time were limited to 15 percent of the firm's Colombian investments; Brazil at times has limited remittances to 10 percent of registered capital. Other countries, such as Argentina and Ghana, with no explicit ceilings on profit repatriation, still limit repatriation through the administration of foreign exchange controls.

Restrictions on multinationals can increase the benefits to host countries only if they do not deter foreign firms from investing. To accompany these policy sticks, most developing countries also offer policy carrots, especially protection from competition and tax incentives. **Protection** includes tariffs and quotas to reduce imports of competing goods, and the outright grant of monopoly control over local markets. Monopoly positions in local markets frequently are sought and sometimes granted, for example, by Kenya, Zambia, and for a time, Indonesia to foreign rubber tire manufacturers. Because import protection and monopoly control create higher domestic prices and profits, they often result in higher direct transfers from host country consumers to the multinationals' foreign stockholders.

The transfer from local consumers to foreign stockholders is even higher if **income tax incentives** are used to induce investment by foreign firms. While the variety of such incentives is almost limitless, the most common is *income tax holidays,* which exempt firms from paying taxes on corporate income, usually for three to six years. Most countries otherwise would tax profits at rates anywhere from 25 percent to as high as 50 percent. For tax holidays to help the multinationals, they must be creditable against income taxes due to their home country governments. Otherwise, if home countries tax firms on worldwide income, as all industrial countries except France do, then taxes foregone by the developing country would simply be transferred to tax revenues of the multinational's home country. Most industrial countries now permit their firms to take credit for tax holidays granted abroad through tax treaties negotiated between host- and home-country governments.

Still, substantial doubt remains that developing countries receive benefits commensurate with the costs of the tax revenues they forgo. Tax holidays can help the foreign investor only if its project is profitable to begin with. Most studies conclude that, for many kinds of FDI, income tax holidays have only marginal effects on multinational investment decisions: They reward the multinationals for doing what they would have done in any case.

13. Vernon, *Storm over the Multinationals,* p. 168.

This is especially true for firms attracted by natural resources or those intending to produce in protected domestic markets of the host countries. Export-oriented, labor-intensive, "footloose" industries, however, may be more sensitive to tax holidays and other incentives.[14] A prominent example is the electronics industry, which utilizes large amounts of unskilled labor to manufacture semiconductor chips, make integrated circuits, and assemble parts of products such as electronic calculators and computers in countries such as Malaysia, Thailand, the Philippines, and Costa Rica.

What, then, are the best ways to attract FDI? To begin with, a country must get some basics right: reliable international transportation and communications facilities, freedom from government regulation, macroeconomic and politic stability, and labor markets in which wages are matched by productivity. One general approach, described in Chapter 5, would be to open up the economy to foreign trade as well as foreign investment, reduce government intervention in the domestic economy, and rely on market forces to both attract foreign investors and regulate their behavior. Where market forces alone are deemed inadequate and some kind of protection is employed, then investment incentives should be reserved for potential export industries, where clear performance targets can be established and profits depend on efficient operation. A study by economists Dennis Encarnation and Louis Wells lends support to this strategy. They performed economic benefit-cost analyses on 50 foreign investment projects in a large Asian country, incorporating shadow prices and using the methods explained in Chapter 12. All the export-oriented projects had social rates of return above 10 percent, which they took to be the opportunity cost of capital. But, in the four industries studied that were oriented to the protected domestic market, 30–70 percent of the projects were socially unprofitable, with rates of return below 10 percent. Moreover, the highest rates of failure were in most heavily protected industries.[15]

Foreign Debt

Foreign borrowing provides several advantages over FDI for developing countries. Most obviously, when a domestic firm borrows abroad, there are fewer of the issues with ownership, profit repatriation, tax holidays, and the like that arise with FDI. In addition, foreign borrowing can be undertaken much more quickly and easily than FDI. However, foreign borrowing gen-

---

14. Louis T. Wells, Jr., "Investment Incentives: An Unnecessary Debate," *The CTC Reporter*, *22* (Autumn 1986), 58–60; and Steven Guisinger et al., *Investment Incentives and Performance Requirements* (New York: Praeger, 1985).

15. Dennis J. Encarnation and Louis T. Wells, Jr., "Evaluating Foreign Investment," in Moran et al., *Investing in Development: New Roles for Private Capital?* pp. 61–85.

erally is not accompanied by as much technology transfer or learning by doing as FDI. Moreover, debts must be paid, even when a project goes bad. Foreign debt has a bad reputation following the debt crises of the 1980s when a large number of developing countries defaulted on their debt payments (discussed in detail later in this chapter). However, prudent borrowing has been an important part of the development strategy of many countries. To simplify only slightly, as long as the rate of return on investment projects exceeds the interest rate on the debt (as described in Chapter 12), foreign borrowing can be a very sensible strategy to augment domestic savings and add to investment. The United States borrowed heavily in international markets in the middle and late nineteenth century to finance its westward expansion (especially the railroads). Most countries in Western Europe, along with Russia, relied on foreign borrowing at one time or another. However, too much foreign borrowing, borrowing of the wrong kind (in terms of currency or maturity), or borrowing to finance consumption or poor investments can lead to trouble. Developing countries that borrow abroad must take care to manage their debt portfolio prudently to ensure that they reap the gains while avoiding the possibility of crisis.

Foreign borrowing in developing countries takes four main forms: official borrowing, commercial bank loans, trade credits, and bonds. Official borrowing from the World Bank, IMF, other multilateral agencies, and other governments (discussed in Chapter 11) were the largest source of development finance until the early 1990s. Commercial bank loans are credits from private banks and other private financial institutions to the government, state-owned enterprises, private corporations, banks, or households. Trade credits typically are short-term loans to importers to carry them from the time they must pay for the imports until they sell the goods. Typically, the original manufacturers, exporters, other suppliers of goods, or banks extend these credits. Bonds can be issued by the government or by private or state-owned enterprises.

COMMERCIAL BORROWING

Commercial bank loans traditionally have been among the largest of all capital flows to developing countries and are those most closely associated with the international debt crisis of the 1980s. The magnitude of commercial bank lending to developing countries has varied widely in recent decades. Bank lending grew sharply in the 1970s, virtually disappeared in the late 1980s after the debt crisis, rebounded in the early 1990s, and then fell off again in 1998 after the Asian financial crisis.

In the 1960s, commercial bank lending was a small but growing component of the resource transfer to developing countries. In 1970, it accounted for about 16 percent of total net transfers. When OPEC raised

TABLE 14–4 LONG-TERM DEBT, ALL DEVELOPING COUNTRIES, 1970–97 (BILLION U.S. DOLLARS)

	1970	1983	1990	1997
STOCKS				
ALL SOURCES	62	633	1206	1,783
OFFICIAL CREDITORS	32	219	607	794
MULTILATERAL	7	79	212	290
WORLD BANK	4	37	212	290
BILATERAL	25	140	395	504
PRIVATE CREDITORS	30	414	599	989
COMMERCIAL BANKS	20	322	336	480
BONDS	2	22	116	405
NET FLOWS				
ALL SOURCES	7.0	49.8	44.3	118.7
OFFICIAL CREDITORS	3.5	21.6	28.5	13.3
MULTILATERAL	0.9	11.0	15.0	21.1
WORLD BANK	0.4	5.7	5.1	6.7
BILATERAL	2.6	10.6	13.5	−7.7
PRIVATE CREDITORS	3.5	28.2	15.8	105.4
COMMERCIAL BANKS	2.3	19.8	3.2	60.1
BONDS	0	1.0	1.2	42.6
OTHER PRIVATE LOANS	1.2	7.4	11.4	2.7

Sources: World Bank, *World Debt Tables 1991 and 1994,* and World Bank, *Global Development Finance, 1999.*

prices in 1973–74 and again in 1979–80, the oil-producing states of the Middle East had large surplus to invest in world markets. One of their favorite investment outlets was bank deposits in the United States and Europe. The international commercial banks, awash in "petrodollars," had to find profitable lending outlets and took renewed interest in lending to developing countries, especially those in South America and East Asia. As a result, commercial bank lending to developing countries mushroomed in the late 1970s and early 1980s. By 1983, annual commercial bank lending to developing countries was eight times larger than it had been in 1970, which represented at least a threefold expansion net of inflation. In 1983, the net value of commercial bank loans accounted for 37 percent of total net resource flows and so exceeded foreign aid as a source of loan finance. The stock of accumulated debt owed by developing countries to commercial banks had expanded 16 times from its 1970 level to reach $322 billion, more than half of all developing country debt, including amounts owed to official creditors (Table 14–4). In effect, the commercial banks channeled petrodollars from the wealthy oil exporters to the middle-income developing countries, a constructive form of intermediation for which they were applauded at the time.

However, the explosion in lending ended in crisis as many countries were unable to repay their debts. In the aftermath of the debt crisis, the international banks sharply reduced their lending to developing countries. By 1990, new commercial bank lending (net of repayments) to developing countries was just $3.2 billion. The total amount of developing country debt outstanding to the commercial banks in 1990 was $336 billion, only slightly larger than in 1983 (and much smaller in real terms). Commercial bank lending had become one of the smallest of all capital flows to developing countries, accounting for less than 3 percent of net resource flows. However, commercial bank lending began to grow again in the 1990s following the resolution of the debt crisis in several key countries, as described later. By 1997, net commercial bank lending reached $60 billion and constituted the second-largest capital flow to developing countries after FDI. But, in late-1997, in the context of the Asian financial crisis (discussed in Chapter 13), commercial banks rapidly withdrew their lines of credit and demanded immediate repayment on many outstanding loans. These withdrawals added significantly to the severity of the crisis. In 1998, net lending amounted to $25 billion, less than half of the 1997 level.

DEBT DYNAMICS

Foreign borrowing, as we have seen, is an accepted and often worthwhile part of economic development. Access to foreign saving permits countries to invest more than they can save and import more than their export earnings otherwise would allow. If the additional investment and imports are put to productive use (factoring in the risks of adverse export and interest rate shocks), they should yield sufficient returns to pay the interest, dividends, and principal on the initial foreign inflows. Under these circumstances (ignoring for the moment issues of currency composition and maturity of the debt), foreign borrowing and growing external debt can be consistent with sustained development. Borrowing for weak investments, however, can lead to debt difficulties.

The basic equations determining the rate of change of debt over time can be described as follows. Recall that foreign savings (F) is equal to the difference between imports and exports of goods and nonfactor services ($M - E$), or roughly the current account of the balance of payments (Chapter 11). For simplicity we assume that all foreign saving is in the form of borrowing. Therefore, the increase in debt in any year is

$$\mathrm{d}D/\mathrm{d}t = iD + M - E \qquad [14\text{--}1]$$

where D = the stock of debt, $\mathrm{d}D/\mathrm{d}t$ = the change in the stock (the first derivative), and i = the average interest rate paid on all foreign inflows, including loans, equity, and grants. The simple differential equation can be solved by assuming that E and M grow at the same exponential rate, g_E. In that case, the stock of debt also will grow exponentially at g_E, and in the long run, the ratio of debt to exports will settle at

$$D/E = a/(g_E - i) \qquad [14\text{--}2]$$

where a = the ratio of foreign saving to exports, $(M - E)/E$, and is a constant assuming that imports and exports grow at the same rate.[16]

Equation 14–2 tells us that the long run ratio of debt to exports depends on the foreign exchange gap, the growth rate of exports, and the interest rate. If g_E is greater than i, the gap can remain positive. If the gap $(M - E)/E$ were 10 percent, the average interest rate were 7 percent (recall that grants and concessional loans have to be averaged in with commercial debt), and the growth of dollar earnings from exports g_E were 12 percent a year, then the ratio of debt to exports would settle at 2, which was about the average for the developing countries in the 1980s. If the growth of exports could be pushed above the growth of imports, the debt-export ratio would fall. If, on the other hand, the growth rate of exports were to fall below the interest rate (either because export growth fell or world interest rates rose), the foreign exchange gap must turn into a surplus to finance the interest payments due on past debt. As we shall see, this is precisely what has happened in the high-debt countries of Latin America. From the perspective of foreign trade, the key to sustaining debt is the ability of the debtor to put the additional resources to productive use in export industries, either directly or indirectly.

Since foreign saving also is equal to the difference between investment and domestic saving, a similar calculation can be made from the investment-saving perspective. The differential equation is

$$dD/dt = iD + I - S_d = iD + vY - sY = iD + (v - s)Y \qquad [14\text{--}3]$$

where Y = GNP, v = the investment share of GNP, and s = the propensity to save out of GNP. As with the trade balance perspective, assume that both debt and GNP grow at the same exponential rate, g_Y. Then the long-run equilibrium ratio of debt to GNP is

$$D/Y = (v - s)/(g_Y - i) \qquad [14\text{--}4]$$

16. Equation 14–1 is solved to yield 14–2 by letting $D/D_0 = E/E_0 = M/M_0 = e^{gt}$ and substituting into equation 14–1, noting that $d(e^{gt}/dt = ge^{gt}$. Then 14–1 becomes $g_E D = iD + M - E$, from which 14–2 can be readily derived. The result is given by Albert Fishlow, "External Borrowing and Debt Management," in Rudiger Dornbusch and F. Leslie C. H. Helmers, *The Open Economy: Tools for Policymakers in Developing Countries* (New York: Oxford University Press, 1988), pp. 220–21.

In this case, if $v - s$ were 3 percent of GNP, i averaged 7 percent on all foreign inflows, and the growth rate of GNP expressed in current dollars were 10 percent a year,[17] the debt-GNP ratio would settle at 1 (or 100 percent). Although some countries reached debt-GNP ratios exceeding 1 during the 1980s, the Latin American debtors' ratios seldom exceeded 50 percent. From the saving-investment perspective, the requirement for sound debt management is to invest in assets that are productive enough to boost the growth rate of GNP and to adopt policies that increase the share of saving in GNP.

At one level, the issue of managing foreign loans and grants to yield high growth rates is simple. If the country behaves as an enterprise, it will borrow only if it can invest in projects that have rates of return above the cost of borrowing. Then loans can be serviced out of the earnings from those investments. For the country there is a further condition, that the project must earn or save sufficient foreign exchange to transfer payments of interest and principal in foreign currency. Seen this way, foreign resources should be sought only if there are productive foreign-exchange-earning investment opportunities for them.

This approach is too restrictive, however. The question is whether the economy as a whole can generate sufficient income and export growth to service the debt. Concern over specific projects is secondary to the larger issue of sound macroeconomic management. If an economy has been well managed and has proven itself able to use its resources productively, the role of foreign resources is to augment the entire investment menu. Precisely how these resources are invested is less important: Additional loans are likely to be productively employed and serviced on schedule. Strong management includes allowing for the risk of a sudden fall in export receipts, higher interest rates, or other adverse shocks. Conversely, if an economy is poorly managed and unlikely to generate sufficient resources to service its debt, then targeting of loans toward specific projects, no matter how productive, is not much protection against default. And, as we shall see later in the chapter, the terms on which the debt is obtained (especially the maturity structure) can have a profound impact on macroeconomic management and vulnerability to a sudden crisis.

THE 1980S DEBT CRISIS

In the early 1980s, borrowing countries, especially in Latin America, faced mounting debt and **debt service** (the payment of interest and principal).

17. This is not as high as it seems. Remember, we are measuring all quantities in current dollars, because that is the basis on which debt is serviced. If the real growth rate is 6 percent a year and the dollar rate of inflation is 4 percent a year, then the g_Y would be 10 percent a year.

TABLE 14–5	DEBT RATIOS, DEVELOPING COUNTRIES, 1970–97 (PERCENT)		
	1970	MAXIMUM 1980–97	1997
ALL DEVELOPING COUNTRIES			
LONG-TERM DEBT TO GNP	14	43	30
LONG-TERM DEBT TO EXPORTS	115	203	116
TOTAL DEBT SERVICE TO EXPORTS	—	33	18
LATIN AMERICAN COUNTRIES			
LONG-TERM DEBT TO GNP	18	60	29
LONG-TERM DEBT TO EXPORTS	149	343	161
TOTAL DEBT SERVICE TO EXPORTS	—	48	34
SELECTED COUNTRIES: TOTAL DEBT SERVICE TO EXPORTS			
ARGENTINA		83	59
BOLIVIA		63	33
BRAZIL		82	57
CHILE		71	20
MEXICO		51	32

Source: Global Development Finance, 1999.

Latin American countries' ratio of long-term debt to GNP rose from 18 percent in 1970 to 25 percent in 1980 and reached 60 percent during the mid-1980s (Table 14–5); the *debt service ratio,* which compares payments of principal and interest to earnings from the export of goods and services, was nearly 50 percent. In Argentina, debt service consumed 80 percent of export earnings; in Bolivia, Chile, and Mexico the ratio was between 50 and 60 percent.

These and other countries, not only in Latin America, began having difficulty generating sufficient government revenue and foreign exchange to service their debt. In the first half of 1982, eight countries had to reschedule their debt payments, compared to six reschedulings in all of 1981 and only three in 1978. In August 1982, Mexico declared a moratorium on the payment of interest on its foreign debt, and the debt crisis was in full cry. In 1985, there were 15 rescheduling packages and in 1987 more than 20 were concluded or negotiated. From 1983 to 1987, more than $300 billion of debt repayments had to be rescheduled.[18]

Once it became clear that many debtors would be unable to meet their obligations, the commercial banks stopped making voluntary loans to the debtors. The only commercial lending that took place after 1982 came as

18. Rudiger Dornbusch, "Background Paper," in Twentieth Century Fund, Task Force on International Debt, *The Road to Economic Recovery* (New York: Priority Publications, 1989), pp. 29–30.

part of elaborate refinancing agreements involving the IMF, the World Bank, creditor governments, the commercial banks, and the debtor governments. Stabilization and structural adjustment packages were part of these agreements, providing official finance to underpin or substitute for commercial bank loans. The commercial banks would make additional loans to service payments on old loans and permit debtors to "capitalize" their interest payments by converting them into additional debt (on which interest was charged), but they demanded that debtors make all their payments in full and on time. (Only later did the banks begin to consider rescheduling the due dates for payments of principal and later still actually reducing the amount of debt owed.) By these means, it was hoped, the debtors could quickly become solvent and the overexposed U.S. banks would not become insolvent. By the late 1980s, however, few banks were interested in further lending. From 1980 to 1982, private creditors sent more than $50 million a year of net resources into developing countries (measured in 1986 prices); in 1987, the net resource flow was negligible.[19]

The impact on the most indebted countries was severe. For a country to turn from being a net borrower into a net repayer of loans, it must reverse the beneficial effects of foreign saving inflows. Instead of investing more than it saves, a country must generate a surplus of saving to be used for the repayment of debt. Instead of importing more than its exports, a repaying country must generate export surpluses because foreign lenders need to be repaid in dollars or other foreign currencies. Where net resource inflows once financed additional growth, net resource outflows from debtors reduce growth. If debtor governments find it difficult to raise more taxes or reduce noninterest expenditures, as most did, they typically resort to inflationary financing that further destabilizes the economy. Capital flight exacerbates the crisis, as domestic savers try to move their assets to more stable financial markets.

These kinds of dramatic changes were clearly evident in Mexico before and after the 1982 crisis, as shown in Table 14–6. In the five years up to and including 1981, imports exceeded exports in Mexico by the equivalent of about 2 percent of GDP, implying capital inflows (or foreign saving) of the same amount. As we know must be the case, total investment exceeded domestic saving by exactly the same amount. Not surprisingly, there was strong growth in investment, GDP, and GDP per capita. The onset of the crisis and the demands by foreign lenders to immediately repay loans required enormous structural changes. Over the five years immediately following the crisis (1982–86), imports fell and exports expanded sharply, providing the trade surplus necessary to generate the capital outflow to pay foreign creditors. The resource balance shifted by a huge 8.3 percent of GDP (from −2 percent to 6.3 percent). Investment fell by over 4 percent

19. World Bank, *World Debt Tables 1989–1990,* Vol. 1, p. 10.

TABLE 14–6	MEXICO BEFORE AND AFTER THE 1982 DEBT CRISIS	
	BEFORE THE CRISIS, 1977–81	AFTER THE CRISIS, 1982–86
EXPORTS OF GOODS AND SERVICES (% OF GDP)	9.6	16.9
IMPORTS OF GOODS AND SERVICES (% OF GDP)	11.5	10.6
RESOURCE BALANCE (% OF GDP)	−2.0	6.3
GROSS DOMESTIC INVESTMENT (% OF GDP)	24.7	20.4
GROSS DOMESTIC SAVINGS (% OF GDP)	22.7	26.7
SAVING INVESTMENT GAP (% OF GDP)	−2.0	6.3
GROSS DOMESTIC INVESTMENT (REAL, AVERAGE ANNUAL GROWTH)	13.0	−12.2
GDP (REAL, AVERAGE ANNUAL GROWTH %)	7.6	−0.6
GDP PER CAPITA (REAL, AVERAGE ANNUAL GROWTH %)	5.0	−2.9
INFLATION, CONSUMER PRICES (AVERAGE ANNUAL %)	23.7	73.2

Source: World Bank, World Development Indicators, 1999.

of GDP, and domestic saving rose by a similar amount, bringing about the 8.3 percentage point shift in the saving-investment gap. Gross domestic investment fell sharply in real terms, as did GDP per capita. The growing budget deficit led to money creation and a sharp increase in inflation, which averaged 73 percent per year between 1982 and 1986.

These kinds of adjustments were not limited to Mexico. Between 1978 and 1981, a group of 15 heavily indebted countries managed to attract sufficient foreign saving to pay the interest and principal due on their debt and still import about $9 billion more of goods and nonfactor services each year than they exported. But from 1983 to 1988, the 15 countries were forced into a reverse transfer—exports exceed imports—of almost $34 billion a year to service their debt.[20] From 1970 to 1981, these countries had enjoyed per capita income growth of 2.7 percent a year, invested 25 percent of their GDP, and tolerated inflation of 39 percent a year on average. During the debt crisis, however, from 1982 to 1988, the same 15 countries suffered declines in per capita income averaging 0.7 percent a year, were forced to reduce their investments to 18 percent of GDP, and inflated their economies by 149 percent a year.[21]

20. Annual average net outflows during the latter period were so much larger than the average net inflows of prior years because of the sharp decline in gross lending after 1982 noted previously. Not only did countries have to repay their old debt, they had to devote their own resources to purchase imports that previously had been financed by foreign borrowing.

21. Dornbusch, "Background Paper," p. 31.

CAUSES OF THE CRISIS

Although nothing inherent in foreign debt causes a repayment crisis, defaults occurred frequently in many Latin American and European countries during the nineteenth century and the 1930s. The crisis of the 1980s was the first since World War II, however. In this instance, several things appear to have gone wrong at once.[22] The fact that so many countries were struck by crisis at the same time suggests that international factors, such as trade prices and interest rates, were at least partly to blame. At the same time, not all countries were affected equally, with some heavily indebted countries (such as Korea and Indonesia) escaping relatively unscathed, suggesting that domestic economic management played an important role.

To begin with, the debt crisis was closely linked to the huge increases in international oil prices of 1973–74 and 1978–80, which caused major disruptions in every economy in the world. Oil importers had to adjust to lower standards of living and oil exporters had to learn to productively manage massive new revenues. Facing plunges in income that sometimes threatened political stability, many governments in oil importing countries tried to compensate by increasing spending. But this strategy, while perhaps politically expedient in the short run, led to growing budget deficits and could not be sustained economically. The countries that followed this path found themselves in deep crisis. The large deficits had to be financed by borrowing either from the central bank, domestic capital markets (which were limited), or abroad. The typical first course of action was to borrow from the central bank, which simply added to the money supply and sparked inflation. Some governments compensated further by maintaining their exchange rates at overvalued levels. This restrained price increases for imports and exportable goods but also discouraged export growth and encouraged capital flight. When recycled petrodollars became available through the international commercial banks, governments grabbed at the chance to finance their deficits, boost investment and prevent declines in consumption. Unfortunately, in many cases, investments were wasteful and there was too much consumption. Resources were not channeled into investments that eventually would pay off the debts with a surplus for the host country.

22. A huge literature examines the 1980s debt crisis. We cite some of the key works here. Jeffrey D. Sachs, ed., *Developing Country Debt and Economic Performance* (Cambridge, MA: National Bureau of Economic Research, 1989–1990): Volume 1, *The International Financial System;* Volume 2, *Country Studies: Argentina, Bolivia, Brazil, Mexico;* Volume 3 (with Susan Collins), *Country Studies: Indonesia, Korea, the Philippines, Turkey;* summary volume, *Developing Country Debt and the World Economy.* William Cline, *International Debt: Systematic Risk and Policy Response* (Washington, DC: Institute for International Economics, 1984) and *International Debt Reexamined* (Washington, DC: Institute for International Economics, 1995). Ishrat Husain and Ishac Diwan, eds., *Dealing with the Debt Crisis* (Washington, DC: World Bank, 1989).

This points to a second major policy difference between the countries that fell into crisis and those that did not: trade orientation. As Harvard economist Jeffrey Sachs pointed out, as the crisis unfolded, most Latin American countries followed an import substitution trade strategy (described in detail in Chapter 18) rather than promoting manufactured exports, as most of the East Asian countries did. Latin America's investments in the 1970s into industries that were producing for the domestic market contributed little to the region's capacity to export and service their debts in the 1980s. By contrast, Asia's investments in export-oriented activities made it much easier to service its debts.[23]

Why did the banks lend to governments that ran large deficits and were not oriented toward exports? The gush of petrodollars left the banks highly liquid, seeking profitable outlets for their deposits. Lending to developing countries seemed to provide an outlet that had not been fully utilized in recent years. Because the debt was **sovereign,** that is, guaranteed by governments, bankers apparently discounted the risk of default, even though history held many examples to the contrary. Once a few banks showed the way, others followed. And once the banks were heavily involved, further lending seemed a sensible way to keep debtor countries liquid enough to continue servicing earlier loans. Banks were encouraged by their own governments, especially the U.S. government, and the international agencies, all of which hoped that the illiquidity of the early 1980s would disappear once the world economy recovered from its instability. Whatever the reasons for the banks' persistence in lending, it is clear that neither they nor their governments foresaw the generalized debt crisis. As with most instances of debt problems, in this case the bankers bore as much responsibility for the crisis as the borrowing countries.

Instability in the world economy precipitated the crisis. The unprecedented rises in oil prices already have been mentioned. Almost as important was the sharp rise in dollar interest rates in the early 1980s. During the latter 1970s, inflation in the United States reached double digits and the Federal Reserve Board tightened the money supply. The immediate consequence was that interest rates soared to a peak of 16 percent in 1981 before settling gradually into a range of 7–9 percent through the second half of the 1980s. Debtor countries were forced to pay the new rates if they had borrowed at flexible interest rates or if they had to refinance old loans now coming due, so their interest payments rose and became unpredictable. For many countries, the impact was substantial. For example, for a group of 15 countries in Central and South America, the rise in interest rates between 1978 and 1981 added over $13 billion to the costs of servicing their debts in 1981 alone. In addition

23. Jeffrey Sachs, "External Debt and Macroeconomic Performance in Latin America and East Asia," *Brookings Papers on Economic Activity,* 1985, no. 2, pp. 523–73.

to higher interest payments, tight money and fiscal stringency in the high-income countries (especially in the United States) led to the world recession of 1981–82. Income in the industrialized economies, having grown by more than 3 percent a year in the preceding years, slowed to 2 percent growth in 1980–81 and declined in 1982. The recession shrank the markets for debtor country exports and caused a decline in a wide range of commodity prices, which on average fell by one third in the early 1980s relative to the prices of manufacturers. These external shocks clearly added to the debt burdens facing developing countries. Note, however, that even in the face of these shocks, not all debtors suffered equally. South Korea and Indonesia were among the world's largest debtors, yet sound economic policies enabled them to service their debt while continuing to grow throughout the 1980s. In particular, these countries responded by reducing their budget deficits, restraining the expansion of domestic demand, and encouraging export production. It took a combination of the deteriorating world economy, poor domestic management, and the myopia of the commercial banks to bring on the crisis.[24]

ESCAPE FROM THE CRISIS

For the international commercial banks and the countries that had borrowed from them, the debt crisis of the 1980s was over by the mid-1990s. For other countries (mainly low-income countries in sub-Saharan Africa, South Asia, and Central America) that had borrowed predominantly from other governments and the international financial institutions, the debt crisis lingered unresolved through the end of the century. The largest Latin American debtor worked out of their insolvency and are now servicing their debt. Table 14–5 shows that, for Latin American countries, debt service ratios have receded from their high levels of the 1980s. The average ratio of debt to GDP in Latin America fell from its peak of 60 percent in the 1980s to 29 percent in 1997. Debt service payments were the equivalent of about one third of export earnings in 1997, down from almost one half in the 1980s. In some countries, the change has been huge. In Chile, for example, the ratio of debt service to exports fell from a peak of 71 percent in the 1980s to just 20 percent in 1997.

The Latin American debtors worked out of insolvency through complex debt relief agreements that involved the debtor governments; the international agencies, specifically the World Bank and IMF; the creditor governments, their treasuries, and aid agencies; and the commercial banks with loans to the debtor countries. Each agreement required a major negotiation

---

24. On the causes of the crisis, see Dornbusch, "Background Paper," pp. 37–47; and John T. Cuddington, "The Extent and Causes of the Debt Crisis of the 1980s" in Husain and Diwan, *Dealing with the Debt Crisis,* pp. 15–44.

among these parties, covering stabilization and structural adjustment programs, new aid and commercial credits, debt rescheduling, and a list of mechanisms for converting or retiring existing debt.

International strategies to resolve the debt crisis evolved slowly in three broad stages during the 1980s. In the first stage, in the years immediately following the eruption of the crisis, the international community was concerned mainly about the health of the commercial banks and, by extension, the international financial system. Banks reduced their lending to the developing countries but expected these countries to make their payments in full and on time. As we have seen, this caused major disruptions in the debtor countries as they quickly shifted from large resource inflows (with $M - E > 0$) to large resource outflows (with $M - E < 0$). It became obvious fairly soon, however, that this strategy was simply undermining whatever residual ability these countries had to repay their debts.

The second stage began in 1985, when U.S. Secretary of the Treasury James Baker announced a new strategy aimed at easing the burdens on the debtor countries. Under the **Baker Plan,** as this strategy came to be known, creditor banks and debtor governments were to renegotiate the debts by stretching out the time frame for repayment (however, the plan included no provisions for actually reducing the amount of debt). In return, the debtor governments would introduce major policy initiatives aimed at regaining macroeconomic stability and reforming the public sector. These **stabilization and structural adjustment programs** contribute to debt reduction by helping reduce deficits in the government budget and the balance of payments, contain inflation, stimulate savings, and generate more resources for investment and debt service. The cost of debt service is borne by citizens of the debtor country in the form of reduced income, higher taxes and fees, reduced services from government, and other adjustments that reduce levels of consumption. These programs were supported by new loans from the IMF, the World Bank, and bilateral aid agencies designed to ease the adjustment burden to some extent by financing imports and investment and, in some cases, by directly financing debt reduction. In addition, loans from creditor governments would be renegotiated by both stretching out the schedule for repayment and reducing the actual amount of debt due. The terms of these bilateral restructurings became progressively easier during the late 1980s. It was hoped that the combination of policy reforms, new financing from the IMF and World Bank, and bilateral debt relief would provide the debtor countries with the wherewithal to fully replay the commercial banks and keep them on sound footing. In the end, however, the Baker Plan proved to be insufficient to resolve the debt crisis.

The breakthrough came in the late 1980s, when a third strategy was unveiled, this time incorporating the idea that the value of the debt would

THE 1982 MEXICAN DEBT CRISIS[25]

By far the two largest debtors in the developing world in the 1980s were Brazil and Mexico, each with over $100 billion of outstanding debt in 1989. It is ironic that Mexico should have been so indebted, because in the later 1970s it benefited from major increases in both oil production and oil prices. However, the Mexican government, like other oil-exporting governments, spent the country's windfall profligately and borrowed heavily against the prospect of a continued oil boom. Mexican debt rose from 12 percent of GNP in 1975 to 53 percent in 1982, the very years that oil exports were booming. By 1982, the ratio of debt-service to exports exceeded 50 percent. Despite the surge in resource flows from oil revenues and foreign borrowing, the Mexican economy actually grew faster, with less inflation, during the 17 years before the oil boom than it did during the boom, as Table 14–7 shows.

When the newly elected government of President Miguel de la Madrid took over in 1982, its finance minister, Silvio Herzog, told creditors that the country could not meet interest payments on its debt. This announcement alarmed the creditor banks, which held about 70 percent of Mexico's debt, and international institutions, not only because of the large Mexican debt but because other countries were likely to follow Mexico's lead. At the time, it seemed quite possible that debtor insolvency across many countries could lead to failures of major U.S. banks and a worldwide financial panic.

To stave off this disaster and help Mexico work out its debt problem, the commercial banks, their governments, and the international agencies put together packages of debt rescheduling, new lending by all institutions, and economic austerity for the Mexican economy. Mexico's trade balance, excluding interest payments, turned from a net inward resource transfer of 4.3 percent of GNP in 1981 to a net outward transfer of 2.4 percent of GNP in 1988; its investment share of GNP fell from 28 to 21 percent. The results of this austerity are evident in Table 14–7 (and shown earlier in Table 14–6): Incomes fell and inflation accelerated. It was starkly obvious that the price of debt repayment would mean deep reductions in the welfare of the Mexican people.

25. Based on accounts by Rudiger Dornbusch, "Mexico's Economy at the Crossroads," *Journal of International Affairs,* 43, no. 2 (Winter 1990), 313–26; and World Bank, *World Debt Tables 1989–1990,* Vol. 1, pp. 28, 52–53.

TABLE 14-7 MEXICAN GROWTH AND INFLATION, 1955-1992 (PERCENT PER YEAR)				
	1955-1972	1973-1981	1982-1988	1988-1992
INCOME PER CAPITA	3.3	2.6	-2.2	2.5
REAL WAGES	3.7	3.1	-5.9	N.A.
INFLATION	5	22	83	21

Sources: Rudiger Dornbusch, "Mexico's Economy at the Crossroads," *Journal of International Affairs*, 43, no. 2 (Winter 1990), 314; and World Bank, *World Tables 1994–1995*, pp. 456–57.

After six years of debt-induced retrenchment that seemed to offer no real relief to Mexico or its creditors, a new debt reduction package was negotiated among all parties in 1989. The commercial banks were offered a menu of options. They could (1) exchange existing debt for new bonds at a 35 percent discount, (2) exchange old debt for new bonds at the same value but a reduced interest rate of 6.25 percent, or (3) make new loans of at least 25 percent of the amounts due them at market rates of interest over 15 years with a 7-year grace period when no principal would be due. In all cases, the new debt was to be considered "senior" to the old, with prior claims on payments, and the Mexican government pledged not to request rescheduling of the new debt. Mexico was also permitted to purchase its own debt at the substantial discounts offered on the secondary market, as long as it was current on its interest payments. Principal and interest payments on the new bonds were guaranteed by a $7 billion fund established by the IMF, the World Bank, and the Japanese government.

By 1990, Mexico's economic situation had improved significantly. In 1987, Mexico was transferring net resources (the surplus of imports over exports of goods and nonfactor services) outward by $8.6 billion a year; from 1989 to 1992, helped by the debt settlement and a resurgence of foreign investment, there was an inward net transfer of $4.8 billion a year. Over that period, income per capita grew by 2.5 percent a year, after seven years of decline. And inflation, which reached 83 percent a year during the debt crisis, was contained at 21 percent a year. The debt settlement was not the only force behind this improvement. The strengthening world economy and Mexico's own economic reforms played major roles in the recovery. Unfortunately, the recovery was accompanied by large amounts of new foreign borrowing (especially after 1992), much of it with short-term maturity structures, that ultimately led to a second crisis in December 1994. The second crisis (described later in this chapter), while very deep, was much more short-lived than the 1982 crisis, and economic growth returned to an average of over 5 percent per year between 1996 and 2000.

be written down and the commercial banks would share in some of the losses. The new U.S. Secretary of the Treasury, Nicholas Brady, announced the broad outlines of the plan in the first months of the Bush administration in March 1989. The **Brady Plan** recognized that debtor countries needed a permanent reduction of their debt burdens to get back on sound economic footing. The strategy called for banks and debtor governments to renegotiate debts on a case-by-case basis from a "menu" of options. Subsequent deals with different countries relied on different combinations of reducing the face value of the debt, reducing the interest rate charged, providing new loans, and other forms of restructuring. The new bonds that were issued to replace the old debt are known as **Brady bonds.** The amount of debt relief encompassed in these deals varied from country to country, depending on their particular situation and the country's ability to repay. Mexico's commercial bank debt was reduced by about 35 percent, whereas Costa Rica received debt reduction of about 65 percent. Later deals were struck with Poland, Ecuador, Venezuela, the Philippines, Brazil, Peru, the Ivory Coast, and several other countries. As with the Baker Plan, the new scheme included stabilization and structural adjustment programs under the auspices of the IMF and World Bank, new lending from these organizations, and bilateral debt relief.

The key to the program was the recognition by the international community and the creditor banks that, by continuing to insist on full repayment, they were undermining the strength of these economies and ultimately receiving less repayment than they would under a negotiated settlement. This condition came to be known as a **debt overhang.** The accumulation of bad debt (the "overhang") reduced the capacity of the country to repay its debts to such a degree that both creditor and debtor could become better off by reducing the value of the debt.[26] (An example of this is shown in the case study on the Mexican debt crisis.)

The extent of the reduction in the value of the debt is reflected by the price at which the banks were able to sell these debts to other investors. The major money markets of the world have active secondary markets in all kinds of debt, public and private, where creditors can sell their claims against debtors at a discount that reflects market expectations about repayment. At the end of 1989, the commercial debt of the 17 most heavily indebted countries sold on the secondary market at only one third of its par value. A buyer of such paper pays $33 to obtain a promise of repayment of $100 plus interest; this reflects the buyer's expectation that the chances of repayment are only about one in three. If the commercial banks believe the

26. Jeffrey Sachs, "The Debt Overhang of Developing Countries," in R. Findlay, G. Calvo, P. Kouri, and J. Braga de Macedo, eds., *Debt, Stabilization and Development: Essays in Honor of Carlos Díaz Alejandro* (Oxford: Basil Blackwell, 1989).

chances of repayment are less than one in three, they may forgo their claim of repayment and sell the loan on the secondary market, realizing a net loss of $67. Debtors, too, can purchase their own obligations on the secondary market, paying $33 to reduce the principal due by $100. Loan agreements normally prohibit borrowers from such **buybacks,** however, because they encourage debtors to default, driving down the price on the secondary market and making it more advantageous to buy back their debt.

Another form of debt restructuring is a **debt-equity swap,** which enables the debtor to pay the creditor in local currency, which can be used only for direct investment in the host country. A bank would accept cruzeiros in exchange for retirement of debt owed by Brazil, and then lend these funds to companies that could use them to finance equity investments. The debtor government has to raise funds on the domestic market, however; this could be inflationary, could squeeze out domestic private investors, or could require tax increases and expenditure reductions. Debt-equity swaps thus solve the problem of the foreign exchange constraint but not the budgetary constraint. Furthermore, many swaps have financed investments that might have been financed in dollars in any case, representing no net gain to the country.[27]

When all forms of debt conversion are added up, the total of debt converted for the five years from 1988 to 1992 was $75 billion. Yet the total long-term debt of developing countries was about $1.3 trillion during those years; in heavily indebted Latin America, debt relief totaled $64 billion against debt of almost $400 billion.[28] Countries that escaped the debt crisis, especially those in Latin America, were helped by debt relief. But they may have been helped even more by the revival of the world economy in the early 1990s and by their own efforts to stabilize and reform their economies. Where the debt crisis hangs on, especially in Africa, continued aid is keeping economies afloat while economic reforms are being put in place.

THE HIGHLY INDEBTED POOR COUNTRIES

Although the debt crisis effectively ended in the early 1990s for most middle-income countries that had borrowed heavily from commercial banks, the crisis continues for many low-income countries, especially many countries in Africa. The IMF and the World Bank refer to these countries (rather awkwardly) as the *highly indebted poor countries* (HIPCs).

27. On the subject of debt relief measures, see Dornbusch, "Background Paper," pp. 67–101; Husain and Diwan, *Dealing with the Debt Crisis,* "Introduction," pp. 1–11; Michel H. Bouchet and Jonathan Hay, "The Rise of the Market-Based 'Menu' Approach and Its Limitations," in Husain and Diwan, *Dealing with the Debt Crisis,* pp. 147–58; and World Bank, *World Debt Tables 1989–1990,* Vol. 1, pp. 21–31.

28. World Bank, *World Debt Tables 1994–1995,* pp. 171, 173, 187, 189.

The debt burdens in many of the HIPCs are very high and their capacity to pay is limited. Total debt outstanding for this group of countries was five times larger than their collective exports in 1990, and nearly four times larger than exports in 1998. Debt service payments consumed over one-third of all government revenues in 1997, which in many cases was three times or more the amount spent on social services.

In contrast to the Latin American countries in the 1970s and 1980s, these countries borrowed heavily from industrialized country governments and the multilateral agencies rather than commercial banks. The HIPCs borrowed in the 1970s and 1980s for many of the same reasons as other developing countries—high oil import prices, low commodity prices, and weak market demand in the industrialized countries. In many of the HIPCs, part of the reason for poor economic performance is a prolonged period of economic mismanagement. Governments kept budget deficits high, erected significant barriers to trade, distorted market prices, and failed to provide basic infrastructure and health and education services. But poor economic management is only part of the story. Many of these countries were hit by substantial declines in export prices and other economic shocks. A large number face very difficult geographical challenges, such as being landlocked, located in the tropics (where disease is much more virulent), or located in or near the Sahara Desert, where rainfall is extremely limited. Several currently are ravaged by the economic and social impacts of the HIV/AIDS epidemic, which further undermines their capacity for sustained economic growth and repayment of debt. In addition, in many cases, industrialized country governments provided these countries abundant funding for poor investments and grandiose consumption projects in an attempt to win them over to one side or the other of the cold war. Some Western loans supported corrupt governments that had little intention or capability of repaying the loans to finance new palaces, showcase steel mills, fleets of cars for the president, and other wasteful expenditures. As new governments have taken over for these old dictators during the 1990s, the debts remain on the books. Mozambique, for example, was devastated by a 16-year-long civil war financed by both East and West as a backdrop to the cold war. In 1992, a democratically elected government took over the ravaged economy and inherited a huge amount of debt that had produced little in terms of productive economic assets. In 1997, Mozambique's debt service owed to international creditors amounted to 5.1 percent of GDP, far more than the 2.9 percent of GDP that the government spent on health care and education.

One factor working in the HIPCs' favor is that, since most of the loans were from official sources, a significant portion of the original debt was issued on concessional terms. The average interest rate on new loans to these countries in 1997 was 2.4 percent, and their loans were due to be repaid over 30 years. In contrast, in 1980, the heavily indebted middle-income countries paid an average interest rate of 10.1 percent and their repayment period averaged 13 years.[29] However, at the same time, since the commercial banks were not major players, a Brady plan-type restructuring is not an option for these countries. Until the late 1990s, the IMF and the World Bank had never written down or written off debts owed to them, even though debt reduction has been an integral part of the resolution of many debt crises in the past (including private sector bankruptcies in most industrialized countries). These agencies have been concerned that a significant debt reduction would impair their own credit ratings, increase their own costs as they borrow in international financial markets, and force them to charge higher interest rates to the countries to which they lend. The extent to which these fears are warranted is a matter of some debate. In any case, since the HIPCs in general have not borrowed heavily from commercial banks, a different strategy is required to alleviate their debt burden.

In the late 1990s, the international community finally began to slowly and partially address the problem. The IMF and World Bank introduced the "HIPC Initiative" in 1996, which was designed to reduce debt burdens of eligible countries to what were deemed to be sustainable levels. However, in the first three years of the initiative, only five countries received partial debt relief—Uganda, Bolivia, Guyana, Mozambique, and Mali. Even in these countries, the debt reduction provided was relatively small: 10 percent of outstanding debt in Mali, 13 percent in Bolivia, 20 percent in Uganda, and 24 percent in Guyana. Only in Mozambique was debt reduction more substantial, reaching 63 percent.

The HIPC initiative was revised in mid-1999 in an attempt to provide more debt relief and provide it more quickly to the highly indebted countries. The "Enhanced HIPC Initiative" program is an improvement over the original, as it should allow more countries to receive greater debt relief in a shorter period of time. To be eligible for debt reduction under the HIPC initiative, a country must first establish a record of good economic policies over a period of three full years, within the context of IMF and World Bank adjustment programs. At the end of the three-year period, the international community determines whether a country's debt burden is sustainable (the "decision point"). The main criterion for determining debt sustainability is the ratio of the net present value (NPV) of debt to exports. In June 1999, the standard for sustainability was reduced to 150 percent from its previous range of 200–250 percent. Several other secondary criteria for certain countries are based on the NPV of debt to fiscal revenues.

If the debt burden is deemed to be sustainable, then no debt reduction is provided, as was the case with Benin and Senegal in 1997 and 1998,

29. World Bank, *Global Development Finance 1999*, pp. 177 and 191.

DEBT RELIEF IN UGANDA[30]

When Uganda gained its independence from Britain in 1962, there was widespread optimism that its vibrant agricultural base and diverse, talented people could provide the basis for sustained economic development. However, political instability in the late 1960s, followed by a coup in 1971 by Idi Amin, ushered in a long period of political terror and economic destruction. By the time President Yoweri Musevini assumed power in 1986, Uganda was one of the poorest countries in the world. Food production had fallen by one third in 15 years, average income had declined by over 40 percent, and life expectancy was just 48 years. The new government embarked on a broad-based economic rebuilding program that focused on rehabilitating infrastructure, restoring macroeconomic balance, lowering barriers to trade, and investing in the social sectors. In the dozen years that followed, the economy staged a remarkable recovery. Average incomes increased by nearly 60 percent and the share of the population living below the poverty line fell from 56 to 44 percent.

30. This information is drawn primarily from the World Bank websites on the HIPC program and the country page for Uganda (www.worldbank.org).

respectively (although under the revised 1999 criteria, both are likely to become eligible). If the debt burden is deemed to be unsustainable, a package of debt relief is identified, including for the first time, a reduction of debts owed to the IMF and World Bank. At the decision point, debts are rescheduled (to provide cash flow relief) but not actually reduced. The country then must go through another period (from a few months to up to three years) of solid economic reform under the tutelage of the IMF and World Bank. If the country is successful, debt reduction is granted at the end of this second period (the "completion point"). Therefore, countries must wait for between three and six years to gain debt reduction under the program, far longer than is the norm in bankruptcy courts or was the case with Brady Plan restructurings. By mid-2000, only one country—Uganda—had finished the entire process and reached its completion point. Five others had reached their decision points. The World Bank expected around 20 countries to reach their decision points by between the end of 2000 and mid-2001.

By the mid-1990s, however, Uganda had accumulated a substantial debt burden. By 1993, total external debt was more than 12 times the value of annual exports, one of the highest such ratios in the world (note that total debt equal to twice the value of exports generally is considered a heavy burden). Two thirds of the debt was owed to multilateral agencies, so that traditional methods for debt relief (for private sector or bilateral debt) had limited potential.

In April 1998, Uganda was the first country to become eligible for debt reduction under the highly indebted poor country (HIPC) initiative. In this first formulation of the HIPC program, Uganda received about $650 million debt relief, reducing its $3.2 billion debt stock by about 20 percent. Two years later, Uganda became the first country to be eligible for the enhanced HIPC program, which offered deeper debt relief to qualifying countries. This second phase reduced Uganda's debts by about $1.3 billion, bringing the total debt reduction under the program to approximately $2 billion. In aggregate, the initiative will reduce Uganda's debt service between 2000 and 2020 by about $80 million per year, or between two thirds and three quarters of debt service payments due. Uganda's early success with the program was encouraging: It doubled the primary school enrollment rate from 50 to 100 percent between 1997 and 2000 and increased investments in farm-to-market roads by 75 percent.

The HIPC initiative has raised many important issues. Should countries be forced to wait so long for debt relief? Should debt relief be granted to all countries or just the best performers, and if the latter, how should that performance be measured? Do the IMF and World Bank use the most appropriate debt sustainability indicators? Are the policy reforms designed by the IMF and World Bank appropriate for the long-term development of these countries? In many countries that have consistently remained on IMF programs, growth has continued to lag, giving rise to criticism that the reform programs are focused too narrowly on macroeconomic stabilization and not enough on providing the foundation for long-term economic growth. Who should finance the debt reduction by the IMF, World Bank, regional development banks, and other international financial institutions? Should these institutions pay for it out of their own paid-in capital (reducing their capacity for future lending), or should member governments make an extra contribution? These issues and many others will need to be addressed both within the debtor countries and in the international agencies and bilateral lenders before the debt crisis finally ends for the poorest countries. (For example, see the case study on Uganda.)

Emerging Market Financial Crises

During the middle and late 1990s, severe financial crises struck a growing number of developing countries, including Mexico, Argentina, Venezuela, Thailand, Korea, Indonesia, Malaysia, Russia, Brazil, and Ecuador. These crises generally were unanticipated and occurred quite suddenly. In several cases they affected countries that previously had strong economic performance and been favorites of the international capital markets. Perhaps the best known are the Mexican peso crisis of late 1994, the Asian financial crises of mid-1997, and the Russian and Brazilian crises of 1998. These crises led to sharp reductions in investment and economic output, major dislocations in trade, widespread unemployment, and increases in poverty. They also led to widespread rethinking of both the role of foreign capital flows (especially short-term flows) and the proper timing and sequencing of financial liberalization in the development process.

At the heart of these crises were huge, sudden reversals of international private capital flows. Economies that had been receiving relatively large amounts of private capital sudden were faced with withdrawals of lines of credit, demands to repay debts, an exodus of portfolio capital, and offshore flight by domestic investors. Table 14–8 shows both the rapid buildup in lending and the depth and speed of the subsequent reversal in capital flows for five of the most severely affected Asian crisis economies: Indonesia, South Korea, Malaysia, the Philippines, and Thailand. Net private capital flows to these five countries more than doubled in just two years from $40 billion in 1994 to $103 billion in 1996. Net commercial bank lending alone nearly tripled from $24 billion to $65 billion. But, in the last six months of 1997, the private capital inflow of $103 billion suddenly turned into an outflow of $1 billion. This net reversal of capital flows of $104 billion was equivalent to about 10 percent of the combined pre-crisis GDPs of these five countries. With a withdrawal of that magnitude in just six months, no wonder these countries were plunged into crisis.

Mexico's crisis in late 1994 followed a similar pattern. Capital inflows into Mexico averaged $30 billion in 1992 and 1993. However, following a political assassination in early 1994, capital began to flow out quickly. By the end of 1994, foreign exchange reserves were nearly depleted and the government was forced to devalue the peso. Massive capital outflows continued in early 1995 and, although they recovered by the end of the year, amounted to more than $10 billion on a net basis for the year as a whole.

TABLE 14–8	FIVE ASIAN ECONOMIES: EXTERNAL FINANCING (BILLION U.S. DOLLARS)					
	1994	1995	1996	1997	1998[a]	1999[b]
CURRENT ACCOUNT BALANCE	−24.6	−41.3	−54.6	−26.3	58.5	43.2
EXTERNAL FINANCING, NET	47.4	80.9	100.6	28.8	−0.5	−1.2
PRIVATE FLOWS, NET	40.5	77.4	103.2	−1.1	−28.3	−4.8
EQUITY INVESTMENT	12.2	15.5	19.7	3.6	8.5	18.7
DIRECT EQUITY	4.7	4.9	5.8	6.8	6.4	14.2
PORTFOLIO EQUITY	7.6	10.6	13.9	−3.2	2.1	4.5
PRIVATE CREDITORS	28.2	61.8	83.5	−4.7	−36.8	−23.4
COMMERCIAL BANKS	24.0	49.5	65.3	−25.6	−35.0	−18.8
NONBANK PRIVATE CREDITORS	4.2	12.4	18.2	21.0	−1.7	−4.6
OFFICIAL FLOWS, NET	7.0	3.6	−2.6	29.9	27.8	3.5
INTERNATIONAL FINANCIAL INSTITUTIONS	−0.4	−0.6	−2.0	22.1	21.6	−2.0
BILATERAL CREDITORS	7.4	4.2	−0.6	7.9	6.1	5.5
RESIDENT LENDING AND OTHER, NET[c]	−17.5	−25.9	−26.8	−35.0	−16.9	−14.9
RESERVES EXCLUSIVE OF GOLD (− = INCREASE)	−5.4	−13.7	+9.3	32.5	−41.1	−27.0

Note: The economies are those of South Korea, Indonesia, Malaysia, Thailand, and the Philippines.
[a]Estimate.
[b]Institute of International Finance forecast.
[c]Including resident net lending, monetary gold, and error and omissions
Source: Institute of International Finance, *Capital Flows to Emerging Market Economies* (Washington, DC: IIF, January 1999).

The two-year reversal in capital flows of $40 billion was the equivalent of about 9 percent of Mexico's 1994 GDP. Similar reversals were seen at the same time in Argentina, Venezuela, and other countries.

As with the earlier debt crises of the 1980s, the reversals in capital flow were immediately reflected in dramatic changes in trade balances, saving-investment gaps, and overall economic activity. For example, in the five Asian crisis countries, current account balances changed from deficits averaging 5 percent of GDP in 1996 to surpluses averaging 5 percent of GDP in 1998. Economic output fell sharply in each of the crisis countries, as shown in Table 14–9. GDP fell either in the year of the crisis or the following year, depending mainly on whether the crisis struck early or late in the year. For example, Argentina's crisis hit early in 1995, and GDP fell 2.8 percent in that year before rebounding by 5.5 percent the following year. Indonesia's crisis hit in late 1997, so it still managed to record growth of 4.7 percent in that year. In 1998, however, the bottom fell out of the economy and it contracted by 13.5 percent. The plunge in GDP

		GDP GROWTH (REAL, %)			
COUNTRY	YEAR OF CRISIS	YEAR PRECEDING CRISIS	YEAR OF CRISIS	YEAR AFTER CRISIS	TWO YEARS AFTER CRISIS
ARGENTINA	1995	5.8	−2.8	5.5	8.1
BRAZIL	1998	3.6	−0.1	−0.4	2.7[a]
INDONESIA	1997	7.8	4.7	−13.5	0.8
KOREA	1997	6.7	5.0	−5.8	8.5
MALAYSIA	1997	8.6	7.7	−7.5	5.0
MEXICO	1995	4.4	−6.2	5.2	6.7
THE PHILIPPINES	1997	5.9	5.2	−0.5	3.3
THAILAND	1997	5.5	−0.4	−10.2	3.3
TURKEY	1994	8.0	−5.5	7.2	7.0
VENEZUELA	1994	0.3	−2.3	4.0	−0.2

TABLE 14–9   GDP GROWTH (REAL) BEFORE AND AFTER CRISIS

[a]*EIU* forecast for 2000.

Source: IMF, *International Financial Statistics Yearbook*, and Economist Intelligence Unit (EIU), various country reports.

growth in Indonesia between 1997 and 1998 is one of the largest one-year reversals anywhere in the world in recent economic history. As usually is the case in such crises, the poor were the most adversely affected. For example, urban day laborers who had previously eked out a subsistence living by loading trucks or working on construction sites suddenly were thrown out of work, with few ready alternatives to earn an income. Poverty rates in Indonesia doubled by official estimates from 12 percent to around 22 percent, with some unofficial estimates suggesting even higher levels.

Almost as striking as the collapse in growth was the speed of the rebound, at least in many of the crisis countries. Argentina, Korea, Malaysia, Mexico, and Turkey all recorded GDP growth of 5 percent or more two years after their respective crises. These economies recovered much more quickly than those affected by the debt crises of the 1980s. As we shall see, this pattern is at least partly a reflection of the central role played by creditor panic in many of these crises.

How did the crises happen? The crisis countries had several important characteristics in common. First, they tended to be middle-income and upper-middle-income countries that had registered several years of rapid economic growth. Second, they all had received large flows of private international capital, much of it with short-term maturity structures. Third, they recently had liberalized their financial systems and had recorded a very rapid—perhaps too rapid—expansion of bank lending and other financial services. Finally, most of the crisis countries had exchange rates heavily controlled by their central banks, often strictly fixed (or pegged) to the U.S. dollar. These similarities suggest that government policies contributed to the crises, especially banking, financial, and exchange rate policies. However, the quick recovery in several countries, the fact that crises struck so many countries in such a short period of time, and the consistent pattern of rapid buildup and then withdrawal of private capital all suggest that international capital markets played an important role as well.

DOMESTIC ECONOMIC WEAKNESSES

Each of the crisis countries had liberalized its financial systems in the late 1980s and early 1990s and had done it in ways that inadvertently left the financial systems fragile and overextended. Entry requirements were eased for banks and other financial institutions, allowing new private banks to open. State-owned banks began to play smaller roles. Governments gave banks more freedom in their lending decisions by removing policies in which the government forced banks to allocate certain amounts of credit to government-chosen firms and investment projects. They also eased controls on interest rates, giving banks much more flexibility to set the rates they charged their customers and reducing the problems arising from negative real interest rates described in Chapter 13. At the same time, banks were given much greater freedom to raise funds through offshore borrowing. In fact, in several countries, banks were actively encouraged by government policies to borrow from foreign banks and relend the funds onshore. As a result, the foreign liabilities of the banking systems of these countries rose sharply. In Thailand, for example, total foreign liabilities of banks and financial institutions rose from 5 percent of GDP in 1990 to 28 percent of GDP in 1995, with most of these liabilities being debts owed to foreign commercial banks. The combination of the increase in the number of domestic financial institutions and their newfound ability to borrow offshore led to very rapid increases in domestic lending activity by banks. Loans from domestic banks to the private sector increased by the equivalent of more than 50 percent of GDP in just seven years in Thailand, Korea, and Malaysia.

Of course, as discussed in Chapter 13, financial liberalization can bring about many benefits to developing countries, including the mobilization of additional resources, reduced intermediation costs, and improved allocation of credit. The problem was not financial liberalization per se but how it was done, especially how rapidly it was done. The speed and magnitude of the expansion of financial activities outstripped the government's ability to prudently regulate and supervise these transactions. The crisis countries liberalized their financial systems too quickly and without giving sufficient attention to establishing strong legal and supervisory institutions to safeguard the system. Central banks did not have supervisors with the skills and authority necessary to determine which banks were vulnerable and to take steps to penalize or close poorly performing institutions. In some cases, supervisors were pressured (or bribed!) to overlook violations by banks with politically influential owners. As a result of this weak supervision, some banks were undercapitalized, nonperforming loans were at high levels, and many prudential regulations (such as banks lending to affiliated companies) regularly were broken with no penalty. Over time, loans tended to go to weaker investment projects and the quality of banks' loan portfolios deteriorated. This left the banks (and the financial systems more broadly) in a vulnerable situation. In Thailand, for example, extensive lending was directed at real estate, construction, and property. When property prices began to fall in late 1996, banks exposed to these markets began to weaken considerably, making these banks' foreign creditors increasingly nervous.

Exchange rate policies added to the problems in the crisis economies. In each of the crisis economies, central banks either held the exchange rate fixed or changed it by small, predictable amounts. None of the crisis economies had fully flexible currencies in which the exchange rate was free to move in response to market supply and demand conditions. Although fixed exchange rates help keep import prices relatively stable and provide a price anchor in a highly inflationary environment, they can create three kinds of problems.

First, they tend to encourage the build-up of short-term capital inflows, which are especially vulnerable to rapid withdrawals by the creditors, as discussed later. With fixed exchange rates, investors believe there is little chance they will lose money from a rapid change in the exchange rate. For example, a foreign investor is more likely to buy a one-month bond denominated in Mexican pesos if the investor believes that there is little chance that the exchange rate will change during the month. By contrast, in countries with flexible exchange rates, foreign investors are more hesitant to buy short-term securities, since a relatively small exchange rate movement quickly could wipe out any gain they realize from higher interest rates.

Second, fixed exchange rates tended to gradually discourage exports and encourage imports. As discussed in more detail in Chapter 18, if an exporter's domestic production costs rise faster than the dollar prices of export sales and if the exchange rate does not shift to make up for the difference, export profitability falls. Partly because of their fixed (or near fixed) exchange rates, the crisis economies generally experienced a slowdown in export growth and a widening of the trade deficit in the years preceding the crisis.

Third, and perhaps most important, once capital withdrawals begin in the early stages of a crisis, fixed exchange rates tend to help accelerate the withdrawals and ultimately contribute to a near depletion of available foreign exchange reserves. With fixed exchange rates, governments are committed to meet all the demand for foreign exchange at the given rate, even when creditors begin to withdraw their lines of credit and demand immediate repayment. In situations where short-term debt exceeds available reserves and the exchange rate is fixed, central banks fight a losing battle. Once investors begin to understand this situation, they begin to speculate against the local currency, betting that the government will have to remove the fixed exchange rate.[31] This speculation adds to the loss of reserves and the pressure on the exchange rate. When the central banks finally exhaust their reserves, they have little choice but to devalue the currency by very large amounts. The Thai baht, for example, jumped from 25 baht to the dollar in July 1997 to 54 baht to the dollar in January 1998 before rebounding later in the year as the crisis passed. Similarly, the Korean won moved from about 900 won to the dollar before the crisis to over 1,900 won to the dollar at the end of 1997 before appreciating back in early 1998.

In sum, several important weaknesses affected the crisis economies, including overextended financial systems, poor supervision, widening trade imbalances, and weakening quality of investment. However, to fully explain the speed and ferocity of these crises, we must turn to the operations of the international capital markets and the actions of the foreign creditors.

SHORT-TERM CAPITAL FLOWS

The surge in capital inflows to emerging markets in the 1990s had its roots in changes in both domestic economic policies and world markets.[32] Internationally, innovations and policy changes in industrial country capital markets (such as new bond and equity mutual funds, new bank syndicates, and increased Eurobond lending) facilitated a greater flow of funds to emerging markets around the globe. In addition, low interest rates in the United States and Japan favored increased outward investment from these countries to Southeast Asia and other emerging markets. Domestically, rapid economic growth gave confidence to foreign investors. In

31. Such speculation takes place along the lines of the following, very simplified example. A foreign investor believes that the Philippine peso will have to be devalued. The investor takes out a short-term loan of 25 million pesos from a bank in the Philippines. The investor then converts the money into dollars using the current exchange rate of 25 pesos to the dollar, yielding $1 million. If the investor is right and the exchange rate moves, fewer dollars will be required to repay the loan. For example, if the exchange rate moves to 50 pesos to the dollar, the investor need convert only $500,000 dollars to get the 25 million pesos needed to repay the loan, allowing the investor to pocket a tidy profit of the remaining $500,000. Note that this kind of speculation itself puts pressure on the exchange rate, since the investor originally borrowed pesos to buy dollars, helping to deplete the Philippines' foreign exchange reserves.

32. The term *emerging markets* became common in the 1990s. Although not precisely defined, the term generally is used in reference to upper-middle-income and lower-middle-income countries that receive significant private capital flows in international markets.

addition, rapid financial deregulation and fixed exchange rates made it much easier for banks and corporations to tap into international capital markets to finance domestic investments.

Perhaps even more important than the size of the capital inflows was its maturity structure. The key reason that so much capital was able to leave these countries so quickly was that a substantial portion of the capital inflows had very short-term maturity structures. A large portion of the loans to the firms, banks, and governments in the crisis countries was scheduled to be repaid in one year or less, and in some cases, loans were designed to mature in just a few months or even weeks. Short-term loans were attractive to both borrowers and lenders for several reasons. For the borrowers, short-term loans generally carry lower interest rates than long-term loans. For the lender, short-term loans carry lower risk (and require less provisioning by the supervisory authorities[33]), since the lender is not exposed over long periods of time. In addition, borrowers were able to use the short-term loans to finance longer-term projects: As long as these economies continued to grow, creditors were happy to roll over or extend the loans when they fell due, allowing borrowers to continue their operations. In other words, as long as things are going well, short-term loans pose few problems. However, as soon as there is any trouble—or more precisely as soon as creditors think there *may* be any trouble—creditors quickly withdraw their lines of credit and demand immediate repayment of loans. This is precisely what happened in East Asia: When Thailand's economy began to noticeably weaken in late 1996 and early 1997, creditors began to close off these lines of credit and demand repayment, setting off a chain of events that led to financial panic and severe economic crisis.

At a general level, economies become vulnerable to a sudden withdrawal of international capital when the short-term foreign exchange *liabilities* of the economy grow rapidly and in excess of short-term foreign exchange *assets*. In that situation, economies can become *illiquid:* Roughly speaking, there may not be enough dollars (or whatever relevant foreign currency) on hand to pay all the international debts falling due. Table 14–10 shows the size of one significant type of foreign liability for the crisis countries: short-term debts (i.e., debts with maturity of one year or less) owed to foreign commercial banks. This figure includes all the short-term debts owed to international banks by the government, state-owned companies, commercial banks, and private corporations in each economy. The

---

33. Central banks require commercial banks to set aside (or provision) a percentage of all new loans to ensure that the bank has some capital on hand in case loans fail. The amount of provisioning varies by the perceived risk of the loan and generally is smaller for short-term loans. In part because banks do not have to provision as much for these loans, short-term loans carry lower interest rates than long-term loans.

TABLE 14–10	SHORT-TERM FOREIGN DEBT AND RESERVES (MILLION U.S. DOLLARS)			
COUNTRY	PERIOD	SHORT-TERM DEBT	RESERVES	SHORT-TERM DEBT/RESERVES
CRISIS COUNTRIES				
ARGENTINA	JUNE 1995	21,509	10,844	1.98
BRAZIL	DEC. 1998	41,038	42,580	0.96
INDONESIA	JUNE 1997	34,661	20,336	1.70
KOREA	UNE 1997	70,612	34,070	2.07
MALAYSIA	JUNE 1997	16,268	26,588	0.61
MEXICO	DEC. 1994	33,149	6,278	5.28
THE PHILIPPINES	JUNE 1997	8,293	9,781	0.85
RUSSIA	JUNE 1998	34,650	11,161	3.01
THAILAND	JUNE 1997	45,567	31,361	1.45
TURKEY	JUNE 1994	8,821	4,279	2.06
VENEZUELA	JUNE 1994	4,382	5,422	0.81
NON-CRISIS COUNTRIES				
CHILE	JUNE 1997	7,615	17,017	0.435
COLOMBIA	JUNE 1997	6,698	9,940	0.67
EGYPT	JUNE 1997	4,166	18,779	0.22
INDIA	JUNE 1997	7,745	25,702	0.30
JORDAN	JUNE 1997	582	1,624	0.36
PAKISTAN	JUNE 1997	3,047	1,249	2.44
PERU	JUNE 1997	5,368	10,665	0.50
SOUTH AFRICA	JUNE 1997	13,247	4,241	3.12
SRI LANKA	JUNE 1997	414	1,770	0.23
TAIWAN	JUNE 1997	21,966	90,025	0.24
ZIMBABWE	JUNE 1997	731	447	1.64

Sources: Bank for International Settlements, *The Maturity, Sectoral, and Nationality Distribution of International Bank Lending* (Basle, Switzerland: various issues) and International Monetary Fund, *International Financial Statistics* (Washington, DC: various issues).

table also shows data for the main liquid foreign exchange asset of an economy: the foreign exchange reserves held by the central bank. The central bank's foreign exchange reserves include its deposits of dollars, yen, deutsche marks, and other currencies held in offshore banks to facilitate international payments, as well as other assets such as U.S. Treasury bills. Note that, just before the crisis in each of these economies, short-term foreign debts exceeded or nearly exceeded the available foreign exchange reserves. In this situation, economies are *vulnerable* to a severe crisis because, in the event that all short-term loans are called in for repayment, not enough foreign exchange will be available to repay every debt. Once creditors begin to call in their loans and reserves begin to dwindle, the price of foreign exchange—the exchange rate—can begin to move quickly as borrowers are forced to pay ever more domestic currency to purchase the dollars or yen they need to repay their debts. Thus, in all of the crisis economies, the exchange rate began to depreciate sharply with the onset of the crisis. In the most severe circumstances, such as Indonesia in 1997 and 1998, domestic borrowers simply could not make the payments and the debts fell into default.

Bear in mind that the short-term bank loans shown in Table 14–10 are just one kind of short-term foreign exchange liability. Other kinds of foreign capital also can be withdrawn quickly, including portfolio equity (i.e., stock purchases), foreign exchange bank deposits, hedging instruments, and long-term loans with clauses that allow accelerated repayment. Moreover, the withdrawals generally are not limited to foreigners: As exchange rates begin to fall, nationals begin to try to convert their assets out of domestic currency and into dollars (or yen), putting further pressure on the exchange rate. Similarly, on the asset side, other foreign assets in addition to reserves may be used to repay creditors. The basic vulnerability arises when total short-term liabilities grow in excess of short-term assets, leaving open the possibility of a sudden shortage of foreign exchange. Longer-term loans and FDI generally cannot be reversed as quickly as short-term loans and therefore are less prone to rapid withdrawals.

CREDITOR PANIC

The financial crises of the mid-1990s to a large extent were the result of what are known as **rational panics** by the creditors, like the panics discussed briefly in Chapter 13. Under certain circumstances, investors may have the incentive to quickly withdraw their money from an otherwise reasonably healthy economy if they believe that other investors are about to do the same thing. The classic example from within one economy is a bank run, in which bank depositors suddenly withdraw their funds and deplete the capital of the bank. The particular conditions under which a rational panic can occur are described in the case study on pages 566–567.

In an international context, two conditions are key for such a panic to occur. The first is a high level of short-term foreign liabilities relative to foreign assets, exactly the circumstances in which these economies found themselves in the months leading up to the crises. In this situation, each creditor begins to recognize that if all creditors demanded repayment, not enough foreign exchange would be on hand to pay everyone. The second is that some event makes creditors believe other creditors may begin to demand repayment. The event could be a military coup, a natural disaster, a sharp fall in export prices, or a fall in property prices that weakens the domestic banking system. Once creditors believe that others might pull out, the only rational course of action for each creditor is to immediately demand repayment and cut off further lending. To not do so risks being the last creditor in line and being left unpaid if foreign exchange reserves are depleted. Hence, the very rapid withdrawals are called *rational* panics. The irony, of course, is that the simultaneous demand for repayment by all the creditors ultimately depletes reserves and brings on the very crisis that all would rather avoid. In this sense, these crises are often referred to as *self-fulfilling*.

In Asia, once Thailand's economy began to slow in late 1996 and early 1997 and banks came under increasing pressure from falling property prices, foreign creditors that had lent heavily to Thai banks began to withdraw their loans. Other creditors came to believe that Thailand might run out of foreign exchange reserves, devalue the baht, or both, and began to withdraw their credits. It became only rational for other creditors to do the same and for domestic investors to begin to convert their assets to dollars. These events ultimately deleted foreign exchange reserves and forced the large depreciation of the baht that began in July 1997. A generally similar chain of events (with differences in the specific details and triggering events) occurred in Mexico in 1994, Indonesia and Korea in 1997, and Russia and Brazil in 1998.

Once a panic begins, it tends to perpetuate itself. This can happen for several reasons. First, as foreign creditors demand repayment and the exchange rate begins to depreciate, nationals in the crisis countries try to convert their financial assets from local to foreign currency, putting additional pressure on reserves and the exchange rate. This was a particularly large problem in Indonesia, Russia, and Brazil in their recent crises. Second, the deprecations wreak havoc on the balance sheets of banks and corporations that had borrowed in foreign currency. For example, as the Indonesian rupiah jumped from about 2,500 rupiah to the dollar in mid-1997 to over 10,000 rupiah to the dollar in early 1998, Indonesian corporations with dollar debts had to come up with *four times* more rupiah than they originally expected to make their debt service payments. The crippling effect of the exchange rate movement was obvious to the creditors, so the more the exchange rate fell, the faster the foreign creditors tried to withdraw any remaining loans, putting even more pressure on the exchange rate. Third, as exchange rates fall in one country, creditors begin to believe something similar will happen in neighboring countries and so start to withdraw their funds from other emerging markets. For example, there was no hint of trouble in Malaysia, Indonesia, and the Philippines until the Thai baht collapsed in July 1997. Within weeks the "contagion" had struck the region, and creditors were withdrawing their money from Thailand's neighbors.

The emerging market financial crises of the 1990s were not new phenomena. As discussed in Chapter 13, similar events have been recurring in slightly different forms since the development of banks and the emergence of international capital flows several centuries ago. Economists have long recognized that financial markets in general (both domestic

SELF-FULFILLING CREDITOR PANICS[34]

Self-fulfilling creditor panics are best understood by beginning with the critical distinction between illiquidity and insolvency. An *insolvent* borrower lacks the net worth to repay outstanding debts out of future earnings. An *illiquid* borrower lacks the ready cash to repay current debt servicing obligations, even though it has the net worth to repay the debts in the long term. A *liquidity crisis* occurs if a solvent, but illiquid borrower is unable to borrow fresh funds from the capital markets to remain current on debt servicing obligations. Because the borrower is solvent, capital markets in principle could provide new loans to repay existing debts with the expectation that both the old loans and the new loans will be fully serviced. The unwillingness or inability of the capital market to provide fresh loans to the illiquid borrower is the core of the problem.

Why might markets fail this way? The primary reason is a problem of collective action. Suppose that each individual creditor is too small to provide all the loans needed by an illiquid debtor. A liquidity crisis results when creditors as a group would be willing to make a new loan, but no individual creditor is willing to make a loan *if the other creditors do not lend as well.* One possible market equilibrium is that no individual creditor is willing to make a loan to an illiquid borrower precisely because each creditor (rationally) expects that no other creditor is ready to make such a loan.

Consider a simple illustration. Suppose that a borrower owes debt D to a large number of existing creditors. The debt requires debt service of θD in period 1, and debt service of $(1 + r)(1 - \theta)D$ in period 2. The debtor owns an investment project that will pay off Q_2 in the second period. (Note that, for the project to be profitable, $Q_2/(1 + r)$ must be greater than the present value of total debt service payments in

34. From Steven Radelet and Jeffrey Sachs, "The East Asian Financial Crisis: Diagnosis, Remedies, Prospects," *Brookings Papers on Economic Activity*, 1998, no. 1, pp. 1–89.

and international) tend to be prone to instability and panic. Early in the twentieth century, industrialized country governments put into place mechanisms and institutions specifically designed to reduce the frequency and severity of financial crises, including lender-of-last-resort facilities at the central bank, deposit insurance, and bankruptcy procedures, making crises much less common in these countries.

However, these key institutions generally do not exist in international financial markets, leaving these markets vulnerable to panics. When

both periods $\theta D + [(1 + r)(1 - \theta)D]/(1 + r)$, which must be equal to D.) The debtor lacks the cash flow to repay θD, since the investment project pays off only in the second period. Moreover, if the debtor defaults, the loan repayments are accelerated (i.e., demanded at once by each of the individual creditors). The investment project then is scrapped, with a salvage value of $Q_1 < D$. In that case, the partial repayment of the outstanding loan from the salvage value is shared among the existing creditors on a pro rata basis.

Typically, this solvent but illiquid borrower would be able to borrow a fresh loan, L, in the first period; use it to repay θD; and then service $(1 - \theta)D + L$ in the second period. Thus, with $L = \theta D$, the total repayment due in the second period is $(1 + r)\theta D + (1 + r)(1 - \theta)D = (1 + r)D$, which by assumption is less than Q_2. In this, then, the project remains profitable. Suppose, however, that each individual creditor can lend at most λ, where $\lambda << D$ (that is, λ is much smaller than D). This lending limit might result from prudential standards imposed on individual bank lenders, which limit their exposure to particular debtors. If only one lender is prepared to lend in the first period, the borrower will be forced into default, since it will be unable to service its debts in the first period. The new creditor lending λ in the first period then would suffer an immediate loss on its loans (indeed, it might receive nothing if repayments are ranked such that all preceding creditors have priority on repayment). Obviously, a first-period loan will require at least n_1 new lenders, where $n_1 = \theta D/\lambda$.

There clearly are multiple rational equilibria in this situation. In the normal case, n_1 lenders routinely step forward, the existing debts are serviced, and the future debts also are serviced. The investment project is carried to fruition. In the case of a financial crisis, each individual creditor decides not to lend, on the grounds that no other creditor is making loans. The debtor is pushed into default. The debt repayments are accelerated and the investment project is scrapped with sharp economic losses, since the salvage value Q_1 is less than $Q_2/(1 + r)$. Each individual creditor, of course feels vindicated in its decision not to lend; after all, the debtor immediately went into default.

central banks face a run on their foreign exchange reserves (akin to a commercial bank facing a depositor run), no international lender of last resort stands ready to supply it with the foreign exchange it needs to remain liquid. Similarly, no international insurance mechanism assures creditors that they will be paid if a borrower defaults. And no international bankruptcy court can call for a mandatory standstill on debt service payments and oversee the distribution of assets of a bankrupt company. On each count, there is extensive debate as to whether these institutions *should* exist, and if so, how they might realistically be designed to operate effectively in an international context where there is no single legal authority. For example, an international agency to insure creditors could lead to excessive lending to weak companies, since the creditor always could rely on an insurance settlement if the company goes bankrupt. In any event, in the absence of these institutions, international financial markets will continue to be prone to rapid oscillations and financial panics.

STOPPING PANICS

Once a financial panic from international capital withdrawals is underway, it is very hard to stop. There are five basic options. First, governments can try to increase the supply of available foreign exchange by borrowing from official sources (such as the International Monetary Fund and World Bank), much like a commercial bank borrows from its central bank in the event of a bank run. The idea is to build up sufficient foreign exchange reserves to allow the economy to operate normally and assure creditors that enough foreign exchange is on hand to pay everyone, if need be. In terms of the ratio of short-term debt to reserves (shown in Table 14–10), the idea is to build up reserves sufficiently that this ratio falls below 1. Second, governments can try to convince foreign creditors and nationals with access to foreign exchange to stop the withdrawals and supply new funding. This approach involves implementing policy reforms aimed at correcting perceived weaknesses in the economy. For example, if creditors are worried about the fundamental strength of the banking sector, reforms to strengthen banks might convince creditors to begin lending again. Third, governments can try to reduce the demand for foreign exchange by tightening fiscal and monetary policies and, perhaps, restricting imports. Fourth, governments can try to stop the rush for loan repayments (and the associated demand for foreign exchange) by restructuring foreign debts so they will be repaid over longer periods of time. This option may include a limited "standstill" period, during which international loan repayments are postponed. Fourth, the government can do nothing (intentionally or unintentionally) and let the panic run its course until all creditors have fled, foreign exchange reserves are exhausted, debts are in default, and the economy is in deep recession. At some point, even in these dire circumstances, some investors will begin to return to take advantage of low asset prices, the foreign exchange market will begin to stabilize (at a greatly depreciated exchange rate), and the economy slowly will begin to recover.

The correct choice of action among these alternatives (or combination of these alternatives) depends on the root causes of the crisis and the perceptions of international creditors. The problem, of course, is that correctly diagnosing a panic and prescribing the right response is very difficult when markets are changing rapidly by the hour, little accurate information is available, and the perceptions and reactions of creditors are impossible to measure. It therefore is not surprising that both the affected countries and the international community often make mistakes when dealing with incipient crises.

The emerging market crises of the 1990s were resolved along the lines of a combination of one or more of the five alternatives just outlined. In most of the affected economies, once the crisis was underway the government turned to the International Monetary Fund for advice and financial assistance. The IMF programs in the crisis economies have been hotly debated, with analysts divided on whether the programs initially helped ease the crisis or unintentionally added to the panic. The IMF's initial set of policy prescriptions centered on tightening both fiscal and monetary policies (to reduce aggregate demand and the demand for foreign exchange) and closing weak financial institutions. For example, Thailand's first IMF program in August 1997 required that the government run a fiscal surplus of 1 percent of GDP, sharply raise interest rates, and immediately suspend the operations of 58 financial institutions.

The basic question is whether these steps reassured investors about the health of these economies (and helped slow capital outflow) or added to investors' negative outlook and thus to the capital withdrawals. These debates are far from fully resolved, but in the case of the Asian crises in 1997, most (but not all) observers now agree that at least parts of the IMF's *original* prescriptions did little to ease the panic.[35] Tight fiscal policies probably added to the economic contraction already underway and made foreign creditors more nervous about future growth in the crisis countries. The IMF's abrupt closure of financial institutions without comprehensive financial restructuring programs in place seemed to add to the panic in several countries. In Indonesia, for example, the closure of 16 commercial banks at the outset of the IMF program was followed by an acceleration of bank runs (since depositors feared their bank would be the next closed)

---

35. For debates on these issues, see Radelet and Sachs, "The East Asian Financial Crisis," pp. 1–90; Jason Furman and Joseph Stiglitz, "Economic Crises: Evidence and Insights form East Asia," *Brookings Papers on Economic Activity* 1998, no. 2, pp. 1–136; Martin Feldstein, "Refocussing the IMF," *Foreign Affairs,* 77, no. 4 (March–April 1998), 20–33; Stanley Fischer, "In Defense of the IMF," *Foreign Affairs,* 77, no. 4 (July–August 1998); David Hale, "The IMF, Now More than Ever," *Foreign Affairs,* 77, no. 6 (November–December 1998); Timothy Lane and others, "IMF-Supported Programs in Indonesia, Korea, and Thailand: A Preliminary Assessment," IMF occasional paper no. 178 (1999); World Bank, *East Asia: The Road to Recovery* (Washington, DC: The World Bank, 1998).

and a collapse of the banking system. The issue of tight monetary policy and high interest rates is more complex. On the one hand, the promise of high interest rates might have attracted some foreign currency and slowed capital withdrawals. On the other hand, foreign creditors might have believed that high interest rates would further weaken banks and corporations, leading them to accelerate their demands for repayment. The empirical evidence on this issue is far from conclusive. In any event, in each of the Asian crisis countries, within a few months, the IMF altered its original programs by calling for less austere fiscal policies and more comprehensive financial restructuring programs.

In addition to misjudgments by the IMF, actions by the governments in several of the crisis economies exacerbated rather than eased the crisis. For example, Thailand's reluctance to float its currency earlier and take steps to address the problems facing banks that were heavily exposed to property markets made the crisis more severe than it otherwise would have been. The Indonesian central bank made huge loans to try to prop up weak banks, ultimately fueling capital flight and further weakening the currency. President Suharto of Indonesia took several actions designed more to protect his family's personal financial interests rather than resolve the crisis, and these steps added to the chaos that ultimately forced him out of office in May 1998.

In addition to policy reforms, the IMF programs included promises of substantial financing from the international community. The purpose of these funds was to augment the foreign exchange reserves of the crisis economies, convince creditors that sufficient funds would be available to repay everyone, and ease pressure on the exchange rate. In several cases, the amount of financing pledged by the international community was extremely large, although the amount actually delivered was much smaller. For example, total commitments for South Korea (December 1997), Brazil (December 1998), and Indonesia (October 1997) were $57 billion, $41 billion, and $40 billion, respectively. In the cases of Mexico in 1994–95 and South Korea in 1997–98, the funds actually made available (over $20 billion in each case) were sufficiently large to help ease the panic. However, given the speed and size of private capital flows in many emerging markets, the amount of funding necessary to stop an investor panic in most cases is huge. It simply is infeasible to expect that the IMF or other agencies could generate the funds necessary to stop a full-blown panic in more than one country at a time. Even if it could, this may not be the best policy. Some analysts believe that the international bailout of Mexico in 1995 made private creditors more relaxed about lending to other emerging markets and so may have contributed to the buildup in capital flows that led to other crises in 1997 and 1998.

In one very important way, the international response to the crisis in South Korea was different from in other countries. South Korea is the clearest example of where the international community supported the fourth broad strategy to stop a panic: a temporary standstill of debt payments. In late December 1997, under pressure from the US government and the IMF, the major creditors to South Korea's banks agreed to reschedule about $22 billion in debts that were scheduled to fall due in the first quarter of 1998. The creditors agreed to exchange the short-term credits for debts with longer maturity (one to three years) and higher interest rates. This step probably was the single most effective action taken to stop the panic in any of the crisis countries. Its effect was immediate: The Korean won began to appreciate and the Korean stock market rebounded the day after the rescheduling was announced. Within weeks, the most intense part of the Korean crisis effectively was over. By April 1998, the situation had calmed sufficiently that international lenders were willing to make new loans to the Korean government. On a net basis, capital flows to Korea again were positive by the end of 1998. After a very sharp contraction of 5 percent in 1998, Korea's GDP expanded by nearly 9 percent in 1999 and returned to its precrisis level.

Debt standstills or rollovers have several advantages in stopping panics. First, rollovers share the burden of adjustment (at least to some extent) more equitably between the creditors and debtors, rather than forcing the debtor to make all the adjustments. As a result, with standstills a realistic outcome, creditors should be less likely to engage in excessive lending, since they will recognize that the international community will not always bail them out. Second, rollovers require less financing by the international community (and its taxpayers) than traditional IMF programs. Third, since rollovers go to the heart of the pressure on the exchange rate (the creditor panic), they can have an immediate salutatory effect. These are exactly the reasons why debt standstills have become the centerpiece of bankruptcy proceedings in most industrialized economies. Unfortunately, many obstacles inhibit establishing the institutions necessary to make standstills a more common approach to international creditor panics, so Korean-type solutions are likely to continue to be the exception rather than the norm.[36]

36. For further discussion of these issues, see Barry Eichengreen and Richard Portes, *Crisis? What Crisis? Orderly Workouts for Sovereign Debtors* (London: Center for Economic Policy Research, 1995); Jeffrey Sachs, "Do We Need an International Lender of Last Resort?" Frank D. Graham lecture, Princeton University April 1995; Steven Radelet, "Orderly Workouts for Cross-Border Private Debt," Harvard Institute for International Development discussion paper no. 721, September 1999.

In other countries where actions by the government or the IMF did not restore confidence and the international community was unable or unwilling to provide sufficient funding or debt rollovers, the effects of the panics were more severe. Panics eventually end, even when little or no actions are taken to stop them, simply because foreign exchange eventually will be depleted, creditors will stop demanding repayment, and debt will fall into default. When this happens, however, the resulting economic contraction is very deep, and the financial system usually is left in a shambles. In Indonesia, for example, where the financial crisis quickly cascaded into a political crisis that led to widespread rioting and destruction of property and ultimately the resignation of President Suharto in May 1998. GDP contracted by about 14 percent in 1998 before the economy finally began to stabilize in 1999. GDP per capita in Indonesia in 1999 was back to about the same level it had been in 1992, and it will take many years for the economy to fully recover.

LESSONS FROM THE CRISES

First, these crises are cautionary tales about rapid financial liberalization in emerging markets. The crisis economies liberalized their financial systems very rapidly without taking care to establish and strengthen the institutions necessary to oversee and regulate financial transactions. Building well-functioning financial systems remains a major challenge in the development process. These crises suggest that governments should proceed more slowly and carefully in liberalizing domestic financial transactions and ensure parallel development of the requisite regulatory institutions.

Second, the crises suggest that governments should focus on liberalizing the rules regulating FDI and other long-term capital flows early in the process and only later fully liberalize short-term capital flows. Long-term capital flows are much less prone to panic and more strongly associated with long-term investment and growth. Since short-term flows create vulnerabilities to a panic, governments could discourage such flows while they are in the process of building the requisite financial institutions. Support is growing for these kinds of measures as a temporary step to protect nascent financial systems, so long as the restrictions are limited to inflows of short-term capital (there is far less support among economists for restrictions on long-term capital or outflows of any kind). Chile has been at the forefront of countries trying to encourage long-term capital flows and discourage short-term flows. For example, Chile requires that foreign investors deposit a share of their investment funds in a non-interest-bearing account for one year, a step that makes short-term investment much less profitable. Such restrictions have reduced short-term capital flows into Chile without reducing aggregate capital flows.[37]

Third, the crises suggests that countries can reduce their vulnerability to financial crises through "self-insurance," by building up sufficient amounts of foreign exchange reserves to be able to withstand financial crises. It is no accident that China and Taiwan were able to avoid serious difficulties while crises swirled around them in 1997 and 1998, even though China, in particular, displays some of the same financial sector weaknesses evident in the crisis countries. Although China had over $30 billion in short-term foreign debt in 1997, its foreign exchange reserves were almost $150 billion, far and away the largest in the world and plenty to assure investors that there was no need to panic. Taiwan, with about $20 billion in short-term debt in 1997, had over $90 billion in reserves, and so also was safe from this kind of crisis.

Fourth, the crises reveal some of the potential pitfalls of relying on a fixed exchange rate. Whether fixed or floating exchange rates ultimately are preferable for long-run growth and development is an open question. Economists have debated the merits of different exchange rate systems for two centuries, and the debate is far from resolved. Fixed rates offer some clear advantages in certain circumstances, since they can reduce volatility in thin foreign exchange markets, provide some certainty to skittish investors, and establish a useful price anchor to halt hyperinflations. But the recent crises indicate that fixed rates can help create vulnerability to a panic and ultimately lead to huge economic adjustments when the exchange rate no longer can be defended. Increasingly, many economists suggest that the choice for developing countries is between a very rigidly fixed rate defended with abundant foreign exchange reserves or a freely floating exchange rate. Debate on fixed exchange rate systems has centered on currency boards and dollarization, as described in Chapter 13. Most economists now tend to believe that currency boards and dollarization are appropriate in only a very limited number of developing countries and that flexible exchange rates generally are the preferred choice. However, the debate on this issue is far from over and is likely to continue in the years to come.

37. For discussions of short-term capital flows, see Richard Cooper, "Should Capital Controls be Banished?" *Brookings Papers on Economic Activity,* 1999, no. 1, pp. 89–141; Jaime Cardoso and Bernard Laurens, "The Effectiveness of Capital Controls on Inflows: Lessons from the Experience of Chile," IMF Monetary and Exchange Affairs Department, 1998; Sebastian Edwards, "Capital Flows, Real Exchange Rates, and Capital Controls: Some Latin American Experiences," Department of Economics, UCLA, 1998; and Felipe Larraín B. ed., *Capital Flows, Capital Controls, and Currency Crises: Latin America in the 1990s* (forthcoming, 2000).

Fifth, the operations of international financial markets and the immediate reactions by the official international community probably added to the severity of the crisis. As a result, there has been widespread discussion about possible reforms to the international financial "architecture." These debates have proceeded on several fronts, including reforming the operations of the IMF itself, strengthening international banking standards, and establishing new international mechanisms for debt standstills and rollovers, but few fundamental changes have been made.[38] In the meantime, few effective international mechanisms are in place to stop similar financial panics from recurring in emerging markets in the future. Unfortunately, this means that financial crises in emerging markets are likely to be a recurring phenomena in coming years.

38. See Barry Eichengreen, *Toward a New International Financial Architecture: A Practical Post-Asia Agenda* (Washington, DC: Institute for International Economics, February 1999); and Morris Goldstein, *Safeguarding Prosperity in a Global Financial System,* report of an independent task force for the Council on Foreign Relations (Washington, DC: Institute for International Economics, September 1999).

PART FIVE

Production and Trade

AGRICULTURE

Understanding the nature of agriculture is fundamental to understanding development. The labor-surplus and neoclassical models presented in Chapter 3 dealt primarily with the nature of the relationship between the industrial and agricultural sectors. The problem of income distribution or extremes of poverty within developing nations discussed in Chapter 4 is substantially a question of how to do something about the rural poor. Nutrition, discussed in Chapter 10, is a question of food production and distribution. And the contribution of exports to development, as treated in Chapters 16 and 18 for many countries, is a question of creating agricultural exports.

Much of this book has been about **rural development,** all those activities that affect the well-being of rural populations, including the provision of basic needs, such as food, and the development of human capital in the countryside through education and nutrition programs. This chapter concentrates on problems that have a direct bearing on raising agricultural production and farmers' income. Indirect measures treated elsewhere in this book, even those as crucial as rural education, will be dealt with only in passing.

In a sense, agriculture simply is one industry among many, but it is an industry with a difference. To begin with, the agricultural sector in a country at an early developmental stage employs far more people than all other industries and sectors put together—60–70 percent or more of the total work force are in agriculture in many of the poorer developing countries, including India and, until the 1990s, China. In contrast, agriculture in developed economies typically employs less than 10 percent of the workforce (3 percent in the United States). Second, agricultural activities have existed for thousands of years, ever since humankind gave up hunting and gathering as its main source of food. Because of this long history, the rural economy often is described as **tradition bound.** Generating electric power or manufacturing automobiles can be done only by means based on modern science and engineering, but crops often are grown using techniques developed hundreds or even thousands of years before the advent of modern science. And the rural societies in which traditional techniques are used often develop customs and attitudes that reinforce older ways of doing things and make change difficult.

A third characteristic of agriculture that separates it from other sectors is the crucial importance of land as a factor of production. Other sectors use and require land, but in no other sector does land play such a central role. The availability of cultivable land, whether relatively plentiful in relation to population, as in the Americas, or scarce, as in much of Asia, fundamentally shapes the kind of farming techniques that can be used. Closely related to the central role of land is the influence of weather. No other sector is as subject to the vagaries of the weather as agriculture. Land, like the weather, differs from place to place so that techniques suitable in one place are often of little use elsewhere. The manufacture of steel must adjust to differences in the quality of iron ore from place to place and similar problems occur in other industries, but the basic techniques in much of manufacturing are similar, at least within and often between countries. In agriculture differences in soil quality, climate, and the availability of water lead to the production of different crops and different ways of raising a particular crop, not only within countries, but even within provinces or counties of a single country.

Finally, agriculture is the only sector that produces food. Humankind can survive without steel or coal or electric power but not without food. For most manufactured products, in fact, there are substitutes, but there is no substitute for food. Food must be either produced within a country or imported.

Agriculture's Role in Economic Development

Agriculture's role in economic development is central because most of the people in poor countries make their living from the land. If leaders are seriously concerned with the welfare of their people, the only ways they can readily improve the welfare for the majority is by helping to raise, first, the farmers' productivity in growing food and cash crops and, second, the prices they receive for those crops. Not all increases in farm output benefit the majority of rural people, of course. The creation of mechanized, large-scale farms in place of small, peasant farms actually may make the majority of the population worse off. Although it is a necessary condition, raising agricultural output is not by itself sufficient to achieve an increase in rural welfare. We return to this problem later.

Most developing countries must rely on their own agricultural sectors to produce the food consumed by their people, although there are exceptions. Countries with large natural-resource-based exports, such as Malaysia or Saudi Arabia, have the foreign exchange necessary to import much of their food. But most developing countries cannot rely so heavily on foreign exchange earnings to feed their populations.

Farmers in developing countries must produce enough to feed themselves as well as the urban population. Hence, as the proportion of the urban population rises, the productivity of farmers also must rise. If productivity does not rise (and in the absence of food imports), the models in Chapter 3 make it clear that the terms of trade will turn sharply against the industrial sector, cut into profits, and eventually bring growth to a halt.

The agricultural sector's size is the characteristic that gives agriculture such an important role in the provision of factor inputs, notably labor, to industry and the other modern sectors. With 70 percent or more of the population in agriculture, the rural sector is virtually the only source of increased labor power for the urban sector. Importation of labor is possible, and usually the urban sector itself experiences population growth, but neither of these sources is likely to be sufficient for the long-term needs of economic growth. If restrictions are placed on the movement of labor out of agriculture, economic development will be severely crippled. Serfs in Russia through the mid-nineteenth century, for example, were tied to their lord's land by law and hence were not free to move to the cities and into industry. Therefore, Russian industry did not begin to grow rapidly until after the serfs were freed. Today such feudal restrictions are increasingly rare, but heavy indebtedness by a farmer to a landlord-moneylender often has the same effect as tying an individual to the land and thus making the individual unavailable to modern industry.

The agricultural sector also can be a major source of capital for modern economic growth. Some writers have even suggested that agriculture is the main or even the sole source of capital in the early stages of development, but this overstates agriculture's role. Capital comes from invested savings and savings from income. However, even in the poorest countries the share of agricultural income in the national product typically is less than half the gross domestic product. Over half the GNP therefore is provided by nonagricultural sectors (industry and services), and these sectors often are important contributors to saving and hence to investment. Furthermore, whereas imports of labor seldom provide a large portion of the domestic labor force, imports of capital, whether in the form of aid or private investment, sometimes do contribute a substantial share of domestic capital formation without drawing on the agricultural sector at all. South Korea is a case in point, where capital formation in the early years of rapid growth was provided mainly by foreign aid and in later years was increasingly paid for from the profits of the industrial sector.

If one treats foreign exchange as a separate factor of production, agriculture has an important role to play in the supply of this factor as well. As indicated in Chapter 16, developing countries' comparative advantage usually lies with natural resources or agricultural products. In only a few cases is the export of manufactures or services the principal source of foreign exchange for a country in the early stages of modern economic growth. Therefore, unless a country is rich in natural resources, such as petroleum or copper, the agricultural sector will play a key role in providing foreign exchange with which to import capital equipment and intermediate goods that cannot be produced at home.

Finally, the farming population of a developing country, in some cases at least, is an important market for the output of the modern urban sector. The qualification "in some cases" must be added because farm populations in some poor countries purchase very little from modern industry. This is particularly likely where the distribution of income is extremely unequal, with most of the country's income, land, and other wealth in the hands of a small urban and rural upper class. In that situation the rural population may simply pay taxes and rents to wealthy urban residents and subsist on whatever is left over. Even cheap cloth from urban factories may be beyond the means of a very poor rural population. If income is less unequally distributed, however, the rural sector can be an important source of demand for industrial products. If a large rural market exists, industries can continue to grow after they have saturated urban demand for their product without turning to foreign markets until they are better able to compete.[1]

SELF-SUFFICIENCY AND DWINDLING WORLD FOOD SUPPLIES

One important aspect of agriculture's role in development typically gets a great deal of attention from economic planners: the degree to which a country wishes to achieve **food self-sufficiency.** *Food self-sufficiency* can take on several different meanings. At one extreme is the view that any dependence on foreign trade is dangerous to a country's economic health,

---

1. A number of good studies treat the role of agriculture in development, including C. Peter Timmer, *Agriculture and the State* (Ithaca, NY: Cornell University Press, 1991); Thomas P. Tomich, Peter Kilby, and Bruce F. Johnston, *Transforming Agrarian Economies: Opportunities Seized, Opportunities Missed* (Ithaca, NY: Cornell University Press, 1995); and Lloyd Reynolds, *Agriculture in Development Theory* (New Haven, CT: Yale University Press, 1976).

TABLE 15–1	WORLD CEREAL EXPORTS (MILLION METRIC TONS)

YEAR	EXPORTS
1962	85
1966	114
1970	113
1974	149
1978	191
1980	216
1985	224
1988	232
1991	234
1992	250
1993	231
1996	234

Source: FAO, Trade Yearbook 1972, 1976, 1978, 1987, 1989, 1993, and 1996 (Rome: Food and Agricultural Organization, 1973, 1977, 1979, 1988, 1990, 1994, 1997).

and dependence on food imports simply is one part of this broader danger. More common is the view that food is a basic or strategic good, not unlike military weapons. If a country is dependent on others for food and hence for its very survival, the suppliers of that food will be in a position to bring the dependent country to its knees whenever it suits the supplier countries' purposes. Others argue that population growth is rapidly eating into the world's food surpluses, and countries relying on food imports soon will find themselves paying very high prices to get what they need from the world's dwindling surplus.

The national defense argument for food self-sufficiency may be valid under certain circumstances. Since a discussion of these circumstances would divert us into an analysis of complex international security issues, suffice it to say that the national defense argument frequently is used to justify policies that have little relationship to a country's real security.

The issue of a dwindling world food surplus cannot be dealt with so easily. History does not support the view that world supplies of exportable food are steadily diminishing. Data on world grain exports are presented in Table 15–1. What these and other data indicate is that, although the world grain export surplus and the corresponding size of the deficit in importing countries fluctuates, the overall surplus is growing, not declining. In 1972, for example, bad weather struck a wide part of the globe, including the Soviet Union, China, India, and Indonesia The resulting surge in demand for grain imports drove prices up sharply in 1973, but prices fell again when production in these deficit areas recovered. The 1972–73 "crisis" was not significantly different in magnitude from other weather-induced fluctuations of the past. After 1973, grain exports rose substantially and prices fell.

Those who speak of an impending world food crisis are implicitly or explicitly forecasting the future. Continued population growth is rapidly pushing people out onto the world's diminishing supply of arable land. In places like Africa's Sahel, agriculture already may have developed beyond the capacity of the land to sustain it. The real issue, however, is not whether the world is running out of surplus land—it is—but whether yields on existing arable land can be raised fast enough to meet the needs of an increasing population with rising per capita incomes. The problem is not one of biology. Research in the plant sciences has shown that yield per acre could be higher than even that of such advanced agricultural systems as Japan's. And most of the world produces food at levels per acre nowhere near those of Japan. Although there is some biological limit to the capacity of the earth to produce food, the planet is not remotely close to that limit today.

The real danger of a long-term food crisis arises from a different source. From a scientific point of view, the countries that could expand food output dramatically may not do so because of internal social and economic barriers to technical progress in agriculture. At the same time, for economic reasons, the world's few food-surplus countries may not be able to continue to expand those surpluses. Therefore, it is possible that the world could face growing food deficits in importing countries that are not matched by rising surpluses in exporting countries. Under such circumstances, food prices would rise sharply, and therefore only countries with large foreign exchange earnings could afford to continue to import sufficient food. Some of the poorest countries, including those where food imports make the difference between an adequate diet and severe malnutrition, may not have the foreign exchange earnings needed to maintain required imports. We must emphasize, however, that while the potential for a disaster of this kind is present, it is not today a reality; many economists believe it will never become a reality.[2] A possible future world food crisis is a weak basis for a country's economic planners to place a high priority on the development of agriculture.

FOOD SUPPLY AND FAMINE

Closely related to the desire for food self-sufficiency is the view that a general nationwide shortage of food is the main cause of devastating **famines** that can lead to millions of deaths within a short period in developing countries. This view sees prevention of famine as primarily an exercise in raising a nation's food production to ensure there are adequate supplies to meet everyone's minimum needs.

---

2. Maldistribution within a country, however, can and does cause severe localized famines, sometimes accompanied by large-scale loss of life. See Jean Drèze and Amartya Sen, *Hunger and Public Action* (London: Oxford University Press [Clarendon], 1989).

But famine is far more a problem of distribution than of food production. Famines often start as a result of some natural phenomenon such as a drought that destroys an entire year's crop in one or more regions of a country. Human-made disasters such as civil wars, however, can have much the same effect. The central issue is not what caused the crop failure but why no one stepped in to assist those who had lost the means to survive. Even in historical times, governments often saw it as their responsibility to maintain stores of grain against just such contingencies. Why have there been such severe famines as recently is the 1990s, when the power of governments to intervene is far greater than it was in the nineteenth century and the means for transporting the grain to the affected areas is readily available. Furthermore, where the government of the famine-affected country is not itself able to mobilize sufficient resources, the international community has stood ready to help out with low-cost or even free supplies of food where necessary. International agencies and nongovernment organizations also sometimes have supplied the means to deliver the food to where it is needed.

Market forces alone often are not adequate to the task of relieving a famine. Large numbers of people in the affected areas have lost most or all their income and are in no position to pay for food. If the famine is in a remote area, as often is the case, transport costs can be high making it unprofitable for private traders to ship grain to the region, even if people there have some income. Nor are these poor farmers in a position to borrow money to tide them over until they do finally receive a good harvest a year or more down the road.

Governments and nongovernment organizations, therefore, must play a central role in situations such as this, but why then do governments sometimes fail to do so? In the words of Jean Drèze and Amartya Sen, the reason often is "negligence or smugness or callousness on the part of the non-responding authorities."[3] In the Chinese famine of 1959–61, during which roughly 30 million people lost their lives, government officials feared the wrath of Mao Zedong if they criticized his radical agricultural policies by pointing out that they had led to a sharp decline in food output, so they kept quiet. Even the statistical authorities were afraid to report what actually was going on and instead published false figures indicating that the harvest in 1959 had been good when the opposite was the case. Famine in Ethiopia in the 1970s and 1980s also resulted from a government unwilling to admit to itself or the international community that it was unable to deal with the severe drought that had affected parts of the country. When the situation got so bad that the international community was called in to help out, the government of that time often tried to

3. Drèze and Sen, *Hunger and Public Action,* p. 263.

withhold food from regions of the country that were in rebellion against the government. In an analogous fashion, food became a weapon in the clan warfare that often wracked Somalia through the 1990s.

As Drèze and Sen have pointed out, famines rarely happen where a nation is democratic or governed by some other form of pluralistic politics. They also rarely happen where there are open channels of communication and criticism such as a free press. An open democratic society will not let its government ignore the plight of starving citizens. As the Chinese and Ethiopian cases illustrate, famines are most likely to occur when a government controls all of the means of communication and uses them to keep itself in unchallenged control.

Once the attention of the government, nongovernment organizations, and the international community focuses on the problem, many mechanisms can be used to end the starvation. Free shipments of food to central distribution points in the affected region are common. Food-for-work programs sometimes can be even more effective, since the food not only allows the individuals receiving it to survive, but the work they do in exchange can build needed infrastructure such as roads or irrigation systems. The basic point, as stated at the outset of this discussion, is that the distribution problem must be dealt with first. Increasing agricultural production, whether to a self-sufficient level or not, also is desirable, but raising production contributes to a long-term solution. It is not an effective way of dealing with the immediate problem caused by a harvest failure and the resulting famine.

Land Tenure and Reform

Before we focus on agricultural production, it is best to explore the problem of land and the way it is owned and organized. Conditions of land tenure set the context within which all efforts to raise agricultural output must operate. Put differently, the property right that matters most in the agricultural sector is the right over the use of land. If that right is well defined as well as exclusive, secure, enforceable, and transferable, then farmers with those rights will have an incentive to invest and work the land efficiently.

PATTERNS OF LAND TENURE

Land tenure and **land-tenure relations** refer to the way people own land and how they rent it to others to use if they choose not to cultivate it themselves. In Europe during the Middle Ages, for example, a local lord owned a piece of land and allowed the local peasants to cultivate it. In exchange for cultivating that land, the peasant family had to deliver a part of the harvest to the lord, and members of the peasant family had to perform labor services in the lord's castle. In most cases, the peasant could not freely leave the land to seek work in the city or with another lord. Peasants did flee, but the lord had the right to force them to return if they could be caught. Serfdom, as this system sometimes is called, was only a modest step up from slavery. Serflike land-tenure relations prevail today in only a few remote and backward areas of the globe. The patterns that do exist, however, are diverse, as the following incomplete listing makes clear.

- **Large-scale modern farming or ranching** usually refers to a large crop- or cattle-raising acreage that uses some hired labor but where many of the activities are highly mechanized. Many such farms are found in the United States, whereas much of Latin American agriculture is characterized by large modern farms that exist alongside small peasant plots.

- **Plantation agriculture** is a system in which a piece of land is used to raise a cash crop, such as tea or rubber, usually for export. Cultivation is by hired labor who are paid wages, and the plantation is run either by the owner or more frequently by a professional manager.

- **Latifundios** is a term used in Latin America and Europe to refer to large estates or ranches on which the hired labor still have a servile (master-servant) relationship to the owner.

- **Family farms or independent peasant proprietors** own plots of land (usually small) and operate them mainly or solely with their own family's labor. This type of tenure is dominant in Asia and Africa and is important in Latin America as well.

- **Tenancy** usually refers to a situation where an individual family farms a piece of land owned by a landlord to whom the farmer pays rent. Much of Asian agriculture is made up of either individual peasant proprietors or tenants.

- **Sharecropping** is a form of tenancy in which the farmer shares the crops with the landlord.

- **Absentee landlords,** who are particularly important in Asia and Latin America, tend to live in cities or other places far away from the land they own. Landlords who live near their land have little to do with it except to collect rents. Some resident landlords provide seeds and certain kinds of capital to tenants.

- **Communal farming** is practiced in parts of Africa, where inhabitants of villages still may own some of their land jointly. Individuals and families may farm plots on communal land, to which they gain access by custom or by allocation from the community's leaders. Europe in an earlier period also had such common lands, which were used, among other purposes, as pasture for the village cows.

- **Collectivized agriculture** refers to the kinds of agricultural systems found for the most part in the states of the former Soviet Union including Russia, China prior to 1981, and Vietnam prior to 1989. Land, except for small family plots, is owned by a cooperative whose members typically are all or part of the residents of a single village. Management is by a committee elected by the villagers or appointed by government authorities, and members of the cooperative share in the output on the basis of the amount of labor they contribute to it.

There are numerous variations within and among these categories, but this list gives some idea of the great range of land-tenure systems that exist in the developing world. The kind of land-tenure system existing in any given country or region has an important bearing on economic development for several reasons. To begin with, prevailing land-tenure arrangements have a major influence on the welfare of the farm family. A family farming only one or two acres of land that must turn over half its main crop to the landlord will have little left over to feed itself or to invest in improvements. Such a heavy rent burden may seem harsh, but half or more of the farmers in some major countries, such as China and South Korea before land reform and parts of Latin America and India today, labor under comparable conditions or worse.

A second important impact of the land-tenure system is on the prevailing degree of political stability. Families that own the land they cultivate tend to feel they have a stake in the existing political order, even if they are quite poor. Because they possess land, they have something to lose from turmoil. Landless farm laborers and tenants who can be pushed off the land at the will of a landlord have no such stake in the existing order. The history of many countries with large landless rural populations often are dotted with periodic peasant rebellions. One such rebellion played a major role in bringing the Communists to power in China. Much of the history of modern Mexico has also been shaped by the revolt of the landless.

TENURE AND INCENTIVE

Land-tenure systems also have a major impact on agricultural productivity. An individual proprietor who has well-defined, exclusive, and secure rights to land knows that increased effort or skill that leads to a rise in output also will improve income. This result does not necessarily follow if the land is owned by someone else and property rights for the farmer are not well defined and secure. Under sharecropping, for example, the landlord gets a percentage share, typically a half of any increase in output. If a tenant's rent contract is only a year or two in length, a rise in output may cause the landlord to threaten eviction of the tenant so that all or much of the increase in production can be captured through a rise in the rent. In some countries, landlords have had to draw up land-rental contracts of many years or even a lifetime's duration, precisely because tenants otherwise would have no incentive to invest in improvements or even to maintain existing irrigation and drainage systems.

Farms with large numbers of hired laborers have an even more difficult incentive problem, compounded by a management problem. Farm laborers are paid wages and typically do not benefit at all in any rise in production. One way around this difficulty is to pay on a **piece-rate basis;** that is, to pay workers on the basis of the number of bushels of cotton or tea leaves they pick. But, although this system works at harvest time, it is virtually impossible to pay on a piecework basis for the cultivation of crops. A laborer can be paid by the acre for planting wheat, but it will be many months before it will be possible to tell whether the planting job was done well or carelessly. In a factory, elaborate procedures can be set up by management to check on the pace and quality of work performed. But work in a factory is much easier to reduce to a routine that can be measured and supervised than work on a farm. A thousand different tasks must be performed on a typical farm; and supervision, even in the hands of a skilled manager, is seldom a good substitute for a farmer motivated by the knowledge that extra effort will lead directly to a rise in income.

Incentives under communal farming suffer in a different way. Property rights in this case are not exclusive because the land is owned in common. Each individual family has an incentive to use the land to the maximum extent possible, but no one has much of an incentive to maintain or improve the land because the benefits of individual improvement efforts will accrue to everyone who uses the land, not mainly to the individual. Economists call this the **public goods** or **free-rider** problem. Everyone agrees that a fire department is necessary if a town is to avoid conflagration, but few people would voluntarily pay what the fire department is worth. Instead each would pay little or nothing in the hope that neighbors would pay enough to maintain the department, but of course the neighbors would not pay enough either. The usual solution to this problem is to turn payment over to the town government and allow that government to assess taxes on everyone in town on an equitable basis. Similar solutions are found in communal agriculture. Certain dates can be set aside when everyone in the village is expected to show up and work on a particular land improvement, such as repair of a fence with a neighboring village. But the incentive to work hard in a common effort relies heavily on community social pressure plus the inner goodwill of each individual. If farmers were saints, goodwill would do the job, but for better or worse, farmers are like the rest of us.

Collectivized agriculture has some of the incentive and management problems of both plantation and communal agriculture, but with important differences. Because rights to the land are held in common, the free-rider problem is present, but its impact is modified by paying everyone "work points" on the basis of the amount of work actually done. At the end of the year, the total number of work points earned by collective members is added up and divided into the value of the collective's output to determine the value of each work point. The individual therefore has a dual incentive to work hard. More work means more work points, and indirectly it leads to higher collective output and hence a higher total income for that individual.

The incentive issue posed by collective agriculture is whether the work-point system is an adequate substitute for the motivation provided on a family farm, where increased output benefits a farmer's own family and only that family. The main problem with the collective system is that an individual sometimes can earn work points by claiming to have worked hard, when in fact that person was sleeping or leaning on a hoe. The solution to the leaning-on-a-hoe problem is to have the leadership of the collective check up on how hard members are working, but that can introduce the supervision or management problem found in plantation labor; namely, it is extremely difficult to supervise many agricultural activities. In general, both the incentive and managerial problems worsen as the collective unit gets larger. In a unit of 20 or 30 families, the size of the Chinese production teams in the 1970s, families can supervise each other and penalize laggards. But in a unit of several thousand families, the size of the Chinese commune in the late 1950s, family members have little incentive to pressure laggards to work harder because no single individual's work, however poorly done, will have much impact on the value of a neighbor's work points. If everyone in the collective thinks this way, of course, the output of the collective will fall. By 1981, the Chinese leadership had decided that even the 20- to 30-family collective unit created incentive and managerial problems, and the leaders introduced reforms that returned Chinese agriculture to a system of family farming.

From an incentive and management point of view, therefore, the family-owned farm would seem to be the ideal system. The analysis so far, however, has left out one very important consideration: economies of scale. In agriculture, economies of scale may exist because certain kinds of machinery can be used efficiently only on large farms. On small farms, tractors or combines may be badly underutilized. Such considerations help explain why many Latin Americans feel that large-scale farming is the most appropriate way to increase agricultural production and exports. Economies of scale may also exist because large collective units are better at mobilizing labor for rural construction activities than individual family farms. We return to the question of scale economies later. Here, all we can conclude is that the question of the ideal type of rural land-tenure system has not been completely resolved.

LAND REFORM

The reform of land-tenure systems can assume many different forms.[4] Here are some typical measures found in many reforms, starting with the least radical:

- **Reform of rent contracts** ensures the tenure of a tenant farmer. Many tenants farm at the will of the landlord and can be removed easily at the end of a season. Laws requiring long-term contracts that restrict the landlord's right to remove a tenant can markedly improve the tenant's willingness to maintain and invest in the land and also introduce a degree of stability into the family's life. In effect, these kinds of reforms strengthen the property rights of tenants at the expense of those of the landlord but do not necessarily involve a transfer of income from owner to tenant.
- **Rent reduction** typically involves a ceiling on the percentage share of the crop that a landlord can demand as rent. If the percentage share is substantially below what prevailed in the past, the impact both on tenant welfare and the tenant family's surplus available for investment can be substantial.
- **Land to the tiller** (the former tenant) **with compensation** to the landlord for loss of land is a measure that can take many different forms. A government can pass a law setting a ceiling on the number of acres an individual can own and so force individuals to sell all land over that limit. Or the reform law can state that only those who actually till the land can own it, and all other land must be sold. A key issue in this kind of reform is whether the former landlord receives full or only partial compensation for the land that must be sold.
- **Land to the tiller without compensation** involves the most radical transformation of rural relations, except for the further step of collectivization. All land not cultivated by its owner is confiscated, and the former landlord receives nothing in return. Frequently, in such reform, the landlord may lose life as well as land.

THE POLITICS OF LAND REFORM

The main motive for undertaking land reform usually is political, not economic.[5] Two types of politics lead to reform. A society with a large tenant and landless laborer population that is controlled by other classes may find

---

4. There are numerous studies of land reform. One of the best-known practitioners was Wolf Ladejinsky. See Louis J. Walinsky, ed., *Agrarian Reform as Unfinished Business: The Selected Papers of Wolf Ladejinsky* (London: Oxford University Press, 1977).

5. Elias Tuma, *Twenty-Six Centuries of Agrarian Reform: A Comparative Analysis* (Berkeley: University of California Press, 1965).

itself faced with increasing rural unrest. In the first type of land reform, to keep this unrest from blowing up into a revolution, bills are passed to reduce the burden on the peasantry and give them a stake in continued stability. In the second type, land reform takes place after a revolution supported by the rural poor has occurred. The main purpose of reform in this case is to consolidate support for the revolution among the rural poor and eliminate the economic base of one of the classes, the landlords, most opposed to the revolution.

The motive behind the Mexican land reforms of the twentieth century, for example, has been largely of the first type. Prior to the Mexican Revolution of 1911, land in Mexico had become increasingly concentrated in large haciendas ranging in size from 1,000 to over 400,000 acres. Although the revolution of 1911 was supported by those who had lost their land and other rural poor, those who took power after the revolution largely were from upper-income groups or the small middle class. This new leadership, however, had to deal with the continuing rural unrest that often was ably led by men such as Emiliano Zapata. To meet the challenge of Zapata and people like him, the Mexican government has periodically redistributed some arable land, most recently under the government of President Luis Echeverria in the 1970s. Mexican land-tenure relations, however, continue to be characterized by large estates existing alongside small peasant holdings. Reform eliminated some of the more extreme forms of pressure for more radical change, but Mexican agriculture still includes a large, poor, and not very productive rural peasant class.

The Chinese land reform of the 1940s and early 1950s under the leadership of the Communist Party was a reform par excellence of the second type. The Communist revolution had been built primarily on the rural poor, and the landlord class was one of the main pillars of support of the existing Kuomintang government. Prior to the reform some 40 percent of the arable land had been farmed by tenants, who typically paid half their main crop to the landlord as rent. The landlord, whether a resident in the village or an absentee, contributed little or nothing other than the land. After the reform, and prior to the collectivization of agriculture in 1955–56, land was owned by the tiller and the landlord received no compensation whatsoever. In fact many landlords were tried publicly in the villages and either executed or sent off to perform hard labor under harsh conditions.[6]

The Japanese land reform that followed World War II was different in important respects from the Chinese experience. Land reform in Japan was carried out by the U.S. occupation forces. The occupation govern-

6. Among the many descriptions of Chinese land reforms is William Hinton's *Fanshen* (New York: Vintage Books, 1966).

ment believed that the landlord class had been an important supporter of the forces in Japanese society that brought about World War II. Small peasant proprietors, in contrast, were seen as a solid basis on which to build a future democratic and stable Japan. Since the Americans had won the war, Japanese landlords were not in a position to offer resistance to reform, and a thoroughgoing reform was carried out. Compensation of landlords was provided for in legislation, but inflation soon had the effect of sharply reducing the real value of the amounts offered. As a result Japanese land reform also amounted to confiscation of landlord land with little compensation.[7]

A second feature of land reform efforts is that land reform legislation is extremely difficult to enforce in the absence of a deep commitment from the government. Most developing countries have some kind of land reform legislation on the books, but relatively few have experienced real reform. In some cases, no serious effort is made to enforce the legislation. In other cases, the legislation is enforced but has little effect because of legal loopholes. India provides examples of both kinds of problems. In the Indian state of Bihar, the government awarded substantial tracts of land to the harijan (former untouchable) caste. But Bihar is a state where much of the real power rests in the hands of so-called higher castes that include many landlords, and these higher castes have forcibly prevented the harijans from taking over the land the government awarded to them. Elsewhere in India, a law limiting the amount of land that can be owned by a single person has been enforced but has had limited real effect. An individual with more land than allowed by law registers the extra land in the name of trusted relatives or associates. For truly enormous landholdings, subterfuges of this kind may be impossible, but most landlords in India possess only several ten or a few hundred acres of land.

LAND REFORM AND PRODUCTIVITY

The impact of land reform on agricultural productivity depends on what kind of system is being reformed as well as the content of the reform measures. Land reform has the greatest positive impact on productivity where the previous system was one of small peasant farms, with high rates of insecure tenancy (for example, one-year contracts) and absentee landlords. Under such conditions reform has little impact on cultivation practices since farms are small both before and after reform. Elimination of landlords also has little effect on productivity because they have nothing to do with farming. On the other hand, turning tenants into owners provides

---

7. There are many studies of Japanese land reform, including R. P. Dore, *Land Reform in Japan* (London: Oxford University Press, 1959).

them with well-defined and secure property rights and hence with a greater incentive to invest in improvements. All the Chinese, Japanese, and South Korean land reforms of the 1940s and 1950s essentially were of this kind.

At the other extreme are reforms that break up large, highly efficient modern estates or farms and substitute small, inefficient producers. In many parts of the developing world, such as Mexico, Kenya, and Malaysia, large, highly mechanized estates using the most advanced techniques have grown up over time. The incentive problems inherent in the use of hired farm labor at least partially are overcome by the use of skilled professional estate managers. Often these estates are major suppliers of agricultural produce for export and hence a crucial source of the developing country's foreign exchange. If land reform breaks up these estates and turns them over to small peasant proprietors who know little about modern techniques and lack the capital to pay for them, the impact on agricultural productivity can be catastrophic. But there also are examples, as in the Kenyan highlands, where the breakup of large estates into small peasant holdings actually increased productivity, mainly because the small holdings were farmed much more intensively than the large estates. In between these two extremes are a myriad of variations with different impacts on productivity, both positive and negative.

LAND REFORM AND INCOME DISTRIBUTION

Land reform will have a major impact on the distribution of income in rural areas only if land is taken from landlords without compensation or at least without anything close to full compensation. If former tenants are required to pay landlords the full market value of the land received, the society's distribution of wealth will be the same as before. The tenant will receive land together with a debt exactly equal to the value of the land, hence no change in net wealth of the former tenants. The former landlord will surrender land but acquire an asset of equal value in the form of a loan to the former tenant. Reform with full compensation may be desirable on productivity grounds because of the advantages of strengthening property rights through owner rather than tenant cultivation, but initially at least, the new owner will be just as poor and the new landlord just as rich as before. On the other hand, if the landlord is compensated with bonds paid for out of general tax revenues, the former tenant's income share may rise, provided the taxes to pay for this do not fall primarily on the tenant. The best-known successful land reforms commonly have involved little or no compensation for confiscated assets of landlords. Such was the case in Russia after 1917 and China after 1949, as well as in the Japanese and South Korean reforms after World War II. This discussion of land-tenure relations and their reform sets the scene for the discussion of agricultural production and how it can be raised. Much of the analysis that follows deals with subjects like agricultural research or the uses of chemical fertilizer. But always keep in mind that, behind the use of better techniques and more inputs, the land-tenure system must provide farmers with well-defined, secure, and enforceable property rights and hence with the incentive to introduce those techniques and inputs, then use them efficiently.

Technology of Agricultural Production

The popular view of traditional agricultural systems is that they are made up of peasants who have been farming the same way for centuries. The implication is that traditional farmers are bound by custom and incapable of making changes that raise the productivity and efficiency of their efforts. Custom, in turn, is reinforced by values and beliefs often closely tied to religion. Change thus becomes doubly difficult because to make a change may involve a rejection of deeply held religious beliefs. In this case, only a revolution that completely overturns the traditional society and all it stands for holds out real hope for agricultural development.

TRADITIONAL AGRICULTURE

Tradition-bound societies of this type exist in the world, but the description does not fit the great majority of the world's peasant farmers. A great accumulation of evidence suggests that these farmers are efficient. They already have made sensible—sometimes complex and subtle—adaptations to their environment, and they are willing to make further changes to increase their welfare if it is clear that an improvement will result with no unacceptable risk of crop failure and hence starvation.[8]

When traditional agriculture is described as *efficient,* the word is used in the same way as it has been used throughout this book. Given existing technology, traditional farmers get the most output they can from available inputs or they get a given level of output with the smallest possible use of inputs. Foreign advisors, regardless of their background, often have to relearn this fact, sometimes at considerable cost. With a little reflection it is hardly surprising that traditional agriculture tends to be efficient within the limits of traditional techniques. The central characteristic of traditional technology is that it changes very slowly. Farmers therefore are not in a position to respond constantly to chang-

8. A classic statement of this point has been made by Theodore W. Schultz, *Transforming Traditional Agriculture* (New Haven, CT: Yale University Press, 1964).

ing agricultural methods; instead, they can experiment over long periods of time with alternative techniques until just the right method for the given technology is found. Long periods of time in this context may refer to decades or even centuries. If a slightly deeper method of plowing or a closer planting of seeds will raise yields per acre, for example, one or two more venturesome farmers eventually are going to give such methods a try. At least, they will do so if they have plows capable of deeper cultivation. If the techniques work, their neighbors will observe and eventually follow suit. Given several decades or a century all farmers in the region will be using similar methods.

This example brings out a closely related characteristic of traditional agriculture. In addition to being efficient, traditional agricultural techniques are not stagnant; they have evolved slowly over time. That peasant farmers in a traditional setting are willing to change if the benefits from a change are clearly perceived has been demonstrated over and over again. Some of the best evidence in support of this willingness to change is that provided by responses to changes in prices. Time and again, as the price of cotton or tobacco or jute has risen relative to other farm prices, farmers—even in some of the poorest countries in the world—have rushed to increase the acreage of these crops. And the reverse has occurred when prices have fallen.

Change in traditional agriculture has involved much more than responses to fluctuations in relative prices. Long before the advent of modern science and its application to farming, there were fundamental advances in all aspects of agricultural technology.

SLASH-AND-BURN CULTIVATION

One of the most fundamental changes, of course, was the conversion of society from groups of hunters and gatherers of wild plants to groups of settled farmers who cleared and plowed the land. Initially settled farming often involved slash-and-burn methods of cultivation. In slash-and-burn agriculture, trees are slashed and fire is used to clear the land. The burnt tree stumps are left in the ground, and cultivation seldom involves much more than poking holes in the ground with a digging stick and dropping seeds into the holes. The original nutrients in the soil plus the nutrients from the burnt ashes make respectable yields possible for a year or two, after which most of the nutrients are used up, weed problems increase, and yields fall off drastically. Farmers then move on to slash and burn a new area, perhaps returning to the first area 20 or 30 years later when the land has regained a sufficient level of plant nutrients. Slash-and-burn agriculture therefore often is referred to as a form of **shifting cultivation** or **forest-fallow cultivation.** This system requires a large amount of land to support a small number of people. Today, the system exists mainly in remote, lightly populated areas, such as in the mountains of Laos and parts of Africa and the Amazon.

THE SHORTENING OF FALLOW

The evolution from slash-and-burn agriculture to permanent cultivation, in which a crop is grown on a piece of land once every year, can be thought of as a process of gradually shortening the period that land is left fallow. The term *fallow* refers to the time that land is left idle to allow the soil to reaccumulate the nutrients essential to successful cultivation. In Europe, the shortening of fallow gradually took place during and after the Middle Ages, and annual cropping did not become common until the latter part of the eighteenth century. In China, the evolution to annual cropping occurred at least a thousand years earlier. In both Europe and China, the driving force behind this evolution was increased population pressure on the land.[9]

The elimination of fallow did not occur automatically or easily. Farmers had to discover ways to restore nutrients in the soil by rotating crops and adding fertilizers such as compost and manure. Ploughs had to be developed to cultivate the land each year yet prevent it from being taken over by grasses. Each of these changes was at least as fundamental as many that have occurred in agriculture in the twentieth century. The difference is that these earlier changes took place over centuries rather than years.

FARMING WITHIN A FIXED TECHNOLOGY

Once fallow was eliminated, increases in agricultural production could be obtained either by increasing yields on annually cropped land or by expanding onto previously uncultivated land. Where population pressure was particularly severe, several centuries ago, grain yields reached levels per hectare higher than those found in many parts of the world even today. In China, for example, two crops a year of rice or of rice and wheat were common before the sixteenth century. By the mid-nineteenth century in both China and Japan, average rice-paddy yields over large areas had passed 2.5 to 3 tons per hectare, whereas in India and Thailand as late as the 1960s average rice yield were under 1.5 tons per hectare. Traditional agriculture was capable of achieving high levels of productivity per unit of land.

What separates traditional from modern agricultural development, therefore, is not the existence of technological progress or the sophistica-

9. Ester Boserup, *The Conditions of Agricultural Growth: The Economies of Agrarian Change and Population Pressure* (Chicago: Aldine, 1965); and Dwight H. Perkins, *Agricultural Development in China, 1368–1968* (Chicago: Aldine, 1969).

tion of the techniques used. Traditional agriculture experienced substantial technological progress, and the techniques used in highly populated areas at least were as sophisticated as many so-called modern techniques found today. The difference between traditional and modern agriculture is in the pace and source of change. In traditional agriculture, change is slow, whereas in modern agriculture, it is rapid. In modern agriculture, scientific research produces most of the new techniques used. In traditional agriculture, new techniques sometimes were the result of the tinkering of individual farmers and at other times new inputs, such as improved seeds, were accidents of nature that led to a variety that produced higher yields or required a shorter growing season.

The principal problem of traditional agriculture, therefore, was that farmers worked most of their lives within a technology that changed very slowly. They could spend their energies raising the efficiency with which they used that technology, but the gains from higher levels of efficient use of a stagnant technique were limited. The improvements in technique that did occur happened over too long an interval of time to have anything but a marginal impact on rural standards of living.

MODERNIZING AGRICULTURAL TECHNOLOGY

Traditional agriculture can be modernized in two ways. The first is technological: specific inputs and techniques can be combined to produce higher agricultural production. Technological modernization deals with such issues as the role of chemical fertilizer and the relationship of fertilizer's impact to the availability of improved plant varieties and adequate supplies of water. These technological issues are the subject of this and the next section. The second approach to modernization concerns the mobilization of agricultural inputs and techniques in developing countries. How, for example, does a country mobilize labor for rural public works or create institutes that will develop new techniques suitable to local conditions? These issues of mobilization and organization are the subject of the following part of this chapter.

There is no universally best technology for agriculture. All agricultural techniques must be adjusted to local soil and climatic conditions and to local factor endowments. Even in industry, technology must be adapted to local conditions, but an automobile assembly plant in Ghana will look much like one of similar size in Indonesia. In agriculture, local conditions are fundamental, not secondary. Students from a developing country can be sent to advanced countries to learn how to develop improved plant varieties suitable to their country, but only occasionally will the plant varieties in the advanced country be directly transferable.

Still, generalizations can be made about the characteristics of modern agricultural technology. The technological development that occurs will differ

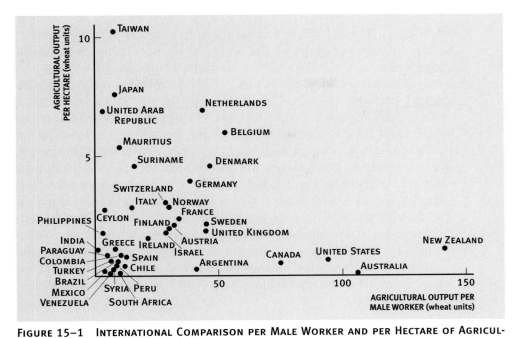

FIGURE 15–1   INTERNATIONAL COMPARISON PER MALE WORKER AND PER HECTARE OF AGRICULTURAL LAND. The dot for the United States indicates that U.S. grain output per farm worker was nearly 100 tons of wheat or its equivalent but U.S. yields per hectare were only about 1 ton. Mauritius, in contrast, had over 5 tons of output per hectare but little more than 10 tons per worker. Output data in the diagram are 1957–62 averages; and labor and land data are for the year closest to 1960.
Source: Yujiro Hayami and Vernon W. Ruttan, *Agricultural Development: An International Perspective* (Baltimore: Johns Hopkins Press, 1971), p. 71.

markedly depending on whether a country has a large area of arable land and a small declining rural population or a large rural population on a very limited amount of arable land. The problem in the former is to get the most output possible out of its limited rural labor force. The latter country also must raise labor productivity. The key to success depends primarily on achieving rapid increases in the productivity of the land.[10] The fundamental difference between these two strategies can be illustrated with a simple diagram, Figure 15–1. As the figure makes clear, the United States and Japan have pursued fundamentally different agricultural strategies, and most other countries fall somewhere in between. In the United States, labor productivity is extremely high but yields per hectare are well below those of many countries, including more than a few of the less developed. In contrast, Japanese labor productivity in agriculture is only a fraction of that in the United States, but land productivity is several times that of the United States.

10. The point is that innovation is induced by perceived needs. See Hans P. Binswanger and Vernon W. Ruttan, *Induced Innovation: Technology, Institutions and Development* (Baltimore: Johns Hopkins Press, 1978).

The difference between the two strategies involves basically different technologies. These different technologies often are called the *mechanical package* (of technologies) and the *biological package.* In the **mechanical package,** tractors, combines, and other forms of machinery are used primarily as substitutes for labor that has left the farm for the cities. In the **biological package,** yields are raised through the use of improved plant varieties such as hybrid corn or the new varieties of rice developed at the International Rice Research Institute in the Philippines. Because of the dramatic effect on yields of some of these new varieties, the phenomenon often is referred to as the **Green Revolution.** But these new varieties raise yields only if combined with adequate and timely water supplies and increased amounts of chemical fertilizer. The basic production functions that describe these two packages therefore are fundamentally different. The isoquants of a production function representing the mechanical package indicate a high degree of substitutability (Figure 15–2), whereas the isoquants for the biological package are drawn in a way to indicate a high degree of complementarity (Figure 15–3). The L-shaped isoquants in Fig-

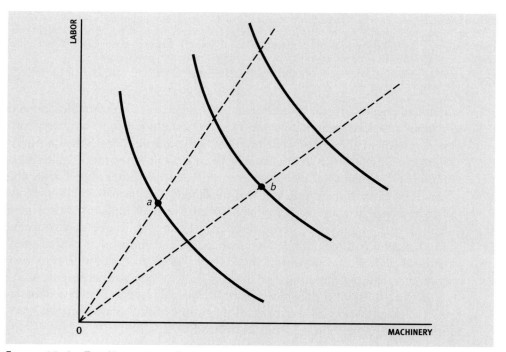

FIGURE 15–2   THE MECHANICAL PACKAGE PRODUCTION FUNCTION. The isoquants in this production function represent increases in agricultural output as one moves out from the point of origin (0). Movement from point *a* to point *b* represents a shift to the use of more machinery, which also involves a rise in agricultural output because machinery is a good substitute for labor.

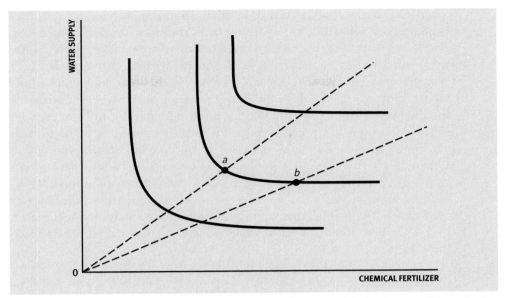

FIGURE 15–3 THE BIOLOGICAL PACKAGE PRODUCTION FUNCTION. The isoquants in this production function also represent increases in agricultural output as one moves out from the point of origin (0), but these isoquants, unlike those in Figure 15–2, indicate little substitutability between inputs. An increase in fertilizer from point *a* to point *b*, for example, does not lead to a rise in agricultural output because the required increase in water supply to make the fertilizer effective has not occurred.

ure 15–3 indicate complementarity because only a limited number of fertilizer and water combinations will produce increases in grain output. Continual increases of only one input, such as fertilizer, will run into diminishing returns and then, where the curve flattens out, no returns. Even the biological package has some substitutability but less than in the case of the mechanical package.

THE MECHANICAL PACKAGE

To someone familiar with the cornfields of Iowa or the wheat fields of Nebraska and the Dakotas, mechanization means the use of large John Deere tractors and combines, metal silos with mechanical loading devices, and numerous other pieces of expensive equipment. Using such equipment, a single farmer with one assistant can farm hundreds of acres of land. But mechanization also can occur profitably on farms of only a few acres. As labor becomes more abundant and land less so, the mechanical package becomes less important in relation to the biological package, but mechanization still has a role to play even in poor, labor-intensive agricultural systems.

Mechanization of agriculture in labor-abundant developing countries primarily is a substitute for labor, just as in the labor-short U.S. Midwest. Even in countries such as China or India, there are periods when the demand for labor exceeds its supply. When two rice crops are grown each year, for example, the first crop must be harvested, fields prepared, and the second crop transplanted—all within a matter of a few weeks. Transporting the harvest to market also takes an enormous amount of labor if goods must be brought in on carts hauled by men or animals or as head loads carried by women, as is still the case in much of the developing world. One driver with a truck can do in a day what might otherwise take dozens of men and women several days to do. Nor can humans or animals working a hand pump or a water wheel move much water to the fields, however hard they work. A small diesel pump can move more water to higher levels than a large number of oxen turning wheels, and oxen cost more to feed than the pump costs to fuel.

Even when labor is extremely inexpensive, therefore, it can be economical to substitute machines for labor in some operations. Over the years manufacturers in Japan and elsewhere have developed whole lines of miniaturized machinery such as hand tractor and rice transplanters to meet this need, and these machines are in widespread use in the developing world. Not all mechanization in the developing world has been economic, however. Frequently tractors and other forms of farm machinery are allowed to enter a country duty free (when other imports have high tariffs) or are subsidized in other ways. Large farmers thus sometimes find it privately profitable to buy tractors and get rid of hired labor when, in the absence of subsidies, they (and the country) would be better off economically using laborers.

A major point of this discussion is that no one agricultural technology is most efficient in all countries. The technology that produces a given level of output at the lowest possible cost in a country with a low per capita income is likely to be very different from the technology that produces the same product at the lowest cost in a country with a high per capita income. The reason is straightforward. Labor in a country with a low per capita income typically is paid much lower wages than in the richer country. Capital conversely often is less expensive in countries with a higher per capita income.

How this works can be illustrated by adding **isocost** lines to Figure 15–2, which is done in Figure 15–4. The isocost lines (*ac* and *bd*) illustrate the various combinations of labor and machinery that can be purchased for a given sum of money, say $1,000 at prices prevailing for machinery and labor in that country. The line *bd* represents the relative costs of these inputs in a high per capita income country, where labor is expensive and capital relatively cheap. The line *ac* represents the situa-

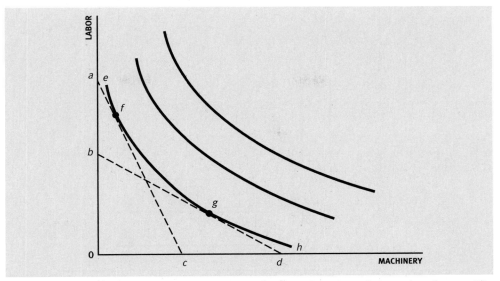

FIGURE 15–4 CHOICES OF TECHNOLOGY WITH DIFFERING COSTS OF CAPITAL AND LABOR. The technology choices here are similar to those in Figure 15–2. Added are the isocost line for the high per capita income country (*bd*) and the low per capita income country (*ac*).

tion in a poorer country, where labor is inexpensive and capital is relatively costly. The objective for the efficient farmer is to produce the most output possible at a given cost (or minimize the cost required to produce a given output). For the country with a low per capita income, that most efficient point is at *f*, where its isocost line is tangent to the isoquant *efgh* of the production function. For the country with the higher per capita income and the relatively expensive labor, in contrast, tangency is achieved at point *g* on that same isoquant. At point *g*, the richer country will use substantially more capital and less labor to produce the same level of output as the poorer country producing at point *f*.

In some cases, however, the capital-intensive technology will be superior regardless of the relative prices of capital and labor. An example would be the use of tube wells with power pumps to replace wells dug by hand with water obtained with a bucket and rope. The latter uses much more labor but saves little or no capital. This situation is illustrated in Figure 15–5. The isocost lines of both the high and low per capita income countries, *ac* and *bd*, are tangent to the production isoquant at almost the same point (*e* is close to *f*). This situation where efficient substitutability is limited also commonly is found with respect to some elements in the biological package, to which we now turn.

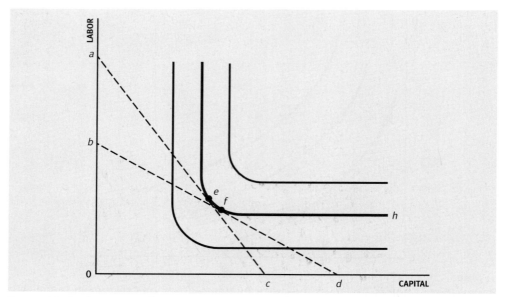

**FIGURE 15–5   CHOICES OF TECHNOLOGY WITH DIFFERING COSTS OF CAPITAL AND LABOR AND LIM-
ITED SUBSTITUTABILITY BETWEEN CAPITAL AND LABOR.** This figure is similar to Figure 15–4 except for
the use of production function isoquants that indicate limited substitutability between capital and labor.

THE BIOLOGICAL PACKAGE AND THE GREEN REVOLUTION

The main impact of the biological package is to raise yields. Nothing is
new about using improved plant varieties in combination with fertilizers
and pesticides to raise yields of rice or corn. The use of modern scientific
laboratories to develop the new varieties dates back half a century and
more. Only since the 1960s, however, have the methods so successful in
the industrialized countries been applied throughout the developing countries. The founding of the International Maize and Wheat Improvement
Center (CIMMYT[11]) in Mexico and the International Rice Research Institute (IRRI) in the Philippines marked the beginning of a truly international effort to develop high-yielding varieties of grain suitable to the
tropical conditions found in so much of the developing world. National
efforts preceded these international centers, and other international centers devoted to the problem of arid and semiarid developing areas have followed. The result has been a steady stream of new, high-yielding varieties
of wheat and rice that have found increasing acceptance in Asia and Latin
America, and to a lesser degree in Africa.

11. The acronym refers to the name in Spanish: Centro Internacional de Mejoramiento de
Maiz y Trijo.

TABLE 15–2 CONSUMPTION OF CHEMICAL FERTILIZER IN DEVELOPING COUNTRIES (1,000 METRIC TONS OF NUTRIENT)				
YEAR	LATIN AMERICA	FAR EAST[a]	NEAR EAST	AFRICA
1948–49 TO 1952–53 (ANNUAL AVERAGE)	116.5	617.2	93.8	32.5
1961–62 TO 1965–66 (ANNUAL AVERAGE)	609.7	1,839.3	379.3	192.2
1969–70	1,171.7	3,546.3	693.9	395.5
1979–80	6,720	9,473	2,831	1,142
1984	7,293	14,442	4,242	1,482
1988	8,807	19,237	5,019	1,694
1992–93	7,908	24,407	4,632	3,780

[a]Far East excludes Asian centrally planned economies.

Sources: FAO, Production Yearbook 1970 (Rome: Food and Agricultural Organization, 1971); Fertilizer Yearbook 1984 (Rome: Food and Agricultural Organization, 1985), p. 121; Fertilizer Yearbook 1989, pp. 88–89; Fertilizer Yearbook 1993, pp. 119–20.

A rapid increase in the use of chemical fertilizers in the developing world had accompanied the increased use of high-yielding and other improved varieties (see Table 15–2). Prior to World War II, modern chemical fertilizers were virtually unknown in the less-developed countries. By the 1970s, they were in widespread use from Brazil to India. Unlike machinery, chemical fertilizers can be purchased in almost any quantity and even very small amounts help yields. Thus, chemical fertilizers are within the reach of even quite poor peasants. The principal limitations on the greater use of chemical fertilizer have not been the conservatism of the peasants or their poverty, but the availability of supplies and the price at which these supplies have been sold. We return to the price question later in this chapter.

A key component of the biological package is water. Improved plant varieties using more chemical fertilizer lead to dramatically higher yields only when there is an adequate and timely water supply. In much of the U.S. Midwest, rainfall provides all the water required and at the right time. In many parts of the developing world, rainfall often is inadequate or comes at the wrong time. In much of India, the difference between a good crop and a harvest failure still depends primarily on when the monsoon rains arrive and in what amount. As a result, efforts to raise yields in the developing world often have focused on measures to extend irrigation systems so that crops are less dependent on the vagaries of the weather.

Extending the irrigated acreage often has been seen as primarily a financial and engineering problem. If a country had enough money in the 1950s and 1960s (from aid or its own resources), it hired a group of engi-

TABLE 15-3	FOOD PRODUCTION PER CAPITA IN DEVELOPING COUNTRIES (INDICES 1989-91 = 100)			
YEAR	WORLD	SOUTH AMERICA	ASIA	AFRICA
1985	98.8	97.8	92.1	97
1989-91	100	100	100	100
1997	106	113.3	123.5	97.1

Source: FAO, *Production Yearbook 1996*, p. 49; *1997*, p. 43.

neers to build a dam to create a reservoir and canals to take water to the fields. As one dam project after another was completed, however, it became increasingly apparent that the irrigation potential of these systems was badly underutilized. Engineers could build the dams and the main canals, but they could not always get the farmer to build and maintain the feeder canals to the fields. Who should do the work and who would reap the benefits of these canals became entangled in the conflicting interests and local politics of rural society. Irrigation extension was as much a social as an engineering and ecological question.

More than anything else, the increased use of inputs from this biological package has made possible the steady, if unspectacular, expansion of agricultural output that has kept the food supply even with, or a bit ahead of, the rise in population (see Table 15–3). In the future, further development of improved varieties and expansion of irrigation systems, together with increased chemical fertilizer production, will remain the major contributors to higher yields. The main function of the mechanical package, in contrast, remains freeing labor from the burden of producing food so that it can do other, ideally more productive, tasks. Whether those tasks in fact will be more productive depends on what is happening in the rest of the economy.

Mobilization of Agricultural Inputs

Although the technology of increasing agricultural output is well understood, the ways in which the relevant inputs can be mobilized are both complex and much less well understood. Some of the problems already have been touched on, both in the discussion of difficulties in expanding irrigation and in the earlier presentation of the relationship between land tenure systems, individual incentives, and management difficulties. Here, we discuss some of these issues further in the context of the agricultural production function. In brief the question is, In what alternative ways can a rural society supply itself with the necessary amounts of labor, capital, and improved techniques?

RURAL PUBLIC WORKS PROJECTS

Mobilizing labor to raise crops is primarily a question of individual and family incentive. The main determinants of such incentive are the nature of property rights over the use of land and the prices paid and received for agricultural inputs and outputs (treated later in this chapter). Mobilization of labor to create rural capital—roads, irrigation systems, and other parts of the rural infrastructure—is the topic of this section.

The creation of a rural infrastructure through the mobilization of rural labor has long been the dream of economic planners in the developing world. The idea is a simple one. In the off-season, labor in the rural sectors of developing countries is unemployed or underemployed. Therefore, the opportunity cost of using that labor on rural public works projects is zero or near zero (although food consumption may go up for people doing heavy construction work).

To use this labor in factories, factories first must be built, and that requires the use of scarce capital equipment. Furthermore, this equipment will lie idle when the rural workers return to the fields to plant and harvest their crops. No such problems exist, however, when off-season unemployed labor is used to build roads or irrigation canals. There is no need to buy bulldozers and other heavy equipment. If there is enough labor, shovels and baskets to carry dirt can accomplish much the same purpose, and farmers already have shovels and baskets or easily can make them. In the ideal situation, therefore, unemployed workers can be put to work, first making crude construction tools, after which they can begin to create roads and canals. The result is a major expansion in the rural capital stock at little or no cost to society other than the reduced leisure time of rural workers.

Effective implementation of rural public works programs using seasonally unemployed labor, however, has proven extremely difficult. The community development programs of India and elsewhere are widely perceived as failures. Time and again, international aid agencies have started pilot public works projects, only to see the project die quietly when aid money ran out. Of all the problems connected with the mobilization of unemployed rural labor, the most basic has been the lack of connection between those who did the work and those who reaped most of the benefits.

When an irrigation canal or a road is built, the main benefits that result take the form of higher yields on land near the canal or easier access to the market for crops grown on land near the road. Land or people living distant from the canal or road receive fewer benefits or none at all. If the people who own the nearby land are also those who did the work constructing a road or canal, then there is a direct relation between effort and reward. Unfortunately, more often than not the people who do the work reap few of the rewards. The extreme case is when the land serviced by the new canal or road is owned by absentee landlords. Absentee landlords are never mobilized for rural public works projects. Rather, landless laborers and tenants do all the work, and the landlords benefit in the form of increased rent. Workers on such projects must be paid wages, and these wages tend to be higher than is justified by their productivity. Rural construction with crude tools, after all, is very low-productivity work. If the wages paid exceed the benefits of the project, it is hardly surprising that these projects come to an end when government or aid agency subsidies run out.

Clearly the problem of mobilizing unemployed labor to build rural infrastructure is more difficult than economists and others first thought. The complexity of successfully sharing the benefits is such that rural public works, though possible, are not the universal solution to the problem of rural development that some once thought them to be.

RURAL BANKS AND CREDIT COOPERATIVES

A second approach to the problem of providing rural areas with sufficient capital for development is to establish rural banks or credit cooperatives that will lend to farmers. In traditional agriculture a farmer has only two sources of credit: members of the family and the local moneylender. Since the interest rates charged by moneylenders typically range from 30 or 40 percent to over 100 percent a year, a farmer goes to a moneylender only when desperate. Peasants do not borrow from moneylenders to buy more fertilizer or a new pump. Only rarely will such investments be productive enough to make it possible to pay off loans with exceedingly high interest charges.

There are numerous reasons why urban commercial banks do not move in and take over from the moneylenders. Because of their location, urban banks lack the knowledge and skills necessary to operate efficiently in rural areas. On the other hand, local moneylenders know the reliability of the people to whom they are lending and the quality of land put up as collateral. Individuals without land, of course, have difficulty getting money even from local moneylenders. Women in particular may have difficulty when they farm land registered in the name of an absent husband, a frequent occurrence in Africa and elsewhere.

Credit cooperatives set up by the small farmers are a potential solution to this problem. The idea is that each farmer is capable of saving a small sum, and if these sums are pooled, one or two farmers can borrow a substantial sum to buy a new thresher or pump. The next year it will be an-

LABOR MOBILIZATION IN CHINESE COMMUNES

Even when land is owned by those who cultivate it, there is a problem of matching effort and reward. A typical project may require the labor of an entire village or several villages, whereas the benefits go primarily to farmers in only one part of the village. The Chinese solution to this problem was to collectivize agriculture by forming people's communes.[12] An entire village owns its land in common. People who participated in public works projects receive work points based on the amount of effort expended, just as if they spend their time cultivating crops. When the project is completed, the land in a part of the village would be more productive, but the higher productivity benefits the entire village. The gap between work and reward in effect has been closed.

The Chinese commune made possible the more or less voluntary mobilization of large amounts of underemployed rural labor. Hills were leveled to create new fields, new reservoirs dotted the countryside, and roads reached deep into the countryside where only footpaths had existed before. But the Chinese ran into the work-reward problem in a different form. As the rural works projects became larger and larger, it became necessary to mobilize labor from two dozen villages, even though the benefits of the project went largely to only one or two of those villages.

The initial solution to this problem was to pool the land of all two dozen into a single commune. Then, increased productivity on the land around a single village would be shared by all 24 villages, and workers in those villages once again had an incentive to participate in the project. This larger commune, made up of two dozen villages, however, immediately ran into all the incentive and managerial problems common to large collective units. The result was that, despite all the construction activity or even because of it, Chinese agricultural output fell; and small collective units called *production teams* replaced the large communes as the basic agricultural management unit, although the latter continued to exist and to perform some functions until China decided to return to household-based agriculture in the early 1980s.

12. When China first collectivized agriculture (1955–57), the Chinese called their rural collectives *producers' cooperatives,* but to simplify the discussion we refer to them as *communes.*

other farmer's turn, and so on. In the meantime, those who put their money in the cooperative will draw interest, and thus be encouraged to save more. But this approach has flaws. Farmers' savings tend to be small, and hence the cooperatives tend to be financially weak. More seriously, farmers in developing countries have little experience relevant to the effective operation and management of the cooperatives. In addition, economic, social, and political conflicts within the village may make it possible to decide something as simple as who will get the next loan.

Because of these and other problems, the establishment of rural credit institutions usually requires significant injections of both money and personnel from outside the village, usually from the government. The entry of the government, however, does not necessarily or even usually, solve the underlying difficulties. A common occurrence is for a rural credit institution to be set up with funds from the central government's budget. These funds then are lent to local farmers not only at rates far below those charged by private credit sources but rates so low that each loan requires a subsidy from the government. Since the rates are low and the credit institutions are run by government personnel, local farmers with political clout have both the incentive and the means to grab the lion's share of the financing available. Corrupt bank officials also may skim off some of the funds, and corrupt officials are seldom among the poorer elements in the village. Equally or more serious is that these loans often are never paid back, so that the new credit institution must be constantly resupplied from the central budget or go out of business. Too frequently, the government personnel running the local bank or cooperative lack the will or the authority to make its clients live up to their contracts.

The problems involved in setting up effective rural credit operations can be overcome. States with well-trained banking personnel and a strong government administration capable of drawing up sensible procedures and enforcing them are certainly able to make rural credit institutions work.

Well-trained personnel and effective government administrators are in short supply in a great many developing countries, but this need not be an insurmountable barrier. The Indonesian state-owned Bank Rakyat Indonesia (BRI; see the case study in Chapter 13), for example, has revamped the incentive systems for its rural lending and savings mobilization personnel. The result has been a manyfold rise in rural lending and an even larger increase in rural savings deposits—all happening at the same time that government subsidies to the BRI rural credit program were eliminated. Millions of farmers and small rural businesses that previously had no access to the banking system were able to obtain loans at rates far below those charged by local moneylenders but high enough to allow the BRI to make a profit. Even the Asian financial crisis beginning in 1997 did not fundamentally undermine the continued expansion and profitability of this rural credit and savings program.

EXTENSION SERVICES

If one key to rapid progress in rural areas depends on the introduction of new inputs and new techniques, it follows that some of the most important rural institutions are those responsible for speeding the transfer of these new techniques to the farmers. **Extension services,** as these institutions usually are called, provide the key link between the research laboratories or experimental farms and the rural population that ultimately must adopt what the laboratories develop.

The key to the effectiveness of the extension worker is contact and trust. Rural education helps increase the channels of contact, because if farmers can read, contact can be made through the written as well as the spoken word. Trust is necessary, because if there is contact, the farmer may not believe what is read or heard. Trust, of course, depends not only on the extension worker's honesty or personality but, fundamentally, on the competence of the extension worker and the research system. Giving a farmer bad advice that leads to crop failure is likely to close the channels of communication for some time. Making contact and establishing trust is further complicated because extension workers usually are men whereas those doing the farming, particularly in parts of Africa, are women.

These remarks make common sense, but they get at the heart of the failure of extension services in many developing countries. Frequently, training for the extension service is seen not as a way of learning how to help farmers but as a way of entering the government bureaucracy and escaping from the rural areas. Some extension workers are government clerks living in town and just as averse to getting their hands dirty as their colleagues in the tax collection bureau or the post office. Even when they do visit the farmers they are supposed to be helping, they know so little about how farmers really operate that they are incapable of pointing out genuinely useful new methods. Too often the extension worker visits the village, tells the farmers what is good for them, and departs; the farmers are left to guess as best they can whether the gain from using the new idea is worth the risk of failure.

At the other end of the spectrum are extension workers who are well-trained and live in the villages and work closely with the farmers when new techniques are being introduced. Chinese communes in the 1960s and 1970s, for example, sent one of their members off for training on the condition that the individual would return to work for the commune. The same can happen in villages where family farms predominate, although the absence of the authoritarian controls found in China makes it more difficult in many places to guarantee that the individual sent will return. Another variation on this theme, tried by CIMMYT among others, is for the basic research to be carried out on farmers' fields rather than in separate experimental stations.

There is much that we do not yet know about the spread of advanced technology in agriculture, but an effective extension service is only a part of the picture. To a large degree, farmers learn from their neighbors. However, if one local farmer owns 30 acres and farms it with a large tractor and the neighboring farmers have only 5 acres and no tractors, the farmers with 5 acres may feel they have little to learn from the experience of their neighbor. More evidence is required, but technology appears to travel more rapidly when neighboring farms in a country or region are much alike. Extremes of inequality thus may impede technological progress as well as being undesirable on equity grounds.

As this discussion of mobilizing rural labor and capital and of accelerating the rate of technical advance makes clear, agricultural development in the developing countries is not solely a scientific or an engineering problem. It also depends on the quality of government administration at both the central and local levels.

THE DEVELOPMENT OF RURAL MARKETS

One common theme in the preceding chapters has been the importance of avoiding major distortions in the structure of prices. Nowhere is an appropriate price structure more important than in the agricultural sector. But, in agriculture as in other sectors, there first must be a market before prices can have widespread effects. And in the rural areas of developing countries the existence of an effectively operating market cannot be taken for granted.

Virtually no areas of the world today still have subsistence farming in its purest form. All farmers specialize to some degree and trade their surplus output on some kind of market. Economic development usually is accompanied by the increasing size and sophistication of this rural marketing network, and in turn that improved network has an important impact on productivity in agriculture. The key to an increasing role for the market is specialization, and specialization depends on economies of scale, low-cost transport, and acceptable risk.

Economies of scale are at the heart of specialization. If everyone could produce everything he or she needed at the lowest possible cost, there would be no need to turn over certain tasks to others. In fact, economies of scale are pervasive. In the most advanced agricultural sectors such as the U.S. Midwest, farmers grow only one or two crops and rely on the market for all their other needs. In developing countries, the single greatest barrier to taking advantage of these economies of scale is transportation costs. The absence of good roads or of trucks to run on them can mean that it can cost as much to move a bulky commodity 50 miles as to produce it in the first place. In the United States, wheat is turned into flour in large mills, and farmers buy bread in the local supermarket like everyone else. In developing countries, only wheat destined for urban consumption is processed in large mills. In rural areas, wheat is processed at home or in village mills, because to take the wheat to a large, distant mill would be prohibitively expensive. In large parts of southern Sudan, to take an extreme but not uncommon example, there are no all-weather roads at all, and large regions are completely cut off from the outside world during the rainy season. Regions such as this cannot readily specialize in crops for sale in the cities or for export abroad.

In large parts of the developing world, therefore, improvements in the transportation system, and hence in marketing, can have a major impact on agricultural productivity. Construction of an all-weather road system in South Korea in the 1970s, for example, made it possible for millions of Korean farmers to increase dramatically their emphasis on vegetables and cash crops destined for urban and export markets. Even the simple device of building paved bicycle paths connecting to the main road made it possible for Hong Kong farmers to expand their vegetable acreage. In the absence of refrigerated transportation, many vegetables spoil quickly, and hence it does not pay to raise them if too much time elapses between the harvest and their sale on the market. Furthermore, enormous amounts of labor are required if the vegetables must be carried every day on human backs across muddy fields. The ability to move the vegetables along a paved path on the back of a bicycle can make the difference between growing vegetables or concentrating on rice, which has to be moved to market only once a year.

Even when the transportation system is adequate, farmers in developing countries may limit their dependence on the market because of the risk it entails. While cash crops can fail due to bad weather or pests, the principal risk from market dependence is that the price of the crop being raised will fall sharply by the time the farmer is ready to sell. For large farmers in advanced economies, a fall in price of their main crop leads to a reduction in their income. If the fall is large enough, that farmer may be forced to borrow from a local bank to tide him or her over until prices rise again. Or the farmer merely may have to draw from the family's savings account. In developing countries, a fall in the price of a cash crop, particularly if food prices are rising simultaneously, may lead to a drop in a farm family's income to a level below that necessary to survive. Credit may tide the family over, but interest rates will be so high that, once in debt, the farmer may never be able to pay off creditors and will lose the land put up as collateral. Most farmers in developing countries avoid becoming dependent on a single cash crop and instead devote part of their land to meeting their family's food requirements. Their average income over the long run might be higher if they planted all their land in cotton or tobacco, but they might not live to see the long run if one or two years of depressed prices wipe them out.

Governments can take measures to reduce both transportation costs (by building roads) and risks (by guaranteeing prices and other similar measures) and thereby develop more efficient markets. But governments also can, and often do, take measures that inhibit the development of rural marketing. Governments around the world seldom have a real understanding of the role of rural traders, of the numerous middle traders who make a marketing system work. Middle traders are seen as exploiters who get between the producer and consumer; they drive down the price paid to the producer and drive up that charged to the consumer to reap huge monopoly profits. In response to political pressures from farmers, governments often have taken over the rural marketing system to improve its operation and eliminate the monopoly profits.[13] The temptation for governments to take this step is particularly strong where the middle traders are of a different race from the majority of the population, as is the case in much of Southeast Asia, where Chinese play a major role in marketing, and in East Africa, where descendants of nineteenth- and early-twentieth-century Indian immigrants now control the wholesale and retail trade.

Although occasionally government involvement improves rural marketing, more often such involvement is based on a wrong diagnosis of the problem. The price at which a farm product is sold in the cities is markedly higher than the price paid to the farmer, but the difference has little to do with monopoly profits. The real cause is the high cost of transportation and a generally rudimentary system of distribution and marketing. It is not that rural traders get paid so much, it is just that it takes so many of them to get the goods to market. When the government takes over, this basic situation does not change. For a high-cost, private rural trading network the government often substitutes an even higher-cost bureaucratic control of the movement of goods.

Agricultural Price Policy

This discussion of agricultural development has stressed the central role of institutional change such as land reform and the creation of effective rural credit, marketing, and extension systems. It also has emphasized the importance of government investment in infrastructure, notably in agricultural research. But the creation of new rural institutions can take a long

13. The problems created by too much government interference in agricultural marketing in Africa are discussed in Elliot Berg et al., *Accelerated Development in Sub-Saharan Africa* (Washington, DC: World Bank, 1981).

time. Needed changes in the land tenure system, in particular, can be blocked by powerful interests for decades and even longer. Nor can an agricultural research system be created in a few years' time. New plant varieties suitable to local conditions may take a decade to develop. If the plant scientists needed to carry out the research have not yet been trained, the process can take longer.

THE MULTIPLE ROLE OF PRICES

In one area, however, government intervention has an immediate and often profound positive or negative impact. Most governments in both industrialized and developing countries intervene in agricultural markets to set prices for both the rural producer and the urban consumer. How they intervene can have a profound effect both on agricultural production and consumption. Specifically, the prices at which grain and other agricultural produce are bought and sold play three, and sometimes four, vital roles:

1. The prices paid to farmers, and the relation of those prices to the prices farmers pay for key inputs, such as fertilizer, have a major impact on what and how much those farmers can produce.
2. The prices paid to farmers, together with the quantity of produce sold, are the primary determinants of farmers' cash income.
3. The prices at which agricultural products are sold in the cities are major determinants of the cost of living of urban residents in developing countries.
4. The prices of agricultural products, particularly in many African countries, often are controlled by government marketing boards, which manipulate them to earn profits for the government, a slightly disguised form of taxation.[14]

Prices have a profound impact on agricultural production because most farmers, even in very poor countries, are interested in raising their income. While some hold that peasants grow particular crops or use particular inputs because that is the way their grandfathers did it, study after study has shown that, when prices change, peasant farmers respond much like any profit-maximizing businessperson operating in a world fraught with uncertainty. If the price of cotton rises relative to, say, corn, farmers will grow more cotton even in very traditional societies.

14. For a full discussion of the multiple role of prices, see C. Peter Timmer, Walter P. Falcon, and Scott R. Pearson, *Food Policy Analysis* (Baltimore: Johns Hopkins Press, 1983); and Isabelle Tsakok, *Agricultural Price Policy: A Practitioner's Guide to Partial-Equilibrium Analysis* (Ithaca, NY: Cornell University Press, 1990).

The most important price relationship from the standpoint of agricultural production is that between farm output and purchased inputs, notably chemical fertilizer. From the farmer's point of view it makes sense to use more chemical fertilizer so long as it increases the value of farm output by more than its cost. (This simply is a manifestation of the profit-maximizing rule that the use of a factor of production should be increased as long as the factor's marginal revenue product exceeds its marginal cost.) The simplest and most-effective ways of increasing rice yields are to raise the price of rice or to lower the price of chemical fertilizer or both. As studies of rice production in Asia have shown, there is a clear relationship between the rice yield per acre in a country and the rice-fertilizer price ratio. Other elements also are at work, but the role of prices is a primary influence. This basic point is illustrated with the diagrams in Figure 15–6.

Part A is a simple one-input–one-output production function. The production function is drawn to reflect diminishing returns. If we know the

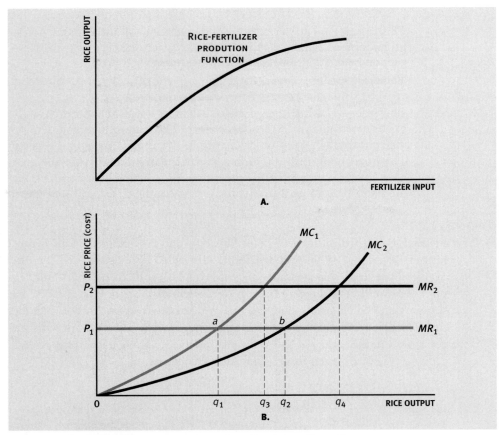

FIGURE 15–6   RICE PRODUCTION AND THE RICE-FERTILIZER PRICE RATIO.

prices of both fertilizer and rice, we easily can derive the marginal cost and marginal revenue curves facing the individual farmer, as is done in Part B.

If the price of fertilizer is lowered, the marginal cost curve will fall from MC_1 to MC_2 and rice production will rise from q_1 to q_2 as farmers maximize their profits at point b instead of point a by increasing the use of fertilizer. Similarly, a rise in the price from P_1 to P_2 while holding fertilizer prices constant will increase rice output from q_1 to q_3.

THE IMPACT OF SUBSIDIES

One of the most persistent problems facing planners and politicians in the developing world is the conflict between urban consumers and rural producers over appropriate agricultural prices. Since food purchases account for at least half the budget of urban consumers in most developing countries, a substantial increase in the price of food will cut sharply into the income of all but the richest urban people. Even governments indifferent to the welfare of their poorer urban residents cannot ignore the political impact of major increases in food prices. From Japan in the 1920s to Zambia in the 1990s, food price rises have triggered massive rioting that has threatened the very existence of particular regimes. (This phenomenon is closely akin to—and often part of—the politically dangerous transition from controlled to liberalized economies discussed in Chapter 5.) Because political leaders themselves live in urban areas and urban residents are in a better position than rural villagers to threaten governments, many states attempt to hold down food prices even during periods of general inflationary pressure. The result is depressed prices for farmers that reduce both farm income and farm output.

Especially (but not exclusively) in some developed countries the political power of the farmers is such that governments raise farm purchase prices to gain rural support. Democracies that still have large or politically powerful rural populations are particularly likely to respond to these pressures. The United States and Japan in the 1950s and 1960s, Japan and the European Union from the 1960s right through 1990s, and South Korea in the late 1960s and early 1970s are examples. The result is that prices are favorable to higher yields, but the income and production benefits of the higher prices may not be equitably distributed. In some countries, richer farmers who market a high percentage of their output gain most from high prices. Small subsistence farmers market little and hence gain little. In other countries, however, all farmers market a high percentage of their crop and all gain from higher prices.

Where both urban and rural residents have considerable political influence, governments sometimes have tried to maintain both low urban food prices and high farm purchase prices. Japan since World War II and South

Korea and Mexico in the 1970s pursued this dual goal. Since the government must pick up the deficit resulting from selling food at prices below what it cost to purchase, only governments with large resources or those willing to forgo other high-priority goals can afford this policy. Thus, there is no single right answer to how high prices to farmers should be. Ultimately, the decision turns on political as well as economic judgment.

One common way to subsidize grain marketing is for the government to absorb the often substantial costs of moving grain from the farm to the urban retail market. Who benefits from this process depends on how the subsidy is handled. Several of the possibilities are illustrated in Figure 15–7, in which marketing costs are represented by the vertical distance between the farmer's grain supply curve and the retail supply curve facing urban residents. These costs are assumed to be a constant amount per unit of grain marketed. In a free market without subsidy, the retail price of grain on the urban retail market would be p_1 and the price received by farmers would be p_2. As this diagram indicates, if the subsidy goes to farmers, the result can be either a rise in grain storage or exports. If the subsidy

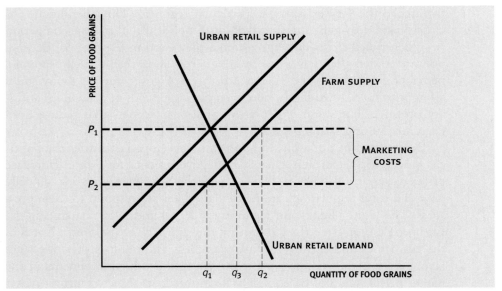

FIGURE 15–7 EFFECT OF A MARKETING SUBSIDY ON SUPPLY AND DEMAND FOR FOOD GRAINS. If farmers receive the marketing cost subsidy P_1P_2, then the farmers' price rises to P_1 and farm output rises from q_1 to q_2. Since food-grain supply now exceeds demand, the excess must be either stored or exported. On the other hand, if urban consumers are given the entire P_1P_2 subsidy, then the price paid by these consumers will fall to P_2 and their demand will rise from q_1 to q_3. The excess in demand then will have to be supplied from imports or the government will have to ration the allocation of food grains to urban consumers.
Source: This diagram is a modified version of that in Timmer, Falcon, and Pearson, *Food Policy Analysis,* p. 198.

goes to urban consumers, on the other hand, the excess demand will lead to a rise in imports.

It is not just foreign trade in grain that is affected by these subsidies. The cost of marketing must be borne by someone, and in these cases it most likely will be an expenditure item in the government's budget. Or the grain marketing authority may borrow from the central bank to cover its costs, but without the ability of ever paying back the loan. The macroeconomic effects of these subsidies can be substantial, particularly in countries where a large portion of marketed agricultural produce is subsidized.

OVERVALUED EXCHANGE RATES

Because the high cost of large subsidies to government marketing boards becomes increasingly obvious to policy makers over time, steps usually are taken to eventually bring these costs under control, even though the political cost can be high. Another way of subsidizing urban consumers or rural producers, however, has a less obvious effect on the government budget but a profound effect on the economy: The use of an *overvalued exchange rate* (see Chapter 18). The impact of an overvalued exchange rate on the grain market is illustrated in Figure 15–8. If, at an equilibrium exchange rate, the world price of grain is P_2, then domestic demand, represented by the curve DD, will be $0q_4$, and the domestic supply of grain will exceed

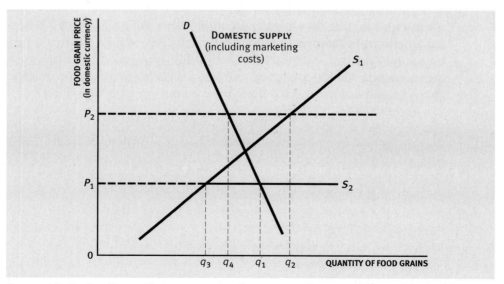

FIGURE 15–8   THE GRAIN MARKET WITH AN OVERVALUED EXCHANGE RATE. If the world price of grain is P_2, then domestic demand (D) will be q_4, and domestic supply ($S_1 S_2$) will be q_2 and result in excess stocks for storage or export. With an overvalued exchange rate, represented by P_1, however, domestic demand (q_1) exceeds domestic supply (q_3) and requires imports or rationing.

demand by the amount $q_4 q_2$. This excess could be either stored or exported. But if this nation's currency becomes overvalued, the world price of grain expressed in terms of domestic currency will fall from P_2 to P_1. Domestic food-grain supply, in this case, will fall to q_3, and the excess of demand at this price, $q_3 q_1$, will be made up with imports or by restricting urban demand through rationing. Therefore, although this method of subsidizing urban consumers does not show up as an expenditure item in the government budget or a loss for the grain marketing board, it has a large negative impact on domestic agricultural production. Domestic agricultural production would fall from q_2 to q_3.[15]

An undervalued exchange rate, of course, will have a positive impact on farm output, but poor urban and rural purchasers of food grain may be forced by high prices to reduce substantially their intake of food; and this may lead to malnutrition and worse. In developing countries, the poor spend a high proportion—over 50 percent—of their budget on food. A price increase for food thus represents a sharp drop in income for these people. They can try to maintain food consumption by cutting back on other items in their budget, but these usually are necessities as well.

Agricultural price policies, therefore, have a profound effect on both agricultural production and the standard of living, and even the basic health, of the poorer segments of a country's people. Since agricultural prices and the exchange rate usually are set by the government in developing countries, it technically is a simple matter to change these prices to reflect the objectives of the government. Price changes involve few of the institution-building or implementation problems connected with developing an effective extension system or mobilizing labor for public works projects. Price changes, however, involve readily apparent costs to those on the receiving end of higher prices. If these people are in a position of influence, the political barriers to effective price policy can be formidable.

---

15. For a study of how trade and macroeconomic policies affect agriculture, see Romeo Bautista and Alberto Valdés. *The Bias against Agriculture: Trade and Macroeconomic Policies in Developing Countries* (San Francisco: ICS Press, 1993).

PRIMARY EXPORTS

International trade is one of the most powerful forces affecting the process of economic development. Trade influences a country's rate of economic growth, income distribution, use of natural resources, and economic and political relationships with the rest of the world. International trade provides firms access to new markets, opens up new opportunities for labor, and gives consumers a much wider and richer array of choices in the goods they buy. Trade allows low-income countries to import the latest machinery and technology without having to develop it on their own and facilitates a much greater flow of information and knowledge between countries. It also creates several challenges for developing countries, including increased competition from foreign firms, instability in world market prices for import and export products, and structural changes inherent in the shift from primary to manufactured products. This chapter begins by describing some general characteristics of exports from developing countries and then explains the concept of **comparative advantage** and its powerful implications for international trade. The bulk of the chapter focuses on countries whose comparative advantage lies in primary commodities: food, agricultural raw materials, timber, metal ores, petroleum, and natural gas. Chapter 18 describes development strategies that attempt to change comparative advantage from primary products to manufactures.

Export Characteristics of Developing Countries

Developing countries export a wide variety of products, including oil and other petroleum products; minerals such as gold, tin, and copper; food and agricultural cash crops; and manufactured products such as textiles, clothing, footwear, electronics, and toys. The diversity of trade patterns among developing countries is shown in Table 16–1. Not surprisingly, countries tend to export products based on their own particular endowments of the basic factors of production (land, other natural resources, labor, and capital). Natural resources dictate the exports of the oil-rich countries of the Persian Gulf, Southeast Asia, and Latin America; copper exporters such as Zambia, Zaire, Chile, and Peru; and timber exporters

TABLE 16–1	EXPORT CHARACTERISTICS OF SELECTED DEVELOPING COUNTRIES, 1996				
COUNTRY NAME	POPULATION (MILLIONS)	GNP PER CAPITA (CUR. INT'L $s)	EXPORT SHARE OF GDP (%)	MAJOR PRIMARY EXPORTS	SHARE OF PRIMARY GOODS IN MERCHANDISE EXPORTS (%)
CHINA	1,215	2,870	21	PETROLEUM	16
INDIA	945	1,580	12	NONE	26[a]
INDONESIA	197	3,310	26	PETROLEUM	49
BRAZIL	161	6,340	7	COFFEE, IRON ORE	46
NIGERIA	115	870	48	PETROLEUM	99
PAKISTAN	125	1,600	17	COTTON, RICE	16
BANGLADESH	122	1,010	14	JUTE GOODS, RAW JUTE	16[c]
MEXICO	93	7,660	32	PETROLEUM	22
THE PHILIPPINES	72	3,550	42	COCONUT PRODUCTS	16
THAILAND	60	6,700	39	RICE, RUBBER, TAPIOCA	27[a]
EGYPT, ARAB REPUBLIC	59	2,860	21	PETROLEUM, COTTON	68
ETHIOPIA	58	500	13	COFFEE, HIDES	99
KOREA, REPUBLIC	46	13,080	32	NONE	8
COLOMBIA	37	6,720	17	COFFEE, FUEL OIL	66
TANZANIA	30	610	22	COFFEE, COTTON	N.A.
KENYA	27	1,130	33	PETROLEUM, TEA, COFFEE	72
PERU	24	4,410	12	COPPER, ZINC, PETROLEUM, LEAD	84
VENEZUELA	22	8,130	37	PETROLEUM	88
MALAYSIA	21	7,410	92	RUBBER, PALM OIL, WOOD, PETROLEUM	24
SRI LANKA	18	2,290	35	TEA, RUBBER, COCONUT	27[b]
GHANA	18	1,790	27	COCOA, WOOD	N.A.
SAUDI ARABIA	19	9,700	43	PETROLEUM	94
CHILE	14	11,700	27	COPPER	85
IVORY COAST	14	1,580	45	COFFEE, COCOA	N.A.
GUATEMALA	11	3,820	18	COFFEE, SUGAR	69
BOLIVIA	8	2,860	20	TIN, GAS, ZINC, SILVER	84
SENEGAL	9	1,650	31	PETROLEUM PRODUCTS, FISH, GROUND NUTS & OIL, PHOSPHATES	50[a]
JAMAICA	3	3,450	55	ALUMINA, BAUXITE, SUGAR	31
ZAMBIA	9	860	38	COPPER	95[b]

[a]1995 data.
[b]1994 data.
[c]1993 data.
Source: World Bank, *World Development Indicators 1998* CD-ROM.

like Malaysia and Ghana. Variations in climate (which may be considered a factor of production) helps explain exports of foods such as coffee, cocoa, bananas, and vegetable oils and raw materials such as rubber and cotton. Countries with abundant labor tend to produce export crops that can be produced efficiently with labor-intensive methods, such as coffee, tea, rice, and tobacco, as well as labor-intensive manufactures such as textiles, clothing, and electronic components. At the same time, developing countries tend to import products that rely on factors of production relatively scarce in their countries, especially highly skilled labor. Therefore, almost all developing countries import machinery and other capital equipment, as well as more technologically advanced intermediate products such as chemicals, refined petroleum products, and metals.

Many developing countries are highly dependent on one or just a few primary commodities for the bulk of their export earnings. The extreme cases of export concentration include many of the major petroleum exporters, Ghana in cocoa, the Ivory Coast in cocoa and coffee, Colombia in coffee and cocaine (not a part of the official data!), Chile and Zambia in copper, and Jamaica in bauxite and alumina. A few countries have a more diversified export base. In three of the cases shown—Bolivia, Malaysia, and Peru—no one product dominates and at least four commodities each account for 5 percent or more of total export earnings. Not surprisingly, very large countries tend to have a greater variety of natural resources and show a much more diversified export pattern.

Large countries also tend to export less of their total production than smaller countries, since there is a bigger domestic market in which to sell their goods. For example, China, India, Brazil, Bangladesh, and Pakistan export a low share of gross domestic product, ranging from 7 to 21 percent in 1996. Economists Moises Syrquin and Hollis Chenery verified this general relationship between country size and exports in their statistical analysis of cross-country patterns of development.[1] They found that, for an average small country with a population of less than 25 million and income per capita of $700 (in 1980 prices), exports of goods and services tend to average about 25 percent of GDP, compared with only 15 percent for a typical large country with the same income. They further found that, as income per capita rose from the neighborhood of $300 to $4,000, the average export share of gross domestic product tended to rise from about 15 to 21 percent. Of course, as with any statistical pattern, there are exceptions to these stylized patterns. Countries of any size that are well endowed with petroleum and other natural resources usually export much

1. Moises Syrquin and Hollis Chenery, "Patterns of Development, 1950–1983," World Bank discussion paper no. 41, 1989, p. 20. Figures are for merchandise exports, excluding the export of services such as tourism and construction.

more: from 37 percent of GDP for Venezuela; around 30 percent for Chile, Indonesia, and Zambia; to 48 percent for Nigeria. Smaller countries lacking rich resource endowments show a wide range of export ratios, from 13 percent for Ethiopia, around 20 percent for Colombia and Tanzania, to around 40 percent for Thailand and Ivory Coast. Malaysia, rich in natural resources but also successful in the transition to manufactured exports, exports an astounding 92 percent of its GDP.[2]

Comparative Advantage

For more than 200 years, trade theorists have tried to explain why nations engage in international trade, what goods and services they trade, and how firms and consumers gain or lose from trade. The workhorse models rely primarily on the **theory of comparative advantage,** which describes trade patterns under assumptions of *static conditions* that hold the factors of production in fixed supply. Comparative advantage has rich implications about the gains from trade. Among the most powerful results are the following: (1) Any country can increase its welfare by trading, because the world market provides an opportunity to buy some goods at relatively low prices. (2) The smaller the country, the greater is this potential gain from trade. (3) A country will gain most by exporting commodities that it produces using its abundant factors of production most intensively, while importing goods whose production requires relatively more of scarcer factors of production.

The first implication is a subtle one that requires elaboration, but is one of the most powerful ideas in all of economics. To reiterate, *any* country can engage in and benefit from international trade, including the world's highest cost and lowest cost producers of any good. To see why, consider the following highly simplified example. Assume that two countries, which can be called Mexico and the United States, both produce only two products, vegetables and computers, and use only one factor of production, labor, in the production process. The labor required to produce each product differs in the two countries, as shown in Table 16–2.

Note that, in this example, it takes fewer labor days to produce either product in the United States. Nevertheless, the United States will be better off if it buys vegetables from Mexico and sells computers in return, even though it can produce vegetables at home with less labor. In the United

---

2. It is worth noting that official export data often are understated in developing countries. Because the data cover only goods exported through official channels, they omit goods exported through parallel markets in countries like Ethiopia, where civil war prevailed until the early 1990s; Tanzania, where inflation and a controlled exchange rate made export unprofitable through the 1980s; and Colombia and Bolivia, where illegal drugs are important exports.

TABLE 16–2	**PRODUCTION COSTS AND COMPARATIVE ADVANTAGE**	
	MEXICO	**UNITED STATES**
LABOR-DAYS TO PRODUCE		
VEGETABLES (1 TON)	5	4
COMPUTERS (1)	30	20
RELATIVE PRICE (TONS OF VEGETABLES PER COMPUTER)	6	5

States, a computer sells for the equivalent of 5 tons of vegetables, since each would take 20 labor-days to produce.[3] In Mexico, however, one computer sells for 6 tons of vegetables, since each would take 30 labor-days to produce. Therefore, the United States would be better off by selling its computers in Mexico and receiving more vegetables in return for home consumption. So, if labor is shifted away from farming and into computer production, U.S. firms can produce enough computers to satisfy domestic demand and export to Mexico, and U.S. consumers can eat more vegetables. But here is the most surprising result: Mexico also is made better off through the trade. Without trade, Mexico would have to produce 6 tons of vegetables to buy one computer in the home market. By selling to the United States, however, Mexico needs to give up only 5 tons of vegetables to get one computer. Thus, Mexico is better off by switching its labor into producing more vegetables and selling them to the United States.

The important point of this example, and the core of comparative advantage, is that both countries can gain from trade whenever the **relative prices** of commodities in each country differ in the absence of trade. Once the two countries begin to trade, the relative prices of commodities will begin to shift until they are the same in the two countries. In the example, the relative price of 1 ton of vegetables in terms of computers would settle somewhere between five and six (the relative prices prevailing before trade in the United States and Mexico, respectively). The final trade price, which can be called the **world price,** will be closer to the initial price in the market of the country whose economy is larger. In our example, the final price in both countries will settle closer to 5 tons of vegetables per computer. One implication is that small countries benefit more from trade because the relative price of commodities shifts more, and therefore the gains from trade are greater. To see this, consider an extreme case in which the U.S. economy is so large and trade with Mexico so small that U.S.

3. If each ton of vegetables requires 4 labor-days to produce, then it takes 5 tons of vegetables to absorb the same labor as one computer, which uses 20 labor-days. This formula for calculating relative prices works in this oversimplified example because labor is the only input into production.

prices do not shift at all. In this case, the United States does not gain from trade (nor does it lose), while Mexico would gain to the full extent of the price difference.

The theory of comparative advantage is posed here in the very simple form developed by David Ricardo during the nineteenth century: two countries, two goods, and only one factor of production (labor). Some of the complexities of the real world can be incorporated into the theory, however. A trading world of many countries can be handled by taking the home country, say, Kenya, and treating the rest of the world as its trading partner. Some of the complexities of many goods will be addressed in Chapter 18. Swedish economists Eli Heckscher and Bertil Ohlin expanded the theory during the first half of the twentieth century to deal with two factors of production, such as labor and capital. Under certain conditions the Heckscher-Ohlin theory can be extended to include more factors of production. The Heckscher-Ohlin model leads to an extremely important result: A country exports products that use its abundant factors of production more intensively and imports products that require relatively more of its scarce factors.

The implications of this more general approach to comparative advantage are encapsulated in Figure 16–1. The economy of the **home country** is divided into **exportable goods,** such as vegetables, that are produced using relatively land- and labor-intensive methods, and **importable goods,** such as computers, produced using relatively capital-intensive methods. As shown in the diagram, the home country is relatively well endowed with land and labor, so the production frontier is skewed to the right, depicting the country's greater capacity to produce vegetables than computers. The country's collective utility in consuming these goods is represented by the community indifference curves.

Without trade, the home country achieves its greatest utility by producing and consuming at point *A*, the tangency of the indifference curve I and the production frontier. The slope at *A* determines the domestic relative price of vegetables in terms of computers. Assume that the rest of the world is better endowed with capital than labor and land relative to the endowments of the home country and that world consumers have tastes broadly similar to those of the home country. Then, in world markets, the relatively higher production of computers compared to the demand for computers will drive its price lower than in the home country; and the relatively lower production of vegetables compared to the demand for vegetables will drive their price higher than in the home country. Since only relative prices matter, these two statements mean the same thing: In world markets, the price of vegetables in terms of computers will be higher than in the home country.

This difference in relative prices between the home country and the rest of the world presents an opportunity for the home country to improve

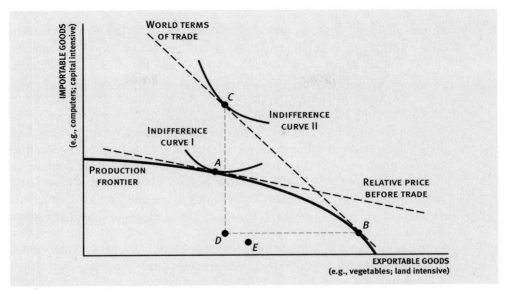

FIGURE 16–1   GAINS FROM TRADE. Before trade, a country both produces and consumes at a point like *A*. With trade, a country produces at a point like *B* and can increase its consumption of both goods and move to a higher indifference curve at *C*.

its welfare through trade. **With trade,** the country, taking advantage of its factor endowment, can produce more vegetables and fewer computers and sell vegetables on the world market at the higher relative price, the world terms of trade in Figure 16–1. In producing more vegetables, the home country moves along the production frontier from *A* to *B*, where the terms-of-trade line is tangent to the production frontier. With vegetables to export, the country then can import computers and consume more of *both* goods. The consumption point *C* is determined by the tangency of the terms of trade line with indifference curve II. The country now exports *BD* of vegetables and imports *DC* of computers, given by the trade triangle *BCD*. As indifference curve II is above and to the right (northeast) of curve I, the country is better off with trade than without it.

The general result is this: Any country, whatever its size and stage of development, can benefit from trade. This is true for large countries like China and India, small countries such as Ghana and Belgium, high-income countries like the United States and Japan, and low income countries such as Mozambique and Haiti. As long as relative prices at home differ from those on world markets, countries can increase their aggregate welfare by engaging in international trade.

However, although every country can gain from trade in the aggregate, *not all individuals or groups within each country necessarily will gain.* In the vegetables-computers example, vegetable producers gain from trade because they sell more vegetables at a higher price. The consumers of computers also gain, because they can consume more at a lower price. But, once trade begins, computer manufacturers face competition from imports and hence sell fewer computers at a lower price than before, while consumers of vegetables must pay higher prices. Comparative advantage theory tells us that the aggregate gains outweigh the losses for the country as a whole, but that may be cold comfort to producers of computers and consumers of vegetables. The losers from trade may share in the gains if suppliers of capital and labor to the computer industry find it easy to shift into the production of vegetables or if mechanisms exist to transfer income from the gainers to the losers. In most countries, neither condition holds to a sufficient degree, especially in the short to medium term. Therein lies the seed of political opposition to policies that promote freer trade, even though all countries gain from it.

However suggestive the theory of comparative advantage may be for developing countries, it is only the beginning of an explanation of development through international trade. The theory fails to explain growth and structural change because it excludes changes over time in the amount of capital, land, and labor available to producers, as well as improvements in the quality or productivity of those factors. The theory provides no mechanism to explain how economies evolve over time and change the composition of their output, consumption, and trade. It also does not capture the two-way relationship between trade and development. In one direction, as we have seen, increased trade can lead to improved welfare and higher incomes. In the other direction, advances in development go hand in hand with more highly skilled labor and higher-quality capital and machinery, opening up new opportunities for increased trade. To better understand how trade and development affect each other, it is necessary to adopt an eclectic approach, using trade theory where it is useful but reverting frequently to other kinds of analysis. The unifying theme is trade strategies: How different approaches to trade, favoring different types of exports and imports, lead to different kinds of economic development. The first such strategy, **primary-export-led growth** is examined in the balance of this chapter.

Primary Exports as an Engine of Growth

Before the 1950s, primary produce exports were seen as central to the development process and as the basic engine for economic growth. For most developing countries, following comparative advantage meant exporting food and raw materials, importing machinery and capital goods, and permitting structural change and income growth to take place as a consequence. The United States, Canada, Australia, New Zealand, Denmark, and other countries had achieved higher levels of income at least partly based on their natural resource endowments; and Argentina had gone quite far in that direction. More recently, many developing countries have tried alternative trade strategies, including import substitution and export of labor-intensive manufactures, both discussed in Chapter 18. Nevertheless, primary product exports have remained central to development strategies in a wide range of developing countries, including Botswana, Colombia, Mexico, Ghana, Nigeria, Indonesia, Malaysia, and the Philippines. Primary-export-led growth brings three broad types of benefits to developing countries: improved utilization of existing factors of production, expanded factor endowments, and linkage effects.

IMPROVED FACTOR UTILIZATION

To begin with, primary-export-led growth can propel an economy both to use more of the available factors of production, and use those factors more efficiently. For example, an isolated country, shut off from world markets, might have substantial amounts of land either being used inefficiently or not at all. We saw in the example in Figure 16–1 how a reallocation of the factors of production in a land-abundant, capital-short country could lead to higher income. In this example, all factors of production are fully employed at the outset, as indicated by production taking place at point A along the production frontier. Even with full employment, however, by reallocating resources to produce and export more land-intensive goods (such as vegetables, rice, or cocoa) and import more manufactures (computers, cloth, or chemicals), the country is able to consume more of both kinds of commodities and increase its welfare. The country moves along its production frontier, from A to B in Figure 16–1. Land, the abundant factor of production, is utilized more intensively with trade in the sense that its productivity (the yield per hectare) rises as labor shifts from manufacturing to agriculture.

If land and labor are not fully employed before trade begins, a country can reap even larger gains from trade. This case is represented in Figure 16–1 by points D and E, both of which lie within the production frontier. Trade helps stimulate the economy by bringing this idle land, labor, and capital into the production process so that the country can produce more of the exportable good and possibly more of the importable good as well. This is represented in Figure 16–1 by the economy moving from point D or E to point B on the production possibility frontier.

This static model of the gains from trade can be applied to the development of several countries (at least with a little imagination and some judicious simplification). In the nineteenth century, the United States and

Canada had abundant land in relation to their endowments of labor and capital. Much of this land was idle, so both countries produced at points within their production frontiers. British demand for cotton and wheat enabled North America to bring this land into production and move toward the production frontier by growing cotton and wheat for export, while importing the manufactured goods it could not produce as efficiently as Britain. Much of the great western migration in both the United States and Canada was essentially a process of bringing large tracts of land and other natural resources into the production process. New Zealand and to some extent Australia followed a similar pattern.

Burmese economist Hla Myint has observed that, when parts of Africa and Asia came under European colonization, the consequent expansion of their international trade enabled those areas to utilize their land or labor more intensively to produce tropical foodstuffs such as rice, cocoa, and oil palm for export. Myint applies Adam Smith's term **vent for surplus** to these cases (as well as the cases of surplus land in the Americas and Australia).[4] The concept applies to a situation in which a country has the capacity to produce more than it can sell on the domestic market. Trade enables the country to employ either land or labor more fully and sell the goods produced with its "surplus" land and labor to the rest of the world.

However, when underutilized land or labor was vented as a result of colonization, as was typical during the nineteenth century, the gains from trade often were purchased at a high cost to the indigenous population. Land that may have been idle or utilized at low productivity frequently was taken by force from its occupiers, whether these were American Indians, the Kikuyu and other peoples of East Africa, or Javanese farmers. Colonizers also used taxation and coercion to keep plantations and mines supplied with low-cost labor in many parts of Africa and Asia. And, especially in British India, the movement along a production frontier toward greater production for export often resulted in cheaper imports that competed directly with traditional handicraft industries, displaying artisans and workers. While the colonial powers could have distributed the gains from trade in ways that benefited indigenous populations enough to compensate them for the losses they bore, often this was not the case.

EXPANDED FACTOR ENDOWMENTS

In addition to helping an economy use its *current* factor endowments more intensively and more efficiently, the expansion of primary product exports can lead to the accumulation of additional factors of production,

4. Hla Myint, "The 'Classical Theory' of International Trade and the Underdeveloped Countries," *Economic Journal,* 68 (1959), 317–37.

especially capital and labor. More specifically, primary-export-led growth can help spur increases in foreign investment, domestic savings, labor, and skilled personnel to complement the fixed factors of production, land and natural resources. In the context of Figure 16–1, the country would be able to produce more of both exportable and importable goods as its entire production frontier shifted out.

Once the profitable opportunities in tropical agriculture or natural resources become apparent, foreign investment is likely to be attracted to the country, first to exploit the country's comparative advantage and, perhaps eventually, to invest in other sectors. The influx of foreign investors has been a familiar story in all mineral-exporting industries and in many tropical-product industries based on plantation agriculture. Well-known examples include Standard Oil in Venezuela, British Petroleum in Iran, Anaconda in Chile, Alcoa in Jamaica, Lever Brothers and Firestone in West Africa, and United Fruit in Central America. Foreign capital frequently has brought migrant labor to the mines and plantations, as occurred in Southern and West Africa, Malaysia, Sri Lanka, and many other places. Both foreign investment and migrant labor, of course, were prominent features in the development in the "new lands" of the Americas and Australia in the nineteenth century. The emergence of new lines of export production also is likely to open up many new profitable outlets for investment that foreign capital will not completely satisfy, whether in the export sector itself or in related industries. These opportunities represent an outward shift in the demand for domestic savings and should induce some supply response and further increase investment in the economy. At least some of the earnings from primary product exports usually are retained as savings (often by the government) that can finance new investment opportunities.

LINKAGE EFFECTS

Another potential benefit from primary product exports is the possibility of stimulating production in other, related sectors. Indeed, the very notion of export-led growth implies that exports would lead to more broad-based economic growth. Several types of linkages to the rest of the economy are possible, including to upstream or downstream industries, increased production of consumer goods, enhanced infrastructure, more widely available skilled labor, and increased government revenues. Albert O. Hirschman coined the phrase **backward linkage** for the situation in which the growth of one industry (such as textiles) stimulates domestic production of an upstream input (such as cotton or dyestuffs).[5] Backward

5. Albert O. Hirschman, *The Strategy of Economic Development* (New Haven, CT: Yale University Press, 1958), Chap. 6.

linkages, which were described in Chapter 3, are particularly effective when the using industry becomes so large that supplying industries can achieve economies of scale of their own, lower their production costs, and become more competitive in domestic or even export markets. The wheat industry worked this way in North America in the nineteenth century; it created sufficient demand for transportation equipment (especially railway rolling stock) and farm machinery that these industries became established in the United States. In Peru, the rapid expansion of the fishmeal industry during the 1950s and 1960s led directly to the production of fishing boats and processing equipment. In fact, Peru's boat-building industry became efficient enough to export fishing craft to neighboring countries. Growth in the processing-equipment industry gave Peru a start on one kind of capital-goods production that can supply a wide range of food-processing industries.[6]

As these examples suggest, one of the most common backward linkages for primary product exports is between food processing for export (rice, vegetable oils, tea) and a processing-equipment industry. Three conditions contribute to these kinds of linkages. First, production initially should take place in small units that use simple technology to give the fledgling equipment industry a change to master production techniques and learn its trade by repetitive production. Second, the export industry should grow steadily over time and thus promise a continuing market for its suppliers. Third, the export sector should be large enough to enable equipment manufacturers eventually to achieve scale economies. These conditions were met in fishmeal and can be met in several agricultural fields. But they generally are not satisfied in mining, which typically requires complex equipment for large-scale investments that must be implemented in the shortest time possible, conditions under which domestic infant industries are unlikely to thrive.

Expanded production of primary products also can stimulate **forward linkages** by making lower-cost primary goods available as inputs into other industries. In many developing countries, agricultural products are used as inputs to the food processing industry. Senegal and the Gambia process raw groundnuts (peanuts) into shelled nuts and oil. In Indonesia, forest products are used in furniture production, and Malaysia exports processed rubber and palm oil stemming from its plantation agriculture. Forward linkages can develop for mining and mineral products (i.e., petroleum refining, plastics, or steel) as well, but the more complex production techniques and demand for highly specialized capital and labor make it difficult for most developing countries to compete in these activities.

6. Michael Roemer, *Fishing for Growth: Export-Led Development in Peru, 1950–1967* (Cambridge, MA: Harvard University Press, 1970).

For example, Venezuela is using its iron ore, natural gas, and hydroelectric power to produce steel, partly for export and partly for domestic use. If, and only if, the domestic steel is cheaper than imported steel, it may stimulate further forward linkages to steel-using industries like construction, transport equipment, processing equipment, and oil derricks.

Consumption linkages develop indirectly as the higher income earned from primary product exports leads to increased demand for a wide range of consumption goods. This type of linkage is most likely to operate if, as a result of expanded exports, a large segment labor force is paid wages above previous levels and increased demand centers on mass-produced consumer goods like processed foods, clothing, footwear, furniture, radios, televisions, packaging materials, and so forth. The North American wheat industry, with its extensive endowment of land, high labor productivity, and egalitarian income distribution based on family farms, successfully stimulated local consumer goods industries. Unfortunately, these conditions are not always present in developing countries. Neither plantation agriculture in Africa, with its large labor force but low wages, nor mining industries, which pay high wages but employ relatively few workers, are able to generate adequate demand to stimulate local consumer goods industries.

Infrastructure linkages arise when the provision of overhead capital—roads, railroads, power, water, telecommunications—for the export industry lowers costs and opens new production opportunities for other industries. The classic example is the railroad in the nineteenth-century United States. Built to connect the East Coast with the grain-producing states of the Midwest, it lowered the cost of transporting both input and output for the manufacturing industry in the wheat-exporting region.[7] Harbors and rail and road networks built to facilitate the export of copper in southern Africa, cocoa and timber in Ghana, tea in India, and beef in Argentina have had similar effects on domestic manufacturing industries. Power projects made economically feasible by export industries, such as the Akosombo Dam in Ghana and the Guri Dam in Venezuela, provide cheap power that may encourage the domestic manufacturing industry.

Primary export sectors also may stimulate **human capital linkages** through the development of local entrepreneurs and skilled laborers. The growth of the Peruvian fishmeal industry, with its many small plants, encouraged scores of new entrepreneurs and trained many skilled workers to operate and maintain equipment. These resources then became available for subsequent development. Rubber, palm oil, and tin production for ex-

7. Albert Fishlow, *American Railroads and the Transformation of the Antebellum Economy* (Cambridge, MA: Harvard University Press, 1965); and Robert W. Fogel, "Railroads as an Analogy of the Space Effort: Some Economic Aspects," in Bruce Mazlish, ed., *Space Program: An Exploration in Historical Analogy* (Cambridge, MA: MIT Press, 1965).

port encouraged entrepreneurs in Malaysia, and small-scale farming for export has proven an outlet for entrepreneurial talent in several African countries.

The best case for petroleum, mining, and some traditional agricultural crops is the **fiscal linkage.** Governments can capture large shares of the economic rents (higher-than-necessary profits) from these exports as taxes or dividends and use the revenue to finance development in other sectors. Governments can choose to spend the revenues on health or education programs or new investment projects, or they can choose to reduce taxes and increase after-tax income. Although a government obviously is better off with than without such revenues, the effectiveness of these revenues in stimulating self-sustaining development in the rest of the economy depends critically on the kinds of programs and interventions the government undertakes.[8]

Recent Empirical Evidence on Primary-Export-Led Growth

Since the 1950s, some economists and the leaders of many developing countries have argued that, despite the possible benefits, primary exports other than petroleum cannot effectively lead the way to economic development. The most common arguments have been that the markets for primary products grow too slowly to fuel growth, the prices received for these commodities have been declining, earnings are too unstable, and linkages do not work. We examine each of these arguments in the next section. Here, we examine the direct empirical question, What has been the relationship between primary exports and economic growth in recent decades? A few resource-rich developing countries have performed relatively well, including Botswana, Malaysia, Indonesia, Tunisia, and Mauritius. However, many others have grown very slowly or not at all, such as Nigeria, Zambia, Argentina, Burma, Egypt, Venezuela, and Colombia. At

---

8. The impact of export industries on economic development through various forms of linkages is the focus of a body of literature called **staple theory,** which tries to explain differing impact by differing characteristics of production technologies. For examples of the genre, see Robert E. Baldwin, *Economic Development and Export Growth: A Study of Northern Rhodesia, 1920–1960* (Los Angeles: University of California Press, 1966); Douglass C. North, "Location Theory and Regional Economic Growth," *Journal of Political Economy,* 63 (1955), 243–85; Roemer, *Fishing for Growth;* and Melville H. Watkins, "A Staple Theory of Economic Growth," *Canadian Journal of Economics and Political Science,* 29 (1963), 141–58. Perhaps the ultimate expression of production characteristics and linkages as determinants of development patterns is the essay by Albert O. Hirschman, "A Generalized Linkage Approach to Development, with Special Reference to Staples," in Manning Nash, ed., *Essays on Economic Development and Cultural Change* (Chicago: University of Chicago Press, 1977), pp. 67–98.

the same time, many of the fastest growing Asian economies are resource poor, including Japan, Korea, Taiwan, Hong Kong, and Singapore. Alan Gelb explored this seeming paradox in the specific case of petroleum exports in *Oil Windfalls: Blessing or Curse?*[9]

Harvard economists Jeffrey Sachs and Andrew Warner went a step further with a systematic econometric exploration of the relationship between primary product exports and economic growth in a sample of 95 countries from around the world between 1971 and 1989.[10] Somewhat surprisingly, they found strong evidence showing that, on average, countries with substantial primary product exports have grown much more *slowly* than resource-poor countries since the early 1970s. More specifically, they found that, on average, an increase of 10 percentage points in the ratio of primary exports to GDP was associated with a 0.7 percentage point slower annual rate of growth of per capita income. Figure 16–2

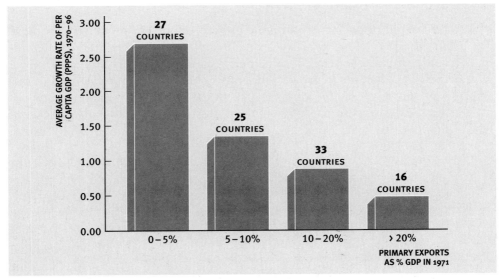

FIGURE 16–2 NATURAL RESOURCE ABUNDANCE AND ECONOMIC GROWTH. Countries with small amounts of primary product exports have grown more quickly than resource-abundant countries.
Source: Updated from Steven Radelet, Jeffrey Sachs, and Jong-Wha Lee, "Economic Growth in Asia," Harvard Institute for International Development, May 1997. Data are from World Bank, *World Development Indicators* (electronic version) and *Penn World Tables* mark 5.6 (website version).

9. Alan Gelb, *Oil Windfalls: Blessing or Curse?* (New York: Oxford University Press for the World Bank, 1988). The disappointing performance of several petroleum-exporting countries also is explored by R. M Auty in *Resource-Based Industrialization: Sowing the Oil in Eight Developing Countries* (New York: Oxford University Press, 1990).

10. Jeffrey Sachs and Andrew Warner, "Natural Resource Abundance and Economic Growth," Harvard Institute for International Development discussion paper 517a, October 1995.

shows the basic negative relationship over a slightly longer time period (1970–96) for 101 countries. For the 27 countries in which primary exports (in 1971) were 5 percent of GDP or less, annual per capita growth averaged 2.7 percent. By contrast, annual per capita growth averaged less than 0.5 percent in the 16 countries with primary exports equal to 20 percent or more of GDP.

How can resource abundance be associated with slower rates of economic growth? After all, primary product exports should raise aggregate wealth and allow a country to increase both its imports and its investment and possibly create some of the linkages described earlier. The next section examines several possible explanations for this apparent puzzle.

Barriers to Primary-Export-Led Growth

SLUGGISH DEMAND GROWTH

In a world of balanced economic growth, exporters of primary products could expect their exports to expand at the same pace as the national income of the countries that import primary products and also expect their own income to grow at that rate. The world is not balanced in this way, however, and economists skeptical of primary export potential have cited structural shifts in the industrial world that seem to condemn third world primary exports to slower growth than industrial world income.[11]

One well-known structural shift, captured by **Engel's law,** is that the demand for staple foods and beverages grows more slowly than income (see Chapter 3). Therefore, as the income of food importers continues to grow, the proportion of their income they spend on food gradually will fall. For high-income countries, the income elasticity of demand for food probably is below one half, implying that the demand for food (including food imported from developing countries) tends to lag far behind income growth.

Technological change in manufacturing also works against the consumption of raw materials, in two ways. First, new technologies and improved machinery help firms reduce wastage so that less raw material is needed in the production process. Modern looms waste less cotton yarn, sawmills turn wood shavings into boards, and so forth. Second, new technologies allow for the substitution of synthetics for raw materials. For example, synthetic rubber has replaced natural rubber, fiber optics

---

11. An early and articulate proponent of this view is Ragnar Nurske, *Equilibrium Growth in the World Economy* (Cambridge, MA: Harvard University Press, 1961), Chaps. 10 and 11.

has substantially reduced the use of copper in wire, and plastic pipes have replaced iron and copper pipe. Metal cans contain less tin, textile production use more synthetic fibers, and automobiles use fiberglass instead of steel.

Aggregate data on primary product production and trade confirm this gloomy picture. From 1963 to 1986, while world industrial production grew by 3.9 percent a year, the consumption of natural raw materials grew by only 1.5 percent a year.[12] The share of nonfuel raw materials and food imports in total industrial-country imports has fallen substantially, from 40 percent in 1965 to about 15 percent in 1996. With imports in the industrial world growing at 11 percent a year in value terms, imports of nonfuel raw materials and foodstuffs have grown by only 7.8 percent a year over more than 30 years, too slow to fuel economic development in primary exporting countries.[13]

Despite the broad trend, there are likely to be encouraging prospects for some primary commodities and some primary product exporting countries. After all, new technologies can *increase* the demand for raw materials. The invention of the railroad substantially increased the demand for iron and steel, and the development of the electric light bulb and other electric appliances led to a boom in the demand for copper. The demand for petroleum, rubber, aluminum, newsprint, plywood, and vegetable oils also received a substantial boost from technological innovation or from high-income elasticities of demand in the early part of the century. Several commodities have experienced substantial export growth rates since 1960: exports of sorghum, wheat, fish, soybeans, vegetable oils, oilseed cake and meal, fertilizers, timber, alumina and aluminum, and nickel all grew by at least 5 percent a year for at least 20 years since 1960, valued at constant prices.[14]

Nevertheless, with slower growth in the industrial countries, the impact of Engel's law, and materials-saving innovations, it seems unlikely that the high-income countries will import enough tropical foods and raw materials to fuel an era of rapid development for primary product exporters over the next few decades. Some commodities will face brisk demand growth and some countries will benefit substantially from producing such exports, but many others will benefit far less.

12. World Bank, *Global Economic Prospects and the Developing Countries* (Washington, DC: World Bank, 1994), pp. 39–40.

13. *World Development Report 1990,* Tables 14 and 15; and *World Development Report 1994,* Tables 13 and 14.

14. World Bank, *Commodity Trade and Price Trends,* 1987–88 ed. (Washington, DC: World Bank, 1988); and World Bank, *Price Prospects for Primary Commodities, 1990–2005* (Washington, DC: World Bank, 1993).

PRIMARY-EXPORT-LED GROWTH IN MALAYSIA[15]

When Malaysia achieved independence in 1957, it was close to the archetypical single-crop economy: Rubber accounted for well over half its export earnings and about a quarter of Malaysia's gross domestic product. The second largest export, tin, earned between 10 and 20 percent of total export revenues. Neither commodity faced a bright future: Demand for rubber was constrained by the availability of cheap synthetic substitutes and the tin market was plagued by production exceeding likely demand. It would have been natural for the new country's planners to fall prey to the dominant export pessimism of the day and build a development strategy around import substitution.

But Malaysia enjoys a rich resource base with a relatively small population, and its development strategy was based on its comparative advantage. The country invested in research to reduce the costs of growing rubber and maintained its competitiveness with synthetic rubber. Measured relative to import prices, rubber export revenues fell by only 4 percent from 1960 to 1987. At the same time, Malaysia invested in planting oil palm and this new export grew in volume by 15 percent a year from 1960 to 1987. Petroleum exports grew by a steady 8 percent a year, and exports of logs and timber expanded by a total of 82 percent from 1960 to 1987. During this period, Malaysia also invested in manufacturing for export. Although primary products earned over 90 percent of export revenues in 1965, by 1998 manufactures has grown sufficiently to account for 79 percent of export revenues. Thanks to investments in both primary and manufactured exports, Malaysia's total export earnings, deflated by import prices (that is, its income terms of trade; see the next section) grew by 7 percent a year for three decades.

As a consequence of its investments in primary and manufactured exports, Malaysia has sustained rapid economic growth, over 6 percent a year from 1965 to 1998. Its per capita income of $8,000 in purchasing power parity terms puts Malaysia on a par with Mexico and Greece, even though, in the mid-1960s, its average income was close to that of Zambia and El Salvador. Malaysia's diversified export base, efficient production, and high income provide the resources for continued rapid development.

15. Data are from the *World Development Report 1990;* World Bank, *World Development Indicators* 2000; and IMF, *International Financial Statistics Yearbook 1990.*

DECLINING TERMS OF TRADE

An influential school of thought, led by Argentine economist Raul Prebisch and Hans Singer of the University of Sussex, has argued that, over the long run, prices for commodity exports on world markets will fall relative to prices of manufactured goods.[16] Since most developing countries export primary products and import manufactured goods, such a shift in relative prices would mean that, over time, developing countries would have to export more primary products to import the same amount of manufactured products. One implication of a fall in relative prices, combined with weak growth in demand for primary products in high-income countries, is that countries relying solely on primary product exports are likely to lag behind in the development process. This prominent view came to be known as **export pessimism** and was the root of arguments in favor of import substitution strategies, discussed in Chapter 18.

Empirical tests of the Prebisch-Singer hypothesis have had mixed results. The most commonly used measure of relative prices of traded goods is the commodity or **net barter terms of trade,** T_n. T_n is a ratio of two indexes: (1) the average price of a country's exports (P_e) and (2) the average price of its imports (P_m). The commodity terms of trade rise if export prices rise relative to import prices. In his 1950 monograph, Prebisch used data on the terms of trade for Great Britain from the 1870s to the 1930s that seemed to support his contention. Prebisch's data were imperfect, however, and inadvertently biased in favor of his hypothesis. In subsequent years, other economists have tried to replicate Prebisch's results using different data sets and various periods of time, with conflicting results.[17] Georgetown University economist John Cuddington and associates used improved data to measure the terms of trade for 24 primary commodities, excluding oil, for the period from 1900 to 1988.[18] Figure 16–3 shows the results. The net barter terms of trade for primary commodities fluctuated widely during the period. Except for a precipitous drop in the early 1920s and again after the mid-1970s, no statistically sig-

16. United Nations (Raul Prebisch), *The Economic Development of Latin America and Its Principal Problems* (Lake Success, NY: United Nations, 1950); Hans W. Singer, "The Distribution of Trade between Investing and Borrowing Countries," *American Economic Review,* 40 (May 1950), 473–85.

17. For a summary of these results, see Bela Balassa, "Outward Orientation," in Hollis Chenery and T. N. Srinivasan, *Handbook of Development Economics,* Vol. 2 (Amsterdam: Elsevier, 1989), pp. 1653–59.

18. The numerator of T_n, P_e, is a geometric average of the price indexes for 24 nonfuel commodities; the denominator P_m is an index of unit values for manufactured goods. See John T. Cuddington and Carlos M. Urzua, "Trends and Cycles in the Net Barter Terms of Trade: A New Approach," *Economic Journal,* 99 (June 1989), 426–42.

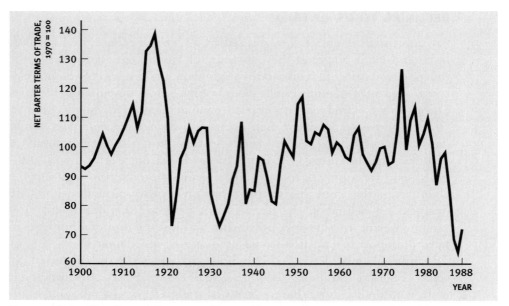

FIGURE 16–3   NET BARTER TERMS OF TRADE, PRIMARY COMMODITIES, 1900–88. A geometric index for 24 commodities, excluding fuels, shows no trend over 88 years, despite wide fluctuations and a sharp drop in 1921.
Source: John Cuddington and Hong Wei, "An Empirical Analysis of the Prebisch-Singer Hypothesis: Aggregation, Model Selection and Implications," in Sir Hans Singer, Neelambar Hatti, and Rameshwar Tandon, eds., *Export-Led versus Balanced Growth in the 1990s,* New World Series, Vol. 13 (Delhi: B. R. Publishing Corp., 1998).

nificant downward trend could be found in the net barter terms of trade.[19] If oil and other fuel prices are included in the index, and there is no reason why they should not be, they would reinforce this conclusion. Some econometricians disagree, however, and, using similar data but different techniques, find significant declines in the net barter terms of trade of at least 0.7 percent per annum.[20]

Although the Prebisch-Singer hypothesis is properly addressed by looking at commodity data, the overall terms of trade for a country (including all export products) is what really matters in its development. Figure 16–4 shows two different measures of the net barter terms of trade since 1950. When oil exporters are included, the terms of trade of developing countries rose dramatically after 1972 and remained high, despite the fall of oil prices during the 1980s and early 1990s. But the terms of trade for non-oil-exporting developing countries declined over the period by over 30 percent. Con-

19. This is the conclusion reached by Cuddington and Urzua.

20. These studies are summarized by David Sapsford and V. N. Balasubramanyam. "The Long-Run Behavior of the Relative Price of Primary Commodities: Statistical Evidence and Policy Implications," *World Development,* 22, no. 11 (November 1994), 1737–45.

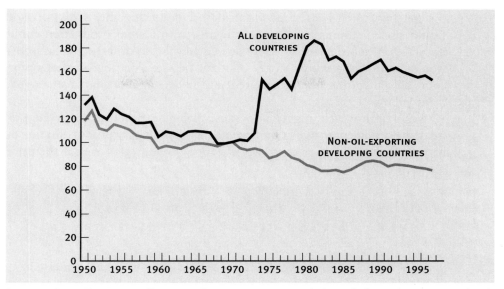

FIGURE 16–4   NET BARTER TERMS OF TRADE, 1950–97. Excluding oil, the net barter terms of trade for developing countries has declined steadily since 1950.
Source: IMF, *International Financial Statistics, 1999.*

clusions about the Prebisch-Singer hypothesis depend critically on the commodities included and the time period under investigation. Although the very long-term trend is not clear, the evidence indicates a steady, gradual decline in the terms of trade for non-oil commodity exporters since 1950.

However, the net barter terms of trade tell us little about income or welfare, which ought to be the basis for judging changes in world trade conditions. A better measure of the income effect of price changes would be the **income terms of trade,** T_i, which measures the purchasing power of exports by comparing an index of export *revenues* to an index of import *prices*. This is equivalent to the net barter terms of trade multiplied by the volume of exports (Q_e), or $T_i = P_e Q_e / P_m = T_n Q_e$. The basic idea is that, if export revenues (not just prices) rise faster than import prices, the exporting country has the capacity to import more goods and is better off. The income terms of trade can behave very differently from the net barter terms of trade if changes in export prices also affect export volumes. If, for example, Zambia increases its copper exports and causes the world price to fall, total copper revenue could increase. This would happen if prices fell less than in proportion to the increase in volume (implying that the absolute value of the demand elasticity for Zambian copper is greater than 1).[21] In this case,

21. The price elasticity of demand for the exports of any one country is $e_i = e_w / s_i$, where e_w is the worldwide price elasticity of demand for the commodity and s_i is the market share of the country. Even if e_w is quite low, say, -0.3, if the country's market share is below 30 percent, which would be quite large, the price elasticity facing that country would be more negative than -1.

the net barter terms of trade would fall, but the income terms of trade would rise. Assuming the resources shifted into copper production could not have produced goods or services of equal value in other sectors, Zambia would be unambiguously better off than before. For non-oil developing countries as a group, the income terms of trade *rose* about 6 percent a year from 1950 to 1997.

Export prices also might fall because of higher productivity in the primary exporting country. An increase in Zambia's copper production due to higher productivity may cause world copper prices to fall. But if the price

GHANA: A CASE OF ARRESTED DEVELOPMENT[22]

At independence in 1957, Ghana probably was the richest country in sub-Saharan Africa, with a per capita income close to $500 (in 1983 prices). By 1983, its per capita income had fallen to $340, below that of Kenya, Sudan, and Pakistan. Many things went wrong for Ghana in that quarter century, but the failure of export policy was crucial.[23] Like Malaysia, Ghana was a one-export country in the late 1950s: Cocoa earned almost 60 percent of export revenues and represented almost a fifth of GDP. In contrast to Malaysia, Ghana under its charismatic leader, Kwame Nkrumah, turned sharply away from its export base to invest in import-substituting industries. In this it failed. Had exports in agriculture, forestry, and mining been maintained, Ghana might have earned sufficient revenue to make a gradual transition to import substitution. But so abrupt was the disinvestment in primary exports that cocoa exports halved in volume from the early 1960s to the middle 1980s, and other exports did not make up that deficit.

Ghana's failure to utilize its generous export base is made more vivid by the performance of its next-door neighbor, the Ivory Coast. With virtually the same resource base, the Ivory Coast invested enough to maintain its coffee exports and then diversified into cocoa (just as Ghana was disinvesting), wood, and other primary products. Over two decades, export volume more than doubled, and per capita GDP grew to nearly twice that of Ghana, despite substantial immigration from less prosperous neighboring countries.

22. *World Development Report 1990;* and World Bank, *World Tables 1989–1990.*

23. On Ghana's development policies, see Michael Roemer, "Ghana 1950–1980: Missed Opportunities," in Arnold Harberger, ed., *World Economic Growth* (San Francisco: ICS Press, 1984), pp. 201–26.

decline is less than the percentage rise in the productivity (Z_e) in copper production, the factors engaged in copper mining would be better off than before. The **single factoral terms of trade,** T_S, measures factor income relative to factor inputs and import prices, or $T_S = (P_e/P_m)Z_e = T_n Z_e$. Note that a rise in either the income or single factoral terms of trade implies an improvement in income or welfare relative to that country's previous situation. But if, as often is the case, either index rises less than export volume, this also implies that exporting countries are sharing part of the potential gains with importing countries, as Prebisch and Singer suggest. Although this measure is intuitively appealing, it rarely is used since data on productivity are not readily available for most developing countries.

FLUCTUATING EXPORT EARNINGS

Not only do the net barter terms of trade show a secular decline, they also fluctuate considerably, as is evident from Figures 16–3 and 16–4. If not well managed, instability in export earnings can be transmitted to the domestic economy and make domestic demand unstable and investment more risky. Fluctuating domestic demand, coupled with uncertain access to imported materials, would discourage investors and reduce economic growth. Export instability may also confuse the signals conveyed by relative prices (since relative prices would regularly fluctuate), so that investors are unsure about the most productive long-term investments. This **signaling effect** raises the capital-output ratio and reduces the growth rate for any given level of investment.

One theory of consumption, the **permanent-income hypothesis** (see Chapter 11), suggests the opposite result, however. Income earners count on some level of relatively certain annual income and try to maintain consumption patterns based largely on that *permanent,* or long-run, income. The more income fluctuates around this permanent level, the more will be saved to maintain the permanent level of consumption through good times and bad.[24] If fluctuating export earnings transmit income instability to households, they will save more, so the country will be able to finance more investment and grow faster. Which effect is likely to dominate?

Economist David Dawe tested these propositions using a measure of export instability that compares deviations in export earnings around a five-year trend to gross domestic product. Among a sample of 85 countries over 15 years (1970–85), Dawe found that export instability corresponds with an increase in the ratio of investment to GDP, consistent with the permanent income hypothesis. However, countries with greater instability have lower

24. Odin Knudsen and Andrew Parnes, *Trade Instability and Economic Development* (Lexington, MA: Heath Lexington Books, 1975), pp. 81–128.

GDP growth rates.[25] The reason, he suggests, may be that the signaling effect is especially strong and so reduces the productivity of all investment, even as the permanent income effect increases the quantity of investment.

This finding poses a dilemma for development strategy. If its comparative advantage lies in primary exports with fluctuating prices in world markets, will a country's growth be enhanced by following comparative advantage more than it is hurt by accepting export fluctuations? Case histories of experience in both Asia and Africa suggest that countries following their comparative advantages, even if they lie in primary exports, grow faster than countries that turn away from this path.[26] The key seems to be how these countries manage their export earnings. For example, the effects of export price instability can be mitigated against by countercyclical fiscal and monetary policies. Moreover, the successful primary exporters diversified their export base, both within primary products and by shifting gradually to manufactured exports, to reduce the instability of total export earnings. They did this by first investing in primary exports, like Malaysia, rather than by turning away from them, like Ghana (see the preceding case studies).

INEFFECTIVE LINKAGES

Another possible explanation for the relatively slow economic growth in primary exporters is that the previously discussed **linkages** with the rest of the economy may have failed to work. For example, the petroleum industry and, with a few exceptions, the mining industry, generally remain *enclaves,* remote from other centers of production and ill adapted to link with the rest of the economy. Neither backward linkages to suppliers of production materials and equipment nor consumption linkages are likely to work. In some instances, railroads and ports built for the mines aid other industries by lowering costs and stimulating investment, but examples of remote or specialized overhead capital also can be found. Liberia's rail and harbor link with its iron mines is poorly placed to stimulate agriculture or other industry, and the pipelines and tanker ports of the petroleum industry have no use outside that sector. Some agricultural export sectors, particularly plantations in colonial Africa, also had few effective linkages, because they use few inputs and pay low wages. However, small-farm, labor-intensive agriculture typically has effective linkages through transport and marketing services and consumer demand by farm families.

Some countries have tried explicitly to encourage forward linkages through taxes or outright bans on the export of primary products. Indone-

25. David C. Dawe, "Essays on Price Stabilization and the Macroeconomy in Low Income Countries," Harvard University, Ph.D. dissertation, May 1993, pp. 50–107.

26. See David L. Lindauer and Michael Roemer, eds., *Asia and Africa: Legacies and Opportunities* (San Francisco: ICS Press, 1994), especially Chaps. 1 and 4.

sia, for example, has banned the export of logs and heavily taxed the export of sawn wood to encourage the plywood and furniture industries. Since export prices are determined in world markets, export taxes and bans reduce the price of the primary commodity in the domestic market. This helps downstream industries, which get the benefit of lower raw material prices. Farmers, loggers, and miners are taxed to provide greater incentives for processors and manufacturing firms. This is one form of *protection,* similar in its effects to protection against imports, the subject of Chapter 18.

These strategies to encourage downstream processing of primary products may succeed in expanding the industrial base and increasing the economic benefits derived from a natural resource. However, resource processing is no panacea for development. Most of the mineral-processing industries share with mining the characteristics of large scale, capital intensity, sophisticated technology, and high wages, so they tend to be extensions of the export enclave and generate little employment and realize few linkages to the rest of the economy. Nor is there much diversification of risk in moving from crude to refined petroleum exports or from bauxite to aluminum.

RENT SEEKING AND CORRUPTION

Another possible explanation for the poor performance of primary exporters is that resource abundance leads to increased corruption and rent seeking, as defined in Chapter 5. Large and relatively easy-to-earn profits can be made by the lucky few that gain control over natural resources. Under these circumstances, entrepreneurial energies are likely to focus on obtaining a larger piece of the existing economic pie, rather than on efforts to enlarge the pie through productivity gains. Economists Philip Lane and Aaron Tornell have developed a formal economic model exploring the relationship between resource riches and rent seeking. They show how a commodity boom can lead to a "feeding frenzy," in which intense competition for the resource rents ultimately leads to inefficiency and waste of the potential windfall. In a country with powerful interest groups and weak government institutions, a commodity boom can worsen the distribution of income and reduce the rate of economic growth.[27] Some developing countries have managed to minimize this problem, but corruption often is a significant problem in resource-rich countries.

DUTCH DISEASE

Booming primary exports may fail to stimulate development for another, more pervasive reason, which has been labeled the **Dutch disease.** This syndrome derives its name from the experience of the Netherlands after 1960,

27. Philip Lane and Aaron Tornell, "Power, Growth, and the Voracity Effect," *Journal of Economic Growth,* 1 no. 2 (June 1996), 213–41.

when major reserves of natural gas were discovered. The ensuing export boom and the balance-of-payments surplus promised new prosperity. Instead, however, during the 1970s the Dutch economy suffered from rising inflation, declining export of manufactures, lower rates of income growth, and rising unemployment. The oil boom of the 1970s and early 1980s produced similar paradoxes in a number of countries, including Saudi Arabia, Nigeria, and Mexico. Economists began to realize that Dutch disease might be a very general phenomenon, applicable to all countries that "enjoy" export booms of primary commodities.[28] Because, as we shall see, the influx of foreign exchange itself causes Dutch disease, the syndrome also can result from large inflows of foreign capital in any form. The import of gold and silver from the Americas, for example, may have helped to retard Spain's growth in the sixteenth century. A surge of foreign investment into the United States probably helped make U.S. industries less competitive in the 1980s. Large foreign aid flows to developing countries can undermine exporting firms' international competitiveness. How can this happen?

The key to this paradox is to understand (1) how export booms affect a country's **real exchange rate** and (2) how the real exchange rate, in turn, affects other industries. The *official* or *nominal exchange rate* simply is the price at which anyone holding foreign exchange, such as dollars, can convert it into local currency, say, pesos in Mexico, naira in Nigeria, or rupiah in Indonesia. Most commonly, the nominal exchange rate is quoted in local currency per unit of foreign currency, say, pesos per dollar. When the exchange rate rises—that is, there are more pesos or naira or rupiah per dollar—the domestic currency is said to *depreciate,* because it takes fewer dollars to buy the same amount of pesos, naira, or rupiah than before.[29] When the exchange rate falls, the domestic currency *appreciates,* because pesos are worth more in dollars than before.

The real exchange rate starts with the nominal exchange rate, and then incorporates the prices of **tradable goods** and **nontradable goods** to analyze how changing prices and exchange rates affect the incentives for production and consumption. Economists call any good that is or could be imported or exported a **tradable.** Prices for tradable goods generally are determined on

28. The Dutch disease has been analyzed from a theoretical standpoint by W. Max Corden and S. Peter Neary, "Booming Sector and Deindustrialization in a Small Open Economy," *Economic Journal,* 92 (December 1982), 825–48. The application of this theory to developing countries is explored by Michael Roemer, "Dutch Disease in Developing Countries: Swallowing Bitter Medicine," in Matts Lundahl, ed., *The Primary Sector in Economic Development* (London: Croom-Helms, 1985), pp. 234–52.

29. The language on exchange rate changes sometimes is confusing. When the nominal exchange rate rises, it takes more domestic currency (naira) to buy foreign currency (dollars). Equivalently, this means that it takes fewer dollars to buy naira. In this latter sense, the naira is said to *depreciate,* or lose value, when the exchange rate rises.

world markets and, in most cases, are not affected by domestic conditions in developing countries. **Nontradables** are goods produced domestically and not imported or exported. Prices for nontradables are determined by supply and demand conditions in the domestic market. Examples of nontradables include transportation, construction, electricity and other utilities, household and other personal services, and manufactures or farm products that are heavily protected and not subject to competition from imports.[30]

The real exchange rate most commonly is defined as

$$\text{RER} = (E_O \times P_T)/P_N \qquad\qquad [16\text{--}1]$$

where RER = an index of the real exchange rate, E_O = an index of the official (nominal) exchange rate, P_T = an index of the prices of tradable goods expressed in foreign currency (e.g., U.S. dollars), and P_N = an index of the domestic price of nontradables. Note that the RER is an index of prices, like the terms of trade, not a price itself. Also note that, since P_T is expressed in foreign currency, by multiplying by E_O the numerator ($E_O \times P_T$) becomes a domestic currency index of tradables prices. Therefore, the RER can be thought of as the ratio of the price of tradable goods to the price of nontradable goods, all expressed in domestic currency. An increase in the RER—because of either an increase in the exchange rate, a rise in the dollar prices of tradable goods on world markets, or a fall in nontradables prices—suggests that the relative price of tradables in domestic markets has risen. Such a shift should encourage more production of tradable goods and discourage consumption of tradable goods. Following the language of nominal exchange rates, a rise in the RER is referred to as a *real depreciation* of the peso or naira, and a decline in the RER is called a *real appreciation*. Official devaluations, which raise the peso price of dollars, cause the real rate to depreciate, at least initially. The same is true for an increase in world tradable prices. An increase in nontradables prices has the opposite effect, causing the RER to appreciate.[31]

The Dutch disease is a wolf in sheep's clothing because it typically starts with what looks like a good thing: A boom in a country's raw material exports. But the boom in exports can cause a sharp appreciation of the RER, in two ways. First, the influx of foreign exchange from higher export earnings creates a surplus of foreign currency. Unless the central bank tries to maintain the official exchange rate at its former level, this shift in supply causes the currency to appreciate in value. Second, higher income from booming primary exports also spurs faster domestic inflation. It does this

30. The definitions of *tradables* and *nontradables* are made more precise in Chapter 19.

31. For a comprehensive discussion of the real exchange rate, see Sebastian Edwards *Real Exchange Rates, Devaluation and Adjustment: Exchange Rate Policy in Developing Countries* (Cambridge, MA: MIT Press, 1991).

because the additional income creates greater demand for all goods and services in the economy. To the extent that this demand spills over into more imports, there is an outflow of foreign exchange but no inflation, because the price of imports is not much affected by demand in a single country. But prices for nontradable goods and services are likely to increase. Due to a limited supply of nontradables, especially in the first months or years of the boom, the greater demand results in higher prices for nontradables (that is, in domestic inflation). From equation 16–1 we know that a rise in nontradable prices causes the RER to decline, or appreciate.

To understand how the real exchange rate becomes the key to the Dutch disease paradox, begin with the impact of the real exchange rate on export industries *other than the booming primary export industry.* Table 16–3 demonstrates that, with a fixed nominal exchange rate, domestic inflation in excess of world inflation (that is, an increase in nontradable prices in excess of tradable prices) causes exporters' profits to decline. This occurs because wages and the prices of domestic inputs rise faster than the prices of exported output. That, of course, is the same thing as a real rate appreciation, since RER would fall in equation 16–1. Note that the same reduction in profitability would follow from an appreciation of the nominal exchange rate, that is, from lowering the peso price of a dollar, which is likely to happen with a commodity export boom. If profits for noncommodity exporters fall, they are likely to produce less for export, and so reduce income and employment in export industries. Exporters' profitability could be restored by a nominal devaluation that offsets domestic inflation, as shown in the last section of Table 16–3.

Now the paradox can be explained: Booming primary exports, by stimulating more rapid domestic inflation and thus causing the real exchange rate to appreciate, render *other* exports less competitive and hence less profitable. Therefore, the "disease" is the deleterious effect of a commodity boom on other export sectors. Producers of tradables, both exporters and import competitors, face rising costs in their purchases of nontradable goods and services, including the wages of their workers. But they cannot charge higher prices because they compete with foreign producers, either as exporters or as import competitors. These farmers and manufacturers face a profit squeeze that will cause some of them to reduce production and employment. The boom in primary exports and nontradables is partly offset by a depression in other tradable industries.

If it is relatively easy to move capital and labor between the booming commodity sector and other activities and if the booming sector can employ all the factors of production released from other, less-profitable activities, then the commodity boom poses no major problem. As prices for the primary export product rise, labor and capital can move into the booming sector, and the economy is better off as a result. If the boom ends, the factors of production can move back to their previous activity. But this usually is not the case. If the booming sector is highly capital intensive (such as petro-

TABLE 16–3	EFFECTS OF INFLATION AND DEVALUATION ON EXPORTERS' PROFITS

TODAY: EXCHANGE RATE = 12 PESOS PER DOLLAR; REAL EXCHANGE RATE = 100

1. EXPORTER SELLS GOODS WORTH	$100,000
2. FOR WHICH EXPORTER RECEIVES LOCAL CURRENCY OF	P1,200,000
3. IF EXPORTER'S COSTS (ALL DOMESTIC NONTRADABLES) ARE	P900,000
4. THEN EXPORTER'S PROFITS ARE	P300,000

THREE YEARS LATER, AFTER THE PRIMARY EXPORT BOOM, BECAUSE OF DOMESTIC INFLATION, NONTRADABLES PRICES HAVE RISEN 33% MORE THAN WORLD TRADABLES PRICES; REAL EXCHANGE RATE APPRECIATED TO 75

1. EXPORTER SELLS GOODS WORTH	$100,000
2. FOR WHICH EXPORTER RECEIVES LOCAL CURRENCY OF	P1,200,000
3. IF EXPORTER'S COSTS (ALL DOMESTIC NONTRADABLES) ARE	P1,200,000
4. THEN EXPORTER'S PROFITS ARE	P0

THREE YEARS LATER, BUT WITH CURRENCY DEVALUED BY 33% TO 16 PESOS PER DOLLAR; REAL EXCHANGE RATE RESTORED TO 100

1. EXPORTER SELLS GOODS WORTH	$100,000
2. FOR WHICH EXPORTER RECEIVES LOCAL CURRENCY OF	P1,600,000
3. IF EXPORTER'S COSTS (ALL DOMESTIC) ARE	P1,200,000
4. THEN EXPORTER'S PROFITS ARE	P400,000
5. WHICH, DEFLATED BY 33% TO YEAR 1 PRICES, AGAIN ARE (IN REAL TERMS)	P300,000

leum), few new jobs will be created, so unemployment may go up (although indirect employment effects of the boom in construction and other activities can mitigate against this effect). More insidiously, when the boom ends (and booms always end), it is likely to be very difficult to move the factors of production back to their previous employment. After all, manufacturing activities cannot just restart overnight. Moreover, at the end of the boom, wages are likely to fall, so workers are unlikely to be happy to move back to lower paying jobs. In addition, the boom can lead to social or migratory shifts that are hard to unwind. Nigeria's oil boom (described in a case study at the end of the chapter) stimulated rural workers to migrate to urban areas to look for new, high-paying construction and civil service jobs. When the oil boom ended, few urban workers wanted to return to rural areas. Many other oil exporters suffered similar fates when petroleum prices fell in the mid-1980s.

Because mineral and other primary sectors typically pay high taxes, commodity booms can lead to a swelling of government revenue. This **fiscal linkage** can be used to stimulate development, especially if the additional revenue is invested in public services, such as infrastructure, education, and health, or to promote efficient investment in tradable sectors, notably agriculture and manufacturing, that have been rendered less competitive by the primary export boom. Although some governments used their fiscal resources effectively during the 1970s oil boom, the record generally was dismal, with significant resources wasted on frivolous projects. Precisely when fiscal resources are generously available do finance ministers have the most difficult time resisting political and social pressures for higher expenditures. Once again, the big difficulties arise when the boom ends, and government must quickly reduce spending and reverse the commitments made during the good times. As discussed in Chapter 14, some countries borrowed heavily from abroad during the commodity booms of the 1970s on the assumption that export prices would remain high and were left with large foreign debts and a significantly reduced capacity to pay when the boom ended.

The depredations of Dutch disease and other problems with primary product exports often are fatal to development aspirations, as the case study of Nigeria illustrates. But this is not necessarily so. Some countries have turned their resource windfalls into sustained development, such as Indonesia, Botswana, Tunisia, Malaysia, and Chile.[32] The negative relationship between primary product exports and economic growth is a tendency, not an absolute straightjacket. Determined governments can take several steps to avoid some of the most difficult problems associated with abundant natural resources.

The best prevention for Dutch disease effects is to avoid or reverse the initial real appreciation of the currency. In most cases, this requires a devaluation of the currency, accompanied by strong restraints on government spending and money creation by the central bank, both aimed at curbing inflation. The government needs to resist demands for expansion and save its new-found revenues until there is time to plan sensible, well-targeted projects with high returns. More generally, the more successful governments have channeled new investments into health, education, and infrastructure development that improves overall well being, enhances productivity, and opens up economic opportunities outside the primary sector. Such an investment policy accomplishes two things. First, it harnesses export windfalls to finance sound, long-term development. Second, by delaying the new expenditures, the government acts *countercyclically* and so helps stabilize the economy by spending less during the most inflationary period of the export boom and more after the boom has faded.[33] These *stabilization measures* are explored in depth in Chapter 19.

For reasons already discussed in Chapter 5, policies of restraint, essential to stabilization, are seldom popular and often vigorously opposed by political pressure groups. Although the judicious use of commodity revenues is easy to prescribe and essential for an economy's health, the advice often is not taken in sufficient doses to effect a cure.

---

32. World Bank economist Alan Gelb has documented six cases of the Dutch disease in *Oil Windfalls*.

33. If, however, the permanent income hypothesis is valid, the households will save much of the windfall and the burden on government is less. David Bevan, Paul Collier, and Jan Gunning, *Controlled Open Economies: A Neoclassical Approach to Structuralism* (London: Oxford University Press [Clarendon], 1990), argue that this was the case in Kenya during the commodity boom of the late 1970s.

NIGERIA: A BAD CASE OF DUTCH DISEASE[34]

In 1973–74, the oil embargo imposed by Arab countries, followed by the activation of OPEC as an effective cartel, quadrupled the price of petroleum on world markets. In 1979–80, the price doubled again, so that by the end of 1980 the terms of trade for oil exports, relative to the price of imports, was nearly seven times the level in 1972. In Nigeria, higher export prices generated an "oil windfall" that added 23 percent to nonmining gross domestic product in the middle 1970s and again in the early 1980s.

Nigeria's political history has been marked by intense competition among ethnic groups—culminating in the Biafran war of the late 1960s—and one of the major battlegrounds of this strife has been the incidence of taxation and government expenditure. Under this kind of pressure, the Nigerian government spent all its oil windfall. Public investment rose from 4 to 30 percent of nonmining GDP and the average pay for civil servants was doubled in 1975. Much of the newfound revenue was squandered on wasteful projects. The second oil windfall only whetted fiscal appetites even more: From 1981 to 1984, the budget deficit averaged 12 percent of nonmining GDP.

Fiscal excesses exacerbated the tendency of export windfalls to create inflation. Prices rose while the central bank kept the nominal exchange rate fixed, so that, by 1984, the real exchange rate had appreciated to nearly three times its level in 1970–72. Over the decade ending in 1984, Nigeria's nonoil exports fell almost 90 percent in nominal terms, a classic if extreme symptom of Dutch disease.

Agriculture suffered worst. Because rural constituencies were politically weak, little of the oil windfall was invested in agriculture, while vast amounts were spent, and wasted, on infrastructure and industry. From 1973 to 1984, the quantity of agricultural exports fell by more than two thirds, while agriculture output per capita and total caloric consumption per capita both declined. From 1972 to 1981, growth in nonmining GDP was a respectable 5.3 percent, but this was only 60 percent of the growth rate during the five years before the oil price boom. It can be argued that Nigeria might have been better off without its oil boom.

34. This account is based on Henry Bienen, "Nigeria: From Windfall Gains to Welfare Losses?" in Gelb, *Oil Windfalls,* pp. 227–60.

INDONESIA: FINDING A CURE [35]

Indonesia was both the poorest and the largest country in the world to receive substantial oil windfalls. At first, the oil boom affected Indonesia much as it did Nigeria. The 1973–74 boom added 16 percent to nonmining GDP and the 1979–80 price surge raised the windfall to 23 percent. Of the first windfall, the government itself spent more than 60 percent. From 1974 to 1978, the real exchange rate appreciated an average 33 percent over its preboom level, a bit more than in Nigeria at that time.

Yet the outcome was very different in Indonesia. Throughout the boom period, the government was required to balance its budget each year, and because all controls had been removed from foreign exchange transfers, stringent management of the money supply was necessary to protect foreign exchange reserves. These self-imposed restraints limited the impact of the windfalls on inflation.

The Indonesian government adopted two policies that took advantage of oil windfalls for national development goals. First, investment in agriculture had a high priority, especially the goal of achieving self-

35. This account is based on Bruce Glassburner, "Indonesia: Windfalls in a Poor Rural Economy," in Gelb, *Oil Windfalls,* pp. 197–226.

sufficiency in rice production. The government financed irrigation systems, encouraged the adoption of new rice varieties, subsidized fertilizer and pesticide sales, provided credit to farmers, invested in rural health and education facilities, and built roads and other infrastructure in rural areas. By the mid-1980s, Indonesia was self-sufficient in rice, and by 1982–83, its total food output per capita was a third above its 1970 level—a performance far above average for all developing and industrial countries over the period.

The second policy was to devalue the exchange rate enough to avoid real appreciation. Major devaluations were imposed in 1978, 1983, and 1986, after which the rate was managed flexibly to maintain its real value. At the end of the oil boom period in 1984, the Indonesian real exchange rate had *de*preciated 8 percent from its 1970–72 average. Consequently, over the period from 1971 to 1984, the quantity of nonoil exports grew by over 7 percent a year, and from 1972 to 1981, nonmining GDP expanded by over 8 percent a year.

Thus shrewd policy played a major role in effecting an early cure for incipient Dutch disease. The government placed great stress on integrating the multitude of ethnic groups of this diverse country, and so avoided the conflicts over fiscal resources that paralyzed Nigeria. Moreover, the country had an important advantage over other oil exporters: Its large labor force, nearly two thirds of it working in rural areas in 1970, dampened any tendencies for surges in wages and thus in domestic prices throughout the oil boom.

INDUSTRY

The concept of development and the process of industrialization often have been treated as synonymous, ever since the Industrial Revolution enabled Britain to raise its industrial production by 400 percent over the first half of the nineteenth century.[1] From then until the present, the dominant criterion for development has been the rise in per capita income brought about largely by industrialization.

Industry as a Leading Sector

From the Chapter 3 discussion of cross-country patterns, we know that higher shares of the gross domestic product generated by industry are closely associated with rising income per capita. Figure 17–1 shows this pattern for manufacturing value added in 1992 for 17 large countries (with populations over 25 million) and 20 small ones. In making such cross-country comparisons, economists conventionally segregate large from small countries. Nations with larger markets are able to develop a wider range of industries sooner in their development because they can take advantage of *scale economies* within the domestic market.[2] Hence, we expect large countries to industrialize faster than small ones.

Both tendencies are evident in Figure 17–1. At any level of income per person, the average for large countries, determined by the regression

1. E. J. Hobsbawm, *The Pelican Economic History of Britain,* Vol. 3, *Industry and Empire* (Baltimore: Johns Hopkins Press, 1969).

2. The concept of *scale economies* is explained later in this chapter.

line, is higher than for small countries. Yet for both sets of countries, a strong correlation is found between industrialization and average income. On average for large countries, as income quintuples from $1,000 to $5,000 per person (in purchasing power parity), manufacturing value added rises from 13 to 22 percent of GDP. In an average small country undergoing the same change in income, the manufacturing share rises more sharply, from about 7 percent to about 17 percent of GNP. A country with per capita income growing at 3 percent a year would take 54 years to make this transition.

Manufacturing share does not grow indefinitely. Somewhere between $10,000 and $20,000 per capita, the ratio of manufacturing value added to GDP begins to decline, as advanced economies move out of manufac-

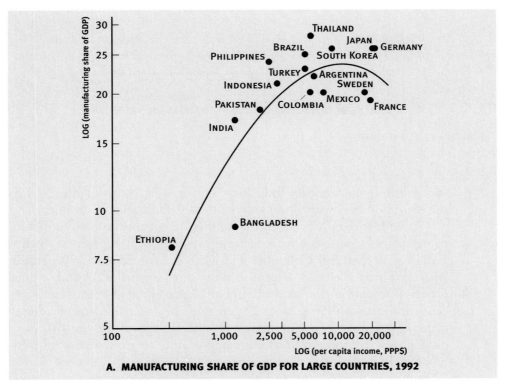

A. MANUFACTURING SHARE OF GDP FOR LARGE COUNTRIES, 1992

FIGURE 17–1   MANUFACTURING SHARE OF THE GDP, LARGE AND SMALL COUNTRIES, 1992. Large countries (with populations over 25 million), on average, are more industrialized than small ones at the same incomes. In both cases, there is a tendency for manufacturing value added to rise as a share of GDP as average income rises, up to a level of about $10,000.
Source: World Development Report 1994 (Washington, DC: The World Bank, 1994), pp. 166–67, 220–21.

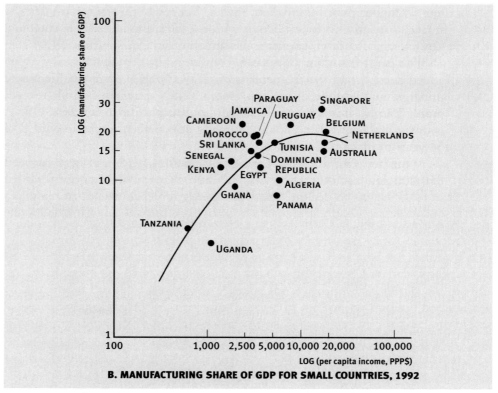

B. MANUFACTURING SHARE OF GDP FOR SMALL COUNTRIES, 1992

FIGURE 17-1   (CONTINUED)

turing into modern service industries. This is indicated in Figure 17–1 by the regression line, which peaks after $10,000 and begins to decline.[3]

But wide variations are evident. Among large countries with similar incomes, Bangladesh has a manufacturing share of only 8 percent, whereas India's is 21 percent; Columbia and Mexico have shares of 20 percent, whereas Thailand's is 28 percent. Among small countries, Uganda's share is only 4 percent in contrast to Kenya at 12 percent, and Panama at 8 percent contrasts with Uruguay at 22 percent. The differences may be due to differing endowments: Columbia's productive agriculture and Mexico's oil deposits give those countries the opportunity to grow with less investment in industry than poorly endowed countries such as South Korea. They may be due to strategy: Thailand and India adopted policies, though

3. The regression equations were of the form $\log MS = a + b \log y + c (\log y)^2$, where MS is the manufacturing share and y is PPP income per capita. The coefficient c was negative and significant in both cases and so gave a curved shape to the regression line.

very different ones, to speed industrialization. Or differences may be due to location and historical circumstance: Uganda is landlocked and suffered prolonged civil war while Kenya is centrally placed to serve a regional market and has enjoyed relative stability.

Cross-country patterns imply that value added in manufacturing ought to grow more rapidly than GDP in the typical developing country. This prediction is partially borne out by World Bank data. For the low- and middle-income countries as a whole, over the period from 1965 to 1990, manufacturing grew by 7.2 percent a year, compared to 4.8 percent a year for GDP. But this average pattern is not observed in most of the individual countries. Of 42 developing countries for which data are available from 1965 through 1990, manufacturing grew at least 1 percent a year faster than GDP in only 19 of them; in most of the others, the differences in growth rates were less than 1 percent a year.[4]

LINKAGES

If manufacturing generally and early developing branches of manufacturing in particular are to lead economic development, they ought to have more **backward linkages** than other sectors, in the sense described by Albert Hirschman and introduced in Chapter 3. There have been several attempts to measure linkages. Those used by Pan Yotopoulos and Jeffrey Nugent seem as easy to understand and useful for our purposes as any.[5] Not surprisingly, linkage formulas depend on input-output tables, which are constructed to display linkages within an economy. A **direct backward linkage** for any industry, j, is measured as

$$L_{bj} = \sum_i a_{ij} \qquad [17\text{--}1]$$

where L_{bj} = the index of backward linkage, and a_{ij} = the Leontief (input-output) coefficient defined in Chapter 3. Thus a measure of backward linkage for any industry is simply the sum of its domestic input coefficients. If, for example, the textile industry adds value equal to 30 percent of its output, and imports inputs equivalent to another 15 percent of output, its backward linkage index L_b will be 55 percent, the share of domestically purchased inputs $(100 - 30 - 15 = 55)$.

---

4. World Bank, *World Development Report 1992* (Washington, DC: The World Bank, 1992), pp. 220–21.

5. Pan A. Yotopoulos and Jeffrey B. Nugent, "A Balanced-Growth Version of the Linkage Hypothesis: A Test," *Quarterly Journal of Economics,* 87 (May 1973), 157–71; reprinted in their text, *Economics of Development: Empirical Investigations* (New York: Harper and Row, 1976), pp. 299–306.

Those who recall Chapter 3 will immediately recognize that this index captures only the direct links. But, if textile production stimulates cotton growing, might not cotton in turn stimulate fertilizer production? It is easy to incorporate these indirect effects by summing the direct and indirect coefficients of the Leontief inverse, designated r_{ij}, to get

$$L_{tj} = \Sigma \; r_{ij} \qquad\qquad\qquad [17-2]$$

where L_{tj} = an index of direct plus indirect or **total backward linkages** from the jth industry.[6]

There is an analogous simple measure of **direct forward linkages:**

$$L_{fi} = \sum_{j} X_{ij}/Z_i \qquad\qquad\qquad [17-3]$$

where L_{fi} = the forward linkage index for the ith industry, X_{ij} = the output of the ith industry purchased by each jth user industry (the row of the input-output table), and Z_i = the production of good i for both intermediate and final use.

Yotopoulos and Nugent use input-output tables for five developing countries (Chile, Greece, Mexico, Spain, and South Korea) to measure the linkage indexes for 18 industries. The results are shown in Table 17–1. For leather, the next-to-last column tells us, for example, that for each additional dollar of leather goods produced, production of all inputs must rise by $2.39. A high index indicates that expansion of the industry will stimulate production in other sectors of the economy. Manufacturing industries dominate the upper ranks of Table 17–1 on the basis of both direct and total backward linkages. The early-developing sectors—leather, clothing, textiles, and food and beverages—represent four of the first five branches ranked by total backward linkages. Primary industries, utilities, and services are low on both lists. Hence, an unbalanced-growth strategy, to stimulate investment in other sectors, should begin with the early-developing industries then move to chemicals and metal products. Advocates of import-substitution strategies find sustenance in these findings.

What do these indices really mean? Should a country base its development strategy on them, even if rapid growth is the principal goal? These particular measurement formulas have been attacked for several reasons, many of them sound. But alternative and more-complicated formulations give similar rankings anyway. The real issue is whether a mechanical summing up of input-output coefficients for one country really tells us anything about the dynamic processes of growth in another country. The textile industry, which ranks high in Table 17–1 according to its total

6. The Leontief inverse matrix is explained in note 11 of Chap. 3.

TABLE 17-1   SECTORAL LINKAGE INDEXES AND RANKINGS IN FIVE LESS-DEVELOPED COUNTRIES

	DIRECT FORWARD LINKAGE INDEX (L_r)	RANK	DIRECT BACKWARD LINKAGE INDEX (L_g)	RANK	TOTAL BACKWARD LINKAGE INDEX (L_r)	RANK
LEATHER	0.645	4	0.683	2	2.39	1
BASIC METALS	0.980	1	0.632	5	2.36	2
CLOTHING	0.025	18	0.621	6	2.32	3
TEXTILES	0.590	8	0.621	7	2.24	4
FOOD AND BEVERAGE MANUFACTURES	0.272	16	0.718	1	2.22	5
PAPER	0.788	3	0.648	3	2.17	6
CHEMICALS AND PETROLEUM REFINING	0.599	7	0.637	4	2.13	7
METAL PRODUCTS AND MACHINERY	0.430	13	0.558	9	2.12	8
WOOD, FURNITURE	0.582	9	0.620	8	2.07	9
CONSTRUCTION	0.093	17	0.543	10	2.04	10
PRINTING	0.508	10	0.509	12	1.98	11
OTHER MANUFACTURERS	0.362	15	0.505	13	1.94	12
RUBBER	0.453	12	0.481	14	1.93	13
MINERALS (NONMETALLIC)	0.870	2	0.517	11	1.83	14
AGRICULTURE	0.502	11	0.368	15	1.59	15
UTILITIES	0.614	6	0.296	16	1.49	16
MINING	0.638	5	0.288	17	1.47	17
SERVICE	0.378	14	0.255	18	1.41	18

Note: The countries are Chile, Greece, South Korea, Mexico, and Spain.
Source: Yotopoulos and Nugent, "A Balanced-Growth Version of the Linkage Hypothesis," Table 2, p. 163.

backward linkage coefficient, may well require input of cotton and synthetic fibers. But whether this additional demand will lead to new investment in farming and chemicals depends on many conditions, none of them reflected in the index. Can cotton be grown in the country at all and, if so, at what cost? It might remain cheaper, and to the country's advantage, to import cotton and use the land to grow more profitable crops. If cotton already is being grown and exported, can output expand to accommodate the textile plant or would it simply divert exports? Reduced exports, of course, would cancel the backward linkage effect.

The potential linkage back to synthetic fibers raises additional issues. Petrochemical industries are subject to substantial economies of scale, and it would take a considerable expansion of the textile industry to justify the very large investment in petrochemicals. If protection is used to keep out imports of synthetic fibers, the textile industry itself would suffer higher costs and perhaps lose its impetus to expand. However, some infant supplier industries may have the potential to reduce costs over time—learning by doing, if they are given a chance.

The requirements for effective forward linkages from manufacturing are even more stringent. To continue the example, textiles have a large forward linkage index, primarily to the clothing industry. But does domestic cloth stimulate the clothing industry? It can if textiles can be produced at costs below the world price of imported cloth. Otherwise, the user industry is better off importing its input. If clothing manufacturers are forced, through tariffs or import controls, to take more expensive domestic cloth, this would discourage, rather than stimulate, the forward linkage.

The static linkage indexes can help direct attention to potential linkages, but detailed studies are required to consider all the relevant conditions and pinpoint the ways in which investment in one industry will lead to investment in others. These studies may well show that some manufacturing sectors can lead growth in certain countries. But some of the references cited in Chapter 16 demonstrated that certain primary sectors also generate effective linkages, and no overwhelming case favors manufacturing on this ground.

URBANIZATION

Since the Industrial Revolution, urbanization and industrialization have moved in tandem. England started the nineteenth century with 30 percent of its people living in cities and ended the century with an urban population share over 70 percent.[7] The trend toward urbanization with industrial development is evident today in cross-country comparisons, depicted in Figure 17–2. As average incomes grow from about $750 per capita (in PPP) to $7,500, both the manufacturing workforce and the urban population grow as shares of the total workforce and population. Beyond $7,500, however, the urban share continues to rise even though manufacturing no longer employs an increasing share of the workers.

What causes rapid urbanization as industrialization proceeds? Several **external economies** (see Chapter 5) benefit manufacturing firms in urban settings. Large populations reduce the firms' costs of recruiting labor of all kinds, but especially skilled workers and technicians. Moreover, in cities, workers usually find their own housing, so firms need not provide it, as they might in rural areas or small towns. **Infrastructure,** including industrial sites, electricity, water, sewage, roads, railroads, and in many cases ports, is provided by the government in the cities at costs that reflect substantial scale economies. Health and education facilities also are more highly developed in the cities.

Each firm also benefits from the **economies of agglomeration** that result from the presence of many other firms, because a wide range of necessary in-

7. Hobsbawm, *Industry and Empire,* Fig. 13.

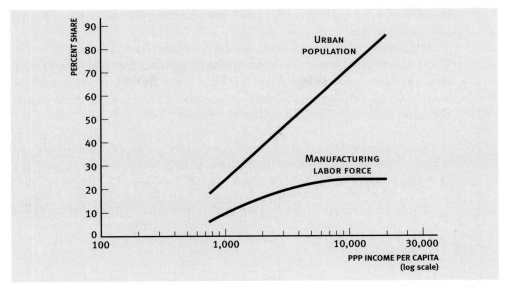

FIGURE 17-2 INDUSTRIALIZATION AND URBANIZATION. Cross-country regressions indicate that as GNP per capita rises up to about $7,500, the manufacturing workforce grows from an average 6 percent of the labor force to 24 percent, while the urban share of the population grows from 18 to 66 percent. But urban growth continues even though manufacturing's share of the workforce levels off.

puts and services becomes available. Manufacturers can reduce transportation costs and shipping delays if they locate near their suppliers. They benefit from the proximity of repair and other industrial services. Financial markets cluster in cities where domestic and international communication facilities are available and cheap. Manufacturers need access to banks and other financial institutions. They also need the city's communications to stay in touch with distant suppliers and markets, especially export markets. When the city in question is a national capital, manufacturers may locate there to gain ready access to government officials who control investment licenses and incentives, import allocations, and a myriad of other policy and administrative devices that affect the profitability of the firm. Finally, the strong preferences of capitalists, managers, and technicians for the amenities of large cities can be a significant reason for locating there.

Once a city is established, its large market creates reinforcing attractions. Distribution costs are minimized when the firm locates near its largest market. If the costs of shipping output weigh heavily in firms' costs, and especially if they are more important than the costs of transporting input, firms will be pulled toward cities. This attraction is particularly strong in developing countries, where intercity and rural-urban transportation networks are sparse or costly. In developed countries, where transportation networks are dense and efficient, manufacturing tends to be

more footloose and seeks out advantages like cheap labor with less regard
for transportation costs.

But urbanization has its costs, as the residents of every large city in the
world observe daily: overcrowding, unsanitary conditions, displacement of
rural migrants, crime. These too have been features of industrialization for
two centuries. During the first half of the nineteenth century, London and
the other growing cities of Britain were dismal places:

> Smoke hung over them and filth impregnated them . . . the elementary public ser-
> vices: water supply, sanitation, street-cleaning, open spaces, and so on, could not
> keep pace with the mass migration of men into the cities, thus producing, espe-
> cially after 1830, epidemics of cholera, typhoid and an appalling constant toll of
> the two great groups of nineteenth-century urban killers—air pollution and water
> pollution, or respiratory and intestinal disease. . . . New city populations . . .
> pressed into overcrowded and bleak slums, whose very sight froze the heart of the
> observer.[8]

Migrants to the large cities of the third world probably need not put up
with conditions as bad as those of early nineteenth-century London, but
cities like Calcutta, Lagos, and São Paulo contain large slums with many
of the same kinds of problems.

Industrializing cities become magnets for rural workers seeking jobs at
higher wages, a pervasive third world phenomenon explored in Chapter 8.
Despite the risks of unemployment and congested living conditions,
urban life may still be attractive to many rural dwellers, relative to the opportunities available at home. The costs of congestion are external diseconomies: Each new migrant will benefit on average but, in so doing, will
reduce the well being of all others, even if only slightly. The social costs
are high, however, because this marginal reduction in well being must be
added up for all residents of the city.

No government feels comfortable with crowded cities, and many have
attempted to stem the flow of migration. Over the long run, this can be
done best by encouraging rural development as actively as industrialization, using the wide range of land tenure, investment, price incentive, and
other policies described in Chapter 15. A complementary approach is to
encourage the dispersal of new industries to smaller cities through the provision of infrastructure, incentives, and controls over location. Spreading
investment reduces congestion and also may reduce the cost of migration.
Migrants will have shorter average distances to travel, so more of them can
search for jobs with no commitment to permanent residence in cities remote from their homes. The decentralization of industry has complemen-

8. Hobsbawm, *Industry and Empire,* p. 86.

tary benefits for agriculture; it distributes urban markets and manufactured supplies more widely among the farming population.

Industrial dispersion has costs, however. Infrastructure costs may be greater in small towns, which have not provided as much of the basic facilities as large cities. To this must be added the higher costs of transportation and other infrastructure required to connect dispersed industrial locations. Even with this wider network of transportation and communications in place, private firms and society incur higher costs of hauling freight (both material input and final output) if they do not locate in the most efficient place. These firms further incur higher costs in communicating with suppliers, customers, and financial institutions, not to mention government officials, and of waiting with idle facilities while parts and repair specialists from distant places arrive to fix broken equipment. Whether the benefits of dispersal justify the costs will depend on the circumstances. Costs will be lower if the population already is dispersed, if several urban centers and connecting infrastructure already exist, and if the new sites have obvious advantages, such as nearby raw materials or abundant water.

Investment Choices in Industry

Chapter 2 introduced the proposition that, because factors of production can be substituted for one another in many production processes, economies were able to conserve capital and get more growth out of a given amount of saving. Chapter 8 used the same analytical device the neoclassical production function to demonstrate that policies to make labor less expensive and capital more expensive could move producers toward investments that employ more labor and less capital for a given level of output. Is there enough variance in production techniques to make such policies effective in conserving capital and creating more employment for a given amount of production? For industry, the answer is yes.

CHOICE OF TECHNIQUE

Table 17–2 illustrates the choice of technology for a single industry, textile weaving. Three alternative technologies are included: an older, semiautomatic loom (T1); a more modern, fully automatic, high-speed loom (T3); and an intermediate technology (T2). More alternatives could have been shown, including handloom weaving, which is still used in some Asian countries. As expected, the three technologies show increasing capital intensity, in the sense that the ratio of capital to output rises, and decreasing labor intensity. The treatment of Chapter 8 has been augmented by the consideration of other operating costs, including rental space, power, and differential

| TABLE 17–2 | CHOICE OF TECHNOLOGY IN TEXTILE WEAVING |

INPUTS (PER MILLION YARDS OF SHIRTING)	ALTERNATIVE TECHNOLOGY[a]		
	T1	T2	T3
1. EQUIPMENT COST ($1,000)	80.0	200.0	400.0
2. LABOR (PERSON-YEARS)	22.0	11.0	5.0
3. OTHER COSTS ($1,000/YEAR)[b]	11.4	9.3	6.7

FACTOR COSTS	RICH COUNTRY	POOR COUNTRY
1. REAL INTEREST RATE (% P.A.)	5.0	10.0
2. PRESENT-VALUE FACTOR (20 YEARS)[c]	12.46	8.51
3. WAGES ($1,000/YEAR)	15.0	1.5

PRESENT VALUE OF COSTS ($1,000)[d]	ALTERNATIVE TECHNOLOGY[a]		
	T1	T2	T3
RICH COUNTRY			
1. CAPITAL CHARGES	80	200	400
2. WAGES	4112	2056	935
3. OTHER COSTS	142	116	83
4. TOTAL	4334	2372	1418
POOR COUNTRY			
1. CAPITAL CHARGES	80	200	400
2. WAGES	280	140	64
3. OTHER COSTS	97	79	57
4. TOTAL	457	419	521

[a]Technologies are T1, semiautomatic loom; T2, intermediate technology; and T3, fully automatic, high-speed loom.
[b]Includes cost of space, power, and wastage of yarn, all of which vary depending on the technology. Excludes the common cost of yarn in the finished product.
[c]Present value of $1 per year for 20 years at the interest rate shown in 1.
[d]Wages and other costs discounted at appropriate interest rate over 20 years using present value factor of factor costs.
Source: Adapted from data in Howard Pack, "The Choice of Technique and Employment in the Textile Industry," in A. S. Bhalla, ed., *Technology and Employment in Industry* (Geneva: International Labour Office, 1975), pp. 153–74.

wastage of the main input, yarn. In many cases modern equipment conserves both energy and material inputs and lowers production costs.

Analysis of the choice of technology is conveniently done using project analysis as described in Chapter 12. Revenues and costs, including the cost of investment, can be discounted over the life of each technology, and the technology with the highest net present value chosen as the most economic. In Table 17–2, for simplicity, we assume that all techniques produce cloth of equal quality and value, so revenue is not brought into consideration. Instead, the present value of costs is minimized.

The second part of the table presents indicative factor costs for a rich country and a poor one: Workers in the rich country are paid ten times the wage of workers in the poor one, whereas the real interest rate in the poor country is twice that of the rich one. Under those conditions, investors in the rich country would minimize costs by choosing the most modern looms, largely because these require so much less labor. Investors in the poor coun-

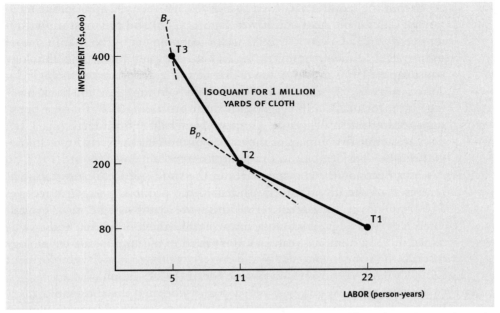

FIGURE 17–3   TECHNOLOGICAL CHOICE IN THE WEAVING INDUSTRY. Three alternative weaving technologies, T1, T2, and T3, are taken from Table 17–2. Each represents a different ratio of capital to labor. Because the industry, or even a single firm, can use any combination of technologies, production could take place at all combinations of labor and capital along T1T2 and T2T3. Thus, an isoquant can be traced from T1 to T2 to T3. The slopes of the budget lines $B_r B_r$ and $B_p B_p$ represent the ratio of wages to capital charges for the rich and poor countries, respectively. They indicate costs will be minimized for the rich country by using the most capital-intensive technology, T3, whereas the poor country should use intermediate technology, T2. Were wages in the poor country only slightly lower relative to capital costs, the most labor-intensive technology, T1, might well be optimal.

try should select the intermediate technology. However, should the annual wage in the poor country be $1,000 a year instead of $1,500, which is a realistic possibility, the oldest and most labor-intensive technology would minimize costs. Figure 17–3 represents these technological choices as a production isoquant similar to those of Figures 2–3 and 8–3, only in a form more realistic for alternative technologies in single industries.

The range of technologies represented in Figure 17–3 is realistic for the weaving industry in a developing country. The scope for technological choice in this industry can be indicated by the range of capital-labor ratios from the most to the least capital-intensive technology. The capital-labor ratio of technology T3 is 22 times that of technology T1. The study from which these figures are taken gives a similar range for cotton spinning, whereas cement-block making in Kenya alone exhibits a ratio of 11 : 1.[9]

9. Howard Pack, "The Choice of Technique and Employment in the Textile Industry," p. 169; and Frances Stewart, "Manufacture of Cement Blocks in Kenya," in Bhalla, *Technology and Employment in Industry,* p. 221.

Even if the scope is narrowed to a choice between the appropriate technology (T2 for the poor country in Figure 17–3) and the most capital-intensive alternative (T3), a wide range of technologies is available in several industries. For shoe manufacturing, the most capital-intensive technology has a capital-labor ratio 2.8 times that of the appropriate technology; for cotton weaving, the ratio is 4.3; for cotton spinning, 7.3; for brick making, 13.8; for maize milling, 3.3; for sugar processing, 7.8; for beer brewing, 1.5; for leather processing, 2.3; and for fertilizer manufacturing, 1.1.[10]

The cumulative impact of the choice of more labor-intensive technologies can be considerable. In one indicative experiment, Howard Pack, an American economist who specializes in the choice of technology, assumes that each of the nine industries listed in the previous paragraph receives $100 million of investment. If all this were spent on the most capital-intensive technology, it would generate employment of 58,000 and a value added of $364 million a year. But, if invested in the appropriate technology instead, the same investment would create over four times the employment (239,000) and 71 percent more value added ($624 million).[11]

Despite the advantages to be gained in both output and employment from using appropriate, more-labor-intensive methods in developing countries, we observe many industrial plants using processes that are too capital intensive. Several possible explanations for this were given in the discussion of the employment problem of Chapter 8 and elsewhere in this text. Market prices of productive factors, for example, typically do not reflect true factor scarcities (opportunity costs or shadow prices) and so distort technology choice. More labor-intensive methods usually are embodied in older models of equipment, frequently available only as used machinery, which may be difficult to learn about, obtain, and maintain; newer equipment may manufacture products of higher quality and value; or managers may not be skilled in handling large labor forces. These factors often are exaggerated. In any case, most of them can be incorporated in present value calculations that reveal least-cost technologies.

These factors probably do not explain the wide range of technologies, many of them apparently inappropriate, that can be observed in a single country or in similar countries. There may be two further explanations for this. First, different firms can face different factor prices. Foreign firms usually have access to cheaper capital than domestic companies can obtain, so their optimal choice of technology is more capital intensive. (However, this may be countered by the multinational firm's greater knowledge of and easier access to machinery using older techniques, some of which may

___

10. Howard Pack, "Aggregate Implications of Factor Substitution in Industry Processes," *Journal of Development Economics,* 11, no. 1 (August 1982), 7.

11. Ibid., p. 10.

be in use in older plants of the same company.) Among domestic companies, small firms, with limited access to formal capital markets, may have to pay more for their capital than large firms. Similarly, small firms may escape both unionization and minimum-wage laws and so are able to employ workers at lower costs. In Indonesia, economist Hal Hill observed four textile-weaving technologies in operation, with a capital-output ratio for the most modern looms over 200 times that for traditional handlooms. Two of these technologies represented least-cost choices for their firms. Surprisingly, these were the two most capital intensive. But when shadow prices were used, only the more labor-intensive of the two techniques remained appropriate.[12]

Second, investors may purchase inappropriate equipment because they and their managers have a strong bias toward the most modern machinery and the highest possible quality of output, with less emphasis on profitability and other economic considerations. Harvard management expert Louis Wells has called this the behavior of "engineering man."[13] If the characteristics of management constrain the choice of technology, the selection may be technique T3 in Figure 17–3, even though the budget line indicates the choice of technique T2. Such noneconomic behavior is more likely to prevail in highly protected, monopolistic situations, where a decision to produce at less than minimum cost will not threaten the firm's existence. State-owned enterprises are particularly prone to inefficiencies of this type.

ECONOMIES OF SCALE

In decisions about alternative technologies, **economies of scale** may be a crucial consideration. Economists at least since Adam Smith have observed that, for many kinds of production, larger facilities may be able to produce at lower unit costs than small ones. For example, steel produced in a mill designed for 2 million tons a year might cost 15 percent less than steel produced in a mill designed for only 1 million tons. As the scale of output rises, the potential average cost falls. (However, if the larger mill produces only 1 million tons, its average cost is likely to be higher than the small mill, because the small one was designed for lower output and the large one was not.) Readers familiar with the theory of the firm will recognize the concept of **long-run average cost,** the potential unit cost of out-

12. Hal Hill, "Choice of Technique in the Indonesian Weaving Industry," *Economic Development and Cultural Change,* 31, no. 2 (January 1983), 337–54.

13. Louis T. Wells, Jr., "Economic Man and Engineering Man: Choice of Technique in a Low-Wage Country," in C. P. Timmer et al., eds., *The Choice of Technology in Developing Countries* (Cambridge, MA: Center for International Affairs, Harvard University, 1975), pp. 69–94.

put when plant size is variable. If the long-run cost curve declines over a range of output relevant to the plant in question, as depicted in Figure 17–4, there are economies of scale.

Scale economies arise for a number of reasons. (1) Some costs, such as research and design efforts or start-up costs, may be fixed over a wide range of output. (2) The amount and cost of materials used in capital equipment will rise with output but not always in proportion. For example, the capacity of a boiler is related to its volume, which for a sphere varies as the cube of its radius, whereas the material used to build it is related to its area, proportional to the square of the radius. (3) The amount of inventory and other working capital does not rise proportionally to output. (4) Greater scale permits greater specialization of both workers and equipment (a point emphasized by Adam Smith), which in turn permits higher productivity. (5) Larger production runs reduce the number of times equipment must be set up or readjusted for each run. For example, a plant that produces two or more products with one machine, such as metal cans of different sizes, could be run more efficiently once it has enough volume to produce each on a separate machine and reduce setup costs. (6) Larger producers may be able to obtain quantity discounts when they procure input. All these economies apply to individual plants. At the level of the firm, further economies may arise in management, transportation, marketing, and finance as more plants are added.

These cost savings can be quite important in manufacturing certain products. Table 17–3 presents data on scale economies for several indus-

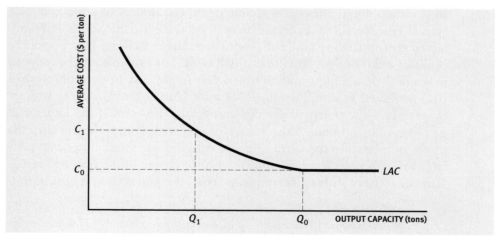

FIGURE 17–4 ECONOMIES OF SCALE. The long-run average cost curve, *LAC*, shows the average cost for plants designed to produce at any capacity. Average cost falls as capacity rises up to Q_0, sometimes called the *minimum efficient scale*. Q_1 is half Q_0. The percentage by which C_1 exceeds C_0 is a measure of the economies to be gained by building plants to a larger scale.

TABLE 17-3	ECONOMIES OF SCALE IN MANUFACTURING		
PRODUCT	PERCENT INCREASE IN AVERAGE COST	PLANT CAPACITY = THIS % OF MES[a]	MES AS % OF U.K. MARKET
REFRIGERATORS	7	33	85
ELECTRIC MOTORS	15	50	60
STEEL	11	33	27
SYNTHETIC RUBBER	15	50	24
PETROCHEMICALS	19	33	23
TIRES	5	50	17
OIL REFINERIES	4	33	14
BEER	5	33	12
KRAFT PAPER	13	50	11
CEMENT	26	33	10
GLASS BOTTLES	11	33	5
DAIRY PRODUCTS	2	67	1
FLOUR	21	67	1

Note: Estimates come from studies of European industries conducted from the late 1960s through the early 1980s.

[a]*Minimum efficient scale* is defined as the output beyond which average costs cease to decline (Q_0 in Figure 17-4) or beyond which no larger plants have been built.

Source: Cliff Pratten, "A Survey of the Economies of Scale," in Commission of the European Communities, *Research on the "Cost of Non-Europe,"* Vol. 2, *Studies on the Economics of Integration* (Luxembourg: Commission of the European Communities, 1988).

tries in Europe in the early 1980s. The **minimum efficient scale** (MES) is defined as a plant large enough so that no further economies can be gained by building a larger facility, Q_0 in Figure 17–4. The first column of the table gives the percentage by which the average cost would be greater if a plant were built to a smaller capacity; the second column shows that capacity (either one third, one half, or two thirds the MES). In practice, if the largest plant in existence does not exhaust the potential scale economies, investigators often take that output as the MES until a larger plant is built.

Some of the cost increases in column 1 are significant: from 11 to 26 percent for electric motors, steel, synthetic rubber, petrochemicals, Kraft paper, cement, glass bottles, and flour. However, this is not very meaningful unless we know how large the MES is relative to the national market. The last column shows how the MES compares to the market in the United Kingdom. For all products except glass, dairy products, and flour, these efficient plants would fill from 10 to 85 percent of British demand for those products. For refrigerators and electric motors, the minimum-efficient-size plant could supply well over half the demand.

The market in the United Kingdom is comparable to that in the largest developing countries if gross domestic product is measured in terms of purchasing power parity. Over a billion people in China, with PPP average income only an eighth of Britain's, have a GDP 2.5 times that in the

United Kingdom; India's GDP is about the same as Britain's; Brazil, Mexico, and Indonesia have economies 60 to 80 percent that of the United Kingdom. But in Nigeria, the largest economy in Africa, the Philippines, and Pakistan, GDP is only a fifth that of Britain. Moreover, in developing countries, it is likely that the effective demand for modern manufactures is considerably smaller than indicated by the comparison of GDPs, because in Britain a much larger share of the population has reached middle-class standards of income. Where markets are much smaller than the minimum efficient scale, unit costs may be much higher than those indicated in the table. Such an industry would remain viable only if protected from imports and given a monopoly.

The characteristics of these large-scale industries shed light on the industrialization process. Those with largest cost savings and the largest potential market shares are all, with the exception of beer, either producer goods (electric motors, steel, synthetic rubber, for example) or consumer durables (refrigerators and others not shown, such as automobiles). Thus, the nondurable consumer goods industries, such as processed foods, textiles, clothing, and footwear, develop early at least in part because economies of scale are no barrier, except in the smallest economies. The barriers to backward integration also are suggested by scale economies in producer goods.

Despite the scale economies, it may be efficient to build small plants in developing countries. A steel plant, for example, should be built when it can produce at a cost below the price of imported steel. This may happen long before the market grows to accommodate a steel mill of minimum efficient scale. Economic size is only one factor that bears on efficiency. All the others mentioned earlier in this text—productivity, opportunity costs of capital and labor, availability of raw materials and complementary inputs, managerial skills, and market organization—also affect the outcome and may outweigh the effects of scale economies. Techniques such as project appraisal (Chapter 12) can be employed to analyze the impact of these elements on profitability.

Moreover, the domestic market is not the only possibility. The "virtuous circle," through which export markets make it possible to attain scale economies, which in turn increase export competitiveness, was one of the forces behind Britain's Industrial Revolution. Indeed, if a domestic industry in a small developing country were efficient enough to compete with foreign plants at any given output, then scale economies would not matter: The home industry could export enough to achieve any scale desired. Developing countries like South Korea and Brazil have achieved scale economies, even in industries like steel and automobiles, with the help of export markets. Economic integration among developing countries may help other countries to do the same.

TABLE 17–4	SHARE OF SMALL ESTABLISHMENTS IN TOTAL MANUFACTURING EMPLOYMENT, 1980S (PERCENT)			
	DISTRIBUTION OF EMPLOYMENT BY SIZE CLASS (%)			
GNP PER CAPITA	1–4 WORKERS	5–19	20–99	100+
$100–500	64	7	4	25
$500–1,000	41	12	10	37
$1,000–2,000	11	13	14	61
$2,000–5,000	8	11	17	64
OVER $5,000	4	6	20	70

Source: Donald R. Snodgrass and Tyler S. Biggs, *Industrialization and the Small Firm: Patterns and Policies* (San Francisco: ICS Press, 1996).

SMALL-SCALE INDUSTRY

Although economies of scale require large plants in some branches of production, in many other industries small- and medium-scale firms can compete effectively with large ones (see Table 17–4). This is especially true in developing countries, where many widely used manufactured items, including most food and tobacco products, textiles, clothing, footwear, furniture and other wood products, cement blocks, bricks, tiles, and various simple metal products, commonly are made by smaller firms.

It often has been argued that developing country governments should promote small-scale industry as either a complement or an alternative to large-scale modern manufacturing. India, probably the postindependence leader in planning for large-scale industrialization, also pursued small-industry development with vigor, a legacy of Ghandi's famous advocacy of small units using traditional technologies. China's use of small-scale rural industry in support of local self-reliance is equally well known. E. F. Schumacher, author of *Small Is Beautiful*,[14] founded a movement of small-industry enthusiasts. Over the years, very few development plans have failed to pay homage to the goal of small-industry development.

Advocates of small-industry promotion promise a wide range of benefits, including accelerated employment creation, income generation for the poor, dispersal of economic activity to small towns and rural areas, and mobilization of latent entrepreneurial talent. They also argue that support for small enterprise and the **informal sector** (see Chapter 8) will create a wider base of political support for capitalism and free-market policies.[15]

14. E. F. Schumacher, *Small Is Beautiful* (London: Sphere Books, 1974).

15. See Hernando deSoto, *The Other Path* (New York: Harper and Row, 1989), and P. N. Dhar and H. F. Lydall, *The Role of Small Enterprises in Indian Economic Development* (Bombay: Asia Publishing House, 1961).

Shortly we assess the potential of small industry to realize these hopes, but first we need to consider what *small industry* really means. There are several different ways to classify manufacturing plants by scale, none perfect. Classifying by the number of workers employed has the advantage that data are widely available. Units with one to four workers (usually a proprietor and family members) can be classified as **cottage shops,** whereas larger plants can be divided into small enterprises (sometimes 5–19 workers), medium enterprises (20–99), and large enterprises (100 or more), respectively. Such distinctions are arbitrary. In a large country or a small industrial one, a plant employing 200 workers would be considered small. Moreover, when plants are classified by other criteria, such as capital invested or technology used, they may shift into different categories.

Cottage shops and small enterprises employ one half to three quarters of all manufacturing-sector workers in many low-income countries. Their share in manufacturing value added is likely to be much lower, however, usually about one fourth the total. This marked discrepancy between the employment share and the value-added share shows that the value added per worker is much lower on average in small plants than in large ones. In part, this reflects the greater labor intensity of small plants.

Since low-income countries typically have abundant labor but little capital, most economists would expect labor-intensive technologies to be efficient in these settings. By this line of reasoning, that small firms usually are more labor intensive sometimes is taken to mean that they are more efficient than large firms. As part of the informal sector, small firms may be exempted from, or escape the enforcement of, taxes, minimum-wage laws, employment codes, and other regulations that raise the costs of larger firms. They also may lack access to subsidized loans, foreign exchange at overvalued (cheap) rates, and controlled imports, which artificially lower the costs of larger firms. It has been theorized that this freedom from many sources of factor-price distortion may induce small firms to use resources more efficiently than large firms. Alternatively, however, they might simply use all resources less efficiently. Attempts to measure the relative efficiency of different-size plants in industries where large and small firms coexist generally have been unable to reach solid conclusions.[16] Such comparisons face many difficulties in any case, not least that product quality may differ greatly between large and small firms. Although cottage shops make cheap plastic sandals, for example, large plants may produce shoes of higher quality.

As a country develops, the average size of its industrial plants tends to rise as implied by Table 17–4. This rise is associated with the expansion of

---

16. Ian M. D. Little, Dipak Mazumdar, and John M. Page, Jr., *Small Manufacturing Enterprises* (New York: Oxford University Press for the World Bank, 1988). They also claim to detect a tendency for medium-size firms to be most efficient.

markets, which permits a few firms in some industries to expand and realize economies of scale and thereby beat out their smaller competitors. A related factor is declining transportation and communication costs, which facilitate the integration of national markets and permit goods to be manufactured in least-cost locations and then shipped to their final markets. Thus, the "natural monopoly" conferred on smaller local firms by high transportation costs and poor communication begins to break down. Industrialization also tends to narrow productivity and wage differentials among units of different sizes, a condition for the efficient allocation of resources.

The presence of many small firms in most poor countries and the many people who depend on them for a living does not necessarily mean that government should promote or subsidize small-scale industry. Most of the cottage shops and small enterprises in low-income countries probably have little capacity for enterprise growth. They typically provide a living for the proprietor and a few family members at a standard above that of peasant farmers but below that provided by efficient modern firms. Like small family farms, most of these "livelihood enterprises" survive as long as no better economic opportunities present themselves, then gradually disappear as the modern sector of the economy develops and workers move on to higher-productivity employment. Only a few small- and medium-scale enterprises have the potential to modernize themselves, upgrade their technologies, and compete successfully with larger firms. To do so, they usually must define some niche of excellence. The small firms that survive in industrial countries tend to be just as capital-intensive and high tech as larger firms in the same economy and to differ from them only in degree of specialization.

Can the promotion of small-scale industry deliver the benefits promised by its advocates? Let us examine the evidence on each of the claims noted earlier.

Small plants generally are more labor intensive than large ones, although there are many labor-intensive large firms as well. Labor intensity contributes to equity in countries where income is distributed very unequally and people often have difficulty finding remunerative employment. The amount a worker earns is more important than merely having a job, however; and the level of pay ultimately is linked to productivity. In small industries in the poorest countries, labor productivity is low and most jobs in small firms provide little more than a chance to share in the general poverty. Government policy should aim not just at raising employment but at helping firms of all scales to develop new markets, adopt new technologies, and raise labor productivity. This is more likely to occur in medium-scale firms than in very small ones.

The claim that small-scale industry promotes regional decentralization also needs considerable qualification. Although many small firms are located in rural areas and small towns, these tend to be traditional "livelihood enterprises" that are likely to lose out in the process of industrialization. Keeping them alive through subsidization might increase equity, but at a high cost to efficiency and long-term growth. Modern small firms, in contrast, cluster in large cities, perhaps even more densely than large firms. Large firms are more self-sufficient and rely on economies of scale to lower production costs. Small firms, however, depend more on economies of agglomeration generated by proximity to firms engaged in similar or complementary activities. Most small producers need access to intermediate material inputs and so prefer to be close to ports and other transport facilities. They are less likely than large firms to train their own workers, so they benefit from being near urban growth centers where skilled workers are located.

Small-scale industry indeed serves as a breeding ground for potential entrepreneurs. Most societies have actual or potential entrepreneurs in farming, retail trading, transportation, and other small-scale activities. Small-scale industry represents a feasible step for these entrepreneurs, who would be blocked from entering manufacturing if large amounts of credit and the ability to manage large-scale enterprises were essential. Small enterprises sometimes can be developed in imitation of earlier entrants and so require less-innovative entrepreneurs. Some small firms have the potential to grow to medium or even large enterprises. It is important, however, not to yield to romanticism. Statistically, very few small firms even survive over long periods of time, let alone grow up to be medium or large enterprises. The rate of business failure is high among small firms in all countries.

Government can assist by providing a legal system, supporting financial and other institutions, and pursuing market-based policies that permit successful enterprises to flourish and require unsuccessful ones to meet market pressures or give way to more efficient alternatives. Most governments can begin by eliminating the many facets of policy that discriminate against small firms. Controlled imports and subsidized credit seldom reach small firms, whereas licensing requirements, health regulations, zoning restrictions, and other measures often are used actively to discourage small enterprises, especially those operating in the informal sector. In the kind of market-based, outward-looking regime described in Chapter 18, small firms should thrive if they have the economic advantages claimed for them by the advocates of small-scale industrialization.

Even in a deregulated, market-oriented economy, however, many feel that small industry needs special help from government to overcome some of its initial handicaps. A fairly standard package of services is used to provide this assistance.[17] It includes credit, usually provided through a small-

17. See Eugene Staley and Richard Morse, *Modern Small Industry for Developing Countries* (New York: McGraw-Hill, 1965).

industry development bank or similar institution; technical advice, organized along the lines of an agricultural extension service; training programs for managers and skilled workers; help in setting up procurement and marketing channels; and industrial estates that provide sites with infrastructure and a focal point for the assistance package. The idea behind this kind of package is to help inexperienced entrepreneurs over their early hurdles, introduce them to regular marketing channels, and eventually make them self-reliant.

However, the package is expensive and often ineffective. It requires government agencies to contact numerous and varied individual entrepreneurs and offer assistance tailored to their specific needs and thus draws heavily on the government's limited managerial and technical resources. Firms served by these programs often find the advice they receive unhelpful and the places in industrial estates that they are offered poorly located or too expensive. Many have failed to repay their loans, and this has sometimes resulted in the bankruptcy of the specialized lending institution. At best, the expense and complexity of small-industry assistance programs limits their outreach to a small fraction of target firms. Nor is it clear that government agencies have the skills and nimbleness required to help small entrepreneurs deal with market situations. Therefore, this approach is no substitute for general economic policies that permit small operators to do what they do best.

INDUSTRY AND DEVELOPMENT GOALS

Industrialization is not a panacea for underdevelopment. But two of its strengths are essential for any development program. As suggested by the Lewis-Fei-Ranis two-sector model (Chapter 3), greater productivity in industry is a key to increased per capita income. And manufacturing provides a much larger menu of possibilities for efficient import substitution and increasing exports than is possible with primary industries alone.

Industrialization and rural development must proceed in tandem. Industry can supply agriculture with inputs, especially fertilizer and simple farm equipment, that raise farm productivity. If manufacturing is efficient, these inputs may be supplied more cheaply than imports. The relationship is reciprocal, because agriculture supplies raw materials for manufacturing, such as cotton and other fibers, rubber, or tobacco. Agriculture and industry also provide reciprocal consumer goods markets. If agricultural incomes grow in an egalitarian fashion, which may require land reform and broad-based rural development, then manufacturing will enjoy a wide and growing market for its consumer goods, one that may enable it to achieve scale economies in both production and marketing. Similarly, the growth of urban incomes, stimulated by industrial expansion, should provide a

TOWNSHIP AND VILLAGE ENTERPRISES IN CHINA

The Chinese have done what appears to be difficult in market economies: They have established modern small- and medium-sized factories in the Chinese countryside. In the first phase of successful development, the emphasis was on the supply of farm inputs, equipment, and consumer goods to communes and other rural customers. Several conditions made possible this early development. China's rural transportation and marketing system was poorly developed, so that rural communities were isolated from urban centers of production. Centralized planning and control of industrial goods intensified this isolation, because communes wanting fertilizer or trucks had to apply to authorities located in urban centers, a process that entailed long delays and often was unsuccessful. It was in the communes' interests for their regions to become self-reliant in agricultural inputs to avoid these delays, and it was also in the planners' interests if local materials, capital, and labor could be used, so that other industrial priorities were not sacrificed. Local industry had the additional advantages of bringing modern technology directly to the countryside and helping narrow the economic and social gaps between farm and city.

This knowledge of technology and how to organize a factory proved to be valuable to China's industrial development effort after market-oriented reforms were introduced in the early 1980s. With the abolition of central planning and the communes, part of the original rationale for these rural industries disappeared, but now these enterprises could buy whatever inputs they wanted and could afford on the open market. Renamed *township and village enterprises,* the factories began producing a wider and wider range of products, not only for the

continuing stimulus to agricultural output and productivity through increasing demand for food. The key to growing food demand is expanding employment and improved urban income distribution.

Industry by itself cannot generate sufficient jobs to absorb the growing number of workers or to equalize income distribution, especially in the poorest countries. Liberalized economies, with reduced controls and market prices closer to scarcity values, can help arrest the tendency toward capital intensity and inappropriate, modern technologies in manufacturing and thus raise job creation in industry. A renewed emphasis on small

countryside but for the urban areas and export as well. Because these enterprises were "owned" locally and relatively small, they were outside of the sphere of control of the central ministries in Beijing and could respond freely to market opportunities. Also, because they were small and, unlike the large state enterprises, lacked access to subsidized bank credit, it was acceptable politically to let loss-making township and village enterprises fail. Local governments had no resources to subsidize their losses, so these industries had to work extra hard to make sure they stayed profitable.

Not all areas of the country benefited equally from the development of township and village enterprises, however. The most dynamic development of this sector was in the coastal provinces of China and in areas within easy reach of cities. Mountainous regions and other areas remote from good infrastructure and urban markets had fewer township and village enterprises. Therefore, agglomeration effects, as indicated elsewhere in this chapter, mattered as much if not more for the smaller-scale township and village enterprises as they did for the large urban manufacturing establishments.

The result of these developments was that employment in township and village enterprises rose from 28.3 million workers in 1978 to 69.8 million in 1985 and 130.5 million in 1997. As a percentage of the total industrial output in China, the share of township and village enterprises rose from 22 percent in 1978 to 32 percent in 1985 and 38 percent in 1997. The share of the large state-owned enterprises, in contrast, fell from 78 percent in 1978 to 65 percent in 1985 and 26 percent in 1997 (the share of foreign joint ventures and outright private firms accounted for the remainder). Particularly during the latter half of the 1980s but throughout the 1990s as well, China's industrial and GDP growth rates would have been significantly lower had it not been for the dynamic growth of the township and village enterprise sector.

industry also may help. Moreover, to the extent that intermediate or innovative technologies are needed to save capital and create more jobs relative to output, an innovative, efficient capital goods industry is an essential part of a development strategy. But, in the final analysis, much of the burden for employment creation and income equalization will lie outside industry, in agriculture and the services.

Industry has been seen as a key to another goal of many developing countries: reduced dependence. If a country wants the ability to do without imports of essential commodities, it must develop both an integrated industrial structure and a productive agriculture. If it wishes to exclude foreign political and cultural influence, it must learn to operate its manufacturing plants without foreign help. Much of the discussion about reduced dependence really is about increasing autarky or self-sufficiency; this implies that a country must produce everything it needs. But an alternative goal suggests the capability of producing a wide variety of goods efficiently enough to trade them on world markets and obtaining some goods overseas when it is advantageous to do so. This leads to the outward-looking strategy discussed in the next chapter.

Behind these considerations lurks a hidden development goal: industrialization for its own sake. Despite advice from many quarters to temper their protective and other industrial policies and instead to promote greater efficiency, employment, and equity, many governments continue to establish the most modern, capital-intensive industries available. This cannot be attributed entirely to misguided policy. The desire to have modern industry may be as great for a country as the desire for a radio or car can be for an individual. To the extent that modern manufacturing is a goal in itself, the best that development economists can do is to point out how much could be accomplished with alternative policies and measure the costs of industrialization in terms of other goals that remain to be achieved.

18

TRADE AND DEVELOPMENT

We have seen in the last two chapters that, for many countries, the process of development is closely linked to a shift from primary products to industry. A country's endowment of the basic factors of production—capital, labor, land, and other natural resources—plays a fundamental role in influencing the precise contours and pace of this process. But comparative advantage is not immutable. Rather, relative factor endowments and comparative advantage tend to change gradually with population growth, degradation of natural resources, capital accumulation, education of the labor force, and the acquisition and adaptation of new technology. In most (although not all) countries, comparative advantage evolves during the process of development away from land- and resource-intensive products toward manufactures: To labor-intensive products first, then to capital-intensive and skill-intensive industries, and eventually to products embodying newer technologies. In some countries, new activities include services, such as tourism, accounting and other basic financial services, and electronic commerce. Within certain broad limits, determined by factor endowments, economic structure, and technology, there is considerable scope for government policies to accelerate (or retard) the pace of structural change and development, alter the mix of economic activities, and influence the technologies employed. Virtually all governments attempt to hasten the gradual shift to a manufacturing or service-based economy. And, depending on the strategy a government adopts, there is some choice about which patterns are followed and even the possibility of marked deviations from the "norms" established by structural change elsewhere.

International trade is at the center of this shift from primary production to manufactures and services. Table 18–1 shows the patterns and pace of change in the composition of both trade and production in recent decades for several developing countries. For some countries, the last third of the twentieth century was a period of rapid growth and change, with dramatic shifts from primary exports to manufactured exports. For example, Malaysia's share of primary product exports fell from 93 percent to 24 percent, matched by a rise in manufactured exports from 7 percent to 76 percent of all exports. At the same time, agriculture's share in total production fell markedly, while industry's share rose. Such dramatic changes can take place only in the context of rapid economic growth, and Malaysia recorded very strong growth of 4.4 percent per capita between 1970 and 1996. To date, such rapid development and structural change has been limited mainly to the well-known success stories of East and Southeast Asia. However, a handful of non-Asian countries are in this group, including Tunisia, Mauritius, and more recently the Dominican Republic. Most other developing countries have seen more modest shifts, and some have seen little change at all. For example, Venezuela's share of primary product exports has changed only slightly, as have its shares of agricultural and industrial production. At the same time, the Venezuelan economy grew very slowly, with population growth exceeding economic growth, so that per capita income actually fell between 1970 and 1996.

Government choices about trade policy for manufactured products can have a substantial impact on the process of structural change and development (primary products were discussed in Chapter 16). Broadly speaking, governments in developing countries have employed two different trade strategies to try to force the pace of changing comparative advantage and to alter the pattern of industrialization: Import substitution and outward-looking development. **Import substitution** is the replacement (or substitution) of imports by products produced by domestic firms. Since new firms in developing countries often are unable (initially) to compete on world markets, import substitution aims to protect domestic firms from international competition by making imported products more expensive or more difficult to purchase. **Outward-looking trade policies** shift the focus from production for the domestic market toward manufacturing for export to foreign markets. This strategy aims to make producers internationally competitive through market forces and supporting institutional arrangements. The core idea behind import substitution is that newly developing industries cannot survive at first without being able to charge higher prices in the home market than those that would prevail in the presence of competition from imports. In contrast, the core idea behind an outward-looking trade strategy is that firms should produce goods in which they can compete internationally to gain access to new

TABLE 18-1   SHIFTS IN THE COMPOSITION OF PRODUCTION AND EXPORTS, 1970–96

COUNTRY	SHARES OF GDP (%)				SHARES OF EXPORTS (%)				GDP GROWTH PER CAPITA (% P.A.)
	1970		1996		1970		1996		
	AGRICULTURE	INDUSTRY	AGRICULTURE	INDUSTRY	PRIMARY	MANUFACTURES	PRIMARY	MANUFACTURES	
KOREA, REPUBLIC	25	29	6	43	23	77	8	92	7.4
SINGAPORE	2	30	0	36	72	28	16	84	6.7
THAILAND	26	25	11	40	95	5	27	73ᵃ	5.3
INDONESIA	45	19	16	43	99	1	49	51	4.7
MALAYSIA	29	25	13	46	93	7	24	76	4.4
MAURITIUS	16	22	10	32	98	2	32	68	3.8
SRI LANKA	28	24	22	25	99	1	27	73ᵇ	3.1
BRAZIL	12	38	14	36	87	13	46	54	3.0
TUNISIA	17	21	14	28	81	19	20	80	2.8
DOMINICAN REPUBLIC	23	26	13	32	96	4	23	77ᵇ	2.7
INDIA	45	22	28	29	48	52	26	74ᵃ	2.6
PAKISTAN	37	22	26	25	43	57	16	84	2.5
MEXICO	12	29	5	26	68	32	22	78	1.7
THE PHILIPPINES	30	32	21	32	93	7	16	84	1.2
MALAWI	44	17	40	21	97	3	93	7ᵃ	1.1
ALGERIA	11	42	13	48	93	7	96	4ᵃ	0.9
HONDURAS	32	22	22	31	92	8	69	31	0.7
ARGENTINA	10	42	6	31	86	14	70	30	0.4
PERU	19	32	7	37	99	1	84	16	0.4
SENEGAL	21	18	18	17	81	19	50	50ᵃ	−0.3
VENEZUELA	6	39	4	47	99	1	88	12	−0.4

Note: Value added in services is not shown, so shares of GDP do not add to 100 percent.

ᵃ1995 data.

ᵇ1994 data.

Source: World Bank, World Development Indicators, 1998 (Washington, DC: World Bank, 1998).

technologies, increase efficiency, and enlarge the scope of their potential market and range of products.

Import Substitution

Import substitution was the principal path to industrialization for almost two centuries following England's emergence as the first industrial power in the Industrial Revolution of the eighteenth century. In the newly independent United States, Alexander Hamilton's 1791 *Report on Manufactures* argued for tariffs to protect U.S. manufacturers from cheap British imports, and President Jefferson unintentionally boosted U.S. manufacturing by the politically inspired Embargo of 1807. Friedrich Lizst, a German economist, espoused protective tariffs as an instrument to industrialize Germany in the mid-nineteenth century. All the major European powers, including Russia (both before and after the Communist revolution), and Japan protected their manufacturing as it became apparent that military strength depended on industrial strength.

In the developing world, import substitution was first explored in Latin America when its primary export markets were severely disrupted, first by the Great Depression of the 1930s and subsequently by the scarcity of commercial shipping during World War II. These events effectively cut off Latin America's trade with the rest of the world, so these countries began to develop their own domestic industrial capacity. Emerging from the war with fledgling industries, countries like Argentina, Brazil, Colombia, and Mexico began systematically to erect barriers against competing imports from the United States and Europe. The export pessimism chronicled by Argentine economist Raul Prebisch, Hans Singer, and others (see Chapter 16) reinforced protectionist sentiment, and Latin America developed import substitution regimes with a multitude of protective techniques that later were emulated by other developing countries. In Asia and Africa, independence following World War II was the stimulus to embark on import substitution, as the newly independent countries wanted to develop their own industrial capacity and reduce their imports from the colonial powers. By the 1960s import substitution had become the dominant strategy of economic development.

The underlying concept of import substitution is simple. First, identify products with large domestic markets, as indicated by substantial imports over the years. Then ensure that local manufacturers can master the production technologies or that foreign investors are willing to supply technology, management, and capital to local firms. This implies focusing on simple technologies that can be mastered quickly, rather than on products requiring more advanced machinery and highly skilled labor. Finally, erect

protective barriers, either tariffs or quotas on imports, to raise the price of competing imports, overcome the high initial cost of local production, and make it profitable for potential investors in the target industries. Tariffs are taxes imposed on imports at the border; quotas are quantitative limits on specified categories of imports. As we shall see, either strategy results in higher prices paid by consumers on domestic markets, which is the most important economic cost of the import substitution strategy.

This stylized approach—focus on relatively simple products with large domestic markets—implies that consumer goods industries, especially processed foods, beverages, textiles, clothing, and footwear, should become the first targets for investment. These products are manufactured with relatively standardized technologies easily accessible to developing country producers, and it was believed that consumers could bear the higher costs of local production without disrupting development. By contrast, capital goods are a less favorable target for import substitution, since they require more sophisticated skills, and raising the cost of capital equipment would discourage investors. Nevertheless, many developing countries have used import substitution to protect steel, machinery, and other capital goods, usually with little success.

Economists find much to criticize in the protective tariffs and quotas that are the sine qua non of import substitution, as this chapter makes clear. But there are valid arguments in favor of protective tariffs, the most compelling of which is the concept of an **infant industry.** Entrepreneurs opening a new production facility in a developing country must compete against firms from industrialized countries that often have long experience in producing the product and have mastered both the production technology and the marketing. The managers and workers of the new, or "infant," industry must learn to use these technologies efficiently by the standards of the industrial countries. In some cases, this may require some engineering adaptation of the technology to suit local conditions. This process of **learning by doing** can take several years. Until these infant industries gain the necessary experience, however, they cannot compete on international markets and are likely to lose out to competing imports on both price and quality. Private investors might finance these near-term losses if the prospects are good for long-term profits. In developing countries, however, domestic capitalists often appear to shun projects with long-delayed returns, partly because capital markets usually are not sufficiently developed to assemble the funds of many savers into large, long-term loans for industry. Without some form of assistance, the argument goes, these investments are unlikely to take place, and developing countries will not be able to learn the skills needed to eventually compete with imports on equal footing. The alternative, almost universally employed, is for government to protect infant industries from competing imports by imposing tariffs or import quotas.[1]

To justify protection or a subsidy on economic grounds, an infant industry must be capable of eventually competing without protection against imports in the home market or, a stronger condition, in export markets. This suggests that, ideally, tariffs should be *temporary* and decline toward zero over time as productivity increases and production costs fall. Eventually, all protection should be removed and the firm should be able to compete with imports with no further assistance. For this strategy to be economically worthwhile, the eventual benefits to society of establishing the new industry (suitably discounted as explained in Chapter 12) must exceed the costs of protection.[2]

All too often, however, these conditions are not met. The industrial landscape is littered with infants that never grew up to compete internationally, from the petrochemical industry of Colombia to the textile industry of Kenya. These kinds of firms require protection indefinitely, at continuous cost to the rest of society. Sometimes, this outcome is due to an initially poor choice to protect the wrong kinds of activities (like steel); often it stems from the reluctance of government officials to remove the comfortable protection given to politically well-connected industrialists.

For reasons that will become apparent, import substitution ultimately is a limited strategy. After an initial burst of industrial output, growth rates typically bog down. Once new industries saturate the domestic market, their growth is constrained by the average growth of the economy. Often firms reach this market limit at production levels that do not achieve economies of scale, so they still are unable to compete with imports. Lack of competition dulls the incentive to increase productivity, especially as profits depend as much on levels of protection as on cost-saving improvements. The contradictory incentives of protection, described later in this chapter, discourage backward integration into intermediate goods industries. The high costs embedded in protected manufacturing make it difficult for firms to switch to exports and compete in markets abroad. And, by reducing their commercial links with the rest of the world, import-substituting countries limit their exposure to new technology and ideas.

Governments use three basic instruments of trade policy to provide higher prices or lower costs at home for selected firms: import tariffs, quotas that restrict import quantities, and production subsidies. A fourth policy

1. One reason most economists consider subsidies to be a superior alternative is because they require a budget outlay that makes clear the cost of protection. Virtually all governments have preferred to use tariffs or quotas and make consumers pay instead.

2. For a complete specification of the infant industry argument, see Harry G. Johnson, "Optimal Trade Interventions in the Presence of Domestic Distortions" in R. E. Caves et al., *Trade, Growth and the Balance of Payments* (Amsterdam: North-Holland, 1965), pp. 3–34.

instrument, the exchange rate, treats all traded goods uniformly, but changes the relationship between traded and nontraded goods. Later in the chapter we show how it is possible to combine all four policy instruments into measures of the extent to which domestic prices are distorted from world prices.

PROTECTIVE TARIFFS

In the early stages of import substitution, when a protective tariff is placed on competing consumer goods imports, the most direct effect is to raise the domestic price of the good, say, cloth, above the world price. For the importing country, the world price of imported cloth is the cost of the cloth landed at the port of entry, usually called the *c.i.f. prices* (including cost, insurance, and freight) or *border price.* With no tariff, the domestic price of cloth would settle at the border price. When a tariff is imposed, however, the price of imported cloth rises above the border price. Domestic prices normally rise by the full extent of the tariff, as long as two conditions hold: (1) The home country's demand for imports does not affect world prices (that is, the world supply is perfectly elastic), and (2) the tariff does not eliminate imports altogether. Any potential manufacturer can charge anything up to the tariff-supported domestic price and still compete with imports, assuming its quality is comparable and domestic consumers do not prefer imports simply because they are foreign.

The increase in domestic prices as a result of the tariff, called the **nominal rate of protection,** is depicted in Figure 18–1. At the world price, P_w (equal to the border price), consumers demand Q_1 of cloth and local producers find it profitable to produce Q_2; the balance, $M_1 = Q_1 - Q_2$, is imported. If an ad valorem (that is, a percentage) tariff t_0 is imposed on imports competing with domestic cloth and if the world supply is perfectly elastic, then the domestic price rises to P_d; this reduces the quantity demanded to Q_3 and increases domestic production to Q_4. Imports are reduced to $M_2 = Q_3 - Q_4$. The increase in domestic output from Q_2 to Q_4 has two effects. First, it increases *producers' surplus* by an amount given by trapezoid *a*, which captures the extent to which producers receive a price (P_d) that exceeds their marginal cost of production, represented by the domestic supply schedule. Second, the increase in production entails a *resource cost,* given by triangle *b*, because factors of production are diverted from more productive uses into import substitution for imported cloth. The government's tariff revenue is equal to the quantity of imports, M_2, multiplied by the tariff rate times the world price, represented by rectangle $c = t_0 P_w M_2$. On the consumption side, consumers pay for protection by the loss of *consumer surplus,* equal to area $a + b + c + d$, generated by both the higher price and reduced consumption. This loss to consumers is only partially compensated by the gains through transfers to either

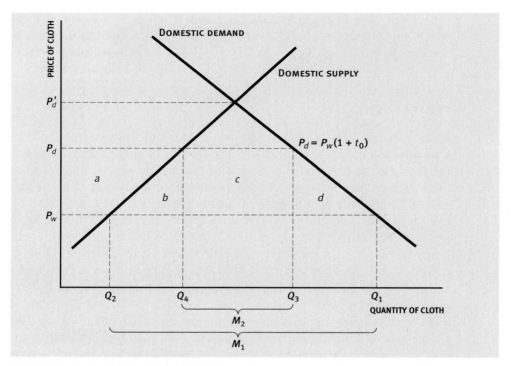

FIGURE 18–1   NOMINAL TARIFF PROTECTION. The imposition of a protective tariff, t_0, causes the domestic price, P_d, to rise above the world price, P_w. Domestic production therefore increases. The resulting loss in consumers' surplus ($a + b + c + d$) is offset by the gain in producers' surplus (a) and tariff revenue for the government (c). The remaining areas b and d represent deadweight losses.

producers (triangle a) or the general public (though the tax revenues represented by rectangle c). Area $b + d$, two triangles representing welfare losses not compensated by gains to anyone, is called the *deadweight loss.* Note that, in this example, the deadweight loss increases along with the tariff rate. A tariff rate that raises the domestic price to P_d' is called a **prohibitive tariff,** since at that point domestic demand equals domestic supply and no cloth is imported.

To see how this might work in practice, let us say that the Philippines decides that it would like to protect its domestic pharmaceutical industry with the intention that domestic firms eventually will be able to compete with imports. The government begins by focusing on the market for aspirin. Initially, total domestic sales of aspirin amount to 10 million bottles each year, of which 2 million are produced domestically. In terms of Figure 18–1, $Q_1 = 10$ million, $Q_2 = 2$ million, and imports (M_1) = 8 million bottles. Aspirin sells for the world (import) price of 50 pesos per bottle, so $P_d = P_w = $ P 50/bottle. The government decides to introduce a 50 percent tariff on imported aspirin ($t_0 = 0.50$), which immediately drives the import price to P 75/bottle (P 50/bottle $\times$ 1.50). Consumers react by purchasing less aspirin, so total sales (Q_3) fall to 9 million. Domestic producers increase their sales price to match the import price, so $P_d =$ P 75/bottle, and the higher price allows them to increase domestic production to $Q_4 = 4$ million bottles. The combined effect of reduced total sales and increased domestic production leads to a drop in imports to $M_2 = Q_3 - Q_4 = 5$ million bottles.

Consumers, of course, bear the burden of the higher tariff, as represented by the loss in consumer surplus, $a + b + c + d$. We can calculate this loss precisely in our example by measuring the area of the trapezoid formed by $a + b + c + d$, which amounts to P 237.5 million.[3] Consumers lose two ways. First, they pay an extra P 25 for each of the 9 million bottles of aspirin they consume (amounting to a loss of P 25 $\times$ 9 million = P 225 million). Second, they reduce their consumption from 10 million to 9 million bottles, reducing their welfare by the area d, which is equal to P 12.5 million.[4] This last amount is not recaptured by anyone in the economy and is part of the total welfare loss from the tariff. Domestic producers, by contrast, gain from the new policy, since they are able to increase their output and charge a higher price for everything they produce. This gain in producer surplus is captured by the area of the small trapezoid a, which in our example is P 75 million.[5] However, the increase in production entails a cost because it uses labor, machinery, and raw materials that could be used to produce something else. This resource cost is captured by the area of triangle b, which is equal to P 25 million.[6] Finally, the government gains from increased revenue collection from the new tariff, amounting to P 25 on each of the 5 million bottles imported, or P 125 million. These gains to the government presumably are shared by society at large, since the government can either reduce other taxes or increase spending. Thus, of the loss in consumer surplus of P 237.5 million, producers gain P 75 million and an additional P 125 million is transferred to the government through higher taxes. The remaining P 37.5 million (equal to $b + d$) is the deadweight

3. The area of a trapezoid is found with the formula $A = \frac{1}{2}h(b_1 + b_2)$, where A is the area, h is the height of the trapezoid, and $b_1 + b_2$ are the lengths of the two bases. In our example, the height of the trapezoid is $P_d - P_w = $ P 25; the bottom base is equal to Q_1, or 10 million; and the top base is equal to Q_3, or 9 million. Therefore, the area of the trapezoid is $A = \frac{1}{2} \times$ (P 25) $\times$ (10 million + 9 million) = P 237.5 million.

4. The area of triangle d is calculated by the formula $A = \frac{1}{2} \times$ base $\times$ height. In the example, $A = \frac{1}{2} \times 1$ million $\times$ P 25, or P 12.5 million.

5. The height of trapezoid a is P 25, the bottom base is equal to $Q_2 = 2$ million, and the top base is $Q_4 = 4$ million. Therefore, the area of a is $A = \frac{1}{2} \times$ (P 25) $\times$ (2 million + 4 million) = P 75 million.

6. $A = \frac{1}{2} \times$ base $\times$ height, where the base is $Q_4 - Q_2 = 2$ million, and the height is P 25. Therefore, $A = \frac{1}{2} \times$ (2 million) $\times$ (P 25) = P 25 million.

loss to society from the higher tariff. Import substitution makes sense economically only if these losses can be compensated by future gains if and when firms eventually become competitive on world markets.

IMPORT QUOTAS

The protective effects of tariffs also can be achieved through restrictions on imports, known as **quantitative restrictions,** *quotas,* or *import licensing.* For both the government and domestic manufacturers, import quotas have the advantage of permitting a known quantity of imports. With tariffs, the quantity of imports depends on the elasticities of supply and demand (reflected by the slopes of the supply and demand schedules), which are known in advance only approximately. A quota that limits imports to the same quantity as a tariff would have many of the same effects. In our example, a quota that limited aspirin imports to 5 million bottles would have some of the same outcomes as the 50 percent tariff. To see this, refer back to Figure 18–1. Instead of the tariff t_0, assume the government limits imports of aspirin to the quantity $M_2 = Q_3 - Q_4$. As with the tariff, the domestic price would still rise to P_d, domestic production would rise from Q_2 to Q_4 and cause a resource cost measured by triangle b, and consumption would fall from Q_1 to Q_3 and add the area of triangle d to the deadweight loss. But, in three important respects, import quotas have different effects than tariffs.

The first difference is that the government no longer collects tariff revenue. Instead the government issues licenses to a limited number of importers, giving them the right to purchase imports of aspirin up to a total of M_2. If the government simply issues the licenses with no fee (which many governments do, using the licenses as patronage for politically well-connected importers), license holders earn a windfall equal to the area of rectangle c. This is because the importer can purchase the goods at price P_w on the world market and sell them at P_d domestically. This windfall, often called a **quota rent** or *premium,* can be substantial, so import licenses are valuable to their recipients. Much effort is expended and large bribes are offered to obtain import licenses, with consequences discussed later in this chapter. Alternatively, the government could retain c as revenue if it were to sell the import licenses at auction. Potential importers would be willing to buy licenses for as much as $P_d - P_w$ per unit of imports. They then could purchase each unit of imported aspirin for P_w, the world price, and break even by selling it at the domestic price, P_d. In that case, the auction price for import licenses would just equal the tariff t_0 that would have led to the same quantity of imports.

The second difference between quotas and tariffs is that quotas can convert a single domestic manufacturer into a monopolist that can charge whatever price maximizes profits. This is not the case with a tariff, since even at a high tariff, goods still can be imported, and domestic producers are forced to compete with imports on the margin at price P_d. But, if the tariff is converted to a quota, even though the same initial quantity of imports is allowed in, domestic producers no longer have to compete with imports. Once the quota has been filled, there is no alternative source of supply to compete with domestic monopolists. Local suppliers then can use their market power to restrict domestic output and charge a monopolist's price above the world price plus tariff, with a consequent loss to consumers and a net loss to the economy.

A third and related difference between tariffs and quotas is how the market outcome changes in a dynamic setting with changes in world prices or domestic supply or demand. Consider, for example, a fall in the world price, P_w. With a tariff in place, both P_w and P_d would fall, giving consumers the benefit of the lower price. Consumption would increase, domestic production would decline, and imports would rise to fill the gap. Under a quota, however, imports could not rise. As a result, domestic production and consumption would remain unchanged, and the domestic price would remain at P_d. The lower world price simply increases the quota rent, with the benefit going directly to import license holders. Put more generally, under most (but not all) circumstances, since tariffs allow imports on the margin, domestic producers and consumers react on the margin to market changes as they would in an open economy; with quotas, they react on the margin as they would in a closed economy. Because of these three consequences of quotas, economists prefer tariffs. As a result, trade reforms and international trade agreements often start with the conversion of quotas to equivalent tariffs, which bears the inelegant name **tariffication.**

SUBSIDIES

Governments also can use subsidies and other preferential treatment to provide the same relative profitability as tariffs. Subsidies can be used to "protect" exports and even nontraded goods, in addition to import substitutes. If textile production receives a 20 percent protective tariff while steel production receives a 20 percent subsidy on output, there is no change in their relative probability. The only difference is that textile consumers pay for that industry's protection through higher domestic prices, while taxpayers, through the government, pay for the steel industry's protection. Figure 18–2 shows the equivalence of tariffs and subsidies.

Economists generally prefer the use of subsidies instead of protective tariffs because, as shown in Figure 18–2, consumers purchase more of a good under a subsidy while society pays no more for production than under an equivalent tariff. Therefore, welfare losses under a subsidy,

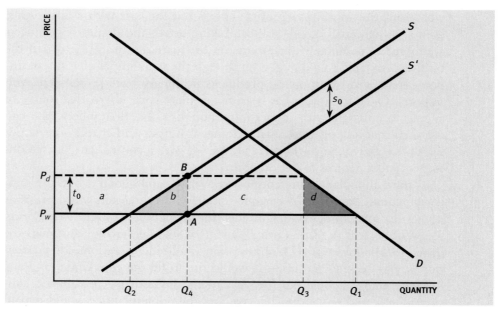

FIGURE 18–2   COMPARISON OF TARIFFS AND SUBSIDIES. If, instead of a tariff, t_0 (see Figure 18–1), the industry were given an equal subsidy, $s_0 = t_0$, the effective supply curve shifts from S to S'. As with the tariff, domestic production is at Q_4 and producers receive the same price, $P_d = P_w(1 + s_0)$. However, consumers now purchase Q_1 instead of Q_3 and pay the world price, P_w, instead of P_d. The subsidy is area $a + b$, paid by taxpayers instead of consumers. The deadweight loss is only triangle b, less than $b + d$ under a tariff. But, if purchasers of the good were taxed at the rate t_0 to pay for the subsidy, the outcome would be identical to that in Figure 18–1.

triangle b, are smaller than those under an equivalent tariff, triangles b plus d.[7] Considering again the aspirin example, with a production subsidy of P 25/bottle, producers still can consume the original 10 million bottles at P 50 bottle, so there is no loss in consumer surplus. Instead, the government (and, therefore, society at large) pays a production subsidy of P 25/bottle. With the subsidy, domestic producers increase production to *4 million bottles, so the subsidy costs P 25 × 4 million = P 100 million. The area of trapezoid a (earlier calculated at P 75 million) accrues to producers as a gain in producer surplus. The net loss is the resource cost of triangle b, which is P 25 million.

Another advantage of subsidies is that, because they usually appear as an expenditure item in the government's budget and must be financed through taxation, there is an annual accounting for the costs of protection offered in this way. The government, therefore, is more restrained in

7. This ignores the additional distortions and welfare losses introduced when the government tries to finance the subsidy by raising additional tax revenue or cutting expenditures. If consumers are taxed to pay the subsidy, the outcome and welfare loss is identical to that with a tariff, as in Figure 18–1.

conferring this kind of protection and correspondingly more likely to adhere to infant industry rules and keep protection moderate and short lived.[8] (Unfortunately, for these same reasons, government officials tend to prefer quotas or tariffs to subsidies.) In addition, subsidies can be targeted more precisely than protective tariffs. Whatever the source of high costs—expensive capital, high wage rates, or lack of trained workers—subsidies can be paid to offset those costs. Protective tariffs, in contrast, can compensate only by raising the domestic price of output.

Export subsidies have been part of several import substitution regimes: In Pakistan, exporters of nontraditional goods got access to licensed imports that carried large quota premiums; in Colombia, exporters were granted certificates entitling them to income tax reductions; and in Ghana, cash subsidy payments were offered. These schemes worked for a time in Pakistan and Colombia, but in most countries such subsidies were weak antidotes to the much stronger incentives to produce for the protected domestic market. And, with the notable exception of the Asian tigers, government officials often made it difficult for exporters to actually collect export incentives, sometimes attempting to collect rents by threatening to withhold payments otherwise.

EFFECTIVE RATES OF PROTECTION

So far, we have examined the effects of tariffs, quotas, and subsidies on output prices and ultimately consumer and producer behavior. However, manufacturers also are concerned with the prices of inputs, and more generally the difference between input and output prices. Trade policies that affect the prices of capital goods and raw material inputs can influence producers just as much as policies that directly affect output prices. A textile manufacturer that imports cotton to spin into yarn and weave into cloth is concerned not only with the price of the cloth but with the margin between the cost of imported cotton (and other imported inputs, such as chemicals and dyes) and the sale price of finished cloth. Within this margin, the manufacturer must pay wages, rents, and interest on borrowed capital and extract profit. The greater is that margin, the more room there is to accommodate higher factor costs and the higher is the potential profit. This margin is the *value added measured in domestic prices*. It can be increased by raising tariffs on competing imports of finished products *or* reducing tariffs on imported inputs (or both). This dual effect of the tariff structure is called *effective protection*. To measure the concept of effective protection, it is necessary to compare two margins: First, the margin

---

8. But not necessarily. The United States and especially the European Community have subsidized their farmers for decades at rates that rival the effective rates protection provided for industry by import-substitution regimes.

between the domestic, tariff-determined prices of inputs and outputs (the value added measured in domestic prices) second, the same margin measured at world or c.i.f. prices, called the *value added measured in world prices*. The fraction by which the first margin exceeds the second is called the **effective rate of protection** (ERP):

$$\text{ERP} = \frac{\text{value added (domestic prices)} - \text{value added (world prices)}}{\text{value added (world prices)}} \qquad [18\text{--}1]$$

Whereas the nominal rate of protection focuses on the effect of trade policies on *prices,* the effective rate of protection examines the impact of trade policies on *value added.* To refine this concept further, note that value added in domestic prices (V_d) is the difference between the potential domestic price (P_d) and the potential domestic cost of material inputs per unit of output (C_d). Further, the potential domestic price is equivalent to the world price (P_w) plus the increase permitted by the ad valorem tariff on competing imports (t_0). The potential domestic cost equals the cost at world prices (C_w) plus any increase permitted by the ad valorem tariff on imported inputs (t_i). The denominator of equation 18–1, the value added measured in world prices (V_w), is the difference between P_w and C_w.[9] Given this, then,

$$\text{ERP} = \frac{(P_d - C_d) - (P_w - C_w)}{P_w - C_w} \qquad [18\text{--}2]$$

$$= \frac{P_w(1 + t_0) - C_w(1 + t_1) - (P_w - C_w)}{P_w - C_w}$$

$$= \frac{P_w t_0 - C_w t_i}{P_w - C_w} \qquad [18\text{--}3]$$

As a last refinement, equation 18–3 can be put in terms of a dollar of output by dividing the fraction through by P_w. The cost of an input for a dollar's worth of output, C_w/P_w, can be designated a, an input coefficient. If we allow for several inputs, each with its own input coefficient, a_i, and its own tariff, t_i, then the formula can be written

$$\text{ERP} = \frac{(t_0 - \Sigma\, a_i t_i)}{(1 - \Sigma\, a_i)} \qquad [18\text{--}4]$$

9. A complication is the cost of inputs, such as electricity and water, that are not traded and therefore have no world price. These can be treated either as a cost of production at zero tariff, in which case they cancel out of the numerator and appear only in the denominator, or be broken down into their local and imported components, with the imported components, such as fuel to generate electricity, treated as traded input and the local costs, such as wages, treated as part of the value added.

To illustrate the workings of effective protection,[10] assume that $100 of cloth, valued at world prices, would require $60 of material inputs, such as cotton and chemicals, also valued at world prices. The value added is $40 at world prices. Consider three stylistic cases of tariff policy: (1) The tariff on output is exactly the same as the tariff on inputs, so $t_0 = t_i$, (2) the tariff on output is higher than the tariff on inputs, so $t_0 > t_i$, and (3) the tariff on output is lower than the tariff on inputs, so $t_0 < t_i$. In the first case, if the government imposes a uniform duty of 10 percent on both competing imports and imported inputs, then from equation 18–3, we see that

$$ERP = 100(0.10) - 60(0.10)/(100 - 60) = 0.10.$$

A uniform tariff, 10 percent, in this case, yields an effective rate of protection of 10 percent, exactly equal to the nominal rate of protection.

In the second case, suppose that, to encourage investment in the textile industry, the government were to permit textile firms to import cotton and chemicals duty free. Then $t_i = 0$ and

$$ERP = 100(0.10)/40 = 0.25.$$

Effective protection now is 25 percent. More generally, if t_0 is greater than t_i, the effective rate of protection (in this case, 25 percent) exceeds the nominal rate of protection (10 percent). Similarly, if the input duty stayed at 10 percent but competing cloth imports were taxed at 20 percent, the ERP would rise to 35 percent. This latter case is illustrated graphically in Figure 18–2. Note, even though only moderate nominal protection is provided, the domestic manufacturer enjoys a large margin of 35 percent over the value added in world prices. Even modest tariffs on competing imports can have substantial effects on the value added. The higher is the effective rate of protection, the greater the incentive to establish the industry in the country, the greater the bias against investment in less protected sectors, and the greater the economic costs of protection.

For the third case, suppose that the government decides to protect cotton yarn producers but not textile manufactures by imposing a 10 percent tariff on cotton and no tariff on textiles. In that case,

$$ERP = 100(0) - 60(0.10)/(100 - 60) = -0.15.$$

Under these circumstances, tariff policy actually *reduces* the value added that can be earned in the textile industry (relative to the value added in world

10. For a complete, although advanced, treatment of effective protection, see W. M. Corden, *The Theory of Protection* (London: Oxford University Press, 1971), especially Chaps. 2 and 3.

prices), significantly undermining the incentives to invest in the industry. While a combination of tariffs that gives rise to a negative ERP may seem unlikely, it actually is fairly common.[11] Two important sectors often face negative protection: Agriculture and exports. Governments usually like to keep food prices low to keep urban consumers happy and so are reluctant to impose duties on food imports. Therefore, any protective tariffs on fertilizer, seeds, or irrigation equipment can undermine the probability of agriculture production and switch investment out of agriculture. In the case of exports, the government cannot use tariffs to raise output prices, since exporters sell on world markets. A tariff on inputs (say, in an attempt to protect yarn used by textile exporters) raises exporters' costs and reduces the value added and the incentives to invest in export industries. This pattern of protection is a critical problem undermining the international competitiveness of exporting firms in many developing countries, a subject we return to later in the chapter.

This last example illustrates another problem with the import substitution strategy: ineffective forward and backward linkages. Once a sector receives import protection, downstream industries are hurt by the higher costs. A tariff on yarn makes it much more difficult to develop a textile industry, unless it too receives tariff protection. But protection also makes it difficult to create backward linkages. Say that the government has put a 10 percent tariff on imported yarn to protect domestic producers and it now would like to support the cotton producers that sell to the yarn makers. The yarn makers, as the most recent recipients of protection, will lobby loudest against giving protection to cotton producers. The reason is simple: Yarn makers have successfully lobbied for a protective tariff to increase their own profits, and they are not about to lose these profits by paying higher prices for cotton. As a general rule, the first to receive protection will strongly resist giving it to others.[12]

Tariff structures in most countries, including most industrial countries, are like the second case described: Duties tend to escalate from low rates on imported industrial inputs to higher rates on imports of finished goods that compete with domestic manufactures. In fact, the levels of protection in the hypothetical examples are modest by world standards. ERPs of 100 percent or more are common in several industries in countries strongly pursuing import substitution. ERPs also can range widely across industries, resulting in severe discrimination against particular kinds of investment.

11. A negative effective rate of protection can have two meanings. If the rate is small, it means that the industry faces high taxes on either its inputs or its own output, as is likely to be true for many primary exporting industries. Alternatively, a very high negative ERP usually indicates that the industry is so inefficient that its inputs cost more in foreign exchange than its output is worth at c.i.f. prices; that is, the value added is negative if measured in world prices. Then, the denominator of equation 18–3 or 18–4 becomes a small negative number.

12. For an early description of this phenomena, see Albert O. Hirschman, "The Political Economy of Import Substitution," *Quarterly Journal of Economics*, 82 (1968), 1–32.

TABLE 18–2	EFFECTIVE RATES OF PROTECTION			
SECTOR	BANGLADESH (1984)	BRAZIL (1966)	THE PHILIPPINES (1965)	NORWAY (1954)
AGRICULTURE	13	46	33	34
MINING	N.A.	−16	−9	−7
MANUFACTURING	114	127	53	9
CONSUMER GOODS[a]	N.A.	198	72	29
INTERMEDIATE GOODS[a]	N.A.	151	45	9
MACHINERY	10	93	24	18
TRANSPORT EQUIPMENT	N.A.	−26	−3	−6

[a]Aggregates for consumer goods and intermediate goods are simple, unweighted averages of constituent industry data.
Sources: For Bangladesh, Thomas L. Hutcheson and Joseph J. Stern, "The Methodology of Assistance Policy Analysis," Harvard Institute for International Development, development discussion paper no. 226, April 1986; and for other countries, Bela Balassa et al., *The Structure of Protection in the Developing Countries* (Baltimore: John Hopkins Press, 1971), p. 55.

The fairly typical pattern of protection is illustrated by the data in Table 18–2 for Bangladesh in 1984 and Brazil and the Philippines in the mid-1960s. The average level of effective protection for manufacturing as a whole ranges from moderate (the Philippines) to high (Brazil). However, the structure within manufacturing is widely skewed. Consumer goods are highly protected and intermediate goods are comfortably protected, although at lower rates. Capital goods industries generally receive less protection, however, since taxes on capital goods discourage investors; rates are especially low in Bangladesh for machinery and in Brazil and the Philippines for transportation equipment (which does not include automobiles, a consumer durable). As a consequence, the incentive to invest in capital goods production is less than in other manufacturing and the development of this sector typically lags behind the others. More damaging in terms of many development objectives, manufacturing as a whole enjoys a substantial advantage over agriculture, which faces effective rates of protection ranging downward from 46 percent to only 13 percent in these examples and, as noted already, is negative in some countries. These biases against investment in agriculture, capital-goods industries, and exports are characteristic of import substitution. Although industrial countries, like Norway in the table, also have used biased protective structures, they were not as extreme as developing countries like Bangladesh (and have been considerably neutralized by the multilateral tariff reforms of the past 30 years).

ERP analysis easily can be extended to incorporate the effect of quotas and subsidies on the value added. This broader view of protection is measured by the **effective rate of subsidy** (ERS). The formula for ERS

TABLE 18–3	EFFECTIVE RATES OF SUBSIDY, 1969 (PERCENT)			
	ALL INDUSTRIES		MANUFACTURING	
	EXPORTS	DOMESTIC SALES	EXPORTS	DOMESTIC SALES
INWARD LOOKING				
ARGENTINA	−17	55	−29	116
COLOMBIA	−12	−1	10	32
ISRAEL	19	79	38	82
OUTWARD LOOKING				
KOREA	9	10	14	7
SINGAPORE	1	8	−1	4
TAIWAN	16	2	21	17

Source: Bela Balassa et al., *Industrial Strategies in Semi-Industrialized Countries* (Baltimore: Johns Hopkins Press, 1982).

is similar to that for ERP (equation 18–4), and its implications are the same. However, the ERS incorporates five elements, two of which are not in the ERP: (1) Tariffs on imports competing with domestic output and on inputs, t_0 and t_i, as under ERP; (2) subsidies on outputs and inputs paid directly to the industry, s_0 and s_i, which could have been included in equation 18–4; as part of the ERP; (3) the premiums due to quota restrictions on imports, q_0 and q_i, which also could have been included in the ERP of equation 18–4; (4) relative subsidies in the form of preferential corporate income taxes that are lower than the average paid by other industries, s_t; and (5) relative subsidies in the form of below-average interest rates on loans, s_b. Because the last two elements are calculated as deviations from average rates of tax or interest, they can be either positive or negative for any industry, although for the entire economy they each must sum to 0. The formula for ERS, derived from equation 18–4, is

$$\text{ERS} = \frac{(t_0 + s_0 + q_0) - \Sigma \, a_i(t_i - s_i + q_i) + s_t + s_b}{(1 - \Sigma \, a_i)} \qquad [18\text{–}5]$$

The ERS is a comprehensive indicator of the extent to which protection affects the relative profitability of various industries. Under import substitution regimes, the ERS is expected to be highest for firms that compete with imports in the domestic market, as is true for the ERP. Under an outward-looking policy regime, however, import-substituting industries should not be favored over export industries: The ERS should be lower, more uniform, and show less variance among industries. Table 18–3 shows the ERS for six economies in the late 1960s. Argentina and Israel display the pattern typical of import-substituting countries: The

ERS for export-oriented industries is much lower than that for industries selling primarily in the domestic market. In contrast, considering all industries, Korea's regime is nearly neutral between exports and domestic sales, while Taiwan's is biased in favor of exports. Within manufacturing, Singapore and Taiwan have nearly neutral regimes, while Korea shows a pro-export bias, the opposite of Argentina.[13] The pattern of the ERS in Korea, and to a lesser extent Taiwan, is less the result of universal low tariffs, quotas, and subsidies than of a more complex pattern of market interventions that actively favored exports, as described later in the chapter.

EXCHANGE-RATE MANAGEMENT

Tariffs, quotas, subsidies, and other interventions are intended to differentiate among different kinds of tradable goods: Industrial import substitutes versus primary exports, capital goods imports versus consumer imports, manufacturing exports versus agricultural exports, and so on. The exchange rate, by contrast, treats all tradable goods uniformly but alters the price between tradables and nontradables (such as local transportation, power and water supplies, personal and household services, and government services). The exchange rate is one of the most pervasive prices in the economy, perhaps affecting more transactions than any other single price. To fully understand the import substitution and outward-oriented strategies, therefore, it is necessary to bring exchange rate policy into play and analyze its interaction with trade policies.

The schedules in Figure 18–3 show exporters' supply of and importers' demand for foreign exchange. The vertical axis is the exchange rate measured in the local currency; for example, pesos per dollar. If the exchange rate is allowed to float, then in the absence of tariffs or quotas, an exchange rate of e_e would just clear the market and be an equilibrium. If tariffs are imposed on imports, the demand curve shifts downward because importers then are unwilling to offer as many pesos per dollar of imports. This lowers the equilibrium peso-per-dollar rate to e_t. Note that, at e_t, not only is import demand reduced, so is the supply of exports, since exporters are unwilling to produce as much for the lower peso revenue. A tariff of any kind, whether to promote industrialization or to raise revenue, thus discriminates against both imports and exports, in favor of production for the domestic market.

13. British political economist Robert Wade calculates, based on the data used to compile Table 18–3, that although Korea's incentive structure appears to be evenhanded between aggregate exports and aggregate domestic sales, the variance within these categories is not very different from those of Argentina, Colombia, and Israel, which on average were more protectionist. See Robert Wade, *Governing the Market: Economic Theory and the Role of Government in East Asian Industrialization* (Princeton, NJ: Princeton University Press, 1990), p. 56.

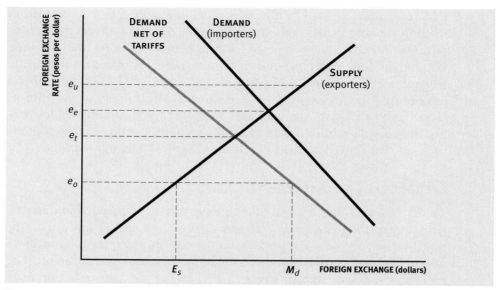

FIGURE 18–3   OVERVALUED AND UNDERVALUED EXCHANGE RATES. The official exchange rate e_o is overvalued: It is too high in dollars per peso or too low in pesos per dollar to balance the demand for foreign exchange with the supply of foreign exchange without high protective tariffs, import quotas, and restrictions on other foreign exchange transactions. Rate e_u, in contrast, is undervalued: It favors exports over imports and generates a trade surplus.

When countries do not leave their exchange rates to market forces but operate **fixed exchange rates,** two other outcomes are possible. Often the official exchange rate e_o is held below e_t. Because the peso price of the dollar is so low, imports increase to M_d and exports decline to E_s; this creates a potential deficit in the current account of the balance of payments. To reduce this deficit, governments typically resort to import quotas, tariffs, and controls over all foreign exchange transactions. This makes some imports relatively cheap (those with no tariffs or quotas) and others more expensive (those with moderate or high restrictions), further distorting the incentives for investment and consumption. The rate e_o is considered **overvalued** in the sense that the dollar price of pesos (the reciprocal of that shown in the diagram) is too high to maintain equilibrium without controls and high tariffs; the peso-per-dollar rate, e_o, therefore is too low. This term often causes some confusion because exchange rates typically are quoted in terms of domestic currency per dollar, while the term refers to the rate in terms of dollars per domestic currency. For example, say that the equilibrium exchange rate in the Philippines is 25 pesos to the dollar, $e_e = \text{P } 25/\$$. This is equivalent to 4 U.S. cents per peso, $0.04/peso. The fixed rate is set at $e_o = \text{P } 20/\$$, which is equivalent to 5 cents per peso, $0.05/peso. With this fixed rate, the peso is said to be overvalued because it costs more dollars to purchase pesos than it would with a floating rate.

Exchange rates become overvalued for a variety of reasons. The genesis of the problem sometimes is a boom in primary exports, which causes appreciation of the real exchange rate, as explained in the discussion of Dutch disease in Chapter 16. Also, as incomes rise with development, fixed exchange rates can become overvalued as the demand for imports rises. Domestic inflation, if it causes domestic prices and costs to rise faster than the world average, also can lead to an overvalued rate, as consumers prefer to purchase relatively cheaper imports as domestic prices rise.

Changing the exchange rate, especially by the large amounts sometimes required, means changing the relative wealth of influential segments of the population. Most obviously, import prices rise with the exchange rate, reducing the welfare of those that purchase imports. Moreover, to prevent domestic prices from rising as much as the currency is devalued, wages and other incomes must be restrained by government policy. Frequently, the politically powerful lose by these measures, especially urban workers, middle-class professionals, the military, civil servants, the upper classes, and others whose consumption depends substantially on imports. On the other hand, devaluation helps the profitability of exporting firms, other earners of foreign exchange, and competitive producers of import substitutes. Since importers tend to have more political power than nascent exporters and consumers like low prices, governments have resisted devaluation; when they have undertaken it, they often devalued by too little in the face of growing demand and continuing inflation. As a result, for much of the period after World War II, most governments maintained fixed exchange rates and were reluctant to risk the destabilizing political effects of devaluation. Until the 1990s, the tendency was for exchange rates to remain overvalued in the developing world.[14] This tendency has been alleviated by the greater flexibility in exchange rates since 1971 and the wave of economic reforms during the 1980s and 1990s, discussed in Chapter 5.

Even though overvalued, exchange rates encourage imports, they were a hallmark of many protectionist regimes that tried to bolster import substitutes. Governments, on the other hand, wanted to keep imports cheap for consumers and, on the other hand, provide protection for domestic firms competing with imports. One fed on the other: The more the exchange rate became overvalued, the larger grew the protection needed by domestic producers to compete with cheaper imports. Industries with no such protection are unlikely to find it profitable to produce for either the home or foreign market. Recall, then, the highly skewed protective structure presented in Table 18–2. Consumer goods and intermediate goods

14. The economic and political difficulties make selective tariffs and quota restrictions even more appealing to governments, despite the allocative inefficiencies such measures entail.

manufacturing can overcome the overvalued exchange rate with their high effective rates of protection from tariffs and import quotas. But agricultural and capital goods manufacturing are more exposed to import competition at the low local currency prices engendered by the overvalued exchange rate.

The second possibility for a fixed rate in Figure 18–3 is an **undervalued** exchange rate, e_u. At this rate, with more pesos per dollar (less dollars per peso) than in equilibrium, exports are favored over imports and there will be a balance-of-trade surplus. Undervalued rates, although not as common as overvalued rates, have been used by pro-export regimes such as that in Taiwan during the 1980s. Despite the success of export-oriented regimes in achieving rapid economic growth, economists like undervalued rates only slightly better than overvalued ones. Export surpluses require either an outflow of capital or a rise in foreign reserves to balance international accounts. Either can be useful in a developing country, as when it is necessary to repay debt or to counter a temporary fall in the terms of trade. Otherwise, foreign investment is made abroad and excess reserves are accumulated at the expense of domestic investment, which is essential to sustain economic development.

To this point we have been concerned about the *level* of the exchange rate. Investors, however, earn returns over several years and are equally concerned with *expected changes* in the exchange rate over time. Investors who perceive that the exchange rate may become overvalued in the foreseeable future will be discouraged from starting or expanding export industries. One important advantage of floating exchange rates is that they are far less likely to become overvalued, so they provide some built-in reassurance to long-term investors. With fixed exchange rates, the government has to establish a history of maintaining the *real value* of the exchange rate over time by ensuring that the nominal exchange rate keeps pace with inflation at home and abroad. Recall from equation 16–1 that the **real exchange rate** (RER) is defined as

$$RER = (E \times P_T)/P_N \qquad [18–6]$$

where E = an index of the nominal exchange rate, P_T = an index of prices of tradable goods expressed in foreign currency, and P_N = an index of the domestic price of nontradables. With a fixed exchange rate, the RER easily can appreciate (decline) and become overvalued if P_N rises more quickly than P_T, which typically is the case when domestic inflation rises faster than world inflation. An appreciation of the RER generally indicates a reduction in the international competitiveness and profitability of firms producing exports or import-competing goods (refer back to Table 16–3 for a numerical example). Therefore, governments that operate a fixed exchange rate must ensure that, first, the exchange rate is set at a level that makes it profitable to invest in exports and efficient import-substitutes, and second, the real exchange rate is maintained at a steady level over long periods.

The central bank, which usually manages the exchange rate, has two instruments to do this. First, if the budget deficit is under control, it can restrict the rate of money creation to restrain domestic price inflation (see Chapter 19). If domestic inflation (approximated by changes in P_N) can be kept no higher than the rate of world price inflation (approximated by changes in P_T), the RER will remain unchanged. However, it is not always within the central bank's power to keep domestic inflation that low. To compensate for domestic prices that rise more rapidly than world prices, it occasionally is necessary to use the second instrument: A devaluation of the official exchange rate. In recent years, many governments have tried to depoliticize exchange rate management by resorting to more frequent and much smaller devaluations when necessary. This technique of flexible exchange rate management, called a **crawling peg,** has been used in many countries with an outward-looking policy regime.[15] In recent years, many exporting countries have moved beyond the crawling peg to floating exchange rates, thereby minimizing the risks of significant exchange rate misalignment.

Although the real exchange rate is widely used as an indicator of the competitiveness of exporters, a more comprehensive indicator is the **real effective exchange rate** (REER). It incorporates both the real exchange rate and an index of nominal protection, N:

$$\text{REER} = E \times N \times P_T/P_P \qquad [18\text{--}7]$$

N, and hence REER, must be defined separately for exportables and importables. In the case of importables,

$$N_m = (1 + t_m + q_m)_k/(1 + t_m + q_m)_0 \qquad [18\text{--}8]$$

where t, s, and q are the average tariff, subsidy, and quota premium rates, respectively, on imports; the subscript m refers to imports; and the subscripts k and 0 refer to the current and base years. For exportables,

$$N_e = (1 - t_e + s_e)_k/(1 - t_e + s_e)_0 \qquad [18\text{--}9]$$

where t and s are the tax and subsidy rates on exports, with subscript e.

In reforming trade regimes to become more outward looking, t_m and q_m are reduced via tariff reform and deregulation. In some cases, t_e is reduced and s_e may be increased to increase profits for exporters. Thus, trade reforms would

15. Both fixed exchange rates and crawling pegs raise other management challenges in the context of open international capital flows, as discussed in Chapters 13 and 14.

cause $REER_e$ to rise and $REER_m$ to decline. After an outward-looking reform, the policy goal is to ensure both that $REER_e$ not appreciate and $REER_e$ stay in line with $REER_m$. Because the index N changes very little except during trade reforms, the real exchange rate, RER, generally is used instead of the more complex and harder-to-measure REER.

IMPORT SUBSTITUTION IN GENERAL EQUILIBRIUM

The process of import substitution in a general equilibrium context is represented in Figures 18–4 through 18–6. Initially (say, in 1970) the country produces at point A and consumes at C in Figure 18–4 under world terms of trade favorable to its export. Imposition of a tariff, presumed here to be uniform on all imports, swings domestic relative prices in favor of importable goods. Production moves toward point B, where more of the importable and less of the exportable are produced. If the country is relatively small and does not affect world prices, trade can take place at the same terms of trade as before on a line parallel to AC, such as BD. Consumption settles at a point such as E, where consumption of both goods is lower than before the tariff, so consumers' well-being has been reduced. Both imports and exports also have fallen, as indicated by the line segment BE (the hypotenuse of the trade triangle, see Figure 16–1), which is shorter than AC. Initially, the shift from free trade necessarily reduces both trade and consumers' welfare. Note that there is no debate that import

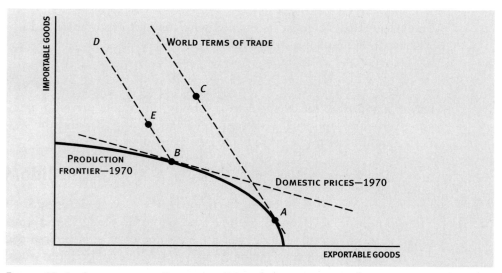

FIGURE 18–4   IMPOSITION OF PROTECTIVE TARIFF (SITUATION IN 1970). A protective tariff increases the relative domestic price of importables and induces a rise in their production from point A to point B. At first, consumption of both goods falls from points C to E.

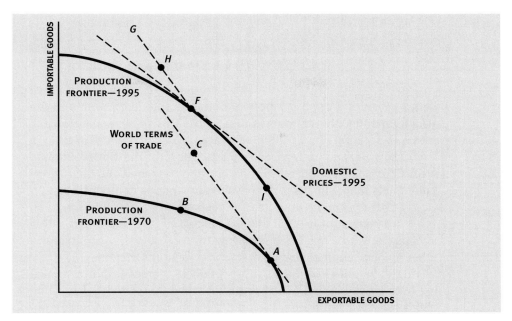

FIGURE 18–5   IMPORT SUBSTITUTION AFTER 25 YEARS OF RAPID GROWTH, 1995. After 25 years of successful import substitution, the production frontier has been shifted outward sufficiently to enable the country to produce at point *F* and to consume at point *H*, on a higher indifference curve than at a point *C* before the imposition of a tariff.

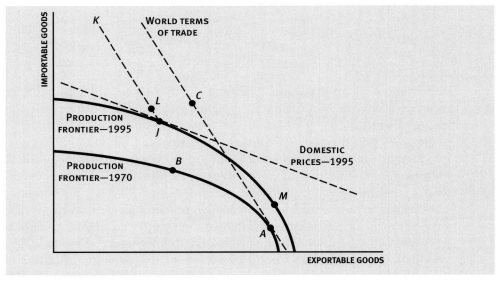

FIGURE 18–6   IMPORT SUBSTITUTION AFTER 25 YEARS OF SLOW GROWTH, 1995. If, instead, import substitution does not move the production frontier outward as substantially as in Figure 18–5, production will take place at a point like *J* and consumption, at *L*, will remain on an indifference curve lower than at the starting point *C*.

IMPORT SUBSTITUTION IN KENYA[16]

Kenya provides a good example of both the potential power and the structural difficulties of import substitution. This small, open economy with a population of 29 million generated a GDP of $360 per capita in 1999 ($975 in purchasing power parity prices of the United States), giving Kenya a total domestic market about 12 percent the size of Colombia's domestic market. Kenya exports goods and nonfactor services equal to 25 percent of its GDP, down from 30 percent in 1970. In 1999, 23 percent of its GDP and 68 percent of its exports came from agriculture, which has been relatively favored by policy compared to other African countries and most import-substituting regimes.

Yet Kenya pursued import substitution as a means of industrializing both before and especially after independence in 1963, utilizing high protective tariffs, quotas, and outright bans on competing imports to attract investors. Effective rates of protection ranged from slightly negative, especially on agricultural processing industries, to levels of 100–500 percent for chemical industries based on simple

16. Data are from *World Development Report 2000/01;* Central Bureau of Statistics, *Economic Survey 1990* (Nairobi: Government of Kenya Printer, 1990); and earlier issues; and unpublished reports.

substitution initially reduces consumer welfare—the only question is whether it lays the foundation for dynamic gains that can compensate for the original loss.

If protection successfully stimulates investment in infant industries and productivity gains such that subsequent growth is substantial, the production frontier will be pushed outward, as in Figure 18–5, and after several years, consumer welfare will have increased. Over time, as more import substitutes become available, their relative domestic price is likely to fall, even if the protective tariff is maintained. So the 1995 domestic price line is drawn with a steeper slope than the 1970 line in Figure 18–4. In 1995, production takes place at a point like *F*, where the domestic price line is tangent to the new frontier. Consumption takes place at a point like *H*, somewhere along line *FG*, drawn parallel to the original world terms of trade (which are presumed not to have changed since 1970). In 1995, consumers are better off at *H* than they had been in 1970 at *C*, since they

last-stage mixing and for the assembly of vehicles and consumer durables. After substantial liberalization in the early 1980s, about a third of imported items, many of them potential competitors with local industry, remained under highly restrictive import licensing. In 1960, Kenya imported over a third of its GDP. By 1999, imports were down to 29 percent of GDP. From 1970 to 1980, manufacturing grew by 10 percent a year, but from 1989 to 1999, the rate had slowed to only 2.5 percent a year. During the peak of import substitution, from 1972 to 1983, the leading industries, with annual growth exceeding 10 percent, were vegetables, clothing, footwear, paper, printing, petroleum refining, rubber products, plastic products, and vehicle assembly; all but the first are typical first-stage import substitution leaders. Also typical of import substitution, the import share of machinery and equipment more than doubled from 11 percent in 1965 to 24 percent in 1983, while the share for nonfood consumer goods fell from 18 to 7 percent.

By the end of the 1970s, it became generally recognized in Kenya that import substitution had run its course. The domestic market was too small to attract many more industries, manufacturing costs generally were too high to permit rapid growth of manufactured exports, and further backward integration into intermediate goods would mean even higher costs for user industries. During the 1980s, economic growth slowed to just over 4 percent a year after its spurt of almost 8 percent a year from 1965 to 1973. Since 1980, Kenya has been shifting, somewhat hesitantly, toward a more outward-looking policy for industry.

are on a higher indifference curve (not shown). There is also less trade than in 1970 (*FH* is shorter than *AC*). Note, however, that consumers' welfare could be improved still more by removing tariffs and reverting to the world terms of trade. If tariffs were removed, producers would move along the 1995 frontier to point *I*, permitting consumption at a point northeast of *H*, on a still higher indifference curve. Trade would be increased compared to the situation at point *F*. This is the desirable result that attracts advocates of import substitution.

The question, of course, is whether or not the production frontier will move out as far as depicted under an import substitution regime. Too often slow or arrested growth is the outcome of protective policies. In that case, trade and consumer welfare may never reach their former levels, as shown in Figure 18–6. With slow growth, producers reach point *J* on the 1990 frontier, but consumption, at a point like *L*, remains below the original point, *C*. Trade is reduced from its 1970 level. Here again, consumption of both goods could be increased if the country reverted to world prices and moved production from *J* to *M* on the new frontier. Note that, once import substitution has taken place a return to free trade always can improve welfare compared to both the protected position and the initial free-trade position.

OUTCOMES OF IMPORT SUBSTITUTION

Import substitution has the potential to be an effective strategy for certain sectors over a limited period of time. It is worth noting again that almost all countries have tried it at one stage or another, and many have achieved some success. But, all too often, the import substitution strategy has been used to protect too many activities and remained in place for too long. Countries introducing import substitution typically record a quick growth spurt during the initial, or *easy phase of import substitution,* as consumer goods industries expand to meet domestic demand. Once the domestic market is saturated, however, growth typically bogs down. Few linkages develop with other domestic industries, as described earlier, and moving up the ladder to products requiring more sophisticated technology proves difficult. Agriculture and manufactured exports tend to grow slowly or not at all. Since most developing countries have relatively small internal markets, import substitution poses a dilemma: Either the number of firms producing a protected good must be small or the size of individual production facilities must be small and may be well below the minimum efficient size. In the first option, limited competition may lead to monopolies that increase costs and reduce quality; in the second option, small production runs raise costs.[17] Therefore, whereas import substitution has had some limited success in bigger countries with large internal markets, at least for a short period of time, it generally has failed in middle-sized or small countries, including most developing countries.

Ironically, many countries that follow the import substitution strategy eventually run into balance of payments problems from growing trade deficits. Even though the strategy is designed to replace some imports with domestic production, not all imports can be replaced (especially capital goods). Since the strategy effectively discourages exports, foreign exchange earnings lag. These problems easily are exacerbated by an overvalued exchange rate, which as described earlier often accompanies the import substitution strategy. In essence, export earnings grow more slowly than the demand for foreign exchange. Therefore, many countries following this strategy have had to borrow heavily and found it difficult to meet their debt service requirements.

17. See Anne O. Krueger, "Why Trade Liberalization Is Good for Growth," *Economic Journal,* 108 (September 1998), 1513–22.

Import substitution incentives also lead to potentially severe misallocations of economic resources. The overvalued exchange rate and low duties on capital and imported inputs encourage producers to use more of these imports than is warranted by scarcities in the economy. Investment is encouraged to be more capital-intensive than is desirable, and the growth realizable from a given amount of saving and limiting employment creation is reduced.

In addition, underlying the protective regime is a set of incentives that reward political astuteness and rent seeking (described in Chapter 5) more than economic competitiveness. When higher domestic costs, reduced import prices, or better-quality foreign goods erode the competitive position of domestic firms, the natural reaction of protected firms is to turn to the government once again for enhanced protection. This option blunts the competitive instincts of entrepreneurs who, in the absence of government support, would have to cut costs, improve quality, and thus raise productivity. In this environment, the most successful managers are those who have the political skills with which to bargain effectively, or simply bribe, officials who administer import quotas and determine tariff rates or have close ties with the political and bureaucratic elite.

Outward-Looking Trade Strategy

To sustain growth and development, it may be necessary to pursue an alternative, **outward-looking strategy,** one that shifts the focus from import substitution for the domestic market toward manufacturing for export to foreign markets. In this strategy, tariff, quotas, and other barriers to trade are reduced or eliminated, so that domestic prices move closer into line with world prices. In addition, governments usually establish institutions such as duty exemption systems, export processing zones, and bonded warehouses to support exporters. In the typical pattern, in the early stages, firms manufacture and export relatively simple labor-intensive products, such as textiles, clothing, shoes, toys, furniture. Some firms assemble (rather than actually manufacture) and export more sophisticated products (such as electronics equipment) as part of a production chain in which the components are manufactured elsewhere. Over time, as workers learn new skills and gain access to improved technology, a country's comparative advantage gradually shifts to manufacturing more-advanced electronics devices, higher-end clothing, and consumer durables. As we shall see, however, until recently, relatively few developing countries had chosen the outward-looking strategy, and fewer still have been at it long enough to make the transition to highly sophisticated manufactured products.

Fifty years ago, few thought that it would be possible for firms from developing countries to compete in world markets for manufactured products. Hans Singer's and Raul Prebisch's export pessimism about primary products (see Chapter 16) led to support for import substitution as a way to develop manufacturing capabilities. In retrospect, it is striking that Prebisch, Singer, and others never seriously considered the possibility that firms from developing countries could compete directly in world markets for manufactured products as an alternative to either primary exports or import substitution. These views began to change in the late 1960s and early 1970s, based on the success of a small number of East Asian manufactured exporters. The 1980s debt crisis, combined with slow economic growth in many countries that were following the import substitution strategy, further reinforced support for export-led growth. By the early 1990s, there was widespread consensus (although not complete agreement) in the advantages of this strategy for developing countries. That view has been tempered somewhat by the financial crises that swept through some of the high-flying Asian economies in late 1997 and 1998. These crises, however, were rooted more in problems with financial development and open capital markets than in trade policy per se (see Chapter 14). By the late 1990s, most developing countries were making at least some attempt to shift to a more outward-looking development strategy.[18]

The evidence supporting the outward-looking strategy is strong, yet not absolute. The most basic evidence is that almost all developing countries that have recorded rapid growth in manufactured exports also have experienced rapid economic growth and vice-versa. Table 18–4 shows the 15 low- and middle-income countries (i.e., those with per capita income measured in purchasing power parity terms of $7,000 or less in 1970, before their period of rapid growth) with the strongest performance in manufactured exports from 1970 to 1996. The table shows the growth rate of non-primary-based manufactured exports (i.e., the analyses exclude manufactured products like diamonds and plywood that are dependent mainly on natural resource endowments) in terms of its contribution to GDP.[19] The top 12 performers (with the exception of Hungary, which was exporting primarily to other Eastern Bloc countries prior to the dissolution of

18. For an engaging overview of the shift in thinking about trade policy and development between the 1960s and 1990s, see Anne O. Krueger's presidential address to the American Economics Association "Trade Policy and Economic Development: How We Learn," *American Economic Review*, 1, no. 87 (March 1997), 1–22.

19. By taking the growth rate weighted by the share of non-primary-based exports in the GDP in the previous year, we avoid the statistical problem that countries with small amounts of manufactured exports can record very high growth rates (with little actual contribution to GDP growth) and those with large amounts of manufactured exports tend to record smaller growth rates.

TABLE 18–4   LOW AND MIDDLE INCOME COUNTRY EXPORTERS OF NON-PRIMARY-BASED MANUFACTURED PRODUCTS, TOP 15 PERFORMERS, 1970–96

COUNTRY	NON-PRIMARY-BASED MANUFACTURED EXPORT GROWTH RATE	AVERAGE GROWTH RATE OF REAL GDP PER CAPITA (PPP$)
SINGAPORE	14.9	7.0
TAIWAN	5.6	6.5
HONG KONG	5.6	5.6
MALAYSIA	4.7	5.4
IRELAND	4.6	3.6
KOREA	4.4	7.4
MAURITIUS	2.9	3.9
HUNGARY	2.0	1.6
CHINA	1.9	5.0
THAILAND	1.9	5.0
PORTUGAL	1.8	3.9
TUNISIA	1.7	3.3
ISRAEL	1.4	2.6
SRI LANKA	1.3	2.7
DOMINICAN REPUBLIC	1.1	2.1

Note: The table shows the top 15 performers from the group of 74 countries with a 1990 population greater than 1 million and a GDP per capita (PPP$) of less than $7,000 in 1970. The non-primary-based manufactured exports weighted growth rate is equal to the annual growth rate of those exports times their share in the GDP in the previous year. The non-primary-based manufactured exports include commodities in from the Standard International Trade Classification system (SITC) categories 5 through 8 except SITC 61, 63, 66, and 68.
Source: Steven Radelet, "Manufactured Exports, Export Platforms, and Economic Growth," Harvard Institute for International Development, CAER discussion paper No. 42, September 1999.

the Soviet Union) all recorded growth rates in per capita income of 3.3 percent or more over the 26-year period. All these 12 countries are among the top 14 fastest-growing low- and middle-income countries in the world over the same period. Only Indonesia and Jordan recorded growth in GDP per capita greater than 3 percent between 1970 and 1996 without being among the top performers in manufactured exports. Note that all 15 countries shown in Table 18–4 (except Hungary) recorded per capita growth averaging 2.1 percent per year or more.

The best known of the high performing countries are from East Asia. Eight Asian economies—South Korea, Taiwan, Hong Kong, Singapore, (collectively known as the "four tigers"), Malaysia, Thailand, Indonesia (the three "little tigers" of Southeast Asia), and China—have set the pace for the rest of the developing world since the 1970s. These countries also have been among the most resolute in pursuing variants of the outward-looking strategy. Rapid export growth, especially in Korea, Taiwan, and Singapore, went hand in hand with growth in per capita income that was two to three times the rate for the average middle-income country over several decades. Many factors—economic, political, geographic, demographic, and cultural—undoubtedly contributed to this strong performance.

For example, the Asian countries invested heavily in human and physical capital, which are central to rapid development. But the focus on manufactured exports clearly played an important role in making educated labor and capital more productive in these economies than they would have been within protected, inward-looking economic regimes.

A growing body of more sophisticated research that controls for the effects of other social, geographic, and economic factors generally supports the close relationship between outward orientation and economic growth. Economists Jeffrey Sachs and Andrew Warner, for example, examined the economic growth performance of 79 countries around the world during the period 1970–89, using a variant of the cross-country growth model described in Chapter 2.[20] After controlling for the effects of nine other variables (including level of income, educational attainment, government consumption, political unrest, and others), they find that the strongest correlate with economic growth is "openness" to trade with the global economy.[21] Per capita income grew about 2 percentage points faster per year in countries that were open to international trade for the entire time period relative to closed economies. Similarly, in a widely read study of the high-performing Asian economies, the World Bank attempted to relate export performance and openness of the economy to the growth in income per capita and the growth in total factor productivity.[22] The bank's analysis, covering more than 50 countries between 1960 and 1985, shows that both income growth and factor productivity growth correlate significantly with the average share (over the entire period) of manufactured exports (in either total exports or gross domestic product). In this study, however, the impact of manufactured export shares on income growth (while positive and statistically significant) is smaller than other factors, such as a country's income relative to the United States in 1960,[23] the rate of primary

---

20. Jeffrey Sachs and Andrew Warner, "Economic Reform and the Process of Global Integration," *Brookings Papers on Economic Activity* 1995, no. 1, pp. 1–118. David Dollar constructs a different index of trade openness and also finds a positive relationship with growth in "Outward-Oriented Developing Countries Really Do Grow More Rapidly: Evidence from 95 LDCs, 1976–85," *Economic Development and Cultural Change,* 40, no. 3 (1992), 523–44.

21. A country was considered to be "open" if it met five criteria: (1) Its average tariff rate was less than 40 percent, (2) its nontariff barriers (e.g., quotas) covered less than 40 percent of imports, (3) the premium on the unofficial parallel market exchange rate did not exceed 20 percent, (4) there were no state monopolies on major exports, and (5) it was not a socialist economy.

22. World Bank, *The East Asian Miracle: Economic Growth and Public Policy* (Washington, DC: World Bank, 1993). The authors use the term *high-performing Asian economies* (HPAE) to cover the seven Asian tigers.

23. The lower is a country's starting income, the easier it is to grow fast by "catching up"; that is, importing equipment and techniques using existing technologies that are nevertheless advanced for the poor country.

enrollment in 1960 (as a proxy for educational endowment), and the average share of investment in GDP. When productivity growth is being explained, manufactured export shares appear to be more important. In a more recent study, UCLA economist Sebastian Edwards examines the relationship between trade policy and total factor productivity growth, using nine different indicators of trade openness to examine the strength of the relationship across these indicators. He finds a strong and consistent positive relationship between trade openness and TFP growth, regardless of which measure of trade openness he uses.[24]

Strong correlations between manufactured exports and rapid economic growth, however, do not prove that the former is the *cause* of the latter, even when researchers carefully control for other factors that could affect growth. At best these correlations indicate a close association between the two. It is entirely plausible that the causation runs the other way: Rapid income and productivity growth, by increasing productive capacity and reducing costs, can make a country more competitive in world markets and lead to faster growth of manufactured exports. Also possible is that both export growth and economic growth are simultaneously caused by something else, such as improved macroeconomic policies, more stable political systems, reduced corruption, or increased savings. Economists Jeffrey Frankel and David Romer partially address the causality issue by tracing the portion of trade due to geographical characteristics (such as country's size, its location, and whether or not it is landlocked), which tend to be weakly correlated or uncorrelated with other possible determinants of growth. They show that this geographical component of trade has a large and robust (albeit only moderately statistically significant positive effect on income.[25] In the end, to a large extent, export growth and economic growth probably support each other in a kind of virtuous circle: Exporting countries have greater access to new machinery and technology that support growth, while faster economic growth provides the means to finance investments in infrastructure and education that support exports.

Skeptics point to potential weaknesses in the methodologies and data used in some of these studies, and they caution that care should be taken to not draw overly strong conclusions. They point out, for example, that studies on the relationship between trade performance and growth (like the Frankel-Romer study) do not directly address the issue of trade *policies*. And studies that examine policies (like the Sachs-Warner and Edwards studies) tend to leave open some questions on precisely how to

---

24. Sebastian Edwards, "Openness, Productivity, and Growth: What Do We Really Know?" *Economic Journal,* 108 (March 1998), 383–98.

25. Jeffrey Frankel and David Romer, "Does Trade Cause Growth?" *American Economic Review,* 89, no. 3 (June 1999), 379–99.

appropriately measure policies, the exact channels through which trade policies affect growth, and the relationships between trade policies and other policies that support growth.[26] The debate, however, mainly is about the magnitude of the relationship and the channels through which trade policies operate. Few of these skeptics conclude that openness to trade is an ill-advised strategy or that trade barriers are conducive to long-run growth.

THE ADVANTAGES OF MANUFACTURED-EXPORT-LED GROWTH

What is it about exports of manufactured products that conveys advantages over import substitution? The first to answer this question was Adam Smith, who, in *The Wealth of Nations,* recognized that export markets would permit factories to produce more of any single item and so to specialize to a greater extent than if they produced only for the home market. Specialization permits each firm to learn more about manufacturing its products efficiently and allows production in greater volumes, which reduces the setup costs of switching from one product to another. International market competition provides the stimulus for firms to move in this direction.

In the two centuries since *The Wealth of Nations,* innovations in both products and technology led to plants that had to be large to be efficient (see Chapter 17). In the production of chemicals, metals, automobiles, and other products, large plants in small home markets needed export markets to achieve economies of scale. If, as economists hypothesize, industrial productivity improves with practice, then learning by doing can be accelerated by increased production through exports. Export markets provide new opportunities for the productive employment of the factors of production. University of Pennsylvania economist Howard Pack points out that, when export markets exist, labor, capital, and even land can be moved rapidly from low- to high-productivity uses without encountering diminishing returns as quickly as with production for the home market.[27] In other words, exports of labor-intensive manufactured exports create large numbers of jobs for low-skilled workers in developing countries, far more jobs than can be created through import substitution. As discussed in Chapter 8, the Asian exporters have been much more successful in creating large numbers of manufacturing jobs than other developing countries.

26. See, for example, Francisco Rodriguez and Dani Rodrik, "Trade Policy and Economic Growth: A Skeptic's Guide to Cross-National Evidence," National Bureau of Economic Research working paper no. 7081 (April 1999); and Ann Harrison and Gordon Hanson, "Who Gains from Trade Reform? Some Remaining Puzzles," *Journal of Development Economics,* 59 (1999), 125–54.

27. These and other observations on the advantages of exports can be found in Howard Pack, "Industrialization and Trade," in H. Chenery and T. N. Srinivasan, eds., *Handbook of Development Economics,* Vol. 2 (Amsterdam: Elsevier, 1989), pp. 333–80.

Exports also provide the foreign exchange necessary to pay for imported raw materials and investment capital goods. As noted previously, one of the great ironies of import substitution is that, even though the strategy is designed to save on imports, the vast majority of countries that followed this strategy eventually ran into balance of payments problems because they could not generate the foreign exchange necessary to pay for the capital goods and raw materials that they needed. By contrast, exporters are better able to pay for a range of imported goods, including capital goods.

Perhaps the most important advantage of manufactured exports is that it provides a channel through which a developing country can gain new technologies and new ideas. The enhanced ability to import capital goods, together with greater exposure to world markets provides exporters with the opportunity to observe the best practices and latest technology used by leading global firms and adopt the technology most appropriate for their own use. Rapid growth in manufactured exports requires close links with multinational firms that provide intermediate inputs, technology, capital goods, and export markets. These links provide a powerful means through which firms can learn about new technology. There is no realistic chance of this occurring if a country is cut off from world markets.

The long-term objective of the outward-oriented strategy is for a country to gradually shift its exports from simple manufacturing into more sophisticated products that will generate higher wages, profits, and income. Labor-abundant, capital-scarce developing economies initially should be internationally competitive in labor-intensive products, such as textiles, apparel, shoes, and toys. Over time, as savings and education deepen the pool of capital and skilled labor and new technology is introduced and adopted, these economies aim to graduate to more capital- and skill-intensive products, such as electronic equipment, refrigerators and other heavy consumer durables, steel, or financial and information services. The idea that countries would move up the technology ladder by following the countries just ahead of them was coined the *flying geese* model of development by Japanese economist Kaname Akamatsu in the 1930s. The Asian countries to some extent have followed this model. Korea, Taiwan, and Hong Kong took over leadership in textiles and apparel in the late 1960s and early 1970s from Japan as Japan moved into electronics, transport, and other capital goods. A decade or so later, Korea and Taiwan moved into electronics components, while the textile and apparel industries moved to Thailand, Indonesia, China, Vietnam, and Mauritius. More recently, Malaysia, the Philippines, and Thailand shifted into electronics production.

To the extent that this shift takes place, it should be reflected by higher wages paid by exporting firms. Critics of the outward-looking strategy often argue that exporting firms tend to pay lower wages than other industries producing for the domestic market, and this often is true, at least in the initial stages of the export strategy. Firms protected by high tariffs or quotas indeed can pay higher wages than exporting firms. However, the employment opportunities in these firms are limited by the constraints of the import substitution strategy, and the wages essentially are elevated artificially by protectionist policies. In other words, the import substitution strategy offers a relatively small number of high-paying jobs for those lucky enough to get them but few opportunities for widespread job creation. Exporting firms initially may pay lower wages than these firms, but they create far more jobs, and tend to pay higher wages than those offered in the informal sector or agriculture, which are the relevant alternatives for many workers. Moreover, wages tend to grow much more quickly over long periods of time in export industries.

To see this, examine the data in Table 18–5, which shows growth rates

TABLE 18–5 GROWTH OF WAGES IN THE MANUFACTURING SECTOR		
COUNTRY	WEIGHTED GROWTH RATE OF MANUFACTURED EXPORTS, 1970–96	CUMULATIVE INCREASE IN REAL WAGES, 1980–96 (%)
FAST GROWTH IN MANUFACTURED EXPORTS		
CHINA	1.9	78
HONG KONG	5.6	81
SOUTH KOREA	4.4	231
MAURITIUS	2.9	41
SINGAPORE	14.9	178
THAILAND	1.9	104[a]
MEDIUM GROWTH IN MANUFACTURED EXPORTS		
INDONESIA	0.6	52
ISRAEL	1.4	43
MEXICO	0.8	−53
SRI LANKA	1.3	−8
SLOW GROWTH IN MANUFACTURED EXPORTS		
ARGENTINA	0.2	9
BOLIVIA	0.2	−13
CHILE	0.3	58
JORDAN	0.3	−18[a]
KENYA	0.1	−28[c]
MALAWI	0.1	−82[a]
THE PHILIPPINES	0.8	26[b]
SOUTH AFRICA	0.5	17[a]
ZIMBABWE	0.4	−29

[a]Indicates 1980–95.
[b]Indicates 1980–93.
[c]Indicates 1980–91.
Source: Steven Radelet "Manufactured Exports, Export Platforms, and Economic Growth." For the calculation of the weighted growth rate of manufactured exports, see the notes to Figure 18–4. Wage data are local currency earnings per worker in manufacturing from the ILO's *Yearbook of Labor Statistics* (Washington, DC: ILO, annually 1980–1996). Nominal wages are deflated by each country's consumer price index, taken from the IMF's *International Financial Statistics* (Washington, DC: IMF, annually 1980–1996).

for real wages (after controlling for inflation) for the manufacturing sector as a whole for a small number of countries for which comparable data were available for the period 1980–96. The data is for the entire manufacturing sector, including firms producing for export and firms producing for the domestic market, which may obscure the picture for some countries. Nevertheless, wage growth generally has been much faster in countries with a strong record of manufactured exports. Manufacturing wages more than tripled in real terms in South Korea and nearly tripled in Singapore, while they more than doubled in China, Hong Kong, and Thailand. By contrast, most of the countries with relatively slow growth in manufactured exports recorded real declines in wages. There are some exceptions to the general relationship, and of course, many other factors affect wage rates. But little evidence suggests that the countries that begin by exporting labor-intensive, low-wage manufactured products become "stuck" at that stage with very low wages, as some fear.

Nevertheless, moving up the production ladder to more skill-intensive products is a difficult challenge and far from automatic. Some exporters have had trouble shifting from garment and textiles to electronics and other products, including Mauritius, Tunisia, Indonesia, and the Dominican Republic. More sophisticated production processes demand better facilities, more reliable infrastructure, and more highly trained workers and managers. To some extent, market forces push this process along, as changes in the relative scarcities of the factors of production—land, labor, natural resources, and capital—lead to changes in comparative advantage. But the experiences of the Asian economies and the other successful manufactured exporters suggest that more than basic market forces are required, as we discuss in the next section.

POLICIES SUPPORTING LABOR-INTENSIVE MANUFACTURED EXPORTS

A government switching from import substitution to an outward-looking strategy has to turn the entire incentive system inside out and make it more profitable for firms to sell overseas while diminishing the profits from sales at home. Neoclassical economists prescribe, not a bias toward exports, but rather a regime that is neutral in its treatment of exports, import substitutes, and nontraded goods. With minimal government interventions and taxes, the market determines most prices and allocations, and it leaves the government to determine the rules of the game and correct for the market failures described in Chapter 5. Hence, private firms, governed by markets, determine what is produced for the home market and for export. This prescription toward more open markets has dominated the literature on development for the past two decades and formed the basis for most programs of structural adjustment toward a more outward orientation.[28] But, in practice, things are not so simple.

Consider, for example, Asia's four tigers, whose success has made them models for less-dynamic economies to emulate. As models, however, these countries pose a problem for the pure neoclassical approach to outward-looking growth. Not only did this group of countries use trade strategies that differed from one another in important respects, some of the strategies were highly interventionist. The extreme cases have been Korea and its model, Japan.[29] Both countries have had stiff protective barriers against certain imports and controlled interest rates at below-market levels, directing cheap credit to favored industries and firms. What has made this approach outward looking is that these interventions were used to induce, and sometimes to force, firms to meet ambitious export targets. In Korea, government-controlled banks loaned to large export firms at preferential interest rates. During the 1960s, when import controls were tight, export firms were given licenses for imported inputs in excess of their needs for export production; the balance would be used to produce for the protected domestic market. Income taxes were lower for export firms, either through lower tax rates or informally, as tax authorities winked at tax evasion by firms meeting their export targets. And the Korean government invested heavily in ports, roads, communications, and other infrastructure required by exporters. In Korea, in contrast to an inward-looking regime, a firm could not take advantage of protection or other market distortions unless it met stringent export targets. In essence, some of the tools of protection were used to help fledgling exporters who were learning by doing: Adopting new technologies, learning how to master them, reducing costs of production, finding and entering markets overseas, and eventually competing on equal terms with foreign firms.

At the other extreme among the Asian tigers has been Hong Kong, which comes as close to the neoclassical, free-trade model as any economy in the world. Singapore, also a very open economy with low protection,

---

28. Four prominent economists who strongly influenced thinking about inward versus outward strategies are Gustav Ranis, "Industrial Sector Labor Absorption," *Economic Development and Cultural Change,* 21 (1973), 387–408; Anne O. Kruegar, *Foreign Trade Regimes and Economic Development: Liberalization Attempts and Consequences* (Cambridge, MA: Ballinger, 1978); Jagdish N. Bhagwati, *Foreign Trade Regimes and Economic Development: Anatomy and Consequences of Exchange Control Regimes* (Cambridge, MA: Ballinger, 1978); and Bela Balassa, "The Process of Industrial Development and Alternative Development Strategies," *Essays in International Finance,* 141 (1980).

29. The revisionist school on Korea, questioning the neoclassical approach, was led by Alice Amsden, *Asia's New Giant: South Korea and Late Industrialization* (New York: Oxford University Press, 1989).

nevertheless diverges from the neoclassical norm in that many of its largest export industries are government-owned service firms in telecommunications, port services, an international airport, and air transport. Taiwan, the three Southeast Asian countries, and China have used a mixed approach. Although protectionist and interventionist in some areas, each employed devices that insulated its export industries from the distortions of the home market and permitted it to buy inputs and sell its output at close to world market prices, as the neoclassical strategy dictates.[30]

What, then, is the essence of the outward-looking strategy as defined in practice by the Asian tigers and other manufactured exporters?[31] Five elements were common to the strategies of all eight high-performing Asian countries, as well as other developing countries that successfully followed the outward-looking strategy, such as Tunisia and Mauritius. It is important to note that these policies not only support exports, they have positive effects on economic growth independent from their effect on exports. Successful trade policy operates in an environment with a range of supporting and complementary policies.

1. Macroeconomic stability was critical to Asia's success. Economies were managed soundly, with small budget deficits, moderate inflation, and convertible currencies with exchange rates that did not stray far from market-determined levels. Economic technocrats were given substantial influence over policy decisions and insulated from political forces. Corruption and rent seeking, although present, generally were kept within limits and ultimately were subordinated to economic growth.

2. Governments invested heavily in physical infrastructure to support exporters (and economic activity more generally). New roads connected remote areas to markets and reduced the cost (and increased the reliability) of inland transportation. New and expanded ports reduced shipping costs and time delays for both imports and exports. Improved power and telecommunication facilities made production more predictable and less expensive and eased communication with suppliers and buyers on world markets.

---

30. Taiwan's interventionist strategy is documented by Robert Wade, *Governing the Market*.

31. For a discussion of the differences in the growth paths of the East Asian countries, see Dwight Perkins "There Are at Least Three Models of East Asian Development," *World Development*, 22, no. 4 (April 1994), 655–61. The common features of Asian growth are explored in David L. Lindauer and Michael Roemer, eds., *Asia and Africa: Legacies and Opportunities in Development* (San Francisco, ICS Press, 1994), especially Chapter 1. The World Bank attempted to reconcile neoclassical and revisionist thinking in its much-discussed book, *The East Asian Miracle: Economic Growth and Public Policy*. A more recent study on Asia's rapid growth and its future prospects (published just before the Asian financial crisis) is the Asian Development Bank's *Emerging Asia: Changes and Challenges* (Manila: Asian Development Bank, 1997).

3. The successful countries developed appropriate education and training institutions to provide the workforce basic skills. Generally, this strategy focused initially on universal primary education, then expanded to older pupils (see Chapter 9). As outlined earlier, providing basic skills then increasing those skills over time is critical to successfully moving up the production ladder. Indeed, one of the great challenges for the future of the more-advanced manufactured exports of East Asia is to upgrade higher education and research institutions so workers can gain the skills needed for more technologically advanced goods and services.

4. In every case of successful manufactured exports, the government established institutions that enabled exporters to import and sell at close to world market prices. Earlier in the chapter (in the discussion of effective rates of protection), we saw how important it is for exporters to have access to capital goods and raw materials at world market prices. Any higher price paid by exporters directly reduces their profitability and international competitiveness, since they cannot raise their sales prices on world markets. (That is, high tariffs on inputs lead to negative ERPs). The neoclassical solution to this problem is simply to remove all import tariffs and quotas, so that domestic prices closely reflect world prices. All the successful exporters took major steps in this direction by lowering tariff rates and removing quotas. The problem is that, for a variety of institutional and political reasons, no country realistically can eliminate all tariffs and quotas immediately. Nor can countries instantly remove all the other handicaps that exporters face, including poor infrastructure, corrupt bureaucracies, and onerous and arbitrary tax systems.

Instead, the successful exporters established a variety of institutions to insulate their fledgling export industries from the controls and price distortions of the protected domestic market.[32] These institutions have taken a variety of forms, including export processing zones, bonded warehouses, duty exemption programs, industrial parks, and science and technology parks. EPZs are enclaves located physically or administratively outside a country's custom's barrier, typically as fenced-in areas near a port, that provide exporters access to duty-free imports and suitable infrastructure. Bonded warehouses essentially are single-factory EPZs. Approved warehouses, usually with a customs officer stationed at the site, can receive duty-free imports of capital and intermediate goods and bypass other customs procedures. Firms usually post a bond as a guarantee against any duties that might be applicable to imports diverted to the domestic market. Duty exemption systems allow qualifying firms, wherever they are located,

32. See Lindauer and Roemer, *Asia and Africa,* especially Chaps. 1 and 11. Also see Steven Radelet, "Manufactured Exports, Export Platforms and Economic Growth," Harvard Institute for International Development, CAER discussion paper no. 42, September 1999.

to import their inputs duty free. Closely related are duty drawback systems, in which exporters initially pay duties on imported inputs then are reimbursed on export of the final product.

Each of these institutions allows exporters to import capital goods and raw materials duty free. Some offer additional advantages such as a high-quality, reliable infrastructure and streamlined customs procedures. All the successful exporting countries established at least one, and in most cases more than one, of these programs. Malaysia relied mainly on EPZs that provided reliable infrastructure and allowed exporters (mainly in electronics) to import and export without being taxed; the government also established bonded warehouses and a duty exemption system for other exporters. Most Korean and Taiwanese exporters used a well-functioning duty exemption and rebate system to obtain inputs at world prices; in addition, a substantial number of firms were set up as bonded warehouses or located in EPZs. Hong Kong and Singapore essentially are citywide EPZs. Indonesia established an agency in the Ministry of Finance that granted exemptions from import licensing restrictions and drawbacks (rebates) for duties paid on imported inputs, and Thailand gave similar privileges to investors who qualified for them. The vast majority of Tunisia's manufactured exporters operate as bonded warehouses, whereas Mauritian exporters are located mainly in export processing zones. China's special enterprise zones are the source of most of its manufactured exports. More recently, the Philippines' remarkable success in establishing a large and rapidly growing electronics industry is at least partially due to the EPZs established at the former Subic Bay naval base and Clark airforce base, where the departing U.S. forces left behind an extensive high-quality physical infrastructure.

5. Factor markets were highly flexible in the Asian countries. In the neoclassical version of the outward-looking strategy, well-functioning labor and capital markets ought to reflect changing factor endowments with changing relative prices and generate such export transitions gradually. Even if the government tries to push industrialization faster than justified by market conditions, fluid factor markets are needed to reallocate labor and investment toward the newly favored industries. The countries of East and Southeast Asia, by and large, have had labor markets in which wages reflected labor abundance and thus encouraged the first stages of labor-intensive, export-oriented industrialization. Once the rapidly growing demand for workers absorbed the labor surplus, market wages began to rise. This occurred in the late 1960s in Korea, the early 1980s in Malaysia, and around 1990 in Indonesia.

Except in Hong Kong and Singapore, however, the Asian tigers intervened in credit markets to keep interest rates suppressed and credit allocations under government influence. In Korea, the government used its control of the major banks to channel credit at below-market interest rates to the large conglomerates, or *chaebol*, that it favored as vehicles to promote later-stage exports. Other, mostly smaller, firms were forced to borrow in the informal credit (curb) market, where interest rates reflected capital scarcity. Real interest rates on loans from banks actually were *negative* for several years during the 1970s, while curb market rates were 15–20 points above bank rates from 1965 to 1985.[33] This two-tiered credit market encouraged the transition into capital-intensive exports, such a steel, ships, and cars, more rapidly than the unrestrained market.

The tendency was reinforced by the Korean government's policies on technology and firm size. The initial spurt of labor-intensive exports such as textiles, clothing, footwear, and plywood took place in a large number of medium-size firms. By the 1970s, however, the government was encouraging the *chaebol* to move into steel, ships, automobiles, electronics, chemicals, and other heavy export industries. All the weapons of state economic power were employed, including subsidized credit, preferential taxes, personal favors, and political sanctions. State firms also were employed as vehicles to obtain new technology, notably in the fertilizer, petrochemical, and steel industries; to train Korean managers and engineers; and in some cases, to spawn new firms once the technology had been mastered. Foreign firms were discouraged from entering these markets, where they would have had a competitive advantage. And, key to the entire strategy, the government made it clear that the ability to export was the ultimate measure of success.[34] The push into heavy industry in the 1970s failed in many instances and was very costly to the economy, but it did result in a range of new export industries and provided a base for reform and expansion in the 1980s. It also accelerated a tendency toward industrial concentration. In 1974, the five largest *chaebol* had combined sales of less than 12 percent of the gross national product; by 1984, their sales exceed 50 percent of GNP.[35]

Taiwan employed a similar mix of policies but stayed closer to the market-based strategy than Korea, a result of politics more than economics. The Kuomintang government, exiles from China's mainland, did not wish to share political or economic power with native Taiwanese, yet wished to

33. Vittorio Corbo and Sang Woo Nam, "The Recent Macroeconomic Evolution of the Republic of Korea: An Overview," World Bank, Economic Research Department, discussion paper DRD 208, 1986.

34. These policies are described by Amsden, *Asia's New Giant,* and Howard Pack and Larry E. Westphal, "Industrial Strategy and Technological Change." *Journal of Development Economics,* 22, no. 1 (June 1986), 87–128.

35. Amsden, *Asia's Next Giant,* p. 116. The same caveat applies here as in the discussion of multinational firms in Chapter 14: Sales and GNP are not comparable measures. But the large rise in this ratio is indicative.

encourage rapid development. A strategy that promoted the growth of small firms reconciled these two goals, and this in turn dictated greater dependence on market mechanisms. From 1966 to 1981, the share of manufacturing workers employed by firms of less than 500 workers actually rose, from 65 to 72 percent; in Korea, by contrast, the share employed in smaller firms fell from 74 to 59 percent. The government used protection, subsidized bank lending, and other interventions to promote the establishment of large-scale, heavy industries that produced intermediate goods. The government (or Kuomintang party) controlled many such firms. But the curb market was efficient in channeling credit to small firms, which were the principal exporters, and for this sector market allocations were more important than government intervention.[36]

In Malaysia, Thailand, Indonesia, and China, the governments also intervened in credit markets, but there seems to be little correlation between this intervention and export success in these countries. Most of this intervention was aimed at firms engaged in import substitution, and there have been few success stories. Malaysia's domestic automobile production, Indonesia's attempts to produce aircraft and steel, and other examples suggest that directed credit, while common in all the Asian countries, was not crucial to export success.

POSSIBLE RISKS

Many of the successful Asian exporters fell victim to the financial crises that swept the globe in 1997 and 1998, which have led some observers to question whether an outward orientation contributed to these problems. As described in Chapters 13 and 14, these crises were related to the sequencing and pace of financial sector liberalization and the related integration with global capital markets. Little direct relationship is found between outward-looking trade policies and these crises.[37] Several of the outward-oriented Asian countries, including Hong Kong, Singapore, Taiwan, China, were not hit by financial crises, although they suffered

---

36. Tyler Biggs and Brian Levy, "Strategic Interventions and the Political Economy of Industrial Policy in Developing Countries," in D. H. Perkins and M. Roemer, eds., *Reforming Economic Systems in Developing Countries* (Cambridge, MA: Harvard University Press, 1991), pp. 365–401. Robert Wade, *Governing the Market,* puts greater stress on government's role in promoting industrialization.

37. Overcapacity in some markets and weakening export earnings probably contributed to the crisis on the margin in some of the Asian countries but does not seem to have been a fundamental cause of the problems. For a discussion, see Steven Radelet and Jeffrey Sachs, "The East Asian Financial Crisis: Diagnosis, Remedies, Prospects," *Brookings Papers on Economic Activity* (1998), 1–90.

through a major recession resulting from their neighbors' miseries. These crises surely are cautionary tales about both rapid financial liberalization and the vagaries of world capital markets, but they do not negate the gains from the outward-trade orientation and related policies reaped by these countries.

A common question is the extent to which the outward-oriented strategy can continue to succeed as more and more countries shift to manufactured exports. The concern is that, if countries around the world, including large countries such as India and China, simultaneously adopt export-oriented strategies, prices for these products will fall and competition will force down wages in all these countries. This easily could happen (and often does happen) in the short run in some specific markets, as new entrants create overcapacity and drive out high-cost producers. For example, prices for semiconductors fell in the mid-1990s as world productive capacity grew rapidly. But the long-term evidence suggests that world trade can expand very quickly and accommodate many new firms. Between 1950 and 1998, world exports grew more than three times more quickly than world output, and exports of manufactured products grew most quickly of all. As more countries trade and transport and telecommunication costs continue to drop, the opportunity for firms to specialize will increase. Global production networks allow firms from many different countries to contribute to the production of one finished good, with each firm specializing in the particular phase of the production process in which it has comparative advantage. Firms in one country are better able to serve niche markets for specialized consumer goods that arise in other countries. Moreover, as developing countries open to world markets, they become markets for other country's exports. Trade is a two-way process. Consider, for example, India and China. As the world's two largest countries continue to integrate with global markets and expand their exports, their imports also expand, so they become enormous markets for capital goods, raw materials, agricultural products, consumer goods, and a wide array of services produced in and exported from other countries.

Perhaps the greatest threat to expanded trade is that greater openness in developing countries could push the industrialized countries toward more protectionist policies. Increased competition from firms in developing countries could exacerbate unemployment in northern countries, at least in some sectors. To the extent that the higher-income countries react by protecting their "sunset industries" and retreating from the world trading system, the prospects for developing country exporters would be dimmed. This is not at all impossible—the last epoch of globalization from 1850–1914 was followed by a closing of the world economic system after World War I and eventually contributed to the onset of the Great Depression. But, despite remaining protection in some sectors, a general resource in the industrialized countries to closing off from the world economy seems unlikely. Trends in recent decades clearly have been in the direction of greater openness, despite the series of oil price shocks, the debt crises of the 1980s, and the more recent financial crises of the 1990s. These shifts have been supported and expanded through world trade arrangements, as discussed in the next section, and seem unlikely to be reversed in the near future.

Nevertheless, the magnitude and speed of the gains recorded by the Asian exporters almost certainly cannot be replicated by all developing countries. The Asian countries surely had an advantage when they began to export, since they had to compete with few countries to attract investment and produce exports. At a deeper level, however, countries with adverse geography will find it much more difficult to compete on world markets. Landlocked developing countries, for example, face huge cost disadvantages relative to similar coastal economies, since they must ship most imports and exports by land over long distances and cross additional international borders. Landlocked countries will find it much more difficult to attract foreign investors and compete on world markets for traded goods, especially goods with relatively low trading margins such as electronics. Similarly, countries with widespread endemic disease or particularly adverse climactic conditions may have less potential for attracting investment and promoting manufactured exports.

Critics of the outward-looking strategy sometimes claim that exporting firms often are "sweatshops" with very low wages and poor working conditions. There is little doubt that, relative to industrialized countries, both wages and working conditions tend to be poor in developing countries. This is true for workers in the agricultural sector, in firms producing for the domestic market, and for exporters. Low wages and poor working conditions tend to reflect the overall low level of development, poor institutional quality (e.g., court systems), and general poverty of many low-income countries. Are these conditions worse in exporting firms? There are two schools of thought. The first suggests that the drive for exports puts countries into a "race to the bottom" in which firms that are competing on world markets will do anything to cut costs, including paying very low wages and imposing harsh conditions on the workforce. Governments trying to attract foreign investment will put in place policies that reinforce these tendencies. The second suggests that the export strategy leads to higher labor productivity and growth in wages. As incomes increase, working conditions tend to improve. In addition, foreign investors tend to be under much closer scrutiny than domestic firms, obliging them to offer better working conditions.

With respect to wages, as was pointed out earlier in Table 18–5, evidence suggests that wages have grown much more quickly in countries that focused on manufactured exports, belying the argument that this strategy leads to a low-wage trap for workers. On labor conditions, unfortunately, very little systematic evidence is found on the issue one way or the other, with most evidence indirect or resting on individual anecdotes. Certainly, many exporting firms engage in poor labor practices; but others consciously have tried to improve conditions and are models for other firms in the country to follow. Many multinational firms responded to adverse publicity about poor working conditions by trying to bring about some improvements. In the countries that have been successful exporters for a long time, such as Singapore, Taiwan, and Korea, working conditions today are much better than they were 30 years ago. While there is no compelling evidence, it seems reasonable to believe that working conditions will tend to improve as incomes grow over long periods of time. To the extent that the outward-looking strategy contributes to sustained growth in per capita income, it probably contributes to improved working conditions over the long run as well.

RECONCILING IMPORT SUBSTITUTION AND EXPORT GROWTH

We have seen how import substitution is ridden with internal contradictions that sap its energy, lead to industrial stagnation, and close the economy out of potential export markets. Yet, if domestic entrepreneurs, managers, and workers are to learn how to manufacture new products using new technology, even if they aim eventually for export markets, they initially may require some form of moderate protection from outside competition.[38] Can the failure of protection be reconciled with the need for it, even as a first step toward outward-looking industrialization?

Theoretically, at least, the answer is yes, and the two actually have been reconciled in a few cases. Most of the Asian countries used limited import substitution strategies, at least early on, and some analysts believe that this may have contributed to their later export success. An outward-looking strategy that accommodates import substitution could have three components:

1. The infant industry concept, strictly interpreted, should guide trade policy. Tariff protection should be granted only to those industries

---

38. Henry Bruton provides a compelling statement of this necessity in "Import Substitution," in Hollis B. Chenery and T. N. Srinivasan, eds., *Handbook of Development Economics,* Vol. 2 (Amsterdam: Elsevier, 1989), pp. 1601–44.

that have some prospect of competing as exporters or import substituters without protection and, then, only if the initial costs of protection are expected to be fully compensated by the eventual benefits of domestic production. Tariffs, or preferably subsidies, should be moderate and temporary, with predetermined rates of decline; quotas never should be used.

2. If the government is capable of doing so, it could follow in the footsteps of Japan and Korea by extending protection and subsidized credit only to firms that achieve agreed-on, ambitious export targets. The likely losses suffered by firms in the early years of exporting would be compensated for by higher profits at home, but firms also would be learning how to compete abroad. This approach is not for all countries, however. Indeed, many countries have tried to follow Korea and Japan's examples, only to find many more difficulties than they anticipated. Targeted interventions require disciplined officials who grant privileged access or other favors on the basis of excellent export performance or other transparent criteria rather than use their power principally for personal gain. Where governments are less determined or less disciplined in their implementation of growth policies, a strategy that depends more on markets and broadly based incentives, minimizing government intervention in detail, is advisable.

3. Industries that are competitive in world markets should not be protected, but encouraged to export instead. This may require special measures to ensure ready access to imports at world market prices, as in Southeast Asia, although the need for intervention diminishes the less protectionist is the grade regime. Domestic firms at first may be incapable of moving directly into export industries. But foreign investors will be able to do so if a liberal investment climate attracts them, as discussed in Chapter 14. This has been the pattern in Southeast Asia, where firms from the industrial countries and, increasingly, from East Asia have played major roles in the manufactured export boom since the mid-1980s.

World Trading Arrangements

With the outbreak of World War I, a long epoch of globalization and rapid growth of world trade came to an end. Many bilateral trade treaties were scuttled, and the industrialized countries began to erect high tariff and nontariff barriers. Their aims were

TRADE REFORM IN MEXICO, 1985–89[39]

Leaders in Mexico, among the most protectionist of nations, recognized by the mid-1980s that shielding the economy from foreign competition had created noncompetitive industries that could not sustain rapid economic growth. In July 1985, as part of a strategy to overcome its debt crisis, the government of President Miguel de la Madrid launched a set of daring trade reforms.

Restrictive licensing of imports was ended for most categories: Whereas 92 percent of domestic production had been protected by licensing before the reform, by the end of 1989, import restrictions covered only 20 percent of production. To compensate, the authorities devalued the peso, so that the real official rate depreciated by over 40 percent through the end of 1986, and raised tariffs from an average 23.5 percent in June 1985 (based on production weights) to 28.5 percent six months later. The additional protection from devaluation and tariff increases helped to keep imports from rising and shielded domestic producers.

39. Based on Adriaan Ten Kate, "Liberalization and Economic Stabilization in Mexico: Lessons of Experience," *World Development*, 20, no. 5 (May 1992), 659–72.

to safeguard industries associated with national security, reduce the demand for foreign exchange, and protect domestic jobs. The onset of the Great Depression accelerated this trend, but the shift toward protectionism only deepened the depression by reducing trade. By 1931, tariff levels on foodstuffs reached 53 percent in France, 66 percent in Italy, and 83 percent in Germany. License and quota restrictions were applied to over one fourth of imports into Belgium and the Netherlands and more than half of imports into Switzerland and France in 1937.[40]

When World War II ended, trade barriers began to fall, and industrial country leaders looked for ways to accelerate and support the process. The perceived failure of the *bilateral* arrangements in effect before World War I gave rise to attempts at **multilateral trade negotiations** (which actually started during the late 1930s). The basic idea behind the multi-

40. Douglas Irwin, "Multilateral and Bilateral Trade Policies," in Jaime de Melo and Arvind Panagariya, eds., *New Dimensions in Regional Integration* (Cambridge: Cambridge University Press, 1995).

In 1986, however, a bold program of tariff reduction was announced and implemented over the following two years. By the end of 1989, the production-weighted average tariff had fallen to 12.5 percent, less than half its level in December 1985. And, after 1986, the real exchange rate began to appreciate and so further exposed domestic industry to import competition. The result was an import boom: Dollar expenditures on merchandise imports doubled from 1987 to 1989, after seven years of decline and stagnation. Under such intense foreign competition, domestic restructuring began to take place.

Mexico's stabilization and structural adjustment have had moderate success. Direct investment from abroad, which had virtually disappeared by the mid-1980s, revived to record levels. Indeed, strong capital inflows of all kinds contributed to the exchange rate appreciation. Merchandise exports, which had been stagnant throughout the 1980s, began growing by more than 9 percent a year from 1988 through 1991. And gross national product, also stagnant throughout the 1980s, began a modest recovery to 4.4 percent a year from 1988 to 1991.

Mexico's reforms have been entrenched. In 1986, Mexico joined the General Agreement on Tariffs and Trade (GATT; see the next section), in effect subjecting its trade reforms to international agreement. During the latter half of the 1980s, it used macroeconomic policies to overcome imbalances, rather than reversing the trade reforms. In 1993, Mexico joined the United States and Canada in the North American Free Trade Agreement, and so further opened its economy.

lateral approach is that, by involving many nations at the same time, each individual country will be better able to overcome narrow interest groups at home that oppose trade liberalization. Although the initial multilateral negotiations made little progress, they led to support for the idea of establishing the **International Trade Organization** in 1948 as a sister organization to the IMF and World Bank. Although the ITO itself was never established, multilateral trade negotiations expanded and ultimately flourished in the ensuing decades through a less formal institution known as the **General Agreement on Tariffs and Trade** (GATT).[41] In addition to these arrangements, since the mid-1980s, some countries have entered into regional trade agreements to complement (and sometimes replace)

41. Although the ITO charter was approved at a UN conference in Havana in 1948, the U.S. Congress refused to ratify the agreement, even though the United States had been one of the driving forces behind the ITO idea. In 1950, the U.S. government announced that it no longer would seek congressional ratification of the UN charter, effectively killing the ITO. See the WTO website (www.wto.org) for details.

TABLE 18–6	GATT TRADE ROUNDS		
YEAR	PLACE AND NAME	SUBJECTS COVERED	COUNTRIES
1947	GENEVA	TARIFFS	23
1949	ANNECY	TARIFFS	13
1951	TORQUAY	TARIFFS	38
1956	GENEVA	TARIFFS	26
1960–61	GENEVA (DILLON ROUND)	TARIFFS	26
1964–67	GENEVA (KENNEDY ROUND)	TARIFFS AND ANTIDUMPING MEASURES	62
1973–79	GENEVA (TOKYO ROUND)	TARIFFS, NONTARIFF MEASURES, "FRAMEWORK" AGREEMENTS	102
1986–94	GENEVA (URUGUAY ROUND)	TARIFFS, NONTARIFF MEASURES, RULES, SERVICES, INTELLECTUAL PROPERTY DISPUTE SETTLEMENT, TEXTILES, AGRICULTURE, CREATION OF WTO	123

Source: World Trade Organization website: www.wto.org.

multilateral trade reform. Some regional trade agreements involve developing countries exclusively, while others have members from both the North and the South. We examine each of these approaches to multi-country trade reform in turn.[42]

MULTILATERAL TRADE REFORM

The GATT began in 1947–48 with a round of negotiations involving 23 countries that resulted in 45,000 tariff concessions affecting about 20 percent of world trade. In the ensuing years, an international agency was created to support the agreement. Both the package of trade rules and tariff concessions and the international agency that supported the rules came to be known as *the GATT.* Between 1947 and 1994, eight rounds of multilateral trade negotiations took place, eventually involving most countries in the world, as shown in Table 18–6. These negotiations often were tedious, time consuming, and difficult, but they yielded significant results. By the mid-1980s, average tariffs in the industrialized countries were down to about 6 percent, substantially lower than their peak in the 1930s. Less progress was made on nontariff barriers, which were not discussed until the Tokyo round of 1973–79. The most recent GATT agreement, the so-called Uruguay round

42. For additional background material on these topics, see Jeffrey A. Frankel, *Regional Trading Blocs in the World Economic System* (Washington DC: Institute for International Economics, 1997); Robert Z. Lawrence, *Regionalism, Multilateralism, and Deeper Integration* (Washington, DC: Brookings Institution, 1996); Jaime de Melo and Arvind Panagariya, eds., *New Dimensions in Regional Integration;* and Jagdish Bhagwati and Anne O. Krueger, *The Dangerous Drift to Preferential Trade Agreements* (Washington, DC: American Enterprise Institute for Public Policy Research, 1995).

(since its initial meeting took place in Punta del Este, Uruguay, in September 1986), was completed in 1994. It was by far the largest trade negotiation ever held, with 123 countries taking part, including for the first time a large number of developing countries. These negotiations further reduced tariffs on manufactured goods by about one third and attacked some trade barriers that had escaped earlier rounds. Agricultural protection, formerly excluded from negotiations, was incorporated for the first time by requiring countries to shift from quantitative restrictions to tariffs *(tariffication)* and by reducing subsidies that enabled industrial countries to cut into the markets of tropical countries. The Multi-Fiber Agreement, which restricted textile and clothing imports in the industrial countries, was scheduled to be phased out over a ten-year period. Trade in services was brought under the GATT for the first time, albeit in a very partial way. Industrial countries, especially the United States, won stricter adherence to *intellectual property rights* that prevent the use of written, recorded, or filmed material and computer programs without permission. The Uruguay round agreement provided developing countries with additional time and flexibility to comply with all of the provisions.

The Uruguay round also resulted in a decision that the organization that had overseen the GATT be superceded by a new organization, the **World Trade Organization,** which was established on January 1, 1995. In some sense, the establishment of the WTO finally brought into existence—in a different form—the ill-fated ITO. The WTO serves as a central institution for global trade negotiations aimed at establishing a system of rules for fair, open, and undistorted competition. It also serves as a forum for the settlement of disputes among member countries. Over three quarters of the member nations of the WTO are developing and transitional economies.

The cornerstone of the GATT and WTO negotiations is the **most favored nation** (MFN) principle: All trading partners enjoy the lowest duty rate an importing country accords to any of its trading partners. Although the term suggests that MFN provides special or preferential status, in fact it is the normal trade status that by international law must be given to all members of GATT. (The United States recently began to use the phrase *normal trade relations* instead of MFN.) In essence, MFN means that whenever a country reduces a tariff or removes a nontariff barrier, it must do so for all of its trading partners. The MFN principle gives the multilateral trade process its power, since it ensures that trade liberalizations will be widespread and not discriminatory.

INTEGRATION IN THE SOUTH

The developing countries, frustrated by their inability to gain wider access to industrial country markets or improve their terms of trade with these markets (especially prior to the Uruguay round), have exhorted

TABLE 18–7	TRADE AMONG DEVELOPING MARKET COUNTRIES		
		1970	1990
VALUE OF INTRA-SOUTH EXPORTS IN BILLION U.S. DOLLARS			
ALL EXPORTS (0–9)		11.9	219.3
MANUFACTURES (5–8)		4.6	143.4
SHARE (%) OF INTRADEVELOPING-COUNTRY TRADE IN			
TOTAL DEVELOPING-COUNTRY EXPORTS[a]			
ALL EXPORTS (0–9)		20.1	28.6
MANUFACTURES (5–8)		27.2	33.5

[a]By current market value.

Source: World Resources Institute, *World Resources 1994–95* (New York: Oxford University Press, 1994), p. 263.

each other to form larger and more meaningful regional trade groups among themselves. Groups of countries have tried to stimulate economic growth by granting preferential access to each other's exports, placing relatively less emphasis on access to industrial country markets. Table 18–7 shows that the value of trade among developing countries multiplied 18 times from 1970 to 1990; correcting for inflation, intrasouth trade grew more than fivefold in real terms. For manufactured exports, the quantity of intrasouth trade expanded ninefold over those two decades. In 1990, manufactured exports were about a third of total developing-country exports. Proponents of regional trade groups hope that greater economic integration among developing countries will increase the importance of intra-developing-country trade to the benefit of all participants.

Three systems of regional trade arrangements (RTAs) can be defined, in increasing degree of economic integration. **Free-trade areas** eliminate tariffs among member countries, although each member is permitted to set its own tariffs on imports from the outside world. The North American Free Trade Agreement among Canada, Mexico, and the United States is a recent example. Because members typically are free to set their own external tariffs, free-trade associations represent a relatively minimal level of cooperation and integration. **Customs unions** also eliminate tariffs among members but go beyond free-trade areas by erecting a common external tariff against imports from the rest of the world. The Preferential Trade Area of eastern and southern African countries, which began in 1984 to reduce internal tariffs for selected commodities, is intended to become a full-fledged customs union. The South African Customs Union (SACU), which includes South Africa, Botswana, Lesotho, Swaziland, and Namibia in its membership, can trace its roots as far back as 1910.

Common markets move several steps closer to full integration. In addition to free trade among members and a common external tariff, common markets either eliminate or substantially reduce restrictions on the movement of labor and capital among member states. They may go further to promote coordinated fiscal, monetary, and exchange-rate policies and may cooperate in many other ways. Both the Central American Common Market and the East African Community had achieved important elements of economic integration until political differences among members destroyed each grouping. The European Union is the most integrated group in the world today. It largely has eliminated tariffs and customs procedures among its member states; harmonized taxes, fees, regulations, and procedures affecting trade; and launched a new common currency (the Euro) on January 1, 1999.

RTAs may benefit their members by conveying **static gains,** in the form of one-time improvements in resource allocations, and by offering **dynamic gains,** stimulating investment in production for export and linked industries. The traditional analysis of the static gains from customs unions makes the distinction between *trade creation* and *trade diversion.* Trade is **created** when an RTA permits one member (country A) to export more to another (country B) by displacing the production of country B's own industries. The import-competing industry in country B presumably was able to sell in the home market because the protective duty shielded it from the exports of more-efficient, lower-cost industries in other countries. When the RTA lowers the duty on imports originating from other member countries, more-efficient industries in those countries can compete with a country's firms in their own markets. More goods are traded than before, hence the term **trade creation.** Although some producers in the importing country are disadvantaged by the change, consumers benefit from lower prices and wider selection. In addition, other firms in the importing country benefit by being able to export more to other member countries as those countries lower their tariffs. Gains from trade creation are analogous to gains from the opening of trade (see Chapter 16), except that they take place within the limited membership of the RTA.

When RTAs discriminate against outside countries (by charging higher tariffs on imports from nonmembers than on imports from member countries), they may cause **trade diversion** by shifting a country's imports away from goods originating in a nonmember country to goods originating in other member countries. If, before the union, country B had an MFN tariff, that is, all countries were treated equally, then the nonmember country's exports must have been cheaper than those of country A, or else country B would have imported from country A in the first place. Once the union is formed, consumers in country B will buy from producers in country A at a lower cost to the consumers, since the tariff is lower than that charged on imports from nonmembers. But this comes at a higher cost in foreign exchange to the country as a whole, since consumers pay more than they would if imports from nonmember were accorded the lower tariff. In addition, part of the tariff revenue previously earned on imports from nonmember countries now is paid to exporters in country A.

For example, say that Bolivia can import telephones either from France for $10 each or from Ecuador for $11 each. With MFN arrangements, it would charge imports from either source the same tariff, say 20 percent. Under these circumstances, Bolivia will import the telephones from France. The importer will spend $10 in foreign exchange and pay the tariff in local currency. With an exchange rate of 5 bolivianos to the dollar, the domestic market price will be 60 bolivianos ($10 × 5 B/$ × 1.20). Say that Bolivia then enters into an RTA with Ecuador in which it lowers all tariffs on trade between the two countries to 5 percent. Importers now will switch to purchasing phones from Ecuador, even though they have to pay $11 for each phone, to take advantage of the lower tariff. The market price in Bolivia for phones will be 57.75 bolivianos ($11 × 5 B/$ × 1.05). Although the market price is lower, the country has paid more in foreign exchange ($11 to Ecuador instead of $10 to France). In addition, government revenue from tariff collection has fallen from 10 bolivianos per phone initially to 2.75 bolivianos. Of this reduction in revenue of 7.25 bolivianos per phone, consumers capture only 2.25 bolivianos through the lower price. The other 5 bolivianos is captured by exporters in Ecuador (through the extra $1 they are paid for each phone). Finally, it is worth noting that the market price for consumers could be even lower still (52.5 bolivianos) if Bolivia charged 5 percent tariff on its imports from France.

From each member country's standpoint the RTA is beneficial if trade creation outweighs trade diversion. This is more likely to be the case if customs union partners have different relative resource endowments or if their consumers have different tastes, so that the members have comparative advantages in the export of different commodities. For example, if Mexico, with comparative advantages in vegetables and petroleum, were to join in an RTA with Colombia, with comparative advantages in coffee and textiles (to oversimplify greatly), trade is likely to be created and both countries would benefit. But, on the whole, neighboring developing countries tend to export similar goods, and there is a presumption that trade diversion would be large. In the old East African Community, for example, much of the trade in manufactured goods came from industries, such as tire manufacturing in Kenya, that could not compete with the outside world. Tanzania and Uganda had to pay higher prices for these manufactures than if they had purchased from outside the market. Note that even if, on balance, trade creation within the RTA exceeds trade diversion, so long as there is some diversion, nonmember countries are losers.

Most advocates of RTAs among developing countries argue that the major gains are not static but dynamic. RTAs widen the market for industries in all member countries, with the attendant benefits noted earlier in this chapter. Economies of scale may be realized by some industries whose output would be too small if confined to the home market. One potentially important, if largely unimplemented, feature of the Andean Pact and the Association of Southeast Asian Nations (ASEAN) is the *complementation agreement,* under which large-scale infant industries are allocated to member countries. In other words, country A would produce all the petrochemicals, country B would produce fertilizer, country C would produce pulp and paper, and so on. Then each member could benefit from starting different industries while all share the costs. The downside to complementation agreements, of course, is that they reduce the potential for competition and the decisions on allocations may be based more on political than economic criteria.

RTAs also increase competition among producers in the member countries. This can be especially important for large-scale industries that otherwise would monopolize home markets at efficient levels of output. But it can have a much more pervasive effect; it can sharpen entrepreneurial and managerial performance in all industries. Intensified competition is thought to have played a major role in stimulating European growth after the formation of the European Common Market and may have contributed to the temporary success of Central American Common Market as well. One manifestation of increased competition is a characteristic pattern of trade in RTAs: Much of the new trade is in similar or even identical products. To some extent this represents specialization in fine detail; for example, one textile firm narrows its products to concentrate on the few things it does especially well. To some extent it may represent more efficient subregional patterns of trade, such as a realignment to take advantage of lower transport costs once borders no longer serve as barriers. But a substantial portion of the trade in similar goods may reflect greater competition and a wider range of choice for consumers. Trade in similar goods belies the trade creation approach, which predicts that countries will gain only if they export dissimilar goods.

Over the long run, these dynamic effects should induce greater investment and hence accelerate growth within the customs union and restructure the economy toward exports of all kinds. Given these advantages, why are there so few examples of successful RTAs in the developing world? One major problem has been the distribution of the gains, whether static or dynamic. When the East African Community was functioning, Kenya (which had moved faster to industrialize) exported more to its neighbors than it imported. Investment flowed into Kenya to take advantage of the industrial infrastructure and the central location of Nairobi. This concentration of gains in Kenya contributed to the demise of the East African experiment and helped to dampen the ardor of countries like Bolivia and Ecuador for the Andean Pact in South America.

The concentration of gains—real or perceived—in the more-advanced member countries leads to political tensions. Conversely, political disagreements among neighbors become much more dangerous when those neighbors are tied together in economic arrangements. Each partner, but especially the economically less advanced ones, can use participation as a whip to threaten other partners if decisions are not taken in its favor. Political tensions among Uganda, Tanzania, and Kenya eventually destroyed the East African Community. Chile withdrew from the Andean Pact over political disagreements with Peru and other countries. The potential for such schisms always exists and substantially increases the risk a country takes when it enters an integration scheme. To achieve the gains of RTAs, each country must develop its economy in ways that may not make much sense in the absence of a union. Malaysia might invest in a fertilizer plant intended to serve the ASEAN countries. But if the free-trade area does not develop or if political arguments make it ineffective, Malaysia has considerably more fertilizer capacity than it can use if it remains a high-cost producer. Does an investor want to take that chance?

To date, attempts at regional trade integration between developing countries generally have been unsuccessful. Trade creation has been relatively small, partially because of the similar factor endowments of the countries involved and partially because the limited size of the market has constrained the potential for specialization. Moreover, some agreements have failed either because some members did not fully implement the accords or because one country was perceived to reap a disproportionate share of the benefits. To be successful, any integration plan must bring the promise of substantial additional investment in the foreseeable future and must provide for a broad and equitable distribution of the benefits of union. Member countries will have to be governed by leaders who recognize common interests and are prepared to cooperate with their neighbors. Larger membership in the RTA tends to reduce these political risks, so that no single country can destroy the arrangement by withdrawing. Finally, and perhaps most important, many RTAs in developing countries have failed because they were inward oriented, designed to give protection to firms in the region and keep out outside competition, rather than as a first step toward integration with the rest of the world. In these cases, the RTA resulted in significant trade diversion, with few of the benefits of trade creation.

TRADING BLOCS

Trading arrangements changed rapidly in the 1990s. While the EU became more integrated and is expanding, the Eastern European trading bloc, COMECON, and the Soviet Union itself disappeared. Canada, Mexico, and the United States are joined in NAFTA, which other Latin American countries are hoping to join. Japanese trade, investment, and aid dominate economic relations among the countries of East and Southeast Asia; this creates a de facto economic sphere of influence, although decidedly not a formal trade arrangement. And the Asia Pacific Economic Cooperation group (APEC), which includes many countries of Asia and the Americas bordering the Pacific Ocean, plans to become a free-trade area in the first two decades of the twenty-first century. These newly emerging trading blocs may begin to supplant the global, multilateral trading arrangements, governed by the GATT and now the WTO, that have guided international trade for almost five decades since World War II. How will the changes affect developing countries?

The answer, of course, depends. The EU always has granted preferential access to exports from its members' former colonies in Africa and the Caribbean and has not been markedly more protectionist toward other developing countries than the United States and Japan. Mexico will be the prime beneficiary under NAFTA, because its much smaller economy now has access to the large U.S. market. Other Latin American countries are likely to benefit eventually, while those left out and the aggressive exporters of East and Southeast Asia, which have depended heavily on the U.S. market, are likely losers. It is doubtful whether Japan could fully replace the United States as an export destination for the latter countries. If, however, the ambitious plans for APEC eventually incorporate Pacific Basin countries in a free-trade area, most of the developing countries of eastern Asia and the Americas will become part of a large and rapidly growing bloc. But the populous countries of South Asia, notably Bangladesh, India, and Pakistan, have not been prominently mentioned as candidates for inclusion in any of the emerging blocs. African countries, although tied to Europe, might be squeezed out of the dynamic markets of Asia and the Americas.

The possible emergence of large regional trading blocs creates uncertainty for many developing countries. The potential exists for substantial trade diversion and an unequal distribution of dynamic gains away from excluded countries, toward those within the new trading agreements. The threat of losses among many developing countries may be a spur to new arrangements to stimulate trade among southern countries, as already is occurring within southern Africa and Southeast Asia. The emerging APEC group, however, is an example of interregional cooperation among so large a group that trade creation and dynamic gains are likely to exceed the loses. Moreover, if regional arrangements go far enough, the habit of more open borders may well boost reforms in worldwide, multilateral trade under the World Trade Organization. The advantages of an outward orientation of both developing and industrial countries argue in favor of multilateral trade reforms in preference to a strengthening of regional trading blocs, however organized.

MANAGING AN OPEN ECONOMY

Economic development takes place in the long term. Most of the processes discussed in the previous chapters, whether improving human welfare or increasing saving or shifting toward manufactured exports, take years and even decades to bear significant results. If policy makers in developing countries gaze only at the far horizon, however, they are unlikely ever to reach it. Much happens in the short term, within a few months or a couple of years, to throw an economy off balance and make pursuing long-term strategies difficult and sometimes impossible. Policy makers need to emulate the ship's captain, who, always steering toward the port of destination, nevertheless must deal decisively with any storms at sea.

Among the most dangerous and likely of these storms are changes in world prices that throw the balance of payments into deficit, excessive spending that fuels inflation, and droughts or other natural disasters that disrupt production. Unless a government counteracts these economic shocks, they create greater uncertainty and higher risk for private producers and investors, who take evasive action that reduces future investment, worsens the crisis, and causes development efforts to founder.

During the 1970s and 1980s, many economies became unbalanced because of unstable world market conditions: Sharp rises in oil prices during the 1970s were followed by equally precipitate declines in the mid-1980s. A cycle began with rising world inflation during the 1970s, followed by corrective policies, especially in the United States, that included monetary restraint and rising interest rates and led to a world recession in the early 1980s. Wide swings in the major exchange rates characterized both decades.

Some governments, especially those in East and Southeast Asia, managed their economies shrewdly enough to overcome and even benefit from these changing conditions. But a larger number of developing countries was unable to cope. Several governments, particularly in Latin America and Africa, made the situation worse. These governments allowed their exchange rates to become overvalued; this contributed to growing deficits in the balance of payments. These deficits were financed by borrowing abroad, so countries accumulated debt that could not be serviced. These governments also ran budget deficits that had to be financed through the banking system, which expanded the money supply and fed inflation. Many governments then intervened in markets to counter the effects of profligate macroeconomic management.

In Chapter 5, we discussed the consequences of such **macroeconomic instability.** Countries with overvalued exchange rates and rapid inflation have been unable to grow rapidly, in contrast to those, especially in East and Southeast Asia, with well-managed economies (recall Figures 5–1 and 5–2). *Stabilization programs,* many funded by the IMF, are intended to correct these macroeconomic imbalances.

In this chapter, we develop a mechanism for analyzing the macroeconomic policies that a developing country should pursue to stabilize its economy and create a climate for faster economic growth. The model developed here incorporates the two main policy approaches for correcting macroeconomic imbalances: *Reductions in expenditure,* such as lower government budget deficits and slower creation of money, and *adjustments in relative prices,* particularly exchange-rate devaluation.

Equilibrium in a Small, Open Economy[1]

Developing economies have two features central to understanding how macroeconomic imbalances occur and can be corrected. First, they are **open economies,** in that trade and capital flow across their borders in sufficient quantities to influence the domestic economy, particularly prices and the money supply. Most economies are open in this sense, especially since economic reforms in China beginning in the late 1970s and the collapse of the Soviet economies in the late 1980s. Today only a few economies, such as Cuba and Burma, are so heavily protected and regulated that they might not qualify as open to trade and finance.

---

1. In developing this and the next two sections, we acknowledge an intellectual debt to Shantayanan Devarajan and Dani Rodrik, who wrote an excellent set of notes for their class on macroeconomics for developing countries at Harvard's John F. Kennedy School of Government in the late 1980s, and to Richard E. Caves, Jeffrey A. Frankel, and Ronald W. Jones, who develop the open economy model in Chapter 19 of *World Trade and Payments: An Introduction* (Glenview, IL: Scott, Foresman, Little, Brown, 1990).

Second, these are **small economies,** meaning that neither their supply of exports nor their demand for imports has a noticeable impact on the world prices of these commodities and services. Economists call these countries *price takers* in world markets. A number of developing countries can exert some influence over the price of one or two primary exports in world markets: Brazil in coffee, Saudi Arabia in oil, Zambia in copper, South Africa in diamonds, for example. But they almost never affect the price of goods they import, and for macroeconomic purposes, it usually is adequate to model even these countries as price takers.[2]

These two qualities—smallness and openness—are the basis for the **Australian model** of a developing economy.[3] Chapters 16 and 18 used simple general equilibrium models to describe comparative advantage (Figure 16–1) and economic growth through import substitution (Figures 18–4 and 18–5). In those models, the two goods were importables and exportables. The Australian model lumps importables and exportables together as *tradables* and distinguishes these from all other goods and services, called *nontradables*. We use this specification in Chapter 16's discussion of the Dutch disease.

Tradable goods and services are those whose prices within the country are determined by supply and demand on world markets. Under the small-economy assumption, these world market prices cannot be influenced by anything that happens within the country and so are *exogenous* to the model (determined outside the model). The domestic price of a tradable good is given by $P_t = eP_t^*$, where e is the nominal exchange rate in local currency per dollar (pesos per dollar for Mexico or rupees per dollar for Pakistan) and P_t^* is the world price of the tradable in dollars. Even if the supply of and demand for tradables changes within an economy, the local price will not change because domestic supply and demand have a negligible influence on the world price. Adjustment of the exchange rate changes the domestic price, however. Because this model simplifies all tradables into one composite good, the price of tradables P_t is best thought of as an index, a weighted average of the prices of all tradables, much like a consumer price index.

Tradables include exportables, such as coffee in Kenya and Colombia, rice in Thailand, beef in Argentina, cattle in West Africa, palm oil in

2. Among developing countries, China and India are large enough that they could become exceptions to the small country rule, given continued growth in China and both greater growth and openness in India.

3. So called because it was developed by Australian economists, including W. E. G. Salter, "Internal Balance and External Balance: The Role of Price and Expenditure Effects," *Economic Record* (August 1959), 226–38; Trevor W. Swan, "Economic Control in a Dependent Economy," *Economic Record* (November 1956), 339–56; and W. Max Corden, *Inflation, Exchange Rates and the World Economy* (Chicago: University of Chicago Press, 1977). Australia also is a small, open economy.

Malaysia and Indonesia, copper in Peru and Zambia, oil in the Middle East, and textiles and electronics in East Asia, and importables, such as rice in West Africa, oil in Brazil or Korea, and intermediate chemicals and machinery in many developing countries.

Nontradables are goods and services, such as transportation, construction, retail trade, and household services, that are not easily or conventionally bought or sold outside the country, usually because the costs of transporting them from one country to another are prohibitive or local custom inhibits trade. Prices of nontradables, designated P_n, therefore are determined by market forces within the economy; any shift in supply or demand will change the price of nontradables. Nontradable prices thus are *endogenous* to the model (determined within the model). P_n, like P_t, is a composite or weighted average price incorporating all prices of nontradable goods and services.

INTERNAL AND EXTERNAL BALANCE

Figure 19–1 depicts equilibrium under the Australian model. The vertical axis represents nontradables (N); the horizontal axis takes both the exportables and the importables of previous diagrams (Figures 16–1, 18–4 and 18–5) and treats them together as tradables (T). The production frontier

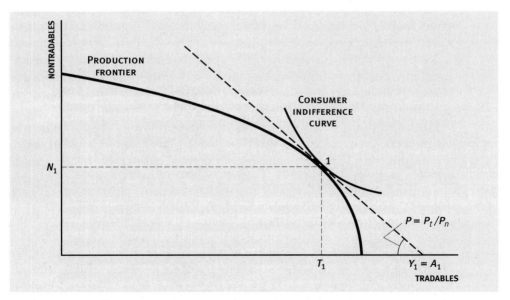

FIGURE 19–1 EQUILIBRIUM IN THE AUSTRALIAN MODEL. With equilibrium at point 1, the tangency of the production frontier and a community indifference curve, the country produces and consumes T_1 of tradables and N_1 of nontradables. The relative price, P, is a measure of the real exchange rate (see text). National income measured in tradable prices is Y_1.

shows the menu of possible outputs of the two kinds of goods, N and T. The community indifference curves show consumer preferences between consumption of tradables and nontradables.

Equilibrium is at point 1, the tangency of a consumer indifference curve and the production possibilities frontier. At this point, the production of tradables, determined by the production frontier at point 1, is T_1, equal to the demand for tradables, determined by the indifference curve at 1; and similarly, for nontradables, supply equals demand at N_1. This is a defining characteristic of equilibrium in the Australian model: At point 1, the markets for both goods are in balance. Put another way, there is **external balance,** because the supply of tradables equals demand, and **internal balance,** because the supply of nontradables equals demand.

The tangency of the indifference curve and production frontier also determines the relative price of tradables in terms of nontradables, $P = P_t/P_n$. The slope of the relative price line P_1 gives this price in Figure 19–1. The relative price, P, is an alternative measure of the **real exchange rate** and is one of the important innovations of the Australian model.[4] This formulation separates out prices that are under the influence of monetary and fiscal policy and domestic market forces, P_n, from prices that can be changed only by adjustments of the nominal exchange rate, $P_t = e\,P_t^*$. Note that P_1 is the only real exchange rate consistent with equilibrium in the model.

If P rises (the price line becomes steeper in the diagram), tradables become more expensive relative to nontradables. Producers then attempt to switch along the production frontier away from N goods, toward T goods. Consumers attempt to switch in the opposite direction, up along the indifference curve to consume less T goods and more N goods. Therefore, a rise in P should work to increase the surplus of T-good production over consumption.

If the production of T goods exceeds consumption of T goods, there is an external surplus, which is identical to a surplus in the balance of trade. To see this, start with the definition of the trade balance as

$$B_t = E - M \qquad\qquad [19\text{--}1]$$

---

4. Chapters 16 and 18 defined the real exchange-rate index as RER $= R_o P_w/P_d$. R_o is an index of the nominal exchange rate, whereas in this chapter we use e, the nominal exchange rate itself. P_w is an index of world prices, often the U.S. consumer or wholesale price index and is similar or identical to P^* as measured in practice. But P_d is a domestic consumer or wholesale price index that includes both tradable and nontradable prices, while P_n is an index of nontradable prices only. Thus, the Australian formulation of the real exchange rate is a more precise definition than those given in the earlier chapters.

where E and M are exports and imports. Because exports are the surplus of supply over demand for exportable goods, while imports are the opposite, a surplus of demand over supply, we can write the balance of trade as

B_t = value of E-goods supply − value of E-goods demand
   − (value of M-goods demand − value of M-goods supply)

   = value of E-goods supply + value of M-goods supply
   − (value of E-goods demand + value of M-goods demand)
   = value of tradables supply − value of tradables demand

or if we let the supply of tradables be X_t and demand be D_t,

$$B_t = P_t X_t - P_t D_t = P_t(X_t - D_t) \qquad [19\text{--}2]$$

In Figure 19–1, with the economy in equilibrium, consumption of tradables is equal to production, so the balance of trade is 0.

The value of income (GNP) also can be found in Figure 19–1. It is the sum of the value of output of N goods (N_1) and T goods (T_1). This value is given by Y_1, the intersection of price line P_1 from point 1 to the T axis.[5] In national income accounting, we distinguish two concepts. Gross national *product,* a measure of the value of output, is given by

$$Y = C + I + E - M \qquad [19\text{--}3]$$

where C and I are consumption and investment by both the government and the private sector. Gross national *expenditure,* often called **absorption,** is

$$A = C + I = Y + M - E. \qquad [19\text{--}4]$$

When, as in Figure 19–1, the economy is in equilibrium, $E = M$ and income equals absorption. Indeed, this is a condition of equilibrium.

This exploration of the Australian model has yielded three results. First, macroeconomic equilibrium is defined as a balance between supply and demand in two markets: Nontradable goods (internal balance) and tradable goods (external balance). Second, to achieve equilibrium in both markets, two conditions must be satisfied: Expenditure (absorption) must equal income, and the relative price of tradables (the real exchange rate) must be at a level that equates demand and supply in both markets (P_1 in Figure 18–1). Third, this also suggests two remedies for an economy that is out of

---

5. Along the T axis, Y_1 is measured in prices of the T good, so $P_t Y_1 = P_t T_1 + P_n N_1$ or $Y_1 = T_1 + (P_n/P_t)N_1$. But $P_n/P_t = \Delta T/\Delta N$, with $\Delta N = N_1$ and $\Delta T = Y_1 - T_1$, the distance along the T axis from T_1 to Y_1. Thus, the value of both goods in T prices is $T_1 + Y_1 - T_1 = Y_1$.

balance: A government can achieve equilibrium—stabilize the economy—by adjusting absorption, the nominal exchange rate, or both. Generally, both instruments must be used to achieve internal and external balance.

THE PHASE DIAGRAM

Using the perspective of trade theory, we tie the small, open economy model of macroeconomic management to the tools of analysis already used in this text. But the principles of stabilization can be explored from a more useful perspective, the **phase diagram.** To develop this approach, consider the markets for tradables and nontradables from the perspective of conventional supply and demand diagrams, as in Figure 19–2.

In these diagrams, we use the real exchange rate, which is the relative price of T goods in terms of N goods (P_t/P_n), as the price in both markets. For tradable goods, that gives a conventional supply and demand diagram: As the price rises, supply increases and demand decreases. But in the non-tradables market, a rise in P means a fall in the relative price of N goods, so supply decreases and demand increases. Note that, in both markets, any increase in expenditure, or absorption, A, causes an outward shift of the demand curve: At any price, consumers will buy more of both goods.

To use these diagrams as a basis for macroeconomic analysis, we need to change the interpretation of the supply curve for tradables. Until now,

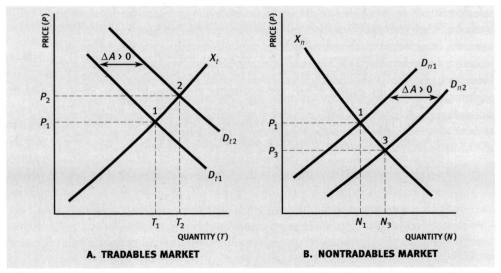

FIGURE 19–2 TRADABLES AND NONTRADABLES MARKETS. Supply is denoted by X and demand by D. The price, P, in both diagrams is P_t/P_n. In part A, the demand and supply curves for tradables X_t and D_t have the conventional slopes. But in Part B the slopes are reversed: X_n falls as P rises (because the relative price of N is falling) and D_n rises as P rises. In both markets, demand increases when absorption (expenditure) increases, shown by an outward shift of D_t and D_n.

we have assumed that all tradables are produced within the home country. But foreign investment and foreign aid can add to the supply of tradables by financing additional imports. Therefore, the supply curve should not be X_t, but $X_t + F$, where F is the inflow of long-term foreign capital in the form of aid, commercial loans, and investment.

Figure 19–2 constitutes a simple model of the small, open economy that is based on two variables: The real exchange rate P on the vertical axis, and absorption A, which determines the position of the demand curves. These, of course, are the conventional variables of microeconomics, price and income. But, in this model, they also are the two main macroeconomic policy tools of government: The exchange rate and the level of expenditure. Because these two variables are central to macroeconomic management, it would be helpful to develop a diagram that uses them explicitly on the axes.

Figure 19–3 does this. It puts the real exchange rate, $P = eP_t^*/P_n$, on the vertical axis, and real absorption, A, on the horizontal axis. The diagram also contains two curves, each representing equilibrium in one of the markets. Along the EB, or *external balance,* curve, the T-goods market is in balance ($X_t = D_t$). Along the IB, or *internal balance,* curve, the N-goods market is in balance ($X_n = D_n$).

The slopes of the two curves, EB and IB, can be derived from Figure 19–2. In the tradables market, when absorption is A_1, equilibrium is at P_1, where T_1 is produced and consumed. This equilibrium point 1 also is shown in Part A of Figure 19–3. If absorption increases to A_2 in Figure 19–2, the

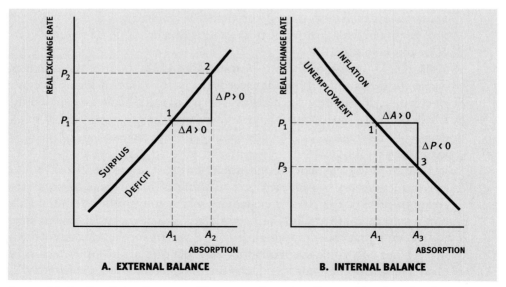

FIGURE 19–3 THE PHASE DIAGRAM. The axes are the main policy variables, the real exchange rate, P, and real absorption, A. The curves show equilibrium in the T-goods market (external balance, EB) and N-goods market (internal balance, IB).

demand curve moves outward and shifts equilibrium to point 2. Note that, with higher absorption, A_2, the real exchange rate, P_2, must be higher to restore equilibrium in the T-goods market. Increased absorption raises the demand for T goods. To meet this demand, it is necessary to raise output, which can be achieved only through a higher relative price of T goods, P_2. This higher price also helps regain balance by reducing the demand for T goods along the new demand curve. Point 2 is transferred to Figure 19–3 at (P_2, A_2).

In the nontradables market, when absorption is A_1, equilibrium is at P_1, where N_1 is produced and consumed. This equilibrium point 1 also is shown in Part B of Figure 19–3. If absorption increases to A_2 in Figure 19–2, the demand curve moves outward and shifts equilibrium to point 3. In the N-goods market, higher absorption, A_2, requires a lower, or appreciated, real exchange rate to restore equilibrium. Increased absorption raises demand for N goods, met by raising output, which can be achieved only through a lower relative price of T goods, P_3. This lower real exchange rate, or higher price of N goods, also helps regain balance by reducing the demand for N goods along the new demand curve. Point 3 is transferred to Figure 19–3 at (P_3, A_2).

Figure 19–3 also shows the **zones of imbalance.** In the T-goods market, Part A, for any given level of absorption, say, A_1, any real exchange rate greater than P_1 would cause external surplus: The production of tradables would exceed the demand for tradables because the relative price, P, would be at a more depreciated level than required for equilibrium. Any real exchange rate below (more appreciated than) P_1 would cause an external deficit, and the demand would exceed the supply of tradables. Therefore, the zone of surplus is northwest of EB and the zone of deficit is southeast.

In the N-goods market, Part B, inflation is to the right of the IB curve, where the demand for N goods exceeds the supply. In that region, for any given real exchange rate, such as P_1, absorption is too high, say, A_3. To the left is the zone of unemployment, where there is an excess supply of N goods. In that region, for any given real exchange rate, say, P_3, absorption is too low, say, A_1.

The meaning of inflation and unemployment is precise in our model but not in the real world. It is best to think of inflation as being an increase in prices faster than is customary in the country in question. That rate would be quite low in Germany, Japan, or China, probably less than 5 percent a year, but quite high in Brazil or Argentina. Unemployment implies not only jobless workers, but also idle capital and other factors of production. In other words, there is unemployment when an economy is inside the production frontier in Figure 19–1. A country may have high levels of labor unemployment but be unable to increase output because it is fully utilizing its capital or land.

EQUILIBRIUM AND DISEQUILIBRIUM

The two balance curves are put together in Figure 19–4. All along the external balance curve the demand for T goods equals the supply produced at home plus any net foreign capital inflow. All along the internal balance curve the demand for N goods equals the supply of N goods. The only point where there is both internal and external balance—equilibrium in both the T- and N-goods markets—is the intersection of the two curves, at point 1. This is sometimes called the *bliss point*. It is the same as the tangency of the indifference curve to the production frontier in Figure 19–1 at point 1. The objective of macroeconomic policy is to adjust the exchange rate and absorption to keep an economy stable, in both external and internal balance at point 1.

Economies spend considerable time in one of the four zones of imbalance shown in Figure 19–4. Zone A to the north of point 1 is a region of external surplus and inflation, where the exchange rate is *undervalued*. In Zone B to the east of equilibrium, the economy faces inflation and a foreign deficit, due principally to excessive expenditure (absorption is greater than income). To the south of point 1 is Zone C, where the exchange rate is *overvalued* (too appreciated) and there is both unemployment and an external deficit. And west of the bliss point the economy is in Zone D, where, because of insufficient absorption, there is unemployment of all resources but a foreign surplus.

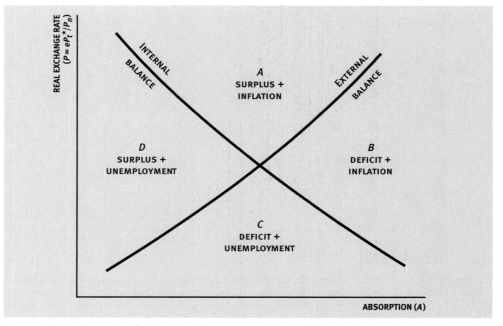

FIGURE 19–4   ZONES OF IMBALANCE. The economy is in equilibrium only at point 1, the intersection of the *EB* and *IB* curves. Zones of imbalance are labeled. For example, in Zone *A* to the north, supply of *T* goods exceeds demand, so there is a surplus, and demand for *N* goods exceeds supply, so there is inflation.

Once in disequilibrium, economies have built-in tendencies to escape back into balance. Figure 19–5 describes them separately for external balance (Part A) and internal balance (Part B). Start with an external surplus, point 1 in Part A. The excess supply of tradables generates two self-correcting tendencies. First, the net inflow of foreign exchange adds to international reserves. If the central bank takes no countermeasures, the money supply will increase and interest rates will fall and induce both consumers and investors to spend more. The increase in absorption moves the economy rightward, back toward external balance. Second, the inflow of foreign exchange will create more demand for the local currency and, if the exchange rate is free to float, will force an appreciation. This is a move downward in the diagram, also toward the *EB* line. The net result of these two tendencies is the resultant, shown as a solid line in the diagram, heading toward external balance. If instead the economy starts in external deficit at point 2, the tendencies are the opposite but the result is the same: A tendency to regain external balance.

The tendency to regain internal balance is shown in Part B. When there is inflation (point 3), it affects both the real exchange rate and real absorption. If the nominal exchange rate remains fixed (or is not allowed to depreciate as fast as inflation), the rise in P_n causes a real appreciation. At the same time, the rise in prices can cause a fall in the real value of absorption, assuming that the central bank doe not take steps to increase

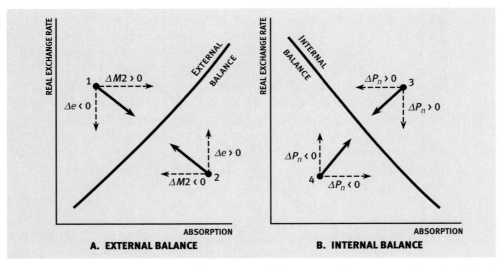

FIGURE 19–5   TENDENCIES TOWARD EQUILIBRIUM. If the economy faces an external surplus (point 1 in Part A), reserves and the money supply tend to rise while the exchange rate tends to appreciate; this drives the economy toward external balance. Conversely for a deficit. If the economy faces inflation (point 3 in Part B), the rise in prices leads to real appreciation of the exchange rate and a reduction in the real value of absorption; this moves conditions toward internal balance. Conversely for unemployment at point 4, but only if prices can fall flexibly.

the money supply to compensate for inflation. Under these assumptions, the economy would move from inflation at point 3 back toward internal balance. Unemployment (point 4) would be self-correcting, also, if prices are able to fall as easily as they rise, but this seldom is the case.

Although these self-correcting tendencies exist, in practice they often fail to work smoothly or quickly enough because of *structural rigidities* in the economy. For instance, exchange-rate changes may take time to affect actual imports and exports, perhaps as long as two years to have a full impact. In economies like Ghana and Zambia, dominated by one or two export products such as cocoa and copper, with long gestation periods for new investment, supply elasticities for tradables may be especially low and foreign deficits can persist for a time despite real devaluations.

Nontradables prices probably rise very quickly when demand exceeds supply, as in Part B of Figure 19–5. But in many developing economies, inflation, once started, may resist corrective policies and prices do not fall so easily when there is unemployment: Unions strike wage bargains that try to maintain real wages by continually raising nominal wages, banks use their market power to keep interest rates high, producers are dependent on imports whose prices are responsive only to exchange rate adjustments, and large firms with monopoly or oligopoly power keep prices up to cover costs that resist downward pressures. Such rigidities have been cited frequently to explain chronic trade deficits and inflation in Latin America, especially in Argentina and Brazil.

However, arguments about structural rigidities can be overstated. There is some flexibility in production for most export industries, even in the short term. And many producer prices are quite flexible, including those of most farm products, those in the large informal sector, and even those of some modern manufacturing firms. Nevertheless, the automatic tendencies toward external and internal balance depicted in Figure 19–5 are likely to be too slow and politically painful to satisfy most governments.

Not all the barriers to adjustment are structural. Sometimes, policies work against adjustment. When foreign reserves fall, for example, the money supply also would fall automatically unless the central bank's policy is to *sterilize* these shifts by expanding domestic credit to compensate for the fall in reserves and keep the money supply from falling. Sterilization prevents the move from points 1 or 2 of Figure 19–5 toward external balance. And nominal exchange rates respond to changing market conditions, as shown in Panel A, only if the exchange rate is allowed to float or the government makes frequent adjustments in the nominal exchange rate to match changing economic conditions.

However, the opposite policy—a fixed nominal exchange rate—is needed if inflation in nontradables prices is to cause a real exchange-rate appreciation, as depicted at point 3 of Figure 19–5. This fixed nominal rate is called an exchange rate *anchor,* because the fixed rate alone can halt the upward drift of prices, as the economy moves due south from point 3 in Part B. Chile used such an anchor to slow inflation during the late 1970s (see the case study later in this chapter). If government devalues the rate to keep up with inflation—Brazil's practice for many years—then real appreciation is thwarted and there is no anchor. Similarly, real absorption falls with inflation only if the government fixes its expenditure and its deficit in nominal terms and allows inflation to erode the real value of the expenditure and if the central bank restrains the money supply to grow more slowly than inflation. More typically, the fiscal authorities adjust the expenditure, while the monetary authorities adjust both the money supply and the nominal exchange rate, to fully compensate for inflation. In that case, rising prices have no impact on the real exchange rate or real absorption and an inflationary economy remains at point 3 in Figure 19–5.

STABILIZATION POLICIES

Whether the barriers to rapid automatic adjustment are inherent in the economic structure or created by policy contradictions, in most cases, governments need to take an active role to stabilize their economies. They have three basic instruments for doing so: exchange-rate management, fiscal policy, and monetary policy.

Alternative **exchange-rate regimes** were introduced in Chapter 13. Governments can vary the exchange rate by having the central bank offer to buy and sell foreign currency at a predetermined or *fixed* official exchange rate (*e* in our nomenclature) that nevertheless can be changed from time to time or by allowing the rate to *float* in the currency market, although the central bank sometimes may intervene to influence the price. An intermediate case is the *crawling peg,* under which the central bank determines the rate but changes it frequently, as often as daily, to ensure that the official rate stays in line with domestic and world inflation; this results in a constant or slowly adjusting real exchange rate (*P*).

Governments have two policies that can influence the level of absorption. **Fiscal policy**—adjusting levels of government expenditure and taxation—directly affects the government's components of consumption and investment. It also influences private expenditure, especially consumption, which depends on *disposable income,* or income net of taxes. **Monetary policy** also affects private expenditure. If the central bank acts to increase the money supply, as described in Chapter 13, it increases the liquidity of households and firms, lowers interest rates, and stimulates private consumption and investment.

The power of the phase diagram is that it indicates the necessary directions for these policies, depending on the state of the economy. Figure 19–6 provides such a policy map. It shows the same external

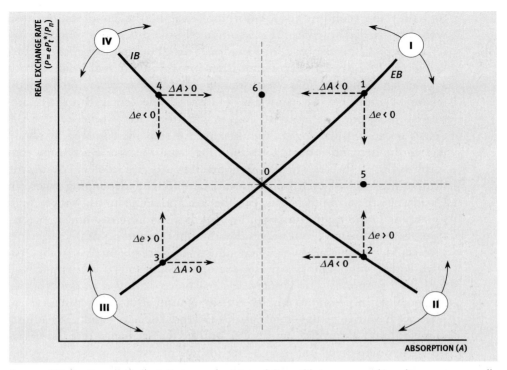

FIGURE 19–6 POLICY ZONES. From any position of disequilibrium, two policy adjustments generally are needed to restore internal and external balance. In each of Quadrants I to IV, a particular combination of exchange rate and absorption policy is prescribed.

and internal balance lines as in the previous diagrams, but adds a new element: four policy quadrants, I to IV, within which the policy prescription always is the same.

Take, for example, point 1, which has been placed on the external balance line but in the inflationary zone. For many years, Brazil was in this situation, with buoyant exports and balance in foreign payments but chronic inflation running from 40 to well over 100 percent a year. Because the demand for nontradables exceeds supply, we know that one necessary correction is a reduction in real absorption—monetary and fiscal *austerity*—that would reduce demand and move the economy due west from point 1. But if that is the only policy taken, the economy would not reach internal balance until point 4, in the zone of external surplus. One imbalance would have been exchanged for another. To avoid generating a surplus, reduced absorption needs to be accompanied by an appreciation of the exchange rate, a move due south from point 1. The result would be a move approximately toward the equilibrium or bliss point, 0.

Note three things about this result. First, this combination of policies, austerity and appreciation, would work from any point within Quadrant I to return the economy to equilibrium. That is, the same combination would be needed whether the economy had inflation with a moderate external surplus or inflation with a moderate deficit, either just above or just below the *EB* line. If the economy starts just below external balance, with a moderate deficit, it may seem strange (*counterintuitive*) to recommend an appreciation that, on its own, would worsen the deficit. But the reduction in absorption, needed to reduce inflation, also would reduce the deficit because it also lowers the demand for tradables. Indeed, it would reduce the demand for tradables too much and throw the economy into surplus; this is the reason that an appreciation is needed. Of course, the relative intensity of each policy would be different, depending where in Quadrant I the economy starts. But the basic principle holds: Anywhere in Quadrant I, the right combination of policies is austerity and appreciation, the combination that moves the economy toward point 0.

Second, in general, two policy adjustments are required to move toward equilibrium. This is a simple example of the general rule enunciated by Dutch economist Jan Tinbergen: To achieve a number of policy goals, it generally is necessary to employ the same number of policy instruments. Here we have two goals—internal and external balance—and need adjustments in both absorption (austerity) and the real exchange rate (appreciation) to reach them both. It is not always necessary to use two goals, however. If the economy lies just to the east of equilibrium at point 5, then a reduction in absorption will achieve internal and external balance simultaneously. And if the initial situation is point 6, due north of 0, then appreciation alone will do the job.

Third, we could view the policy prescription in either of two ways. Austerity is needed to reduce inflation (move west) and appreciation is used to avoid surplus (move south). Or appreciation can be targeted on internal balance (move south toward point 2) but alone would cause a deficit, so that austerity then is required to restore external balance. Therefore, no logic in macroeconomics suggests that one particular policy should be assigned to one particular goal. Economic institutions often do this anyway. In practice, the central bank might use the exchange rate to achieve external balance while the finance ministry uses the budget for internal balance. But, if these two approaches are not coordinated, they may well fail to reach equilibrium.

With these principles established for Quadrant I, it is fairly routine to go around the map in Figure 19–6 and see what policy responses are required:

- In Quadrant II at a point like 2, with an external deficit but internal balance, exchange-rate devaluation is needed to restore foreign balance but taken alone would push the economy into inflation. Fiscal and monetary austerity also are needed to avoid inflation and reach equilibrium. We could have reversed this assignment of policies and used austerity to achieve external balance and devaluation to stimulate the economy. Many African countries were in this situation during the 1970s and early 1980s, with low inflation but an insufficiency of export earnings and foreign investment to pay for the imports required for economic development.

- In Quadrant III at point 3, an expansionary fiscal-monetary policy would eliminate unemployment but at the cost of a foreign deficit, so devaluation is needed to reach equilibrium. Or devaluation could stimulate employment and so require expansion to eliminate the resulting surplus. This is the situation of a mature industrialized economy during a recession, with unemployed labor and capital, but it is not so common in developing countries.

- In Quadrant IV at point 4, exchange-rate appreciation can eliminate the external surplus while fiscal expansion prevents unemployment. Or fiscal expansion can end the surplus while appreciation prevents the resulting inflation. A few countries in Asia, such as Taiwan (see the case study at the end of this chapter) and Malaysia in the 1980s, have been in this situation.

So the principles of macroeconomic stabilization are simple: If policy makers know where to place their economy on this map, they know how to move toward equilibrium. But how do policy makers know where they are? The answer lies partly in measurement, partly in art. Regularly available data on the balance of payments and changes in reserves and on inflation can help locate an economy with respect to the external and internal balance lines. Data on the nominal and real exchange rates, on the budget deficit, and on the money supply can indicate movements from one policy quadrant to another. In principle, econometric models can locate the economy and indicate the policies needed to balance it. In practice, especially but not only for developing economies, such models can be too imprecise and too unstable to be wholly dependable. The art of stabilization policy comes in knowing just how hard to push on each component of policy and how long to keep pushing. In this, experience in managing a particular economy is as important a guide as the models estimated by economists.

Tales of Stabilization

Throughout this book we have referred to different kinds of economic problems that are associated with developing countries, including Dutch disease, debt crises, terms-of-trade shocks, foreign exchange shortages, destructive inflation, and droughts or other natural catastrophes. The Australian model and its phase diagram can be used to show how these and other shocks affect macroeconomic balance and how they should be handled.

THE DUTCH DISEASE

Chapter 16 described the strange phenomenon of the Dutch disease, in which a country that receives higher export prices or a larger inflow of foreign capital may end up worse off than without the windfall. The Dutch disease was first analyzed by Australian economists Max Corden and Peter Neary, using a version of the open economy model.[6] Figure 19–7 traces the impact of a windfall gain using the phase diagram.

An economy in equilibrium at point 1 suddenly begins to receive higher prices for its major export or is favored by foreign aid donors or foreign investors. All the oil producers, from Saudi Arabia to Indonesia to Mexico, were in this position in the 1970s, as were coffee (and many other commodity) exporters during the boom of the mid-1970s. Egypt and Israel were rewarded with large aid programs by the United States after the Camp David accord of 1978, as was Ghana by the World Bank and others during its stabilization of the 1980s. Both Chile in the late 1970s and Mexico after its stabilization in the late 1980s received large inflows of private capital, much of it a return of previous flight capital. Foreign exchange windfalls are more frequent than sometimes is supposed.

When the windfall occurs, the supply of tradable goods rises at any given price. This can be shown as a rightward shift in the supply curve in Figure 19–2A. In the phase diagram of Figure 19–7, there is a rightward shift in the EB curve. At point 1, for example, which had been in external equilibrium along EB_1, the economy now is in surplus, so the new EB curve must be to the right; for example, at EB_2. The economy cannot remain at point 1 because the inflow of reserves increases the money supply; this adds to demand and, because the windfall will increase private income and government revenue, leads to greater expenditure. So absorption rises—a move from point 1 toward point 2. This moves the economy off its internal balance, into inflation.[7]

The resulting rise in P_n has two effects: a reduction in real absorption that partially corrects the initial rise in A and, assuming the official rate is fixed, a real appreciation of the exchange rate. (The real rate also would ap-

6. W. Max Corden and J. Peter Neary, "Booming Sector and Deindustrialisation in a Small Open Economy," *Economic Journal*, 92 (1982).

7. If the windfall is an inflow of capital, this treatment is precise. In the case of a rise in export prices, however, the move from point 1 to 2 is an approximation. Strictly speaking, a rise in export prices should raise P_t^*, a depreciation of the real exchange rate that moves the economy upward from point 1, after which the economy moves east toward EB_2.

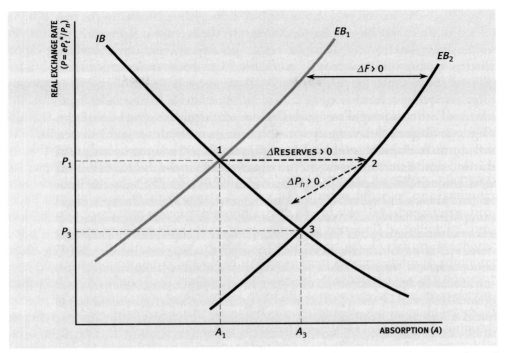

FIGURE 19–7   THE DUTCH DISEASE. An export boom or capital inflow shifts the *EB* curve rightward and leaves the economy at point 1 in surplus. As reserves accumulate and the money supply rises (or as the government and consumers spend the windfall), absorption rises and the economy moves eastward, into inflation. As nontradable prices rise, the real exchange rate appreciates. At the new equilibrium, point 3, because *P* is lower, the supply and demand is balanced with less production of *T* goods and more output of *N* goods than before. The loss of tradable output is what makes this a "disease."

preciate if the nominal rate were floating, because the greater supply of foreign currency would drive the price of foreign currency down.) Therefore, the economy would first move from point 1 toward 2 in Figure 19–7 and then begin to head in the general direction of the new equilibrium, point 3. In this case, market forces are likely to be sufficient to reach the new equilibrium unless the authorities prevent appreciation and maintain real absorption and so keep the economy in an inflationary posture like point 2.

What, then, is the problem? The economy is at a new equilibrium; its terms of trade have improved; its currency has appreciated and so citizens have more command over foreign resources; people are spending and consuming more without having to work any harder. There are two flaws in this otherwise idyllic picture. First, such windfalls generally are temporary. When export prices fall or the capital inflow dries up, the *EB* curve will shift back and a costly adjustment will be necessary. We analyze that process in the next section.

The second problem is that, in shifting from the old to the new equilibrium, there have to be adjustments in the economy. The real exchange rate P is lower, so X_t has fallen, while X_n has risen. Because the booming export sector will not retrench, nonboom tradables bear the brunt of the adjustment. Frictions in the labor market are likely to mean at least temporary unemployment as workers switch from tradable to nontradable production. If the tradable sector includes modern manufacturing, then long-term development may be set back because manufacturing is the sector likely to yield the most rapid productivity growth in the future. And if tradable industries close, it will be more difficult to make the inevitable adjustment back toward point 1 when the windfall is over. This decline in nonboom-tradable production turns a foreign exchange windfall into a "disease."

What can be done to cure the disease? The government could try to move the economy back toward the old (and probably future) equilibrium at point 1. Its tools are the official exchange rate, which would have to be devalued against the tendencies of market forces, and expenditure, which would have to be reduced through restrictive fiscal and monetary policies that also reduce inflation (lower P_n or at least its growth). The resulting buildup of reserves and bank balances would have to be sterilized through monetary policy so they would be held as assets and not spent. It is a neat political trick to manage an austere macroeconomic policy in the face of a boom, because all the popular pressures are for more spending. Not too many countries have managed it. Indonesia is among the few that have; we discussed Indonesia's therapy for Dutch disease in a case study in Chapter 16.

DEBT REPAYMENT CRISIS

When Mexico announced in 1982 that it could no longer service the debt it acquired during the oil boom of the 1970s, many other developing countries followed Mexico's lead and the financial world entered a decade of debt crisis (Chapter 14). Most Latin American countries largely have overcome their debt problems, but many African countries continue to struggle to repay the money they have borrowed, mostly from aid agencies. Although debt service insolvency encroaches gradually on an economy and can be foreseen, it often appears as a national crisis because economic management has been inept.

The formal analysis of a debt crisis is similar to that of another common phenomenon, a **decline in the terms of trade** that leads to a foreign exchange shortage, which in turn is simply the reverse of the Dutch disease. Therefore, the oil exporters, such as Indonesia, Nigeria, and Venezuela, faced a similar kind of crisis once oil prices began falling in the 1980s.

Figure 19–8 captures this process. An economy in balance at point 1 needs to find additional resources to repay its foreign debt or needs to

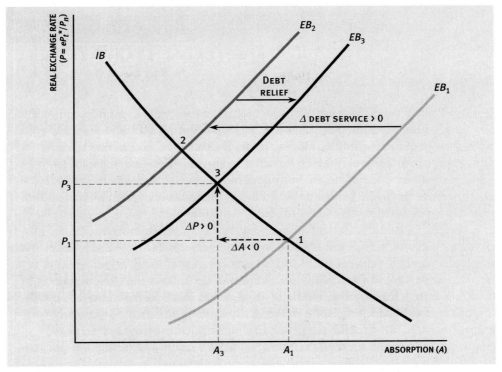

FIGURE 19–8   DEBT CRISIS OR DECLINING TERMS OF TRADE. An economy in equilibrium at point 1 suddenly needs to repay its debt (or faces falling export prices). External balance shifts from EB_1 to EB_2, although debt relief or increased foreign assistance might reshift the balance line back to EB_3. If policies accommodate the fall in reserves and income, absorption will decline. A devaluing exchange rate, via central bank action or market forces, will help the economy move to its new equilibrium at point 3. With more tradables produced and less consumed, the surpluses can be used to repay the debt.

adjust to falling terms of trade. The supply of tradables therefore shifts to the left in Figure 19–2A; in the phase diagram, the EB curve also shifts leftward to EB_2.[8] If the crisis leads to debt relief or additional foreign aid, the curve would move less far and might settle at EB_3.

Now in foreign deficit, the economy will begin losing reserves. If the government has to repay some of the debt or if falling export prices cut into its revenues, the government needs to reduce its expenditures as well. Both cause a reduction in absorption. These actions move the economy toward external balance but also into unemployment. To gain the new equilibrium at point 3, it also is necessary to devalue the currency. This could be done by the central bank under a fixed rate or by the foreign exchange market under a floating rate. At the new equilibrium, the country

8. Strictly speaking, we cannot analyze the fall in export prices this way, but it is a reasonable approximation for many situations. See note 7.

PIONEERING STABILIZATION: CHILE, 1973–84[9]

In the last year of the Salavatore Allende regime in Chile, when the public sector deficit soared to 30 percent of GNP and was financed mostly by printing money, inflation exceeded 500 percent a year. In 1973, General Augusto Pinochet overthrew Allende and established an autocratic regime. An early goal of his government was to stabilize the economy. It proved to be a difficult task of many years, with important lessons for later stabilizations in Latin America.

Faced by rapid inflation and unsustainable external deficits, the government imposed a fiscal and monetary shock on the economy. The budget deficit was cut to 10.6 percent of GNP in 1974 and again to 2.7 percent in 1975. Monetary policy was tight: From the second quarter of 1975 through the middle of 1976, it has since been estimated, households and firms were willing to hold more money than was in circulation. But inflation persisted; consumer prices nearly doubled in 1977.

Despite draconian measures, prices continued to rise for two reasons. First, the peso was aggressively devalued to improve the foreign

9. Based on the account by Vittorio Corbo and Andrés Solimano, "Chile's Experience with Stabilization Revisited," in Michael Bruno et al., *Lessons of Economic Stabilization and Its Aftermath* (Cambridge, MA: MIT Press, 1991).

is producing more and consuming less tradables, because P has risen. This, of course, is a loss of welfare for the populace. The surplus of X_t over D_t is used to repay the debt or simply compensates for reduced export prices.

Debt crises, and the hardships they cause, are not an inevitable consequence of borrowing to finance development. If the borrowed resources are invested productively, they will increase the potential output of both tradables and nontradables. Added production will increase income and generate the capacity to repay the debt out of additional income, without a crisis and an austerity program. Countries such as Korea and Indonesia have been large international borrowers, but prior to the financial crisis of 1997–1999, they escaped debt crises.

balance, the more so because of the 40 percent fall in copper prices in 1975. In 1977, the peso was worth about one- 80th its 1973 value against the dollar. Second, wages in the formal sector were determined by rules that permitted adjustments based on the previous year's rate of inflation—a rule that helped to perpetuate the higher rates of earlier years. It also was argued by some that the monetary policy was not stringent enough.

In 1978, the government switched gears and began using the exchange rate as its main anti-inflation weapon. At first a crawling peg was adopted with preannounced rates, the *tablita,* that did not fully adjust to domestic inflation. In 1979, the rate was fixed at 39 pesos to the dollar for three years. The appreciating real exchange rate, or *anchor,* helped control inflation, which was down to 10 percent by 1982. But it also discouraged export growth and contributed to a growing current-account deficit. At the same time, Chile liberalized its controls over foreign capital flows and attracted large inflows of loans: Net long-term capital rose from negligible amounts before 1978 to average over $2 billion a year in the next five years, equivalent to 8 percent of GNP in 1980. This inflow not only financed the growing current deficit but contributed to the real appreciation of the exchange rate.

Not until after 1984 did Chile finally achieve a semblance of both internal and external balance. It did so through a large real devaluation, approaching 50 percent, supported by tighter fiscal and monetary policies. After a decade and a half of falling income per capita, Chilean incomes grew by 5.8 percent a year from 1985 to 1991.

STABILIZATION PACKAGE: INFLATION AND A DEFICIT

External shock is not the only way an economy gets into trouble. Reckless or misguided government policies often are to blame. Impatient with sluggish development or intent on benefiting its constituencies, a government expands its spending and incurs a budget deficit. Unable to finance the deficit by borrowing from the public, the ministry of finance sells short-term bills to the central bank; this adds to the money supply. The economy drifts into inflation and a foreign deficit, at a point like point 1 in Figure 19–9, far from equilibrium at point 2 on the economy's original external balance curve EB_1. When economies become unstable in this way, private investors get skittish and try to invest in nonproductive assets like land or, more often, invest abroad; this deepens the external deficit. The government, recognizing the error of

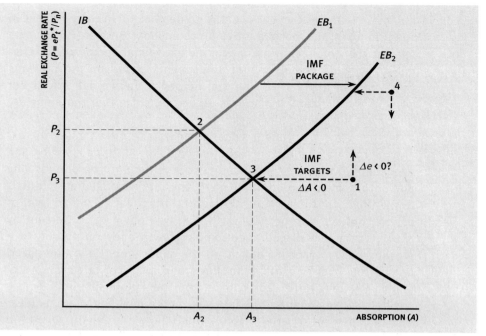

FIGURE 19–9 STABILIZATION FROM INFLATION AND A DEFICIT. An economy at point 1, far from equilibrium at point 2, above all needs to reduce absorption through austerity: reduced budgetary deficits and slower growth of the money supply. An IMF and donor package of aid might bring equilibrium closer by shifting the external balance to EB_2, but the aid package will be conditional on the austerity program. Whether any exchange rate action is required depends on the precise initial position, point 1.

its ways or just hoping for some outside help to avoid painful adjustment, calls in the IMF.

The core IMF stabilization program consists of a reduction in the government's budget deficit and programmed targets for domestic credit that, in effect, cap the growth of the money supply. Together, these measures reduce absorption in the economy and move it westward from point 1, closer to external and internal balance. IMF packages frequently include an exchange rate devaluation as well. Whether this is needed or not depends on the precise location of the economy (point 1) relative to equilibrium (point 2). In some cases, the reduction in absorption will be sufficient to reach both internal and external balance. As pictured in Figure 19–9, a small devaluation would be needed to reach point 2 and avoid unemployment.

However, IMF programs usually come with substantial aid attached, not only from the fund, but from the World Bank and bilateral donors. The aid package, by adding to the economy's capacity to buy tradables, would shift the EB curve to the right, to EB_2 in the diagram, and move equilibrium to point 3. Note two things about this aid package. First, it reduces the need for austerity to some extent, as A_3 is greater than A_2. Second, it reduces the need for devaluation of the exchange rate. Indeed, as shown, there is little or no need to devalue to move from 1 to 3. Donors and the IMF nevertheless frequently insist on devaluation. Sometimes, that may be a requirement just to reach a point like 3. In other cases, donors and the IMF may have in mind a self-sustaining stabilization that will be valid even after aid is reduced and the external balance curve moves back toward EB_1. Whatever the motive, it is important to realize that aid itself is a partial substitute for both devaluation and austerity. In essence, the aid does what higher production of tradables otherwise would have to do and it finances expenditures that otherwise would have to be cut. Ghana's experience, which fits this description, is discussed in the next case study.

Another kind of stabilization also can be illustrated with Figure 19–9, **rapid** (or **hyper-**) **inflation.** In Bolivia's hyperinflation of the mid-1980s (see Chapter 5) or the chronic inflations in Brazil and Argentina, external balance is a secondary consideration or not a major problem. Point 4 in the diagram depicts this situation. Austerity still is required to move toward equilibrium at point 2 or 3 (if there is an aid package). But devaluation would only intensify inflation. Instead, the currency must be appreciated, which also dampens inflation. One way to achieve this would be to fix the nominal rate and let the continuing (if decreasing) inflation in nontradable prices (P_n) appreciate the real rate P. This is the *exchange rate anchor,* a device used often in Latin America, especially in Chile during the late 1970s, in Bolivia during the mid-1980s, and in Argentina during the 1990s. It has the disadvantage that a lower real rate discourages export growth. Yet investment in new exports may be part of a strategy to open the economy, diversify exports, and move the external balance curve to the right.

DROUGHT

The human tragedy of drought or other natural disasters in places such as Ethiopia, the West African Sahel, and India before the Green Revolution dwarfs issues of macroeconomic management. But the adept management of an economy racked by natural disaster is essential to reduce the misery of starving or displaced people. Drought, for example, reduces a country's capacity to produce food, export crops, and in some countries, generate electricity from hydropower. At the same time, income is lower because farmers and others have less product to sell. Government then needs to provide social safety nets; this means spending more on the provision of food, transportation, health services, and sometimes shelter. Foreign governments often provide financial, food, and technical aid under these situations.

RECOVERING FROM MISMANAGEMENT: GHANA, 1983–91[10]

In 1983, after a decade of economic mismanagement, Ghana's gross national product was 20 percent below its 1974 peak, investment was only 4 percent of GNP, exports had sunk to 6 percent of GNP, and inflation rocketed to 120 percent for the year. After a decade of economic decline, Ghana's military government, headed by Flight Lieutenant Jerry Rawlings, was ready to undertake drastic measures to stabilize the economy and restart economic development.

Working closely with the International Monetary Fund, Ghana focused on three deep-seated problems: Exchange-rate reform, fiscal adjustment, and monetary policy. At first, the government maintained its fixed exchange rate but drastically devalued the cedi from 2.75 to the dollar in 1983 to 90 by 1986. In 1986, Ghana adopted a restricted floating currency, using periodic auctions to determine the rate. The official exchange market was broadened in 1988, when many foreign exchange bureaus were authorized to trade currencies and virtually absorbed the parallel market in currency; by 1990, the banks were empowered to trade in an interbank currency market. This completed the move to a floating rate regime. By the end of 1992, the cedi traded at 520 per dollar.

In 1983, with fiscal revenues less than 6 percent of GNP, the urgent need was to restore revenues and control expenditures. The deficit was cut from 6.2 to 2.7 percent of GNP in the first year of austerity, and by 1985, the government had begun a major public investment program to stimulate growth. By 1988, the government had restored total expenditures to 15 percent of GNP, 20 percent of which was investment, and was running a surplus of nearly 4 percent of GNP.

Throughout the period, the money supply was constrained but inflation remained stubbornly above 20 percent a year until 1991, when it was reduced to 16 percent and real interest rates finally became positive. Because food prices play a large role in the consumer price index, investment in food production was seen as an important component of any long-run attack on inflation.

The aid donors responded handsomely to Ghana's stabilization and the accompanying economic reforms: The sum of net official transfers

10. This account is based on Ishan Kapur, et al., *Ghana: Adjustment and Growth, 1983–91* (Washington, DC: International Monetary Fund, 1991).

and net long-term capital rose from just over $100 million in 1983 to $585 million in 1991.

Stabilization helped restore economic growth. From the depression of 1983–91, GNP grew by 5.1 percent a year and investment rose to 17 percent of GNP. The improvement, although dramatic in relation to the early 1980s, still left Ghana with a lot to be done: In 1991, income per capita remained 25 percent below its 1973 level.

The macroeconomic reflection of a drought is depicted in Figure 19–10. The economy begins in equilibrium at point 1. Drought reduces the economy's capacity to produce both nontradables (some foods, hydroelectricity, water supplies) and tradables (export crops, importable foods, some manufactures). We show this as a leftward shift in both the

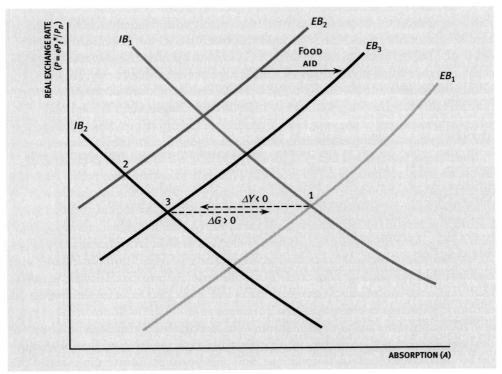

FIGURE 19-10 DROUGHT. Drought or another natural disaster reduces the capacity to produce both non-tradables and tradables, so the curves shift to the west. Disaster relief from abroad augments the external balance curve and shifts it to $EB_3 2$, with equilibrium at point 3. Remaining temporarily at point 1, the economy becomes inflationary. The reduction in output and therefore in income reduces absorption, but the government's need to spend more on relief tends to offset this move toward equilibrium. The outcome could be continued inflation.

ACCUMULATING RESERVES: TAIWAN, 1980–87[11]

By 1980, Taiwan had established an economic growth record that was being cited as a model for other developing countries. The government's macroeconomic policy always had been conservative. When the second oil crisis hit in 1979–80 and as Taiwan began to lose diplomatic standing while China regained its place in the official world order, macroeconomic policy was tightened further.

The central bank began to undervalue its exchange rate and became more restrictive in its monetary policy. The Taiwan dollar was depreciated from 36 per U.S. dollar in 1980 to 40 in 1983, while the real rate depreciated 15 percent against an average of the U.S. dollar, yen, and Hong Kong dollar, representing Taiwan's major trading partners. (Hong Kong trade was destined mainly for China.) From 1980 to 1984, increases in the money supply as a share of GNP were below the long-term trend. Fiscal policy was neutral, however: Both expenditures and revenue fell as shares of GNP and left the deficit roughly constant. The results of exchange rate and monetary policies were dramatic. While exports rose moderately as a share of

11. The data for this case comes from the Republic of China, *Taiwan Statistical Data Book 1993* (Taipei: Republic of China, 1993).

IB and *EB* lines: Reduced output of X_n at any given price means a larger zone in which D_n exceeds X_n; this is inflationary. Similarly for X_t; and this enlarges the area of deficit. The new external balance curve, EB_2, may be augmented (shifted back to the right) by foreign aid to EB_3, in which case, the new equilibrium is point 3.

The economy, still at point 1, is inflationary. The fall in incomes creates a tendency for absorption to shrink on its own and move the economy leftward toward the new equilibrium. At the same time, the government tries to spend more to relieve hunger, disease, and other problems. The outcome depends on the relative force of these tendencies. The impact of most natural disasters is temporary, typically lasting a year, although some African droughts have been much longer. It is appropriate to try to ride out such shocks with minimal adjust-

GNP, imports plunged from about 45 percent of GNP in 1980 to 35 percent in 1986. Reserves rose from under 15 percent of GNP in 1980 to over 60 percent by 1987.

From the national income accounts, a current-account surplus must be matched by a surplus of saving over investment: $S - I = E - M$. The necessary savings surplus was generated by both a rise in saving, from around 30 to almost 40 percent of GNP, and a fall in investment, from over 30 to under 20 percent of GNP. The savings surplus was generated in part by structural factors and in part by the rise in real interest rates caused by monetary stringency. Real interest rates on loans, which had been slightly negative in 1980, rose to a range of 8–10 percent a year from 1982 to 1986. Furthermore, domestic credit was tight. The central bank sterilized the rise in foreign reserves by forcing a sharp drop in the increments to private domestic credit: Net new loans fell to only 5 percent of GNP by 1986.

A price was to be paid for accumulating reserves. The unemployment rate, which had been 1.2 percent in 1980, rose to 2.9 percent in 1985. The growth rate of GNP, which was nearly 10 percent a year from 1970 to 1980, was a little below 7 percent from 1980 to 1985, after which it recovered to about 8 percent a year. Still, measured against most other countries' performances, this was an enviable record. By the mid-1980s, informed opinion in Taiwan turned against mercantilist policies while the U.S. government exerted pressure on Taiwan to reverse its policies. The real exchange rate was appreciated 25 percent, fiscal and monetary policies became more expansionary, and the days of large surpluses and unrestrained reserve accumulation were over.

ment, especially if foreign aid can bear much of the burden. Therefore, for example, even if an exchange-rate adjustment is called for to reach equilibrium, it is unlikely to work very well during a drought and probably should be resisted. This could be said for fiscal austerity, too, except that the rise in prices can deepen the suffering of those already hurt by the drought. If the government is able to shift its expenditures so that a greater portion goes into alleviating the impact of the drought, it may be able to relieve the worst suffering while restricting the rise of total expenditures and containing inflation.

Bibliography and Additional Readings

CHAPTER 1. INTRODUCTION

Fatimah Daud. *"Minah Karan": The Truth about Malaysian Factory Girls.* Kuala Lumpur: Berita Publishing, 1985.

Simon Kuznets. *Modern Economic Growth.* New Haven, CT: Yale University Press, 1966.

Angus Maddison. *Monitoring the World Economy 1820–1992.* Paris: Organization for Economic Cooperation and Development, 1995.

Kamal Salih and Mei Ling Young. "Changing Conditions of Labour in the Semiconductor Industry in Malaysia," *Labour and Society,* 14 (1989), 59–80.

World Bank. *World Development Report.* New York: Oxford University Press, annual.

Obstacles to Development

Alexander Gerschenkron. *Economic Backwardness in Historical Perspective.* Cambridge, MA: Harvard University Press, 1962.

Karl Marx. *Das Kapital.* 1867.

W. W. Rostow. *Stages of Economic Growth,* 2d ed.; New York: Cambridge University Press, 1971; 1st ed., 1960.

Historical Heritage and Economic Development

Paul Collier and Jan Willem Gunning, "Explaining African Economic Performance," *Journal of Economic Literature,* 37, no. 1 (March 1999), 64–111.

Keith Hart. *The Political Economy of West African Agriculture.* New York: Cambridge University Press, 1982.

Albert O. Hirschman. "Ideologies of Economic Development in Latin America." In *A Bias for Hope.* New Haven, CT: Yale University Press, 1971.

Anthony G. Hopkins. *An Economic History of West Africa.* New York: Columbia University Press, 1973.

David Landes. *The Wealth and Poverty of Nations: Why Some Are So Rich and Some So Poor.* New York: W. W. Norton, 1998.

E. S. Mason, Mahn Je Kim, Dwight H. Perkins, Kwang Suk Kim, and David C. Cole. *The Economic and Social Modernization of the Republic of Korea.* Cambridge, MA: Harvard University Press, 1980.

D. H. Perkins, ed. *China: Asia's Next Economic Giant?* Seattle: University of Washington Press, 1986.

CHAPTER 2. ECONOMIC GROWTH:
THEORY AND EMPIRICAL PATTERNS

Obstacles to Development

Alexander Gerschenkron. *Economic Backwardness in Historical Perspective.* Cambridge, MA: Harvard University Press, 1962.

W. W. Rostow. *Stages of Economic Growth.* 2d ed. New York: Cambridge University Press, 1971; 1st ed., 1960.

Income Levels and Economic Growth around the World

Angus Maddison. *Phases of Capitalist Development.* Oxford: Oxford University Press, 1982.

———. *Monitoring the World Economy 1820–1992.* Paris: Organization for Economic Cooperation and Development, 1995.

Robert Summers and Alan Heston. *Penn World Tables, Mark 5.6* (website version). Philadelphia: University of Pennsylvania.

World Bank. *Global Development Indicators 1999.* Washington, DC: World Bank, 1999.

The Harrod-Domar Growth Model

Evsey Domar. "Capital Expansion, Rate of Growth, and Employment." *Econometrica* (1946), 137–47.

———. "Expansion and Employment." *American Economic Review,* 37 (1947), 34–55.

Roy F. Harrod. "An Essay in Dynamic Theory." *Economic Journal* (1939), 14–33.

Joan Robinson. *The Accumulation of Capital.* London: Macmillan, 1956.

The Solow (Neoclassical) Growth Model

Charles I. Jones. *Introduction to Economic Growth.* New York: W. W. Norton, 1998.

Joan Robinson. *Essays in the Theory of Economic Growth.* London: Macmillan, 1962.

Robert Solow. "A Contribution to the Theory of Economic Growth." *Quarterly Journal of Economics,* 70 (February 1956), 65–94.

———. "Technical Change and the Aggregate Production Function," *Review of Economics and Statistics,* 39 (August 1957), 312–20.

Empirical Evidence on Economic Growth

Irma Adelman and Cynthyia Taft Morris. *Society, Politics, and Economic Development— A Quantitative Approach.* Baltimore: John Hopkins University Press, 1967.

Robert Barro. "Economic Growth in a Cross Section of Countries." *Quarterly Journal of Economics* 106, no. 2 (May 1991), 407–43.

William J. Baumol. "Productivity Growth, Convergence, and Welfare: What the Long-Run Data Show." *American Economic Review,* 76 (December 1986), pp. 1072–85.

Bradford DeLong and Lawrence Summers. "Equipment Investment and Economic Growth." *Quarterly Journal of Economics* 106; no. 2 (May 1991), 445–502.

John Gallup and Jeffrey Sachs. "Geography and Economic Development." In Boris Pleskovic and Joseph Stiglitz, eds., *World Bank Annual Conference on Development Economics 1998.* Washington, DC: World Bank, 1998, pp. 127–178.

Robert Hall and Charles Jones. "The Productivity of Nations." National Bureau of Economic Resarch working paper no. 5812, November 1996.

Ross Levine and David Renelt. "A Sensitivity Analysis of Cross-Country Growth Regressions." *American Economic Review,* 82, no. 4 (September 1992), 942–63.

Gregory Mankiw, David Romer, and David Weil. "A Contribution to the Empirics of Economic Growth." *Quarterly Journal of Economics* 107, no. 2 (May 1992), 407–38.

Steven Radelet and Jeffrey Sachs. "Shipping Costs, Manufactured Exports, and Economic Growth." Harvard Institute for International Development, January 1998.

Jeffrey Sachs and Andrew Warner. "Economic Reform and the Process of Global Integration." *Brookings Papers on Economic Activity* 1 (1995), 1–118.

Xavier X. Sala-i-Martin. "I Just Ran Two Million Regressions." *American Economic Review,* 87, no. 2 (May 1997), 178–83.

Jonathan Temple. "The New Growth Evidence." *The Journal of Economic Literature* 37, no. 1 (March 1999), 112–56.

Beyond Solow: New Approaches to Growth

Susan Collins and Barry Bosworth. "Economic Growth in East Asia: Accumulation versus Assimilation." *Brookings Papers on Economic Activity,* 2 (1996), 135–203.

Robert Lucas. "On the Mechanics of Economic Development." *Journal of Monetary Economics,* 22 (January 1988), 3–42.

Paul Romer. "Endogenous Technological Change." *Journal of Political Economy,* 98 (October 1990), S71–S102.

———. "Increasing Returns and Long-Run Growth." *Journal of Political Economy,* 94 (October 1986), 1002–37.

Alwyn Young. "The Tyranny of the Numbers: Confronting the Statistical Realities of the East Asian Growth Experience." *Quarterly Journal of Economics,* 110, no. 3 (August 1995), 641–80.

CHAPTER 3. STRUCTURAL CHANGE

The Changing Structure of Output

Hollis B. Chenery, Sherman Robinson, and Moshe Syrquin. *Industrialization and Growth: A Comparative Study.* London: Oxford University Press, 1986.

Hollis B. Chenery and Moises Syrquin. *Patterns of Development, 1950–1970.* London: Oxford University Press, 1975.

Hollis B. Chenery and Lance J. Taylor. "Development Patterns: Among Countries and over Time." *Review of Economics and Statistics,* 50 (November 1968), 391–416.

Edward F. Denison. *Accounting for United States Economic Growth, 1929–1969.* Washington, DC: Brookings Institution, 1974.

Irving Kravis, Alan Heston, and Robert Summers. *International Comparisons of Real Product and Purchasing Power.* Baltimore: Johns Hopkins Press, 1978.

Dale Jorgenson, Frank Gallop, and Barbara Fraumeni. *Productivity and U.S. Economic Growth.* Cambridge, MA: Harvard University Press, 1987.

Simon Kuznets. *Economic Growth and Structure.* New York: W. W. Norton, 1965.

———. *Modern Economic Growth.* New Haven, CT: Yale University Press, 1966.

Dwight H. Perkins and Moshe Syrquin. "Large Countries: The Influence of Size." In Hollis B. Chenery and T. N. Srinivasan, eds., *Handbook of Development Economics,* Vol. 2. Amsterdam: Elsevier, 1989.

W. W. Rostow. *Theorists of Economic Growth from David Hume to the Present.* London: Oxford University Press, 1990, Part III.

Moshe Syrquin. "Patterns of Structural Change." In Hollis B. Chenery and T. N. Srinivasan, eds., *Handbook of Development Economics,* Vol. 1. Amsterdam: Elsevier, 1988.

Two-Sector Models

John C. Fei and Gustav Ranis. *Development of Labor Surplus Economy.* Homewood, IL: Irwin, 1964.

Dale W. Jorgenson. "Testing Alternative Theories of the Development of a Dual Economy." In I. Adelman and E. Thorbecke, eds., *The Theory and Design of Development.* Baltimore: Johns Hopkins Press, 1966.

W. Arthur Lewis. "Economic Development with Unlimited Supplies of Labor." *The Manchester School,* 22 (May 1954), 139–91.

———. *The Theory of Economic Growth.* Homewood, IL: Irwin, 1955.

Balanced versus Unbalanced Growth

Albert O. Hirschman. *The Strategy of Economic Development.* New Haven, CT: Yale University Press, 1958.

Ragnar Nurkse. *Problems of Capital Development in Underdeveloped Countries.* New York: Oxford University Press, 1953.

Paul N. Rosenstein-Rodan. "Problems of Industrialization of Eastern and Southeastern Europe." *Economic Journal* (June–September 1943); reprinted in A. N. Agarwala and S. P. Singh, eds., *The Economics of Underdevelpoment.* New York: Oxford University Press, 1963.

Interindustry and General Equilibrium Models

Hollis Chenery and Paul Clark. *Interindustry Economics.* New York: Wiley, 1959.

Kemal Dervis, Jaime de Melo, and Sherman Robinson. *General Equilibrium Models for Developing Countries.* London: Cambridge University Press, 1982.

Robert Dorfman, Paul Samuelson, and Robert Solow. *Linear Programming and Economic Analysis.* New York: McGraw-Hill, 1958.

Graham Pyatt and Erik Thorbecke. *Planning Techniques for a Better Future.* Geneva: International Labor Office, 1976.

Sherman Robinson. "Multisectoral Models." In Hollis B. Chenery and T. N. Srinivasan, eds., *Handbook of Development Economics,* Vol. 2. Amsterdam: Elsevier, 1989, pp. 885–947.

CHAPTER 4. DEVELOPMENT AND HUMAN WELFARE

Concept and Measures

Gary S. Fields. *Poverty, Inequality and Development.* London: Cambridge University Press, 1960.

Allen C. Kelley. "The Human Development Index: Handle with Care." *Population and Development Review,* 17, no. 2 (1991), 315–24.

Dudley Sears. "The Meaning of Development." In Charles K. Wilber, ed., *The Political Economy of Development and Underdevelopment.* New York: Random House, 1973.

Amartya K. Sen. *On Economic Inequality.* New York: W. W. Norton, 1973.

United Nations Development Program. *Human Development Report.* New York: Oxford University Press, annually 1990–1999.

Wouter van Ginneken and Jong-goo Park, eds. *Generating Internationally Comparable Income Distribution Measures.* Geneva: International Labor Office, 1984.

Patterns of Inequality and Poverty

Irma Adelman and Cynthia Taft Morris. *Economic Growth and Social Equity in Developing Countries.* Stanford, CA: Stanford University Press, 1973.

Irma Adelman and Sherman Robinson. *Income Distribution Policy in Developing Countries. A Case Study of Korea.* Stanford, CA: Stanford University Press, 1978.

Montek S. Ahluwalia. "Inequality, Poverty and Development." *Journal of Development Economics,* 3 (1976).

Klaus Deninger and Lyn Squire, "A New Data Set Measuring Income Inequality." *World Bank Economic Review,* 10, no. 3 (September 1996), 565–91.

Gary S. Fields. "Changes in Poverty and Inequality in Developing Countries." *The World Bank Research Observer,* 4, no. 2 (July 1989), 167–85.

Deon Filmer, Elizabeth M. King, and Lant Pritchett. "Gender Disparity in South Asia: Comparisons between and within Countries," World Bank Policy research paper no. 1967, 1999.

John Luke Gallup, Steven Radelet, and Andrew Warner. "Economic Growth and the Poor." Harvard Institute for International Development, 1998.

Frida Johansen. "Poverty Reduction in East Asia. The Silent Revolution," World Bank discussion paper no. 203, 1993.

Simon Kuznets. "Economic Growth and Income Inequality," *American Economic Review,* 45, no. 1 (March 1955).

Susan M. Randolph and William F. Lott. "Can the Kuznets Effect Be Relied on to Induce Equalizing Growth?" *World Development,* 21, no. 5 (May 1993), 829–40.

World Bank. *World Development Report 1990* [special issue on poverty]. New York: Oxford University Press, 1990.

Theories of Inequality and Poverty

William R. Cline. "Distribution and Development: A Survey of the Literature." *Journal of Development Economics* (1975), 359–400.

W. Arthur Lewis. "Economic Development with Unlimited Supplies of Labor." *Manchester School,* 22 (May 1954).

Strategies for Growth with Equity

Entisham Ahmad and Yan Wang. "Inequality and Poverty in China: Institutional Change and Public Policy, 1978–1988." *World Bank Economic Review,* 5, no. 2 (1991), 231–58.

Hollis Chenery et al., eds. *Redistribution with Growth.* London: Oxford University Press, 1974.

Giovanni Andrea Cornia, Richard Jolly, and Frances Stewart, eds. *Adjustment with a Human Face,* 2 vols. London: Oxford University Press (Clarendon), 1987.

International Labor Office. *Employment, Growth and Basic Needs: A One-World Problem.* New York: Praeger, 1977.

John Mellor. *The New Economics of Growth: A Strategy for India and the Developing World.* Ithaca, NY: Cornell University Press, 1976.

Rati Ram. "The Role of Real Income Level and Income Distribution in Fulfillment of Basic Needs." *World Development,* 13, no. 5 (May 1985), 589–94.

T. N. Srinivasan, "Development, Poverty and Basic Human Needs: Some Issues." *Food Research Institute Studies,* 16, no. 2 (1977), 11–28.

CHAPTER 5. GUIDING DEVELOPMENT: MARKETS VERSUS CONTROLS

The March toward Markets

Bela Balassa. "Exports and Economic Growth: Further Evidence," *Journal of Development Economics,* 5, no. 2 (1978), 181–89.

Jagdish Bhagwati. *Foreign Exchange Regimes and Economic Development: Anatomy and Consequences of Exchange Control Regimes.* Cambridge, MA: Ballinger Press, 1978.

Henry J. Bruton. "The Import Substitution Strategy of Economic Development." *Pakistan Development Review,* 10 (1970), 123–46.

Anne O. Krueger. *Foreign Exchange Regimes and Economic Development: Liberalization Attempts and Consequences.* Cambridge, MA: Ballinger Press, 1978.

———. "The Political Economy of Rent-Seeking." *American Economic Review,* 64, no. 3 (1974), 291–303.

Ian M. D. Little. *Economic Theory, Policy, and International Relations.* New York: Basic Books, 1982.

———, Tibor Scitovsky, and Maurice Scott. *Industry and Trade in Some Developing Countries.* London: Oxford University Press, 1970.

Ragnar Nurkse. *Equilibrium Growth and the World Economy.* Cambridge, MA: Harvard University Press, 1961.

Jeffrey Sachs and Andrew Warner. "Economic Convergence and Economic Policies." Harvard Institute for International Development, Development discussion paper no. 502, March 1995.

Theodore W. Schultz. *Transforming Traditional Agriculture*. New Haven, CT: Yale University Press, 1964.

Hans W. Singer. "The Distribution of Trade between Investing and Borrowing Countries." *American Economic Review,* 40 (1950), 470–85.

Moshe Syrquin and Hollis Chenery. "Three Decades of Industrialization." *World Bank Economic Review,* 3, no. 2 (1989), 145–81.

United Nations (by Raul Prebisch). *The Economic Development of Latin America and Its Principal Problems*. Lake Success, NY: United Nations, 1950.

World Bank. *The East Asian Miracle: Economic Growth and Public Policy*. Oxford: Oxford University Press, 1993.

Implementing Market Reforms

Maxim Boyco, Andrei Shleifer, and Robert Vishny. *Privatizing Russia*. Cambridge, MA: MIT Press, 1995.

Armeane M. Choksi and Demetrius Papageorgiou, eds. *Economic Liberalization in Developing Countries*. New York: Blackwell, 1986.

Sebastian Edwards and Sweder van Wijnbergen. "Disequilibrium and Structural Adjustment." In Hollis Chenery and T. N. Srinivasan, eds., *Handbook of Development Economics,* Vol. 2. Amsterdam: Elsevier, 1989, pp. 1481–533.

Stanley Fischer. "The Role of Macroeconomic Factors in Growth." *Journal of Monetary Economics,* 32 (1993), 485–512.

Tony Killick, ed. *The Quest for Economic Stabilization: The IMF and the Third World*. London: Heinemann, 1984.

Janos Kornai. *The Road to a Free Economy*. New York: W. W. Norton, 1990.

———. *The Socialist System: The Political Economy of Communism*. Princeton, NJ: Princeton University Press, 1992.

David Lindauer and Michael Roemer. *Asia and Africa: Legacies and Opportunities in Development*. San Francisco: ICS Press, 1994.

Juan Antonio Morales and Jeffrey D. Sachs. "Bolivia's Economic Crisis." In J. D. Sachs, ed., *Developing Country Debt and the World Economy*. Chicago: University of Chicago Press, 1989, pp. 57–79.

Barry Naughton. *Growing out of the Plan: Chinese Economic Reform, 1978–1993*. Cambridge: Cambridge University Press, 1995.

Joan M. Nelson. "The Political Economy of Stabilization: Commitment, Capacity and Public Response." *World Development,* 12, no. 10 (1984), 983–1006.

——— et al. *Fragile Coalitions: The Politics of Economic Adjustment*. Washington, DC: Overseas Development Council, 1989.

———, ed. *Economic Crisis and Policy Choice: The Politics of Adjustment in the Third World*. Princeton, NJ: Princeton University Press, 1990.

Mancur Olsen. *The Rise and Decline of Nations*. New Haven, CT: Yale University Press, 1982.

Theodore Panayotou. *Green Markets: The Economics of Sustainable Development*. San Francisco: ICS Press, 1993.

Dwight H. Perkins. "Reforming China's Economic System." *Journal of Economic Literature,* 26, no. 2 (June 1988), 601–45.

———. "Completing China's Move to the Market." *Journal of Economic Perspectives,* 8, no. 2 (Spring 1994), 23–46.

——— and Michael Roemer. *Reforming Economic Systems in Developing Countries*. Cambridge, MA: Harvard University Press, 1991.

———, Richard Pagett, Michael Roemer, Donald R. Snodgrass, and Joseph J. Stern. *Assisting Development in a Changing World: The Harvard Institute for International Development, 1980–1995*. Cambridge, MA: Harvard Institute for International Development, 1997.

Jeffrey D. Sachs. "The Bolivian Hyperinflation and Stabilization." *American Economic Review,* 77, no. 2 (May 1987), 279–83.

Andrei Shleifer and Daniel Treisman. *Without a Map: Political Tactics and Economic Reform in Russia.* Cambridge, MA: MIT Press, 2000.

Edward Steinfeld. *Forging Reform in China: The Fate of State-Owned Industry.* Cambridge: Cambridge University Press, 1998.

Paul Streeten. "Structural Adjustment: A Survey of the Issues and Options." *World Development,* 15, no. 12 (December 1987), 1469–82.

Lance J. Taylor. *Varieties of Stabilization Experience: Toward Sensible Macroeconomics in the Third World.* London: Oxford University Press (Clarendon), 1988.

Raymond Vernon, ed. *The Promise of Privitization: A Challenge for American Foreign Policy.* New York: Council on Foreign Relations, 1988.

John Williamson, ed. *IMF Conditionality.* Washington, DC: Institute for International Economics, 1983.

World Bank, *Accelerated Development in the Sub-Saharan Africa.* Washington, DC: World Bank, 1981.

———. *Adjustment in Africa: Reforms, Results and the Road Ahead.* Oxford: Oxford University Press, 1994.

———. *World Development Report 1989* (on financial systems reform). New York: Oxford University Press, 1989.

———. *World Development Report 1991.* London: Oxford University Press, 1991.

Daniel Yergin and Joseph Stanislaw. *Commanding Heights: The Battle between Government and the Marketplace That Is Remaking the Modern World.* New York: Simon and Schuster, 1998.

CHAPTER 6. SUSTAINABLE DEVELOPMENT

Jeffrey Sachs and Andrew Warner. "Natural Resource Abundance and Economic Growth." Harvard Institute for International Development discussion paper 517a, October 1995.

World Bank. *World Development Report 1992: Development and the Environment.* Washington, DC: World Bank, 1992.

Market Failures

Edward B. Barbier. *Economics, Natural Resource Scarcity and Development.* London: Earthscan, 1989.

John M. Hartwick and Nancy D. Olewiler. *The Economics of Natural Resource Use.* New York: Harper and Row, 1986.

Harold Hotelling. "The Economics of Exhaustable Resources." *Journal of Political Economy,* 39 (1931), 137–75.

Tom Tietenberg. *Environmental and Natural Resource Economics,* 4th ed. Glenview, IL: Scott Foresman, 1988.

———. *Environmental and Natural Resource Economics,* 5th ed. New York: Addison-Wesley, 2000.

Policy Solutions

Asian Development Bank. *Emerging Asia: Changes and Challenges.* Manila: ADB, 1997.

Randall Bluffstone and Bruce A. Larson, eds. *Controlling Pollution in Transition Economies.* Cheltenham, UK: Edward Elgar, 1997.

Robert Bohm, Chazhong Ge, Milton Rusell, Jinnan Wang, and Jintian Yang. "Environmental Taxes: China's Bold New Initiative." *Environment,* 40, no. 7, September 1998.

Gunnar Eskeland and Shantayanan Devarajan. *Taxing Bads by Taxing Goods: Pollution Control with Presumptive Charges.* Washington, DC: World Bank, 1996.

Theodore Panayotou. *Instruments of Change: Motivating and Financing Sustainable Development.* London: Earthscan, 1998.

A. Shah and Bruce Larsen. "Carbon Taxes, the Greenhouse Effect, and Developing Countries." Policy research paper no. 95. Washington, DC: World Bank, 1990.

Tom Tietenberg. *Environmental and Natural Resource Economics,* 5th ed. New York: Addison-Wesley, 2000, pp. 372 and 453.

Jeffrey R. Vincent, Rozali Mohamed Ali, and associates. *Environment and Development in a Resource-Rich Economy: Malaysia under the New Economic Policy.* Cambridge, MA: Harvard Institute for International Development, 1997.

Policy Failures

Shakeb Afsah and Jeffrey Vincent. "Putting Pressure on Polluters: Indonesia's PROPER Program." Available at www.worldbank.org/nipr/work-paper/vincent/index.htm, February 1997.

Sheoli Pargal and David Wheeler. "Informal Regulation of Industrial Pollution in Developing Countries: Evidence from Indonesia." *Journal of Political Economy,* 104, no. 6, (December 1996), 1314–27.

Jeffrey Vincent and Scott Farrow. "A Survey of Pollution Charge Systems and Key Issues in Policy Design." In Randall Bluffstone and Bruce A. Larson, eds., *Controlling Pollution in Transition Economies.* Cheltenham, UK: Edward Elgar, 1997.

Measuring Sustainability

Yusuf J. Ahmad, Salah E. Serafy, and Ernst Lutz, eds. *Environmental Accounting for Sustainable Development.* Washington, DC: World Bank, 1990.

Stavros Georgiou, Dale Whittington, David Pearce, and Dominic Moran. *Economic Values and the Environment in the Developing World.* Cheltenham, UK: Edward Elgar, 1997.

Ernst Lutz, ed. *Toward Improved Accounting for the Environment.* Washington, DC: World Bank, 1993.

David Pearce and Giles Atkinson, "Capital Theory and the Measurement of Sustainable Development: An Indicator of 'Weak' Sustainability." *Ecological Economics,* 8 (1993), 103–8.

David Reed. *Structural Adjustment, the Environment, and Sustainable Development.* London: Earthscan, 1996.

Jeffrey Vincent and Rozali bin Mohamed Ali. "Natural Resources, Environment, and Development in Malaysia: An Economic Perspective." Unpublished manuscript, 1994.

World Bank. *World Development Report 1994: Infrastructure for Development.* Washington, DC: World Bank, 1994.

Global Sustainability

Kenneth Arrow et al. "Economic Growth, Carrying Capacity, and the Environment." *Science* (April 28, 1995), 520–21.

Robin Broad. "The Poor and the Environment: Friends or Foes?" *World Development,* 22, no. 6 (June 1994), 811–22.

Gene Grossman and Alan B. Krueger. "Economic Growth and the Environment." *Quarterly Journal of Economics* (May 1995), 353–77.

———. "Environmental Impacts of a North American Free Trade Agreement." In Peter Garber, ed., *The US-Mexico Free Trade Agreement,* Cambridge, MA: MIT Press, 1993, pp. 13–56.

Hettige, Hemamala, Robert Lucas, and David Wheeler. "The Toxic Intensity of Industrial Production: Global Patterns, Trends, and Trade Policy." *American Economic Review,* 82, no. 2 (May 1992).

Adam Jafee et al. "Environmental Regulation and the Competitiveness of US Manufacturing: What Does the Evidence Tell Us?" *Journal of Economic Literature,* 33, no. 1 (March 1995), 132–63.

Dale Jorgenson and Peter Wilcoxen. "Environmental Regulation and US Economic Growth." *Rand Journal of Economics,* 21, no. 2 (Summer 1990), 314–40.

———. "Impact of Environmental Legislation on US Economic Growth, Investment, and Capital Costs." In Donna Brodsky, ed., *US Environmental Policy and Economic Growth: How Do We Fare?* Washington, DC: American Council for Capital Formation, 1992.

Martin McGuire. "Regulation, Factor Rewards, and International Trade." *Journal of Public Economics,* 17, no. 3 (April 1982), 335–54.

Irving M. Mintzer, ed. *Confronting Climate Change.* London: Cambridge University Press, 1992.

Theodore Panayotou. "Financing Mechanisms for Agenda 21." Harvard Institute for International Development, March 1994.

Theodore Panayotou and Jeffrey Vincent. "Environmental Regulation and Competitiveness." In *World Competitiveness Report 1997.* Geneva: World Economic Forum, 1997, pp. 64–73.

Rudiger Pethig. "Pollution, Welfare, and Environmental Policy in the Theory of Comparative Advantage." *Journal of Environmental Economic Management,* 1975, no. 2, 160–69.

Michael Porter, "America's Green Strategy." *Scientific American* (April 1991), 168.

——— and Claas van der Linde. "Toward a New Conception of the Environment-Competitiveness Relationship." *Journal of Economic Perspectives,* 9, no. 4 (Fall 1995).

Robert Repetto. "Jobs, Competitiveness, and Environmental Regulation: What Are the Real Issues?" World Resources Institute, March 1995.

Horst Seibert. "Environmental Quality and the Gains from Trade." *Kyklos,* 3 no. 4 (1975), 657–73.

Mary Tiffen and Michael Mortimore. "Malthus Controverted: The Role of Capital and Technology in Growth and Environment Recovery in Kenya." *World Development,* 22, no. 7 (July 1994), 997–1010.

David Wheeler and Ashoka Mody. "International Investment Location: The Case of US Firms." *Journal of International Economics,* 33, nos. 1–2 (August 1992), 57–72.

World Commission on Environment and Development (the Brundtland Commission). *Our Common Future.* New York: Oxford University Press, 1987.

World Resources Institute. *World Resources 1992–1993.* New York: Oxford University Press, 1992.

Policy Solutions and Policy Failures

Robert Coase. "The Problem of Social Cost." *Journal of Law and Economics,* 3 (October 1960), 1–44.

John A. Dixon and Maynard M. Hufschmidt, eds. *Valuation Techniques for the Environment.* Baltimore: Johns Hopkins Press, 1986, pp. 121–40.

Bjorn Larsen and Anwar Shah. "World Fossil Fuel Subsidies and Global Carbon Emissions." World Bank working paper WPS 1002, October 1992.

Theodore Panayotou. *Green Markets: The Economics of Sustainable Development.* San Francisco: ICS Press, 1993.

———. "Conservation of Biodiversity and Economic Development: The Concept of Transferable Development Rights." *Environmental and Resource Economics,* 4 (1994), 91–110.

David W. Pearce and R. Kerry Turner. *Economics of Natural Resources and the Environment.* Baltimore: Johns Hopkins Press, 1990.

Paul R. Portney. "The Contingent Valuation Debate: Why Economists Should Care." *Journal of Economic Perspectives,* 8, no. 4 (1994), 3–17.

Robert Repetto and Malcolm Gillis, eds. *Public Policies and the Misuse of Forest Resources.* London: Cambridge University Press, 1988.

Jeffrey Vincent. "The Tropical Timber Trade and Sustainable Development." *Science,* 256 (1992), 1651–55.

CHAPTER 7. POPULATION

A Brief History of Human Population

Lester R. Brown. *In the Human Interest.* New York: W. W. Norton, 1974.

Carlo Cipolla. *The Economic History of World Population,* 7th ed. New York: Barnes and Noble, 1978.

Massimo Livi-Bacci. *A Concise History of World Population,* 2nd ed. Malden, MA: Blackwell Publishers, 1997.

The Demographic Future

Joel E. Cohen. *How Many People Can the Earth Support?* New York: W. W. Norton, 1996.

Thomas W. Merrick. "World Population in Transition." *Population Bulletin,* 41, no. 2 (January 1988), 8–16.

World Bank, *Population and Development: Implications for the World Bank.* Washington, DC: World Bank, 1994.

The Causes of Population Growth

Gary Becker. *A Treatise on the Family.* Cambridge, MA: Harvard University Press, 1981.

John C. Caldwell. "The Soft Underbelly of Development: Demographic Transition in Conditions of Limited Economic Change." *Proceedings of the World Bank Annual Conference on Development Economics 1990.* Washington, DC: World Bank, 1991, pp. 207–69.

———. "Toward a Restatement of Demographic Transition Theory." *Population and Development Review,* 2, nos. 3–4 (September–December 1976), 225–55.

Richard Easterlin. "Modernization and Fertility: A Critical Essay." In R. Bulatao and R. Lee, eds., *Determinants of Fertility in Developing Countries,* Vol. 2. New York: Academic Press, 1983, pp. 562–86.

Michael S. Teitelbaum. "Relevance of Demographic Transition Theory for Developing Countries." *Science,* 188 (May 2, 1977), 420–25.

Analyzing the Effects of Rapid Population Growth

Nancy Birdsall. "Economic Approaches to Population." In Hollis B. Chenery and T. N. Srinivasan, eds., *Handbook of Development Economics,* Vol. 1. Amsterdam: North-Holland, 1989, pp. 477–542.

David E. Bloom and Jeffrey G. Williamson. "Demographic Transitions and Economic Miracles in Emerging Asia." *World Bank Economic Review,* 12, no. 3 (September 1998), 419–55.

Ester Boserup. *Economic and Demographic Relationships in Development.* Baltimore: Johns Hopkins Press, 1990.

Colin Clark. "The 'Population Explosion' Myth." *Bulletin of the Institute of Development Studies* [Sussex, England] (May 1969).

———. "The Economics of Population Growth and Control: A Comment." *Review of Social Economy,* 28, no. 1 (March 1970).

Ansle J. Coale and Edgar M. Hoover. *Population Growth and Economic Development in Low-Income Countries: A Case Study of India's Prospects.* Princeton, NJ: Princeton University Press, 1958.

Rati Ram and Theodore W. Schultz. "Life Span, Savings, and Productivity." *Economic Development and Cultural Change,* 27, no. 3 (April 1979), 394–421.

Julian Simon. *Theory of Population and Economic Growth.* Oxford: Blackwell, 1986.

———. *The Ultimate Resource.* Princeton, NJ: Princeton University Press, 1981.

Population Policy

Nick Eberstadt. "Recent Declines in Fertility in Less-Developed Countries and What 'Population Planners' May Learn from Them." *World Development,* 11, no. 3 (March 1985), 113–38.

"Fertility and Family Planning Surveys: An Update." *Population Reports* series M, no. 8 [Baltimore, Johns Hopkins Press] (September–October 1985).

Marshall Green. "The Evolution of US International Population Policy, 1965–92: A Chronological Account." *Population and Development Review,* 19, no. 2 (June 1993), 303–21.

W. Parker Mauldin and Bernard Berelson. "Conditions of Fertility Decline in Developing Countries, 1965–75." *Studies in Family Planning,* 9, no. 5 (1978).

National Academy of Sciences. *Population Growth and Economic Development: Policy Questions.* Washington, DC: National Academy Press, 1986.

John A. Ross, W. Parker Mauldin, S. R. Green, and E. Romana Cooke. *Family Planning and Child Survival Programs as Assessed in 1991.* New York: Population Council, 1992.

World Bank. *World Development Report 1984.* New York: Oxford University Press, 1984, pp. 51–206.

CHAPTER 8. LABOR'S ROLE

Analyzing Employment Issues

George A. Akerlof and Janet L. Yellen, eds. *Efficiency Models of the Labor Market.* Cambridge: Cambridge University Press, 1986, "Introduction," pp. 1–21.

Albert Berry. "The Labor Market and Human Capital in LDCs." In Norman Gemmell, ed., *Surveys in Development Economics.* Oxford: Blackwell, 1987, pp. 205–35.

——— and R. H. Sabot. "Unemployment and Economic Development." *Economic Development and Cultural Change,* 33, no. 1 (October 1984), 99–116.

Peter Gregory. "An Assessment of Changes in Employment Conditions in Less Developed Countries." *Economic Development and Cultural Change,* 28, no. 4 (July 1980), 673–700.

Lawrence F. Katz. "Efficiency Wage Theories: A Partial Evaluation." *NBER Macroeconomics Annual 1986.* Cambridge, MA: National Bureau of Economic Research, 1986, pp. 235–76.

Dipak Mazumdar. "The Urban Informal Sector." *World Development,* 4, no. 8 (August 1976), 655–79.

Mark Rosenzweig. "Labor Markets in Low-Income Countries." In Hollis B. Chenery and T. N. Srinivasan, eds., *Handbook of Development Economics,* Vol. 1. Amsterdam: North-Holland, 1989, pp. 713–62.

Joseph E. Stiglitz. "Economic Organization, Information and Development." In H. Chenery and T. N. Srinivasan, *Handbook of Development Economics,* Vol. 1. Amsterdam: North-Holland, 1989, pp. 93–160.

Labor Reallocation

Jagdish Bhagwati and Martin Partington. *Taxing the Brain Drain: A Proposal.* Amsterdam: North-Holland, 1976.

John R. Harris and Michael P. Todaro. "Migration, Unemployment and Development: A Two-Sector Analysis." *American Economic Review,* 60 (March 1970), 126–42.

Ragnar Nurkse. *Problems of Capital Formation in Underdeveloped Countries.* Oxford: Blackwell, 1957; first published in 1953.

Jeffrey G. Williamson. "Migration and Urbanization." In H. Chenery and T. N. Srinivasan, eds., *Handbook of Development Economics,* Vol. 1. Amsterdam: North-Holland, 1989, pp. 425–65.

Employment Policy

Henry Bruton, "Technology Choice and Factor Proportions Problems in LDCs." In Norman Gemmell, ed., *Surveys in Development Economics.* Oxford: Blackwell, 1987, pp. 236–65.

S. J. Burki et al. "Public Works Programs in Developing Countries: A Comparative Analysis." World Bank staff working paper no. 224, February 1976.

Edgar O. Edwards, ed. *Employment in Developing Nations.* New York: Columbia University Press, 1974.

Richard B. Freeman. "Labor Market Institutions and Policies: Help or Hindrance to Economic Development?" In *Proceedings of the World Bank Annual Conference on Development Economies 1992.* Washington, DC: World Bank, 1993, pp. 117–44.

Howard Pack and Larry E. Westphal. "Industrial Strategy and Technological Change: Theory versus Reality." *Journal of Development Economics,* 22 (1986), 87–128.

Lyn Squire. *Employment Policy in Developing Countries: A Survey of Issues and Evidence.* New York: Oxford University Press for the World Bank, 1981.

Frances Stewart. "Technology and Employment in LDCs." In Edgar O. Edwards, ed., *Employment in Developing Nations.* New York: Columbia University Press, 1974, pp. 83–132.

Susumu Watanabe. "Exports and Employment: The Case of the Republic of Korea." *International Labour Review,* 106, no. 6 (December 1972), 495–526.

Louis T. Wells. "Economic Man and Engineering Man: Choice of Technology in a Low-Wage Country." In C. Peter Timmer et al., eds., *The Choice of Technology in Developing Countries: Some Cautionary Tales.* Cambridge, MA: Harvard University Center for International Affairs, 1975, pp. 69–93.

Larry E. Westphal. "Fostering Technological Mastery by Means of Selective Infant-Industry Protection," in Simon Teitel, ed., *Trade, Stability, Technology, and Equity in Latin America.* New York: Academic Press, 1982, pp. 255–79.

———, Linsu Kim, and Carl J. Dahlman. "Reflections on the Republic of Korea's Acquisition of Technological Capability." In Nathan Rosenberg and Claudio Frischtak, eds., *International Technology Transfer: Concepts, Measures, and Comparisons.* New York: Praeger, 1985, pp. 167–221.

CHAPTER 9. EDUCATION

Importance of Education

George Psacharopoulos and Maureen Woodhall. *Education for Development: An Analysis of Investment Choices.* New York: Oxford University Press, 1985.

Theodore W. Schultz. "Investment in Human Capital." *American Economic Review,* 51 (January 1961), 1–17.

World Bank. *World Development Report 1980.* New York: Oxford University Press, 1980.

Trends and Patterns

M. Blaug, R. Layard, and M. Woodhall. *Causes of Graduate Unemployment in India.* Harmondsworth, UK: Penguin Press, 1969.

Martin Carnoy. "Rates of Return to Schooling in Latin America." *Journal of Human Resources* (Summer 1967), 359–74.

Russell Davis. "Planning Education for Development." Harvard Institute for International Development, development discussion paper no. 60, June 1979.

World Bank. *Primary Education. A World Bank Policy Paper.* Washington, DC: World Bank, 1990.

Education's Role in Development

Mark Blaug. "The Empirical Status of Human Capital Theory: A Slightly Jaundiced Survey." *Journal of Economic Literature,* 14, no. 3 (September 1976), 827–55.

M. Boissiere, J. B. Knight, and R. H. Sabot. "Earnings, Schooling, Ability, and Cognitive Skills." *American Economic Review,* 75, no. 5 (December 1985), 1016–30.

Philip H. Coombs with Manzoor Ahmed. *Attacking Rural Poverty: How Nonformal Education Can Help.* Baltimore: Johns Hopkins Press, 1974.

Ronald Dore. *The Diploma Disease. Education, Qualification and Development.* Berkeley: University of California Press, 1976.

Philip J. Foster. "The Vocational School Fallacy in Development Planning." In C. A. Anderson and M. J. Bowman, eds., *Education and Economic Development.* Chicago: Aldine, 1966, pp. 142–63.

Paolo Freire. *Pedagogy of the Oppressed,* translated from the Portuguese by Myra Bergman Ramos. New York: Seabury Press, 1970.

Robert H. Haveman and Barbara L. Wolfe. "Schooling and Economic Well-Being: The Role of Nonmarket Effects." *Journal of Human Resources,* 19, no. 3 (Summer 1984), 377–407.

Ivan Ilich. *Deschooling Society.* New York: Harper and Row, 1970.

Emmanuel Jiminez. "The Public Subsidization of Education and Health in Developing Countries. A Review of Equity and Efficiency." *World Bank Research Observer,* 1, no. 1 (January 1986), 111–29.

John B. Knight and Richard H. Sabot. *Education, Productivity, and Inequality. The East African Experience.* New York: Oxford University Press for the World Bank, 1990.

Herbert S. Parnes. *Forecasting Educational Needs for Economic Development.* Mediterranean Regional Project. Paris: Organisation for Economic Cooperation and Development, 1962.

George Psacharopoulos. "Education and Development: A Further International Update and Implications." *Journal of Human Resources,* 20, no. 4 (1985), 583–604.

———. "Education and Development: A Review." *World Bank Research Observer,* 3, no. 1 (January 1988.).

———. "Returns to Investment in Education: A Global Update." *World Development,* 22, no. 9 (September, 1994); 1325–43.

T. Paul Schultz. "Education Investments and Returns." In Hollis B. Chenery and T. N. Srinivasan, eds., *Handbook of Development Economics,* Vol. 1. Amsterdam: North-Holland, 1989, pp. 543–630.

Theodore W. Schultz. "The Value of the Ability to Deal with Disequilibrium." *Journal of Economic Literature,* 13, no. 3 (September 1975), 837–46.

Jan Tinbergen and H. C. Bos. "A Planning Model for the Educational Requirements of Economic Development." In *Econometric Models for Education.* Paris: Organisation for Economic Cooperation and Development, 1965.

UNESCO. *Statistical Yearbook 1999.* Paris: UNESCO, 1999.

United Nations Programme. *Human Development Report 1993.* New York: Oxford University Press, 1994, "Overview," pp. 1–8, and "Assessing Human Development," pp. 10–20.

World Bank. *Financing Education in Developing Countries. An Exploration of Policy Options.* Washington, DC: World Bank, 1986.

———. *World Development Report 1991.* New York: Oxford University Press for the World Bank, 1991, pp. 42–51, 52–69.

CHAPTER 10. HEALTH AND NUTRITION

Health in Developing Countries

Samuel H. Preston. "The Changing Relationship between Mortality and Level of Development." *Population Studies,* 29, no. 2 (January 1975), 231–48.

———. *Mortality Patterns in National Population, with Special Reference to Recorded Causes of Death.* New York: Academic Press, 1976.

Amartya Sen. "More than 100 Million Women Are Missing." *New York Review of Books* (December 20, 1990), pp. 61–66.

———. *Development as Freedom.* New York: Alfred A. Knopf, 1999.

United Nations Children's Fund (UNICEF). *The State of the World's Children.* New York: Oxford University Press, annual.

World Bank. *Health Sector Policy Paper,* 2d ed. Washington, DC: World Bank, 1980.

Effects of Health on Development

Jere R. Behrman. "Health and Economic Growth: Theory, Evidence, and Policy." In *Macroeconomic Environment and Health.* Geneva: World Health Organization, 1993, pp. 21–61.

Jere R. Behrman and Anil B. Deolalikar. "Health and Nutrition." In Hollis B. Chenery and T. N. Srinivasan, eds., *Handbook of Development Economics,* Vol. 1. Amsterdam: North-Holland, 1989, pp. 631–711.

Selma Mushkin. "Health as an Investment." *Journal of Political Economy,* 70, no. 5, part 2 (Supplement, October 1962), 129–57.

C. Peter Timmer. "Food Policy, Food Consumption, and Nutrition." Harvard Institute for International Development, development discussion paper no. 124, October 1981.

Malnutrition

Jere R. Behrman, Anil B. Deolalikar, and Barbara L. Wolfe. "Nutrients: Impacts and Determinants." *World Bank Economic Review,* 2, no. 3 (September 1988), 299–320.

Alan Berg. *The Nutrition Factor: Its Role in National Development.* Washington, DC: Brookings Institution, 1973.

———. *Malnutrition. What Can Be Done? Lessons from World Bank Experience.* Baltimore: Johns Hopkins Press for the World Bank, 1987.

——— and James Austin. "Nutritional Policies and Programs: A Decade of Redirection." *Food Policy,* 9, no. 4 (November 1984), 304–12.

Thomas T. Poleman. "Quantifying the Nutritional Situation in Developing Countries." *Food Research Institute Studies,* 18, no. 1 (1981), 1–58.

Shlomo Reutlinger. "Malnutrition: A Poverty Problem or a Food Problem?" *World Development,* 5, no. 8 (August 1977), 715–24.

——— and Marcelo Selowsky. *Malnutrition and Poverty: Magnitude and Policy Options.* World Bank occasional papers no. 23, Baltimore, Johns Hopkins Press, 1976.

Amartya Sen. "Ingredients of Famine Analysis: Availability and Entitlements." *Quarterly Journal of Economics,* 96, no. 3 (August 1981), 433–64.

C. Peter Timmer, Walter P. Falcon, and Scott R. Pearson. *Food Policy Analysis.* Baltimore: Johns Hopkins Press, 1983.

Medical Services

Frederick Golladay. "Health Problems and Policies in Developing Countries." World Bank staff working paper no. 412, August 1980.

James Kocher and Richard Cash. "Achieving Health and Nutritional Objectives within a Basic Needs Framework." Harvard Institute for International Development, development discussion paper no. 55, March 1979.

Michael Lipton. *Why Poor People Stay Poor: Urban Bias in World Development.* Cambridge, MA: Harvard University Press, 1977.

CHAPTER 11. CAPITAL AND SAVINGS

Investment Requirements for Growth

World Bank. *World Development Report 1999/2000.* Washington, DC: World Bank, 1999.

Sources of Saving

Robert Barro. "Are Government Bonds Net Wealth?" *Journal of Political Economy* (November–December 1979).

Sebastian Edwards. "Why Are Saving Rates So Different across Countries? An International Comparative Analysis." National Bureau of Economic Research working paper no. 507 (April 1995).

Stanley Please. "Saving through Taxation: Reality or Mirage?" *Finance and Development,* 4, no. 1 (March 1967), 24–32.

Steven Radelet, Jeffrey Sachs, and Jong-Wha Lee. "Economic Growth in Asia." Harvard Institute for International Development, May 1997.

Luis Servén Schmidt-Hebbel and Andrés Solimano. "Saving and Investment: Paradigms, Puzzles, and Policies." *World Bank Research Observer* no. 11, 1 (February 1996), 87–117.

Determinants of Private Saving

Alberto Aldo and Franco Modigliano. "The Life-Cycle Hypothesis of Saving: Aggregate Implications and Tests," *American Economic Review* (March 1963).

Ansley J. Coale and Edgar M. Hoover. *Population Growth and Economic Development in Low-Income Countries.* Princeton, NJ: Princeton University Press, 1958.

Angus Deaton. "Saving in Developing Countries: Theory and Review." *Proceedings of the World Bank Annual Conference on Development Economics.* Washington, DC: World Bank, 1989.

———. *Understanding Consumption.* Oxford: Clarendon Press, 1992.

Robert H. Frank. "The Demand for Unobservable and Other Non-Positional Goods." *American Economic Review,* 75 (March 1985).

M. Gersovitz. "Savings and Development." In Hollis Chenery and T. N. Srinivasan, eds., *Handbook of Development Economics,* Vol. 1. Amsterdam: North-Holland, 1988.

Nicholas Kaldor. "Problems Economicas de Chile." *El Trimestre Economico,* 26, no. 102 (April–June 1959), 193, 211–12.

P. Masson, T. Bayoumi, and H. Samiei. "International Evidence on the Determinants of Private Saving." IMF working paper no. 51, 1995.

Franco Modigliano and Richard Brumberg. "Utility Analysis and the Consumption Function: An Interpretation of Cross-Section Data." In K. Kurihara, ed., *Post Keynesian Economics.* New Brunswick, NJ: Rutgers University Press, 1954.

F. Modigliani, R. Brumberg, and A. Ando. "Life Cycle Hypothesis of Savings: Aggregate Implication and Tests." *American Economic Review,* 52, no. 3 (1963).

Roger S. Smith. "Factors Affecting Saving, Policy Tools and Tax Reform: A Review." International Monetary Fund working paper no. 89/47, May 23, 1989, Table 2.

T. N. Srinivasan. "Saving in the Development Process." In James H. Gapinski, ed., *The Economics of Saving.* Norwell, MA: Kluwer Academic Publishers, 1993.

Foreign Saving

Donald Snodgrass and Tyler Biggs. *Industrialization and the Small Firm: Patterns and Policies.* San Francisco: ICS Press, 1996.

International Monetary Fund. *Balance of Payments Statistics Yearbook 1998.* Washington, DC: International Monetary Fund, 1998.

World Bank. *Global Development Finance 1999.* Washington, DC: World Bank, 1998.

Foreign Aid

Craig Burnside and David Dollar. "Aid, Policies, and Growth," World Bank policy research working paper no. 1777, June 1997.

Paul Collier and David Dollar. "Aid Allocation and Poverty Reduction." World Bank, 1998.

David Dollar and William Easterly. "The Search for the Key: Aid, Investment, and Policies in Africa." World Bank, 1998.

Mark McGillivray and Akhter Ahmed. "Aid, Saving and Investment Reexplored: The Cases of Bangladesh, India, Nepal, Pakistan, and Sri Lanka." *Asian Economic Review* 36, no. 3 (December 1994).

Richard Reichel, "Development Aid, Saving and Growth in the 1980s: A Cross-Section Analysis." *Saving and Development* 19, no. 3 (1995).

World Bank. *Assessing Aid: What Works, What Doesn't, and Why?* Washington, DC: World Bank, 1998.

CHAPTER 12. FISCAL POLICY

Expenditure Policies and Public Saving

Anita Bhatia. *Military Expenditures and Economic Growth.* Washington, DC: World Bank, 1987.

Malcolm Gillis. "Tacit Taxes and Sub-Rosa Subsidies," in Richard Bird (ed.), *More Taxing Than Taxes.* San Francisco: ICS Press, 1991.

Peter Heller. "Underfinancing of Recurrent Development Costs." *Finance and Development,* 16, no. 1 (March 1979), 38–41.

Norman Hicks. *Expenditure Reductions in Developing Countries.* Washington, DC: World Bank, 1988.

International Monetary Fund. *Government Finance Statistics Yearbook 1994.* Washington, DC: IMF, 1994, pp. 46–47.

R. P. Short. "The Role of the Public Enterprises: An International Statistical Comparison." IMF dept. memo 83/34, 1983.

Project Appraisal

Arnold Harberger. *Project Evaluation: Collected Papers.* Chicago: Markham, 1974.

I. M. D. Little and James A. Mirrlees. *Project Appraisal and Planning for Developing Countries.* New York: Basic Books, 1974.

Michael Roemer and Joseph J. Stern. *The Appraisal of Development Projects.* New York: Praeger, 1975.

———. *Cases in Economic Development.* London: Butterworths, 1981.

United Nations Industrial Development Organization by P. Dasgupta, S. Marglin, and A. Sen. *Guidelines for Project Evaluation.* New York: United Nations, 1982.

Tax Policy and Public Saving

James Alm, Roy Bahl, and Matthew Murray. "Tax Base Erosion in Developing Countries." *Economic Development and Cultural Change,* 39, no. 4 (July 1991), 849–72.

Richard Bird and Oliver Oldman, eds. *Readings on Taxation in Developing Countries,* 3d ed. Baltimore: Johns Hopkins Press, 1975.

John F. Due. "Some Unresolved Issues in Design and Implementation of Value-Added Taxes." *National Tax Journal,* 42, no. 4 (December 1990), 383–98.

——— and Raymond Mikesell. *Sales Taxation: State and Local Structure and Administration.* Baltimore: Johns Hopkins Press, 1983.

Malcolm Gillis. "Federal Sales Taxation: Six Decades of Experience." *Canadian Tax Journal* (January–February 1985).

———. "Tacit Taxes and Sub-Rosa Subsidies." In Richard Bird, ed., *More Taxing Than Taxes.* San Francisco: ICS Press, 1991.

——— and Charles E. McLure, Jr. "Taxation and Income Distribution: The Colombian Tax Reform of 1974." *Journal of Development Economics,* 5, no. 3 (September 1978), 237, 249.

Omkar Goswami, Amal Sanyal, and Ira N. Gang. "Taxes, Corruption and Bribes: A Model of Indian Public Finance." In Michael Roemer and Christine Jones, eds., *Markets in Developing Countries: Parallel, Fragmented and Black.* San Francisco: ICS Press, 1991, pp. 201–13.

Arnold C. Harberger. "Principles of Taxation Applied to Developing Countries: What Have We Learned?" In Michael Boskin and Charles E. McLure, Jr., eds., *World Tax Reform: Case Studies of Developed and Developing Countries.* San Francisco: ICS Press, 1990.

IFPRI Report [International Food Policy Research Institute], 8, no. 1 (January 1986).

International Monetary Fund. *Government Finance Statistics Yearbook.* Washington, DC: International Monetary Fund, various years, country tables.

Glenn P. Jenkins. "Tax Reform: Lessons Learned." In Dwight H. Perkins and Michael Roemer, eds., *Reforming Economic Systems in Developing Countries.* Cambridge, MA: Harvard Institute for International Development, 1991.

———. "Economic Reform and Institutional Innovation." Unpublished paper, April 11, 1995.

Dwight R. Lee and Richard B. McKenzie. "The International Political Economy of Declining Tax Rates." *National Tax Journal,* 42, no. 2 (March 1989), 79–87.

Richard A. Musgrave et al. *Fiscal Reform in Bolivia: Final Report and Staff Papers of the Bolivian Mission on Tax Reform.* Cambridge, MA: Harvard Law School, International Tax Program, 1981.

Joseph A. Pechman, ed. *World Tax Reform: A Progress Report.* Washington, DC: Brookings Institute, 1988, "Introduction," p. 13.

Robert Repetto and Malcolm Gillis, eds. *Public Policies and the Misuse of Forest Resources.* New York: Cambridge University Press, 1988, "Conclusions," Chap. 10.

Harvey Rosen, *Public Finance.* Homewood, IL: Irwin, 1985.

Carl Shoup. "Choosing among Types of VAT." In Malcolm Gillis, Carl Shoup, and Gerry Sicat, eds., *Value-Added Taxation in Developing Countries.* Washington, DC: World Bank, 1990.

Carlos A. Silvani and Alberto H. J. Radano. "Tax Administration Reform in Bolivia and Uruguay." In Richard M. Bird and Milka Casanegra de Jantscher, eds., *Improving Tax Administration in Developing Countries.* Washington, DC: International Monetary Fund, 1992, pp. 19–59.

Joseph Stiglitz. *Economics of the Public Sector.* New York: W. W. Norton, 1988.

Alan A. Tait. *Value-Added Tax.* Washington, DC: International Monetary Fund, 1988, Chap. 1.

Vito Tanzi. "Quantitative Aspects of Tax Systems in Developing Countries." In David Newberry and Nicholas Stern, eds., *The Theory of Taxation for Developing Countries.* London: Oxford University Press, 1987.

World Bank. *World Development Report 1988.* New York: Oxford University Press for the World Bank, 1988, pp. 43–185.

George J. Yost III, ed. *1994 International Tax Summaries, Coopers & Lybrand International Tax Network.* New York: Wiley, 1994.

Income Distribution

Richard M. Bird and Luc Henry DeWulf. "Taxation and Income Distribution in Latin America: A Critical View of Empirical Studies." *International Monetary Fund Staff Papers,* 20 (November 1975), 639–82.

Alejandro Foxley, Eduardo Aninat, and J. P. Arellano. *Redistributive Effects of Government Programs.* Elmsford, NY: Pergamon Press, 1980, Chap. 6.

Malcolm Gillis. "Micro and Macroeconomics of Tax Reform: Indonesia." *Journal of Development Economics,* 19, no. 2 (1986), 42–46.

Donald R. Snodgrass. "The Fiscal System as an Income Redistributor in West Malaysia." *Public Finance,* 29, no. 1 (January 1974), 56–76.

CHAPTER 13. FINANCIAL POLICY

Maxwell J. Fry. *Money, Interest and Banking in Economic Development,* 2d ed. Baltimore: Johns Hopkins University Press, 1995, pp. 162–69.

International Monetary Fund. *International Financial Statistic.* Washington, DC: IMF, various issues, 1970–1994.

Ronald I. McKinnon. *Money and Capital in Economic Development.* Washington, DC: Brookings Institution, 1973.

Inflation and Savings Mobilization

Yaw Ansu. "Comments." In Arnold C. Harberger, ed., *World Economic Growth.* San Francisco: ICS Press, 1984.

Arnold C. Harberger. "A Primer on Inflation." *Journal of Money, Credit and Banking,* 10, no. 4 (November 1978), 505–21.

Albert O. Hirschman. *Journeys toward Progress: Studies of Economic Policy-Making in Latin America.* New York: Twentieth Century Fund, 1963, pp. 208–9.

Michael Roemer. "Ghana, 1950 to 1980: Missed Opportunities." In Arnold C. Harberger, ed., *World Economic Growth.* San Francisco: ICS Press, 1984, pp. 201–30.

George M. von Furstenberg. "Inflation, Taxes, and Welfare in LDCs." *Public Finance,* 35, no. 2 (1980), 700–10.

Interest Rate and Saving Decisions

Michael J. Boskin. "Taxation, Savings and the Rate of Interest." *Journal of Political Economy,* 8b, no. 2, part 2 (April 1978), 3–27.

Alberto Giovanni. "The Interest Elasticity of Savings in Developing Countries." *World Development,* 11 (July 1983), 601–8.

Larry Summers. "Capital Taxation and Capital Accumulation in a Life-Cycle Growth Model." *American Economic Review,* 71 (September 1981), 533–44.

Colin Wright. "Savings and the Rate of Interest." In Arnold C. Harberger and Martin Bailey, eds., *The Taxation of Income from Capital.* Washington, DC: Brookings Institution, 1969.

Financial Development

David C. Cole and Betty F. Slade. *Building a Modern Financial System.* Cambridge: Cambridge University Press, 1996.

Sebastian Edwards. "Stabilization with Liberalization: An Evaluation of Chile's Experiment with Free-Market Policies 1973–1983." *Economic Development and Cultural Change,* 27 (September 1985), 224–53.

Sergio Pereira Leite. "Interest-Rate Policies in West Africa." *International Monetary Fund Staff Papers,* 29, no. 1 (March 1982), 48–76.

Steven C. Leuthold. "Interest Rates, Inflation and Deflation." *Financial Analysis Journal* (January–February 1981), 28–51.

Yung Chul Park. *Financial Liberalization and Opening in East Asia: Issues and Policy Challenges.* Seoul:Korea Institute of Finance, 1998.

Richard H. Patten and Jay Rosengard. *Progress with Profits: The Development of Rural Banking in Indonesia.* San Francisco: ICS Press, 1991.

Marguerite Robinson. "Rural Financial Intermediation: Lessons from Indonesia." Harvard Institute for International Development, development discussion paper no. 434, October 1992.

A. Wahid. *The Grameen Bank: Poverty Relief.* Boulder, CO: Westview Press, 1993.

World Bank. *Global Economic Prospects 1998/99.* Washington, DC: World Bank, 1999.

———. *World Development Report 1989.* Washington, DC: World Bank, 1989.

———. *World Development Report 1999/2000.* Washington, DC: World Bank, 1999.

Monetary Policy and Price Stability

Arnold Harberger. "A Primer on Inflation." *Journal of Money, Credit and Banking,* 10, no. 4 (November 1978), 505–21.

Anne O. Krueger. *Exchange Rate Determination.* New York: Cambridge University Press, 1983, pp. 123–36.

John Williamson. *The Open Economy and the World Economy.* New York: Basic Books, 1983, pp. 238–41.

CHAPTER 14. PRIVATE FOREIGN CAPITAL FLOWS, DEBT, AND FINANCIAL CRISES

Development Assistance Committee of the OECD. *Development Cooperation in the 1990s.* Paris: OECD, 1989.

International Monetary Fund. *Balance of Payments Yearbook 1990,* Vol. 44, part 2. Washington, DC: International Monetary Fund, 1993.

———. *International Financial Statistics Yearbook.* Washington, DC: International Monetary Fund, annual.

United States Agency for International Development. *Congressional Presentation.* Washington, DC: U.S. Agency for International Development, annual.

World Bank. "International Factors Reducing Poverty: Aid and Poverty." *World Development Report 1990.* Washington, DC: World Bank, 1990, p. 131.

———. *Global Development Finance.* Washington, DC: World Bank, annual.

Foreign Aid

Robert L. Ayres. *Banking on the Poor.* Cambridge, MA: MIT Press, 1984.

Robert Cassen et al. *Does Aid Work?* London: Oxford University Press, 1986.

Jonathan Eaton. "Foreign Public Capital Flows." In Hollis B. Chenery and T. N. Srinivasan, eds., *Handbook of Development Economics,* Vol. 2. Amsterdam: North-Holland, 1989, pp. 1305–86.

Joint Ministerial Committee of the Boards of Governors of the World Bank and the International Monetary Fund. *Aid for Development: The Key Issues.* Washington, DC: World Bank and IMF, 1986.

Paul Mosley. "Aid, Savings and Growth Revisited." *Oxford Bulletin of Economics and Statistics,* 42 (May 1980), 79–91.

Foreign Investment and the Multinationals

Eduardo Borensztein, Jose de Gregorio, and Jong-Wha Lee. "How Does Foreign Direct Investment Affect Economic Growth?" *Journal of International Economics* 45 (June 1998), 115–35.

"The Fortune Global 500 Ranked by Performance," *Fortune* (August 2, 1999).

Theodore H. Moran. "Foreign Direct Investment and Development: The New Policy Agenda for Developing Countries and Economies in Transition." Washington, DC: Institute for International Economics, 1998.

UNCTAD. *Transnational Corporations,* 7, no. 3 (December 1998), 131.

UNCTAD. *World Investment Report 1999,* Annex Table A.I.7.

Romain Wacziarg. "Measuring the Dynamic Gains from Trade." World Bank policy research working paper no. 2001, November 1998.

Multinationals' Investment Patterns

Jack N. Behrman and William A. Fischer. *Overseas R&D Activities of Transnational Corporations.* Cambridge, MA: Oelgeschlager, Gunn and Hair, 1980.

Fred C. Bergsten, Thomas P. Horst, and Theodore H. Moran. *American Multinationals and American Interests.* Washington, DC: Brookings Institution, 1978.

Thomas L. Brewer. "Foreign Direct Investment in Developing Countries." World Bank working paper WPS 712, June 1991, p. 9.

Eliana Cardoso and Rudiger Dornbusch. "Foreign Private Capital Flows." In Hollis B. Chenery and T. N. Srinivasan, eds., *Handbook of Development Economics,* Vol. 2. Amsterdam: Elsevier, 1989, pp. 1387–1439.

Dennis J. Encarnation and Louis T. Wells, Jr. "Evaluating Foreign Investment." In Theodore H. Moran et al., *Investing in Development: New Roles for Foreign Capital?* Washington, DC: Overseas Development Council, 1986, pp. 61–85.

David Goldsborough. "Foreign Direct Investment in Developing Countries." *Finance and Development* (March 1985).

Joseph M. Grieco. "Foreign Investment and Development: Theory and Evidence." In Theodore H. Moran, *Investing in Development: New Roles for Foreign Capital?* Washington, DC: Overseas Development Council, 1986, pp. 47–48.

Steven Guisinger et al. *Investment Incentives and Performance Requirements.* New York: Praeger, 1985.

G. K. Helleiner. "Transnational Corporations and Direct Foreign Investment." In Hollis B. Chenery and T. N. Srinivasan, eds., *Handbook of Development Economics,* Vol. 2. Amsterdam: Elsevier, 1989, pp. 1441–80.

Theodore H. Moran, ed. *Multinational Corporations.* Lexington, MA: Lexington Books, 1985.

——— et al., *Investment in Development: New Roles for Foreign Capital?* Washington, DC: Overseas Development Council, 1986.

Charles P. Oman. "New Forms of Investment in Developing Countries." In Theodore H. Moran et al., *Investing in Development: New Roles for Foreign Capital?* Washington, DC: Overseas Development Council, 1986, pp. 131–55.

John Stopford. *The World Directory of Multinational Enterprises 1982–1983.* Detroit: Gale Research Company, 1982.

United Nations Centre for Transnational Corporations (UNCTC). *Transnational Corporations in World Development.* New York: United Nations, 1988.

Raymond Vernon. *Storm over the Multinationals: The Real Issues.* Cambridge, MA: Harvard University Press, 1977.

Louis T. Wells, Jr. "Investment Incentives: An Unnecessary Debate." *The CTC Reporter,* 22 (Autumn 1986), 58–60.

The 1980s Debt Crisis

Rudiger Dornbusch. "Background Paper." In Twentieth Century Fund, Task Force on International Debt, *The Road to Economic Recovery.* New York: Priority Publications, 1989.

———. "Mexico's Economy at the Crossroads." *Journal of International Affairs,* 43, no. 2 (Winter 1990), 313–26.

Albert Fishlow. "External Borrowing and Debt Management." In Rudiger Dornbusch, F. Leslie, and C. H. Helmers, *The Open Economy: Tools for Policymakers in Developing Countries.* New York: Oxford University Press, 1988, pp. 187–222.

Ishrat Husain and Ishac Diwan, eds. *Dealing with the Debt Crisis.* Washington, DC: World Bank, 1989.

Carol Lancaster and John Williamson, eds. *African Debt and Financing.* Washington, DC: Institute for International Economics, 1986.

Jeffrey Sachs. "The LDC Debt Crisis." *NBER Reporter* (Winter 1986), 15–16.

Foreign Debt

Guillermo Calvo, Ronald Findlay, Pentii Kouri, and Jorge Braga de Macedo, eds. *Debt, Stabilization, and Development: Essays in Honor of Carlos Diaz-Alejandro.* Oxford: Basil Blackwell, 1989.

William Cline. *International Debt: Systemic Risk and Policy Response.* Washington DC: Institute for International Economics, 1984.

———. *International Debt Reexamined.* Washington, DC: Institute for International Economics, 1995.

Jeffrey Sachs. "External Debt and Macroeconomic Performance in Latin America and East Asia." *Brookings Papers on Economic Activity,* 1985, no. 2, pp. 523–73.

———. "The Debt Overhang of Developing Countries." in R. Findlay, G. Calvo, P. Kouri, and J. Braga de Macedo, eds., *Debt, Stabilization and Development: Essays in Honor of Carlos Diaz Alejandro.* Oxford: Basil Blackwell, 1989.

———, ed. *Developing Country Debt and Economic Performance.* Chicago: University of Chicago Press for NBER, 1989.

Gordon W. Smith and John Cuddington. *International Debt and the Developing Countries.* Washington, DC: World Bank, 1985.

Emerging Market Financial Crises

Jaime Cardoso and Bernard Laurens. "The Effectiveness of Capital Controls on Inflows: Lessons from the Experience of Chile." IMF Monetary and Exchange Affairs Department, 1998.

Richard Cooper. "Should Capital Controls Be Banished?" *Brookings Papers on Economic Activity,* 1999, no. 1, pp. 89–141.

Sebastian Edwards. "Capital Flows, Real Exchange Rates, and Capital Controls: Some Latin American Experiences." Department of Economics, UCLA, 1998.

Barry Eichengreen. *Toward a New International Financial Architecture: A Practical Post-Asia Agenda.* Washington, DC: Institute for International Economics, February 1999.

——— and Richard Portes. *Crisis? What Crisis? Orderly Workouts for Sovereign Debtors.* London: Center for Economic Policy Research, 1995.

Stanley Fischer. "In Defense of the IMF." *Foreign Affairs* 77, no. 4 (July–August 1998).

Martin Fledstein. "Refocusing the IMF." *Foreign Affairs* 77, no. 2 (March–April 1998), 20–33.

Jason Furman and Joseph Stiglitz. "Economic Crises: Evidence and Insights from East Asia." *Brookings Papers on Economic Activity,* 1998, no. 2, pp 1–136.

Morris Goldstein. *Safeguarding Prosperity in a Global Financial System.* Report of an Independent Task Force for the Council on Foreign Relations. Washington, DC: Institute for International Economics, September 1999.

David Hale. "The IMF, Now More than Ever." *Foreign Affairs,* 77, no. 6 (November–December 1998).

Institute of International Finance. *Capital Flows to Emerging Market Economies.* Washington, DC: Institute for International Finance, January 1999.

Timothy Lane and others, "IMF-Supported Programs in Indonesia, Korea, and Thailand: A Preliminary Assessment." IMF occasional paper no. 178 (1999).

Felipe Larraín B., ed. *Capital Flows, Capital Controls, and Currency Crises: Latin America in the 1990s* (forthcoming, 2000).

Steven Radelet. "Orderly Workouts for Cross-Border Private Debt." Harvard Institute for International Development discussion paper No. 721, September, 1999.

Steven Radelet and Jeffrey Sachs. "The East Asian Financial Crisis: Diagnosis, Remedies, Prospects." *Brookings Papers on Economic Activity* 1998, no. 1, pp. 1–90.

Jeffrey Sachs. "Do We Need an International Lender of Last Resort?" Frank D. Graham lecture, Princeton University, April, 1995.

World Bank. *Global Development Finance 1999.* Washington, DC: World Bank, 1999, pp. 177 and 191.

World Bank. *East Asia: The Road to Recovery.* Washington, DC: World Bank, 1998.

CHAPTER 15. AGRICULTURE

Agriculture's Role in Economic Development

Carl Eicher and John Staatz. *Agricultural Development in the Third World,* 2d ed. Baltimore: Johns Hopkins Press, 1990.

Bruce F. Johnston and Peter Kilby. *Agriculture and Structural Transformation.* London: Oxford University Press, 1975.

J. W. Mellor and B. F. Johnston. "The World Food Equation: Interrelations among Development, Employment, and Food Consumption." *Journal of Economic Literature,* no. 22 (1984).

J. Mohan Rao. "Agriculture in Recent Development Theory." *Journal of Development Economics,* no. 22 (1986).

Lloyd Reynolds. *Agriculture in Development Theory.* New Haven, CT: Yale University Press, 1976.

Theodore W. Schultz. *Transforming Traditional Agriculture.* New Haven, CT: Yale University Press, 1964.

Erik Thorbecke, ed. *The Role of Agriculture in Economic Development.* New York: Columbia Press, 1969.

C. Peter Timmer. "The Agricultural Transformation." In Hollis B. Chenery and T. N. Srinivasan, eds., *Handbook of Development Economics,* Vol. 1. Amsterdam: North-Holland, 1988.

————, ed. *Agriculture and the State.* Ithaca, NY: Cornell University Press, 1991.

World Bank. *World Development Report 1982.* New York: Oxford University Press, 1982.

Self-Sufficiency in Food

R. Barker, E. Bennagen, and Y. Hayami. "New Rice Technology and Policy Alternatives for Food Self-Sufficiency." In International Rice Research Institute, *Economic Consequences of the New Rice Technology.* Los Banos, Philippines: International Rice Research Institute 1978, pp. 337–61.

Lester Brown. *By Bread Alone.* New York: Praeger, 1974.

Jean Drèze and Amartya Sen. *Hunger and Public Action.* London: Oxford University Press (Clarendon), 1989.

Richard Goldman. "Staple Food Self-Sufficiency and the Distributive Impact of Malaysian Rice Policy." *Food Research Institute Studies,* 14, no. 3 (1975), 251–93.

Land Reform

Ronald P. Dore. *Land Reform in Japan.* London: Oxford University Press, 1959.

William Hinton. *Fanshen.* New York: Vintage Books, 1966.

Elias Tuma. *Twenty-Six Centuries of Agrarian Reform: A Comparative Analysis.* Berkeley: University of California Press, 1965.

Louis J. Walinsky, ed. *Agrarian Reform as Unfinished Business: The Selected Papers of Wolf Ladejinsky.* London: Oxford University Press, 1977.

Technology of Agricultural Production

Hans B. Binswanger. "Agricultural Mechanization: A Comparative Historical Perspective." *World Bank Research Observer,* 1, no. 1 (January 1986).

———— and Prabhu Pingali. "Technological Priorities for Farming in Sub-Saharan Africa." *World Bank Research Observer,* 3, no. 1 (January 1988).

———— and Vernon W. Ruttan. *Induced Innovation: Technology, Institutions and Development.* Baltimore: Johns Hopkins Press, 1978.

Ester Boserup. *The Conditions of Agricultural Growth.* Chicago: Aldine, 1965.

Dana G. Dalrymple. *Development and Spread of High Yielding Wheat Varieties in Developing Countries.* Washington, DC: Agency for International Development, 1986.

Yujiro Hayami and Vernon W. Ruttan, *Agricultural Development: An International Perspective.* Baltimore: Johns Hopkins Press, 1971.

Dwight H. Perkins. *Agricultural Development in China, 1368–1968.* Chicago: Aldine, 1969.

Mobilization of Agricultural Inputs

S. J. Burki, D. G. Davies, R. H. Hook, and J. W. Thomas. *Public Works Programs in Developing Countries: A Comparative Analysis,* World Bank staff working paper no. 224, February 1976.

Uma Lele. *The Design of Rural Development: Lessons from Africa.* Baltimore: Johns Hopkins Press, 1975.

Dwight H. Perkins and Shahid Yusuf. *Rural Development in China.* Baltimore: Johns Hopkins Press, 1984.

Agricultural Price Policy

Hussein Askari and John Cummings. *Agricultural Supply Response: A Survey of the Econometric Evidence.* New York: Praeger, 1976.

Romeo Bautista and Alberto Valdés. *The Bias against Agriculture: Trade and Macroeconomic Policies in Developing Countries.* San Francisco: ICS Press, 1993.

Elliot Berg et al. *Accelerated Development in Sub-Saharan Africa.* Washington, DC: World Bank, 1981.

Walter P. Falcon and C. Peter Timmer. "The Political Economy of Rice Production and Trade in Asia." In L. Reynolds, ed., *Agriculture in Development Theory.* New Haven, CT: Yale University Press, 1975.

Raj Krishna. "Agricultural Price Policy and Economic Development." In H. M. Southworth and B. F. Johnston, eds., *Agricultural Development and Economic Growth.* Ithaca, NY: Cornell University Press, 1967.

C. Peter Timmer, Walter P. Falcon, and Scott R. Pearson. *Food Policy Analysis.* Baltimore: Johns Hopkins Press, 1983.

Isabell Tsakok. *Agricultural Price Policy: A Practitioner's Guide to Partial-Equilibrium Analysis.* Ithaca, NY: Cornell University Press, 1990.

Rod Tyers and Kym Anderson. *Disarray in World Food Markets: Quantitative Assessment.* London: Cambridge University Press, 1992.

CHAPTER 16. PRIMARY EXPORTS

Comparative Advantage

Richard E. Caves, Jeffrey A. Frankel, and Ronald W. Jones. *World Trade and Payments: An Introduction,* 5th ed. Boston: Little Brown, 1990.

Export Characteristics of Developing Countries

Moises Syrquin and Hollis Chenery. "Patterns of Development 1950–83." World Bank, discussion paper no. 41, 1989.

Primary Exports as an Engine of Growth

Robert E. Baldwin. *Economic Development and Export Growth: A Study of Northern Rhodesia, 1920–1960.* Los Angeles: University of California Press, 1966.

David C. Dawe. "Essays on Price Stabilization and the Macroeconomy in Low Income Countries." Harvard University, Ph.D. dissertation, May 1993.

Albert Fishlow. *American Railroads and the Transformation of the Antebellum Economy.* Cambridge, MA: Harvard University Press, 1965.

Robert W. Fogel. "Railroads as an Analogy to the Space Effort: Some Economic Aspects." In Bruce Mazlish, ed., *Space Programs: An Exploration in Historical Analogy.* Cambridge, MA: MIT Press, 1966.

Arnold Harberger, ed. *World Economic Growth.* San Francisco: ICS Press, 1984.

Albert O. Hirschman. *The Strategy of Economic Development.* New Haven, CT: Yale University Press, 1958, Chap. 6.

———. "A Generalized Linkage Approach to Economic Development, with Special Reference to Staples." In Manning Nash, ed., *Essays on Economic Development and Cultural Change.* Chicago: University of Chicago Press, 1977, pp. 67–98.

Stephen R. Lewis, "Primary Exporting Countries." In Hollis B. Chenery and T. N. Srinivasan, eds., *Handbook of Development Economics,* Vol. 2. Amsterdam: North-Holland, 1989, pp. 1541–1600.

David Lindauer and Michael Roemer, eds., *Asia and Africa: Legacies and Opportunities for Development.* San Francisco: ICS Press, 1994.

Hla Myint. "The 'Classical Theory' of International Trade and the Underdeveloped Countries." *Economic Journal,* 68 (1959), 317–37.

Douglass C. North. "Location Theory and Regional Economic Growth." *Journal of Political Economy,* 63 (1955), 243–85.

Michael Roemer. *Fishing for Growth: Export-Led Development in Peru, 1950–1967.* Cambridge, MA: Harvard University Press, 1970.

Melville H. Watkins. "A Staple Theory of Economic Growth." *Canadian Journal of Economics and Political Science,* 29 (1963), 141–58.

Barriers to Primary-Export-Led Growth

R. M. Auty. *Resource-Based Industrialization: Sowing the Oil in Eight Developing Countries.* New York: Oxford University Press, 1990.

Bela Balassa. "Outward Orientation." In Hollis B. Chenery and T. N. Srinivasan, eds., *Handbook of Development Economics,* Vol. 2. Amsterdam: North-Holland, 1989, pp. 1645–89.

John T. Cuddington and Carlos M. Urzua. "Trends and Cycles in the Net Barter Terms of Trade: A New Approach." *Economic Journal,* 99 (June 1989), 426–42.

W. Max Corden and S. Peter Neary. "Booming Sector and Deindustrialization in a Small Open Economy." *Economic Journal,* 92 (December 1982), 825–48.

Sebastian Edwards. *Real Exchange Rates, Devaluation and Adjustment: Exchange Rate Policy in Developing Countries.* Cambridge, MA: MIT Press, 1991.

Alan Gelb. *Oil Windfalls: Blessing or Curse?* New York: Oxford University Press for the World Bank, 1988.

Odin Knudsen and Andrew Parnes. *Trade Instability and Economic Development.* Lexington, MA: Heath Lexington Books, 1975.

Philip Lane and Aaron Tornell. "Power, Growth, and the Voracity Effect." *Journal of Economic Growth,* 1 no. 2 (June 1996), 213–41.

Ragnar Nurkse. *Equilibrium Growth in the World Economy.* Cambridge, MA: Harvard University Press, 1961.

Michael Roemer. "Resource-based Industrialization: A Survey." *Journal of Development Economics,* 6, no. 6 (June 1979), 163–202.

———. "Dutch Disease in Developing Countries: Swallowing Bitter Medicine." In Matts Lundahl, ed., *The Primary Sector in Economic Development.* London: Croom-Helms, 1985.

———. "Ghana 1950–1980: Missed Opportunities." In Arnold Harberger, ed., *World Economic Growth.* San Francisco: ICS Press, 1984, pp. 201–26.

Jeffrey Sachs and Andrew Warner. "Natural Resource Abundance and Economic Growth." Harvard Institute for International Development discussion paper 517a, October 1995.

David Sapsford and V. N. Balasubramanyam. "The Long-Run Behavior of the Relative Price of Primary Commodities: Statistical Evidence and Policy Implications." *World Development,* 22, no. 11 (November 1994), 1737–45.

Hans W. Singer. "The Distribution of Trade between Investing and Borrowing Countries." *American Economic Review,* 40 (May 1950), 470–85.

Robert Summers and Alan Heston. *Penn World Tables, Mark 5.6,* 1994 (website version at www.upenn.edu/econ/faculty/index/Heston_Alan.html).

United Nations (Raul Prebisch). *The Economic Development of Latin America and Its Principal Problems.* Lake Success, NY: United Nations, 1950.

World Bank. *Price Prospects for Primary Commodities, 1990–2005.* Washington, DC: World Bank, 1993.

———. *Global Economic Prospects and the Developing Countries.* Washington, DC: World Bank, 1994, pp. 39–40.

———. *World Development Indicators 1999.* Washington, DC: World Bank, 1999.

———. *Commodity Trade and Price Trends.* Washington, DC: World Bank, annual.

CHAPTER 17. INDUSTRY

Industry as a Leading Sector

E. J. Hobsbawm. *The Pelican History of Britain,* Vol. 3, *Industry and Empire.* Baltimore: Penguin, 1969.

David S. Landes. *The Unbound Prometheus: Technological Change and Industrial Development in Western Europe from 1750 to the Present.* London: Cambridge University Press, 1969.

Stanford Research Institute et al. *Costs of Urban Infrastructure for Industry as Related to City Size in Developing Countries: India Case Study.* Menlo Park, CA: Stanford Research Institute, 1968.

Moises Syrquin and Hollis Chenery. "Three Decades of Industrialization." *The World Bank Economic Review,* 3, no. 2 (1989), 141–81.

Pan A. Yotopoulos and Jeffrey B. Nugent. "A Balanced-Growth Version of the Linkage Hypotheses: A Test." *Quarterly Journal of Economics,* 87 (1973), 157–71.

Investment Choices in Industry

American Rural Small-Scale Industry Delegation. *Rural Small-Scale Industry in the People's Republic of China.* Berkeley: University of California Press, 1977.

William Byrd and Qingsong Lin. *Rural Industry.* Oxford: Oxford University Press, 1990.

Ranadev Banerji. "Average Size of Plants in Manufacturing and Capital Intensity." *Journal of Development Economics,* 5 (1978).

P. N. Dhar and H. F. Lydall. *The Role of Small Enterprises in Indian Economic Development.* New York: Asia Publishing House, 1961.

Hal Hill. "Choice of Technique in the Indonesian Weaving Industry." *Economic Development and Cultural Change,* 31, no. 2 (January 1983), 337–54.

International Labor Office. *Employment, Income and Equality: A Strategy for Increasing Productive Employment in Kenya.* Geneva: International Labor Office, 1972.

Ian M. D. Little, Dipak Mazumdar, and John M. Page, Jr. *Small Manufacturing Enterprises.* New York: Oxford University Press for the World Bank, 1988.

Alan S. Manne, ed. *Investments for Capacity Expansion: Size, Location and Time Phasing.* Cambridge, MA: MIT Press, 1967.

Keijiro Otsuka, Deqiang Liu, and Naoki Murakami. *Industrial Reform in China: Past Performance and Future Prospects.* Oxford: Clarendon Press, 1998.

Howard Pack. "The Choice of Technique and Employment in the Textile Industry." in A. S. Bhalla, ed., *Technology and Employment in Industry.* Geneva: International Labor Office, 1975.

———. "Aggregate Implications of Factor Substitution in Industry Processes." *Journal of Development Economics,* 11, no. 1 (August 1982).

C. F. Pratten. *Economies of Scale in Manufacturing Industry.* London: Cambridge, University Press, 1971.

E. F. Schumacher. *Small Is Beautiful.* London: Sphere Books, 1974.

Donald R. Snodgrass and Tyler Biggs. *Industrialization and the Small Firm: Patterns and Policies.* San Francisco: International Center for Economic Growth and the Harvard Institute for International Development, 1996.

Eugene Staley and Richard Morse. *Modern Small Industry for Developing Countries.* New York: McGraw-Hill, 1965.

Hernando de Soto. *The Other Path.* New York: Harper and Row, 1989.

William F. Steel. *Small-Scale Employment and Production in Developing Countries: Evidence from Ghana.* New York: Praeger, 1977.

Joseph Stern, Ji-Hong Kim, Dwight H. Perkins, and Jung-ho Yoo. *Industrialization and the State: The Korean Heavy and Chemical Industry Drive.* Cambridge, MA: Harvard Institute for International Development, 1995.

Frances Stewart. "Manufacture of Cement Blocks in Kenya." In A. S. Bhalla, ed., *Technology and Employment in Industry.* Geneva: International Labor Office, 1975.

Louis T. Wells, Jr. "Economic Man and Engineering Man: Choice of Technique in a Low-Wage Country." In C. P. Timmer et al., eds., *The Choice of Technology in Developing Countries.* Cambridge, MA: Center for International Affairs, Harvard University, 1975, pp. 69–74.

Jeffrey Williamson. "Regional Inequality and the Process of National Development: A Description of Patterns." *Economic Development and Cultural Change,* 13 (1965), 3–45.

CHAPTER 18. TRADE AND DEVELOPMENT

Import Substitution and Outward Orientation

Bela Balassa et al. *The Structure of Protection in the Developing Countries.* Baltimore: Johns Hopkins Press, 1971, p. 55.

Jagdish Bhagwati. *Protectionism.* Cambridge, MA: MIT Press, 1988.

Henry J. Bruton. "The Import Substitution Strategy of Economic Development." *Pakistan Development Review,* 10 (1970), 123–46.

———. "Import Substitution." In Hollis B. Chenery and T. N. Srinivasan, eds., *Handbook of Development Economics,* Vol. 2. Amsterdam: Elsevier, 1989, pp. 1601–44.

W. M. Corden. *The Theory of Protection.* London: Oxford University Press, 1971, especially Chaps. 2 and 3.

Albert O. Hirschman. "The Political Economy of Import Substitution." *Quarterly Journal of Economics,* 82 (1968), 1–32.

Outward-Looking Trade Strategy

Narongchai Akrasanee, David Dapice, and Frank Flatters. *Thailand's Export Growth: Retrospect and Prospects.* Bangkok: Thailand Development Research Institute, 1990.

Alice Amsden. *Asia's New Giant: South Korea and Late Industrialization.* New York: Oxford University Press, 1989.

Asian Development Bank. *Emerging Asia: Changes and Challenges.* Manila: Asian Development Bank, 1997.

Bela Balassa. "Outward Orientation." In Hollis B. Chenery and T. N. Srinivasan, eds., *Handbook of Development Economics,* Vol. 2. Amsterdam: Elsevier, 1989, pp. 1645–89.

———— et al. *Industrial Strategies in Semi-Industrialized Countries.* Baltimore: Johns Hopkins Press, 1982.

Jagdish N. Bhagwati. *Foreign Trade Regimes and Economic Development: Anatomy and Consequences of Exchange Control Regimes.* Cambridge, MA: Ballinger, 1978.

Tyler Biggs and Brian Levy. "Strategic Interventions and the Political Economy of Industrial Policy in Developing Countries." In D. H. Perkins and M. Roemer, eds., *Systems Reform in Developing Countries.* Cambridge, MA: Harvard University Press, 1991, pp. 365–401.

Vittorio Corbo and Sang Woo Nam. "The Recent Macroeconomic Evolution of the Republic of Korea: An Overview." World Bank, Economic Research Department, discussion paper DRD 208, 1986.

David Dollar. "Outward-Oriented Developing Countries Really Do Grow More Rapidly: Evidence from 95 LDCs, 1976–85." *Economic Development and Cultural Change,* 40, no. 3 (1992), 523–44.

Sebastian Edwards. "Openness, Productivity, and Growth: What Do We Really Know?" *Economic Journal,* 108 (March 1998), 383–98.

Jeffrey Frankel and David Romer. "Does Trade Cause Growth?" *American Economic Review,* 89, no. 3 (June 1999), 379–99.

Ann Harrison and Gordon Hanson. "Who Gains from Trade Reform? Some Remaining Puzzles." *Journal of Development Economics,* 59 (1999), 125–54.

Helen Hughes, ed. *Achieving Industrialization in East Asia.* Cambridge: Cambridge University Press, 1988.

Adriaan Ten Kate. "Liberalization and Economic Stabilization in Mexico: Lessons of Experience." *World Development,* 20, no. 5 (May 1992), 659–72.

Anne O. Krueger. *Foreign Trade Regimes and Economic Development: Liberalization Attempts and Consequences.* Cambridge, MA: Ballinger, 1978.

————. "Trade Policy and Economic Development: How We Learn." *American Economic Review,* 1, no. 87 (March, 1997), 1–22.

————. "Why Trade Liberalization Is Good for Growth." *Economic Journal,* 108 (September 1998), 1513–22.

David L. Lindauer and Michael Roemer, eds. *Asia and Africa: Legacies and Opportunities in Development,* San Francisco, ICS Press, 1994, especially Chaps. 1 and 11.

Lawrence J. Lau, ed. *Models of Development: A Comparative Study of Economic Growth in South Korea and Taiwan.* San Francisco: ICS Press, 1990.

I. M. D. Little, Tibor Scitovsky, and Maurice Scott. *Industry and Trade in Some Developing Countries.* London: Oxford University Press, 1970.

Mancur Olson. *The Rise and Decline of Nations.* New Haven, CT: Yale University Press, 1982.

Howard Pack. "Industrialization and Trade." In Hollis B. Chenery and T. N. Srinivasan, eds., *Handbook of Development Economics,* Vol. 2. Amsterdam: Elsevier, 1989, pp. 333–80.

———— and Larry E. Westphal. "Industrial Strategy and Technological Change." *Journal of Development Economics,* 22, no. 1 (June 1986), 87–128.

Dwight Perkins. "There Are at Least Three Models of East Asian Development." *World Development,* 22-4 (April 1994), 655–61.

Steven Radelet. "Manufactured Exports, Export Platforms, and Economic Growth." Harvard Institute for International Development, CAER project discussion paper no. 42, September 1999.

———— and Jeffrey Sachs, "The East Asian Financial Crisis: Diagnosis, Remedies, Prospects." *Brookings Papers on Economic Activity,* 1998, no. 1, pp. 1–90.

Francisco Rodriguez and Dani Rodrik. "Trade Policy and Economic Growth: A Skeptic's Guide to the Cross-National Evidence." National Bureau of Economic Research working paper no. 7081 (April 1999).

Jeffrey Sachs and Andrew Warner. "Economic Reform and the Process of Global Integration." *Brookings Papers on Economic Activity* 1995, no. 1, pp. 1–118.

Robert Wade. *Governing the Market: Economic Theory and the Role of Government in East Asian Industrialization.* Princeton, NJ: Princeton University Press, 1990.

World Bank. *The East Asian Miracle: Economic Growth and Public Policy.* Washington, DC: World Bank, 1993.

World Trading Arrangements

Jagdish N. Bhagwati and Anne O. Krueger. *The Dangerous Drift to Preferential Trade Agreements.* Washington, DC: American Enterprise Institute for Public Policy Research, 1995.

Jeffrey A. Frankel. *Regional Trading Blocs in the World Economic System.* Washington, DC: Institute for International Economics, 1997.

Douglas Irwin, "Multilaterial and Bilateral Trade Policies." In Jaime de Melo and Arvind Panagariya, eds., *New Dimensions in Regional Integration.* Cambridge: Cambridge University Press, 1995.

Harry G. Johnson. *Money, Trade, and Economic Growth.* London: Allen and Unwin, 1962, Chap. 3.

————. "Optimal Trade Interventions in the Presence of Domestic Distortions." In R. E. Caves et al., *Trade, Growth, and the Balance of Payments.* Amsterdam: North-Holland, 1965, pp. 3–34.

Robert Z. Lawrence. *Regionalism, Multilateralism, and Deeper Integration.* Washington, DC: Brookings Institution, 1996.

Jaime de Melo and Arvind Panagariya, eds. *New Dimensions in Regional Integration.* Cambridge: Cambridge University Press, 1995.

United Nations. *Yearbook of International Trade Statistics.* New York: United Nations, annual.

Jacob Viner. *The Customs Union Issue.* New York: Carnegie Endowment for International Peace, 1950.

World Trade Organization website: www.wto.org.

CHAPTER 19. MANAGING AN OPEN ECONOMY

Equilibrium in a Small, Open Economy

Pierre-Richard Agenor and Peter J. Montiel. *Development Macroeconomics,* 2nd ed. Princeton, NJ: Princeton University Press, 1999.

Richard E. Caves, Jeffrey A. Frankel, and Ronald W. Jones. *World Trade and Payments.* Glenview, IL: Scott, Foresman, Little, Brown, 1990, Chap. 19.

Rudiger Dornbusch. *Open Economy Macroeconomics.* New York: Basic Books, 1980.

W. Max Corden. *Inflation, Exchange Rates and the World Economy.* Chicago: University of Chicago Press, 1977.

W. E. G. Salter. "International Balance and External Balance: The Role of Price and Expenditure Effects." *Economic Record* (August 1959), 226–38.

Trevor W. Swan. "Economic Control in a Dependent Economy." *Economic Record* (November 1956), 339–56.

Tales of Stabilization

Michael Bruno et al. *Lessons of Economic Stabilization and Its Aftermath.* Cambridge, MA: MIT Press, 1991.

W. Max Corden and J. Peter Neary. "Booming Sector and Deindustrialization in a Small, Open Economy." *Economic Journal,* 92 (1982).

Ishan Kapur et al. *Ghana: Adjustment and Growth, 1983–91.* Washington, D.C.: International Monetary Fund, 1991.

Mark Lindenberg and Noel Ramirez. *Managing Adjustment in Developing Countries.* San Francisco: ICS Press, 1989.

I. M. D. Little et al. *Boom, Crisis and Adjustment: The Macroeconomic Experience of Developing Countries.* Washington, DC: World Bank, 1993.

David E. Sahn, ed. *Adjusting to Policy Failure in African Economies.* Ithaca, NY: Cornell University Press, 1994.

World Bank. *The East Asian Miracle: Economic Growth and Public Policy.* Oxford: Oxford University Press, 1993a.

———. *Adjustment in Africa: Reforms, Results and the Road Ahead.* London: Oxford University Press, 1993b.

Index

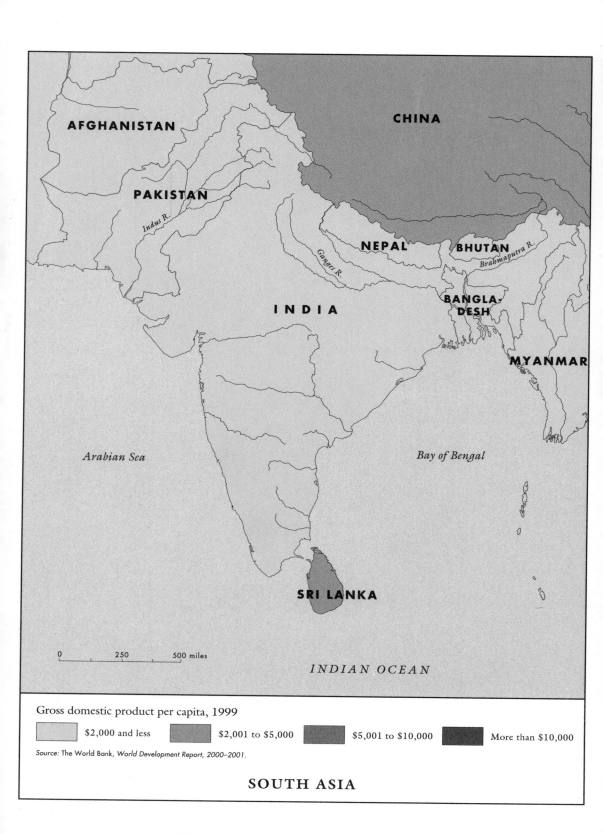

AFGHANISTAN

CHINA

PAKISTAN

Indus R.

NEPAL

BHUTAN

Ganges R.

Brahmaputra R.

BANGLA-
DESH

INDIA

MYANMAR

Arabian Sea

Bay of Bengal

```
0        250        500 miles
```

SRI LANKA

INDIAN OCEAN

Gross domestic product per capita, 1999

$2,000 and less $2,001 to $5,000 $5,001 to $10,000   More than $10,000

Source: The World Bank, *World Development Report, 2000–2001.*

SOUTH ASIA